# RELIGION
# CASTE AND POLITICS
# IN INDIA

CHRISTOPHE JAFFRELOT

Columbia University Press
New York

Columbia University Press
*Publishers Since 1893*
New York   Chichester, West Sussex
© Christophe Jaffrelot, 2011
All rights reserved

Published by arrangement with PRIMUS Books, Higher Academic Division
of Ratna Sagar P Ltd, New Delhi, India.

Library of Congress Cataloging-in-Publication Data

Jaffrelot, Christophe.
  Religion, caste, and politics in India / Christophe Jaffrelot.
    p. cm.
  Includes bibliographical references and index.
  ISBN 978-0-231-70260-7 (cloth : alk. paper)
  ISBN 978-0-231-70261-4 (pbk. : alk. paper)
  ISBN 978-0-231-80015-0 (eBook)
  1. Hinduism and politics—India. 2. Hindutva. 3. Caste—India.
  4. India—Religion. 5. Hinduism—Relations—Islam.
  6. Islam—Relations—Hinduism. 7. Ethnic conflict—India.
  8. India—Politics and government. 9. India—Social conditions.
  10. India—Foreign relations. I. Title.

BL1215.P65J34 2011
322'.10954—dc22

                    2010050539

*For Vadim*

# Contents

## III. COMMUNAL VIOLENCE

## IV. THE RISE OF THE LOWER CASTES

## V. THE POLITICAL CULTURE (OF VOTING) IN INDIA

## VI. INDIA AND THE WORLD

# Preface

In my twenty years as an academic I have authored several books and edited numerous collections of essays. However, when I was asked by my publishers to put together my articles and chapters from my previous published works for this volume, I was faced with a different kind of dilemma, and it has taken me a significant amount of time to find a solution to it: how to establish a common thread that will link my work over the last two decades.

Though my research has spanned a wide spectrum, I have also had fairly clear-cut areas of interest. The first ten years of my career—including my doctoral work—was devoted to the study of Hindu nationalism. During the following decade, I concentrated on analysing lower caste politics, with special reference to the Dalit movement, including Dr. Ambedkar and the Ambedkarite movement. These two fields of research contribute most to this book, together with the ramifications pertaining to communal violence and the politics of pilgrimage as well as procession.

Keeping the dynamics of nationalism and caste politics in perspective, I also explored other, more or less related topics, such as Pakistan's politics and theoretical and comparative reflections on nationalism, ethnicity and democracy, which I have not included here. In the present volume I have concentrated on the functioning of India's democracy on the one hand, and the way India relates to the world on the other. The trajectory is obvious for the former since I have studied it from the point of view of its political culture where caste and religion play a major role. As far as the second theme—the way India relates to the world—is concerned, I see it as an interaction between domestic politics and foreign policy, especially when the latter is examined from a sociological perspective. While the Indo-American rapprochement harks back to some extent to the Indian middle class' fascination with the US, the affinities of the Indian diaspora in the West with Hindu nationalist movements also suggests that we cannot divorce the internal and the external dynamics any more.

I consider myself to be standing at the crossroads of history and anthropology and *Religion, Caste and Politics in India* offers a good illustration of the multidisciplinary dimensions of my methodology: carrying out fieldwork and working in the archives. At the same time, empirical research needs conceptual frameworks and I have constantly tried to test theoretical models, while building some myself—an attempt confined primarily to my books, but sometimes spilling over to shorter pieces of writing too.

Reading the articles and chapters of this volume years after having written them, I have sometimes been tempted to edit them. But I have resisted this temptation to appropriate wisdom through hindsight, and have restricted myself to making minor changes, mainly in titles and subtitles, simply to make the contents more readable. There is a certain value in staying with the original point of view, even if it seems a little skewed today and I hope the reader will share this feeling while turning the pages that follow.

Before I end, I wish to thank Savi Savarkar for allowing me to use one of his paintings for the cover of this volume. Nothing could have been more appropriate: the Brahman in the lower half recalls the pot the Dalits were made to carry around their necks. However, the Brahman is still screaming after the Dalit who does not dare to respond as yet, but prefers to look the other way as if embarrassed by so much vulgarity. The noble character is not the Brahman—who is not only losing ground, but also his temper—anymore. We are in this transitional phase that I have elsewhere termed a 'silent revolution', where religion (represented by the swastika on the Brahman's face) continues to interfere with caste, while the instrumentalization of Hinduism—especially by the proponents of Hindutva politics—is expected to submerge social divisions along caste lines.

I would also like to extend my gratitude to Yogesh Sharma who introduced me to Primus Books. This book is dedicated to my last son, Vadim who is but two years old, the only one among my four children who has not visited India yet and, of course, to Tara, my guiding star.

*Paris*                                                      CHRISTOPHE JAFFRELOT

# Acknowledgements

The author and publishers are grateful to the following copyright owners for permission to reproduce the essays in this volume. Every endeavour has been made to contact copyright owners and apologies are expressed for any omissions:

*Asian Survey* for 'Sanskritization vs. ethnicization in India: changing identities and caste politics before Mandal', appearing in Vol. 60, No. 5, September-October 2000, pp. 756–66.

*Cambridge Review of International Affairs* for 'India and Pakistan: interpreting the divergence of two political trajectories', appearing in Vol. 15, No. 2, July 2002, pp. 251–68.

*Comparative Studies of South Asia, Africa and the Middle East* for 'The Bahujan Samaj Party in north India: no longer just a Dalit party?', appearing in Vol. 18, No. 1, 1998, pp. 35–52.

Curzon Press, Richmond for 'The rise of Hindu nationalism and the marginalization of the Muslims in India today', in *The Post-Colonial States of South Asia*, eds. A. Shastri and A.J. Wilson, 2001, pp. 141–57.

C. Hurst & Co., London for 'Voting in India: electoral symbols, the party system and the collective citizen', in *Cultures of Voting: The Hidden History of the Secret Ballot*, eds. R. Bertrand, J.L. Briquet and P. Pels, 2007, pp. 78–99.

*Economic and Political Weekly* for 'Gujarat: the meaning of Modi's victory', appearing in its issue of 12 April 2008.

*India Quarterly* for 'The India-US rapprochement: state-driven or middle class-driven?', appearing in Vol. 65, No. 1, 2009, pp. 1–14.

*India Review* for 'Indian democracy: the rule of law on trial', appearing in Vol. 1, No. 1, January 2002, pp. 77–121; 'India's Look East policy: an Asianist strategy in perspective', appearing in Vol. 2, No. 2, April 2003, pp. 35–68; 'The impact of affirmative action in India: more political than socioeconomic', appearing in Vol. 5, No. 2, April 2006, pp. 173–89.

*Indian Journal of Social Science* for 'Hindu nationalism, strategic syncretism in ideology-building', appearing in Vol. 5, No. 42, August 1992, pp. 594–617.

*The Indo-British Review* for 'The genesis and development of Hindu nationalism in the Punjab: from the Arya Samaj to the Hindu Sabha (1875–1990)', appearing in Vol. 21, No. 1, 1995, pp. 3–39.

*International Political Sociology* for Christophe Jaffrelot with Ingrid Therwath, 'The Sangh Parivar and the Hindu diaspora in the west: what kind of "long-distance nationalism"?', appearing in Vol. 1, No. 3, September 2007, pp. 278–95.

*The Journal of Asian Studies* for 'The rise of the Other Backward Classes in the Hindi belt', appearing in Vol. 59, No. 1, February 2000, pp. 86–108.

L'Ecole Française d'Extrême Orient for 'Militant Hindus and the conversion issue (1885-1990): from *shuddhi* to *dharm parivartan*: politicization and diffusion of an "invention of tradition"', in *The Resources of History, Tradition and Narration in South Asia*, ed. J. Assayag, 1999, pp. 127–52.

Manohar Publishers (New Delhi) for 'The Hindu nationalist movement in Delhi: from "locals" to refugees—and towards peripheral groups?', in *Delhi: Urban Space and Human Destinies*, eds. V. Dupont, E. Tarlo and D. Vidal, 2000, pp. 181–204.

M.E. Sharpe for 'The subordinate castes' revolution', in *India briefing: Quickening the pace of change*, eds. A. Ayres and P. Oldenburg, 2002, pp. 121–58.

*Mondes* for 'The cardinal points of Indian foreign policy', appearing in No. 1, Autumn 2009, pp. 200–11.

*Nations and Nationalism* for 'The Hindu nationalist reinterpretation of pilgrimage in India: the limits of *yatra* politics', appearing in its issue of 2008, pp. 1–19.

Oxford University Press (New Delhi) for 'The idea of the Hindu race in the writings of Hindu nationalist ideologues in the 1920s and 1930s: a concept between two cultures', in *The concept of race in South Asia*, ed. P. Robb, 1995, pp. 327–54; 'The politics of processions and Hindu-Muslim riots', in *Community conflicts and the state in India*, eds. A. Kohli and A. Basu, 1998, pp. 58–92; 'Hindu nationalism and democracy', in *Transforming India: Social and Political Dynamics of Democracy*, eds. F. Frankel, Z. Hasan, R. Bhargava and B. Arora, 2000, pp. 353–78; 'The Vishva Hindu Parishad: a nationalist but mimetic attempt at federating the Hindu sects', in *Charisma and Canon: Essays on the Religious History of the Indian Subcontinent*, eds. V. Dalmia, A. Malinar and M. Christof, 2001, pp. 388–411; 'From Indian territory to Hindu *bhoomi*: the ethnicization of nation-state mapping in India', in *The Politics of Cultural Mobilization in India*, eds. John Zavos, Andrew Wyatt and Vernon Hewitt, 2004, pp. 197–215; 'Introduction', in *The Sangh Parivar: A Reader*, ed. C. Jaffrelot, 2005, pp. 1–22.

Penguin India (New Delhi) for 'The BJP in Madhya Pradesh: networks, strategies and power', in *Hindus and Others: the question of identity in India today*, ed. G. Pandey, 1993, pp. 110–45.

Permanent Black (New Delhi) for 'Introduction: The invention of an ethnic nationalism', in *Hindu nationalism: A Reader*, ed. C. Jaffrelot, 2006 and 2007, pp. 3–26.

Routledge, London for 'The 2002 pogrom in Gujarat: the post-9/11 face of Hindu nationalist anti-Muslim violence', in *Religion and violence in South Asia*, eds. J. Hinnels and R. King, 2006, pp. 173–92; 'Introduction', in *Rise of the plebeians? The changing face of Indian legislative assemblies*, eds. Christophe Jaffrelot and Sanjay Kumar, 2009 (Coll. 'Exploring the political in South Asia'), pp. 1–23; Christophe Jaffrelot with Waheguru Pal Singh Sidhu, 'Does Europe matter to India?', in

*European Security in a Global Context: Internal and External Dynamics,* ed. Thierry Tardy, 2009.

Sage (New Delhi) for 'The changing identity of the Jats in north India: kshatriyas, *kisans* or backwards?', in *Thinking social science in India: essays in honour of Alice Thorner,* eds. Jasodhara Bagchi, Sujata Patel and Krishna Raj, 2002, pp. 405–21; 'Composite culture is not multiculturalism: a study of the Indian Constituent Assembly debates', in *India and the Politics of Developing Countries: essays in Memory of Myron Weiner,* ed. A. Varshney, 2004, pp. 126–49; 'The BSP in Uttar Pradesh: party of the Dalits or of the Bahujans—or catch-all-party?', in *The Dalits of India,* ed. M. Sebastian, 2007, pp. 260–86; '"Why should we vote?": the Indian middle class and the functioning of the world's largest democracy', in *Patterns of middle class consumption in India and China,* eds. C. Jaffrelot and P. Van der Veer, 2008, pp. 35–54.

*SAMAJ* for 'Hindu nationalism and the (not so easy) art of being outraged: the *Ram Setu* controversy', appearing in its special issue, No. 2, '"Outraged Communities": Comparative Perspectives on the Politicization of Emotions in South Asia' (http://samaj.revues.org/document1372.html).

Till the final proof stage the copyright permission for some of the above had not arrived. If and when they do, we shall mention the courtesy extended by them as well.

CHRISTOPHE JAFFRELOT

# Introduction: India's twenty-first century began in the 1990s

It is usual for historians of Europe to assert that the twentieth century began in 1914, with the traumatic event that was the First World War. And for the commentators of the American affairs, the infamous 9/11 is the marker for the official commencement of the twenty-first century, even though the event took place one year into the new century. In India, I am prepared to argue that the twenty-first century was born ten years earlier. Indeed, the 1990s, the decade during which most of the essays reproduced in this book have been written, appear as the major turning point in India's post-independence history. The 1990s was the time when the Nehruvian model was put into question in a more decisive manner than never before. The Nehruvian model which persisted till the 1980s relied on four pillars: (1) state-driven economy, (2) secular but, (3) conservative democracy, and (4) non-alignment (with some pro-USSR tilt after the 1970s). These pillars have been revisited in one way or another in the 1990s.

While the Constitution of India, promulgated in 1950, did not refer to 'socialism'—the word was introduced in its Preamble in 1976—Nehru, Indira Gandhi and the left-wing of the Congress, in the 1950s and 60s, believed in a combination of fabianism and socialism that led to the nationalization of key sectors of the economy (including the banks and insurance companies), the creation of the Planning Commission, the regulation of the private sector through the 'licence raj', protectionism and the rejection of multinationals. Certainly the Indian economy was not state-owned, but it was state-driven.

So far as the political regime is concerned, the Constituent Assembly opted not only for the parliamentary brand of democracy that the political elite had been initiated into during the British Raj, but also granted equal rights to its citizens and recognized (almost)[1] all religious and linguistic communities. In the 1950s this orientation translated into linguistic federalism and in 1976 the Indian Republic was not only officially associated to socialism, but also secularism, the word being introduced in the Preamble of the Constitution. However. the democracy of India was not as progressive as the terms of the Constitution suggested since the Nehruvian system relied far too heavily on the *Congress* system, a fundamentally conservative socio-political construct. Certainly, Nehru and after him Indira Gandhi, embodied leftist principles at the top, but many regional barons—including Chief Ministers—were staunch conservatives—and in any case, to win elections, the Congress needed the support of local notables who did not favour social reforms at all. As a result, land reform remained unachieved and the social profile of the political class retained its original elitist character for decades.

Being a socialist (or rather social-democratic) and a multicultural parliamentary democracy, India, as the first decolonized free country of Asia, charted its own path in the world that was unique in many ways. It valued its liberty so much that it could not be part of the communist camp, and it resented inequality and dominance (resulting particularly from imperialism) to such an extent that it could not join hands with the US either. India became the torch-bearer of the Non-Aligned Movement (NAM) not only because of this neither-nor approach, but also because it believed it had a message for the world drawing from Mahatma Gandhi's legacy. This Third-Worldly equidistance was somewhat tarnished by India's pro-Soviet tilt in the 1970s in reaction to the US-Pakistan-China rapprochement, but also because of Indira Gandhi's socialist credo.

The mainstays of state-driven economy, secularism, the political hegemony of traditional elites and the anti-American defence of non-alignment, which began to erode in the 1980s, were practically wiped out in the 1990s and after. In 1990–2 a number of symbolic events occurred in quick succession which significantly altered the old Nehruvian legacy: the 'Mandal affair', the demolition of the Babri Masjid in Ayodhya, economic liberalization and the India-US rapprochement. These are the issues around which this book is built. This introduction provides me an opportunity to discuss how these developments pertaining to different spheres are interconnected and also to update the analysis of the subsequent chapters.

## From the Rise of the OBCs to the Dalitization of Indian Politics

In August 1990, Prime Minister V.P. Singh announced the implementation of the Mandal Commission Report which had recommended that 27 per cent of the jobs in the state administrations and the Public Sector Undertakings (PSUs) should be reserved for the lower castes belonging to the Other Backward Classes. This decision to boost positive discrimination resulted in massive protests from upper caste students who objected to the shrinking of their opportunities. It was precisely a turning point in terms of the democratization of Indian politics since the 'Mandal affair' forced the lower castes to join hands in order to defend their common interests as OBCs against the resistance of the upper castes. By the turn of the 1990s, OBCs tended to vote together and for their own people, leading to a plebeianization of politics symbolized by the rise to power of Mulayam Singh Yadav in Uttar Pradesh and Laloo Prasad Yadav in Bihar. The former became Chief Minister for the first time in 1989, the latter in 1990. But their reign—labelled the 'Yadav raj' by the media—ended in the first decade of the century, at a time when the 'OBC phenomenon' began to decline. The Other Backward Classes are an administrative category which made common political cause when the castes composing these 'classes' joined hands and formed political parties to defend their interests. But this sense of urgent solidarity eroded when mainstream parties began to endorse their claims.

## FROM MANDAL I TO MANDAL II

Gradually, the Congress appropriated the post-Mandal agenda, as is evident from its policy regarding reservations in the university system. To begin with, this new concern of the ruling party was brought in partly by the United Progressive Alliance's (UPA's) partners, including the communists. The Common Minimum Programme that the components of the new coalition negotiated after the 2004 elections stated: 'The UPA Government is very sensitive to the issue of affirmative action, including reservations in the private sector.'[2] But instead of pushing the very delicate private sector dimension of this issue, the Manmohan Singh government began to focus on the one aspect of the Mandal Commission Report that had been ignored so far. Mandal had not only recommended a 27 per cent quota in jobs of public sector, but also 'in all scientific, technical and professional institutions run by the Central as well as State Governments' (Government of India 1980: 59). On 5 April 2006, Arjun Singh, the Human Resource Development Minister announced that he was in favour of reservations for the OBCs in the universities, the IITs and the IIMs (Ramakrishnan 2006). Other heavyweights of the governments—including Kapil Sibal—expressed reservations and an Oversight Committee, whose president was Veerappa Moily, was formed to finalize the reforms as well as an ad hoc Group of Ministers (GoM) was set up. The Central Educational Institutions (Reservations in Admission) Bill which was concocted by these bodies was not as radical as the leftist had planned. Reservations were not to be implemented in the private institutions and the universities, IIMs and IITs would have three years to adjust to the new rules of this game (especially to expand their capacity by 54 per cent so as not to penalize the non OBC/SC/ST students). Some institutions, like the Mumbai-based Homi Bhabha National Institute would permanently remain out of its perimeter, but one more step towards the systematization of reservations in favour of the OBCs had been taken.

## THE DECLINE OF OBC SOLIDARITY

In spite of these successes, but also because of them since there were no battles left to fight, the political unity of OBCs has decreased after Mandal I. Moreover, the OBC sense of solidarity was affected by the tactical moves of the mainstream parties and by the increase of *jati*-based rivalries. The Congress and the Bharatiya Janata Party (BJP), upper caste-dominated national parties, became adept at co-opting OBC leaders or at promoting those they already had in their ranks, as is evident from the following examples. In Rajasthan, Ashok Gehlot, a Mali, was made chief minister after the 1998 and 2008 state elections. In Madhya Pradesh, all the BJP chief ministers have been OBCs since 2003: Uma Bharti, Babulal Gaur, Shivraj Singh Chauhan. This strategy stands in stark contrast to the situation prevailing in Uttar Pradesh where the party was handicapped by the reluctance of the upper caste lobby—made of Kalraj Mishra, Lalji Tandon and Rajnath Singh— to let the most popular OBC leader of the BJP, Kalyan Singh become the strongman of the party.

Besides rivalries between upper castes and lower castes within national parties, the OBC *jatis* lost their post-Mandal strategic unity in the late 1990s. In Uttar Pradesh, where the Lodhs traditionally supported the BJP, the Yadavs and the Kurmis tended to join hands with Mulayam Singh Yadav's Samajwadi Party. This rapprochement could not withstand the appeal of the Bahujan Samaj Party (BSP) to the Kurmis and by Beni Prasad Varma, one of Mulayam's Kurmi lieutenants, shifting his loyalty to the Congress. In Bihar, the political divorce between the Kurmis and the Yadavs took a more dramatic turn when the Janata Dal disintegrated: Laloo Prasad Yadav formed the Rashtriya Janata Dal while Nitish Kumar, a Kurmi leader, joined hands with the Janata Dal (United). The JD(U), not only became the arch-rival of the RJD but also an ally of the upper caste dominated BJP. This coalition won power for the first time in 2005, sealing the fate of Laloo's plebeian politics.

The Yadavs tried to revive the lure of the Mandal years, two decades later, when they initiated a fourth front during the 2009 general elections—which failed miserably—and even more clearly when they launched a transparty OBC protest against the Congress project of reserving 33 per cent of the Lok Sabha seats for women in 2010. This move too was short-lived.

OBC politics is certainly declining compared to the late 1990s, but let us repeat that this is to some extent because its promoters are victims of their successes and because the Congress and the BJP have been forced not to ignore the lower castes any longer.

## THE COMING OF AGE OF AMBEDKARISM?

While OBC politics seems to be on the wane, the Dalit-dominated party that is the BSP continues its march forward. Certainly, the party has resorted to many tactical devices to rise to power. First, it has made alliances with politicians sharing no ideological affinities with Ambedkarism, be they from the Congress or the BJP. Second, it has tapped the plus vote of the upper castes by nominating a large number of Brahman and Vaishya candidates at the time of elections, a tactic which enabled the BSP chief, Mayawati, to win an absolute majority in 2007 in Uttar Pradesh. But beyond these stratagems, the main lesson one may draw from the last two decades of continuous growth of the BSP lies in its capacity to remain first and foremost a Dalit party.

In its most important state, Uttar Pradesh, the BSP is no longer the party of a single *jati* only. Here, it can be called a Dalit party because it not only attracts 85 per cent of the Jatavs, but also 64 per cent of the second largest Dalit *jati*, the Pasis (or Dusadhs) and 61 per cent of the other Dalit *jatis*. As a whole, the Dalit support for the BSP registered an 8 percentage points increase in UP. This is a new development in a state where non-Jatav Dalit groups used to vote massively for the Congress and even the BJP (for example, the Balmikis).

As is evident from Tables 1 and 2, the BSP—which has become the third largest political party in India, coming in before the CPI(M)—has consolidated its position within the Dalits. It now attracts large portions of caste groups which used to vote for mainstream parties or the Republican Party of India (RPI) (like the Buddhists in Maharashtra). While the OBC phenomenon prompted drastic adjustments within the Congress and the BJP in the 1990s, the rise of the Dalits has already led the ruling party to include ten Scheduled Castes members in Manmohan Singh's second government. Whether such a tactic will succeed in bringing back Dalit voters to the Congress fold remains to be seen.

TABLE 1: PERCENTAGE OF VOTES POLLED BY THE BSP
IN SEVEN GENERAL ELECTIONS

| Year | Candidates | Winning candidates | % of valid votes |
| --- | --- | --- | --- |
| 1989 | 246 | 3 | 2.07 |
| 1991 | 231 | 2 | 1.61 |
| 1996 | 117 | 11 | 3.64 |
| 1998 | 251 | 5 | 4.7 |
| 1999 | N.A. | 14 | 4.2 |
| 2004 | 435 | 19 | 5.33 |
| 2009 | 500 | 21 | 6.17 |

*Sources:* Election Commission of India 1990: 7; n.d.: 9; 1996; Narasimha Rao and Balakrishnan 1999; Yadav and Kumar 1999: 120–6; and Yadav and Palshikar 2009: 33.

TABLE 2: THE DALIT VOTES FOR THE BSP IN SEVEN STATES

| States | Dalit votes (%) |
| --- | --- |
| Chhattisgarh | 27 |
| Delhi | 23 |
| Haryana | 57 |
| Madhya Pradesh | Jatavs: 27 |
| | Other Dalits: 6 |
| Maharashtra | Mahars: 15 |
| | Buddhist Dalits: 37 |
| | Other Dalits: 9 |
| Punjab | 21 |
| Uttar Pradesh | Jatavs: 85 |
| | Pasis: 64 |
| | Other Dalits: 61 |

*Source:* Verma 2009.

The first lesson one may draw from the most recent developments on the Indian political scene pertains to the continuation of the democratization of Indian politics that had started in the 1990s and that has probably been the most important achievement of the last 20 years.

## From Hindu Nationalist Mobilization to Marginalization of the Religious Minorities—Towards an Ethno-democracy

On 6 December 1992, the Ayodhya movement reached its culmination point with the demolition of the Babri Masjid by Hindu nationalist activists who had the blessings—and probably much more—of BJP leaders. Almost 20 years later, this unlawful act, which has remained unpunished, stands as a powerful symbol of the communalization of the Indian nation. The Nehruvian system was accused of being 'pseudo-secularist' by Hindu nationalists because of the way the minorities were 'pampered' by Nehru, Indira Gandhi and her son Rajiv. Post-1990s, India has become, to some extent, an ethno-democracy given the impact of Hindu majoritarianism, which has reduced certain religious minorities to the status of second class citizens. This is evident from the fact that most of the communal riots which took place in the 1990s (particularly in Gujarat and Orissa—against the Christians in the latter state—during the following decade) never resulted in truly convincing legal action, the inquiry commissions being either politically motivated or useless.

The relation between Mandal and Mandir is now well-established: the movement in favour of the (re)building of the Ram Temple (Mandir) was largely a reaction to Mandal, aiming to reunite a Hindu community that had been divided along caste lines by the reservation issue. Not only was Advani's *Rath yatra*, in September 1990, intended to dilute the impact of V.P. Singh's announcement the month before, but the communal riots which proliferated in the late 1980s-early 1990s (see Table 3) were supposed to crystallize collective identities along religious lines, low caste Hindus and Dalits, especially, being subcontracted for the killing and looting of Muslims in large numbers. This polarization of the Indian society contributed to the electoral success of the BJP in the late 1990s. After that, except in some states like Gujarat where Modi reactivated the politics of fear among the Hindus for electoral reasons, communal violence was probably no longer required and the ruling BJP was, anyway, more anxious to show that it knew how to maintain law and order after 1998, when it came to power for the first time at the Centre.

Not only did communal riots cease to be the order of the day—except in Gujarat—but when the BJP lost power in 2004 and the Congress-led UPA formed the government, it seemed bound to restore the secular politics of the yesteryears. Certainly, the saffronization of the state—including education—is not on the agenda of the ruling elite any more, but the minorities continue to suffer—especially in the BJP-ruled states like Gujarat, but not only. The Christians of Orissa have

TABLE 3: HINDU/MUSLIM RIOTS IN POST-INDEPENDENCE INDIA

| Year | Number of riots | | Number of deaths | |
|------|------------------------------|----------------------------------------|-------------------|-------------------------------|
| | *Various sources (see below)* | *Varshney-Wilkinson dataset[3]* | *Various sources* | *Varshney-Wilkinson dataset* |
| 1950 | | 50 | | 167 |
| 1951 | | 7 | | 10 |
| 1952 | | 13 | | 7 |
| 1953 | | 23 | | 27 |
| 1954 | 83 | 17 | 34 | 10 |
| 1955 | 72 | 13 | 24 | 12 |
| 1956 | 74 | 12 | 35 | 29 |
| 1957 | 55 | 11 | 12 | 8 |
| 1958 | 41 | 2 | 7 | 0 |
| 1959 | 42 | 1 | 41 | 0 |
| 1960 | 26 | 10 | 14 | 13 |
| 1961 | 92 | 32 | 108 | 112 |
| 1962 | 60 | 16 | 43 | 27 |
| 1963 | 61 | 4 | 26 | 8 |
| 1964 | 1,070 | 34 | 1,919° | 146 |
| 1965 | N.A. | 6 | N.A. | 6 |
| 1966 | 133 | 8 | 45 | 33 |
| 1967 | 209 | 14 | 251 | 56 |
| 1968 | 346 | 10 | 133 | 55 |
| 1969 | 519 | 38 | 674 | 718 |
| 1970 | 521 | 33 | 298 | 216 |
| 1971 | 321 | 10 | 103 | 28 |
| 1972 | 240 | 11 | 70 | 33 |
| 1973 | 242 | 14 | 72 | 35 |
| 1974 | 248 | 14 | 87 | 21 |
| 1975 | 205 | 10 | 33 | 15 |
| 1976 | 169 | 3 | 39 | 0 |
| 1977 | 188 | 10 | 36 | 17 |
| 1978 | 219 | 27 | 108 | 76 |
| 1979 | 304 | 6 | 261 | 124 |
| 1980 | 427 | 38 | 375 | 203 |
| 1981 | 319 | 22 | 196 | 105 |
| 1982 | 474 | 44 | 238 | 98 |
| 1983 | 500 | 26 | 1,143# | 84 |
| 1984 | 476 | 44 | 445 | 342 |
| 1985 | 525 | 42 | 328 | 158 |
| 1986 | 764 | 108 | 418 | 243 |
| 1987 | 711 | 75 | 383 | 230 |
| 1988 | 611 | 14 | 223 | 88 |
| 1989 | 706 | 48 | 1,155 | 521 |

TABLE 3 (*continued*)

| Year | Number of riots | | Number of deaths | |
|------|------------------|------------------|------------------|------------------|
| | *Various sources* (see below) | *Varshney/Wilkinson dataset*[3] | *Various sources* | *Varshney/Wilkinson dataset* |
| 1990 | 1,404 | 107 | 1,248 | 596 |
| 1991 | 905 | 41 | 474 | 161 |
| 1992 | 1,991 | 76 | 1640 | 1,337 |
| 1993 | 2,292 | 32 | 952 | 750 |
| 1994 | 179 | 9 | 78 | 35 |
| 1995 | 40 | 7 | 62 | 11 |
| 1996 | 728 | | 209 | |
| 1997 | 725 | | 264 | |
| 1998 | 626 | | 207 | |
| 1999 | N.A. | | N.A. | |
| 2000 | 26 | | 23 | |
| 2001 | 34 | | 52 | |
| 2002 | 21* | | 2,032** | |
| 2003 | 52 | | 21 | |
| 2004 | 11 | | 34 | |
| 2005 | 45 | | 31 | |
| 2006 | 28 | | 31 | |
| 2007 | 27 | | 17*** | |
| 2008 | 28 | | 152**** | |
| 2009 | 28 | | 23 | |

|  |  |
|---|---|
| * | The Gujarat violence is considered here as one riot only. |
| ** | Including 2,000 casualties in Gujarat. |
| *** | Anti-Christian riots that occurred in Kandhamal District and that claimed 12 lives are not counted here. |
| **** | Anti-Christian riots that occurred in Kandhamal District and that claimed more than 50 lives are not counted here. |
| # | Including Nellie riots in Assam. |
| ° | Including 985 casualties in Orissa. |
| *Sources:* | For 1954-85, Brass 1990: 168; for 1986-8, figures released by the government in Parliament and published in *India Today*, 15 October 1990: 24 and 15 January 1991: 26; for 1989 and 1990, see *National Mail* (Bhopal), 18 July 1991; for 1991 and 1992, *Muslim India* 1994; for 1993 and 1994, *Muslim India* 1995: 558; for 1995, Engineer 1995: 3267-9; for 1996, 1997 and 1998, see *Muslim India* 1999: 161; for 2000, Engineer 2001; for 2001, Engineer, see http://www.indianmuslims.info; for 2002, Engineer 2003: 280-2; for 2003, Engineer 2004: 15-18; for 2004, Engineer 2004: 1241-3; for 2005, see Indian Social Institute (http://www.isidelhi.com); for 2006, Engineer, see PUCL Bulletin at http://www.pucl.org/Topics/Religion-communalism/2007/review.html; for 2007, see Engineer at http://indianmuslims.in/communal-riots-report-2007; for 2008, see Engineer, 'Communal Riots 2008' at http://indianmuslims.in/communal-riots-2008; for 2009, see Engineer, 'Communal Riots 2008' at http://www.sacw.net/article1315.html. |

Nota Bene: Krishna 1985: 71, Saksena 1990, Rajagopal 1987.

been at the receiving end of the Hindu militants and the Muslims suffer from an increasingly institutionalized marginalization.

## THE BAJRANG DAL MILITIA AND THE CHRISTIANS*

In spite of the Congress being back in office, Hindu activists working in armed militias continue to harass the minorities. The Bajrang Dal, the militant wing of the Vishva Hindu Parishad, is a case in point. Its activists attacked Christians in Orissa on a large scale in 2008. The situation was already tense when, in December 2007, tribal Christians decided to erect a Christmas Gate in front of a Hindu place of worship in a village called Brahmanigaon. The local Hindus, a minority, alerted the VHP leader, Swami Laxmananda Saraswati, who rushed to the place. His car was attacked by Christian tribals and the clashes left 10 dead. Eight months later, on 23 August 2008, the Swami's ashram was celebrating Janmasthami when about 30-40 assailants wearing masks attacked the place with revolvers and four AK-47. They killed the Swami and 4 of his aides and disciples. The VHP and the Bajrang Dal orchestrated a retaliation which resulted in the killing of 9 people, the demolition of 30 churches and orphanages (*The Times of India*, 28 August 2008), the burning of 300 villages and the destruction of 4,104 houses of Christian families. About 50,000 Christians left their homes to seek shelter in relief camps in cities (*The Statesman*, 7 September 2008). The Hindutva militants then declared that only refugees who converted to Hinduism would be allowed to return to their villages (*The Indian Express*, October 2008).

## THE MARGINALIZATION OF THE MUSLIMS

The general impression that the Muslim community was seriously losing ground gained momentum at the turn of the century after the unprecedented wave of communal riots of the 1990s, the rise to power of Hindu nationalist forces in 1998 and the Gujarat pogrom of 2002. In June 2005, one year after the Congress-led coalition, the UPA, took over from the BJP-led NDA, Prime Minister Manmohan Singh appointed a High Level Committee to report on the situation of the Muslim minority and suggest remedies for its deteriorating condition. This was an unprecedented move, reflecting a sense of urgency. So far, only Scheduled Castes, Other Backward Classes (which turned out to be castes too) and tribes had been surveyed in this fashion. The report that was submitted by the committee—that came to be called 'the Sachar Committee' after its chairperson—showed that only 8 per cent of urban Muslims were part of the formal sector whereas the national

---

*This section draws from 'The Militias of Hindutva: Communal Violence, Terrorism and Cultural Policing', in *Armed Militias of South Asia: Fundamentalists, Maoists and Separatists*, ed. Laurent Gayer and Christophe Jaffrelot, London: Hurst, New York: Columbia University Press, New Delhi: Foundation Books, 2009, pp. 199–236.

average was 21 per cent for Indian city dwellers (*Social, Economic and Educational Status of the Muslim Community of India: A Report* 2006: 91–6) and that Muslims were also poorer than average Indians. According to a survey conducted by the National Sample Survey Organization, the average monthly expenditure of urban Muslims was Rs. 800 a month; that is, the same as that of the Dalits and *adivasis* and much less than that of upper caste Hindus (Rs. 1,469). The Sachar Committee Report made seventeen-page-long recommendations and included the following: 'Incentives to private sector to encourage diversity in the work force' (ibid.: 242) and efforts 'to increase the employment share of Muslims amongst the teaching community, health workers, police personnel, bank employees and so on' (ibid.: 252). The only precise recommendation, perhaps, was the following: 'A special assistance package for the development of these districts (where Muslims are more than 25 per cent) should be launched' (ibid.: 250). No substantial measure has been implemented so far.

In addition to socio-economic decline, the Muslims of India also suffer from political marginalization. In the Lok Sabha, their under-representation is more and more evident (see Table 4). In 1980, the percentage of Muslim MPs in this assembly was almost proportional to their share in the population (9 per cent compared to 11.4 per cent according to the 1981 census). Then they experienced a steady erosion which accelerated from the late 1980s till the late 1990s, when the BJP-led NDA (which did not appoint many Muslim candidates) came to power. Things started to improve significantly in 2004 with the electoral defeat of the BJP. But in 2009, the percentage of Muslim MPs decreased again in spite of the electoral victory of the Congress-led UPA. The situation, in fact, is as bad as it was in the late 1990s when Muslim MPs represented only 5.1 per cent of the house members, whereas Muslims constituted 12.1 per cent of the Indian population according to the 1991 Census. Today Muslim MPs make up 5.5 per cent of Lok Sabha MPs, whereas Muslims comprise 13.4 per cent of the population according to the 2001 census.

TABLE 4: Muslims Among Lok Sabha MPs Since 1980

| Year | Seats | Muslim candidates | Muslim MPs | Percentage of the MPs | Success rate (%) |
|------|-------|-------------------|------------|-----------------------|------------------|
| 1980 | 542 | 131 | 49 | 9 | 37 |
| 1984 | 542 | 123 | 46 | 8.4 | 37 |
| 1989 | 543 | 133 | 33 | 6 | 25 |
| 1991 | 543 | 149 | 28 | 5.1 | 19 |
| 1996 | 543 | 140 | 28 | 5.1 | 20 |
| 1998 | 543 | 146 | 28 | 5.1 | 19 |
| 1999 | 543 | 175 | 32 | 5.8 | 18 |
| 2004 | 543 | 168 | 35 | 6.4 | 21 |
| 2009 | 543 | 832 | 30 | 5.5 | 3.6 |

*Sources*: Hasan 2008: 257 for 1980–2004 and Election Commission of India for 2009.

A state-wise survey shows that states like Gujarat, Jharkhand, Karnataka, Delhi, Rajasthan, and, last but not least, Maharashtra do not have even one Muslim MP.[4] The situation is fairly similar in state assemblies, none of them having the same percentage of Muslims MLAs as they have of Muslim voters. Their deprivation rate is below 20 per cent, on an average over the period 1952–2004, but it is above 50 per cent in Rajasthan, Andhra Pradesh, Maharashtra, Madhya Pradesh, and Karnataka. It is 79.27 per cent in Gujarat (Ansari 2006: 370).

At the local level, the Muslims of India are also experiencing a process of ghettoization which began to accelerate with the wave of communal riots in the 1990s. Not too long ago they embodied the urban core of great cities—Hyderabad, Ahmedabad, Bhopal, etc.—but today either these old cities are crumbling or the Muslims are leaving them out of fear, to set up ghettoes at the periphery, like in Juhapura (Ahmedabad), a place that many local Hindus call 'Little Pakistan'.

## From Liberalization to Inequalities—and Naxalism

In 1991, the Narasimha Rao government—in which Manmohan Singh played a key role as minister of finance—reacted to the economic crisis that affected India by implementing ambitious liberal reforms. The public sector remained almost intact, but the 'licence raj' was dismantled, the Planning Commission lost some of its major prerogatives, import quotas and tariffs which had made India into a protectionist country were either reduced or removed completely, and the inflow of foreign investments became easier in most sectors. This liberalization policy— after some time—helped the country grow at an unprecedented rate of 7–8 per cent a year. But this new prosperity was far from being evenly distributed. The small and marginal peasants did not profit from it. Its main beneficiaries were the 'nouveaux riches' of a new kind of middle class, a social category very much interested in consuming and showing off, that was simply not part of the equalitarian Nehruvian system. For this new middle class, the liberal turn of 1991 was the right antidote to the Mandal affair: while additional quotas reduced the traditional opportunities of the upper caste elites in the public sector, the liberalization of the economy opened new ones in the private sector.

Liberalization not only led to greater social inequality, but also to the emergence of unprecedented regional disparities within states (rural areas lagging behind urbanized ones) and between states. Socio-economic maps of India, indeed, show that the gap between the southern and the western parts of India and the northern and eastern parts was widening. Map 1 is very revealing of this evolution. In 1993–4, the Indian countryside was almost uniformly poor: less than 10 per cent of the rural dwellers could afford to spend Rs. 560 or more a month. Ten years later, the only parts of India where less than 25 per cent of the peasants can spend more than Rs. 580 a month were in Bihar, Jharkhand, Orissa, Chhattisgarh,

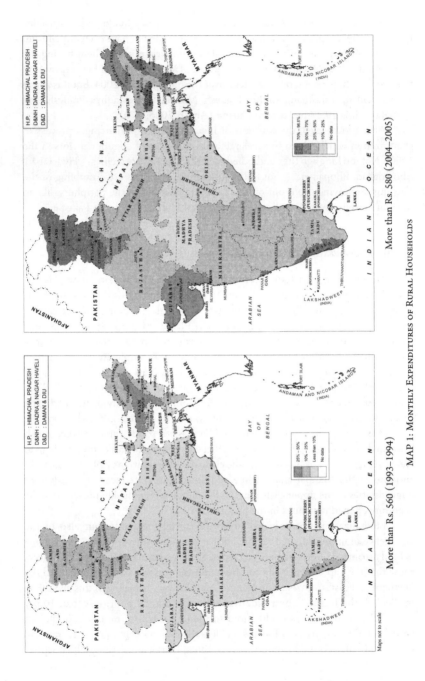

Maps not to scale

More than Rs. 560 (1993–1994)

More than Rs. 580 (2004–2005)

MAP 1: MONTHLY EXPENDITURES OF RURAL HOUSEHOLDS

and Madhya Pradesh. These were also some of the states where Naxalism has spread rapidly over the last ten years.

Not only do the maps of mass poverty and of Maoist control seem to overlap, but these large pockets of growth without development are also located in the tribal belt of India which is at the periphery of society in cultural terms but also in terms of infrastructure. Undoubtedly, the Naxalites have benefited from the lack of roads and thick forests in these areas. They could strike more easily than elsewhere, especially when big companies started to dislodge *adivasis* to exploit the rich mineral resources underground, like in Chhattisgarh and Orissa.

According to different estimates, the 'Naxals' (as they are called in the Indian media) number only about 50,000. Besides their 6,000–7,000 firearms (including some AK-47s), they use Improvised Explosive Devices (Chakravarti 2008: 3). While they killed about 500 people (mostly state officers and policemen) a year till the late 1990s, this figure doubled by the last years of the following decade (see Table 5).

TABLE 5: Casualties in the Seven States which are
the Most Affected by Maoism in India (2006–10)

| Year | 2006 | | | 2007 | | | 2008 | | | 2009 | | | 2010 (> June) | | |
|---|---|---|---|---|---|---|---|---|---|---|---|---|---|---|---|
| Categories | C* | P# | M° | C | P | M | C | P | M | C | P | M | C | P | M |
| Andhra | 18 | 7 | 127 | 24 | 4 | 45 | 28 | 1 | 37 | 10 | 0 | 18 | 6 | 0 | 5 |
| Bihar | 16 | 5 | 19 | 23 | 21 | 5 | 35 | 21 | 15 | 37 | 25 | 16 | 29 | 6 | 6 |
| Jharkhand | 18 | 47 | 29 | 69 | 6 | 45 | 74 | 39 | 50 | 74 | 67 | 76 | 35 | 11 | 18 |
| Chhattisgarh | 189 | 55 | 117 | 95 | 182 | 73 | 35 | 67 | 66 | 87 | 121 | 137 | 53 | 107 | 62 |
| Maharashtra | 13 | 3 | 33 | 9 | 2 | 8 | 2 | 5 | 7 | 12 | 52 | 23 | 6 | 2 | 1 |
| Orissa | 3 | 4 | 16 | 13 | 2 | 8 | 24 | 76 | 32 | 36 | 32 | 13 | 26 | 18 | 13 |
| West Bengal | 9 | 7 | 4 | 6 | 0 | 1 | 19 | 4 | 1 | 134 | 15 | 9 | 234 | 33 | 38 |
| TOTAL | 266 | 128 | 348 | 240 | 218 | 192 | 210 | 214 | 214 | 391 | 312 | 294 | 389 | 177 | 144 |
| TOTAL PER YEAR | 742 | | | 650 | | | 638 | | | 997 | | | 710 | | |

*Notes:* C*-Civilians; P#-Policemen and paramilitary; M°-Maoists
*Source:* South Asia Terrorism Portal, http://www.satp.org/satporgtp/countries/india/maoist/data_sheets/fatalitiesnaxal.asp (accessed on 1 July 2010).

Prime Minister Manmohan Singh has admitted that the Naxals posed the most serious threat to internal security. This devastating increase in their striking capacity is due to the increasing sophistication of their arms and also in some measure because of the way they intermingled (and sometimes even inter-marry) with tribals. Well entrenched in the tribal belts of India, the Naxals have 'liberated' new territories in the course of time. By 2004 they were present in 55 districts of 9 states (Andhra Pradesh, Bihar, Maharashtra, Orissa, Madhya Pradesh, Chhattisgarh, Jharkhand, West Bengal, and Uttar Pradesh). By 2005, the number of 'Naxal infested' districts—to use the official terminology—had risen to 76, and in 2006 to 165 (out of 602) spread over 14 states, Karnataka, Kerala, Tamil Nadu, Uttarakhand, and Haryana being the new additions (ibid.: 9–10).

In reaction to the rise of this revolutionary movement, the state has oscillated between a variety of strategies. It has allowed the formation of a private self-defence militia in Chhattisgarh, Salwa Judum, something the Supreme Court has strongly disapproved of, arguing that citizens were not supposed to become the law enforcers. It has tried to start peace negotiations, unsuccessfully so far, and finally it has had to resort to the use of force. But the deployment of troops in Chhattisgarh has resulted in many more casualties—75 Central Reserve Police Force (CRPF) men were killed in May 2010 in an ambush—without guaranteeing the needed security. India may embark on a proper counter-insurgency operation if talks fail, but that would mean years of more or less civil war in the Indian heartland.

Congressmen are aware that the only way out is development. The UPA government has already started to pay more attention to the rural poor, as evident from the passing of the National Rural Employment Guarantee Act (NREGA) in February 2006. By this Act, rural houeholds affected by umemployment are to be given work for 100 days a year or some form of financial support for 100 days. The payment should not represent less than 25 per cent of the minimum wage during the first month and not less than 50 per cent afterward. This scheme was implemented in 200 districts among the poorest sections of India during the first year, and has been extended gradually, such that it covered most of India by 2008–9, when about 45 millions jobs for an average duration of 48 days per household have been registered. In 2009–10, the NREGA budget represented Rs 39,000 crore (8 billion dollars), that is about 1 percentage point of the Indian GDP. While the central government covers three-fourths of this expenditure, the state governments—which decide the level of the allowance cover the remaining one-fourth. Undoubtedly, the NREGA has been a milestone in India's fight against rural mass poverty. But whether it means more than assistance remains to be seen. After all, development may require investments too, especially in the domain of irrigation.

## From the India-US Rapprochement to the India-US Estrangement?

Besides these domestic developments, India also made some significant diplomatic moves in the early 1990s too. While she took most of the national initiatives mentioned earlier, as far as diplomacy was concerned, she was judiciously more passive, adjusting to the major international changes of the post-cold war years. Her moves were also more discrete—almost invisible—in the initial stages. But by 1991, it was clear that India needed to distance herself from Russia and to diversify her strategic and economic partnerships. Asia was the first choice of the Narasimha Rao government, but his country was not yet welcome in the ASEAN, an organization India was able to join in 1995 in the framework of its Look East policy. Besides, India's real objective seemed to be the US, as suggested by her rapprochement with Israel, Tel Aviv being the most sensible detour to reach Washington. In 1991, India opened an embassy in Israel and vice versa, a move that had been rather downplayed at that time. Why this new craze for America? Not only because economic relations intensified with American multinationals investing massively in India, but also because the new Indian middle class was fascinated by the 'American way of life', a trend boosted by the Indian diaspora in the US—a country where many elite families sent their sons and daughters for further studies. The Indo-American rapprochement peaked during George W. Bush's second term when both countries concluded a path-breaking agreement on nuclear civil energy.

The momentum of the Indo-American relations has not been sustained after the Obama administration took over in 2009. The new American President did not pay as much attention as his predecessor to India; he seemed to be more willing to engage with China—a country much more important to the US than India from an economic point of view. Second, Obama's emphasis on de-nuclearization was bound to indispose India, which owes some of its international importance to its de facto nuclear status and which fears that the nuclear deal it made with Bush may be in jeopardy. Last but not the least, Obama, in spite of the surge in Afghanistan seems to be prepared to subcontract the war (and the peace) to Pakistan in order to start the withdrawal of American troops from that area as early as 2011. Though Indo-American relations have not been significantly damaged, they seem to have reached a plateau.

India would never be an *ally* of the US anyway—she is too particular about her sovereignty and too independent-minded. But she may look for alternatives and cultivate other relations even more actively as the US has disappointed her. It may re-launch old Indo-Russian links, not only in the military domain, but also for nuclear energy. More importantly, India may try to play a leading role among the emerging countries. It has already been one of the founder members of IBSA (a consortium organizing yearly summits which gathers together India, Brazil and South Africa). It is also an active member of BRICs—Brazil, Russia, India and China—four countries which hold a yearly summit since 2009. India is not content with joining hands with emerging countries in such fora; she does the same in multilateral contexts where these emerging countries do not spare the West. In the WTO these countries—which have otherwise diverging interests—have marred the Doha cycle with major setbacks. In Copenhagen, India joined hands with China and Brazil against the conference agenda which failed (with the tacit support, if not the active nuisance, of President Obama). More recently, instead of helping the West to isolate Iran, India maintained good relations with Tehran. This emphasis on the solidarity with other emerging countries against the West may not mean that India is back to its Third-Worldly roots. The Indian elite is too closely associated with the West to allow the reversal of gears to that extent. But this evolution may reflect the coming of age of a major power that is likely to be on its own, like any other emerging country, in the near future.

From 1990 onwards, the plebeianization of politics, the ethnicization of democracy, liberalization (cum inequalities) and the rapprochement with the US—these four developments have transformed India in less than 20 years as substantially as the Nehruvian system in the previous four or five decades. These trends tended to mutually reinforce each other, partly because they went well together (like liberalization and the rapprochement with the US), partly because they were locked in dialectic relations (like Mandir and Mandal). None of these new mainstays of contemporary India have been decisively put into question during the last ten years. However, they have started to transform themselves. First, so far as the plebeianization of politics is concerned, the distribution of accent has gradually shifted from OBCization to Dalitization and second, the ethnicization process does not rely on overt violence as much as when the BJP was on the rise or was in office at the Centre, but results in the marginalization of religious minorities, including the Muslims. In addition to this, liberalization has fostered inequalities and unleashed the appetite of the corporate sector—including the mining companies—in such a way that the Indian government has tried to mitigate its effect through corrective mechanisms like the NREGA. These were supposed to bring the state back into the picture, but have not been successful in defusing tension in the Maoist-dominated areas. And finally, though India-US relations have not deteriorated in any significant way, yet they have at least reached a plateau which has reconfirmed India in its need for further diversification of its international partnerships, especially among the emerging countries.

The transformation of these parameters will influence India's journey to modernity and power. The marginalization of Muslims may be an additional factor in the crystallization of new forms of violence (including terrorism, in relation to Pakistan-based groups). The rise of inequalities may make the Maoist problem difficult to contain. These developments may take India on the road to a security state. This scenario is not the most probable because of the resilience of the rule of law and the capacity of the political system—including the most plebeian parties—to endorse the claims of the poor, as evident from the introduction of the NREGA, which may be further extended. Hopefully, India will pursue a more balanced trajectory across the twenty-first century which—for her—has started early.

## Notes

1. A few groups have been overlooked, including minor linguistic groups and the Sikhs and the Jains who have been assimilated into Hinduism.
2. Available at <http://india.eu.org/1822.html> (accessed on 13 June 2006).
3. Varshney, Ashutosh and Wilkinson, Steven, Varshney-Wilkinson dataset on Hindu-Muslim violence in India, 1950–1995, Version 2. [Computer file]. ICPSR04342-v1.

Ann Arbor, MI: Inter-university Consortium for Political and Social Research [distributor], 2006-02-17. doi:10.3886/ICPSR04342. Based on the archives of *The Times of India* from January 1950 to December 1995. http://dx.doi.org/10.3886/ICPSR04342.
4. For a more detailed analysis, see Christophe Jaffrelot with Virginie Dutoya, Radhika Kanchana and Gayatri Rathore 2009: 43–8.

# References

Ansari, Iqbal A. (2006), *Political Representation of Muslims in India (1952-2004)*, New Delhi: Manak.

Brass, P. (1990), *The Politics of India since Independence*, Cambridge: Cambridge University Press.

Chakravarti, Sudeep (2008), *Red Sun: Travels in Naxalite Country*, New Delhi: Penguin.

Election Commission of India (1990), *Report on the Ninth General Elections to the House of the People in India, 1989*, New Delhi: Government of India Press.

——— (1996), *Statistical Report on General Elections, 1996 to the Eleventh Lok Sabha*, Vol. 1, New Delhi.

——— (n.d.), *Report on the Tenth General Elections to the House of the People in India, 1998*, New Delhi.

Engineer, A.A. (1995), 'Communalism and Communal Violence in 1995', *Economic and Political Weekly*, 23 December.

——— (2001), 'Communal Riots, 2000', *Economic and Political Weekly*, 27 January.

——— (2001), 'Communal Riots, 2001', available at <http://www.indianmuslims.info>.

——— (2003), 'Communal Riots in 2002: A Survey', *Economic and Political Weekly*, 25 January.

——— (2004), 'Communal Riots, 2003', *Muslim India*, Vol. 22, No. 2, January.

——— (2004), 'Communal Riots, 2004', *Muslim India*, Vol. 22, Nos. 11/12, November-December.

——— (2006), 'Communal Riots, 2006: A Review', *PUCL* (People's Union for Civil Liberties) *Bulletin*, available at <http://www.pucl.org/Topics/Religion-communalism/2007/review.html>.

——— (2007), 'Communal Riots, 2007', available at <http://indianmuslims.in/communal-riots-report-2007/>.

——— (2008), 'Communal Riots, 2008', Centre for the Study of Society and Secularism, Mumbai, available at <http://indianmuslims.in/communal-riots-2008/> and < http://www.sacw.net/article1315.html>.

Government of India (1980), *Report of the Backward Classes Commission, First Part*, Vols. I & II, New Delhi.

Hasan, Zoya (2008), *Politics of Inclusion: Castes, Minorities and Affirmative Action*, Delhi: Oxford University Press.

*India Today*, 15 October 1990, 15 January 1991.

Jaffrelot, Christophe with Virginie Dutoya, Radhika Kanchana and Gayatri Rathore (2009), 'Understanding Muslim Voting Behaviour', *Seminar*, No. 602.

Krishna, Gopal (1985), 'Communal Violence in India', *Economic and Political Weekly*, 12 January.

*Muslim India* (1994), No. 134, February.

———— (1995), 'Ministry of Home Affairs, Note for Consultative Committee Meeting on Communal Situation', No. 156, December.

———— (1999 ), 'Lok Sabha questions', No. 110, 23 February, reproduced in No. 196, April 1999.

Narasimha Rao, G.V.L. and Balakrishnan, K. (1999), *Indian Elections: The Nineties*, Delhi: Har-Anand.

*National Mail* (Bhopal) (1991), 'Communication from the Minister of State for Home before the Rajya Sabha', 18 July.

Rajagopal, P.R. (1987), *Communal Violence in India*, New Delhi: Uppal Publishing House.

Ramakrishnan, Voir V. (2006), 'Examining Reservation', *The Hindu*, 5 May. Available at <http://www.hinduonnet.com/fline/stories/20060505004600400.htm>.

Saksena, N.S. (1990), 'Communal Violence in India', Noida: Trishul.

*Social, Economic and Educational Status of the Muslim Community of India: A Report* (2006), Prime Minister's High Level Committee, Cabinet Secretariat, Government of India, November.

Verma, Rahul (2009), 'Dalit Voting Patterns', *Economic and Political Weekly*, 26 September, Vol. XLIV, No. 39.

Yadav, Y. and Kumar, S. (1999), 'Interpreting the Mandate', *Frontline*, 5 November.

Yadav, Y. and Palshikar, S. (2009), 'Between *Fortuna* and *Virtu*: Explaining the Congress' Ambiguous Victory in 2009', *Economic and Political Weekly*, 26 September, Vol. XLIV, No. 39.

# I

## Secularism at Stake
### The birth and rise of Hindu nationalism

# Chapter 1

# Composite culture is not multiculturalism: a study of the Indian Constituent Assembly debates

In his article on 'India's minorities', Myron Weiner refers to the American pattern of multiculturalism where 'Italian-Americans, Irish-Americans, Polish-Americans and Jews [who] once regarded themselves as minorities . . . are now seen by others (and sometimes by themselves) as "ethnics"' (Weiner 1989: 43). The terms used by Weiner recall those of Michael Walzer who used the phrase 'hyphenated Americans' to refer to the peculiar melting pot that is the United States (Walzer 1992). This pattern partly relies on affirmative action programmes, which may help 'minorities' to become 'ethnics'. More generally speaking, the Anglo-Saxon concept of multiculturalism emphasized the need of officially granting protections to underprivileged groups (Dunne and Bonazzi 1995). This is one of the institutionalized dimensions of multiculturalism. Another method for dealing with ethnic diversity in the democratic context is the consociational way, theorized by Arend Lijphart since the 1960s, and which has been recognized as one means of surmounting communal cleavages in the Netherlands and even Lebanon before the 1980s (Lijphart 1975: 129). Whether it has recourse to positive discrimination or not, multiculturalism emphasizes the need to recognize communities whose rights cannot be protected through the individually available human rights alone.

On the other hand, the French notion of national identity largely ignores the multiculturalist recipes and its implications in terms of affirmative action—even though a debate is now evolving in France on that issue because of the growing population of immigrants (Kymlicka 1989; Taylor 1994). The main objective of the French Republic is still to assimilate the allogene groups according to the famous pattern of *integration republicaine,* which implies that they give up the public manifestations of their cultural identity[1]—including the scarf for the Muslim girls attending school. The French language has also remained in a purely monopolistic position for a long time—since the 1990s regional languages are also taught in the education system but they play a very marginal role. This quest for uniformity in the public sphere has much to do with the Republican Utopia of a secularized individualism and the post-1789 discourse on equality. It goes hand in hand with the Jacobin notion of a strong, centralized State that is in charge of building a united nation (Audard 1999:116-37). Rajeev Bhargava, while he distinguishes republicanism and liberal individualism, underlines that both 'are equally blind to the importance of multiculturalism and altogether evade multicultural issues'.[2]

The Indian notion of national identity, to my mind, combines elements of both models, the multicultural one and the Jacobin one. After independence, India used a form of positive discrimination for the Scheduled Castes and Scheduled Tribes, but not for religious minorities. While religious communities were acknowledged from a cultural point of view, they were not given official recognition in social and political terms. In 1966 the Punjab was bifurcated, officially, not on the basis of religious criteria—even though it was a response to the Sikh movement—but because of linguistic considerations: the new Punjab spoke Punjabi while Haryana was looked at as part of the Hindi belt (Brass 1974). As a rule, as underlined by Myron Weiner, the 'Government of India has ... consistently refused to extend reservations to religious groups on the grounds that it would be divisive' (Weiner 1989: 67). The reluctance of the Government of India towards any official protection of the religious minorities reflected a more general attitude: its emphasis was as much on national unity as on multiculturalism. The most common phrases, during the Constituent Assembly debates were 'unity in diversity' or 'composite culture'. One can explain this reluctance vis-à-vis religious pluralism by the trauma of Partition. However, these circumstances may not explain everything. The place of the minorities in the Indian nation, as formulated by the Constituent Assembly also reflects long-term ideological trends.

## Types of Nationalism

The Indian nationalist movement, embodied since 1885 by the Indian National Congress, rapidly split into two currents. Towards the end of the nineteenth century, the Moderates and the Extremists in the Congress began putting forward conflicting definitions of the nation: the former conceived of the nation in a universalist perspective, free from any reference to ethnicity, while the latter lay claim to a prime status for the Hindu community.

After the 1920s, however, there was a further branching off of the first school of thought. Gandhi advocated the kind of multiculturalism which recognized the right of existence of all religious communities in public life. In fact, in his eyes, the Indian nation was a collection of religious communities, all on an equal footing. His views about the national flag are highly revealing in this respect:

Any nation needs a flag. . . . [In the Indian flag] the white strip would represent the other religions [other than Hinduism and Islam]. It would come first since they are in smaller numbers. The colour of Islam [green] would follow and the Hindu red [saffron] would come last to show that the strongest must protect the weak. . . . And to show that the weak is equal to the strong, the three strips would have the same size. (Gandhi 1924: 198-9)

While Gandhi represented a major variant of Indian nationalism, Nehru embodied another one. The progressive intelligentsia epitomized by Nehru, attempted to prune the role of religious communities in political life, advocating that the individual was the basic unit of the nation[3]—an outlook shared by representatives of the lower castes and particularly by the Dalit leader B.R. Ambedkar, who endeavoured to use the process of nation-building in order to challenge the hierarchical principles of a caste-based society.

The Hindu nationalists and the Hindu traditionalist wing of the Congress opposed this twofold—Gandhian and Nehruvian—current. Although less extreme than the Hindu nationalists, the Hindu traditionalists' position was characterized by the fact that it sought to protect Hindu culture in the widest sense of the term (Ayurvedic medicine, Sanskrit, etc., were thus viewed as elements of a legacy to be preserved).[4] This trend further strengthened its position as separatism gained ground amongst an increasing number of Muslims. Founded in 1906, the Muslim League succeeded in acquiring a separate electorate for the Muslims in 1909. Its leader, M.A. Jinnah further propounded the theory according to which Hindus and Muslims constituted 'two nations'. It was by virtue of this theory that the League demanded the formation of Pakistan in 1940.

In 1947, India's independence and its Partition were concurrent events. What form would nation-building assume in this context? Constituent Assembly debates revealed the intentions of the various players. The Constituent Assembly had been elected in 1946 under British rule, who saw it playing a major role in the transition towards the granting of an independent status to their colony. Debates thus spread over the entire period from 9 December 1946 to 1949, ending with the proclamation of one of the longest Constitutions in the world on 26 January 1950. All aspects of public life were covered in the debates with the national issues being at the forefront. However, the dark clouds of Partition, which took place more than eight months after the debates had begun, hovered clearly over them. Each and every current on the political scene which had evolved over the colonial period was, nonetheless, in its element and played its part. Apart from the Hindu nationalists, whose political parties seemed, in any case, fragmentary, the Gandhian representation too was fairly weak in the Constituent Assembly debates. Gandhian influence declined to a large extent after the death of the Mahatma in January 1948.

## A Paradoxical Convergence

The main players, therefore, were proponents of universalist nationalism and the Hindu traditionalists. Both groups conceded that national unity should be given greater importance than cultural diversity. The former's ideology had much in common with the traditionally dominant French view of the nation, a Jacobin ideology that is well known for its emphasis on unity and integration, as evident from Marcel Mauss' definition of the nation:

We regard as forming a nation a society materially and morally integrated, with a stable and permanent centralized political power, well established borders, a relative moral, mental and cultural unity of its inhabitants who consciously adhere to the state and its laws. (Mauss 1953 [1920]: 588)

This definition rules out the presence of any intermediary bodies, be they castes or religious communities.[5] Nehru identified with this perspective when he rejected the notion of a nation based on ethnic feelings or with religious communities, as propounded by Hindu nationalists or the Muslim League. In the mid-1930s, he had strongly criticized the ethnic brand of nationalism, while recalling the political situation in India in the 1920s:

The general Muslim outlook was thus one of Muslim nationalism or Muslim internationalism, and not of true nationalism. For the moment the conflict between the two was not apparent.

On the other hand, the Hindu idea of nationalism was definitely one of Hindu nationalism. It was not easy in this case (as it was in the case of the Muslims) to draw a sharp line between this Hindu nationalism and true nationalism. The two overlapped, as India is the only home of the Hindus and they form a majority there. It was thus easier for the Hindus to appear as full-blooded nationalists than for the Muslims, although each stood for his own particular brand of nationalism.

Third, there was what might be called real or Indian nationalism, which was something quite apart from these two religious and communal varieties and, strictly speaking, was the only form which could be called nationalism in the modern sense of the word. In this third group there were, of course, both Hindus and Muslims and others. (Nehru 1989: 720)

Thus, in Nehru's eyes, the values of individualism were an embodiment of modernity and constituted the very pillars of nationalism, while anything that smacked of tradition was further perceived as pertaining to the universe of *gemeinschaft* (as opposed to that of *gesellschaft*), and doomed to disappear.[6]

While the French, universalist brand of nationalism and the ethnic— supposedly German or 'oriental'—one are often presented as poles apart (Plamenatz 1973), they can be regarded as two versions of the same phenomenon, primarily because of their emphasis on unity. Traditional-type social bonds have no real place in ethnic nationalism, for the forging of this kind of nation implies that the accent is on the homogeneity of the group, and equality—a value of modernity—is often one of the bases for this unity. The concern for unity can certainly rely on pure organicism, on a hierarchical-type complementarity, but ethnic nationalism, more often than not, rules out any return to the old order of things.

The territorial/universalist version of nationalism and the ethnic one give both greater importance to unity as compared to the profusion of cultures and social differentiation. In this, they differ from Gandhi who sought to preserve the socio-cultural diversity of India. Certainly, the convergence of universalists *à la* Nehru and certain Hindu traditionalists must not be excessively exaggerated for they continued to oppose each other on a number of issues. Nevertheless, these two ideological poles are responsible for the emphasis placed on national unity in the Indian Constitution at the expense of a true multiculturalism as envisioned by Gandhi.

## Circumscribed Multiculturalism

### A JACOBIN REJECTION OF COMMUNITIES

The ambiguity of the allegedly universalist, modern discourse of Congress comes from the anxiety of its representatives to promote the unity of the nation. This objective took the form of rejection of communities insofar as they saw intermediary bodies as weakening national cohesion. This ambivalence was discernible in a number of Congressmen. G.B. Pant, the then chief minister of Uttar Pradesh, made a revealing speech in January 1947 before the Constituent Assembly:

It is not for me to attempt any dissertation on the various aspects of minorities or fundamental rights. I cannot however refrain from referring to a morbid tendency which has gripped this country for the last many years. The individual citizen who is really the backbone of the State, the pivot, the cardinal centre of all social activity, and whose happiness and satisfaction should be the goal of every social mechanism, has been lost here in that indiscriminate body known as the community. We have even forgotten that a citizen exists as such. There is the unwholesome, and to some extent a degrading habit of thinking always in terms of communities and never in terms of citizens (Cheers). (*Constituent Assembly Debates* [hereafter *CAD*], 1989, Vol. I: 332)

Pant establishes a strong relationship between, on the one hand, the need for the minorities—and especially the Muslims[7]—to get integrated, to merge with the nation—as individuals—and, on the other hand, the pre-condition of this process, the dissolution of the religious communities. The stress on the individualist dimension of nation-building lends itself quite naturally to a unitarian interpretation. Recognizing an undifferentiated individual as being the basis of the nation obviously implied pleading for a culturally uniform nation. B.R. Ambedkar, law minister in Nehru's government and the chairperson of the Constitution Drafting Committee, declared in the same vein: 'Our difficulty is how to make the heterogeneous mass that we have today take a decision in common and march on the way which leads us to unity' (ibid.: 101). Ambedkar extolled equality and individualist principles in the Western sense of the term. There is little place for cultural diversity and even for decentralization in the ideal of a strong nation that such leanings may generate.[8] In the same perspective, S. Radhakrishnan, later made president of the Indian Republic in 1962 by Nehru himself, suggested, that the following be included in the preamble to the Constitution:

In stating the decisions which we have made, we might add one or two sentences by way of preamble 'with a view to develop a homogeneous, secular, democratic State, the devices hitherto employed to keep minorities as separate entities within the State be dropped and loyalty to a single national State developed'. While this should be our recognized aim, we do not wish to ignore altogether our recent past, so for a period often years the following recommendations are intended to secure adequate representation for the minorities. Before we put down the decisions, let us have some introductory sentences and make it clear that it is not our desire in this House to have these minorities perpetuated. We must put an end to the disruptive elements in the State. What is our ideal? It is our ideal to develop a homogeneous democratic State. (*CAD*, 1989, Vol. V: 283)

This provision was undoubtedly aimed at the Muslims, with the result that some of Nehru's supporters joined up with the Hindu traditionalists during the debates on constitutional guarantees to be granted to the Muslim minority.

## THE PLACE OF THE MUSLIMS IN QUESTION

The birth and rapid development of the 'two-nation theory' culminating in the formation of Pakistan had always been attributed by a number of Congress members to the introduction of separate electorates by the British.[9] The Minority Committee, appointed by the Constituent Assembly to prepare minority-related articles, hastened to abolish this system.

This stance was all-received by most of the Muslim representatives, who argued that their community should be rewarded and reassured since they had chosen to remain in India rather than go to Pakistan and had suffered a great deal from the post-Partition riots. They were desperately looking for institutional protection against the overwhelming domination of the Hindu majority.[10] They demanded that the status quo be maintained as regards separate electorates, or failing that, that they be granted a system of reserved seats where only those candidates who obtained at least 35 per cent of their community's votes would be declared elected.[11] The majority opposition to these safeguards led them to support the cause of proportional representation in assemblies, in the government and administration.

In response to these demands, the Congressmen requested the Muslims to forget about their religious identity. Pant told the Muslim representatives: 'Your safety lies in making yourselves an integral part of the organic whole which forms the real genuine State' (ibid.: 223). His approach was close to that of Hindu traditionalists such as K.M. Munshi, an influential member of the Constitution Drafting Committee, who, believed that the Partition was a foregone conclusion, and declared in July 1947, 'We have now a homogeneous country. . . [*sic*]' (*CAD*, 1989, Vol. I: 546). Sardar Patel, who headed the Minority Committee, gave an even more scathing reply, indeed what were probably veiled threats, to the Muslims' demand for a separate electorate: 'Do you want now peace in this land? If so, do away with it; you can do no harm either to Pakistan or India or anything, but only you will have all over the country what is happening in this country near about us; if you do want it, you can have it' (ibid.: 226).

These words, spoken on 27 August 1947, probably alluded to the communal riots that took place at that time in India, and particularly Delhi, in which Muslims were the main victims. The debate took off again the next day when the Muslims reiterated their demand for a separate electorate. Patel's rebuttal was:

Those who want that kind of thing have a place in Pakistan, not here (Applause). Here, we are building a nation and we are laying the foundations of One Nation, and those who choose to divide again and sow the seeds of disruption will have no place, no quarter, here, and I must say that plainly enough. (Hear, Hear) (ibid.: 271)

Within the Minority Committee, Patel had not objected to a quota of reserved seats for the Muslims. Their contrariness, however, had made him regret this concession. Eventually, this clause was deleted from the Constitution draft. The crucial episodes of this story took place within the Minority Committee, where a group of people led by H.C. Mookerjee, a Christian leader, and including Rajkumari Amrit Kaur, opposed the granting of reservations to the Muslims and to the Scheduled Castes. The former moved a motion for the dropping of the clause on reservation of seats in the legislature. Unexpectedly, some Muslim members, including Tajamul Husain, a representative from Bihar, who was first in favour of reservations, had changed their mind and supported this resolution (*CAD*, 1989, Vol. III: 270). Therefore in May 1949, Patel introduced an amendment cancelling the reservation of seats for the Muslims. During the Constituent Assembly plenary session, one of the representatives from the Muslim League strongly objected that this modification did not reflect the general feeling of the Muslim community and argued:

Unity really means harmony, the adjustment of things which are different with different groups of people not only in this country but also in other parts of the world. Harmony is possible only when all sections of people are satisfied, are contended. (ibid.: 278)

But other Muslim representatives expressed dissonant views. Z.H. Lari, a socialist from Uttar Pradesh, rejected reservations because he did not want to consider the minority 'as a separate indifferent entity but as a welcome part of the organic whole' (ibid.: 283). Naziruddin Ahmad, from West Bengal considered that the demand for reservations reflected a post-Partition 'fear-complex' which was disappearing, now that 'the situation has vastly improved and is daily improving' (ibid.: 296). Tajamul Husain spoke along similar lines against any kind of protection, such as separate electorates whose demand amounted to 'asking for charity':

The majority community will never trust you then. You will never be able to exert yourself. You will be isolated, you will be treated as an alien and your position will be the same as that of the Scheduled Castes. You are not poor. Like the Scheduled Castes, you are not weak; you are not uneducated; you are not uncultured; you can always support yourself. You have produced brilliant men. So do not ask for protection or safeguard. You must have self-confidence in you. You must exert yourself. You must get into the Assembly by open competition. The times have changed. Adjust yourself. (ibid.: 334)

Such a speech exemplifies the responsiveness of minority leaders to the prospect of building a new nation along secular lines. Moreover, Nehru, the symbol of this enterprise, who had spoken just before Husain, had considered the abolition of reservations for the minority an 'historic turn in our destiny' (ibid.: 329) and strongly argued in favour of it:

[In] a full-blooded democracy, if you seek to give safeguards to a minority, and a relatively small minority, you isolate it. Maybe you protect it to a slight extent, but at what cost? At the cost of isolating it and keeping it away from the main current in which the majority is going,—I am talking on the political plane of course—at the cost of forfeiting that inner sympathy and fellow-feeling with the majority. (ibid.: 330)

Nehru and a majority of the Muslim speakers seemed to share the same project of a new India. In doing so they were forgetting about the socio-political reality: Muslims were not as poor as the Scheduled Castes in 1950, but Partition had left the community without any elite; the communal antagonism was less evident than in 1947 but the 'inner sympathy' Nehru refers to was not very prominent among the Hindu traditionalists who governed northern Indian states. We will return to these handicaps. It is sufficient to say here that they would have justified some kinds of protection which, eventually, were removed from the Constitution on behalf of the need for national unity, a concern the Universalists *à la* Nehru shared with the Hindu traditionalists.

The unexpected convergence between Jacobin Indians and Hindu traditionalists was exemplified by the debate on the protection of minority cultures. In April 1947, the Assembly had stated in a very important article: 'Minorities in every unit shall be protected in respect of their language, script and culture, and no laws or regulations may be enacted that may operate oppressively or prejudicially in this respect' (*CAD*, 1989, Vol. VII: 893). The Constitution Drafting Committee had rewritten it in the following terms: 'Any section of the citizens residing in the territory of India or any part thereof having a distinct language, script and culture of its own shall have the right to conserve the same' (ibid.). A Muslim member, Z.H. Lari, raised an objection against what he considered to be the toning down of the text (ibid: 893). Ambedkar then justified the rewording of the article (ibid.: 922) in the same terms as Hindu traditionalists like Thakur Das Bhargava, who refused even the mention of 'communities' summed up by the word 'minorities' in the original version (ibid.: 899). The debate took a bitter turn when Muslims mentioned the government's neglect of Urdu. An anonymous speaker retorted: 'You may go to Pakistan' (ibid.: 918). In the Congress benches, only Hirday Nath

Kunzru sided with the Muslims, arguing that 'The dissatisfaction of the minorities has risen to a dangerous pitch only in those countries where their just claims in respect of the preservation and promotion of their culture have been denied' (ibid.: 899).[12] Kunzru's plea was, however, to no avail.

These constitutional debates show how limited Indian multiculturalism was, particularly because the Muslims had lost the 'privileges' they had enjoyed for decades, in terms of political representation on behalf of the nation-making process. The restrictions placed on multiculturalism were largely due to the rejection of communities in the institutional framework, on the one hand, by Hindu traditionalists who considered 'communities' to be synonymous with religious minorities, and on the other, by the supporters of the Jacobin State for whom the individual constituted the basis of the nation. Nehru himself mitigated his commitment to cultural diversity in the name of national unity. His speech commenting upon the first draft of the Constitution submitted by Ambedkar was very significant in this regard:

... while it is our bounden duty to do everything we can to give full opportunity to every minority or group and to raise every backward group or class, I do not think it will be a right thing to go the way this country has gone in the past by creating barriers and by calling for protection. As a matter of fact nothing can protect such a minority or a group less than a barrier which separates it from the majority. It makes it a permanently isolated group and it prevents it from any kind of tendency to bring it closer to the other groups in the country. (ibid.: 323)

There was a definite tilting of the scales in favour of unity. On other occasions Nehru remained protective of cultural diversity as is evident from the debates on the national language, the civil code, the code of nationality and the national symbols.

## Unity in Diversity

### THE MOST UNIVERSALLY ACCEPTABLE
### NATIONAL SYMBOLS

The Indian Union, which was born with the proclamation of the Constitution on 26 January 1950, maintained the neutrality of the State against the aspirations of the Hindu traditionalists for a 'Hinduization' of the Republic. The debates on the issue of national symbols are very revealing in this perspective. Hindu traditionalists such as Seth Govind Das and H.V. Kamath wanted to call the national flag, 'Sudarshan' ('fine-looking' in Hindi and Sanskrit)—the phrase normally used to describe the *chakra* or Vishnu's disc, which is used as a weapon, and to have the Swastika, a vedic symbol par excellence, inscribed on it (*CAD*, 1989, Vol. I: 742). Seth Govind Das also wanted India to be officially called Bharat, after the first

Aryan invader in Hindu mythology (*CAD*, 1989, Vol. VII: 223) and H.V. Kamath wanted *Vande Mataram* (Salute to the Motherland) to be made the national anthem (*CAD*, 1989, Vol. I: 953). This text had first appeared in Bankim Chandra Chatterjee's novel *Anand Math* (1882) as the war song of Hindu ascetics fighting the Muslim 'invaders' in the eighteenth century. It had been sung at the 1896 Congress session incurring the ire of many a Muslim.

The debates that ensued ended in compromises which were mostly unfavourable to the Hindu traditionalists. So far as the naming of India is concerned, after long discussions (*CAD*, 1989, Vol. VII: 430–3), it was finally decided to use the well known formula of the first article of the Constitution: 'India, that is Bharat, shall be a Union of States'. Insofar as the national anthem was concerned, *Vande Mataram* was rejected in favour *Jana Gana Mana*, a composition by Rabindranath Tagore, struck up at the 1911 Congress session, which sings praises of India's unity in spite of its regional diversity.

The national flag and emblem also ended up avoiding overtly Hindu connotations. The Indian Republic drew on its Buddhist legacy, giving itself both Indian and yet neutral official symbols and thereby ensuring that no single religious community would be able to stake claims to them. The tri-coloured flag bore the *chakra* (wheel of Dharma) and the official emblem was the great Buddhist Emperor Ashoka's lion capital. Nehru took care to underline that the *chakra* was 'a symbol of India's ancient culture' (*CAD*, 1989, Vol. I: 740) and that one should not look for any cultural significance in the flag's colours. Such a stand contrasted revealingly with the position of Gandhi. S. Radhakrishnan tried to give merit to Nehru's interpretation by presenting the orange strip at the top as a symbol of renunciation, the white strip in the middle with the *chakra* as representing truth and the green strip at the bottom as an allegory of the nourishing earth (ibid.: 746). In spite of these explanations, both Christians and Muslims were delighted to see white and green respectively in the choice of colours, since, in their eyes, the flag represented the best example of Indian multiculturalism (ibid.: 749). The outcome of the debate on the definition of citizenship was, in fact, a much more substantial step forward in this direction.

## *JUS SANGUINIS* VERSUS *JUS SOLI*: TWO APPROACHES TO CITIZENSHIP

The definition of citizenship led to an intense debate on the floor of the Constituent Assembly. The draft submitted by the committee in charge of preparing a list of fundamental rights, citizenship being one of them, accorded the status of Indian citizen to whosoever was born in India. The extremely generous character of citizenship by place of birth appeared even more liberal in the context of the Partition. Because, not only did it allow refugees from Pakistan to become Indian citizens in their own right, but it also gave the right to citizenship to all those persons born in India before August 1947 (ibid.: 417). The president of the assembly, Rajendra Prasad—known for his Hindu traditionalist leanings—broke his silence to worry about a clause 'so wide that every one born in this country will be a citizen of the Union . . .' (ibid.: 423). But Patel was concerned that the slightest of leeway could, if one were to resort to citizenship by blood, lead to the introduction of a 'racial phraseology in our Constitution' (ibid.). An expert committee was asked to look into the issue, but its report was later rejected, leading to a new text that was finally submitted by the Constitution Drafting Committee. It suggested that the following would be considered Indian citizen, at the time of the proclamation of the Constitution: (*a*) A person born in India; (*b*) A person with at least one parent born in India; (*c*) A person who has been residing in India for at least five years; and (*d*) The case of persons having migrated to Pakistan at the time of Partition was considered separately. Those who returned to India before 19 July 1948 were automatically Indian, while those who returned after this date, which also marked the establishment of a residence permit system, had to apply for naturalization.

These provisions led to another very animated debate, thus making the issue of citizenship the most discussed subject after those relating to languages and ownership rights. P.S. Deshmukh, a Congress member of the assembly from central India, felt that they 'would make Indian citizenship the cheapest on earth', considering the ease with which it could be acquired (*CAD*, 1989, Vol. DC: 353). He spoke in favour of citizenship by blood suggesting that references to territory be replaced by criteria of ancestry and that Indian nationality should be granted to all Hindus and Sikhs, whatever their place of residence. He criticized the facilities being offered for naturalization, comments which were, in fact, aimed at immigrants coming from Pakistan:

. . . he might be a fifth columnist: he might have come with the intention of sabotaging Indian independence. . . . Is it wise that we should throw open our citizenship so indiscriminately? I do not see any ground whatsoever that we should do it, unless it is the specious, oft-repeated and nauseating principle of secularity of the State. I think that we are going too far in this business of secularity. Does it mean that we must wipe out our own people, that we must wipe them out in order to prove our secularity, that we must wipe out Hindus and Sikhs under the name of secularity, that we must undermine everything that is sacred and dear to the Indians to prove that we are secular? (ibid.: 354)

Deshmukh added later on that Pakistan 'was established because the Muslims claimed that they must have a home of their own and a country of their own. Here we are an entire nation with a history of thousands of years and we are going to discard it, in spite of the fact that neither the Hindu nor the Sikh has any other place in the world to go to. . . . If the Muslims want an exclusive place for themselves called Pakistan, why should not Hindus and Sikhs have India as their home?' (ibid.: 355–6).

It was, however, left to Thakur Das Bhargava, one of the pillars of the Hindu traditionalist milieu, to suggest an amendment totally at odds with the spirit of the bill. Considering that the Muslims who had migrated to Pakistan had 'forfeited their right to become citizens of this country' (ibid.: 381), he asked that access to Indian citizenship be reserved for victims of violence or for persons fearing for their security, a clause that applied a priori to Hindus who remained in Pakistan (ibid.: 383).

The following day, Nehru retaliated by first making a statement of fact: a number of 'nationalist Muslims'—as he continued to call Muslims who had not supported Pakistan's ideological drive—had crossed over the border fearing for their lives during the communal riots of 1947; those keen on returning were few in number and, in any case, the government had already started the process of granting them a residence permit; they were, thus, already here. The prime minister went on to speak about principles:

One word has been thrown about a lot. I should like to register my strong protest against that word. I want the House to examine the word carefully and it is that this Government goes in for a policy of appeasement, appeasement of Pakistan, appeasement of Muslims, appeasement of this and that. I want to know clearly what that word means. Do the honourable Members who talk of appeasement think that some kind of rule should be applied when dealing with these people which has nothing to do with justice or equity? I want a clear answer to that. If so, I would only plead for appeasement. This Government will not go by a hair's breadth to the right or to left from what they consider to be the right way of dealing with the situation, justice to the individual or the group.

Another word is thrown up a good deal, this secular State business. May I beg with all humility those gentlemen who use this word often to consult some dictionary before they use it? It is brought in at every conceivable step and at every conceivable stage. I just do not understand it. It has a great deal of importance, no doubt. But, it is brought in in all contexts, as if by saying that we are a secular State we have done something amazingly generous, given something out of our pocket to the rest of the world, something which we ought not to have done, so on and so forth. We have only done something which every country does except a very few misguided and backward countries in the world. Let us not refer to that word in the sense that we have done something very mighty. (ibid.: 400–1)

All the amendments contrary to the spirit of the initial article were withdrawn when they were put to vote. Nehru's vigilance bore fruit in yet another fundamental debate, on the question of the national language.

## THE NATIONAL LANGUAGE ISSUE

The language problem came up in the Constituent Assembly right at the beginning, when some members began speaking in vernacular languages understood by only a few of their fellow-members (*CAD*, 1989, Vol. I: 27, 833; Vol. V: 151). Out of sheer habit and for convenience's sake, the debates took place mostly in English;

but this incurred the displeasure of Hindu traditionalists like Seth Govind Das who raised the question of the language in which the Constitution should be written and he, very naturally, spoke in favour of Hindi (Austin 1972: 297; *CAD*, 1989, Vol. III: 222). This attitude provoked uneasiness amongst members from south India where Hindi was hardly spoken and where English seemed to be the preferred idiom at the national level.[13] Nehru agreed that there should be a Hindi version of the Constitution but he preferred that it be first voted in English. He strongly opposed Rajendra Prasad on this issue (Austin 1972: 285).

The controversy finally broke out in September 1949, after it had been put off a number of times in the hope of reaching a consensus, when the question of choosing the official language of the country came up. G. Ayyangar, an eminent Congress member of the Constitution Drafting Committee, proposed a compromise formula: while the official language must be Hindi in Devanagari script, English would be used at the same time at the national level for a period of 15 years which could be extended by the Parliament. India would use international figures. The country's laws would be written in English which would also be the language of the courts. A list of 13 vernacular languages concluded Ayyangar's amendment, a sure sign of respect towards regional languages. The list was preceded by a paragraph which expressed the same concern:

It shall be the duty of the Union to promote the spread of Hindi and to develop the language so as to serve as a medium of expression for all the elements of the composite culture of India and to secure its enrichments by assimilating without interfering with its genius, the forms, style and expressions used in Hindustani and in the other languages of India, and drawing, wherever necessary or desirable, for its vocabulary, primarily on Sanskrit and secondarily on other languages. (*CAD*, 1989, Vol. DC: 1,323)

The letter and spirit of the clause strongly brings to mind Nehru's views on the subject (Nehru 1989 [1946]: 54–5). There was a definite emphasis on Hindustani—a mixture of Hindi and Urdu—a language dear to Gandhi. Ayyangar's amendment quite naturally aroused opposition in the Hindu traditionalist camp which wanted a faster transition to Hindi. Seth Govind Das, P.D. Tandon—the Congress leader in Uttar Pradesh—and Ravishankar Shukla—the chief minister of Madhya Pradesh—to name only a few prominent personalities, were amongst the most aggressive. Their amendments to Ayyangar's text called for the reduction of the 15-year period to only five years, allowing the states in the Hindi-belt to use Hindi in legal texts and courts, and the use of Sanskrit figures. No mention was made of a 'composite culture' as an objective or even of regional languages. Seth Govind Das was the first to take the floor and his speech was a clear reflection of the anti-Muslim bias of the Hindu traditionalists:

I do agree that many Hindu poets and scholars have also created outstanding literature in Urdu. Despite this, I cannot help saying that Urdu has mostly drawn inspiration from outside the country. . . . It is true we have accepted our country to be a secular State but we never thought that that acceptance implied the acceptance of the continued existence of heterogeneous cultures. India is an ancient country with an ancient history. For thousands of years one and the same culture has all along been obtaining here. This tradition is still unbroken. It is in order to maintain this tradition that we want one language and one script for the whole country. We do not want it to be said that there are two cultures here. (*CAD*, 1989, Vol. DC: 1,328)

The following day, Nehru spoke at length in support of Ayyangar's amendment and gave a fitting reply to Seth Govind Das without actually naming him. As often in the past, whenever he feared a strong opposition, he relied on Gandhi's legacy to bail him out: he said it would be a betrayal of the 'Father of the Nation' not to adopt an idiom that 'should represent that composite culture which grew up in Northern India', as taught by Gandhi (ibid.: 1,411), as the official language.

People talk about culture, about Sanskriti, etc., and rightly, because a nation must have a sound basis of culture to rest itself, and as I have said that culture must inevitably have its roots in the genius of the people and in their past. No amount of copying and imitation, however good the other culture may be, will make you truly cultured because you will always be a copy of somebody else. . . . Nevertheless, when you are on the threshold of a new age, to talk always of the past and the past, is not a good preparation for entering that portal. Language is one of these issues, there are many others.

There are many types of culture. There is the culture of a nation and of a people which is important for it, there is also the culture of an age, the yuga dharma, and if you do not align yourself with that culture of the age you are out of step with it. It does not matter how great your culture is if you do not keep step with the culture of the age. . . . There is a national culture. There is an international culture. There is a culture which may be said to be—if you like—absolute, unchanging, with certain unchanging ideals about it which must be adhered to. There is a certain changing culture which has no great significance except at the moment of at that particular period or generation or age but it changes and if you stick on to it even though the ages change, then you are backward and you fall out of step with changing humanity. (ibid.: 1,412)

That was undoubtedly a barely concealed plea by Nehru in favour of English, commensurate with his universalist, nay cosmopolitan leanings. It was not, however, enough to make the champions of Hindi give up. Ravishankar Shukla immediately retaliated, while at the same time confessing his embarrassment at having to oppose Nehru who undoubtedly enjoyed great moral authority. Indeed, the roughly 400 amendments to Ayyangar's text submitted in the Assembly basically modified only four aspects of it which were nonetheless quite important— the Parliament could, 15 years after the promulgation of the Constitution, officially recognize figures originating in Sanskrit; Hindi could be used in regional courts with the approval of the President of the Republic; legal texts could be promulgated in regional languages as long as an English translation was provided; Sanskrit would be added to the 13 languages officially recognized in the initial list.

In practise, English remained the language of the elite and of inter-state relations. In 1959, Nehru, still prime minister, suggested that English remain in common use along with Hindi. In 1963, with the 1965 deadline approaching, the Parliament reviewed the issue and the Official Languages Act upheld the situation prevailing since 1950 with English becoming the 'associate official language'. After a final attempt by supporters of Hindi which spurred a number of demonstrations in south India, a 1967 amendment dispelled the fears of non-Hindi speaking states by clarifying that this arrangement would not be challenged as long as even one of them remained attached to it.

THE QUESTION OF THE CIVIL CODE

Nehru's intervention was required on yet another issue regarding the personal law of each community. Muslims had, in fact, expressed their attachment to the *Shariat* quite early in the Constituent Assembly debates. Hindu traditionalists such as K.M. Munshi were, however, in favour of a uniform civil code and invoked the need to 'consolidate and unify our personal law in such a way that the way of life of the whole country may in course of time be unified and secular' (*CAD*, 1989, Vol. I: 547).

Nehru should have been sensitive to this argument. His universalist-modernist leanings should have made him opt for the same kind of rapprochement with Hindu traditionalists as the one which took place when the question of separate electorates came up, because the same principles applied: communities should not play any role in public life. Incidentally, Nehru and Ambedkar introduced a Hindu Code Bill in the Constituent Assembly with a view to reform the Hindu customary law so as to bring it in line with Western norms. In the case of the Shariat, however Nehru preferred to let the Muslims themselves choose the path of reform at will. He feared that any action by the State may cause tension among the Muslims whom he wanted to feel at home in India since they had chosen not to go over to Pakistan (Gopal 1984: 172). Finally, Article 44 of the Constitution merely stated: 'The State shall endeavour to secure for the citizens a uniform civil code throughout the territory of India'. This very vague phrasing did not commit the State into taking any drastic action.

Nehru's tolerance was, in a sense, a victory for multiculturalism. However, it left itself open to criticism from the Hindus since the majority community's personal law had been reformed but not that of the minorities. In a way, giving the Muslims a special status with regard to the civil code seemed an attempt to balance the abolition of separate electorates. Indeed, the ruling party resorted to a sort of 'trade-off' after independence with different groups enjoying specific benefits, which it used as potential bargaining counters and which it could either threaten to withdraw or promise to enhance. In the case of the Muslims, the *Shariat* became a symbol of electoral calculations. For instance, in 1985, Rajiv Gandhi reinstated it as the source of Muslim civil law by getting a law passed in Parliament which removed the Muslim community from the ambit of the penal code clause relating to divorce. Thus, if the intent of the abolition of separate electorates was integration of the Muslims in the Indian nation, the official acknowledgement of their specific cultural character was tantamount to leading them to vote in favour of the party allegedly most deeply committed to its defence.

At first sight, the Indian Constituent Assembly debates echo the old cleavage, within the Congress Party, between two conceptions of the nation. On the one hand, Nehru, less isolated than it seemed because of his charisma and the correlative vast silent coalition behind him, embodied a liberal, individualist variety of nationalism which gained for itself the respect of minorities. On the other hand, Hindu traditionalists advocated a nation-building process that was to be based on the culture of the majority community.

We need, however, to qualify the opposition between these two camps. They do not stand in such a stark contrast when they come to the question of a religion-based multiculturalism. In fact they share the same aim, that is to exclude religious communities from the public sphere, the former in the name of individualist values and the latter by virtue of their concern to see Indian identity embodied in Hindu culture. A certain amount of overlapping thus emerges, with theoretical implications that could lead to a situation where the oft-evoked dichotomy between 'ethnicism' and 'universalism' in nationalism, if seen from a particular angle, becomes relative. In a country where one ethnic group is in majority, promoters of a secular nation-state would try to subordinate, indeed, dissolve, cultural communities, and would, in the process, receive the support of those in favour of a certain amount of ethnicity in nation-building from within the majority population. For them, the advantage of the liberal approach was, in fact, the possibility it offered to avert the perpetuation of minority communities capable of eroding national unity; and if the 'official' nationalism had no ethnic basis in the texts, it could nevertheless hold true in practice. Universalist options go hand in hand with the implementation of a form of democracy that responds to the logic of 'one man, one vote', which the cultural majorities could use to their advantage. In India's case, as undoubtedly in others, 'traditionalists' could hope that, one day, the political majority would coincide with the cultural majority or, to be more precise, that the cultural majority would also become the political majority, initially on the strength of its ethnic identity within the political sphere, and that it could then give a new direction to national life.

Even in present-day India, the confluence between universalism and ethnicism can easily be seen, especially in two demands Hindu nationalists have made. On the one hand, they are demanding that a Human Rights Commission replace the Minority Commission, an official body responsible for the protection of minorities' rights, and on the other hand, they want to promulgate a uniform civil code. These measures would help flush the communities out of the political sphere—in the name of universalist values. Such demands—the result of a political strategy, no doubt—thus substantiate the existence of an overlapping between two apparently antithetical approaches.

The convergence between the secular Jacobins and the Hindu traditionalists of the Congress that we have noticed during the Constituent Assembly debates have much in common with the French scenario where some obsessive leftist Republicans and the Nationalist right have joined hands against any cultural recognition of the Muslim culture of the immigrants. However, in France, there has never been any tradition of multiculturalism. In India, there was one, well represented by Gandhi, but it was squeezed by the two other schools of thought. Yet, it is largely to this legacy that India owed its circumscribed multiculturalism and its specific variety of secularism based, in theory at least, on the equidistance of the state vis-à-vis all the religions, something very different from the French *laïcité*.

## Notes

1. See the response of Pierre Birnbaum to Charles Taylor, in Birnbaum 1995: 129-39 and the books of Wieviorka (1996) and Amselle (1996).
2. Rajeev Bhargava (1999), 'Introducing Multiculturalism', p. 48. About liberal individualism, Bhargava convincingly argues that 'By denying the importance of practices and cultural traditions the liberal individualist is unable to even notice the systemic bias and domination of these practices' (ibid.: 49).
3. This typology draws from the one established by Gyanendra Pandey (1990). Ashutosh Varshney (1993) has suggested another typology about contemporary Indian politics; he distinguishes secular nationalism from Hindu nationalism and from separatist nationalism (the Sikh movement for Khalistan, for instance). So far as the first category is concerned, he further distinguishes Indira Gandhi's 'secular arrogance' from Rajiv Gandhi's 'secular innocence' (Varshney 1993: 247).
4. I have borrowed this definition of Hindu traditionalism from B. Graham (1990).
5. Indeed, Mauss adds that 'Everything, in a modern nation, contribute to transform its members into uniform individuals. It is as homogeneous as a primitive clan that is supposed to be made of equal citizens' (Mauss 1969: 588).
6. This approach can be found among scholars too. Louis Dumont applied a similar dichotomy in his definition of nationalism as compared to 'communalism' (religious nationalism in Nehru's words) (Dumont 1966: 378).
7. The fact that Pant hinted at the Muslims is evident from the previous paragraph of his speech: 'Let not the minorities look to any outside power for the protection of their rights. This will never help them. Let not the lesson of history be lost. It is a lesson which should be burnt deep in the hearts and minds of all minorities that they can find their protection only from the people in whose midst they live and it is on the establishment of mutual goodwill, mutual trust, cordiality and amity that the rights and interests not only of the majorities but also of the minorities depend. This lesson of history, I hope, will not be forgotten' (*CAD*, 1989, Vol. I: 332).

8. Ambedkar later declared: 'I am glad that the Draft Constitution has discarded the village [so much praised by Gandhi] and adopted the individual as its unit [in the final text tabled, of which he was the main writer]' (*CAD*, 1989, Vol. VII: 39).
9. See, for instance, the book of Rajendra Prasad, the president of the Constituent Assembly (Prasad 1947).
10. They particularly feared a reversal in legislation concerning the use of Shariat.
11. Ambedkar supported the same demand for the Scheduled Castes but had to give up because of the strong hostility of most of the Congressmen.
12. Kunzru, like Nehru, as a Kashmiri Brahman, belonged to a milieu which had traditionally served the successive rulers of north India ever since the Middle Ages and which drew a certain cosmopolitanism from this legacy (*India Who's Who*, 1970: 153).
13. T.T. Krishnamachari, from Madras, denounced the 'linguistic imperialism' of the Hindi-speaking north (in Austin 1972: 234).

## References

Amselle, Jean-Loup (1996), *Vers un multiculturalisme français: l'emprise de la coutume*, Paris: Aubier.
Audard (1999), 'French Republicanism and "Thick" Multiculturalism', in R. Bhargava, A.K. Bagchi and R. Sudarshan (eds.), *Multiculturalism, Liberalism and Democracy*, Delhi: Oxford University Press.
Austin, Granville (1972), *The Indian Constitution: Cornerstone of a Nation*, Bombay: Oxford University Press.
Bhargava, Rajeev (1999), 'Introducing Multiculturalism', in R. Bhargava, A.K. Bagchi and R. Sudarshan (eds.), *Multiculturalism, Liberalism and Democracy*, Delhi: Oxford University Press.
Birnbaum, Pierre (1995), 'Du multiculturalisme au nationalisme', *La Pensée Politique*, 3.
Brass, Paul (1974), *Language, Religion and Politics*, Cambridge: Cambridge University Press.
*Constituent Assemby Debates* (1989), Vols. I, V, VII and VIII, New Delhi: Lok Sabha Secretariat.
Dumont, Louis (1966), *Homo Hierarchicus*, Paris: Gallimard.
Dunne, Michael and Tiriano Bonazzi (1995) (eds.), *Citizenship and Rights in Multicultural Societies*, Keele: Keele University Press.
Gandhi, M.K. (1924), 'Le drapeau national', *Young India*, 13 April 1921, in M.K. Gandhi, *La Jeune Inde*, Paris: Stock.
Graham, Bruce (1990), *Hindu Nationalism and Indian Politics*, Cambridge: Cambridge University Press.
Gopal, S. (1984), *Jawaharlal Nehru*, Vol. 3, London: Jonathan Cape.
Gutman, A. (1994) (ed.), *Multiculturalism*, Princeton: Princeton University Press.
*India Who's Who 1970* (1970), New Delhi: INFA.
Jaffrelot, Christophe (2005), *Dr. Ambedkar and the Untouchables: Analysing and Fighting Caste*, New Delhi: Permanent Black.
——— (1999), *The Hindu Nationalist Movement and Indian Politics, 1925–1990s*, Delhi: Penguin India.

Kymlicka, W. (1989), *Liberalism, Community and Culture,* Oxford: Clarendon.

Lijphart, Arendt (1975 [1968]) (ed.), 1975 (2nd edn), *The Politics of Accommodation: Pluralism and Democracy in the Netherlands,* Berkeley: University of California Press.

Mauss, Marcel (1969), 'La nation' [1920], *Oeuvres,* Tome 3, Paris, Minuit.

Nehru, Jawaharlal (1989 [1934–1935]), *Glimpses of World History,* Delhi: Oxford University Press.

——(1989 [1946]), *The Discovery of India,* Delhi: Oxford University Press.

Pandey, Gyanendra (1990), *The Construction of Communalism in Colonial North India,* New Delhi: Oxford University Press.

Plamenatz, John (1973), 'Two Types of Nationalism', in E. Kamenka (ed.), *Nationalism: The Nature and Evolution of an Idea,* London: Edward Arnold.

Prasad, Rajendra (1947), *India Divided,* Bombay: Hind Kitabs.

Taylor, Charles (1994), 'The Politics of Recognition', in A. Gutman (ed.), *Multiculturalism,* Princeton: Princeton University Press.

Varshney, Ashutosh (1993), 'Contested Meanings: India's National Identity, Hindu Nationalism, and the Politics of Anxiety', *Daedalus,* Summer.

Walzer, Michael (1992), *What it Means to Be American,* New York: Marislio.

Weiner, Myron (1989), 'India's Minorities: Who are They? What do They Want?', in Myron Weiner [ed. A. Varshney], *The Indian Paradox: Essays in Indian Politics,* New Delhi: Sage.

Wieviorka, Michel (1996), *Une Société Fragmentée? Le Multiculturalisme en Débat,* Paris: La Découverte.

# Chapter 2

# From Indian territory to Hindu *bhoomi* the ethnicization of nation-state mapping in India

The Indian political tradition as it is expressed, for example, in the *Arthashastra* (the treatise of *Artha,* meaning, the sphere of politics and economy) gives an ambiguous and subordinate place to the notion of territory: the king rules over the *janapada,* that is to say 'a country' meaning by it, population and territory. In this conception, territory and human beings are not differentiated: power holds sway over the territory endowed with humans for allowing the ruler to preserve order (seen as social and cosmic). By implication 'a perfect king is by definition a universal ruler' (Biardeau 1982: 33). Madeleine Biardeau emphasizes, moreover, that 'the ritual of royal consecration is preceded by a conquest of cardinal points' and that 'the king acquires prestigious titles as if he ruled over the universe'. As a result, the Hindu kingdoms were perceived as 'as many cosmos' (ibid.).

These ancient characteristics were subsequently blurred by the setting up of state machineries: in the sixteenth century, the Mughal Empire initiated a process of administrative control of the subcontinent in which many of the Hindu kingdoms were gradually absorbed. The British went one step further. Even though their philosophy of indirect rule led them to grant some autonomy to the princely states, they changed territorial management in the direction of even more pronounced centralization. This process was perfected after independence, with the formation of the Indian Union, certainly federal, but all the same controlled by a strong centre which came to head a whole cascade of administrative entities.

The view of the territory underlying the Constitution of 1950 reflected Weberian conceptions of a uniform rational-legal state. The organization did not meet historical or cultural criteria but those of administrative efficacy. However, under the pressure of regionalist movements the territory of India was gradually differentiated in the 1950s according to a particularist criteria: language. Subsequently, the rational-legal conception of territory was put into question by Hindu nationalists, who, in a way, drew some of their inspiration from the Hindu classical patterns mentioned earlier.

## The Indian Union: From Uniformity to (Caste-based) Linguistic Particularism

After independence, the provinces of India were divided into three categories: Class A grouped together all those regions which belonged to British India; Class B regions were those born out of the fusion of princely states; and Class C were those directly administered by New Delhi. This administrative division reflected rational-legal conceptions from two points of view. First, none of these regional entities met any cultural or ethnic criteria (such as that of language, religion, caste, or tribe). The British provinces were very often multicultural and the states of the Indian Union that were born in 1950 remained as such. Second, these states were subdivided according to the same non-ethnic administrative rationale: they were constituted of several divisions (*vibhag*) which themselves got split into districts (*zilas*), and these got further sub-divided into smaller units called *tehsils* or *talukas*, which contained many villages directed by their own council (*panchayat*). This *panchayat* did not rule over one village only but over the grouping of several villages.

At all levels situated on top of the village an officer of the central government or the state government represented the administration. The most important local unit was the district where the District Magistrate (DM), trained by the Indian Administrative Service (the elite of the Indian administration), played a key role in the centralization of the state machinery. The DM is like a prefect. The Indian district has obvious affinities with the French *département* because frontiers do not meet any criterion other than that of administrative efficacy: they represent the essential network of an impersonal grid system.[1] The administrative design installed by the Indian Constitution of 1950, then, relies a lot for its essentials on bureaucratic principles—which accounted for the cultural heterogeneity of the Indian provinces. But these principles were increasingly questioned, especially by movements which wanted a redrawing of regional frontiers based on linguistic criteria.

## NEHRU AND THE LINGUISTIC STATES ISSUE

The Congress Party was from an early stage affected by internal tensions regarding the administrative map of India. In 1920, during the Nagpur session where Mahatma Gandhi asserted his dominance over the party, regional branches of the Congress were restructured according to linguistic criteria: the Provincial Congress Committees thereafter corresponded to linguistic regions and so sent Marathi, Tamil or Gujarati delegates to the annual session of the Congress Party. This organization reflected in part the Gandhian conception of the Indian nation, defined as a collection of cultural and linguistic as well as religious communities. In April 1920, Gandhi, sketching out the profile of a future independent India, wrote in his journal, *Young India*, that 'the actual division of the provinces is a factor that equally goes on to do a lot of harm to the cause of indigenous languages. A new division of the provinces based on the language criterion will be followed by a reorganization of the Universities [after the attainment of Swaraj]' (Gandhi 1948: 52).

Inside the Constituent Assembly, elected in 1946, the partisans of a reshaping of the Indian map according to linguistic criteria were to protest in a sporadic fashion. The majority amongst them was enlisted from the Telugu-speaking elected members who wanted to separate their region from the Presidency of Madras, dominated by Tamil speakers (see, for example, the plea made by N.G. Ranga in *Constituent Assembly Debates* [hereafter *CAD*], 1989, Vol. VII: 351). Nehru opposed this type of agitation for three reasons: first, in contrast to Gandhi, he wanted the Indian nation to be built on the aggregation of individual allegiances and feared that a recognition of linguistic particularisms would weaken the country. Second, he combined this universalism with a profound attachment to the idea of cultural synthesis. In his view, the 'genius' of India lay in its capacity to practise unity in diversity. The structuring of states according to linguistic criteria risked breaking this achievement by homogenizing the fundamental administrative entities. In his well known biography of Nehru, S. Gopal underlined this fact:

> The British might have established composite provinces for their own reasons but such provinces had other virtues too. A province like Hyderabad, with people speaking various languages, including Urdu, appealed to Nehru as a potential centre of composite culture in south India, while Bombay had built up a rich cosmopolitan tradition which it would be vandalistic to throw away. (Gopal 1979: 262)

Nehru was lastly anxious to preserve the map of India as it existed because he considered that other problems had to be treated on priority. In his Constituent Assembly speech of 8 November 1948 he called upon the supporters favouring the redrawing of the Indian map according to linguistic criteria to suspend their mobilization until a more favourable moment (*CAD*, 1989, Vol. VII: 320–1). Many of the elected members were to side with the arguments of Nehru and contented themselves with announcing that they would suspend their agitation for the time being (ibid.: 326).

A crisis was above all averted, however, because of the nomination on 17 June 1948 of a Parliamentary Commission, the *Dhar Committee*, charged with examining the question of revising the administrative map. Many of the parliamentarians decided to await the report of the Commission before joining the debate in earnest. The Commission pronounced itself against the formation of states on the basis of linguistic criteria but admitted to the idea of the creation of the province of Andhra—the Telugu-speaking zone of the presidency of Madras—that had numerous solid supporters. (Parthasarathi 1987: 27)

The notion of linguistic states nevertheless gained support inside the branches of the Congress Party. In several regions opinion was mobilized around cultural identities of which language was often a crucial element. In many of the cases, language also concealed a sense of belonging based on caste.

## CASTE AND TERRITORY

In India the frontiers of linguistic zones correspond very often to the area of spread of a dominant caste—that is, the caste which is the most numerous and which owns most of the land locally (for a more detailed definition of 'dominant caste', see Srinivas 1972)—because the matrimonial relations required by the endogamous caste alignments imply the usage of the same language: one has to marry in one's own caste and speak the same language so as to conclude a marriage. Maharashtra is a good example of this phenomenon because the Marathas—a caste of cultivators of intermediate status, like most of the dominant castes—represented approximately one-third of the population. But most of the other linguistic regions have their dominant castes: the Reddys in the Telugu-speaking area, the Lingayats in the Kannada-speaking zone and so on. While caste had progressively lost its legitimacy (since the penetration of Western ideas of equality and liberty endorsed in the Constitution) as the relevant unit for making any territorial claim,[2] the linguistic criteria has not suffered from the same type of opprobrium. Therefore it was instrumentalized by certain caste groups for extracting a restructuring of administrative frontiers: the agitation for a linguistic state concealed, then, the will of a dominant caste to have the political frontiers coinciding with their area of influence, in order to better control the levers of power at the state level.

The strategy of the dominant caste was denounced by Ambedkar before the Dhar Committee. Chairman of the Drafting Committee of the Indian Constitution, Ambedkar was primarily a leader of the Dalits of the Bombay Presidency. He had very early warned his caste—the Mahars—against the division of Bombay into two linguistic states, Maharashtra (where the Marathas would constitute a relative majority) and Gujarat, of which Gujarati would be the language and where the Anavil Brahmans and the Patidars—a dominant caste of this province—could then 'reduce all other communities to a subordinate status' (Ambedkar 1979: 123).

The presidency of Madras offered a comparable case. The Telugu-speaking Brahmans had more and more difficulty in accepting an inferior rank to the Tamil-speaking Brahmans, notably in the administration whose head offices were located in Madras, in the Tamil country. The Telugu Brahmans were, therefore, in the front rank of the agitation in favour of a linguistic state and they very soon received the support of the two dominant castes of the 'Telugu country', the Reddys and the Kammas who aspired to enhance their influence in an administrative entity where their demographic weight would be much more important (Harrison 1968: 110–11).

The caste logic underlying the agitation for a linguistic state is also very evident from the case of the Princely States. In Mysore (the heart of today's Karnataka), the Lingayats—the principal dominant caste—had struggled since 1927 in favour of a regrouping of the Kannada-speaking districts, which belonged, to the states of Mysore and Hyderabad and to Bombay Presidency. The movement in favour of a new Kannada-speaking state, Karnataka, would actually allow the Lingayats to spread their influence (ibid.: 112).

Obviously, the regional mobilization in favour of linguistic states reflected caste interests. This is an additional reason—besides the vindication of ethno-linguistic identities—for considering that the redrawing of the Indian map according to linguistic criteria fundamentally put into question the rational-legal conception of territory. Moreover, some Indian leaders explicitly opposed these particularist movements in the name of universal values. Ambedkar in his deposition before the Dhar Committee declared thus:

> The linguistic provinces would come back to create as many nations as there are groups which would be proud of their race, their language and their literature . . . . No one could have envisaged such a situation with equipoise. It could lead to the disintegration of India. (Ambedkar 1979: 102)

A commission consisting of Nehru (the Prime Minister), Vallabhbhai Patel (the Deputy Prime Minister) and Pattabhi Sitaramayya (a Telugu Brahman, then president of the Congress) was constituted to defuse tensions and reconsider the issue. Its report, drafted by Nehru, was made public in April 1949. It recommended that this debate be shelved for ten years, while admitting that the case of Andhra Pradesh—demanded by the Telugu-speaking population—could be examined if all the parties would come to an accord.

## THE CREATION OF THE LINGUISTIC STATES

On 19 October 1952, Potti Srisamallu, a Gandhian who was agitating for the formation of the province of Andhra, undertook a fast unto death and died on 15 December in Madras, provoking a large number of angry demonstrations by the Telugu-speaking population. Nehru resigned himself to announcing the formation, on 19 December 1952, of Andhra Pradesh. On 18 January 1953, giving in to the pressure of the Congress delegates, he was obliged to accept a resolution favourable to the establishment of linguistic states during the annual session of the Congress Party. He decided, therefore, on 22 December 1953, on the formation of a commission responsible for establishing 'the broad guidelines following which the states should be reorganised' (Parthasarathi 1987: 373).

Nehru received the report of the States Reorganization Commission on 30 September 1955. It recommended the replacement of the 27 states by three territories of the Union directly administered by New Delhi and 16 states of which three were created on the basis of linguistic criteria (the other state entities were a response to a socioeconomic logic and took into account the means of communication as much as language): Kerala (where Malayalam is spoken by a large majority), Karnataka (where Kannada is the dominant language) and Vidharba (which should have been constituted from the Marathi-speaking districts of Madhya Pradesh but which never came into existence). Assam, the Punjab, and the Province of Bombay were not to be affected by this type of reorganization, the Commission said, considering that the economic prosperity of these regions required that their frontiers of 1947 should be maintained. This decision provoked violent protests. In the Punjab, the Sikhs of the Akali Dal (the party which posed itself as the representative of this community since the 1920s) agitated for the formation of a Punjabi-speaking state—Punjab being their language—while the States Reorganization Commission had recommended the formation of a greater Punjab including the Punjab of 1947, the Patiala and East Punjab States Union (PEPSU) and Himachal Pradesh, a project that was bound to enable the Hindi-speaking populations of these regions to be in an overwhelming majority. In Maharashtra, where the Marathi-speaking population wanted to emancipate itself from the domination of the Gujaratis (especially in Bombay), a similar movement emerged. In 1955–6, Nehru was repulsed by these agitations in which he saw very well the role of other factors—such as caste—as well as language:

Whether it is caste or provincialism, we still live in a tribal age. Religion was exploited to break up our unity [alluding here to Partition] and now language, which should be a binding and ennobling factor, works in the same way. Meanwhile, caste remains to separate us and to encourage narrow groupings. (ibid.: 367, letter dated 10 May 1956)

Finally, the reorganization of the large majority of the states on a linguistic basis was achieved in 1956. This reform put into question the rational-legal arrangement to a certain extent: at a sub-regional level, the bureaucratic system remained the same (with the District Magistrate and the panchayats playing the same key roles) but the provinces acquired an ethnic identity based on language and even caste. However, since the 1960s, not only caste but also tribes and religious communities have been the root cause of a new drive for linguistic states.

## BEYOND LINGUISTIC GROUPS: TRIBES, RELIGIOUS COMMUNITIES AND CASTES

In 1956, Assam was 'amputated' from the North-East Frontier Agency which was placed under the direct administration of New Delhi. Many local tribes agitated at the same time for a state which would be their own. In 1963, the Nagas, a collection of largely Christianized tribes, obtained a Nagaland. In 1966, it was the turn of the Mizos (aborigines of Tibetan-Burmese origin) to obtain an autonomous Union Territory which became Mizoram in 1972. In the same year Meghalaya became a state separated from Assam. These new administrative entities conformed a priori to the criteria applied in 1956 because the movements which had agitated for them—and which sometimes had gone as far as to demand independence but without success—had argued on the basis of their linguistic specificity. In fact, the linguistic unity of these regions was far less clearcut than of those states founded in 1956, so much so that English had to be designated as the official language of Nagaland and Meghalaya; in addition these regions often have one or many subsidiary official languages. Language served again as an alibi for less legitimate movements founded on a complex ethnic identity, of which language was only one component. In the 1980s, the demand for Gorkhaland, a little further west in the region of Darjeeling, followed the same logic: the Gorkhas argued that their language—Nepali—was the basis for agitating for separate status, but they constituted an ethnic group on another basis too, most notably because they had been considered a 'martial race' by the British. They finally obtained some autonomy inside the state of West Bengal in the late 1980s.

A similar scenario took place in Jharkhand over a much longer period: founded in the 1940s, the 'Jharkhand movement', named after a territory including different tribes in south Bihar, in north Orissa and in east Madhya Pradesh, agitated for a separate state for many decades. Here the linguistic alibi could not be advanced. Therefore the supporters for autonomy openly justified their claim by their attachment to the territory and the cultural specificity of the local tribals. In 2000, after decades of more or less intense struggle, the state of Jharkhand was finally realized. At the same time, another tribals-dominated region, Chhattisgarh, was also granted the status of a state.

The states or autonomous zones that tribal populations have obtained in the course of the last 50 years, therefore, have been very loosely based on linguistic criteria and relied more than before on the ethnic basis—in fact many of these movements could not even hide behind the issue of language. A parallel process was observed in the case of the territorial demand of some religious communities and castes.

Sikh nationalism is a good example. Punjab was very early established as a model state because of its agricultural dynamism, and the Sikhs have benefited from these economic achievements. On the other hand, Punjabis—and in particular the Sikhs—came increasingly to resent the fact that their agricultural produce should be 'exported' in its raw form, because New Delhi hesitated to industrialize a border zone which would serve as a target, in case of war, for Pakistan. The rich Sikh peasantry—very often of Jat caste—were discontented about the level of agricultural prices at which the government bought their grain for feeding the other states and also the constant reduction of the funds that New Delhi allocated to Punjab because the state was becoming richer and hence self-sufficient. Certain leaders of the Akali Dal—a party dominated by the Sikh Jats—came to think that greater independence would allow them to manage economic growth in the province more effectively. For this reason a section of the Sikhs came to agitate for a state of their own under the guise of linguistic particularism.

In 1966, the Sikhs of the Akali Dal started an agitation for having the frontiers of Punjab correspond to that of the Punjabi-speaking zone. The Punjabi language (whose script is Gurumukhi) was the language of the Sikhs and this agitation clearly aimed at giving a state to the Sikhs. Language, here, served as a screen for a communal demand par excellence. This Punjabi Suba movement resulted in 1966 in the division of Punjab into two parts: a Hindi-speaking Haryana and a Punjab where the Sikhs represented 71 per cent of the population in 1971.[3]

In addition to tribes and religious communities, castes got their state too in the post-Nehruvian period, without having to resort to the linguistic alibi. Indeed, the creation of Uttaranchal in 2000—along with that of Jharkhand and Chhattisgarh—was mainly due to caste-based demands. In this hilly region of Uttar Pradesh, in the 1990s, upper castes have always been a majority whereas Other Backward Classes (OBC) represented 2 per cent of the population only. In 1993 the OBC-dominated government of Mulayam Singh Yadav in Uttar Pradesh decided to implement the recommendations of the Mandal Commission report and reserve 27 per cent of the posts in the local administration for 2 per cent of OBCs. Upper castes, inhabitants of Uttaranchal, mobilized, demonstrated and clashed with the police. Politicization of caste cleavages led then to demands for a separate state. The Hindu nationalist party, the Bharatiya Janata Party (BJP) endorsed this claim. It took over power in Uttar Pradesh in 1997 and at the Centre in 1998 and decided to create a separate state of Uttaranchal in 2000. For the first time, a new state was created in favour of caste groups without the alibi of language.

To sum up, the Nehruvian ideal of a rational-legal state, so far as the territory issue is concerned, was put into question as early as the 1950s by agitations with ethnic connotations—either linguistic movements or movements having a tribal, religious or caste basis and language as an alibi. This early ethnicization of the territory reflected itself in the naming of certain new states such as Tamil Nadu (Tamil country) or Andhra Pradesh (the province of Andhras). This ethnicization process did not put into question the bureaucratic arrangement so far as the district units and its subdivisions were concerned. It was not as negative as Nehru feared either. It did not lead to the disintegration of the country. On the contrary, it enabled the Centre to accommodate regional identities with the required flexibility. The federal structure of the Indian Union turned out to be most resourceful. In a way, the redrawing of the administrative map reflected India's ability to maintain unity in diversity. However, this trend acquired a new dimension in 2000 when states were created for tribal groups (Jharkhand and Chhattisgarh) and caste groups (Uttaranchal) without taking the trouble of invoking the linguistic argument. More important, at the same time, the old rational-legal framework has been exposed to a new threat which puts this multiculturalism into question: the rise of Hindu nationalism which defends an ethnic conception of territory but in opposition to all particularisms, linguistic as well as religious.

## The Hindu Nationalist Territory

The Hindu nationalist ideology, as it crystallized between the end of the nineteenth century and beginning of the twentieth century, carries a conception of space in part inherited from the classical views of ancient India. In the *Dharmashastra*, Bharat (India) is described as 'the land of *dharma* and as such, she has a unique ritual, religious and magical status' (Halbfass 1990: 177). This 'country' is said to spread out between the Himalayas and the sea. Its core is made of Aryavarta, the land of the Aryas, enclosing in itself the section of the territory that is found between the Himalayas and the Vindhya mountains. The Aryas are the twice-born, that is to say the members of the three superior social orders: Brahmans, Kshatriyas and Vaishyas. Hence, the caste system, in a way, defines the territory.

The Arya Samaj, a proto-nationalist Hindu movement founded in 1875 by Swami Dayananda Saraswati, was the first Hindu proto-nationalist movement to reinterpret this conception and to emphasize the entrenchment of the Aryan sovereignty in the sacred land. It presented the so-called ancestors of the Hindus, the Aryas of the Vedic epoch, as an elected people: descended from Tibet into Aryavarta—a so-called virgin zone—sometime after the Creation, they allegedly used this base for becoming 'the sovereign masters of the earth' (Dayananda 1940: 288). For Dayananda, the Aryavarta was both the cradle of a civilization, of which the Hindus were the caretakers, and the primordial place from where humanity originated.[4]

## HINDU NATIONALISM AND THE CULT OF *BHOOMI* (LAND)

The ideology of Hindu nationalism was really codified by V.D. Savarkar in the 1920s. In 1923, in his book, *Hindutva: Who is a Hindu?*, he defined Hinduness (Hindutva) as the sense of belonging to an ethnic community possessing a territory and presenting the same racial characteristics. So far as territory is concerned, Savarkar proceeds to a subtle reinterpretation of the word Hindu, or Sindhu (the H and S are interchangeable in Sanskrit): Sindhu, in Sanskrit, does not signify only Indus but also the sea—which surrounds the southern peninsula—so much so that this word alone, Sindhu, designates, almost in one go all the frontiers of the country. Therefore, writes Savarkar, '*Hindustan* has come to mean the whole continental country from the Shindu to Shindu from the Indus to the sea' (Savarkar 1969: 32). For Savarkar, a Hindu is first of all one who lives in the zone between the rivers, the seas and the Himalayas, 'so strongly entrenched that no other country in the world is so perfectly designed by the fingers of nature as a geographical unit' (ibid.: 82). It is because of the way they were entrenched in this land that the first Aryas, as early as the Vedic period, 'developed a sense of nationality' (ibid.: 5). For Savarkar, this land is sacred: Hindustan is the Hindus' holy land.

This conception of territory was further developed by the Rashtriya Swayamsevak Sangh (RSS) that came into existence in 1925. This movement was very much inspired by V.D. Savarkar, as is evident from the prayer which its members recite during its sessions for ideological and physical training which are daily held by its local branches:

I bow before you for all times, Oh mother earth (*matribhoomi*) my beloved! That my life be offered for thy cause, Oh great pure earth (*punyabhoomi*) that I worship. I bow before you again and again.

This mystique of the motherland was further exacerbated after the Partition of India in 1947 when the Congress was accused of having presided over 'the vivisection of Mother India'. Nathuram Godse, the murderer of Gandhi, who had belonged to the RSS and was a disciple of Savarkar, explained his act as a punishment that one must inflict on the Mahatma for this trauma.

Still today, the Hindu nationalists are more interested in the earth—perceived in an organicist perspective—than in territory in the sense of an anonymous space defined by an administrative grid. This option is well in tune with their devalourization of the state vis-à-vis the nation: for them, the form of power and its administrative incarnation has lesser importance than the nation, a spiritual principle, which reflects the soul of the people in their eternity. The frontiers of the state are not, moreover, those that they respect the most. For instance, they regard the Nepalese as members of the Hindu nation, because their ruler belongs to their faith. An RSS publication gives a good illustration of this worldview:

In the majority of the nations of the world, the state is the first, . . . the nation is circumscribed by the territorial jurisdiction of the state. . . . In this viewpoint, Bharat is in a particular situation because the foundation of this ancient nation has always been culture and not politics. On our land, numerous states have come into existence and gone by, some times many states, from republics to monarchies, have co-existed. . . .

The pillars of national unity of Bharat are found in a big way in its history, its geography, its religion, its philosophy and its culture. The sight and the meeting of the rivers on the banks on which our ancestors have created a literature which has become the standard of the human civilization. The caves of the mountains which have been honoured by the retreat of the sages and the lakes, which testify to their spiritual realization, washing the spirit and the body of all sin and suffering. One visit to these places of pilgrimage, allows one to have a general survey of the remote places in four corners of the country, and also allows one to become conscious that every part of the country is sacred. Similarly such a visit allows one to share the sentiment of closeness with one's compatriots and partake of the observation of the existence of the same cultural attitude across the country, such as, found in the assembly of people from all over India in big religious gatherings of the Kumbh Mela. The spiritual awakening prompted by the saints and preachers who tour all over the country and the common values followed by all across the country—all this makes our country an immortal nation.

For making every one conscious of this reality, it is necessary that each citizen of Bharat familiarizes with its rivers and its mountains which are the boon of nature and also with the places of pilgrimage and with the great memorials of the ancestors. (Sharma 1993: 3–4)

This text opposes territorial nationalism to an ethnic conception of the nation where the definition of the 'Indian earth' reposes exclusively on the Hindu culture. Ritual places are credited with a national value. The Hindu nationalists exploit here a conception of Indian territory that is very widespread in their community because of the key role of pilgrimages in Hinduism. The Hindu pilgrims sketch in fact a sacred geography in which the participants see the 'true India'. Diana Eck, on the basis of field enquiries in the Himalayan border regions, even points out that, 'all the Indian earth constitutes, in the eyes of the Hindu pilgrims, a sacred geography' (Eck 1985).[5]

In the text of the RSS cited earlier, *Punyabhoomi Bharat*, the rivers figure as the first markers of identity of the Indian space, probably because water has a particular purificatory value in Hinduism and many of the water courses are regular objects of pilgrimage. Next comes, for similar reasons, the lakes, which according to the author 'have inspired all the people of Bharat to rise above the differences of caste and of region and create a strong nation'. Then it is the turn of the mountains which concludes the 'natural' set. The set of 'cultural' signs opens with the four *Dhams* (lit. the places of residence, in this case of the Hindu gods) situated in Badrinath in the Himalaya, Rameshwaram in the extreme south, Dwarka in the west, and Puri in the east, that correspond expediently to the cardinal points. On this account, the places of pilgrimage are presented as the anchoring points of the unity of Bharat since time immemorial. The author illustrates the same principle based on the seven sacred cities of Hinduism that are traditionally perceived as the privileged places for attaining eternal peace, *moksha:*

Ayodhya, Mathura, Haridwar, Kashi (Benares), Kanchipuram, Avantika (Ujjain) and Dwarka are the seven cities which are reputed to confer Moksha. These seven cities were situated in different directions and in different regions acting as the links in a chain which unites the nation. Each citizen of Bharat, whatever his caste, his sect or his province, always feels the desire to pay a visit to these cities as a devotee. (Sharma 1993: 29)

The twelve *jyotirlingas*—stalagmites worshipped as the phallic symbol of the god Shiva—which are places of important pilgrimages in Hinduism are described in the same fashion: 'As they are distributed across the country, they symbolize the unity of the nation'. The map of India that these descriptions sketch reposes on the sacred geography of traditional India. But the entire process constitutes, of course, an invented tradition. The Hindu nationalist ideologues want to establish a fallacious continuity between their view of India and a mythic past.

COUNTERING CENTRIFUGAL FORCES ON
BEHALF OF THE HINDU EARTH

As early as 1952, *The Organiser,* the official organ of the RSS, opposed federalism and the making of the provinces as an intermediary government structure: 'In our ideal, we would wish to abolish the provinces and wish to establish a unique and a unified administration in our country' (*The Organiser,* 29 December 1952: 3). As the demand for a linguistic state intensified in Tamil Nadu, the Jan Sangh— founded in 1951 and dominated by the RSS—began to act against this sign of separatism of 'Dravidistan' (*The Organiser,* 10 October 1955: 7). Then it denounced the linguistic states as soon as they took shape in 1956 because of 'their regionalist connotations and their dangerous tendency towards separatism' (*The Organiser,* 26 January 1956: 5).

Subsequently, the multiplication of the linguistic states and the development of separatist movements in Punjab and Kashmir led to a reassertion by the Hindu nationalists of their conception of the 'Hindu earth'. They rejected the notion of territory because it implied a division of this primordial earth according to administrative schema—which prepared the ground for separatist movements. At the beginning of the 1980s, the promotion of a Hindu nationalist conception of India took a more militant turn. The notion of earth then was used to displace that of a segmented, administrative territory. The *Ekatmata yatra* launched by the Vishva Hindu Parishad (VHP) in 1983 sought, for example, to manipulate the symbols of the 'Hindu earth' with the aim of popular mobilization. Three caravans rallied from Kathmandu to Rameshwaram (Tamil Nadu), Gangasagar (Bengal) to Somnath (Gujarat) and Haridwar (Uttar Pradesh) to Kanyakumari (Tamil Nadu), on which converged 69 other caravans starting from the interior, distributing the waters of the Ganga (50 centilitres for 10 rupees) and provisioning the holy waters from the local temples or the other sacred rivers that they met on their way. This show of mixing of the waters was aimed at symbolizing the Hindu unity; all the caravans converged moreover on to Nagpur, the headquarters of the RSS and the geographical centre of India, before separating once again (for the map of the route followed by the *Ekatmata yatra,* see Assayag 1998: 147).

The modus operandi of the *Ekatmata yatra* played clearly on the perceptions that Hindus have of their territory across the rivers and other places of pilgrimage. Formally, the *Ekatmata yatra* reproduced the modus operandi of a pilgrimage. For instance, its main halts were sacred places. The religious geography of the Indian space was therefore harnessed for the ends of an ideological mobilization.

The same phenomenon was observed in 1989 in the course of the movement for the construction of the Ram Temple. This divinity was born, according to the legend, at Ayodhya (Uttar Pradesh). His birthplace was said to have been occupied by a temple until it was replaced by a mosque the 'Babri Masjid', in the sixteenth century on the orders of the first Mughal emperor, Babur. From 1984, the VHP demanded a restitution of this site to the Hindus. In 1989, it organized during the summer, with the logistical support of the RSS, the *Ram Shila Pujan,* that consisted of honouring in a devotional manner bricks (*shila*) inscribed with the name of Ram. These consecrated bricks were to be used for the construction of the new temple dedicated to Ram. Consecration took place across India. In the second stage, all these bricks were dispatched to Ayodhya where they were exhibited with the markings of their place of origin. Some amongst these came from foreign countries such as the United Kingdom or the United States, but the operation was aimed above all at mobilizing the Hindu population in India. This was reiterated in the ceremony of the placing of the first stone (*shilanyas*) on 9 November 1989:

at the exact time of *shilanayas*, all Hindus were called upon to turn towards Ayodhya and make an offering of flowers.

The Hindu nationalists searched in this way to exalt Ayodhya as a sacred place at the centre of Hinduism, by endowing this religion with a centre comparable to that of the 'Semitic religions'—an expression often used by Hindu nationalists with derogatory overtones. The ceremony of 9 November calling upon all the Hindus to turn towards Ayodhya, for example, seemed inspired more or less consciously by the Muslim prayers facing Mecca.

In 1990, the VHP launched a *Ram Jyoti yatra*. At Ayodhya, the fire of a Vedic sacrifice gave birth to a torch that served to light up two others in Benares and in Mathura (the birthplace of Krishna), the two cities where mosques were also supposed to have been constructed in place of temples. These flames were lit and spread all over the country to light the small lamps that every Hindu family has in its home for the feast of Diwali (the festival of lights), with which this operation very judiciously coincided. In 1992, a comparable manifestation, the *Ram Paduka yatra*, consisted of touring the sandals of Ram that, according to the legend, his brother—to whom the kingdom was given—had installed on the throne during the exile of Ram in the forest.

Thus, since 1983, the VHP has endeavoured to mobilize 'the Hindu nation' by utilizing forms of mass mobilization derived from a religious style of procession or pilgrimage. This formula was appropriated and adapted after 1990 by the BJP. In 1990, the then president of the BJP, L.K. Advani, travelled nearly 10,000 km from Gujarat to Ayodhya (passing through Andhra Pradesh) on a Toyota on which was placed an epic chariot. This mobilization was to continue till the start of the construction of the temple, but Advani was arrested in Bihar before he could enter Uttar Pradesh.

The popular success met by the agitation around the Ayodhya site is revealing of the new form of ethnicization of the Indian territory: an increasing number of Hindus came to recognize each other in the cultural version of the territory that was proposed to them, even accepting Ayodhya as the centre of the nation. Jackie Assayag emphasizes that the first video cassette produced by the VHP 'showed the sacred land whose capital is Ayodhya' (1998: 130). After linguistic states questioned the rational-legal model of the nation, another form of ethnic movement is experiencing considerable success.

The conception of territory that Nehru, Ambedkar and other Indian leaders sought to promote after independence drew its inspiration from the same values as that of the Weberian rational-legal state. This ideal was questioned as early as the 1950s with the demand for linguistic states which often reflected caste demands. The creation of the first linguistic states in the 1950s was followed by other changes of the administrative map of India that responded to the same logic—language serving more and more as a pretext for the creation of new territorial entities that were in fact wanted by tribes or religious communities. Gradually, the 'alibi' of language was not even utilized by groups agitating for autonomy. The history of post-independence Indian territory is then above all a success of ethnic forces over the rational-legal framework of the state. However, this ethnicization process had some very positive connotations: it showed the capacity of the Indian federal system to accommodate centrifugal forces. In a way, this respect for regional entities was the territorial counterpart to secularism in the realm of communal relations. Both contributed to a form of multiculturalism.

The ethnicization process due to the rise of Hindu nationalism is supported by a very different logic, as this movement tries to project the culture of the majority community as the embodiment of Indian identity. In their view, the minorities can only stay in India if they give up the public dimension of their faith (that has to be confined to the private sphere) and if they pay allegiance to Hindu symbols as national symbols. The Hindu nationalist view of India *as land* exemplifies this: India is not a territory defined by an administrative map. It is a *bhoomi*, earth, defined by Hindu ritual places: rivers, lakes, *lingams*, mountains. As a result, its borders do not coincide with those of the Indian state but with the spread of such ritual places. While in most ethnic brands of nationalism, land is a secondary factor, here it plays a major role. Not as the anonymous space of the classical territorial nationalisms *à la* Congress;[6] but as the sacred *bhoomi* of the Hindus. This view partly derives from the old notion of Aryavarta, the land on which the Aryas had settled and established their ritual norms.

However, this tradition has been substantially reinterpreted in the framework of Hindu nationalist ideology and, therefore, it carries contradictions due to the ideological attempts at reconciling perceptions which are poles apart. Hindu nationalists have aspired since 1947 to reunify India, Pakistan and Bangladesh and re-establish *Akhand Bharat*. This project reflects an extreme valourization of land, but it contradicts the definition of the nation as based on Hindu culture.

## Notes

1. However, the notion of historical territory—what we would call 'terroir' in French—is not entirely absent in the Indian context. The frontiers of a district are, for example, very often inherited from those of a Princely State or those defined by the colonial state, which were themselves derived from the mould of administrative design of the Mughal empire. Now the provinces of British India were not entirely devoid of all particularist connotations: Bihar—which was first associated with Bengal until 1912 and later with Orissa—was largely born of separatist movements based on linguistic differences— Sindh was also separated from the Bombay Presidency in 1934 because the local Muslims wanted their own administrative unit.
2. Just after Partition, the Jats had tried to carve out a 'Jat land' in the Jat-dominated areas of Uttar Pradesh, Punjab and Rajasthan, but they failed.
3. See Singh 1984: 44. In the next census of 1981, however, their share of the population had fallen to 52 per cent while that of the Hindus increased from 40 per cent to 48 per cent, mainly because of the migration of agricultural labourers. This erosion of the

demographic weight of the Sikhs was one factor in the revival and radicalization of the autonomy movement, but the Indian state was not prepared to make any new concessions to explicitly communal movements.

4.  The second aspect has shaped the Hindu nationalists' worldview. Jackie Assayag underlines that the first video cassette produced by the Vishva Hindu Parishad, an offshoot of the RSS, showed 'the cosmic big bang turning into a saffron-coloured map, that of Akhand Bharat; then Ayodhya—the navel of Hinduism—progressively appears bathed in light. India is conceived of, in this way, less as a geographical entity than as a cosmological and theological product born at the same time as Rama. . . .' (Assayag 1998: 130). Not only does Hindu nationalism present India as a spiritual guide of Humanity; it also considers the Hindu diaspora as the living proof of the ubiquitous character of the Hindu presence. The Vishva Hindu Parishad is committed to implanting itself in foreign countries by using 'diasporic' bridgeheads.

5.  The Hindu imagination of space has given birth to certain metaphors which could have helped in the crystallization of Hindu nationalist constructs. For instance, a monk of southern India wrote that 'the land of the fatherland is to the nation as the physical body is to a yogi' because the seven sacred cities of Hinduism seemed to be laid out as the sensitive centres (*chakras*) of the *kundilini*, that one must untie by yoga as to attain a spiritual awakening (Chidbhavananda 1985: 136).

6.  The relations between the conception of territory by the Hindu nationalists and the Congress is quite interesting. Since the 1920s, Hindu nationalists have criticized the Congress and call their nationalism artificial because it is territorial. All communities in the frontiers of British India, then of the Indian Union, must riot to their viewpoint be considered as Indian on an equal footing. They defend an ethnic nationalism by considering that the Hindus alone embody the Indian nation and Hindu culture sums up the essence of Indian culture. But, at the same time, the Hindu nationalists defend a vision of the nation where space is greatly valued. Simply, the frontiers which they call for are not those—arbitrary from their viewpoint—of the British Raj but the natural limits defined by a version of Hindu geography.

## References

Ambedkar, B.R. (1979 [1948]), 'Maharashtra as a linguistic province, Statement submitted to the Linguistic Provinces Commission', in *Dr Babasaheb Ambedkar: Writings and Speeches*, Vol. 1, Bombay: Government of Maharashtra.

Assayag, J. (1998), 'Ritual Action or Political Reaction?: The Invention of Nationalist Processions in India During the 1980s', *South Asia Research*, Vol. 18, No. 2.

Biardeau, M. (1982), 'Dharma et frontieres politiques en Inde', in J.P. Charnay et al. (eds.), *Le bonheur par l'empire ou le rêve d'Alexandre*, Paris: Anthropos.

Chidbhavananda (1985), *Facets of Brahman or the Hindu Gods*, Tiruchirapalli: Sri Ramakrishna Tapovanam.

*Constituent Assembly Debates* (1989), Vol. VII, New Delhi: Lok Sabha Secretariat.

Dayananda, Swami (1940), *Sathyarth Prakash: Le livre de l'Arya Samaj*, Paris: Maisonneuve.

Eck, D. (1985), *Darsan: Seeing the Divine Image in India*, Chambersburg: Anima.

Gandhi, M.K. (1948), 'La cause des langues indigènes' (21 April 1920)', in Gandhi, *La Jeune Inde*, Paris: Stock.

Gopal, S. (1979), *Jawaharlal Nehru: A Biography, Vol. 2 (1947–56)*, London: Jonathan Cape.

Halbfass, W. (1990 [1981]), *India and Europe: An Essay in Philosophical Understanding*, Delhi: Motilal Banarsidass.

Harrison, S. (1968 [1960]), *India: the Most Dangerous Decades*, Delhi: Oxford University Press.

Parthasarathi, G. (1987) (ed.), *Jawaharlal Nehru: Letters to Chief Ministers, 1947–64, Vol. 3 (1952–4)*, Delhi: Oxford University Press.

Savarkar, V.D. (1969 [1923]), *Hindutva: Who is a Hindu?*, Bombay: S.S. Savarkar.

Sharma, J.K. (1993), *Punyabhoomi Bharat (Introduction to map of the sacred land Bharat)*, New Delhi: Keshav Kunj.

Singh, Gopal (1984), 'Socio-economic bases of the Punjab crisis', *Economic and Political Weekly*, 7 January.

Srinivas, M.N. (1972), *Social Change in Modern India*, New Delhi: Orient Longman.

# Chapter 3

# The invention of an ethnic nationalism

The Hindu nationalist movement started to monopolize the front pages of Indian newspapers in the 1990s when the political party that represented it in the political arena, the Bharatiya Janata Party (BJP), rose to power. From 2 seats in the Lok Sabha, the lower house of the Indian Parliament, the BJP increased its tally to 88 in 1989, 120 in 1991, 161 in 1996—at which time it became the largest party in that assembly—and to 178 in 1998. At that point it was in a position to form a coalition government, an achievement it repeated after the 1999 mid-term elections. For the first time in Indian history, Hindu nationalism had managed to take over power. The BJP and its allies remained in office for five full years, until 2004.

The general public discovered Hindu nationalism in operation over these years. But it had of course already been active in Indian politics and society for decades; in fact, this *ism* is one of the oldest ideological streams in India. It took concrete shape in the 1920s and even harks back to more nascent shapes in the nineteenth century. As a movement, too, Hindu nationalism is heir to a long tradition. Its main incarnation today, is the Rashtriya Swayamsevak Sangh (RSS), founded soon after the first Indian communist party, and before the first Indian socialist party. In fact, Hindu nationalism runs parallel to the dominant Indian political tradition of the Congress Party, which Gandhi transformed into a mass organization in the 1920s. Indeed, Hindu nationalism crystallized as an ideology and as a movement exactly at the time when the Congress became imbued with Gandhi's principles and grew into a mass movement. It then developed an alternative political culture to the dominant idiom in Indian politics, not only because it rejected non-violence as a legitimate and effective modus operandi against the British in the wake of the discourse of Bal Gangadhar Tilak (1856–1920) and his apologia in favour of a Hindu tradition of violent action (Jaffrelot 2003: 299–324; Cashman 1975), but also because it rejected the Gandhian conception of the Indian nation.

Mahatma Gandhi looked at the Indian nation as, ideally, a harmonious collection of religious communities all placed on an equal footing. He promoted a syncretic and spiritual brand of the Hindu religion in which all creeds were bound to merge, or converge. Even though the leaders of India's minorities—especially Muslims—resisted this universalist appeal—in part because Gandhi articulated his views in a thoroughly Hindu style—the Mahatma insisted till the end that he spoke on behalf of all communities and that the Congress represented them all. In the early 1920s he even presided over the destiny of the Khilafat Committee, which had been founded to defend the Khilafat, an institution challenged after the defeat of the Ottoman empire in the First World War (Minault 1982).

Gandhi's universalist definition of the Indian nation echoed that of the man he regarded as his guru in politics, Gopal Krishna Gokhale (1866–1915), and, more generally speaking, of the first generation of Congress leaders. For the founders of Congress, the Indian nation was to be defined according to the territorial criterion, not on the basis of cultural features: it encompassed all those who happened to live within the borders of British India. Therefore, it was not perceived as being within Congress' purview to deal with religious issues which, in fact, were often social issues—such as child marriage and widow remarriage—all such issues being those that came under the personal laws of different denominations. Moreover, the early Congress had started for this latter purpose a National Social Conference which met at the same time and in the same place as Congress did, during its annual session, but as a separate body. In contrast with the founders of Congress, Gandhi acknowledged religious identities in the public sphere, even as he viewed the nation as an amalgamation of many different communities. In the 1920s and after, however, the legacy of the first-generation Congress leaders was still pursued and deepened by major Congress Party figures: the Nehrus, i.e. Motilal Nehru (1861–1931) and his son, Jawaharlal Nehru (1889–1964), who advocated a liberal nation-building process based on individuals, not groups. For Motilal, who was elected president of the Congress in 1919 and 1928, and for Jawaharlal, who—before independence—occupied the same post in 1929, 1936, and 1946, and who was to become Gandhi's spiritual son, the construction of the Indian nation could only be rooted in secular, individual identities. The Nehrus represented a variant of the universalist standpoint, quite different from that embodied by Gandhi.

Hindu nationalism, like Muslim separatism (a movement which in India was formed around the same time), rejected both versions of the universalist view of nationalism articulated by Congress (on this typology, see Pandey 1990). This ideology assumed that India's national identity was summarized by Hinduism, the dominant creed which, according to the British census, represented about 70 per cent of the population. Indian culture was to be defined as Hindu culture, and the minorities were to be assimilated by their paying allegiance to the symbols and mainstays of the majority as those of the nation. For Congressmen like Nehru this ideology—like that of the Muslim League or of Sikh separatists—had nothing to do with nationalism. They branded it with the derogatory term 'communalism'. But in fact the doctrine that was to become known by the name 'Hindutva, fulfilled the criteria of ethnic nationalism' (Jaffrelot 1999). Its motto, 'Hindu, Hindi, Hindustan', echoed many other European nationalisms based on religious identity, a common language, or even racial feeling.

All the same, the essential characteristics of Hinduism scarcely lent themselves to such an *ism*. This is, first, because Hinduism has no 'book' which can truly be said to serve as a common reference point. As Louis Renou points out, in Hinduism 'religious books can be described as books written for the use of a sect' (Renou 1972: 50). Moreover, Hinduism has often been described not as a religion but as a 'conglomeration of sects' (Thapar 1989: 216). In fact the term 'Hindu' derives from the name of a river, the Indus; it was used successively by the Achaemenids, the Greeks, and the Muslims to denote the population living beyond that river (Frykenberg 1989: 30), but till the medieval period it was not appropriated by the people themselves (O'Connell 1973: 340–4). A 'Hindu' consciousness apparently found its first expression in the seventeenth and eighteenth centuries in the empire of Shivaji, and then in the Maratha confederacy. But the conquests of the Marathas in the direction of the Gangetic plain 'did not imply the existence of a sense of the religious war based on ethnic or communal consciousness' (Bayly 1985: 187); they resulted from a motivation that was ritual in character—to restore to the Hindus certain holy places, such as Varanasi, which were revered throughout India. The development of Hindu nationalism is, therefore, a modern phenomenon that has developed on the basis of strategies of ideology-building, and *despite* the original characteristics of a diverse set of practices clubbed under the rubric of Hinduism.

## An Ideological Reaction to the Other: From Reform to Revivalism, in the Nineteenth Century

The first expression of Hindu mobilization emerged in the nineteenth century as an ideological reaction to European domination and gave birth to what came to be known as 'neo-Hinduism' (Jones 1989; Copley 2000). To begin with, Europeans fascinated the local intelligentsia. In Bengal, where the British first settled, the East India Company used the services not only of *compradores* but also of the local literati, who came from the Hindu upper castes—these *bhadralok*, were mostly Brahmans and, as a result, a new elite of upper caste British-trained white-collar workers took shape (Broomfield 1968). This intelligentsia often admired Britain for its remarkable scientific, technical, legal, and social achievements.

Yet most members of this intelligentsia also regarded the West as a threat. They were inclined to reform their traditions along modern lines but not to the extent that they would abandon or even disown them; in fact they often wanted to reform these traditions in order to save them. Reformists, therefore, became revivalists by pretending that, in emulating the West, they were only restoring to pristine purity their own traditions via eliminating later accretions.

Within the Hindu milieu this transition from reform to revivalism took place in the course of the nineteenth century. This is well illustrated by the contrast between the Brahmo Samaj and a later—but not unrelated—organization, the Arya Samaj. The former was founded in 1828 by Rammohun Roy (1772–1833), the renowned Bengali Brahman who had been employed by the East India Company and who looked at the British presence in India as a providential development

(Collet 1962). Roy supported Western reformist ideas, including the abolition of *sati*. At the same time, he was very critical of the proselytizing work of Western missionaries. He steadfastly vindicated Hinduism against Christian expansionism, though in the reformist way. He admitted that missionaries were right when they stigmatized polytheism, the caste system and the condition of Hindu women. But he argued that these retrograde practices were latter accretions in Hinduism, that in its original form Hinduism did not lay itself open to such opprobrium.

It had ignored idol worship—in fact it was even more monotheistic than Christianity, which admitted the Trinity—and it was an egalitarian creed emphasizing unmediated access between the individual and God. Roy argued that he had discovered all these virtues in the Upanishads—a late addition to Vedanta, the most recent part of the Veda (Robertson 1995). He suggested that, according to these sacred texts, each man is endowed with an *atma*, which is nothing other than a part of Brahma—the divine substance that supports the world. Therefore, the Vedic religion relied on an unmediated relation between man and God. He fought with Unitarian missionaries to hammer home this point during long public debates. The notion of a Vedic 'golden age' when Hinduism was superior to Christianity can be seen to crystallize at this time (Saikai 1928). This idea was embodied in the doctrine of the Brahmo Samaj, the organization he founded in 1828 and which survived Roy's death in 1833 (in London, where he had travelled as the first major Hindu reformer) (Kopf 1969 and 1979).

The Brahmo Samaj attracted Hindu reformists from various regions, including the Bombay Presidency. This was the region from which Swami Dayananda Saraswati came. Dayananda was a Gujarati Brahman who had embraced *sanyas* (asceticism). He travelled to Calcutta in 1873, meeting Keshub Chandra Sen—the most famous Brahmo Samaji leader of the time—who had just returned from England and was; especially critical of the moral decay of that otherwise modern country (Borthwick 1977). Sen promoted the idea that India was technically less advanced but spiritually superior (Raychaudhuri 1988).

Dayananda Saraswati capitalized on the intellectual legacy of Roy and Sen in the 1870s, but he also took it several steps further, and in a somewhat different direction. While the Brahmo Samaj is focused on the religious dimension of the Vedic 'golden age', Dayananda argued that, in addition to its spiritual glory, Indian antiquity was imbued with cultural and social greatness. The Vedic epoch was, in his construction, no longer embodied only in spirituality but also in a people—in its culture and its land. Dayananda maintained that the 'Aryas' of the Vedas formed the autochthonous people of Bharat, the sacred land below the Himalayas. They had been endowed by their god with the most perfect language, Sanskrit, the mother of all languages. This claim was strengthened by British Orientalism, whose most famous eighteenth-century exponent William Jones argued that it was the fount of an Indo-European family of languages. The idea that Europe's languages originated in Sanskrit had by this time become widespread (Marshall 1970; Halbfass 1988). Last, but not least, Dayananda depicted Aryan society as endowed with robust egalitarian values. He did not ignore the caste system, but he reinterpreted it, arguing that, to begin with, this social system did not rely on hereditary hierarchical relations but on a merit-based division of labour, each *varna* fulfilling complementary functions. In the original Aryan society, for Dayananda, children were assigned to different *varnas* by their gurus according to their aptitude and inclination, a novel idea which reflected the influence upon him of Western individualism.

In fact, Dayananda's revivalism inaugurated a specific combination of stigmatization and emulation of the threatening 'Other'. In contrast to the old reformists *à la* Rammohun Roy, Dayananda did not look upon British colonialism as a providential development but rather as posing a threat to Hindu civilization, including its caste system. In order to defuse this threat Dayananda recommended some emulation of the West. In this respect he followed Roy. His idea of reform was not to make India like the West, but to make its standards acceptably Western. His effort was to dissuade the British from changing Hindu customs by law, as well as to dissuade Hindus from admiring the West and/or converting to Christianity. This was best done by arguing that what fascinated Hindus about the West existed already, deeply buried, in their own ancestral traditions. Dayananda's interest was thus to emulate the West in order to more effectively resist its influence.

It followed that the conversion of Hindus—including the Untouchables—to Christianity was perceived by Dayananda as a challenge to Hinduism. By the end of his life he introduced a ritual of reconversion—something no one could find in the Hindu scriptures as having previously existed. For this purpose he adapted the old ceremony of *shuddhi,* by which upper caste Hindus who had been defiled could reintegrate with their caste. *Shuddhi* was therefore a purification procedure which Dayananda transformed into a reconversion technique, drawing inspiration from Christianity (Ghai 1990). Dayananda presided over the 'shuddhization' of a few Christian converts who wished to return to Hinduism during his lifetime, but even at that time, and more so after his death, the prime target of the *Shuddhi* movement's disciples were Muslims and Sikhs (Jones 1973).

Dayananda founded the Arya Samaj in 1875, in Punjab, the province where Hindus, more than anywhere else, felt a strong sense of vulnerability because of their demographic weakness vis-à-vis Muslims (51 per cent of the local population) and Sikhs (7.5 per cent). After Dayananda's death the Arya Samaj continued to develop in Punjab and became politicized (Jones 1976; Rai 1914; Gupta 1991; Vable 1983; Pandit 1975; Dua 1999).

## The Political Turn: The Hindu Sabha Movement

In Punjab the Arya Samaj attracted upper caste notables who were involved in trade and commerce. This social milieu appreciated the sect's reformist creed because it did not recognize any sort of supremacy by Brahmans—on the contrary it denied the role of Brahmans as intermediaries between man and God. Hitherto,

Brahmans had here claimed to occupy the upper rungs of society, even though the merchant castes had, in fact, become the dominant force in society. The merchant castes had indeed become so powerful that they played the role of moneylenders for the entire Punjab peasantry. When debtors failed to pay their dues, as often happened, merchant castes bought their land. This phenomenon accelerated by the late nineteenth century to such an extent that the British—who wanted to protect rural society as it had supported their rule—introduced in 1901 the Punjab Alienation of Land Act, a piece of legislation protecting 'rural tribes' from such transfer of property (Barrier 1966). The British further antagonized the Hindu elite in 1906 when Lord Minto promised a Muslim delegation—which was to spawn the Muslim League by the end of the year—that the Muslim minority of India would be granted a separate electorate. This announcement did not materialize all over British India until 1909, in the framework of the Morley-Minto constitutional reforms, but in Punjab it led the Hindu urban elite to organize as early as 1907: Hindu Sabhas (Hindu associations) that were formed throughout the province, mostly under the impulse of Arya Samaj leaders, including Lal Chand, who formulated the standard expression of Hindu anxiety regarding British policy in 1909, in a series of articles in *The Panjabee* (Rai 1967).

While Arya Samajis, thus far, did not view themselves as 'Hindus' but as followers of the Vedas—so much so that they did not declare themselves 'Hindus' in the census—British policy convinced them to give up this claim and join hands with the other streams of Hinduism, including the orthodox, who paid allegiance to Sanatan Dharma, which had criticized the reformist zeal of Arya Samajis against idol worship, the caste system, and Brahman priesthood (Chand 1904).

The Sanatanis had developed major strongholds in the United Provinces (the region rechristened Uttar Pradesh after independence), this being the crucible of Hindu orthodoxy and home to holy cities such as Haridwar and Varanasi, where the Arya Samaj only had substantial pockets of influence in the western areas. Sanatanis were therefore primarily responsible for the formation of the Hindu Sabha of the United Provinces in the mid-1910s, which happened as a reaction against the extension of a separate electorate in favour of Muslims at the municipal level. The leader of this Hindu Sabha, Madan Mohan Malaviya, was a well known Sanatani, famous for his orthodoxy and his interest in educational matters. Malaviya is indeed best remembered as having initiated the foundation of the Banaras Hindu University (BHU) in 1916 (Dar and Somaskandan 1966).

The Hindu Sabha movement spread beyond Punjab and the United Provinces into Bihar, Bengal, the Central Provinces and Berar, and into the Bombay Presidency. Some of these regional branches sent delegates to Haridwar for the founding of Hindu Mahasabha in 1915. But this intended umbrella organization was still-born, not only because of persisting difficulties between Arya Samajis and Sanatanis over social reform, but also over British rule: the latter continued to pay allegiance to the British in spite of everything, while Arya Samajis resented their politics and even indulged, sometimes, in radical forms of resistance.

## The Hindu Sangathan Movement: Hindu Nationalism Crystallizes

The Hindu Mahasabha was rekindled in the 1920s. At this time the ideology of Hindu nationalism was codified and acquired its distinctive features. This development followed the same logic as the initial stages of socio-religious reform movements: Hindu nationalism crystallized in reaction to a threat subjectively felt if not concretely experienced. This time the threatening Other was neither Christian missionaries nor colonial bureaucrats, but Muslims, not only because of their special equation with the British—as evident from the separate electorates issues—but also because of their mobilization during the Khilafat Movement.

This movement had developed in the wake of World War I as a sequel to the peace treaties which abolished the Muslim Khilafat—a word deriving from the title 'Khalifa' (Caliph), held till then by the Ottoman sultan, one of the defeated rulers. In India, Muslims demonstrated against the British, who had naturally taken part in the post-War negotiations. But their mobilization also affected Hindus, who were a more accessible target, and with whom they sometimes happened to be locked in socioeconomic conflicts locally. In the early 1920s riots multiplied, including in south India, where inter-communal relations had been traditionally much less tense. In fact the first large riot occurred in what is now Kerala, caused by economic frustrations among the Mappilas or Moplahs (Muslim peasants) vis-à-vis Hindu landlords (Hardgrave 1977).

The wave of riots which spread over India in the early 1920s fostered a Hindu reaction that resulted in a relaunching of the Hindu Mahasabha. While the movement had stopped organizing regular sessions after 1919, it met again at Haridwar in 1921 and became the crucible of the collaboration between Arya Samajis and Sanatanis, who now agreed that Muslims were posing such a threat to Hindus that they could not afford to fight each other any more. This convergence found expression in the collaboration between Malaviya and Lajpat Rai, the latter being one of the most important Arya Samaji leaders in Punjab.

Hindu Sabhaites then emphasized the need for an organization (*sangathan*) for the majority community. However, for the Arya Samajis *sangathan* meant something more than it did to Sanatanis. For Swami Shraddhananda, for instance, the *Shuddhi* Movement needed to be revived and directed more towards Untouchables to make them feel better integrated in society once they had been 'purified'. This was something Sanatanis continued to accept reluctantly, as a temporary response to Muslim militancy (Thursby 1972).

The Hindu Mahasabha was not a party in its own right but a sub-group of Congress members. It worked as a lobby within Congress (Gordon 1975). Such a position weakened its general stand—especially after Gandhi rose to power in Congress—introduced a more centralized decision-making process, and made it embody a broad-based Hindu brand of politics. Because his style and programme were based on a universalist and reformist Hinduism, Gandhi did not leave the Hindu Sabhaites much room for manoeuvre in the Congress and, more generally, in the Indian public sphere. Eventually, therefore, the Hindu Mahasabha had to part company with Congress. It became a full-fledged party in the late 1930s under the leadership of V.D. Savarkar, who made its ideology so radical that Congress leaders like Nehru were not prepared to cohabit with what they saw as a communal and fundamentalist variety of politics. Savarkar was a Maharashtrian Brahman from Nasik; but even before he took over as president of the Hindu Mahasabha, the centre of gravity had shifted from north to central India, more especially to the Central Provinces and Berar, and to the Bombay Presidency.

## THE MAHARASHTRIAN CRUCIBLE OF HINDU NATIONALISM

Hindu nationalism as we know it today was born in Maharashtra in the 1920s, in the context of reaction to the Khilafat Movement. Its ideology was codified by Savarkar much before he joined the Hindu Mahasabha. A former anti-British revolutionary, his book *Hindutva: Who is a Hindu?* written in the early 1920s while still a prisoner of the British at Ratnagiri in Maharashtra was the first attempt at endowing what he called the 'Hindu Rashtra' (Hindu nation) with a clear-cut identity: namely Hindutva, a word coined by Savarkar and which, according to him does not coincide with Hinduism. Declaring himself an atheist, Savarkar argued that religion was only one aspect of Hindu identity, and not even the most important. In fact he draws his definition of Hindu identity out of Western theories of the nation. The first criterion of the Hindu nation, for him, is the sacred territory of Aryavarta as described in the Vedas, and by Dayananda, whose book *Satyarth Prakash* Savarkar read extensively (Keer 1988: 29).[1] Then comes race: for Savarkar the Hindus are the descendants of 'Vedic fathers' who occupied this geographical area since antiquity. In addition to religion, land and race, Savarkar mentions language as a pillar of Hindu identity. When doing so he refers to Sanskrit but also to Hindi: hence the equation he finally established between Hindutva and the triptych: 'Hindu, Hindi, Hindustan'. Hindu nationalism appears for the first time as resulting from the superimposition of a religion, a culture, a language, and a sacred territory—the perfect recipe for ethnic nationalism.

For Savarkar, who invented this new doctrine in the wake of revivalists *à la* Dayananda, Hindu Sabhaites, and Sangathanists, the Indian identity is epitomized by Hindutva: the majority community is supposed to embody the nation, not only because it is the largest but also because it is the oldest. Hindus are the autochthonous people of India, whereas the religious minorities are outsiders who must adhere to Hindutva culture, which is the national culture. In the private sphere they may worship their gods and follow their rituals, but in the public domain they must pay allegiance to Hindu symbols. This applies especially to Muslims and Christians, the proponents, in his view, of truly un-Indian religions. Buddhists, Jains, and Sikhs are not considered non-Hindus by Savarkar—they are followers of sects closely linked to Hinduism.

Because Savarkar wrote *Hindutva* in reaction to the pan-Islamic mobilization of the Khilafat Movement, most of his thought derives from his deep-rooted hostility to Islam and its followers. For Savarkar the Muslims of India constituted fifth-columnists whose allegiance was to Mecca and Istanbul (the political capital of the Ummah until the 1920s). Though in a minority, Muslims were a threat to Hindus because of their pan-Islamism, and because, being more aggressive and better organized, they could outmanoeuvre Hindus, who remained effete and divided into many castes and sects.

While Savarkar provided Hindu nationalism with an ideology, he did not outline a plan of action by which Hindus ought to react to the Muslim threat, or reform and organize themselves. This task was taken up by another Maharashtrian, Keshav Baliram Hedgewar (1889-1940), who paid a visit to Savarkar in the mid-1920s and then founded the RSS in his hometown, Nagpur (Deshpande and Ramaswamy 1981). This organization was intended not only to propagate the Hindutva ideology but also to infuse new physical strength into the majority community.

To achieve this twofold objective the RSS adopted a very specific modus operandi. Hedgewar decided to work at the grassroots in order to reform Hindu society from below: he created local branches (*shakhas*) of the movement in towns and villages according to a standard pattern. Young Hindu men gathered every morning and every evening on a playground for games with martial connotations and ideological training sessions. The men in charge of the *shakhas*, called *pracharaks* (preachers), dedicated their whole life to the organization; as a part of RSS cadres they could be sent anywhere in India to develop the organization's network. At the time of India's independence there were also about 600,000 *swayamsevaks* (volunteers) (Curran 1951). The RSS soon became the most powerful Hindu nationalist movement, but it did not have much impact on public life in India simply because it remained out of politics. M.S. Golwalkar, who succeeded Hedgewar as *sarsanghchalak* (head) of the organization in 1940, had made apoliticism a rule. Savarkar, who revived the Hindu Mahasabha after being released by the British in 1937, asked Golwalkar for support at a critical juncture—when the Mahasabha left Congress and became a full-fledged party, but in vain (Andersen and Damle 1987).

However, soon after independence, the RSS leaders realized they could not remain out of politics. In January 1948 Mahatma Gandhi was killed by a former RSS *swayamsevak*, Nathuram Godse, and Prime Minister Jawaharlal Nehru immediately imposed a ban on the organization, whose leaders then realized that they could not expect help from any party in the political arena. A section of the movement's leaders who were already favourably inclined towards involving the

RSS in politics now argued that this state of things justified the launching of a party of its own by the RSS. Though reluctant, Golwalkar allowed them to discuss the matter with Shyama Prasad Mookerjee, who had been president of the Hindu Mahasabha. These negotiations resulted in the creation of the Bharatiya Jana Sangh (forerunner of the present Bharatiya Janata Party or BJP) in 1951, on the eve of the first general elections.

## THE SANGH PARIVAR TAKES SHAPE

At its inception, the Jana Sangh was Janus-faced, with former Hindu Sabhaites like Mookerjee and RSS members like Deendayal Upadhyaya at its helm (Graham 1990). After the untimely death of the former in 1953, Upadhyaya took over the party organization and eliminated the Hindu Sabhaites. Upadhyaya, however, was not only an organization man: he was first and foremost an ideologue, probably the last major Hindu nationalist ideologue. In the 1960s his doctrine of 'Integral Humanism' became the official platform of the Jana Sangh. Not only did Upadhyaya draw inspiration from the Hindutva ideology of Savarkar, his eulogy of the organic unity of the *varna* system harked back to Dayananda: a century of ideology-building then culminated in Upadhyaya's conservative thought.

The xenophobic dimensions of the Jana Sangh were, however, more evident in the writings of Balraj Madhok, president of the Jana Sangh in the late 1960s. Madhok's views echoed those of Savarkar and Golwalkar inasmuch as he exhorted minorities to 'Indianize'—meaning they should adopt Hindu cultural features and assimilate into a 'Hindian' nation (Fox 1987; Frykenberg 1987).

The Jana Sangh was only one of the front organizations set up by the RSS, the latter's aim no longer being merely to penetrate society only through *shakhas* but also to establish organizations working within specific social categories. Thus in 1948 RSS cadres based in Delhi founded the Akhil Bharatiya Vidyarthi Parishad (ABVP), a student union whose primary aim was to combat the communist influence on university campuses. (The ABVP currently ranks first among student unions in terms of membership.) In 1955 the RSS gave itself a workers' union, the Bharatiya Mazdoor Sangh (BMS) whose primary mission was also to counter the 'red unions' in the name of Hindu nationalist ideology, this being a doctrine that also sought to promote social cohesion over class struggle. (In the 1990s the BMS became India's largest trade union.)

In addition to these unions the RSS developed more targeted organizations. In 1952 it founded a tribal movement, the Vanavasi Kalyan Ashram (VKA),[2] which aimed above all to counter the influence of Christian movements among the aboriginals of India, proselytism and priestly social work having resulted in numerous conversions. The VKA applied itself to imitating missionary methods and thus achieved a number of 'reconversions'.

In 1964, in association with Hindu clerics, the RSS set up the Vishva Hindu Parishad (VHP), a movement responsible for grouping the heads of various Hindu sects in order to lend this hitherto unorganized religion a sort of centralized structure. Here too, Hindu nationalists took Christianity, particularly the notion of 'consistory', as a model. For a long time the VHP only attracted gurus who had founded their own ashrams. Such gurus used the VHP as a soapbox, even a form of legitimacy, with the main sect leaders remaining purposefully at a distance (Jaffrelot 2001).

Another subsidiary, Vidya Bharati, was established in 1977 to coordinate a network of schools first developed by the RSS in the 1950s on the basis of local initiatives. Lastly, in 1979 the RSS founded Seva Bharati to penetrate India's slums through social activities (free schools, low-cost medicines, etc.). Taken together, these bridgeheads are presented by the mother organization as forming the *Sangh Parivar*, or 'the family of the Sangh', that is, of the RSS (Jaffrelot 2005).

## HINDU NATIONALISM AND POLITICAL STRATEGY

The Jana Sangh always wavered between two strategies: one, moderate, involved positioning itself as a patriotic party on behalf of national unity, as the protector of both the poor and of small privately-owned businesses, deploying a populist vein. The other line, more militant, was based on the promotion of an aggressive form of 'Hinduness', symbolized by the campaign to raise Hindi to the level of India's national language and protecting of cows (by banning cow-slaughter). The cow being sacred for Hindus but not for Muslims. The latter were in fact the implicit target of an agitation against slaughtering cows set off in 1966, in the context of the fourth general elections campaign.

Although the militant strategy was more in keeping with RSS wishes and the feelings of its activists, it ran up against India's constitutional rules of secularism and prevented the Jana Sangh from broadening its base and striking up alliances with other parties. This strategy changed in the 1970s. In 1977 the Jana Sangh resigned itself to following a moderate line and merged with the Janata Party, which had just defeated Indira Gandhi's Congress Party. However, the former Jana Sangh had not broken with the RSS, to the great displeasure of some of its new partners in power, particularly the socialists. This latter group, associated with the government's second-in-command Charan Singh (who sought to destabilize Prime Minister Morarji Desai—all the better to take his place), drew their argument from an upsurge in Hindu-Muslim riots within which RSS activists were involved, to demand that the former Jana Sanghis break with the RSS. The Jana Sanghis' refusal precipitated the break-up of the Janata Party, paving the way for Indira Gandhi's return.

In 1980 the former Jana Sangh leaders started a new party, the Bharatiya Janata Party (BJP), which remained faithful to the moderate strategy. The BJP, which had Atal Behari Vajpayee as its first president, diluted the original ideology of the Jana Sangh in order to become more acceptable in the Indian party system and to find allies in this arena. This more moderate approach to politics was considerably resented by the rest of the *Sangh Parivar*.

The RSS kept its distance from the BJP and made greater use of the VHP to rekindle ethno-religious political activism. This more militant strategy found its main expression in the launching of the Ayodhya Movement in the mid-1980s.

The BJP rallied to the call of this ethno-religious mobilization strategy and even participated in the processions which took place all over India: the agitation contributed to its success at the polls, taking it from 2 to 88 parliamentary seats and from 7.4 to 11.6 per cent of the votes cast. In 1990, while the party was a major component of the coalition in power that had just ousted the Congress Party, its president, L.K. Advani, went on a 10,000 km 'chariot-journey' or *Rath yatra* that was to culminate in the construction of the Ram Temple in Ayodhya. Advani was stopped before entering Uttar Pradesh and during the repression of activists who attacked the mosque some dozen were left dead. This episode reinforced the champion-of-Hinduism image that the BJP had been trying to acquire among the majority community. The 1991 general elections actually enabled the party to win 20.08 per cent of the vote and 120 seats in the Lok Sabha. Paradoxically, its success in Uttar Pradesh, where the BJP was able to form the state government, did not enable it to solve the Ayodhya temple issue.

Hindu nationalist militants put an end to this deadlock by demolishing the mosque on 6 December 1992. This operation and the ensuing Hindu-Muslim riots—1,200 dead within a few days—prompted New Delhi to take a number of repressive measures, including the dissolution of assemblies in states where the BJP was in power (Uttar Pradesh, Madhya Pradesh, Himachal Pradesh, and Rajasthan), and a ban on the RSS and the VHP. These proved temporary measures and did not affect the *Sangh Parivar*.

By the mid-1990s the BJP reverted to its moderate line, discarding the manipulation of religious symbols for political ends in favour of touting more legitimate issues such as national unity and economic independence. This was not only because it had lost elections in UP, MP, and HP in 1993—the voters obviously punishing the party for violent excesses related to the Ayodhya affair—but also because *Sangh Parivar* leaders admitted they could not acquire power unless the BJP formed political alliances with regional parties. Moreover, Advani, the party's president, allowed Vajpayee to take the forefront once again because Vajpayee was less marked by Hindu nationalist activism.

The BJP was able to build a coalition of more than fifteen parties in the late 1990s. This 'National Democratic Alliance' enabled Vajpayee to form a government after the 1998 and 1999 elections. The arrangement forced the BJP to put on the backburner contentious issues—such as the construction of a temple in Ayodhya; restrict Article 30 of the Indian Constitution guaranteeing the right of religious and linguistic minorities to establish educational institutions; abolish Article 370 of the Constitution granting a partially autonomous status to Jammu and Kashmir; promulgate a uniform civil code, primarily to put an end to the possibility given to Muslims to follow Islamic Law (*sharia*).

Once in office, the BJP implemented some of the traditional items of the Hindu nationalist programme. Vajpayee's first major decision was the nuclear test of May 1998. The policy of the minister for human resource development, Murli Manohar Joshi, was also well in tune with Hindu nationalist leanings: he appointed personalities who had been close to the *Sangh Parivar* as heads of the directive body of the Indian Council of Historical Research (ICHR),[3] the Indian Council of Social Science Research (ICSSR), and the search committee for faculty appointments in the National Council of Educational Research and Training (NCERT) which was entrusted with the task of designing a new school curriculum. One of Joshi's priorities was to create new textbooks—including those dealing with Indian history—rewritten in a vein more in line with Hindu nationalist ideology.

But the BJP distanced itself from several other traditional mainstays of its ideology, such as economic nationalism—a notion encapsulated by the word 'swadeshi'. The government in fact opened new sectors to foreign investment. This new, sympathetic approach of 'liberalization' caused some concern within the *Sangh Parivar*. The Swadeshi Jagran Manch—a newly created offshoot of RSS— and the Bharatiya Mazdoor Sangh complained to the RSS, whose governing body, the Akhil Bharatiya Pratinidhi Sabha, passed a resolution in March 2000 supporting an 'India-centric and need-specific' model of development (Hansen and Jaffrelot 2001).

In May 2004, during the parliamentary elections, the NDA government led by the BJP was surprisingly defeated and replaced by a Congress-led coalition. The defeat was considered by most components of the *Sangh Parivar* to be that of the Vajpayee moderate line. The VHP leaders were especially vocal. For them the BJP-led government had betrayed the Hindus by not building the Rama temple they longed for in Ayodhya. The compulsions of coalition politics had stymied the Hindutva agenda. Former socialists and other self-proclaimed secularist allies of the BJP-led coalition would not allow Hindutva-oriented objectives such as the building of a Rama Temple in Ayodhya (Jaffrelot 2005b). The BJP had become adept at coalition-making, to stay in power, but the rules of the coalition game had diluted the agenda.

As a result, Hindutva forces are today deeply divided. The BJP leaders consider that any return to a radical brand of Hindu nationalist politics by the party will alienate its allies and postpone *sine die* its comeback to the helm of political affairs in the country. The RSS and VHP leaders assume that the BJP lost the 2004 elections because the Vajpayee government had disappointed too many Hindus. They fear that any further dilution of the ideology of the party would widen the gap between the BJP and the rest of the *Sangh Parivar*. When such differences emerge between the political sector of the *Sangh Parivar* and the rest, the political wing eventually falls in line. In the late 1980s, for instance, Advani succeeded Vajpayee for the second time and took the party towards the Hindutva direction, as desired by the RSS. Undoubtedly, Advani's departure as president of the BJP on the eve of new year's day 2006 was largely perceived as being at the behest of the RSS. The tensions between the RSS and the BJP cannot be taken lightly anyway. They affect two mainstays of the self-perception—and indeed the identity—of the Hindutva Movement. First, while the *Sangh Parivar* claims to form a 'family', with its members playing complementary parts, the RSS and the BJP (and the VHP and the BJP) appear to be at cross purposes (Jaffrelot 2005a).

Second, the experiment of the Vajpayee government has shown that the RSS could not really exert the influence it wanted over power, even when the BJP was in office. This failure, once again, puts into question a key element of the *Sangh Parivar's* identity. Certainly, the RSS aspires to reshape society in its own image at the grassroots level in a long-term perspective. But it also wants to be the 'Raj guru', the mentor of government. The Vajpayee government episode has demonstrated that such an objective is very difficult to achieve. This realization may force the *Sangh Parivar* to change its functioning.

## Notes

1. While in England in 1906–10 Savarkar stayed at India House, a guesthouse founded by Shyamji Krishna Varma, who had been a close disciple of Dayananda.
2. Hindu nationalists translate 'indigenous peoples' as *vanavasi*, literally 'those who live in the forest', instead of the more commonly used term throughout India, *adivasi*, in 'other words those who were there first'. From the Hindu nationalist ideological standpoint the initial inhabitants of the country were 'Aryans' and not aboriginals: the latter they argue were driven away or conquered by Aryan invasions.
3. In February 2000 the ICHR 'suspended' two volumes of its series called 'Towards Freedom', namely those edited by Sumit Sarkar and K.N. Panikkar, both known for being highly critical of the *Sangh Parivar*.

## References

Andersen, W. and Damle, S.D. (1987), *The Brotherhood in Saffron: The Rashtriya Swayamsevak Sangh and Hindu Revivalism*, New Delhi: Vistaar Publications.

Barrier, N.G. (1966), *The Punjab Alienation of Land Bill of 1900*, Durham: Duke University Press.

Bayly, C.A. (1985), 'The Pre-History of "Communalism"? Religious Conflict in India 1700-1800', *Modern Asian Studies,* Vol. 19, No. 2.

Borthwick, M. (1977), *Keshub Chandra Sen: A Search for Cultural Synthesis*, Calcutta: Minerva Associates.

Broomfield, J.H. (1968), *Elite Conflict in a Plural Society: Twentieth-century Bengal*, Berkeley: University of California Press.

Cashman, R. (1975), *The Myth of the Lokmanya*, Berkeley: University of California Press.

Chand, Lal (1904) (2nd edn), *Sanatana Dharma: An Advanced Text Book of Hindu Religion and Ethics*, Benares: Central Hindu College.

Collet, S.D. (1962), *The Life and Letters of Raja Ram Mohan Roy*, Calcutta: Sadharan Brahmo Samaj.

Copley, A. (2000) (ed.), *Gurus and their Followers: New Religious Reform Movements in Colonial India*, Delhi: Oxford University Press.

Curran, J.A. (1951), *Militant Hinduism in Indian Politics: A Study of the RSS*, N.P.: Institute of Pacific Relations.

Dar, S.L. and Somaskandan, S. (1966), *History of the Banaras Hindu University*, Benares: BHU.

Deshpande, B.V. and Ramaswamy, S.R. (1981), *Dr Hedgewar: the Epoch Maker*, Bangalore: Sahitya Sindhu.

Dua, V. (1999), *The Arya Samaj in Punjab Politics*, New Delhi: Picus Books.

Frykenberg, R.E. (1987), 'The Concept of "Majority" as a Devilish Force in the Politics of Modern Asia', *The Journal of Commonwealth and Comparative Politics*, Vol. 15, No. 3, November 1987.

———— (1989), 'The Emergence of Modem Hinduism as a Concept and as an Institution: A Reappraisal with Special Reference to South India', in C.D. Sontheimer and H. Kulke (eds.), *Hinduism Reconsidered*, Delhi: Manohar Publications, p. 30.

Fox, R.G. (1987), 'Gandhian Socialism and Hindu Nationalism: Cultural Domination in the World System', *The Journal of Commonwealth and Comparative Politics*, Vol. 25, No. 3, November 1987.

Ghai, R.K. (1990), *Shuddhi Movement in India*, New Delhi: Commonwealth Publishers.

Gordon, R. (1975), 'The Hindu Mahasabha and the Indian National Congress 1915 to 1926', *Modern Asian Studies*, Vol. 9, No. 2.

Graham, B. (1990), *Hindu Nationalism and Indian Politics: The Origins and Development of the Bharatiya Jana Sangh*, Cambridge: Cambridge University Press.

Gupta, S.K. (1991), *Arya Samaj and the Raj*, New Delhi: Gitanjali Publishing House.

Halbfass, W. (1988), *India and Europe: An Essay in Philosophical Understanding*, New York: State University of New York.

Hansen, T. and Jaffrelot, C. (2001) (eds.) (2nd edn), *The BJP and the Compulsions of Politics in India*, Delhi: Oxford University Press.

Hardgrave, Jr. R.L. (1977), 'The Mappilla Rebellion, 1921: Peasant Revolt in Malabar', *Modern Asian Studies*, Vol. 11, No. 1.

Jaffrelot, C. (1999), *The Hindu Nationalist Movement and Indian Politics*, New Delhi: Penguin.

———— (2001), 'The Vishva Hindu Parishad: A Nationalist but Mimetic Attempt at Federating the Hindu Sects', in Vasudha Dalmia, Angelika Malinar, and Martin Christof (eds.), *Charisma and Canon: Essays on the Religions History of the Indian Subcontinent*, Delhi: Oxford University Press.

———— (2003), 'Opposing Gandhi: Hindu Nationalism and Political Violence', in D. Vidal, G. Tarabout, and E. Meyer (eds.), *Violence/Non-Violence: Some Hindu Perspectives*, Delhi: Manohar-CSH, pp. 299-324.

———— (2005a) (ed.), *The Sangh Parivar: A Reader*, Delhi: Oxford University Press.

—— (2005b), 'The BJP and the 2004 Elections: Dimensions, Causes and Implications of an Unexpected Defeat', in Katharine Adney and Lawrence Saez (eds.), *Coalition Politics and Hindu Nationalism*, New York: Routledge.

Jones, K. (1973), ' "Ham Hindu Nahin": Arya-Sikh Relations', 1877–1905, *Journal of Asian Studies*, Vol. 32, No. 3, May 1973.

—— (1976), *Arya Dharm: Hindu Consciousness in Nineteenth-Century Punjab*, Berkeley: University of California Press.

—— (1989), *Socio-Religious Reform Movements in British India*, Cambridge: Cambridge University Press.

Keer, D. (1988), *Veer Savarkar*, Bombay: Popular Prakashan, p. 29.

Kopf, D. (1969), *British Orientalism and the Bengali Renaissance*, Calcutta: Firma K.L. Mukhopadhyay.

—— (1979), *The Brahmo Samaj and the Shaping of the Modern Indian Mind*, Princeton: Princeton University Press.

Marshall, P.J. (1970) (ed.), *The British Discovery of Hinduism in the Eighteenth Century*, Cambridge: Cambridge University Press.

Minault, Gail (1982), *The Khilafat Movement: Religious Symbolism and Political Mobilization in India*, New York: Columbia University Press.

O'Connell, J.T. (1973), 'The Word "Hindu" in Gaudiya Vaishnava Texts', *Journal of the American Oriental Society*, Vol. 93, No. 3, pp. 340–4.

Pandey, Gyanendra (1990), *The Construction of Communalism in Colonial North India*, Delhi: Oxford University Press.

Pandit, Saraswati (1975), *A Critical Study of the Contribution of the Arya Samaj to Indian Education*, Delhi: Sarvadeshik Arya Pratinidhi Sabha.

Parmanand (1985), *Mahamana Madan Mohan Malaviya: An Historical Biography*, 2 Vols., Varanasi: BHU.

Rai, Lajpat (1914), *The Arya Samaj: An Account of its Aims, Doctrine and Activities, with a Biographical Sketch of the Founder*, New Delhi: D.A.V. College.

—— (1967), *A History of the Arya Samaj*, Bombay: Orient Longman.

Raychaudhuri, T. (1988), *Europe Reconsidered: Perceptions of the West in Nineteenth-Century Bengal*, Delhi: Oxford University Press.

Renou, L. (1972) (2nd edn), *Religions of Ancient India*, New Delhi: Munshiram Manoharlal, p. 50.

Robertson, B.C. (1995), *Raja Rammohun Roy: The Father of Modern India*, Delhi: Oxford University Press.

Saikai, H.C. (1928) (ed.), *English Works of Raja Rammohun Roy*, Vol. 1, Calcutta: Brahmo Samaj Centenary Committee.

Thapar, R. (1989), 'Imagined Religious Communities? Ancient History and the Modern Search for a Hindu Identity', *Modern Asian Studies*, Vol. 23, No. 2, p. 216.

Thursby, G.R. (1972), 'Aspects of Hindu-Muslim Relations in British India: A Study of Arya Samaj Activities, Government of India Politics, and Communal Conflicts in the Period 1923–1928', Ph.D. dissertation, Duke University.

Vable, D. (1983), *The Arya Samaj: Hindu without Hinduism*, New Delhi: Vikas.

# Chapter 4

# Hindu nationalism, strategic syncretism in ideology-building

Schematically, the origin and development of ethnic movements in India have been approached in the main from two opposing theoretical positions: the 'primordialist' and the 'instrumentalist'. While the former tends to analyse the cultural specificity as leading naturally to some form of ethnic consciousness, the latter considers cultural identities perfectly malleable and explains such movements as stemming from the manipulation of identity symbols by elites willing to mobilize 'their' community with some socio-political interest in view (Brass 1974: 121). The main weakness of these two approaches seems to lie in their attitude toward the nationalist ideology: either the question vanishes because of a more or less implicit equation between ideology and culture, or ideology is considered as a mere means of mobilization manipulated by èlites.[1]

This essay suggests a third intermediate perspective on the basis of a case study, the genesis and development of Hindu nationalism as an *ideology*. Ideology is defined by Geertz as a 'symbolic strategy' evolved in a society undermined by the modernization processes (Geertz 1973: Ch. 8: 193–254). The term, according to this perspective, refers 'to that part of culture which is actively and explicitly concerned with the establishment and defence of patterns of value and belief' (Fallers 1961: 677–8). Nationalism is obviously an ideology par excellence according to this definition. This theoretical perspective emphasizes the 'instrumentalist' idea of manipulative reinterpretations of cultural material; nevertheless the model remains predominantly 'cultural' since the major aim of the reinterpreters is to adjust the outward expression of ideology while preserving the basic values and identity of the society.

This theoretical framework seems to be relevant in throwing light on the emergence of the Hindu nationalist ideology in terms of 'invention of the tradition'.[2] My hypothesis is that it is even possible to analyse it as a sub-category of this invention process, a sub-category that can be called 'strategic syncretism' because the content of this ideology has been drawn to a large extent from material derived from the cultural values of groups which were seen as antagonistic towards the Hindu community. This 'syncretism' proved to be 'strategic' because it underlay an ideology aiming to dominate the others, in terms of prestige as well as on a

*This chapter draws from a paper prepared for presentation at the Conference of the British Association for South Asian Studies, 10–12 April 1992, Birmingham.

concrete socio-political plane. I shall test this hypothesis by focusing on three significant and cumulative (in terms of ideology-building) episodes, the shaping of socio-religious reform movements, the birth of the Hindu Mahasabha in the wake of the Khilafat Movement and the ideological development of the 'RSS complex'.

## The Western Challenge and the Nineteenth Century Socio-Religious Reform Movements

In the nineteenth century, a number of socio-religious reform movements attempted to gather support amongst Hindus. These movements represented primarily a reaction to the threat of Western domination and especially to a twofold cultural challenge—the utilitarian reformism and Christian proselytism. Both relied mainly on the criticism of idol worship as being polytheistic superstitions and of the caste system as 'a degrading and pernicious system of subordination' (Mill quoted in Stokes 1989: 54). Such a discourse appeared all the more dangerous for the cultural equilibrium of Hindu society as it could find expression in legislative reforms 'from above' (such as the Age of Consent Bill, 1891) or lead to conversions (in Punjab, the first census revealed a steady erosion of the proportion of Hindus partly due to this phenomenon—from 43 per cent in 1891 to 36.3 per cent in 1911).[3]

### THE INVENTION OF A GOLDEN AGE: THE BRAHMO SAMAJ AND THE DEBATE AROUND MONOTHEISM

The first significant socio-religious reform movement, the Brahmo Samaj, emerged in this context in 1828 in Calcutta, the city where western ideas had first taken hold. Rammohun Roy, the founder, aspired to reform Hinduism whose shortcomings he acknowledged, especially with regard to idol worship. Moreover, the Brahmo Samaj expression of devotion took the form of prayers to 'the One True God'. At the same time, Roy argued that idol worship was a late corruption of the most perfect antiquarian religion in which God was worshipped as the pure Absolute. His main sources were the Upanishads, the latest texts of Vedic literature where *Brahman* is indeed described as a 'spiritual essence' sustaining the whole of creation, individual souls included.[4] His study of the Upanishads, however, proved to be influenced by 'a more rigid monotheism of the people of the Book' (Miller 1987: 181) since the philosophy of 'the speculative brahman' tended to be replaced by a rather rational theism.

In fact, Roy selected the Upanishads and reinterpreted them in that way, because of his desire to confute the missionaries whose propaganda 'abus[ed] and ridicul[ed] the gods and saints of [Hinduism]'[5] (which he felt eventually deserved some respect!). One of his main intellectual activities—the translation and interpretation of the Upanishads—was systematically justified as a means of enlightening the Westerners:

> Such benevolent people will perhaps, rise from a perusal of them [these translations] with the conviction, that in most ancient times the inhabitants of this part of the globe (at least the more intelligent class) were not unacquainted with metaphysical subjects; that allegorical language or description was very frequently employed to represent the attributes of Creator, which were sometimes designated as independent existence; and that, however, suitable this method might be to the refined understanding of men of learning, it had the most mischievous effect when literature and philosophy decayed, producing all these absurdities and idolatrous notions which have checked, or rather destroyed, every mark of reason, and darkened every beam of understanding.[6]

That this evocation of a monotheistic original religion was intended to strengthen the standing of Hinduism in relation to Christianity is confirmed by Roy's alacrity in exposing the idolatrous doctrine of the Trinity[7] by contrast, implicitly, with his upanishadic religion.

Roy's approach is syncretic because he endeavours to reform Hinduism by resorting to the precepts of Christianity and Western rationalism; but this syncretism proves to be strategic since he claims that he draws this neo-Hinduism from a purely indigenous Golden Age which enables him to rehabilitate the Hindu identity scoffed at by the Europeans. This is one of the first building blocks of a pre-nationalist ideology evolved to resist foreign aggressions seen as most dangerous for the native cultural equilibrium. However, this process enters its maturity phase after the emergence of another socio-religious reform movement, the Arya Samaj.

## THE INVENTION OF A GOLDEN AGE: THE ARYA SAMAJ
## AND THE DEBATE AROUND THE CASTE SYSTEM

The Arya Samaj was founded in 1875 by Swami Dayananda who came into contact with the Brahmo Samajists in Calcutta in the early 1870s. Even though he disapproved of their complaisance towards Christianity, Dayananda followed in their wake inasmuch as he institutionalized the idea of a Vedic monotheism and joined in the criticism of the idolatry of popular Hinduism raised by Christian missionaries. He entered into theological arguments all over north India with missionaries, for instance. The form of worship propagated by the Arya Samaj is supposed to rehabilitate the one prevailing during the Vedic Age even though its *Agnihotra* (fire sacrifice), performed when the sun rises and sets, omits most of the typically Vedic ritualism because of its deliberately abstract monotheism.

More importantly, Dayananda added a social dimension to the myth of a Golden Age in the making. The so-called Vedic caste system was presented by him as much more flexible than the one then prevailing in India. Indeed, he maintained that *jati* (hereditary, endogamous and hierarchical castes copiously criticized by the Westerners) did not exist in the Vedic times but the prevalent social organization then was a *varna* system.

References to the four *varnas* do exist in the *Rig Veda*, the earliest of the Vedic texts, in hymn X-90 relating a famous foundation myth allegory, to have born out of the sacrifice of the primordial Man (*Virat Purusha*): 'the Brahman (priest) was his mouth, his arm was made the Kshatriya (warrior), his thighs became the Vaishya and from his feet the Shudra (servant) was made'. This fourfold schema is an ideal, normative one, whose relationship to social practise is not very well known, but it clearly implies a hierarchical structure based upon ritual distinctions: as in the *jati* system, the brahman and the shudra stand poles apart in the social organization.

Dayananda described these four Vedic 'classes' as merely born out of the collectivity's needs in terms of socioeconomic complementarity, claiming further that status distinctions came at a later stage. He contended that originally, therefore, children were placed in each *varna* according to their individual qualities:

The fixture of the *varna* according to merits and actions should take place at the sixteenth year of girls and twenty-fifth year of boys. Marriages also should take place in their own *varna*, i.e., a brahman man should be married to a brahman woman; a kshatriya to a kshatriya, a vaishya to a vaishya, and a shudra to a shudra. This will maintain the integrity of each *varna* as well as good relations.[8]

By such reasoning, Dayananda substituted the prevailing, illegitimate *jati* system, in comparison with Western social values, by a more prestigious *varna* system whose reinterpretation enabled him to rehabilitate a social system of ritual hierarchy (a pillar of Hindu cultural equilibrium) since it can be favourably compared to the individualistic values which the Europeans pride themselves: Dayananda can now question the Western superiority by arguing that his civilization was respectful of the justice principle much before the West.

Thus, on the one hand Dayananda reinforced the myth of a Vedic Golden Age through which a segment of the Hindu intelligentsia regained its self-esteem in its confrontation with European domination; on the other hand, he legitimized the caste system under the garb of a so-called ancestral *varna* incorporating certain individualistic values. Dayananda's reformism, far from contesting the social system, tried to protect its equilibrium, as his recommendation relating to the strict endogamy of *varna* testifies. It is easy to recognize here the same process of ideological reconstruction theorized by Geertz and Fallers: the Arya Samaj tries to evolve an ideology likely to vindicate an identity threatened by the criticism against one of its major pillars—such as the caste system—or, generally speaking, by the negation of its 'cultural quality'. Here, the building of a tradition through the invention of a Golden Age seems to be the natural formulation of a pre-nationalist ideology.

## 'STRATEGIC SYNCRETISM' AND HINDU PRE-NATIONALISM

*'Strategic syncretism' as a variant of the building of tradition process*: This 'invention of tradition' by the socio-religious reform movements is of a special type because it is provoked by and modelled on the antagonist's culture in its *raison d'être* and in its content. Rammohun Roy and Dayananda 'discover' in the Veda what they need to resist Western influences. This is an ideology of 'strategic syncretism': 'syncretism' because there is a strong intention to reform one's society through the assimilation of Western values consistent with the Hindu cultural equilibrium; and 'strategic syncretism' since the equilibrium in question remains the prime concern. This strategy combines two dimensions, the first directed towards 'psychological' demands, and the second concerning 'mimetic' aspects of ideology building.

(*a*) Recovering one's self-esteem: In claiming that Vedic society was at least as monotheistic and as respectful of the individual as the Christian West, the socio-religious reform movements attributed—syncretic phase—to their history the prestigious values the Europeans were so proud of—first strategic moment—and try to legitimize at the same time—second strategic moment—cultural institutions like the caste system under the idealized garb of *varna*.

Underlying these arguments, a major aspect of the reformers' message was: there was no need to leave Hinduism, because of rationalist scepticism or to be converted, since this religion, in its pristine purity, had the same virtues as Christianity and modern science. The only relevant objective is to reestablish this Golden Age of Hinduism, and especially its *varna* system.

The sociological basis of this ideological strategy is easy to trace. Among the Hindus, individuals most willing to protect the cultural equilibrium belong to the high caste élite, not only because they aspire to preserve a privileged position but also because they alone seem to have an overall view of their society. The *varna* model expounded in the Veda, with its organicist emphasis on the harmony of a complementary social system is most probably a brahmanic creation. Indeed, the leaders of the socio-religious reform movements were mainly from the high caste intelligentsia (Roy was a Brahman whose knowledge of English enabled him to work in the East India Company administration and Dayananda, a Gujarati brahman, came from an orthodox milieu).[9]

(*b*) Borrowing cultural features from the aggressor: The syncretism of this movement is strategic also because it involves assimilating the Other's practises to resist him more effectively. As we will see, this aspect became dominant during the twentieth century. In the nineteenth century, it found its first expression in the *Shuddhi* Movement. Originally, the purification ritual of *Shuddhi* served to restore to their status persons of high castes who had been polluted.[10] The ritual was converted from an internal to an external purpose. From the mid-1890s onward, Arya Samajist preachers (*upadeshak*) undertook to (re)convert individuals and their families in north India, especially in the Punjab where the movement was widespread. In 1901, their movement had 8,259 members who were drawn mainly from the intelligentsia and the urban merchant castes.[11]

This imitation of missionaries' techniques is on a par with the Arya Samajist endeavour to endow Hinduism with a Book. For Dayananda (1981: 633, 689), the Veda was such a scripture; he used it as a basis for preaching and it was strong enough to counter the missionaries' use of the Bible. Moreover, he claimed its superiority—coming from its anteriority, scientificity and universality—to persuade Muslims and Christians to conversion! As Romila Thapar (1985: 18) put it, the socio-religious reform movements 'attempted to defend, redefine and create "Hinduism" on the model of the Christian religion. They sought for the equivalent of a monotheistic God, a Book, a Prophet or a Founder and congregational worship with an institutional organisation supporting it'[12] which is often themselves (the Arya Samaj was, for instance, described by some of its leaders as a 'Vedic Church' (Lajpat Rai 1967: 120). This construction of a Hindu identity through emulation and imitation of the Other, the dominant, is inherent to 'strategic syncretism'. This process led to the formation of a true nationalism.

*A first ethnic nationalism*: The socio-religious reform movements' attempts at cultural vindication incorporated a form of nationalism not only because it resulted, by the turn of the century in an aggressive *Shuddhi* Movement, but also because its strategic 'invention of tradition' *implied* a historical enquiry into the original civilization. This research led to the 'discovery' of a Vedic Golden Age, a myth which constituted the touchstone of the first ethnic nationalism in India. The Vedic Aryas were indeed described by Dayananda as a primordial and elect people to whom the Veda had been revealed by God and whose language— Sanskrit—was said to be the 'Mother of all languages' (Dayananda 1981: 249). These Aryas would have migrated in the beginning of creation from Tibet—the first emerged land—towards the Aryavarta. This territory, the homeland of the Vedic Civilization, covered the Ganga basin. From this basis, the Aryas would have dominated the whole world till the war of the Mahabharata—an epic now historicized. The national renaissance implied precisely for Dayananda an inversion of the decline process—the root cause of India's subjugation by the British—and a return to the Vedic Golden Age. The Hindu nationalist identity clearly resulted from traditional criteria of nationalism: a glorious past, a prestigious language and a historical land. This new 'historicism'[13] was the touchstone of nationalism because it provided a powerful lever by which Hindus sought to regain their lost self-esteem vis-à-vis the Europeans.[14]

Thus, the Western challenge has had a catalytic effect, provoking a specific process of cultural reform—what I termed 'strategic syncretism'—from which stemmed a paradoxical ethnic nationalism.[15] Indeed, it borrows many features from the cultural dominant it is supposed to fight, true, under the guise of a return to the Vedic Golden Age. This paradox stems from the original dual objectives of nationalism: on the one hand it had to legitimize endangered institutions like the caste system ('saved' at the cost of an individualist reinterpretation), and on the other hand, it should assimilate cultural characters—like proselytism—which seemed to underlie the European superiority. This mimetic dimension of the Hindu nationalist ideology-building process reached a new development in the 1920s, during the confrontation with another 'aggressor', namely, the Muslim.

## The Confrontation with Militant Islam and the Political Crystallization of Hindu Nationalism

### THE HINDU SABHA MOVEMENT

In the Punjab, it is easy to observe a filiation of ideas between the Arya Samaj and the first political exponents of Hindu nationalism, the Hindu Sabhaites, as early as the first decade of this century. The Punjab Hindu Sabha was formed between 1907 and 1909 by the Arya Samajists. It reacted to the perceived pro-Muslim bias of the British authorities; especially to the institution of a separate electorate for Muslims throughout India—even in areas such as the Punjab where Muslims formed a majority.[16] The Hindu Sabhas functioned as interest groups. They were established to pressurize the British as well as the Indian National Congress, from inside or from outside the party. The text that can be considered as the Hindu Sabhaites' ideological charter was written in 1909 by an Arya Samajist leader, Lal Chand. Its title, *Self Abnegation in Politics* referred to the exceedingly passive attitude of the Indian National Congress.

Founded in 1885, the Congress aspired to represent the whole of the Indian nation. This did not mean that the religious communities were overlooked. In fact, 'India, and the emerging Indian nation, was conceived of as a collection of communities: Hindu + Muslim + Christian + Parsi + Sikh and so on' (Pandey 1990: 210). But these communities were considered more or less as equal and the Hindu majority was expected to make some sacrifices in the interest of national integration. The founding of the Muslim League in 1906, the year in which a delegation of Muslims had appealed to the British for separate electorates, had aroused a fear that minorities might indulge in separatism; hence the complaisancy of the Congress regarding the institution of separate electorates. Protesting vehemently against this attitude, which deprived the Punjab Hindus from a political protector, Lal Chand (1938: 103) justified the development of the Hindu Sabha and the statement of its specific ideology in the following words: '. . . patriotism ought to be communal and not merely geographical. . . . The idea is to love everything owned by the community. It may be religion, it may be a tract of country, or it may be a phase of civilization'.

This nationalism drew heavily upon the earlier cultural revivalism of the Arya Samaj. The Arya Samajist background made them proud of the Vedic Golden Age whose setting had been the early Punjab, the first place which the Aryans had occupied. As early as 1909 an Arya Samajist *upadeshak*, Bhai Parmanand (1982: 36) advocated the partition of north-west India to reserve this piece of land for the Hindus.

The Hindu nationalism[17] evolved by these Arya Samajists, as an ideology, reached its maturity in the 1920s[18] within the Hindu Mahasabha whose formation shows most clearly 'strategic syncretism' at work.

## THE HINDU MAHASABHA: AN IMITATIVE NATIONALISM

Though the Hindu Sabhas adopted a federal structure in the second decade of the twentieth century in north India, the Hindu Mahasabha was effectively launched, as an ideological pressure group within the Congress Party in 1922, largely as a reaction to the Hindu-Muslim riots that broke out in the wake of the Khilafat Movement.[19] In 1921, on the Malabar coast the Moplahs (Muslim descendants of ninth century Arab merchants) instigated violence and forcible conversions that had a traumatic (and catalytic) effect on the Hindu Sabhaites—especially on leaders of the Arya Samaj. A context of aggression somewhat similar to the one created by Western penetration, provoked an analogous reaction.

Indeed, the ideological discourse propagated from the Hindu Mahasabha tribune until the mid-1920s, during the Hindu Sangathan Movement, reproduced the 'strategic syncretism' mechanism. At this stage, Hindu nationalists were inclined to identify certain values which they regarded as the basis of Muslim strength and solidarity, such as an avoidance of sectarian divisions, an emphasis on social cohesion, and to insist that these values could also be established within the sect and caste-ridden Hindu community whose members continued to be described by the British as weak (see Bamford 1985: 111). But this process of assimilating aspects of the Other was adopted under the cover of reestablishing a mythical Golden Age and it remained subordinated to a hierarchical view of society.

The report by B.S. Moonje (1923), leader of the Central Provinces Hindu Sabha, on the Malabar riot constitutes a 'paradigmatic text' in this respect. One of Moonje's explicit aims was to 'remove the docility and the mildness from the temper of the Hindus and make them imbibe the aggressiveness of their neighbours'. His comparison between the two communities led him to diagnose three main Hindu weaknesses: (*a*) Attributing Muslims' virility, their 'readiness to kill and to be killed' above all to their diet and the Islamic practise of sacrifice, Moonje advocated ending 'the un-vedic principle of *ahimsa*' (dispensing vegetarianism) and rehabilitating 'the vedic institution of Yajnathag [seen as an animal sacrifice] accustoming a Hindu to the sight of spilling blood and killing'. This proposal is plausible since during the Vedic times, before the emergence of Buddhism and Jainism, India was familiar with sacrifices and ignored vegetarianism, (*b*) Moonje's main concern, however, was the lack of unity among Hindus compared to the Muslims from a religious as well as a social point of view. First, Moonje lamented, the absence of a common meeting place in the Hindu polity for the castes from the highest to the lowest on perfectly equal terms, just as the Mahomedan has in his Masjid [Mosque] ... [where Muslims] vividly visualise and imbibe the feeling of oneness and the identity of their social and religious interest. ... During vedic times there was the institution called *Yajnasamarambh* where all the four *varnas* used to meet together, for listening to Shastric discourses on religion, sociology, Ayurveda and other sciences then known to them; but it has long since disappeared. Cannot our temples be made to serve the purpose which the Masjid does for the Mahomedan?

*Yajnasamarambh* refers literally to the beginning of the sacrifice. The acceptance of the word as designating a sort of sacrificial assembly would in any case have been a fiction since Vedic sacrifices were performed on behalf of a single sacrificer.[20] Moreover, Moonje abandoned the idea of reintroducing it and instead suggested the transformation of Hindu temples. Shraddhananda endorsed this suggestion in 1926.[21] In this instance the process of 'strategic syncretism' remains incomplete; while Moonje mentions a prestigious 'vedic institution' this reference is not used to cover his mimetic attitude towards Islam. By contrast, he complies fully with the model when he dwells on the most crucial disease of the Hindus: (*c*) Social disunity.

The Hindus are divided into so many watertight compartments, each having a social culture and life of its own, that there is hardly any association between them in the wider field of social activities and amenities of the community as a whole . . .; so that if one section happens to come in conflict with Mahomedans, the other section hardly ever consider it worth their while to run to its help. . . . The Mahomedans on the other hand, form one organic community, religiously well-organized and disciplined, so that any injury done to any part of the community anywhere, is felt as keenly all through out. In a word, there is a living communal feeling in them and it is so high and overpowering that they can hardly think of any public movement unless in terms of their communal interests.

Moonje's proposals to remedy this deficiency were justified by another free interpretation of the *varna* system:

. . . if the Chaturvarnya, which is a distinctive feature of the Aryan civilisation as compared with other systems of civilisation in the world is to be maintained and to prosper as I believe it should, and yet union and solidarity is to be evolved it must give up its system of water-tight compartments of castes and bring about a real organic unity between the four sections of the society which can be done by again bringing into vogue the system of marriage on what are called the *Anuloma* and *Pratiloma Paddhati* as provided in our *Dharmashastra* [religious law treatises] with a view to bind the four sections of the society in blood connections and thus bring about organic unity out of the very diversity of sociological functions allotted to these four original varnas or castes.

Although the so-called Vedic 'custom' (*paddhati*) of *Anuloma* and *Pratiloma* inter-caste marriages (that is, when the male's status is higher than the female's and vice versa) is mentioned in the treatises, this does not mean, of course, that they approve of it. The code of Manu, the main *Dharmashastra*, describes it in the tenth chapter as the root-cause of the mixture of castes that led from the ideal *varna* system to the confused pattern of *jatis*. However, as far as Moonje was concerned, this reference provided a sufficient basis for the validation of his 'invention of tradition'.

His report illustrates a pervasive discourse among the Hindu nationalist leaders[22] whose ideology is a typical version of 'strategic syncretism'. Compared with the socio-religious reform movements, their aim was not so much to protect Hinduism from the cultural influence and prestige of the Other as to identify those aspects in which this aggressor was worthy of imitation in order to cope with his practical superiority. But the technique remains the same: it consists in assimilating the cultural features that threaten the Hindus and, in claiming that they belonged to the Vedic Golden Age to revive them. The most interesting single aspect of this 'invention-protection' of a Hindu identity is the efforts undertaken to preserve the hierarchy through the reinterpretation of the *varna* system.

This reinterpretation is supposed to preserve a major pillar of the Hindu identity—the hierarchy—and to supply the Hindu community with a *national* framework. Indeed, the organicist reading of the *varna* system offers an indigenous sociological pattern of the nation, equivalent to the communitarian (Muslim) and individualistic (European) versions of this political institution. Praising the functional interdependence of the *varna* system, Bhai Parmanand (1936: 126), who presided over the Hindu Mahasabha after Moonje (1927–33) in 1933, asked: 'How could a nation hope to live after lost sight of this aspect of Dharma?' The aim was to maintain the principle of hierarchy while matching the degree of communal solidarity which had apparently been achieved by Indian Muslims. Moreover, many patrons and even leaders of the Hindu Mahasabha were orthodox Brahmans, landlords and even *maharajahs* who found in its reinterpretation of the *varna* a legitimation of the caste system at large. The marginal position of the Hindu Mahasabha inside and then outside the Congress came mainly from this social conservatism which the RSS partially managed to eschew.

## The Uses of 'Strategic Syncretism' by the 'RSS Complex'

### THE RSS AS A NATIONALIST SECT

Like the Hindu Mahasabha, the RSS emerged in response to Hindu-Muslim riots. Its aim was also to consolidate the Hindu nation through psychosocial reform involving some assimilation of the Other's equalitarian values. The method which it used, however, appeared to be much more relevant. For Hedgewar, such an assimilation could not be achieved within the framework of a reinterpreted *varna* system since it was still a division—true, fourfold only—of the Hindu nation,[23] so it attempted to create an ethic of selfless individualism which could provide the basis for a more inclusive and cohesive form of Hindu nationalism. The RSS was thus supposed to become a sort of Hindu nationalist spearhead based on individual solidarity. Its 'syncretism' (the import of egalitarian values typical of European nationalism and the Muslim communal fraternity) was 'strategic' because it aimed at building a Hindu nation strong enough to resist these 'foreigners' and because it was seen as a mere elaboration of the familiar, indigenous sectarian pattern. Since the 1920s, the distinctive feature of the RSS has been the *shakha,* the local branch of the movement where 50 boys and male adults at the maximum meet daily for a highly ritualized physical and ideological training. This latter aspect is symbolized by a Sanskrit prayer the *swayamsevaks* of a *shakha* offer to the saffron flag, representing the 'Hindu Rashtra' and the RSS 'guru'. The most interesting point, for our thesis, is the presence within the *shakha* of members of the backward castes and Untouchables which bears testimony to its social inclusiveness. This aspect reflects the very objective of the RSS: the *shakha* is intended to be a sort of melting pot, a microcosm of the Hindu nation, which implies the eradication of caste divisions on behalf of an universal model and individualistic type solidarity. The Western form of national fraternity has obviously been selected as a model.

But its implementation employs purely Hindu frames and values like the sectarian institution and world renouncement as testifies the status of the organization's cadre, the *pracharaks* (publicists and full-time organizers). Most of them have foregone opportunities to pursue a professional career and build up a family to devote their entire time and energy to the cause.[24] Their main mission consists in establishing *shakhas* and supervising the functions all over their 'zone', a town, a tehsil, a district, a division, a state: the RSS network relies mostly on the *pracharak* at each level of its hierarchy. The way the *pracharaks* work, their abnegation and even sometimes austerities make them look like world-renouncers, inside and even sometimes outside the RSS. This ethic of self-effacement is the root cause of their prestige in their locality. Such a position explains the way some young *swayamsevaks* recognized their *pracharak* as their guru.

World-renouncers in India hold a special status. The ethic of renunciation put them outside the social system; they embody a form of 'anti-structure' in the sense of Victor Turner (1969). Thus situated, they can transcend the caste differentiations and identify with like-minded individuals. They are 'out-of-the-world individuals'.[25] Considered collectively, the world-renouncers gathered around sects whose doctrine and singular divinity cult are shared by all of them (Dumont 188–9):

The Indian sect is a religious grouping constituted primarily by renouncers, initiates of the same discipline of salvation, and secondarily by their lay sympathizers any of whom may have one of the renouncers as a spiritual master or guru.... In theory, for the man-in-the-world adherence to a sect is an individual matter, superimposed on caste observances, though not obliterating them, and the sect respects these observances even though it relativizes them and criticizes worldly religion from the point of view of individualistic religion. Moreover, the sect, springing from renunciation, has the power to recruit irrespective of castes.

Drawing from the works of Turner and Dumont, Gross defines the sect among which he worked assiduously as fraternal 'communitas' and 'institutionalized liminalities': first, the sect, and especially the sub-unit made one guru's disciples, forms a sort of brotherhood ignoring the caste status and even a family, kin terms being omnipresent here; second, the sectarian organization appears to be very rigorous, geographical space being so strictly cut out as all the monasteries of a given area should be under the responsibility of a 'zonal patron'.[26]

Thus, it seems that the RSS resorted to the familiar sectarian pattern to acclimatize the individualistic forms of solidarity perceived as the root cause of the Europeans and Muslims' cohesion and strength. Indeed, from a sociological point of view the elementary unit of the nation is the individual,[27] and the sect is the only Hindu social institution where individualism is prominent, the holistic caste system being kept at bay. Thus the RSS embodies indissolubly a sort of 'brotherhood in saffron' to use the title of a recent study (Andersen and Damle 1987) (if we put the emphasis on the sectarian dimension) and the 'Hindu Rashtra in miniature' as Hedgewar said in his last speech of 1940 (Deshpande and Ramaswamy 1981: 185–6) stressing the nationalist dimension of his movement.

This organization satisfies the main criteria of 'strategic syncretism'. First, it aims at assimilating with Hinduism at large these cultural feature: of the others (Muslims as well as British) which have made them formidable antagonists—a capacity to national or communal solidarity based on some equalitarian values; second, it resorts, to make these 'imports', to a Hindi pattern that is not the *varna* system any more but the Hindu sect, the only institution where some individualistic values can be found in the Hindu universe. This substitution renews the original perspective of the 'strategic syncretism' process since the defence of hierarchy seems not to remain a priority any more.

This appreciation must be shaded because the equalitarian project of the RSS is a millenarian one, a dream that would come true once the organization and the Hindu society are 'completely identical'.[28] According to Golwalkar, the second *sarsanghchalak* (supreme chief) who presided over the destinies of the RSS from 1940 to 1973, this triumph of equality presupposes that 'all persons in the society [would] . . . have realised the Soul and have transcended wordly bonds'.[29] In the meantime, the ideal social pattern remains an organicist version of the *varna* system, which has been defended by the chief ideologues of organizations closely affiliated with the RSS since the 1950s such as the Bharatiya Mazdoor Sangh (BMS), a trade union, and the Bharatiya Jana Sangh (BJS). D. Thengadi, the founder of the BMS insisted on the need to restore a 'vertical arrangement'[30] of society and D.

Upadhyaya (1965: 43), who was General Secretary of the BJS from 1953 to 1967, explained that:

In our concept of four castes, they are thought of as analogous to the different limbs of *Virat-Purusha* [the primordial man whose sacrifice is described in the Rig -Veda].... These limbs are not only complementary to one another, but even further, there is individuality, unity. There is a complete identity of interest, identity of belonging. . . . If this idea is not kept alive, the castes instead of being complementary can produce conflict. But then this is distortion. . . . This is indeed the present condition of our society.

Thus, the RSS fronts born to operate in the 'real' society continued to refer to the *varna* system as an ideal indigenous social structure useful to assimilate the Others' forms of community feeling based on individuals, and simultaneously, legitimize a hierarchical organicist pattern.

While the *varna* system and the Hindu sect are considered by different organizations within the RSS complex as alternative patterns of socio-national unity, the problem of religious unity requires special treatment.

## THE VHP: A HINDU CHURCH?

Along with the division into castes, the multiplicity of religious currents within Hinduism has been a source of constant complaint by Hindu revivalists.[31] Abortive attempts had been made by Dayananda to convene an assembly of *pandits* 'to hold a discussion as to which was the true faith.'[32] The Vishva Hindu Parisad (VHP), was the first organization formed under the auspices of the RSS to provide a unifying framework for the diverse elements of organized Hinduism (ancient sectarian traditions). As such, it constitutes another example of 'strategic syncretism'.

The VHP was founded as a reaction to the continuing activities of the Christian missionaries. Some months before its founding conference, the granting of Nagaland (a new federate state in north-east India) to christianized tribes had been criticized by the Hindu nationalist leaders who saw it as the result of a 'denationalization' (i.e. conversion) process that threatened national unity. S.S. Apte (1964: 15), a former RSS *pracharak,* who had been appointed General Secretary of the VHP by Golwalkar, justified the creation of his new organization in the following terms:

The declared object of Christianity is to turn the whole world into Christendom—as that of Islam is to make it 'Pak'. Besides these two dogmatic and proselytising religions there has arisen a third religion, communism. . . . The world has been divided into Christian, Islamic and Communist, and all these three consider the Hindu society as a very fine rich food on which to feast and fatten themselves. It is therefore necessary in this age of competition and conflict to think of, and organise the Hindu world to save itself from the evil eyes of all the three.

With this objective in view, the day the VHP was founded, it was decided to organize an International Hindu Conference:

> It was decided to have symposium, and conferences of the learned of all the various sects, an exhibition of the rise, growth and glory of the Hindu civilization through the medium of pictures and sculptures right from Vedic times of our own day, and such other programmes and functions as will engender a sense of oneness and unity underlying the apparent diversities.[33]

This proposed gathering was intended to prepare the way for providing Hinduism with an ecclesiastical structure similar to that which had given the Christian churches such apparent strength. Those attending were expected to constitute an embryonic religious council which could be recognized as a central authority by all Hindus. Moreover, a sub-committee was appointed in order 'to evolve a code of conduct which would promote and strengthen Hindu *samskara* [*rites de passage* of any Hindu's life] in society.[34] The claim to form a sort of Hindu supreme body became more legitimate—though still fallacious—after the Second International Conference (1979) and the organization of a Dharma Sansad from 1984 whose sessions demanded through voted resolutions, amongst other things, the rebuilding of temples on sites where mosques had been constructed during the Mughal period as in Ayodhya or Mathura. The representative character of the VHP tended to increase steadily though most prestigious religious figures kept their distance from it.

For our purpose, the most interesting aspect of this attempt at giving Hinduism a centralized form of ecclesiastical organization, matching a more subtle standardization of doctrines and ritual practices, lies in its promoters' efforts to legitimize it with reference to Hindu traditions. All the above 'conferences' are said to be modern versions of the one convened by the last Hindu Emperor, Harsha, in AD 648 at Kannauj.[35] However, this assembly, which in fact took place at the end of AD 642, was associated with Buddhism, a creed which had deeply influenced Harsha and which generated this sort of ecclesiastical organization (Devahuti 1970: 96, 157). Once more a historical myth had been constructed to justify the borrowing of cultural features from rival communities, this time 'semitic religions' perceived in an undifferentiated way.

The examples of ideological construction selected from the history of Hindu nationalism converge towards a sort of core definition of 'strategic syncretism' as well as two common conclusions.

Syncretism effect: The Hindu nationalist identity born out of the strategic syncretism process is not very Hindu. Paradoxically, the Hindu nationalist ideology emerged and developed by a process of assimilating external values and notions (monotheism, a solidarity based—more or less—on equalitarianism, a centralized ecclesiastical structure) which *appeared*[36] to endow the rival and antagonistic groups with prestige and strength. The whole process is determined by a nationalist perspective and this quest for a national cohesion leads to a homogenizing action which is contrary to the pluralistic and hierarchical essence of Hinduism.

This syncretism served strategic purposes for three related reasons: It enabled Hindus to use the Europeans' methods (such a proselytism) against them—this is the 'mimetic' dimension; it strengthened the self-esteem of Hindus by convincing them that the new prestigious values and ideas derived from their Golden Age— this is the 'psychological' dimension; and it remained partial—which is part of the strategy of cultural vindication—since Vedic precedents were also reinterpreted to *legitimize* certain cherished institutions such as socio-ritual hierarchy in the case of the *varna*.

This model complies with the formula of Fallers since it analyses the construction of the Hindu nationalist ideology as a process primarily intended to vindicate a threatened culture. Simultaneously, the 'primordialist' and 'instrumentalist' approaches are questioned: on the one hand, nationalism appears to be built up through the invention of the traditions and on the other, the manipulation of identity symbols do not play any significant role in the formation of the Hindu nationalist movement as an ideological movement. My hypothesis is that this manipulation is especially relevant in the political arena where, it enables leaders to mobilize masses. But, this elite resorts at that stage to symbols evolved or selected throughout the ideology-building up process. Thus, my hypothesis is that this construction comes first and stems from cultural motivations, even though socioeconomic factors may intervene: the frustration of the Punjabi Hindus was a major factor in the decision of launching Hindu Sabhas but their promotees were mostly Arya Samajists, and not any frustrated Hindus.

## Notes

1. See, for instance, Robinson, and also Brass (1977: 215–34). More recently, Van der Veer's (1987: 283) quick criticism of Louis Dumont illustrates the same type of theoretical antagonism. The latter assumes that Hindus and Muslims were radically irreconciliable in terms of religious values and norms (Dumont 1966: 382), whereas the former stresses the necessity not to divorce 'these values and sentiments from the political arenas in which they are shaped'.
2. This term refers to Kothari's concept of 'building of tradition' (1968: 273–93) that I applied to the case of Hindu nationalism.
3. *Punjab Census Report 1911*: 99. On this question cf. Jones (1981: 87–92). On the Arya Samaj at large, see the reference book by Jones (1975).
4. S.N. Das Gupta writes:
   The Upanishad again and again reiterate the fact that this spiritual essence is incognizable by any of the sense organs—by eye or by touch—that it is beyond the reasoning faculties of man and is therefore unattainable by logic, and that it is indescribable in speech and unthinkable in thought. The apperception of it is not of an ordinary cognitive nature,

but is an apperception of the essence of our beings ('Philosophy' in Basham 1975: 112).

5. 'The brahmanical magazine or the missionary and the brahmun being a vindication of the Hindoo religion against the attacks of Christian missionaries—Calcutta 1821' in *English Works of Raja Rammohun Roy*, Vol. 1, 1928: 159.

6. Preface to 'Translation of the Cena Upanishad, one of the chapters of the Sama Veda; according to the gloss of the celebrated Shancaracharya establishing the unity and the sole omnipotence of the supreme being and that he alone is the object of worship—Calcutta 1823', ibid.; 36. For other prefaces on the same pattern, see ibid.: pp. 2, 47.

7. 'Even idolaters among Hindoos have more plausible excuses for their polytheism' (ibid.: 193) he ventures to write by inviting Christian writers in entering upon 'a minute investigation of the comparative merits of our respective religions . . .' (ibid.: 201).

8. Swami Dayananda (1981: 115). In the first version of *Sathyarth Prakash* (Light of Truth), Dayananda recommended that 'the allocation of a *varna* should be made by the state, after due examination of the graduates from the schools' (Jordens 1978: 116).

9. Moreover, according to Thapar (1989: 229) 'Hindu identity was defined by those who were part of this national consciousness and drew on their own idealized image of themselves resulting in an upper caste, brahmana-oriented identity'.

10. An overview of *Shuddhi* is given by Ram Bhaj Dutt in *Punjab Census Report 1911*: 150.

11. *Punjab Census Report, 1901*: 116.

12. See also, Nandy (1983: 24–5). This cultural adjustment under Western influences found expression in the repression of 'indecent' forms of worship, such as 'fertility rites' in Punjab. See Jones (1988: 51).

13. I use this notion in the sense of Smith (1981: Ch. 5).

14. Here, the book of an Arya Samajist, Har Bilas Sarda (1906) suggests that the first cycle of ideological building up had been achieved by the turn of the twentieth century.

15. I developed this interpretation of the first phase of Hindu nationalism in Jaffrelot (1988: 555–75).

16. In the Punjab, the mobilization of Hindu merchants and intelligentsia stemmed also from socioeconomic grievances in the 1900s, the British tried to protect the Muslim population, mostly rural, by preventing the Hindu moneylenders from acquiring land (Anti-Land Alienation Act, 1901) and by restricting the Hindu intelligentsia's access to administration (see the Memoranda of the Hindu Sabha, National Archives of India, New Delhi, Home Department (Political Part A), Proceeding Nos. 29–31 and 50–3, December 1909).

17. To dispel any doubt about the existence of such an ideology as early as 1909, one can quote another prominent Arya Samajist-Hindu Sabhaite leader's (Lajpat Rai) speech before the 1909 Punjab Provincial Hindu Conference:
    It may be that the Hindus by themselves, cannot form themselves into a nation in the modern sense of the term, but that is only a play on words. Modern nations are political units. . . . That is the sense in which it is or can be used. In fact the German word 'Nation' did not necessarily signify a political nation or a State. In that language it connoted what is generally conveyed by the English expression 'people' implying a community in possessing a certain civilisation and culture. Using it in that sense, there

can be no doubt that Hindus are a 'nation' in themselves because they represent a civilisation all their own . . . . In the present struggle between Indian communities, I will be a Hindu first and an Indian afterwards, but outside India or even in India against non-Indians I am and shall ever be an Indian first and a Hindu afterwards (cited in Kelkar 1941, Vol. 1: 277).

18. This decade is considered as a landmark by G. Pandey (1990: 260–1) too, since it was the time when arose a new contest between two different conceptions of nationalism— one that recognized the giveness of 'pre-existing' communities which were to form the basis of the new India, and another that challenged this view of history, past and present. Alongside these there developed yet another kind of 'nationalism' 'communalism' that sought to establish a hierarchy of cultures of India (and, indeed, particular regions of India) and to assign to one or another a primary place in the future of the society.

19. This Muslim mobilization started when the post-First World War peace treatises were under discussion. It looked as though Turkey was going to lose the Arab Provinces and other territories with the result that the Sultan of Turkey would no longer be the Caliph of the Islamic world.

20. I am indebted for this analysis to Charles Malamoud who accepted to read and comment upon Moonje's report.

21. 'The first step I propose is to build one *Hindu Rashtra Mandir* in every city and important town, with a compound which could contain an audience of 25,000 (the size of the Delhi Great Mosque according to him) and a hall in which *Katha* (religious stories in prose) from *Bhagavad Gita*, the *Upanishads* and the great epics *Ramayana* and *Mahabharata* could be daily recited. . . . While the sectarian Hindu temples are dominated by their own individual deities, the Catholic Hindu Mandir would be devoted to the worship of the three mother-spirits the Gaumata (Mother Cow), the Saraswati (Goddess of Knowledge)-mata and the Bhumi-mata (Mother Land) . . ' (see Shraddhananda 1926: 140–1).

22. Previously the 'sanatanist' (orthodox) wing of the Hindu Mahasabha, led by M.M. Malaviya had already produced similar 'manifestos' through the projects of the Banaras Hindu University, for instance, cf. Sundaram (1942: XIX–XX).

23. This view has also been promoted by the most reformist wing of the Arya Samaj, the *Jat Pat Torak Mandal*. (Letter from Sant Ram to V.D. Savarkar, dated 8 January 1938, *Savarkar Papers*).

24. This analysis relies mostly on interviews of the RSS, the BJP and the VHP cadres and sympathizers in Delhi and Madhya Pradesh quoted in my thesis (1991: 632, 997, 1124).

25. This interpretation refers to Louis Dumont's analysis of the Hindu sects as the sphere of individuals-outside-of-the-world. Dumont (19: 238) and in the appendix '*Le renoncement dans les religions de l'Inde*', pp. 348–9.

26. This analysis is especially relevant in the case of the orders founded by Shankara in reaction to the development of Buddhism and their Naga warrior-monks wing formed at the time of Muslim invasions (Gross 1979: Chs. 2, 4 and 6).

27. Cf. Mauss, 'La Nation' (*L' Année Sociologique* 3e série 1953–4) where the persistence of any intermediate institution is said to be inconsistent with the emergence of a true nation since this process implies complete 'moral integration'.

28. Quote of Golwalkar's annual speech *Hitavada*, 31 December 1947: 6.
29. *The Organiser*, 1 December 1952: 7.
30. *The Organiser*, 24 October 1955: 6.
31. Very often, this regret was on a par with the attempt to promote a 'Hindu Book', still in the view of resisting the Semitic religions in imitating them. The Vedas were promoted in this perspective by Varma (1917: 9–10).
32. Sarda (1946: 162). Interestingly, Dayananda's guru had already failed to convene such an assembly—comprising learned pandits and Maharajas—to 'establish fully that the Vedic Dharma is the only true and eternal Faith' (ibid.: 33).
33. *The Organiser*, 7 September 1964: 16.
34. *The Organiser*, 30 January 1966: 2.
35. *The Organiser*, '*Hindu Vishva*' Special Number, Second World Hindu Conference, March-April 1979: 26.
36. It is necessary to underline the subjective dimension of the process: what is at stake is the *perceived* strength of the other. For instance, the limits of the Muslim community homogeneity are shown by Marc Gaborieau (1986).

# References

Anderson, W. and Damle, S. (1987), *The Brotherhood in Saffron: The Rashtriya Swayamsevak Sangh and Hindu Revivalism*, New Delhi: Vistaar Publications.

Apte, S.S. (1964), 'Why Vishva Hindu Parishad', *The Organiser*, Divali Special Issue.

Bamford, P.C. (1985/1925), *Histories of the Non-Cooperation and Khilafat Movements*, K.K. Books.

Basham, A.L. (1975), *A Cultural History of India*, Delhi: Oxford University Press.

Brass, P. (1974), *Language, Religion and Politics in North India*, Cambridge: Cambridge University Press.

—— (1977), 'A Reply to Francis Robinson', *Journal of Commonwealth and Comparative Politics*, Vol. 15, No. 3, November.

Chand, Lal (1938), *Self Abnegation in Politics*, Foreword by Bhai Parmanand, Lahore: The Central Hindu Yuvak Sabha.

Deshpande, B.V. and Ramaswamy, S.R. (1981), *Dr Hedgewar: the Epoch Maker*, Bangalore: Sahitya Sindhu.

Devahuti, D. (1970), *Harsha: A Political Study*, Oxford: Clarendon Press.

Dumont, Louis (1966), *Homo Hierarchicus: The Caste System and its Implications*, Delhi: Oxford University Press.

*English Works of Raja Rammohun Roy*, 1946, Vol. 1 (edited by Nag and Burman), Calcutta: Sadharma Brahmo Samaj.

Fallers, L.A. (1961), 'Ideology and Culture in Uganda Nationalism', *American Sociologist*, Vol. 3, No. 4, August.

'Forcible Conversions in Malabar', *Moonje Papers*, New Delhi: Nehru Memorial Museum.

Gaborieau, Marc (1986), 'Hiérarchie sociale et mouvements de réforme chez les musulmans du sous-continent indien', *Social Compass*, Vol. 39, Nos. 2–3.

Geertz, C. (1973), *The Interpretation of Culture*, New York: Basic Books.

Gross, S.L. (1979), *Hindu Asceticism: A Study of the Sadhus of North India*, 2 Vols., Berkeley: University of California, doctoral dissertation.

Jaffrelot, Christophe (1988), 'L'émergence des nationalismes en Inde. Perspectives théoriques', *Revue Française de Science Politique*, Vol. 4, No. 38.

——— (1989), 'La place de l'Etat dans l'idéologie nationaliste hindoue—éléments pour l'étude de l'invention de la tradition politique', *Revue Française de Science Politique*, Vol. 39, No. 6, December.

——— (1991), *Des nationalistes en quête d'une nation: les partis nationalistes hindous au XXème siècle*, Paris: Institut d'Etudes Politiques, Doctoral thesis.

Jones, K. (1988), 'Socio-religious Movements and Changing Gender Relationships among Hindus of British India', in J.W. Björkman (ed.), *Fundamentalism, Revivalists and Violence in South Asia*, New Delhi: Manohar.

——— (1975), *Arya Dharm, Hindu Consciousness in 19th Century Punjab*, Berkeley: University of California Press.

——— (1981), 'Religious Identity and the Indian Census', in N.G. Barrier (ed.), *The Census in British India*, New Delhi: Manohar.

Jordens, J.T.F. (1978), *Dayananda Sarasvati: His Life and Ideas*, Delhi: Oxford University Press.

Kelkar, G.V. (1941), 'The All India Hindu Mahasabha', *The Indian Annual Register*, Vol. 1.

Kothari, R. (1968), 'Tradition and Modernity Revisited', *Government and Opposition*, Summer.

Mauss, M., 'La Nation', *L' Année Sociologique*, 3e série 1953–4.

Mill, James (1989), 'History of British India', in E. Stokes, *The English Utilitarians and India*, Delhi: Oxford University Press.

Mitter, P. (1987), 'Rammohun Roy and the New Language of Monotheism', in F. Schmidt (ed.) *The Inconceivable Polytheism*, London: Harwood Academic Publishers.

Nandy, A. (1983), *The Intimate Enemy: Loss and Recovery of Self under Colonialism*, Delhi: Oxford University Press.

Pandey, G. (1990), *The Construction of Communalism in Colonial North India*, Delhi: Oxford University Press.

Parmanand, Bhai (1982), *The Story of My Life*, New Delhi: S. Chand & Co.

——— (1936), *Hindu Sanghathan*, Lahore: The Central Hindu Yuva Sabha.

Rai, Lajpat (1967/1915), *A History of the Arya Samaj*, New Delhi: Orient Longman.

Robinson, F. (1977), 'Nation Formation: The Brass Thesis and Muslim Separation', *Journal of Commonwealth and Comparative Politics*, Vol. 15, pp. 215–30.

Sarda, Har Bilas (1906), *Hindu Superiority: An Attempt to Determine the Position of the Hindu Race*, Ajmer: Rajputana Printing Works.

——— (1946), *Life of Dayanand Saraswati*, Ajmer: P. Bhagwan Swarup.

*Savarkar Papers*, 'Letters from Sam Ram to V.D. Savarkar dated 8 January 1938', Nehru Memorial Museum and Library, Microfilm Section, Reel No. 1, File No. 3.

Swami, Dayananda (1981), *The Light of Truth* (*Satyarth Prakash*), Allahabad: Dr. Ratna Kumari Svadhyaya Sansthana.

Shraddhananda, Swami (1926), *Hindu Sanghatan: Savour of the Dying Race*, Delhi: Arjun Press.

Smith, A.D. (1981), *Ethnic Revival*, Cambridge: Cambridge University Press.

Stokes, E. (1989), *The English Utilitarians and India*, Delhi: Oxford University Press.

Sundaram, V.A. (1942) (ed.), *Benaras Hindu University 1916-1942*, Benaras: Tara Printing Works.

Thapar, Romila (1989), 'Imagined Religious Communities? Ancient History and the Modern Search for a Hindu Identity', *Modern Asian Studies*, Vol. 23, No. 2.

—— (1985), 'Syndicated Moksha', *Seminar*, September.

Turner, V. (1969), *The Ritual Process, Structure and Anti-Structure*, Chicago: Aldine Publishing House.

Upadhyaya, D. (1965), *Integral Humanism*, New Delhi: Bharatiya Jana Sangh Publication.

Van der Veer, P. (1987), 'God Must be Liberated! A Hindu Liberation Movement in Ayodhya', *Modern Asian Studies*, Vol. 21, No. 2.

Varma, K.C. (1917), *Regeneration of the Hindus*, Madras.

# Chapter 5

# The genesis and development of Hindu nationalism in the Punjab from the Arya Samaj to the Hindu Sabha (1875–1910)

Schematically, the origins and development of ethnic movements in India have been approached in the main from two opposing theoretical positions: the 'primordialist' and the 'instrumentalist' one. While exponents of the primordialist approach assume that the cultural specificity of a regional or ethnic group leads naturally to a national consciousness, those favouring the instrumentalist approach take the view that cultural identity and outlook can be constructed by an elite which has mastered the techniques of manipulating the symbols and myths of 'their community' (Brass 1974: 121). Both approaches tend to reduce the expression of nationalist ideology to a single process; on the one hand, it is represented as an unmediated statement of an immutable underlying culture and on the other it is treated as no more than an artefact, designed by elites as a means of arousing mass support and manipulated by them to that end (Robinson 1977: 215–34).[1]

This essay intends to suggest a third perspective on the basis of a case-study, the genesis and development of Hindu nationalism as an *ideology* and then a political movement in the Punjab. Ideology is defined by C. Geertz as a 'symbolic strategy' evolved in a society undermined by modernization processes (Geertz 1973: Ch. 8, 193–254). The term, in this perspective, refers 'to that part of culture which is actively and explicitly concerned with the establishment and defence of patterns of value and belief' (Fallers 1961: 677–8). Nationalism is obviously an ideology par excellence according to this definition. This theoretical perspective emphasizes the 'instrumentalist' idea of manipulative reinterpretations of cultural material, nevertheless the model remains predominantly 'cultural' since the major aim of the reinterpreters is to adjust the outward expression of ideology while preserving the basic values and identity of the society.

This theoretical framework can be used to examine the emergence of the Hindu nationalist ideology in terms of 'invention of the tradition'.[2] My hypothesis is that it is even possible to analyse it as a sub-category of this process of invention,

---

*I am most grateful to Bruce Graham and Ian Talbot for their comments on an earlier version of this article.

a sub-category that can be called 'strategic syncretism' because the content of this ideology has been supplied to a large extent by material taken from the cultural values of groups who were seen as antagonistic towards the Hindu community. This 'syncretism' proved to be 'strategic' because it underpinned an ideology which aimed at dominating the 'Others'.

In the nineteenth century, a number of socio-religious reform movements attempted to gather support amongst Hindus. These movements represented primarily a reaction to the threat of Western domination and especially to the twofold cultural challenge presented by utilitarian reformism and Christian proselytism. Both relied mainly on criticism of idol worship as arising from polytheistic superstitions and of the caste system as 'a degrading and pernicious system of subordination' (Mill 1989: 54). Such discourse appeared all the more dangerous for the cultural equilibrium of Hindu society at it could find expression in legislative reforms 'from above' (such as the Age of Consent Bill, 1891) or lead to conversions.

The Brahmo Samaj took shape in this context in 1828 in Calcutta. Rammohun Roy, the founder, aspired to reform Hinduism whose shortcomings he acknowledged, especially with regard to idol worship. Moreover, the Brahmo Samaj expression of devotion took the form of prayers to 'the One True God'. At the same time, Rammohun Roy argued that idol worship was a corrupt practise which had deformed an originally pure monotheistic religion in which God had been worshipped as an absolute value. His main sources were the Upanishads, the latest texts of Vedic literature in which Brahman is indeed described as a 'spiritual essence' sustaining the whole of creation, individual souls included.[3] His reading of the Upanishads, however, proved to be influenced by 'a more rigid monotheism of the people of the Book' (Mitter in Schmidt 1987: 181) since the philosophy of 'the speculative brahman' tended to be replaced by a rather rational theism.

In fact, Roy chose to work from the Upanishads and reinterpreted them in this way, because of his wish to refute the missionaries whose propaganda 'abus[ed] and ridicul[ed] the gods and saints of [Hinduism]' (*English Works of Raja Rammohun Roy* [hereafter *English Works*], 1928, Vol. 1: 159). One of his main works—the translation and interpretation of Upanishad—was justified as a means of enlightening the Westerners:

Such benevolent people will perhaps, rise from a persual of them [these translations] with the conviction, that in most ancient times the inhabitants of this part of the globe (at least the more intelligent class) were not unacquainted with metaphysical subjects; that allegorical language or description was very frequently employed to represent the attributes of Creator, which were sometimes designated as independent existence; and that, however suitable this method might be to the refined understanding of men of learning, it had the most mischievous effect when literature and philosophy decayed, producing all these absurdities and idolatrous notions which have checked, or rather destroyed, every mark of reason, and darkened every beam of understanding (*English Works* 1928, Vol. 1: 36).[4]

That this evocation of a monotheistic original religion was intended to strengthen the standing of Hinduism in relation to Christianity is confirmed by Roy's concern to represent the Christian notion of the Trinity of God (*English Works* 1928, Vol. 1: 201) as a retreat from the idea of an abstract unity which he believed, the Upanishads had sustained.

His approach is syncretic because he endeavours to reshape Hinduism by investing it with selected principles from Christianity and Western rationalism; but this syncretism proves to be strategic since Roy claims that he has derived this neo-Hinduism from a purely indigenous Golden Age which enables him to rehabilitate the Hindu Identity scorned by the Europeans. This is one of the first building blocks of a pre-nationalist ideology designed to withstand the aggressive attacks by outsiders on values which were at the centre of Hindu cultural identity. However, this essential project was taken further by a later socio-religious reform movement, the Arya Samaj.

The assumption of continuity between the Brahmo Samaj and the Arya Samaj does not mean that they represent the same philosophy: obviously, the former was more liberal, penetrated by Christian influences and the latter was, since its inception, more revivalist. The continuity lies in the method they adopted to cope with the West: both resorted to the same 'strategic syncretism', under different garbs and the graduation from reformist to revivalism reflects to a certain extent, the inner logic of this strategy which aims at reasserting the indigenous identity on behalf of a pseudo-historicism.[5]

The Arya Samaj was founded in 1875 by Swami Dayananda who met the Brahmo Samajists in Calcutta in the early 1870s. Even though he disapproved of their interest in Christianity, Dayananda followed their example to the extent that he institutionalized the idea of a Vedic monotheism and criticized the idolatry of popular Hinduism raised by Christian missionaries. The form of worship promoted by the Arya Samaj was intended to rehabilitate that which was said to have existed during the Vedic Age, even though its *Agnihotra* (fire sacrifice), performed when the sun rises and sets, omits most of the typically vedic ritualism because of its deliberately abstract monotheism.

More importantly Dayananda added a social dimension to the myth of a Golden Age in the making. The so-called vedic caste system was presented by him as much more flexible than the one then current in India. Indeed, he maintained that *jati* (hereditary, endogamous and hierarchical castes copiously criticized by the Westerners) did not exist in the Vedic times but that the prevalent social organization then was a *varna* system.

The first references to the four *varna* appear in *Rig Veda*; in the hymn X-90 relating to the origin of mankind, the social order derives from the sacrifice of the primordial Man (*Virat Purusha*): 'the Brahman (priest) was his mouth, his arm was made the Kshatriya (warrior), his thighs became the Vaishya and from his feet the Shudra (servant) was made'.

Dayananda assumed that this system of four vedic 'classes' was merely born out of the collectivity's needs in terms of socioeconomic complementarity, claiming further that status distinctions came at a later stage. Originally, therefore, contended Dayananda, children were placed in each *varna* according to their individual qualities.[6]

The national renaissance implied for Dayananda a reversal of the process of decline—the root cause of India's subjugation by the British—and a return to this Vedic Golden Age. At this point the essential elements of Hindu nationalist ideology were present; the origin of the Hindus has been assigned a clear location in the past, when the organic link between a people, a spirit, a language of high culture, and a sacred territory had been forged.

The Arya Samaj took root in the Punjab more deeply than anywhere else, from the last quarter of the nineteenth century. The point I would like to make on the basis of this local case-study is that our understanding of the formation of the Hindu nationalist movement, first embodied in the Hindu Sabhas, requires primarily a cultural analysis in terms of 'strategic syncretism' and then an 'instrumentalist' approach: the latter is necessary to explain the 'transition to politics' (the entry into the political arena) but this process follows and builds upon an ideological construction that we can explain primarily in terms of 'strategic syncretism'.

## The Birth of Hindu Cultural Nationalism in the Punjab

While, consequent to the tours undertaken by Dayananda, some regional branches of the Arya Samaj were set up all over north India during the final years of the nineteenth century (North-West Provinces: 1886, Rajputana: 1888, Bengal and Bihar: 1889, Central Provinces: 1889) (Jones 1989: 98), the first of these was the one in the Punjab and it was the one which underwent the most rapid development.[7] Its success was very probably due to the characteristics of Hinduism in one of the regions of India which had continually been disturbed by movements of peoples and armies and whose local communities had been subject to systematic religious, social and political pressures. Situated on the strategically important zone between the valleys of the Indus and the Ganga, the Punjab had always been vulnerable to military and political incursions from the west and the east. The Muslims had come through this pathway in order to reach the fertile agricultural regions around Delhi and Agra, which became the core of the conversions to Islam from the eleventh century onwards, and the rise of Sikhism in the region was in part a militant warrior-like response to the dislocation of local community life by a succession of invaders. Whereas the structures and practices of Hinduism survived the loss of Hindu political control in the upper and central regions of the Ganga Valley, in the Punjab Doab they were steadily eroded, until Hinduism was reduced to the family religion of a chain of trading communities and resilient agricultural groups, such as the Jats. The temples declined and the Brahmans lost much of their social and ritual status (Talbot 1988: 26). The census figures for 1881 show that Hinduism had been reduced to minority status in a region which was very close to its heartland: 40.7 per cent of the population were Hindus as against 51.3 per cent Muslims and 7.5 per cent Sikhs. These facts were conducive to proto-nationalist ideas and were in keeping with the anti-Brahmanical message of the Arya Samaj.

The minority status of the Hindus, was most obvious in the western and central districts where the population in the countryside was Muslim and Sikh: the Hindus in these areas were gathered together in the cities where they controlled trade, as in Lahore, former capital of Mahmud of Ghazni and Ranjit Singh. The Hindus were also concentrated in newer commercial centres such as Multan. Insulated within these urban limits, the Hindus of West and Central Punjab had always possessed a sense of insecurity, partly shared by their co-religionists in the cities of East Punjab where the Hindu Jat peasants were larger in number but had joined forces with their Sikh and Muslim counterparts against the merchant classes on whom they depended for the marketing of their products and for loans (ibid.: 28–9). This feeling of insecurity was heightened after the annexation of Punjab in 1849. Though the last region to be conquered by the British on account of the resistance offered by the Sikh army, this strategic province went on to benefit from an exceptionally dynamic British administration which carried out irrigation works, built the infrastructure (transport network) for promoting trade and developed a bureaucracy which opened up new avenues of employment for the Hindu community in the urban areas from which soon arose the entire intelligentsia. But simultaneously, the British authorized Christian missions to undertake their activities in the region which, within the logic of 'strategic syncretism', promoted the rise of the Arya Samaj; the British then sought allies amongst the Muslim landed classes and the Hindu and Sikh agriculturist, a move which precipitated the 'transition to politics' by the Arya Samajists through the formation of a Hindu Sabha. The intention here is therefore to show that this political movement, whose formation fulfils the criteria of 'instrumentalism', is associated with an earlier movement, the Arya Samaj, which was already a vehicle for what was virtually Hindu nationalism, constituted in accordance with the logic of a cultural analysis.

## HINDU PROTO-NATIONALISM: THE SECTARIAN MODEL

My argument is that the Hindu nationalism of the Punjab Hindu Sabha is an overtly political version of the earlier communitarism of the Arya Samaj. This argument rests upon the following propositions:

1. that the Arya Samaj, in defining its outlook, was engaged in the same process of 'strategic syncretism' which had produced the outlook of the Brahmo Samaj;

2. that the Arya Samaj was a blend of old and new characteristics within the social traditions of Hinduism, in the sense that it resembled a sect (in its reinvention of religious truth, and its stress on the equality of believers) but also had many of the features of a political association (a hierarchy and uniformity of units, an ability to influence and manipulate legal and political structures, and a developed ideology); and

3. that the ideology of the Arya Samaj contained a concept of the Hindu nation, and of its historical development, which indicated an awareness of the political utility of Hindu nationalism.

## Brahmos then Aryas

The manner in which the Arya Samaj followed the Brahmo Samaj can be observed in the Punjab itself, because the Brahmo Samaj was established in the territory by Bengali middle class immigrants who had been encouraged by the British to settle there in order to contribute to the setting up of the administration in Punjab after its annexation in 1849, at a time when Bengal possessed the most Westernised system of education and the largest number of the intelligentsia. Under the impetus of these Bengalis, the first Brahmo Samaj was set up in 1863 in Lahore (Oman 1991 [1934]: Ch. VI), the cultural capital of the Punjab; others were created later at Rawalpindi (1867), Amritsar (1873) and Multan (1875) (Jones 1966: 379). Prominent brahmos such as Debendranath Tagore (in 1856–7) and Keshub Chandra Sen (in 1867) had come to the Punjab to develop their movement (Gopal No. XLVI: 3, 5).

From 1877 however, the Brahmo Samaj found its place being taken over by the Arya Samaj. Dayananda undertook a tour of the Punjab from April 1877 till July 1878 in the course of which he set up nine branches of his movement which developed in those very places where the Brahmo Samaj had established itself some decades earlier and which now became the strongholds of the Arya Samaj: in 1901, the male members of the movement (the names of women members were not registered), were the most numerous in Lahore (1,331), Sialkot (936), Gujranwala (649), Gujarat (622), Gurdaspur (512), Amritsar (492) and Jullundur (428).

In all these branches, the excessively high representation of the intelligentsia from the administrative departments or from the professional classes, was testified by the fact that the day for worship (restricted to Vedic hymns) was fixed on Sunday, which was their weekly holiday (*Punjab Census Report 1891*: 177). In these circles, the Arya Samaj distinctly succeeded the Brahmo Samaj within a logic of 'strategic syncretism' as is seen in the example of Lahore and particularly of the student circles of the Government College: the leaders of the Arya Samaj during the 1880s, the time when the new movement supplanted the old one, were later to be recruited from among those students adhering to the Brahmo Samaj. Lala Sain Das, the President of the Arya Samaj of Lahore right from 1877, was a member of the Brahmo Samaj before he met Dayananda (Rai 1965: 48). He himself was not a member of the intelligentsia, not having had a Western education, but his work (translator from English into Urdu in the law courts) brought him in contact with these circles among whom he started looking for potential candidates[8] and that was how he recruited from the Brahmo Samaj those who became the main leaders of the Arya Samaj during the subsequent decade; Pandit Guru Dutt, future ideologist of the Arya Samaj; Hans Raj, the driving force behind the future Dayananda Anglo-Vedic College; Lajpat Rai, the future Arya Samajist political leader; and Munshi Ram, who was later to establish a gurukul at Haridwar, were all members of the Brahmo Samaj before 1880 (ibid.: 49).[9]

From the point of view of these members of the intelligentsia who were still students when they joined the Arya Samaj, the Brahmo Samaj was deficient in two respects: first, they were sufficiently orthodox to resent its radical criticism of Hindu society (negation of the caste system, widow remarriage), and second, they were offended by its religious universalism, even reverence for Christianity, which was particularly emphasized by Keshub Chandra Sen, who came to Punjab in 1867 and again in 1873. It did not allow in the eyes of the intelligentsia for the total rehabilitation of the culture of the country confronted by the challenge presented by the Europeans. Now, it was in the Punjab that this challenge was most forcefully evident from the steady advance seen in the number of conversions, which from 3,912 in 1881 had gone up to 19,750 in 1891 and to 38,513 in 1901 (*Punjab Census Report 1901*: 158).

These figures reflect both the connivance of the British authorities (who readily offered irrigated land for the establishment of Christian communities) (Talbot 1988: 70) as well as the particularly assertive initiatives taken by the Punjab missions. These which were based in Ludhiana had been waiting since 1834, to enter this final territory which had remained unconquered (Jones 1989: 85). Right from the 1860s, the Christian missions established a network covering the entire province. They had perfected their methods, since in addition to opening schools and homes for orphans, they started proselytism in the bazars, in an attempt to reach out to women in purdah, and they set up model Christian colonies in the Lahore district, in 1868, on land newly opened up to cultivation as a result of irrigation. It was precisely the geographic concentration of the initiatives and conversion more than the number of persons affected which caused concern: in 1881, 2,168 of the 3,912 converts were found to be in the districts of Lahore, Amritsar, Sialkot and Delhi. They were generally Untouchables benefiting from the social services deployed by the missions (in 1901 in Gujranwala, four-fifths of the 2,681 Christians were 'sweepers', a proportion which the census official, in the absence of figures for the other districts, considered as being fairly representative) (cited in Jones 1989: 383).

As a means of dealing with this threat, the reformism of the Brahmo Samaj was judged to be inadequate. The Punjabi intellectuals wanted to highlight the positive aspects of Hinduism and to defend it by showing that in its original form, it incorporated all the virtues which Europeans valued in their own religion. The 'revivalism' of the Arya Samaj enabled the transition to this new stage in the formation of an apparatus in the defence of culture, initiated by the Brahmo Samaj. Analysing in his memoirs the reasons for the failure of the Brahmo Samaj in Punjab, Bipin Chandra Pal felt that it lacked:

a direct message of monotheism on the authority of the Vedas, because such a message would place the modern Hindu religion on the same plane as Christianity or Islam, and it was this more perhaps than any spiritual need that moved the youthful intelligentsia of the Punjab in those days. The Brahmo Samaj by its universalism and particularly by its open appreciation of Christian ethics and piety did not meet this need of the Punjabee mind. This is why the message of the movement of Pandit Dayananda had such large, if not almost universal acceptance of the intellectual classes of the Punjabee Hindu (ibid.).

The internal process of thought of Lajpat Rai, a young representative of the intelligentsia of Punjab, attracted towards the Brahmo Samaj before he became one of the main Arya Samajists leaders in the 1900s, then a Hindu nationalist in the 1920s, is indicative of the psychological and ideological factors which were of importance for this rise of the Arya Samaj. Lajpat Rai came from a family having complex religious convictions; while his mother was an orthodox Sikh, his father, under the influence of a maulvi was attracted to Islam when he was very young. Till he was forty he observed the *namaz* and the fasting of the Ramazan, without however getting converted. He then became a supporter of Syed Ahmed Khan, his allegiance towards a reformed Islam going hand in hand with a deep aversion for Hindu rites and particularly for idol worship which he had, besides, denounced in the published organ of the Brahmo Samaj of Lahore. His father's influence therefore predisposed the young Lajpat Rai to an attraction towards the Brahmos whom he met when he came to Lahore at the age of 14 to study there.[10] In 1885 he became a member of the Brahmo Samaj. But the very next year he was won over by the speeches made by his Arya Samajist comrades of the Government College, Guru Dutta and Hans Raj (Rai 1965: 26). He therefore left the Brahmo Samaj for the Arya Samaj at the end of very significant intellectual journey which he retraced twenty years later:

. . . The Brahmo Samaj at that time was considered to be a sort of reformed, or refined, Christianity, resembling more the Unitarian church than the monotheism of the Vedas or the Vedicism . . . the Brahmo Samaj had ceased to be an effective shield for the protection of, Hindu theism. . . . (Rai 1967 [1914]: 102)
    By contrast against the current belief about India's sordid past, he (Dayananda) delved deep into literature and tradition and painted a golden age. . . . [W]ith Dayananda's shrugging off the accretion of centuries, an older past seemed to be faintly visible in which Indians could take pride. (ibid.: 197)

Lajpat Rai's action was in line with the logic of 'strategic syncretism'; in order to put up a fight against the danger of Christianity, it was no longer enough to bring reforms into Hinduism in accordance with Christian canons (starting off with monotheism); it had to be asserted that these prestigious characteristics had been part of the original religion, if the Hindu identity was to be rehabilitated.

That the Arya Samaj developed in the Punjab following this logic of 'strategic syncretism' is also brought out by the way in which it sought, on the one hand, to reform Hinduism, under cover of a return to the Vedas, according to Western criteria, and on the other hand to assimilate the method of work at the basis of the success of the mission: for one thing, the Arya Samaj fought for widow remarriage, decried idol worship, child marriages, ostentatious wedding ceremonies, and fertility rites considered obscene by the British,[11] precisely in order to counter their criticisms—not without success moreover, as is seen in the comments of the administrative authorities who were attracted to this 'Hindu Protestantism', incorporating many 'European ideas on religion and science' (*Punjab Census Report 1891*: 179).[12]

Besides, the Arya Samaj set up a network of orphanages (one at Ferozepur, the other at Biwani), and schools [(in 1911 it accounted for two colleges, one of them being for girls alone, three gurukuls, sixteen High Schools and numerous primary schools, fifty of these being reserved for girls) (*Punjab Census Report 1911*: 135)] explicitly conceived to thwart the designs of the Christian missions: during the famine of 1897, Lajpat Rai made use of the Ferozepur orphanage dating back to 1877 to gather together 300 children who would otherwise come under the charge of the missionaries (Rai 1978: 88–9); the first High School for girls was similarly opened in 1896, in Jullundur, by Munshi Ram (and his brother-in-law Devraj) when his daughter returned from school singing 'Christ is my anchor. He is my Krishna' (Kishwar 1986: WS 10).

The strategic dimension of the Arya Samajist imitative action is particularly clear with regard to its *stricto sensu* missionary activity: from 1897, under the impetus of Munshi Ram, a movement of *Veda Prachar* (Propagation of the Vedas) was launched, relayed by 73 *upadeshaks* 'constantly travelling throughout the province, preaching (particularly during large fairs) and inspecting the local branches of the Arya Samaj' (cited in *Census of India 1911* [1913]: 124).

This portrayal of the movement in socio-religious terms presents, however, the problem of its pre-Nationalist Hindu nature.

Lajpat Rai recalls the years he spent at College when he crossed over from the Brahmo Samaj to the Arya Samaj as foreshadowing his commitment to Hindu nationalism. 'It was in those two years, I became wedded to the idea of Hindu nationality. It was in those two years I learnt to respect the ancient Aryan culture which became my guiding star for good' (Rai 1965: 28).

But is this not an *a posteriori* reconstruction connected with the political involvement of the author at the time he wrote this? Is not the Arya Samaj of the end of the nineteenth century primarily a movement of a sectarian nature, dedicated to carrying out socio-religious reforms like so many other sects before it, and simply more ambitious, as was for example the plan of Shankara from whom it drew its inspiration? The evolution of the movement during the decade from 1890-1900 seems to testify to the validity of this hypothesis.

## A Sect or a Pre-nationalistic Movement?

Louis Dumont analyses the reformist and 'revivalist' movements which appeared in the nineteenth century as complying with the same logic as the Hindu sects: 'Finally, Hinduism remained untouched, it was only new sects that were created (Dumont 1966: 246). This interpretation of the socio-religious reform movements deserves to be examined closely in the case of the Arya Samaj. Apart from the reformist vocation of the Arya Samaj, two phenomena present themselves to prop up this hypothesis: on the one hand the fact that a whole current of opinion in the Arya Samaj turned Dayananda—who had always refused this status—into a guru, and on the other hand, the ritual nature of the stakes which divided the movement under the pressure of this current.

This latter was first directed by Guru Dutt (1864–90). Coming from a large Arora family of Multan (his grandfather had been the ambassador of the State of Bahawalpur to Kabul), he had become a member of the Arya Samaj in 1881 before coming to Lahore in 1882. In 1883, he had been sent by the Arya Samaj of this city to Dayananda who lay dying in Ajmer. He returned transformed by this experience. From 1883 onwards, he started interpreting Dayananda's writings in a very religious light: he thus turned him into a *rishi* and the *Satyarth Prakash* into a scripture (Jones November 1966: 44). His main disciple and lieutenant, Munshi Ram, who was a contemporary of Lajpat Rai whom he followed also into the Hindu nationalist movement, enables an assessment to be made of the importance of the spiritual motivations which incited him to join the Arya Samaj.

Munshi Ram had also experienced a disturbed youth and family background. He was the son of a particularly devout police official of the Khatri caste who did not adhere to the rigidness of the caste system on account of his constant tours. At the age of 15 he was distressed when some policemen prevented him from entering the Vishwanath Temple in Benares because the Rani of Rewa was performing her *puja* there: unable to explain to himself why God had tolerated the exclusion of a worshipper from his temple, he was forced to question the grounds of his religious beliefs and to suffer a crisis of faith, similar to that which Dayananda had experienced before running away from his parental home. Munshi Ram considered becoming a Christian and later turned to atheism (Jambunathan 1961: 18). As a student in Benares, Munshi Ram spent his time reading English Literature (Scott, Locke, Bacon), gambling and in drinking alcohol, a habit which he could not manage to overcome. An initial meeting with Dayananda did not calm his troubled religious sentiments: he remained an atheist (ibid.: 63. cf. 84). Having come to Lahore to sit for his exams after several failures, Munshi Ram was attracted towards the Brahmo Samaj whose literature he had read; but they reminded him of the words of Dayananda and he sat down to read the *Satyarth Prakash:* it came as a revelation to him; he immediately offered his services to Lala Sain Das who appointed him to head the Arya Samaj at Jullundur. Thereafter his life underwent a total change, particularly after his meeting with Guru Dutt: 'I felt that there was at least one soul with whom I could be in communion' (ibid.: 31–3); though a Kshatriya, he became a vegetarian and immersed himself in reading the Vedas so as to be able to hold his own in the face of orthodox pandits during oratorical debates which he organized to popularize the beliefs of the Arya Samajists (ibid.: 72-4). Munshi Ram's route was therefore different from that of Lajpat Rai's to the extent that his motivation in joining the Arya Samaj was essentially spiritual in nature, and the guru-disciple relationship which he had established with Guru Dutt was strengthened.[13] Moreover, in 1902, he entered into *vanaprastha* and in 1917 he took *sanyas* under the name of Swami Shraddhananda.

The sectarian aspect of the Arya Samaj was evident in the emphasis on ritual definition and maintenance by those of its intellectuals who identified themselves strongly with its spiritual mission. In 1887, Guru Dutt introduced a strictly Arya Samajist funeral rite; from 1886 to 1890, he promoted the most sober forms of Hindu marriage (Jones 97–8; Das 1897: 3) and, more than anything else, he instigated an internal debate, the ritual in question recalling sectarian conflicts: in 1899, he protested against the opening of a special building of the D.A.V. College for non-vegetarians (Jambunathan 1961: 117; Vedananda Thirta n.d.: 332).

The first Dayananda Anglo-Vedic College had been set up in 1886 with the aim, as its name indicates, of offering to the youth of the Hindu elite an education which, in keeping with the syncretism of the Arya Samaj, carved out a place for 'national' values overshadowed by the Western establishments, while at the same time imparting a 'modern'[14] education. Vegetarianism and the management of the D.A.V. College went on to become the centre of a long domestic quarrel which continued for three years: in Guru Dutt's view, distorting the principle of vegetarianism amounted to betraying Dayananda, whereas for Mulk Raj (brother of Hans Raj), giving up a meat diet meant repeating the error of the Buddhist and Jain heresies whose attachment to the principle of *Ahimsa* had deprived India of all its manhood. Guru Dutt, and after his death, his disciple Munshi Ram, moreover demanded that the teaching of Sanskrit be included in the first years of the courses at the D.A.V. College.

Hans Raj, the Principal of the College since its creation (he remained Principal till 1911) and Lal Chand, the President of the Managing Committee, refused to give English a secondary place as compared to Sanskrit (Rai 1965: 55–7). The accumulation of these lines of division led to the schism of 1892: the Lal Chand-Hans Raj clan, which Lajpat Rai joined, controlled the D.A.V. College (hence its being known as the 'College faction' or 'Cultured faction') whereas the supporters of Munshi Ram (starting with the group of missionaries set up by Guru Dutt in 1888) kept the main local branches of the Arya Samaj of Punjab, which ensured to it a majority of the votes in the Arya Pratinidhi Sabha, the managing body of the movement in which the local delegates held office since 1886. The rivalry of these two factions (the second was called the 'Vegetarian section' or 'Mahatma section') gave rise to a competition for the development of concurrent local branches: there was bitter rivalry, particularly till 1897, and the rift was institutionalized. In 1903, in fact, the College faction endowed itself with a managing body parallel to the Arya Pratinidhi Sabha, called the Arya Pradeshik Pratinidhi Sabha; the preceding year, Munshi Ram had set up the educational institution that Guru Dutt was already yearning for: this gurukul (a name derived from the traditional Hindu schools in which the guru teaches the Vedas to young Brahmans) was constructed near the holy city of Haridwar. It aimed at 'reviving the old institution of Brahmacharya'[15] on the model of the universities of olden times, such as the one at Taxila. The institution ended up finally giving only a mediocre education and did not match that of the D.A.V. College.[16]

The schism, followed by the continuance of the two tendencies within the Arya Samaj, did indeed stem from a conflict that is typical of the history of Indian religions or sects in which one current secedes in order to strictly adhere to the word of the guru who founded it. However, while acknowledging that in these respects the Arya Samaj did resemble a sect, we also need to consider those features of its activity which conformed to other models of organization and doctrinal expression. One measure is provided by the plans of Dayananda himself, who was not concerned simply to create one more sect within the framework of Hinduism. While the organization plan mentioned in his testament has only a theoretical value, the one adopted in practice at least needs to be examined. Now, while the local unit at the base of the local Arya Samaj is called the mandir, the premises are not considered as sacred even though during the weekend some Vedic rites (such as the *havan*) are in fact performed there, as it is used also as the place where the simple meetings of an association are held. To join the Arya Samaj, the non-Hindus need to perform a *shuddhi* purification ceremony but, in case of Hindus—at least from high castes—there was no provision for initiation ritual: 'signing the declaration of faith is sufficient' (Rai in Oman 1991[1934]: 176). Membership of the Arya Samaj mandir is open to people in their individual capacity on payment of a subscription equivalent to 1 per cent of the person's income; a President, Vice-President, Secretary, Propaganda Secretary, Treasurer, Librarian and priest, are elected. The General Assembly of this basic unit then elects one delegate for every ten members (the minimum number required for forming a mandir), to the provincial bodies; we have seen that there was one of these for each faction. These bodies are in charge particularly of assigning the *upadeshaks* (preachers), who are sometimes paid a salary, to the mandirs which need them most.[17] The implicit organizational model here is that of a secular association with a uniform branch structure and elementary rule for maintaining a hierarchy of central and regional executive and plenary bodies.

Assimilating the Arya Samaj to a simple sect needs to be considered with circumspection on the ideological and sociological planes from which L. Dumont views it. On the sociological plane, the sectarian nature of the movement appears to be fortified when considering the manner in which it dug out a place for itself in Indian society: it penetrated furtively into the world of castes without questioning the hierarchical values which, in fact, enabled the conclusion to be arrived at that 'Hinduism has remained untouched' by the reform movements. But did the Arya Samaj deliberately confine itself to the non-social world? It would seem more as if it was forced to do so by society all around while it was the messenger of a strong. Hindu cultural nationalism, shared by the 'vegetarian' branch as well as the college faction, as is testified by its viewpoint on history.

The hypothesis drawn from the combination of the social and ideological levels amounts to defining the Arya Samaj as avant-garde, if not wholly as a nationalist sect, i.e. dedicated to personifying a knitted Hindu nation.

## Arya Samajist Nationalism

### Bringing an ideology into history

The basic element of the ideological corpus of the Arya Samaj lies in its concept of the Other as an enemy, and in an interpretation of history in which we can see the touchstone of national identity. This set purpose brings us back to the chain postulate advanced by P. Ricoeur according to which:

the knowledge of the self is an interpretation—the interpretation of the self in turn, finds a choice intermediary in narration, among other signs and symbols—and this medium borrows as much from history as from fiction, making the history of a life into a fictional story, or if we prefer, a historical fiction, comparable to the biographies of great men in which history and fiction are found mixed together. (Ricoeur 1988: 295)

This hypothesis is presented as being valid both for individual and for collective identities. In the case of pioneers of Hindu nationalism such as Lajpat Rai and Shraddhananda, authors of early autobiographies, the two dimensions are closely knit. Admitting that he was never 'overly fond of religious studies and research' (Rai 1965: 76), Lajpat Rai relates the fact that the book that marked his youth was *Gasis-i-Hind* by Maulvi Muhammad Husain, in which he 'learnt for the first time to admire the courage of the Hindu and to be proud of the Hindus'[18] thanks to the accounts of the exploits of the Rajputs. Although Munshi Ram entered the Arya Samaj keeping in mind its religious perspective, he, more than anyone else, devoted himself to codifying the vision of history inherited from Dayananda. He contributed towards institutionalizing a Hindu nationalistic vulgate of capital importance for the consolidation and the propagation of this identity, insofar as it implants the myth of a primordial, sovereign and chosen people;

. . . The Veda was revealed in the beginning of creation for all races. It contains germs of all sciences—physical, mental and psychical. But it cannot be denied that the glorious period of the supreme achievements of the Vedic Church was the bright period of Indian History. When India was the centre of Vedic propaganda and missionaries were sent from it to different parts of the world, it was also the seat of a world-wide empire, and Indian kings exercised direct sovereignty over Afghanistan, Baluchistan, Tibet, etc., and Indian colonists colonized Egypt, Rome, Greece, Peru and Mexico. (Jambunathan 1961: 155–6)

This assertion of the primary role of India as the centre of a universal Vedic civilization in the beginning of time is an unchanging element of the Arya Samaj. In 1926, Munshi Ram, renamed Shraddhananda after his vows of renunciation in 1917, justifies this antecedence by the fact that:

the plateau of Tibet was the first to come out of water and therefore the revelation of the Vedas was imparted to early humanity at the sacred soil. Mankind was then divided into the good or virtuous and the bad or vicious. The first were named 'Aryas' and the latter 'Dasyus' in the Veda itself. (Shraddhananda 1926a: 71)

The decline which gradually followed the Golden Age of Indian Domination is explained in the words of Dayananda, and before him, in those of all socio-religious reforms movements, by the deterioration that came into spiritual practices (polytheism replacing monotheism, idol worship) and in social institutions (child marriage, forbidding remarriage of windows, multiplication and insulation of castes whose system becomes hereditary, introduction of untouchability, lowering of the position of women). During the Vedic period, 'caste in India was a form of industrial and social organisation which is the equivalent of the modern industrial "class" society': Lajpat Rai calls to witness the authority of Senart to show that it was a social system convenient for purposes of production and whose rules in the field of marriage were as flexible as those of the Greek 'genos' which Senart compares moreover to the Indian *gotra* in the framework of a reconstitution of an Indo-European structure that comes in very handy for rehabilitating the image of India (ibid.: 128–9).

It was in order to return to this Golden Age, or at least to reverse the movement toward decadence, that the Arya Samaj put its energy into promoting marriages of adults or adolescents[19] and inter-caste marriages (Munshi Ram thus arranged for his daughter—Khatri by caste—to marry an Arora, and he arranged marriages between Brahmans and non-Brahmans).[20] This concept of national revival was expressed in two complementary ways according to the branch of the Arya Samaj concerned. The College wing set itself the task of reforms in the certainty that India could only regain her lost supremacy by being self-reliant. The call in favour of India depending on her own resources was an important element of Arya Samajist culture, and Lajpat Rai states this forcefully:

. . . [T]he first duty of the Hindus was to get strong enough to stand on their own legs; they ought to imbue lessons of self-help, self-confidence and self-respect and cease looking towards others. (Rai 1965: 88)

Socio-cultural reform hence consisted here in using the weapons of the colonizer against himself—again under cover of a return to the Vedas—in order rapidly to restore the greatness of the nation. As for the 'vegetarian' current, it placed itself in a far more ancient perspective. Munshi Ram was convinced that Dayananda was a *rishi* who had 'reawakened the dormant and dying spirit of the motherland' (Ram 1893: 7–8): the national revival seemed here to emerge in an almost automatic fashion from the reactivation of past virtues, without any deliberate effort. In both cases, the Arya Samajists convey a concept of history reflecting the deep-rootedness of the nationalist identity invented by Dayananda. This was all the more firm for being increasingly constituted against 'the Muslini Other' barely mentioned by Dayananda at the end of the *Satyarth Prakash*. The interpretation of the Hindu decline furnished by Munshi Ram testifies to this evolution.

The date of the decline is fixed by the latter in a fanciful manner: his biographer, J.T.F. Jordens points out that in his first pamphlet, in 1893, he differed from Dayananda who considered the disintegration of Indian society to date back to the Mahabharata war, since he for his part, saw in it a consequence of Muslim invasions (Jordens 1981: 38). Generally, Shraddhananda asserted both things at the same time: in 1926, he acknowledged that 'in the plains of Kurukshetra the spirit of Indian bravery was crushed and Brahman domination was unleashed reducing the other Varnas to servitude' (Shraddhananda 1926a: 79). The way was thus opened up for all the social ills that were to bring about a degeneration from which India had not yet recovered; yet, in the same work, the author does not detect any of these ills till the time of Harsha, at the head of the last Indian Empire in the eighth century, therefore, undeniably long after the Mahabharata war: true, the castes were tending to become hereditary but they were not yet too fragmented, child marriages were only just starting to develop and more than anything else—a finally decisive criterion for Shraddhananda—till the time of Harsha 'no non-Aryan community lived in India and if some non-Aryans did come and settle down there, they were absorbed in the Hindu community. . .' (ibid.: 5–6). It was later, after the Muslim invasions, that the decline was hastened: apart from the massacres and the construction of mosques in place of temples (ibid.: 38), the Hindus were then subjected to wholesale campaigns of forced conversion (ibid.: 30), the paroxysm being reached in the reign of Aurangzeb (ibid.: 34) in accordance with a technique which was to be followed later by the agents of Saint Francois-Xavier.[21]

Lajpat Rai also simultaneously with his admiration for the exploits of the Rajputs, acquired a hatred for the Muslims: while he was an adolescent, he had in fact discovered Indian history through a school textbook entitled *Waqiate-i-Hind* which gave him 'the feeling that the Muslims had subjected the Hindus to great tyranny' (Rai 1965: 77).

This evolution towards an ideological anti-Islamism constitutes another side of the formation of national identity: parallel to the appropriation of national history, it is a question of reinforcing the definition of this long term 'We' against a 'Them' which serves as a traditional foil. The Arya Samaj hence appears to be indeed the vehicle of an ethnic nationalism. This statement of fact necessarily reflects on the analysis of its sociological status which can be defined by the words 'nationalist sect' on the basis of the *Shuddhi* Movement which was a reaction against the conversions which continued to weaken Hinduism to the 'benefit of Christianity and Islam'.

## The *Shuddhi* Movement

The Arya Samaj saw the Hindu decline not only in term of quality but also in those of quantity: from 1881 till 1911, the number of Hindus declined from 9,252,295 to 8,773,621, i.e. from 43.8 per cent it fell to 36.3 per cent of the population of the Punjab, as against increases from 11,662,434 to 12,275,477 (50.7 per cent), and from 33,699 to 199,751 (0.8 per cent) respectively for Muslims and Christians (*Census of India 1891*: 93; *Census of India 1911*: 99). In 1911, those in charge of the census were of the view that since 1901, 40,000 Hindus had been converted to Islam and 120,000 to Christianity, the majority being from the castes of Untouchables (*Census of India 1911*: 100).

The introduction of such enumerations and the increasing publicity given to them, heightened the hitherto vague feeling of a decline in numbers which, by this means, became an obsession. We read from 1881 in the Arya Samajist press some accounts displaying alarm in the place of these trends right from the time of their publication. Associating the deterioration in quality with the decline in numbers, the Arya Samajists gave credit to the explanation of the Europeans according to which the lower castes were giving up Hinduism for other religions in order to improve their condition; hence the idea of countering the offensive of the missionaries by adopting their methods of proselytism, as also by better integrating the untouchable and the lower castes into Hindu society.

These are the two directions in which the *Shuddhi* Movement advanced, typical of 'strategic syncretism', since they are tantamount to assimilating a technique which constituted the strength of the Europeans, and in this process establishing a community—a nation in the making—on the model of the dominant power: the former is noteworthy particularly on account of the deepening of the division 'We'/'They', the latter on account of the egalitarian social integration that it implies.

### A NEW PROSELYTISM

The method adopted by the Arya Samajists having an enthusiasm for proselytism was the one that Dayananda is said to have used for bringing back to the 'Aryan' fold a Hindu converted to Christianity and another converted to Islam (Sarda 1968: 196–7; Shraddhananda 1926a: 86).

The insistent manner in which these episodes were brought to the fore by his disciples leads one to see them as reference points for legitimizing a fairly non-Hindu procedure of reconversion, which Dayananda himself never talked about: this was the *Shuddhi*. Literally the word means 'purification' and indicates a ritual meant to purify members of the high castes of any serious defilement that they may have fallen victim to. It is found used in this sense in numerous ancient treatises, as is pointed out by P.V. Kane (Kane, Vol. 4, 1953: 117, 267–333, 828–30). A *Devalasmriti* also had reportedly been formulated, after the first Muslim raids, in order to codify the conditions for reintegration of Hindu converts to Islam, but this text seems to have become rapidly obsolete, as was testified by the reticence of Brahmans to use this kind of procedure [(in 1850, the Brahman family of a child who had attended a Christian school in Bombay was ostracized by the other Brahmans in spite of purificatory baths in Benares)] (Thursby 1972: 40; Jordens 1977: 146). Some writers maintain that Hinduism was always potentially proselytical; hence J.F. Seunarine asks: 'Did not Sankaracarya himself in a sort of "Home Missions" effort travel far and wide to spread his teaching?' (Seunarine 1977: 2).

True, but this was precisely the beginning of the Brahmanic reaction to Buddhist and Jain proselytism; and just as Shankara appropriated the method of these rivals, the Arya Samaj seems to borrow from the Semitic religions procedures which did not come to it naturally. Moreover, Seunarine acknowledges, on reading Kane, that *Shuddhi* indicates, particularly in the Smriti, a procedure aimed at restoring ritual purity and that, in the case of the annulment of a conversion forced by *mlecchas,* it is more the *paravartana* rite which is used (ibid.: 29-30). In the logic of 'strategic syncretism', the Arya Samaj had given to the idea of *Shuddhi* a specific significance which amounted to adding on a missionary dimension to Hinduism. This reinterpretation contributed towards bringing disturbance into its relationships with the other religions in the Punjab.

Right from 1884, the Arya Samaj began to apply the *Shuddhi* rite to Hindus recently converted to Islam and to Christianity. The organization took care to use the services of an orthodox *pandit* as is reported by the organizer of this movement within the Arya Samaj, Ram Bhaj Datt, a Mohyal Brahman, the son of a rich *zamindar* of Gurdaspur who was an advocate in Lahore (Sen 1973: 394):

The first organised effort towards the Shuddhi or reconversion of the converts to Islam or Christianity was made by the Amritsar Arya Samaj. It must, however, be acknowledged that much of its success was due to the help and cooperation of one Pandit Tulsi Ram, the most orthodox of the orthodox and one of the most learned, revered and renowned Brahmans of Amritsar. The Arya Samaj used to make the repentant go through a ceremony of Tonsure, Horn, Yagyopavit (investiture with the sacred thread) and the Gayatri (initiation in to the Vedic Dharm) and thus admitted him in their fold. Thereupon Pandit Tulsi Ram used to send the purified to Haridwar with his letter called Shuddhi Patra, where he was duly purified once more by a dip in the Ganges. This went on for years. From all parts of the Province, people were sent to Amritsar (*Punjab Census Report 1911*: 150).

These were the orthodox techniques of purification for the high castes who may have been exposed to a ritual pollution (just like the sacred thread, the *Gayatri mantra*—prayer from the *Rig Veda* conceived in this case as an initiation into the Vedic religion—is reserved for the 'twice-born' Brahmans, Kshatriyas, Vaishyas).

These ceremonies concerned only a small population till 1894: the Amritsar branch which was the most dynamic in this field 'dealt' with only 39 cases in 1884 and 55 in 1885 (Jones 1976: 131). The phenomenon went on to acquire a new dimension simultaneous to the change in its nature brought about under the impetus of Munshi Ram.

His faction first found its *Shuddhi* operations being curbed by the opposition from the D.A.V. College faction, which was anxious not to rouse the hostility of other groups (orthodox Hindus as well as Muslims); but after the schism of 1892–3, Munshi Ram was able to fully involve himself in this activity; he developed the *Shuddhi Sabha* formed in the early 1880s in Lahore with the *Singh Sabha*, a Sikh association set up in 1879. This *Shuddhi Sabha* reconverted 226 persons in 1896, compared to 14 in 1895 (Jones 1966: 50): this was the pointer to the transition from the conversion of individuals to that of families, even of entire sub-castes. This evolution led however to the snapping of ties between Arya Samajists and Sikhs, since in 1896,[22] the swelling in the numbers of those converted by the Arya Samaj was due to the entry of Sikh sub-castes, such as the Sikh Rahtiyas, a caste of weavers:

The first mass purification, reports Munshi Ram, began with the SHUDDHI OF RATHIAS, a sect of Sikhism who were not allowed to sit on the same carpet even by the Khalsas . . . . In the middle of 1896 AD they applied for their Shuddhi and within the next few months a thousand and more were taken into the Arya Samaj as brethren, entitled to full social and religious rights. (Shraddhananda 1926a: 87; Pareek 1973: 136)

From 1885 onwards, Sikhism, which Dayananda considered as a sectarian current within Hinduism, was being subjected to criticism by the Arya Samajists who reproached it with indulging in the same superstitions and idolatry as Hinduism. Hence, at the end of the nineteenth century, the Sikhs were incited to distance themselves from the Arya Samaj and to evolve in their defence their own 'revivalist' organizations (Jones 1973: 457–75).

However, the development of *Shuddhi* brought acrimony particularly into the relations with Muslims. In 1849, the Muslims had resisted the British by launching a Jehad under the leadership of Sayad Ahmad Shahid; subsequently, they had developed a movement whose 'revivalist' nature brought to mind the Arya Samaj. Like the latter it looked like a tightly knit sect which was considered heterodox. Mirza Ghulam Ahmad outraged orthodox opinion—especially among the Deobandis—by his challenge to the fundamental Islamic doctrine of 'Khatmi-nabuwwat' that Muhammad is the last of Prophets.[23] Mirza Ghulam Ahmad started preaching sermons around 1879 but did not gain renown in the Punjab till the end of the 1880s[24] at the time when the Arya Samaj was intensifying the practice of individual *Shuddhi* [(whose main targets were particularly Muslim converts) (Jones 1966: 50)] and a little before the integration of the Muslim Bhangis and the Rathias (Shraddhananda 1926a: 88) when the movement changed in scale. During the years 1907-10, the Rajput Muslims became the target of the Arya Samajists in the North-Western provinces: 1,052 of them were thus reconverted (*Census of India 1911*, Vol. XV: 134). Large scale operations in this area however only took place ten years later.

The Arya Samajist/Muslim antagonism was symbolized for years by the extremely violent exchanges between Mirza Ghulam Ahmad and Lekh Ram, a *pandit* of Peshawar who had joined the Arya Samaj in 1880 and was resolutely anti-Muslim; these were fostered through the press by means of pamphlets; from 1887 till 1890, in his capacity as the editor of the *Arya Gazette*, followed by pamphlets such as *Jihad* (1892) which relates the atrocities connected with the Muslim invasions in India, he contributed towards aggravating feelings of hatred (Jones 1976: 148–51). This practice of blasphemous denigration of the sacred symbols of the other religion—N.G. Barrier has compiled a material in this connection (Barrier 1974: 172–81)—came to a head when a Muslim assassinated Lekh Ram in 1897. This followed the sacrilegious articles in which this publicist had specialized. His funeral procession was joined by 7,000-8,000 Hindus (Oman 1991[1934]: 171), a fact which indicated that the communal antagonism was crystallizing.

The *Shuddhi* Movement represented a major stage in the effort of the Arya Samaj to constitute a community against the 'other', through an imitation of his assets—in this case his proselyte technique—for purposes of an increase in numbers. (It should be noted that the enemy, here was the Muslim; very few cases are noted of reconversion to Hinduism of those who had become Christians, probably because the time was not yet ripe for grappling with the religion of the ruling power). Added to the 'revivalist' tones of the Arya Samajist concept of History, this new proselytism tended to invalidate the possibility of a pure and simple assimilation of the Arya Samaj to a sectarian movement; the aggressiveness complied more with the logic of nationalism, yet, the very modalities of *Shuddhi* bring to mind sectarian practises: initiation firstly, which defines the sect insofar as it establishes a direct link with the founder *guru*, and secondly the integration of the low castes which constitutes a decisive factor for qualifying the movement as a 'nationalist sect' on the sociological plane.

## A NATIONALIST SECT

From 1900, the redirection of the *Shuddhi* operations—which began with the Rathias—in the direction of the low castes, was taken farther. The 1911 enumeration recorded only 147 and 10 conversions or reconversions of Muslims and Christians respectively, while the low castes or Untouchables were subjected to the *Shuddhi* rites in tens of thousands all over Punjab in order to raise them to the rank of the 'twice-born': this was case with 2,000 to 3,000 Ods in 1901–2, particularly in Multan, 30,000 Meghs (weavers and leather workers) along the Kashmir border in 1903, and 30,000 Jats in Karnal, who thus found themselves theoretically incorporated into the network of social relations (commensality, marriage rules) reserved for the upper castes. The Meghs thus received the services of an *upadeshak,* often a Brahman, for performing their rituals. At the same time as the Arya Samaj was questioning the rules of hierarchy through these 'purifications', it was freeing itself from the tutelage of the orthodox *pandits* by simplifying the ritual as is explained by Ram Bhaj Datt, who had become the President of the *Shuddhi Sabha:*

The ceremony is everywhere the same. In all cases the person to be reclaimed has to keep Brat (fast) before the ceremony (a part of which consists in putting on the sacred thread). In some cases where the fall was due to passion, the number of Brats is increased by the persons who are to perform the ceremony. The very act of their being raised in social status makes them feel a curious sense of responsibility. They feel that they should live and behave better and that they should act as Dvijas. It has thus, in the majority of cases, a very wholesome effect on their moral, social, religious and spiritual being. As to treatment, the Arya Samaj treat the elevated on terms of equality. (*Punjab Census Report 1911*: 110)

This is an idealized description insofar as *Shuddhi* tended to be reserved for the less impure castes—even among the Untouchables—and particularly insofar as the majority of the Arya Samajists had reservations about challenging the caste system in favour of which an active minority was militating. The ideal type of social relations that this avant-garde devised however has the characteristic of integrating the sectarian and nationalist dimensions of the Arya Samaj within the logic of 'strategic syncretism'.

The expansion of the *Shuddhi* Movement on the basis of an egalitarian ethic gave it the appearance of being a sect. In contrast to the practice of rigid social ordering in the Hinduism of caste distinctions, the sect, at least theoretically, recruits its members independently of their social status because, by joining it, the devotee becomes an individual-outside-the-world, who renounces all the qualifications of the caste world (Dumont 1966: 238). The sect is thus a *communitas,*[25] the only place in Indian society in which we observe a form of individualism and of equality, both going hand in hand. And these are precisely the values which define the nation on the sociological plane. The institution is in fact characterized by social inclusiveness, by the incorporation of all its groups, including those of low status, a 'moral integration' which does not allow for intermediary bodies, according to the categories of M. Mauss (Mauss 1952–4: 7–68) following which L. Dumont defines the nation as 'a collection of individuals'.[26] The hypothesis which proceeds from the parallel thus drawn can be set forth thus: in the framework of the process of 'strategic syncretism' in which reformist-revivalists borrow from the rulers the cultural traits which constitute their strength in the perspective of the reaffirmation of their identity, the Arya Samajists, after having acquired a nationalist conscience based on a reinterpretation of history, had found in the sect a sociological counterpart to the Western nation.

This hypothesis is derived from the attention given by the *Shuddhi* Movement to the low castes. The magnitude of the phenomenon confers on the Arya Samaj a dimension which exceeds the bounds of sectarian logic. If the Hindu sect is, in the typology of Victor Turner, a 'normative *communitas*', the Arya Samaj appears, here, as an 'ideological communitas', one of the 'utopian models of societies based on existential *communitas*' (Turner 1977: 132). Its objective visibly was not to superimpose itself on a caste-ridden society, but indeed to transform it, even to absorb it, by abolishing the differences of status, in short to form the avant-garde of a nation in sociological terms. This perspective is clearly brought out in the plan of certain Arya Samajists of structuring their organization into a new caste destined to encompass the whole of society.[27] This position, however, remains a minority one as compared to the one set out by Dayananda which aimed at rehabilitating the system of the Vedic *varnas*, reinterpreted in such a way as to make room for the individualist values of equality and merit, but implying the maintenance of a hierarchical framework. The 'vegetarian' current, which puts into practice a sectarian logic, reinserts it, as a matter of principle, in the framework sketched by Dayananda: Ram Bhaj Datt thus concludes the earlier mentioned account by indicating that the low castes 'purified' by *Shuddhi* are simply raised to the rank of the 'twice-born', their classification as Brahmans, Kshatriyas or Vaishyas will depend on their individual conduct.

\* \* \*

The Arya Samaj of the beginning of the century comprised thus two potential models of the nation formulated within the logic of 'strategic syncretism': confronted with the danger of the 'Semitic religions' which Munshi Ram considered explicitly as one unit with the opposition to the 'Aryan idea of Dharma' (Shraddhananda 1926b: XXXVII-XXXVIII), the Arya Samajists had acquired a nationalist ideology through the rediscovery of a Golden Age already exalted by the Brahmo Samaj. They had asserted the separate character of their identity through limitation of the proselytical methods of the 'ruling powers' and devised a sociological model of their nation by borrowing the egalitarian and unitarian values of the latter. This imitativeness was strategic not only insofar as it consisted in turning the very weapons of the 'Other' against himself, but because it aimed at rehabilitating a culture which constituted a total 'world vision'. The sociological models of the nation—the system of the *varnas* as the sect—are perfectly indigenous models of the nation. The second, which appeared at a later date, did not however involve the preservation of the social hierarchy as if some of the Arya Samajists had given it up in order to put up a better resistance against the individualism and solidarity of 'the Others'. This option could not but give rise to many reservations on the part of the upper castes in Punjab: far from being acknowledged as the avant-garde of the Hindu nation, the Arya Samaj was considered till the turn of the century as a 'heresy'. The vitality of a sectarian mode of behaviour had much to do with this and explains the limits of a 'Hindu solidarity'.

The Arya Samajists were the first to stress on their specificity with relation to Hinduism, which was seen as a degraded form of the Vedic religion. In 1891, the leadership of the movement called on its members to declare themselves as 'aryas' and not as Hindus at the time of the census (Jones 1981: 87), just as Dayananda had recommended in 1881 (Vable 1983: 60).[28] Simultaneously, the 'traditionalist' Hindus, disparaged by the Arya Samajists, saw them as veritable enemies against whom they were ready to join with the Muslims.

The practice of *Shuddhi* did indeed have serious repercussions within what the British, with their predisposition towards reasoning in terms of social entities, too hastily called the Hindu community. Right from the mid-1880s, the *pandits,* guardians of orthodoxy, reacted by taking recourse to the traditional weapons of the *Shastrarth,* a public debate on controversial religious themes ( Jones 1976: 109). Then they used the channel of the press and organized themselves within a Bharat Dharm Mahamandal (Grand Society for India's Religion) in 1887.

The prime mover behind this enterprise was Deen Dayal Sharma, a Gaur Brahman having the title of *pandit* who was also anxious to protect Hinduism from the reforms of the colonizers (such as the Age of Consent Bill), the development of christian schools (hence the initiative he took to set up a Hindu College in 1899 in Delhi) and the proselytism of the missionaries in general: the Bharat Dharm Mahamandal developed as a reaction, a network of local Sanatan Dharma Sabhas serving as a base for paid *upadeshaks* ( Jones 1989: 77–80). This structure brings to mind that of the Arya Samaj and the logic of 'strategic syncretism' except that, as its name indicates, its ideology was that of the Sanatan Dharma, defined first of all by the value it gives to the traditional caste system and the absence of sectarian affiliation replaced by respect for the *shastras.*[29]

The Sanatanists (i.e. the 'traditionalists' or the 'orthodox') denounced in particular the socio-religious reforms of the Arya Samaj when the latter, through *Shuddhi* challenged the social order by trying to incorporate low castes or Untouchables into the category to the twice-born. The Arya Samaj met here, in fact, with a major obstacle. Potentially, it aspired to form a well-knit community whose internal solidarity would enable a resistance to be put against assaults from outside (Rai 1965: 88). But it seemed impossible to execute this nationalist project on account of the very structure of Hindu society. Thus, in 1903, when the Arya Samaj of Sialkot undertook to perform the *Shuddhi* ceremony for almost 50,000 Megh Untouchables, it was seen that 'even the Muslim joined the (orthodox) Hindus in their work of persecution of the new Arya Mahashyas [title of respect conferred on these new "twice-born"; literal meaning Gentlemen]' (Shraddhananda

1926a: 88). In order to prevent these Meghs from being subjected to the retaliatory measures of the orthodox upper castes (which often took the form of a social ostracism), the Arya Samajists undertook to endow the community with its own schools, dispensaries and temples. The dispute between the Arya Samajists and Sanatanists however continued to grow worse as the former successively sought to free themselves from the ritual rules of orthodoxy, including those of *Shuddhi* right from 1890, ceremonies were conducted to do away with the costly journey to Haridwar, then the Arya Samajists dispensed with the help of *pandits* and performed on their own, rituals which became more and more specific to themselves (Jones 1976: 134). (In 1900, a candidate desiring to join the Arya Samaj had to live on a milk diet for a period of fifteen days which was quickly reduced to three days. Then he had to declare in public his adherence to the Ten Principles of the Arya Samaj. A big *Homa* sacrifice was then undertaken and passages from the Vedas were recited) (*Census of India 1901*, Vol. XVI: 87).

Thus far I have shown the extent to which a cultural analysis serves to explain how the Arya Samaj developed a view of Hindu Society which anticipated many of the elements of Hindu nationalism. We have seen that the process involved degrees of myth construction and assimilation of certain virtues attributed to the Other which were seen as a source of strength and will-power. We must now consider circumstances in which the presentation of Hindu nationalist ideas was undertaken quite deliberately by leaders who wished to demonstrate that they had a measure of popular backing for their concrete demands for policy changes by the authorities, that is, situations in which leaders and groups adopt an instrumental approach to the promotion of Hindu proto-nationalism and to the creation of political Hindu nationalist associations based upon it.

## Emergence of a Hindu Political Forum in the Punjab

The formation of a Hindu front and its 'transition to politics' is explained firstly by a recourse to the categories of the 'instrumentalist' approach insofar as the endangering of the socioeconomic and political interest of the Hindus by the British was at the origin of the process which culminated in the creation of a Hindu Sabha in the form of socioeconomic pressure group.

### INTELLIGENTSIA AND TRADER CASTES: BASES OF THE ARYA SAMAJ

The Arya Samajist' 'transition to politics' derived first of all from its sociological composition dominated by a 'hard core' intelligentsia descended from the merchant castes, and the more or less intense support of trader circles (Khatri—originally kshatriyas—, Arora and Agarwal).

## The Weight of the Intelligentsia

Like all socio-religious reform movements, the Arya Samaj first recruited its members from among youth who had received a Western style education but who had their roots in their own culture.[30] Now, this intelligentsia was at the height of its development in the Punjab at the end of the nineteenth century.

The recourse to Bengali 'babus' being just a makeshift arrangement, the Government of Punjab, during the last one-third part of the nineteenth century, applied itself to the task of training its own officers for its rapidly expanding administration. It encouraged, to this end, the development of schools and itself set up in 1870 the Punjab University (or Government College) in Lahore; this institution which crowned the new anglicized educational structure produced an intelligentsia of which Lahore remains the capital, the majority of its members coming from the Hindu upper castes. The latter, basically city dwellers with the traditional vocation of taking charge of administrative duties had in fact, lost no time in entering these anglicized establishments, aware of the benefits they could draw from them. The literacy rate is in this case a good indicator of the advance made by certain Hindu castes: while 44 per cent of the Punjab's population was Hindu, the latter constituted 65 per cent of the literate in 1881, as against 20 per cent Muslims and 10 per cent Sikhs. Among the Hindus, the castes having the highest literacy rates were the Khatris, the Agarwals and the Aroras. Their eagerness to enter into the educational system is brought out clearly in the memories of P.D. Tandon, himself the son of a Khatri Arya Samajist:

> The Punjabi Khatris had for generations been deprived of their right to administration; and now suddenly opportunities were thrown before them, anyone's to pick up. The Khatris and soon the other castes ran forward to grasp them . . .; soon they spread all over the Punjab Government list, the medical service of the army—the first commissioned service open to Indians—and the professions of lawyers, barristers, doctors, scientists and professors. Many rose from the lowest ranks through sheer integrity hard work and self-teaching. (Tandon 1972: 28)

Here again, the experience of Lajpat Rai serves as a characteristic example: the son of a teacher in the Government Middle School of Rupar (Ambala district) of the Agarwal caste, he was sent in 1881 to the Government College of Lahore from where he graduated in 1883 to become a *Vakil* in Hissar after having joined the Arya Samaj (Rai 1965: 26–7). The college in Lahore fulfilled the dual function of delivering to upper caste Hindus a certificate for entry into the administration (particularly the judiciary) and in a large number of cases of being initiated into the Arya Samaj. Apart from Guru Dutt and Munshi Ram, another future Arya Samajist leader of the Punjab Hindu Sabha, Hans Raj was in the same class in college as Lajpat Rai and had been led to join the movement in a similar way. Descended from a Khatri family of Hoshiarpur district, it was when he joined Government College that Hans Raj met Lala Sain Das, the President of the Arya

Samaj in Lahore and became chief editor of the local journal, *Regenerator of Aryavarta* (Sen 1944: 112), before offering to serve as the Principal of the D.A.V. College without remuneration.

This Arya Samajist intelligentsia was concentrated moreover in Lahore where it ended up by being continually replicated through the Dayananda Anglo-Vedic College which gave a very good preparatory training for the exams enabling entry into the administration. This intelligentsia of the Arya Samaj, however, only constitutes the avant-garde of trader castes which more generally were sympathetic towards the movement.

## The Membership of the Merchant Castes

Within Hindu circles, the trader castes occupy the front ranks in the Punjab on account of the decline of the Brahmans and the Rajputs since the time of the Muslim invasions and the Sikh domination. The Kshatriya castes had indeed seen their power being taken away by the Sikhs (Dungen 1968: 75) and the Brahmans, deprived of patrons, had moreover to take recourse to the support of trader circles which consisted predominantly of the Hindu trading castes:[31] these found themselves in a situation that was all the more comfortable as the British allowed them to extend their economic dominance and to translate it in socio-cultural terms, through education (ibid.: 81). Hence, the attraction exercized on the trader castes by the Arya Samaj whose reformism enabled a ritual status to be recognized for them, in keeping with their new prosperity and their situation within new intellectual professions. In 1891, more than half the 9,105 male members of the movement belonged to the Khatri and Arora merchant castes (*Census of India 1901*: 101). This sociological composition reflected the same socio-cultural logic as in Gujarat where Dayananda had set up the Arya Samaj with the support of traders 'seeking a better status more in keeping with their new prosperity' (Jordens 1978) linked with the economic advance of British India; in the Punjab, his movement developed along the same lines among the merchant castes which felt that they could aspire all the more legitimately to the leadership of their community as the Brahmans and Kshatriyas, who are hierarchically superior to them, had been marginalized. Barrier hence explains the attraction that the Arya Samaj exercized over the merchant castes by the fact that:

Dayananda's claim that caste should be determined primarily by merit not birth, opened new paths of social mobility to educated Vaishyas who were trying to achieve social status commensurate with their improving economic status. (Barrier 1967: 364)

Even if its growth [(from 14,000 members in 1891 to 22,929 in 1901 and to 100,846 in 1911) (*Census of India 1891*: 172; *Census of India 1901*, Vol. 1A: 110; *Census of India 1911*: 138)] was the result particularly, from 1901, to the integration of members of the low cast [(the Meghs becoming its major component with 22,115 members) (*Census of India 1911*, Vol. 1: 124)], Khatris, Aroras, Agarwals and Brahmans represented around half the strength of the Arya Samaj in the Punjab (37,007 out of 76,839) in 1911. Among these merchant and Brahman castes, who continued all the same to dominate the organization, a distinction should however be made, between those (such as Guru Dutt, Lajpat Rai, Munshi Ram, Hans Raj, . . .) who had had the benefit of a modern education and belonged to the intelligentsia which founded the Arya Samaj, and the traders, more apt to financially support the movement than to lead it. But this support was essential and its incentives as well as its modalities deserve to be studied.

## Collaboration between the Intelligentsia and the Arya Samajist Merchants

The trader circles appreciated in the Arya Samajist creed the notion of 'self-help' which, a certain way, suited their spirit of enterprise and perhaps arose out of it. These Arya Samajists in fact set about developing business with the help of merchants: they were the first, in the 1890s, to set up indigenous enterprises which were the precursors of the Swadeshi Movement.[32] Exasperated by the imposition in 1893 of an 'excise tax' on Indian cottons, Mul Raj, the founder president of the Lahore Arya Samaj set up associations selling only *deshi* (made in India) clothes in response to a nationalist desire to become free of the economic dominance of the English (Rai 1965: 96). The following year, he initiated the first bank with purely Indian capital (Tandon 1989: 152-4). This institution was officially established collectively with other Arya Samajist leaders (such as Lal Chand), some Brahmos (Kali Prosanna Roy) and a Sikh *rais* (Sardar Dayal Singh Majithia). Its management was entrusted to Harikishen Lal (an advocate trained at Cambridge who became a magnate) and to Dalpat Rai (brother of Lajpat Rai). The following year, the same group created the Bharat Insurance Company (Chand 1978: 99).

The relationship between the Arya Samajist intellectuals and merchants as a group provided the conditions for a form of clientelism in which a young Arya Samajist professional man could find that support and approval of notables at the district level. Lajpat Rai had the advantage such a relationship; having qualified as a *vakil*, in 1886 he took up residence in Hissar, where in a court case he conducted the defence of Lala Ramji Das, a rich merchant and landowner, who was also, like Lajpat Rai, an Agarwal. His association with Lajpat Rai persuaded Ramji Das to abandon his prejudice against Westernized young men (Rai 1965: 36) and to support Lajpat Rai in his efforts to establish a branch of the Arya Samaj in Hissar. The bond between patron and client was built into the leadership structure of that branch: Chandu Lal, the son of Ramji Das, served as the president of the branch until 1909 and Lajpat Rai remained as its secretary. Chandu Lal is described as being a veritable *rais* ('the most respected and the most powerful personality of his region') (Nanakchand 1946: 7), combining the qualities of the trader and the authority of the man of (orthodox) learning and of power:

> He was an expert in Hindi book-keeping and was regarded an authority in indigenous usage of *hundis* (bills of exchange, etc.). He had a reputation in an ability to manage an estate and landed property . . . . He was aristocratic by birth and temperament and had an expensive style of living. (Rai 1965: 158)

Indeed the Deputy Commissioner of the area mistakenly considered him as the 'Raja of the District' (ibid.: 37). It is difficult to explain the support *rais* such as Chandu Lal gave to the Arya Samaj. However, their traditionalism would indicate that the *rais* saw themselves as offering patronage of a religious association (and even, in doing so, defending the Hindu religion) as eminent Hindus had done in the past as a means of gaining merit. This cooperation between 'publicists' from the intelligentsia and *rais* or notables seems to be similar to the one analysed by C. Bayly as the basis of local politics in Allahabad at the turn of the century (Bayly 1973; 1975).

Apart from this association between a member of the intelligentsia and distinguished local family, it should be noted that Lajpat Rai was able to obtain the services of one of the rare Jats of Hissar with a Western education; this was Dr Ramji Lal whose influence contributed towards popularizing the movement among the Hindu Jats of the districts of Hissar, Rohtak—where they are found in large numbers—and Delhi, as his patients travelled long distances from these places, to consult him (Nanakchand 1946: 7). The Arya Samaj of this period enjoyed the advantage of the support of rich trading groups, and was recruiting some of its members from the farming castes, which till then had remained on the periphery of the movement. However, this social base began to break up when the interests of the urban and rural populations came into conflict with each other.

## THREATS TO HINDU URBAN CIRCLES

The Hindu trading castes dominated industry and commerce (in 1911, the Baniya, Khatri and Arora castes possessed 79 per cent of the non-agricultural wealth) and used their economic power to gain control of landed property: their near monopoly over moneylending operations too enabled them, when the debts were not reimbursed, to acquire the land of the debtor. The moneylenders were all the more ruthless as the land whose possession had always been an important element in the status and in the *izzat* (honour) of the upper castes, was becoming more productively valuable as a result of the dynamism of the agricultural economy, under the effect of irrigation works and of growing monetization (Talbot 1988: 54-5).

The supremacy and the prosperity of the intelligentsia and of the trading circles from which it originated were however endangered at the turn of the century.

## The Legislation on Land

The efforts of the British to protect the economic interests of landed groups affected the situation of the Hindu traders and merchants in the cities. More so than in other provinces of India, the British administrators in the Punjab equated political stability with the strength of the agrarian society; in particular they wanted to retain the allegiance of the zamindars and the peasant castes (the relative majority being Jats) reputed for their warrior-like qualities (ibid.: 49 and following). This strategy, which reflected the belief that some landed groups had stood by the British at the time of the Mutiny, was given concrete shape in paternalistic legislation for protecting the countryside against external threats, the most important being the greed of the urban moneylenders. The main component of this policy was the Punjab Alienation of Land Act of 1901 which, in the utilitarian logic of the transformation of society by law, prohibited any landowner from selling or mortgaging his land without the permission of the administrator of the district: in practice, this law was meant to prevent the transfer of land of the 'agrarian' to the 'non-agrarian' classes (the moneylenders essentially); the government set itself the task of drawing up a list of these tribes (Barrier 1966). The Hindu trading casts not having protested too virulently, the British gave a further push to this system by the Punjab Pre-Emption Act of 1902 (even distant relatives and others farmers of the village became owners when they purchased land from a villager seller) and by the Agricultural Debt Limitation Act of 1904 [(the time limit granted to the debtor before legal action could be taken for non-reimbursement of a debt was extended from the three years to six) (Barrier 1967, Vol. I: 355)]. This legislation had the advantage of ensuring to the British a very wide rural base within which the Muslim and Hindu peasants (of the Jat caste) found themselves making common cause with each other.

## The 'Race for Positions'

As for the Hindu intelligentsia, it had simultaneously to face a restriction of the job opportunities from which it had benefited since the 1880s in the administration and the professions. The number of people trained within the framework of the Anglicized educational system exceeded the capacity of recruitment to the administration. But this phenomenon was also magnified by the emergence of Muslim and Sikh competitors, who had been finally attracted to an educational system which they had not used much till then through conservatism (the Muslims remaining attached to the madrasa system) and for lack of money or of affinity with 'scholarly' activities. The proportion of the Hindus among the literate fell to 61 per cent in 1901, while that of the Muslims rose to 21 per cent and that of the Sikhs to 12 per cent.

The rate of growth of literacy of the Muslims was 28.4 per cent as against 13.4 per cent for the Hindus from 1891 to 1901, which led K. Jones to conclude: 'Competition between an expanding Muslim educated elite and the entrenched

Hindus became a bitter issue during the last years of the century, fuelled as it was both by Muslim competence and governmental employment policies. Muslims still faced the reality of educated Hindus already in control of much of the Punjab's wealth and many of its economic opportunities'.

The second factor of frustration of the Hindu intelligentsia was the preferential treatment the Muslims, by dint of protesting to the British, finally obtained for themselves.

## Discrimination in Favour of Muslims

The British authorities in the Punjab, in spite of the religious diversity of the region, had received instructions from 'founder-fathers', John and Henry Lawrence, just after the annexation to maintain religious neutrality. They adhered to this advice until the time when some commissions set up by the English government itself for investigating the problems of the colonial administration throughout India stirred up an avalanche of complaints from the Muslims: by launching, in this way, forums for discussion, the British were exposing themselves to a hardening of opposition from different communities over the rules of access to varied professional and administrative positions (Barrier 1968, Vol. 17: 523–39).

In 1881, the Hunter Education Commission was the occasion of a confrontation between Muslims who, being under-represented in the educational system, asked for more scholarships and the Hindus, who opposed a concession of this type and demanded, on the other hand, that Urdu be replaced by Hindi as the official language in the secondary school system and in the law courts. In spite of the agitation organized by both parties, the authorities gave in to neither party. However, the Aitchison Commission of 1886, entrusted with investigating the recruitment of officers, revived antagonism: the Hindus demanded the simultaneous holding of the competitive examinations for recruitment to the administration, in London and in India, so as to increase the chances of success of Indian candidates, but the Muslims opposed this as they were certain that this system would be more advantageous to the Hindus who were better prepared. This Commission remained neutral, but Lyall, the Governor of Punjab, proved to be all the more receptive to the demands of the Muslims as the 1880s were years marked by a succession of Hindu-Muslim riots (fifteen occurred between 1883 and 1891, often connected to the slaughtering of cows): desiring to restore peace and order, and disturbed by the evidence that Hindu officials almost never appointed Muslims to subordinate posts, Lyall modified his policy in favour of the Muslims between 1887 and 1889.

The circulars recommending that priority be given to the recruitment of Muslims, were kept secret, but this practice became systematic from 1889 under the impetus of S.S. Thorburn, the new Financial Commissioner, who undertook to apportion equitably the number of Muslims and Hindus in the posts in the judicial, executive and college educational services. In 1904, the existence of the circulars became known, and both sides began to organize more openly their efforts to influence the recruitment process.

Aware that their interests were affected in such ways by the policies of the British authorities, the trader circles, the Hindu intelligentsia and its Arya Samajist avant-garde reacted by developing a style of nationalism which could be used to increase their bargaining power in provincial politics.

## IN SEARCH OF AN ORGANIZATION FOR THE DEFENCE OF HINDUS

### On the Fringes of the 'Moderate' Congress

The Hindu intelligentsia of the Punjab had at first ignored the Indian National Congress, but they now turned to it as the most convenient channel of communication with the British administration. In particular they used the Congress to express their opposition to the Punjab Alienation of Land Bill (Barrier 1967: 367).

The consolidation of the 'Extremist' sentiment behind Tilak presented the Arya Samajists with an opportunity of identifying themselves with a nationalism which was both Hindu and activist (as indicated by the article of faith in *Swadeshi*). The participation of Lajpat Rai in the Congress session in Bombay in 1904 marked his promotion to the rank of a national leader; the Swadeshi Movement of 1905 then reinforced the adherence of the Arya Samajists to the Congress. In 1907, at the time of the Surat split, Lajpat Rai, the leader of the Congress in Punjab, preferred to attempt a mediation between the 'Moderates' and the 'Extremists'. But the exclusion of the 'Extremists' by the 'Moderates' incited the Arya Samajists, who had openly aligned themselves with Tilak during the 1906 Congress, to consider themselves as being outside the Congress.

At the provincial level, also, the Arya Samajists had chosen to act alone; in 1907, finding that the Congress was unwilling to take up the cause of the urban Hindus, they directed their attacks against the British and cited the defence of their Hindu nationality as well as their economic interest as the basis for their action.

### A Revolt against Pro-Muslim Discrimination

In 1907, the Punjabi peasantry launched into a violent agitation against a draft bill stiffening the conditions for cultivating the zones of the Chenab and the Bari Doab, opened up to colonization in 1887, within the framework of an intensive irrigation policy: the regulations affecting the transfer and inheritance of holdings were made more rigid in order to prevent the dispossession of the agrarian tribes and the subdivision of land amongst heirs; in addition, the tenancy rates were revised (Barrier 1967, Vol. I: 353–83). Announced at the same time as an increase in the rates of irrigation water in the wake of several bad harvests, this proposal aroused the indignation of the zamindars who assembled together as many as 10,000 people during a meeting in Lyallpur. Since this measure was only meant to rectify the defects in a model colony, the English, convinced that the peasants concerned would credit them with good intentions, formed the conclusion that it was the nationalists of the Arya Samaj who were responsible for this agitation, as they had been for the Swadeshi Movement: Lajpat Rai and Ajit Singh (the Jat chief of a terrorist organization) were therefore deported to Mandalay for having given an impetus to the popular agitation by holding huge meetings, and Arya Samajists in the administrative services were placed under surveillance. The Viceroy, Lord Minto, however, took the view that the Punjab authorities had made a mistake and therefore ordered the bill to be shelved. There was an immediate return to order but the Hindu intelligentsia, and particularly the Arya Samajists became aware of the extent to which the government mistrusted them and considered them as a potentially seditious body.

Suspected by the government and being outside the Congress, the Arya Samajists kept to themselves, all the more so as the experience of repression of the movement of 1907 persuaded many Arya Samajists that a return to lawful politics was necessary with the result that the 'Moderates' were able to regain power within the Congress, in the Punjab as elsewhere: in 1908, following his release from detention Lajpat Rai was disposed to allow Harikishen Lal to take control of the Punjab unit of the Congress from which the Arya Samajists (and the Hindu intelligentsia in general) had moved away in order to restore their standing with the government. As early as June 1907, their leaders published a letter in the press asserting that 'the Arya Samaji [was] an apolitical organization, and as such [had] no links with any kind of political agitation' (Morley Collection MSS, 21). This step, which was aimed also at proving the innocence of Lajpat Rai was ineffective; in July 1907, F.A. Robertson (judge in the High Court of Punjab), giving an account of his field enquiry, wrote to the Lieutenant-Governor of the Punjab:

The Aryas are possibly correct in stating themselves to have been in the inception a purely religious body, but that one section has been much mixed up with political agitation, and has used its organisation for its furtherance, hardly admits of doubts. And this section has been in the van in its dislike for Europeans and English rule and administration, and has been marked by a strong animus against Christianity. (ibid.: 59)

Robertson added that according to his informers, Lajpat Rai was at the centre of the political agitation of the Arya Samajists in 1907.

However, the most interesting element in Robertson's report lies in the interpretation of the agitation which is brought out from conversations with certain Arya Samajists:

The Mahommedans of late years have been getting far more than their fair share. The Government is afraid of the Mahommedans. Let us make the Government afraid of us, and they will give us, if not all our wants, much more than we get now, and much more than the Mahommedans are now usurping. . . . The Extremists did not believe that they could turn the British out, or put anything in their place, but they believed that they would frighten the Government into practical surrender, as a result of which, protected by British bayonets, they would enjoy the loaves and fishes. (ibid.: 60)

This belief that the British were discriminatory in favour of the Muslims fuelled the grievances of the 'educated and trader classes' (who asked for 'a treatment displaying greater sympathy and recognition') (ibid.) towards the Land Alienation Act and its successive amendments. This feeling of being a victim of the pro-Muslim bias of the British was strengthened in a decisive manner by a historic decision of the Central government: this was the institution of separate electorates which various Muslim organizations were demanding, and which, in the Punjab, threatened to endanger the political domination of the Hindus of the urban areas. Although in the minority, the latter did indeed tend to control the political arena in the municipalities (such as in Multan, Amritsar, Sialkot and Lahore where the Municipal Council established in 1867 had 9 representatives for 35,000 Hindus and 7 for 60,000 Muslims) (Tinker 1954: 49), which were the only ones open to competition till the reform of 1909.

## The 1906-9 Turning Point

In October 1906, the Viceroy, Lord Minto, who was preparing to bring in some constitutional reforms, had received a pan-Indian delegation of the not yet officially constituted Muslim League; to the Muslims who had demanded measures of 'positive discrimination' (such as separate electorates) keeping in mind both the backwardness of their community in terms of education, its minority status and its importance both from the demographic as well as the historical point of view, the Viceroy had replied that he was convinced:

that any electoral representation in India would be doomed to mischievous failure which aimed at granting a personal enfranchisement regardless of the traditions of the communities composing the population of this continent. (Koss 1967: 383)

In August 1907, constitutional reforms were announced which were later promulgated in 1909. The British granted to the Muslims the principle of separate electrorates, i.e. that the number of representatives of their community that they elected thereafter was proportional to their demographic strength, both countrywise as well as on the level of the provinces. The legislative councils of the Punjab, Bengal and Assam were hence made up of the majority of elected Muslims, while those of the United Provinces, the Bombay Presidency, Bihar and Orissa included four each. But in each of these it was a question of a minimum as the Muslim electors were also authorized to vote in the framework of 'general' constituencies from which Muslim candidates could present themselves. This dual vote clause was accepted by Morley in January 1909, under the pressure of the Muslim League, obviously to gain the support of the Muslims at a time when the Swadeshi Movement was attracting certain Hindu groups (Jha 1976: 41).

In the Punjab, this strategy of dividing to rule was being objected to even within the British administration, as is indicated in a report of the Deputy Commissioner of Lahore suggesting in 1909 that certain demands of the Hindus be granted (starting with nomination of Lal Chand to the Legislative Council) because:

> The Muslims, though keen, are apt merely to talk and to get nothing done. The Muslims must stick to us for their own sakes and should receive consideration accordingly; but under their present petting they are beginning to take the line conversation that we cannot get on without them . . . . Much as I dislike the policy of divide and rule, if it is to be followed, I would far sooner hold the balance even as between the Hindus and Muslims, and divide as between Hindus and Hindus or Muhammadans and Muhammadans. (Morley Collection MSS, 60A)

In spite of these recommendations, the authorities in the Punjab conformed their pro-Muslims bias during the following years again partly on account of their fear of the Hindu nationalists, as is testified by the surveillance to which they subjected the Arya Samajists suspected of having affinities with the Congress and particularly with terrorist movements.

Thereafter, all Hindu circles in the cities were constrained to unite, the Arya Samajists giving up their particular interests in order to lead the fight. Arya Samajist leaders suggested the creation of Hindu Sahayak Sabhas, associations founded in 1906 to promote the unity of the Hindu sects, into political organizations, so as to counter the action of the Muslim League of the Punjab which, founded in December 1906, was putting pressure on the government to obtain more scholarships and seats for Muslims in the Legislative Council (*Confidential Proceedings* (Political) 1909: 986–7). Spearheading this initiative was Ram Bhaj Datt (1866–1923) who had acquired the authority of a leader within the 'College faction' by guiding the agrarian agitation of 1907 with Ajit Singh and Lajpat Rai, who had withdrawn into the background after his sojourn in prison. Lal Chand (1852–1912), another leader of the 'College branch' (he headed the D.A.V. College succeeding Hans Raj, from 1884 till 1904) who was also judge in Lahore and one of the founders of the Punjab National Bank, resisted Ram Bhaj Datt, alleging that in the situation as it prevailed at the time, the Arya Samajists should abstain from any activism; but he came round to adopting the opinion of the others, in the spring, after a Muslim (Shaha Din) had been appointed to the High Court in Punjab instead of himself.

The Hindu Sabha of the Punjab was founded in 1907 and during 1908 and 1909 Sabhas were established within each district. The central office of the provincial Sabha was located in Lahore. Credit for its achievement was given to the D.A.V. College branch of the Arya Samaj and to its principal leaders, Lajpat

Rai and Lal Chand. The inheritance of the new organization was twofold; in one respect, it marked a further application of the cultural method of developing Hindi nationalism, to the extent that its basic doctrines derived from those of the Arya Samaj, with its emphasis on the adaptation of traditional ideas to take account of the challenge represented by British rule and Christian proselytism; yet in another respect, it exemplified the instrumentalist strategy since the founding of this Hindu Sabha was the reaction of a frustrated elite who considered that their socioeconomic and political interests were threatened by the British policy. This methodological statement is confirmed by the fact that *action* of this Hindu Sabha was expressed in conformity with the 'instrumentalist' logic.

## THE HINDU SABHA, A PRESSURE GROUP FOR PROMOTING HINDU 'NATIONAL' INTERESTS

### An Interest Group

The Hindu Sabha made itself known to the government in April 1909 through a letter from its General Secretary, Shadi Lal (an Agarwal judge who went on to become Chief Justice in the Punjab High Court), to the Viceroy, Lord Minto, who had just received a delegation of the Muslim League:

The Hindu community humbly submits that while every reasonable precautions may be adopted to safeguard the interests of the minorities where they are likely to be jeopardised, no case has been made out for any special concession to any community on the score of its alleged historical or political importance and that the claim of excessive representation— advanced in certain quarters, in connection with the Reform Scheme, is opposed to the principles of justice and fair play . . . in the matter of giving appointments in the public services, merit is often overlooked for class consideration with the result that the Hindus suffer thereby. The Government, on the annexation of the province started schools and colleges, and the Hindus flocked to these institutions which their rulers had thrown open to the benefit of all classes and sections of the people. If other communities, in the race for progress, did not keep pace with them, that is no fault of theirs. (NAI Home Department (Political Part A) December 1909)

In July 1909, the Hindu Sabha of Lahore communicated to the Punjab government another memorandum against the Pre-Emption Act, demanding as a minimum concession the extension of the right of preemption to the non-agrarian tribes in the case of land sold by members of non-agrarian tribes. In addition, they expressed their indignation at the fact that Brahmans and Khatris, whose attachment to their holdings was long-standing, had not been classified among agrarian tribes, while this had been done in the case of all Muslim castes.[33]

The Hindu Sabha also expressed its anxiety over the new composition of the Provincial Council provided for in the constitutional reforms. The number of representatives in it went up from 24 to 30, but to the detriment of the Hindus in relative numbers (NAI Home Department (Political Part A), December 1909). The very fact that the Hindu Sabha had appeared at the juncture when the Morley-Minto reforms were being formulated, at the time when the Hindus of the cities in the Punjab were already considering themselves as victims of discrimination in their province, is enough to point to its character as an interest group.

However, this dimension should not obscure the relationship of continuity which binds it to the Arya Samaj. Its ideology had only been slightly reoriented here to serve the purposes of interest, in keeping with 'instrumentalist' logic. Hence the transition from an Arya Samajist nationalism to a Hindu nationalism was a rapid and irrevocable one.

## A Hindu Version of the 'Two-nation Theory'

Jinnah, the main architect of Pakistan, is generally considered as the author of a 'theory' according to which the Hindus and the Muslims of India constituted two nations by virtue of their primordial socio-cultural characteristics. This ideological construction has been analysed as the rationalization of a separatism motivated by the will of an elite to acquire its own territory. Now, this interpretation can apply as much to the Hindu Sabha of the Punjab which, as a reaction to the threats of the interests of the Hindu minority of the region, also displayed separatist inclinations in the framework of an older cultural nationalism.

The ideological charter of the Punjab Hindu Sabha was published from February 1909 onward by Lal Chand in the form of letters to the *Punjabee* (the newspaper founded by Lajpat Rai) under the generic title 'Self Abnegation in Politics'. Considered by later members of the Hindu Sabha as a foundation text, it was republished in 1938. In fact, the problems that Lal Chand addressed in it included some which had preoccupied the Arya Samaj, and others concerning the socioeconomic defence of the Hindu nation, which were new.

It betrayed an anxiety over the demographic decline of the Hindus, which dated back to the conversion activities of the Christian missionaries, and also over the teaching of Persian—a language then still used by the administrative authorities. The opposition to Persian was motivated both by considerations of cultural nationalism ('thousands of Hindus who should be familiar with the truths of the Upanishads and of the *Bhagavad Gita* . . . were irremediably forced to have a knowledge of foreign dogmas and doctrines') (Chand 1938: 38) as well as by considerations of interest (the handicap that the necessity of learning a new language represented, for those who were trying to entry gain to the administrative service under difficult circumstances). Lal Chand stressed the way in which the discriminatory policy of the government had worked against Hindus:

Being driven away from their livelihood on the land, they (the Hindus) are also being gradually ousted from the Government service as a means of living. And, barring law and medicine, the only remaining source left is trade and industry where they are making a struggle. (ibid.: 4)

On the political plane, the focus of Hindu anxieties continued to be the Morley-Minto Reform measures and their provision for separate voting rights of the Muslims, which were likely to give them representation within the regional power structure (ibid.: 30): this reform had been accepted by the moderate Congress elite. As a result, Congress was now being described as 'a veritable source of weakness for purely Hindu interests' (ibid.: 2) and as an organization which was prepared to make concessions in the hope of strengthening the bond between the Hindu and Muslim communities. According to some Hindu nationalist leaders, however, Muslim nationalism was to some extent inspired by pan-Islamic sentiment and could therefore be explained as a projection into Indian politics of a powerful international force and a cause for concern amongst the Hindus of north-western India.[34] This line of reasoning could lead to the conclusion that concessions by the Hindus to Muslim separatism would end in failure. Lal Chand argued that the best response to this situation was for Hindus to recover pride in themselves:

The point I wish to urge is that patriotism ought to be communal and not merely geographical.... Therefore what is necessary and required is to bear the communal interest always in mind and this will solve the many difficulties which now present themselves.... The idea is to love everything owned by the community. It may be religion, it may be a tract of country, or it may be a phase of civilisation.... This then is the fire I wish to rekindle. Here in politics, in the sense I have explained, the desire is to secure better political advantages and to safeguard the universal interests of the community as a whole.... (ibid.: 103)

This programme formulated in pragmatic terms the interests of the community and testified to the emergence of a Hindu nationalist conscience imbued with a political vocation. Arya Samajists such as Bhai Parmanand, a young *upadeshak* very close to Lajpat Rai, considered right from 1909, the possibility of the partition of North-West India, the Muslims being granted Sindh and the North-West Frontier Province (NWFP), and the Hindus keeping the Punjab, along with all that this plan involved in terms of migration (Parmanand 1982: 36).

This is where we reach the point at which interest and ideology are hinged on each other because, while it was indeed the threat that weighed on the Hindus at this juncture which gave rise to this communalist reaction, the substance of this communalism existed in the latent state in the form of the Arya Samajist creed. However, we are confronted here with more than just a reactivation of the Arya Samajist ideology as it is here a matter of protecting all Hindus, since it is this category which was affected by what it considered as an insufficient political representation and by the 'quotas' granted for entry into the administration. The impact of the separation of 'communities' invented by the census operations was found considerably magnified by the introduction of separate electoral lists under the terms of the 1909 reforms: seeing that the number of seats to be filled per 'communal' electoral college was proportional to the demographic strength of this 'community' such as defined by the census, the numerical strength of this latter naturally roused an increased interest among the elite—in the meaning of Paul Brass—of this 'community' (or of what it claimed to be its 'community'), as the elite in question would always have a tendency to want to push back its frontiers as far as possible.

## The Impact of the Censuses on Hindu Unity

The statistical definition of the Hindus as held by the British, led to homogenization which became all the greater as the census figures took on a political hue. Confronted with the complexity of Hinduism whose socio-religious structure often led the persons whose enumeration was being undertaken, to declare themselves as members of one or another caste, or devotees of a particular sect, before calling themselves Hindus as the census agents expected, the latter decided to define them thus by default, as is indicated by Ibbetson who supervised the census of 1881 in the Punjab:

... every native who was unable to define his creed, or described it by any name other than that of some recognized religion, or the sect of some such religion, was held to be classed as a Hindu. (*Census of India Report 1881*, Vol. 1: 19)

This method later came to be refined further by the joining of additional criteria for discrimination, such as respect for the cow and the Brahman (*Census of India 1911*, Vol. XV: 120), but when in 1901, the authorities took in hand the task of enumerating the sects, they had to soon abandon the project, particularly on account of the impossibility of taking account of this 'bewildering maze of sects which overlap in the most extraordinary fashion' (*Census of India 1911*, Vol. 1: 115). The homogenizing effect of this approach remained latent till the time when the numerical strength of the 'community' thus defined was to become a political issue within the framework of the the constitutional reforms of 1909.

In view of the census operations of 1911, E.A. Gait, the Commissioner of the Census, had, in 1910, sent a circular to the provincial census superintendents suggesting that the definition of the Hindus be made stricter in such a way as to eliminate animists and the lower castes; the main criteria to verify in order to be counted among the Hindus were the worship of the 'great Hindu gods', 'authorisation to enter Hindu temples' and not being 'the cause of pollution[1]' through touch of simple proximity (*Modern Review*, Vol. 8, 1910: 683). The Hindu intelligentsia reacted strongly to this instruction which would result in an amputation of the numerical strength of 'its' community. In Bengal, the *Modern Review* founded by a Brahmo Samajist militant, Ramananda Chatterji, denied to the British the right to decide who was a Hindu and who was not, which involved primarily the Untouchables:

For non-Hindus must never forget that it is an essential characteristic of the existing Hindu Social organism that some members are considered higher and some lower, some clean and some unclean. One may call this sort of social constitution irrational, unjust, self-destructive, fatal to national solidarity and progress, wanting in humanity, etc. but one is bound to recognise the fact as a fact. (ibid.)

In other words, the reformers—Bengali Brahmos in this case—gave up their pursuit of being detractors of Hinduism in order to, on the contrary, defend it against external aggressors by federating its different components.

The same phenomenon is observed in the Punjab where the Arya Samaj had not protested against the separate enumeration of the Sikhs right from the second 1868 census (whereas they had been considered as Hindus during that of 1853) (Jones 1981: 79). But in 1910, the Circular sent by Gait, according to Lajpat Rai himself, produced a new Hindu solidarity motivated by the new political implications of demography.[35] Apart from its clauses concerning the Untouchables which incited the Arya Samaj to relaunch the *Shuddhi* Movement among them, the Gait circular provided for widening the definition of the 'Sikhs' at the expense of the Hindus (the *keshdharis*—unshaven Sikhs—no longer being the only ones to be recognized as Sikhs, as was the case for the 1901 census: it was to be any one who called himself a Sikh) (*Punjab Census Report 1911*: 100). The Arya Samajists took up this challenge. During the second Punjab Hindu Conference of November 1910, the Presidency was invested in a Sikh spiritual leader, Baba Gur Baksh Singh Bedi, who declared that the Sikhs, Arya Samajists and Brahmos were all Hindus, by virtue of a nationalist territorial definition:

Indian Muslims who go to Arabia on pilgrimage are called Hindus there. All inhabitants of India who visit the United States of America are there called Hindus . . . . We think, therefore, that all persons of Hindu extraction whose spiritual 'ideals', cultures and exercises are mainly Hindu in character and origin and whose special social and domestic life and ideals conform generally to the Hindu type may be called 'Hindus'. (*Modern Review*, 1910, Vol. 8: 571)

We find here the appropriation by one of the definition of the 'name' that the 'other' offered, on account of its strategic relevance in terms of self-interest. It was in this perspective that the Arya Samajists campaigned for a wider definition of the category of Hindus both by the British and by the population during the census operations. In the United Provinces, where the Arya Samaj had been active since the turn of the century, the census agents observed in 1911 that:

. . . there was at the time a good deal of agitation of a political nature, which in one form was directed to urging the inclusion of all Hindus by race in the category of Hindus by religion. This was undoubtedly responsible for the numerous entries such as Hindu Jain and Hindu Arya and Hindu Sikh. (*Census of India 1911*, Vol. XV: 120)

The Arya Samajists were driven to adopt an inclusive definition of the Hindu community by two closely related imperatives, that of confronting the doctrine of electoral representation by community which formed the basis of the constitutional reforms of 1909 and that of challenging the exclusive definition of the Hindu category by the census authorities. Interestingly, under these difficult circumstances, a large number of Hindu leaders rallied around the reformism of the most radical current among the Arya Samajists, still dominated by Munshi Ram: his sectarian model of an egalitarian Hindu nation carved out by means of *Shuddhi* appeared as the best means to give substance to the inherent solidarity of the Hindu community. The Sanatanist leaders eventually accepted this approach, even though in 1909 they had been prepared to organize a social boycott of the *Chamars* (Untouchables handling leather) on whom the Arya Samajists had performed the *Shuddhi* rite in Hoshiarpur (Jones 1976: 308). The *Shuddhi* campaign which started in 1910 in the framework of preparing for the coming census, was aimed primarily at the Muslim Rajputs of the Malkana caste, particularly in the western district of the United Provinces: the Rajput Shuddhi Sabha, constituted in 1909 under the patronage of Munshi Ram, reconverted 1,052 'Muslim Rajputs' in three years (*Census of India 1911*, Vol. XV: 134). In 1910–12, Ram Bhaj Datt reportedly performed the rite on 100,000 Doms (a sweep caste) in his district of Gurdaspur at the border with Jammu and Kashmir, where the members of the Arya Samaj also numbered 1,047 in 1911 (*Census of India 1921*, Vol. 1: 119). In 1913, another 9,000 Untouchables, from Jammu, were 'purified' in the same way. In the Punjab, in 1912, the Meghs of Sialkot became the subject of a new *Shuddhi* campaign undertaken on around 36,000 persons (Jones 1976: 308; Jordens 1977: 156).

The fact that the Sanatanists had given up their prejudice towards *Shuddhi* in the context of the census, testifies to the spread of a collective Hindu conscience; this is all the more so as symetrically, the Arya Samajists who, till then, were loath to be encompassed within an idolatrous and hierarchical Hinduism, declared themselves fully as being not 'Aryas' as they said previously, but 'Hindus' during the 1911 census. The organizers of the census noted moreover a rapprochement between 'Arya Samajists' and 'Sanatanists'.

Owing to lapse of time, the opposition of the Sanatanists to the Arya Samaj has become feeble and with the marked change in the ideas of the majority of the educated Hindus, a great many of the Arya Samaj propaganda have been, accepted by the Hindu community, while, on the other hand, the Arya Samaj have moderated their tone of criticism and begun to show more respect to some of the orthodox Hindu institutions. The result is that greater harmony now prevails between the Arya Samajists and the orthodox Hindus, particularly the more advanced section of the latter: and the two communities now work together in several lines, such as the revival of ancient festivals, the promotion of the study of Sanskrit and Hindi, the spread of female education and the introduction of social reform. (*Punjab Census Report 1911*: 134)

Undoubtedly this rapprochement was a tactical one, conditioned by the situation arising out of the application of reforms on the basis of the census. The Arya Samajists' approach was 'instrumentalist': their propaganda was directed to persuade the Hindus to declare themselves as such during the census (particularly when they were Sikhs or Untouchables) because they had realized how important it was for them, as an urban Hindu elite, to enlarge the ranks of 'their' community, in order to strengthen their leadership over it, especially in the perspective of the new electoral politics.

But far from proceeding out of corporatist motivations alone, the ideology of the new Hindu Sabha is founded to be a kind of extension the Arya Samajist nationalism. Proof of this lies in the fact that Lajpat Rai, at the Punjab Provincial Hindu Conference of October 1909, after having insisted on the necessity of constituting a 'Hindu Congress' in order, notably, 'to make a protest against these confidential circulars of the government which aim at giving preferential treatment to the other communities at the expense of the Hindus' (Ketkar 1941: 277), laid stress on the status of nationhood integral to the Hindus by invoking the same characteristics of ethnic nationalism (history, culture, . . .) as the founders twenty years earlier, of the Arya Samajist nationalism:

It maybe that the Hindus by themselves, cannot form themselves into a nation in the modern sense of the term, but that is only a play on words. Modern nations are political units . . . . That is the sense in which the expression is used in connection with the body called the 'Indian National Congress' . . . . But that is not the only sense in which it is or can be used. In fact, the German word 'Nation' did not necessarily signify a political nation or a State. In that language it connoted what is generally conveyed by the English expression 'people' implying a community in possessing a certain civilisation and culture. Using it in that sense, there can be no doubt that Hindus are a 'nation' in themselves, because they represent a civilisation all their own. In the present struggle between Indian communities, I will be a Hindu first and an Indian afterwards, but outside India or even in India against non-Indians I am and shall ever be an Indian first and a Hindu afterwards.[36]

This declaration which was tantamount to a statement certifying the birth of Hindu nationalism—as a sub-assembly of Indian nationalism—testifies all the more to the relationship of continuity existing between this ideology and that of the Arya Samajists of the 'College faction', its promoters, since it drew its inspiration explicitly from an article written by Lajpat Rai in the *Hindustan Review* (Allahabad) in 1899, at a time when the Arya Samajists had not yet proclaimed themselves officially as being Hindus. The Hindu Sabha, over and above the nationalist ideology of the Arya Samajists, also adopted the sociological model of the nation developed by the Arya Samaj, as suggested by Lal Chand while transferring it simply on the political plane:

Weak and disunited we are and divided into various sects. But the remedy ties in bringing the sections on a common political platform where they should realise that they are merely branches of the same stock and community . . . (Chand 1938: 118)

The aim was very much that of awakening a national Hindu conscience by erasing the divisions between sects and castes, a task in which the Arya Samaj had already been engaged for three decades: this objective was found to be placed in the same perspective as its social reformism and that explains how the Arya Samaj was a pioneer among movements for a Hindu nationalism both sociological as well as ideological.

The formation of the Hindu Sabha of the Punjab around an Arya Samajist nucleus illustrates the manner in which the 'cultural' and the 'instrumentalist' analyses of nationalism can hinge on each other: it is indeed on the basis of a nationalist ideology formulated by the Arya Samaj in the logic of 'strategic syncretism' that a Hindu Sabha movement took shape at the time when the interests of this group of people (wider than the one represented by the Arya Samaj) found itself endangered. The Hindu solidarity born out of this process proved to draw its strength from the intensity of the external threat.

\* \* \*

Interestingly, the same phenomenon was observed in the United Provinces. In this region the Hindu Sabha was founded in 1915, mainly in reaction to the introduction of separate electorates for the Muslim community at the municipal level (Lutt 1977; Gordon 1974: 151; Robinson 1973). This measure added to the bitterness felt by some Hindu leaders on account of the grant of a separate electorate for the Muslims in 1909. Even before, the Hindu-Muslim antagonism had crystallized around the issue of the official language: in the last third of the nineteenth century, Hindu leaders such as Madan Mohan Malaviya had intensified their campaign on behalf of the recognition of Hindi as a court language, along with Urdu. This reform was demanded in order to enable the Hindu youth to find a job more easily (Malaviya 1897: 20–1). As suggested by Paul Brass, this movement motivated by a race for jobs in the administration (Brass 1974: 132) was probably a landmark in the development of Hindu militancy.

It is the case that the issues generated by the institution of separate electorates for Muslims and by the maintenance of Urdu rather than Hindi as the language of the law courts and the administration were taken up by educated Hindus as matters of material interest, affecting their career paths and their social standing, and to that extent an instrumentalist interpretation of the shift towards Hindu nationalism is justified. However, it was also the case that their reaction was inspired by an ideological view of themselves as the owners of a particular cultural heritage. The personalities eager to protect the Hindu interests through the United Provinces Hindu Sabha were already active in socio-religious movements where the Hindu militant ideology had been developed. M.M. Malaviya, for instance, had been a member of the Hindu Samaj, an organization founded at Allahabad in 1880 to protect and promote Hindu institutions, such as the local Magh Mela whose idolatry was criticized by the missionaries (Chaturvedi 1972: 12). In the 1890s, he played a leading role in the development of the Bharat Dharma Mahamandal, the chief Sanatanist movement in north India (Parmanand 1985: 243; Farquhar 1967: 317). In 1904, he conceived the first draft of what became in 1916 the

Banaras Hindu University, an institution dedicated to the rehabilitation of Hindu traditions and knowledge (Sundaram 1942: VIII).

Therefore, as in the Punjab, we observe an interesting sequence where the transition to politics, through Hindu Sabhas, takes place in accordance with the 'instrumentalist' model but in the wake of a cultural mobilization embodied by the Sanatanist movement which appears, here, like a counterpart to the Arya Samaj in the Punjab. The birth of Hindu nationalism, at least in the Punjab and the United Provinces cannot be explained as a product of cultural givens or instrumentalist strategies alone. The more complex explanation seems to lie in a sequence combining first a cultural reaction (from which derived in ideology the 'strategic syncretism' perspective which is more elaborate than the 'primordialist' view) and second would suggest a political mobilization by ideologically Hindu minded elites whose interests have been threatened or needed to be promoted.

## Notes

1. P. Van der Veer's quick criticism of Louis Dumont illustrates the same type of theoretical antagonism. The latter assumes 'l'hétérogénéité sociale définitive des deux communautés' Hindu and Muslim, in terms of religious values and norms (1966: 382), whereas the former stresses the necessity not to divorce 'these values and sentiments from the political arenas in which they are shaped' (1987: 283).

2. This term refers to Kothari's concept of 'building of tradition' (1968: 273–93) that I applied to the case of Hindu nationalism (1989: 829–51).

3. The Upanishads, writes S.N. Das Gupta, 'again and again reiterate the fact that this spiritual essence is incognizable by any of the sense organs—by eye or by touch—that it is beyond the reasoning faculties of man and is therefore unattainable by logic and that it is for their comments on an earlier version of this indescribable in speech and unthinkable in thought. The appreciation of it is not of an ordinary cognitive nature, but is appreciation of the essence of our beings' (Basham 1975: 112).

4. For other prefaces on the same pattern, see *English Works* 1928, Vol. 1: 2, 47.

5. A.D. Smith insists on the role of this historicism in the birth of nationalism (1981). The notion of 'strategic syncretism' owes much to the last chapter of his first book (1971).

6. In the first version of *Satyarth Prakash*, Dayananda recommended that 'the allocation of a *varna* should be made by the state, after due examination of the graduates from the schools' (Jordens 1978: 116).

7. In 1909, there were seven provincial branches of the Arya Samaj to each of which the following number of sub-associations were affiliated: Punjab: 260; United Provinces: 212; Rajputana: 36; Bengal and Bihar: 45; Central Provinces and Berar: 45; Bombay: 35; Burma: nor recorded (Gupta 1991: 26).

8. 'He used to come to the hostel in search of converts and followers' recalls Lajpat Rai, one of his followers (Rai 1965: 26).

9. Hans Raj's brother, Lala Mulk Raj remained a Brahmo but he enabled, thanks to his financial support, his brother to gain responsibilities inside the Arya Samaj (he succeeded to Sain Das as the chief the branch of Lahore in 1890) (ibid.: 53).

10. 'My father always condemned the Hindu religion, and Hindu customs and ritual, and sometimes he used extremely harsh language about the Hindu gods and goddesses' (Rai 1965: 15).
11. Here, the Arya Samaj inherited an older tendency (Jones 1988: 51).
12. The Deputy Commissioner of Gurgaon says of the Arya Samaj in 1901: 'One great result of its spread has been the diminution in expenditure on marriages and other occasions which is a move in the right direction' (*Punjab Census Report 1901*: 116).
13. For instance, he entered in his diary, on 20 July 1988: 'Saw Pandit Guru Dutt had a long discussion about salvation. Found both of us agreed on all subjects . . . with the acquaintance of Guru Dutt my faith (religion) grew in strength' (Jambunathan 1961: 100).
14. The preamble of the founding character indicated:
    'The primary object will therefore be to weld together the educated and uneducated classes by encouraging the study of the national language and vernaculars; to spread a knowledge of moral-spiritual truths by insisting on the study of classical Sanskrit; to assist the formation of sound and energetic habits by a regulated mode of living; to encourage sound acquaintance with English literature; and to afford a stimulus to the material progress of the country by spreading a knowledge on the physical and applied sciences' (Rai 1967[1914]: 136–7).
15. *The Gurukula Through European Eyes* 1917: I. The regulation of the gurukul indicates: 'On entering, the boys take a vow of poverty, chastity and obedience for 16 years, and this vow they renew at the end of the tenth years. The pupils are not allowed to visit their home during this long period of training' (ibid.: 15).
16. It seems most of the graduates could only become *upadeshaks* in the Arya Samaj (NAI Home Political F. 549–52/1915).
17. For the organization wanted by Dayananda, see (Munshi Ram and Rama Deva 1910: 230–1); for the actual organization, see (Dua 1970: 34–5).
18. Rai 1965: 77. '*Qasis-i-Hind* often moved me to tears and I began to feel that both my mind and my ears were fascinated by accounts of the valorous deeds of the Rajputs. This feeling became stronger everyday till at last it developed into an irresistible passion' (ibid.: 78).
19. Rai 1930: 128–9. This enterprise was far from being fully successful: in 1911, the Census Report of the United Provinces showed that the proportion of married girls, below 10 years and between 10 and 15 years, was respectively 0.92 per cent and 4.42 per cent compared to 1.57 per cent and 6.02 per cent among the Hindus (cited in Gupta 1991: 47).
20. Pareek 1973: 132. Lajpat Rai acknowledged that inter-caste marriages remained 'quite experimental' and took place 'occasionally' (Oman 1991[1934]: 177).
21. Shraddhananda, himself supervised the reprint of the book by O.C. Wood on the Assassins to acquaint the Indian public with this sect: 'It is well known to student of modern History that Islam was mostly propagated by open-violence and compulsion, but that secret dagger also played a great part in silencing its enemies or that cunning devices came into play. In gaining the blind faith of the heathens is not so well known. *The History of the Assassins* gives us an idea of what was done by Nazaris in order to propagate their ideas of Islam and the extracts which I have already culled from the the History of the Jesuits throw ample light on the secret dagger service of a Christian

sect in order to defend (as they thought) their own blind faith from the onslaught of others' (Shraddhananda 1926b: XIX–XX).

22. K. Jones gave a later date, 1900, and R.S. Pareek an intermediate one, 1899 (1973: 136).

23. I am grateful to Ian Talbot for drawing my attention to this point.

24. Jones 1976: 148. More typical of Muslim 'revivalism' than the Ahmadiyah, the Anjuman-i-Himayat-i-Islam was founded in 1884. Like the Arya Samaj, it published tracts against Christian missionaries and established schools and colleges such as the Islamia College (Lahore) which played a similar role to D.A.V. College in inspiring a generation of activists who moved from social reform to politics (Gilmartin 1989).

25. This *communitas* is defined by Victor Turner as 'a relationship between concrete, historical, idiosyncratic individuals' (1977: 131). Interestingly, one of the main features of *communitas* is 'the persisting adhesion between equality and absence of property' (ibid.: 134).

26. Dumont 1966: 379. E. Gellner exposed a similar point of view in his analysis of Renan's theory: 'Renan believed nations to be a peculiarity of Europe as it developed since Charlemagne. He correctly singled out one, perhaps the, crucial trait of a nation: the anonymity of membership. A nation is a large collection of men such that its members identify with the collectivity without being acquainted with its other members and without identifying in any important way sub-groups of that collectivity. Membership is generally unmediated by any really significant corporate segments of the total society. Sub-groups are fluid and ephemeral and do not compare in importance with the 'national' community. Links with groups predating the emergence of the nation are rare, tenuous, suspect, irrelevant' (Gellner 1987: 6).

27. Jordens 1977: 155. Recently, I applied this schema to the Rashtriya Swayamsevak Sangh (1993).

28. In 1891, out of 9,510 male *aryas*, 8,103 were returned as belonging to the 'arya sect' of the 'Hindu Religion' (*Punjab Census Report 1891*: 178).

29. Farquhar 1967: 316. The vagueness of the term 'Sanathan Dharma' is clearly expressed by one of the census agents in 1911: 'For want of a later name covering all the orthodox forms of worship, the term Sanatan Dharma was used to designate the followers of the orthodox Hindu schools other than the religious orders. In other words all orthodox Hindus, not included in one of the sects enumerated above, have been classed as *Sanatan Dharmis* . . . . That enjoined by the Vedas, the Smritis, the Puranas, etc. is the Sanatan (Ancient) religion. But it must not be presumed that every one of the persons registered as Sanatan Dharmi is orthodox. The term includes all shades of belief, from the punctilious observance of Agnihotra (daily fire sacrifice), or worship of a particular God, down to the mere belief in the utility of adhering to the orthodox section of the Hindu society, without observing any, or at least many of the restrictions essential to the carrying out of the orthodox observances' (*Punjab Census Report 1911*: 124–5).

30. Attending the second anniversary of the Lahore Arya Samaj in 1879, Oman observed that 'he was surrounded by several of those bright-faced intelligent youths to be found at the present day in every town of British India who, under the stimulus of Western education, are in a state of intellectual restlessness, eager for reforms and innovations in what they feel is a backward state of society, and who, with the generous ardour and confidence of boys, hope to be able to recast, upon an improved model, institutions

which are the outcome of a hundred influences operating through many an eventful century' (Oman 1991[1934]: 153).

31. 'With us the Brahmans were an unprivileged class and exercised little or no influence of the community . . . without erudition and because of their daily dependence on the other castes, there was a touch of mild derision towards the Brahmans. The very addresses "oh Pandita" or "oh Brahmana" had gentle sarcasm about it' (Tandon 1972: 77). This peculiar despise for brahmans in Punjab is probably one factor of the success of the Arya Samaj, traditionally opposed to the brahmanical orthodoxy.

32. According to Lajpat Rai, 'Lala Sain Das clad himself in nothing but Swadeshi cloth and preached Swadeshi, even in 1881' (Rai 1965: 88).

33. NAI Home Department (Political Part A), December 1909. The Hindu Sabha simultaneously continued to assure the British of its loyalty. In 1910, Munshi Ram wrote a long plea asserting the exclusively religious nature of the Arya Samaj during the trial of 84 Arya Samajis arrested on charges of sedition in the State of Patiala, after A. Grey, at the head of the Punjab Chief Court Bar had likened the Arya Samaj to a political organization in 1909 (Ram and Deva 1910). The *Arya Pratinidhi Sabha* of the United Provinces of Agra and Oudh, anxious to dispel the image of the Arya Samaj as reflected in the remarks of A. Grey, stressed during its Lucknow session in February 1910 that the movement had never 'given a call for disloyalty in British India or in the princely States' [NAI Home Department (Political Part B), April 1910].

34. 'Mohammedans have Constantinople being their back, not to speak of other Mohammedan States which more or less British statesmanship have deal . . . British Statesmen, therefore, not only desire to conciliate muslim opinion, but are seriously nervous lest they should give any offence to it' (Chand 1938: 1).

35. 'The Gait circular had a quite unexpected effect and galvanized the dying body of orthodox Hinduism into sympathy with its untouchable population' (Rai 1967[1914]: 124).

36. Ketkar 1941: 277. Lal Chand was even more explicit: '. . . a Hindu should not only believe but make it a part and parcel of his organism, of his life and of his conduct that he is a Hindu first and an Indian after. Here I wished to reverse the dominant idea propounded by the Congress that we are Indians first and Hindus next' (1938: 70).

# References

Barrier, N.G. (1966), *The Punjab Alienation of Land Bill of 1900*, Duke University.

—— (1967), 'The Arya Samaj and Congress Politics in the Punjab: 1894–1908', *The Journal of Asian Studies*, Vol. 26, No. 3, May.

—— (1967), 'The Punjab Disturbances of 1907: The Response of the British Government in India to Agrarian unrest', *Modern Asian Studies*, Vol. I, No. 4.

—— (1968), 'The Punjab Government and Communal Politics, 1870–1900', *Journal of Asian Studies*, Vol. 17, No. 3, May.

—— (1974), *Banned-Controversial Literature and Political Control in British India (1907–1947)*, Columbia: University of Missouri Press.

Bayly, C.A. (1973), 'Patrons and Politics in Northern India', *Modern Asian Studies*, Vol. 7, No. 3.

———— (1975), *The Local Roots of Indian Politics: Allahabad 1880–1920*, Oxford: Clarendon Press.

Brass, P. (1974), *Language, Religion and Politics in North India*, Cambridge: Cambridge University Press.

———— (1977), 'A reply to Francis Robinson', *Journal of Commonwealth and Comparative Politics*, Vol. 15, No. 3, November.

*Census of India 1881*, Vol. 1.

———— *1901*, Vol. XVI, 'North West Provinces and Oudh', Part 1, Report by R. Bum.

———— *1901*, Vol. 1A, Part II.

———— *1911*, Vol. XV, 'United Provinces of Agra and Oudh', Part I, Report by E.A.H. Blunt.

———— *1911*, Report by E.A. Gait, Vol. 1, Part 1, Calcutta, 1913.

———— *1921*, Vol. 1, Part I, Report by J.T. Marten.

———— *1891, Punjab Census Report*

———— *1901, Punjab Census Report.*

———— *1911, Punjab Census Report.*

Chand, Lal (1938), *Self Abnegation in Politics*, Foreword by Bhai Parmanand, Lahore: The Central Hindu Yuvak Sabha.

Chaturvedi, S. (1972), *Madan Mohan Malaviya*, Delhi: Government of India.

Das, Jivan (1897) (ed.), *Works of the late Pandit Guru Datta Vidhyarthi*, Lahore: Punjab Economical Press.

Das Gupta, S.N. (1975), 'Philosophy', in A.L. Basham (ed.), *A Cultural History of India*, Delhi: Oxford University Press.

Dayananda, Swami (1981), *The Light of Truth* (*Satyarth Prakash*), Allahabad: Dr Ratna Kumari Svadhyaya Sansthana.

Dua, V. (1970), 'Social organisation of Arya Samaj: a study of two local arya centres in Jullundur', *Sociological Bulletin*, Vol. 19, No. 1, March.

Dumont, L. (1966), 'Nationalisme et "Communalisme"', Appendix D, *Homo Hierarchicus*, Paris: Gallimard.

*English Works of Raja Rammohun Roy* (1928), 'The brahmanical magazine or the missionary and the brahmun being a vindication of the Hindoo religion against the attacks of Christian missionaries—Calcutta 1821', in Vol. 1, Calcutta.

———— Preface to 'Translation of the Cena Upanishad, one of the chapters of the Sama Veda: according to the gloss of the celebrated Shancaracharya establishing the unity and the sole omnipotence of the supreme being and that he alone is the object of worship—Calcutta 1823', Vol. 1, Calcutta.

Fallers, L.A. (1961), 'Ideology and Culture in Uganda Nationalism', *American Anthropologist*, Vol. 3, No. 4, August.

Farquhar, J.N. (1967), *Modern Religious Movements in India*, Delhi: Munshiram Manoharlal.

Feroz, Chand (1978), *Lajpat Rai: Life and Work*, Delhi: Ministry of Information and Broadcasting.

Geertz, C. (1973), 'Ideology as a Cultural System', in *The Interpretation of Culture*, New York: Basic Books.

Gellner, E. (1987), *Culture, Identity and Politics*, Cambridge: Cambridge University Press.

Gilmartin, O. (1989), *Punjab and Islam: Punjab and the Making of Pakistan*, University of California Press.

Gopal, M., 'The rise and fall of Brahmo Samaj in Punjab', Occasional Papers on History and Society—2nd series, No. XLVI, Nehru Memorial Museum and Library.

Gordon, R. (1974), 'The Hindu Mahasabha and the Indian National Congress: 1915 to 1926', *Modern Asian Studies*, Vol. 9, No. 2

Gupta, S.K. (1991), *Arya Samaj and the Raj*, New Delhi: Gitanjali Publishing House.

Jaffrelot, C. (1989), 'La place de l'Etat dans l, idéologie nationaliste hindoue – éléments pour l'étude de l' invention de la tradition politique', *Revue Française de Science Politique*, Vol. 39, No. 6, December.

—— (1993), *Les nationalistes hindou: Ideologic, implantation et mobilisation des années 1920 aux années 1990*, Paris: Presses de la FNSP.

Jambunathan, M.R. (1961) (ed.), *Swami Shraddhananda (Autobiography)*, Bombay: Bharatiya Vidya Bhavan.

Jha, P. (1976), *Political Representation in India*, Meerut: Meenakshi Prakashan.

Jones, K. (1966), 'The Bengali elite in Post-Annexation Punjab: an example of Inter-Regional Influence in 19th Century India', *The Indian Economic and Social History Review*, Vol. 3, No. 4, December.

—— (1966), 'Communalism in the Punjab: The Arya Samaj contribution', *The Journal of Asian Studies*, Vol. 28, No. 1, November.

—— (1973), ' "Ham Hindu Nahin": Arya Sikh relations 1877-1905', *The Journal of Asian Studies*, Vol. 32, No. 3, May.

—— (1976), *Arya Dharm: Hindu Consciousness in Nineteenth Century Punjab*, Berkeley: University of California Press.

—— (1981), 'Religious Identity and the Indian Census', in Barrier, Gerald N. (ed.), *The Census in British India: New Perspectives*, Delhi: Manohar.

—— (1988), 'Socio-religious movements and Changing Gender relationships among Hindus of British India', in J.W. Bjorkman (ed.), *Fundamentalism, Revivalists and Violence in South Asia*, Delhi: Manohar.

—— (1989), *The New Cambridge History of India III-1: Socio-Religious Reform Movements in British India*, Cambridge: Cambridge University Press.

Jordens, J.T.F. (1977), 'Reconversion to Hinduism, the Shuddhi of the Arya Samaj', in G.A. Oddie, *Religion in South Asia*, London: Curzon Press.

—— (1978), *Dayananda Sarasvati: His Life and Ideas*, Delhi: Oxford University Press.

—— (1981), *Swami Shraddhananda: His Life and Causes*, Oxford: Oxford University Press.

Kane, P.V. (1953), *History of Dharmashastra*, Vol. 4, Poona Bhandarkar Oriental Research Institute.

Ketkar, G.V. (1941), 'The All India Hindu Mahasabha', *The Indian Annual Register*, Vol. 1.

Kishwar, Madhu (1986), 'Arya Samaj and Women's Education: Kanya Mahavidyalaya, Jalandhar', *Economic and Political Weekly*, Vol. 29, No. 17, 26 April.

Koss, S.E. (1967), 'John Morley and the Communal Question', *The Journal of Asian Studies*, Vol. 26, No. 3, May.

Kothari, R. (1968), 'Tradition and modernity revisited', *Government and Opposition*, Summer.

Lütt, J. (1977), 'Indian Nationalism and Hindu Identity: the beginnings of the Hindu Sabha Movement', Communication to the Seventh International Conference of the Association of Historians of Asia, Bangkok, 22–6 August 1977.

Malaviya, M.M. (1897), *Court Character and Primary Education in the North-West Provinces and Oudh*, Allahabad: Indian Press.

Mauss, M. (1952–4), "La Nation", *L' Année Sociologique*, Troisième série.

Mill, J. (1989), 'History of British India', in E. Stokes, *The English Utilitarians and India*, Delhi: Oxford University Press.

Mitter, P. (1987), 'Rammohun Roy and the new language of Monotheism', in F. Schmidt (ed.) *The Inconceivable Polytheism*, London: Hardwood Academic Publishers.

*Modern Review* (1910), Vol. 8, No. 5, November.

―― (1910), Vol. 8, No. 6, December.

*Morley Collection*, MSS EURD 573(12), IOLR.

Nanakchand, Pandit (1946), *Autobiography*, Nanakchand Papers (typed), NMML Manuscript section.

NAI Home Department, Confidential Proceedings (Political), Proceeding No. 155, October 1909, IOLRP/8153.

NAI Home Department (Political Part A) Proceeding Nos. 29–31, December 1909.

―― (Political Part A) Proceeding Nos. 50-3, December 1909.

―― (Political Part B) Proceeding Nos. 69-70, April 1910.

NAI Home Political F. 549–552/1915.

Oman, J.C. (1991[1934]), *Cults, Customs and Superstitions of India*, Delhi: Indian Bibliographies Bureau.

Pareek, R.S. (1973), *Contributions of Arya Samaj in the Making of Modern India 1875–1947*, New Delhi: Sarvadeshik Arya Pratinidhi Sabha.

Parmanand, Bhai (1982), *The Story of My Life*, New Delhi: S. Chand & Co.

―― (1985), *Mahamana Madan Mohan Malaviya*, Vol. 1, Benares: Banaras Hindu University.

Rai, L. Lajpat (1930), *L'Inde malheureuse –réfutation du livre de Miss Mayo "Mother India"*, texte français de Mme M. Girette, Avant-propos de Romain Rolland, Paris: Rieder.

―― (1967 [1914]), *A History of the Arya Samaj*, Bombay: Orient Longmans.

―― (1965), *Autobiographical Writings*, (ed.) Vijaya Chandra Joshi, Delhi and Jullundur: University Publishers.

Ram, Munshi (1893), *The Future of the Arya Samaj*, Lahore: Virajanand Press.

―― and Deva, Rama (1910), *The Arya Samaj and its Detractors: A Vindication*, Dayanandabad.

Ricoeur, P. (1988), *L' identité narrative*, *Esprit*, Juil. Août 1988.

Robinson, F. (1973), 'Municipal Government and Muslim Separatism in the United Provinces, 1883 to 1916', *Modern Asian Studies*, Vol. 7, No. 3.

―― (1977), 'Nation formation: The Brass thesis and Muslim separatism', *Journal of Commonwealth and Comparative Politics*, Vol. 15, No. 3, November.

Sarda, Har Bilas (1968), *Life of Dayanand Saraswati*, Ajmer.

Sen, N.B. (1944) (ed.), *Punjabi's Eminent Hindus*, Lahore: New Book Society.

Sen, S.P. (1973) (ed.), *Dictionary of National Biography*, Vol. 1, Calcutta: Institute of Historical Studies.

Seunarine, J.F. (1977), *Reconversion to Hinduism through Shuddhi*, Madras: The Christian Literature Society.

Shraddhananda (1926a), *Hindu Sangathan: Saving of the Dying Race*, Delhi: Arjun Press.

―― (1926b), 'Introduction', in O.C. Wood, (tr.), *The History of the Assassins*, Benares: Gyanmandal Press.

Smith, A.D. (1981), *Ethnic Revival,* Cambridge: Cambridge University Press.

——— (1971), *Theories of Nationalism,* London: G. Duckworth.

Sundaram, V.A. (ed.), *Banaras Hindu University: 1916–1942,* Benares.

Talbot, I. (1988), *Punjab and the Raj 1849–1947,* New Delhi: Manohar.

Tandon, P. (1972), *A Punjabi Century,* Delhi: Hind Pocket Books.

——— (1989), *Banking Century—A short history of banking in India and the pioneer: Punjab National Bank,* New Delhi: Penguin Books.

*The Gurukula through European eyes*—Reprint from the Pioneer of the notable articles of M.H. Phelps, with an introduction by Mahatma Munshi Ram, Kangri, Gurukul Press, 1917.

Thursby, G.R. (1972), 'Aspects of Hindu Muslim relations in British India: a study of Arya Samaj activities, Government of India politics, and communal conflicts in the period 1923–1928', unpublished Ph.D. thesis, Duke University.

Tinker, H. (1954), *The Foundation of Self-Government in India, Pakistan and Burma,* London: Athlone.

Turner, Victor (1977), *The Ritual Process,* Ithaca: Cornell University Press.

Vable, D. (1983), *The Arya Samaj: Hindu without Hinduism,* New Delhi: Vikas Publishing House.

Van der Veer, P. (1987), '"God must be liberated!" A Hindu Liberation Movement in Ayodhya', *Modern Asian Studies,* Vol. 21, No. 2.

Van Den Dungen, P.H.M. (1968), 'Changes in status and occupation in nineteenth century Punjab', in D.A. Low (ed.) *Soundings in Modern South Asian History,* Berkeley: University of California Press.

Vedananda Tirtha, Swami (n.d.), *Wisdom of the Rishis or Complete Works of Pandit Guru Dutt,* Hindi Electric Press.

# Chapter 6

# The idea of the Hindu race in the writings of Hindu nationalist ideologues in the 1920s and 1930s a concept between two cultures

Students of early Indian history and the Great Tradition indicate that at that time autochthons' ideas about the Other were based on cultural and linguistic rather than racial distinctions and that these differentiations were blurred. Wilhelm Halbfass emphasizes that in ancient India 'the *mlecchas* are nothing but a faint and distant phenomenon at the horizon of the indigenous tradition. They do not possess an "otherness" against which one's own identity could be asserted or in which it could be reflected' (Halbfass 1988: 187). This peculiar 'xenology' stems mainly from the fact that the society is seen, in the Brahmanical tradition, as maintaining a relationship of homology with the *dharma* as a universal norm. This theme is very clear, for instance, in the *sloka* of the *Rig Veda* narrating the sacrifice of the primordial man (*Virat Purusha*) (Renou 1956: 99).

This organicist and self-universalizing view of society explains partly why the racial criterion has been downplayed in this tradition. According to Romila Thapar, the *mleccha* were discriminated against because they did not observe the rules of the *varna vyavastha* and the vedic rituals, being ignorant of the language (Sanskrit) in which the latter were performed (Thapar 1978: 155). The discrimination was a function of the degree of ritual purity rather than ethnicity and the 'Aryas' were taken to be a 'noble people' rather than a racial group. Therefore, the frontier between the Aryas and the *mlecchas* was a relatively open one: the progeny of inter-caste unions formed a new caste included in the social system, in the Shudra category (ibid.: 157) and foreigners could also be integrated if they accepted the ritual rules of which the Brahmans were the custodians. The successive invaders (the Greeks, Shakas and Huns who adopted local religious beliefs and practises) were thus recognized as Kshatriyas. As a result, 'from about the ninth century onwards references to large numbers of indigenous peoples as *mlecchas* beg[a]n to decrease' (ibid.: 173).

The inner logic the caste system demonstrates here is its capacity for assimilation of the Other at a subordinate level: insofar as its hierarchy reflects a graduation of status based on the concept of ritual purity, any group can be attributed a rank according to its degree of purity, orthopraxy or conformity with the social rules (Dumont 1966: 242). This assimilation-and-subordination is more than an opportunity: it is a necessity, because the 'traditional Indian xenology', as Halbfass terms it, does not enable the Aryas to conceive anything beyond them; every community is supposed to be integrated to their social system to maintain the cosmic order. This world view, however, is primarily promoted by the Brahmanical order whose attitude, according to Sheldon Pollock, citing Geissen, amounts to a 'pre-form of racism' (Pollock 1993: 107), as evident in the exclusion of the Shudras from knowledge of the Vedas. Yet the author emphasizes the absence of eugenic grounds for this exclusion in the *Mimamsa:*

While a biogenetic disqualification is sometimes adduced elsewhere, sudras and other despised communities are here not excluded from vedic literacy on the grounds of physical or intellectual inferiority. On the contrary, 'sudras are as capable of learning as the twice-born are'; in the matters of this world, aryas and mlecchas have equal capabilities [according, respectively, to Kacaspati and Kumarila]. (ibid.: 110)

As a result, Pollock describes the restrictions on high-culture literacy as part of 'a program of domination' (ibid.: 111). This assessment, combined with the idea of a 'pre-form of racism', is close to the notion of 'upper caste racism'—a term coined by Gyanendra Pandey (Pandey 1993: 252)—which I shall try to apply to key Hindu nationalist ideologues. In effect, these men drew some of their inspiration from the 'Great Tradition'.

However, these ideologues had also been exposed to many European ideas about race. Interestingly, philosophers and sociologists working on racialism sustain that the racial theory was born in an article of 1664 by François Bernier, a French doctor who travelled extensively in India. This article, entitled *Nouvelle division de la terre, par les différentes espèces ou races d'hommes qui l'habitent,* was the first attempt to divide the world according to the racial criterion (Toth 1988: 23). But, though Bernier's travelogues were translated into English as early as 1671, this article apparently was not; and, therefore, the first proto-racialist theories evolved by Europeans using the English medium must probably be located in the late eighteenth century. In 1792, William Jones had deduced from the discovery of the Indo-European linguistic family the notion of a common, original race whose branches had migrated towards Europe and India (Marshall 1970: 15). This theory was developed during the nineteenth century by many German philologists such as Albrecht Weber, R. Roth, A. Kuhn and J. Mohl (whose books were published in the 1840s and 1850s). In their writings appear the notions of 'Sanskritic race' or 'vedic people'. These speculations reached India from the late 1850s onwards through Max Müller, who tended to be somewhat more cautious, and William Muir who published, in 1860, a study on 'The trans-Himalayan origin of the Hindus, and their affinity with the western branches of the Aryan race'.[1]

The first Hindu revivalist thinkers were clearly influenced by these European reconstructions of the past. Swami Dayananda Saraswati, according to Jordens, 'did his best to keep abreast of what European scholars were publishing' (Jordens

1978: 170). In 1868 or 1869 he employed a Bengali to read to him Max Müller's translation of the *Veda*, about which his knowledge seems to have been rudimentary till then (ibid.: 56–7). The theses of the Western orientalists about the vedic period probably shaped the views he expressed in *Satyarth Prakash* (The Light of Truth), few years later. In this book, the vedic Aryas are described by Dayananda as a primordial and elect people to whom the Veda has been revealed by God and whose language—Sanskrit—is said to be the 'Mother of all languages' (Dayananda 1981: 249). They would have migrated in the beginning of the world from Tibet—the first land to emerge from the Oceans[2]—towards the Aryavarta. This territory, homeland of the vedic civilization, covered the Punjab, Doab and Ganges basin. From this position, the Aryas would have dominated the whole world till the war of the Mahabharata, a watershed opening a phase of decadence. The national renaissance implied precisely, for Dayananda, a coming back to the vedic Golden Age. The Arya Samaj is probably the first movement in India defining nationalism in terms of ethnicity: in Dayananda's writings, the Hindu are clearly the descendants of the Aryas, even if he called his followers not to register themselves as Hindus—because of the decadent shape of Hinduism—before the census of 1881. This stance was reversed by his successors before the census of 1911.

The idea of world domination by the Hindus was elaborated around that time by another Arya Samajist based in the Rajasthani British enclave of Ajmer, Har Bilas Sarda (1867–1955).[3] In the second chapter of *The Hindu Superiority* (1906), entitled 'Hindu colonization of the world', this author rejects the Central Asia theory of emigration (a point to which I shall return) and asserts that the Aryavarta was the birthplace of a race which spread and settled in Egypt, Ethiopia, Persia, Asia Minor, Greece, Rome, Turkistan, Germany, Scandinavia, Hyperborean countries, Great Britain, Eastern Asia and America (Sarda 1975: 109–63). This geography is precisely the one suggested from another point of view by W. Jones: beyond the linguistic links between the Greek, the Gothic, the Celtic, the Persian and the Sanskrit, Sarda indicated that the Scythian, Hyperborean and Scandinavian philosophies and mythologies might have been introduced or shaped by 'a foreign race' from the East (Jones 254–5). As far as America is concerned he adds:

It is very remarkable that the Peruvians, whose Incas boasted of the same descent, styled their greatest festival Ramasitoa; whence we may suppose, that South America was peopled by the same race, who imported into the farthest parts of Asia the rites and fabulous history of Rama. (ibid.: 256)

The similarities in the inscriptions on Abyssian, Ethiopic and Indian monuments led Jones to conclude that 'Ethiopia and Hindustan were peopled or colonized by the same extraordinary race' (ibid.: 257). Har Bilas Sarda, who quotes Jones abundantly along with Colebrooke, Kuhn, Muir, Müller, Roth, A. Weber and the Theosophists, uses such claims to prove that most of the civilizations originated in the Hindus-Aryas, a race which colonized the whole world before the Mahabharata war.

The same themes appeared at the same time in the second book by Bal Gangadhar Tilak, *The Arctic Home in the Vedas* (1903). The author, known for his Hindu nationalist leanings, claimed that the Aryans had their original home near the North Pole in palaeolithic times and that they migrated from this place southwards into Asia and Europe because of changes in the climatic conditions (Karandikar 1957: 193). Interestingly, Tilak refers often to Muir and Müller to substantiate his theory (Leopold 1970: 275).

Obviously, the first Hindu nationalist ideologues of the late nineteenth century and early twentieth century borrowed heavily from the European orientalists. Among other themes, the one they used assiduously related to the common racial origin of the European and Indian peoples, and its corollary, the southward migration which they interpreted to prove that the Hindus were the first race and that they once dominated the whole world. This myth helped the first Hindu revivalists to regain a certain self-esteem by claiming that then-ancestors were the first inhabitants of the world. But the argument was not developed beyond this point. It seems that these authors hesitated to resort to the themes of racial purity as such, and this is the issue I would like to analyse now, especially because this attitude proved to be perennial.

A similar kind of ambiguity in the use of racial theories can be observed in the case—on which I shall focus—of Hindu nationalist ideologues of the 1920s and 1930s, when such theories were so much in vogue in Europe. The reason for this restraint seems to lie in the contradiction between the Western influences and the 'traditional Indian xenology': the leaders of the inter-war period inherited an hierarchical but integrative view of society into which the racial theories did not fit easily.

## The Hindus as a Race and the Western Influence

V.D. Savarkar was probably the most influential ideologue of Hindu nationalism in the 1920–40 period. His book *Hindutva: Who is a Hindu?* has been recognized as a treatise of Hindu identity by many followers. It was one of the influences which prompted Hedgewar to create the Rashtriya Swayamsevak Sangh in 1925. This book shares the perspective of those written by Swami Dayananda and Tilak. Savarkar had been given a grant to study in England thanks to the recommendation of the latter (Anand 1967; Chitragupta 1987 [1926]), and the hostel where he lived between 1905 and 1910 in London, India House, was being looked after by a staunch Arya Samajist from Bombay, S.K. Verma,[4] whose interest in Herbert Spencer's theories was evident in his journal, *The Indian Sociologist* (Yajnik 1950: 103–19). Savarkar inherited the Hindu revivalist ideas of the late nineteenth and early twentieth centuries, but he extended them and developed their racial aspects.

Near the end of *Hindutva*, Savarkar offers the following definition of the Hindu:

A Hindu, then is he who feels attachment to the land that extends from Sindhu to Sindhu as the land of his forefathers—as his Fatherland; who inherits the blood of the great race whose first and discernible source could be traced from the Himalayan altitudes of the Vedic Saptasindhus and which assimilating all that was incorporated and ennobling all that was assimilated has grown into and come to be known as the Hindu people; and who, as a consequence of the foregoing attributes, has inherited and claims as his own the Hindu sanskriti [culture], the Hindu civilization, as represented in a common history, common heroes, a common literature, common art, a common law and a common jurisprudence, common fairs and festivals, rites and rituals, ceremonies and sacraments. (Savarkar 1969: 100)

Obviously, Savarkar attaches most importance to the concepts of territory and race. The first draws its name, Hindustan, from the fact that it is girdled by the sea and seven rivers (*sapta sindhus*, mainly the Indus and the Brahmaputra). The second, coming from the mountains where these rivers have their source, is said to have settled in this land at the dawn of the world. Savarkar insists on this primacy and ascendancy of the Hindus: 'They are not only a Nation but also a race-jati. . . . All Hindus claim to have in their veins the blood of the mighty race incorporated with and descended from the vedic fathers. . . ' (ibid.: 84–5).

The myth of the vedic Golden Age is reactivated and reinterpreted to the extent that Savarkar puts the emphasis more on its racial dimension than on the cultural or religious aspects which are presented as derivative. This emphasis seems to be easy to explain: Savarkar tries desperately to demonstrate that an original unity underlies and orders the cultural diversity of the Hindus:

And no word can give full expression to this racial unity of our people as the epithet, Hindu does. Some of us were Aryans and some Anaryans; but Ayars and Nayars [according to the South India terminology]—we were all Hindus and own a common blood.[5] Some of us are Brahmans and some Namashudras or Panchamas [untouchable castes]; but Brahmans or Chandalas [one generic term for the Untouchables]—we are all Hindus and own a common blood. Some of us are Daxinatyas [from the South] and some Gauds; but Gauds or Saraswatas [*smarta*—orthodox—Brahmans]—we are all Hindus and own a common blood. Some of us were Rakshasas [demonical beings perceived as the original settlers of India] and some Yakshas [supernatural beings having some elements of divinity]; but Rakshasas or Yakshas—we are all Hindus and own a common blood. Some of us were Vanaras [inhabitants of the forest, tribals as well as monkeys] and some Kinnaras [denizens of the *antariksha* or atmospheric region]; but Vanaras or Naras—we are all Hindus and own a common blood. Some of us are Jains and some Jangamas [shaivite sect]; but Jains or Jangamas—we are all Hindus and own a common blood. Some of us are monists, some pantheists; some theists and some atheists. But monotheists or atheists—we are all Hindus and own a common blood. We are not only a nation but a Jati, a born brotherhood. Nothing else counts, it is after all a question of heart. We *feel* that the same ancient blood that coursed through the veins of Ram and Krishna, Buddha and Mahavir, Nanak and Chaitanya, Basava and Madhava, of Rohidas and Tiruvelluvar courses throughout Hindudom from vein to vein, pulsates from heart to heart (Savarkar 1969: 89).

This incantatory piece of rhetoric is indicative of the whole ideological strategy of Savarkar: belonging to a community divided into many castes and sects, he tries to imbue it with a nationalist consciousness by arguing that beyond all the visible differences there exists an invisible bond—blood. (However, he acknowledges that the reality of this common blood is less important than the *feeling* of its national meaning, a point to which we shall return in the second section.)

The way in which Savarkar employed a racial criterion stemmed probably from Western influences which we must now analyse. During his stay in England, Savarkar had obviously been exposed to evolutionary theories. In his autobiography, books by Darwin, Spencer, Tyndall, Haeckel and Huxley are mentioned: they were among his readings in the Andamans prison where he was kept for anti-British activities between 1911 and 1921, and where he conceived *Hindutva*.[6] All these writers share a common interest in evolutionist theories. The work of the German zoologist, Ernst Haeckel, even belongs to the bio-evolutionist school of thought, since he justified the domination of races considered to be incapable of progress (Taguieff 1987: 335). In the late 1930s, soon after his liberation from jail in 1937, Savarkar expressed a certain attraction for European fascism. In 1938, the year after he became president of the Hindu Mahasabha, he congratulated Hitler during a public meeting at Delhi for having 'liberated' the Sudetans who shared the 'same blood and same tongue' (*Hindu Outlook*, 12 October 1938: 13) as the Germans. At the same time, *Hindu Outlook* (the Hindu Mahasabha mouthpiece) and *Mahratta* (one of Tilak's newspapers, edited by N.C. Kelkar, an active Hindu Sabhaite) praised Franco (ibid., 2 November 1938: 5) and Mussolini (ibid., 30 November 1938: 7), as well as Hitler (*Mahratta*, 6 January 1939: 10).

Some Hindu Sabhaites had had direct contacts with European fascists since the early 1930s. When Moonje (Tilak's lieutenant at Nagpur, who became president of the Hindu Mahasabha in 1927) journeyed to London to attend the first Round Table Conference, he went to Italy in order 'to see the working of the Ballila movement'.[7] It seems that he met Hitler and had an interview with Mussolini, who was pleased to show him his military institutions (*Dharmaveer: Dr. B.S. Moonje Commemoration Volume* 1972: 25). After coming back to India, Moonje laboured to establish a military school. It opened in 1938 at Nasik, thanks to the support of many maharajas (letter from Moonje, *Moonje Papers* 1936).

But the main Hindu movement generally perceived as stemming from European inter-war fascism is the Rashtriya Swayamsevak Sangh. In fact, its foundation took place in 1925 before the first contacts of Hindu nationalist leaders with European fascists, and its model was more the sect than the totalitarian party (Jaffrelot 1995: Ch. 1). However, the ideological influence seems to have been real, as indicated by the use of the concept of race in *We, or our nationhood defined*, the first central text of the RSS written in 1938 by M.S. Golwalkar, who became head of the organization in 1940. Drawing his inspiration explicitly from 'Western political scientists' (Golwalkar 1947: 21), this author distinguished five criteria as defining a nation: land, race, religion, culture and language. Among those, by contrast with Savarkar's *Hindutva*,[8] the racial factor is given more prominence than the territorial.

This emphasis on the racial criterion stems clearly from the influence of the Nazi model which attracted attention in the 1930s:

The ancient Race spirit which prompted the Germanic tribes to over-run the whole of Europe, has re-risen in modern Germany. With the result that the nation perforce follows aspirations, predetermined by the traditions left by its depredatory ancestors. Even so with us: our Race spirit has once again roused itself as is evidenced by the race of spiritual giants we have produced, and who today stalk the world in serene majesty. (Golwalkar 1947: 39–40)

The concept of 'race spirit' used by Golwalkar corresponds most probably here to the German notion of *Geist*. It refers to a conception of the nation based on ethnic qualities: the nation bears a special genius expressed in its culture and its language. This kind of nationalism had been developed by Herder and Fichte without racial references; and, apparently, Golwalkar, in the wake of the Hindu revivalist writers, took it over and added the word 'race'. However, another passage of his book would appear to indicate that Golwalkar borrowed more than an ethnic model of nationalism from the German national socialism:

German pride has now become the topic of the day. To keep up the purity of the Race and its culture, Germany shocked the world by her purging the country of the Semitic Races— the Jews. Race pride at its highest has been manifested here. Germany has also shown how well nigh impossible it is for Races and cultures, having differences going to the root, to be assimilated into one united whole, a good lesson for us in Hindusthan to learn and profit by. (ibid.: 43)

Here, Golwalkar draws from the eugenic core of the European fascism. He openly suggests that minorities can hardly be assimilated and, therefore, must be eliminated. The trouble with this often quoted passage is that it is the only place, so far as I know, where Golwalkar refers to racial purity. He does not seem to have evolved a systematic racial theory based on eugenic or biological principles. This is probably largely due to the fact that Golwalkar drew most of its inspiration from European writers who cannot be termed 'racist' in biological terms. Among the 'political scientists' quoted by Golwalkar we find 'Hole-Combe' (in fact Arthur Norman Holcombe), 'Bluntsley' (in fact Johann Kaspar Bluntschli), 'Gumplovic' (in fact Ludwig Gumplovicz) and Burgess (John W. Burgess).[9] None of these writers was a hard-core eugenist. Holcombe, in the very book quoted by Golwalkar,[10] writes that 'modern anthropologists and ethnologists have not succeeded in classifying mankind upon the evidences of relationship by blood, so as to enable the political scientist to identify nations with particular races' (Holcombe 1923: 129). This assertion is somewhat shaded by the polysemy of the word 'race' in Holcombe's writings (like in so many others at that time). About 30 pages later, he writes that:

in general, Oriental nationalism is blended with the larger problems arising out of the rivalries of races. The doctrine of self-determination may be understood, not as the self-determination of nations, but as racial self-determination. It has been so understood, for instance, by the more radical leaders of the movement for self-government in India. (ibid.: 161)

Despite this lack of conceptual rigour, Holcombe remained an exponent of a non-ethnic form of nationalism. By contrast, Gumplovicz, who wrote *Der Rassenkampf* in 1883, was influenced by Gobineau's theories. However, he also criticized the idea of classifying races—none of them being pure—and did not consider races as primary elements but as constructs, products of the fight between groups striving for domination (See *La lutte des races* 1893: 179–92; Taguieff 1987: 577, and Horowitz 1963: 10–17). In addition, Golwalkar mentions Gumplovicz en passant. He quotes more extensively 'the famous German writer', 'Blunstley', a passage (its origin not indicated by Golwalkar) which comes from Bluntschli's *The Theory of the State* which was published in English in 1885 and republished in 1892, 1895, 1897, 1898, 1901 and 1921. The excerpt selected by Golwalkar is revealing of the influences to which he was most receptive:

[A nation] is a union of masses of men of different conceptions and social states, in hereditary society of common spirit, feeling and race bound together especially by a language and customs in a common civilization which gives them a sense of unity and distinction from all foreigners, quite apart from the bond of the state. (Bluntschli 1885: 86 in Golwalkar 1947: 21)

This definition is chiefly illustrative of the German kind of 'ethnic nationalism' based on inherited cultural features. 'Race' appears here as one criterion among others. The racial dimension was emphasized by other writers as early as the late nineteenth century, but Golwalkar did not borrow primarily from them.

More generally, no other Hindu nationalist ideologue has been able to assimilate the biological logic underlying the fascist version of racialism. This must be scrutinized, not to congratulate oneself on this incapacity, but in order to identify the Hindu nationalist variety of racism, which is probably less dramatic but more enduring than the eugenic or biological one. This particular racial theory seems to be rooted in the 'traditional Indian xenology' and to have been adapted to the specific needs of ideologues such as Savarkar and Golwalkar in terms of (Hindu) nation-building.

## Social Racism Rather than Bio-Racism or the Persistence of the Traditional Xenology

The historical account of the formation of the Hindu people by Savarkar excludes the notion of a pure race. True, to emphasize the uniformity of the Hindu blood throughout the society, he invokes the legality of inter-caste marriages through the customs of *anuloma* and *pratiloma* (Savarkar 1969: 85), and, on the same reasoning, he denied that the Shakas and the Huns were integrated in the Hindu matrix: they were opposed straightaway (ibid.: 21). But as mentioned, his Hindu race includes Aryans as well as non-Aryans. This is an implicit acknowledgement of the way the former conquered the subcontinent. As the Aryans penetrated the subcontinent, 'different peoples of other highly developed types began to be incorporated into their culture' (ibid.: 11).

Savarkar rejects even the idea of a pure Hindu race:

After all there is throughout this world so far as man is concerned but a single race—the human race kept alive by one common blood, the human blood. . . . Even as it is, not even the aborigines of the Andamans are without some sprinkling of the so-called Aryan blood in their veins and vice versa. Truly speaking all that any one of us can claim, all that history entitles one to claim, is that one has the blood of all mankind in one's veins. The fundamental unity of man from pole to pole is true, all else only relatively so. (ibid.: 90)

This repudiation of the very idea of a Hindu race, so strongly stressed elsewhere by Savarkar can be explained from two points of view: first, the Aryan theory was not thought nationalistic enough; and, second, that social integration which dominates the hierarchical view of the world in Brahmanical Hinduism, remained a very strong priority for the Hindu nationalist ideologues.

(1) *The Aryan theory is not nationalistic enough.* The Aryan theory had been very much used by Indian writers, in order to regain their lost self-esteem, from the end of the nineteenth century till the beginning of the twentieth century. Alleging racial links with the dominant white power and invoking the colonization of the world by Indian Aryans were factors nourishing nationalist pride. But in the 1930s and 1940s, the Aryan theory seems to have been counter-productive from this very same Hindu nationalist view point.

First, it seems it was not able to unite the Hindu nation beyond the castes, sects and regionalisms (as Savarkar tried to show in some parts of his book) because it introduced a division between the Aryans and the peoples who used to live in India before the Aryan migration, mainly the Dravidians and tribals whom Savarkar considered part of the Hindu nation from other points of view such as culture and geography. According to Joan Leopold, this divisive impact of the Aryan theory had been the main cause of its rejection by many nationalist writers even before Savarkar (Leopold 1970: 281). In Savarkar's nationalism the emphasis is put above all on the land. The territory being the main basis of Hindu nationalism, the pre-Aryan tribes are automatically recognized as Hindus, independently of their race:

Therefore, the Santals, Kolis, Bhils, Panchamas, Namashudras and all other such tribes and classes are Hindus. This Sindhustan is as emphatically if not more emphatically, the land of their forefathers as of those of the so-called Aryans; they inherit the Hindu blood and the Hindu culture; and even those of them who have not as yet come fully under the influence of any orthodox Hindu sect, do still worship deities and saints and follow a religion however primitive, are still purely attached to this land, which therefore to them is not only a Fatherland but a Holyland. (Savarkar 1969: 121)

For authors such as H.B. Sarda or Golwalkar, the Aryan theory was not nationalist enough because it assumed that the Aryans were not the first inhabitants of India. Obviously, Hindu nationalist leaders could not appreciate the writings of Aryanists in which it was said that the Hindus were 'like their English masters, foreigners who entered the country at an earlier date' (Leopold 1974: 589). This was another motive for rejection related to the importance of territory. Refusing the idea of an Aryan invasion, Golwalkar maintains that the 'Hindus come into this land from nowhere, but are indigenous children of the soil always, from time immemorial and are natural masters of the country'. In order to make this point without contradicting prestigious predecessors such as Tilak, Golwalkar concedes that the 'Aryans, i.e., the Hindus, lived in the region of the North Pole'. But he argues that modern palaeontological researches demonstrate that the North Pole is not stationary, and that 'quite long ago it was in that part of the world, we find, is called Bihar and Orissa at the present'.[11]

Its transnational connotations are the third motive for the resistance shown towards the Aryan theory by Hindu nationalist ideologues, especially because some Orientalists and Theosophists used it precisely as a lever for their universalism: the idea that the dominant European and the Indians belong to the same racial family, which used to be appreciated as a means to recover one's self-esteem, is now dismissed because it might inhibit nationalism.

Savarkar's emphasis on the territory opportunately reduced the transnational connotations of Aryanism: this concept does not refer any longer to the 'racial links' with the dominant white power, but only to the Hindus of India in a purely nationalistic perspective. This aspect of Savarkar's thought was probably due to his reading of Arya Samajist ideologues such as Guru Datt Vidyarthi who wrote for instance: 'I do not use the word Arya in the sense in which it is taken by the modern Europeans: on the other hand, I mean by it the inhabitants of Aryavarta and Aryavarta only'.[12]

Finally, the racial criterion is not the most relevant one to distinguish the Hindus from the community perceived as their main aggressor, the Muslims, many of whom were converts. Taking the case of a Bohra or a Khoja, Savarkar explains that: 'He possesses—in certain cases they do—pure Hindu blood; especially if he is the first convert to Mohammedanism he must be allowed to claim to inherit the blood of Hindu parents' (Savarkar 1947: 101). In this case, Savarkar admits that the division is not a racial but a cultural one:

It is clear that though their original blood is thus almost unaffected by an alien adulteration, yet they cannot be called Hindus in the sense in which that term is actually understood, because we Hindus are bound together not only by the tie of the love we bear to a common fatherland and by the common blood that courses through our veins and keeps our heart throbbing and our affections warm, but also by the tie of the common homage we pay to our great civilisation—our Hindu culture, which could not be better rendered than by the word Sanskriti. (ibid.: 92)

This reference to the major role of culture in the definition of a nation leads us to the main point: race cannot be over emphasized by Savarkar because he has inherited a 'xenology' where the racial criterion was downgraded vis-à-vis the cultural attitude.

(2) *Hierarchical integration versus racism.* As we have seen with Halbfass and Thapar, traditionally culture not race was the factor of exclusion in India; therefore, this exclusion was not insuperable. The Hindu nationalist leaders maintain this tradition. For Savarkar, Sister Nivedita (the Irish disciple of Vivekananda) was a true Hindu: 'For she had adopted our culture and come to adore our land as her Holyland. She felt she was a Hindu and that is, apart from all technicalities, the real and the most important test' (ibid.: 130). Therefore, the preponderance of the relation with the land and the culture allows a sort of subjective 'raciality'—the contradiction in terms already noticed earlier.

Interestingly, Golwalkar himself defined race in cultural terms:

Race is a hereditary Society having common customs, common language, common memories of glory or disaster; in short, it is a population with a common origin under one culture. Such a race is by far the most important ingredient of a Nation (Golwalkar 1947: 26).

Race is not a primary identity to which people would belong—or be excluded from—because of their genes; it is a society whose culture is shaped by history. Further, some passages of Golwalkar's book suggest that the race spirit itself can be shaped by traditions of the people:

The aspirations of the individual, as also of the Race are conditioned by its mental frame. As is the mould in which the Racial mind is thrown—of course by its agelong traditions—so are its desires, its aspirations. It is the Race Consciousness awakening to march further on, but it must tread the road into which its past traditional way has led it. (ibid.: 39)

This subordination of the genetic heredity to the work of culture in the long term is incompatible with biological racism. Interestingly, Golwalkar can only enjoin the Muslims to integrate to the Hindu nation by renouncing their culture:

Culturally, linguistically, they must become one with the National race; they must adopt the past and entertain the aspirations for the future, of the National race; in short, they must be 'Naturalised' in the country by being assimilated in the Nation wholly (ibid.: 54).

The term 'race', if we define it on the basis of biological criteria, becomes more and more inadequate here since the Muslims are supposed to be able to change their race even when they are not converts but descend from the stock of invaders of the Arab or Turanian races (a notion much in vogue at the beginning of the century). In fact, the use of the concept of race is here close to that of 'ethnic nation' since the Other is required to adopt the culture, the language, the historical legacy and the aspirations of the Hindus. If he does not, he will not be eliminated but will be treated statutorily as an inferior. P.A. Taguieff's typology, contrasting the racisms of domination and extermination, is useful at that stage. In the latter case, the obsession with racial purity makes the elimination of the Other, who *cannot* be integrated, a necessity; whereas, in the former case, ethnic groups are ordered hierarchically but they can entertain relationships: the Other is thinkable, at a subordinate rank (Taguieff 1987: 174). The following quote from Golwalkar illustrates this racism of domination because in it non-Hindus are enjoined to become Hindus—which marks the rejection of the biological logic—but if they chose to remain 'aliens', they can only occupy a position of inferiority. He writes:

the non-Hindu people in Hindusthan must either adopt the Hindu culture and language, must learn to respect and hold in reverence Hindu religion, must entertain no idea but those of glorification of the Hindu race and culture, i.e. they must not only give up their attitude of intolerance and ungratefulness towards this land and its agelong traditions but must also cultivate the positive attitude of love and devotion instead—in one word they must cease to the foreigners, or may stay in the country, wholly subordinated to the Hindu nation, claiming nothing, deserving no privileges, far less any preferential treatment—not even citizen's rights. (Golwalkar 1947: 55–6)

This alternative is consistent with the core of the 'traditional xenology', according to which alien groups were required to integrate the autochthonous society of the *varnas* at a rank necessarily inferior to the Brahmans who were the custodians of the social as well as ritual order. Moreover, Golwalkar considered as *mlecchas* 'those who do not subscribe to the social laws dictated by the Hindu Religion and Culture'.[13] Simultaneously, he praised the *varna vyavastha* as the best social system.[14]

This cultural inheritance is however blended with foreign influences. Golwalkar obviously borrows his distinction between 'citizens' and the other nationals from Bluntschli, who considered that the former were entitled to exert political rights forbidden to the latter (Bluntschli 1881: 197). He was also probably impressed by the book of J. Burgess from which he borrowed one of its definitions of nationalism, and in which one finds a strong plea in favour of homogeneous ethnic nations. Referring to Bluntschli, Burgess writes:

The reigning nationality is in perfect right and pursues, from a scientific point of view, an unassailable policy when it insists, with unflinching determination, upon ethnical homogeneity here. It should realise this, of course, through the peaceable means of influence and education, if possible. When however, these shall have been exhausted in vain, then force is justifiable. It may righteously deport the ethnically hostile element in order to shield the vitals of the state from the forces of dissolution, and in order to create the necessary room for a population sufficient in numbers, in loyalty and capacity to administer the empire and protect it against foreign powers. (Burgess 1890: 42)

Such ideas foreshadowed developments which took place in Europe a few decades after their formulation. They undoubtedly influenced Golwalkar in the way he dealt with Muslims. However, he did not follow Burgess on deportation: physical elimination was not explicitly part of his programme in 1938, and he still favoured a form of integration of the minorities in a hierarchical framework.

We can see this approach at work more obviously in an anonymous pamphlet, *Grave Danger to the Hindus*, written by a Savarkarite.[15] Here, the author invites the Muslims to join the Hindu mainstream at a subordinate but quite high level:

You behave as if you are living in a country with which you have no concern, just as travellers live in a way side inn for a few days and go away. . . . Once you begin to have that natural feeling of human beings, that love of the dear Motherland, that moment we will take you into our fold and christen you Kshatriyas! Then within a generation you will all become Muslim-Hindu-Kshatriyas, without, in any way going against the important teaching of the Holy Prophet. . . . After all Religion is a personal one and a man who wears a dress and calls himself a Muslim does not become one if he does not behave according to the broad tenets of Islam. Hence dear Brethren—most of you were Hindus once and just because you have changed your religion you cannot become foreigners—call yourself proudly Kshatriyas and begin to act like Kshatriyas. . . . I tell you that once you call yourself Kshatriyas, that moment the Hindu-Moslems problem will vanish like mists before the powerful sun. Come on brothers, become Kshatriyas. ('An Obscure Hindu', *Grave Danger to the Hindus*, 1940: 75–6)

This kind of discourse conforms with the 'traditional xenology': the Hindu elite is willing to integrate any community to the extent that it respects an orthopraxy fixed by the Brahmanical order, irrespective of racial origin. True, the author emphasizes that most of the Indian Muslims are of Hindu or Aryan descent, but it does not make any difference for the others. Some Indian Muslims are not Aryans in any—necessarily subjective—taxonomy: there are people of Mongol, Touranian and Arab origins among them, for instance. But the urging to integrate applies to them too.

Such a text testifies how hollow must have been the influence of the biological racial theories, especially among the second-rank leaders from which it emanates. The eugenic logic is obviously incompatible with the 'traditional xenology' in which the caste system is the regulating agency. Moreover, Bhai Parmanand, cannot see in Hitler's 'lesson for India', anything other than the primitive caste system:

The message that he sent on the Annexation [Of Austria] in which he described himself as a tool in the hands of the Lord of Destiny for the unification of Germany reminded me of the assurance of Lord Krishna that whenever the world has need of him, He manifests

Himself. Is the unity of India complete? I submit not. British India and Indian India to use the common parlance, are divided from each other. They are one and indivisible in every respect except politically. Where is the Hitler who will bring about their unification? ... Hitler's theory is National Socialism. ... I find a great affinity between Hitler's National Socialism and the Varnashrama of the Hindus. (*Hindu Outlook*, 12 October 1938)

This analysis is indicative of the partiality of the Hindu nationalists' understanding of fascism: they play down its eugenic content and focus on its authoritarian and hierarchical corporatist organization of society, which they assimilate to the most familiar, organic *varna* system of the 'traditional xenology'. In this perspective, when G. Pandey characterized Golwalkar's praise of the *varna vyavastha* as 'an upper caste racism' (Pandey 1993: 252), he summarized the ambivalence of Hindu nationalism. Savarkar and Golwalkar were probably as much influenced by the Brahmanical *Weltanschauung* of the 'Indian traditional xenology' as by the European notion of biological racism. Hindu nationalist ideologues, in my interpretation, did not look beyond the evolutionist authors and become acquainted with eugenic, fascist writers; this was because they felt profound affinities with the outlook of the former: an organicist theory based on concepts of physics and zoology. Haeckel and Huxley were zoologists; Darwin was a naturalist and Tyndall a physicist; and Herbert Spencer applied the latters' evolutionist and organicist ideas to society (for instance in *Social Statics*, 1851). Interestingly, students of natural science were always strongly represented in the RSS. Hedgewar was a doctor; Golwalkar studied and taught zoology; Rajendra Singh, who took over the organization in 1994, graduated in physics and taught that subject; and H.V. Seshadri, the movement's general secretary, graduated in chemistry.

The affinities between Hindu nationalism and some Western applications of natural science to society, hark back to the Hindu view of the world. In a way it is zoological since the universe is described as being formed of *jatis*. In itself, this vision inhibits the development of a eugenic form of racism. Savarkar as well as Golwalkar translates race by *jati* or vice versa;[16] this terminology must be taken literally. As Olivier Herrenschmidt suggests, the true meaning of *jati* is species (Herrenschmidt 1989: 252), a definition Monier-Williams had already given in his Sanskrit dictionary. There are animal as well as human *jatis* along a continuum, each with a special *dharma*. Therefore, there cannot be one Hindu race opposed to other races. There can exist only one Hindu culture defining the social rules implemented by a certain human community in which different species co-exist in a hierarchical relationship. This society cannot but be open to the other species who adopt these rules. And the ones who do not are necessarily the lowest groups, in practice, Muslims are considered as Untouchables in many Indian localities. The hierarchical view of the caste system is thus extended to the other species: hierarchical principles regulate not only the Hindu social system, but also of course the whole society and even the universe—and upper castes, primarily Brahmans, occupy a prominent position in this schema. The fact that the Hindu nationalist ideologues remained more interested in social, hierarchical unity than in racial purity is confirmed by their interpretation of the Hindu decline.

## The Cause of the Hindu Decline is Not Racial But Social

In the late nineteenth and early twentieth century, many of the European theoreticians of decline explained this phenomenon as a racial degeneration caused by interbreeding.[17] Even though one of the first exponents of this theory, Gobineau, was a Frenchman,[18] his ideas reached England, along with those expressed in a very similar vein in the United States by Samuel G. Morton.[19] But none of the Hindu nationalist ideologues cites him or other English writers who developed similar theses, such as Charles B. Davenport, Madison Grant, Louis Agassiz and of course Houston Stewart Chamberlain.

The idea of decline has been very prominent in the discourse of the Hindu intelligentsia from an early stage. M.G. Ranade (1842–1901) stated: 'All admit that we have been deformed'.[20] But during the nineteenth century the Hindu socio-religious reform movements attributed this decline to social causes more than to any racial degeneration. Rammohun Roy, as early as 1821, blamed the 'division into castes, which has been the source of want of unity. . .' (*English Works of Raja Rammohun Roy*, 1928, Vol. 1: 160). The physical defects of the Hindu population were certainly emphasized, echoing the criticism of effeteness expressed by the British, especially with regard to Bengal.[21] But the racial weakness of the Hindu was not considered as such. The emphasis, as in the Arya Samajist ideology, remained on the sociological origins of Hindu decline.

Dayananda ascribed it to the gradual deterioration that followed the Golden Age of Indian Domination. It occurred in spiritual practises (polytheism replacing monotheism; idol worship; and so on) and in social institutions—child marriage, forbidding remarriage of widows, multiplication and insulation of castes whose system becomes hereditary, introduction of untouchability, lowering of the position of women. Dayananda's goal was to re-establish the so-called original vedic social system based on *varna*, because of its organic unity and flexibility.

In the 1920s and 1930s, the way Munshi Ram—renamed Shraddhananda after his vows of renunciation in 1917—addressed the question of Hindu decline is quite revealing. He strongly adhered to the myth of a primordial vedic race but attributed its decline to social defects.

Shraddhananda contributed towards institutionalizing a Hindu nationalistic vulgate of capital importance for the consolidation and the propagation of this identity, insofar as it implanted the myth of a primordial, sovereign and chosen people:

the Veda was revealed in the beginning of creation for all races. It contains germs of all sciences—physical, mental and psychical. But it cannot be denied that the glorious period of the supreme achievements of the vedic Church was the bright period of Indian History. When India was the center of vedic propaganda and missionaries were sent from it to different parts of the world, it was also the seat of a world-wide empire, and Indian kings exercised direct sovereignty over Afghanistan, Baluchistan, Tibet, etc. and Indian colonists colonised Egypt, Rome, Greece, Peru and Mexico. (Jambunathan 1961: 155–6)

This assertion of the primary role of India as the centre of a universal vedic civilization in the beginning of time is an unchanging element of the Arya Samaj. In 1926, Munshi Ram justifies this antecedence by the fact that:

the plateau of Tibet was the first to come out of water and therefore the revelation of the Vedas was imparted to early humanity at the sacred soil. Mankind was then divided into the good or virtuous and the bad or vicious. The first were named 'Aryas' and the latter 'Dasyus' in the Veda itself. (Shraddhananda 1926: 71)

Notwithstanding this emphasis on the ancient value of the Aryas, the Hindus have become a 'dying race' because of social defects. The date of the decline is fixed, as in Dayananda's book, after the Mahabharata war, but Shraddhananda elaborates this point in referring to the disintegration of the *varna* system: 'in the plains of Kurukshetra the spirit of Indian bravery was crashed and Brahman domination was unleashed reducing the other Varnas to servitude' (ibid.: 79).

The way was thus opened up for all the social ills that were to bring about a degeneration from which India had not yet recovered; yet, in the same work, the author does not detect any of these ills until the time of Harsha, at the head of the last Indian Empire in the eighth century and, therefore, undeniably long after the Mahabharata war: true, the castes were tending to become hereditary but they were not yet too fragmented, child marriages were only just starting to develop and more than anything else—a finally decisive criterion for Shraddhananda—till the time of Harsha, 'no non-Aryan community lived in India, and if some non-Aryans did come and settle down there, they were absorbed in the Hindu community. . .' (ibid.: 5–6). It was after the Muslim invasions that the decline was hastened because they did not assimilate into the social system.

The fragmentation of an organic social system is thus perceived as the root cause of the decline, while the idea of a racial degeneration is simply omitted. The same phenomenon is obvious in the writings by Savarkar, Golwalkar and Bhai Parmanand in the 1920s and 1930s. These three authors consider the development of Buddhism as the first cause of decline, because of its sociological implications. Savarkar, in *Hindutva*, considers the promotion of 'ahimsa and spiritual brotherhood' (Savarkar 1969: 20) as a major factor of the invasion by the Huns and the Shakas, not only because the Hindus had lost their martial values, but also because they had been taught to consider their enemies as part of the same humanity from a universalistic point of view (ibid.: 21).

Golwalkar's and Parmanand's analysis is more sociological. The former explains that the introduction of renunciation as the ultimate goal of religious life led to a new individualistic spirituality, something the ritualistic vedism did not know:

Over-individualisation in the field of religion followed and the consequence was that the individual became more prominent than the society, the nation. For those whom the spirit of true religion did not touch intensely, this was another name for self-seeking, even at the cost of the welfare of the whole. (Golwalkar 1947: 14)

The interchangeability of the words society and nation deserves to be noticed here because it is the key to Golwalkar's argument: the Hindu national decline began when the social corporate structure of the original *varna* system disintegrated under the impact of Buddhist principles. This argument is formulated in a more explicit manner by Bhai Parmanand. In his book *Hindu Sangathan,* the rise of Buddhism is again described as the origin of the Hun invasion because 'the rosary could not be a match for the sword' (Parmanand 1936: 21). Besides, its sociological implications were utterly destructive:

The ideal of personal salvation is the root-cause of our selfishness and this alone has been responsible for the downfall of our nation. It is diametrically opposed to the idea of social duties. . . . Instead of drawing the people's attention to their real duties under the caste and ashrama system [the *varnashrama vyavastha*] and trying to remove their defects [Buddha] wrongly concluded that these systems alone were responsible for all social evils. . . . The abolition of castes and ashramas cut at the very root of social duties. How could a nation hope to live after having lost sight of this aspect of Dharma? 'Equality for all' is an appealing abstraction; but the nation could not long survive the rejection or destruction of Dharma. (ibid.: 126–7)

Hindu degeneration is thus constantly interpreted as resulting primarily from the decline of a so-called vedic social order characterized by the organic solidarity and complementarity of hierarchized *varna*. In this process, the quest for individual salvation, initiated by Buddhism and the development of hereditary *jatis*, invented by the Brahmans, are seen as the main factor of the degradation. In this perspective, the aim of the Hindu nationalist movement is to remedy this situation by restoring the so-called original society whose organic unity designated it as a perfect nation model. The appeal to 'Hindu Sangathan', the organization and unity of the Hindus, largely stemmed from this approach.

Thus, in the Hindu nationalist ideology, the idea of decline is not related to the loss of racial purity. And the quest for revival does not imply any racial purification. On the contrary, the consolidation of Hindu society is presented as a preliminary stage likely to enable the Hindus to absorb the Muslims (descendents of non-Aryan invaders as well as 'natives').[22] The conception of decline expressed by the Hindu nationalist leaders of the 1920s and 1930s confirms a certain indifference towards racial purity compared to social unity.

The main conclusion of this enquiry seems to lie in the ambivalent response of the Hindu nationalist ideologues of the 1920s and 1930s to the European biological theories. These ideologues had inherited a 'traditional xenology' where the racial criterion was minimized compared to the degree of orthopraxy: the caste system reveals here its integrative capacity inasmuch as everybody can find a place in it according to one's rank. All in all, the hierarchical principle of the caste system makes the eugenic criterion of elimination difficult to apply: the exclusion can only be partial; it takes the form of a rejection at the periphery but not outside the whole of the society.

This does not mean that the Hindu nationalist ideologues did not expound a racial theory. They did so, but it was more a racism of domination than a racism of extermination. This specificity was again in accordance with the 'traditional xenology': the Other is not excluded but he can be only integrated at a subordinate rank. The members of minorities who refuse to become Hinduized are bound to remain statutory second-rate citizens from the Hindu nationalist point of view. This kind of discrimination is, indeed, nothing but a form of 'upper caste racism'.

## Notes

1. I am most grateful to Bruce Graham for the information contained in this paragraph which he developed in still unpublished chapters; see his book on the Jana Sangh where the argument is summarized in one page (Graham 1990: 44).
2. The idea that the Tibet, and more generally the Himalaya, was the birth place of the Aryan race was first developed by European writers. Originally, geographers of the eighteenth century, alleging the effects of the Deluge, explained that the ancestors of humanity could only come from high mountains. Since the highest mountains surrounded Tibet, philosophers such as Kant and Herder evolved this thesis, obviously borrowed by Dayananda from European authors. See Poliakov 1987 [1971]: 210–13.
3. This Arya Samajist leader—who organized the celebration for Dayananda's birth centenary in 1924—became a Hindu Sabhaite in the 1920s. See Gopal 1935.
4. Home Department (Political) Proceedings for the year 1914, P/9460, 1 December 1914, Pro. no. 169, IOLR. During his stay in London, he introduced a nationalist pledge that the inmates of India House would collectively repeat every night a bedtime prayer in which the word 'race' appeared along with five other concepts: 'One God, one nation, one language, one race, one form, one hope' (Srivastava 1983: 64). At that stage, 'race' was not used to designate a special community but, as in many European writings at that time, as a rather loose synonym for 'nation'. In the India House, Arya Samajists such as Har Dayal and Bhai Parmanand, and Muslim leaders like Asaf Ali and Sikandar Hayat Khan, shared the same type of non-religious, revolutionary nationalism.
5. I shall return to this contradiction in terms in the second part of the chapter.
6. Savarkar 1984: 269–70. The references are to Charles Darwin (1809–82), Herbert Spencer (1820–1903), John Tyndall (1820-93), Ernst Heinrich Haeckel (1834–1919), and Thomas Henry Huxley (1825–95).

7. M.N. Ghatate (a prominent RSS worker at Nagpur, and Moonje's secretary during his European tour), *Dharmaveer: Dr. B.S. Moonje Commemoration Volume* 1972: 68–9.

8. However, it seems that *We, or our nationhood defined* is an abridged version of an essay by the eldest brother of V.D. Savarkar; see Andersen and Damle 1987: 43.

9. He also mentions a certain 'Getel'; in fact Raymond Garfield Gettell who published an *Introduction to Political Science* in 1910.

10. Golwalkar cites the following definition of nationalism by Holcombe by omitting the words of the original in parentheses: 'Nationality (regarded as a force in modern politics) is a corporate sentiment, a kind of fellow feeling or mutual sympathy relating to a definite home-country (and binding together the members of a human group, irrespective of differences in religion, economic interests, or social position, more intimately than any other similar sentiment). It springs (as Lincoln eloquently suggested) from a common heritage of memories, whether of great achievements and glory or of disaster and suffering' (Holcombe 1923: 133). This definition largely borrows from Renan's universalistic definition of nationalism—which Holcombe himself cites; but Golwalkar omitted an interesting part of it.

11. Golwalkar 1947: 13. Interestingly, this theory has been introduced in the history textbooks in the states controlled between 1990 and 1992 by the Bharatiya Janata Party, the political front of the RSS.

12. Cited in Leopold 1969: 293. For a biographical sketch of Vidyarthi, see Tirtha n.d.: i-iv.

13. Cited in Pandey 1993: 258. (The quotation probably comes from *Bunch of Thoughts* rather than from *We, or our nationhood defined*).

14. We can read, in a compilation of Golwalkar's speeches and writings: 'The Hindu people, they ['our forefathers'] said, is the Virat Purusha, the Almighty manifesting Himself . . . . this means that the people who have this fourfold arrangement [the *varna* system], i.e., the Hindu people, is our God'; Golwalkar 1966: 49.

15. The author of this text is S.R. Narayana Ayyar, a *vakil* from Coonoor who announced to Savarkar that he wanted to write a pamphlet with the same title 'Grave Danger to the Hindus' in 1938 (*Savarkar Papers*, NMML, Reel no. 1, File no. 5, letter dated 16 May 1938).

16. See for instance the Hindi version of Savarkar, *Hindutva*, (n.d.) 30.

17. This school of thought, though not prominent, was represented in India (Leopold 1974: 593).

18. For a superb though concise analysis of Gobineau's theory, see Schlanger 1971: 184.

19. In 1911, Earl Finch opened his lecture at the first Universal Congress of Races in London with these words: 'The disciples of Gobineau in France and the ones of Morton in America have stressed that interbreeding has had and can only have disastrous consequences' (Taguieff 1987: 338).

20. Bary 1964, Vol. 2: 135. In the address he delivered at the Indian National Social Conference of 1897, Ranade declared: 'In the case of our society especially, the usages which at present prevail among us were admittedly not those which obtained in the most glorious periods of our history. On most of the points which are included in our programme, our own records of the past show that there has been a decided change for the worse. . . .' (Ranade 1902: 168).

21. The development of gymnasia was part of the socio-religious reform programme (Rosselli 1980: 121–48).

22. In this respect the view of Bhai Parmanand is similar to the one of Savarkar and Golwalkar which we studied in the second section (Parmanand 1936: 188).

## References

An Obscure Hindu (1940), *Grave Danger to the Hindu*.

Andersen, W. and Damle, S. (1987), *The Brotherhood in Saffron: the Rashtriya Swayamsevak Sangh and Hindu Revivalism*, New Delhi.

Anand, V.S. (1967), *Savarkar: a study in the evolution of Indian nationalism*, London.

Bluntschli, M. (1881), *Théorie générale de l'Etat*, Paris.

Bluntschli, J.K. (1885), *The Theory of the State*, English translation from the 6th German edition, Oxford.

Chitragupta, (1987 [1926]), *Life of Barrister Savarkar*, Bombay.

Dayananda, Swami (1981), *Satyarth Prakash* (The Light of Truth), Allahabad, translated and introduced by Ganga Prasad Upadhyaya.

*Dharmaveer: Dr. B.S. Moonje Commemoration Volume* (1972), 'Reminscences of V.G. Deshpande', Nagpur.

Dumont, L. (1966), *Homo Hierarchicus: le système des castes et ses implications*, Paris.

*English Works of Raja Rammohun Roy* (1928), 'The Brahmunical magazine or the missionary and the Brahmun being a vindication of the Hindoo religion against the attacks of Christian missionaries', Vol. 1, Calcutta.

Ghatate, M.N. (1972), 'Dr. B.S. Moonje: tour of European countries', in *Dharmaveer: Dr. B.S. Moonje Commemoration Volume*, Nagpur.

Golwalkar, M.S. (1947), *We, or our nationhood defined*, Nagpur.

———, (1966), *Bunch of Thoughts*, Bangalore.

Gopal, R. (1935), 'Har Bilas Sarda, a sketch', in H.B. Sarda, *Speeches and Writings*, Ajmer.

Graham, B. (1990), *Hindu Nationalism and Indian Politics: the origins and development of the Bharatiya Jana Sangh*, Cambridge.

Halbfass, W. (1988), *India and Europe: An essay in understanding*, New York.

Herrenschmidt, O. (1989), *Les meilleurs dieux sont hindous*, Paris.

*Hindu Outlook*, 12 October 1938.

———, 2 November 1938.

———, 'A Great Dictator: Signor Mussolini at work', 30 November 1938.

Holcombe, A. (1923), *The Foundation of the Modern Commonwealth*, New York.

Home Department (Political) Proceedings for the year 1914, P/9460, 1 December 1914, Pro. no. 169, IOLR.

Horowitz, I.L. (1963), 'The sociology of Ludwig Gumplowicz (1838–1909)', Introduction to L. Gumplowicz, *Outlines of Sociology*, New York.

*Hymnes spéculatifs du Veda* (1956), 'Rig Veda X-90', Notes and Introduction by Louis Renou, Paris.

Jaffrelot, C. (1996), *The Hindu Nationalist Movement and Politics in India c. 1925–1993: Identity-building, implantation and mobilisation*, London, Hurst, Ch.1.

Jambunathan, M.R. (1961) (ed.), *Swami Shraddhananda* [Autobiography], Bombay.

Jones, William (1970), 'On the Hindus', in P.J. Marshall (ed.), *The British Discovery of Hinduism in the Eighteenth Century*, Cambridge: Cambridge University Press.

Karandikar, S.L. (1957), *Lokamanya Bal Gangadhar Tilak: the Hercules and Prometheus of modern India*, Poona.

*La Lutte des Races* (1893), Paris.

Leopold, J. (1970), 'The Aryan theory of race', *Indian Economic and Social History Review*, Vol. 7, No. 2, June 1970.

——— (1974), 'British applications of the Aryan theory of race to India', 1850-1870, *English Historical Review*, Vol. LXXXIX, No. 352, July 1974.

*Maharatta*, 6 January 1939, p. 10.

Marshall, P.J. (1970), 'Introduction', in Marshall (ed.), *The British Discovery of Hinduism in the Eighteenth Century*, Cambridge.

*Moonje Papers*, 'Letter from Moonje to Appasahib Kelkar, 25 February 1936', Nehru Memorial Museum and Library, Microfilm section, Reel no. 10.

Pandey, G. (1993), 'Which of us are Hindus?', in Pandey (ed.), *Hindus and Others: the question of identity in India today*, New Delhi: Viking.

Pareek, R.S. (1973), *Contributions of Arya Samaj in the Making of Modern India 1875–1947*, New Delhi.

Parmanand, Bhai (1936), *Hindu Sangathan*, Lahore: The Central Hindu Yuva Sabha.

Poliakov, L. (1987 [1971]), *Le mythe aryen. Essai sur les sources du racisme et des nationalisms*, Bruxelles.

Pollock, S. (1993), 'Deep orientalism? Notes on Sanskrit and power beyond the raj', in C.A. Breckenridge and P. Van der Veer (eds.), *Orientalism and the Postcolonial Predicament*, Philadelphia.

Ranade, M.G. (1902), 'Revival and reform', in *Religious and Social Reform*, Bombay.

——— (1964), 'Revivalism versus reform' in W.T. De Bary (ed.), *Sources of Indian Tradition*, New York.

Rosselli, J. (1980), 'The self-image of effeteness: physical education and nationalism in nineteenth-century Bengal', *Past and Present*, No. 86.

Sarda, Har Bilas (1975), *Hindu Superiority: An Attempt to Determine the Position of the Hindu Race in the Scale of Nations*, New Delhi: Rajdhani Granthaghar.

Savarkar, V.D. (1969), *Hindutva: Who is a Hindu?*, Bombay: S.S. Savarkar.

——— (1984), *My Transportation for Life*, Bombay: Veer Savarkar Prakashan.

*Savarkar Papers*, Narayana Ayyar, S.R., *Grave Danger to the Hindus*, NMML, Reel no. 1, File no. 5, letter dated 16 May 1938.

Schlanger, J.E. (1971), *Les métaphores de l'organisme*, Paris: Vrin.

Shraddhananda (1926), *Hindu Sangathan: Saviour of the Dying Race*, Delhi: Arjun Press.

Srivastava, H. (1983), *Five Stormy Years: Savarkar in London*, New Delhi.

Taguieff, P.A. (1987), *La force du préjugé: Essai su le racisme et ses doubles*, Paris, La Découverte.

Thapar, R. (1978), 'The image of the barbarian in early India', in Thapar, *Ancient Indian Social History*, New Delhi: Orient Longman.

Tirtha, Swami Vedananda (n.d.) (ed.), *Wisdom of the Rishis or Complete Works of Pandita Guru Datta Vidyarthi*, Lahore.

Toth, L. (1988), 'Existe-t-il une doctrine traditionnelle de la race?', *Politica Hermetica*, No. 2.

Yajnik, I. (1950), 'Herbert Spencer Lectureship', Chp. IX of *Shyamaji Krishnavarma: Life and Times of an Indian Revolutionary*, Bombay: Lakshmi Publications.

# Chapter 7

# Militant Hindus and the conversion issue (1885︎1990) from *shuddhi* to *dharm parivartan* politicization and diffusion of an ︎nvention of tradition︎

Classical Hinduism ostensibly ignores conversion since one is born a Hindu, one does not become a Hindu. Yet, it incorporates procedures of purification and initiation which have certain similarities to what is designated by the term 'conversion' in the religions of the Book, that is, to put it briefly, the fact to join a body of believers and to adhere to a new faith. First, certain rites of expiation and purification enable Hindus, who have been ostracized by their castes as a result of a breach of orthodoxy or orthopraxy to be reintegrated. These procedures reflect the rules of functioning of a caste society. In fact, caste mediates the religious identification of the individual; one cannot be a Hindu in the social world without being situated somewhere in the caste system. Whoever loses one's caste by transgressing the rules of the system must, therefore, be able to be reintegrated after having performed suitable rites of expiation and purification. In a way, these rites are equivalent to conversion. Second, initiation into a Hindu sect other than that with which one may have been associated since childhood through the family cult can also be compared to a conversion, in that a profound change in the nature of the worship practised by the devotee is involved and, should the latter not be a simple lay disciple, but would have embraced the career of renunciation and become a monk, a passage from the social world to a life outside that world is also entailed.

The idea of 'conversion to Hinduism' is thus doubly problematical. On the level of doctrine, one does not observe adherence to Hinduism in general, but rather to particular sects, the worship and philosophy of which can be very contrasted. On the social level, integration into a community of believers is much less significant than caste allegiance. Hinduism could, therefore, only be recalcitrant

*A slightly different version of this article has been already published in French: 'Les (re)conversions à l'hindouisme (1885-1990): politisation et diffusion d'une "invention de la tradition"', *Archives de sociologie des religions,* No. 87, July-September 1994, pp. 73–98. I am most grateful to Shail Mayaram for her comments on an earlier version of this article.

as regards the notions of conversion and reconversion. These ideas were introduced lately in the nineteenth century by militant reform movements in order to counter the influence of proselytizing religions.

Paradoxically, it was this milieu with xenophobic inclinations which was to introduce procedures of (re)conversion, to a large extent alien to Hinduism.

The Arya Samaj was probably the first to develop a new form of (re)conversion. This procedure, the *shuddhi,* was inspired by features of classical Hinduism, such as just described. However, its originators also attempted to introduce proselytizing techniques particular to Islam and Christianity. The *Shuddhi* Movement which began at the end of the nineteenth century can only be explained in relation to the activities of Christian missionaries. It was more or less a mimetic reaction: certain features of Christian proselytism were emulated in order to protect the numerical strength of the Hindu community—as enumerated in the census and, for the same reason, some orthodox Hindus suppressed their disagreement. (For the sake of convenience, I shall designate with the term 'orthodox' those who are also the principal supporters of orthopraxy, the 'Sanatanists'—I shall use both terms as synonyms).

This reaction, however, was conditioned by the persistence of a so-called Muslim and/or Christian 'threat.' As soon as the latter appeared to diminish in strength, in the second half of the 1920s, opposition to the *Shuddhi* Movement arose among the orthodox leaders. This movement subsequently lost momentum. It had, nevertheless, contributed to the crystallization of conflicts between religious communities and, in particular, to the formation of the Hindu nationalist movement.

After independence, this movement remained hostile towards the conversion of Hindus to religions which originated outside of India. The movement could not, however, revive a substantial programme of (re)conversions until the 1980s, in reaction to the conversion of Untouchables to Islam, although only a limited number were involved. Far from being a common practise, (re)conversion appeared then as one of the operations orchestrated by the Hindu nationalist movement in response to the systematically exaggerated 'threat' of the 'Semitic religions'. The counter-offensive of the 1980s seems, however, to have started a banalization of (re)conversion to Hinduism in a form closely related to Christian and Muslim conceptions according to a mimetic process which had already been initiated by the Arya Samaj. This routinization found expression in a certain simplification of the (re)conversion ritual and in the winning over of orthodox Hindu figures to the Hindu nationalist ideology.

## Inventing a Hindu Proselytism?

Founded by Dayananda Saraswati, the Arya Samaj rapidly became the main socio-religious reform movement in north India. It was particularly well established in the Punjab at the end of the nineteenth century. Its reformist aims were to rid Hinduism of practises and beliefs already criticized by the British, such as idol worship, child marriage, etc. It was, for Dayananda, a question of the symptoms of a decline of Indian civilization, the hour of glory of which he situated in the Vedic period.

In the eyes of the Arya Samaj, the Hindu decline was manifested not only in qualitative, but also in quantitative, terms. In fact, from 1881 to 1911, the Hindu population in the Punjab went down from 9,252,295 to 8,773,621, or from 43.8 per cent to 36.3 per cent, as opposed to an increase from 11,662,434 to 12,275,477 (50.7 per cent), and from 33,699 to 199,751 (0.8 per cent, but over 593 per cent) for Muslims and Christians respectively. Between 1901 and 1911, 40,000 Hindus were converted to Islam and 120,000 to Christianity, the majority among them from the untouchable castes (*Punjab Census Report 1911*: 100).

The introduction of censuses and their increasingly wide diffusion amplified the sentiment, until then quite vague, of a demographic regression; in this way, an obsession with numbers was engendered. From the 1881 census onwards, the Arya Samaj publications commented in an alarmist manner on the decennial censuses (Jones 1981: 186). In 1909, a Bengali, who was to be widely read in the Punjab, U.N. Mukherji, published a pamphlet entitled, 'Hindus, a dying race', in which he asserted, allegedly on the basis of censuses, that within 420 years the Hindus would have disappeared from the face of the earth, mainly as a result of conversions (Datta 1993). The Arya Samaj undertook to counter the offensive of the missionaries by drawing their inspiration from their proselytizing methods, but also by trying to more adequately integrate Untouchables and low castes into Hindu society, as the missionaries, quick to denounce the condition of the latter in their sermons, had focused on them as a primary target.

## THE *SHUDDHI* AS A MIMETIC REACTION

In an earlier period, from roughly 1885 to 1895, the Arya Samaj was only concerned to reconvert Hindus who had 'gone over' to Islam or Christianity. The method which the Arya Samajists called upon in support of proselytism was that which had been employed by Dayananda—who died in 1883—to bring back in the 'Aryan' fold a Hindu converted to Christianity, and another who had converted to Islam (Sarda 1946 [1968]: 196–7). The perseverance with which these episodes have been subsequently recalled by his disciples suggest an effort at legitimatizing a procedure of reconversion quite uncharacteristic of Hinduism, and of which Dayananda himself never spoke: the *shuddhi*.

The literal meaning of this term is 'state of purity'; it designates a group of rites meant to rid members of high castes of impurities with which they may have been tainted by a polluting contact. The *shuddhi* is mentioned in several Sanskrit treatises, as noted by P.V. Kane (1953: 117, 267–333, 828–30). A *Devalasmriti* was also evolved following the first Muslim raids, in order to codify the conditions of reintegration of Hindus converted to Islam (Seunarine 1977); however, the text would appear to have fallen into disuse and did not lessen the reservations on the part of the most orthodox regarding this type of procedure. In 1850, for example, the Brahman family of a child who had attended a Christian school in Bombay was ostracized by other Brahmans, notwithstanding expiations and purificatory bathing in Benares (Thursby 1972: 40; Jordens 1977: 146). This case, which roused the indignation of the Indian intelligentsia, illustrates how the logic of the caste system, limits the possibilities of conversion, and even of reconversion, to Hinduism: aspirants are readily rejected because of their impurity.

In the late nineteenth century, the Arya Samaj tried to overcome these obstacles by reinterpreting the rite of *shuddhi*. This reinterpretation is a good example of the 'invention of tradition'. For Eric Hobsbawm, this expression designates an effort to establish a fictive continuity through an ideological construction (Hobsbawm and Ranger 1983: 1–14), while Rajni Kothari resituates this strategy in the context of a society subject to an outside cultural aggression and describes it, on that basis, as an attempt to legitimate the imitation of prestigious characteristics of the other by presenting them as analogous to elements of indigenous tradition, or virtually contained in them (Kothari 1968: 273–93).

The latter analysis seems to be more relevant in the case of the Arya Samaj, even if it can be further refined. As regards the reinterpretation of the *shuddhi* by this movement, one can in fact speak of a veritable strategic mimetism, not only copying the dominant Western characteristic so as to equal it in prestige, but also to turn against it its own weapons—in this case, that of proselytism—always in the guise of allegiance to a purely local tradition. The Arya Samaj did, call upon traditions, in order to render innovations more readily acceptable.[1]

Their approach would have been true to tradition if it had fulfilled two criteria: first, if the Arya Samaj had contented itself with 'purifying' members of upper castes who had converted (or, descendants of those who had); and, second, if this organization had acted solely as a sect and (re)converted people in the form of initiation. However, the ambition of the Arya Samaj was much greater, and this contributed to the disruption of its relations with other religions in the Punjab and to the triggering off of hostility among orthodox Hindus.

Earlier, beginning in 1884, the Arya Samaj was content to practise the *shuddhi* rites in a classic form for members of high castes who had left Hinduism. The organization took care to resort to the services of an orthodox *pandit*, as recounts the organizer of this movement in the Arya Samaj, Ram Bhaj Datt, a Brahman from Gurdaspur and advocate in Lahore (Sen 1973: 394):

> The first organized effort towards the *suddhi* or reconversion of the converts to Islam or Christianity was made by the Amritsar Arya Samaj. It must, however, be acknowledged that much of its success was due to the help and co-operation of one Pandit Tulsi Ram,

the most orthodox of the orthodox and one of the most learned, revered and renowned Brahmans of Amritsar. The Arya Samaj used to make the repentant go through a ceremony of Tonsure, Horn, *Yagyopavit* (investiture with the sacred thread) and the *Gayatri* (initiation into the Vedic Dharm) and thus admitted him in their fold. Thereupon Pandit Tulsi Ram used to send the purified to Haridwar with his letter called *Shuddhi Patra* [literally, letter certificate][2], where he was duly purified once more by a dip in the Ganges. This went on for years. From all parts of the Province, people were sent to Amritsar. (*Punjab Census Report 1911*: 150)

The author describes here the orthodox purification techniques for upper castes having been exposed to ritual pollution. Indeed, the sacred thread and the *Gayatri mantra*—a prayer in the *Rig Veda* understood here as an initiation formula into the Vedic religion—were reserved for the 'twice-born', Brahmans, Kshatriyas and Vaisyas. These ceremonies only involved a limited number of individuals, until 1884: the Arya Samaj in Amritsar only 'dealt with' thirty-nine cases in 1884, and fifty-five in 1885 (Jones 1976: 131). The phenomenon nevertheless acquired a new scale at the same time as it changed in nature under the impetus of Munshi Ram.

Munshi Ram was at the head of the most purist group of the Arya Samaj, which refused education in English and confined itself to a strict vegetarianism.[3] In the second half of the 1890s, Munshi Ram further developed the Shuddhi Sabha, which had been formed in the early 1880s in Lahore. This organization is said to have carried out 226 reconversions in 1896, as opposed to 14 in 1895 (Jones 1966: 50): this is an indication of the transition from the conversion of individuals to that of families, or indeed, of entire sub-castes. This evolution provoked great tensions between Arya Samajists and Sikhs, as the growth of numbers of those converted by the former was comprised increasingly of Sikh sub-castes, such as the Rahtias, a caste of weavers:

The first mass purification began with the *suddhi* of Rathias (*sic*), a sect of Sikhism who were not allowed to sit on the same carpet [i.e. Untouchables]. In the middle of 1896,[4] they applied for their *suddhi* and within the next few months a thousand and more were taken in the Arya Samaj as brethern, entitled to full social and religious rights. (Shraddhananda 1926: 87)

Since 1885, Sikhism, which Dayananda viewed as a sectarian current in Hinduism, was the object of criticism by the Arya Samajists, who reproached it for the same sins of superstition and idolatry as committed by Hinduism. At the end of the nineteenth century, the Sikhs were also induced to separate themselves from the Arya Samaj and to develop their own 'revivalist' defence organizations (Jones 1973: 457–75).

However the development of the *shuddhi* affected above all the relations with Muslims, among whom a movement arose which was an explicit counterpart of the Arya Samaj. The founder of this Ahmadiya, Mizra Ghulam Ahmad, began his preaching around 1879 at the time when the Arya Samaj intensified a practise of individual *shuddhi* (the particular targets of which were Muslim converts) and shortly before the collective conversion of Muslim Bhangis (Untouchables).[5]

Beginning in 1900, the reorientation of the *shuddhi* campaigns directed towards the low castes, and initiated by the conversions of the Rahtias, was accelerated soon after. Numerous Arya Samajist discourses justified this development by citing the necessity of improving the condition of the Untouchables so as to preclude that the latter continued to be the primary target of the missionaries. Lajpat Rai thus wrote in 1909:

> The Hindus are going down in numbers. Your insolence towards the lower classes of Hindus is paid back by the latter turning their back on you. Mohammedanism and Christianity are extending their arms to embrace them and indications are not wanting of the readiness of the lower classes of Hindus to accept the hospitality of non-Hindu religions and social systems. Why? The reason is obvious. As a Hindu you won't touch him; you would not let him sit on the same carpet with you, you would not offer him water in your cups, you would not accept water or food touched by him; you would not let him enter your temples, in fact you would not treat him like a human being. (Rai 1986: 302)

The reorientation of the *Shuddhi* Movement towards Untouchables and low castes was to improve their condition so as to dissuade them from converting to Christianity and Islam. The Arya Samaj movement, notwithstanding this shift, thus remained true to its calling, namely the fight against non-Hindu proselytism. It is, however, significant that the objective of reconversion, in terms of 'migration' from one religious community to another, was so rapidly pushed in the background. This reorientation reflected the reservations in the Hindu milieu as regards the reintegration of persons having forsaken Hinduism: *shuddhi* continued to refer, not to the idea of conversion, but rather to that of purification within the caste system. However, the practise of the *shuddhi* in the case of Untouchables expressed no less a modern reinterpretation, as it was not a matter of the purification of high castes having lost their status, but of elevating those who were situated at the bottom of society to the rank of 'twice-born'. The heretical character of this project eventually condemned it.

The census of 1911 registered in the Punjab only 147 and 10 conversions of Muslims and Christians respectively, whereas non *dvijas* and Untouchables who underwent the *shuddhi* rites to raise them to the rank of 'twice-born' were to be counted in the tens of thousands across the Punjab. This ceremony was performed for 2,000 to 3,000 Ods in 1901–2, above all in Multan, and for 30,000 Meghs (weavers and leather workers) along the Kashmir border in 1903, and for 30,000 Jats (a peasant caste of intermediate status) in Karnal. The *shuddhi* was to enable the integration of low castes into the network of social relations (commensality, marriage rules, etc.) reserved for the 'twice-born', as Ram Bhaj Datt, who had become president of the Shuddhi Sabha, noted:

The ceremony is everywhere the same. In all cases the person to be reclaimed has to keep Brat (fast) before the ceremony [during which the sacred thread is given]. In some cases where the fall was due to passion, the number of Brats is increased by the persons who are to perform the ceremony. The very act of their being raised in social status makes them feel a curious sense of responsibility. They feel that they should live and behave better and that they should act as Dvijas [twice-born]. It has thus, in the majority of cases, a very wholesome effect on their moral, social, religious and spiritual being. As to treatment, the Arya Samaj treat the elevated on terms of equality. (*Punjab Census Report 1911*: 150)

The Meghs thus received the services of an *upadeshak* ('preacher', in the Arya Samaj), often a Brahman, for the accomplishment of their rituals. This integration of the lower castes and Untouchables in the social network of the upper castes was to have precluded the temptation for them to convert to Islam or, above all, to Christianity. However, such an undertaking gave rise to the opposition of orthodox Hindus and even of some Arya Samajists who were loathe to accept the calling into question of caste hierarchy. In fact, the performance of the *shuddhi*—whether in relation to Untouchables or non-Hindus—was only generally accepted, for socio-political reasons, when Hinduism appeared to be under threat.

THE *SHUDDHI*:
AN EXCEPTIONAL PROCEDURE IN PERIODS OF CRISIS

From 1909 onwards the efforts of the Arya Samaj to swell the ranks of the Hindu community reflected political considerations, which were to forestall the opposition of the orthodox. In 1909, the British granted to the Muslims a separate electorate and a political representation in proportion to their numerical strength. This measure further exacerbated the obsession with censuses among the Hindu minority in the Punjab. In addition, in view of the census operations of 1911, E.A. Gait, the Commissioner of the Census, had sent to the Provincial Census Superintendents a circular proposing to make the definition of Hindu more strict, so as to exclude animists and Untouchables. The main criteria to be established in order to be registered as a Hindu were to worship 'the great Hindu gods', to be authorized to enter Hindu temples, and to not 'cause pollution' by contact or simple proximity (*Modern Review*, 1910: 683). The Hindu intelligentsia reacted sharply to this directive, the effect of which would be to drastically reduce the numerical strength of the Hindus.

The creation of separate electorates and Gait's circular induced a general rallying to the stance of the most radical Arya Samajists. The orthodox resigned themselves to it. Whereas in 1909 they had gone so far as to organize a social boycott of the Chamars (Untouchables working with leather) with whom the Arya Samajists had conducted the *shuddhi* rite in Hoshiarpur (Jones 1976: 308), they changed their views on the following year. From 1910 onwards, the *shuddhi* movement acquired a new dimension. It could now include Untouchables without encountering too strong an opposition from the most conservative Arya Samajists and the Sanatanists. However, one must distinguish among the latter the leaders such as the promoters of the Sanatan Dharma Sabha or of orthodox (upper) castes associations and the local notables. At the grass-root level, the Arya Samaj had always met strong reluctance from upper caste orthodox, simply because the 'shuddhization' of Untouchables put into question the caste hierarchy. In 1903, the Rajput strongly objected to the *Shuddhi* Movement launched among the Meghs by the Arya Samaj (Ghai 1990: 72). However, this kind of resistance was easily overcome when Sanatanist leaders considered that *Shuddhi* was necessary and supported it.

From 1910 to 1912, Ram Bhaj Datt administered the *shuddhi* ritual to 100,000 Doms (a caste of garbage collectors) from his district of Gurdaspur on the Jammu and Kashmir borders (*Census of India 1921*, Report by J.T. Marten: 119). In 1913, a further 9,000 Untouchables in Jammu were 'purified' in the same manner. In the Punjab, in 1912, the Meghs of Sialkot were the object of a new *shuddhi* campaign concerning some 36,000 persons.[6] However, one of the most important *shuddhi* campaign that had begun in 1910 in the framework of preparations for the census was focused primarily on the Muslim Rajputs from the Malkana caste, notably in the west of the present state of Uttar Pradesh. The Rajput Shuddhi Sabha, formed in 1909 under the patronage of Munshi Ram, is said to have reconverted 1,052 'Muslim Rajputs' in a period of three years (*Census of India 1911*, Report by E.A.H. Blunt: 134).

On the whole, the *shuddhi* had acquired in the 1910s a legitimacy which was largely due to the political context. The orthodox themselves rallied around it, whether it was concerned with Muslims, Christians or Untouchables, out of the apprehension of seeing a depletion of the Hindu ranks. To sum up: the Arya Samaj elaborated a hybrid procedure whose characteristics are explained by diverse influences of which it is the product, but also by the mission which it carried out. The *shuddhi* inherited its ritual from traditional techniques of purification but was inspired by the modus operandi of the missionaries and had to serve to elevate the status of the low castes likely to forsake Hinduism, as well as integrating the converts. It was for its authors, therefore, a question, of a functional innovation, a characterization which no doubt applies to any 'invention of tradition'. However, the Arya Samaj did not provide Hinduism with a veritable conversion procedure and did not transform it into a proselytizing religion. In fact, the *shuddhi* was not institutionalized, but remained an exceptional procedure intended to meet crisis situations, such as that arising of the intrusion of Christian missionaries, or when communal tensions were exacerbated. The intensified recourse to the *shuddhi* and its subsequent desuetude in the course of the 1920s is a good illustration of this phenomenon.

The question of conversions to Islam and reconversions to Hinduism became one of the main issues structuring the religious groups in antagonistic communities in the early 1920s. The phenomenon was to be observed not only in the Punjab, or even north India, but also in the south, in the framework of the Khilafat Movement.

From 1920–1 onwards, part of the Indian Muslims mobilized themselves to defend the status of Caliph of the Ottoman Sultan, which the Allied Powers— including the British—threatened to abolish in the peace treaties following the First World War. This mobilization at times degenerated into violence, of which the Hindus, doubtlessly because they constituted a more accessible target than the British, were on several occasions victims. On the Malabar Coast, the Moplahs— peasants descended from Muslim traders settled in India since the eighth century— set off a cycle of riots which resembled the Jacquerie as much as the Jehad. The latter dimension was, however, expressed by the—ephemeral—establishment of a 'Khilafat Kingdom', in which Islam was raised to the official religion, and particularly found expression in the forced conversions of Hindus (Wood 1987: 215).

The Arya Samaj reacted vehemently. *Upadeshaks* were sent from Punjab to effectively manage reconversion campaigns (Hardgrave, 1977: 92). Other Hindus, sometimes from the ranks of the Congress Party, went to the area to militate in favour of the reconversions. One of them, Moonje, a native of Nagpur, spoke out for the return to Hinduism of those who had not been converted by force. He had been appointed by a religious leader, the Shankaracharya of the Karweer Pith, representative of an orthodox milieu until then largely hostile to a reintegration in the Hindu fold of persons made impure by conversions [Moonje (1922–3)]. This convergence of very different personalities towards the positions which had, until then, been defended by the Arya Samaj, clearly illustrates the salient feature of the issue of conversions at a time—the 1920s—when 'communal' identities crystallized in India.

Congress members, moreover, revived in 1922 the Hindu Mahasabha. The final objections of the orthodox leaders were removed by one of them, M.M. Malaviya, who presided over the Hindu Mahasabha between 1922 and 1924. The latter invoked a verse from the *Dharmasastra Mahaprabandha* to legitimize the recourse to the *shuddhi,* but he particularly justified the use of this technique by spreading rumours according to which Muslim Mullahs would have collected five million rupees to finance the conversion of Hindus, and the Khojas (Muslim merchant community) would have converted 100,000 Hindus (*Indian Annual Register* 1923: 133).

The reconversion of the Malkana Rajputs, interrupted after the movement of 1907–10, was re-initiated in the Agra region by *rajahs* representing the aristocratic and conservative èlite whose orthodoxy had, until then, prevented them from subscribing to the procedures of reconversion (Thursby 1972: 47). The Rajput Upkami Mahasabha, a caste association took the lead in late 1922 (Sharma 1989). Shraddhananda was invited to associate himself with their campaign at a meeting held in February 1923, at the conclusion of which he founded the Bharatiya Hindu Shuddhi Sabha, of which he was president and Mahatma Hans

Raj, another Arya Samajist, vice-president (Jordens 1981: 132). Shraddhananda published a pamphlet exhorting Hindus to save their 'dying race', thus taking up terms already employed by U.N. Mukherji, whom he had known since 1909; films were shown portraying the aftermath of the Moplah rebellion [Thursby 1972: 49 (footnote)]. During the year 1923, 30,000 Malkana Rajputs were said to have been reconverted (Jordens 1981: 132).

In addition to the amplitude of the phenomenon, its salient feature resides in the active rallying of the orthodox to the principle of reconversion. While local caste associations had taken the lead in 1922, at the grass-root level, many Rajput panchayats resisted the idea of reintegrating the Malkanas in their original sub-caste, as they were demanding. Their reluctance was overcome by resorting to the service of orthodox Pandits applying strictly the *shuddhi* rituals and because of the full support extended to the movement by another category of orthodox, the Rajput caste associations, including the All India Rajput Sabha. In 1927, *The Tribune* could write in an editorial that 'The *shuddhi* . . . propaganda is no longer the exclusive concern of the Arya Samaj: an overwhelming majority of the Hindus are now identified (with it).' (cited in Sikand 1997: 71)

However, this does not mean that Hinduism had suddenly become open to 'religious migrations': the (re)conversions were still only accepted by the orthodox under the pressure of events and as purificatory procedures complying to the injunctions of the caste system. The reconversions of the Malkana Rajputs had precisely not been too difficult to carry out because these Muslims had preserved Hindu features. For example, Shraddhananda marvelled at their respect for the cow and their vegetarianism, which was, in fact, astounding (Jordens 1981: 132). The purificatory rituals could therefore be used more easily to reintegrate the concerned persons into their castes.[7] Moreover, the Sanatanists won over to the principle of reconversion contributed thereto through an association whose name was a programme in itself, the Hindu Punah Saṃskar Sabha, that is the Association for the Re-acquisition of Hindu *Saṃskars*. *Saṃskar,* in Hinduism, denotes the moral influences which mould the personality to make one comply with one's *dharma* (one's own and that of one's caste); this term also designates the rites of passage which accompany the life of a Hindu (Kapani 1992). *Saṃskar* thus constitute the pillars of Hindu orthopraxy. That the orthodox members of the Hindu Mahasabha had considered the respect of orthopraxy as a major condition of any reconversion is also to be read in the resolution passed by the movement regarding this subject, in 1923. It declared that it was:

by all means proper and desirable to reclaim and admit in our society, after prayaschitta according to Shastras, all those Malkanas who are for some years called neo-Muslims, who follow the principal customs of Hindus. . . (*Indian Annual Register* 1923: 136)

The reference, not to the *shuddhi* procedure, but to those of the *prayaschitta*[8] contained in the *shastras* is an additional indication of the orthodox concern to clearly situate the reconversions in a traditional framework.

When the so-called 'Muslim threat' appeared to be less serious, in the second half of the 1920s, numerous orthodox leaders dissociated themselves from the *Shuddhi* Movement, and in particular from its efforts to reintegrate Untouchables into caste society. In 1925, Lajpat Rai, in a speech he delivered as president of the Hindu Mahasabha, qualified as 'suicidal' the orthodox attitude which consisted in neglecting the Untouchables whom the Christians and Muslims wanted to convert (*Indian Quarterly Register* 1925: 380). However, in 1926, most of the orthodox leaders left the organization in response to a draft resolution by Shraddhananda concerning access of Untouchables to schools and wells. Reservations on the part of the leadership of the movement—in the front ranks of which figured the very conservative Malaviya—regarding his propositions led Shraddhananda to also leave the Hindu Mahasabha. Henceforward, he no longer militated for the 'Hindu Sangathan', but rather for the 'Arya Sangathan' (Jordens 1981: 159), that is, the organization (in the sense of unification) no longer of Hindus, but of Arya Samajists. He thus returned to his first adherence.

Shraddhananda's defection suggests a more general lesson. In the early period, the Arya Samaj had endeavoured to resist the missionaries (and to a lesser extent the Muslims) by reinterpreting the *shuddhi* in such a way as to make it a procedure analogous to that of the 'rival religions'. This effort awakened the support of the orthodox insofar as it was a matter of reintegrating individuals into their caste in a perspective which Hinduism had long known and insofar as the 'threat' represented by the 'Others' appeared to be strong. When the latter became less prominent, the application of the *shuddhi* and the upliftment of low caste people were generally rejected by the orthodox leaders. At the grass-root level, members of the upper castes had always tended to show reluctance towards this process. By the same token, Arya Samajists who supported the *shuddhi* returned, like Shraddhananda, to their first adherence. The Arya Samaj thus evolved to the status of a mere sect of Hinduism which no longer followed the calling to spread its egalitarian ideal throughout society. Certainly, the Arya Samaj contained lay disciples, but when they succeeded in establishing an egalitarian community, it was, like the sect, outside the world.

In 1912, for example, the Meghs for whom the *shuddhi* had been performed were settled in a colony created exclusively for them and provided with a hospital, schools, and so on (Jones 1976: 308). The *shuddhi* was reduced to the level of a rite of initiation into the Arya Samaj, which then looks like a sect. From the 1890s onwards, the ceremonies, which obviated the journey to Haridwar and consisted for the candidate to openly declare his adherence to the ten principles of the Arya Samaj (Jones 1976: 134; *Census of India 1901*, Report by R. Burn: 87). This organization had, therefore, not succeeded in becoming—on the social plane, if not in the sphere of ideas, where its impact was considerable—more than a sect which was in particular attractive to members of low castes, whose Sanskritization it facilitated.[9]

In sum, the movements sustained in the name of the *shuddhi* by the Arya Samaj, and then the Hindu Mahasabha, between the 1880s and the 1920s, were largely conditioned by the socio-political context, in particular by the crises arising from the activities of Christian missionaries and from the growth of communalisms. While the *Shuddhi* Movements did contribute to the crystallization of religious antagonisms, they did not find expression in the emergence in Hinduism of a genuine (re)conversion procedure. In this respect, traditional principles continued to prevail. First the orthopraxy of the caste system stood opposed to the purification of Untouchables and to a form of proselytism permitting the integration of new arrivals into a community of believers which does not exist, at least, not outside crisis periods, when Hindu solidarity is emphasized. Second, conversion in the sense of individual adherence to a new belief is only really to be observed in the sectarian framework—the only place where a community of believers can exist—as the destiny of the Arya Samaj testifies.

After independence, Hindu nationalist movements continued to inveigh against Christian or Muslim proselytizing activities, arguing henceforth that all conversion was synonymous with denationalization. The conversion of Untouchables to religions which were born in India (Sikhism or Buddhism) never aroused hostility. By contrast, the Hindu nationalists undertook ambitious (re)conversion campaigns, as of the 1980s, in reaction to a limited recrudescence of Muslim proselytism. However, they could only do it when communal antagonisms reached their peaks.

## (Re)conversion Against 'Denationalization'

After independence, conversion to Christianity and Islam was more often described as a process of 'denationalization'. Many Congress members wanting to eradicate all traces of British colonization spoke out for a restriction of the activities of the missions. The question was debated in the Constituent Assembly when it discussed the formulation of the right to 'propagate' one's faith in Article 19 (on religious freedom) of the Fundamental Rights in the first Draft Constitution. The word 'propagate' was here a euphemism for 'proselytizing activity' and even 'conversion', terms whose emotional charge was too great. Loknath Misra, a representative from Orissa, elected on the Congress ticket, criticized vehemently the use of this term:

... article 19 is a Charter for Hindu enslavement. I do really feel that it is the most disgraceful Article, the blackest part of the Draft Constitution. I beg to submit that I have considered and studied all the constitutional precedents and have not found anywhere any mention of the word 'propaganda' as a Fundamental Right, relating to religion. . . . You know that propagation of religion brought India into this unfortunate state and India had to be divided into Pakistan and India. If Islam had not come to impose its will on this land, India would have been a perfectly secular State and a homogeneous State. There would have been no Partition. Therefore, we have rightly tabooed religion . . . . If you accept religion, you must accept Hinduism as it is practised by an overwhelming majority of the people in India. . . . This unjust generosity of tabooing religion and yet making propagation of religion a fundamental right is somewhat uncanny and dangerous. Justice demands that the ancient faith and culture of the land should be given a fair deal, if not restored to its legitimate place after a thousand years of suppression. . . . In the present context what can this word 'propagation' in article 19 mean? It can only mean paving the way of the complete annihilation of Hindu culture, the Hindu way of life and manners. Islam has declared its hostility to Hindu thought. Christianity has worked out the policy of peaceful penetration by the back-door on the outskirts of our social life. This is because Hinduism did not accept barricades for its protection. (*Constituent Assembly Debates*, Official Report, 1989: 822–4)

This speech is a good reflection of the thinking of Congress traditionalists[10] and even of Hindu nationalists. In these milieux, Partition was attributed to Muslims and Hindus were portrayed as victims who had suffered as a consequence of their lack of organization and of their 'appeasement' of religious minorities. Now that India had become more than before the land of the Hindus, it was a question of protecting Hinduism—always perceived as vulnerable, despite a population consisting of 82 per cent of the Indians in 1991—and of not conceding new privileges to the minorities, such as the recognition of the right to propagate one's faith, which would above all serve missionary religion such as Christianity and Islam. Some even went to the extent of advocating an official recognition of Hinduism which, in their eyes, constituted the matrix of national culture, and which would not contradict the 'secular' calling of the government, given that they viewed its profound tolerance as its major characteristic.

These positions were marginalized in the Constituent Assembly, notably because of the influence exerted by Nehru. The latter was anxious to reassure the minorities—in particular, the roughly 10 per cent Muslims who had chosen to remain in India. The arguments of another participant in the debate, T.N. Krishnamachari, a Congress member as well, also deserves close attention:

Sir, objection has been taken to the inclusion of the word 'propagate' along with the words 'profess and practise' in the matter of religion. Sir, it does not mean that this right to propagate one's religion is given to any particular community or to people who follow any particular religion. It is perfectly open to the Hindus and the Arya Samajists to carry on their *shuddhi* propaganda as it is open to the Christians, the Muslims, the Jains and the Buddhists and to every other religionist, so long as he does it subject to public order, morality and the other conditions that have to be observed in any civilised government. (Graham 1989: 836)

This type of discourse implicitly exhorted Hindus to align themselves with members of other religions in the context of a competition for souls and, in certain respects, this was the evolution to be observed in the course of the following decades.

Article 19, which became Article 20 in the Constitution passed in 1950, finally stated:

Subject to public order, morality and health; and to the other provisions of this part, all persons are equally entitled to freedom of conscience and the right to freely profess, practise and propagate religion.

Although the concern with religious tolerance was brought within the compass of the central power, Hindu militant attitudes persisted in the states, the most significant case no doubt being that of Madhya Pradesh. This province of Central India in 1991 included 23 per cent Tribals (as against the national average of 7.8 per cent), a population among which the missions had been most active since the nineteenth century. In 1954, following a so-called intensification of activity by Christian missionaries in the tribal zones (more than 4,000 Tribals were allegedly converted in 1952 and 877 in 1953, compared with 40 in 1951 in the district of Surguja alone) (*Report of the Christian Missionary Activities Enquiry Committee 1957*: 21), the state government appointed, in 1954, a commission of inquiry headed by B.S. Niyogi and including G.S. Gupta, a veteran of the Arya Samaj. This commission discovered that the number of missionaries officiating in India had risen, between 1951 and 1955, from 4,377 to 4,877, of which 480 were in Madhya Pradesh, nearly half of whom were American (ibid.: 108). Furthermore, the funds received from abroad by the missions, between 1950 and 1954, amounted to Rs. 2.9 million, two-thirds of which came from the United States. These funds had previously been utilized to build schools, orphanages and hospitals, where conversions had at times been fraudulently achieved according to the Niyogi Report (ibid.: 99–135). The conclusion drawn by the author of the report was that:

Evangelization in India appears to be a part of the uniform world policy to revive Christendom for re-establishing Western supremacy and is not prompted by spiritual motives. The objective is apparently to create Christian minority pockets with a view to disrupting the solidarity of the non-Christian societies, and the mass conversions of a considerable section of *adivasis* with this ulterior motive is fraught with danger to the security of state. (ibid.: 137)

The so-called 'separatism' of the tribals in Jharkhand—a partially Christianized area of south Bihar which had been aspiring to have its own state since the 1940s—was viewed in this perspective. The conversions were thus analysed mainly in political terms and denounced as a threat to national integrity. On this account, the 'Niyogi Report' recommended the establishing of quotas on foreign missionaries, or even their expulsion.

The arguments of this report was used, after its publication in 1957, by militant Hindu movements. In 1958, a Hindu Mahasabha MLA from the Madhya Pradesh Assembly introduced a bill in the state assembly which took up the terms of the Niyogi Report, 'in view of prohibiting fraudulent conversions.'[11] This text, which was under discussion until 1961, was finally rejected by the Congress majority in the name of religious freedom. While expressing his shock at the practices of foreign missionaries, Nehru always refused to expel them. Their number simply declined (there were 4,800 missionaries in 1959) because of a more stringent issuance of visas (ibid.: 108). The accommodating attitude of the Indian authorities towards Christians was confirmed in 1964, when the President of the Indian Union, Radhakrishnan, went to Bombay to receive Pope Paul VI, who had come to take part in the International Eucharistic Conference (Gopal 1989: 335). With this tolerant attitude, the Congress Party made it possible for Hindu nationalists to attempt to politically exploit the conversions.

## THE SELECTIVE OPPOSITION OF HINDU
## NATIONALISTS TO CONVERSIONS

The Hindu Mahasabha had been constituted as an independent political party in the 1930s, when its defence of the Hindus had been deemed incompatible with the ideology of the Congress, of which it had until then been a sub-group. From the 1930s onwards, the Hindu Mahasabha can be described as a 'Hindu nationalist' party, to the extent that its leaders considered Indian identity to be epitomized in Hindu culture (which according to them, as to the Arya Samaj, went back to the Vedic Golden Age), and enjoined religious minorities to restrict the expression of faith to the private sphere and to give public allegiance to symbols of Hindu identity considered to be 'national' (Jaffrelot 1996: Ch. 1). Failing that, conversion was denounced as a process of 'denationalization', which is allegedly evidenced by the change of names undertaken by Hindus when they converted to Islam or Christianity (*Hindu Vishva*, 1988: 16–20).

The use of the word 'denationalization' is revealing of the status of religion in the ideology of the militant Hindus. A number of them were not practising Hindus and even scorned certain rituals, which they perceived as superstitious. They were foremostly nationalists and, in that respect, modern. Religion for them was first a mark of national culture, a collective attribute acquired since socialization within the family cell. This conception, which fits in the framework of an ethnic nationalism, precludes the consideration of conversion as a decision involving only the individual.

The religions brought under attack by the nationalists Hindu were, moreover Islam and Christianity; Sikhism and Buddhism did not arouse the same animosity because they had their origin on Indian soil, as the reactions of Hindu nationalists to the conversions of Untouchables to Sikhism and Buddhism testify.

## THE NON-ISSUE OF CONVERSIONS TO
## SIKHISM AND BUDDHISM

These conversions began in the 1930s under the impetus of Ambedkar, who considered, when his hopes of socio-political reform were disappointed, that the only way for the Untouchables to free themselves from caste hierarchy resided in conversion. He announced this idea for the first time, in 1935, at Yeola. Immediately following this speech, the Hindu Mahasabha brought together 1,000 delegates in a special session held in Bombay, under the chairmanship of Malaviya. Their first moves were quite symbolic: Malaviya 'purified' Untouchables in Benares with the *Mantra Dikṣa* ceremony (the revealing of a sacred formula which generally takes place in the sectarian context at the time of initiation), and the Shankaracharya of the Karweer Pith assured Ambedkar that he would found a new sect if there was need to guarantee Untouchables an equal status with the other 'sections' of Hinduism (*Indian Annual Register* 1935: 30).

The revival of Ambedkar's movement in favour of the mass conversion of Untouchables, in 1936, nevertheless awakened the activity of the Hindu Mahasabha. Above all, the eventuality of Untouchables going over to Islam aroused in their milieux the obsessive fear of 'being exterminated in one's own land' (*The Times of India*, 14 April 1936). This apprehension, which had already been felt at the beginning of the century because of the divergent demographic evolution of Hindus and Muslims, thus re-emerged in a new form. It was fostered by the certainty of a Muslim plot: the Nizam of Hyderabad was said to have offered forty million rupees to Ambedkar in the case of conversion to Islam (ibid.). Moonje—the leader of the Hindu Mahasabha most directly concerned by this initially Maharashtrian problem—entered into negotiations with Ambedkar, under pressure from figures such as the businessman J.K. Birla (ibid., and *Moonje Papers* 1936), in order to find a compromise.

Significantly, Moonje at once viewed matters from the same perspective as Ambedkar, according to whom it was illusory to expect a reform in orthodox Hinduism. He proposed, with the approbation of the Shankaracharya of the Karweer Pith, that Ambedkar 'join the Sikhs or the Arya Samaj, which had completely eliminated the caste system' (*The Times of India*, 14 April 1936). This option made it possible to retain the Untouchables within 'Hindu culture'. Ambedkar gave serious thought to the possibility of a conversion to Sikhism. Moonje undertook, successfully, to obtain the assent of the Maharaja of Patiala—the major Sikh princely state in the Punjab—whom he viewed as representative of the Sikh community, to the purpose of having an accord between Ambedkar and Sikh dignitaries ratified (*Moonje Papers*, 28 June and 8 July 1936). Following these negotiations and confronted with the reservations of Muslim leaders, Ambedkar announced, in August 1936, that he rejected the principle of mass conversion of Untouchables to Islam, which Moonje viewed as a great personal victory (ibid.: 23 August 1936). However, Ambedkar also abandoned the idea of converting to Sikhism.

Twenty years later, he revived his conversion movement. In 1956, he converted to Buddhism, taking with him from 300,000 to 600,000 Untouchables, according to estimates (Zelliot 1992: 126). This did not arouse vehement protests on the part of Hindu nationalists, as they considered also Buddhism to be a national religion, given that it originated on the Indian soil.

## THE HINDU NATIONALIST FIGHT AGAINST
## CONVERSIONS TO ISLAM AND CHRISTIANITY

By contrast, Christians and Muslims continued to arouse hostility. After independence, the RSS imposed itself as the major movement favouring (re)conversion to Hinduism. The opposition of the RSS to conversions to Islam and Christianity was, however, particularly endorsed by its three affiliates, the Vishva Hindu Parishad (VHP), the Vanavasi Kalyan Ashram (VKA) and the Bharatiya Jana Sangh (BJS).

Created in 1964, the VHP general secretary, a member of the RSS leadership, justified the creation of this organization in the following terms:

The declared object of Christianity is to turn the whole word into Christendom—as that of Islam is to make it Pakistan. Besides these two dogmatic and proselytising religions there has arisen a third religion, communism. . . . The world has been divided into Christian, Islamic and Communist, and all these three consider the Hindu society as a very fine rich food on which to feast and fatten themselves. It is therefore necessary in this age of competition and conflict to think of, and organize, the Hindu world to save itself from the evil eyes of all the three. (Apte 1964: 15)

The main example to which the author alluded in support of his argumentation was the 'separatism' of the Naga tribes in the north-east who had, in 1963, obtained their own state, Nagaland. This 'separation' was ascribed to the 'denationalization' of the tribes—four-fifths of whom were Christianized—by the missions, which clearly figured as the main adversaries.

One means to fight the Christian missions which the VHP acquired rapidly consisted in a nucleus of religious propagandists. Among its first 'aims and objectives' was, in fact:

To establish an order of missionaries, both lay and initiate, for the purpose of propagating dynamic Hinduism representing the fundamental values of life. . . .and to open, manage or assist seminaries or centres for training such missionaries. (Sikand and Kajju 1994: 2217)

The use of the term 'missionaries' is not irrelevant: its militants, following the example of the Arya Samaj's *upadeshaks* during the *Shuddhi* Movement, sought to countervail the influence of the Christian missions by adopting their own weapons. Their activity consisted primarily in establishing orphanages, schools, student hostels and dispensaries to compete with those developed by the Christian missions, in particular among the tribes in the north-east, in order to reclaim persons who had left Hinduism for Christianity.[12] In the 1970s, Muslims constituted a target which was at least as important as the Christians. It was a matter, as in the case of the Malkanas, of former Rajputs, the history of which the VHP re-wrote in an edifying manner (Sikand and Kajju 1994: 2217). In the midst of the tribal populations, the same social activities and reconversions were reserved for the VKA which, gradually extended its sphere of activity throughout India.

Parallel to this effort to rival the Christian missions by imitating their techniques, the Hindu nationalists, through their party, strove to have laws passed which would place restrictions on conversions. In Madhya Pradesh, to continue with this example, the Jana Sangh, when it came to power by means of a short-lived coalition in 1967-9, had a law passed called *Dharm Swatantra* (religious freedom) which foresaw a punishment of two years imprisonment for persons involved in conversions which did not strictly comply with the principle of voluntary participation (*The Statesman Weekly*, 21 December 1968: 8). When, in 1977, members of the Jana Sangh returned to state power through the Janata Party, Christians had reason to complain about questionnaires from the government concerning the circumstances of their conversion and the age at which family members had converted. Conversions which had been influenced, or in which minors were implicated, would have led to prosecution in the framework of the 1968 law (*Link*, 4 June 1979).

In 1977–80, Jana Sangh members were also involved in the central power in New Delhi and attempted to profit therefrom to have a law with national scope passed in Parliament. One of their deputies, a militant Arya Samajist, introduced in 1978 a 'Freedom of Religion Bill' which aimed at preventing anyone from 'converting or attempting to convert, directly or otherwise, a person from one religious faith to another by the use of force or by fraud or blackmail or deception, or by whatever other fraudulent means' (*The Times of India*, 26 April 1979). This text was inspired by a comparable law which had gone into effect earlier the same year in Arunachal Pradesh (a Union Territory in the North-East under the direct administration of New Delhi); for in this zone inhabited by tribals, the implementation of such a bill would have given place to attacks against churches. Christian MPs derived their argument from this to criticize the 'Freedom of Religion Bill' which, in the end, was not passed (*Lok Sabha Debates*, 1979, Vol. XXIV: Col. 245).

In sum, from 1947 to the 1980s, Hindu nationalists attempted to fight against conversions, not to Sikhism or Buddhism, but to Christianity and Islam, in which they perceived a denationalization process undermining India's integrity. Their efforts, however, had an only mitigated success. The issue of conversions began to assume an entirely different importance in the early 1980s following the conversion of groups of Untouchables to Islam. The subsequent Hindu nationalist mobilization marked a certain *routinization* of reconversion, as the heads of orthodox sects associated themselves on a long-term basis with it, not at all manifesting the reservations which could be observed in the 1920s. This evolution proved to be inseparable from the growing politicization of an issue, the social and religious character of which was still less manifest than at times during the *Shuddhi* Movements.

## THE CONVERSIONS OF 1981 AND THE HINDU
## NATIONALIST MOBILIZATION

On 19 February 1981, roughly 1,000 Untouchables from the village of Meenakshipuram (Tirunelveli district in Tamil Nadu) converted to Islam. This was outwardly manifested by the adoption of the skullcap, the wearing of a more costly *longi* (garment attached around the waist), as well as by the changing of the name of their village to Rehmatnagar (Mathew 1982: 1031). This community, following an upward socioeconomic movement, had long hoped to convert in order to be free from caste hierarchy (Mujahid 1988). This collective conversion was only the first in a series in the course of the next seven months during which some 3,000 Untouchables went over to Islam. The chain of conversions was approved by Muslim political leaders, who did not hesitate to at times patronize, or supervise, conversion ceremonies, the building of mosques, etc. (*The Hindustan Times*, 22 July 1981).

These developments fostered a renewed sentiment of vulnerability among many Hindus, who were prompt to accuse transnational Islamic forces. The Baudhik Pramukh (chief ideologue) of the RSS inveighed against yet another 'denationalization' campaign, and other Hindu nationalists incriminated the financial strength of the countries on the Persian Gulf (Sudarshan 1986: 277–90 and Goel in ibid.: 197–216). Reports in newspapers, which could not be suspected of Hindu nationalism were also primarily interested in the amounts which would have been paid to those who had converted (as much in some cases, it was said, as 500 rupees) (*The Hindu Awakening*: 21–2), the money supposedly having come from Arab countries (*The Times of India*, 18 July 1981). Thus arose the conviction as to an international conspiracy, illustrated in an article which appeared on the front page of *The Times of India*, entitled 'International Islamic conspiracy for mass conversion of Harijans' (Ibid.: 21 March 1981).

The author referred to an account published in the *Arab Times* (Kuwait) regarding a report from the Islamic Cultural Centre (London) which announced the conversion of 80 to 120 million Hindus thanks to the Gulf money and to the so-called appeal by the president of the Jamaat-al-Islami, made during its February session in 1981, to double the demographic strength of the Muslim community.[13] These apprehensions appeared out of proportion with the diminutive character of the Jamaat-al-Islami, the size of which was only slowly increasing (2,792 members in 1981, as compared with 2,157 in 1974). The reality of danger, however, mattered less than the subjectivity of the Hindus who felt threatened.

In response to the conversions of 1981 in Tamil Nadu, the Vishva Hindu Parishad intensified its reconversion activities. In 1981 and 1982, it announced the return to the Hindu fold of 8,279 Christians and 13,921 Muslims (*The Hindu Awakening*: 21–2). It was as if the pattern of the 1920s—during which the *Shuddhi* Movement had been extensively revived by the forced conversions in Malabar— would be repeated, apart from the fact that the ritual employed was no longer that of the *shuddhi* and that there were scarcely any reservations among the orthodox leaders regarding the idea of reconversion.

### SIMPLIFICATION AND ROUTINIZATION?

Instead of *shuddhi,* Hindu nationalists employed henceforth the terms *dharm parivartan*—change of religion, *dharm prachar*—diffusion, propagation of religion, or *pratyavartan*—return, understood as a return to the fold of Hinduism. This semantic shift suggests a distancing from the classic categories of Hinduism. It expresses a devalourization of the ritual hierarchy which had until then induced— for example, in the *Shuddhi* Movement—a conception of conversion as a purification, or as an initiation into a sect. Henceforth, the terms utilized refer less to the Hindu social structure and more to the migration of individuals from one religious community to another.

This evolution reflects in part a gradual Western influence on Indian society in which the notions of ritual purity and impurity were becoming less prominent, particularly in the cities. More specifically, the Hindu nationalists, even should they always allude to a Golden Age in which an ideal society corresponded to organicist and hierarchic principles wanted to form a Hindu nation by eroding the factors of division, or at least of differentiation, which castes represented. They perpetuated the strategic mimetism practised by the Arya Samaj by attempting to introduce the—Western—concept of nation, corresponding to a mentality which is basically individualistic and egalitarian and which, in their case, was not without affinity with the notion of a 'community of believers'.

One of the consequences of this ideological imitation is seen in the fact that the rituals of (re)conversion were much simpler in 1980 than they had been in 1880s, as this description of the reconversion of 600 Christians in Andhra Pradesh demonstrates:

> The ceremony began with the hoisting of the saffron OM flag by Sri Sadajeevat Lalji, Central Treasurer, Vishva Hindu Parishad, After Go-Puja [cow worship] and Havana [form of Vedic sacrifice] these 600 people assumed new Hindu names. Afterwards they went into the temples and performed pujas. (*Hindu Vishva,* 1992: 44–7)

Significantly, this account fails to mention the intervention of a priest, which remained necessary. Nevertheless, the modalities of this ceremony contrast with the more elaborate *shuddhi* ritual, even after the reinterpretation by the Arya Samaj. The OM (syllable associated with spiritual awakening in Hinduism), the colour saffron (the colour of renunciation), the cow and the Vedic sacrifice, are symbols which the RSS and its affiliates endeavoured to promote because they have the advantage of transcending differences of caste and sect. Reconversion was, therefore, seen primarily as a reinforcement of the Hindu nation, also shown by the recourse to the saffron flag, which is that of the RSS and which the latter wanted to have raised to the national standard.

Not only had the modalities of reconversion been simplified and become more ideological than at the beginning of the century, but, in addition, the religious leaders, orthodox of repute, no longer opposed the 'conversion' of Untouchables and tribals, even when they have no part in these ritual procedures.

In Madhya Pradesh, one of the main protagonists of the (re)conversions of tribals who had gone over to Christianity was the son of a maharaja who, until then, had merely patronized the Vanavasi Kalyan Ashram. In 1992, he reconverted, doubtlessly with the assistance of a priest, roughly 1,300 tribals (of whom a sizeable number were, however, not Christians, but declared themselves to be 'animists') in the district of Raigarh, where missionaries, active since the end of the nineteenth century, had little by little brought the proportion of Christians to 10 per cent. Here, the ritual was very cursory, its major part residing in *havans* performed by the converts under the guidance of a priest and in the ablutions which the Maharaja did at the feet of the tribals. He himself spoke not of (re)conversion, but of 'nationalization' (*Sunday*, 1992: 44–7). This programme has been going on for years: in 1997, *The Organiser* announced the reconversion of 870 Tribal Christians according to the same procedure (*The Organiser*, 1997: 15).

(Re)conversions are, however, generally a matter for religious figures, heads of sects or monasteries, or mere founders of ashrams. In south India, since 1981, the latter had undertaken mass *dharm parivartan*. In Karnataka, for example, Vishvesh Tirth, the Madhavacharya of Udipi, reconverted 1,000 Christians (Seshadri 1983: 123). The absence of opposition to (re)conversion among religious figures, reputedly the most orthodox, represents a new factor. The latter seem indeed to have abandoned their prejudice regarding the inclusion in Hindu society of persons who had never belonged to it, or who, having left it, had broken with orthopraxy. This evolution is congruent with the forsaking of the notion of the *shuddhi* and reflects a diminished consideration of the notions of purity and impurity.

Thus, (re)conversions to Hinduism were henceforward more comparable to those of other religions, as more stress was placed on communitarian culture than on the modalities of social integration, that is, caste. However, they were perhaps still to be distinguished to the extent that the highlightening of communitarian culture was practised at the cost of the individual and, certainly, spiritual dimension of conversion. The evolution of the Hindu attitude involved in the (re)conversion campaigns was inseparable from the increasingly evident political objectives of this (counter-)proselytism, as it was first a matter of strengthening 'one's' community in terms of numbers. In distinction to the situation which prevailed in the 1920s, the rallying of religious figures does not, however, appear to be due only to circumstances. Numerous religious figures seem, in fact, lastingly integrated in the Hindu nationalist movement. They subscribe to its ideology, in which their orthodoxy is evidently diluted.

Whether a question of the *Shuddhi* Movements in the late nineteenth and early twentieth centuries, or of the (re)conversion campaigns in the 1980s, it appears that this type of action was only practicable in Hinduism as a reaction to the threat of proselytizing religions, the techniques of which were emulated. For a long time, conversions only took place in the context of limited counter-offensives, as Hindu society, nothwithstanding the efforts of the Arya Samaj, the Hindu Mahasabha and the RSS-VHP combine remained hostile towards the integration, or reintegration, of individuals who did not provide all the guarantees required by orthodoxy and orthopraxy, beginning with ritual purity. The history of the Arya Samaj suggests that the *shuddhi,* in the case of Untouchables, was really successful only in a sectarian framework, the preferred place for any conversion in Hindu society.

However, it seems that the Hindu nationalist response to the conversion of Untouchables to Islam in the early 1980s has been a milestone for a greater acceptance in Hindu milieux of (re)conversion in a sense closer to that which the majority of other religions give this word, that is, as the transition from one community of believers to another. There would thus have been a kind of 'semiticization' of conversion in the Hindu milieu, resultant of a process which had been continuous following a century of imitation of the Other in the guise of allegiance to tradition.

These changes must be analysed in the context of the Hindu mobilization symbolized by the claiming of the Ayodhya site. Never had a Hindu nationalist agitation caused such long-lasting tension in communal relations; and, the context then created was, of course, advantageous for a re-evaluation of (re)conversion as a procedure of '(re)nationalization', since the boundaries between rival groups hardened, and only (rival) communities of believers being seen.[14] Sect and caste differentiations like any other cleavages within the Hindu 'community' tended to occupy the back seat.

## Notes

1. For more details concerning the notion of 'strategic mimetism', see Jaffrelot 1993: 517-24.

2. Traditionally, persons having undergone a *prayaschitta* rite (vide *infra*) received a certificate of the same type (I am grateful to Catherine Clémentin-Ojha for this information).

3. On Munshi Ram—who became Swami Shraddhananda after he had embraced the career of a world-renouncer—see Jordens 1981.

4. K. Jones gives a later date, 1900, and R.S. Pareek an intermediate date, 1899 (Pareek 1973: 136). This inconsistency is explained by the fact that the Rahtias asked Shraddhananda to be admitted to the Arya Samaj through the *shuddhi* procedure in 1896, but that the latter could only take place several years later, and, on two occasions,

because of opposition from numerous members of the Arya Samaj to the admission of Untouchables into their movement (Jordens 1981: 52).

5. The antagonism between the Arya Samajists and Muslims was symbolized for years by exchanges of unheard violence which were carried on by press and pamphlets, between Mirza Ghulam Ahmad and Lekh Ram, a *pandit* from Peshawar who joined the Arya Samaj in 1880. From 1887 to 1890, as editor of the *Arya Gazette,* then through pamphlets such as *Mad* (1892), which related atrocities connected with Muslim invasions in India, Lekh Ram contributed to the exacerbation of hatred. This antagonism reached its height when a Muslim assassinated Lekh Ram, in 1897, subsequent to sacrilegious articles.

6. (Jones 1976: 308; Jordens 1977: 156). Concerning the (re)conversions of the Jats in the Punjab in the 1920s, see *The Diaries of Dr. Ramjilal Hooda 1989*: 245–67.

7. Despite their criticism of the caste system, the Arya Samajists presented the (re)conversions as the restoration of former Rajputs to their caste. They did not hesitate, so as to convince reluctant Malkanas, to propagate an edifiant account of their 'original caste' and to promise a 'reintegration' into the networks of commensality of the twice-born (Sikand and Katju 1994: 2215).

8. The term *prayaschitta* denotes a ritual of expiation. It means literally 'thought of propitiation.'

9. Concerning the Sanskritization of Untouchables through the Arya Samaj, vide Mahar 1960; Sebring 1972; Rowe 1968.

10. I borrow this category from Bruce Graham who carefully distinguishes Hindu traditionalism from Hindu nationalism: The former 'stressed the need to preserve Hindu religious beliefs and social practices and to foster the study of the Hindi and Sanskrit languages and their literatures. While a Hindu traditionalist might devote much of his public life to cultural associations and institutions dedicated to the promotion of Hinduism, he might well support the Congress as the expression of a purely political nationalism with clearly defined representative and constitutional objectives. On the other hand, the more uncompromising Hindu nationalist was concerned not simply to conserve Hinduism but to develop the latent power of the Hindu community and thus to promote Hindu *sangathan*. . .' (Graham 1989: 174).

11. The law recommended by the report stated: 'Any attempt, by force or fraud, or threats of illicit means or grants of financial or other aid, or by fraudulent means of promises, or by moral and material assistance, or by taking advantage of any person's inexperience or confidence, or by exploiting, any person's necessity, spiritual (mental) weakness or thoughtlessness, or, in general, any effort (whether successful or not), directly or indirectly to penetrate into the religious conscience of persons (whether of age or underage) of another faith, for the purpose of obtaining their religious conscience or faith, so that to agree with the ideas or convictions of the proselytising should be absolutely prohibited' (*Report of the Christian Missionary Activities Enquiry Committee 1957*: 170).

12. In 1981, the VHP claimed to have 3,000 branches covering 437 of the 534 districts of India, 150 full-time activists, 442 boarding schools, orphanages and schools, 150 medical centres and 10 newspapers (Andersen and Damle 1987: 134).

13. This was, in fact, a baseless rumour. See Graff 19.

14. The increased strength of the Hindu nationalists favours not only (re)conversions to Hinduism; it calls into question possibilities of 'leaving' this religion. Parallel to the

activities of the VHP, Hindu nationalists redoubled efforts, beginning in the 1980s, to use their power against again a good example. In 1985, when Congress governed the state, eight foreign missionaries were faced with deportation until this decision was suspended and five-year visas granted due to the intervention of the Supreme Court and Rajiv Gandhi—to the detriment of the VHP. In 1990, the Bharatiya Janata Party, which succeeded the Jana Sangh as the political front of the RSS, won the elections in Madhya Pradesh. It then issued deportation orders against two missionaries—a Belgian and an American—from the district of Surguja, where the number of Christians had gone from 545 in 1951 to 28,000 in 1981.

# References

Andersen, W. and Damle, S. (1987), *The Brotherhood in Saffron: The Rashtriya Swayamsevak Sangh and Hindu Revivalism*, New Delhi: Vistaar Publications.

Apte, S.S. (1964), 'Why Vishva Hindu Parishad', *The Organiser*, Divali Special.

*Census of India 1901*, Vol. XVI, *North West Provinces and Oudh*, Part 1, Report by R. Burn.

*Census of India 1911*, Vol. 15, *United Provinces of Agra and Oudh*, Part 1, Report by E.A.H. Blunt.

*Census of India 1921*, Vol. 1, Part 1, Report by J.T. Marten.

*Constituent Assembly Debates—Official Report* (1989), Vol. VII, 4 November 1948–8 January 1949, New Delhi: Lok Sabha Secretariat.

Datta, P.K. (1993), 'Dying Hindus: Production of Hindu Communal Common Sense in early 20th Century Bengal', *Economic and Political Weekly*, 19 June 1993.

Ghai, R.K. (1990), *Shuddhi Movement in India*, New Delhi: Commonwealth Publishers.

Goel, S.R. (1986), 'Money-Power and Politics of Conversion', in D. Swaroop (ed.), *Politics of Conversion*, New Delhi: Deendayal Research Institute.

Gopal, S. (1989), *Radhakrishnan: A Biography*, Delhi: Oxford University Press.

Graff, V., 'La Jamaat-al-Islami Hind', in O. Carré and R. Dumont (ed.), *Radicalismes islamiques*, Paris: L'Harmattan.

Graham, B.D. (1989), 'The Congress and Hindu Nationalism', in D.A. Low (ed.), *The Indian National Congress*, Delhi: Oxford University Press.

Hardgrave Jr., R.L. (1977), 'The Mapilla Rebellion, 1921: Peasant Revolt in Malabar', *Modern Asian Studies*, Vol. 11, No. 1.

*Hindu Vishva*, December 1988.

———, March-April 1992.

*Hindustan Times*, 22 July 1981.

Hobsbawm, E. and Ranger, T. (1983) (eds.), 'Introduction: Inventing Traditions', in *The Invention of Tradition*, Cambridge: Cambridge University Press.

'Home coming', *The Organiser*, 16 March 1997.

*India Annual Register* (1923), Calcutta, Vol. 2.

——— (1935), Vol. 2.

*Indian Quarterly Register*, (1925), Vol. 1.

Jaffrelot, C. (1993), 'Hindu Nationalism: Strategic Syncretism in Ideology-Building', *Economic and Political Weekly*, 20–27 March.

————— (1996), *The Hindu Nationalist Movement and Indian Politics,* New Delhi: Viking.

Jones, K. (1966), Communalism in the Punjab: The Arya Samaj Contribution, *The Journal of Asian Studies,* Vol. 28, No. 1, November.

————— (1973), '"Ham Hindu Nahin" [We are not Hindus]: Arya-Sikh Relations 1877-1905', *Journal of Asian Studies,* Vol. 32, No. 3, May.

————— (1976), *Arya Dharm: Hindu Consciousness in 19th Century Punjab,* Berkeley: University of California Press.

————— (1981), 'Religious Identity and the Indian Census', in N.G. Barrier (ed.), *Census in British India,* New Delhi: Manohar.

Jordens, J.T.F. (1977), 'Reconversion to Hinduism, the Shuddhi of the Arya Samaj', in G.A. Oddie (ed.), *Religion in South Asia,* London: Curzon Press.

————— (1981), *Swami Shraddhananda: His Life and Causes,* Delhi: Oxford University Press.

Kane, P.V. (1953), *History of Dharmashastra,* Vol. 4, Poona: Bhandarkar Oriental Research Institute.

Kapani, L. (1992), *La notion de Samskara,* Vol. 1, Paris, Collège de France—De Broccard.

Kothari, R. (1968), 'Tradition and Modernity Revisited', *Government and Opposition,* Summer.

*Link,* 4 June 1979.

*Lok Sabha Debates,* New Delhi: Lok Sabha Secretariat, Vol. XXIV, 27 March 1979, Col. 245.

Mahar, P. (1960), 'The Changing Religious Practices of an Untouchable Caste', *Economic Development and Cultural Changes,* Vol. 8, No. 3.

Mathew, G. (1982 ), 'Politicisation of Religion: Conversions to Islam in Tamil Nadu', *Economic and Political Weekly,* 19 June.

*Modern Review,* Vol. 8, No. 6, December 1910.

*Moonje Papers* (1922-3), B.S. Moonje, 'Forcible Conversions in Malabar (1923)', Nehru Memorial and Museum Library, Manuscript Section, Sub-file no. 12, 21 pages.

—————, Letter from Moonje to Kelkar on 18 June 1936, NMML (Microfilm Section), Reel no. 11.

—————, Letter from Moonje to the Maharaja of Patiala on 28 June and 8 July 1936, NMML (Microfilm Section), Reel no. 1.

—————, Letter from Moonje to Malaviya from 23 August 1936, NMML.

Mujahid, Abdul Malik (1988), *Conversion to Islam,* Chambersburg: Anima Books.

Parekh, R.S. (1973), *Contributions of Arya Samaj in the Making of Modern India 1875–1947,* New Delhi: Sarvadeshik Arya Pratinidhi Sabha.

*Punjab Census Report 1911.*

Rai, Lala Lajpat (1986), 'The Depressed Classes', *The Modern Review,* July 1909, reproduced in D. Swaroop (ed.), *Politics of Conversion,* New Delhi: Deendayal Research Institute.

*Report of the Christian Missionary Activities Enquiry Committee* (1957), Vol. 1, Gwalior: Government Regional Press.

Rowe, W.L. (1968), 'The New Cauhans: a Caste Mobility Movement in North India', in J. Silverberg (ed.) *Social Mobility in the Caste System of India,* La Haye: Mouton.

Sarda, Har Bilas (1968), *Life of Dayananda Saraswati,* Ajmer (1946).

Sebring, J. (1972), 'The formation of new castes: a probable case from North India', *American Anthropologist*, Vol. 173, No. 3.

Sen S.P. (1973) (ed.), *Dictionary of National Biography*, Vol. 1, Calcutta: Institute of Historical Studies.

Seshadri, H.V. (1983), 'The Hindu renaissance: A brief survey of the Hindu response to the major internal and external challenges facing the Hindu society', *Manthan*, Vol. 5, No. 1, May.

Seunarine, J.F. (1977), *Reconversion to Hinduism through Shuddhi*, Madras: The Christian Literature Society.

Sharma, Ram (1989), *Mahatma Hans Raj*, New Delhi: D.A.V. Publications.

Shraddhananda, Swami (1926), *Hindu Sangathan: Saviour of the Dying Race*, Delhi: Aryan Press.

Sikand, Y.S. (1997), 'The Fitna or Irtifad: Muslim missionary response to the Shuddhi of Arya Samaj in early twentieth century India', *Journal of Muslim Minority Affairs*, Vol. 17, No. 1.

Sikand, Y., and Kajju, M. (1994), 'Mass conversions to Hinduism among Indian Muslims', *Economic and Political Weekly*, Vol. 29, No. 34, 20 August.

Smith, D.E. (1963), *India as a Secular State*, Princeton, NJ: Princeton University Press.

Sudarshan, K.S. (1986), 'Conversion or denationalisation', in D. Swaroop (ed.), *Politics of Conversion*, New Delhi: Deendayal Research Institute.

*Sunday*, 12 April 1992.

*The Diaries of Dr. Ramjilal Hooda* (1989), Hisar: Modern Book.

*The Statesman Weekly*, 21 December 1968.

*The Times of India*, 14 April 1936, 26 April 1979, 21 March 1981, 18 July 1981.

Thursby, G.R. (1972), 'Aspects of Hindu-Muslim relations in British India: a study of Arya Samaj activities, government of Indian Politics and communal conflicts in the period 1923-1938', Unpublished Ph.D. thesis, Duke University.

Vishva Hindu Parishad, (n.d.), The *Hindu Awakening: Retrospect and Promise*, New Delhi: Vishva Hindu Parishad.

Wood, C. (1987), *The Moplah Rebellion and its Genesis*, New Delhi: People's Publishing House.

Zelliot, E. (1992), *From Untouchable to Dalit*, New Delhi: Manohar.

# Chapter 8

# The rise of Hindu nationalism and the marginalization of Muslims in India today

India, the 'largest democracy of the world' has also been known after 1947 for its attempts at establishing a secular regime and its success—quite exceptional—in maintaining it for decades despite ups and downs. Even though Indira Gandhi had the notion of secularism inserted in the Indian Constitution in 1976, almost twenty years after independence, the political system set up during the reign of her father, Jawaharlal Nehru, was already designed along those lines. Secularism has been understood in India not as a synonym for the French word *laïcité*, which implies separation between church and state; rather, it designates the equidistance of the state vis-à-vis all religions and an equally positive attitude towards them all. For instance, Article 25 of the Constitution emphasizes that 'all persons are equally free to profess, practice and propagate religion', and Article 30 states that 'All minorities, whether based on religion or language, shall have the right to establish and administer educational institutions', which can also receive subsidies from the state.

Paradoxically, to provide an added sense of security to the religious minorities, specifically the Muslims (12 per cent of the population in the 1991 census) and the Christians (about 2 per cent) were also entitled to use their personal law for regulating their community life, whereas the Hindu majority forming 82 per cent of the population had to submit to the Hindu Code Bill which, in the 1950s–60s, reformed the traditional practises regarding divorce, inheritance and adoption in the light of Western law. This is something that most militant Hindus still regard today as unbalanced treatment of the different religious groups.

The relationship between the Hindus and the religious minorities has always been in the form of a dialectic. Authorities such as Paul Brass, Gyanendra Pandey and Sandria Freitag have argued that economic factors and the emergence of a proto-democratic political arena during the British Raj (Brass 1974; Freitag 1990; Pandey 1990) gradually led all the communities to reshape their identity along ethno-nationalist lines to give birth to what is known as *communalism* in India.

While these elements need to be highlighted, I would like to stress the subjective aspects of the Hindu-Muslim relationship by focussing on the largely irrational feeling of vulnerability in certain segments of the Hindu community. The sentiment that Muslims pose a threat to the majority community was the root cause for the crystallization of a form of Hindu nationalism about one hundred years ago, its reactivation in the 1920s and 1930s, and most recently in the 1980s and 1990s. This last episode unfolded itself while the Muslim community, which was never in a strong position in post-independence India, has been further marginalized.

## The Birth and Rise of Hindu Nationalism: Stigmatizing and Emulating 'Threatening Others'

In the past, the word 'Hindu' primarily designated those who lived to the east beyond the river Sindhu, or Indus, not the followers of a creed. In fact, Hinduism can hardly be considered to be a religion since, although it sanctions a strong orthopraxy as embodied in the caste system, it does not contain real orthodoxy. It has no Book which can serve as a common reference to its adherents; the relevant books have been written by gurus for their sects (*sampradayas* or *panths*) which, indeed, represent the basic units of the Hindu world (Stienencron 1989: 20). The only approximate form of 'ecclesiastical structure' (Thapar 1985: 17) was created by Shankara who in the eighth century established monasteries in the four corners of India. Interestingly, he did so as a way of countering the growing influence of Buddhism which threatened to displace the Brahmans as the religious elite. The heads of the four monasteries were ordained to exercise a spiritual authority comparable to that of the Buddhist clergy: a Hindu pattern of reaction to exterior threats was taking shape which consisted, for the Brahmanical elite, in imitating those who were perceived as posing a threat to them in order to resist them more efficiently.

This modus operandi was again at work, in a way, in the nineteenth century in the context of European colonization. Upper caste Hindus reacted to the British utilitarian administration and Christian missions which shared an aversion to Hinduism for its idolatrous polytheism and caste system. They invented a Vedic golden age in which God was presented as unique (as propounded by Raja Rammohun Roy, the founder of the Brahmo Samaj in 1928 in Calcutta) and in which the Aryans were deemed to occupy positions in the social system according to their merits (as advocated by Swami Dayananda Saraswati, founder of the Arya Samaj in 1875 in Bombay). The nineteenth century socio-religious reform movements tended to modernize Hinduism along Western lines—they protested against child marriage and the *sati*, militated in favour of female literacy, etc.—but they also emulated the British in order to fight their influence more effectively. For instance, the Arya Samaj reinterpreted the old notion of *shuddhi*, a ritual which traditionally enabled an upper caste Hindu to purify himself when he has been soiled by some polluting contact, and transformed it into a reconversion procedure, thereby making Hinduism a proselytizing creed, more similar to Christianity and Islam.

The Muslims' attitudes precipitated the next stage in the formation of a Hindu nationalist identity. The peace negotiations following the First World War made Indian followers of Islam apprehend that the Caliphate, hitherto embodied in the person of the Ottoman Sultan, would be suppressed. In 1919, some of their leaders launched a 'Khilafat Movement' against the British who were taking part in the negotiations (Minault 1982). This mobilization degenerated in some instances into Hindu-Muslim riots, especially on the Malabar coast in 1921. It triggered a cycle of violence which lasted till the late 1920s in north India and reinforced a sense of vulnerability among many Hindus. In response, Hindu activists launched the movement Hindu *Sangathan*. Hindu nationalism crystallized in this context into an ideology and a political movement.

## The Hindutva Movement: An Ethno-Religious Nationalism

The Hindu nationalist ideology was first thoroughly codified in 1923 by Vinayak Damodar Savarkar (1883–1966) in *Hindutva: Who is a Hindu?* In this work, a Hindu is primarily someone who lives in Hindustan, the land beyond the Indus, between the Himalayas and the Indian Ocean. But Savarkar does not believe in territorial nationalism, a notion that implies a universalistic world view. For him, the historical place of the Hindus is remarkable because of rootedness south of the Himalayas. Due to this, the first Aryans, in Vedic times, were immune from foreign influences and intermarried in such a way that all Hindus 'can claim to have in their veins the blood of the mighty race descended from the Vedic fathers . . .' (Golwalkar 1939). In addition to geographical and ethnic unity, Savarkar, paradoxically emphasizes India's linguistic unity by arguing that Sanskrit is set up as the referent of all the subcontinental languages. Thereafter, every political programme based on the Hindu nationalist ideology—and especially those of the Hindu Mahasabha, the political party headed by Savarkar in 1937–42—would call for recognition of Sanskrit or Hindi, the vernacular language closest to Sanskrit, as the national language.

The tenets of Hindu nationalist ideology were subsequently revised by the Rashtriya Swayamsevak Sangh which soon became the leading organization in the Hindutva Movement. Golwalkar, who succeeded Hedgewar as chief of the RSS in 1940, gave the movement its ideological charter in 1938 with his book *We, or Our Nationhood Defined*, in which religious minorities were called upon to pledge allegiance to Hindu symbols of identity as the embodiment of the Indian nation (ibid.). With Hindu culture embodying the essence of Indian identity, religious minorities were requested to limit expressions of community distinctiveness to the private sphere.

The concept of *chiti* or 'race-spirit' in the writings of Savarkar, and later of Golwalkar, conveys the idea of the soul of the nation rather than biological connotations (Jaffrelot 1995). This conception allows, in fact insists upon, the integration of minorities by means of acculturation and at a subordinate level, whereas the tenets of biological racism, reasoning in eugenic terms, could well have incorporated an idea of total exclusion. This difference reflects the importance of social categories in Hinduism, a civilization that has always been characterized by an ability and a determination to assimilate the Other at a subordinate level as part of the organicist, hierarchical rationale of a caste-based society. Golwalkar considered as *mleccha* (barbarian) foreigners 'who do not subscribe to the social laws dictated by the Hindu religion and culture' (Golwalkar 1966: 62), a definition which closely coincides with the traditional usage of this term. In ancient India, a *mleccha* was someone on the fringe of the orthopraxy specific to the caste society dominated by Brahmanical values.[1]

## The Hindu Nationalist Network

The Hindu nationalist network first spread among the high castes of northern India and is still largely confined to this area. This geographical situation can be explained in two ways. First, the Sanskrit Great Tradition on which the ideology is based is closely related to the Hindi-speaking north. Second, this is a region inhabited by a large proportion of high caste Hindus who are attracted to the Hindutva Movement because, with its emphasis on social organic unity, it seems well equipped to protect them from the increasing demands of the low castes.

The Hindu nationalist movement, especially the RSS that is its backbone, has always regarded itself as destined to encompass the whole of India. This being so, it determined at a very early stage to spread throughout Indian society. First, it developed a network of *shakhas*. The RSS' ultimate ambition was to reach all the cities and villages of India in this way. Its membership rose from 10,000 in 1932 to 600,000 in 1951 and today stands at around 2 million, divided among 27,264 branches (*shakhas*) and 39,175 sub-branches (*upshakhas*) (Barthval 1998: 16). The *upshakhas* are the RSS' real basic units since the number of *shakhas* simply indicates the places where the movement is present—thus a town may contain several sub-branches.

After independence, this effort to cover the territory of India was supplemented by an effort to develop a network of sectoral affiliates. The aim here was not to penetrate society directly by means of *shakhas*, but to let up unions or organizations to defend specific social categories. These organizations give the Hindu nationalist movement a foothold in most sectors of society, where they work hand in glove with the *shakha* network. All these bridgeheads are presented by the mother organization as the *Sangh Parivar*, 'the family of the Sangh' (i.e. the RSS).

In 1948, Delhi-based RSS officials founded the Akhil Bharatiya Vidyarthi Parishad (ABVP), a students' union which was primarily intended to counter communist influence on university campuses. Today it is the student union with the largest membership—about one million students. A few years later, in 1955, the RSS set up a trade union, the Bharatiya Mazdoor Sangh (BMS) primarily to oppose the 'Red unions'. In the name of Hindu nationalist ideology and in line with organicist principles, the BMS attaches greater importance to social cohesion than to class struggle, hence its references to Gandhi's political philosophy and economics. By the late 1980s, the BMS had become India's biggest trade union. While the Congress-backed Indian Trade Union Congress (INTUC) came first with 2.2 million members in 1980 against 1.2 million workers affiliated to the BMS, it had only 2.7 million members in 1989 while the BMS stood at 3 million.[2]

Along with these unions, the RSS developed a number of more specialized organizations including the Vanavasi Kalyan Ashram (VKA)[3] whose purpose was primarily to counter the influence of the Christian missionaries among the tribals of central India where their evangelization and social work had led to conversions. The VKA imitated the techniques of the missionaries by developing dispensaries and schools to bring about a number of 'reconversions'. The strategy of stigmatization and emulation of the so-called 'threatening others' was still at work.

## The VHP, A Hindu Consistory?

In 1964, in association with Hindu religious figures, the RSS launched the Vishva Hindu Parishad (VHP), a movement designed to bring together the different Hindu sect leaders and provide this loosely organized religion with some kind of centralized structure (Jaffrelot 1999a: 191–212). The VHP succeeded in gathering together the heads of different Hindu sects on a covertly political platform.

Till the 1960s, few heads of traditional sects had joined the Hindu nationalist movement. Digvijay Nath, the Gorakhpur-based chief of the Naths, had been returned to the Lok Sabha on an Hindu Mahasabha ticket.

Before that, Swami Karpatriji, one of the most influential ascetics of Varanasi had founded the Ram Rajya Parishad in 1948 in order to fight the Hindu Code Bill which, according to him, went against Hindu traditions. He received the support of several maharajas in Rajasthan and Madhya Pradesh where he maintained pockets of influence till the 1960s. He then played a key part in the 1966 cow protection movement, which aimed at prohibiting cow-slaughter through the constitution itself, something Nehru had refused out of respect for the non-vegetarian communities. Large numbers of sadhus took part in this movement, the biggest that had been held in Delhi till then. At that time, the VHP was instrumental in bringing many more religious figures into the Hindu nationalist movement.

The ground had been prepared for this task by the profound change Hindu ascetics were undergoing. These *sadhus* were generally known as itinerant individuals absorbed in the solitary quest for God, even when they belonged to monk orders. However, even before independence, the urban middle class had been a favourable milieu for the emergence of new kinds of sadhus who, even though they were initiated in traditional orders, preached in English and downplayed their individual relationship with their disciples in comparison to imparting 'mass enlightenment'. In fact, they specialized in the collective healing of the psychological distress of the middle class, which suffered from stress and urban anomie. Even today their teaching aims more at making life a success than at spiritual salvation. The modern sadhus almost ignore their sectarian affiliation and, by contrast, emphasize their 'Hinduness'. They develop so-called philanthropic activities and establish their reputation via lucrative travels in the West. Many of them eventually joined the Hindu nationalist movement. Swami Chinmayananda, a 'modern guru' who established his *ashram*, the Sandypani Academy, in Bombay in 1963 was one of the founders of the Vishva Hindu Parishad.

The VHP was founded in his ashram, but under the auspices of the RSS which seconded one of its *pracharaks*, Shiv Shankar Apte, to become its General Secretary. Since then the objective of the movement has been to strengthen Hinduism by endowing it with a centralized organization. For the Hindu nationalists, there is an urgent need for federating the sects of their religion which otherwise appears to be at the mercy of the minorities. The circumstances of the founding of the VHP are illuminating in this respect. The movement was launched in Bombay just before the visit of the Pope who, it had been announced, would convert a large number of Hindus to Christianity. Once again, Hindus feeling threatened by a 'semitic' creed, responded by imitating its centralized structure specifically the Catholic notion of 'consistory'. Moreover, it then tried to evolve a Hindu catechism, to standardize the Hindu rituals, and to deploy its own preachers in the regions where the missionaries were operating. It thus implemented the strategy of stigmatization and emulation in its own way.

## The Ayodhya Movement

The Vishva Hindu Parishad became the spearhead of Hindu nationalism in the early 1980s, primarily because the RSS decided to make it the principal means of action after it had distanced itself from the BJP. The BJP, from the RSS' point of view, had shown itself to be too prompt to dilute its Hindu nationalist character, primarily so that it could form electoral alliances with parties of different persuasions, as evident from its aborted Janata phase in 1977–80.

The *Sangh Parivar* benefited from the reactivation of a Hindu sentiment of vulnerability consequent to the conversions of Meenakshipuram. In that village in Tamil Nadu, several hundred Untouchables had converted to Islam in 1981. These conversions were interpreted by *Hindu Vishva*, the official organ of the VHP, as constituting 'part of a long-term plan intended to transform the [Muslim] minority into a majority' (*Hindu Vishva*, March–April 1982: 7). The VHP sponsored Hindu Solidarity Conferences all over India to awaken solidarity among Hindus, for *jana jagaran,* according to the common expression, which tended to replace the RSS slogan of Hindu *Sangathan.*

The VHP also organized the *Ekatmata yatra* (literally, 'pilgrimage of unity') from the same perspective in 1983. Three caravans connecting Kathmandu and Rameshwaram (Tamil Nadu), Gangasagar (West Bengal) and Somnath (Gujarat), and Haridwar (Uttar Pradesh) and Kanyakumari (Tamil Nadu), distributed water from the Ganges and provided themselves with sacred water from local temples or from other sacred rivers encountered on the way. This mingling was intended to symbolize Hindu unity and, indeed, all the caravans converged in Nagpur, the headquarters of the RSS and the geographical centre of India. The Ganges, the river of salvation, was a shrewd choice since, just like the cow, it represents a symbol venerated by all Hindus.

The manipulation of religious symbols appeared even more distinctly in the Ayodhya movement. In Ayodhya in the sixteenth century, the Mughal emperor Babur had a mosque built on a site which many Hindus believed to be the birthplace of the god Ram. In 1984, the VHP started a movement claiming the retrocession of the *Ramjanmabhoomi* (birthplace of Ram) to the Hindus. In May–June, the VHP provided itself with an organization, which assembled young Hindu militants, the Bajrang Dal.[4] Its founder, Vinay Katiyar, had until then been a *pracharak* of the RSS. However, the Bajrang Dal proved to be less disciplined than the RSS and its violent utterances as well as actions were to precipitate many communal riots.

In September 1984 the VHP conducted a march beginning in Sitamarhi (Bihar) in the name of the 'liberation' of the Ayodhya temple, the site of which was reached on 7 October. In accordance with its interest in acting as a pressure group, the march set out to convey a petition to the government in Lucknow and then took the route to Delhi, which it should have reached in December, shortly before the elections foreseen for January 1985. However, in the meantime, the assassination of Indira Gandhi completely transformed the political atmosphere and led the VHP to change its plans.

The Ayodhya movement underwent a new stage of development in 1989 when the VHP decided to build a temple at Ram's birthplace. Its *Ram Shila Pujan* programme consisted in taking the bricks with which the temple was supposed to be built to thousands of towns and villages in order to have them consecrated by sadhus and to collect donations. More importantly, this campaign surcharged the atmosphere with communal feelings, which were to influence the results of the late 1989 elections. The BJP joined the Ayodhya movement at that stage, realizing its growing popularity among the Hindus of north India. It registered a significant electoral advance, winning 88 seats in the 1989 election as opposed to only two in 1984. This gain was further strengthened in 1991 when it won 119 seats, of which six were won by 'modern gurus'. In September 1990, Hindu militants tried to take by storm the Babri Masjid. The mosque's domes were damaged but the militants were successfully repressed by the authorities. A dozen or so of the casualties amongst the militants enhanced the cause of the so-called 'Hindu martyrs'.

The Ayodhya movement which took shape in the context of this new reaction to the perception of 'threatening others' was of far greater magnitude compared to previous ethno-religious mobilizations triggered by Hindu nationalists. Paradoxically at that time the Muslims looked more marginalized than ever.

## Muslims as Second Class Citizens

The constitutional dispositions, which were intended to found a multicultural polity after independence, remained largely non-implemented because Hindu traditionalists from the Congress were well-entrenched in the north Indian states. These leaders, exemplified by S. Sampurnanand, the chief minister of Uttar Pradesh in 1954–60; and Ravishankar Shukla, the chief minister of Madhya Pradesh in 1947–56; were known for a staunch attachment to Hindu culture which found expression in the promotion of Hindi, Ayurvedic medicine and protection of the cow (Indian National Congress 1988). Their prejudice against Muslims was expressed in their bias against Urdu and their low levels of recruitment to the bureaucracy and the police (Hasan 1990: 52). In 1964, only 7.7 and 5.5 per cent of those in the bureaucracy of Uttar Pradesh and Bihar respectively were Muslims, two states where they constituted 15 and 14 per cent respectively of the population. Nehru promoted Muslim leaders such as Maulana Azad and Rafi Ahmad Kidwai as his ministers in the national cabinet and Zakir Husain as vice president in 1962 (who later became president in 1967–9). But at the state level, Muslims often did not reach such posts of responsibility.

The hiatus between New Delhi's policies and politics at the state level was specially striking in the linguistic domain. In 1963, the Official Languages Act established English as an 'associated official language', to the chagrin of Hindu nationalists who wanted Hindi to be the only official language. In the states of the Hindi belt, where almost half of the Muslims live and where traditionalist Hindu Congressmen were in command, the latter's policy put Urdu, the language recognized by the Muslims as an identity symbol, in jeopardy. Hindi was considered as the official language by the states of this area after 1947. In Uttar Pradesh, the government of G.B. Pant declared that Hindi was the language to be used in courts and by the administration, whereas Urdu had been an official language during the British Raj. The Anjuman-e-Taraqqi-e-Urdu (Academy for the Promotion of Urdu) organized a protest movement in the form of a signature campaign, and in 1958 Nehru demanded that the Urdu-speaking population of the state be allowed to be educated in their language. The reluctance of the state authorities to amend the education policy, which was in the state's domain of competence, was such that Urdu continued to lose ground, so much so that today Muslim institutions have the Koran printed in Devanagari (the script used for writing Hindi) in order to reach their co-religionists. Urdu newspapers are also developing Hindi editions, but this effort does not enable them to resist the general trend very efficiently, as

Table 8.1 shows. The Muslims of Uttar Pradesh had to wait until the 1989 election campaign before the Congress state government declared Urdu as the second official language. This decision was obviously taken with an eye on the Muslim vote.

TABLE 8.1: Hindi and Urdu Media (Numbers of Each)

| | Dailies | | Weeklies | | Bi-monthlies | |
|---|---|---|---|---|---|---|
| | 1958 | 1990 | 1958 | 1990 | 1958 | 1990 |
| Hindi | 73 | 1381 | 233 | 4669 | 60 | 1652 |
| Urdu | 44 | 344 | 117 | 903 | 24 | 261 |

*Sources:* Hasan 1994: 32–73.

Such a tactical move was not new. Muslims supported the Congress after independence because, as a secular party, it promised to protect their interests better than any other party. Nehru especially was regarded as a custodian of Muslims' interests. The Congress maintained this relationship even after his death, but it tended to assume a more and more clientelistic form. The ruling party was eager to co-opt and patronize Muslim leaders who often turned out to exert a conservative influence over their community, especially when they were religious leaders. Gradually, the notion of secularism got perverted because of them and their association with the Congress Party.

The conservative leadership of the Muslim community erected the *Shariat* (the Muslim legal code) as a symbol of Muslim identity and of India's multiculturalism, whereas they did not show much tolerance themselves. This complex issue was well illustrated during the Shah Bano affair. Shah Bano, a Muslim woman, had been divorced by her husband according to the Shariat. On appealing to the courts, she was granted some alimony by the High Court of Madhya Pradesh where she lived, but her former husband appealed the decision before the Supreme Court which reconfirmed the judgement in 1985. Immediately, Muslim leaders started an agitation with 'Shariat in danger' as the standard slogan and went to Rajiv Gandhi, the prime minister. Gandhi, who did not want to alienate them, had the Congress Party vote an amendment in Parliament in order to exclude the Muslim community from the article of the Code of Criminal Procedure on the basis of which the Supreme Court had pronounced its judgement. This move was strongly disapproved of by the *Sangh Parivar* which saw it as a sign of the 'pseudo-secularism' of the Congress and of its pampering of the most obscurantist Muslims. The Shah Bano affair prepared the ground for the Hindu mobilization around Ayodhya.

The attitude of Rajiv Gandhi was in tune with the way his mother had tended to communalize politics after her comeback in 1980. On the one hand, she recognized the long-awaited status of autonomy for the Aligarh Muslim University in 1981 (Graff 1990: 1771–81), and on the other hand, she multiplied her visits to Hindu temples and let one of her lieutenants, C.M. Stephen, declare in 1983 that the Congress culture was on the 'same wavelength' as Hindu culture. Simultaneously, she gave indirect support to the Sikh extremist Sant Bhindranwale in order to destabilize the more moderate factions of the Akali Dal, the main rival of the Congress in Punjab. The second reign of Indira Gandhi was thus marked by an erosion of secularism which had been the dominant ideology of the Congress leadership at the Centre.

Similarly, Rajiv Gandhi did not choose one community over another but admitted the legitimacy of communal considerations in the public sphere. In 1986, he tried to balance his decision in the Shah Bano affair by accepting the demand of the VHP concerning the unlocking of the Babri Masjid, so that the Hindus could worship there. This concession, far from defusing the Hindu nationalist agitation re-launched it. Similarly, in 1989, he accepted that the first stone of the temple envisioned by the VHP was laid in front of the mosque, on disputed land. Rajiv Gandhi even started his election campaign from the neighbouring town of Faizabad, 'Ram's land' as he called it. He was obviously trying to hijack some of the Hindu mobilization which were boosting the BJP's electoral prospects. In fact, his tactic was responsible for removing all inhibition regarding the use of communal discourse in politics and prepared the ground for the unleashing of Hindu nationalism in the Ayodhya affair.

The Muslims were the first victims of this mobilization. As Table 8.2 shows, the average number of communal riots per annum jumped from 400 in 1980–5 to about 700 in 1986–9 and rose from 1,000 to 2,000 between 1990 and 1993. Rioting was especially intense before the elections, when the *Sangh Parivar* used communal violence as a means for polarising the electorate along religious lines. In 1989, out of the 88 constituencies where the BJP won the seat, 47 had just been affected by communal riots (Chiriyankandath 1992: 69). However, the worst riots took place after Hindu militants destroyed the Babri Masjid on 6 December 1992. At that time, Muslims demonstrated in the streets and attacked symbols of the state to protest against the leniency of the Congress government which, according to them, should have averted the demolition. Police forces and then Hindu activists retaliated. The toll was especially high in Bombay, Surat and Bhopal. The BJP was, in effect, punished for these excesses during the 1993 state elections when it lost Uttar Pradesh, Madhya Pradesh and Himachal Pradesh. The party then shifted from its strategy of ethno-religious mobilization to a more moderate approach in politics. As Table 8.2 shows, the number of riots started to decline at that time.

TABLE 8.2: HINDU-MUSLIM RIOTS (CONTINUED)

| Year | Number of riots | Number of deaths |
|------|-----------------|------------------|
| 1954 | 83 | 34 |
| 1955 | 72 | 24 |
| 1956 | 74 | 35 |

*(Table 8.2 continued)*

| Year | Number of riots | Number of deaths |
|------|-----------------|------------------|
| 1957 | 55 | 12 |
| 1958 | 41 | 7 |
| 1959 | 42 | 41 |
| 1960 | 26 | 14 |
| 1961 | 92 | 108 |
| 1962 | 60 | 43 |
| 1963 | 61 | 26 |
| 1964 | 1,070 | 1,919 |
| 1965 | 173 | 34 |
| 1966 | 133 | 45 |
| 1967 | 209 | 251 |
| 1968 | 346 | 133 |
| 1969 | 519 | 674 |
| 1970 | 521 | 298 |
| 1971 | 321 | 103 |
| 1972 | 240 | 70 |
| 1973 | 242 | 72 |
| 1974 | 248 | 87 |
| 1975 | 205 | 33 |
| 1976 | 169 | 39 |
| 1977 | 188 | 36 |
| 1978 | 219 | 108 |
| 1979 | 304 | 261 |
| 1980 | 427 | 375 |
| 1981 | 319 | 196 |
| 1982 | 474 | 238 |
| 1983 | 500 | 1,143 |
| 1984 | 476 | 445 |
| 1985 | 525 | 328 |
| 1986 | 764 | 418 |
| 1987 | 711 | 383 |
| 1988 | 611 | 223 |
| 1989 | 706 | 1,155 |
| 1990 | 1,404 | 1,248 |
| 1991 | 905 | 474 |
| 1992 | 1,991 | 1,640 |
| 1993 | 2,292 | 952 |
| 1994 | 179 | 78 |
| 1995 | Not available | 62 |
| 1996 | 728 | 209 |
| 1997 | 725 | 264 |
| 1998 | 626 | 207 |

*Sources:* Jaffrelot 1999(b): 552; for 1993–4, 'Ministry of Home Affairs' Note for Consultative Committee Meeting on Communal Situation', *Muslim India*, No. 156, December 1995, 558; for 1995, Engineer 1995: 3267–9; for 1996, 1997 and 1998, *Lok Sabha Questions*, Nos. 110, 23 February 1999, reproduced in *Muslim India* 1999: 161.

If the number of communal riots have returned to the level of the 1950s and 1960s, it does not mean that India is back to the situation that was prevailing then. The rise of the BJP is accompanied by a banalization of the Hindu nationalist discourse as testified by the Supreme Court verdict of December 1995. The judges had been asked to decide over the legality of the communal propaganda displayed by BJP and Shiv Sena leaders. Their utterances were obviously at odd with the Representation of the People Act which prohibits all references to religion during election campaigns. Surprisingly, the judges concluded that there was nothing wrong in canvassing on the theme of Hindutva (Hinduness) since this notion, like that of 'Hinduism', referred to 'a way of life', not to a religion.

Similarly, many communal riots have not been investigated seriously, like that of Bhopal in which there were 120 casualties in 1992. Nor have the reports of commissions of investigation been tabled before the assemblies or followed through in any way. The Bhagalpur riot, which resulted in about 1,000 casualties in 1989, the worst toll since 1947, was investigated by a commission but its report was made public almost eight years later and the judicial procedures followed were erratic:

The 142 cases filed in court accused 1,932 people of participating in incidents of violence and looting. Six years later, 87 cases against the 901 accused were still pending. Of the 55 cases decided, 11 have ended in convictions in which 50 people have been punished. Of the 406 people accused in murder cases, the court has decided on 95 people, of whom 94 have been acquitted. (*Economic and Political Weekly* 1996: 1057)

The growing under-representation of the Muslims in elected bodies also bears testimony of their relegation to the status of 'second class citizens'. As my computations show in Table 8.3, the gap between the percentage of the Muslims

TABLE 8.3: MUSLIMS IN THE LOK SABHA

| Year | Muslim MPs (No.) | Total MPs (No.) | Muslim MPs (%) | Muslims in population (%) |
|---|---|---|---|---|
| 1952 | 22 | 489 | 4.5 | 9.5 |
| 1957 | 26 | 494 | 5.3 | 9.5 |
| 1962 | 23 | 494 | 4.6 | 10.7 |
| 1967 | 30 | 520 | 5.7 | 10.7 |
| 1971 | 30 | 518 | 5.8 | 11.2 |
| 1977 | 32 | 542 | 5.9 | 11.2 |
| 1980 | 47 | 529 | 8.9 | 11.2 |
| 1984 | 47 | 542 | 8.7 | 11.4 |
| 1989 | 32 | 544 | 5.9 | 11.4 |
| 1991 | 27 | 544 | 5.0 | 12.1 |
| 1996 | 21 | 544 | 3.8 | 12.1 |
| 1998 | 27 | 544 | 4.9 | 12.1 |

*Sources:* Data compiled by author.

in the Indian population and their share of the Lok Sabha has never been so pronounced as in the 1990s. Not only does the BJP, which has become the largest party in Parliament since 1996, not give tickets to many Muslim candidates, but the Congress has been doing the same because the general atmosphere makes their chances of winning very slim.

The under-representation of Muslims in the administration and the police continues to be very pronounced. In 1991 they represented only 4.9 per cent of the police force in Uttar Pradesh (where they formed 17.3 per cent of the population), 4.2 per cent in Maharashtra, 6.2 per cent in Gujarat and 2.3 per cent in Delhi (Hasan 1997: 294). At an all-India level, Muslims represent only 5.5 per cent of the Central Reserve Police Force and 4.4 per cent of the central administration (forming less than 3 per cent of its elite group, the Indian Administrative Service) (*India Today*, 31 January 1993: 31-7). In the private sector, a survey of the eight largest Indian firms in 1984 showed that the share of Muslims among the executives varied between zero and 5.6 per cent (Hasan 1988: 2470)·

In the rural areas also, data collected by the National Sample Survey Organisation has shown that in 1987–88 Muslims on average owned less land than Hindus, as highlighted in Table 8.4.

TABLE 8.4: Land Ownership Among Hindus and Muslims (In %)

| Size of Plot of Land | Hindus | Muslims |
|---|---|---|
| Landless | 28.0 | 34.7 |
| Less than 1 acre | 17.3 | 24.4 |
| 1-2.5 acres | 18.3 | 17.5 |
| 2.5-5 acres | 16.3 | 12.9 |
| More than 5 acres | 20.1 | 10.5 |

*Sources: Muslim India* 1994: 378.

The same survey also highlighted the backwardness of Muslims in terms of education. The illiteracy rates are 42.4 and 59.5 per cent for Muslim men and women respectively, and 25.3 and 42.2 for Hindu men and women. In keeping with the pattern, in rural India 58.2 per cent of the males and 76.1 per cent of the females are illiterate amongst Muslims, as against 51.3 per cent and 75 per cent respectively for the Hindus (*Muslim India* 1994: 378). This lack of education is in part due to the anti-Urdu policies of the states but also due to the archaic system of the Koranic schools favoured by many Muslims. In turn, it partly explains the under-representation of Muslims in the administration.

The secular regime that was enshrined in the Indian constitution half a century ago still remains far short of its expectations. Nehru's dream of multiculturalism has largely turned sour. One might argue that he should be considered responsible for this state of affairs, that he prepared the ground for the Hindu backlash since he failed to impose the same treatment such as a common civil code for instance on people of all creeds. Yet, as this essay argues, communal tensions in post-independence India have much deeper roots.

The interaction between the religions of India has gradually transformed them into something different. The worldly non-spiritual aspect of them has acquired a political and ideological dimension. Hinduism has probably undergone the most profound change of all in recent times after ideologues have attempted to endow what they regarded as an amorphous and quietist collection of sects with a proselytizing mission and disciplined organization. Paradoxically, in this process, they have tended to imitate the 'semitic religions' they professed to stigmatize.

The resulting ideology of Hindu nationalism has been supported by a network of organizations—the *Sangh Parivar*—whose strength has no equivalent. In addition to their deep-rooted implantation in certain segments of the society, Hindu nationalists have now captured the state apparatus and are attempting to use it to propagate their views.

The first casualties of this trend have been the Muslims who already suffered the prejudice of many Congress leaders in the states in north India. Their continuing, and even growing, marginalization in the administration, in elected bodies and in the economy jeopardize the very multiculturalist aspirations of 'the largest democracy in the world'.

Indian Muslims, however, are beginning to develop alternative strategies. While some of their leaders have adopted defensive postures by asking for quotas in the administration, members of the intelligentsia are trying to emancipate their community from the influence of obscurantist religious leaders. More importantly, Indian Muslims have started to use their main asset—their numbers—so precious at the time of elections to consolidate an alliance with opponents to the *Sangh Parivar*, to be found not only among the religious minorities, such as the Christians who have also suffered atrocities during the Vajpayee governments, but also the lower castes who are fighting the Hindutva movement because it is directed by 'twice-born Hindus'.

## Notes

1. Romila Thapar explains that this exclusion is not based on a racial criterion; it is social and ritual and hence can be overcome via acculturation and recognition of the superiority of the Brahman. See, Thapar 1978: 165, 169 and 179.
2. *Lok Sabha Debates* 1990: 633. For more details, see Jaffrelot 1992: 251–70. Today, the BMS has about 4.5 million members.
3. The Hindu nationalists translate 'indigenous peoples' by *vanavasi*, literally 'those of the forest' and not, as is generally the case in India, by *adivasi*, i.e. 'those who were there before', because from their point of view, the country's first inhabitants were the 'Aryans' and not the autochthonous populations which were driven back or conquered by the Aryan invaders, from whom today's tribes are descended.
4. *Hindu Vishva*, 21 March 1986: 30. The term 'Bajrang' is generally attached to the name of Hanuman (the monkey leader and head of the armies of Ram) to characterize his strength.

# References

Barthval, H. (1998), *Rashtriya Swayamsevak Sangh: Ek Parichay*, New Delhi: Suruchi Prakashan.

Brass, P. (1974), *Language, Religion and Politics in North India*, Cambridge: Cambridge University Press.

Chiriyankandath, J. (1992), 'Tricolour and Saffron: Congress and the New Hindu Challenge', in S.K. Mitra and J. Chiriyankandath (eds.), *Electoral Politics in India: A Changing Landscape*, New Delhi: Segment Books.

*Economic and Political Weekly* (1996), 'Recalling Bhagalpur: Aftermath of 1989 Riots', 4 May.

Engineer, A. A. (1995), 'Communalism and Communal Violence in 1995', *Economic and Political Weekly*, 23 December.

Freitag, L.S. (1990), *Collective Action and Community: Public Arenas and the Emergence of Communalism in North India*, Delhi: Oxford University Press.

Golwalkar, M.S. (1939), *We, or Our Nationhood Defined*, Nagpur: Bharat Prakashan.

—— (1966), *Bunch of Thoughts*, Bangalore: Jagaran Prakashan.

Graff, V. (1990), 'Aligarh's Long Quest for "Minority" Status: AMU (Amendment) Act, 1981', *Economic and Political Weekly*, 11 August.

Hasan, M. (1988), 'In Search of Integration and Identity: Indian Muslims since Independence', *Economic and Political Weekly*, November.

—— (1990), 'Adjustment and Accommodation: Indian Muslims after Partition', *Social Scientist*, Vol. 18, Nos. 8–9, August-September.

—— (1994), 'Minority Identity and its Discontents: Ayodhya and its Aftermath', *South Asia Bulletin*, Vol. 14, No. 2.

—— (1997), *Legacy of a Divided Nation: India's Muslims Since Independence*, London: Hurst.

*Hindu Vishva* (1982), March-April.

—— (1986), 21 March.

*Indian National Congress* (1988), Delhi: Oxford University Press.

*India Today* (1993), 31 January.

Jaffrelot, C. (1992), 'Note sur un syndicat nationaliste hindou: le travail et les travailleurs dans l'idéologie et les stratégies du Bharatiya Mazdoor Sangh', in G. Heuzé (ed.), *Travailler en Inde, Purushartha*, No. 14, Paris: EHESS.

—— (1995), 'The Idea of the Hindu Race in the Writings of Hindu Nationalist Ideologues in the 1920s and the 1930s: A Concept Between Two Cultures', in P. Robb (ed.), *The Concept of Race in South Asia*, Delhi: Oxford University Press.

—— (1999a), 'The Vishva Hindu Parishad: Structures and Strategies', in J. Haynes (ed.), *Religion, Globalisation and Political Culture in the Third World*, London: Macmillan.

—— (1999b), *The Hindu Nationalist Movement in India*, New Delhi: Penguin.

*Lok Sabha Debates* (1990), Third Session, Col. 8, No. 2, New Delhi: Lok Sabha Secretariat.

*Lok Sabha Questions* (1999), No. 110, 23 February 1999, reproduced in *Muslim India*, No. 196, April.

Minault, G. (1982), *The Khilafat Movement: Religious Symbolism and Political Mobilization in India*, New York: Columbia University Press.

*Muslim India* (1994), No. 140, August.

Pandey, G. (1990), *The Construction of Communalism in Colonial North India*, Delhi: Oxford University Press.

Stienencron, H. von (1989), 'Hinduism: On the Proper Use of a Deceptive Term', in G.D. Sontheimer and H. Kulke (eds.), *Hinduism Reconsidered*, New Delhi: Manohar.

Thapar, R. (1978), *Ancient Indian History*, New Delhi: Orient Longman.

―――― (1985), 'Syndicated Moksha', *Seminar*, September.

# II

## The *Sangh Parivar*

# Chapter 9

# The *Sangh Parivar*: how cohesive is this family?

The *Sangh Parivar* means the family of the Sangh, that is the family of the Rashtriya Swayamsevak Sangh. This organization, better known as the RSS, is the last *avatar* of a series of Hindu militant movements ranging from the Arya Samaj to the Hindu Mahasabha. Born in 1925, the RSS has drawn most of its ideological inspiration from Vinayak Damodar Savarkar who was to take over the Hindu Mahasabha in 1937. In his book, *Hindutva: Who is a Hindu?* (1923), Savarkar considers that the Indian national identity is embodied in the Hindu culture, which encompasses not only Hinduism—as a religion—but also a language, Sanskrit (and its main vernacular derivative, Hindi), the worship of Hindustan as a sacred land and the cult of the Vedic Golden Age. His motto was 'Hindu, Hindi, Hindusthan!' In Savarkar's views the religious minorities are requested to pay allegiance to this dominant identity and to hold back the manifestations of their faith within the private sphere.

The RSS was founded by one of Savarkar's admirers, Keshav Baliram Hedgewar in a very specific context. Indeed the 1920s were marked by a pan-Islamic mobilization, the Khilafat Movement, which aimed at vindicating the status of Caliph held by the Ottoman Sultan. This movement targeted first the British—who were among the victors of the First World War and who were eager to punish Turkey for its role during the war—but it affected Hindus too. Hindu-Muslim riots took place in different places, including today's Kerala. Hindu nationalist leaders then proclaimed that their community needed to organize itself in order to resist its aggressors: they cashed in on a new Hindu feeling of vulnerability and Hedgewar reacted to it and exploited it by launching the RSS.

## The RSS: A Pervasive Network

In contrast to most of the other nationalist movements, including the fascist ones, the RSS did not look at the conquest of state power as its priority. In fact, it preferred to remain aloof from the political arena for decades—it even resisted the attempts by Savarkar to enrol its activists in the electoral campaigns of the Hindu Mahasabha in the last years of the British Raj. For its first *sarsanghchalak*, Hedgewar, and his successor, M.S. Golwalkar who took over from him in 1940,[1] the priority work was to reform the Hindus, to reframe Hindu society from below—not from above through the state apparatus. They both looked at the Hindus as weak and vulnerable vis-à-vis the Muslims. They were also apprehensive of the new militancy of the lower castes and feared the growing appeal of Gandhi's brand of Hinduism which emphasized non-violence. They aspired, on the contrary, to restore—and even create—a martial brand of Hinduism and to reshape the mind and the body of the Hindus in order to make them warrior-like.

In order to achieve this objective, Hedgewar initiated a very specific modus operandum epitomized by the *shakha*. *Shakha* means 'branch': in the RSS arrangement it still designates the basic unit of the whole edifice. It is both a place and a social group: every day the members of one *shakha* meet at the same place for accomplishing physical exercises and to listen to ideological sermons. Children are the main targets of the RSS because they like to exercise and they are more intellectually malleable. To attract them towards the *shakhas* the physical part of the daily programme is given more importance and includes many games—many *swayamsevaks* have often joined the RSS to play *kho-kho* or *kabaddi*. Gradually, these games prepare the ground for more muscular activities—including the plying of the *lathi*—and men to more disciplined drills, marches, and the ceremonial saluting of the flag, the 'saffron *dhwaj*' that the RSS regards as its guru. So far as the ideological propaganda is concerned, daily sessions in the *shakhas* are marked by oriented commentaries of the most topical issues and historical perspectives ranging from recollections of the Vedic golden age to the heroic deeds of Shivaji or other Hindu warriors who fought against 'Muslim invaders'. The *shakhas* are intended to include Hindus from all castes and classes. They are the 'Hindu Rashtra' in miniature, the crucible of the ethnic nation.

For decades, the main aim of the RSS has been to expand the *shakhas'* network. Hedgewar decided to train a special body of *swayamsevaks* to this effect, the *pracharaks*. The members of this avant-garde, were supposed to dedicate their whole life to the RSS. Even though they were often well-educated, they gave up the idea of embracing a professional career. They did not marry either. Instead, the RSS became their family, a sort of 'brotherhood in saffron' as suggested by Walter Andersen and Shridhar Damle (1987). Their sacrifice for the higher cause of the nation was sublimated in the RSS discourse through the religious idiom of the world-renouncer: the *pracharaks* were described as *karma yogis*, saintly characters who emulated the key figures of the *Mahabharata*, Arjun, and Krishna who acted in society for the benefit of the whole world.

As a result, the network of the RSS *shakhas* expanded steadily. Its epicentre was in Nagpur, where Hedgewar had founded the movement. It grew rapidly in the north. The Hindi belt laid itself more open than any other region to such an expansion. First, it spoke the language that the RSS regarded as the national language par excellence. Second, it coincided with the birthplace of the Aryan civilization—the Aryavarta—according to the Hindu nationalist ideologues. Third, the Hindi belt was also the region where the upper castes 'twice-born' were in largest numbers. In the United Provinces—post-independence Uttar Pradesh— they represented one-fifth of the population with about 10 per cent Brahmans, whereas these *dvijas* accounted for less than half this proportion in most of the rest of India. Now, the RSS ideology had strong affinities with the ethos of the Hindu upper castes. The *pracharaks* drew most of their inspiration from what the RSS calls the Hindu *saṃskars,* that is the orthopraxy of the brahmanical way of life and inculcated these values in the youths in these *shakhas.* In fact, parents often appreciated that their children attended the *shakha* because it helped them to learn good manners and to comply with the dominant social code.

In 1939, the RSS had 40,000 members distributed in about 500 *shakhas* and in 1943, 76,000—including 35,000 in the then Central Provinces, 20,000 in Bombay Presidency, and 14,000 in Punjab ('Note on the Volunteer Movement in India') where the growing tensions between Hindus and Muslims made the RSS more attractive for the former who looked at it as a militia providing self-defence techniques. The context of Partition enabled the RSS to make further inroads in north India: in 1948, there were about 600,000 *swayamsevaks,* mostly in north India (Andersen and Damle 1987: 50). The movement suffered from a severe setback in 1948–9 because of the assassination of Mahatma Gandhi by one of its former members, Nathuram Godse. Jawaharlal Nehru had the RSS banned and 20,000 *swayamsevaks* arrested, but things returned to normalcy in early 1950 after the movement adopted a Constitution that was supposed to avoid such extreme acts of violence in the future. In 1951, the RSS was back to its 1948 pattern: it had 600,000 *swayamsevaks,* most of them concentrated in central and northern India, The regions where the movement was the strongest were Uttar Pradesh (200,000 members), Madhya Pradesh (125,000), the greater Punjab (Delhi and Himachal Pradesh included, 125,000), Bombay Presidency (60,000) and Bihar (50,000) (Curran 1951: 14, 43).

The RSS network continued to grow rather steadily in the 1950s–60s. It registered a second setback in 1975–6 because of another ban during the Emergency. But the Janata phase, during which Hindu nationalist leaders including Atal Behari Vajpayee and Lal Krishna Advani were part of the Union Government, was marked by a vigorous growth: the number of *shakhas* jumped from 10,000 in 1977 to 13,000 in 1979. The number of *swayamsevaks* then crossed the 1 million landmark (*The Hindustan Times,* 19 April 1977; *The Organiser,* 12 March 1978; *The Indian Express,* 15 May 1978 and Deora n.d.: 7, 32). The expansion continued at the same pace in the early 1980s: the number of *shakhas* rose to 17,000 in 1981 (*The Organiser,* 5 April 1981, 14 February 1982: 4), 20,000 in 1985 (*The Organiser,* 10 November 1985) and 25,000 (in 18,890 localities since many cities now had more than one *shakha,* which came to be called *upshakhas*) in 1989, that is 1.8 million *swayamsevaks* (*India Today,* 30 June 1989: 40–3). The development of *shakhas* was less vigorous in the 1990s. According to RSS sources there were 27,264 *shakhas* and 39,175 *upshakhas* in 1998 (Bathval 1998: 16). At the same time, the weekly magazine *Outlook* gave almost the same figure—39,301 *upshakhas*—and a very interesting regional break up: Uttar Pradesh still came first, with 9,000, but Kerala came second with 4,149, before Maharashtra (4,000), Rajasthan (3,500), Madhya

Pradesh (3,230), Karnataka (2,305), Bihar (2,300), Andhra Pradesh (1,660), West Bengal (1,500), Delhi (1,500), Orissa (1,481) and Tamil Nadu (1,051).[2] In 2001, in his annual report before the Akhil Bharatiya Pratinidhi Sabha (ABPS) of the RSS, the General Secretary of the organization indicated that it had 30,053 *shakhas* and 43,535 *upshakhas* (*The Organiser*, 25 March 2001: 20). In 2003, he gave the figures, respectively, of 32,075 and 46,000 and in 2004, 33,758 and 48,329 (ibid., 28 March 2004: 11). From 10,000 *shakhas* in the 1970s to 30,000 in 2000, by and large, the network of the RSS has tripled while India's population had doubled, from 548 millions in the 1971 census to about one billion in 2000.

The RSS is a very rare example of an organization which remained faithful to the same method for 80 years. In 2000, its Joint General Secretary, Mohanrao Bhagwat reasserted this stand in explicit terms:

Our endeavour is to reach out to each and every person in the society, widen our approach and raise the level of consciousness of the common man. And for this man-making nation-building mission we have chosen shakha as the instrument . . . . We believe that individual is the best instrument to effect change in society. And shakha is the best medium to create such individuals. (ibid., 19 March 2004: 4)

Yet, in addition to its *shakha*-based network, the RSS has developed several fronts and given shape, thereby, to the *Sangh Parivar*.

## The Matrix and its Affiliates

When Laxmibai Kelkar, a woman who admired his work, came to Hedgewar in order to know how women could benefit from the RSS work, he advised her to set up a parallel organization for women. This is how the Rashtra Sevika Samiti was born in 1936, and was based on the RSS model. It has now about 3,500 branches all over India. The creation of the Rashtra Sevika Samiti on the same pattern 11 years after that of the RSS is revealing of Hedgewar's obsession with the establishment of a network covering the whole of the Indian society. In his last speech he urged his followers to continue the work he had started in unambiguous terms: 'Remember, we have to organise the entire Hindu society from Kanyakumari to the Himalayas' (Deshpande and Ramaswamy 1981: 188).

However, Hedgewar's successor, Golwalkar gradually realized that the RSS modus operandum would not be sufficient to achieve the ultimate aim that was to cover and permeate the whole of society. He reaffirmed that goal in emphatic terms in his first speech to the ABPS after independence in late 1947: 'Continuously expanding amongst the Hindu society we hope to reach a stage where the Sangh and the entire Hindu society will be completely identical. This is bound to happen in the course of time for there is no escape' (*Hitavada*, 31 December 1947: 55).

Such an objective did not imply only the criss-crossing of the territory by *shakhas*. Society also got organized in many different ways, through unions and interest groups whose ideologies sometimes went against those of Hindu nationalism. How could the RSS counter these social forces? The stakes were especially high after independence because of the growing activism of the communists. Not only had the insurgency in Telangana worried the RSS leaders, but the ground work of student unionists on the university campuses showed them that the Left might be posing a continuous threat to their own activities. At that time, the RSS had convinced itself that the Congress was bound to disappear and that it was destined to remain face to face with the Left (*The Organiser*, 6 June 1950: 5). In reaction, an RSS activist, Balraj Madhok, launched in Delhi the first front organization of the RSS in July 1948, the Akhil Bharatiya Vidyarthi Parishad (ABVP). In contrast to the 'red unions' the ABVP was not formed to foster student power but to bring about collaboration between all those involved in university education since 'the teachers and the taught are both wheels of the same car' (*The Organiser*, 6 November 1948: 5). Such a philosophy was to pervade all the creations of unionist fronts by the RSS: the aim was to resist the proponents of class struggle and to promote a conflict-free society. The ABVP relayed the RSS influence on many campuses of north India. It was at the forefront of agitational politics in the 1970s during the JP movement, which resulted in the coming together of many student activists in Bihar and Gujarat. The ABVP drew rich dividend from this mobilization after the Emergency. Its membership reached 170,000 students and teachers in 1977 and jumped to 250,000 in 1982 (Andersen and Damle 1987: 215). The growth of the ABVP continued in the 1990s, a decade during which it became the largest student union of India. In 2003, it was still the first student union with 1,101,000 members (<http://www.abvp.org>).

Logically enough, the RSS launched a network of schools soon after targeting the students: its aim had always been the reshaping of the youth's mind, as well as the strengthening of his body. It was therefore quite natural that in addition to the ABVP and the *shakhas* network, *pracharaks* start an educational movement. An exceptionally dynamic *pracharak*, Nanaji Deshmukh, a Maharashtrian Brahman who had been sent to Gorakhpur, in Uttar Pradesh, initiated the first component of this new front of the RSS in 1952 under a very evocative name, the Saraswati Shishu Mandir. These 'Mandirs' were federated and put under an umbrella organization called Vidya Bharati in 1977 with its headquarters in Delhi. At that time, Vidya Bharati ran 700 schools (*The Organiser*, 19 November 1978: 1). In the early 1990s, the organization was responsible for managing 5,000 schools with 1.2 million pupils enrolled and 40,000 teachers employed (Khanna 1991: 22-3). In 2003 it had 14,000 schools, 73,000 teachers and 1.7 million pupils (<http://www. rss.org/New_RSS/parivaar/History.jsp>). The expansion of the RSS in the field of education was made easier by the growing demand of education everywhere in India, including the villages, and the growing disaffection of the middle class with the ill-managed and underfunded public system.

Among the first components of the *Sangh Parivar* was also a political party. Till the 1950s the RSS chiefs had all preferred to remain aloof from politics, considering that the political game could only exert a corrupt influence on the mind of the *swayamsevaks*. In any case they did not want to conquer power; they wanted to conquer society in order to gain power as a ripe fruit. Golwalkar therefore used to dismiss political activities: 'We aspire to become the radiating centre of all the age-old cherished ideals of our society—just as the indescribable power which radiates through the sun. Then the political power which draws its life from that source of society, will have no other [goal] but to reflect the same radiance' (Golwalkar 1966: 103). Golwalkar changed his mind in 1948–9 for tactical reasons. After Gandhi's assassination, the RSS was banned and nobody came out to argue its case in Parliament. Senior *swayamsevaks* then considered that the movement needed some political branch. In December 1949, K.R. Malkani wrote in the RSS mouthpiece, *The Organiser:*

Sangh must take part in politics not only to protect itself against the greedy designs of politicians but to stop the un-Bharatiya and anti-Bharatiya policies of the Government and to advance and expedite the cause of Bharatiya through state machinery side by side with official effort in the same direction . . . Sangh must continue as it is, an *ashram* for the national cultural education of the entire citizenry, but it must develop a political wing for the more effective and early achievements of its ideals. (*The Organiser*, 1 December 1949: 7–14)

The idea of the *Sangh Parivar* was taking shape: RSS leaders now thought in terms of creating wings' of the organization to reach out to domains in which they were not active, like party politics. In this case, however, the RSS did not create a party alone, but co-founded one with Shyama Prasad Mookerjee, the president of the Hindu Mahasabha who was more than happy to receive the support of the Sangh for launching a more dynamic political organization. The Bharatiya Jana Sangh was established just before the first general election in 1951. Mookerjee died in 1953 and the RSS leaders who had been seconded to the party apparatus—among whom Deendayal Upadhyaya was the more prominent— immediately took over power and marginalized the old lieutenants of Mookerjee.

Upadhyaya was not the president of the party but its General Secretary. Presidents were better known public figures, but they never remained in office for very long and they had little authority over the party apparatus. Upadhyaya gained most of the power within the party structure. Gradually, he appointed RSS-trained party members at key posts, at the national level as well as at the state level. These *swayamsevaks* usually occupied the position of *sangathan mantris*, that is 'organising secretaries'. They formed the party's steel frame. The party-building pattern which crystallized under Upadhyaya therefore enabled the RSS to exert a strong influence over the Jana Sangh simply because of the relationship between the party cadres and their mother organization.

This pattern was systematically resorted to when the RSS initiated new front organizations. In 1952, Vanavasi Kalyan Ashram was founded in Jashpur (today's Chhattisgarh) by R.K. Deshpande, an RSS man who wanted to counter the growing influence of the Christian missionaries among the *adivasis*. The main objective of the VKA was to reconvert those who had become Christians. To attract the tribals the VKA established free hostels, hospitals, and schools. In fact, the VKA imitated the Christian missions which were adept at this kind of philanthropic work in order to counter them more effectively. The former Maharaja of Jashpur supported the VKA in the 1960s and then joined the Jana Sangh. His son, Dilip Singh Judeo took over from him in both capacities in the 1980s: as patron of the VKA he launched operations of reconversion in the tribal belt and as politial leader he contested elections on the BJP ticket—before becoming Union Minister in the Vajpayee government. The VKA, by then, was run by another *pracharak*, Bhaskarrao, who had come to Chhattisgarh from Kerala in 1984.

The *Sangh Parivar* arrangement, therefore, associated notables—be they political notables occupying the post of party president in the Jana Sangh or former Maharajas patronizing the VKA—with RSS workers, who did all the organization work.

The same modus operandum applied in the case of the fifth component of the *Sangh Parivar*, the Bharatiya Mazdoor Sangh (BMS). Once again, *pracharaks* were given a mandate to open a new front while emulating enemies of the RSS to counter them more efficiently. In the late 1940s, Golwalkar, who worried about the communist influence among the working class, asked D.P. Thengadi, a Maharashtrian *pracharak*, to infiltrate 'red' labour unions in order to gain the experience he would need in order to form a workers' branch of the RSS. He therefore joined the INTUC (the labour union affiliated to the Congress), revived its Madhya Pradesh branch and then set up his own union, the BMS (interview with G. Prabhakar, General Secretary of the BMS, 5 December 1990, Bhopal). During the BMS inaugural conference which took place in Bhopal, Thengadi declared Communism his 'enemy number one' (*The Organiser*, 1 August 1995: 13) and entrusted the union with the task to fight the ideology of class struggle. Instead, the BMS was intended to favour the collaboration of all the social components of society and to restore the supposedly lost harmony by promoting a corporatist socio-political arrangement.

The BMS has been increasingly successful, so much so it became the largest labour union in the 1990s. In 2000, according to the RSS website the BMS had about 3,400 unions with a 4.5 million membership across the country (<http://www.rss.org.parivar>).

In the 1960s, an attempt at organizing the peasants (*kisans*) was initiated in Vidarbha by RSS *pracharaks*, including Bhau Sahab Bhuskhute—once again a Maharashtrian Brahman. This endeavour was repeated in Uttar Pradesh in 1972 and finally, in 1979, an all India session was organized for the official launch of the Bharatiya Kisan Sangh. The main objectives of the BKS are the development of 'research work for agricultural development' and 'to determine and settle the profitable rates for the agricultural producer' (<http://www.rss.org/New_RSS/

parivaar/History.jsp>). Like the BMS, the BKS is opposed to radical forms of agitation: as the RSS website says, 'BKS not only thinks of its interest but also broods for the country's interest as well'. In 2000, according to the RSS website the BKS was active in 301 districts and 11,000 villages with a membership of 250,000 peasants (<http://www.rss.org>).

The seventh major component of the *Sangh Parivar*, the Vishva Hindu Parishad, was founded in 1964. The usual pattern applied once again: the RSS seconded a senior *pracharak*, Shiv Shankar Apte, one more Maharashtrian Brahman, to create a new front in the religious domain, a domain that the *Sangh* had left untouched so far. This need for organizing the Hindu religious sects, again was determined by some feeling of vulnerability—and its manipulation. RSS leaders pointed out that the Hindu sects represented innumerable rival schools of thought. And this division was perceived as the root cause for the weaknesses of Hinduism vis-à-vis other religions, including Christianity, whose missionaries were described as converting Hindus en masse. The VHP was therefore created to endow Hinduism with a church-like centralized structure and to use this new ecclesiastical apparatus to counter Christian proselyte activities. Like other components of the *Sangh Parivar*, the RSS cadres who were despatched to the VHP worked hand in hand with notables—former Maharajas, businessmen, respectable politicians—who formally presided over the organization as prestigious patrons. What was new, of course, was the involvement of a third group, the religious heads of several Hindu sects and monastries who were bridging the ideological world of the *Sangh Parivar* and the religious world of the *ashrams* and *maths*. In the 1980s–90s these saffron-clad religious figures were to be at the forefront of the VHP's Ayodhya movement.

The Rashtra Sevika Samiti, the ABVP, the Saraswati Shishu Mandirs, the Jana Sangh, the VKA, the BMS, and the VHP were the first components of the *Sangh Parivar* and have considerably developed in the course of time.[3] In the 1990s, the BJP—the political heir of the Jana Sangh—has even become the largest party in Parliament; the ABVP the largest student union and the BMS the largest labour union. All the components of the *Parivar* were clearly intended to prolong the work of the RSS since the aim remained the same: to penetrate society in depth, at the grassroot level, and to convert it to Hindu nationalism. Simply, the fronts of the RSS could accomplish its work in a more subtle way. They projected themselves as social, political or religious organizations, not as RSS subsidiaries. Therefore, they could attract those who disapproved of the RSS para-military style and its anti-minority discourse. They were like masks of the RSS. Second, in their respective fields, they emulated the opponents that the RSS had identified as its primary targets in order to counter them more effectively—be they communist unionists or Christian missionaries. Third, they systematically relied on the collaboration of RSS *pracharaks* and respectable notables who patronized the organizations.

## How Coherent and Remote-Controlled are the Components of the *Sangh Parivar*?

Officially, each component of the *Sangh Parivar* is completely autonomous and RSS leaders deny the very idea that they form a network. In the 1980s-90s BJP leaders like L.K. Advani and K.N. Govindacharya had 'fashioned the idea of the *Parivar* as a harmonizer of divergent though not always conflicting interests' (*India Today*, 11 November 2002: 30), but the *sarsanghchalak* who took over from Rajendra Singh in 2000, K.S. Sudarshan challenged this interpretation:

We don't call it *Parivar* at all. In the media it is called a *Parivar*. We say *Sangh* and allied organisations. Allied in the sense that we take inspiration from the Hindu thought process, but each organisation is independent.

What's meant by a *Parivar*? That there is a head who can impose his will. We can't thrust our decisions on anyone, we can only suggest. Our *swayamsevaks* decide where the suggestion is valid and get it accepted by the particular organisation. They try and ensure that this balance and cooperation is maintained. (Ibid.: 34)

### CONCEALING AN ILLEGITIMATE RELATION

This reading of the inner functioning of the *Sangh Parivar* can be interpreted in two different ways. One can argue that it is purely tactical; that it aims at hiding a highly centralized modus operandi. Such a dissimulation may be part of the RSS attempt at attracting in its nebulae new members who do not adhere to its ideology but may join one of its affiliates without any problem. This dissimulation may be especially significant in the case of the political wing of the RSS. This component of the *Sangh Parivar* is altogether different from the others, simply because parties belong to the public arena and when their members occupy official charges in assemblies or governments they must honour the people's mandate, not go by the diktat of a secret organization like the RSS which has no democratic legitimacy. This issue came to the fore in the late 1970s when *swayamsevaks* from the Jana Sangh joined hands with other opposition parties, merged into a new party, the Janata Party—which won the 1977 elections—and when two of them, A.B. Vajpayee and L.K. Advani, became ministers at the Centre. Other Janata Party leaders who did not come from the Jana Sangh objected that these *swayamsevaks* divided their loyalty between two different organizations, the party and the RSS. Indeed, the RSS appeared proactive in political matters behind the scene. It had offered its help to the government in tasks aimed at 'raising the national and social consciousness of our people' (*The Organiser*, 28 May 1977: 1) and non-Jana Sangh members of the Janata Party feared that it should become an 'extra-constitutional authority' (Goyal 1978: 196), hence the dual membership controversy. This episode is one of the grimmest chapters of the RSS story. Some of the ex-Jana Sanghis of the Janata Party, including A.B. Vajpayee, were deeply disturbed by the controversy. Vajpayee suggested that the *swayamsevaks* who were in politics should distance themselves from the RSS (Jaffrelot 1999: 310). But no compromise could be found and the Janata Party broke in 1979 and in 1980 the ex-Jana Sanghis founded the BJP.

Therefore, the RSS may be especially concerned with the concealing of its links with the BJP in order to avoid the re-enactment of a controversy similar to the dual membership episode. This preoccupation was very obvious when the National Democratic Alliance, the BJP-led coalition took over power in 1998. The BJP then down played its Hindu nationalist ideology because most of its allies professed some secular ideology. The party even placed contentious issues such as the building of a Ram Mandir in Ayodhya on the back burner. And the RSS *sarsanghchalak*, Rajendra Singh declared immediately:

We will not hold the government on a leash, nor turn the heat on it. There is nothing common between the BJP and us, we only share an ideology. The only thing we would expect is that the government will not hinder our activities like Indira Gandhi or the Communist government in Kerala. (Interview with Gautham Machaiah in *The Times of India*, 28 March 1998)

Two years later, the General Secretary of the BJP, Venkaiah Naidu, declared that the party had no 'organic link' with the RSS, which was a 'cultural and social' organization. He insisted that the very notion of *Sangh Parivar* was a creation of the media (*The Hindu*, 13 February 2000). But in September 2002, the same man, who had just been appointed President of the BJP emphatically declared, 'We are proud of our connections with the RSS' (*Central Chronicle*, 5 September 2002), as if things could be told, at last. Indeed, it seems that the inhibitions which affected the *Sangh Parivar* so far as the RSS/BJP relation was concerned have been lifted. The turning point, in this process, was the 2002 Gujarat riots. It then turned out that the NDA allies were prepared to remain associated with the BJP even though the Chief Minister of Gujarat, Narendra Modi, an RSS man, had displayed a staunch Hindu communal bias. The BJP could be frank about its core identity—including its relationship with the RSS—since its NDA allies were not as concerned with secularism as those of the Janata Party 20 years ago: none of the big ones left the ruling coalition or even protested somewhat vehemently.

The rapprochement of the BJP and the RSS found expression in the growing interest of the latter in administration and electoral matters. The BJP let the RSS invest in the political arena more and more directly. In 2003, after the party's victory during the Madhya Pradesh state elections, the RSS decided to have one of its cadres, Anil Dave, appointed special advisor to the new Chief Minister, Uma Bharti. Soon after, one of her ministers, a BJP leader, declared: 'If the RSS really intervenes in the administration, then it will be good and result in curbing rampant corruption' (ibid., 22 December 2003). The 2004 election campaign reconfirmed the growing eagerness of the RSS to exert some control over the BJP. The Sangh explicitly disapproved of the import of leaders from other parties—especially those who had defected from the Congress. It was anxious, not only to have committed *swayamsevaks* among the party cadres, but also, for the first time, among the party candidates. According to reliable press reports, the RSS leaders have indicated that at least one winnable seat in every district of northern and western states should have a committed RSS activist as the candidate (*The Hindu*, 10 March 2004): the RSS was willing to be represented in the Parliamentary party to monitor it.

To sum up: for years the RSS played down the existence of a *Sangh Parivar* in order to conceal its special relationship with the BJP. The bad memory of the dual membership controversy largely explains this tactic. But in reality, the RSS is not reducing, but strengthening its links with the BJP.

However, the way the RSS minimizes the idea of a *Sangh Parivar* can be interpreted in a different manner, that is, in spite of regular meetings with all its affiliates, the RSS has not been able to maintain their cohesion.

## INTERNAL CONFLICTS

The RSS became aware of the need to create new structures for ensuring the cohesion of its affiliates in the 1970s. In 1977 it 'established forums called *samanvaya samitis* (coordination committees) designed to bring together full-time workers from the RSS and from the affiliates at the district and state levels' (Andersen and Damle 1987: 142). In addition to these local developments, the leaders of the RSS and its main affiliates started to meet rather secretly.[4] To begin with, the leaders of the components of the *Sangh Parivar* went to the RSS headquarters in Nagpur in order to discuss their own strategies and take some of their orders. The RSS therefore plays a role in coordinating its family—one of its senior officers, by the way, is in charge of this coordination work. Incidentally, the RSS headquarters has gradually been transferred, de facto from Nagpur to Delhi, in the Jhandewalan office, because it was easier to keep in touch with the leaders of the major components of the *Sangh Parivar*—including the BJP—which were all based in Delhi, or had to come to the capital to pressurize the state.

During these meetings, the main components of the *Parivar* are usually represented by their leaders. For instance, in May 2003, a three-day conclave gathered together 55 top leaders of the *Sangh Parivar*. K.S. Sudarshan was in the chair. The BJP was represented by A.B. Vajpayee, L.K. Advani, Venkaiah Naidu, Murli Manohar Joshi, Arun Jaitley and other general secretaries—interestingly senior ministers without any RSS background were not invited. The RSS was represented by senior functionaries, H.V. Seshadri, Mohan Bhagwat and Madan Das Devi—the RSS man in charge of coordination among the *Sangh* affiliates. The VHP was represented by Ashok Singhal and Praveen Togadia. The BMS, the Bharatiya Kisan Sangh, the ABVP, Vidya Bharati, and the VKA were also represented by senior leaders. The aim of the meeting was to hammer out 'a common perspective' on national issues. The Prime Minister spoke last. He 'welcomed the successful effort to coordinate *Sangh Parivar* activities and was elated enough by the success of the show to wish increased frequency of such conclaves . . . .' (ibid., 4 May 2003).

In spite of this meeting, the relations between major components of the *Sangh Parivar* continued to deteriorate. The problem was especially acute regarding the relations between the VHP and the BJP. In 1998, the former was naturally very pleased that the BJP-led coalition could form the government. Certainly, the VHP leaders recognized that the BJP had been obliged to remove the issue of the Ram Janmabhoomi from its agenda in order to convince its secular allies to join the NDA, but it expected from the new Prime Minister that he should facilitate the building of a Ram Mandir in Ayodhya anyway. The VHP exerted as much pressure as it could over the Vajpayee government, but the BJP leaders were not willing to create fissures in the NDA by addressing this issue—which they probably did not regard as a priority. As a result, the VHP became more and more vocal. By early 2003, its leaders did not spare the Prime Minister any more. Acharya Giriraj Kishore, the VHP General Secretary, described him as a 'pseudo-Hindu' (*The Hindu*, 3 January 2003). In April 2003, Ashok Singhal, the International Executive President of the VHP, arraigned L.K. Advani—who had been spared so far—by accusing him of betraying the Hindutva cause after having ridden to power in the name of Ram (ibid., 25 April 2003).

The *samanvay baithak* mentioned earlier—in which Prime Minister Vajpayee took part—occurred soon after in May. It made no difference. In July, Singhal repeated strong attacks against Vajpayee. He declared that he should resign if his government could not bring in legislation to enable the construction of a Ram Temple in Ayodhya (ibid., 4 July 2003). Togadia went further. He accused Vajpayee and Advani of being 'inebriated with power' (ibid., 16 October 2003). Then, in October 2003, he attacked the Prime Minister for his recent peace initiative vis-à-vis Pakistan. He described it as an 'abject surrender' to a 'terrorist state' (ibid., 24 October 2003). In the face of such direct attacks, the BJP leaders told the RSS to restrain the VHP (ibid., 14 February 2003). This was precisely one of the objectives of the three-day *baithak* which took place in May 2003. But it proved unsuccessful, as we have seen. Therefore, the RSS appeared to be powerless and had no other solution but to impress upon the BJP that 'it should keep a direct channel of communication open between itself and the VHP, rather than going through the RSS' (*Central Chronicle*, 8 September 2003).

It appears, therefore, that the *Sangh Parivar* does not form a very centralized family, simply because the RSS is not always in a position to impose a compromise between affiliates which are locked in a conflict. It may even abstain to intervene of hot take side, even if such an attitude results in more bickering. The tensions between the BJP and the VHP are not the only ones at stake. The BJP has also been attacked by the BMS and the Swadeshi Jagran Manch (SJM) which both denounced its economic policy. As early as September 1998, the SJM accused the

Vajpayee Government of pursuing an 'anti-swadeshi and anti-people's economic agenda' (*The Hindustan Times*, 2 September 1998). In November, the BMS criticized the BJP-led government of selling eight public sector units to the private sector (*Central Chronicle*, 15 November 1998). Things became even worse as time passed. In 2001, D.P. Thengadi, the senior BMS leader declared that the Minister of Finance, Yashwant Sinha was 'a criminal' and Murlidhar Rao, the SJM convenor, went to the extent of saying 'that government is not being led by political leadership but by people who are insensitive to national interest' (*The Hindu*, 7 July 2001). The RSS, again, abstained from intervening in this debate.

We can, therefore, interpret Sudarshan's plea about the non-reality of the *Sangh Parivar* as a purely descriptive proposition: there is nothing like a family of the RSS because the RSS is not in a position to impose its will like a *pater familias*. It is not even in the position of a referee. Naturally, this problem was especially acute when the BJP was in office. On the one hand, the RSS' natural inclination is in favour of the doctrinal purity, which affiliates like the VHP, the BMS, and the SJM embody, but on the other hand it does not want to make things even more complicated for the BJP, as it considers the party in office role to be extremely precious.

The specific role of the BJP, indeed, is largely responsible for the cleavages affecting the *Sangh Parivar*. As a political party, the BJP is inevitably different from the rest of the RSS affiliates. A party has to adjust, even to a small extent, to the expectations of the voters and needs to make compromises with its potential allies. The Jana Sangh and then the BJP could not stick rigidly to their original ideology, otherwise they would have taken the risk of alienating the voters and their potential allies. The BJP, therefore, oscillates between a strategy of ethno-religious mobilization, which is in tune with the RSS natural inclination, as it did between 1989 and 1993, when it took part in the Ayodhya movement along with the VHP, and a more moderate approach of politics which prevails when it seeks allies (like in the 1980s under Vajpayee's leadership) or when it takes part in coalitions (like during the NDA government). During the phases when the BJP follows the latter, more pragmatic strategy, it tends to dilute its ideology and to distance itself from the RSS and the other components of the *Sangh Parivar*. Tensions emerge in this context and the notion of *Sangh Parivar*, indeed, seems to be much less relevant. For instance, in the early 1980s, when the BJP, which had just been founded under the presidentship of Atal Behari Vajpayee, distanced itself from the ethno-religious brand of Hindutva nationalism and embraced a more moderate political line it even adopted 'positive secularism' and 'Gandhian socialism' as its mottos. The RSS leaders resented very much this dilution of its ideology and in the 1984 elections, the movement supported the Congress in different parts of India and even launched a new political party, Hindu Munnani, in Kerala and Tamil Nadu, two states where the BJP was very weak anyway: it was a very effective warning signal. Interestingly, in the first half of the 1980s, no representative of the BJP attended the *samanvya samitis* (Andersen and Damle 1987: 142).

The very fact that the BJP could distance itself from the RSS shows that the notion of *Sangh Parivar* has lost some of its value. It means that the party has tended to gain a growing autonomy while it grew. Certainly, the RSS may exert some direct influence on the BJP, for instance, for solving faction fights. For the BJP leader, L.K. Advani, this influence reflects the moral authority of the RSS cadres: 'After all there are thousands of *pracharaks* who are our peers, our equals in all respects, who never aspired for any office. Therefore we respect them' (interview with L.K. Advani, 11 February 1994, New Delhi). But the BJP has become a mass party, which is in a stronger position vis-à-vis the diktats of the Sangh. For instance, in the late 1990s, the RSS itself disapproved of the economic policy of the Vajpayee Government regarding the opening up of the Indian economy to multinationals, but the government hardly amended its line of conduct and the RSS was not in a position to impose its doctrine. Similarly, the RSS was very critical of non-RSS leaders like Jaswant Singh or Brajesh Mishra who were close to Vajpayee, but their career has not been affected by this hostility.[5]

Obviously, the components of the *Sangh Parivar*—and more especially the BJP—have gained a very substantial autonomy. This state of things results primarily from the principles which guides the despatching of RSS cadres to different affiliates. These senior *swayamsevaks* are systematically sent to the front organizations with whom they have affinities; they are therefore bound to cultivate a specialization that they can call their own. They are supposed to run their organization autonomously in their field of predilection, within the framework of the RSS ideology. Their strategy has to fit in this framework, but they have room to manoeuvre so far as tactics are concerned. In case of conflict with the Sangh leaders, the chiefs of the different fronts of the *Parivar* are in a rather strong position to argue their case.

To sum up, the notion of *Sangh Parivar* needs to be qualified from two points of view: First, the components of this nebulae are more autonomous than one may think at a glance. Second, the RSS complex hardly form a family given the latent or explicit tensions between the BJP and the rest of the *Parivar*. These tensions, however, must not be over-emphasized. The *Sangh Parivar* has never broken. The bond between its components is very strong, largely because it comes from below: not only the RSS seconds *swayamsevaks* to its affiliates, but these *swayamsevaks* are easily transferred from one affiliate to another, so much so that they help to keep the network together. For instance, the leader of the Bajrang Dal, Vinay Katiyar became president of the Uttar Pradesh unit of the BJP in 2002.

Incidentally, to publicize the inner differentiation of the *Sangh Parivar* can be a very well thought out strategy for attracting supports from many different— even antagonistic—quarters of society. Indeed, the RSS may cultivate a real division of labour between the different components of the *Sangh Parivar* which represent different social milieus (labour, students, tribals, . . .) and ideological sensibilities (economic liberalizers, religious nationalists, etc.). From a tactical point of view, the *Sangh Parivar* leaders have everything to gain to promote VHP militant Hindu nationalists who may attract citizens entertaining extremist views as well as BJP mainstreamized politicians who may woo the moderates. The *Sangh Parivar,* therefore, must not be seen only as covering different social sectors of the Indian society, but also as covering a large spectrum of the different streams of the public opinion, the RSS monitoring its different fronts tactfully.

## From 'Parivar' to Constellation

The core group of the components of the *Sangh Parivar* represents either major arenas of the public sphere (the political domain with the Jana Sangh, the religious domain with the VHP, etc.) or targets macro-sociological categories (women with the Rashtra Sevika Samiti, students with the ABVP, workers with the BMS, tribals with the VKA, etc.). The second generation of the *Sangh's* affiliates tend to focus on much more specific causes or social groups.

The first affiliate of this kind was the Bharat Vikas Parishad which was founded in 1963 by Lala Hansraj Gupta, a Delhi-based RSS worker and a successful businessman who was to become mayor of the Indian capital. The organization was intended 'to involve entrepreneurs and well off sections of the society in national service and for protecting Bharatiya values' (<http://www.rss.org/New_RSS/Parivaar/History.jsp>). In 2000, the organization had 500 branches and 20,000 members, a clear indication of its elitist orientation.

True to its will to attract the cream of the society, in addition to the entrepreneurs and the university students, the RSS has created a special branch for scientists, Vigyan Bharati. Its main aim is to convince the scientists to 'promote the use of swadeshi technologies and encourage indigeneous scientific endeavours' (*Outlook,* 27 April 1998: 19). Besides, Vigyan Bharati is eager to raise private funds for financing scientific research in India.

At the exact opposite of this elitist body, Seva Bharati was founded in 1979 for the downtrodden. This organization has been designed for carrying out social work in slums and resettlement colonies. It provides free medical assistance, free education as well as vocational training to populations which have no access to these facilities. In addition to that the RSS has also established Samajik Samrasta Manch 'to eradicate the social evils like casteism, inequalities, untouchability, etc.' (<http://www.rss.org/New_RSS/Parivaar/History.jsp>).

The ex-armymen form a completely different group, which has also been targeted by the RSS in the last few years. In 1993, the Purva Sainik Seva Parishad (PSSP) was launched in Uttar Pradesh to look after the interests of this group. In addition, in 1994, the RSS has sponsored the Forum of Reared Defence Officers (FORDO), which had been created for ex-armymen but has also become a circle of reflection on defence matters.

In fact, the RSS has become adept at launching think tanks which are designed for one specific group or issue. Historically, the first think tank which emerged was the Deendayal Research Institute which was established in Delhi in

1972 in the memory of the late Deendayal Upadhyaya. Then the RSS created the Akhil Bharatiya Sahitya Parishad 'to promote such literature which may be in tune with the ethic of the nation and its eternal values' (ibid.). In the same vein, the Bharatiya Itihas Sankalan Yojna was launched for developing 'the research and writing history of the last 5,000 years of Bharat' (ibid.). Another think tank of the RSS, the Akhil Bharatiya Adhivakta Parishad (ABAP), which was established in 1992, deals with justice-related issues. It wants 'to work constantly for the improvement and evolution of a judicial system which is in harmony with the genius of the nation and in consonance with Bharatiya traditions, values and sense of justice and to make the justice delivery system more efficient' (*Outlook*, 27 April 1998: 19). The ABAP has offices in practically all courts of the country.

In addition to the organizations which target specific groups, new, micro components, have also been launched to promote very precise causes. For instance, when the Sikh separatist movement gained momentum in the 1980s, creating a big rift between Sikhs and Hindus, the RSS formed the Rashtriya Sikh Sanghat 'for promoting greater cordiality between the Sikh community and the rest of the Hindu society' (<http://www.rss.org/parivar/>). This organization was officially established in 1987. Similarly, the RSS created the Swadeshi Jagran Manch in November 1991, a few months after the Indian government initiated a new economic, liberal policy. The chief target of the Manch are the multinationals but it fights more generally against globalization and privatization.

Besides the development of affiliates in charge of distinctive groups and specific issues, the RSS has developed a strong presence in the media. As early as 1946, the RSS realized the need to create its own publishing house. Thus, Bharat Prakashan Trust launched an English weekly, *The Organiser,* in 1947. In the 1990s, the RSS had seven publishing houses based in Lucknow, Bangalore, Delhi, Nagpur, Jaipur, Pune, and Cochin. The RSS publish a dozen weeklies in English, Hindi, Marathi, Bengali, Malayalam, Kannada, Tamil, Telugu, and Assamese. So far as dailies are concerned, the RSS newspapers are half a dozen and are published in four languages, English, Hindi, Marathi, and Malayalam.

Even though the *Sangh Parivar* is not as coherent as it used to be, its components need to be seen in their inter-relations: the RSS and its affiliates form a complete network. In fact, the creation of new fronts ranging from labour union, to think tanks extended the initial achievements of the *shakha* network.

Yet, one point needs to be clarified in this respect. The *shakhas* were intended to be the crucible of a completely homogeneous 'Hindu Rashtra', whereas the non RSS components of the *Sangh Parivar* recognize the socioeconomic and cultural specificity of many different milieus. It seems that there is a contradiction between the initial project and this subsequent development, simply because the Hindu Rashtra can hardly be a collection of distinctive groups.

In fact there are two routes to the 'Hindu Rashtra'. The *shakha*-based one, which relied on the socio-psychological reforms of individuals and the *Sangh*

Parivar one, which intends to reframe fully constituted groups and to incorporate them in a new socio-political arrangement. This project calls to mind the corporatist model followed by authoritarian regimes such as the regime of Salazar in Portugal. Here unity does not derive from the transformation of individuals along a systematic and standardized pattern, but from the integration of complementary groups in a fixed social structure. This corporatist arrangement has strong affinities with the organicist overtone of the Hindu nationalist ideology.

This project is eminently political and the Sangh Parivar may indeed try to assume a new political role in the future. During the May 2003 conclave, which brought together 55 leaders of the Sangh Parivar 'it was suggested that a committee of BJP MPs be set up for each of the critical ministries and these committees should "hold a dialogue" with the minister concerned and with RSS organizations working in related areas to explain and discuss policy, and fine tune, if necessary' (The Hindu, 2 May 2003). If one day the BJP wins an absolute majority in Parliament the components of the Sangh Parivar may well form, in their area of expertise, 'shadow ministries' which will be in charge of guiding the work of the 'critical ministers'.

## Notes

1. Five leaders have successively occupied the post of sarsanghchalak, K.B. Hedgewar (1925–40), M.S. Golwalkar (1940–73), Balasaheb Deoras (1973–94), Rajendra Singh (1994–2000) and K.S. Sudarshan (2000–).
2. Outlook, 27 April 1998: 17. In this press report, the number of shakhas in Gujarat is incredibly low, 900.
3. Their expansion has not been linear, though. In 1956, the RSS leaders had decided to stop seconding pracharaks to affiliates because the mother organization could not afford doing it any more. The loaning of pracharaks to affiliates was resumed in 1962 and systematized when Balasaheb Deoras became General Secretary in 1965 (Andersen and Damle 1987: 113–14).
4. Things changed only after the Vajpayee Government was formed. For example, the Agra meeting, in 2000 had benefited from an extensive press coverage that had only been possible because the RSS leaders had no inhibition to go public with their proceedings (see Frontline, 10 November 2000: 115–20).
5. In 2001, Sudarshan spotted out B. Mishra as his favourite target, to no avail (see his interview in Outlook, 9 April 2001: 38–9).

## References

Andersen, W. and Damle, S. (1987), The Brotherhood in Saffron: The Rashtriya Swayamsevak Sangh and Hindu Revivalism, New Delhi: Vistaar Publications.

Balasaheb Deoras (n.d.), With Delhi Newsmen in the Press Club of India, 12 March 1979, New Delhi: Suruchi Sahitya Publications.

Bathval, Dr Harichandra (1998), *Rashtriya Swayamsevak Sangh: Ek Parichay*, New Delhi: Suruchi Prakashan.

*Central Chronicle*, 15 November 1998, 5 September 2002, 8 September 2003, 22 December 2003.

Curran, J.A. (1951), *Militant Hinduism in Indian Politics: A Study of the RSS*, Institute of Pacific Relations.

Deshpande, B.V. and Ramaswamy, S.R. (1981), *Dr Hedgewar: the Epoch Maker*, Bangalore: Sahitya Sindhu.

*Frontline*, 10 November 2000.

Golwalkar, M.S. (1966), *Bunch of Thoughts*, Bangalore: Jagarana Prakashana.

Goyal, D.R. (1978), *Rashtriya Swayamsevak Sangh*, New Delhi: Radhakrishna Prakashan.

*The Hindu*, 13 February 2000, 7 July 2001, 3 January 2003, 14 February 2003, 25 April 2003, 2 May 2003, 4 May 2003, 4 July 2003, 16 October 2003, 24 October 2003, 10 March 2004.

*The Hindustan Times*, 19 April 1977, 2 September 1998.

*Hitavada*, 31 December 1947.

http://www.abvp.org

http://www.rss.org

*India Today*, 30 June 1989, 11 November 2002.

Interview with L.K. Advani, 11 February 1994, New Delhi.

Interview with G. Prabhakar, General Secretary of the BMS, 5 December 1990, Bhopal.

Jaffrelot, C. (1999), *The Hindu Nationalist Movement and Indian Politics*, New Delhi: Penguin.

Khanna, N. (1991), 'Education: the RSS Way', *Sunday*, 1 December 1991.

'Note on the Volunteer Movement in India', prepared by the Intelligence Bureau, 27 January 1940 and August 1940, in L/P & J/Coll. 17-C18, India Office Library and Records, London.

*The Organiser*, 6 November 1948, 1 December 1949, 6 June 1950, 28 May 1977, 12 March 1978, 19 November 1978, 5 April 1981, 14 February 1982, 10 November 1985, 1 August 1995, 25 March 2001, 19 March 2004, 28 March 2004.

*Outlook*, 27 April 1998, 9 April 2001.

*The Indian Express*, 15 May 1978.

*The Times of India*, 'Interview with Gautham Machaiah', 28 March 1998.

# Chapter 10

# Hindu nationalism and democracy

No wing of the Hindu nationalist movement, whether the militant youth of the Bajrang Dal or political parties like the Jana Sangh or its successor, the Bharatiya Janata Party, has ever been really attracted by the fascist, putschist strategy. The Rashtriya Swayamsevak Sangh and its offshoots probably never promoted a coup d'état because they did not regard state power as the most important object of conquest—they preferred to work at the grassroots level with a long-term perspective.[1] They could have stayed out of the institutional framework or even the political domain, as many RSS leaders argued they should in the late 1940s to early 1950s. However, the Jana Sangh and the BJP, and before them the Hindu Mahasabha, have always played the game of electoral politics. The Jana Sangh distanced itself somewhat from the elections in the 1970s, when Atal Behari Vajpayee considered that it was 'becoming increasingly difficult to dislodge the Congress by the ballot-box since elections proved to be an unequal battle, since the Congress has money power' (*The Hindu*, 16 September 1974). But this stand was not uncommon then—as the JP (Jayaprakash Narayan) movement was to testify—and, in any case, the Jana Sangh continued to contest elections.

Does this rejection of putschist strategies mean that Hindu nationalism fully adheres to democracy? This chapter proposes to give some answers to this question by analysing how the *Sangh Parivar* and the Hindu Mahasabha have approached this political system even before independence, by studying the kind of democracy they tended to favour and by highlighting the limits of their democratic credentials.

## The Hindu Nationalist Ideology of Democracy

### INDIA, A DEMOCRACY FROM TIME IMMEMORIAL

Even before Hindu nationalism crystallized in the inter-war period, Hindu revivalists were not averse to the notion of democracy. On the contrary, they argued that democracy was not alien to India. Aurobindo even claimed that democracy was born in India; it was merely returning via the British after a long journey. All that was needed was to free it from the foreign elements which were now affecting it (Aurobindo 1970, Vol. 1: 767–9). This discourse naturally reflected a nationalist strategy: the British prided themselves on being democrats, and members of the

Indian intelligentsia (and among them, Hindu revivalists) did not want to see their country lagging behind. The Hindu nationalists inherited this conception from the revivalists in the 1920s and 1930s.

As did many others (Jaiswal 1924; Prasad 1928: 170), the first Hindu nationalist ideologues emphasized the existence of a democratic precedent in India. This they generally situated in Buddhist institutions, the village, and the ancient 'republics'. Radha Kumud Mookerji, a professor of history at Lucknow University in the inter-war period, was one of the intellectuals of the Hindu Mahasabha who advocated such ideas.[2] In *Hindu Civilization*, the first edition of which came out in 1936, he explains that the monarchy of Vedic times was far from absolute: 'Within the framework of autocracy, there were operative certain democratic elements, the significance of which should not be missed' (Mookerji 1950: 99). For instance, Mookerji found that 'the *Atharva Veda* has several passages indicative of the people choosing their king' (ibid.). But the republics were naturally seen by the author as the main embodiments of democracy in ancient India:

> The growth of republics as a feature of Indian political evolution implied that of the necessary democratic procedure by which their working was regulated and governed. It is a remarkable testimony to the popular republican instincts and traditions of the times that democratic procedure was applied in every sphere of life, political, economic and even religious. The Pali texts furnish interesting information on the working of the Buddhist Samghas in strict and minute conformity with genuine democratic principles. The essence of democracy is government by decision based on discussion in public meetings or assemblies. The Pali texts describe the meetings of religious assemblies or Samghas in all their stages. (ibid.: 209)

Mookerji emphasizes the role of voting in the making of decisions within the Buddhist Samgha (ibid.: 214). So-called democratic procedures typical of a religious body, the Buddhist community, were used to substantiate the claim that ancient India knew political democracy.

This kind of discourse was not confined to the Hindu Mahasabha. Hindu traditionalist Congressmen made assiduous use of it, as the 1946–50 Constituent Assembly debates testify. When the question of regime type arose in the Assembly, many of them declared that India could choose only democracy because that is what she had always known (before she was conquered by 'foreigners'). To substantiate this claim, soon after the opening session of the Constituent Assembly, Purushottam Das Tandon, well known for his Hindu traditionalist leanings,[3] established a parallel between this Assembly and an illustrious Buddhist precedent:

> After centuries, such a meeting has once more been convened in our country. It recalls to our mind our glorious past when we were free and when assemblies were held at which the Pundits met to discuss important affairs of the country. It reminds us of the Assemblies of the age of Asoka [the third Emperor of the Maurya dynasty who lived and ruled till 232 BC]. (*Constituent Assembly Debates* [hereafter *CAD*], 1989, Vol. 1: 65)

The assemblies presented here as the precursors of the Constituent Assembly were in no way political: the pundits evoked by Tandon were Brahmans versed in Sanskrit scriptures who could have debated questions of theology or ritual, but even for these purposes, they were not representatives of society. As far as the assemblies convened by Ashoka are concerned, they also undoubtedly had a religious vocation: the Emperor, it seems, had indeed convened the third Buddhist Council and thus contributed to the building of the canon of the religion to which he had been converted.

Like many Congressmen, and especially Hindu traditionalists such as Tandon, Hindu nationalist ideologues were not hostile to democracy insofar as it appeared to be rooted in Indian soil and culture. To that extent, it was a prestigious feature adding to the country's glory.

## AN ANTI-INDIVIDUALISTIC CONCEPTION OF DEMOCRACY

Even though Hindu nationalists have generally praised democracy and appreciated its advent in India, they have tended to distinguish their conception of democracy from the Westminster model borrowed from Britain in the 1950 Constitution. This argument was made clear during the 1975 Emergency. At that time, the RSS and its affiliates projected themselves as being at the forefront of the fight against Indira Gandhi, but this claim needs to be qualified. First, the RSS fought less for democracy than for regaining a right to legal existence. (The then RSS chief, Balasaheb Deoras, proposed to Indira Gandhi that she accept its collaboration. The RSS launched its anti-Emergency agitation after she refused.) (Jaffrelot 1996: 273). Second, Hindu nationalists suggested that the democracy for which they fought was not necessarily that of the parliamentary system. For instance, D. Thengadi, who was one of the main RSS leaders underground, declared:

The Constituent Assembly imposed British-type institutions on the people. India too has had a democratic tradition, a tradition of thousands of years, and the temperament of the Indian people can be easily moulded accordingly. But the Indian democratic system has been different. Its nature is different from that of the British democratic system. (Thengadi 1991: 45)

Thengadi does not explain here what the differences are, but he is more explicit in other writings, borrowing heavily from the organicist world view of his mentor, Golwalkar.

## IN DEFENCE OF SOCIAL ORGANICISM

Golwalkar's favourite political arrangement combined territorial representation (election by constituencies) with functional representation, where each corporate body nominates delegates at the request of both its local branches and the central organization. This mechanism was described as merely giving concrete shape to what was already practised in ancient India, where each of the *varnas* chose its representative for its village council (*gram panchayat*) and thence to the royal council (Golwalkar 1966: 37–8). Golwalkar did not hesitate to demand, if necessary, a revision of the Constitution to put this plan into action.

This programme looks like an Indian variant of the corporatist state, since the group, not the individual, is regarded as the relevant unit; this group can be the family, the village, the *varna*, but also the 'industry'. Indeed, Thengadi, who was the founder of the Bharatiya Mazdoor Sangh in 1955, proposed a parallel system from the trade unionist point of view:

> Bharatiya culture believes that the 'Nation', and not the 'class', is the basic unit of human society. Horizontal division of the world is a fiction. Vertical arrangement of it is a fact. . . . [In ancient India] like a family, the community had its life based upon mutual love and confidence, and consequently, its horizontal division could not even be dreamt of. It was further realized that the various communities are but different limbs of the same organism, i.e., the Bharatiya Nation. The Bharatiya social order thus implied the industry-wise arrangement and not class-wise arrangement. (*The Organiser*, 24 October 1955: 6, 12)

Thengadi not only dealt with 'economic democracy', he also criticized the foreign inspiration of parliamentary democracy, in comparison with the Indian version of democracy, because 'Unlike the western form of democracy, which is more intellectual, the Indian alternative—the dharmic system—is based on human values' (*The Organiser*, 5 January 1995). Thengadi even suggested constitutional reform because 'checks and balances provided by the Constitution and our legal systems can be effective only if they are supplemented by checks and balances in human, social mind as a result of appropriate *samskaras*[4] of dharma' (Jaffrelot 1996: 48). Thengadi's discourse bears testimony to the latent hostility of Hindu nationalists towards a secular form of democracy, a political system separated from religious notions such as the most all-embracing one, dharma, which also underlies social organicism.

Thus, Hindu nationalist leaders disapprove of parliamentary democracy because it is alien to religious (*dharmic*) notions and does not fit into their non-individualistic view of society. Today, these conceptions are propagated not only by old-timers or more or less sidelined leaders such as Thengadi, but also by mainstream ideologues. In the BJP, K.N. Govindacharya for instance, has adopted the same perspective in a recent assessment of India after 50 years of independence:

> The Constitution is not the product of our soil; a minimum addition is required to make it more responsive. Consensus, instead of majority-minority concept, suits the country better. Occupational representation (participation of various social groups based on their occupation) in the system will deliver the goods. Such a system will be in conformity with our traditions and ethos. . . .

It is clear the system has to be rooted in our soil. Public and political education are essential ingredients for our evolution. M.K. Gandhi, Aurobindo Ghosh and M.N. Roy had reservations about the System right since its inception. There was skepticism about the efficacy of adopting the parliamentary system of democracy. Dr. B.R. Ambedkar emphasized the need of having an Indian Union—a true reflection of our ethos—instead of federation. Jayaprakash Narayan favoured party-less democracy. RSS founder M.S. Golwalkar considered 'unanimity' as the mode of elections, with an added component of functional representation as the best model of governance.

I feel Golwalkar's view is best suited for our society. In the process of evolution, the system is bound to tend towards this goal. As of now, I am not pessimistic about the survival of our system. We need improvement, not change in the system ('Agenda', *The Pioneer*, 6 April 1997).

Like his predecessors, Golwalkar and Thengadi, Govindacharya does not reject democracy, but displays a strong inclination for a reformed version of parliamentary democracy. Interestingly, he does not draw his inspiration from Golwalkar alone but also from Gandhian views. Indeed, this variant of the Hindu nationalist conception of democracy overlaps with ideas propagated by Gandhi and his disciples.

## DOES HINDU NATIONALISM ECHO GANDHIAN VIEWS?

It is well known that Gandhi's first and only book, *Hind Swaraj* (1908), is not only an indictment of Western, modern materialistic civilization, but also of parliamentary democracy:

The condition of England at present is pitiable. I pray to God that India may never be in that plight. That which you consider to be the Mother of Parliaments is like a sterile woman and prostitute. Both these are harsh terms, but exactly fit the case. That Parliament has not yet of its own accord done a single good thing, hence I have compared it to a sterile woman. The natural condition of that Parliament is such that, without outside pressure, it can do nothing. It is like a prostitute because it is under the control of ministers who change from time to time. (Gandhi 1922: 26)

Gandhi agrees with one of the main ideas of the opponents of parliamentary democracy, namely that deputies are too corrupt to represent the voters, that they waste their time in useless debates and that they stick to their parties' programme without thinking for themselves. The Mahatma, then, preferred the reign of 'a few good men' (ibid.: 27). This stand reflected a strong distrust of the people who allegedly are not able to make up their minds; they live under the influence of the press and populist leaders.

In a book professing to be a reflection on 'democratic values', Vinoba Bhave opposed *raj-niti* (power politics) to *lok-niti* (democratic ethics). This view implied the dissolution of parties and the relinquishing of any electoral system aimed at reaching a consensus. Bhave's anti-individualism encompassed a germ of authoritarianism. He wrote that social harmony would reign if everyone fulfilled his or her duty in the social order: 'if every limb were to function smoothly, the whole body would function properly' (Dalton 1982: 186).

The main work of Jayaprakash Narayan (JP) (another Gandhian leader mentioned by Govindacharya), *A Plea for Reconstruction of Indian Polity,* is also an indictment of parliamentary democracy which, as he saw it, implied excessive centralization of power and systematically betrayed the wishes of the people. In parliamentary democracy, the electors are 'manipulated by powerful, centrally controlled parties, with the aid of high finance and diabolically clever methods and super media' (Narayan 1959: 66). In setting forth his political ideal, JP also claimed he drew upon models from ancient India, and particularly from the interpretation of these models provided by Aurobindo who, like Gandhi, was one of his sources of inspiration. Going back to the thesis of this author about a century later, JP maintained that the political order of ancient India was based 'on the system of the self-governing village community', which only British colonization was able to destroy (ibid.: 22). Ancient India, therefore, held the key to 'an organically self-determining communal life', and for JP, the challenge at hand was just 'a question of an ancient country finding its lost soul again' (ibid.: 26).

Obviously, JP opposed parliamentary democracy because he wanted a democracy expressed through a truly decentralized system of governance. Gandhi's political ideal was already a network of independent villages, drawing its inspiration from the orientalist stereotype of the 'village republics':

My idea of Village Swaraj is that it is a complete republic, independent of its neighbours for its vital wants, and yet interdependent for many others in which dependence is a necessity. . . . The government of the village will be conducted by the Panchayat of five persons, annually elected by the adult villagers, male and female, possessing minimum prescribed qualifications. These will have all the authority and jurisdiction required. Since there will be no system of punishments in the accepted sense, this Panchayat will be the legislature, judiciary and executive combined to operate for its year of office. (Gandhi 1967: 186)

The RSS and its offshoots were also in favour of a decentralized state. As early as the 1950s, the Jana Sangh proposed in its election manifestoes to divide the Indian territory into about one hundred large districts, or *janapadas*. These would be much smaller than the states and would, it was argued, promote village autonomy. In its 1954 election manifesto, the party committed itself to make the village councils, or panchayats, 'the foundation of administration', granting them an increase in financial resources and (re)establishing the so-called traditional rule that their members would be elected unanimously (Bharatiya Jana Sangh 1973: 62). However, the Hindu nationalists' emphasis on the unity of Indian society led them to advocate a unitary rather than a federal state, a move which reflected their basic difference with the Gandhians, that is, their rejection of diversity. While the latter have always stressed pluralism, Hindu nationalists cannot accommodate the notion of a plural society.

## The Limits of the Hindu Nationalists' Commitment to Democracy

### DEMOCRACY:
### THE MOST CONVENIENT REGIME FOR A MAJORITY

Hindu nationalists favoured democracy before independence not only because of the prestige they could draw from the claim that India had been a democracy since its antiquity; they also espoused it as early as the 1930s because this regime relied on the notion of majority rule. Hindu nationalists were increasingly obsessed by demographic figures from the late nineteenth century onwards, when the first censuses showed a limited but steady erosion in the proportion of Hindus in the population of India. This sensitivity led them to over-emphasize the fact that Hindus formed a majority in India, and that it was their nation for this reason. In addition, they could claim to be its first inhabitants. Democracy has suited them more than any other regime because it relies on the principle of 'one man, one vote'.

This first became clear in the speeches of Veer Savarkar after he took over as chief of the Hindu Mahasabha. In the presidential address delivered at the 1937 session of the party he declared, 'Though we form an overwhelming majority in the land we do not want any privileges for our Hindudom' (*Indian Annual Register*, 1938, Vol. 1: 420). In fact, Savarkar did not want any privileges for any community because the Hindus were in a majority. From this perspective, he added:

Let all citizens of Indian States be treated according to their individual worth, irrespective of their religious or racial percentage in the general population. Let their language and script be the national language and script of the Indian State which is understood by an overwhelming majority of the people, as happens in every other State in the world. Let no religious bias be allowed to tamper with that language and script. Let 'one man, one vote' be the general rule irrespective of caste, creed, race or religion. (ibid.)

Savarkar was favourably inclined towards democratic principles, because they guarantee the domination of the 'over-whelming majority', that is, the Hindus—a logic which would enable Hindi to become the national language. The universalistic discourse of democracy was evidently hijacked in order to promote communal interests.[5] The Hindu Mahasabha leaders seem to have been deeply convinced that they could make their point through the use of universalistic values, so much so that the party's working committee decided to refer the Hindu-Muslim question to the League of Nations in 1940 (*Indian Annual Register*, 1940, Vol. 1: 10).

This discourse heralded the present-day propaganda of the RSS and its offshoots in favour of the disbanding of the Minorities Commission. Even though this Commission was established by the Janata Party, of which the former Jana Sangh was a component, the Hindu nationalist movement quickly criticized it as an institution responsible for the 'division of the nation'. The BJP, the Jana Sangh's successor, proposed to replace it with a Human Rights Commission,[6] which would have enabled it once again to use the language of universalism for particularistic ends. The aim was to remove some of the protections granted to the minorities because of their vulnerability and, in effect, to assert the strength of the Hindu majority.

The BJP shaped the notion of 'minorityism' in the same perspective. The term was first used by L.K. Advani after he took over as BJP president in 1986. In January 1987, in an address to the BJP's National Council, he referred to the 'dangers of minorityism' in an obvious allusion to the Congress government's concern to protect certain interests of the Muslims, as exemplified in the Shah Bano controversy (Advani 1987: 8–9). Advani had specifically condemned the Muslim Women's (Protection of Rights in Divorce) Bill on behalf of modern, universalistic values. Addressing the plenary session of the BJP as the party's incoming president, he stated in 1986 that in the Shah Bano affair some Muslim leaders had acted as 'obscurantists' and 'fanatics' because they disregarded the rights of their community's wives (Advani 1986: 465).

Hindu nationalism has thus become adept at promoting the interests of the majority community in the guise of universalistic values that are pillars of liberal democracy. In reality, Hindu nationalists appreciate the majority rule of democracy because it means that Hindus can never lose power, provided they vote *en bloc*, which is indeed their chief objective. As Sudipta Kaviraj has suggested, the main enemies of democracy in India are those who would like to merge democracy and 'majoritarianism', as if both things would mean the same. They do not oppose democracy openly; on the contrary, 'they are in fact the greatest supporters of majority rule. But they do not want democratic government to be a complex arrangement in which majority rule is counterbalanced by a system of secure enjoyment of minority right.' (Kaviraj 1994: 123).

This analysis can be applied to different categories, including the Other Backward Classes (OBCs) and the Hindi-speaking population, but, of course, it is especially relevant in the case of Hindu nationalism. Savarkar's reaction to the abolition of separate electorates by the Constituent Assembly is very significant in this respect. In May 1949, soon after Sardar Patel made this decision known, Savarkar sent him the following telegram:

I heartily congratulate you and the Constituent Assembly on leading and adopting the resolutions doing away with separate electorates, reservations and weightages based on invidious racial or religious distinctions and on having thus vindicated the genuinely national, character of our Bharateeya state. (Savarkar and Joshi 1967: 224)

Savarkar did not reject a religion-based state to promote an individualistic civil space; he opposed separate electorates and reservations because they hindered his efforts to equate democracy and majoritarianism, that is the pursuance of 'a permanent unbeatable majority which would place [large groups] in power forever' (Kaviraj 1994: 124). But in a true democracy, 'Large majorities are bearable only if there is a random element in them, if individuals and groups are sometimes in the winning and sometimes in the losing group' (ibid.).

Thus, while the Hindu nationalists look at democracy as something that is not alien to India, and furthermore, as an element of its historical prestige, they have promoted a non-individualistic version of it, and they have been especially interested in this political system because it is a convenient way to establish the domination of the majority community.

## THE *SANGH PARIVAR* AND DEMOCRATIC PROCEDURE

Since independence, the RSS has not been able to claim to represent the people because it did not contest elections, but its democratic credentials have been affected by its desire to influence those in power. In his attempts to transform the RSS into a kind of advisor to the government, Golwalkar drew his inspiration from the classic connection between temporal power and spiritual authority:

The political rulers were never the standard-bearers of our society. They were never taken as the props of our national life. Saints and sages who had risen above the mundane temptations of self and power and had dedicated themselves wholly for establishing a happy, virtuous and integrated state of society, were its constant torch-bearers. They represented the *dharmasatta* [religious authority]. The king was only an ardent follower of that higher moral authority. (Golwalkar 1966: 92–3)

Golwalkar was invoking the Hindu tradition of the king's guru (*raj guru*) and, because of the RSS' emulation of the values of renunciation—the *pracharaks* are known for their ascetic lifestyle—he proposed for his organization the traditional function of 'dharmic' counsellor to state power:

We aspire to become the radiating centre of all the age-old cherished ideals of our society— just as the indescribable power which radiates through the sun. Then the political power which draws its life from that source of society, will have no other [goal but] to reflect the same radiance. (ibid.)

Golwalkar's successor, Deoras, tried to play the role of the *raj guru* during the Janata phase when he met Morarji Desai, Charan Singh, and Jayaprakash Narayan in order to influence power from outside. This activity, as noticed by D. R. Goyal, tended to turn the RSS into a 'supra party' and an 'extra-constitutional authority' (Goyal 1978: 196) that was incompatible with the logic of democracy, simply because this centre of power was not subject to the verdict of the polls.

The problem became even more acute after the BJP came to power in 1998. Even though the new prime minister, Atal Behari Vajpayee, was known for not being as close to the RSS as, for instance, Lal Krishna Advani, the then BJP president, he had been trained in this organization and still regarded it as his 'family' (*The Organiser*, 1998: 28–9). He praised the 'RSS ethos' in general and the way it 'change[d]. . . the collective mind'. While in power, the BJP enabled the RSS to exert a stronger influence over Indian politics. Sangh leaders regularly met the prime minister and key ministers such as Advani. In July 1998, two meetings were convened by the RSS chief, Rajendra Singh, for interacting with the 180-odd BJP MPs. Vajpayee and Advani attended parts of this event. Such meetings had been organized previously, but this time the BJP MPs were the pillars of the ruling coalition (*The Hindustan Times*, 21 July 1998). More importantly, in Uttar Pradesh, Rajendra Singh was allowed to address a group of about 55 top bureaucrats, including the chief secretary and the director general of police, on 'how they could emerge as ideals before the public' (ibid.: 27 July 1998). The meeting took place in the presence of ministers of Kalyan Singh's government; bureaucrats could hardly miss Rajendra Singh's message since their political bosses were obviously supporting what he said.

The RSS and its offshoots have traditionally been apprehensive about elections, which they never really regarded as the legitimate procedure for filling posts of responsibility. The Jana Sangh and then the BJP have professed that they were more democratic than other parties. For one thing, they limited the number of terms of the party chief (as in the BJP today, where the term of the president can only be renewed once); for another, they held party elections often. Through these elections local committees designate state units, which then nominate delegates to an all-India council, which in turn elects the party president. The Jana Sangh and the BJP have certainly held party elections more often than other parties, but in contrast with what has happened in the latter, there have been very few contested elections. Most of the time, there has been one candidate per post, because the very notion of contested elections is rejected as divisive (Jaffrelot 1996: 149ff).

Inner democracy is not very evident in any other Indian political party or organization. During the 1920s, the Congress had been given a more representative AICC by Gandhi; even so, it suffered from the Mahatma's interference, as testified by the 'dismissal' of Netaji Subhas Chandra Bose in 1939. After independence, Nehru forced P.D. Tandon to resign and, more importantly, there were no party elections for the 20 years between 1972 and 1992. However, this was largely due to factionalism which was a form of pluralism that is rejected by the BJP today. When the BJP itself was affected by groupism and factionalism as a result of its coming to power in several states in the early 1990s, it preferred not to conduct party elections in several regional party branches, such as Madhya Pradesh.

The limited role of elections in the functioning of the Jana Sangh and the BJP is well in tune with what happens in their mother organization, the RSS. The latter was obliged to draft a constitution after its ban in the wake of Gandhi's assassination. This document required local branches of the RSS to elect provincial assemblies whose members would nominate the delegates to the Akhil Bharatiya Pratinidhi Sabha (ABPS). This body was empowered to elect the general secretary, who in turn appointed the executive committee. In practice, there have never been more candidates than posts to be filled, and the general secretary has more or less been free to nominate, transfer, or even suspend the *pracharaks*. Similarly, the *sarsanghchalak*, the RSS chief who embodies supreme authority, cannot be voted out. He remains at the helm until his death or until he resigns. He is not elected, but designated by his predecessor, as in 1940 and 1973, when Hedgewar and Golwalkar, respectively, designated their successors.

The taste for personalizing power that is evident in the structure of the RSS and its offshoots partly explains the interest of the Hindu nationalists in the presidential system. Whereas members of a parliamentary cabinet are responsible to Parliament, in the presidential system, members of the executive are any persons chosen by the president, and are responsible to the president alone.

## PARLIAMENTARY DEMOCRACY OR PRESIDENTIAL SYSTEM?

The BJP reaffirmed its faith in a presidential form of government in 1991, as a means to guarantee a stronger Centre (*The Statesman*, 16 January and 2 February 1991). Several of its top leaders elaborated on this point while assessing the achievement of India after 50 years of independence. Vajpayee went into this question more deeply than any other BJP leader. In the Thirteenth Desraj Chowdhary Annual Memorial Lecture which he delivered on 11 November 1996, he declared that 'the present system of parliamentary democracy has failed to deliver the goods and that the time has come to introduce deep-going changes in our structure of governance' (Vajpayee 1996: 4). Among the 'ills of the present system of parliamentary democracy . . . fashioned after the British model nearly five decades ago',[7] Vajpayee highlighted the incapacity of Parliament to satisfactorily exert its legislative function and to launch serious debates. As a remedy, he envisaged, first, the presidential system; or second, proportional representation (PR); or third, the strengthening of democracy within the political parties. While everybody will agree with the third proposal, the first two are debatable; they seem to be contradictory, since the presidential system is intended to concentrate the authority of the state, while the main asset of the electoral system known as PR lies in its capacity to represent different opinions.

However, the strengthening of the president's role was obviously favoured by Vajpayee, and a subsequent interview suggests that this process would have authoritarian implications:

It's 50 years since independence and time we reviewed the functioning of our institutions. I have made a few suggestions. For example, I feel that where political parties are unable to form a government at the Centre, the President should carry on the administration with the help of advisers. (*India Today*, 15 May 1997)

Such a schema, which amounts to extending a kind of president's rule to the Centre, has clear anti-democratic consequences. First, the president would acquire significant prerogatives even though he would not be elected by the people, but by members of Parliament and of the legislative assemblies. Second, it would be very difficult to assess 'where political parties are unable to form a government'— the president could interpret the situation according to his personal inclinations. Third, the president would be free to choose his advisors, and not necessarily from among elected politicians whose legitimacy derives from universal suffrage. Vajpayee's formula reflects a certain fascination for strong, personalized power, which is well in tune with the middle-class craving for the replacement of politicians by bureaucrats and technicians.

After the 1998 elections, the BJP and its coalition partners evolved a National Agenda for Governance, in which one of the items read: 'We will appoint a Commission to review the Constitution of India in light of the experience of the past 50 years and to make suitable recommendations.'[8] In April 1998, L.K. Advani, the home minister, virtually spelt out the terms of reference of such a commission: whether the political system needed to be decentralized, whether to continue with the parliamentary system, and whether the electoral system needed to be reformed (*The Organiser*, 29 March 1998: 29). A few days later, during the BJP National Council session, he explained that the proposed commission would go into the 'merits and demerits' of the parliamentary system and the presidential system to make recommendations, but he pointed out that parliamentary democracy was not among the basic features of the Constitution which could not be changed (*The Hindu*, 27 April 1998).

The presidential system is not necessarily opposed to democracy, even though it reflects an inclination towards concentration (even personalization) of power. In fact, the growing attention that is paid to this system is not limited to the Hindu nationalist milieu. Several Congressmen, for instance, have been toying with this idea for some time (ibid., 5 May 1998), and it is even referred to by many politicians who are concerned with the need to reform the state. Yet, the form that presidentialization of the regime would take under the auspices of the BJP appears to be more threatening than it would under other parties, because of the BJP's ideological background and the way in which the RSS and its offshoots function.

## The *Sangh Parivar*: Stronghold of Social Status Quo?

### THE BJP: STILL THE PARTY OF AN ELITE

One of the major changes on the Indian political scene since the late 1980s has been the rise of the Other Backward Classes (OBCs) and the Dalits. The share of the former among the MPs of the Hindi belt—where the BJP won most of its seats and where social change was much slower than in the south—has increased from less than five per cent in the 1950s to about 25 per cent in the 1990s. For the first time, the Lok Sabha harbours a large proportion of agriculturists (many of them from the lower castes), whereas it used to be a stronghold for lawyers and other professionals. In many respects, this trend represents a democratization of Indian democracy. However, the BJP, until recently, did not participate in this process.

Classifying Lok Sabha members according to their profession is difficult because of the large number of those who declare agriculture as their profession, even though they may have some land but do not cultivate it themselves. In Table 10.1, which analyses Uttar Pradesh, Bihar, Madhya Pradesh, Rajasthan, Haryana, Himachal Pradesh, Chandigarh, and Delhi, the MPs who, in *Who's Who in the Lok Sabha,* have given agriculture as their profession but hold an LL.B. have been classified as lawyers. Nonetheless, the 'agriculturalists' category remains very heterogeneous, since it encompasses landlords as well as tenants. In spite of these caveats, it is noteworthy that the share of the agriculturalists among the BJP MPs has tended to increase, while that of the lawyers has been on the decline. However, the group composed of traders and industrialists represents about one-fourth the total member of BJP MPs in the 1990s—compared to less than four per cent for the Janata Dal and six per cent for Congress—a clear indication that in parliament the BJP still represents the business community to a greater extent than do other parties.

The proportional over-representation of upper caste MPs among the BJP members elected from the Hindi belt and Gujarat, where the party won most of its seats, was evident from 1989. Their percentage declined in the 1996 election, but remains prominent and much more important than in the Congress and the Janata Dal. Interestingly, in 1996 the erosion of the upper castes' share benefits the MPs from the Scheduled Castes, who are largely elected by non-SC voters, as much as those from the OBCs. In fact, very few Dalits vote for the BJP, as testified by the exit poll made by the Centre for the Study of Developing Societies in 1996. This poll also shows that the upper castes are still over-represented among the BJP electorate, while the Scheduled Tribes are significantly under-represented. The OBCs are also under-represented, but to a lesser extent.

The forward castes' votes polarize in favour of the BJP in Maharashtra, Uttar Pradesh, and Bihar, where respectively 50, 64, and 67 per cent of the upper castes preferred this party. The BJP also remains a predominantly urban party. Thirty-two per cent of the urban dwellers voted for it, as against 19 per cent of the people living in rural constituencies. As for the upper caste graduates living in towns and cities, 52 per cent of this category opted for the BJP in 1996.

## THE UPPER CASTE MIDDLE CLASS AND THE BJP

The upper caste middle class has always been over-represented within the Hindu nationalist movement, to such an extent that the Jana Sangh was known as a 'Brahman-baniya' party. The *Sangh Parivar* held some attraction for these milieus

TABLE 10.1: OCCUPATIONAL DISTRIBUTION OF HINDI-BELT MPs
OF THE THREE MAIN PARTIES

| Occupation | 1989 | | | 1991 | | | 1996 | | |
|---|---|---|---|---|---|---|---|---|---|
| | BJP | Cong | JD | BJP | Cong | JD | BJP | Cong | JD |
| Agriculturalist | 14 | 13 | 34 | 16 | 23 | 19 | 35 | 10 | 10 |
| | 21.8% | 37.1% | 32.3% | 18.6% | 38% | 35.8% | 28.8% | 29% | 40% |
| Lawyers | 15 | 5 | 20 | 9 | 12 | 8 | 18 | 6 | 1 |
| | 23.4% | 14.2% | 19% | 10.4% | 20% | 15% | 14.8% | 17.6% | 4% |
| Traders | 5 | 2 | 3 | 12 | 3 | 1 | 19 | 2 | 1 |
| | 7.8% | 5.7% | 2.8% | 13.9% | 5% | 1.8% | 15.7% | 5.8% | 4% |
| Industrialist | 2 | 0 | 0 | 6 | 0 | 1 | 5 | 0 | 0 |
| | 3.1% | | | 6.9% | | 1.8% | 4.1% | | |
| Ex-Civil Servant | 2 | 0 | 0 | 2 | 0 | 0 | 4 | 0 | 0 |
| | 3.1% | | | 2.3% | | | 3.3% | | |
| Ex-Army | 1 | 0 | 1 | 5 | 2 | 1 | 4 | 1 | 1 |
| | 1.5% | 2.8% | | | 1.6% | | | 2.9% | |
| Policeman/Pilot | 1 | 1 | 0 | 0 | 1 | 0 | 0 | 1 | 0 |
| | 1.5% | 2.8% | | | 1.6% | | | 2.9% | |
| Journalist | 2 | 0 | 6 | 1 | 1 | 2 | 1 | 1 | 0 |
| | 3.1% | 5.7% | 1.1% | | 1.6% | 3.7% | 0.8% | 2.9% | |
| Writer & Artist | 0 | 0 | 2 | 1 | 0 | 0 | 2 | 2 | 3 |
| | | | 1.9% | 1.1% | | | 1.6% | 5.8% | 12% |
| Teacher | 5 | 3 | 9 | 5 | 5 | 6 | 9 | 2 | 3 |
| | 7.8% | 8.6% | 8.6% | 5.8% | 8.3% | 11.3% | 7.4% | 5.8% | 12% |
| Doctor | 4 | 0 | 2 | 6 | 0 | 0 | 7 | 1 | 0 |
| | 6.25% | | 1.9% | 6.9% | | | 5.7% | 2.9% | |
| Engineer | 0 | 0 | 2 | 1 | 0 | 3 | 0 | 2 | 3 |
| | | | 1.9% | 1.1% | | 5.6% | | 5.8% | 12% |
| Trade Unionist | 0 | 2 | 1 | 0 | 0 | 2 | 0 | 0 | 1 |
| | | 5.7% | 0.9% | | | 3.7% | | | 4% |
| Social Worker | 4 | 2 | 3 | 6 | 0 | 3 | 10 | 2 | 2 |
| | 6.25% | 5.7% | 2.8% | 6.9% | | 5.6% | 8.2% | 5.8% | 8% |
| Political Worker | 5 | 5 | 19 | 3 | 10 | 5 | 1 | 1 | 0 |
| | 7.8% | 14.2% | 18% | 3.4% | 11.6% | 9.4% | 0.8% | 8% | |
| Former Ruler | 2 | 1 | 0 | 2 | 1 | 0 | 2 | 2 | 0 |
| | 3.1% | 2.8% | | 2.3% | 1.2% | | 1.6% | 5.8% | |
| Religious Figure | 2 | 0 | 2 | 8 | 0 | 1 | 3 | 0 | 0 |
| | 3.1% | | 1.9% | 9.3% | | 1.8% | 2.4% | | |
| Sportsman | 0 | 0 | 0 | 2 | 2 | 1 | 0 | 0 | 0 |
| | | | | 2.3% | 3.3% | 1.8% | | | |
| Other, Not known | | 1 | 1 | 1 | 0 | 0 | 1 | 1 | 0 |
| | | 2.8% | 0.9% | 1.1% | | | 0.8% | 2.9% | |
| TOTAL | 64 | 35 | 105 | 86 | 60 | 53 | 121 | 34 | 25 |
| | 100% | 100% | 100% | 100% | 100% | 100% | 100% | 100% | 100% |

| Castes and communities | 1989 | | | 1991 | | | 1996 | | | 1998 | | |
|---|---|---|---|---|---|---|---|---|---|---|---|---|
| | BJP | Cong | JD | BJP | Cong | JD | BJP | Cong | JD | BJP | Cong | JD +SP +RJD |
| Upper castes | 46.67 | 34.21 | 28.45 | 51.40 | 27.69 | 16.99 | 42.75 | 27.27 | 14.28 | 43.26 | 22.22 | 15.22 |
| Brahman | 17.33 | 15.79 | 6.90 | 24.30 | 10.77 | 1.89 | 19.57 | 15.91 | 4.76 | 18.44 | 6.67 | – |
| Rajput | 16.0 | 7.89 | 14.66 | 17.76 | 6.15 | 13.21 | 13.77 | 4.55 | 7.14 | 12.77 | 2.22 | 15.22 |
| Bhumihar | – | – | 1.72 | – | 3.08 | 1.89 | 1.45 | – | – | 1.42 | 2.22 | – |
| Baniya/Jain | 6.67 | 2.63 | 1.72 | 3.74 | 3.08 | – | 5.07 | 4.55 | – | 4.96 | 6.67 | – |
| Kayasth | 2.67 | 5.26 | 2.59 | 1.87 | 3.08 | – | 2.17 | – | 2.38 | 2.13 | 2.22 | – |
| Other* | 4.0 | – | 15.52 | 9.35 | 13.85 | 1.89 | 7.97 | 20.45 | – | 8.51 | 2.22 | – |
| Intermediate | 8.0 | 7.89 | 15.52 | 9.35 | 13.85 | 1.89 | 7.97 | 20.45 | – | 8.51 | 2.22 | – |
| Castes | | | | | | | | | | | | |
| Jat | – | 2.63 | 11.21 | 2.80 | 10.77 | 1.89 | 4.35 | 13.64 | – | 4.26 | 11.11 | – |
| Maratha | 1.33 | 2.63 | – | 0.93 | 1.54 | – | 0.72 | 2.27 | – | 0.71 | 2.22 | – |
| Patidar | 6.67 | – | 4.31 | 5.61 | 1.54 | – | 2.90 | 4.55 | – | 3.55 | 4.44 | – |
| Bishnoi | – | 2.63 | – | – | – | – | – | – | – | – | 4.44 | – |
| OBC | 16.0 | 5.26 | 26.72 | 14.02 | 13.85 | 39.62 | 18.1 | 11.36 | 54.76 | 17.02 | 8.89 | 50.0 |
| Yadav | 1.33 | – | 14.66 | – | 1.54 | 22.64 | 1.45 | – | 33.33 | 1.42 | 2.22 | 21.74 |
| Kurmi | 5.33 | 5.26 | 4.31 | 7.48 | 4.62 | 9.43 | 5.80 | – | 4.76 | 7.09 | – | 10.87 |
| Lodh | 2.67 | – | 0.86 | 2.80 | – | – | 2.90 | – | – | 2.13 | – | – |
| Other | 6.67 | 6.90 | 6.90 | 3.74 | 7.69 | 7.55 | 7.97 | 11.36 | 16.67 | 4.26 | 6.67 | 17.39 |
| SC | 16.0 | 18.42 | 18.10 | 16.82 | 15.38 | 24.53 | 21.01 | 11.36 | 14.29 | 15.60 | 11.11 | 17.39 |
| ST | 9.33 | 23.68 | 3.45 | 4.67 | 21.54 | – | 7.97 | 22.73 | – | 6.38 | 26.67 | – |
| Muslim | 1.33 | 5.26 | 6.9 | – | 4.62 | 13.2 | – | 4.55 | 14.29 | 0.71 | 4.44 | 13.04 |
| Sikh | 1.33 | – | – | 0.93 | – | – | 0.72 | – | – | 0.71 | – | – |
| Christian | – | 2.63 | – | – | – | 1.89 | – | – | 2.38 | – | – | 2.17 |
| Sadhu | – | – | – | 1.87 | – | – | – | – | – | – | – | – |
| Unidentified | 1.33 | 2.63 | 0.86 | 0.93 | 3.08 | 1.89 | 1.45 | 2.27 | – | 7.80 | 4.44 | 2.17 |
| TOTAL | 100.0 | 100 | 100 | 100 | 100 | 100 | 100 | 100 | 100 | 100 | 100 | 100 |
| | N = 75 | N = 38 | N = 166 | N = 107 | N = 65 | N = 53 | N = 138 | N = 44 | N = 42 | N = 141 | N = 45 | N = 46 |

* Khattri, Amil Tyagi.

for two main reasons. One was its sanskritized style and defence of social hierarchy; the other was its economic liberalism and defence of the 'middle world', a world, according to Bruce Graham, composed of 'the provincial professions, small industry, and country trading and banking' (Graham 1990: 158). The affinity between Hindu nationalism and these categories was particularly noticeable in the towns of the Hindi belt. Since the late 1980s, however, the BJP has benefited from the growth of a new middle class that has emerged largely as a result of economic liberalization. The system of values of this rising social category is based, in theory at least, on merit gained through hard work. Its members thus show little concern for the poor (Kothari 1988) and disapprove of reservation systems in principle. These views overlap with those of the BJP. The party advocates a more vigorous liberalization of the domestic economy. It also expresses apprehensions about caste-based reservations, though publicly it has to moderate its stand so as not to alienate the OBC voters. In fact, the Mandal affair was probably as important as the Ayodhya movement in rallying upper caste middle class support around the BJP in the early 1990s.

This middle class not only shares the BJP's concern about the rise of new groups (the OBCs and the Dalits)—that is, its apprehension regarding the social dimension of democracy— they also have in common with it a growing questioning of parliamentary government. In 1993, an opinion poll conducted in Mumbai, Delhi, Kolkata, Chennai, and Bangalore revealed that 58 per cent of interviewees agreed with the following proposition: 'If the country is to progress, it needs a dictator'. (*The Times of India*, 28 December 1993: 1, 11). The anti-parliament attitude underlying this stand reflects the opprobrium affecting politicians. The survey conducted by the Centre for the Study of Developing Societies during the 1996 elections showed that only 22 per cent of the interviewees thought that their MP cared for the people (as against 27 per cent in 1971) (*India Today*, 31 August 1996: 31). The authoritarian option, however, seems to be considered by the urban middle class alone. Among the interviewees of the 1993 survey, 68 per cent declared that they belonged to the 'middle class' (as against eight per cent to the 'lower-middle class', nine per cent to the 'upper-middle class', and 10 per cent to the 'working class'). Indeed, the masses continue to regard the act of voting as useful, as testified by the fact that ordinary people vote more than the elite groups.[9]

The urban middle class obviously aspires to a more orderly day-to-day life and a kind of discipline that is regarded as a precondition for economic progress. This is one of the reasons for the attraction the BJP holds for this group, since it is known for its RSS background. The urban middle class also approves of the BJP's crusade against corruption, a theme that it has cashed in on despite allegations that some of its leaders had been involved in corruption. The common assumption is that parliamentary democracy not only needs to be disciplined; it also needs to be purified.

Historically, the Hindu nationalists have supported democracy largely because, in contrast to today's advocates of 'Asian values' in South East and East

TABLE 10.3: CASTE BACKGROUND OF THE PARTIES' ELECTORATES

| | Cong(I) | BJP | NF/LF | BSP | State Parties | Others |
|---|---|---|---|---|---|---|
| Forward | 29 | 33 | 17 | 1 | 10 | 10 |
| OBC | 25 | 23 | 25 | 2 | 18 | 7 |
| SC | 31 | 11 | 21 | 16 | 14 | 7 |
| ST | 47 | 17 | 15 | 2 | 7 | 12 |

Source: *India Today,* 31 May 1996: 27.

Asia, for whom democracy is an import from the West, they have regarded it as a national regime. According to them, India was always a democracy—before foreign invasions—and to say so was a good means for regaining one's self-esteem in front of the British. This 'traditional' democracy, however, does not meet the criteria of parliamentary or liberal democracy, since Hindu nationalists have tended to be favourably inclined towards an organicist arrangement. This approach is not fundamentally different from the Gandhian view of democracy.

The democratic credentials of Hindu nationalists can be questioned for other reasons. First, they supported democracy as the most convenient regime for establishing a permanent Hindu domination, since Hindus were a majority. Second, the RSS has been keen to exert some influence on the political domain even though it has not contested elections itself. Third, even though the BJP holds internal elections more often than most other organizations and parties, the RSS and its offshoots are not ruled by democratic procedures, since there is often only one candidate for one post and the personalization of power, as well as the repression of any dissent, are commonplace. Today, these authoritarian leanings find expression in a more or less openly declared interest in a presidential system of governance.

The fourth factor affecting the credibility of the Hindu nationalist commitment to democracy lies in its sociological composition: the movement is still identified with the upper castes, since a large number of its leaders, militants, and voters belong to this milieu. Though the BJP is gradually promoting low caste cadres within the party apparatus, it still does not contribute to the present-day (social) democratization of Indian (political) democracy.

## Notes

1. I have developed this point in the first chapter of my book (1996).
2. R.K. Mookerji belonged to the Bengal Hindu Sabha and was one of the opponents of the Communal Award in 1932. See Chatterji 1994: 26-7.
3. In the late 1940s, he was closely associated with Hindu nationalist leaders (such as Shyama Prasad Mookerjee), for his fight on behalf of Hindi and the refugees from East Bengal.
4. Here, the notion of *samskaras* does not refer to 'rites of passage' but, as often in the RSS' discourse, to all the good influences which can be exerted on the formation of character (Jaffrelot 1996: 48).

5. Savarkar reiterated this stand in even more explicit terms in his 1938 presidential address: 'The Hindu Sannathanist Party aims to base the future Constitution of Hindusthan on the broad principle that all citizens should have equal rights and obligations irrespective of caste or creed, race or religion, provided they avow and owe an exclusive and devoted allegiance to the Hindusthani State. . . . No attitude can be more National, even in the territorial sense than this and it is an attitude in general which is expressed by the curt formula "one man, one vote"' (*The Indian Annual Register,* 1939, Vol. 2: 325).

6. See, for instance, the party's election manifesto in 1996 (Bharatiya Janata Party 1996).

7. Vajpayee reiterated his attacks on the foreign origin of parliamentary democracy on several occasions. Delivering the M.S. Golwalkar Memorial Lecture organized by the Deendayal Research Institute on 22 February 1997, he considered that the low level of the socioeconomic development in India resulted from 'the present system of parliamentary democracy, which we borrowed blindly from the British' (*The Organiser,* 9 March 1996).

8. Digvijay Singh, the Chief Minister of Madhya Pradesh, for instance, advocated a presidential form of government (*National Mail,* 21 October 1996).

9. Among those who voted more, one finds the 'very poor' people (+2.9 point above the average turnout), the Scheduled Castes (+1.9 point), and the villagers (+1.1 point). Among those whose turnout is below the average, one finds the upper castes (−1.6 point), urban dwellers (−3 point), and graduates and post-graduates (−4.5 point) (*India Today,* 31 August 1996: 30–9).

# References

'Agenda', *The Pioneer,* 6 April 1997.

Advani, L.K. (1986), *Presidential Address,* BJP Plenary Session, 9 May.

—— (1987), *Presidential Address,* 9th National Council Session, 2–4 January.

Aurobindo, Sri (1970), 'Bande Mataram' (article dated 20 March 1908), in *Collected Works,* Vol. 1, Pondichery: Sri Aurobindo Ashram Trust.

Bharatiya Janata Party (1996), *For a Strong and Prosperous India: Election Manifesto 1996,* New Delhi.

Bharatiya Jana Sangh (1973), 'Manifesto-1954', in *Party Documents,* Vol. 1, New Delhi: BJS.

Chatterji, J. (1994), *Bengal Divided: Hindu Communalism and Partition, 1932–1947,* Cambridge: Cambridge University Press.

*Constituent Assembly Debates* (1989), Vol. 1, New Delhi: Lok Sabha Secretariat.

Dalton, D. (1982), 'The Concept of Politics and Power in India's Ideological Tradition', in A. Jeyaratnam Wilson and Dennis Dalton (eds.), *The States of South Asia: Problems of National Integration,* London: Hurst.

Gandhi, M.K. (1922) (5th edn), *Indian Home Rule,* Madras: Ganesh and Co.

—— (1967), 'The Kingdom of Rama', in K. Satchidananda Murty (ed.), *Readings in India History, Politics and Philosophy,* London: George Allen and Unwin.

Golwalkar, M.S. (1966), *Bunch of Thoughts,* Bangalore: Jagrana Prakashan.

Goyal, D.R. (1978), *Rashtriya Swayamsevak Sangh*, New Delhi: Radhakrishna Prakashan.

Graham, B. (1990), *Hindu Nationalism and Indian Politics*, Cambridge: Cambridge University Press.

*The Hindu*, 16 September 1974, 27 April 1998, 5 May 1998.

*The Hindustan Times*, 21 July and 27 July 1998.

*Indian Annual Register*, 1938, Vol. 1.

———, 1939, Vol. 2.

———, 1940, Vol. 1.

*India Today*, 31 August 1996, 15 May 1997.

Jaffrelot, C. (1996), *The Hindu Nationalist Movement and Indian Politics, 1925-1990s*, New Delhi: Viking.

Jaiswal, K.P. (1924), *Hindu Polity: A Constitutional History of India in Hindu Times*, Calcutta: Butterworth.

Kaviraj, S. (1994), 'Democracy and Development in India', in A.K. Bagchi (ed.), *Democracy and Development*, London: Macmillan.

Kothari, R. (1988), 'Class and Communalism in India', *Economic and Political Weekly*, 3 December.

Mookerji, R.K. (1950), *Hindu Civilization: From the Earliest Time up to the Establishment of the Maurya Empire*, Bombay: Bharatiya Vidya Bhavan.

Narayan, Jayaprakash (1959), *A Plea for Reconstruction of Indian Polity*, Kashi Akhil Bharat Sarva Seva Sangh.

*National Mail*, 21 October 1996.

*The Organiser*, 24 October 1955.

———, 'Adhivakta Parishad wants checks and balances through Dharma in Constitution', 5 January 1995.

———, Interview with A.B. Vajpayee, 'Sangh is My Soul', May 1995, reprinted in *Communalism Combat*, February 1998.

———, A.B. Vajpayee, 'Challenges to Democracy in India', 24 November 1996.

———, *Varsha Pratipada Special*, 'National Agenda for Governance', 29 March 1998.

———, 'Vajpayee Advocates a Change in Our System of Governance', 9 March.

Prasad, Beni (1928), *The State in Ancient India*, Allahabad: The Indian Press.

Savarkar, S.S. and Joshi, S.S. (1967) (eds.), *Historic Statements: V.D. Savarkar*, Bombay: Popular Prakashan.

*The Statesman*, 16 January and 2 February 1991, Delhi.

Thengadi, D.P. (1991), 'Lamp at the Threshold', Preface to P.G. Sahasrabuddhe and M.C. Vajpayee, *The People versus Emergency: A Saga of Struggle*, New Delhi: Suruchi Prakashan.

*The Times of India*, 28 December 1993.

# Chapter 11

# The Vishva Hindu Parishad: a nationalist but mimetic attempt at federating the Hindu sects

> Remember, it is the VHP that has given these sants legitimacy and exposure. Their only audience consisted of old men and women. Now they have a large audience. — A vice-president of the BJP, *India Today*, 1995: 35

> The leaders have let us down too many times. If the sants and sadhus had not called us, we would not have come this time.
> — A *karsevak* who went to Ayodhya to prepare for the construction of the Ram temple, *The Times of India*, 1992

The Vishva Hindu Parishad (VHP) can only be understood in relation to the Rashtriya Swayamsevak Sangh (RSS). Not only does the movement draw its ideology from the RSS, its structure is also derived from it. Indeed, the backbone of the VHP is embodied in the figure of the *pracharak*, a full-time 'preacher' and organizer of the RSS. These *pracharaks* are specially trained in Instructors' Training Camps and then at the Officers' Training Camps of the RSS. Though they are often well educated they renounced career and family life to devote themselves more completely to the cause of Hindu nationalism. Besides, they are bound to an itinerant life because their mission is to pervade the network of RSS *shakhas*.

*Pracharaks* conceive of their mission, their self-denial and austerity, in a manner similar to renouncers. They are perceived as such by several young *swayamsevaks* of the *shakhas,* who may even regard their *pracharak* as a guru. The RSS thus constitutes a kind of nationalist sect.[1] It presents itself both as a 'brotherhood in saffron'[2] inspired by the Hindu sect pattern, and in the words of its founder Hedgewar, in his last speech delivered in 1940, as the 'Hindu Rashtra in miniature'.[3]

The affinities that the RSS *pracharaks* entertain with the Hindu sects are especially important for their activities in the VHP since this organization has been created to bring together the largest possible number of religious figures. However, the VHP does not draw its inspiration from the traditional Hindu sect, except for the self-professed asceticism of its *pracharaks*. Interestingly, it has undertaken its mission by imitating the ecclesiastical structure characteristic of 'Semitic religions', Christianity and Islam, so as to more effectively resist these very religions—which it perceives as posing a threat to Hinduism.

## RSS *Pracharaks* and 'Modern Gurus'

The first project director of the VHP was Shiv Shankar Apte, a Maharashtrian Brahman born in Baroda. Apte studied law in Bombay before becoming an advocate in the sphere of influence of K.M. Munshi, a Congress leader known for his traditionalist Hindu positions.[4] Attracted by journalism, Apte collaborated for a time with the United Press of India, but his encounter with Golwalkar, head of the RSS from 1940 to 1973, led him to embrace the career of *pracharak* (*Shraddhanjali Smarika*: 28). In 1961, Apte published three articles in *Kesari* (a paper founded by B.G. Tilak) on the need to hold a meeting to bring together all the currents of Hinduism in order to create greater coherence.[5]

Soon after, an article by Swami Chinmayananda echoed his thoughts:

> It seemed to me, in a way that was still vague, that it was time to call for a *World Hindu Council* [the English name which the Vishva Hindu Parishad gave itself] by inviting to Delhi or Calcutta delegates from throughout the world to discuss the difficulties and needs concerning the survival and development of Hindu culture. In this Council, we would elaborate the plans and programmes making it possible to bring the family of Hindu dharma together. (*Hindu Vishva* [hereafter *H.V.*], 1980: 19)

Chinmayananda was a disciple of Swami Shivanand, founder of the Divine Life Society in Haridwar. Coming from a respected family in Kerala, he attempted to pursue his studies in Chennai but, not able to enrol at the university, he left to study law in Lucknow in the early 1940s. He then became a journalist in Delhi. It was in this capacity that, in order to investigate *sadhus* whom he suspected of deception, he went to the Himalayas and eventually became a disciple of Swami Shivanand. After having been initiated into the Adi Shankaracharya order at the *math* in Sringeri by his guru, Swami Tapovanand, he gave lectures on *jnana yajna* (the sacrifice of knowledge) in the 1950s. He described these sermons as a metaphor for Vedic sacrifice. He assembled five pandits around the *kund*, where the fire is lit, who were responsible for making sacrificial offerings (*ahuti*). Thereby, the human body is the *kund*, its five senses replace the priests, their perceptions are the offerings of the soul—the kindling of which is analogous to the flame.[6] The verve with which Chinmayananda described the 'sacrifice' bears testimony to his rhetorical ability. It was the latter to which he owed unforeseen popular success; his lectures attracted thousands of disciples and he began to make all India tours in the 1950s. The social milieu which he wished to address most was the middle classes, whom he described as 'modern educated illiterates'. This was without doubt the reason why he established his ashram, the Sandypani Academy, in Bombay, the gateway to Westernized India. He soon awakened the hostility of the 'orthodox'— starting with his guru and the monastery with which he was affiliated, Sringeri— by promoting English as the medium of communication and acknowledging Hindus of all castes, irrespective of gender, and allowing them all access to spiritual knowledge. His sermons attracted, primarily, disciples from the middle class, not only in India but also in South-East Asia and the United States. Van der Veer thus sees him as a precursor of the 'modern guru'[7] a category which can be defined on the basis of a few of Chinmayananda's characteristics. His spiritual practise rested on a discourse which valorized individual development and a moral code as a factor in social success. To these themes the middle class in Western countries and in India were responsive.

Second, he did not fit into a precise sectarian tradition; the sectarian affiliation diminished in value relative to the 'Hindu' allegiance. He founded his own ashram. He began quite early to increase his lecturing throughout the world, and this was well in tune with the form he had chosen for his teaching, for in his arena the personal relation of master to disciple became less significant than public discourse. Swami Chinmayananda, moreover, did not initiate his *shishyas* (disciples) by whispering a mantra in their ears. He held such practice to be obsolete because they were elitist. He gave his mantra 'from the dais' to the entire audience. From this perspective, Chinmayananda was heir to neo-Hindu socio-religious reform movements. Ramakrishna too did not initiate disciples, either, and they too were recruited precisely from the Westernized middle class (Sarkar 1992: 1543–66).

S.S. Apte was of course interested in the article written by Swami Chinmayananda in 1963. The encounter of these two men is significant because they are representative of the two categories which were to form the keystone of the Vishva Hindu Parishad: Hindu nationalists and the modern guru. Apte, in effect, undertook to contact the greatest possible number of sect leaders with a view to founding the VHP in 1964, but he primarily rallied modern gurus. He travelled for nine months throughout India to find people interested in his project. He was in communication with roughly 800 people, of whom 150 were guests at the inaugural conference of the VHP (*H.V.*, September-October 1980: 19).

## The VHP: Council of 'Hinduism'?

Apte saw in the VHP an instrument of consolidation through the unification of Hinduism. Its foundation ensued mainly from the sentiment that Christian proselytism[8] constituted a threat to Hinduism, and that it was therefore necessary to emulate its techniques so as to offer more effective resistance. Indeed the VHP gives a good illustration of what I have called the Hindu nationalist strategy of the stigmatization and emulation of so-called threatening others. For the RSS leaders and their followers, Hindus are vulnerable to Muslims and Christians because these communities are supported from outside India and because they then expand (through conversions or high birth rates), but also because they believe Hindus are weak and divided into too many castes and sects. One of the remedies lies in imitating their 'threatening others', mainly Christians, in the view of the VHP.

Even though the project of such an organization developed over a long period, its formation was precipitated in 1964 because of the Pope's visit. The Pope announced, in August, that the International Eucharistic Conference was to be held in Bombay in November. The organ of the RSS, *The Organiser*, spoke out against this 'invasion' after the announcement had been made, maintaining that 'Catholicism [was] not only a religion, but a formidable organisation allied with certain foreign powers . . . . The conversion of tribals on a large scale in the industrial heart of India [in Bihar] constitute[d] a threat for national security because, in the case of conflict between their country and the church, the allegiance of Catholics [would] always be foremostly to the Pope!'⁹ This image of an enemy whose strength was derived from organizational rigour and its transnational dimension underlies the objective of Hindu nationalists to provide their religion with the ecclesiastical form of a church. This sheds light on the task and structure assigned to the VHP.

S.S. Apte˜ explained the foundation of the movement in the following terms:

> The declared objective of Christianity is to transform the entire world into Christendom, just as it is that of Islam to make a Pak[istan]. Beside these two dogmatic and proselytising religions, a third has appeared, Communism . . . . The world has been divided into Christian, Islamic and Communist [zones], and these three consider Hindu society to be a very good and very rich food upon which they feast and grow fat. It is therefore necessary, in this age of competition and conflict, to think of organising the Hindu world to save it from the evil eyes of these three. (*The Organiser*, Divali Special, 1964: 15)

The main example offered by the author in support of his argument was the 'separatism' of the Naga tribes in the north-east which had just been granted Nagaland in 1963. The RSS attributed this move to the 'denationalization' of the aborigines by the missions.¹⁰ The RSS decided to react to this 'aggression' by using the weapons of the 'aggressors': the Hindus had to borrow Christians' techniques to resist them more efficiently. Hence the church-like structure of the VHP, for it is intended to be a centralized federation of the sects of Hinduism. S.S. Apte was explicit on this point in his opening speech at the founding conference of the VHP:

> Vishnuites, Saivites, Lingayats, Advaits, Dalits, Vishnuite-Dvaits, Sikhs, Jains, Buddhists— in fact all the *panth* denominations of our very diverse society, as well as the people [Hindus] living in foreign countries, can make their difficulties disappear and come together to recognise the unity behind the diversity. Our effort is to promote a harmonious mutual understanding and a new order in accordance with the genius and spirit of our ancient noble heritage, while answering to the exigencies of the modern scientific age. (*H.V.*, September-October 1980: 4)

The founding conference brought together representatives of different sects—for example Tara Singh and Gyani Bhupendra Singh, the president of the SGPC¹¹—which constituted for the Hindu nationalists a current of Hinduism. In addition, the VHP provided itself with an 'advisory council grouping the shankaracharyas, the holy leaders and the gurus of all the Sampradayas and Panths'

(*The Organiser,* Divali Special, 1964: 15). It was also decided to organize a large international conference in Allahabad on the occasion of the Kumbh Mela in 1966, in which 'the learned of all sects' were to participate.[12]

To bring the different *shankaracharyas* together into the VHP was all the more difficult as they traditionally argued over pre-eminence. The First World Hindu Conference in Allahabad, which was given the old Sanskrit name Prayag, on 22-4 January 1966, suffered from the defection of *shankaracharyas* from Badrinath and Sringeri. Among 25,000 delegates, at least as many founders of ashrams or heads of modern associations were to be found as were spiritual masters initiated and invested, according to the rules of sects, with an ancient tradition. Among the former, the presence of two individuals in particular should be mentioned.

Prabhu Dutt Brahmachari had participated in the independence movement, attracted by Gandhi and by Hindu traditionalists such as M.M. Malaviya, P.D. Tandon and Sampurnanand. In the 1920s, these traditionalists invited him to join the editorial staff of *Aaj,* a Hindi paper in Benares. Shortly thereafter, however, he became a renouncer and founded his ashram in Jhuri, near Allahabad, where he participated in the organization of the Kumbh Mela. In 1948, the head of the Allahabad RSS, Rajendra Singh, who became chief of the RSS almost 50 years later, made his acquaintance. M.S. Golwalkar also drew close to him. During the 1951-2 elections, he followed the suggestions of these men and stood against Nehru in the name of cow protection and in opposition to the Hindu Code Bill (*The Organiser,* 26 October 1990: 9). Prabhu Dutt Brahmachari was the true exemplar of the category of 'modern guru'—sadhus who had founded their own ashrams and were active in politics.

Another important modern Hindu leader present at the first VHP conference was Sant Tukdoji. As president of the Bharat Sadhu Samaj, Sant Tukdoji was more representative of the 'Hindu traditionalist' current of the VHP.[13] He attributed his going over to the VHP to the need to protect Hinduism against Christianity and Islam, as well as against the anti-Hindu stance of the government (*The Organiser,* 26 December 1965).

Among the representatives of historical religious currents, the most significant was Swami Vishvesh Tirth of Pejawar *math* (Udupi, Karnataka), the spiritual leader of the Vishnuite Madhva sect (*The Organiser,* 30 January 1966: 1; 3 May 1981: 4). Born in 1931, he had been initiated to this order at the age of seven, and subsequent to apparently rigorous studies, notably of the Vedanta; he was named head of the Sri Krishna *math* in Udupi in 1951. He then established his reputation as a defender of Hindu culture through the Madhva Mahamandal, an institution principally active in the area of education (for the promotion of the learning of Sanskrit and the *shastras*) (*H.V.,* May 1981: 39).

The under-representation of spiritual masters at the head of prestigious sects suggests that the VHP attracted, above all, swamis who sought additional legitimacy or a valourizing platform. This was a question of weakness but not necessarily of an insurmountable handicap insofar as the authority of a Hindu spiritual master can be derived from a source other than official investiture at the head of a recognized sect. Knowledge of spiritual texts, an ascetic discipline, and rhetorical talent can compensate for these and help make it possible to proclaim oneself as a religious spokesman.

Despite its poor representativeness, the meeting in Allahabad was intended to be a kind of parliament[14] and repository of Hinduism. A subcommittee was designated to 'elaborate a code of conduct suitable to promote and strengthen the Hindu *samskars*' (*H.V.*, 30 January 1966: 2). This Vidvat Parishad then met to simplify the rites of purification, to give an official status to five principal festivals of the Hindu calendar, and above all to elaborate the much-vaunted code of conduct. Significantly, the process was accomplished in reference to Christianity and Islam:

Christians and Muslims generally observe in a strict and scrupulous manner certain rules of religious conduct. Every Christian and Muslim, moreover, possesses outward symbols indicative of his religion. The Parishad has felicitously arrived at a 'code of conduct' which is suitable for all sects and beliefs. It has decided that the *pratashnan* (morning ablutions) and the *ishwarsmaran* (the reciting of the name of god) would constitute the minimal rules of conduct. (*H.V.*, 11 June 1967: 14)

Beyond these efforts to enact a code of conduct, the VHP also sought to establish its central authority over an entire religious network which was scattered through monasteries and temples. Priests were thus called upon at the Prayag assembly to make these latter places centres for the 'propagation of dharma and sanskriti' (*H.V.*, 30 January 1966: 15).

At the end of January 1979, a Second World Hindu Conference was held in Allahabad under the auspices of the VHP. As in 1966, this conference was intended to be a comprehensive gathering, but in a more credible manner, considering the number (estimated at 100,000) and representativeness of the delegates. The 'different currents' of the 'Hindu nation' were, in effect, represented: Buddhism by the Dalai Lama, who inaugurated the conference; the Namdhari Sikhs and the Jains by two dignitaries from those communities; the disciples of Shankara by the *shankaracharya* of Badrinath; the 'dualists' by two Jagadgurus from Udupi; and the Nimbarkis, the Vallabhis, the different schools and disciples of Ramanuja, the Ramanandis, the disciples of Chaitanya, those of Kabir, the Naths of Gorakhpur, the Arya Samajists, the Ramakrishna Mission and the Divine Life Society by various personalities.

The logic of these unitarian efforts remained that of a strategic mimetism: Hinduism was threatened by the proselytising religions which imperilled its majority status.[15] This implied the eradication of untouchability, which was a factor in conversions, and the unification of Hinduism via a coherent whole. These two remedies were once again proposed by reference to the cultural characteristics of Christian and Muslim 'aggressors'.

From this perspective the VHP again proposed a 'minimum code of conduct for the daily life of every Hindu', the objective of which was once again the unification of religious practices and references. Article 1 called for the veneration by all, morning and evening, of the sun; Article 2 for the systematization of the symbol 'om' (on lockets, visiting cards, etc.). Article 3 was yet more explicit: 'The Bhagavad Gita is the sacred book of Hindus, regardless of their sect. It contains the essence of Hindu philosophy. All Hindus should have a copy in their home' (*H.V.*, March-April 1979: 89). Notwithstanding the number of delegates present in Prayag in 1979, those endowed with real authority were either absent (such as the more important *shankaracharyas*), or not very active in the VHP (such as the *shankaracharya* of Badrinath). The main religious figures significantly involved were not recognized as sect leaders, but as heads of their own ashrams, such as a newcomer who was to become a pillar of the VHP, namely Satyamitranand Giri.

Born in Agra in 1932 into a Brahman family, Satyamitranand Giri pursued his studies in the establishments of the Arya Samaj and the Hindi Sahitya Sammelan until receiving his M.A. in Hindi literature. He then embraced the calling of a renouncer and made his way to the Himalayas. Initiated in Rishikesh by the *shankaracharya* of Jyotirmath, he accepted, at the age of twenty-eight, the directorship of the Bhanpura *math* (Mandsaur district in Madhya Pradesh), the foundation of which is attributed to Shankara. He assumed this responsibility for three years as *shankaracharya*, then resigned so as to travel more freely. His journeys to southern Africa and the United States showed him that the spiritual addresses asked of him in these regions were more highly valued and lucrative than what he made by teaching his Indian disciples, despite their becoming increasingly numerous, particularly among the Patels of Gujarat.[16] One year, after having given up the office of *shankaracharya*, Satyamitranand Giri participated in the foundation of the VHP, which had offered him a prestigious platform.[17] However, he only joined the core influential people in the organization a few years later, after constructing a Bharat Mata Mandir with a pedagogic aim in Haridwar.[18]

Among the most active sect leaders in the VHP now figured Mahant Avaidyanath who, in the 1970s, had succeeded his guru Digvijay Nath as head of the sect of Naths in Gorakhpur. Like his father, he was invested with important responsibilities in the Hindu Mahasabha, a small Hindu nationalist party. He was elected MLA from the district of Gorakhpur in 1962, 1974 and 1977, then to the Lok Sabha in 1970, 1989 and 1991 (Parliament of India 1992: 43). At the same time, he occupied positions at the head of the Congress-backed Bharat Sadhu Samaj of the region in the 1960s.[19]

From its foundation in 1964 to the 1970s, the VHP thus endeavoured to group together the largest possible number of religious figures so as to provide Hinduism with an ecclesiastical structure. This undertaking attracted, above all, modern gurus who sought a valourizing platform, indeed legitimization, while the heads of 'historical sects', not having the same needs, showed more reserve—a few personalities excepted—in relation to the type of organization which was until then unknown to Hinduism, and which would undermine their independence.

When the VHP was founded, Apte was aware of the need to introduce new principles into Hinduism in order to defend the idea of a greater organization of sects: 'modernisation is a *sine qua rum* for the continuity and eternal survival of a society.'[20] Swami Chinmayananda recognized that the very idea of the VHP was at odds with Hinduism:

I know that religious organisation is contrary to the very principle of Hinduism, but we must evolve with our times . . . . If one remains unorganised, one has neither strength nor vitality. Consequently, in the spiritual domain, even if progress and development are accomplished on the individual level, religion must also organize itself to serve society . . . . If we do not organise ourselves, there will be no integration. And that is a matter of urgency. If we are not integrated despite the 82% of the population which we represent, our voices will never be heard. While the 18% [*sic*] Christians and Muslims are well organized. Their demands and their needs are well taken care of by the democratic government . . . (*Shraddhanjali Smarika* n.d.: 69)

Chinmayananda thus justifies the organization of Hinduism by means of the VHP on the basis of the threat which the Muslim and Christian minorities represent.

This change was thus legitimized by the higher stakes involved, also by the so-called Hindu tradition. Apte declared during the founding conference of the VHP:

It has been our tradition, since Vedic times, to come together in moments of crisis to reform society and cure its disorders. There were Jain assemblies, Buddhist councils and gatherings of the Sikh Panth, in which we sought solutions to the scourge which encroached more and more on society. If I had to, I would say that there has not been a united and representative gathering of all the *panths* and sects of our multi-petal society since the epoch of Harsha. We have today the possibility to create it. (*H.V.*, September-October 1980:19)

The VHP also compared the conferences of 1966 and 1979 to that called by Emperor Harsha in the seventh century. At Prayag he had brought together representatives of different religious currents in India to induce them to live on good terms. This practise, however, reflected the Buddhist influences to which Harsha had been exposed (Devahuti 1970: 96, 157). But the relevance for Hindu nationalists lay in finding a 'national' reference suitable for legitimizing this type of gathering which was not really in character with Hinduism. A prestigious past was evoked so as to present a cultural import—the principle of an ecclesiastical structure. The mimetic aspect of the VHP's mindset had to be concealed somehow, even though it was more or less acknowledged by Apte himself.

Soon after its creation in 1964, the VHP succeeded in implanting its network throughout India, notably by employing on the one hand the ideological affinities which associate the *pracharaks* and the sadhus as variants of the figure of the renouncer and, on the other hand, the relationship between the notable-cum-patron (*rais*, *jajman*) and the religious figure (brahman, sadhu).

## The *Swayamsevak*, the Notable and the Sadhu

The Vishva Hindu Parishad is not only inscribed in the Hindu nationalist project of the RSS, but is also part of the strategy of the movement. In addition to its purpose of becoming a council of Hinduism, the organization is intended to enable the structure of the Hindu nationalist movement to pervade national and local levels by bringing together notables and sadhus imbued with its ideology.

Succeeding each other as general secretaries of the organization were senior *pracharaks* who ensured a liaison with the leadership of the RSS, located in Nagpur. In 1982, the VHP was assigned a new general secretary, Har Mohan Lal, a diamond merchant from Agra and *swayamsevak* since 1947.[21] Most significantly, a secretary, Ashok Singhal, an Arya Samajist from Aligarh and former *pracharak* of the RSS for the Kanpur region, was appointed. Singhal became general secretary at the death of Har Mohan Lal in April 1986, and his office of deputy general secretary fell to Acharya Giriraj Kishore, *swayamsevak* since 1940 and then *pracharak*.[22] The preponderance of men from the RSS at the head of the VHP is confirmed and reinforced by the action of Moropant Pingle, a member of the general staff of the RSS who, as a 'trustee' of the VHP, exercized a strong influence on the conduct of the organization from the 1980s onwards.

These men benefited from the patronage of notables who often held positions as 'trustees', generous members who were benefactors. Eminent people linked with land or business affairs were attracted to this organization for the defence of Hinduism. These activities conform with their traditional function of providing patronage to Hindu institutions.[23] Thus, the Maharaja of Mysore presided over the VHP before being replaced by the Maharaja of Udaipur in 1968 (*The Organiser*, 12 April 1968: 6). Another princely figure actively involved in the direction of the VHP, Vijaya Raje Scindia, never occupied an official position other than that of 'trustee', but as such she made numerous donations to the organization. Apart from princely families, notables patronizing the VHP were above all recruited from among Marwari industrialists: V.H. Dalmia—elder son of Jaidayal Dalmia (1904-93), founder of an industrial group who also patronized the VHP's cow-protection activities,[24] is president of the VHP; S.B. Somayya is one of the former vice-presidents, and G.H. Singhania is a 'trustee' of the organization. The presence of these eminent personalities serves to enhance the respectability of the VHP. The VHP also benefits from the patronage of retired Congress members,[25] or of former reputable advocates.[26] It has also attracted the patronage of retired policemen and armymen: its former vice-president S.C. Dixit was director-general of police in Uttar Pradesh from 1980 to 1984 and joined the movement subsequent to his retirement. He was also vice-president of the Lucknow branch of the Chinmaya Mission, the institution founded by Swami Chinmayananda (Parliament of India 1992: 198). Once again, patronage appears to be addressed to the VHP, as also to other institutions of which the purpose is more religious than ideological; however, it is precisely this distinction which becomes blurred.

While members of the RSS occupy governing positions in the VHP and notables occupy the more honorary posts, sadhus have places in the deliberative areas of the organization's structure. The organizers' endeavour is to woo them in order to institutionalize the collaboration of Hindu nationalist militants and religious leaders. In 1981 the VHP strengthened its Central Margdarshak Mandal (central circle of those 'who show the way'), the members of which were 'to conduct and guide religious ceremonies, morals and ethics of Hindu society'.[27] The members in question, numbering thirty-nine, represented quite comprehensively the sects of Hinduism: four *shankaracharyas* were at the head, then the Nimbarki, Ramanuji, Ramanandi and Goswami Jagadgurus, as well as other minor *acharyas*. Parallel to this instance, the VHP founded a Sadhu Sansad (Parliament of Sadhus), of which the seventeen sadhus were to enable the 'power (*shakti*) of the sadhus [to] play a greater role in the activities of national construction' (*H.V.*, September-October 1980: 30–1).

These institutions evolved over the years; the Margdarshak Mandal, strengthened in its status as permanent organization, was raised to two hundred members who were called upon to meet twice yearly to the purpose of 'advising the VHP in socio-religious domains'.[28] The Sadhu Sansad became, in 1984, a Dharma Sansad comprising hundreds of participants and meeting to discuss 'vital problems' of the country at very irregular intervals. This informal character is found in the Sadhu Sammelans (assemblies) which are called at random.

Parallel to the effort of structuring the religious milieu connected with the VHP, the movement attempted to branch out to the local level. The basic unit of the movement, similar to that of the RSS and BJP, but called *upakhanda*, corresponds to a territory of 2,000 inhabitants; then there are the *khanda* (20,000 inhabitants), the *prakhand* (100,000 inhabitants), the district, division, and finally the state. The *pracharaks* provided by the RSS numbered 150 in 1982, but the VHP also undertook to train its own *dharma pracharaks*; one hundred among them were 'initiated' by the heads of the seven *akharas* in Haridwar, in July 1982 (*The Organiser*, 28 November 1982: 11; 1 August 1982: 1). They were primarily active at the levels of district, division and state. The cadres of the VHP attempted to rally religious leaders at these different levels so as to form equivalent substitutes for the Margdarshak Mandal of the district, division and state. The example of Ujjain in Madhya Pradesh suggests that the main-spring of this enterprise was also constituted at the local level by activists trained by the RSS and receiving the patronage of notables. In this town, the presidency of the local VHP was occupied until 1984 by a former town mayor and member of the Congress. In 1984, the post of president went to a Baniya from the Agarwal caste, Babulal Har Lavaka, who owned an electronic components shop in the town's centre. This man did not belong to a party but was known for his activity in a religious association with philanthropic connotations, the Gayatri Parivar.[29] It was by virtue of his status as a notable patronizing certain forms of social work with Hindu accents that the local RSS leaders asked him to preside over the Ujjain VHP.[30] He never belonged to the RSS and even disapproved of 'certain activities' of the movement.

Lavaka was assisted by a secretary from the *soni* (silversmith) caste, who came from the RSS. He was active for twenty years in the Jana Sangh and the BJP before losing interest in political matters, preferring to work in the VHP.[31] His transfer to this organization corresponds to the desire of RSS leaders to appoint its cadres to offshoots of the movement with which they have the greatest affinities. In addition to the office of secretary in the local VHP, that of *sangathan mantri* is also occupied by a member of the RSS. The *sangathan mantri* supervises six districts around Ujjain. There is, however, no doubt that he represents the kingpin in the organizational structure of the local VHP insofar as he is the favoured correspondent in the hierarchy of the movement.

Compared to the poles constituted by notables and activists, the milieu of religious figures is by far the most interesting in the Ujjain VHP. Ujjain, no doubt by virtue of its status as a 'holy town' alongside a river which is much venerated by Hindus, shelters numerous monasteries. One of the main monasteries, the Sandipani Ashram, is considered by the Vallabhis to be the seventy-third seat of Vallabhacharya, who is said to have held a discourse and to have planted a pipal tree there in the sixteenth century. Ujjain also assumes a particular importance for the Naths. One finds on the periphery of the town the caves where Gorakhnath and Matsyendranath are said to have stayed, as well as the tomb of the latter (Rath n.d.). Despite the significance of the Vallabhi, Nath and Udaisin monasteries, no member of these *sampradayas* participated in the activities of the VHP at the time of our field-work in the early 1990s.

The sadhu representing the religious pole in the local VHP, Swami Shanti Swaroopanand, did not belong to a traditional order. In 1984 he took over the administration of the ashram which had been founded in the 1930s by Swami Akhandanand. Apparently he had been initiated, like Sadhvi Rithambara, by Swami Parmanand in Haridwar. He was thus trained in an activist practice of 'monkhood' centred on propaganda. It was during a tour—which he compared to those by Vivekananda—intended to 'awaken and organize' (*jagaran aur sangathan*)[32] Hindus that he discovered Ujjain and settled at the Akhand Ashram.

Shanti Swaroopanand no doubt represents a category of sadhus who have chosen the career of renouncer less because of the discipline and doctrine of a sect than for ideological reasons. Like the majority of these sadhus, he came from a well-off, educated milieu. The son of a Rajput family, he received his M.A. in philosophy. He initially became interested in 'monkhood' by listening to the sermons (*prachans*) of sadhus passing through his village. Shanti Swaroopanand was clearly attracted by the very ideological discourses held by Swami Parmanand and it is by way of his own rhetorical capacity (which is, in fact, remarkable and in a heavily Sanskritized Hindi) that he was solicited by leaders of the VHP. The ideology which he propounds is in no way distinguishable from the Hindu nationalism of the RSS and its affiliates. Anti-Islamic xenophobia appeared at once as the central motif in his discourse. He invokes the desecrations and persecutions of the Mughal Empire, the separatism of Kashmiri Muslims, and generally those in India who support the Pakistani cricket team and give their allegiance to Arabian countries. The Muslim threat ensues not only from this transnational position but also from the demographic growth of this minority, the males of which, according to Swami Shanti Swaroopanand, marry four times and have on average twelve children. He demands the nationalization of this community, which is to take place through the adoption of a uniform civil code and the recognition of an ancient Hindu culture as the national culture—which does not prohibit the practice of Islam in the private sphere.

Faced with what he considers the Muslim threat, he holds the entrance of sadhus into politics to be a matter of urgency for, on the one hand, awakening and organizing Hindus, and on the other to oblige politicians in New Delhi to desist from serving the minorities in exchange for their votes, but rather to recognize the preponderance of Hindus.

All these arguments have been codified by the RSS and adopted by the VHP decades ago, so that Swami Swaroopanand cuts a much better figure as 'swayamsevak in saffron' than as renouncer. This is all the more so the case as he shows only scorn for sadhus who have withdrawn to the mountains or ashrams, while the real fight, in his eyes, is in the world. This inclination for a life in the world can be inferred from his publicity equipment. He travels in a Maruti van upon which is mounted a loud speaker. His interest in the West is another indication of this and one of his disciples in the ashram, an American, discussed it with him. He was concerned about the price of airline tickets to Europe, where he hoped to be able to hold a few paid lectures on yoga.

This type of sadhu is not only distinguished from renouncers of traditional *sampradayas* by worldly activities, but also through the devalorization of sectarian adherence. He acknowledges being Saivaite in the Paramahans tradition (*parampara*), but wants above all to be 'Hindu'. In addition to his seat in the Margdarshak Mandal, Shanti Swaroopanand is the Pramukh Dharmachari of Madhya Bharat and the patron (*sanrakshak*) of the VHP in Ujjain.

On the whole, the VHP has branched out to the local level on the basis of a potentially influential sociological trilogy, the innovation residing above all in the rallying of religious figures who had previously been more on the margin of the RSS. The network thus formed made possible the meeting of the first Dharma Sansad on 7–8 April 1984 in Delhi, assembling 528 religious representatives of the different currents in Hinduism—in the wider sense as understood by the Hindu nationalists (*H.V.*, August 1990:15).

The important fact to be emphasized regarding the last two or three decades is the increase in the number of 'modern' sadhus who do not all have the status of guru. Most of them have been trained by men of the generation of Swami Chinmayananda, Satyamitranand Giri, Brahma Dutt Brahmachari and Swami Parmanand. Shanti Swaroopanand was trained that way by the latter, like the famous Sadhvi Rithambara. This daughter of a Punjabi farmer belonging to the Kshatriya caste is reputed to have attained 'nirvana' at 16 years of age during a visit by Swami Parmanand to her village. Having followed the latter to his ashram in Haridwar, she was primarily instructed in oratory, like her co-disciple Shanti Swaroopanand. In 1986, at 23 years of age, she developed the art of the *dharmik pravachans* and was soon engaged in agitation for the VHP—with which her guru had links—and then for the BJP in 1989.[33] However, her discourses were apparently presented as being those of another sadhvi, Uma Bharti, whose career had been comparable.

Coming from a low caste (Lodh) family, Bharti was noticed in her village in Madhya Pradesh for her oratory in matters of a religious nature when she was 6 years old. Rajmata Scindia, whose guru lived in a neighbouring district, having been impressed by her sermons, encouraged her to present herself for the 1984 elections as a candidate for the BJP (*Sunday,* 1 September 1991: 27). This attempt was, however, unsuccessful. Uma Bharti only began to show what she could achieve in 1989. During the electoral campaigns of 1989 and 1991 her speeches (apparently made by Sadhvi Rithambara when first recorded on cassettes) revealed a fervent capacity to manipulate religious symbols to political ends.[34] Elected as a member of parliament from Khajuraho, where she is sometimes venerated as a *devi,* at the age of 30 she declared herself a 'religious missionary' by profession in *Who's Who in the Lok Sabha* (Parliament of India 1992).

Significantly, this profession was claimed by three other sadhus elected on the BJP ticket in 1991, with sometimes the additional comment *dharmacharya* or 'social worker' (ibid.: 776–8). These indications confirm that the differences between this kind of religious figure and militant Hindu nationalists, who readily designate themselves in the same way, are very tenuous, all the more so as Uma Bharti and others like her were not initiated into any sect before their entry into the VHP.

## The Infiltration of Religious Institutions

So far, the VHP has not been able to make exceptional inroads among the leadership of orthodox Hinduism; the *shankaracharyas,* for instance remain aloof from the organization, while it recruits its main supporters among 'modern gurus'. However, the movement is deploying a strategy of infiltration regarding temples as well as religious festivals.

One of the departments of the VHP is devoted to the training of *pujaris, purohits* and *pracharaks.* The people responsible for these activities in Madhya Pradesh justify them by alluding to the deterioration of services rendered by priests. Their practice being routinized, they no longer know the meaning of the formulas they recite and have lost all vocation as intermediaries between the devout and god. They are accused of being primarily concerned with earning the money necessary to support their families, and sometimes more.[35] This diagnosis led the VHP towards involvement in the training of priests. To this end the organization has engaged the services of Sanskritists responsible for collecting knowledge from old *pujaris,* and to subsequently open *gurukuls* where children are taught. At the same time, sessions of 'professional training' are offered to priests who are already in service.

This plan of action enables the VHP to enter the temples. Its presence can be observed, apart from the ideology of the priests, in physical terms, as witnessed at the Mahakal temple in Ujjain.

This temple shelters one of the twelve *jyotirlingas* of Mahadev and constitutes as such a highly regarded place of pilgrimage. The procession of the deity Mahakal also attracts dense crowds every year. Vijaya Raje Scindia patronizes the procession from the top of the Gopal Mandir[36] which the Scindia family constructed in 1848-56. She is, in fact, heiress of the dynasty which patronized the religious events and institutions of Ujjain at a time when the town was part of Gwalior State. Daulat Rao Scindia, founder of the dynasty, had the authority to sanction the temples' management to a family of Tailanga Brahmans (Verma and Guru 1982: 373). One sees here the advantage which the VHP can derive from the presence in its ranks of princely notables such as Vijaya Raje Scindia.

Her influence, moreover, is not irrelevant to the presence of the VHP in the Mahakal temple itself. One of the buildings on the side of the tank of the temple was transformed into a *dharamsala,* the immense hall of which is used by the VHP for its meetings.[37] This infiltration into a sacred space by an ideological movement aroused no objection on the part of the roughly fifty *pandits* officiating at the temple. One of them, who underscores, his adherence to the same *biradari* as Madan Mohan Malaviya, considers the VHP to be the base of Hindustan. Hinduism constitutes the national culture of India and should be recognized as such.[38] Another, the descendant of a prestigious lineage of Vallabhi gurus,[39] himself came from the RSS and was elected as municipal councillor on the Jana Sangh ticket before occupying the presidency of the BJP in Ujjain.[40] He too emphasizes the generosity of the Scindia family's official patronage of the temple, and this is a factor in his allegiance to the Rajmata. This individual, Vishwanath Vyas, is a member of a Brahman caste association, as well as president of a Panda Samiti which includes numerous *pujaris* and *purohits,* among whom he can expound the Hindu nationalist ideology.[41]

In addition to infiltrating temples, the VHP uses festivals. Hindu festivals constitute advantageous moments, from the point of view of the VHP, to spread its message as, in most cases, all sects are represented on these occasions. It is keen, then, to prevent the reassertion of differences and rivalries between *sampradayas,* and to promote the notion of Hindu festivals as crucibles of national unity.

To this end, the VHP, developed a department for the coordination of Hindu festivals (*hindu parva samanvaya*), to which was assigned the objective of awakening love of Hinduism. Festivals, from this (ideological) point of view, should be vehicles of national fervour which alone will eliminate the weaknesses of Hindu societies which originated with its enslavement (*goulami*) by the Muslim conquest, and later, colonization.[42] Its priority is the standardization of festivals in such a way that they become national festivals (*rashtriya tyohar*). It is thus necessary to combat the diversity which the 'jatis, sampradayas, panths, mohalles, pradeshes' bring to each celebration, so that all celebrate these festivals in unison (*sammilit*). To do this, the VHP establishes societies for the co-ordination of festivals (*hindu samanvaya samiti*) in as many places as possible/and primarily in places of pilgrimage. Significantly, the model of national festivals spontaneously evoked by Santosh Trivedi, the man in-charge of these questions in the VHP, is the Muslim prayer:

The Muslims perform *namaz,* and one thus sees Islam, a thousand Muslims who bow down and rise up; it is the strength of Islam which one sees. In our festivals, one does not see the identity [in English in the original] of the Hindu, one does not see the strength of the Hindu. This is why the first thing to accomplish is a Hindu reawakening [Hindu *jagaran*] during the festivals so as to bring about mobilization. [in English in the original][43]

This type of discourse well illustrates the process of strategic mimetism involved in the emulation of cultural traits which are supposedly the source of the strength of the Other, the Muslim in this case, in order to more effectively combat it. In this practice the VHP attempted to exploit the calendar of festivals without really succeeding in playing the role of pan-Hindu co-ordination. The organization was founded on the date of Krishna's birth and, above all, it organized its first World Hindu Conference on the occasion of the Kumbh Mela in Allahabad. Afterwards, the sessions of the Dharma Sansad were held quite regularly during the Kumbh Melas in Haridwar and Allahabad, or during the Magh Mela organized every year in that town. During the Kumbh Mela in Allahabad in 1989, the VHP strove to exploit the presence of a very popular sadhu, Devraha Baba. This hermit from Vrindavan, who was quite readily ascribed an age of 300 years, was visited by such dignitaries as Indira Gandhi, who came to seek his blessings, bowing and touching her head to the feet of Baba, who used to be perched on a platform on the bank of the Yamuna. The VHP succeeded in having Devraha Baba on their tribune at the beginning of the Kumbh Mela, in front of a captivated audience (Tully 1992: 100).

The example of Ujjain—another large place of pilgrimage where the VHP attempted to exploit the festivals—illustrates the range, as well as the limitations, of this strategy.[44]

The participation of the VHP in the Mahakal procession would appear to be very revealing in this regard; concerned to affirm their presence, the cadres of the organization took part in the march, clad in their distinctive caps and ochre scarves. But in so doing they appeared to be one of the components in the Hindu mosaic, just like the other *akharas,* and not like an encompassing force. This contradiction emerges yet more clearly from the action of the Hindu nationalist camp during the Kumbh Mela at Ujjain in April 1992.

This festival, organized every twelve years and called Simhastha because it is celebrated when Jupiter enters the house of Lion (*Simha*), is the only Kumbh Mela to have been organized in a town that belonged to a princely state until 1947. And the Scindias, because they financed half the expenses incurred during this event, derived a prestige which continues today to be reflected on Vijaya Raje Scindia. The Simhastha attracts millions of devotees and thousands of sadhus each time it is held. In 1968, some one hundred *akharas* representing 30,000 sadhus are said to have participated (Verma and Guru 1982: 379). In 1992, approximately ten million pilgrims went to Ujjain, from 17 April to 16 May, for a simple bath on a particularly auspicious date, or for a longer stay (*National Mail*, 15 and 17 May 1992). The gathering, of course, represents a prime target for the VHP, which participated there in several forms.

Vijaya Raje Scindia, who presided over the committee responsible for the organization of the Simhastha, supervised the preparation of the festival for several months (*National Mail*, 12 March 1992). Hindu nationalists participated in a Sanskrit Sammelan, opportunely organized at the time of the Simhastha and presided over by Karan Singh.[45] The VHP also made use of this occasion to hold annual sessions of the Bajrang Dal and the Durga Vahini of the Madhya Bharat. The latter, located near the Mahakal temple, was inaugurated by Satyamitranand Giri, who took advantage of the situation to 'reconvert' some hundred tribals to Hinduism.[46] Above all, the VHP employed the framework of the Simhastha to convoke a Sant Sammelan presided over by Avaidhyanath. The latter reaffirmed the determination of his movement regarding the construction of the temple in Ayodhya where the Babri Masjid was to be destroyed nine months later. Ashok Singhal, who dominated the meeting, specified that the Ram Temple would be completed in two years' time and he called upon all the sadhus present to spend the next *chatur mas* (four months around the monsoon season when sadhus are not supposed to travel) in Ayodhya to continue to exert pressure on the government.[47]

The reactions of some sadhus to the presence of Hindu nationalists at the Simhastha cast light on the limitations of the VHP strategy. Isolated individuals, such as Swami Yogeshwar Videhi Hariji, denounced the political dimension of the movement in favour of the Ram temple (*National Mail*, 10 May 1992). Above all, sadhus took umbrage at the collusion of certain religious leaders with the BJP government of Madhya Pradesh, a collusion in which the VHP was instrumental.

The organization of the Simhastha had been entrusted to a minister in the BJP government in Bhopal, Babulal Jain, a member of the state assembly from Ujjain district and member of the RSS since childhood. This man also had a seat in the committee over which Vijaya Raje Scindia presided. It appears that they together managed the few hundred million rupees which the state government allotted to the Simhastha from 1990 to 1992. The VHP made use of this formidable ally to further 'its' sadhus, a majority of whom were Saivaites. But the Saivaites were in a minority compared to the total number of sadhus present. When they asked that there be only one *shahi snan*, to which the authorities agreed, the Vishnuites protested, saying that their traditions prescribed the organization of three baths; Babulal Jain had to find a compromise (*National Mail*, 19 March 1992). The simple fact that this kind of conflict can still arise is an indication of the weakness of the VHP in representing all sadhus and, above all, is a sign of its inability to neutralize ancestral rivalries. It would once again appear as one group among various others, and that is why the organization needed the support of the government.

This process was again to be observed at the concluding ceremony of the Simhastha. The responsible officials, Babulal Jain and Vijaya Raje Scindia, invited different sect leaders to the Grand Hotel. However, they did not respect the order of precedence. Sadhus close to the VHP were given place in the first rows, while prestigious *mahants* were not even offered a seat. The latter protested and left the hall, taking their *mandaleshwars* with them. Babulal Jain and Vijaya Raje Scindia were obliged to extend their apologies to these outraged *mahants*.[48]

In this study of the Vishva Hindu Parishad, I have tried to show that this organization applies a form of strategic mimetism through its efforts to erect an ecclesiastical structure and to hold pan-Hindu festivals on the model of Christian and Muslim 'aggressors' in order to unify Hinduism and thereby offer greater resistance to rival religions. The VHP is, in this respect, only to a certain extent Hindu, even if it seeks to legitimize its innovations by claiming to replicate the assemblies of the time of Harsha. Its organization has, all the same, reproduced a traditional sociological articulation between the notable-cum-patron and the sadhu which is to be found at local and national levels. This configuration has been converted to strategic ends to make the establishment of the movement easier at the local level. However, the VHP has been more successful in recruiting 'modern gurus' than important sect leaders. It is trying hard to rally more orthodox and prestigious leaders around its cause but the strategy of infiltration, which consists of the VHP penetrating temples and festivals, shows its limitations, as many religious figures disapprove of the methods of the movement and fear for their own independence.

## Notes

1. For more details on this interpretation, see Jaffrelot (1996).
2. To employ the title of the book by Andersen and Damle (1987).
3. Quoted in Deshpande and Ramaswamy 1981: 185–6.
4. After independence, he became one of the proponents of the reconstruction of the Somnath temple—destroyed by Mahmud of Ghazni (Van der Veer 1992: 89–93).
5. See *Hindu Vishva* (*H.V.*), September-October 1980: 18.
6. Interview with Swami Chinmayananda in Puteaux, 10 June 1993.
7. See Van der Veer in Marty and Appleby (1994).

8. Andersen and Damle 1987: 133–4. One of the VHP's objectives, assuming a prominent place in its statutes, concerned the establishment 'of an order of missionaries, both laymen and initiates', as well as the opening and management of 'seminaries or training centres for these missionaries' (*H.V.*, September-October 1980: 27).

9. The obsessive fear of Christian 'separatism' continued until the 1980s, to which this excerpt from the 'opinion column' in the *Hindu Vishva*, organ of the VHP, bears witness: 'The Christian rebels, after having formed a separate state named Mizoram with a special status, are now preparing to extend their terrorist activities to Orissa, Bihar and Madhya Pradesh so as to form new theocratic states named Kolham and Jharkhand' (*H.V.*, June 1987).

10. Four-fifths of the people included in the census declared themselves Christians, which is an indication of the extent of conversions.

11. Shiromani Gurudwara Prabhandhak Committee, the committee for the management of Sikh temples.

12. *The Organiser*, 21 June 1969. S.S. Apte repeated in 1969 his will to promote 'the integration and unification without rift of all strata, castes, communities and sects, in such way as to make of this multi-petal [*sic*] society a great living organism.'

13. This institution, in Nehru's mind (he presided over it in the year of its foundation: *The Statesman*, 27 March 1957: 4) was intended to lead the sadhus to participate in economic development through *shramdan* (voluntary work) (*Hitavada*, 15 April 1956: 4). This project revealed above all the mark of Gandhian values, as shown by the themes of *bhoodan*, of the prohibition of alcohol and cow protection (*Hitavada*, 2 March 1956, 1 May 1956: 5, 24 September 1956: 7 and 25 September 1956: 6).

14. *H.V.* (Republic Day Special Number 1966: 9). S.S. Apte considered his members to be 'representatives' of Hindus dispersed throughout the world and of different persuasions.

15. According to an old fear which the 1971 census had already 'revived'. See for example Misra (1973). The census of 1971 showed a diminution in the proportion of Hindus from 83.4 per cent in 1961 to 82.7 per cent, while the Muslims went up from 10.7 per cent to 11.2 per cent.

16. This biography draws from chapter 5 of the thesis by McKean (1992).

17. Satyamitranand Giri contributed to the introduction of the VHP in Anglo-Saxon countries, beginning in the 1970s (*H.V.*, March 1978: 55).

18. Each of its seven storeys contains figures symbolizing one aspect of the Hindu nation (Jaydee 1984: 39–41). This 'temple' was inaugurated in the presence of Indira Gandhi in 1983.

19. *Who's Who in the UP Legislative Assembly 1962–1967* (1993: 10).

20. World Hindu Conference (n.d.: 95).

21. *Shraddhanjali Smarika*, 13 April 1986: 2.

22. Interview with Acharya Giriraj Kishore on 18 November 1989 in New Delhi and *H.V.*, July 1982: 34.

23. Regarding patronage of the Puri temples by the rajas, see Kulke 1978: 133.

24. *The Times of India*, 10 March 1993.

25. Such as K.M. Munshi and Shivnath Katju, son of a minister of Nehru and president of the VHP prior to Dalmia.

26. Such as the former Chief Justice of Calcutta High Court, who became working president of the VHP in 1966, older brother of Shyama Prasad Mookerjee and son of Ashutosh Mookerjee, vice-chancellor of the University of Calcutta from 1906 to 1914

244    *Religion, Caste and Politics in India*

and 1921 to 1923, and illustrative representative of the bhadralok elite (*Shraddhanjali Smarika*, 13 April 1986: 56).

27. Vishva Hindu Parishad (n.d.: 28). 'First the Margdarshak Mandal was defined in the constitution of the VHP as a simple "advisory council" comprising *dharmgurus*, saints, scholars and philosophers of different sects of Hinduism to advice the Board of Trustees every now and then on points of philosophy and the code of conduct when their opinion was sought' (*H.V.*, September-October 1980: 30). Its role would at present appear to be much more active.

28. Interview with Acharya Giriraj Kishore in New Delhi, 10 October 1991.

29. Founded in Haridwar by Acharya Shri Ram Sharma and his wife, the Gayatri Parivar combined an enthusiasm for ancient India and an admiration for science, which is described as deriving from spirituality and Brahmanic ritualism. His ascetic ethics were deliberately orientated towards the world, as this organization maintained it provided through its discipline, spiritual realization and material success. See McKean (1992).

30. Interview with Babulal Har Lavaka in Ujjain, 25 August 1992.

31. Interview with Hari Narayan Soni in Ujjain, 25 August 1992.

32. Interview with Shanti Swaroopanand in Ujjain, 24 August 1992.

33. *The Times of India*, 19 July 1992:13. Sadhvi Rithambara attempted to found her own ashram, between Vrindavan and Mathura, on land which the BJP government had ceded at a throw away price, notwithstanding prevailing laws (*Frontline*, 12 March 1998: 100).

34. Regarding the special effects which lend these cassettes an almost superhuman intensity, see Sarkar (1992), as also the essay in this volume by Tanika Sarkar.

35. Interview with Dinesh Vaidya in Ujjain, 25 August 1992.

36. She only comes down for the *puja* to the deity Mahakal, who arrives at the end of the procession. Formerly, she saluted and threw *malas* to various *akharas* who marched past her for several hours (observations made on 26 August 1992).

37. I attended the celebration of the anniversary of the local VHP on 23 August 1992. All the speeches and pamphlets distributed at the entrance focused on Hindu nationalist themes.

38. Interview with Jai Shankar Sawalji in Ujjain, 23 August 1992.

39. His grandfather was the Raj Guru of the Maharaja of Dewas, and his father a *purohit* of repute, to whom the Birlas, as *jajman*, gave the building bordering another side of the temple tank.

40. Interview with Vishwanath Vyas, 26 August 1992.

41. As regards the opinion of a few priests chosen at random, the majority of whom favour the construction of a temple in Ayodhya. See *Sunday*, 8 February 1993: 32–3.

42. Interview with Santosh Trivedi in Indore, 28 August 1992.

43. Ibid.

44. The same phenomenon could be illustrated by the participation of the VHP at the Mahamaham festival in Tamil Nadu. In 1992, the VHP seems to have wanted to install its tribune at the centre of this festival, which is organized every twelve years, notwithstanding police opposition (*Sunday*, 8 March 1992: 72).

45. *National Mail*, 5 May 1992. Karan Singh, former maharaja of Jammu and Kashmir and minister under Indira Gandhi, had been close to the VHP since the 1980s. For more details on this point, see Jaffrelot 1996: Ch. 10.

46. *National Mail,* 12 April and 9 May 1992. The Shiv Sena also organized an exhibition, near the Datta Akhara, in which the corruption involved in the organization of the Simhastha was denounced in images (*National Mail,* 21 March 1992).
47. *National Mail,* 14 May 1992. Singhal also announced on this occasion that the VHP availed of eighty million rupees in the bank for the construction of the temple.
48. Interview with Shanti Swaroopanand, 25 August 1992.

## References

Andersen, W. and Damle, S. (1987), *The Brotherhood in Saffron: The Rashtriya Swayamsevak Sangh and Hindu Revivalism,* New Delhi: Vistaar Publications.

Deshpande, B.V. and Ramaswamy, S.R. (1981), *Dr Hedgewar: the Epoch Maker,* Bangalore: Sahitya Sindhu.

Devahuti, D. (1970), *Harsha: A Political Study,* Oxford: Clarendon Press.

*Dharma Marg,* January 1984.

Dumont, L. (1966), *Homo Hierarchicus,* Paris: Gallimard.

*Frontline,* 12 March 1993.

Gross, R.L. (1979), 'Hindu Asceticism: A Study of the Sadhus of North India', Ph.D. dissertation in anthropology, Vol. 2, Berkeley: University of California.

Hayat, S. (1984), 'Hindu Revivalism: Genesis and Implications', *Regional Studies,* Vol. 2, No. 4.

*Hindu Vishva (H.V.),* 30 January 1966, Republic Day Special Number 1966, 11 June 1967, March 1978, March-April 1979, September-October 1980, May 1981, July 1982, June 1987, August 1990.

*Hitavada,* 2 March 1956, 15 April 1956, 1 May 1956, 7 September 1956, 24 September 1956, 25 September 1956.

*India Today,* 30 April 1995.

Jaffrelot, C. (1993), *Les nationalistes hindous: Idéologie, implantation et mobilisation des années 1920 aux années 1990,* Paris: Presses de la FNSP.

―――― (1996), *The Hindu Nationalist Movement and Indian Politics,* Delhi: Viking.

Jaydee (1984), Bharat Mata Mandir, *Dharma Marg,* Vol. 1, No. 4, pp. 39–41.

Kulke, Hermann (1978), 'Royal Temple Policy and the Structure of Medieval Hindu Kingdoms', in *The Cult of Jagannath and the Regional Tradition in Orissa* (ed.), A. Eschmann, H. Kulke and G.C. Tripathi, pp. 125–37, New Delhi: Manohar.

Mauss, M. (1953-4), 'La nation', *L'année sociologique,* 3ème série, pp. 5–68.

McKean, M. (1992), 'Towards a Politics of Spirituality: Hindu Religious Organizations and Indian Nationalism', Ph.D. dissertation in anthropology, Sydney: University of Sydney.

Parliament of India (1992), *Tenth Lok Sabha Secretariat.*

Rath, S. [n.d.], *Temples of Ujjain,* Ujjain: Devasthan Administration.

*The Organiser,* Divali Special 1964, 26 December 1965, 30 January 1966, 12 April 1968, 3 May 1981, 1 August 1982, 28 November 1982, 26 October 1990.

Sarkar, S. (1992), '"Kaliyuga", "Chakri" and "Bhakti": Ramakrishna and his Times', *Economic and Political Weekly,* 18 July, pp. 1543–66.

Seshadari, H.V. (1981), *Warning of Meenakshipuram,* Bangalore: Jagarana Prakashan.

——— (1988) (ed.), *RSS: A Vision in Action*, Bangalore: Jagarana Prakashan.

*Shraddhanjali Smarika* [n.d.], New Delhi: Vishva Hindu Parishad.

*Sunday*, 1 September 1991, 8 March 1992, 8 February 1993.

*The Statesman*, 27 March 1957.

*The Times of India*, 19 July 1992.

———, 5 December 1992.

Tully, M. (1992), *No Full Stops in India*, New Delhi: Penguin.

Turner, V. (1969), *The Ritual Process, Structure and Anti Structure*, Chicago: Aldine Publishing House.

Van der Veer, P. (1992), 'Ayodhya and Somnath: Eternal Shrines, Contested Histories', *Social Research*, Vol. 59, No. 1.

——— (1994), 'Hindu Nationalism and the Discourse of Modernity: The Vishva Hindu Parishad,' in *Accounting for Fundamentalisms*, M. Marty and S. Appleby (eds.), Chicago: University of Chicago Press, pp. 653–68.

Verma, R. and Guru, S.D. (1982), *Madhya Pradesh District Gazetteers: Ujjain*, Bhopal: District Gazetteers Department.

Vishva Hindu Parishad [n.d.], *The Hindu Awakening: Retrospect and Promise*, New Delhi: Vishva Hindu Parishad.

*Who's Who in UP Legislative Assembly 1962-1967*, Lucknow: UP Legislative Assembly Secretariat.

*World Hindu Conference* [n.d.].

# Chapter 12

# The BJP in Madhya Pradesh
## networks, strategies and power

With some exceptions, most studies of post-independence Hindu nationalism have focused on its ideological and organizational dimensions at an all-India level (Curran 1951; Baxter 1971; Andersen & Damle 1987, and Jaffrelot 1989). Only a few authors have drawn attention to the regional or local reality of this movement[1] even though the Bharatiya Jana Sangh (BJS) and then the Bharatiya Janata Party (BJP) established themselves as the main rivals to the Congress in Delhi, Himachal Pradesh, Rajasthan and Madhya Pradesh. In Madhya Pradesh, this achievement is all the more interesting as, first, by contrast with Rajasthan it led to a quasi-perfect two-party system and, second, unlike Delhi or Himachal Pradesh, Madhya Pradesh is a huge state of 4,43,446 sq. km.

The BJP's capture of power in Madhya Pradesh in 1990 was partly a consequence of a general reaction against the Congress, but it was also due in large part to its techniques of mobilization and to the work of its local activists and organizers for years. My main concern is to analyse the character of these strategies and party-building methods that enabled this political force to spread its influence all over the state and eventually gain power.

## A Specific Party-Building Pattern:
### Sangathanists, Notables and Princes

Schematically, the 'classical' theory of party-building in India tends to place the emphasis on the ability of political leaders to obtain the support of local notables whose followers or clients would vote according to their instructions and therefore constitute 'vote banks'. The process of building a party consists mainly, in these terms of analysis, in accumulating sufficient votebanks to ensure electoral majorities in the constituencies and the return of pledged candidates to legislative assemblies and the Lok Sabha. This theory was developed mainly with reference to the Indian

*This essay draws from my doctoral dissertation ('Des nationalistes en quête d'une nation—Les partis nationalistes hindous au XXe siècle', Directeur: Jean Leca, Institut d'Etudes Politiques de Paris, 1991, 1793). I am most grateful to Bruce Graham for his comments on an earlier version of this essay.

National Congress, whose methods were described by Myron Weiner in the 1960s as follows:

[Congress] does not mobilize, it aggregates. It does not seek to innovate, it seeks to adapt. Though a few Congressmen dream of transforming the countryside, in practice most Congressmen are concerned simply with winning elections. In its efforts to win Congress adapts itself to the local power structures. It recruits from among those who have local power and influence (Weiner 1967: 15; Bailey 1963: 60–3, 138, 149–53).

As early as 1970, G.A. Heeger suggested that this party-building pattern did not apply in the case of the Jana Sangh in Punjab; in general terms, he pointed out that:

Parties can be more than aggregates put together to form a winning coalition. As might be surmised from the term 'party' itself, they can reflect the claim by the party that it—a part—addresses itself correctly to and for the nation as a whole . . . . For the Jan Sangh leadership, their party is to be a microcosm of an ideal India (Heeger 1970: 864–5).

Heeger's assumption that the development of the Jana Sangh represented such a special pattern rested on the further claim that it was the political projection of the Rashtriya Swayamsevak Sangh (RSS) which helped to establish the party in 1951. Formed in 1925, the RSS was conceived by its founder K.B. Hedgewar as 'the Hindu Rashtra in miniature' (Deshpande and Ramaswamy 1981: 185–6), because it was intended to be free of caste and sectarian divisions and dedicated to Hindu nationalism. In its internal culture, the RSS was expected to embody the ideal form of 'Hindu Rashtra' and its *pracharaks* were in charge of spreading this model throughout the society.[2] Just after independence this ultimate purpose of the movement was described in the following terms by M.S. Golwalkar, who had succeeded Hedgewar in 1940: 'Continuously expanding ourselves amongst the Hindu society we hope to reach a stage when the Sangh and the entire Hindu Society will be completely identical. This is bound to happen in the course of time for there is no escape' (*Hitavada*, 31 December 1947: 6).

Such sentences reflect the millenarian and virtually totalitarian aspiration of the RSS to become coterminous with the Hindu society in order to transform it in the process into a 'Hindu Rashtra' (Shri Guruji 1964: 9). Its mission was not to accommodate itself to the structure of Hindu society but to reshape that structure so that Hindus would accept a greater sense of community. To use its own terminology, the RSS wanted to bring about Hindu *Sangathan*, the Organization of Hindu Society. It was this voluntarist purpose which Heeger detected in his work on the Punjab Jana Sangh.

In Madhya Pradesh, the Jana Sangh and then the BJP seemed to combine both methods of expansion, the 'aggregative' and the *sangathanist* which put the emphasis here not only on the strengthening of Hindu society, but also on the need of a solid party organization—one pre-condition of the former aim. However, my hypothesis is that the party-building partem, forty years after the founding of the Jana Sangh, remains predominantly *sangathanist*, especially in Madhya Bharat.

Before concentrating upon this combination of two types of development, we would take stock of the regional pattern which confronted the party's organizers when the modern state of Madhya Pradesh was established in 1956. The following regions may be distinguished, surveying the State from west to east. In the west, adjacent to Rajasthan, were the territories which had once constituted the small State of Madhya Bharat. In the north-east, on the southern border of Uttar Pradesh, were the remote regions which had composed Vindhya Pradesh. In the centre were the districts of what had once been the Mahakoshal region of the old Central Provinces. To the east, adjoining Orissa, was the hilly region of Chhatisgarh (see Table 12.1, Appendix A, for a district-wise presentation). Each of these regions had its own distinctive history and cultural background. The Congress was most secure in Mahakoshal, where its networks of activists and local leaders had been built up steadily during the British period, when the party had initially established its foothold in the Central Provinces and Berar. It was weaker in Madhya Bharat and Vindhya Pradesh, two regions which had been dominated by princely states, where it entered at a later stage. And in Madhya Bharat, what were disadvantages for the Congress proved to be advantages for the Hindu nationalist parties.

## Madhya Bharat: The Stronghold

First, the Hindu Mahasabha, then the Jana Sangh and later the BJP established widely distributed bodies of support in the Madhya Bharat region. The election map for the Legislative Assembly poll of May 1980 shows the BJP entrenched in this area (see Appendix B). I shall try to show first that this stronghold is the legacy of a dual party-building process combining the *sangathanist* approach in the south (Malwa) and the 'aggregative' one in the north (the core of the former Gwalior State).

The strong position achieved by the party in Malwa was mainly a function of a long-standing and extensive network of the RSS *shakhas* of the organization. Supervised by *pracharaks,* these *shakhas* hold daily meetings where its members (mostly young men and boys) are involved in physical and ideological activities contributing to the *sangathanist* work. In Malwa, the first *shakha* had been founded by Hedgewar himself in Indore and Dewas as early as 1929, when the organization was still mainly confined to the Nagpur area.[3] Afterwards, the *shakha* network has expanded steadily through the impetus of Hedgewar's uncle, *swayamsevaks* coming from Nagpur to pursue their studies or find a job, and then *pracharaks* whose deployment marked a turning point.

Among them the most prominent figure was Prabhakar Balwant Dani, from Umred (Nagpur district), who had been sent to the Banaras Hindu University in the early 1930s and subsequently became general secretary of the RSS between

1946 and 1956 and from 1962 till his death in 1965. He worked as the *prant pracharak* till 1945 from his headquarters of Indore. The first team of his *pracharaks* was formed during the training camp of Khandwa in 1942. Then, they were sent all over Malwa (Manohar Rao Moghe from Indore to Ujjain, Kushabhau Thakre and Haribhau Wakankar from Dhar respectively in Mandsaur-Ratlam division and Kukshi while Moreshwar Rao Gadre stayed at Indore).

These *pracharaks* developed the RSS network, first in the district towns and then in the *tehsil* headquarters and even in some villages. In the Ujjain area, for instance, there were around sixty *shakhas* in 1950, half in Ujjain town and half in the rural periphery (interview with Manohar Rao Moghe). In Indore district, there were around one hundred *shakhas* before the assassination of Mahatma Gandhi, and this level was regained in the mid-1960s when seventy branches were functioning in the city and twenty-five in the rural area.[4] In 1970, the Madhya Bharat regional unit of the RSS represented 100,000 *swayamsevaks,* most of them belonging to the Malwa region.[5] In 1992 Madhya Bharat had 11,000 *shakhas* and 15,000 *upshakhas.* Around 170 *pracharaks* were active in the region, an average of 5.7 per district.[6]

From the very foundation of the Madhya Bharat unit of the Jana Sangh in Indore in 1951, the party relied on this RSS network in Malwa. The leaders of this Jana Sangh unit were RSS cadres who had been seconded from their own organization. Moghe, the Madhya Bharat *prant pracharak* between 1945 and 1950, became the first state *sangathan mantri* of the Jana Sangh in 1951. He was succeeded in 1953 by Kushabhau Thakre who remained the most important figure of the party. A *swayamsevak* since 1938, he had operated as an RSS *pracharak* in the 1940s in Ratlam (Chittor) and Mandsaur districts. He served as a *sanagathan mantri* for the Jana Sangh from 1951 for Malwa and from 1953 for Madhya Bharat. He was replaced by Moreshwar Rao Gadre and then Pyarelal Khandelwal—two other *pracharaks,* bachelors like him—when he became *sangathan mantri* in 1956 for the newly-established State of Madhya Pradesh (interview with Kushabhau Thakre). The state *sangathan mantri*—who was ex-officio member of the national council— was the most powerful officer in a Jana Sangh unit, and thus Kushabhau Thakre was virtually in charge of the Madhya Pradesh Jana Sangh, whose successive presidents tended to be mere figureheads.

This arrangement corresponded to that which an RSS *pracharak* would expect to have in relation to his unit's *sanghchalak,* who was usually a leading citizen serving as a patron and a more or less distant guide of the local activities of the movement. For instance, the *pracharak* sent from Nagpur to Gwalior in the 1940s, P.R. Sahasrabuddhe, worked in collaboration with a leading local advocate, the father of N.K. Shejwalkar.[7] The *prant sanghchalak* for Madhya Bharat, from the late 1950s till his death in 1979, has been Ram Narain Shastri, a famous Ayurvedic practitioner of Indore.[8] The RSS *sangathanist* pattern relied on this collaboration of activists and notables imbued with the ideology of militant Hinduism, and the Jana Sangh and then the BJP tended to imitate it.

Moreover, Thakre's party-building technique was similar to that used by the RSS in extending its own organization. His priority was to establish a dense network of local committees by utilizing the existing RSS network and sending *sangathan mantris* into the countryside (in the same way as the first RSS *pracharaks* were sent out from Nagpur).[9] In both cases, RSS men-turned-party activists were supposed to use their militant potential, in terms of personal energy and following, to reach the people and make them aware of the Jana Sangh as well as assist them as social workers. This task was easier to accomplish in the urban setting and among the middle class elements (shopkeepers, professionals and clerks), which constituted the basic milieu of the RSS cadres.[10]

One of the best illustrations of this process is Ujjain, one of the holy centres for Hindus and a part of the old Gwalior State, where the RSS *pracharaks* recruited among the Jain community, for instance.[11] But the case of Ujjain is all the more interesting, as the Jana Sangh's strategy produced results also in less favourable milieus such as urban labour sectors. In this town, where the textile mills employed most of the 42,224 industrial workers in 1961 (Verma and Guru 1982: 128–31), *shakhas* had been established in the factory areas as early as 1935 when Digambar Tijare, a Brahman mill worker from Vidarbha, had been sent as a missionary— *swayamsevak* by Nagpur to work in a textile factory.[12] Babulal Mehere, a textile worker and cofounder of the Bharatiya Mazdoor Sangh ran four *shakhas* at that time. Simultaneously he contributed to a labour co-operative bank along with other RSS men.[13] Among his colleagues was Hukum Chand Kacchwai, another textile worker affiliated to BMS who had taken part in the famine relief operation in Jhabua district and had assisted refugees from West Pakistan. He was one of the first of his group to stand for election and was returned for the local reserved Lok Sabha constituency in 1962 and 1967, when the Jana Sangh also won the local Legislative Assembly seat (*Who's Who in the Lok Sabha* 1967: 219–20). Since then, the Ujjain reserved constituency of the Lok Sabha has been lost by the Hindu nationalist parties only once, in 1984. In 1980, 1989 and 1991, S.N. Jatiya, another BMS activist, won the seat, with his image of being a man close to the people, and even to the Muslims, at least till 1989.[14] In 1990, Babulal Mehere entered electoral politics and became an MLA from a predominantly labour constituency, Ujjain south.

Similar local traditions can be found in some rural pockets. The most significant example I encountered was in the Gwalior region, in Shivpuri constituency. Here, the assembly ticket has been given since 1957—except in 1977 and 1980—to Sushil Asthana, a *swayamsevak* from childhood (he joined the RSS in 1942), who used to keep a shop in the town and whose simplicity as well as accessibility were the main sources of his popularity, among certain sections of the population at least a backward caste kisan from Piparsod, a small village situated 17 km. away from the town, provides this testimony: 'Go anyday to the leader Sushil, he will at once make you sit beside him with great attention. And he will come with you, whatever be your problem .... He is a pure man, and very austere;

he is a *devta admi* [noble soul]'.[15] Asthana has been re-elected MLA for the third time in 1990.[16]

These local examples suggest an *ideal, typical* party-building process based on the groundwork of RSS-trained militants. The main achievement of this *sangathanist* pattern was the creation of 'safe seats' all over Malwa as early as 1962. The most revealing example, from this point of view, is the parliamentary constituency of Shajapur where the Jana Sangh has always had outsiders returned, such as the Mumbai-based pressman, Baburao Patel (MP in 1967) and the all-India leader from south India, Jagannath Rao Joshi (MP in 1971). This stronghold remained when the constituency was declared reserved for the Scheduled Castes in 1977: since then, Phool Chand Verma, a *swayamsevak* from Indore, where his father had joined the RSS in the late 1930s as a mill worker, has been elected four times. This safe seat is primarily due to the local activity of the RSS network.[17]

As a matter of fact, this *sangathanist* party-building pattern relied heavily on the pre-existing RSS network. But this network was unevenly distributed, even in Madhya Bharat. To solve this problem, the Jana Sangh had to extend the *sangathanist* method in two ways: first, it launched agitational campaigns to exploit issues of general concern and thus to compensate for local gaps in the RSS network; second, it co-opted local notables in the list of election candidates, provided they were generally sympathetic to the party cause.

In west Nimar district for instance, the party built a base among the tribals by recruiting an advocate from Sanver and ex-Congress freedom fighter, Ram Chandra Bade, through whom it helped to organize the tribals' protest against the State administration, which wanted to dislodge them from illegally occupied land. In 1960, Balchandra Bagdare, an advocate and founder of the RSS unit in Khargone in 1939, sent his activists into forest tracts to befriend *adivasis*, to know their problems.[18] Later on, he led with Bade a tribal delegation to Bhopal where the issue was temporarily settled, this displacement of the tribals being suspended (*The Hindustan Times*, 11 July 1962: 5; *The Times of India*, 16 July 1962). In 1962, the four reserved constituencies of the district were won by the Jana Sangh and Bade was elected as the MP for Khargone, a success which he repeated in 1971.

A similar case of co-operation between a party activist and a notable gave birth to another stronghold in Dewas district, where the Jana Sangh made its presence felt early in the countryside, whereas the Congress Party's influence was initially confined to the town (Mayer 1962: 272–3). Kailash Chandra Joshi, who joined the RSS of his village, close to Hatpipalya, in 1943, was elected MLA of Bagli with the help of the ex-jagirdar who owned seventy villages in the former Gwalior state and whom he had unsuccessfully supported in 1957. He has held the seat since 1962.[19]

However, the most significant example of this specific party-building pattern emerged in Mandsaur district where Thakre had already strengthened the RSS network. On the one hand, two active RSS men, Virendra Kumar Sakhlecha (an advocate trained in Indore) and Sunder Lal Patwa (*pracharak* in the late 1940s) were elected MLAs for the first time in 1957, in the constituencies of Javad and Manasa respectively. On the other hand, this early pocket of strength arose also because of the support of local notables. As early as 1952, Vimal Kumar Choradia, who belonged to an influential Jain family of Bhanpura, known for its involvement in the Praja Mandal of the former Indore state, was approached to stand on the Jana Sangh ticket. He twice won the Garoth seat in the Legislative Assembly. Another source of strength came from the sizeable Rajput community, who had been affected by the Abolition of Jagirs Act (1951). In 1962, the party MLA from the Mandsaur constituency of Sitamau, Thakur Kishor Singh Sisodia, was an ex-jagirdar of the former Gwalior state and an active member of the Ram Rajya Parishad (like quite a few other ex-landlords). He had been *sarpanch* of three *gram panchayats* before presiding over the Mandsaur Marketing Society (Madhya Pradesh Vidhan Sabha 1964: 22).

Besides these local illustrations, the party seems to have acknowledged the necessity of co-opting local notables to broaden its base throughout Malwa. From the 1960s, the pattern of growth of the Jana Sangh, and then the BJP, in this area shows RSS men providing the core of wider clusters of support and representation which expanded in each district, thanks to the recruitment of notables. This method of expansion, which may be termed the 'cluster technique', appears as the most common variant of the *sangathanist* model. In 1962, out of twenty-three Jana Sangh MLAs from Malwa for whom detailed biographical data is available, almost one-third can be classified as notables (i.e. heirs of the traditional rural elite and/ or members of local authority committees or heads of such local bodies as co-operative banks, Mandi Samitis).[20] In 1967, the figures were six out of seven, and, in 1972, three out of six.

This tendency was reversed in the state elections of 1977 when the composite Janata Party was returned to power: out of fifty-five MLAs in Malwa, at least twenty-six had an RSS background. Most of them had served terms as political prisoners during the Emergency: the repression which these *swayamsevaks*—many of whom had not taken part in electoral polities—before 1977—had just endured and the underground resistance which some of them had undertaken during the Emergency, had increased their prestige while the popularity of the ruling Congress had reached its lowest ebb. Therefore, the ex-Jana Sangh leaders were able to nominate their activists and dispense with their earlier use of local notables as an electoral auxiliary.[21]

The oscillation between 'notable' and 'activist' MLAs stabilized during the 1980s in favour of the *swayamsevaks*-turned-BJP workers (see Table 12.1). However, since the 1950s, many of them had managed to enter municipal councils or co-operative management boards, an evolution which was likely to limit the need to resort to local notables. For instance, Patwa became president of the Neemuch Central Cooperative Bank in 1967, Bagdare entered the municipal council of Khargone and Kailash Chandra Joshi presided over the municipality of Hatpipalya between 1955 and 1960. If this 'notabilization' tends to bring the BJS and BJP leaders into line with those of other parties, the possession of an RSS background nevertheless remains a major criterion for gaining responsibilities inside the BJS/BJP, and even for re-selection as a party candidate.

In general, therefore, the party-building method, and especially the 'cluster technique', used by the Jana Sangh and BJP in the Malwa region was mainly *sangathanist,* that is, it was based on the assumption that the foundation of electoral success was the exposition of a particular philosophy (Hindu nationalism in association with a sense of social work) and the nomination of RSS activists as election candidates and exemplars of that philosophy. The 'aggregative' method was used only to the extent of co-opting as candidates local notables who were, like the *sanghchalaks,* known to be sympathetic to the Hindu nationalist cause.

Hindu nationalist politics followed a different logic in northern Madhya Bharat, where the former princely house of Gwalior remained a powerful source of influence. During the 1950s and 1960s, the Hindu Mahasabha survived in various parts of this region partly thanks to the support of the Gwalior family, whose patronage of its activities was already evident in the 1930s.

Maharaja Jivaji Rao Scindia (1916–61) had been willing to patronize a movement which invoked the Maratha empire with pride,[22] and he valued it as a means of counteracting Congress influence in his state.[23] The main support of the Hindu Mahasabha was, however, the principal jagirdar of the state, Chandrojirao Angre, a descendant of the eighteenth-century Maratha admiral, Kanhoji Angre, whose exploits were narrated by V.D. Savarkar. In fact, Savarkar visited Gwalior as early as 1938, the year of foundation of the first local Hindu Sabha, in which the son of Chandrojirao, Sambhajirao Angre, was involved.[24]

In 1951, Chandrojirao Angre, who was still general secretary of the All India Landowners and Jagirdars Association—a charge he held from the 1930s—was appointed zonal organizer of the Hindu Mahasabha for Madhya Bharat. In the first general elections, the party managed to have eleven of its candidates elected as MLAs and two as MPs, thanks in great part to the influence of 'forty jagirdars and petty rulers' (*Hindu Mahasabha Papers,* Letter from Indra Prakash to Mahant Digvijay Nath) owing allegiance to the Scindias. Apparently to reduce this Hindu Sabhaite pocket, Jawaharlal Nehru asked Vijaya Raje Scindia, Gwalior's Maharani, to stand on a Congress ticket in 1957, to dispel the rumours alleging some links between Gwalior house and the Hindu Mahasabha (Scindia with Malgonkar 1988: 171–3). Despite this forced affiliation, the Hindu Sabhaites still managed to return seven MLAs and one MP in Madhya Bharat in 1957 and 1962, not least because of the informal support which the Angre family gave to these candidates.[25] Dependent to a large extent on the support of locally influential notables, this persistence of the Hindu Mahasabha in this region is typical of the 'aggregative' pattern.

While it seems relevant to analyse the politics of Hindu nationalism in northern and southern Madhya Bharat through the categories, respectively, of the 'aggregative' and *sangathanist* party-building patterns, one of the most interesting aspects of these processes was the way in which the two patterns combined after 1967.

The palace of Gwalior decided to oppose D.P. Mishra, the Congress Chief Minister (who had tried to reduce the local influence of the Scindias), and to make a deal with the Jana Sangh shortly before the 1967 elections. The resultant adjustment of seats enabled the Jana Sangh to emerge as a significant force in the Gwalior region. At last, RSS men like Asthana in Shivpuri, Raghavji in Vidisha, Jagdish Prasad Gupta (a trade unionist in a textile mill), Naresh John (a former *pracharak* who had been appointed *sangathan mantri* in the Gwalior area) and Shitla Sahai (an advocate then mostly known as an educationist and a social worker) in Gwalior, managed to get elected as MLAs. The Scindias also reasserted their authority, in their own territory by nominating specially chosen candidates including ex-Hindu Sabhaites (like Laxmi Narayan Gupta, Pichhore MLA since 1952), ex-landlords or rulers (like Raghubir Singh Machhand, Ron MLA in 1967) along with personalities like Ram Nath Goenka (Vidisha MP in 1971). Members of the Scindia family formally joined the Jana Sangh in the early 1970s.[26] They were followed by other princes from Madhya Bharat, like Bhanu Prakash Singh of Narsinghgarh, who contested as a Jana Sangh candidate in 1971 when Indira Gandhi's proposal to abolish privy purses was a major issue. The party profited from these entrants, especially in northern Madhya Bharat where most of the seats, eleven, were won again in 1972 by former landlords such as Mahendra Singh of Kalukheda, or by other candidates who had the backing of the Scindias.

However, by contrast with other princes who returned to the Congress as early as 1971, or oscillated between different parties, Vijaya Raje Scindia remained in the Hindu nationalist fold to become an all-India party leader. She formally joined the Jana Sangh in 1972, two months after conducting a satyagraha of the party against the Simla Accord (*The Motherland*, 19 October 1972: 1; 2 August 1972: 1). In 1974, she became a vice-president of the Jana Sangh (a post she held in the BJP from 1980 to 1991). In competition with her son, Madhav Rao Scindia, who joined the Congress in December 1979 and whose performance as Minister of Railways and then of Civil Aviation and Tourism benefited his home area, she represented a 'super notable' who has at her disposal a major 'vote bank'.[27] However, this status does not imply any reduction in the importance of party ideology or discipline. Vijaya Raje Scindia and Sambhajirao Angre—her aide since the 1950s—regularly canvassed all over 'their' constituencies and displayed a strong commitment to Hindu nationalism, as evident from the activity of Vijaya Raje Scindia in support of the Vishva Hindu Parishad (VHP).

Thus, in the Malwa region, Hindu nationalist parties had to build up areas of support by the *sangathanist* approach, while employing the 'aggregative' approach as an auxiliary method; on the other hand, in the Gwalior region they achieved substantial electoral strength by accepting the patronage of the Scindia family. However, Vijaya Raje Scindia had identified herself with the Hindu nationalist ideology and with the concepts of party discipline at an early stage. Therefore, the

Jana Sangh and BJP building pattern in Madhya Bharat appears predominantly *sangathanist*.

## Towards the 'Conquest of the East'

The same type of combination of *sangathanist* and 'aggregative' techniques was resorted to by the party leadership to conquer the eastern regions of Madhya Pradesh where the Jana Sangh network was much weaker than in Madhya Bharat (*The Organiser*, 13 August 1950: 38). For instance, it counted only a hundred local committees in Vindhya Pradesh against 203 in Madhya Bharat (twenty at Ujjain, seventeen at Indore, fifteen at Gwalior, and five at Bhopal) in 1965. By 1958 it had managed to open a party unit in each district and by 1962 in each *tehsil*. The last target—a committee in each *panchayat*—was nearly achieved by the BJP in the late 1980s, when 10,000 out of 14,000 *panchayats* were covered, Durg and Rajnandgaon remaining probably the two 'weakest' districts. As in Malwa, these advances reflected first of all the work of RSS men seconded to the domain of political activity, either in their own localities *or* as itinerant *sangathanist mantris*.

The first case is best illustrated by the situation in Bhopal district, the heart of a Muslim state where the RSS ran less than ten *shakhas* in the early 1950s.[28] In its rural part, in Berasia *tehsil*, Laxmi Narayan Sharma and Gauri Shankar Kaushal, two teachers with RSS backgrounds who had worked on behalf of the villagers, have in turn held the constituency since 1967.[29] Just as the labour areas of Ujjain were receptive to Hindu nationalist appeals, so the labour constituency of Govindpura in Bhopal has been loyal to Babulal Gaur, an active trade unionist who first won this seat in a by-election in 1974 and has retained it ever since. He had helped to run many *shakhas* around a textile mill where he worked between 1947 and 1966. He benefited also from the work of RSS militants in the Bharat Heavy Electricals Limited (BHEL) area. In this township of 90,000 inhabitants today, the RSS founded many *shakhas* in the 1960s.[30] The BMS opened a free Ayurvedic dispensary there, and from 1988 the BJP's *Jhuggi Jhonpri Mahasangh* has been trying to improve the living conditions of slum-dwellers by installing pumps. It also built a Vishvakarman Mandir.[31] Gaur was also helped by the fact that the town of Bairagarh, where Sindhis had settled after Partition, was part of his constituency.[32]

In Vindhya Pradesh too the first areas of influence for the Jana Sangh were created thanks to local RSS men deputed to party work. Hukum Chand Jain, who used to be a *pracharak* in Satna, became *sangathan mantri* for Vindhya Pradesh (see *Shyama Prasad Mookherjee Papers*). Ram Hit Gupta, a cloth merchant and RSS *pracharak* replaced him at a later stage, before entering the electoral fray: he was returned as MLA from Amarpatan in 1957, and has lost the seat on only two occasions since that date. Sukhendra Singh, a Rajput advocate from Satna and a *swayamsevak* since 1945, was elected MLA of his hometown in 1962, 1967 and 1972 and then MP, in 1977 and 1989.

By contrast with the situation of Vindhya Pradesh, in Mahakoshal and Chhattisgarh the party had to send organizing secretaries from Madhya Bharat. Though pockets of influence had taken shape around Raipur and Bilaspur because of the work of local RSS men active in the Jana Sangh, like Yashwant Rao Meghawale in Dhamtari (Raipur district), the Chhattisgarh unit of the party was given a dynamic structure after Moreshwar Rao Gadre, the Jana Sangh *sangathan mantri* for Madhya Bharat was despatched there from Indore in 1964.[33]

A similar scenario occurred in Mahakoshal. The RSS organization had been reinforced in the late 1930s by Eknath Ranade, a *pracharak* from Maharashtra who subsequently replaced Prabhakar Balwant Dani as general secretary in 1956. But its network remained mostly confined to a few urban centres like Jabalpur, from where RSS men seconded to the Jana Sangh right from 1951 (Badri Prasad Gupta, *sangathan mantri,* and Baburao Paranjpe, an ex-Hindu Sabhaite and member of Subhas Bose's Indian National Army did not manage to expand the party organization substantially). Therefore, Narayan Prasad Gupta, an ex-*pracharak* from Bhopal, was sent there in 1973, as *sangathan mantri* for the divisions of Jabalpur and Sagar. Before that, he had been despatched in 1962 to Betul where he had worked primarily among tribals,[34] whose votes have since that date gone sometimes to Congress candidates and sometimes to Hindu nationalist nominees. Here the Jana Sangh also relied on G. Khandelwal, a city advocate and ex-Congressman, who remained a strong contender for the Betul city seat throughout the 1960s and 1970s.

Altogether, beyond the Madhya Bharat 'frontier', the party expansion depended more clearly on enlisting the support of sympathetic notables (see Table 12.1). In this respect, the most significant elections are those of 1985, when the BJP broke through in Vindhya Pradesh and especially in Chhattisgarh (see Appendix C). In this latter area, seven out of thirteen of its MLAs may be classed as local notables—in most cases *sarpanchs* without a clear-cut ideological affiliation—even if these figures must be qualified for two reasons.

First, most of the seats (eight out of thirteen) were won in tribal constituencies where militants have been working for years. In northern Chhattisgarh, the Vanavasi Kalyan Ashram (VKA), has since 1952 been trying to counter the proselytizing work of Christian missionaries (*The Organiser*, 14 January 1990), and preaching among Christianized tribals by emphasizing the status of Hanuman as a Hindu tribal god.[35] Simultaneously, militants such as Larang Sai (Samri MLA from 1967 and then MP from Surguja in 1977 and 1989) and Baliram Kashyap (MLA of Jagdalpur and then Bhanpuri—in Bastar district—since 1972) had built strong pockets of influence by defending certain interests of the tribals. In 1966, Larang Sai's mobilization of opposition against the nationalization of forest products was a local landmark, for instance. Therefore, the 1985 electoral success in Chhattisgarh reflects also the impact of such long-term propaganda and activity.

Second, as in Madhya Bharat, the main rural leader supporting the BJP in this area is a prince with Hindu nationalist leanings, Dilip Singh Judeo, the heir of the Jashpur estate whose father patronized the VKA as a Ram Rajya Parishad officer and, from 1966, as a Jana Sangh office-bearer.[36] Dilip Singh Judeo's willingness to espouse Hindu nationalism, and to take risks, was revealed by his fight against Arjun Singh (previously Union Minister for Human Resource Development) during the June 1988 by-election for the Kharsia seat. At that time, his campaign seemed to have been financed by Lekhi Ram Aggarwal, an industrialist and *tendu* leaf contractor based at Kharsia whose family has interests in Bilaspur and Raipur, but who is also an ardent RSS member [he joined the movement in 1946, because of the 'Direct Action Day' organized by the Muslim League and the riots that followed in Calcutta (interview with L.R. Aggarwal)].

In Vindhya Pradesh, the Maharaja of Panna, Narendra Singh, played a role similar to Dilip Singh Judeo. Close to Vijaya Raje Scindia, he stood, like her, on the party ticket throughout the 1970s and 1980s because of ideological affinities. A senior party leader acknowledges that he was helpful in developing the Hindu nationalist electoral strength in Panna district and in two constituencies of Satna and Chhatarpur districts. Since the late 1980s, he has been patronizing the local VHP while leaving the electoral side of the work to his son, Lokendra Singh, who became an MP from Damoh in 1989.[37]

Clearly, the party-building pattern evolved in Madhya Bharat, which combined activists, notables, and a few ideologically-minded ex-princes, tended to be exported towards the eastern part of the state, even though the dependence on rural leaders is more important in this zone and the maharaja involved happened to be less reliable (Lokendra Singh shifted to the Congress (I), before the 1991 elections, for instance).[38] The net overall result remains a predominantly *sangathanist* approach which is bound to underline the strategies advocated and implemented by the Madhya Pradesh BJP unit.

## Strategies and Power: The 1980s in Perspective

At the time of its inception under Vajpayee's presidentship in 1980, the BJP was presented as the Janata Party's political heir. The corollary dilution of the ex-Jana Sanghi ideology—testified by 'commitments' such as 'positive secularism' and 'Gandhian socialism'—was intended to broaden the party's base. The Madhya Pradesh BJP unit, dominated by Kushabhau Thakre and Vijaya Raje Scindia, could only feel apprehensive about this new strategy.[39]

The Janata experience had just confirmed their reluctance to diverge from the *sangathanist* pattern and its emphasis on party discipline. The small socialist group had been overlooked by the ex-Jana Sangh dominated government and the state Janata Party president, Kushabhau Thakre, because of its eagerness to debate or dissent,[40] but also because, by definition, the *sangathanist* pattern excludes co-operation with other groups: since the organization is expected to become coterminous with the whole nation, there is no place for other groups. Party discipline and ideological commitment had been two prerequisites of any politician's recruitment since the 1950s. Anyone satisfying these criteria was welcome in the party fold, as was evident from the gradual absorption of the Hindu Sabhaites[41] and the adhesion of socialists such as Arif Beg, a Muslim MLA from Indore, in 1973, and Brij Lal Verma, from Raipur who joined the party in 1972 and became a minister in Morarji Desai's government in 1977.

In the first half of the 1980s, the liberal BJP high command's strategy appeared too indiscriminate when judged by standards of the ex-Madhya Pradesh Jana Sangh, since it implied more the 'aggregation' than the absorption of politicians from other schools of thought. The Madhya Pradesh BJP unit, true to its discipline, implemented the strategy. It attracted leaders like the Gwalior District Congress President, Dr Dharmaveer, in 1985. However, these recruitments were not very numerous and remained fairly precarious, especially in the case of Muslim leaders. Hamid Qureshi, a Janata Party minister, remained in the BJP in 1980 and another Muslim, Hasnat Siddiqui, entered the party in 1984 to be elected as the MLA of south Bhopal in the following year. But both of them left between 1984 and 1986, even before the party had amended its policy under L.K. Advani's presidentship.[42]

The Madhya Pradesh unit of the BJP welcomed the change under Advani, which stemmed partly from the report of a working group appointed in 1985, under Vajpayee's presidentship, after the 1984 rout (when the BJP managed to send only two MPs to the Lok Sabha). This inquiry committee measured how the grassroots and regional cadres—and among them the ones from Madhya Pradesh— were disturbed by ideological dilution as well as organizational compromises (electoral alliances included).[43] Advani's leadership was quickly appreciated amongst the party workers because of his clear-cut doctrine as well as his reactivization of the network of organizers. Thakre had already left to Kailash Chandra Joshi the post of party president—theoretically the most important in the BJP structure—to return to organizational tasks without losing an ounce of his authority, all the more as he had been appointed one of the all-India secretaries in 1982 and one of the party's vice-presidents in 1986.

His party unit was now free to make use of its activist strength within its original twofold strategic frame, directed towards social and religious mobilizations.

## Mobilization Techniques: The Political Use of Socio-Economic and Religious Issues

Agitation for social causes had always been part of the *sangathanist* pattern. We have so far noted only its local significance, in west Nimar for instance, but BJS/BJP's main asset—its activist network—enabled it to use this method on a large scale very early. By the end of the 1950s, the BJS was organizing massive demonstrations against Nehru's Cooperative Farming Scheme, claiming that it alienated the kisans' independence. 5,000 villages were covered and the party's veterans look back to this campaign as the initial stimulus of the party's growth in Madhya Pradesh.[44] Since then, the party has become adept at exploiting various social issues such as the Rationalization of Land Revenue Bill and the Compulsory Deposit Scheme of 1963 which concerned mainly the middle classes (*Madhya Pradesh Chronicle*, 27 June 1963: 1; 1 October 1963: 3). It campaigned effectively against inflation in the 1970s and more recently against power cuts affecting the irrigation system.[45]

In the 1980s, the Madhya Pradesh BJP, applied the recommendations of the 1985 national working group which enjoined the State units to multiply cells as 'projections of the party to penetrate [certain] sections [of society].'[46] In keeping with this guidance, the party established or strengthened front organizations to cater to the interest of women, peasants, youth, slum-dwellers and Harijans.

In the late 1980s, some of these front organizations orchestrated major social mobilization programmes. In autumn 1988, the BJP's youth wing, the Bharatiya Janata Yuva Morcha (BJYM) organized a campaign called *Kranti Mashal* whose main theme was the defence of the right to work—which implied, among other things, the suppression of English as a compulsory subject in certain competitive examinations.[47] BJYM processions left from the outlaying districts of Morena, Sidhi, Raigarh, Raipur and Jhabua, and after proceeding from town to town in the course of a month, reached Bhopal. There Sunder Lal Patwa—the party President since 1985—and Vijaya Raje Scindia presided over the final meeting after which between 25,000 and 70,000 activists gheraoed the Vidhan Sabha.[48]

The efforts to reach the rural people were less dramatic but probably more efficient. In 1986, the party entrusted Pyarelal Khandelwal with the responsibility of a three-year *Gram Raj Abhiyan* whose main slogan was *rin mukti*, the waiving of villagers' loans. Around 2,000 party workers took part in this campaign at one stage or another and reached 40,000 villages out of 70,000.[49] During the electoral campaign of 1989, *dharnas* were organized in *tehsil* towns, while in every *gram panchayat* BJP workers held meetings as well as tried to discuss villagers' problems.[50] This activity should be emphasized because the socioeconomic dimension of the BJP electoral campaign tended to be overshadowed in the press by the simultaneous movement on behalf of the Ayodhya movement. Nevertheless, the impact of this latter agitation has been crucial and deserves to be scrutinized at the local level.

The Madhya Pradesh Hindu nationalist network was not unfamiliar with manipulation of religious symbols to strengthen the Hindu consciousness and to effect political mobilization. Before the 1967 elections, for instance, the RSS complex was associated with the cow protection movement. In Indore, Ram Narain Shastri led a procession of 5,000 people in support of it.[51] Satyamitranand Giri, the *shankaracharya* of Bhanpura *Peeth* (Mandsaur district), presided over the State Sarvadaliya Goraksha Maha Abhiyan Samiti and canvassed for Jana Sangh MLAs.[52] However, the part played by the Vishva Hindu Parishad in the 1989 movement was of much greater significance.

The Madhya Pradesh VHP unit, whose head office is in Indore, had been reactivated by the early 1980s. Like the other enterprises of the RSS complex in the state, its key workers are old *swayamsevaks*. Its general secretary, Gulab Chand Khandelwal, elder brother of Pyarelal Khandelwal, joined the RSS in 1939 while he was a student at Indore and the *prant sangathan mantri* for Madhya Bharat, Hukum Chand Sawala, is an ex-*pracharak* from Bhanpura.[53] This core group benefits from patronage in the merchant community as indicated by the background of its president (Bhagwan Das Toshnewal, an industrialist from Indore) and of its working president (Ajmera, an ex-Hindu Sabhaite who owns a motor-garage in Bhopal). Besides this typical combination of activists and notables, the VHP supplied Hindu nationalism with a third, religious network whose main figure at the state level was Swami Divyanand—the new *shankaracharya* of Bhanpura *Peeth* from 1988 and the president of the Madhya Pradesh Kar Seva Samiti till 1991—and then Shanti Swaroop Maharaj. A disciple of Swami Paramanand (who is also the guru, based in Haridwar, of Sadhvi Rithambara), Shanti Swaroop Maharaj heads a small *akhara* in Ujjain as well as the regional Margdarshak circle of the VHP.[54] The VHP managed to establish this tripartite combination made of one activist, one notable and one sadhu throughout Madhya Pradesh, at the district level or even below.

For instance, in Shivpuri, the main activist is an ex-student leader from the RSS, Vinod Garg, whose brother owns a small oil-mill and patronizes a local temple where the Ram *shila* was stored. The president of the district unit since 1983 is a retired district judge, V.D. Saxena, and one local sadhu called Jay Prakash Das Ramayani who takes part in the VHP activity. One sadhu from the adjacent district of Guna, where he has a small ashram, Pagel Baba, comes over for the functions requiring a strong orator.[55] Commenting upon the role of the sadhus in the organization, one of the chiefs of the VHP in Shivpuri explained: 'Whenever we need them, we call them'.

In 1989 the VHP conducted the *Ram Shila Pujan* as part of the Ram Mandir campaign: activists and sadhus went to a large number of urban localities and villages to consecrate the bricks brought in processions and to collect an average donation of Rs. 1.25 per household (this was the standard donation expected in order to build the projected temple in Ayodhya). There were 22,732 *Ram Shila Pujans* all over Madhya Pradesh which would have produced an income of Rs. 7.9 million (*Hindu Vishva* 1990: 63-4). The movement had a powerful impact throughout the state: 3,000 *Ram Shila Pujans* took place in Bastar and Raipur divisions (where Rs. 400,000 were collected—Rs. 60,000 from Raipur city alone). In Mahakoshal, 5,000 devotees of Jabalpur took part in a procession carrying the Ram *shilas* to a local temple and in Hoshangabad district there have been 400 *pujans* (forty-three to seventy-five per block).[56] But Madhya Bharat remained the most highly mobilized area: 10,000 *Ram Shila Pujans* had already been performed there by the beginning of October (*The Times of India*, 7 October 1989: 6). Villagers of a very remote area in Rajgarh district gave Rs. 100: from the district as a whole, Rs. 300,000 were collected (*Dainik Bhaskar*, 22 November 1989: 1; 13

November 1989: 1). The local coordinator of the campaign, Pyarelal Khandelwal, was also the Rajgarh Lok Sabha candidate. Moreover, the BJP candidates were in most cases associated with the Ram Mandir campaign and the religious personalities conducting it (when they were not sadhus themselves or perceived as such like the Khajuraho MP, Uma Bharti). In Bhopal, the local BJP candidates stood on the dais with Swami Divyanand when he came for a *maha yajna* performed at the time of the *shilanayas* (*Madhya Pradesh Chronicle*, 11 November 1989: 9).

The legitimacy acquired by the BJP candidates through their association with the cause of the Ram Mandir was one factor in the electoral success of the BJP in 1989 and 1990 (see Appendix D). Moreover, a large number of the 219 BJP MLAs were militants who had taken an active part in this campaign. Of the 170 for whom detailed biographical information is available, 100 were activists associated with the RSS or organizations belonging to the RSS complex, and only seventy can be classed as local notables. In Chhattisgarh, nineteen out of fifty-one, and in Mahakoshal, twenty-five out of fifty-seven were notables (*Madhya Pradesh Vidhan Sabha Parichay* 1991). The tendency to rely on activist recruits helps to explain the relatively young age of the BJP MLAs: nearly one-fourth of them were under thirty-five years of age.

Referring to the Lok Sabha elections of 1989, Sunder Lal Patwa declared that, 'the key voters like the heads of various communities in villages, or zamindars, etc., who were able to influence the voting trend, had now become redundant . . .' (*Madhya Pradesh Chronicle*, 28 October 1989: 1). The BJP leaders were convinced that, as in 1977, the context enabled their activists to face the electorate with a good chance of success in most of the constituencies, without the help of as many leading citizens or rural leaders as before. By contrast with 1977, however, they managed to *create* a wave in their favour by resorting mainly to Hindu nationalist themes. Thus, their success in 1989 and 1990 suggests the emergence of a 'Hindu vote'. Does this mean that the BJP mobilized voters throughout the Hindu community regardless of social status?

Traditionally, the lists of MLAs returned by the BJS/BJP contained large proportions of people with high caste, urban professional, or merchant backgrounds.[57] The set of candidates selected by the BJP for the last State election still has these biases: in 1990, fifteen per cent of BJP candidates had a commercial background [against 6.9 per cent for the Congress (I)] and 16.8 per cent (against the Congress' 13.11 per cent) were lawyers or medical practitioners.[58]

Nevertheless, this social characteristic has not prevented the BJP from recruiting backward and low caste activists with increasing effectiveness. In the beginning, partly because the affiliation to the RSS was perceived as a means of Sanskritization, the *shakhas* were instrumental in attracting Scheduled Caste youth who could in time become trade unionists and/or Jana Sangh leaders. From the 1960s, most of the successful candidates whom the Jana Sangh fielded repeatedly in reserved constituencies had an RSS background. These included: H.C. Kachhwai and S.N. Jatiya at Ujjain, B.L. Phirozia at Gohad, N. Ahirwar at Maharajpur,

N. Kesri at Ashta, Gaurishankar Shejwar at Sanchi, G. Yatav at Sarangpur, Phool Chand Verma in Shajapur, S.P. Patel at Pandanha, and C. Arya at Suwasra.

For these men the Hindu nationalist affiliation is not perceived as contradicting their commitment to the cause of the Untouchables because of the RSS social reformism which is part of its *sangathanist* nationalist vocation; S.N. Jatiya stresses the convergence between this reformism and Dr B.R. Ambedkar's work in the following terms: 'He has given the thought but we are applying it practically in RSS. Because there, is no caste and no religion there. The only religion is Bharat Mata and we want to serve the nation'.[59] It should be noted that Jatiya, though highly educated and even Sanskriticized—says he has learnt Sanskrit and he belongs to Sanskritists' associations—is perceived as a labour and low caste leader. Thus, the Hindu nationalist parties have gradually penetrated the low castes, thanks to the individuals from this milieu who had been attracted by the *shakhas*.

In the 1980s, this long-term expansion among low castes through the RSS network has been amplified and given a rural dimension by the campaign on behalf of the Ram Mandir, a movement which enabled the BJP to reach villagers on an unprecedented scale.

For instance, in Piparsod (the village of Shivpuri district mentioned earlier) where an RSS *pracharak's* recent attempt to create a *shakha* had failed, the BJP consolidated its position after V. Garg organized a successful *Ram Shila Pujan*. The ground for the villagers' mobilization was prepared by the broadcasting of the epics, *Ramayana* and *Mahabharata,* on national television, which led the villagers to purchase forty-five TV sets in two years (Chambard 1991: 125). Although Garg's main local aide was a Brahman textile merchant educated at Shivpuri, agriculturists sympathized with the Hindu nationalist cause. Among the four villagers who tried to go to Ayodhya as *karsevaks* in October 1990, two were Gaur Brahmans who had long been members of the BJP, while the others were a Chowkidar and a Kirar (backward—though regionally dominant—caste) who were deeply moved by the religious nature of the enterprise. Indeed a majority of the 1,500 *karsevaks* from Shivpuri district were said to come from backward castes in the villages.

The momentum of this movement did not appear to have been affected by V.P. Singh's promise to implement the Mandal Commission Report. First, the Janata Dal has always been weak in the state. Second, the backward castes do not seem well organized or particularly conscious of what is at stake. In 1984, Madhya Pradesh had the lowest proportion of Shudra MPs: five per cent (Frankel and Rao 1989: 423), most of them concentrated in some northern districts adjacent to Uttar Pradesh. But even in this area, the backward castes tend to support BJP leaders such as Uma Bharti (a Lodh, MP of Khajuraho and vice-president of the BJP Madhya Pradesh Kisan Morcha) and R.K. Kusmariya (a Kurmi, MP of Damoh and president of the BJP Kisan Morcha). The situation may become different in Chhattisgarh, where Sahu associations have mobilized for the implementation of the recommendations made by the Mandal Report (*National Mail,* 5 January 1992).[90] Third, the Janata Dal's programme was not likely to provoke factional tensions in the BJP ranks. The Madhya Pradesh BJP—which counts only a dozen MLAs from the backward castes[60]—does have some backward caste representatives among its leaders. It has even set up a 'Pichhre Varg Mahasangh'. However, its leader, Babulal Bhanpur, an ex-textile mill worker from Bhopal, who joined the RSS in 1946 and is one of the co-founders of the BMS, though he approves of the spirit of the Mandal Report, subscribes fully to the party's official stand according to which reservations must have an economic basis.[61]

This is indicative of the discipline of the BJP, even though its capacity to mobilize on a broader basis, its access to power and the difficulties inherent in the government work have nourished personal ambitions and factional dissidences.

## Power, Dissensions and Discipline

The 1990 electoral victory enabled the party in the state to form a government on its own for the first time. During its two-and-a-half years in office, its system of governing showed an interesting way of dealing with dissent which cannot be dissociated from the *sangathanist* party-building pattern.

There have, in the past, been clashes of interest and personality among the state leaders of the Madhya Pradesh BJP. At one level, prominent local figures, such as Shitla Sahai and R.H. Gupta (who were members of the Janata government in 1977–80 and became important ministers again in 1990) have been prone to resent the extent to which the top posts in the party and in the government have tended to be monopolized by the same leaders all originating from its oldest stronghold, Malwa. In 1985, they expressed their protest—Sahai being then the dissidents' candidate for the state unit presidentship—at the convention of Bina. But eventually, after Sahai withdrew, Patwa replaced Joshi as party president and the latter succeeded the former as Leader of the Opposition in the Vidhan Sabha.[62]

At another level, there have been rivalries between these leaders from Malwa themselves. The tension between Kailash Chandra Joshi and Virendra Kumar Sakhlecha crystallized in the late 1970s, when the former had to resign as Chief Minister because of ill-health and was succeeded by the latter in January 1978. Sakhlecha, later took exception of his replacement in January 1980, by Sunder Lal Patwa who had kept aloof from the two previous governments. The antagonism between Sakhlecha and Patwa worsened after cases of corruption were registered against the former in 1982 and the latter in 1984.[63]

Ten years after the Janata Party experiment, the position of the three former chief ministers is instructive. In March 1990, Patwa became Chief Minister. Joshi refused to join the new government in order, he said, to take care of the party organization.[64] Eventually, however, eight months later, he agreed to accept the post of Minister of Industry and Energy. Interestingly, Sakhlecha's recent career has followed a somewhat parallel evolution: having been expelled from the BJP for breach of discipline in 1984, he created his own party but failed to make an impact; he then applied for, and was granted, readmission to the BJP in 1989. He became a member of the BJP National Council in December 1990. However, he was not given any election ticket.

The first motivation underlying the decisions by Joshi and Sakhlecha to 'return to the ranks' is probably a negative one. They realized that outside the party or on the margin of its mainstream they were losing influence, since most of their strength had derived not so much from their personal appeal or following, as from a *sangathanist* network of activists now likely to become indifferent or even hostile to their ambitions. The second motivation seems to come from the constant pressure from the party organizational leaders—who control this activist network—to work unitedly for the party cause without regard for personal gain.

This dual power structure, comprising on one hand organizational leaders and on the other elected or ministerial figures, is an important factor in promoting the cohesion of the party and the government. The 'infrastructure' is mainly embodied in the organizing cadres whose effective manager is Kushabhau Thakre. These men are not supposed to face the electorate.[65] They are expected to devote themselves almost exclusively to organizational work and to resist the temptation of a legislative or ministerial career. They thus provide an example of self-restraint which makes them, rather than the BJP members of the legislature and government, the role model for party workers. Kushabhau Thakre, for instance, is a bachelor who lives in a small room at the party's office building. This example of self-denial is a source of moral authority, as Babulal Gaur's testimony indicates: 'Kushabhau Thakre is our great man. He organized the whole party for the last forty or thirty years. He knows each and every worker from tehsil to city . . . . He is the Bhishma Pitamah of our party. He is very simple. He lives in a small place, just like a small *takht* . . . . Unmarried . . . . Donated his whole life to Nation, to RSS . . . . If he thinks that I am not good and I am not working in the interest of the party or nation, he will first guide me. Slowly, slowly he will say do this, do this for our party. When someone will not go according to the party lines, then he will say, all right, thank you.'[66]

Such moral prestige is likely to weigh against some divisive tendencies inside the party or the government. Interestingly, Vijaya Raje Scindia and Sambhajirao Angre tend to play similar roles. They have never accepted ministerial portfolios or other official responsibilities. Rather they work behind the scenes for 'party solidarity', and Vijaya Raje Scindia constantly exhorts the BJP MLAs and ministers to adhere to a 'value-based code of conduct'. In 1985, Shitla Sahai seems to have withdrawn from the fray in Bina because of pressures from her quarter.

After the formation of the Patwa government, Sambhajirao Angre, Kushabhau Thakre and a few others have participated in meetings of what is known as a 'core group', established to supervise the working of the government (*National Mail*, 30 November 1990: 1). Usually the chief minister took part in these meetings to enable the party organizers 'to know what are his limitations'.[67] In many ways, the influence of the core group reinforces that of the RSS whose organs remain watchful too. For instance, in 1990 the editor of *Swadesh*, Rajendra Sharma, criticized Patwa's ostentatious commemoration of his father's sixth death anniversary—a function to which V.P. Singh, the then Prime Minister, had been invited.[68]

However, the advantages of this dual power structure must not be over-estimated. First the sense of discipline, imposed from 'outside' or acquired by the public leaders in their youth inside the RSS, has some negative implications: few charismatic personalities are likely to emerge from the RSS' party's ranks—the most popular crowd pullers remain Vijaya Raje Scindia and Uma Bharti. Moreover, one of the aims of the men in charge of power at Bhopal between 1990 and 1992 has been to improve the presence of their party at the local level. A major decision of Sakhlecha's government in 1978-79 was the organization of *panchayat* and municipal elections (*The Times of India*, 21 June 1978). Patwa made a similar move in 1990, passing a law approving the holding of *panchayat* elections on a party basis (Madhya Pradesh Panchayati Raj Adhiniyam, p. 1668). The aim was to provide the party with an opportunity to gain control of the local power structure just as the Communist Party of India (Marxist). CPI(M) has done in West Bengal, which might have been viewed by the Madhya Pradesh BJP as a model. This strategy confirms the still high priority granted to the *sangathanist* pattern, since it recalls the efforts of *swayamsevaks* having entered the political arena to win positions of authority in local institutions.

Second, 'king makers' like Thakre and Vijaya Raje Scindia cannot easily control the behaviour of those leaders who are not part of the formal leadership structure and who feel frustrated, like Sakhlecha. In the party elections in early 1991 Sakhlecha polled sixty-eight votes even though he stood against Lekhi Ram Aggarwal, the 'official' candidate for the party presidentship who won with 123 votes [132 delegates abstained from voting (*National Mail*, 31 December 1990: 1)]. So far, this expression of dissent differs from the factionalism of other parties in that once a resolution has been passed or an office-bearer elected, the opponents accept the outcome with discipline. The risk of defection is also limited because dissenters know that they could be marginalized inside the party, or even excluded from it, if they overstep the mark.

But dissensions, if not factional tensions, may increase, especially in the event of repeated political failures. The recriminations against Patwa provoked by the setback of the BJP in the 1991 Lok Sabha elections[69] indicates this tendency. In July 1992, Sakhlecha also exploited the issue of the killing by the police in Bhilai of sixteen demonstrators of the Chhattisgarh Mukti Morcha (the trade union founded by Shankar Guha Niyogi): the demonstrators were demanding the implementation of labour laws and the arrest of the persons named by Asha Niyogi as the murderers of her husband (*Kriti Parichay* (Hindi), August 1992: 16–18).

Beyond the rivalries between politicians, the 'infrastructure' of the party has also been affected after the BJP came to power. The formation of the 'core group' was on a par with a questioning of the old collective mode of leadership. Senior leaders like Narayan Prasad Gupta and Pyarelal Khandelwal were thus sidelined;

and they expressed public resentment of Kushabhau Thakre's defence of Patwa whose resignation was being asked for by other party workers after the elections of 1991.[70]

These tensions reflect a more general source of potential dysfunction which is inherent in the dual power structure of the BJP: while government leaders tend to be cut off from the party cadres to a certain extent, the latter, the whole time organizers as well as the MLAs, cannot but be unhappy with the style of functioning and the performances of the government. These causes of discontent need to be scrutinized.

After the inception of the government, the ministers tended to adopt a different manner. Frequently, because of their new activity as well as their positions at the head of the state government which provided them new channels of authority, they became cut-off from the activist network. The feeling of being neglected by the ministers, and especially by Patwa, underlaid many of the party workers' criticisms of the latter after the Lok Sabha elections in 1991 (*National Mail*, 20, 21 and 29 July 1991). These considerations had even led some of them not to 'do their job whole-heartedly'[71] during the 1991 electoral campaign.[72]

The main achievement publicized by the government during its years in office was the waiving of rural loans for an amount of Rs. 600–700 crores.[73] This was greatly appreciated but some party workers regretted that the ceiling was established at Rs. 10,000, a limit not mentioned during the *Gram Raj Abhiyan*. The impossibility of fulfilling expectations that the BJP had helped to arouse, particularly regarding unemployment, annoyed party activists too, even though it stemmed mainly from financial constraints; the deficit budget amounted to Rs. 480.29 crores in 1992. In the Vidhan Sabha, backbenchers from the ruling party did not hesitate to arraign senior ministers about the inadequate number of teachers or the shortage of *tendu* leaves for beedi workers (*National Mail*, 18 February 1992 and 13 March 1992). To rectify this sort of situation, a three-day training camp was announced during the summer of 1992 to 'acquaint the participants—Members of the Parliament and the Legislative Assembly—with the role of MLAs of the ruling party' (Ibid., 14 June 1992).

The promptness of the BJP organizers and MLAs in criticizing the government is revealing of their political culture: the party activists are bound to oppose any government because their aim, inherited from the RSS training, is to change the whole society and also because they tend to ignore the financial and administrative constraints,[74] their work being mainly organizational. This is clearly the other side of the medal in the dual power structure of the BJP.

Some RSS and BJP leaders are also worried about the incapacity of certain MLAs to resist the temptation of corrupt practices. This is the usual outcome of the access to power, but it may be seen also as a somewhat 'rational' reaction. Since the government is not able to fulfil the promises made to the voters, some MLAs are sceptical about their re-election and prepare for their future accordingly. Therefore, the asset that was the clean image of the BJP is likely to be eroded if the efforts of its more idealistic leaders from the organizational wing to retain the status of 'a party with a difference' are not effective.

*

The first conclusion suggested by this study of the BJP in Madhya Pradesh is to confirm the party's specificity, which originates mainly from its filial link with the RSS. This relation helps to explain its reliance on the *sangathanist* party-building pattern, an unusual degree of party discipline and the crucial role of the activists' network, used to mobilize the electorate by exploiting religious symbols and socioeconomic issues as well as to perform social work at the local level. When it was formed in 1980, the BJP inherited from the Jana Sangh these structural assets. They enabled it to maintain for ten years the level of valid votes the Jana Sangh had reached since 1967 (around thirty per cent). In 1989–90, the BJP's share of the vote rose to around forty per cent, mainly thanks to the Ram Mandir agitation. But this expansion and the attaining of State power posed a new challenge to the party, that of a decline in militancy and discipline amongst the party workers.

The relative demobilization of the activists' network was one important factor contributing to the BJP's electoral setback in the State in 1991. The inner constraint of the *sangathanist* party-building pattern was then easy to perceive: since the strength of the BJP lies predominantly in its network of activists, it cannot afford to alienate this group even to a small extent. Therefore, the future of the BJP in Madhya Pradesh depended before the dismissal of Patwa's government upon its performances in power, but also in large part upon its capacity to reconcile the government with the activist network. The national party leaders had asked the Chief Minister to change his style of functioning[75] and apparently he had complied with their views.[76] But the years of the BJP's existence in office have revealed another contradiction which may be inherent in the *sangathanist* model. While the Hindu-nationalist complex, deriving from a 'non-political' and oppositional movement the RSS, is born to reform the society in its image, this radical idealism—very strong among the activists—may hardly survive into a period of political power since this new context inevitably reveals the difficulties of any policy implementation. This is one of the reasons why the government tended to concentrate on ideological measures which please the party workers without putting a strain on the Budget, such as the promotion of Hindi, the rewriting of history textbooks and the recognition of Vidya Bharti, the educative front of the RSS.[77]

## Notes

1. The most notable exceptions are for Uttar Pradesh, see Burger 1969; for Delhi, see Puri 1980, and, more recently, for case studies relating to several regions of north India, Graham 1990.

2. Usually, *pracharaks* have foregone opportunities to pursue a professional career and, temporarily at least, to build up a family, in order to devote their whole time and energy to this task.

3. According to his biographers, K.B. Hedgewar founded these atypical units when he accompanied his aunt to Indore for medical treatment, see Deshpande and Ramaswamy 1981: 110.

4. Interview with Pyarelal Khandelwal who was *pracharak* in Indore district from 1955 to 1964.

5. *The Hindustan Times*, 6 August 1970. Ram Narain Shastri stated that the regular participants in the *shakhas* numbered about 6,000. In 1963, he had indicated that in the Ujjain *shakhas*, some of them functioning since 1935, accounted for 4,000 *swayamsevaks* (*Madhya Pradesh Chronicle*, 5 November 1963: 6).

6. Interview with Uttam Chand Israni, Madhya Bharat *prant karyavah* since 1979.

7. Interview with N.K. Shejwalkar who has been one of the makers of the Jana Sangh in Gwalior.

8. Interview with Vimal Kumar Choradia who succeeded him as *prant sanghchalak*.

9. For instance, Haribhau Joshi, a *pracharak* who used to be in charge of the Ujjain Akhil Bharatiya Vidyarthi Parishad (student union belonging to the RSS complex) in the early 1950s and who became teacher in Maharashtra afterwards was dispatched to Susner in Shajapur district in 1957. After twice being elected MLA he chose to return to organizational work and went to Chhattisgarh for some time in the late 1960s (Ali 1987: 360).

10. The police reports on the repression of the satyagraha launched by M.S. Golwalkar in protest of the RSS ban after Gandhi's murder underline the high percentage of 'advocates, teachers, students and civil servants' among the 1,444 *swayamsevaks* arrested by mid-January 1949, one month after the first demonstration (*Madhya Bharat Cabinet Papers*).

11. By example, Babulal Jain, the chief organizer of the Jana Sangh in Ujjain in the 1960s joined the RSS in his village of Maksi in 1945.

12. Interview with Moghe. The workers of Indore textile mills were approached by *swayamsevaks* as early as the mid-1930s too.

13. Interview with Babulal Mehere.

14. Ujjain Qazi's brother stated in 1989: 'Maybe we will vote for Jatiya who has an impeccable record as a leader of workers and the downtrodden. He has faced police lathis for the labourers' (*The Indian Express*, 22 November 1989: 4).

15. Interview with N.P. Dhakar. For a detailed study of Piparsod, see, Chambard (1980) to whom I am grateful for 'introducing' me to the village.

16. But after two years of the BJP in office, the local chief of the VHP deplored that most of the BJP MLAs are not incorruptible any more, an issue I have addressed in the last section.

17. Interview with P.C. Verma.

18. Interview with Balchandra Bagdare.

19. Interview with Kailash Chandra Joshi.

20. This socio-political category corresponds partly to what A. Mayer has termed 'rural leaders', members of the local elites who managed to dominate the institutions of the Panchayati Raj or the co-operative system, a position that gave them 'opportunities to gain power as patrons and as brokers', see, Mayer 1963: 103.

21. Out of the 147 ex-Jana Sanghi MLAs in 1977, at least six had been underground workers and seventy-four had spent between seventeen and twenty-two months in jail (*Madhya Pradesh Vidhan Sabha* 1977). Almost all of the 1,800 Maintenance of Internal Security Act (MISA) political prisoners in Madhya Pradesh would have been Jana Sangh members (*The Hindu*, 23 January 1977; *The Hindustan Times*, 18 February 1977).

22. As a sign of these ideological affinities, the Maharajah inaugurated first Moonje's 'Nasik Military School' in 1938 (*Hindu Outlook*, 30 March 1938: 1). But he had desisted from doing the same for the Hindu Mahasabha Bhawan (*Savarkar Papers*, Letter from Ganpat Rai dated 25 August 1937).

23. This consideration became more important in the 1940s, after the Quit India Movement had affected the state (*Gwalior State Papers*, Foreign and Political Department, File no. 7, C/99).

24. Interview with Sambhajirao Angre.

25. Ibid.

26. Madhav Rao Scindia joined the party in 1970 (*The Organiser*, 28 February 1970: 1).

27. The fervour she awakened in a town as far from Gwalior as Ujjain, as patron of the Mahakal Sawari for instance, was a sign of her popularity.

28. Interview with U.C. Israni who was one of the 12,000 Sindhis who settled in Bhopal after the Partition.

29. Interviews with L.N. Sharma and G.S. Kaushal.

30. Interview with Giriraj Kishore, a BHEL worker and one of the main promoters of these *shakhas*.

31. For more details on this point, see Jaffrelot 1991: 251–70. The day of Vishvakarman is intended by the BMS to rival the Leftists' May Day.

32. In 1961, the Sindhi-speaking population of Bhopal district had reached 23,870, see Shrivastav and Guru 1989: 99. Like most of the displaced persons, this Sindhi community has pro-Hindu nationalist leanings.

33. Interview with V.R. Meghawale who was elected MLA of Dhamtari constituency in 1962 and 1967.

34. Interviews with Baburao Paranjpe (Jabalpur MP in 1982–4 and 1989–91) and N.P. Gupta.

35. Whence the multiplication of Hanuman temples in this tribal belt. For the activity of the VKA among women, see, Sen 1990.

36. He became a Jana Sangh Rajya Sabha member in 1970. In 1962, the Madhya Pradesh RRP had half of its ten MLAs elected in Raigarh and Surguja districts, the other princely supports being the family of Dewas Senior and Kawardha states whose 'vote banks' were captured by the Jana Sangh in 1967. In 1990, the scion of Dewas Senior House was elected as a BJP MLA. He was already active in the party as head of the district Bharatiya Janata Yuva Morcha, the youth wing of the BJP founded in 1978.

37. Interview of R.H. Gupta who was the Finance Minister in the State Government of Bhopal in 1967–9, 1977–80 and 1990–2.

38. Interview with Lokendra Singh. Despite this defection, the BJP kept the seat of Damon, which may a sign that the party did not need the princely patronage any more. This evolution is also likely to happen in Gwalior area: after having grown in the shadow

of Vijaya Raje Scindia, the Hindu nationalist organizations may be able to stand by themselves.

39. Vijaya Raje Scindia, then one of the party vice-presidents, circulated a text opposing 'Gandhian socialism' and favouring Deendayal Upadhyaya's 'Integral Humanism' among the delegates of the first session of the BJP in Mumbai (*The Hindustan Times*, 27 December 1980). The then secretary of Madhya Pradesh BJP, Kailash Sarang, also expressed some reservations towards 'Gandhian socialism' (*National Herald*, 28 January 1981).

40. Interview with Shitla Sahai, the then Health Minister. He commented upon the socialists' behaviour as follows: 'They were few people, one thing. And secondly, since more members were out of the stock of the Jan Sangh, so we were smoothly working in the government and delivering the goods to the people of Madhya Pradesh. Socialists, they are in the habit of debating, of criticising people who are in front of them . . . . So that was actually not the matter for consideration...'

41. From 1962–3, Hindu Sabhaites joined Jana Sangh by waves (*Madhya Pradesh Chronicle*, 25 October 1963: 6).

42. H. Siddiqui left the BJP in August 1986 because he disapproved of the party's campaign in favour of a uniform civil code in the wake of the Shah Bano case, an affair which originated in Indore and helped the Hindu nationalist forces a great deal in Madhya Pradesh. (Interview with N. Rajan, editor of the *National Mail*, to whom I owe this information among others.)

43. BJP Working Group Report, presented to the National Executive, Bhopal, 20 July 1985.

44. At that time, Kushabhau Thakre attributed the growth from twenty-nine mandal committees in 1959 to forty-nine (i.e., 500 local committees and 23,000 members) in 1961 to this agitation which 'gave the Jana Sangh workers an opportunity of establishing contact with the peasants' (*The Organiser*, 2 January 1961: 7).

45. 4,000 militants courted arrest on this issue all over Madhya Bharat (*The Statesman* [Delhi], 17 January 1982).

46. BJP Working Group Report, presented to the National Executive, Bhopal, 20 July 1985: 28.

47. Interview with the Madhya Pradesh BJYM organizing secretary, Vipin Dixit.

48. The highest estimation is supplied by *Free Press Journal* (8 October 1988) and the lowest by *Madhya Pradesh Chronicle* (10 October 1988). The party newspaper, *Move on*, published from Bhopal provides the Honouring figures: Sagar (5,500), Damoh (3,600), Tikamgarh (2,132), Satna (2,690), Morena (2,570), Indore city (3,600), Indore rural (2,715), Ujjain (1,278), Sidhi (1,800), Bilaspur (1,200), Raipur (1,882), Raigarh (1.167), Rajnandgaon (1,209), Guna (968), Jhabua (1,570), Bastar (778), Durg (337)—(25 October 1988: 5).

49. Interview with P. Khandelwal.

50. Dhyanendra Singh, Vijaya Raje Scindia's brother, worked for instance in his constituency of Morar (Interview). See also, *India Week*, 16 June 1989: 11.

51. *Madhya Pradesh Chronicle*, 8 November 1966: 3. Another demonstration took place in November in Indore (ibid., 27 November 1966: 3) but except for this city, Khandwa was the only place witnessing a notable mobilization (ibid., 24 December 1966: 3).

52. Ibid., 19 October 1966: 3.

53. Interview with G.C. Khandelwal and H.C. Sawala.

54. Interview with Shanti Swaroop.
55. Interviews with V. Garg and V.D. Saxena. The same structure prevails in Ratlam where B.L. Bhati, an ex-*pracharak* in Kota who settled in Ratlam as teacher of the Gujarati school in 1958, reactivated the VHP in the mid-1980s (under the patronage of the affluent Gujarati and Jain communities who had given the movement its first presidents) *and* with the help of sadhus, one of them being Bhati's brother (interview with B.L. Bhati).
56. *Madhya Pradesh Chronicle*, 11 November 1989: 5; 7 October 1989: 5 and 15 September 1989: 5.
57. Moreover a substantial number of Guptas, Khandelwals, or Aggarwals, are found amongst the cadres of the party and its MLAs or MPs. The proportion of Jains is especially high amongst the party functionaries as well as the patrons of the Hindu nationalist movements. Sakhlecha, Patwa, Raghavji, Johri, Sawala, Choradia, H.C. Jain, Babulal Jain, Ajmera belong to this community for instance.
58. The agriculturists were 756.7 per cent against 67 per cent among Congress candidates, (Chief Electoral Officer, *Vidhan Sabha General Election 1990 Analytical Tables* 1990, p. 59).
59. Interview with S.N. Jatiya.
60. The BJP candidates' list for the Legislative Assembly included only twenty-five backward castes' contestants (*Dainik Bhaskar*, 1 February 1990).
61. Interview with Babulal Bhanpur. Babulal Gaur, an *Ahir* whose personal prestige could have enabled him to emerge as a backward caste leader shares the same view.
62. Another type of inter-regional tension emerged after the formation of the BJP government in the early 1990s, when the leaders from Madhya Bharat were accused of being over-represented. One senior MLA from Jabalpur, Jaishree Banerjee, protested that the other areas were neglected (*National Mail*, 17 March 1992). Some MLAs from Chhattisgarh expressed the same criticism and argued that if this trend continued, they would be left with no alternative but to support the demand for separate Chhattisgarh (ibid., 15 July 1992). Four members of Patwa's government only came from this area and among them there were two Marwaris, one Bihari Brahman and only one Sahu, whose caste is yet important in the province (interview with P. Khandelwal).
63. It seemed that the background of these charges was partly rooted in their rivalry (*The Statesman* [Delhi], 7 November 1982: 7; 14 November 1984: 6).
64. In fact, his disappointment as contender for chief ministership appeared clearly when he desisted from attending the swearing-in ceremony of Sunder Lal Patwa (*Dainik Bhaskar*, 6 March 1990: 1, 3).
65. Kushabhau Thakre contested only twice in Khandwa—the first time for a by-election in 1979, at a critical juncture when the Janata Party had to be boosted. N.P. Gupta contested in 1952, 1977 and 1980 and Pyarelal Khandelwal in 1989 and 1991. It must be remembered that, for instance, the general secretary of the Jana Sangh from 1953 to 1967, Deendayal Upadhyaya contested only once in a by-election.
66. Interview with Babulal Gaur who became Minister for Law, Gas Relief and Local Self-Government in 1990. I recognize here the emphasis on the disciplined activist network which is perceived as the key to success in the long term, from the *sangathanist* point of view.

67. Interview with Kushabhau Thakre.
68. *India Today*, 31 July 1990: 14. *Swadesh* expressed similar criticisms during the year 1990. See also, *The Sunday Observer*, 16 December 1990: 4.
69. The parry won only twelve seats—eight of them in Madhya Bharat—compared with the yield of twenty-seven in 1989 and its share of valid votes increased from 39.66 per cent in 1989 to 41.88 per cent in 1991 mainly because he fielded seven more candidates (40 against 33).
70. These two leaders justify their move in significant terms: 'It is for the first time in 40 years that we have gone to Delhi and complained to the top leadership of the BJP and the RSS regarding our internal matters . . . so long we have been living like a family with Mr Thakre as the elder brother. But there is a limit to tolerating the whims of someone . . . . We cannot be mute spectators if someone destroys the work of our lifetime' (cited in *The Times of India*, 23 September 1991: 4).
71. *National Mail*, 23 June 1991 and 16 May 1991 on 'sabotage from within the party' in Jabalpur constituency.
72. This 'revolt' at the grassroot level had already been reflected in the voting pattern of the last party elections in 1991. In these, Sakhlecha performed creditably because of his long background as an activist whereas L.R. Aggarwal was probably perceived as a 'notable' whose support was confined to the high ups of the party.
73. Another outcome advertised by the government was the provision of ownership rights (*pattas*) of about 89,000 hectares of land to more than 70,000 forest land encroachers—mostly tribals—by the end of June 1992 (*Free Press*, 25 August 1992).
74. Some ministers complained that the administrative apparatus was sometime reluctant to energetically implement certain measures.
75. See, for instance, the recommendations expressed by Bakht in *National Mail*, 1 July 1991: 1.
76. See, for instance, the certificate of satisfaction delivered to him by L.K. Advani (*The Times of India*, 10 May 1992).
77. In May 1992 the state government decided to constitute a separate board for conducting the class five and eight examinations of schools run by Vidya Bharti (*National Mail*, 1 June 1992).

# References

Ali, Ashfaq (1987), *Bhopal: Past and Present*, Bhopal: Jai Bharat Publishing House.
Andersen, W. and Damle, S.D. (1987), *The Brotherhood in Saffron: The Rashtriya Swayamsevak Sangh and Hindu Revivalism*, New Delhi: Vistaar Publications.
Bailey, F. (1963), *Politics and Social Change: Orissa in 1959*, London: University of California Press.
Baxter, C. (1971), *The Jana Sangh: A Biography of an Indian Political Party*, Bombay: Oxford University Press.
BJP Working Group Report (1985), presented to the National Executive, Bhopal, 20 July.
Burger, A. (1969), *Opposition in a Dominant Party System*, Berkeley: University of California Press.

Chambard, Jean-Luc (1980), *Atlas d'un village indien*, EH ESS, Paris.

——— (1991), 'La chanson de la terre qui tremble ou la punition du roi qui avait voulu regner sans sa reine', *Cahiers de Litterature orale*, No. 29.

Chief Electoral Officer (1990), *Vidhan Sabha General Election 1990 Analytical Tables*, Bhopal.

Curran, J.A. (1951), *Militant Hinduism in Indian Politics: A Study of the RSS*, Institute of Pacific Relations.

*Dainik Bhaskar*, 13 and 22 November 1989, 1 February and 6 March 1990.

Deshpande, B.V. and Ramaswamy, S.R. (1981), *Dr Hedgewar: the Epoch Maker*, Bangalore: Sahitya Sindhu.

Frankel, F. and Rao, M.S.A. (1989) (eds.), *Dominance and State Power in Modern India: Decline of a Social Order*, Delhi: Oxford University Press, Vol. I.

*Free Press*, 25 August 1992.

Graham, Bruce (1990), *Hindu Nationalism and Indian Politics: The Origins and Development of the Bharatiya Jana Sangh*, Cambridge: Cambridge University Press.

*Gwalior State Papers*, Foreign and Political Department, File no. 7, C/99, Madhya Pradesh State Archives, Bhopal.

Heeger, G.A. (1970), 'Discipline versus Mobilization: Party Building and the Punjab Jana Sangh', *Asian Survey*, 12 October.

*Hindu Mahasabha Papers*, Letter from Indra Prakash to Mahant Dig Vijay Nath, 4 October 1951, C-189, Manuscript Section, Nehru Memorial Museum and Library.

*Hindu Outlook*, 30 March 1938.

*Hindu Vishwa: Vishva Hindu Parishad Silver Jubilee Special Issue 1989–90* (1990), Vol. 25, No. 12, August.

*Hitavada*, 31 December 1947.

*The Indian Express*, 22 November 1989.

*India Today*, 31 July 1990.

*India Week*, 16 June 1989.

Jaffrelot, C. (1989), 'La place de lEtat dans l'idéologie nationaliste hindoue', *Revue Française de Science Politique* , Vol. 39, No. 6, December.

——— (1991), 'Note sur un syndicat nationalist hindou—Le travail et les travailleurs dans l'idéologie et les stratégies du Bharatiya Mazdoor Sangh', in G. Heuzé (ed.), *Purushartha*, No. 14.

*Kriti Parichay* (Hindi), August 1992.

*Madhya Bharat Cabinet Papers*, File 505/48, Madhya Pradesh State Archives, Bhopal.

*Madhya Pradesh Chronicle*, 27 June, 1 and 25 October, 5 November 1963, 19 October, 8 and 27 November, 24 December 1966, 15 September, 28 October and 11 November 1989.

*Madhya Pradesh Vidhan Sabha Sadasyon ka Sankshipt Parichay: 1962* (1964), Bhopal: Madhya Pradesh Vidhan Sabha Sachivalay.

*Madhya Pradesh Vidhan Sabha (navan) Sadasya Parichay* (1991), Bhopal: Madhya Pradesh Vidhan Sabha Sachivalay.

Mayer, A. (1962), 'System and Network: An approach to the study of political process in Dewas', in T.N. Madan (ed.) *Indian Anthropology: Essays in Memory of D.N. Majumdar*, Bombay: Asia Publishing House.

——— (1963), 'Some political implications of Community Development in India', *Archives Europiennes de Sociologie*, Vol. IV.

*The Motherland,* 19 October 1972, 2 August 1972.

*National Mail,* 30 November and 31 December 1990; 16 May, 23 June, 20, 21 and 29 July 1991; 5 January, 18 February, 13 March, 1 and 14 June 1992.

*The Organiser,* Jana Sangh Special Issue, 13 August 1950.

*The Organiser,* 2 January 1961, 28 February 1970, 14 January 1990.

Puri, G. (1980), *Bharatiya Jana Sangh: Organisation and Ideology,* New Delhi: Sterling Publishers.

*Savarkar Papers* (1937), Letter from Ganpat Rai dated 25 August, Microfilm Section, Reel no. 3, File no. 1, Nehru Memorial Museum and Library.

Scindia, Vijaya Raje with Malgonkar, M. (1988), *Princess: The Autobiography of the Dowager Maharani of Gwalior,* New Delhi: Time Books International.

Sen, Ilina (1990), 'Women and proselytisation: a case study of Christian missionary and Hindu revivalist attitudes towards women in Raigarh district of Madhya Pradesh', paper presented at the International Congress of Sociology, Madrid, July.

Shri Guruji (1964), 'Yes, RSS wants to dominate every walk of national life', *The Organiser,* Divali Special.

Shrivastav, P.N. and Guru, S.D. (1989), *Madhya Pradesh District Gazetteers: Bhopal and Sehdre,* Bhopal: Directorate of Gazetteers.

*Shyama Prasad Mookherjee Papers,* Manuscript section, File no. 173, Nehru Memorial Museum and Library.

Sikander Bakht, *National Mail,* 1 July 1991.

*The Statesman* [Delhi], 17 January and 7 November 1982, 14 November 1984.

*The Hindu,* 23 January 1977.

*The Hindustan Times,* 11 July 1962, 6 August 1970, 18 February 1977.

*The Sunday Observer,* 16 December 1990.

*The Times of India,* 16 July 1962, 21 June 1978, 7 October 1989, 23 September 1991, 10 May 1992.

Verma, R. and Guru, S.D. (1982), *Madhya Pradesh District Gazetteers: Ujjain,* Bhopal: District Gazetteers Department.

Weiner, M. (1967), *Party Building in a New Nation: The Indian National Congress,* Chicago: Chicago University Press.

*Who's Who in Lok Sabha 1967* (1967), New Delhi: Lok Sabha Secretariat.

# Appendices

## Appendix A

TABLE 12.1: Madhya Pradesh: Numbers of Notables and Activists Amongst BJS and BJP MLAs by Regions for 1957–1990

| | 1957 | 1962 | 1967 | 1972 | 1977 | 1980 | 1985 | 1990 |
|---|---|---|---|---|---|---|---|---|
| % of valid votes | 9.9 | 16.7 | 28.3 | 28.5 | 47.3* | 30.3 | 32.5 | 39.7 |
| Total number of seats (seats won) | 288(10) | 288(41) | 296(50) | 296(77) | 320(215)*-147-** | 320(60) | 320(58) | 320(219) |
| **Gwalior Area (Districts: Morena, Bhind, Gwalior, Datia, Shivpuri, Guna, Vidisha)** | | | | | | | | |
| Seats (seats won) | 35(0) | 35(0) | 35(19) | 35(21) | 39(39)*-20-** | 39(11) | 39(9) | 39(29) |
| Notables*** | — | — | 10 | 13 | 2** | 4 | 3 | 11 |
| Activists*** | — | — | 7 | 5 | 13** | 7 | 4 | 14 |
| **Malwa Area (Districts: Rajgarh, Shajapur, Ujjain, Indore, Dewas, Khargone, Dhar, Jhabua, Ratlam, Mandsaur)** | | | | | | | | |
| Seats (seats won) | 56(8) | 56(26) | 57(27) | 57(6) | 62(55)*-40-** | 62(23) | 62(8) | 62(50) |
| Notables | 2 | 8 | 6 | 3 | 3** | 4 | 3 | 13 |
| Activists | 5 | 15 | 11 | 3 | 26** | 17 | 4 | 33 |
| **Bhopal Area (Districts: Sehore, Bhopal, Raisen)** | | | | | | | | |
| Seats (seats won) | 9(0) | 9(0) | 11(7) | 11(2) | 12(8)*-6-** | 12(7) | 12(5) | 12(11) |
| Notables | — | — | 2 | — | 0** | — | 1 | 1 |
| Activists | — | — | 2 | 2 | 5** | 4 | 4 | 7 |

Vindhya Pradesh (Districts: Tikamgarh, Chhatarpur, Damoh, Panna, Satna, Rewa, Sidhi, Shahdol)

| Seats (seats won) | 41(2) | 41(5) | 42(1) | 44(4) | 44(36)*-15-** | 44(2) | 44(9) | 44(21) |
|---|---|---|---|---|---|---|---|---|
| Notables | — | 2 | — | 2 | 3** | 1 | 5 | 7 |
| Activists | 2 | 2 | 1 | 2 | 8** | 0 | 3 | 11 |

Chhattisgarh (Districts: Surguja, Raigarh, Bilaspur, Raipur, Bastar, Durg, Rajnandgaon)

| Seats (seats won) | 81(0) | 81(5) | 84(9) | 84(10) | 90(54)*-22-** | 90(6) | 90(13) | 90(51) |
|---|---|---|---|---|---|---|---|---|
| Notables | — | 1 | 5 | 1 | 5** | 2 | 7 | 19 |
| Activists | — | 2 | 1 | 2 | 9** | 2 | 3 | 16 |

Mahakoshal (Districts: Narsimhapur, Balaghat, Mandla, Jabalpur, Chhindwara, Hoshangabad, Betul, Khandwa, Sagar, Seoni)

| Seats (seats won) | 66(0) | 66(5) | 66(14) | 66(7) | 71(39)*-25-** | 71(11) | 71(14) | 71(57) |
|---|---|---|---|---|---|---|---|---|
| Notables | — | 1 | 4 | 2 | 5** | 4 | 8 | 25 |
| Activists | — | 1 | 5 | 3 | 14** | 6 | 2 | 19 |

*Sources:* Election results published by the Madhya Pradesh Chief Electoral Officer (Bhopal) and *Madhya Pradesh Vidhan Sabha Sadasyon ka Sankshipt Parichay*, Bhopal, 1961, 1964, 1970, 1972, 1977, 1980, 1985 and 1991.

\* : Figures of the Janata Party.

\*\* : Figures of ex-Jan Sangh members elected as Janata Party candidates.

\*\*\* : 'Notables' designates leading citizens without formal ideological commitment to Hindu nationalism and especially rural leaders elected as members of *gram pachayants, janapad sabhas, zila parishads* or of the boards of co-operative institutions. Marketing Societies and Mandi Committees. In urban contexts, this term refers also to members of municipal councils, big merchants or prestigious advocates.

'Activists' implies an ideological commitment testified by fidelity to the same party over a long period and an active involvement in at least one of the branches of the 'RSS complex' other than the BJP. 'Activists' acquiring a local leadership through their elections or appointments to influential posts are still considered as representatives of this category and not as 'Notables'.

## Appendix B

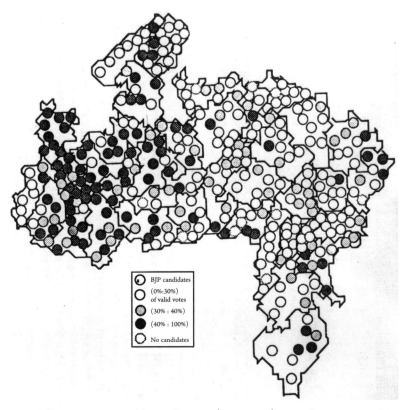

THE BJP's PERFORMANCE IN MADHYA PRADESH (REGIONWISE) IN THE ELECTIONS OF 1980

# Appendix C

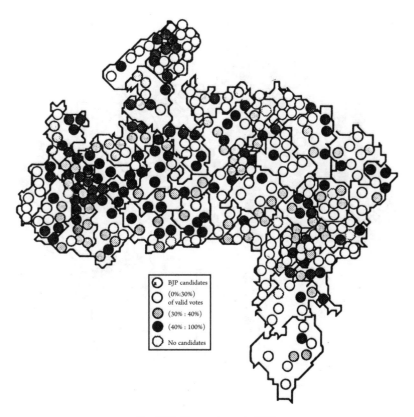

**Legend:**
- BJP candidates
- (0%:30%) of valid votes
- (30% : 40%)
- (40% : 100%)
- No candidates

THE BJP's PERFORMANCE IN 1985

# Appendix D

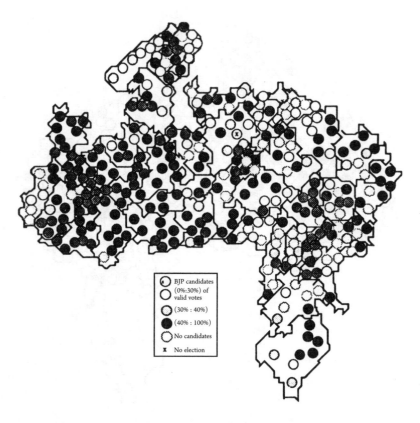

The legend reads:

- BJP candidates
- (0%:30%) of valid votes
- (30% : 40%)
- (40% : 100%)
- No candidates
- No election

THE BJP's PERFORMANCE IN 1990

# Chapter 13

# The Hindu nationalist movement in Delhi from ⬚locals⬚to refugees⬚ and towards peripheral groups?

The Bharatiya Janata Party (BJP) suffered a major setback during the 1998 assembly elections in Delhi when it won only 15 seats to Congress' 51. However, this defeat can be attributed largely to the then growing unpopularity of Vajpayee's Government at the Centre. Not long before, during the last two general elections, held in 1991 and 1996, the BJP had recorded its highest ever scores in Delhi (49.6 per cent and 53 per cent respectively) and its popularity was not a new phenomenon. In fact, in contrast to the adjoining states, Delhi is perhaps the oldest electoral stronghold of the Hindu nationalist movement. As early as the autumn of 1951, the Bharatiya Jana Sangh emerged as the main rival to the Congress during the Delhi municipal elections with 25 per cent of the valid votes as against Congress' 33 per cent (*The Statesman*, 29 September 1954: 1). And during the 1952 assembly elections, it still performed reasonably well, taking 22 per cent of the valid votes (*Delhi Gazetteer*, 1976: 972). Since then, the Jana Sangh and later the BJP have continued to be the main challenger to the Congress or even the ruling party in Delhi (see Tables 13.1 and 13.2).

The exceptional strength of the Hindu nationalist parties in Delhi has often been attributed to the circumstances and implications of Partition: communal feelings were exacerbated in a city which had been badly affected by Hindu-Muslim riots and which harboured so many refugees from Pakistan.

This approach can be substantiated by facts but it needs to be supplemented and refined. First, the Hindu nationalist movement had already some support before 1947 in Delhi, as suggested by the pre-independence development of the RSS, which relied on the collaboration between local notables (who were often big merchants) and activists from the intelligentsia (who, originally, were Maharashtrian Brahmans). Second, the influx of so many Punjabis who resented the Congress' so-called 'appeasement' policy towards Muslims did help the Jana Sangh, but this was partly because many of the refugees had already imbibed Hindu nationalism in the Punjab. Furthermore, while the Jana Sangh depended on the refugees (for its organization as well as at the time of elections), it did not become the party of the refugees. In fact, refugees voted in large numbers for the Congress while it was the local business community who provided strong support for the Jana Sangh, and the BJP. In a way, these parties were primarily representative of

TABLE 13.1: Party-Wise Composition of Delhi Municipal Corporation

| Party | 1958 | 1962 | 1967 | 1971 |
|---|---|---|---|---|
| Congress | 42 | 73 | 42 | 44 |
| Jana Sangh | 25 | 9 | 52 | 53 |
| Communists | 7 | 2 | 2 | 1 |
| Others | 1 | - | 2 | 1 |
| Independents | 9 | 3 | 3 | 3 |
| TOTAL | 84 | 87 | 101 | 102 |

*Source: Delhi Gazetteer, 1976.*

TABLE 13.2: Percentage of Votes Polled in State Elections and
Delhi Metropolitan Council Elections

| Year of elections | Congress | BJS/BJP | Swatantra/Janata Party |
|---|---|---|---|
| 1952 | 52.1 | 21.9 | — |
| 1972 | 48.5 | 38.5 | 0.1 |
| 1977 | 36.1 | — | 52.6 |
| 1983 | 47.5 | 37.0 | 3.7 |

*Source: D. Gupta 1996: 37.*

the 'middle world'. The BJP has retained this social profile today even though it tries to reach the rural periphery of Delhi.

## The RSS Organization-Building Pattern in Delhi

The RSS was not the first Hindu nationalist organization in Delhi. Kenneth Jones considers that Delhi 'became the centre of a new type of Hinduism—organized, structured Hinduism' (Jones 1993: 203) as early as the late nineteenth century, especially after Dayananda founded a branch of the Arya Samaj there in 1878 and after Deen Dayal Sharma established the headquarters of the Bharat Dharm Mahamandal, a Sanatanist (orthodox) association in 1890, followed by the founding of the Hindu College in 1899. In 1909 the Arya Samaj also transferred its main office to Delhi with the creation of the Sarvadeshik Arya Pratinidhi. The Delhi Provincial Hindu Sabha was later founded by Arya Samajists and Sanatanists in 1918 and the headquarters of the Hindu Mahasabha was transferred from Benares to Delhi in 1925, after Lajpat Rai became its president. The Hindu Sabha movement was never a mass movement in Delhi—it polled only 179 votes, as against Congress' 6,261 during the 1945 Legislative Assembly elections when the winning candidate and his runner-up were both Muslims (Gupta 1997: 21). But its modest resources helped the RSS take root in Delhi in the 1930s.

In its formative phase, the RSS developed its network by sending *pracharaks* from Nagpur to most cities, in particular to those with substantial student populations since the educated youth was its priority target (and the *pracharaks* could approach students after registering themselves as students). As K.R. Malkani explains, 'In town after town the Sangha *pracharak* would arrive with a few letters of introduction to the local leaders, whether belonging to Congress, Hindu Mahasabha, Arya Samaj or whatever. He would put up in the local Bhavan of any of these organisations or in a temple or with any well-wisher' (Malkani 1980: 43). This modus operandi is well illustrated by an example from Delhi in the 1930s.

The *pracharak* who was sent to Delhi was Vasant Rao Oke. A Chitpavan Brahman from Nagpur, he had joined the RSS in 1927 and had served as secretary to Hedgewar for sometime. He had completed his Instructors' Training Camp (ITC) in 1929–30 and his Officers' Training Camp (OTC) in 1931 and organized the first OTC outside of Nagpur in Poona in 1934 (interview with Vasant Rao Oke 12 August 1992). After this he was sent to Delhi where he received the support of Padam Raj Jain, a notable from the Hindu Mahasabha. This Marwari from Calcutta had been impressed by the Nagpur *shakha* which he had visited after the session of the Hindu Mahasabha in Poona in 1935. He told Hedgewar how much he appreciated his 'silent but highly important work' (Letter of 27 July 1936, *Savarkar Papers*) and suggested that the RSS start a branch in Delhi. Vasant Rao Oke was sent there in November 1936 and as general secretary of the Hindu Mahasabha, P.R. Jain helped him establish the Delhi *shakha* by authorizing him to set up his general headquarters—and the first *shakha*—in the central office of the Mahasabha (letter of Padam Raj Jain to Savarkar, 29 November 1936 and interview with V.R. Oke, ibid.).

This office was close to Birla Mandir and Jugal Kishore Birla who patronized the temple extended his help to Oke.[1] The latter found his first recruits in the premises of the temple. One of them recalls:

We used to go to Birla Mandir to play and once Vasant Rao Oke was on the road. He was on the lookout for young people to start the *shakha*. He saw us play. He called us and asked why we were playing there and would we want to learn how to wield a *lathi* [stick], to wield a sword. We said, 'Yes'. We went to the *shakha* and got enrolled there, in 'Hindu matri bhavan'. It was the first branch in Delhi. It was opened in 1936. (interview with Ratan Bhattacharya, 6 November 1997)

In 1937, there were six *shakhas* in Delhi but ten years later, at the time of Partition, there were as many as one hundred, according to Oke who had become *prant pracharak* (in charge of the Delhi province) in 1938 and kept this position for ten years. It was a big unit, compared to others in Uttar Pradesh and elsewhere. Oke was especially successful at attracting government servants, students from the three main colleges (Hindu College, St. Stephen's and Ramjas) and Banias, as the social profile of his patrons testifies.

Each branch of the RSS used to benefit from the support of local patrons who were soon referred to as *sanghchalaks* (literally, directors). They functioned mostly as counsellors or even guides and conferred a certain respectability to the movement by sponsoring the *pracharaks'* activities. In Delhi, Padam Raj Jain could not play this part for long because of the deteriorating relations between the RSS and the Hindu Mahasabha, especially after Madhav Sadashiv Golwalkar took over as *sarsanghchalak* of the RSS in 1940. This role was played in 1937–40 by Prakash Dutt Bhargava, an advocate who had met Golwalkar at the Banaras Hindu University (BHU) when he was a student but who was originally from Ajmer and was not very influential—not even a notable in the true sense of the word.[2] For these reasons he could not fulfil the conditions for being a good *sanghchalak* and ended up contacting Lala Harichandra Gupta, who was to become the first Delhi *sanghchalak* in 1940. As a *zamindar* (landlord) who owned orchards in Uttar Pradesh, and a rich businessman with a factory in Delhi, Gupta had 'a social public life' (interview with V.R. Oke) and had been elected to the Municipal Council. An RSS old timer described him as a *rais*, a wealthy notable. When he came to Delhi, Golwalkar would stay in Lala Harichandra Gupta's house situated in Sitaram Bazaar.[3]

A bigger *rais*, Lala Hans Raj Gupta, became *prant sanghchalak* in the late 1940s. Though he had an M.A. and an LL.B. degree, Hans Raj Gupta never practised law because he had joined his father-in-law's business in the mid-1920s and had soon after inherited important firms from both him and his own father. He had settled in Delhi in the 1930s when his father had already built a bungalow at 20 Barakhamba Road. The family made a fortune from the steel industry and by renting sugar cane crushers to the peasants of western Uttar Pradesh. In 1937, the responsibility of the iron syndicate fell on him and he started an iron forgery, a distillery in Meerut as well as factories making cycles and fans in the 1940s (Mishra 1972: 1–11). He looked after the Delhi-based business of M. Vishveshwarya, a civil engineer from Mysore who had built a big dam there and was the founder president of the All India Manufacturers' Association of Delhi, an institution of which Hans Raj Gupta was made the chairman in 1945 (H.R. Gupta 1972: 26 and interview with his son, Rajendra Gupta, 25 February 1995).

In addition to his business, Hans Raj Gupta had inherited ideological inclinations from his father. The latter had been a staunch Arya Samajist who had sent his son to Arya Samaj prayer meetings every Sunday as well as Arya Samajist schools. One of his teachers, Mohan Singh Mehta, had initiated him into the scout movement and Hans Raj Gupta remained supportive of the Hindustan Scouts Association all his life. In 1935 he joined the Congress but he soon considered that its so-called 'appeasement policy' towards Muslims was responsible for Jinnah's militancy and he shifted to the RSS in 1944–5. Oke contacted him first:

I met Hans Raj Gupta because in every area we used to arrange meetings with good people [*sic*]. In Barakhamba Road there were several good people: some businessmen, some contractors. From every house we used to call on one man every month at one place where I would go to address them about the Sangh's ideas. They were invited to visit at least one *shakha* to see our work. (interview with V.R. Oke)

Hans Raj Gupta was thus requested to visit a *shakha* and then to preside over the RSS function of Raksha Bandhan in 1945. These details are revealing of the way the RSS penetrated the establishment of Delhi. In 1946, Gupta attended an ITC in Vrindavan, where he met Golwalkar. He became the *prant sanghchalak* in 1947, and in 1948 chairperson of Bharat Prakashan, the publisher of the RSS mouthpieces, *The Organiser* and *The Motherland* (in the 1970s).

As a true notable, succeeded in occupying posts of responsibility without contesting elections. He became the mayor of Delhi in 1967 after being selected as one of the six eldermen by the hundred elected members of the Municipal Corporation. He was re-elected up to 1973 and his son, Rajendra Gupta, reached the same position in 1977–9. By then, Hans Raj Gupta had given up party politics in order to devote more time to what he called 'social work'. In fact, he patronized caste associations (he supported the Aggarwal Sabha's efforts to organize this merchant caste and reform its social habits) and educational institutions (he was chairman of the D.A.V. (Dayananda Anglo-Vedic) Higher Secondary School of Yusuf Sarai and gave financial assistance to Indraprastha College, Hindu College, Bal Bharati Public School, etc.). He also contributed to the scout movement (in the 1970s he was still director of the Delhi branch of the Bharat Scout and Guides). Rather than social, these activities were more akin to philanthropy than social work. They were in fact well in tune with the traditional function of the *rais* (Haynes 1987).

In his work on Allahabad, C.A. Bayly suggests that the Indian National Congress was first established at the local level thanks to the collaboration of *rais* and publicists—educated Brahmans (or Kayasthas) fluent in English and able to present the claims of the *rais* to the British (Bayly 1973: 349–88). The *rais* would support the publicists in their efforts to defend Hindu society and culture (especially festivals such as the Magh Mela of Allahabad) from British interference. Bayly points out that the publicists gradually emancipated themselves from the *rais* after the reforms of 1909 and 1919 and became full-fledged politicians (Bayly 1975). However, such a schema still seems relevant to the study of the RSS even after 1947. In this case, the publicists were primarily *pracharaks* whose main purpose was to propagate the ideology of the movement. Most were educated Brahmans who seemed more prepared than 'modern' Congressmen to seek the guidance of conservative notables whose patronage they needed.

In Delhi, the *rais*-publicist combination was successively embodied first by the pair formed by Lala Harichandra Gupta and Vasant Rao Oke; then by Hans Raj Gupta and Oke, and from the mid-1950s onwards, by Hans Raj Gupta and Madhav Rao Muley. The latter, again a Chitpavan Brahman, had been sent from Nagpur to Lahore in 1940 to occupy the newly created post of *prant pracharak* for the Punjab province which included Delhi according to the RSS map of India (*The Organiser*, 1979: 13). In this capacity, Muley tended to eclipse Oke, especially after the latter developed a keen interest in the creation of the Jana Sangh despite Golwalkar's initial reservations about the implication of *pracharaks* entering party politics.

Thus, one of the main assets of the RSS in Delhi was the support which it gathered from *rais* of the business community. Besides the elite of this milieu, many other Delhi Banias took an interest in the movement. Kanwar Lal Gupta was one of them. This rich merchant, educated at Delhi University in the 1940s, joined the RSS, and later became the first general secretary of the Delhi Pradesh Jana Sangh in 1951. He was elected to the Delhi Vidhan Sabha in 1953, to the Municipal Corporation in 1958 and to the Lok Sabha from Sadar constituency—its base—in 1967 (B.R. Gupta 1975: 85). Another Bania, Shyam Charan Gupta, an Arya Samajist who joined the RSS in 1940, was also president of the Delhi branch of the Boy Scouts Association and of the Delhi Provincial Aggarwal Sabha. He was elected MLA (Member of the Legislative Assembly) on a Jana Sangh ticket in 1952 and was then made Municipal Councillor in 1967 and 1972 (ibid.: 130). In fact, the merchant castes were well represented among the RSS and Jana Sangh leadership both before and after Partition, something which can be explained in various ways.

First, the Arya Samaj had prepared the ground for Hindu nationalism. In 1931, out of about 400,000 Hindus there were more than 50,000 Arya Samajists in Delhi (*Census of India, Delhi* 1933: 120). Most of them probably belonged to the merchant communities; in the Punjab the merchant castes (Khatris, Aroras, Agarwals) and Brahmans together represented about half of the 100,846 Arya Samaj members in 1911 (*Census of India* 1891: 172; 1911: 138). The merchant castes appreciated the Aryas' notion of 'self-help' which suited their sense of enterprise and perhaps even stemmed from it. Arya Samajists were the first to set up indigenous undertakings such as the Punjab National Bank and the Bharat Insurance Company in the 1890s (Tandon 1989: 152-4).

The Arya Samaj's success story in the Punjab had a lot to do with the specific social structure of the province. The Kshatriyas who had seen their power being taken away by Sikhs and Brahmans and felt deprived of patrons, had to take recourse to the support of the merchant castes (Dungen 1968: 75). The Banias came to occupy the forefront of Hindu society more and more exclusively as the British allowed them to extend their economic dominance and to translate it into socioeconomic terms through education (ibid.: 81). Barrier argues that the Arya Samaj's attraction to the Banias stemmed from the fact that in spite of all these changes the Banias remained the last of the 'twice born': 'Dayananda's claim that caste should be determined primarily by merit not birth, opened new paths of social mobility to educated Vaishyas who were trying to achieve a social status commensurate with their improving economic status' (Barrier 1967: 364). Dipankar Gupta has suggested more convincingly that the Arya Samaj gained much support in the Punjab, especially from Banias, because the local society was free from brahmanical control and orthodoxy.[4]

While the Arya Samaj had prepared the ground for Banias joining the RSS in Delhi as it had in the Punjab, there were some Delhi Banias who joined the RSS without having any Arya Samaj background. One RSS veteran, who admits the over-representation of Banias in the RSS, considers that it provided a good opportunity for Banias to practise sports in the light of the fact that they spent most of their time sitting down in their shops: 'Businessmen would join the RSS,' he argued, 'because it would give them something in terms of exercise' (interview with Rajendra Gupta). The need for physical strength was even more acutely felt in the 1940s when Muslim organizations demanding the creation of Pakistan, began to acquire a similar para-military dimension.

Thus Delhi's magnates such as Hans Raj Gupta and, more generally, a number of local Banias, contributed to the growth of the Hindu nationalist movement in the city, even before independence. However, the main factor influencing the rise of the RSS and later the Jana Sangh after independence was the influx of refugees from the Punjab.

## Ambivalence of Refugees' Support

Partition and the influx of thousands of refugees into Delhi in 1947 enabled the Hindu nationalist movement to organize mass mobilizations in the city for the first time. In 1947 about 450,000 people from west Punjab settled in Delhi. They composed almost one-third of the urban population (Datta 1993: 288). Many of them had lost everything and some had been victims of communal violence. The Hindu Mahasabha and the RSS presented themselves as organizations catering to their needs and exploited their resentment.

On 7 December 1947, about 50,000 people attended a meeting held by the two organizations. The main speakers were the Maharaja of Alwar, Gokul Chand Narang and Jugal Kishore Birla, both close to the Hindu Mahasabha and Golwalkar who eulogized the role of his movement in protecting Hindus in Punjab. He also criticized the 'satanic' attitude of Nehru's government for its 'appeasement' policy vis-à-vis Pakistan (Report of the Commission of Inquiry 1970: 66). Refugees had already openly expressed their resentment of Gandhi on several occasions,[5] especially when he announced what was to be his last fast in January 1948. Immediately, refugees demonstrated in front of Birla House, shouting slogans such as 'Blood for blood!' and 'Let Gandhi die!' (Report of the Commission 1970: 141). In addition to Rs. 550 million for Pakistan, Gandhi wanted local representatives of the different communities to sign a 'peace-pledge' before he suspended his fast. Interestingly, Hans Raj Gupta did so on behalf of the Hindus. However, on 25 January, the Hindu Mahasabha and the Delhi branch of the Arya Samaj organized a procession against Gandhi's fast and two days later the Hindu Mahasabha held a meeting, allegedly attended by 50,000 people, in which Gandhi and the Congress were aggressively accused of being responsible for Partition (Ibid.: 57; *Hindu Mahasabha Papers* 1948). A few days later, on 30 January 1948, Mahatma Gandhi was assassinated in Birla House by Nathuram Godse.

Besides orchestrating the refugees' protest and exploiting their resentment, the Hindu Mahasabha and RSS tried to project themselves as their benefactors. The Hindu Mahasabha Bhawan was opened to refugees and food as well as clothes were distributed while the Hindu Mahasabha established a refugee camp near the railway station (interview with Hardayal Devgun, 17 October 1995). However, it was short of funds and after some time the Mahasabha contented itself with having lists of job seekers circulated among local businessmen.

The *Sangh Parivar* or the *Sangh* family played a more important part after the ban imposed on the RSS because of its links with Gandhi's assassin, was lifted in 1949. In fact, it could by this stage appear more convincingly as the protector of the refugees because most of its leaders, especially in the newly created Jana Sangh, came from Punjab. While Oke, Muley and 'locals' such as Hans Raj Gupta remained at the helm of the RSS, an increasing number of Punjabis were taken on as their lieutenants and the Delhi unit of the Jana Sangh recruited most of its cadres from this milieu. Men such as Balraj Madhok, Bhai Mahavir, Vijay Kumar Malhotra, Kedarnath Sahni and Hardayal Devgun were among the most prominent figures and they shared a similar background.

Madhok came from a Jammu-based Khatri family with Arya Samajist leanings (interview with B. Madhok, 10 November 1990). He joined the RSS in 1938 while he was studying in D.A.V. College in Lahore. According to him, 'the Arya Samajists were closest to Dr Hedgewar's way of thinking' (Madhok 1985: 23). He became a *pracharak* in 1942 and was sent to Kashmir in this capacity. Bhai Mahavir, the son of Bhai Parmanand, a staunch Arya Samajist who had been President of the Hindu Mahasabha in 1933, was one of his fellow-students in D.A.V. College in Lahore and he joined the RSS at the same time (interview with Bhai Mahavir, 4 September 1992). He too was a Khatri. He had spent a couple of years, from 1942 to 1944, as a *pracharak* in Julundhur before working as office secretary of the RSS in Lahore from 1944 to 1947. After 1947 he settled down in Julundhur and then in Karnal where he worked as a lecturer. He came to Delhi in 1956 when he was offered a job in Panjab University College, an institution specially created for Punjabi refugees, where Madhok was already teaching. Madhok had come to Delhi soon after Partition. He had taken part in the foundation of the Praja Parishad[6] in Jammu in November 1947 and had been expelled from Jammu and Kashmir soon after because of his political activities. In 1948 he settled in Delhi.

The moving spirit behind the creation of the Jana Sangh was Shyama Prasad Mookherjee but his colleagues in this enterprise were either Delhi-based Hindu nationalists or refugees from Punjab. After he resigned from Nehru's government because of the Liaqat-Nehru Pact in April 1950, he was given a welcome ceremony by a group of prominent Delhi citizens, including Hans Raj Gupta, Vasant Rao Oke, Mauli Chandra Sharma (the son of Deen Dayal Sharma, a co-founder of the Hindu Mahasabha, who worked in the administration of several Princely States before settling in Delhi) (Oral History Transcript, interview with M.C. Sharma, 154, 162 and 175) and Lala Yodhraj Bhalla, the son of Hans Raj, one of the founders of D.A.V. College in Lahore and the president of the Punjab National Bank. Mookerjee immediately launched a campaign for the defence of refugees which culminated in July with an All India Refugee Conference which attracted

15,000 participants in Delhi (*Sunday News of India*, 30 July 1950: 1, 3). Several months later, in January 1951, Mookerjee discussed the possibility of founding a new party with the same group: Madhok, Bhai Mahavir, Dharmavir (Bhai Parmanand's son-in-law, a former lecturer in English in Lahore and the Punjab *prant pracharak*), Balraj Bhalla (Yodhraj's brother) and Mahasha Krishnan (an Arya Samajist who edited *Pratap* in Lahore before Partition and who continued to do so in Delhi after 1947) (Madhok 1985: 50). On 27 May 1951, one month after the creation of the West Bengal branch of the Jana Sangh by Mookerjee, a meeting was held in Julundhur at the instigation of Madhok, to launch the Jana Sangh which would represent Punjab and Delhi (*The Organiser*, 10 September 1951: 14). Balraj Bhalla was elected its first president, Mauli Chandra Sharma its vice-president and Balraj Madhok as secretary (Puri 1980: 27).

Madhok and Bhai Mahavir were appointed to important posts in the All India Jana Sangh which was founded in Delhi on 21 October 1951, with Bhai Mahavir becoming general secretary and Madhok a member of the working committee (and in 1958 national secretary in-charge of north India). However, they continued to play a part in the party-building process in Delhi too—with Madhok presiding over the local branch of the Jana Sangh in 1959 and winning the Lok Sabha seat for New Delhi in a bye-election in 1961. Other refugees were also very active in the local party apparatus.

Refugees with an RSS background gradually took over the party apparatus in the 1950s and displaced leaders who either had no RSS background—like the Hindu Sabhaites—or were not from west Punjab. The turning point occurred in 1954 when Vaid Guru Dutt, the president of the Delhi Jana Sangh, expressed his resentment of RSS interference in party affairs. An Arya Samajist and teacher of History in the Government College, Lahore, before he migrated to Delhi where he became a writer and practised Ayurvedic medicine, Guru Dutt had no links with the RSS. Ironically enough, K.L. Gupta, vice-president of the Delhi Jana Sangh, and V.R. Oke, its organizing secretary, supported him, even though they were from RSS cadres. This local conflict crystallized at the same time that similar developments were occurring in the party central headquarters where M. Sharma, who had succeeded Mookerjee as party president in 1953, also objected to RSS interference, but in vain. Eventually, like Dutt, Gupta and Oke, he resigned. The Delhi Jana Sangh was dissolved (*The Times of India*, 5 January 1955: 3) and then re-constituted with former RSS *pracharaks* from Punjab at the helm. While Madhok was president, he had so many responsibilities at the national level that the day to day affairs fell to Kedarnath Sahni's share.

Sahni had just settled in Delhi in 1954. He came from Julundhur where he had worked as *pracharak*. A native of Punjab, he was born in Rawalpindi and studied in Multan Arya Samaj School. Like Madhok, he considers that in Punjab, the 'Arya Samaj prepared the ground for the RSS to work'. He had been sent to Kashmir as a *pracharak* in 1946 and later to east Punjab after having been expelled from Jammu and Kashmir in 1948 (interview with K.N. Sahni, 20 November 1990). In 1954 he was appointed to the key post of organizing secretary of the Delhi Jana Sangh. He became general secretary four years later when Lal Krishna Advani took over from him. Advani was not from Punjab, but was a refugee from Sindh, like another RSS figure in Delhi, Kewalram Ratanmal Malkani.[7] Advani had joined the RSS in Hyderabad (Sindh) in 1942, had been sent to Karachi as a *pracharak* in 1947 and had migrated to Rajasthan, where he worked as *pracharak* after Partition (interview with L.K. Advani, 11 February 1994). He came to Delhi in 1957 and became secretary and later vice-president of the Delhi Jana Sangh. Thus, the key posts of the party unit were gradually occupied by refugees with an RSS background. In addition to this sociological change, the *Sangh Parivar* worked for the cause of refugees—or pretended to do so.

Hans Raj Gupta initiated a Hindu Sahayata Samiti which worked almost as a front for the RSS. Though it was especially active in Delhi, it also had some existence elsewhere in India—in Gwalior for instance. Its main work consisted of distributing clothes and blankets in refugee camps and enrolling children in the new Hindu Sahayata Samiti schools (*The Organiser*, 1 January 1948: 7; 8 January 1948: 9 and *Hitavada*, 9 January 1948). However, the refugees gradually became less concerned with emergency measures and more interested in issues such as the cost of rent and the rate of loans. In the *Sangh Parivar*, Vijay Kumar Malhotra devoted comparatively more time to these issues in the framework of a 'welfarist tactic' well in tune with the RSS tradition of selective relief-work: its activists' network has always enabled the *Sangh Parivar* to do a kind of social work which, in fact, was intended to help the movement to build pockets of influence among poor, displaced persons and the like.

Malhotra had a profile similar to Madhok and Mahavir: a Khatri by caste, he had joined the RSS in Lahore while in the 7th grade at D.A.V. College and had been sent to Jammu as a *pracharak* in 1947. Not long after, he had come to Delhi to study at Panjab University College—the college specially created for Punjabi refugees. He later taught there—like Madhok and Mahavir he was a teacher by training—till the college closed down in 1958 (interview with V.K. Malhotra, 24 November 1990). Malhotra then joined D.A.V. College. As a student leader he became secretary of Delhi University Students' Union (DUSU) in 1951 and later all India organizing secretary of the Akhil Bharatiya Vidyarthi Parishad (ABVP) till 1952 when he shifted to the 'refugees front'. He was then the founder-president of the Kendriya Chamarti Sabha and one of the three convenors of the United Refugees Front, the two others being Balraj Khanna (then a member of the Hindu Mahasabha) and Bishamdar Kapur (close to an ex-Hindu Sabhaite from the Congress, Mehr Chand Khanna). This organization, which had been set up 'under the initiative of Delhi Pradesh Jana Sangh' (Puri 1980: 63) lobbied in favour of the refugees. It fought against the elevation of rents in government-built residential quarters and shops in refugee colonies in Delhi like Lajpat Nagar, Kingsway Camp, Malaviya Nagar, Moti Nagar, Ramesh Nagar and so forth. The Delhi Jana Sangh supported the agitation of the United Refugees Front against the government decision to recover full payments on refugees' properties within three years—Kedarnath Sahni asked for 30 years.

Being a party with refugees at its helm and defending the cause of refugees from Punjab, the Jana Sangh was well placed for getting the refugees' votes. A study of refugees from the Dehra Dun district shows that about 40 per cent of them remained very hostile to Muslims and considered that the Congress had done no good for the country. In a place like Rishikesh, this attitude combined with support for the RSS and Jana Sangh (Saksena 1961: 21). Gita Puri came to a similar conclusion in her study of the Jana Sangh in Delhi. Among the four Jana Sangh MLAs elected in Delhi in 1952 were G.D. Salwan, the president of the Refugees Relief Committee in Jhandewalan (where the RSS headquarters was situated and where so many refugees had settled), Shyam Charan Gupta in Daryaganj (again a constituency with many refugees) and Ranajang Bahadur Singh (in Kingsway Camp—a former refugee camp). During the 1954 elections to the Municipal Corporation, the Jana Sangh won 10 of its 15 seats in refugee-dominated constituencies (Y. Puri 1993: 186), and during the 1958 elections to the Municipal Corporation, the Jana Sangh won 16 (out of 25) seats in refugee-dominated constituencies (G. Puri 1980: 154). In the 1962 municipal elections, when the party suffered a severe setback, it won 6 of its 9 seats in constituencies with a substantial percentage of refugees. In 1967, 23 of its 52 seats and in 1971, 23 of its 53 seats were won in Punjabi-dominated constituencies.

However, to consider the Jana Sangh of Delhi as 'the party of refugee people' (Pandit 1984: 58) is incorrect. First, Punjabis probably voted for the Jana Sangh not only because of the hardships they suffered as refugees but also because of their backgrounds: many of them were already supporters of the RSS before 1947. Indeed, the movement saw a dramatic increase in the 1930s and 1940s in eastern and western Punjab as well as in Delhi. In fact, of all the Indian provinces, Punjab was the one state where the RSS developed most quickly. While the first *shakhas* had started there in 1935 with the help of Arya Samajists-turned-Hindu Sabhaites (like Bhai Parmanand), the movement swelled in greater Punjab (Delhi and Himachal Pradesh included, but west Punjab excluded) to reach 14,000 members by 1940 ('Notes on the Volunteer Movement in India', Intelligence Bureau, 27 January and 23 August 1940) and 125,000 members by 1951 (Curran 1951: 14, 43). The fortunes of the RSS in Punjab were undoubtedly linked to the rise of separatism among local Muslims. At that time, the organization tended to function as a militia for both offensive and defensive purposes.[9]

More important, the Jana Sangh cannot be considered the party of the refugees, not only because its strength in the city-capital was not purely based on refugee support, but also because there were refugees who did not vote for this party. A large number of refugees did in fact remain close to the Congress, not least because they already saw it as a Hindu party even before Partition. Almost since its inception in the late nineteenth century, there had been a strong Hindu traditionalist current in the Punjab Congress. Lala Lajpat Rai epitomized this school of thought till his death in 1928, as did several other extremists from the Arya Samaj. One of his lieutenants, Gopichand Bhargava, took over from Rai in the 1930s, and after Partition, Gopichand's brother, Thakurdas Bhargava, became one of the main advocates of Hindu traditionalism in the Constituent Assembly. He objected to the recognition of religious minorities as 'communities' (*Constituent Assembly Debates*, 1989, Vol. VII: 899) and to the granting of rights of citizenship to non-Hindu immigrants from Pakistan. He was also one of the staunchest advocates of cow-protection and the promotion of Hindi as a national language (Sen 1973, Vol. l: 175).

Many Delhi-based Punjabi Congressmen had similar Hindu leanings. Jagat Narain, who had been a student of Bhai Parmanand and remained a staunch Arya Samajist, was a Congressman. He was the editor of *Milap*, an Arya Samaj paper with a strong inclination towards the Congress.[10]

In addition to this tradition, Mehr Chand Khanna, the key figure of Hindu politics in the North-West Frontier Province before 1947, was co-opted into the central government soon after Partition. Khanna—Rai Bahadur since 1927—was a *rais* of Peshawar who had been elected to the Municipal Council as early as 1922 and who was appointed by the British to the NWFP (North-West Frontier Province) Franchise Committee in 1932. He had been elected to the Legislative Council in 1933 on a Hindu Mahasabha ticket (letter from Moonje to the Secretary of the Joint Select Parliamentary Committee, 10 July 1933, *Moonje Papers*). He shifted to the Congress after Partition and worked first as an advisor for the Ministry of Rehabilitation and later as its minister. At the same time, he was at the helm of a powerful refugees' lobby, the Delhi Refugees Federation. In 1962, Khanna was the Congress candidate for the prestigious Lok Sabha seat of New Delhi against Madhok (who had wrested it from the Congress in 1961) and he won with 57 per cent of the valid votes, as against Madhok's 38 per cent. He had been nominated owing to the support of other refugee representatives within the Congress, notably Jag Pravesh Chandra.[11]

Generally speaking, the refugees from the North-West Frontier Province tended to maintain their allegiance to the Congress Party. They had been close to the party before Partition, not least because Muslim politics in this area had been dominated by Abdul Ghaffar Khan, the so-called 'Frontier Gandhi', rather than the Muslim League.

Interestingly, the percentage of members of the Metropolitan Council of Delhi (MCD) who came from west Punjab did not fluctuate in accordance with Jana Sangh election results: in 1967 when the party won a majority, 34 per cent of its members were from Pakistan; in 1972 when it lost heavily, refugees still represented 33 per cent of the metropolitan councillors; in 1977 when the Janata Party (of which the former Jana Sangh was a major component) swept the polls, the proportion of refugees in the MCD dropped to 26 per cent and in 1983 when the Congress Party won the elections the proportion of refugees stabilized at 25 per cent (Seth and Malhotra 1989: 127).

The Congress retained strong support among Punjabi refugees partly because it was perceived as a Hindu party, but also because Nehru's government helped them a lot. The Ministry of Rehabilitation, established on 6 September 1947, set up three refugee camps: Kingsway, Tibia College (in Karol Bagh) and one in Shahdara. The number of inmates started to decline by mid-1948, which meant that the refugees were finding new jobs and places to live (Datta 1993: 290), largely due to the government's policy. While 190,000 refugees were accommodated in houses which had been left by Muslims, 1.2 million were given new houses. Parallel to these special measures, 4,752 shops and stalls were built by the government and local bodies (ibid.: 292). In 1948, a loan of Rs. 42,62,075 was sanctioned for refugees and by March 1952, 1,800 of the displaced secured jobs through the employment exchange set up by the government (ibid.: 294). The refugees who benefited from this rehabilitation scheme were naturally grateful to the Congress government. Malkani himself admits that Nehru's government was very helpful to refugees:

The government has done relatively well. I would not attack the government on this. There was only one problem: the government was not firm enough with Pakistan. They should have asked for more compensation because the property the Hindus left there were about ten times the property left by the Muslims. But apart from that, the government did well. I had no particular grievance. (interview with K.R. Malkani)

Some refugees therefore voted for the Congress because they were not unhappy with the government's policy, but also because they depended on Congressmen for getting things done. Since many of them were traders, they had to ask the government for licences, electricity connections and so on. In Delhi as elsewhere, the Congress could rely on its bargaining power and operated within a framework of clientelism.

The Jana Sangh was thus not 'the party of the refugees' because refugees did not vote only for this party and because the party did not recruit its support only from refugees. This point was made as early as 1951 during the first local elections to the Delhi Municipal Corporation: although the refugees were just settled and could not take part in great numbers in the poll, the Jana Sangh won one-quarter of the valid votes. This figure reflected the influence the *Sangh Parivar* had gained among 'locals' after 25 years of groundwork in Delhi. Not surprisingly, its following was especially strong among traders. In the Chandni Chowk unit of the party, where, in the 1970s, three-quarters of the office bearers were 'locals', 55 per cent of them were Banias and 29 per cent Kshatriyas—probably Khatris working as businessmen (G. Puri 1980: 80–1). The Jana Sangh had indeed a strong following among 'locals' and if it won a majority of its seats to the Municipal Corporation in refugee-dominated constituencies, a substantial number of them were obtained in 'local' Hindu dominated constituencies: 3 out of 9 in 1962, 18 out of 52 in 1967—the first elections after K.L. Gupta (still very influential in Delhi Sadar), rejoined the Jana Sangh in 1964—and 15 out of 53 in 1974 (ibid.: 158–75). In the 1967 municipal elections in the Sadar district the Jana Sangh won more votes than the Congress (43 per cent as against 41 per cent) in the Hindu 'local'-dominated wards, partly because it was able to nominate 'local' candidates (Saini and Andersen 1971: 1084-1100).

In fact, the Jana Sangh was weak only in the rural and the reserved constituencies where the Congress, in contrast, was very strong. One of its main leaders, Brahm Prakash Choudhury, a Yadav, who had been Chief Minister of Delhi in 1952, was elected to the Outer Delhi seat of the Lok Sabha four times successively from 1962 onwards. The Jana Sangh, by contrast, did not win any rural seat to the Municipal Corporation in 1958 (for the good reason that it had not even fielded a candidate), and won only one in 1962 in Alipur where, interestingly, more than half of its office-bearers were Punjabi refugees with an urban background. In 1967 it won 4 seats and in 1971, 2 seats (ibid.: 84, 92, 158-75). The urban bias of the party was still evident in the 1983 elections.

So far as reserved seats were concerned, the Jana Sangh could not win any seats in Karol Bagh in the 1958 municipal elections largely because it could not attract Scheduled Caste voters in this Dalit-dominated constituency. This weakness affected its prospects for a long time since it could win only 4 reserved seats in the elections to the Delhi Municipal Corporation in 1971. Even in the reserved constituencies where it won, the Jana Sangh owed its success mainly to non-Scheduled Caste voters as Saini and Andersen have shown in their detailed study of the voting pattern for the Scheduled Caste seat of Sadar Bazaar (Saini and Andersen 1969: 266-76). The only Jana Sangh representative elected in a reserved and rural constituency in the 1971 municipal elections, S.P. Sumnaskar, defected to the Congress Party in 1975 because 'high caste members dominated the Jana Sangh and displayed superiority complex and wanted to keep Scheduled Castes members at a distance'. He considered that there was 'no opportunity for those who [were] outside this Punjabi-Banya alliance' (G. Puri 1980: 80-1). The only Scheduled Caste leaders who remained in the Jana Sangh had an RSS background and had inherited an impulse to 'Sanskritize' from their training. Its successful candidate in Karol Bagh in 1967 (and its unsuccessful candidate in 1971) was an advocate advisor to the All India Scheduled Castes Uplift Union, but with an RSS background and the second Jana Sanghi who, after Sumnaskar succeeded in winning a reserved and rural seat, Kalka Dass, had a similar profile. He had joined the RSS in 1946 in Mehrauli, his birth place, while his father—the headman of several villages—was close to Ambedkar (he called himself a Jatav). For Kalka Dass, who won the Mehrauli Municipal Council seat in 1977 and 1983 and the Karol Bagh parliamentary seat in 1989 and 1991 on a BJP ticket, the *Sangh Parivar* was the only movement fighting against the caste system on behalf of nationalistic—and therefore supposedly egalitarian—values (interview with Kalka Dass, 23 November 1990). The Jana Sangh failed to attract Scheduled Caste leaders who had not been trained in the RSS mould and who were truly representative of their group.

One may conclude from the aforesaid argument that the Jana Sangh was not so much 'the party of the refugees' as the party of the urban Hindu middle classes. Punjabi refugees did not vote exclusively for the Jana Sangh and when they did, it was not only because they were refugees but also because of the political culture they had acquired before 1947 and their ethos and interests as businessmen. Meanwhile many 'locals' voted for the Jana Sangh because of an ideological background they had acquired before Partition, and because of their professional activities as merchant castes. Instead of looking at the Jana Sangh as 'the party of the refugees' it may then be more relevant to study it as the party of businessmen, provided one includes within this category anybody independently involved in trade, industry (including cottage-industries) and other manufacturing.

## From the 'Middle World' to the 'Outer World'?

The distinction between 'locals' and refugees is probably less important than the one between businessmen and others. In his study of the 1972 elections to the Delhi Metropolitan Council, Raj Chandidas emphasizes that 'the Jana Sangh draws heavily for its support on petty traders and small businessmen' (Chandidas). This description was also true of the Jana Sangh candidates to the Delhi Municipal Corporation and the Delhi Metropolitan Council among whom Banias and Khatris, both merchant castes, represented 42.5 to 44.5 per cent of the total. While 20 per cent of the members of the council were businessmen (as against 22 per cent in 1967),[12] 47 per cent of the Jana Sangh candidates had this background.

Many Jana Sangh candidates in 1971 and 1972 were probably Punjabi refugees since most of them were businessmen. The 1971 Census indicates that 31 per cent of these refugees were involved in 'trade and commerce', 16 per cent in 'manufacturing, processing, servicing and repairs (other than household industry)', and 11 per cent in 'transport, storage and communication' (*Census of India–Delhi* 1971: 96). In 1971, almost 60 per cent of the Punjabi refugees (and even more if one takes into account 2 per cent involved in 'construction') belonged to what Bruce Graham has called 'the middle world'—the middle classes, threatened from above by the state's intervention and from below by an increasing awareness of the backward classes (Graham 1990: 165). Therefore, the Jana Sangh's relative success in Delhi may have less to do with the large refugee population than with its social profile. The 'middle world'—whether among 'locals' or refugees— voted for the party because it defended their interests. Indeed, Deendayal Upadhyaya, the general secretary of the Jana Sangh from 1952 till his death in 1968, never ceased to criticize the Nehruvian view of a state-owned economy and the Congress' priority towards industrialization. In 1958 he wrote that 'By taking up programmes of heavy industries the [Planning] Commission intended to bring about a structural change in our society. . . . But we cannot build a pyramid from the top downwards' (Upadhyaya 1958: 258). He criticized the lack of investment in 'decentralized small scale industry' which, in his view should have been the main route to economic development (ibid.: 268). From 1951, the Jana Sangh advocated a division of tasks between the state (which would run heavy industry) and the private sector: the production of consumer goods, for instance, would be reserved for the latter, and the state would be required to prevent economic conglomeration so that family enterprises might flourish (Bharatiya Jana Sangh 1973, Vol. 1: 52).

TABLE 13.3: CASTE AND COMMUNITY OF THE JANA SANGH
CANDIDATES TO THE DELHI MUNICIPAL CORPORATION IN 1971
AND TO THE DELHI METROPOLITAN COUNCIL IN 1972

| Castes and communities | 191 | % | 1972 | % |
|---|---|---|---|---|
| Upper Castes | 54 | 62 | 32 | 59.3 |
| Brahman | 11 | 12.6 | 7 | 13.0 |
| Bania | 18 | 20.7 | 11 | 20.4 |
| Khatri | 19 | 21.8 | 13 | 24.1 |
| Arora | 5 | 5.7 | – | – |
| Other | 1 | 1.1 | 1 | 1.8 |
| Intermediate Castes | 2 | 2.3 | 2 | 3.7 |
| Jat | 2 | 2.3 | 2 | 3.7 |
| Other Backward Classes | 11 | 12.6 | 5 | 9.3 |
| Gujjar | 5 | 5.7 | 2 | 3.7 |
| Yadav | 4 | 4.6 | 2 | 3.7 |
| Saini/Mali | 1 | 1.1 | – | – |
| Julaha | 1 | 1.1 | 1 | 1.8 |
| Other | – | – | – | – |
| Scheduled Castes | 6 | 6.9 | 2 | 3.7 |
| Sikh | | – | 1 | 1.9 |
| Muslim | 1 | 1.2 | 1 | 1.9 |
| Europeans/Anglo-Indians | – | – | – | – |
| Non-Identified/Other | 13 | 15 | 11 | 20.4 |
| TOTAL | 87 | 100 | 54 | 100 |

*Sources:* Interviews with BJP and Jana Sangh old-timers.

The Jana Sangh tried to defend 100,000 small-scale enterprises of India in a very concrete way. It objected to the imposition of sales taxes which hampered the functioning of these enterprises. In 1958, merchants were forced to accept the establishment of state control over the grain trade, a measure intended to reduce inflationary shortages by promoting a centralized regional distribution of the produce. The Jana Sangh condemned this decision, arguing that it would lead to the nationalization of small businesses (*The Hindustan Times*, 8 March 1959: 1–2) and the disappearance of 30,000 wholesalers and 3 millions retailers (*Party Documents*, 1958, Vol. 2: 163). Thus, those who belonged to the 'middle world' could be attracted to the Jana Sangh simply because of its right-wing agenda.

TABLE 13.4: OCCUPATIONAL BACKGROUND OF THE JANA SANGH
CANDIDATES TO THE DELHI MUNICIPAL CORPORATION IN 1971

| Occupation | Absolute numbers | % |
|---|---|---|
| Agriculturist | 6 | 6.9 |
| Lawyer | 4 | 4.6 |
| Medical profession | 4 | 4.6 |
| Business | 41 | 47.2 |
| Executive/employee | 4 | 4.6 |
| Teacher/Principal | 6 | 6.9 |
| Journalist | 3 | 3.5 |
| Trade unionist/Social worker | 2 | 2.3 |
| Politician/*Pracharak* | 2 | 2.3 |
| Landlord | 1 | 1.2 |
| Unknown | 13 | 14.9 |
| TOTAL | 87 | 100 |

*Sources:* Interviews with BJP and Jana Sangh old-timers.

TABLE 13.5: OCCUPATIONAL BACKGROUND OF THE BJP MEMBERS OF
THE DELHI MUNICIPAL CORPORATION ELECTED IN 1983

| Occupation | BJP | % |
|---|---|---|
| Agriculturist | 3 | 8.6 |
| Lawyer | 2 | 5.7 |
| Business | 21 | 60.0 |
| Ex-civil servant | 1 | 2.9 |
| Teacher | 4 | 11.4 |
| Trade unionist/Social worker | 2 | 5.7 |
| Unknown/Other | 2 | 5.7 |
| TOTAL | 35 | 100 |

*Sources:* Interviews with local cadres and office-bearers in the office of the Delhi Pradesh BJP.

The over-representation of the 'middle world' in the ranks of the Hindu nationalist party remained true in 1983 within the Delhi Municipal Corporation: while this institution had 20 per cent of businessmen, the BJP group had 60 per cent.

Ten years later, the over-representation of the upper castes in the BJP was still very much in evidence, as testified by the large number of upper caste candidates, especially Banias and Khatris, fielded by the party during the 1993 state assembly elections. While the Congress nominated almost as many upper caste candidates (though more Brahmans than Banias) as the BJP, it also nominated a larger number of Jat candidates, a sign of the rural reach of the Congress in outer Delhi.

TABLE 13.6: CASTE AND COMMUNITY BACKGROUND OF THE BJP AND
CONGRESS CANDIDATES TO THE ASSEMBLY ELECTIONS IN 1993

| Castes and communities | BJP | Per cent | Congress | % |
|---|---|---|---|---|
| *Upper Castes* | 33 | 47.1 | 26 | 35.7 |
| Brahman | 8 | 11.4 | 11 | 15.1 |
| Rajput | 3 | 4.3 | – | – |
| Bania | 11 | 15.7 | 4 | 5.5 |
| Khatri | 9 | 12.9 | 9 | 12.3 |
| Arora | – | – | 1 | 1.4 |
| Other | 2 | 2.9 | 1 | 1.4 |
| *Intermediate Castes* | 9 | 12.9 | 15 | 20.5 |
| Jat | 9 | 12.9 | 15 | 20.5 |
| *Other Backward Classes* | 7 | 8.6 | 5 | 6.8 |
| Gujjar | – | – | 2 | 2.7 |
| Yadav | 1 | 1.4 | 3 | 4.1 |
| Jhangi | 4 | 5.7 | – | – |
| Soni | 1 | 1.4 | – | – |
| Other | 1 | 1.4 | | |
| *Scheduled Castes* | 13 | 18.6 | 13 | 17.8 |
| *Sikh* | 1 | 1.4 | 1 | 1.4 |
| *Muslim* | 3 | 4.3 | 1 | 1.4 |
| *Europeans/Anglo-Indians* | – | – | – | – |
| *Non-Identified/Other* | 5 | 7.1 | 12 | 16.4 |
| TOTAL | 70 | 100 | 73 | 100 |

*Sources*: Interviews in the party offices.

The larger number of Jat candidates in the Congress is of course congruent with the larger proportion of agriculturists among its assembly candidates. However, the share of businessmen—by far the largest—is slightly more important within the Congress, whereas in the BJP, the teachers are second to the businessmen with more than 11 per cent (see Table 13.7).

The social composition of the BJP Delhi State Executive suggests that the party is slowly promoting Jats in its apparatus since the Jat share of seats grew slightly between 1993 and 1995 at the expense of the upper castes. The erosion of high caste seats is especially marked among the Brahmans. However, the proportion of Other Backward Classes and Scheduled Castes in the party structure remains nominal.

The social profile of the office bearers of the district and local units of the BJP and the Congress show a similar picture. All in all, the BJP remained slightly more Punjabi, more urban and more elitist (from the caste point of view at least) than the Congress, and by and large as business-oriented as the latter but then the differences between both parties are often not significant.

After winning the 1993 assembly elections, the BJP appointed Madan Lal Khurana as chief minister, who was clearly representative of this milieu. Khurana

TABLE 13.7: OCCUPATIONAL BACKGROUND OF THE BJP AND
CONGRESS CANDIDATES TO THE ASSEMBLY ELECTIONS IN 1993

| Occupation | BJP | % | Congress | % |
|---|---|---|---|---|
| Agriculturist | 8 | 11.4 | 10 | 14.3 |
| Lawyer | – | – | 3 | 4.3 |
| Medical profession | 4 | 5.7 | 2 | 2.9 |
| Business | 28 | 40.0 | 29 | 41.4 |
| Ex-civil servant/Service/Engineer | 3 | 4.3 | 4 | 5.7 |
| Teacher/Principal | 8 | 11.4 | 3 | 4.3 |
| Journalist/Writer | 1 | 1.4 | 3 | 4.3 |
| Trade unionist/Social worker | 5 | 7.2 | 13 | 18.6 |
| Politician | 6 | 8.6 | – | – |
| Landlord | 1 | 1.4 | – | – |
| Unknown/Other | 6 | 8.6 | 3 | 4.3 |
| TOTAL | 70 | 100 | 70 | 100 |

*Sources*: Interviews in the party offices.

joined the RSS in 1943, in Lyallpur in west Punjab, even before he was a teenager. His family, Khatri by caste, migrated to Jammu after Partition and then settled in Delhi. M.L. Khurana, who used to live in Paharganj, started his career as a teacher with a modest income of Rs. 400 per month till 1967, the year when he was first elected member of the Metropolitan Council. He then set up a goods truck transport and bus company (Devgun (n.d.): 6 and interview with M.L. Khurana, 8 December 1990). Khurana is, therefore, typical of the post-Partition *Sangh Parivar* leadership, made up of upper caste teachers and/or businessmen from Punjab. He became general secretary of the Delhi Jana Sangh in 1965 and kept this charge till 1975. In 1977 he was elected executive councillor of Delhi and in 1980, general secretary of the Delhi branch of the BJP of which he became the president in 1985. He was succeeded by Om Prakash Kohli, another Khatri teacher from Punjab, but in 1993 was elected chief minister when the BJP won the elections.

Khurana had to resign in February 1996 owing to his alleged involvement in the 'hawala affair'. His successor, Sahib Singh Verma, was from a different background. An RSS activist since childhood, he had worked as a college librarian till 1993. Verma, a Jat from the periphery of Delhi and unlike most Jats not a farmer, was put in-charge of rural development and education in Khurana's cabinet. While Verma was probably appointed for a variety of other reasons such as power equations within the party; the Delhi BJP certainly chose him partly in order to expand its social base in Outer Delhi where it used to be very weak. In August 1997, Verma commissioned a survey to identify more OBCs in Delhi. Press reports suggested that it was aimed at trying to include new castes, such as the Jats and the Jaiswals in this category (*The Times of India*, 25 July 1997). Indeed the BJP

TABLE 13.8: CASTE BACKGROUND OF THE BJP DELHI STATE EXECUTIVE
AND OF THE DELHI CONGRESS PRADESH COMMITTEE

| Castes and communities | BJP 1993 | % | BJP 1995 | % | Congress 1992 | Congress 1994 |
|---|---|---|---|---|---|---|
| Upper Castes | 99 | 70.8 | 63 | 69.2 | 11 | 6 |
| Brahman | 33 | 23.6 | 12 | 13.2 | 3 | 2 |
| Rajput | 2 | 1.4 | 3 | 3.3 | 1 | – |
| Bania | 28 | 20.0 | 21 | 23.1 | 4 | 1 |
| Khatri | 32 | 22.9 | 21 | 23.1 | 3 | 3 |
| Kayastha | 3 | 2.1 | – | – | – | – |
| Other | 1 | 0.7 | 6 | 6.6 | – | – |
| Intermediate Castes | 5 | 3.6 | 8 | 8.8 | 2 | 2 |
| Jat | 5 | 3.6 | 8 | 8.8 | 2 | 2 |
| Other Backward Classes | 12 | 8.6 | 3 | 3.3 | – | – |
| Gujjar | 6 | 4.3 | – | – | – | – |
| Saini | | | 1 | 1.1 | – | – |
| Julaha | – | 0.7 | – | – | – | – |
| Other | – | – | ● 1 | 1.1 | – | – |
| Scheduled Castes | 12 | 8.6 | 6 | 6.6 | 5 | 1 |
| Sikh | 3 | 2.1 | 1 | 1.1 | 1 | – |
| Muslim | 4 | 2.9 | 7 | 7.7 | 3 | 1 |
| Non-Identified/Other | 5 | 3.6 | 3 | 3.3 | – | – |
| TOTAL | 140 | 100 | 91 | 100 | 26 | 10 |

*Sources:* Interviews in the party offices.

may well be tempted to play 'the OBC card', from which it might be able to derive electoral dividends in the post-Mandal context.

While the coming to Delhi of hundreds of thousands of refugees after Partition helps to explain the Jana Sangh's electoral fortunes in the capital as early as 1951, it is not in itself a sufficient explanation. Many of the Punjabis who settled in Delhi may well have voted for the Jana Sangh because they had lost everything after Partition, a catastrophe they attributed to the Congress. But others, especially those from the NWFP, still preferred the ruling Congress Party because they perceived it as a Hindu party anyway and depended on it for rehabilitation. The Punjabi refugees who opted for the Jana Sangh often did so because they had already been won over by the RSS in Punjab where the movement had grown rapidly in the 1940s. In other words, the trauma of Partition acted not to convert them to right-wing Hindu politics but to reconfirm their existing inclination.

More important, the base of the Jana Sangh was never confined to Punjabi refugees. The party also recruited strong support from 'local' businessmen, partly because of the early groundwork of the RSS and, before that, the Arya Samaj. In fact, the Jana Sangh and the BJP were probably less parties of refugees than parties of traders—Banias and Khatris (a caste whose members are often engaged in commercial activities). This interpretation is all the more convincing as about one-third of the refugees started businesses in Delhi. However, the social profile of the BJP cadres and MLAs is not significantly different from that of the Congress equivalents, even though the Jana Sangh and the BJP have perhaps been more consistently and constantly elitist.

Today, the BJP seems eager to expand its base in the rural periphery of the Delhi state where the Hindu nationalist movement has always been weak. The selection of a Jat, Sahib Singh Verma as chief minister in 1996, may be analysed in this perspective and the inclusion of his archrival, M.L. Khurana, in Vajpayee's government might have been an attempt to remove him from the local scene. However, Verma's own dismissal shortly before the 1998 state assembly elections and his replacement by Sushma Swaraj (a Brahman) have antagonized the rural voters of the Delhi state. The resignation of Khurana from Vajpayee's government in early 1999 had also heralded his return to local Delhi politics. In October-November 1999, he contested an MP seat. Interestingly, Sahib Singh Verma was also nominated by the BJP to contest in Outer Delhi, a Jat-dominated constituency where the party had only fielded upper caste candidates till then. Both of them won their seat. In fact all the BJP candidates won the seven seats of Delhi for the first time, a reconfirmation of the party's traditional influence in this old stronghold of Hindu nationalism.

## Notes

Research for this essay would not have been possible without financial support from the ORSTOM-CNRS programme and the constant help of Mrs Bhalla from the Centre of Human Sciences (New Delhi) who collected some of the data presented in the last part of this essay. I am also most grateful to Dipankar Gupta for his comments as discussant of my paper. Certain nuances and insights can be attributed to him. I would also like to thank Dirubhai Seth for his constructive remarks following the oral presentation of this paper.

1. In fact, the building of this office was, like the temple, financed by Jugal Kishore Birla who acted as a traditional patron in both cases.
2. Max Weber convincingly defines notables as persons, '(1) whose economic position permits them to hold continuous policy-making and administrative positions in an organization without (more than nominal) remuneration; (2) who enjoy social prestige of whatever derivation in such a manner that they are likely to hold office in virtue of the members' confidence, which at first is given and then traditionally accorded' (1988: 290).
3. Interview with Ratan Bhattacharya. He was elected in the Lal Darwaza-Suiwalan ward on a Jana Sangh ticket in the 1958 Delhi Municipal elections.
4. I am grateful to Dipankar Gupta for this comment.
5. In Kingsway Camp, for instance, he had been criticized for reading excerpts of the Koran to refugees (Pyarelal 1957: 441).
6. An organization supported by the RSS and close to the Dogras (Hindu landlords), the Praja Parishad was the first incarnation of the Jana Sangh in Jammu and Kashmir.

7. Malkani, a *swayamasevak* since 1942, had settled in Delhi in January 1948, arriving from Hyderabad (Sindh). He joined the *The Organiser* in October 1948. Interviews with K.R. Malkani, 16 November 1989 and 11 August 1992.

8. The *Sangh Parivar* was especially active and reasonably successful among students of Delhi University after Partition. In July 1948, Madhok founded the Akhil Bharatiya Vidyarthi Parishad in Delhi, which became the first affiliate of the RSS.

9. Hardayal Devgun, who was to be elected MP in east Delhi in 1967 on a Jana Sangh ticket and who had joined the RSS in Lahore to become a *pracharak* in 1940, said that 'he organized the Hindus against Muslim rioters' but underlines that his 'people attacked Muslim shops and so on' when they heard a false rumour suggesting that he had been killed (interview with H.D. Devgun).

10. The Arya Samaj people at large distanced themselves from the Jana Sangh in the 1950s. Immediately after Partition, the RSS and the Arya Samaj had advocated the formation of a Greater Punjab, amalgamating PEPSU (Patiala and East Punjab States Union), Himachal Pradesh and east Punjab, with Hindi as its official language—something the Sikhs could not accept. The Delhi-Punjab unit of the Jana Sangh adopted a much more moderate position by conceding that Punjabi and Hindi should be recognized as the languages for education and administration. Furthermore, in support of the notion of a Greater Punjab, the party alleged that Punjabi, which the Akali Dal considered peculiar to the west of the province—a region they wanted to separate off for themselves—was in fact spoken throughout. This cause and its supporting arguments were highly unpopular with the Arya Samajists who regarded Hindi as the sole language of the eastern part of the province where they were in a majority and who at times aspired to hive off this region from the western half of Punjab and have Delhi as its capital. The Delhi Jana Sangh could attract strong public support from the Arya Samaj only in 1967 when its president, Hardayal Devgun, persuaded R.S. Shawlwale, a prominent local Arya Samajist, to contest in Chandni Chowk as a Jana Sangh candidate.

11. Jag Parvesh Chandra, who arrived in Delhi on 17 August 1947 from Lahore where he had worked as a journalist since 1938, was inducted into the ruling party by Rajendra Prasad. He was elected to the Legislative Assembly in 1952 and ended up as Chief Executive Councillor from 1983-90.

12. Seth and Malhotra 1989. Kilawat gives somewhat different figures: 33 per cent of businessmen and 15 per cent teachers in the 1972 Delhi Metropolitan Council (n.d.): 268.

## References

Barrier, N.G. (1967), 'The Arya Samaj and Congress Politics in the Punjab: 1894–1904', *The Journal of Asian Studies*, Vol. 26, No. 3, May.

Bayly, C.A. (1973), 'Patrons and Clients in Northern India', *Modern Asian Studies*, Vol. 7, No. 3.

—— (1975), *Local Roots of Indian Politics*, Oxford: Clarendon Press.

Bharatiya Jana Sangh (1973), 'Manifesto: 1951', in *Party Documents*, Vol. 1, New Delhi.

——, 'Resolution passed at the party's annual session, 28 December 1958', in *Party Documents*, Vol. 2.

*Census of India, Punjab Census Report,* 1891.

*Census of India,* 1911.

*Census of India, 1933—Delhi,* Vol. 16, Lahore: Civil and Military Gazette Press.

————, *1971—Delhi,* General Report.

Chandidas, R., 'Elections to Delhi Metropolitan Council: An Analysis of Electoral and Ecological Variables', *Economic and Political Weekly.*

*Constituent Assembly Debates* (1989), Vol. VII, New Delhi: Lok Sabha Secretariat.

Curran, J.A. (1951), *Militant Hinduism in Indian Politics: A Study of the RSS,* Institute of Pacific Relations (duplicated).

Datta, V.N. (1993), 'Panjabi Refugees and the Urban Development of Greater Delhi', in R.E. Frykenberg (ed.), *Delhi Through the Ages,* Delhi: Oxford University Press.

*Delhi Gazetteer* (1976), New Delhi: Delhi Administration.

Devgun, Hardayal (n.d.), *Corruption and Bharaliyajanata Party,* New Delhi: Democratic Vigilance Committee.

Dungen, P.H.M. Van Den (1968), 'Changes in Status and Occupation in 19th Century Punjab', in D.A. Low (ed.), *Soundings in Modern South Asian History,* Berkeley: University of California Press.

Graham, B. (1990), *Hindu Nationalism and Indian Politics,* Cambridge: Cambridge University Press.

Gupta, B.R. (1975), *The Aggarwals,* New Delhi: S. Chand & Co.

Gupta, D. (1997), *The Context of Ethnicity,* Delhi: Oxford University Press.

'Hans Raj Gupta's reminiscences', in *Vinay Aur Vivek,* Delhi: Sri Hansraj Gupta Abhinandan-Prant Samaroh Samiti Prakashan.

Haynes, D.E. (1987), 'From Tribute to Philanthropy: the Politics of Gift Giving in a Western Indian City', *The Journal of Asian Studies,* Vol. 46, No. 2, May.

*Hindu Mahasabha Papers,* NMML, Manuscript section, C-160 Press Statement, dated 18 January 1948.

*Hitavada,* 9 January 1948.

Interviews with K.R. Malkani, 16 November 1989 and 11 August 1992, New Delhi.

Interview with B. Madhok, 10 November 1990, New Delhi.

Interview with K.N. Sahni, 20 November 1990, New Delhi.

Interview with V.K. Malhotra, 24 November 1990, New Delhi.

Interview with Kalka Dass, 23 November 1990, New Delhi.

Interview with M.L. Khurana, 8 December 1990.

Interview with Bhai Mahavir, 4 September 1992, New Delhi.

Interview with Vasant Rao Oke, 12 August 1992, New Delhi.

Interview with L.K. Advani, 11 February 1994, New Delhi.

Interview with Hans Raj Gupta's son, Rajendra Gupta, 25 February 1995, New Delhi.

Interview with Hardayal Devgun, 17 October 1995, New Delhi.

Interview with Ratan Bhattacharya, 6 November 1997, Agra.

Jones, K. (1993), 'Organized Hinduism in Delhi and New Delhi', in R.E. Frykenberg (ed.), *Delhi Through the Ages,* Delhi: Oxford University Press, 1986, rpt.

Kilawat, S.C. (n.d.), *The Government of the Federal Capital of India (Delhi),* Jaipur: Publication Scheme.

Madhok, B. (1985), *RSS and Politics,* New Delhi: Hindu World Publications.

Malkani, K.R. (1980), *The RSS Story,* New Delhi: Biblia Impex.

Mishra, Ramashankar (1972), 'Jivan vritt', in *Vinay Aur Vivek,* Delhi: Sri Hansraj Gupta Abhinandan-Prant Samaroh Samiti Prakashan (Hindi).

*Moonje Papers,* Letter from Moonje to the Secretary of the Joint Select Parliamentary Committee (dated 10 July 1933), NMML, Microfilm Section, Reel no. 9.

'Notes on the Volunteer Movement in India', prepared by the Intelligence Bureau, 27 January 1940 and 23 August 1940, in L/P&J/Coll. 17—C81 IOLR.

Oral History Transcript, interview with M.C. Sharma (Hindi), NMML.

Pandit, V.L. (1984), *Elites and Urban Politics: A Case Study of Delhi,* New Delhi: Inter-India Publications.

Puri, G. (1980), *Bharatiya Jana Sangh—Organisation and Ideology: Delhi, A Case Study,* New Delhi: Sterling.

Puri, Yogesh (1993), *Party Politics in the Nehru Era: A Study of Congress in Delhi,* New Delhi: National Books Organisation.

Pyarelal (1957), *Mahatma Gandhi: The Last Phase,* Vol. 2, Ahmedabad: Navajivan Publishing House.

*Report of the Commission of Inquiry into Conspiracy to Murder Mahatma Gandhi* (1970), Part 1 and Part 2, New Delhi: Government of India.

Saini, M.K. and Andersen, W. (1971), 'The Congress Split in Delhi', *Asian Survey,* Vol. 11, No. 11, November 1971.

Saini, N.K. and Andersen, W. (1969), 'The Basti Julahan bye-election', *The Indian Journal of Political Science,* July-September 1969.

Saksena, R.N. (1961), *Refugees: A Study in Changing Attitudes,* Bombay: Asia Publishing House.

*Savarkar Papers,* Letter of 27 July 1936, Reel no. 3, File no. 1, NMML (Nehru Museum and Memorial Library).

———, Letter of Padam Raj Jain to Savarkar, 29 November 1936, Reel no. 4, File no. 1.

Sen, S.P. (1973) (ed.), *Dictionary of National Biography,* Vol. l, Calcutta: Institute of Historical Studies.

Seth, K.N. and Malhotra, G.C. (1989), *Delhi Metropolitan Council: A Study (1966–1989),* Delhi: Metropolitan Council.

*Sunday News of India,* 30 July 1950.

Tandon, P. (1989), *Banking Century. A Short History of Banking in India and the Pioneer: Punjab National Bank,* New Delhi: Penguin Books.

*The Hindustan Times,* 8 March 1959.

*The Organiser,* 10 September 1951, 1 January 1948, 8 January 1948, Varshapratipada Special, 1979.

*The Statesman,* 29 September 1954, Delhi.

*The Times of India,* 5 January 1955, 25 July 1997.

Upadhyaya, D. (1958), *The Two Plans: Promises, Performances, Prospects,* Lucknow: Rashtradharma Prakashan.

Weber, Max (1988), *Economy and Society,* New York: Bedminster Press.

# Chapter 14

# Hindu nationalism and the (not so easy) art of being outraged
## the *Ram Setu* controversy

Religious outrage has triggered collective violence in pre-modern India, as C. Bayly has shown in his seminal work on the 'pre-history of communalism' (Bayly 1985): heads of pigs were found in mosques, followers of Islam offered cows in sacrifice during Id, Hindu processions passed by mosques while playing music during the prayer time. . . . The meaning of such 'rituals of provocation'—to use Marc Gaborieau's expression (Gaborieau 1985)—changed with the crystallization of communal ideologies. Then, these stratagems acquired a political dimension. They were still used to provoke riots but the polarization of society they were intended to create was often supposed to translate into votes, for instance. In this essay I shall address this issue not from the point of view of violence, but from that of mobilization by asking one (twofold) question: how can the Hindutva movement shape or manipulate religious forms of outrage in order to attract supporters and is the sacred dimension of the outrage the most critical one?

Hindu nationalists cultivate the art of being outraged when elements of their religion are affected. They promptly denounce 'attacks' against sacred symbols of Hinduism: any disrespect can be portrayed as blasphemy and lay itself to popular mobilizations—which may translate into votes. Hindu nationalist politicians have always been eager to instrumentalize so-called outrageous situations at the time of elections. Agitations against cow-slaughter in 1967 and for (re)building the Ram Temple in Ayodhya in 1989, a few months before general elections in both occurrences, are cases in point. In 1967, the *Sangh Parivar*—through the VHP and its party, the Jana Sangh—mobilized thousands of demonstrators in New Delhi to protest against the outrage to Hinduism that cow-slaughter represented, a practise still legal in a few states and which the *Sangh Parivar* accused the Muslims to indulge in at the time of Bakr Id (Graham 1990: 147–55). In 1989, the same groups orchestrated a similar campaign in defence of Ram, in the form of the Ayodhya movement.

A purely instrumentalist interpretation, however, is not sufficient. The Hindu nationalist culture of outrage cannot be understood irrespective of its psychological context. It is part of a discourse of victimization which is the very matrix of Hindu nationalism (Jaffrelot 1996). This ideology was shaped in the late nineteenth century as a reaction to a strong sense of vulnerability. Hindus, though in a majority, were seen by its proponents as weak, compared to the Muslims, because of their inner divisions along caste and sectarian lines. This majoritarian complex of inferiority made Hindu nationalist leaders prompt to outcry as soon as some of their sacred identity symbols were 'under attack' because of religious minorities, be they Muslim or Christian.

The controversy about the *Ram Setu,* the last 'outrage' to date affecting Hinduism (from the point of view of the *Sangh Parivar*) exemplifies this pattern. But it complexifies it since the Hindutva leaders appear to be less concerned by the sacred character of this identity symbol than by its historical quality. It also shows that the enemy responsible for the victimization of the Hindus may not be Muslims or Christians, but the State and the lower castes—then, fighting the so-called outrage may be more complicated. Last but not least, it is revealing of the Hindu nationalists' quest for non-religious (and even non-historical) reasons for defending an object of outrage: the *Ram Setu* also had to be defended for economic and strategic reasons.

## The *Ram Setu* Controversy: Outraging the Sacred— Popular Agitation and the Victimization Discourse

*Ram Setu* is the name of the bridge that is supposed to link south India to Sri Lanka since the *Ramayana*. According to this epic, it was built by Hanuman, the chief of Ram's army, in order to cross over the ocean and rescue Sita who had been abducted by Ravana. As early as the nineteenth century, the British made plans to dredge this channel in order to enable big ships to navigate along the Indian coast or to travel between the eastern side of India towards the Arabian Sea to use it. In 1838 efforts were made to this end for the first time, but they did not succeed in making the passage navigable for big ships. Another plan was made in 1860 but it was never implemented.[1]

Almost one century later, in 1955, independent India constituted the Sethusamudram Project Committee to examine the feasibility of dredging the canal connecting the Gulf of Mannar with the Palk Bay. The Committee recommended that the canal project be linked with the Tuticorin Harbour Project and that both projects be undertaken simultaneously. In 1963, the Government of India sanctioned the Tuticorin Harbour Project in order to transform this deep sea port into a major maritime hub. But the Sethusamudram Project was not taken further.

Tuticorin became a big harbour, but nothing compared to Colombo which developed into a major container port. Colombo reached its full handling capacity in 1992 because it could receive big international cargos and be used as a transhipment port.[2] Tuticorin could not replicate this success story because it could not be approached by big ships, though it experienced a 17 per cent per annum growth rate in the early 2000s.[3] And the smaller ones which reached it from the East coast of India had to go around Sri Lanka, travelling 500 extra kilometres and spending large amounts in fuel and crew charges. This state of things also raised a security problem since India was one of the few sovereign countries which did not have a continuous navigable route for big ships in its own territorial water.

The supporters of the Sethusamudram Project also argued that it would help developing backward districts of Tamil Nadu such as Tirunelveli and Ramanathapuram. The Project was revived in 1983—to no avail—and again in 1994 when the government of Tamil Nadu updated the project and detailed it. The Vajpayee government, which was formed in 1999 with the support of the National Democratic Alliance, a coalition led by the BJP, took it up under pressure of its local ally, the All India Anna Dravida Munnetra Kazhagam (AIADMK). In the 2000-1 budget, Yashwant Sinha, the then Union Finance Minister, allocated Rs. 4.8 crore for a feasibility study of the Sethusamudram Project. The Project then begun in 2004, under the NDA regime, when the Vajpayee government approved a Rs 3,500 crore budget to create a shipping channel. The first concrete step, though, was taken after the NDA lost the 2004 elections to the Congress-led United Progressive Alliance, by Prime Minister Manmohan Singh who inaugurated the project on 2 June 2005. Dredging started in July 2006. Six dredgers worked between the mouth of the channel in Palk Straits: Dredger XVI owned by Dredging Corp. of India Ltd., Pacifique, owned by Belgium-based Dreging International, Banwari Prem and Triloki Prem owned by Mumbai-based Vector Shipping Services Pvt. Ltd., Darya Manthan owned by Hong Kong-based Chellaram Shipping Ltd., and Prof. Gurjanov owned by the Russia-based Baltdraga Ltd. (Narain 2008). By July 2007, 17.57 per cent of the Sethusamudram Project had been achieved according to the official Sethusamudram Project government website. The completion rate reached 24.76 per cent in September 2007.

Hindu nationalists immediately denounced an attack against a sacred site.[4] One of them, Subramanian Swamy, went to the Supreme Court with a written petition. The government then filed a counter affidavit questioning the very existence of the *Ram Setu* which, according to them, was purely mythical and legendary:

contents of the Valmiki Ramayana, the Ramcharitmanas by Tulsidas and other mythological texts, which admittedly formed an important part of ancient Indian literature . . . cannot be said to be historical record to incontrovertibly prove the existence of the characters, or the occurrence of events depicted therein. (*The Indian Express* 2008)

This argument prepared the ground of a stronger reaction. Hindu nationalists built a whole campaign of agitation based on the usual feelings of being outraged and their old discourse of victimization.

'RAM UNDER ATTACK'

The weekly mouthpiece of the *Sangh Parivar, The Organiser,* devoted its Divali special issue to the *Ram Setu* controversy late in 2007. The 21 articles it contained perfectly illustrate the Hindu nationalist rhetoric that was articulated at that time. Gautam Sen, one of the *Sangh Parivar* leaders in England, set the tone:

The dredging of the *Ram Setu* channel on the grounds that there was neither Ram nor any historic bridge is simply outrageous. It is the equivalent of orphaning an entire civilisation by denying the well-springs of its foundation. (Sen 2007: 17)

What was at stake, of course, was the religious identity of Hindus. This point was made at length by Sunita Vakil few pages afterwards:

It is quite saddening that the ruling party, by casting aspersions on the name of Ram, a strong symbol of Hindu faith, is trying to destruct India's rich cultural heritage and all [what] it stands for. By denying the existence of Lord Ram armed with a non descript affidavit in the apex court, the Congress leaders have dealt a heavy blow to the collective Hindu psyche besides reducing a sacred epic that defined Hindu identity and nationhood for ages, to a mere work of fiction. (Vakil 2007: 52)

The words used to denounce the government's disregard for such sacred symbols as Ram and the *Ram Setu* were always the same: outrage, insult, humiliation, blasphemy, etc. And these attacks against Ram and the *Ram Setu* were equated with attacks against Hindus at large, and even against their country. Among the contributors to the Divali special issue of *The Organiser,* a Sanskrit scholar, Dr Indulata Das writes: 'Insult of Ram is an insult to India' (Das 2007: 36).

Naturally, the religious figures who had been invited to contribute to this special issue emphasized the sacred dimension of the *Ram Setu* even more. Swami Nischalanda Saraswati, the Shankaracharya of Puri wrote for instance:

We are really shocked that the existence of Sri Ram and the *Ramayan* is being disputed on this sacred land where this great hero took birth. It is not only meant for the demolition of the *Ram Setu* but also backed by a ploy to outrage the reputation, honour and self-pride of Hindu society. (Saraswati 2007: 55).

Swami Dayananda Saraswati, another safron-clad 'saintly' figure, was even more explicit about the implications of the sacredness of the *Ram Setu* in his fascinating speech as chief guest of the function organized for the release of Subramanian Swamy's book, *Ram Setu: a Symbol of National Unity,* on 20 April 2008:

Any destruction to the sacred Sethu would hurt the sentiments of crores of Hindus. Any sentiment is sacred. No sentiments needs any logic, and sentiment is above all. Therefore, we don't need to give any reason for our attitude, that has been inherited since generations. (Rath 2008: 9)

The sacredness of the *Ram Setu* was reason enough to denounce the outrageous attitude of the government.

Those who insisted most on the sacredness of the *Ram Setu*, though, were activists specializing in popular mobilizations—be they religious figures or politicians. Ravi Shankar Prasad, the Bharatiya Janata Party (BJP) national spokesperson, regarded the government's affidavit as an 'humiliating insult to Lord Ram' (Prasad 2007: 76) and Sadhvi Rithambara, one of the most vocal VHP saffron-clad leaders, denounced its 'blatant disregard toward the religious sentiments of [the] majority community' (Rithambara 2007: 62).

## LOOKING FOR POPULAR MOBILIZATION

The protest against so-called sacrilegious attacks against symbols of Hinduism generally translates into calls to agitate. Indeed, the VHP leaders launched a mobilization campaign under the aegis of Sadhvi Rithambara and Satyamitranand Giri. The former considered that 'the campaign to save *Ram Setu* should be of vital importance to any cultured person, without any connection to political identity or ideological stand' (Rithambara 2007: 63). The latter launched his 'most ardent appeal to the Indian society to embark once again upon the path of satyagraha in order to protect the very existence of the Hindu culture which is under serious threats. Let us all be prepared to lay down our lives if the need arises to achieve this most sacred cause' (Giri 2007: 65).

The RSS created a new organization only devoted to the defence of the *Ram Setu*, the Rameshwaram *Ram Setu* Raksha Manch. This organization initiated an agitation campaign in Tamil Nadu. In September 2007, for instance, it resulted in the arrest of activists belonging to this movement and to the arrest of other activists belonging to another offshoot of the RSS, the Hindu Janajagriti Samiti.[5] The agitation reached its culmination point in late December 2007 when the Rameshwaram *Ram Setu* Raksha Manch organized a huge rally in Rohini (Delhi) on the Swarna Jayanti Udyan grounds. It was attended by VHP leaders—including Ashok Singhal (International President) and Pravin Togadia (International General Secretary) as well as saffron-clad saintly figures, BJP leaders—including the entire top brass of the party as well as the Chief Ministers of Madhya Pradesh, Rajasthan, Chhattisgarh, Uttarakhand and Himachal Pradesh—and RSS leaders, amongst whom was K. Sudarshan, the *sarsanghchalak* (*The Economic Times* 2007).

## THE PSYCHOLOGICAL CONTEXT: A VULNERABILITY SYNDROME

Outrage to the sacred is usually instrumentalized by ethno-political entrepreneurs from the BJP and the VHP who attempt to mobilize—and gain followers—for a crucial cause. But this particular mobilization and the motivations of its initiators have to be analysed in the context of a general feeling of vulnerability. Traditionally, those who suffered from this syndrome considered that it was Muslims who posed the greatest threat to Hinduism; in the case of the *Ram Setu,* the Congress-led government was their first target because it was accused of always appeasing the minorities at the expense of Hindus.

## Hindus 'Under Threat'

Sadhvi Rithambara, in the aforementioned article about the 'attack' against the *Ram Setu* writes: 'The current assault on our Hindu dharma is nothing new but an extension of centuries of unprovoked assaults. Hindu history is replete with accounts of the most atrocious attacks perpetrated on the peace loving Hindus in India' (Rithambara 2007: 62). For the *Sangh Parivar,* Hindus are—and have always been—victims of external assailants. Over the years, this reading of history percolated and now finds some echo among ordinary citizens who become thus sympathizers of the Hindutva forces. One of the letters reproduced in the 'readers' forum' of *The Organiser* illustrates this very well and deserves to be quoted at length:

Tolerance is a great quality but not at the cost of wiping out the great religion [that is Hinduism]. *Ram Setu* is just another episode in this vilified and dangerous campaign. It is high time that some permanent solution is put up to mitigate the sufferings of Hindus. Delhi Metro's route alignment was changed so that Qutub Minar is not harmed; the Taj industrial corridor project is under legal stay so as to preserve Taj Mahal and there are several other typical cases where minority card is being played. But when it comes to a Hindu thought, psyche, religion or anything associated with Hindu, there is a lot of demeaning, defamation, hurting the religious sentiments, etc. (*The Organiser,* 2007: 80)

Another reader wrote: 'The Hindu in India is faced with a unique situation. While he is theoretically part of a majority, he is so fractured into various ideological groups that he is virtually powerless to influence the politics of the country' (*The Organiser,* 2007: 80).

In contrast, according to Hindu nationalists, minorities form blocks which the political parties are always keen on 'pampering'. The Hindutva leaders traditionally argue that the Congress plays votebank politics and is especially keen to make concessions to Muslims in order to get their support at the time of elections. But in the case of the *Ram Setu,* Muslims were not involved and so their discourse had to be different.

## Hindus Against Low Caste Dravidians?

Subramanian Swamy argued that 'the UPA is an anti-Hindu government. Because Karunanidhi is an atheist, and UPA's puppeteer Ms. Sonia Gandhi is a Christian fundamentalist, they together thought that they can demoralise the ordinary Hindu by demolishing the *Ram Setu*' (Swamy 2007: 69).

Sonia Gandhi's rise to power, since she became president of the Congress Party in 1997, has been followed with great suspicion by the Hindu nationalists who predicted that she would betray the Indian nation, not only because of her foreign origin, but also because of her Catholic background. The myth of an anti-Hindu conspiracy of the minorities has crystallized in this context and has been reactivated during the *Ram Setu* movement. Referring to the government's affidavit, Gautam Sen considered for instance that:

The subjection of their beliefs and history to some allegedly superior investigative forensic science is merely an Islamo-Christian conspiracy signifying complete bad faith . . . . It is a diabolical intrigue that threatens to subjugate Hindus politically as the prelude to a final solution that will impale them on the beliefs of their imperialist conquerors. (Sen 2007: 17)

In the case of Karunanidhi, the accusation of being anti-Hindu is more complicated. He is certainly 'anti-Brahman'! This Dravidian leader is the heir of a long Tamil tradition of Brahman-bashing harking back to Periyar, the author of a corrosive book entitled *The Ramayana: A True Reading* in 1959. In this book, that was banned in some parts of India, Periyar made statements which were much more provocative than those of Karunanidhi's, especially when the former referred to Ram's morality. But his anti-Ram stances were in tune with the south Indian version of the *Ramayana*. In the Dravidian states, Ram has never been such a popular deity. In fact, he has always been seen there as a north Indian import and a symbol of the Aryan invasions. The Brahmans, who brought Hinduism to the south, were accused of subjugating indigenous people and subjecting them to a foreign civilization. In contrast, in Tamil Nadu at least, Ravana is a heroic son of the soil, a Vedic scholar and an epitome of morality. Unlike Ram who questioned Sita's chastity, Ravana is presented in the Dravidian movement as a refined man—a connoiseur of music— who abstained from manhandling Sita. Besides his deliberately anti-Brahman tirades, Periyar fought for *Pahutu arivu*, that is rationalism against *Mooda nambikai*, superstitions. This is why Swamy accuses him of being an atheist.

During the *Ram Setu* controversy, Karunanidhi followed a purely Dravidian vein and argued that Ram could not be an historic person and that the *Ram Setu* could not be an ancient man-made bridge. During the celebration of Periyar's ninety-ninth birth anniversary, he declared at a public meeting at Erode: 'Some say there was a person over 17 lakh years ago, his name, Ram. And we should not touch the bridge (*Ram Setu*) he built. Who is this Ram? From which engineering college did he graduate? Is there any proof of this?'[6] A few days later, on 20 September, he said that 'Ram is a big lie' and then that, according to Valmiki himself he was a drunkard.[7]

The *Sangh Parivar* could not put up with such a discourse. On the other hand, its leaders could not react to it in the way they had reacted to a minority leader like Sonia Gandhi. In fact, the *Ram Setu* controversy shows how difficult it is for the *Sangh Parivar* to identify and cash in on pan-Hindu symbols. While Ram is a popular symbol in the north among almost all caste groups it is not that prestigious in the Dravidian south, especially among the lower castes. By activating this identity symbol, the *Sangh Parivar* risks alienating other Hindus instead of unifying the majority community. Incidentally, this is why the notion of a 'Hindu race' was never used by the ideologues of the Hindutva movement as it would have introduced a line of cleavage between 'Aryans' and 'Dravidians' (Jaffrelot 1995: 327–54).

However the *Sangh Parivar* is certainly not shy of alienating some Hindus. It has been fighting physically against communists in Kerala for decades, the RSS/ CPI(M) violence leaving dozens of people dead every year. The Bajrang Dal is also implementing a form of cultural policing directed against Hindu artists. In February 2004, activists from the movement filed a complaint against canvasses painted by a Hindu artist, Shail Choyal, for an information campaign of the NGO 'CARE' devoted to providing care for newborns. They particularly criticized the painter's depiction of Hindu divinities such as Ganesh and Krishna. On February 10, their complaint was registered by the police who, in the company of some 50 Bajrang Dal militants, searched the offices of the director of the Udaipur Lok Kala Mandal, the art centre where the canvasses were stored, seized the paintings and put the director and the painter behind bars. They were later released on bail, but the Bajrang Dal organized a protest march during which their effigies were burned.[8]

This cultural police's wrath is not merely brought down on famous painters: it even hunts down amateur artists at the local level. For instance, in Gwalior (Madhya Pradesh), the Bajrang Dal and the Durga Vahini—the youth wing and the women wing of the VHP—accused an employee of the Indian Institute of Tourism and Travel Management of having staged a play, *Kal, Aaj aur Kal*, that showed disrespect for Sita, Ram and Laxman. On 14 March 2004, members of these two organizations burst into the employee's home to blacken her face in public as punishment. Her father as well as her brothers and sisters stepped in. They were beaten and thrown out of their house, while their home was ransacked, all under the passive gaze of police officers (Tripathi 2004: 41).

The depiction of the role of women in society by Hindu film-makers has also resulted in strong-arm tactics by the Bajrang Dal. In 2000, Canada-based director Deepa Mehta chose to make a film entitled *Water* on the life of Hindu widows in Varanasi in the 1930s. At that time—and even now to a lesser extent—these women were condemned to celibacy and begging. Usually they gathered together in 'homes' where they lived on public charity and eked out a living by making fuel out of cow dung. The screenplay showed an 'illicit' relationship between a Brahman widow and an untouchable and the rape of a child widow. The VHP president immediately declared that the film insulted 'ancient Indian culture and traditions' (*The Hindu*, 5 February 2000) and threatened 'more violent protest' if Deepa Mehta tried to shoot in India. She nevertheless, did after having secured all the necessary authorizations from the central government and the authorities of Uttar Pradesh. The set that was built on the banks of the Ganges was totally ransacked by Bajrang Dal militants and the damage added to the delays accumulated on the shooting led to colossal losses (65,000 US dollars) for the producer.

Deepa Mehta then decided to continue shooting in Madhya Pradesh where she could not have been more warmly welcomed by the head of government at that time, Digvijay Singh. But here again, the Bajrang Dal resorted to force to prevent the shooting from taking place. Deepa Mehta's previous film, *Fire,* had already ignited the anger of Hindu nationalists, as it picturized two women falling in love. The same theme was taken up in *Girlfriend,* a Bollywood film, which sparked an even more violent Bajrang Dal campaign in 2004: posters were torn down and screenings were prevented in most of Mumbai's theatres, a sign that this organization saw itself as a vice squad allegedly protecting Hindu values.

Obviously, the *Sangh Parivar* has targeted Hindus outraging Hinduism before. But the *Ram Setu* controversy is different. For the first time, *Sangh Parivar* leaders seem to have identified an outraged symbol whose defence could divide Hindus in a big way. What is at stake is not a handful of artists but sections of the Dravidian movement. Certainly, the BJP is not too concerned by the feelings of the DMK voters given its weak electoral basis in Tamil Nadu, but attacking the Dravidian tradition might have repercussions throughout India among the Dalit and Other Backward Classes (OBC) leaders who regard Periyar as one of their heroes—especially since Mayawati and the Bahujan Samaj Party (BSP) tried to establish a pan-Indian presence by touring south India over the last 2-3 years. This is probably one of the main reasons why, eventually, the *Sangh Parivar* put the *Ram Setu* issue on the back burner after a couple of demonstrations, one of them resulting in the infamous ransacking of the flat of Karunanidhi's daughter by Hindu nationalist activists in Bangalore. Interestingly, instead of entrusting the VHP with the task of exploiting the *Ram Setu* controversy, the new body's very name, the Rameshwaram *Ram Setu* Raksha Manch, downplays the whole exercise: it has to be a local issue rooted in the concerns of the local people.

The fact that sections of the Dravidian movement did not recognize Ram as a sacred figure also explains why the *Sangh Parivar* looked for other good reasons to be outraged: what was at stake, for the organization, had to be the historical quality of the *Ram Setu.* This attempt at historicizing myths was part of the Hindu nationalist ideology anyway.

## The Historicization of Myth: Searching for the root cause of outrage

While BJP and VHP leaders insist on the sacred character of the *Ram Setu* in order to mobilize people on the street, for the *Sangh Parivar* dignitaries who really matter—the RSS leaders—this 'bridge' needs to be preserved for other, more nationalist reasons.

One contributor to *The Organiser* Divali special issue downplays the question of historicity and of its corollary, the scientific proof of the existence of Ram and the *Ram Setu*: 'True, when one is writing human history, tangible evidence is important. But when one is dealing with the divine, faith is overriding. And faith has been overwhelming when it came to Lord Ram' (Goralia 2007: 40). In other words: there is no need to prove the existence of Ram (and the *Ram Setu*) with scientific tools since every follower of Hinduism believes in him as a sacred figure of their religion. This argument is not put forward by any RSS leader. Even when they emphasize the sacred nature of Ram and the *Ram Setu*, they make a point to stress their historical quality too.

## HISTORY AS A KEY ELEMENT OF ETHNO-NATIONALISM

RSS leaders have not been outraged by the government's treatment of the *Ram Setu* as a religious symbol, but as a *historical* symbol. For these pro-Hindutva ethno-nationalists the main pillar of the Hindu identity lay in the Vedic golden age, an historical foundation phase which is well described in the *Ramayana*. Since Golwalkar, the RSS doctrine has been distinguishing Hinduism as a religion from Hinduism as a *national* way of life. The former is considered as an element of the latter, which matters much more, in spite of its worldly character. That is why the historical features of ancient India are so important. Ram Madhav, the former spokesman of the RSS and a member of its executive committee, made it clear about the *Ram Setu* controversy: its historicity had to be demonstrated because what was at stake was the very historicity of Ram, a fundamental element of the Hindu nationalist identity:

Denial of historicity of Ram is denying the very identity of this nation. That may not do any harm to our religion because as a religion we Hindus are not much bothered about this historicity question. . . . Hindus are not a people driven by history. Hinduism will survive any onslaught [regarding the historicity of its gods]. But as a nation we will pay a very heavy price for questioning the existence of Ram, the Imam-e-Hind [*sic*]. (Madhav 2007: 45)

For the RSS leaders the preservation of Hinduism is not enough and the real objective is the building of the 'Hindu Rashtra'. To achieve this goal, they rely on the Vedic golden age, a civilizational founding moment that simply has to be revived. RSS leaders are keen to cite Swami Dayananda, one of the key ideologues in the making of this myth of a Vedic golden age, and some of his epigones, like Benjamin Khan who wrote:

We find that Valmiki depicts a society where women are held in honour, a society which is free from the horrors of the Sati system, a society in which child-marriage is unknown and maidens are free to chose their husbands. It was a society with political and economical freedom where men had their proper occupations . . . . The caste system had not assumed the rigidity it acquired later; it was only an economic device and not a birth-principle. . . . Valmiki did not hesitate to condemn the doctrine of Fate, which was rendering the nation impotent. He ridiculed all those who pinned their faith to destiny and lowered the value of human efforts. For him, it is human will which is the spring of all human action and even if there is anything like destiny, it can be made to change its course by man's prowess. (Khan 1983; Balanshankar, 2007: 9)

This reading of the Vedic period is a clear invention of the past emulating the mainstays of the West: the underlying values which are referred to in this excerpt are those of Western individualism.

## RAM, AS THE ALTER EGO OF JESUS AND MOHAMMED

Suffering from a deep sense of vulnerability, the Hindutva leaders have always tried to imitate the cultural features of Others—including the West—which would confer prestige and/or a reputation of effectiveness on them. While child marriage and the caste system suffered from an unanimous opprobrium, individual freedom was universally revered and therefore the Vedic golden age had to incorporate this quality. This reasoning is a core element of the Hindu nationalist strategy of stigmatizing and emulating strong Others, including those who represent a threat to Hindus. Ram Madhav's plea in favour of the historicity of Ram must be seen in this very perspective: Ram has to be revered as a historical figure because the religions displaying the greatest dynamism today, i.e. Christianity and Islam according to him, are based on the teachings of historical men, Jesus Christ and Mohammed: 'Remove historicity from Jesus's life or remove Bethlehem and Jerusalem from his history, Christianity will collapse. Remove historicity from Prophet Mohammed, Islam will collapse' (Madhav 2007: 45).

In fact, all the Semitic religions are seen as role models, including Judaism, a creed rooted in history and supporting a committed nation-state. Visiting Israel during the *Ram Setu* controversy, Madhav was struck by the emotional and political weight given by the government placed to the historical religious sites. He contrasted this with the attitude of the United Progressive Alliance (UPA) rulers: 'Here is a nation that I am visiting—proud of its Millenia old history and heritage; and here is the nation to which I belong—writhing in self-denial and self-hate' (ibid.: 44). Here/there, us/them. . . the strategy of stigmatization and emulation of Others relies on repetitive, even obsessive, comparisons. Though Jews have become role models for the proponents of Hindutva, given their remarkable resilience in the midst of an Islamic hostile milieu, emulating Christians and Muslims remains more relevant since they are seen as a direct threat to Hindus who thus need to borrow from them in order to counter them. Now, these two religions cash in on the historicity not only of religious figures but also of sacred sites like Bethlehem, the Vatican, Medina and Mecca. For the RSS leaders, Hinduism must similarly recognize the historicity of sacred places such as the *Ram Setu*.

## IN QUEST OF SCIENTIFIC PROOFS

The first set of proofs mobilized by the Hindu nationalists are 'the archaeological findings [. . . which] substantiate historicity of Lord Ram' (Gupta 2007: 12). O.P. Gupta enlists sixteenth century coins embossed with figures of Lord Ram, Egyptian tablets depicting 'stories similar to those in the *Ramayana*' (ibid.: 12) and Maya tablets of the same kind—as if that was enough to establish the historicity of Ram.

The second set of proofs comes from the British writings. Dinesh Chandra Tyagi, the General Secretary of the Hindu Mahasabha, another Hindu nationalist party—the oldest one in fact—bluntly writes:

As far as the historicity of *Ram Setu* is concerned, it is proved in *Madras Presidency Glossary* edited by C.D. Maclean and *Survey of India* (1767). *Ram Setu's* name was changed to Adam Bridge but the documentary proof given by the British Library and Glossary claim that this bridge connects Ceylon to Peninsula of India and it really joined the two countries until 1480, when a breach was made through the rocks during a storm. Length of the Sethu about 30 miles, breadth 1.25 miles, direction South-West South-East to North-West is depicted in the document, partly above and partly below water, but usually 4 feet above the sea level was visible mostly. Thus the proof is visible and uncontroversial but politically-closed eyes of the UPA leaders could not see it. (Tyagi 2007: 79)

Dr. S. Kalyana Raman, the Director of the Saraswati Research Centre and the President of the Rameshwaram *Ram Setu* Raksha Manch, refers to the travelogue of Alexander Hamilton, entitled *A New Account of the West Indies* which, in 1744 describes on page 338 his visit to Ceylon by crossing the bridge. Raman also refers to another edition of Maclean's book (1903: 2440) where he read that the bridge 'really joined Ceylon to India until 1480, when a breach was made through rocks during a storm. A subsequent storm enlarged this and foot traffic then ceased' (Raman 2007: 22). The importance somewhat naively attached to Western sources—that I noticed in my essay on the emulation of the Western criteria of 'what is a nation' by the Hindu nationalists—is confirmed here. His Holiness Swami Chidanand Saraswati even writes: 'The bridge clearly exists and has earned even a place in the Encyclopaedia Britannica' (Saraswati 2007: 58).

The third set of proofs derives from satellite photographs. The (re)discovery of the *Ram Setu* by Hindu nationalists seems to have taken place in 1997 when one old-timer of the RSS, Chamanlal, saw a picture of a current NASA's photo exhibition in Delhi that showed 'the picture of *Ram Setu*'. He then contacted Uma Bharti, the then Union Minister of Coal and Mines who sent a team of scientists from her administration. They went to Rameshwaram and 'confirmed the underwater formation of rocks attached to each other and described those rocks as old as one lakh years' (Bharti 2007: 74). These 'two scientific sources'—to use the words of Subramanian Swamy—have been quoted *ad nauseam* afterwards: the NASA's photographs have been repeatedly presented as establishing 'the Sethu's existence as a chain of shoal stones' and the Department of Earth Science of the Government of India stated that these stones had been 'deliberately placed there' (Swamy 2007: 70). Of the two, the NASA photographs, have been referred more often. For instance, the website of Hindu Janajagriti Samiti, an offshoot of the *Sangh Parivar* explains:

Pictures taken by NASA (USA) from space show the remains of what appears to be an age old man-made bridge between Rameshwaram and Sri Lanka. According to Hindu scriptures and belief, Lord Ram and his *vanaar sena* had built a bridge from Rameshwaram to Sri Lanka about 17 lacs [*sic*] 25 thousands years ago. The discovery of Shri *Ram Setu* by NASA confirms that Hindu scriptures and belief are correct in this matter and that Ramayana is history and not 'mythology' as is often construed.[9]

The NASA had to clarify repeatedly that these photographs had been misinterpreted by the *Sangh Parivar*. The NASA spokesman, Michael Braukus declared: 'Some people have taken pictures by our astronauts to make their claim. No position can be taken on the basis of these photographs in any way.' In 2002, Mark Hess, a NASA official, had already stated that 'the mysterious bridge was nothing more than a 30 km long, naturally-occurring chain of sandbanks called "Adam's bridge". NASA had been taking pictures of these shoals for years. Its images of these shoals had never resulted in any scientific discovery in the area.'[10]

But Hindu nationalists do not care. Mixing Sanskrit and 'scientific' sources, Subramanian Swamy concludes: 'The *Ram Setu* formation is as if it was constructed in the manner described in the *Ramayana* authored by Valmiki, Kamban and Tulsidas. The bridge formation by placing these stones one by one, according to the Earth Science Department of the government is not less than 9,000 years.'[11]

In short, the main outrage felt by the Hindu nationalists in the *Ram Setu* controversy is not due to the sacred nature of this 'bridge', but to its historicity. For them, the denial of a prestigious past is more problematic because it questions the chief foundation of their political project: the revival of the 'Hindu Rashtra' of the Vedic Golden Age. Such an attitude is not new. During the *Ramjanmabhoomi* Movement, which focused on the 'liberation' of Ram in Ayodhya from the mid-1980s till 1992, the *Sangh Parivar* had tried hard to prove that a Ram temple had existed in place of the Babri Masjid, by looking for archaeological vestiges below its foundations.

## The Efficiency Argument

### ON THE UTILITY OF *RAM SETU*

According to the Hindu nationalist leaders, the *Ram Setu* had to be preserved for practical reasons too. None of these leaders mention its sacred and historical nature as a sufficient reason for preserving it. For O.P. Gupta, 'it is common sense that a breach in the *Ram Setu* will allow tsunamis to make direct hits at the Kerala and southern Tamil coasts with full force inflicting more casualties and more loss of lives than without the breach' (Gupta 2007:11).

Gautam Sen refers to the 'unknown and potentially huge environmental costs that the project might impose on future generations' (Sen 2007: 17). His Holiness Swami Chidanand Saraswati argues along the same lines that 'even from a strictly environmental perspective, to destroy the bridge and open the area for sea traffic is paving the way for environmental disaster' (Saraswati 2007: 59).

His Holiness Sadhvi Rithambara gives the longest lists of reasons why the *Ram Setu* needs to be saved:

Apart from its spiritual significance, *Ram Setu's* other attributes are more scientific and have a significant security value for the nation as it contains rich reserve of thorium, which is used as a nuclear fuel. Over the centuries, *Ram Setu* has served as a natural barrier against tsunamis. When the waves of the last tsunami were swallowing up the residents of the islands and India's coastal areas, it was this *Ram Setu*, which stopped the dangerous waves from reaching Tamil Nadu and beyond. By far the greatest feature of *Ram Setu* has to be its strategic location, which has provided a natural security cordon against enemy ships as it prevents anti-Indian terrorists from entering Indian ports undetected. (Rithambara 2007: 63)

Uma Bharti—who shared the VHP dais so often during the *Ramjanmabhoomi* Movement—cashes in on similar arguments but adds an economic one:

The destruction *of Ram Setu* is not only an insult to Indian culture, but it will also deprive lakhs of fishermen of their livelihood and will also present a grave threat to our national security. Most of the cadres of LTTE, who cross over to Tamil Nadu from Sri Lanka posing as refugees, reside in the nearby areas of Rameswaram. They indulge in the smuggling and sell their weapons to Islamic terrorists. (Bharti 2007: 74)

The economic argument remains unconvincing since the correlation between the dredging of the *Ram Setu* and the decline of the fishing activities is not clear at all, but such an argument is nonetheless common in the Hindu nationalist rhetoric.

THE ANTI COW-SLAUGHTER MOVEMENT REVISITED

Hindu nationalists have usually found it important to substantiate their claim regarding a sacred symbol by underlying its practical—and especially its economic—utility. For instance, the cow-protection movement relied on sacred elements and a strong plea in favour of the economic assets of this animal, as if its sacredness was not a sufficient reason for protecting it. This ambivalence is evident from the attitude of the Jana Sangh during the 1966–7 anti cow-slaughter campaign.

In 1966, VHP leaders created the Sarvadaliya Goraksha Maha-Abhiyan Samiti (SGMS) in order to mobilize Hindus in the street and force the Congress-led government to reform the Constitution by making cow-slaughter illegal. Saffron-clad leaders gathered with a huge crowd of 100,000 people in front of Parliament in order to put pressure on the MPs. Once again, the VHP demonstrated its skill for tapping popular sentiments.

The Jana Sangh adopted a more complex strategy. On the one hand, it supported the VHP's argument that allowing cow-slaughter was an insult to Hinduism. But it underlined the economic dimension of the issue. That remained its standard attitude for years. In 1954 already, its election manifesto read:

Cow is our point of honour, and the eternal symbol of our culture. Since immemorial times it has been protected and worshipped. Our economy too, is based on the cow. Cow-protection, therefore, is not only a pious duty but an indispensable need. It is impossible to protect and improve cattle so long as its slaughter continues. (Bharatiya Jana Sangh 1973: 68)

The 1951 manifesto already said: 'The party stands pledged to the prohibition of cow-slaughter. Special steps will be taken to improve the breeds of cow to make it an economic unit in our agricultural life' (ibid.: 52). In the 1957 manifesto, the relevant paragraph starts with the same ambivalent wording: 'Respecting the sentiments of the people of Bharat, and taking into consideration the economic importance of the cow, Jana Sangh will try to get Central legislation enacted to ban cow-slaughter throughout the country' (ibid.: 119). In the 1962 manifesto, the first 21 lines of the paragraph entitled 'Cow-protection and animal husbandry' are devoted to cattle breeding, milk production and marketing of dairy products. The only mention of the need to legally forbid cow-slaughter came in the last 2 lines, and almost as a matter of fact (ibid.: 135–6). Naturally, the 1967 manifesto returns to a more balanced approach by stating: 'The cow is our national point of honour. It is also the basis of India's agriculture. Bharatiya Jana Sangh will amend the Constitution and impose a legal ban on the slaughter of the cow and its progeny' (ibid.: 163).

The constant oscillation of the Jana Sangh between the argument of sacredness and others pertaining to the economic repertoire is very revealing of the fact that, even for the holy cow, the religious motivations were not enough: to be complete, the Hindu nationalist response to an outrage needs to address practical dimensions too. This is even more remarkable in this case since the economic rational would in fact have led to the slaughter of the old and sick cows which had become useless.[12]

Hindu nationalists have become experts in the art of being outraged. In pre-modern India, the blasphemous attitude of Muslims and Christians provoked violent reactions by the majority community (and vice versa). After the crystallization of ethno-nationalist ideologies during the British Raj, Hindu nationalists, who articulated a deep rooted inferiority complex, have tried hard to catch minorities out while insulting the sacred symbols of their religions. To denounce a disrespectful behaviour or to give some substance to one's complaints on the basis of rumours enabled the *Sangh Parivar* members to polarize society along communal lines and to mobilize new followers. Such a process was likely to trigger riots and to translate into votes for the Hindu Mahasabha, the Shiv Sena, the Jana Sangh and then the BJP, the main Hindu nationalist parties. This standard scenario worked rather well in the case of the *Ramjanmabhoomi* Movement when the Hindu nationalist leaders denounced the way the birthplace of Ram had supposedly been colonized by Muslim invaders who were also accused of having destroyed the temple built there before and of keeping Ram prisoner of the Mosque that replaced it. During the first phase of the *Ramjanmabhoomi* Movement, in 1984, VHP activists started a procession from Ayodhya in Uttar Pradesh to Sitarmahi in Bihar with a lorry bearing large statues of Ram and Sita behind bars (Van der Veer 1987). Five years later, the *Sangh Parivar* orchestrated dozens of communal riots during the *Ram Shila Pujas*—ceremonial consecrations of bricks named after Ram; and in the 1990s, the BJP surfed on the 'saffron wave', to use Thomas Blom Hansen's metaphor.

However, a purely instrumentalist interpretation of the Hindu nationalist use of outrage would be too simplistic. First, the sentiment of vulnerability is such among Hindu nationalists that they sometimes really feel victimized. Second, and more importantly, the use of sacred symbols is not that easy, as this case study reveals. The *Ram Setu* movement shows that the *Sangh Parivar* finds it more difficult to mobilize followers when the culprits are not Muslims—then, they must at least be Christians as the attack against Sonia Gandhi mentioned earlier suggested. It also shows that the exploitation of the outrage is more complicated when its instigators are born Hindus. *Sangh Parivar* members have already attacked other Hindus—be they communists or 'deviant' artists—but in the case under study, they had to face sections of the Dravidian movement associated with Dalits whom the Hindu nationalists cannot afford to alienate. This social caveat harks back to a geographical one: not only is it difficult to mobilize against Hindus but it is also difficult to mobilize Hindus who do not regard the identity symbol that the *Sangh Parivar* was manipulating as sacred: in Tamil Nadu, Ram is not as popular as in the north and there are indeed very few pan-Hindu symbols.

In any case, sacredness is not the only source of the outrage 'felt' by the Hindu nationalists. This is the second series of conclusions I would draw from the *Ram Setu* story. Ideologues of the RSS are prompt to highlight the historical dimension of Ram and its *Setu:* they do not care so much for their sacredness. Their historicity matters more because it is the foundation stone of Hindu nationalism—which, like any ethno-nationalism, needs real heroes—and it is the only way to be on a par with competing civilization whose key figures—Jesus and Mohammed—are located in human history.

The holy character of the outraged symbol is not enough: it has to be historical; and it has to be useful too. The *Ram Setu*, therefore, is also defended for economic and strategic reasons, even by saffron-clad leaders who may have found it sufficient to consider that it was a sacred cause. Such a modus operandi was also observed during the anti cow-slaughter movement in the 1960s. It suggests that the Hindu attitude vis-à-vis sacredness is not the same as the one we see in other cultures where nobody feels the need to invoke non-religious arguments. In Islam, for instance, the sacredness of Mecca is self-sufficient and its defence does not need to be supported by additional arguments.

The Congress-led government withdrew the affidavit it had filed with the Supreme Court after the start of the *Sangh Parivar* agitation in order to defuse any such mobilization in a sensitive election year. Instead, it has left it up to the Court to validate or not the Sethusamudram Project as of July 2008.

## Notes

1. See 'History', <http://sethusamudram.info/content/view/18/26>.
2. 'Tuticorin Port vs Colombo Port', <http://sethusamudram.info/content/view/26/30>.
3. 'Tuticorin port has potential to be global container hub – PricewaterhouseCoopers', <http://sethusamudram.info/content/view/25/30>.
4. They were not the first one to mobilize. Swami Avimukteshwaranand Saraswati, one of the main disciples of the Shankaracharya of Dwarka and Jyotirpith, launched a campaign with his own, limited means. (Personal communication of an unpublished letter sent on 29 September 2007 to *India Today* and *Outlook* by Alvara Enterria, Publications Director of Indica Books, Varanasi).
5. On the protests orchestrated by the Hindu Janajagriti Samiti, see <http://www.hindujagruti.org/activities/campaigns/religious/ramsetu/>.
6. 'Tamils celebrate Ravana as a hero and Rama as the villain', *Outlook,* cited in <http://sethusamudram.info/content/view/42/26>.
7. To quote Karunanidhi fully, in response to L.K. Advani, the BJP leader, who asked him to apologize after his initial statements, the DMK chief said: 'I have not said anything more than Valmiki, who authored the *Ramayana.* Valmiki has even stated that Ram was drunkard. Have I said so?' (Cited in 'Cong chants "Ram, Ram" on Sethu row', *The Economic Times,* 22 September 2007).
8. 'PUCL, Cultural policing by Bajrang Dal and the Rajasthan police', <http://www.pucl.org/Topics/Religion-communalism>.
9. 'What is Setu (Sethu) Samudram Project', <http://www.hindujagruti.org/activities/campaigns/religious/ramsetu/>.
10. 'Space photo no proof of Ram Sethu: NASA', <http://sethusamudram.info/content/view/ 66/26>.
11. Ibid.
12. This is exactly the reason why the Supreme Court had considered that it would be unreasonable to ban cow-slaughter in the Constitution of India in its 1958 decision.

## References

Balanshankar, R. (2007), 'A lesson of history', *The Organiser,* Divali Special, 11 November.
Bayly, C.A. (1985), 'The pre-history of "Communalism"? Religious conflict in India 1700-1800', *Modern Asian Studies,* Vol. 19, No. 2.

Bharatiya Jana Sangh (1973), *Party Documents, 1951-1972*, Vol. 1, New Delhi: Bharatiya Jana Sangh.

Bharti, Uma (2007), 'Sri Ram and History of Ram Sethu', *The Organiser*, Divali Special, 11 November.

Das, Indulata (2007), 'Insult of Ram is an insult to India', *The Organiser*, Divali Special, 11 November.

Gaborieau, Marc (1985), 'From Al-Beruni to Jinnah', *Anthropology Today*, Vol. 1, No. 3.

Giri, Swamy Satyamitranand (2007), 'The epitome of national unity and integrity', *The Organiser*, Divali Special, 11 November.

Goralia, Prafull (2007), 'Historicity, ASI and Ram', *The Organiser*, Divali Special, 11 November.

Graham, Bruce (1990), *Hindu Nationalism and Indian Politics: The Origins and Development of the Bharatiya Jana Sangh*, Cambridge: Cambridge University Press.

Gupta, O.P. (2007), 'Demolition threat to Ram Sethu and IPC', *The Organiser*, Divali Special, 11 November.

Jaffrelot, Christophe (1995), 'The idea of the Hindu race in the writings of Hindu nationalist ideologues in the 1920s and 1930s: a concept between two cultures', in Peter Robb (ed.), *The Concept of Race in South Asia*, Delhi: Oxford University Press, pp. 327–54.

——— (1996), *The Hindu Nationalist Movement and Indian Politics*, New York: Columbia University Press.

Khan, Benjamin (1983), *The Concept of Dharma in Valmiki Ramayana*, New Delhi: Munshiram Manoharlal.

Maclean, C.D. (1903), *Manual of the Administration of the Madras Presidency*, 3 Vols., AES, New Delhi.

Madhav, Ram (2007), 'Ram in Hindu belief: immortality is historicity', *The Organiser*, Divali Special, 11 November.

Narain, Priyanka P. (2008), 'Informal Hindu alliance starts fussing over Sethusamudram', *Mint*, 10 July.

*The Organiser*, Divali Special (2007), 11 November.

Prasad, Ravi Shankar (2007), 'Ram Setu is sacred like Ayodhya and Chitrakoot', *The Organiser*, 11 November.

Raman, Dr. S. Kalyana (2007), 'Ram Sethu: A question of security of the nation', *The Organiser*, Divali Special, 11 November.

Rath, Deepak Kumar (2008), 'Swamy's book on Ram Sethu released: Abandon Ram Sethu Project', *The Organiser*, 4 May.

Rithambara, Sadhvi (2007), 'An assault on the soul of India', *The Organiser*, Divali Special, 11 November.

Saraswati, Swami Nischalanda (2007), 'Save Ram Sethu', *The Organiser*, Divali Special, 11 November.

Sen, Gautam (2007), 'An attempt to orphan an entire civilisation by denying the wellsprings of its foundation', *The Organiser*, Divali Special, 11 November.

Swamy, Dr. Subramanian (2007), 'This is a war between Ram bhaktas and Ravan chelas', *The Organiser*, Divali Special, 11 November.

*The Economic Times* (2007), 'Massive rally against Ram Sethu Project', 31 December.

*The Hindu* (2000), 5 February.

*The Indian Express* (2008), 26 February.

Tripathi, P.S. (2004), 'A law unto itself', *Frontline*, 23 April.

Tyagi, Dinesh Chandra (2007), 'Historicity of Sri Ram and Ram Sethu not contentious', *The Organiser*, Divali Special, 11 November.

Vakil, Sunita (2007), 'UPA assaults Hindu Dharma', *The Organiser*, Divali Special, 11 November.

Van der Veer, Peter (1987), 'God must be "liberated"! A Hindu liberation movement in Ayodhya', *Modern Asian Studies*, Vol. 2, No. 1.

# Chapter 15

# The Hindu nationalist reinterpretation of pilgrimage in India the limits of *yatra* politics

*Yatra:* a journey, a procession, a pilgrimage, an expression which reflects an ancient Indian tradition that has emerged over millennia. *Yatra:* an organized and often angry politico-religious march which has an enormous potential for turning incendiary, which risks further widening the communal divide and which is invariably conducted with a cynical eye on vote-gathering and elections. No prizes for guessing which definition finds favour with the BJP and the *Sangh Parivar.*[1]

The notion of pilgrimage—*yatra* in Sanskrit and in many Indian vernacular languages—is one of the mainstays of Hinduism which has undergone substantial nationalist reinterpretations in the course of time. The newspaper editorial from which the text above is excerpted juxtaposes two versions of it which seem to be poles apart. In India today, when someone uses the word *yatra*, he may indeed refer to a religious institution, namely a pilgrimage or a procession, or to an ethno-religious demonstration of strength by some Hindu militant organizations. But these two meanings are like the two faces of the same coin, and sometimes it is not so easy to distinguish one version from the other. The traditional Hindu pilgrimage lent itself to political uses for two reasons: because of its territorial dimension which could be reinterpreted in ethno-nationalist terms in the case of pan-Indian *yatras* and because of its egalitarian quality which has affinities with the sociology of nations—even when they are based on ethno-religious criteria, nations do not admit intermediate bodies such as castes and tribes. The reinterpretation of the *yatra* by Hindu nationalists is, therefore, a good example of the reshaping of traditions by political entrepreneurs. But this instrumentalization is limited in one respect. While the Hindutva leaders have tried to exploit *yatras* for mobilizing popular support, the masses have not always taken part in *yatra* politics for the reasons they were supposed to.

## Pilgrimage as the Crucible of *Communitas* and National Space

The anthropology of pilgrimage outlined in Victor Turner's work likened such ritual to a *communitas*. In contrast to social structures organized according to categories of class, caste, tribe or any other status group, the *communitas* forms a liminal entity based on 'a directly personal egalitarian relationship' (Turner 1975: 201). Pilgrimages constitute *communitas* because they are undertaken by individuals acting of their own free will and also because they are nevertheless highly codified rituals that abide by an orthodoxy (ibid.: 177).

Pilgrimage thus defined is the archetypal *communitas*: both a collection of individuals transcending internal group status divisions and, at the same time, a binding category adhering to a particular identity. On one hand, pilgrimage 'liberates the individual from the obligatory everyday constraints of status and role, defines him as an integral human being with a capacity for free choice, and within the limits of his religious orthodoxy presents for him a living model of human brotherhood and sisterhood' (ibid.: 207); and on the other hand pilgrimage can generate,

. . . the kind of fanaticism which, in the Middle Ages, led to their Christian reformulation as Crusades and confirmed the Muslim belief in the spiritual necessity of a *jihad* or holy war, fought for custody of the pilgrimage shrines of the Holy Land. When *communitas* becomes force rather than 'grace', it becomes totalism, the subordination of the part to the whole instead of the free creation of the whole by the mutual recognition of its part. (ibid.: 206)

Beyond that, Turner gives an ideological content to the pilgrimages he has studied throughout the world. To him they are 'both instruments and indicators of a sort of mystical regionalism as well as of a mystical nationalism' (ibid.: 212).

The other reason for which pilgrimage can be a vehicle for nationalism has to do with the geographic localization usually occupied by the places visited by the faithful: they are usually in liminal areas, on the periphery of civilizational areas and they thus often delimit the territory of the ethnic nation as its ideologues define it.

## HINDU *TIRTHAS* AND THE DEMARCATION OF A SACRED SPACE

In India, the calendar of pilgrimages punctuates the life of the faithful, whether he is Hindu, Muslim, Christian, Buddhist or Jain. Some of these rituals are shared by the faithful of several confessions (Assayag 2004), but most of them have become community-specific (Morinis 1984) in the course of time because of the essentializing effect of British colonialism and the growing communal divide.

Hindus, who represent 80 per cent of the Indian population, naturally supply the largest hordes of pilgrims. In their case, places of pilgrimage are not only related to holy figures—as is the case for Muslims or Buddhists who pay visits to the tombs of Pirs or *bhoddisatvas*—but also and above all holy sites called *tirthas*. *Tirtha*, derived from the Sanskrit verb *tr/tarati*, 'to cross', refers to a ford: a *tirtha* is a holy place that provides special access to a god. Water being the prime vehicle of the sacred, the word *tirtha* also refers to a pool or bathing place (Eck 1981: 325). The typology of Hindu *tirthas* suggested by Diana Eck moreover begins with rivers such as the Ganges, Yamuna or Godavari, and places through which these waters flow, that figure among 'the greatest of India's sacred crossing' (ibid.: 334): Benares, Haridwar, Gaya, Prayag (Allahabad). Then come the mountain *tirthas*, those of the Himalayas being the most famous—Badrinath, Kedarnath, Amarnath, and so on. In the third place are the coastal *tirthas*, the foremost among which are Puri in the east, Chidambaram and Rameshvaram in the south and Dwarka and Somnath in the west. The forest *tirthas* may constitute a more heterogeneous ensemble, but the city *tirthas* are easily identifiable, because they are the seven holy cities of Hinduism where access to *moksha* (spiritual liberation) is reputedly easier: Ayodhya, Mathura, Haridwar, Benares, Kanchipuram, Ujjain and Dwarka. Lastly, the *jyotirlingam* are *tirthas* found both in the mountains and on the plains because they are stalagmites worshipped as *lingam* (phallic symbol representing Shiva). The most famous of them is in the Amarnath Cave in Kashmir to which there is an annual pilgrimage.

In addition to these *tirthas*, known throughout India, are naturally those whose influence is limited to a single province; but in that event, it is often the case that a legend or the high deeds of a mythical hero links them to 'national'—or 'civilizational'—places of pilgrimage. The network of *tirthas* thus sketches out a holy geography covering the entire space of Hindu civilization. It should be pointed out in this regard that many anthropologists see these pilgrimages as vectors integrating 'little traditions' into some 'great traditions'—to use Redfield's categories—starting with M.N. Srinivas, the father of Indian ethnology for whom 'Every great temple and pilgrim centre was a source of Sanskritisation [in other words, of emulating the great Brahmanic tradition], and the periodic festivals or other occasions when pilgrims gathered together at the centre provided opportunities for the spread of Sanskritic ideas and beliefs' (Srinivas 1967: 74).

The notion of *tirthas*, indeed, reflects a conception of space codified by the Brahmanic tradition. In the Puranas, it is written that the earth forms a disk centred on Mount Meru in the Himalayas and surrounded by a belt of mountains (the Lokaloka). Seven continents lie between the two. The southern part of the one that is closest to the centre is called Bharatvarsha, after the name of the first king, Bharat, to have ruled on this earth. This kingdom stretched from the Gulf of Bengal to the Indian Ocean, to the Arabian Sea and the Tibetan Plateau. The divinities watching over this land and its four cardinal points were said to have been 'imported' from the Lokaloka to settle in Puri to the east, Rameshwaram to the south, Dwarka to the west and Badrinath to the north. Undoubtedly, the four cardinal points are all equally represented on purpose. In the *Dharmashastra*, Bharat is described as a *karmabhoomi*, in other words the ideal ground on which to exercise rituals that enable men to affect their *karma* with the gods. As Halbfass emphasized, 'According to the sacred cosmography of Hinduism, only Bharat is fit for ritual performances and soteriological activities' (Halbfass 1990 [1981]: 177).

Logically then, the ultimate pilgrimage consists in 'encircling the universe' by touring India through Puri, Rameshwaram, Dwarka and Badrinath. Ascetics are the first to volunteer for this feat. Richard Burghart, who studied the renouncers of the Ramanandi order, notes that 'Renouncers frequently state to one another that it is their solemn vow to visit all four quarters (*dham*) at least once in their lifetime' (Burghart 1983: 371). In practice, in the course of the eight months of the year that their journey lasts (the monsoon months being very inauspicious for travel), most of them settle for going to Benares, Hariharkshetra (at the confluence of the Ganges and the Gandaki), Janakpur (where Ram and Sita married) in Nepal, and the Ganges Delta and Bengal before staying in Ayodhya for the rainy season. But Diana Eck points out that (i) beyond this already very long journey, 'The circumambulation of the land of Bharat includes the ... seacoast *tirthas*' (Eck 1981: 335) and that (ii) before taking rest in Benares 'Pilgrims have circumambulated the whole of India, visiting hundreds of *tirthas* along the way, bringing water from the Ganga [Ganges] in the north to sprinkle the *lingam* of Rameshwaram in the far south and returning north with sands from Rameshwaram to deposit in the riverbed of the Ganga' (ibid.: 334).

Hindu pilgrimages thus meet an important criterion of Victor Turner's model which holds that, since holy places are on the periphery of the sacred domain, the routes followed by the faithful enable them to embrace the entire sacred space. It also corroborates Turner's theory likening these rituals to *communitas*.

The pilgrimage of Pandharpur (Maharashtra) where, twice a year, thousands of Hindus come to worship the god Vithoba (a form of Vishnu) is a case in point. The bank of the river where the pilgrims establish their camp at the end of their journey is known as 'walwanti ekata', the 'sand of unity'[2] because people mix freely, irrespective of caste. Professor Karve, who gave a very comprehensive account of this pilgrimage in the 1960s, suggests that, on the road, women tend to forget about their status to the point of having lunch together, be they Brahman—like her—or of the Maratha caste (a dominant peasant caste considered less pure than the upper castes) (Karve 1962: 19). Karve emphasizes the happiness that radiates from the pilgrims despite the fatigue and suffering endured during the journey—particularly due to fasting—to such an extent that she describes them as being 'intoxicated with happiness' (Karve 1988: 159), a feeling conducive to the formation of *communitas*, a group in the process of bonding.[3]

Pandharpur also corroborates Turner's interpretation with regard to the sacred geography of pilgrimage. The town is located at the southern limit of Marathi-speaking territory. It is thus on the periphery of the territorial and cultural unit that it defines, as are most places of pilgrimage. And twenty different pilgrimage routes converge towards Pandharpur, each leaving from a holy place associated with a poet of Maharashtra reputed for his high spiritual deeds. As Courtright points out, these 'religious traditions have contributed immeasurably to the Maharashtrian sense of cultural unity' (Courtright 1985: 204).[4]

Other studies instruct us about how *communitas* are formed in the course of pilgrimage, and particularly the conditions in which individuals emerge in their own right and aggregate within a new moral community. Louis Dumont's analysis according to which, in Hinduism, individuals could only be 'outside of the world' (1966: 324–50), applies here because of the asceticism to which the faithful are bound. The Aiyappan pilgrimage in Kerala, for instance, requires that 41 days before departure the faithful refrain from sexual intercourse, observe a vegetarian diet and sleep on the ground. Through this asceticism, 'the pilgrim begins to be weaned away from society' (Daniel 1984: 247), explains Valentine Daniel who participated in the pilgrimage. The trek itself is one of the most difficult because the pilgrims go barefoot on a forced march to optimize their merits—but they hum religious chants that add to their fervour. Although this display of asceticism is not to the taste of Brahmans who generally remain on the sidelines of pilgrimage, it is conducive to the development of a genuine sense of fraternity among men from different castes, upper and lower.

The preparation phase for the Aiyappan pilgrimage, in particular, involves practising brotherhood, as Lars Kjaerholm, who followed this phase in a Tamil Nadu village, points out: pilgrims 'must treat each other as social equals . . . Psychologically what happens is an effort to efface the usual social identities, and an attempt to merge them with the divine identity' (Kjaerholm 1986: 132). On their return, pilgrims seem to be transformed by the experience of collective fervour: 'They all appeared to be immensely happy with the trip they had made. The joy of expectation had now become transformed into uninhibited joy . . .' (ibid.: 136).

Maharashtrian pilgrimages to worship Vithoba and Keralite pilgrimages to worship Aiyappa still remain regional rituals. But in Hinduism there are of course many 'national' pilgrimages that crisscross all of India. The best known are naturally those that lead to the holy places located on the edges of the subcontinent. Ann Gold studied from within a group of Rajasthani pilgrims who decided to go to Puri on the Orissa coast. This pilgrimage also displays features of a *communitas*. Among 63 participants, about a dozen were from the Brahman caste, the rest of the troop being peasants from various castes. The journey to Puri—which lasts about ten days—was marked by intense group fervour and once they arrived at the Indian Ocean, in Puri, the faithful bathed 'with remarkable abandon and togetherness' (Gold 1988). On the way, the pilgrims stopped at Gaya to scatter into a tributary of the Ganges the ashes of relatives for whom they hoped thus to improve the chances of salvation. On the way back, they stopped at Haridwar, the place where the Ganges leaves the mountains and enters the plains, where they bought bottles of river water. Once back home, they drank this water during a final ritual, the Celebration of the Ganges, an indication that the essential aim of the pilgrimage that they had just accomplished was to make a tour of this most sacred river. But instead of doing such a tour on foot like their ancestors, they did it by bus, in 30 days, stopping at high tourist spots such as Agra.

From the monographs discussed earlier, it emerges that not only do Hindu *tirthas* mark out a sacred geography delimiting a civilization, but also that the groups of pilgrims taking part in them form a *communitas* in Turner's sense. This second feature is explained by the very nature of *tirthas* which, as Eck points out, are places open to all, including 'to Shudras, outcastes and women, who are excluded from Brahmanical rites' (Eck 1981: 338);[5] but more importantly, it has to do with the sociological alchemy of pilgrimage that manages to emancipate the individual from the status that the social structure assigns him, elevating him to the position of a person[6] after a detour via ascetic values: the rules of pilgrimage require of the pilgrim the discipline of an ascetic, so much so that 'The lay pilgrim becomes a *sannyasin* [an ascetic] of sorts, leaving the household behind and taking up the privations and hardships of the road' (Eck 1981: 340). This is because the pilgrim, like the ascetic, is moved by one single aim: the quest for salvation.[7] On the way, 'each person, whatever his language, his country, his caste, is there for himself, in a private, individual capacity, not as a rightful member of any group. The individual is in the universal and asserts himself there, quite simply, as a Hindu, over and above the particularity of sociological determinations' (Herrenschmidt 1989: 145). Having become an ascetic for the time this ritual lasts, the pilgrim achieves the status of an individual whose behaviour no longer depends on the orthopraxy of caste but on his relationship either to a guru[8] and/or the group of which he is a part. For taking a detour via the condition of an ascetic, the pilgrim is able to join a new community, Turner's *communitas*. But this socio-psychological construct is fleeting: it does not last longer than the ritual itself.

An increasing number of Hindus partake of this social and religious phenomenon that is pilgrimage. As Chris Fuller observes, 'Pilgrimage has always been a vital part of Hinduism, but never more so than in the modern era as ever-increasing numbers of pilgrims set out on longer and longer journeys' (Fuller 1992: 204). This evolution of course has to do with the modernization of means of communication that, in less than half a century, have made pilgrimages easier. In the early twentieth century, as M.N. Srinivas noted in his study of the village of Rampur in Karnataka, making a pilgrimage to Benares was a privilege reserved for a handful of inhabitants. Fifty years later, the same thing has become extremely common, and long sightseeing stops are scheduled along the way for all pilgrimages to the holy places of the north. This popular dimension of pan-Indian pilgrimages made this ritual institution even more attractive to the Hindu nationalists who had already tried to use religious processions. In fact they have attempted to utilize both dimensions of pilgrimage, its *communitas* features and its territorial symbolism.

## Hindu Nationalism and the Politics of *Yatra*

The codification of Hindu nationalism goes back to the 1920s, and more precisely to the publication of an ideological charter entitled *Hindutva: Who is a Hindu?* by

Veer Savarkar in 1923.[9] In it, the author presents Hindus as forming a nation in and of themselves by the fact of their ethnic heritage (they descend from the first Aryans), their religious culture, their language Sanskrit—and also the sacred land (*punyabhoomi*) they inhabit. For Savarkar, a Hindu is first of all someone who is born in the area lying between the Indus River, the Indian Ocean and the Himalayas, an area 'so strongly entrenched that no other country in the world is so perfectly designed by the fingers of nature as a geographical unit' (Savarkar 1969: 82). Paradoxically, the ethnic nationalism that Hindutva embodies thus places considerable emphasis on territory. But there is no real contradiction therein because this regard for space does not refer to any sort of *jus soli*, but rather reflects the importance of the land in what remains a closed conception of political identity.[10]

The extremely strong emphasis on Hindu territory is again found in the RSS which set itself the aim of reforming (and strengthening) the Hindu community— 70 per cent of Indian society at the time—to enable it to resist the Muslims—24 per cent—by developing a network of local cells (*shakhas*) the members of which have met, over the past 80 years, every evening or every morning, theoretically irrespective of caste, for ideological and physical training sessions. The prayer at a time when the Hindu nationalist movement was increasingly divided between its political party, the Bharatiya Janata Party (BJP), which tried to project a moderate brand of Hindu politics—and the RSS, which promoted an undiluted version of Hindutva. *Yatra* politics became part of the latter's strategy.

The RSS offshoot that implemented it was the Vishva Hindu Parishad (VHP), which had been created to federate the various sects of Hinduism and that the RSS entrusted with creating a new nationalist dynamic in the early 1980s, including in the political field. The VHP's strategy was intended to solicit a 'Hindu vote' that should force the parties—starting with the BJP—to take this community into account.

This strategy relied on the manipulation of religious symbols. The VHP was better armed than any other to do so, given the many *mahants* (priests) and sadhus or *sannyasins* (ascetics) that it counted among its ranks, be they modern gurus having created their own ashram or heirs of historic and prestigious *sampradayas* (these spiritual currents claim to descend from a founding guru sometimes dating back to Indian antiquity). In 1983, the VHP inaugurated a new type of pilgrimage, the *Ekatmata yatra*, which started from three high places of Hindu civilization: the northern cortege went from Kathmandu to Rameshwaram in Tamil Nadu in the south, the eastern cortege went from Gangasagar in Bengal to Somnath in Gujarat in the west, and the northwestern cortege went from Haridwar to Kanyakumari again in Tamil Nadu. These columns were joined on the way by 69 other, purely regional, corteges before converging on Nagpur, the birthplace and headquarters of the RSS, as well as the geographic centre of India, and then going on their way.[11] The main architect of the *Ekatmata yatra* was the Joint General Secretary of the VHP, Acharya Giriraj Kishore, whose trajectory exemplifies the key role of the RSS cadres in keeping the *Sangh Parivar* (the nebula of the RSS offshoots) together. A *pracharak* since 1943, he had been appointed secretary of the ABVP (the student wing of the RSS in 1960) and then of the Rajasthan unit of the Jana Sangh—the ancestor of the BJP—in 1971, before joining the VHP.[12]

For the promoters of the *Ekatmata yatra*, this 'pilgrimage' epitomized the necessary mixing of populations of India that was seen as the best possible way to strengthen the country's unity. It pursued the metaphor on a daily basis because each cortege distributed water from the Ganges (at ten rupees for a half-litre) and at the same time got fresh supplies from the rivers that it crossed and the temple basins it flowed along on the way in order to manifest the blending of the waters of India and their fundamental unity. This symbolism met with considerable resonance given the great significance of the water from the Ganges and water in general for Hindus.

Goddess Ganga Mata—Mother Ganges—was in fact represented in her usual form of a mother goddess, and was carried on a palanquin. The VHP thus reinserted processional features into the context of a pilgrimage, borrowing some of its elements—such as the central role of water—from traditional rituals. For the planners of the *Ekatmata yatra*, the issue was thus to instrumentalize Hindu symbols and practices for purposes of nationalist mobilization. They made no secret of their intentions, as attests the presentation of their 'programme' published in the RSS' weekly, *The Organiser:*

When the yatras reach their destination at Rameshwaram and Somnath, the *khumba* [jars] will contain water from all the sacred places, namely the four *Dhams* [Badrinath, Puri, Rameshwaram and Dwarka], the twelve *jyotirlingam* . . . and hundreds of sacred rivers lakes and wells. (*The Organiser*, 23 October 1983: 15)

The commentary of VHP Secretary-General, H.V. Seshadri, was, in a way, even more explicit:

The countless spots of pilgrimages, temples and ashram, which have been now looked upon mainly as symbols of our *Punya Bhoomi*—a holy land—have now acquired a new and vital emphasis: they are symbols of a common *Matri Bhoomi* [motherland] as well. (ibid., 15 January 1984: 7)

The VHP achieved its objective beyond all hopes because the *yatra* took on the dimension of a nationwide mass demonstration. According to its figures, 312 corteges instead of the 90 initially planned joined the movement and 4,323 meetings instead of the 1,800 planned were organized. In all, 531 of the 534 districts in the country were affected (ibid., 12 February 1984: 6). Thousands of bottles of water from the Ganges and images of the *Bharat Mata* were sold along the way.[13] The Hindu nationalists apparently played successfully on the religious heartstrings of the faithful. The *Ekatmata yatra* inaugurated a new brand of ethno-religious engineering likely to become more and more political over the course of time.

## THE 1990 *RATH YATRA*: A NATIONAL PILGRIMAGE

The *yatras* that followed, indeed, stood out by their increasingly explicit ideological tone. The one held in 1990, the *Rath yatra*, in this regard performed a transition. Its aim was political. L.K. Advani, the president of the BJP, stated on 12 September that he would undertake this *yatra* between 25 of that month and 30 October to 'mobilise public opinion' (*About Us* [BJP bulletin], Vol. 7). But its form was religious: the term *Rath yatra* in the Hindu religion generically refers to processions with chariots (*Rath*) that punctuate the life of all sacred places. Unlike the *Ekatmata yatra*, the *Rath yatra* had only one main cortege that was supposed to cover the 10,000 km between the two high places of Hinduism, Somnath (Gujarat)—an already very politically connoted *tirtha*[14]—and Ayodhya (Uttar Pradesh). The cortege regalia also strove to exhibit religiosity, the *Rath* being escorted by activists dressed as Hanuman and women performing the dances of the *gopis* (cowherds that accompany the god Krishna, a major divinity of Vishnuism), all of this taking place in a highly charged atmosphere amid religious songs and slogans chanted in unison. The 'pilgrims' were few, given the small number of those passage on the roadside and took part in the meetings held at its halting places were involved in the same collective fervour.

Mixing religion and politics, Advani, the man in the *Rath*—a Toyota converted into an epic chariot—pursued two Hindu nationalist aims through this mass mobilization. First, the final destination, Ayodhya, had become the symbol of the majority community's humiliation 'under the yoke' of the Muslim minority. Second, he aspired to unify all the Hindus in a context of increased divisions. In August 1990, Prime Minister V.P. Singh had announced the introduction of a 27 per cent quota in the state commission, a decision that had fostered resentment among the upper castes and even unprecedented inter-caste tensions. Mobilizing Hindus around the Ayodhya issue by using the *Rath yatra* was first of all supposed to enable the BJP to reunite the Hindus, its potential electorate, against the Muslim Other. As it was, the *Rath yatra* was marred by numerous communal riots which were triggered by Hindu nationists (Jaffrelot 1998).

The *Rath yatra* was one of the greatest mass movements in independent India, so much so that its organizers even compared it to Mahatma Gandhi's Salt March. In Gujarat, the *Rath yatra* went through 600 villagers and some 50 rallies were held, some of them displaying excessive activism. In Ahmedabad, for instance, a young Hindu nationalist placed a *tilak* (religious mark indicating what sect the devotee belongs to) on Advani's forehead made of his own blood, and in Jetpur (Rajkot district), hundreds of others gave him a jar full of their blood as a sign of sacrifice to the Cause. These blood offerings transpose into a Hindu context a Shia practice used in the Moharram ritual. Therein is an additional example of the way the Hindu nationlists end up imitating the Other, the one they stigmatize the most, all the better to rival him.[15]

In Maharashtra, the frenzy was all the greater since Advani held a rally alongside Bal Thackeray, the leader of Shiv Sena, a Hindu nationalist party with local roots and a radical discourse. He then went to Hyderabad, the capital of Andhra Pradesh, an indication that the movement intended to penetrate into the south where it had little footing. From there the caravan went up to Madhya Pradesh, one of the most rural states in India where peasant mobilization was reported by the local press in terms that betray their surprise:

Massive crowds turned up at all the places including hamlets and villages to give a warm and vociferous welcome to the Rath Yatra. The people defied the torrential rains and eagerly awaited the arrival of Advani. On both sides of the road thick crowds were standing cheering the Yatra. Many people had come with Trishul [tridents, symbol of Shiva indicating a form of activism that borders on aggressivity] and reverentially bowed before the Yatra. Slogans were raised expressing their full support to the building of the Ram temple. (*National Mail*, (Bhopal), 8 October 1990)

One of the slogans invented by the crafters of this movement had particular resonance: 'Say with pride that we are Hindus!' (Garv se kaho, ham Hindu hein!). In Rajasthan, where the caravan next went, a new slogan appeared: 'Advani, you drive us! We're with you. Begin the building of the temple! We are your hands'.

Little by little, special envoys for the national press even began to gauge the scope of popular mobilization. Sent to Haryana, a state neighbouring Delhi, the correspondent of *The Indian Express* reported in one of his articles:

At every village all along its route . . . crowds ranging from hundreds to thousands turned out to see him. In the towns they clambered on to roofs to catch a glimpse of the bespectacled man on the 'Rath'. In villages they perched on trees, conches blew and brightly decked women performed repeated 'arti' [ritual accomplished with a lamp]. (*The Indian Express*, 14 October 1990)

Advani never arrived at Ayodhya, for on 23 October 1990, Prime Minister V.P. Singh authorized the head of the Bihar government, Laloo Prasad Yadav, a lower caste leader who had campaigned in favour of quotas, to arrest him when he crossed the border to enter the neighbouring state of Uttar Pradesh. This decision reinforced the determination of many activists. Some approximately 40,000 of them—made it to Ayodhya despite the police barricades. They stormed the mosque, prompting law-enforcement agents to severe repression that left about 30 dead.

The martyrs' ashes were carried in procession throughout India during an *Asthi Kalash yatra* (pilgrimage of ashes and bones) that was punctuated by many riots. At the same time, Rajmohan Gandhi, grandson of the Mahatma, organized a *Sadhbhavana yatra*, or pilgrimage for harmony among religious communities. *Yatras* were becoming a permanent element in the Indian political landscape.

The BJP has tried to cash in on the success of the *Rath yatra* to make, *yatra* politics a permanent feature of its strategy. Advani's successor as BJP president, Murli Manohar Joshi, organized in 1991 an *Ekta yatra*, 15,000 km long from Kanyakumari (at the southern tip of India) to Srinagar where he raised the Indian flag to demonstrate Kashmir's attachment to *Bharat Mata* (Mother India). Then the *Janadesh yatra* took four top leaders of the party from Mysore, Porbandar, Calcutta and Jammu to Bhopal in 1993. Three years later, Advani's *Suraj Rath yatra* crossed India for 35 days. The following year his *Rashtra Bhakti ki Teerth yatra* lasted two months. Finally, the *Suraksha yatra* was organized in early 2006, again by Advani, to protest against the government's powerlessness in the face of Jehadists' attacks. The religious features in which *yatra* politics was previously cloaked gradually eroded away.

None of these *yatras* was as successful as the *Ekatmata yatra* and the *Rath yatra*. This decline in popularity may be attributed to a certain fatigue vis-à-vis an overworked formula. But it also had something to do with the religious overtone of the two most popular *yatras* so far, in a context, that is true, dominated by anti-Muslim resentment and the anti-Mandal agitation. Certainly, the Hindutva forces had been able to recast an old institution—the pilgrimage—in a more attractive way when religious symbols were at stake. Yet, one must not exaggerate the impact of such an instrumentalization either.

## The Limits of Instrumentalization

Hindu nationalist leaders have developed a strategy of political pilgrimage to mobilize the masses behind them by manipulating religious symbols that carry a strong emotional potential. They do not make any mystery of it and even look at this strategy as being as old as India. Narrating Advani's 'Patriotic Pilgrimage', one of his lieutenants, Sudheendra Kulkarni, makes it clear:

For the common folk, *yatra* was a religious obligation through which they *unconsciously* became aware of the bond that held them together. For the spiritual seers, social reformers and often, progressive political leaders, it was a *conscious* medium of people's education and mobilization. (Kulkarni 2004: 19-20; italics as in the original)

According to Kulkarni, *yatra* politics was a deliberate attempt at creating nationalist sentiments in the people by manipulating religious feelings.

In the course of fieldwork I did in 1990 in northern India I noticed that many villagers had joined the *Rath yatra* in order to participate in building the temple to Ram, in the *karseva*. Interviews I conducted in 1991 in the village of Piparsod in Madhya Pradesh, which I had already visited three times over the preceding years, allowed me to confirm that peasants from the lower castes (including Untouchables) and Brahmans had joined the *Rath yatra* 'for Bhagwan Ram' (Lord Ram). One of the lower caste peasants who had done so for this reason had participated *mandir ke nirman ke lye* (in order to build the temple), whereas he did not even vote for the BJP. In the nearby town, Shivpuri, one of the VHP cadres exhibited a stone from the Babri Masjid that he called *prasad* (leftover of the sacred food offered to god) in front of fascinated sympathizers.

Alongside these 'devotees', many Hindus participated in the *Rath yatra* out of a taste for adventure and out of a desire for social recognition, to defy the authorities and accomplish a sacred—and therefore prestigious—exploit by the religious nature of this undertaking. The case of women is especially interesting. The Indian press has, in retrospect, underscored the massive participation of women in the *Ekatmata yatra* (*The Organiser*, 27 November 1983: 13) and the *Rath yatra* [*The Statesman* (Delhi), 18 and 19 May 1991]. Journalists have systematically attributed it to the religiosity of Hindu women who, certainly, are still the custodians of tradition in India. This interpretation is probably valid to a great extent. But one should not neglect the a-religious and nevertheless deep motivations of some of the women who took part in the *Rath yatra*. To many of them, this event provided a unique occasion to act in a public space to which Hindu women generally do not have access (Gold 1988: 304). While Hindu women are generally confined to the domestic sphere, this time they could legitimately take to the street, using as an argument the sacred nature of the focus of the procession-like demonstration, Ram. They could thereby gain an unprecedented slice of freedom, especially when they were members of one of the organizations that the Hindu nationalists had created to mobilize women. As early as 1936, the RSS had founded a woman's branch the Rashtra Sevika Samiti, whose conservative ethos primarily promoted women's role as the pillar of the traditional joint family. In the 1980s, the VHP also created a women's wing which aimed to attract young Hindu women, the *Durga Vahini*, the Durga Brigades, from the name of the goddess Durga, the goddess of destruction often represented with a necklace of skulls, tongue hanging, crimson, bloodied weapons in hand and riding a tiger. These *Durga Vahini* recruited young Hindu women who harboured some taste for action. The movement's members moreover underwent training in martial arts and could even be versed in the use of firearms on the pretence of self-defence training (against possible attackers, naturally Muslims).

According to Tanika Sarkar, the Hindu nationalist movement, while continuing to promote women's maternal role, also offers them other channels of expression and real means of emancipation. It 'does enable a specific and socially crucial group of middle class women in moving out of their homebound existence, to reclaim public spaces and even to acquire a political identity and gives them access to serious intellectual cogitation' (Sarkar 1993: 24).

Taking a more specific interest in the activist youth from the urban middle class to which Sarkar refers here, Paola Bacchetta goes further, drawing on a field study conducted in Ahmedabad (Gujarat). The young woman she describes in detail in a well known article 'was attempting to create for herself a new structural position to occupy: that of a perpetually single but tough and respected woman who would impose herself in the public space without definite sexual, gender, or (Indian) regional connotations' (Bacchetta 1993: 43). The impact of the Hindu nationalist movement on the women of the majority community was naturally amplified by the action of some of this movement's leaders. Two sadhvi (women ascetics), Sadhvi Rithambara and Uma Bharti, disciples of famous gurus and wearing the saffron robe, were ardent champions of the agitation in the 1980s and 1990s in favour of the Ayodhya Temple. For Amrita Basu,

It may be liberating for women, who are continuously enjoined to be decorous, to be praised for their good citizenship when they deliver loud, angry and coarse public speeches . . . [T]heir use of vulgar expression and their ability to' address men with familiarity and condescension transgress traditional gender roles and expresses both their anger and their power. (Basu 1993: 29)

In such a context, the *Rath yatra* acted as a catalyst. It was easy for Hindu women to mobilize and gather on the roadside as a cortege went by or at the foot of the tribunes meeting after meeting. There they found a space of liberty and developed a new sociability. And to prove that all that was possible thanks to Ram, the sacred aim of the movement, they made it a point of honour to offer their *mangalsutra* to L.K. Advani.[16] Beyond that, the *Rath yatra* was the opportunity to give unprecedented praise for the audacity shown by women implicated in the Hindu nationalist movement. Thus the movement's leaders celebrated the escape of Uma Bharti, placed under house arrest after she had attempted to break through the barricades blocking access to the roads of Ayodhya.[17] Some women used this new margin for manoeuvre by emulating such heroic achievements. In Madhya Pradesh, the VHP leader told anyone who would listen that on the way to Ayodhya he had met a group of female villagers aged 35 to 40 who had asked him with much determination the way to *parikrama*, literally the 'circumambulation' by which the Ayodhya pilgrimage ends every year. Moonje gave it to them. A few days later, he saw them again, having turned back. They then told him that they had come under fire from the police guarding the Babri Masjid and helped those who had been wounded. And now, he said to conclude his story, they were returning home to take care of their children.[18] One of the women who had gone to Ayodhya for the *karseva* was decorated by the BJP government in Madhya Pradesh for her bravery [*Dainik Jagaran* (Hindi), 16 November 1990: 10].

If so many women took part in the *Rath yatra* and some of them even in the final assault against the Babri Masjid, they sometimes mobilized for reasons other than merely worshiping Ram—to gain a certain autonomy. But this use of pilgrimage was only possible due to the quality of *communitas* attached to the Hindu pilgrimage. This feature translates not only through the erasure of caste distinctions, but also by the erosion of gender-related statuses. More precisely, women are justified in participating in this public activity that is pilgrimage because in these circumstances they enjoy religious legitimacy. Owen Lynch thus notes that at the pilgrimage to Mathura,[19] Krishna's birthplace, 'Women often come without male relatives to chaperone them' (1988: 174). The traditional pilgrimage offered a certain space of relative liberty for women, and the Hindu nationalist *yatras* attracted some of them not only for their religious content and their political message, but for personal motivations.

The attitude of the Shiv Sena women of Bombay can be analysed in the same way. As Atreyee Sen convincingly argues, 'poor women in the slums of Mumbai who supported the political right were not Hindu fundamentalist women passively mobilised by a party into the ascendant nationalist wave' (2007: 41); they had their 'own rationale for supporting the pan-Indian cause of Hindutva, which was related to their growing aspiration to maintain links with rural women [those of their family with whom they did not have much left in common except religion], legitimize female militancy in their localities and carve out a visible public role for women' (ibid.: 23). They asserted themselves in this manner at the time of the Ayodhya Movement, like the *Durga Vahini* volunteers.

The mobilizing potential of Hindu nationalist *yatras* such as the *Ekatmata yatra* and the *Rath yatra* can first be explained by the affinities these political events have with traditional pilgrimages, bearing out the essential criteria of Turner's model: Hindu pilgrimage defines a sacred space that is also a civilizational area and those who partake in them form a *communitas*, within which differences in social status are blurred for a certain, limited time, to make way for solidarity among individuals. These two features clearly lend themselves to a Hindu nationalist usage. By characterizing Indian territory on the basis of Hindu *tirthas*, the Hindu nationalists put forth an ethnic definition of the nation at odds with the universalistic doctrine enshrined in India's Constitution. Inventing a form of Hindu individualism by bringing together pilgrims having shed intermediary bodies such as caste, an impediment to the birth of a 'Hindu Rashtra', supplies the heralds of the Hindutva with the raw material that enables them to build the sort of nation they aspire to, all the more so since the pilgrims on their *yatras*, like those who participate in traditional pilgrimages and processions, are driven by a particular fervour that recalls the radicalism mentioned by Turner with regard to the Crusades and the Jehad: grace can change into violence, and Hindu corteges have certainly been the preferred vehicles for communal riots.

Although Hindu nationalists have sought to use features of pilgrimage that could help them get people out in the street, the analysis should not stick to this strictly instrumentalist interpretation, for citizens do not always shift into action for the same reasons for which instigators seek to mobilize them. In the case at hand, participants in the *Ekatmata yatra* and the *Rath yatra* took part for reasons other than those contemplated by the organizers. Some women, in particular, were there not by virtue of any religious or ideological sentiment, but to seize the occasion to appear for ostensibly legitimate reasons in a public space from which they are often banned. The autonomy of these 'subalterns' partly explains that once the Hindu nationalist *yatras* took on an increasingly open secular dimension, they ceased to attract masses of citizens.

## Notes

1. 'Chariot of fire', editorial in *The Hindu*, 23 August 2002.
2. I am most grateful to Hema Rairkar for this information.
3. Guy Deleury's account regarding the same pilgrimage bears out this interpretation (1960: 103).
4. See also Feldhaus (2003).

5. Eck fittingly adds: 'Although in practice the egalitarianism one finds in the text has not invariably been upheld, it remains the ideal of the *Dharmashastra* tradition' (Ibid.: 339).

6. It should moreover be pointed out that at major pilgrimage sites, the faithful have their name—a mark of individuality if there is one—recorded in huge ledgers so that their merits can be recognized (Bharati 1963: 138).

7. Such quest can take various forms. The purpose of the pilgrimage to Benares, for instance, is primarily to expiate one's sins (Parry 1981: 345).

8. Peter Van der Veer's study on the Ayodhya pilgrimage is very instructive here. The author points out that such activity 'depends on a network of *guru-disciple* relations, which are not based upon caste-distinctions, but on free, personal choice' (Van der Veer 1984: 65).

9. I have studied the genesis of Hindu nationalism in the first chapter of Jaffrelot (1996).

10. For more details on this point, see Jaffrelot (2004).

11. Olivier Herrenschmidt (1989) has aptly shown that Brahmans and Untouchables never take part in a procession together: one or the other is always missing and so there are only 'partial totalisations'.

12. Interview with Acharya Giriraj Kishore, 11 February 1994, New Delhi.

13. Along the road from Kathmandu to Rameshwaram alone, 6,000 representations of *Bharat Mata* and 70,000 bottles of water were sold (*Dharma Marg,* October 1984: 40).

14. The Somnath Temple had been sacked and destroyed by Muslim invaders during the Muslim era before being restored by the Indian government on the initiative of Deputy Prime Minister Vallabhbhai Patel in a spirit of Hindu activism. In 1951, the President of the Indian republic, Rajendra Prasad, another Hindu traditionalist, had placed a *jyotirlingam* in the sacrosanct heart of the temple.

15. On this strategy of stigmatizing and imitating the Other, see Chapter 1 of Jaffrelot (1996).

16. The *mangalsutra* is the necklace Hindu women receive as part of the marriage ceremony.

17. Uma Bharti's partisans pointed out that her cutting her hair better to go unnoticed was further proof of her determination (Datta 1991: 62).

18. Interview with M. Moonje, 12 October 1991, in Bhopal.

19. The *caurasi kos parikrama* is a circumambulation of Braj, an area around Agra, Mathura and Vrindavan.

# References

Assayag, Jackie (1998), 'Ritual action or political reaction? The invention of Hindu Nationalist processions in India during the 1980s', *South Asia Research,* Vol. 18, No. 2, pp. 125–46.

——— (2004), *At the Confluence of Two Rivers: Muslims and Hindus in South India,* Delhi: Manohar.

Bacchetta, Paola (1993), 'All our goddesses are armed: religion, resistance and revenge in the life of a militant Hindu nationalist woman', *Bulletin of Concerned Asian Scholars*, Vol. 25, No. 4, pp. 38–51.

Basu, Amrita (1993), 'Feminism inverted: the real women and gendered imagery of Hindu nationalism', *Bulletin of Concerned Asian Scholars*, Vol. 25, No. 4, pp. 25–36.

Bharati, Agehananda (1963), 'Pilgrimage in the Indian tradition', *History of Religion*, Vol. 3, No. 1, pp. 135–67.

Burghart, Richard (1983), 'Wandering ascetics of the Ramanandi sect', *History of Religions*, Vol. 22, No. 4, pp. 361–80.

Courtright, Paul (1985), *Ganesha: Lord of Obstacles, Lord of Beginnings*, New York: Oxford University Press.

Daniel, Valentine (1984), *Fluid Signs: being a Person the Tamil Way*, Berkeley: California University Press.

Datta, P.K. (1991), 'VHP's Ram', *Economic and Political Weekly*, 2 November 1991, pp. 2517–26.

Deleury, Guy (1960), *The Cult of Vithoba*, Poona: Sangam Press.

Dumont, Louis (1966), 'Le renoncement dans les religions de l'Inde', Appendix B *Homo hierarchicus, Le système des castes et ses implications*, Paris: Gallimard, pp. 324–50.

Eck, Diana L. (1981), 'India's *Tirthas*: "Crossing" in Sacred Geography', *History of Religions*, Vol. 20, No. 3, pp. 323–44.

Feldhaus, Anne (2003), *Connected Places: Region, Pilgrimage, and Geographical Imagination in Maharashtra*, New York: Palgrave Macmillan.

Fuller, C. (1992), *The Camphore Flame*, Princeton, NJ: Princeton University Press.

Gold, Ann (1988), *Fruitful Journeys: The Ways of Rajasthani Pilgrims*, Los Angeles/Berkeley: University of California Press.

Halbfass, Wilhelm (1990 [1981]), *India and Europe: An Essay in Philosophical Understanding*, Delhi: Motilal Banarsidass.

Herrenschmidt, Olivier (1989), *Les meilleurs dieux sont hindous*, Lausanne: L'âge d'homme.

Jaffrelot, Christophe (1996), *The Hindu Nationalist Movement in India*, New York: Columbia University Press.

——— (1998), 'The politics of processions and Hindu-Muslim riots', in A. Basu and A. Kohli (eds.), *Community Conflict and the State in India*, Delhi: Oxford University Press, pp. 58–92.

——— (2004), 'From Indian territory to Hindu Bhoomi: the Ethnicization of Nation-State Mapping in India', in John Zavos, Andrew Wyatt and Vernon Hewitt (eds.), *The Politics of Cultural Mobilization in India*, Oxford/New York: Oxford University Press, pp. 197–215.

Karve, I. (1962), 'On the road: a Maharashtrian pilgrimage', *The Journal of Asian Studies*, Vol. 22, November, pp. 13–29.

——— (1988), 'On the road: a Maharashtrian pilgrimage', in E. Zelliot and M. Bersten (eds.), *The Experience of Hinduism: Essays on Religion in Maharashtra*, Albany: State University of New York, pp. 142–73.

Kaur, Raminder (2004), 'Fire in the Belly: the political mobilization of the Ganapati festival in Maharashtra', in John Zavos, Andrew Wyatt and Vernon Hewitt (eds.), *The Politics* of *Cultural Mobilization in India*, Oxford/New York: Oxford University Press, pp. 37–70.

Kjaerholm, L. (1986), 'Myth, pilgrimage and fascination in the Aiyappa Cult', in A. Parpola and B.S. Hansen (eds.), *South Asian Religion and Society*, London: Curzon, pp. 121–61.

Kulkarni, S. (2004), *Lal Krishna Advani's Patriotic Pilgrimage*, New Delhi: Ocean Books.

Lynch, Owen M. (1988), 'Pilgrimage with Krishna, sovereign of the emotions', *Contributions to Indian Sociology*, Vol. 22, No. 2, pp. 337–65.

Morinis, Alan E. (1984), *Pilgrimage in the Hindu Tradition*, Delhi: Oxford University Press.

Parry, Jonathan P. (1981), 'Death and cosmogony in Kashi', *Contributions to Indian Sociology*, Vol. 15, Nos. 1-2, pp. 171–94.

Sarkar, Tanika (1993), 'Women agency within authoritarian communalism: the Rashtrasevika samiti and Ramjanmabhoomi', in G. Pandey (ed.), *Hindus and Others*, Delhi: Viking, pp. 24-45.

Savarkar, Vinayak Damodar (1969 [1923]), *Hindutva: Who is a Hindu?*, Bombay: S.S. Savarkar.

Sen, Atreyee (2007), *Shiv Sena Women*, London: Hurst.

Sharma, J.K. (1993), *Punyabhoomi Bharat (Introduction to map of the sacred land Bharat)*, New Delhi: Keshav Kunj.

Srinivas, M.N. (1967), 'The cohesive role of Sanskritisation', in P. Mason (ed.), *India and Ceylon: Unity and Diversity*, London: Oxford University Press, pp. 67–82.

Turner, Victor (1975), 'Pilgrimages as social processes', in V. Turner (ed.) *Dramas, Fields, and Metaphors: Symbolic Action in Human Society*, Ithaca and London: Cornell University Press, pp. 166–230.

Van der Veer, Peter (1984), 'Structure and anti-structure in Hindu pilgrimage to Ayodhya', in Kenneth Ballhatchet and David Taylor (eds), *Changing South Asia: Religion and Society*, Hong Kong: Asian Research Service/School of Oriental and African Studies, p. 59.

# III

---

## Communal Violence

# The politics of processions and Hindu-Muslim riots

Why should we not be able to convert large religious festivals into political mass rallies? Would it not be possible for the political activities to in this way penetrate the most humble village?

– editorial of the *Kesari* in 1896, cited in Cashman 1975: 79

The series of communal riots which broke out in the late 1980s and early 1990s amidst the Ayodhya controversy were, judged by the number of casualties, the worst since Partition. Many of these explosions of violence originated in Hindu processions. The fact that religious processions could be a vector of tension and even violence between communities is not new. In his essay on the prehistory of communalism, C.A. Bayly shows that riots occurred because of, or in the wake of, religious processions in the late eighteenth and early nineteenth centuries (1985: 198–9). Nor is such a phenomenon peculiar to India, as Natalie Davis' account of the sixteenth-seventeenth century conflicts between French Catholics and Protestants demonstrates. According to Davis, 'Much of the religious riot is timed to ritual, and the violence seems often a curious continuation of the rite' (1987: 170); baptisms and religious services are two common occasions for riots. She underlines, however, that 'these encounters are nothing compared to the disturbances that cluster around processional life' (Davis 1987: 171).

There is no doubt that the correlation between processions and riots results from certain features of this social and ritual institution. First of all, processions are one of the procedures by which a community delimits its territory. In her study of nineteenth century British India, Sandria Freitag convincingly argues that religious processions define the 'sacred space' of the community. This attribute was naturally conducive to violence in certain contexts, since 'when one group's space overlapped another's . . . these circumstances often prompted riots' (Freitag 1990: 134–5). In his study of the 1893 riots in Bombay, Jim Masselos also shows that communal violence pitched in opposition groups whose territories had previously been demarcated by religious festivals (1993: 187). Second, processions also constitute potential vehicles of communal violence because of their capacity for

---

*A shorter version of this chapter has been published in French in Vidal, Tarabout and Meyer 1994.

homogenizing identities. The participants in a procession necessarily downplay the internal divisions of their community and place more value on their sense of belonging to a religious group.

Though each group of participants might remain distinct from its neighbours, they shared involvement in the same observance for the same ostensible object. Community connections must have been felt at their most tangible and concrete, fostered by these very specific influences which were physical, spatial and temporal in nature. As long as the impact of all these influences still operated, the overarching nature of group identification based on religious community appeared utterly convincing. *Threats to community values during these occasions of integrative collective activities could prompt immediate and vehement response.* (Freitag 1990: 138, emphasis added)

Freitag's analysis is drawn from the concept of *communitas* as elaborated by Victor Turner to designate circumstances, such as processions, in which a social 'structure', necessarily heterogeneous in terms of status, constitutes an *undifferentiated whole* (Turner 1974: 237). These notions appear to be particularly applicable to the Hindu milieu, given its extreme social differentiation along caste and other lines, and the manner in which religious processions transcend such distinctions.[1] The procession, by virtue of its encompassing and homogenizing qualities, will be particularly apt to oppose itself to the 'other', primarily the Muslims.

This approach has recently been taken by Sudhir Kakar (1996; see also 1990: 143) in a book based on the 1990 Hindu-Muslim riot in Hyderabad. One of the key concepts Kakar uses is that of 'physical group' which he defines as 'a group represented in the bodies of its members rather than in their minds, a necessary shift for a group to become an instrument of actual violence' (1996: 45). Further elaborating on this notion, he writes:

The individual is practically wrapped up in the crowd and gets continuous sensual pounding through all avenues that one's body can afford. The consequence is a blurring of the body image and of the ego, a kind of self-transcendence that is reacted to by panic or exhilaration as individuality disappears and the 'integrity', 'autonomy' and 'independence' of the ego seem to be wishful illusions and mere hypothetical constructs. (1996: 45)

According to Kakar, religious processions 'perhaps produce the most physical of all groups' (1996: 46):

Rhythms of religious ritual are particularly effective in breaking down social barriers between the participants. They produce a maximum of mutual activation of the participants and a readiness for action, often violent. This is why violence, when Muslim-initiated, often begins at the end of Friday afternoon prayers when congregants, who have turned into a congregation, stream out of the mosque, into the street in a protesting procession. Processions at Muharram for the Muslims and Dusshera (and increasingly Ganesh

Chaturthi) for the Hindus are almost certain recipe for violence when they are preceded by a period of tension between the communities and when a precipitating incident has just occurred.

The idea that a religious procession is an 'almost certain recipe for violence' implies that certain communal riots find their origin in crowd psychology. Such an interpretation echoes the well known approach of Gustave Le Bon in *La Psychologie des Foules* (1895). By studying communal violence from this perspective, one tends to exaggerate the spontaneity and the autonomy of the crowd involved in rioting. Moreover, when he considers the role leaders can play in a crowd, Kakar highlights their restraining influence. According to him, 'Without the rituals which make tradition palpable and thus extend the group in time by giving assurances of continuity to the beleaguered ego, and without the permanent visibility of leaders whose presence is marked by conspicuous external insignia and who replace the benign and loving functions of the superego, religious crowds can easily turn into marauding mobs' (1990: 143).

Other students of religious riots, however, have often emphasized the role of leaders in triggering violence. Thus when writing about the riots between Catholics and Protestants, Davis highlights the role of clerics and local notables whose premeditated involvement is demonstrated by the manner in which they identified targets in advance (1987: 182, 184). She logically concludes that 'crowds do not act in the mindless way' (1987: 186). Similarly in his study of communal violence in South Asia, Stanley Tambiah notes that processions often degenerate into rioting as a result of manipulation by leaders who wish to bring about ideological and political mobilization:

Processions can be precursors of violence as well as actually develop into riots, and both politicians and religious leaders, who are often both, know their histrionic value as well as their instrumental efficacy in defining and inscribing the region or territory being claimed as an ethnic group's homelands (1996: 241).

The notion of premeditation is not unknown either. The houses of the targeted 'others' are sometimes marked in advance. In fact, riots caused by processions constitute the modus operandi of what Paul Brass calls ' "institutionalized riot systems" in which known actors specialize in the conversion of incidents between members of different communities into "communal riots" ' (Brass 1997: 9). As we shall see, processions can easily offer such 'incidents' to these 'known actors', whom Brass defines as 'a network of persons who maintain communal, racial, and other ethnic, relations in a state of tension, of readiness for riots' (1997: 126), and among whom Hindu nationalists figure quite prominently. Mass processions can entail a loss of rationality when they drift towards a status of *communitas*, but it is precisely for this reason—notably for the sociological homogenization inherent in this phenomenon—that leaders can attempt to utilize them as striking forces or potential instruments. Kakar recognizes this fact but chooses not to pursue it:

That the physical and cultural groups sometimes coincide and that it is the endeavor of those who use and manipulate symbols of cultural identity to bring the cultural group closer to the psychological state of a physical group is a subject which I will not pursue here. (Kakar 1996: 45)

By contrast, I advance the hypothesis that the instrumentalization of religious processions by ideologically minded leaders largely explains the way these rituals have become conducive to communal riots. To overlook this fact is to miss the key aspect of the complex relationship between processions and communal violence. Indeed, Kakar's interpretation based on crowd psychology itself implies the intervention of ideological factors: it presupposes that religious processions do not comprise members of more than one community although traditional Hindu processions included Muslims and vice versa. Just as Hindu groups often participated in Muharram, Muslims would perform as musicians at certain Hindu festivals. The gradual (and partial) exclusion of these 'others' is a political process which evolved over an extended period of time.

The manipulation of religious processions by political leaders is an old phenomenon. On the Hindu side, on which I focus in this chapter, it appears along with the crystallization of militant Hinduism in the late nineteenth century. It was primarily aimed at mobilizing the Hindu community against what was perceived by some Hindu leaders as the Muslim 'threat'. I shall explore this claim by looking at some of the most important examples. Tilak's re-interpretation of processions in honour of Ganesh beginning in the 1890s, represented an anti-Muslim unitarian mobilization. In the 1920s, following the Khilafat Movement, the same logic operated.

However, processions also became vehicles of violence when local power politics was at stake. The relative democratization of the political system, which followed the Government of India Act of 1919, favoured the emergence of a political class which was attentive to the sensibilities of the electorate and was concerned, therefore, with defending religious institutions such as processions. Over the years, a twofold pattern of procession-based riots has emerged, for ideological and electoral reasons. The growing importance of elections in a democratic framework and the increasingly tense relations between Hindus and Muslims from the 1970s onwards largely explain this development.

In the late 1980s and early 1990s, however, the two aspects of the politics of procession were increasingly integrated: Hindu nationalist leaders used processions and riots to mobilize supporters more and more frequently, especially at the time of elections, when it was particularly useful for them to polarize the electorate along religious lines.

# Religious Processions and Riots in British India

## THE 'NEW' HINDU PROCESSIONS AS
## ANTI-MUSLIM MOBILIZATIONS

I have attempted to show elsewhere (Jaffrelot 1996: Ch. 1) that a sense of cultural vulnerability was prompted in certain Hindu circles by the activities of Christian missionaries after the 1820s. Even though they criticized them publicly, members of the Hindu elite took to imitating these *firangis* (foreigners) in order to resist them more efficiently. In order to cope with the missions' proselytizing, the Arya Samaj adapted the Christian notion of conversion through the reinterpretation of a traditional ritual of purification called *shuddhi*. In other words, some of the most militant Hindus developed a strategy of stigmatization and emulation of the so-called 'threatening others'. Starting in the late nineteenth century, and especially in the early twentieth century, at the time of the Khilafat Movement, they came to regard Muslims as the main threat to Hindus. Some Hindu leaders, more or less consciously, began to imitate the congregational aspects of Muslim festivals, deliberately using processions as a means of mobilizing their community. While these aspects of communal relations have been amply examined by historians, the fact that a large number of Hindu-Muslim riots found their origin in processions must be emphasized and explored in greater depth.

## The Ganesh Festival Reinterpreted

The capacity of Hindu processions to transcend certain social distinctions constituted a valuable asset for those who deplored divisions within the majority community, a weakness to which they imputed the boldness with which Muslims assaulted Hindus. Such considerations formed the background of the reinterpretation of the Ganesh festival in the late nineteenth century.

In 1893, a procession organized in Yeola in honour of Balaji was attacked by Muslims as it passed by a mosque; the Muslims had been disturbed by the music. Seeking a means to strengthen Hindu communitarian consciousness, B.G. Tilak, one of the chief Hindu traditionalist leaders of the Indian National Congress in Bombay Presidency, called upon all Hindus to desist from participating in Muharram processions. It was in this context that he decided to reinterpret Ganesh Chaturthi, the festival that is organized every year on the occasion of the birth anniversary of Ganesh (or Ganapati) (Kelkar 1967: 182). Tilak thus transferred the celebration from the private sphere to the public domain in order to mobilize and unite Hindus.[2]

This reinterpretation of the Ganesh festival is a good illustration of the strategy of stigmatization and emulation of 'threatening others' that militant Hindus adopted. Tilak, faced with the Muslim 'threat', envisaged the incorporation into Hinduism of a practice he perceived as a strength of Islam—assembly and worship as a community of equals. Moreover, as an editorial in *Kesari*, one of Tilak's newspapers, shows, he did not conceal the mimetic dimension of this approach:[3]

Religious thoughts and devotion may be possible even in solitude, yet demonstration and *eclat* are essential to the awakening of masses. Through this nationalist appeal, the worship of Ganapati spread from the family circle to the public square. The transition is noteworthy since (despite some exceptions) Hindu religious worship is largely a matter of individual or family worship. Congregational worship as that in Christianity or Islam is not common. But nationalism provided the necessary social cement in this case. (Quoted in Jog 1979: 44–5)

The Ganesh festival henceforth consisted of a long celebration of ten days which coincided with Muharram and concluded with a procession in the course of which militant chants were sung before the idol of the god was immersed.[4] The pageant held during the new Ganesh festival included choirs of young men clad in the uniform of Shivaji's soldiers; their main 'patriotic' theories were directed as much towards the British as towards the Muslims. In Poona in 1894, Tilak's supporters defied the orders of the District Magistrate not to take a procession past a mosque, and thereby precipitated a riot. The following year, the procession again ignored the route fixed by the authorities to take the same 'detour'; this time, however, 400 Muslims had stocked weapons in the mosque and were awaiting its arrival (Michael 1986: 191–2). These events mark the emergence of a particular pattern of communal rioting which has subsequently been repeated and amplified. Initially, this model was, composed of three sequential elements: (i) the development of a sentiment of vulnerability among Hindu militants following an outbreak of rioting, the initiative of which was attributable to the Muslims; (ii) a unitarian reaction involving a recourse to processions which comprised only one community by excluding Muslims from the Hindu processions (the purpose of the processions was to symbolize Hindu solidarity and, thereby, serve as instruments of political mobilization); and finally, (iii) the instigation of a riot following a change of route by the new Hindu procession, which the Muslims perceived as blatant incitement. This pattern retained several elements of earlier procession-based riots. The change of route, for instance, has long served as a provocation; it is designed to assert one's presence over a large territory or to infringe on the other community's space. Since the late nineteenth century, however, with the construction of communal identities, the processions have been reinterpreted and used as provocation by the new, ideologically-oriented leaders. Over time, the protagonists became accustomed to preparing for the rioting, notably by arming themselves; this gradually became characteristic of this pattern of violence. While this schema took shape in the late nineteenth century, a period marked by one of the first waves of communal violence, it became more prevalent in the 1920s during the series of riots which broke out in conjunction with the Khilafat Movement.

## Processions and Riots in Nagpur in the Context of the Khilafat and Hindu Sangathan Movements

In the early 1920s, Hindu sentiments of vulnerability vis-à-vis the Muslims were reactivated by the Khilafat Movement. This Muslim mobilization degenerated into riots on several occasions, in particular on the Malabar coast, where the Mapillas (or Moplahs), Muslim tenants who had in the past led numerous peasant revolts (Dale 1975: 85–97), attacked the British administration and Namboodari landowners (some of whom had been forcibly converted).[5]

This rioting appears as the first (and among the most significant) of a series which continued up to 1927. A number of these violent acts were incited when a Hindu procession insisted on playing music while passing in front of a mosque—a practice which Muslims, especially those participating in the Khilafat Movement, did not tolerate.[6] The bloody rioting in Calcutta in 1924 and, above all, in 1926, broke out over the same issue.[7]

Muslim sensitivity to this problem was to be used by militant Hindu members of the Indian National Congress to mobilize their community. A number of them, associated with the Hindu Mahasabha, which acted as a kind of pressure group in the Congress, had viewed the Hindu-Muslim riots in the early 1920s as cause for deep concern.[8] This was true in the case of B.S. Moonje, a former lieutenant of Tilak (who died in 1920) in Nagpur.[9]

After having investigated the violence in Malabar, Moonje wrote a report in which he underlined the necessity of strengthening the Hindu community by removing caste distinctions, by restoring the Vedic practice of animal sacrifice to recapture the physical courage displayed by the Muslims and by establishing congregational forms of worship, also practised by Muslims. The latter represented one of the axes of the 'Hindu Sangathan' movement which was launched by the Hindu Mahasabha in 1922 (Prakash 1938). Moonje's strategy of simultaneous stigmatization and emulation of the Muslims had an aggressive dimension, as his tactics in Nagpur testify.

In September 1923, the small Muslim minority in Nagpur, as elsewhere, protested that Hindu processions, accompanied by music, were being taken past their mosques. On 30 October 1923, the authorities prohibited all processions. To challenge this decision, Moonje orchestrated a protest movement which rallied approximately 20,000 persons (Andersen and Damle 1987: 32). Having proved his point, in November, he organized a procession which involved music and passed several mosques. Since both camps had been armed beforehand, the subsequent riot entailed heavy casualties. The following year, the local Hindu Sabha claimed the right for its participants to carry *lathis* (sticks) in the Ganesh Chaturthi procession.[10]

The RSS was founded in 1925 in Nagpur by one of Moonje's lieutenants, K.B. Hedgewar, who shared his concern for strengthening the Hindus vis-à-vis the Muslims. As a veteran of the Nagpur RSS, Vasant Rao Oke, who joined the movement shortly after its formation, explains, the aggressive defence of processions occupied a major place in the RSS strategy:

In 1927 there were riots in Nagpur. Hindus were defensive. [In the past], Muslims stopped the Ganesh processions when they passed before a mosque with music. However, in 1927 Dr. Hedgewar came in front of the [Ganesh] procession, from the beginning, on the mosque road till the tank while beating the drums. Because of him all the others also came along beating the drums. They had the courage then [to follow the procession].[11]

Political leaders with Hindu militant leanings invested this procession with the purpose of strengthening the majority community *against* the Muslims. It was a matter of confirming its collective identity by establishing the Hindus' claim on urban space—aggressively, if need be—and of exploiting the mobilizing virtues of the procession to rally followers. The procession as a technique of mobilization was thus increasingly employed by political leaders, precisely *because* potential violence made it possible to assert in the streets the dominant status of the Hindu community with regard to the minorities. A further dimension to inter-communal conflict was provided by the representative politics which developed around electoral and parliamentary institutions provided under the Government of India Act of 1919. The political system then became increasingly influenced by the role of elections and factionalism.

## POLITICAL COMPETITION, PROCESSIONS AND RIOTS: THE CASE OF THE RAM LILA IN ALLAHABAD

The political framework of British India was significantly transformed in 1919 when the Montague-Chelmsford Reforms extended the right to vote to a new strata of the population and stimulated political competition by endowing provincial governments with new power. Party leaders bent upon appealing to the voters tended to resort to arguments drawn from the religious repertoire.

As Bayly has shown, until the turn of the century, local politics had been dominated by *rais* (notables), who typically belonged to merchant or landlord milieus, and were considered by the British to be 'natural leaders'. Their patronage of religious institutions represented an important source of social respect, and it was with these leaders that the British negotiated the route to be followed by processions. The 'patrons' used educated young men, whose learning gained them acceptance as intermediaries with the British (Bayly 1973: 349–88). However, from the time of the constitutional reform of 1909, these publicists began to emancipate themselves from the tutelage of the *rais* and to use the Indian National Congress as a vehicle for their political ambitions. This process was accentuated following the 1919 reforms (Bayly 1975: 273). Politicians of the 'publicist' type then became rivals of the *rais*, not only for elected posts, but also for more symbolic functions providing prestige such as the patronage of religious ceremonies like processions. 'Publicists' inducted into politics vied with them for this office and then endeavoured to arrogate it to themselves, sometimes for electioneering purposes (Freitag 1990: 76, 200).

In Allahabad, the political game was dominated during the 1920s by the rivalry between Motilal Nehru and Madan Mohan Malaviya, who were poised to supplant the local *rais*. The former called for a secularism of British inspiration, while the latter, who came from a very orthodox family,[12] valued the defence of Hindu interests. Since 1880, Malaviya had participated in the Hindu Samaj, an organization formed under the patronage of *rais* in reaction to the threat which Christian missionaries brought to bear on the annual Magh Mela (Bayly 1975: 106). Above all, since 1904, he had worked towards the foundation of a Benares Hindu University which finally opened in 1916 and, in his eyes, was to be the vehicle of a Hindu renaissance (Sundaram 1942: XLI). The first public clashes between Nehru and Malaviya took place in 1915-16, after the former supported a law which accorded Muslims in the United Provinces a separate system of electorates at the municipal level (Robinson 1973: 427–32). In response, Malaviya then participated in a major agitational campaign[13] and in the formation of a regional Hindu Sabha (Gordon 1975: 151). In 1923, the conflict between the two factions took a more radical turn after the Swaraj Party, newly constituted by Motilal Nehru and C.R. Das, gained a majority in the Allahabad Municipal Council, and won 31 seats in the legislative council as opposed to six by Malaviya's group. Malaviya exploited the tense relations between Hindus and Muslims to regain ascendancy at the local level.[14]

The Malaviya family, traditionally versed in the Vedas and known for its strict observance of *smarta* (traditional, orthodox) rites, enjoyed a particular prestige by virtue of which it bore responsibility for the annual Ram Lila (festival celebrating various events of Ram's life) which assumed notable eminence in Allahabad (Parmanand 1985, Vol. 2: 684). After its electoral defeat at the local level, Malaviya's group[15] sought to reassert its sway over the Allahabad Hindus by offering itself as the defender of Hinduism and probably, also, exploiting communal tensions. A serious riot broke out in 1924 after members of the Ram Lila procession engaged in provocative behaviour. The exclusion of Muslim musicians from the procession, for which Malaviyas' followers were probably responsible, prepared the ground for this communal flare up in which twelve were killed and hundreds injured. Whereas in the past, the presence of Muslim musicians had ensured that music was not played before mosques, on this particular occasion, the Hindu processionists organized a demonstration in front of the Jama Masjid or local Grand Mosque. The Malaviyas' strategy became clear during the 1925 Ram Lila, which occurred a few weeks prior to municipal elections: they refused to commit themselves to desisting from music when their procession passed before the Jama Masjid. The District Magistrate, who banned the Ram Lila procession, stated that he was convinced that their objective was 'to show the Nehru family that they do not rule the Allahabad Hindus' (Parmanand 1985, Vol. 2: 83; Pandey 1978: 119–20). Indeed, the Malaviyas regained control of the municipal council in the subsequent elections.

In 1926, the electoral stakes were much higher, as approximately 1.3 million voters were called upon to send new representatives to the legislative council of the United Provinces. With this contest in mind, Malaviya formed a new political group within the Congress, the Congress Independent Party, and was more zealous than ever in his defence of the Ram Lila procession. The British authorities, however, made their approval of the procession dependent on a guarantee from the organizers that no music would be played when the marchers were passing a mosque. Presiding over a meeting of 10,000 people on 5 October, Malaviya indignantly retorted: 'If music is to be stopped before every one of the sixteen or seventeen mosques it will be a mourning procession, not a Ram Dal (group celebrating Ram)' (quoted in Parmanand 1985: 688). He then addressed a telegram to the British authorities which began thus:

> The Hindu residents of Allahabad assembled at a public meeting, record their strong protest against the attitude of the district authorities in refusing licences even this year for the Ram Lila procession in conformity with the long-established local custom. (*Indian Quarterly Review* (hereafter *IQR*) 1926, Vol. 2: 104)

Malaviya called for a show of determination even though rioting had broken out the previous month in the centre of Allahabad on the occasion of the Dadkhando (anniversary of Krishna), causing two deaths, and the situation remained tense (*IQR* 1926, Vol. 2: 81). The defence of processions at the risk of precipitating a riot appears here to be doubly connected with electoral competition. On the one hand, processions played a part in political propaganda, promoting Malaviya as the protector of 'his' community and disqualifying the adversary;[16] on the other hand, communal tensions (and even violence in 1924) dramatically divided the electorate along religious lines, in such a manner that the Hindu voter valued this particular identity and voted in conformity with it.[17] The procession assumed a key function here as a vehicle of rioting. *The Leader*, published from Allahabad, founded by Malaviya, read:

> The religious processions . . . ha[ve] in recent years . . . been devoted largely to the display of weapons and physical force by both Mohammedans and Hindus. . . . Weapons and ammunitions were purchased in large quantities by the inhabitants [of Allahabad] in September [1924]. (Quoted in Freitag 1980: 202)

The Ram Lila procession was banned in Allahabad by the British administration during 1925–36. In 1937, however, when the first elections under the 1935 Act were held, one observes in Allahabad as in many other towns, an attempt to establish this ritual as a show of force. The Hindu Mahasabha campaigned not only for the lifting of the ban on the Ram Lila but also for the right to play music before mosques at any time (Kesavan 1990:13) Eventually, a riot occurred in 1938 after participants of the Holi procession (celebrated at the end of winter, during the Holi festival) indulged in provocative colour throwing. According to Kesavan, 'the Holi procession was evidently looking for trouble because it counted two to three hundreds lathis in it, vastly more than normal' (1990: 16).

During the colonial period, militant Hindus found in the religious processions of their community an institution which would prove most useful for their ideological project of promoting Hindu interests. It was a means of mobilizing the majority community in the face of so-called Muslim 'threats' and an ideal instrument for instigating violence with the aim of reasserting Hindu supremacy in a most radical manner. It was not difficult, amidst tensions, to transform the fervour of the procession into aggression, even to add to it an armed gang. In the 1920s, in addition to this strategy, the politics of processions acquired an electoral dimension in the framework of growing political competition. A new element of election-oriented religious populism came to exacerbate communal tensions at the local level. The pattern of procession-based riots initiated by the new Ganesh festival, with its three sequences identified above persisted, but the motivations of the political entrepreneurs orchestrating them changed. The Hindu leaders who used the processions to mobilize their community against the Muslims were no longer alone. Growing political competition and the increasingly important role of elections in determining leadership led some political leaders to consider processions and riots as resources.

## Towards the Routinization of a Pattern

After independence and the riots related to Partition, communal violence became a marginal phenomenon. On average, there were fewer than 100 riots a year between 1954 and 1964 (Jaffrelot 1996: 552). The trauma of 1947 and Nehru's vigilant secularism are among the main explanations for this state of things. The frequency of communal riots began to increase in the late 1960s and again in the late 1970s. The model we have used so far remains relevant in explaining certain forms of this communal violence as suggested by isolated cases, such as the riot of Bhiwandi in 1970 and Jamshedpur in 1979. Similarly, some of the procession-based riots of the early 1980s retain features of the anti-Muslim mobilization of the 1920s. The ever-increasing politicization of processions, however, gradually introduced one significant difference: in the end, the religious element almost disappeared from them; they were converted into demonstrations of strength, pure and simple.

## FROM BHIWANDI TO JAMSHEDPUR

In the 1970s, two instances of violence, the magnitude of which justified the appointment of commissions of inquiry, bear testimony to the persistence of the old pattern of procession-led riots but also of its progressive transformation into a more blatantly political phenomenon. In Bhiwandi, relative communal harmony still prevailed in the early 1960s partly because of socioeconomic reasons. While the textile mills, the main source of employment in the town, belonged primarily to Muslims, their suppliers and moneylenders were mainly Marwaris (Hindu merchant caste from Marwar); the working force comprised Muslims as well as Hindus. This economic interdependence made possible an arrangement whereby Hindu and Muslim representatives alternated as heads of the municipal council. The deterioration in relations between the two communities in the second half of the 1960s, may be attributed to the organization of processions of a political nature. Indeed, Hindu nationalist activists gave an aggressive turn to Shiv Jayanti (the festival celebrating the anniversary of Shivaji).

Tilak had initiated this festival to celebrate the birthday of Shivaji. While the purpose of the procession was not to attract devotees; the distinctive features of the religious procession had been preserved: the image of Shivaji was conveyed on a palanquin and the march was accompanied by the same musical instruments. It was a political procession in religious garb. However, since the time of Tilak, Shiv Jayanti had not been used to mobilize Hindus in the street as systematically as the Ganesh procession which appeared to be more suited to this purpose because of its religious appeal.[18] Until 1964, this festival continued to be celebrated privately in Bhiwandi by members of the RSS. That year, however, the members of this movement and of its political front, the Jana Sangh, constituted a 'Shiv Jayanti Utsav Samiti' which would be responsible for organizing a public commemoration of Shivaji's anniversary. Three thousand people, including many young men, marched, throwing *gulal* (a coloured powder used during Holi) and chanting provocative slogans, in particular, 'Akhand Hindusthan Zindabad' (Long live Undivided India!) and 'Hindu Dharmacha Vijay Aso' (Let the Hindu religion be victorious!) (Madan n.d.: 163–4). A similar demonstration involving 6,000 people passed in front of the Grand Mosque of Nizampura. In 1966, *gulal* was thrown at a mosque in an expression of greater militancy. The 1967 procession reproduced the same scenario, but with still greater ostentation: two images of Shivaji, one showing him mounted on horseback and the other surrounded by his court, were carried in the procession (Madan n.d.: 166–71). The impending municipal elections were not irrelevant to this elaboration of the demonstration; furthermore, all those who took an active part therein—some of them from the newly created Shiv Sena—were elected.

In 1968, the more moderate elements in both communities went to great lengths to marginalize the radicals in the Shiv Jayanti Utsav Samiti and organized a Shiv Jayanti procession which reintegrated numerous Muslims. It was the same in 1969, but that year nineteen militant Hindus, fifteen of whom belonged to the Jana Sangh, resigned from the Shiv Jayanti Utsav Samiti to form a 'Rashtriya Utsav Mandal' (Madan n.d.: 179). The latter took charge of the organization of the Shiv Jayanti and the procession, to which it attracted, between 3,000 and 8,000 villagers from the surrounding areas (out of a total of roughly 10,000 participants) (ibid.: 145). The processionists were armed with *lathis* at the end of which hung saffron flags. At one point, the procession struck up anti-Muslim slogans, compelling the Muslim participants to walk out. Then, it slowed its progress while traversing Muslim quarters, provoking retaliation in the form of stone throwing. Members of the procession immediately attacked Muslim stalls and dwellings, as well as their inhabitants. On 7 May, rioting caused 43 deaths—15 Hindus and 28 Muslims. Despite a curfew, the rioting continued the next day leaving 22 dead, 8 Hindus and 14 Muslims, and for the four following days, during which 8 Muslims were killed.

This violent outcome reveals the increasing politicization of the pattern initiated by the 'new' Ganesh festival. First, the procession used for mobilizing Hindus in the street did not have a religious character; it no longer seemed necessary to make instrumental use of the devotees' emotion as had been done earlier in celebrating the Ganesh festivals. Second, the Shiv Jayanti procession was manipulated with political and even electoral objectives in mind. The Jana Sangh, evidently eager to promote the idea that its local branch sought to defend the Hindu community, was prepared to encourage activism within the procession even at the risk of causing a riot. In fact, the Shiv Jayanti procession provided the Jana Sangh and the Shiv Sena with a vehicle for communal aggression. The testimony of one of its militants after the violence of 1970 is most revealing in this respect:

Every organisation which demands public support always tries to make a show that it has a following. . . . It is true that by collecting so many villagers for the Shiv Jayanti procession, the constituents of the RUM, namely, the Jana Sangh-minded and the Shiv Sena-minded leaders thereof wanted to show their strength. (Cited in Madan n.d.: 157–8)

Another element of the original model, the Hindu feeling of vulnerability, which amounted to a paradoxical inferiority complex on the part of the majority community, is also to be found in the Bhiwandi riots. Shortly after the events, *Sobat,* a Marathi weekly of Hindu nationalist inspiration published in Poona, carried an article in which the following point was made:

A Hindu boy grows up hearing the news of terrible atrocities done by the Muslims. Feelings of inferiority complex are created in his mind throughout his life, directly or indirectly. The boy growing today at Ahmedabad, Baroda or Bhiwandi-Thana will not grow to be of that type. He has seen Hindus thrashing Muslims, he has seen and heard Hindus destroying the Dargahs and mosques wherein arms were kept hidden. (ibid.: 113)

The other large riot resulting from a Hindu procession in the 1970s took place in Jamshedpur in 1979. This iron and steel centre in Bihar, where the Muslim minority represents roughly a fifth of the population, had already experienced communal tensions in April 1978, when the Ramnavami procession deviated from the authorized route to pass through Muslim quarters. In March-April 1979, the *akhara* (gymnasium, generally attached to a temple) responsible for this annual procession asked the authorities for permission to follow the same route. The District Commissioner refused and entered into negotiations with the representatives of the two communities with the intention of reaching a compromise. But on 7 April, a leaflet was distributed in the town announcing the determination of the Hindu militants to pass through Muslim quarters; this threat was carried out, forcing the police to intervene and arrest some of the activists. The RSS, which in Jamshedpur numbered between four and five hundred regular members divided into fifteen *shakhas*, was clearly at the root of these initiatives, acting through an organization known as the Ramnavami Akhara Samiti. Moreover, Deoras, the head of the RSS, had arrived on 1 April to preside over a meeting in Jamshedpur; in front of an audience of 2,000 persons, he denounced the fact that Hindus could not freely organize processions in their own country.

The direct involvement of local Hindu nationalists was evident throughout this crisis. On 10 April, while negotiations between representatives of the two communities were being pursued at a police station in the town, the Muslims gave way so as to defuse the Hindu mobilization. This unanticipated concession perceptibly upset the plans made by the Hindu nationalists: there was now a chance that the procession would pass through the Muslim quarters without clashes. The following day, the procession had covered half its planned route when Dina Nath Pandey, a former Jana Sanghi, stopped it near a Muslim quarter; he demanded that the authorities immediately release sympathizers arrested on 7 April. This demand, which had not been made earlier in such terms, was unacceptable to the Superintendent of Police. The impasse exacerbated latent tensions, particularly as 2,000 persons armed with knives suddenly joined the procession. The Muslims then began to throw stones at the marchers, precipitating a riot in the course of which militant Hindus used home-made bombs, confirming the premeditated character of the violence. Of the 108 dead, according to official estimates, 79 were Muslims. The report drawn up by the commission of inquiry concluded without circumlocution that Hindu nationalists in general, and Pandey in particular, were responsible for what had transpired.[19]

In contrast to the Bhiwandi riot, the Jamshedpur disturbance proceeded from the manipulation of a traditional religious procession. However, one again finds therein the determining role of Hindu nationalists acting *ex officio* or through an *akhara*. By and large, these two case studies bear testimony to the persistence of the politics of procession in which the psychology of crowds is less decisive than the part played by political leaders. The procession-based riots of the early 1980s recall even more precisely the communal violence of the 1920s.

## PROCESSIONS AND RIOTS AS MEANS OF TRANSCENDING CASTE BARRIERS

The early 1980s were marked by a reactivation of a feeling of vulnerability within Hindu nationalist circles. The process was probably set in motion by the conversion to Islam of about 3,000 Untouchables in Tamil Nadu in 1981 (Mathew 1982: 1028–31). This presented an opportunity to transform their sense of ineffectiveness induced Hindu nationalists by caste divisions into a struggle for unity in communal conflicts with Muslims. This was the chain of reaction, similar to the Sangathan movement, that the Hindu nationalists were trying to create in the 1980s. From 1981 to 1983, the RSS and VHP, organized 'Hindu Solidarity Conferences', which culminated in rioting on several occasions. Although some violent acts affected Christians,[20] most were directed towards Muslims.

In Poona, a fifteen-day campaign orchestrated by the RSS concluded on 14 February 1982 with a procession named *Vishal Hindu Aikya Yatra*. The route of this procession had been fixed by the local authorities but was changed so as to enter a Muslim quarter where militants of the VHP trigerred off acts of violence; hotels and shops, for example, were set on fire. The procedure was repeated the following day in Sholapur when a similar procession became a show of force with cries of 'Ek dakha aur do, Pakistan tor do' (Give another shove and shatter Pakistan) and 'Vande Mataram gana hoga nahin to Hindustan chorna hoga' (Sing the Vande Mataram, or leave India). Shops in the Muslim area were also set on fire. The procession in Poona carried three large bells which were supposed to 'symbolically toll for the death of Untouchability'[21] and giant portraits of Ambedkar, Phule, Gandhi and Golwalkar, as well as a copy of the 'Laws of Manu' (Engineer 1984: 135). They, therefore, seem to have appeared as a means of reinforcing the cohesion of the Hindu community *against* the Muslim Other.

The 1982 riot in Meerut saw the participation of Bhangis (sweepers, removers of night-soil), whom Hindu nationalist propaganda encouraged to consider themselves as descendants of Valmiki, the legendary author of the *Ramayana* (Ibid., 1982: 1003). This participation by the Bhanghis would certainly have resulted from some sort of negotiation; according to testimonies gathered by Engineer, Rs 200 were paid for each crime committed. This tactic was effective during the 1987 riots in Meerut when 'Chamars and Bhanghis joined upper caste Hindus to loot and burn down' Muslim shops and houses in return for money and alcohol (Ibid., 1988: 29). It was also employed in riots in Ahmedabad and Delhi.

In the 1980s, the policy of reservations implemented by the Gujarat government hardened social relations in Ahmedabad. In 1981, the granting of additional quotas to Untouchables for certain classes of medical colleges provoked violent acts of retaliation on the part of the upper castes. These developments favoured a rapprochement between the movements of the Untouchables and Muslims (Bose 1981: 713–16). In 1985, the announcement of an increase in quotas prompted new acts of particularly fierce violence—180 people were killed—directed first against the lower castes and then the Untouchables (Patel 1985: 1175). However, VHP militants were soon despatched to the quarters of Untouchables affected by the rioting in order to distribute funds and dissuade those who threatened to convert to Islam.[22] Above all, Ahmedabad represented a favourable context for the strategy of forging Hindu unity using violence instigated through processions.[23]

Slogans advocating caste unity were written on walls in the Untouchable quarters. The *Rath yatra* (procession of the Hindu festival of Lord Jagannath during which his image is taken in a chariot to be dipped in the sea) soon provided an occasion to actualize these appeals. The procession numbered 100,000 participants and was one and a half kilometres in length. It was intended as a show of Hindu force and the customary involvement of Untouchables in the *Rath yatra* provided an ideal vehicle for the sentiment of *communitas*. The ten-hour procession passed through seven Muslim quarters, shouting disparaging, indeed obscene, slogans. Stones were thrown at the procession, inciting a riot which many Untouchables, who had been brought in lorries, joined.

Thus the first half of the 1980s, as earlier in the 1920s, was the setting for the reaction of militant Hindu movements to the 'Muslim threat'. The former aimed at strengthening the cohesion of the majority community, notably by means of the procession as a form of *communitas* and the violence which such shows of force, sometimes inevitably, provoked. It was a matter of creating Hindu unity (including Untouchables) against the Muslim Other. In the second half of the decade, the upsurge of rioting responded to an analogous logic but once again electoral considerations played an important part.

## An All-India Anti-Muslim, Election-Oriented Politics of Processions?

The most important change affecting the politics of procession and rioting probably took place in the late 1980s to early 1990s, during the wave of riots induced by the Ayodhya affair. At that time, the two dimensions of the communal use of processions—anti-Muslim mobilization and election-oriented use of shows of strength and violence—merged to a great extent. The Hindu nationalist strategy still entailed the use of processions and riots as a means to react to so-called Muslim threats; however, communal violence was also utilized to polarize voters along communal lines. That such politics came to acquire an all-India dimension was also a new phenomenon.

From the mid-1980s, relations between Hindus and Muslims in the public sphere were dominated by the controversy site of the Ayodhya. In 1984, the VHP started an agitation campaign for the 'liberation' of a site which Hindu nationalists claimed to be *Ramjanmabhoomi* (Van der Veer 1987: 298). This step was intended to rally 'the Hindu nation' around a common symbol. The major riots occurred because of, or in the wake of, pseudo-religious processions organized by the VHP on the occasion of *Ram Shila Pujan*. Even though the Bharatiya Janata Party (BJP) was not at the forefront, its leaders, especially at the local level, took part in the *Ram Shila Pujan* in order to gain political advantage from these popular mobilizations before the campaign for the Lok Sabha elections which were scheduled to take place in late 1989.

## THE *RAM SHILA PUJAN* AND THE 1989 ELECTIONS

The VHP had announced in January 1989 that it would lay the foundation stone of a temple dedicated to Ram at the site of his birth on 9 November, that is to say, with great likelihood, in the middle of the electoral campaign. In the meantime, beginning that summer, the VHP undertook to consecrate bricks stamped with the name 'Ram' (*Ram Shila*) in as many urban quarters and villages as possible. This ceremony comprised a *puja* during which militants or officiating priests collected donations—and a procession carrying the 'sanctified' bricks. We find here the utilization of ritual forms borrowed from Hinduism to raise the value of a political symbol in a pre-electoral context. These processions became increasingly similar to shows of force as the election date drew closer, rapidly fostering a cycle of rioting.

The appeals surrounding the *Ram Shila Pujan* contained some strong language and invited the audience to think in terms of confrontation and aggression. A typical example is the following extract from the text contained in a standard propaganda cassette:

> The blood of foreigners, of traitors who do not venerate the ancestors, will flow. . . . The *Ram Shila* will be the protectors of Hindu culture. . . . The foreign conspiracies [an allusion to conversions allegedly financed with money from Arab countries] will no longer succeed. The *Ram Shila* will be the death of those who call Mother India by the name of sorceress.[24]

According to official estimates, 706 riots took place in 1989.[25] One reliable source claims that '1,174 people died in different parts of the country in riots that followed the passage of *Ram Shila* processions through the states'.[26] Violence was particularly fierce in Gujarat, Rajasthan, Madhya Pradesh, Uttar Pradesh and Bihar, but some southern states, mainly Karnataka and, to a lesser extent, Andhra Pradesh were also affected. The typical development of the riots is very clearly illustrated by those that occurred in Bhagalpur which, by far the most violent, saw about 1,000 people dead, of whom 900 were Muslims.[27] In October 1989, the VHP organized *Ram Shila* processions which were to pass through the rural parts of Bhagalpur district for a period of five days before converging on 24 October in the town. On that day, the procession—which initially numbered from 1,000 to 3,000 persons,[28] but after a few kilometres swelled to 10,000 participants—struck up such slogans as 'Hindi, Hindu, Hindusthan, Mullah bhago Pakistan' (Hindi, Hindu, for India;

Muslim clerics must flee to Pakistan) (Bharti 1989: 2643). It was stopped by roughly 300 Muslims at the approach to the Muslim-dominated area of Tartarpur 'which was not on the route sanctioned by the official licence issued to the procession'.[29] Marchers, among whom were VHP, BJP and RSS members according to witnesses audited by the subsequent inquiry commission, then started to shout slogans such as 'Long live mother Kali [a Hindu goddess], Tartarpur will be empty' and 'We will avenge the insult inflicted by Babar on her children' (Engineer 1996: 1729). At that stage, according to the majority report of the inquiry commission: 'a large portion of the majority of the processionists were peaceful and totally devotional in their attitude and were dedicated to the task they were performing but there were also persons who were armed and there were persons who were shouting slogans' (cited in Engineer 1996: 1730).

The procession in this case had grown beyond expectations and the crowd was behaving in a hysterical manner. One participant described what had happened in the following terms:

There seemed to be some sort of a madness in the procession of Mahadev Singh. It was as if everyone believed that it would be a great victory for Hinduism if the procession passed through Chattarpur [sic]. The crowd seemed to be intoxicated with its power and was shouting anti-Muslim slogans with fervour.[30]

This group followed its route with police escort when a home-made bomb exploded, triggering off the riot. It lasted several days and spread to 250 villages spanning 15 of the 21 blocks of Bhagalpur district. The duration and intensity of the violence were partly the responsibility of the police who, along with BJP activists, participated in rioting and looting. A mosque was partially destroyed and residents belonging to certain student hostels figured among the victims of the first day of violence. Rioting continued more or less sporadically for over a month and spread to the rural periphery of Bhagalpur where the pattern of communal violence resembled that of the urban areas.

Thus the wave of rioting in the autumn of 1989 was provoked by militant Hindu nationalists employing processions to mobilize their community and instigate communal violence. The novel features concern the organization of pseudo-religious processions such as the *Ram Shila Pujan*, the triggering of pre-electoral riots and the pan-Indian use of this strategy. First the Hindu nationalist movement has invented pseudo-religious processions from the *Ekatmata yatra* in 1983 to the *Rath yatra* in 1990. For the *Sangh Parivar*, it obviously makes more sense to design their own rites in order to promote their ideology; it is also easier to use them as they wish, including as vehicles of aggressive behaviour. The invention of new political rites, however, does not imply major changes in the inner logic of these processions: many of them combine people motivated by ideology with devotees following their religious emotion, as was evident in the case of the *Ram Shila Pujan* of Bhagalpur.

Second, the hypothesis that communal riots tend to polarize the electorate in such a way that the Hindu majority, feeling 'more Hindu', would be more inclined to vote for the BJP, is confirmed by the outcome. Out of 88 constituencies in which the BJP won in the 1989 Lok Sabha election, 47 were in areas where there had been rioting during the autumn, thus confirming that 'an atmosphere of communal polarization contributed to the strength of the party's showing' (Chiriyankandath 1992: 69). In their interviews with Paul Brass after the 1991 elections, both BJP and Janata Dal leaders in Uttar Pradesh acknowledged 'that the fomenting of violence both to win votes and to ward off defeat by arousing communal sympathy and animosities is part of the standard repertoire of contemporary political practises in north India politics' (Brass 1993: 274).

Third, for the first time, riots broke out simultaneously in all the northern states on the basis of the same issue. In the past, rioting remained more or less localized, and was most often caused by particular socioeconomic rivalries and political conflicts, while the pretexts for violence would usually be specific to the place concerned. The unleashing of communal violence on a general scale was made possible by the use of the pan-Indian symbol of Ram by a Hindu nationalist network which could itself cover the entire Indian territory to organize *Ram Shila Pujans*. These were performed in 297,705 different places.[31]

The Ayodhya Movement alone, however, did not account for the riots. The nationalization of communal violence, remained incomplete. Riots probably occurred for both national as well as local reasons. In the villages around Bhagalpur which were affected by communal riots, local economic rivalries partly explain the violence, even though the *Ram Shila Pujan* was a catalyst. As Tambiah suggests, the process of nationalization needs to be complemented by an analysis in terms of 'parochialization' since local configurations (socio-ethnic and caste cleavages, the outcome of local history, etc.) give different meanings to issues such as the Ayodhya Movement (Tambiah 1996: 257). Nevertheless, the nationalization of communal conflicts had probably never had such an impact relative to the local factors. There were certainly local explanations for most of the riots but they were generally less important than national explanations for communal violence. The endeavour to 'nationalize' Hindu-Muslim antagonism by organizing processions with violent implications undoubtedly reached its height on the occasion of the *Rath yatra* of L.K. Advani in the autumn of 1990. In fact, in the early 1990s, the politics of procession acquired a new shape, that of 'yatra politics', which was characterized primarily by an attempt to cover larger territories.

## YATRA POLITICS AND COMMUNAL RIOTS: *RATH YATRA,*
## *RAM JYOTI YATRA* AND *ASTHI KALASH YATRA*

For the president of the BJP, the *Rath yatra* entailed covering 10,000 km. in the space of one month, from the Somnath temple in Gujarat to Ayodhya in Uttar

Pradesh, where the VHP had announced that the construction of the temple would commence on 30 October 1990. Advani stood in a DCM-Toyota, decorated to replicate the model of Arjun's chariot which had appeared in the televised version of the *Mahabharata* broadcast from 1988 to 1990. He covered between 100 and 250 km. each day, halting time and again to hold meetings.

The distance travelled and the nature of the point of arrival evokes the comparison of the *Rath yatra* with a pilgrimage, rather than with a procession. Thousands of people went to witness the passing of the *Rath yatra* through their quarters or their villages, greeting it with marks of religious fervour and joining it as if it were a procession; women, for example, offered their *mangalsutra* (the necklace received by a woman upon marriage and meant to be worn at all times) and coconuts, or performed the Rass Garba, a dance characteristic of Krishna and his *gopis* (milkmaids; in the *Mahabharata*, they are Krishna's lovers).

Parallel to this enormous procession, the VHP organized the *Ram Jyoti yatra* also in preparation for the *karseva* due to commence on 30 October: 'the *Ram Jyoti* (*yatra*) was conceived as a surrogate for Advani's *Rath yatra*, and was intended to help form processions wherever he personally could not go' (Chakravarti et al. 1992: 952). The plan of action, beginning on 29 September, involved lighting with a torch from Ayodhya other torches in Mathura and Varanasi and, from there, in all districts in order to symbolize the reawakening of the worshippers of Ram—potentially all Hindus. Once again, processions were the medium of choice; this time, the object being carried was a flame. In Karnail Ganj, a small town in the district of Gonda, adjacent to Faizabad district where Ayodhya is located, the *Ram Jyoti yatra* forcibly joined the Durga Puja (festival in honour of the Hindu goddess Durga) procession, despite efforts by the police to keep the two apart; and it was the larger procession thus formed which broke into anti-Muslim slogans when passing through sensitive parts of town. This resulted in stones and Molotov cocktails being thrown; the riot later spread to Muslim quarters. Five days of violence caused the death of 45 persons.[32] Hindu zealots had taken advantage of the fervour of the participants in the Durga Puja procession to turn it against the Muslims.[33]

The riots connected with the *Ram Jyoti yatra* confirmed the increasingly all-India character of communal violence: they occurred in many different settings, including localities in Karnataka. At Channapatna, located 70 km. south-west of Bangalore, the *Ram Jyoti yatra* proceeded without incident under heavy police escort. Five days later, however, the local procession commemorating the birth anniversary of Muhammad came under attack; thirteen of the seventeen victims were Muslims. In another town in Karnataka, Davangere, the *Ram Jyoti yatra*, numbering 15,000 to 20,000 participants, provoked a riot after successfully negotiating with local authorities to deviate from the original route and enter a Muslim quarter.[34]

Advani was arrested when his *Rath yatra* entered Bihar. Hindu nationalists immediately declared a 'Bharat Bandh' which soon degenerated into rioting, notably in places through which Advani had passed—in the same way that reprisals would occur when a local procession was attacked. In two days of violence, prompted sometimes by the unwillingness of some Muslim merchants to close their shops, 42 people died in Rajasthan, 7 in Gujarat, 6 in Karnataka, 5 in West Bengal and 1 in Andhra Pradesh.

In spite of massive arrests and severe controls at the borders of Uttar Pradesh, tens of thousands of VHP militants appeared on 30 October at the mosque in Ayodhya to accomplish the announced *karseva*. They assaulted the site twice, obliging the forces of law and order to open fire in order to repel them. This provoked anti-Muslim riots in nearly all the states; in five days the violence caused, 66 deaths in Karnataka, 63 in Gujarat, 50 in Uttar Pradesh, about 20 in Madhya Pradesh and in Bihar, and at least 10 in Andhra Pradesh.[35]

The *karsevaks* who died in Ayodhya were immediately hailed as martyrs by the *Sangh Parivar*. Urns containing their ashes became the object of further processions (the *Asthi Kalash yatra*), which travelled through several districts. These corteges no longer retained anything but the form of Hindu processions, with the object of veneration being related even more indirectly to a religious ritual than in the case of the *Ram Shilas*. Once again, however, it was a matter of arousing the fervour of *communitas* through discourses which combined songs and speeches.[36] As such, the *Asthi Kalash yatra* served to incite new outbreaks of rioting. A procession in Agra, apparently comprising no more than 50 persons, ignored the guidelines of the local authorities and entered a Muslim quarter. Stone-throwing in those areas precipitated a new riot in which militant Hindu nationalists made use of more sophisticated arms than usual: later searches found one of the militants in possession of 60 high-powered home-made bombs and 80 litres of acid.[37]

Scholars such as Sandria Freitag and Sudhir Kakar argue that religious processions are occasions which lend themselves to the outbreak of communal rioting because the participants have an intricate relation to space and an exceptionally strong sense of belonging to their community. However, available evidence suggests that these conditions that are necessary but not sufficient for collective aggression. In most of the cases cited in this essay, such potential energy exploded when it was directed and even sparked off by ideologically-minded leaders. Indeed, as processions have become increasingly politicized, they have become more directly correlated with riots.

The pattern of procession-based riots which emerged in the late nineteenth century with the reinterpretation of the Ganesh festival was initiated by Hindu leaders eager to unify and mobilize Hindus—allegedly in reaction to Muslim assaults. This type of ideological procession, as a vehicle for recurrent acts of violence, was to be found again in the 1920s in Nagpur. At that time, the democratization of the political system brought forth a small political class which, divided as it was into parties and factions, was all the more inclined to exploit the religious sentiments of the electorate. In this context, the defence of processions became an issue in electoral contests that zealots such as Malaviya promoted at the risk of inciting riots. In fact, the transformation of Hindu processions into shows of force and the triggering of communal violence were sometimes seen as a means of polarizing the voters along religious lines. Thus in the cases of pre-independence riots that I have selected, Hindu processions were related to communal antagonism from two points of view, as anti-Muslim mobilizations and as elements of political, or even electoral, strategies. In both situations, local leaders, Hindu nationalist activists or politicians, played a crucial part. This twofold pattern persisted after independence; more precisely, it was one of the scenarios followed by communal riots when Hindu-Muslim conflicts became virulent. Initially, the dimension of mobilization had been more significant than the electoral one. One of the main changes to come about in the late 1980s and early 1990s involved the manner in which both aspects combined, many procession-based riots serving as anti-Muslim mobilizations in the framework of electoral campaigns: Another significant change lay in the partial nationalization of the Hindu-Muslim conflict, as promoted by 'yatra politics'.

In concluding, three additional questions might be raised: Do communal riots find their origin only in *Hindu* processions? What has been the response of the state to these kinds of riots and to riots in general? Is it still relevant to study the procession-related riots in the 1990s given that, first, the 1992–3 communal violence did not follow this pattern and, second, the incidence of not only procession-based riots but all sorts of communal riots is on the wane?

## The Politics of Riots and Processions

The outburst of communal violence which followed the demolition of the Babri Masjid in Ayodhya on 6 December 1992 and which was responsible for about 1,250 casualties was not 'instigated' by processions: there was no need to mobilize people in that manner because Hindu-Muslim antagonism had already been sufficiently exacerbated. This does not mean that this cycle of violence was not orchestrated in a ritualized way: often in reaction to Muslim protests in the streets, Hindu nationalist activists (from the *Sangh Parivar* or the Shiv Sena) led the offensive and resorted to processional forms, using 'rituals of confrontation', to borrow a phrase coined by Marc Gaborieau (1985). Sudhir Chandra remarks that the activities of the rioters who took part in the communal violence which occurred in Surat after the demolition of the Babri Masjid were indeed 'like rituals':

The arson they indulged in then resembled the community bonfire organised on the occasion of the Holi festival. It bore an even more bizarre resemblance—one with sacrificial *yajnas*—as some of the rioters threw into the rising flames, as oblation, live human beings, including children. (Chandra 1996: 84)

In Bombay in January 1993, the Shiv Sena organized *Maha Aartis* (a grand version of the Hindu ritual of worship performed at sunset) which, in contrast with the usual *aartis* performed in the temples, assumed a mass congregational character. They were intended to compete with the Muslims' *namaz* (literally, prayers; in this context, congregational prayers held in mosques) in which the Shiv Sainiks probably saw impressive gatherings and which they criticized for spilling out from the mosque onto the streets. Once again, the stigmatization of the Other is associated with an effort to emulate him. These *Maha Aartis* prepared the ground for riots in a way similar to the processions, as suggested in the following account by Masselos:

> The experiences enforced ideas of separate identity from Muslims and bonded those present to activity of antagonism. . . . [T]hey provided physical gathering points and emotional rallying spaces from which gangs moved out to attack Muslim targets. (Masselos 1996: 116)

Since early 1993, the number of communal riots has steeply declined from 1,601 (with 1,681 people killed) in 1992 and 2,292 (952 killed) in 1993 to 179 (78 killed) in 1994.[38] According to Engineer, 62 people died in such violence in 1995 and 24 in 1996 (Engineer 1995a, 1995b, 1996). This pattern clearly stems from several contradictory factors: militant Hindus believe that the Muslims have been 'taught a lesson' (to quote a phrase often heard in the *Sangh Parivar*) with the demolition of the mosque and the subsequent riots; secular activists have worked against communalism at the grassroots level and large sectors of the population are aware of the manner in which such turmoil can affect their daily lives and businesses. In 1993, especially after the electoral defeat of the BJP in Uttar Pradesh, Madhya Pradesh and Himachal Pradesh, the Hindu nationalist organizations realized that communal violence had alienated many voters, especially in the rural constituencies; they began to soft-pedal the issue of Ayodhya and relinquished the idea of mobilizing Hindus against Muslims through politico-religious processions. A major reason for the declining number of riots no doubt lies in this altered strategy.

Yet this pattern of communal mobilization has not disappeared, as conditions in several south Indian cities testify. In Hyderabad and Madras, Ganesh processions still lead to riots, as in 1995 when the processionists deliberately slowed down in order to pass by mosques at the time of the Friday prayer. In Hyderabad, the riot left five people dead. In Madras, the Hindu Munnani, an RSS affiliate clearly orchestrated such provocation.[39] Indeed, riots related to Hindu processions are probably more numerous in south India today possibly because some members of the RSS combine feel the need to crystallize a militant identity within the majority community of that region—something that has already been partly accomplished in the north.

## Muslim Processions and Riots

While Hindu processions are more often at the origin of a communal riot since they fit well in the Hindu nationalist strategy of ethno-religious mobilization used by the *Sangh Parivar* in the late 1980s-early 1990s, Muslim processions can also be used for similar purposes. Instances of this are available as far back as in Penderel Moon's testimony in the 1940s[40] as well as in some of the most recent riots. In May 1996, for example, Calcutta was affected by a riot resulting from a controversy about the Muharram procession:[41] one of the processions bearing a *taziya* (replica of the cenotaphs of Hasan and Hussain, the grandsons of the Prophet Muhammad) insisted on passing through a Hindu area, whose inhabitants mobilized to such an extent that they pelted the procession with stones. The ensuing riot was responsible for five casualties and the army had to intervene to restore peace and order. As usual, politicians were involved: although this Muslim pocket of Calcutta has traditionally been a stronghold of the Left Front—Kalimuddin Shams, one of Jyoti Basu's ministers had been elected from there in the past—a Congressman had won the recent elections and become the champion of the local Muslims. 'The heretic voters deserved punishment', commented M.K. Dhar in *The Hindustan Times*. In addition, the local mafia was looking for an opportunity to have the local administrators transferred because they had stopped several illegal constructions and put bootleggers behind bars. Thus one finds the same ingredients in this riot originating from a Muslim procession as in those deriving from Hindu ones.

Today, Hindus and Muslims are engaged in fierce competition over processions. Since 1978 in Hyderabad, a large procession has been organized in honour of Muhammad to coincide with the Ganesh procession (Engineer 1991: 273–4). Also to be observed, on the part of the Hindus, is a multiplication of processions. In Maharashtra, 68 *Rath yatras* alone were registered in the first half of 1986, compared to four in 1985, and 944 Shivaji Jayanti celebrations were held, compared with 656 in 1985 (Rajgopal 1987: 133). What can the state do about this disturbing development?

## The Role of the State

The fact that a growing number of processions serve as vehicles of communal rioting will no doubt be difficult to counter, as the authorities have inherited from the Raj the principle of non-interference in religious celebrations.[42] N.S. Saksena, a veteran of the Indian police, gives an interesting testimony in this respect:

In all Police Training Colleges the trainees are told about the main festivals of Hindus and Muslims; then they are told as to what precautions have to be taken to maintain peace. One important aspect of this instruction is to explain to them how all religious processions have to be regulated and controlled. In order to do this job successfully it is incumbent on all Station House Officers to maintain an exhaustive record of all religious processions—the route which is customarily followed by them, the equipments, including ceremonial weapons, which are carried, the timings of the start and finish of the procession, etc. *No one ever contemplated or should contemplate banning of these processions.* (Saksena 1990: 84, emphasis added)

There has been a general failure to ban even ideologically motivated processions for very long. Shiv Jayanti, banned in Bhiwandi subsequent to the 1970 riots, resurfaced at Kalyan (located 10 km from Bhiwandi) in 1982. The participation of Bal Thackeray, head of the Shiv Sena, and of Congress ministers from Maharashtra, suggests that the party in power can expect a certain recognition from the electorate for this symbolic gesture.[43] In 1984, Shiv Jayanti was the occasion of a new riot in Bhiwandi, where the procession had once again received authorization.

The attitude of the state towards processions needs to be analysed within the broader context of its policy vis-à-vis communal mobilizations and conflicts at large. Today, the agencies of the government rarely remain neutral during communal riots. Ideally, the government, the administration and the police should aim only at re-establishing civil peace through repression and, possibly, negotiation; most of the time they have other things in mind. Several scenarios illustrating the role of the state, or some of its agencies, in communal riots need to be analysed.

Let us first consider the situation which arises when a political group aims to discredit the government in a particular state. It may choose to foment or exploit a communal riot to support the claim that the ruling faction (or party) is incapable of maintaining law and order. Such a chain of events developed in Madhya Pradesh in 1989, when the *Ram Shila Pujan* led to a riot in Indore. Reliable informers alleged that supporters of the head of one of the Congress factions had orchestrated the outbreak of violence in order to cause trouble for the incumbent chief minister, Motilal Vora, the head of another Congress faction. The primary objective of his opponents was to undermine his efforts to win endorsement for his followers as the party's election candidates.[44] While taking *Ram Shilas* in procession had generated a lot of communal tension, the magnitude of the 1989 riot in Indore can be partly explained by factional fights within the ruling party. A similar situation arose in Hyderabad with the riot which occurred in December 1990 in the wake of the *Rath yatra* and led to the death of 120 people. It was alleged that members of the chief minister's own party, the Congress, had instigated the rioting in order to discredit him, and he felt obliged to resign from office shortly after the disturbance.

In such cases, however, state power is involved only to the extent that it is coveted by dissidents in the ruling party. The state can of course play a part on its own. Obviously, a government may often interfere with the action of the security forces. In some cases, its main aim is to delay their intervention in order (i) to 'teach a lesson' to a community whose vote was 'misguided' in the past; (ii) to let the victims suffer in order to appear as its protector—a stratagem which the Congress is alleged to have used vis-à-vis the Muslims; (iii) or even to let a minority which has just been subjected to severe humiliation or even violence, take its revenge in the streets. (This would explain the duration of the 1990 Hyderabad riot, given the fact that the aggressors were primarily Muslims of the old town.)

The two other scenarios can be illustrated by the riots of Meerut. In 1982 and 1987 Congress leaders, including the then chief minister, are alleged to have let the riot develop against the Muslims partly because they did not vote the right way in the previous elections (Engineer 1982: 1804; see also 1988: 22). According to some press reports, the management of communal violence was especially in evidence in Congress-ruled states before the 1989 elections. At that time, the Congress(I) used riots to appear as the saviour of the Muslims and to divide the opposition since the BJP and the Left could less easily work together in the context of communal polarization. And it was more difficult to foment riots in opposition-ruled states.[45]

Police officers often invoke political interference to explain the duration of riots, whether they have been provoked by processions or not. In early 1995, a senior police officer of Uttar Pradesh completed a study on the 'Perception of Police Neutrality during Communal Riots' at the National Police Academy of Hyderabad. From a study of ten major riots, he reached the conclusion that 'no riot can last for more than 24 hours unless the state administration wants it to continue'.[46] Yet he admitted that the prolongation of riots was not only due to the (in)action of governments; he found a deep anti-Muslim bias within the police itself. In Uttar Pradesh, such bias is on a par with the under-representation of Muslims in the state police, especially the Provincial Armed Constabulary (PAC), where they account for a mere 4 per cent, as against 17.3 per cent in the state population.[47] This imbalance partly explains why Hindu-Muslim riots have increasingly tended to pitch Muslims against the police since the late 1970s. One of the first examples of this evolution is probably to be found in the Varanasi riot of 1977 (Banerjee 1990: 56).

While the police is vulnerable to such criticism, it is not prevented, not even dissuaded from reprehensible behaviour by the State. After the 1987 Meerut riot, which can well be described as a police assault on Muslims, the only government sanction consisted of suspending the local chief of the PAC. Amnesty International then objected that such leniency would suggest that the police enjoyed complete impunity (Noorani 1987: 2140).[48] Similarly, after the beginning of the Bhagalpur riot in 1989, Rajiv Gandhi visited the place and cancelled the transfer of the local Superintendent of Police, whose anti-Muslim prejudice had publicly found expression during the events; this was obviously because the man was very popular with the Hindu community, which the Congress Party could not afford to alienate before the elections.[49] Many of the worst crimes took place after that; it was as though the rioters had gained total immunity.

The capacity of the state administration, even in Bihar, to control the communal bias of the police has been illustrated by the way Laloo Prasad Yadav, as soon as he took over as chief minister in 1990, successfully threatened police officers with systematic sanctions in case of riots in their district. However, the state administration has not really penalized police officers who have been found guilty by the majority report of the inquiry commission about the Bhagalpur riot: the Inspector General of Police in Bhagalpur at the time of the riot has simply been transferred. Nonetheless, the situation in West Bengal—an obvious degeneration since the late 1980s notwithstanding—suggests that communal peace does, to a great extent, depend on political will. Despite the high proportion of Muslims (23.1 per cent in 1991), Hindu-Muslim tensions are very rare, except in districts where Bangladeshi immigration is high (such as Murshidabad) and in parts of Calcutta. Surely such an exceptional situation must be attributed to the secular policies of West Bengal's Left Front government, which has been dominated by the CPI(M) since it attained power in June 1977.

Largely because of the state governments' attitude—whatever the party in command—the inquiry commissions investigating communal riots are rendered ineffectual. Most of the time, politicians interfere with their work; as a result, their reports tend to be delayed and, in any case, there is seldom any follow-up by the criminal justice system. After the Bhagalpur riot in 1989, the Congress government of Bihar appointed a one-man commission of inquiry whose communal bias appeared so apparent that Laloo Prasad Yadav, felt compelled to add two more members to the commission; the original member remained chairman. Five years after the event, the chairman finally submitted a minority report exonerating the Hindu nationalist forces and the police officers while his colleagues produced a completely different report. Parallel to that, the judiciary, whose work is independent of that of the inquiry commission, has not achieved very much in its treatment of riots related to the Ayodhya controversy. The 142 cases filed in the court accused 1,392 people of participating in incidents of violence and looting. Six years later, 87 cases against 901 accused are still pending. Of the 55 cases decided, 11 have ended in convictions in which 50 people have been punished. Of the 142 cases, 38 cases relate to murder of which 12 cases have been decided and 1 resulted in conviction. Of the 406 people accused in murder cases, the court has decided on 95 people, of whom 94 have been acquitted.[50]

## Notes

1. This process is never entirely realized, however, because 'the Brahman excludes from his procession Untouchables and excludes himself (or is excluded) from theirs . . . . Only partial totalisations occur' (Herrenschmidt 1989: 193).
2. Numerous editorials by Tilak in *Kesari* bear witness to this. For instance on 3 September 1895, he wrote: 'If Hindus, even in one province, unite to worship the same God at least for ten days every year, it is an event of no mean significance' (quoted in Karandikar 1957: 124).
3. His lieutenant, the editor of *Kesari*, said: 'Tilak himself admitted that the arrogance of the Moslems gave rise to the idea of the festival which was obviously intended to draw all the Hindus around a central national function. Tilak often justified it by remarking

that there was nothing wrong in providing a platform for all the Hindus of all high and low classes to stand together and discharge a joint national duty' (Kelkar 1967: 284).

4. The first public celebration took place in Girgaum, near Bombay, under the auspices of, among other personalities, the father of Bal Thackeray, the founder of the Shiv Sena. It was there that the centenary of this institution was celebrated with great pomp in 1992 (*Sunday*, 20–6 September 1992: 47–9).

5. The number of Hindus forcibly converted would have been between 1,000 and 1,500 (Wood 1987: 215; see also Hardgrave 1977: 82).

6. In Akola, in the Central Provinces, Muslims obtained in 1924 the banning of Ganesh processions, introduced in 1907 and accompanied by music only since 1923, without doubt under the influence of the local Hindu Sabha, which militated in vain for a lifting of the prohibition by the British authorities. National Archives of India, New Delhi, Home Political Department, F-179 & KW (1926).

7. *Indian Quarterly Register* (*IQR*) 1924, Vol. 2: 30 and Dutta (1990: 38–47). The violence in Calcutta in 1926 caused 110 deaths and left 975 wounded.

8. See, for instance, the reaction of the Arya Samajist Lajpat Rai (Rai 1966: 173).

9. Moonje established himself in Nagpur in 1901 as a surgeon specializing in ocular problems (*Dharmaveer: Dr. B.S. Moonje Commemoration Volume*, 1972: 26). The first organization which he introduced locally was the Rashtriya Mandal, a circle of Brahman intelligentsia founded in 1906, which supported the cause of the 'Extremists' until they were banned by the British in 1909. From 1917, Moonje was considered to be the dominant figure in the Provincial Congress Committee in the Central Provinces (Baker 1979: 54). Although a Deshastha Brahman, he ate meat and was devoted to hunting (NMML, microfilm section, Moonje Papers, Roll no. 7, letter of 30 October 1927 to Maharaja Scindia). He said of himself that he was 'perhaps Kshatriya by temperament' (ibid., Roll no. 11, letter of 18 May 1936 to Rajah Ichalkarang). In addition, he developed shooting clubs which were intended to actualize the *akhara* traditions during the Second World War for the massive enlisting of Hindus in the British army, because the training of his community in military techniques was more important than anti-colonial non-cooperation.

10. Baker (1979: 101) and *Moonje Papers*, Sub-file no. 13, Letter of the General Secretary of the Hindu Sabha of Nagpur to local papers, 3 September 1924.

11. Interview with V.R. Oke, 12 August 1992, in New Delhi.

12. His father was accorded the title of 'Vyas' in recognition of his knowledge of the *Bhagawata* (Chaturvedi 1972: 1).

13. *Meston Papers*, Mss Eur F (IOLR) and Home Political Department, File no. 56, Deposit Fortnightly Report of UP (September 1915).

14. Studying 'the connection between political ambitions at the provincial level and the growth of communal antagonism in the localities' (Page 1982: 77), David Page underlines that in Allahabad, 'Malaviya's party exploited religious passion as a means of displacing their opponents' (Ibid.: 80–1).

15. The distinction between M.M. Malaviya and his group, more involved than himself in the riots of 1924–6, is underlined by the local British authorities (Parmanand 1985, Vol. 2: 678).

16. In 1926, Motilal Nehru wrote to his son: 'Publicly I was denounced as an anti-Hindu and pro-Mohammedan, but privately almost every individual voter was told that I was

a beef-eater in league with the Mohammedans to legalise cow-slaughter in public places at all times' (Nehru 1960).

17. The ICP took twelve seats, as against sixteen for the Swaraj Party (which amounted to scarcely half its result in 1923).

18. In 1927 the celebration of the tricentenary anniversary of Shivaji in Surat was an interesting exception. The procession of Shiv Jayanti, which was led by leaders of the local Hindu Sabha, was under close scrutiny by the District Magistrate who gave the following account:

> When the procession consisting of about 1,000 persons and with five parties of *bhajanwallas* [singers and musicians] playing *manjiras* [cymbals] and singing religious songs, came to Parsi Sheri, it came to a halt owing to the menacing attitude of about 20 to 25 Muhammedans with *lathis* in front. A parley took place between the few Muslims and the advanced guard of the procession led by Dr Raiji [leader of the Hindu Sabha] and others. The Muslims requested that the music should stop near the mosque. It appears that either Dr Raiji definitely refused to accept such a request, or that his attitude was interpreted to mean that. The Muslims got excited. Brickbats and pieces of road metal were flourished in the air . . . the City Magistrate asked the leaders of the procession to disperse the procession or to change the route as the attitude of the Muslims was threatening. It however appears that the leaders were divided over the question . . . when the armed party had been lined up across the road, the constables as well as the procession advanced a little towards the mosque. This was immediately interpreted by the Muslims as the decision of the police to conduct the procession past the mosque with the protection of the armed constables, and with music playing. This was unfortunate as it led to an infuriate attack. . . . (Report of K.L. Panjabi, District Magistrate of Surat, to the Secretary to the Government of Bombay, Confidential Proceedings in the Political Department for the year 1927, India Office Library and Records.)

This narrative, if one accepts it as a reliable source, illustrates the key role played by Hindu nationalist leaders within processions directed against the Muslims.

19. *Report of the three-member Commission of Inquiry headed by Shri Jitendra Narain, former Judge, Patna High Court, to inquire into the communal disturbances that took place in April 1979, in and around Jamshedpur*, Patna, Superintendent Secretariat Press, 1981, p. 41.

20. One example is Kanyakumari, a district in which the RSS had developed some hundred *shakhas* so as to better combat the influence of Christianity (Mathew 1983: 415).

21. *The Organiser,* 28 February 1982: 7.

22. *India Today,* 31 May 1986: 35.

23. The local VHP paper, *Vishwa Hindu Samachar,* stated in July 1985: 'All Hindus should unite against *vidharma* [those who practise another religion]. Outmoded feudal values still prevail in our villages which have kept the caste pollution intact and has thus resulted in friction within the Hindu fold. . . . Savarna Hindus [upper castes] should now become alert and not widen the gap between the castes and compromise with *dalit* and should not continue to remain selfish' (quoted in Engineer 1986: 1343).

24. A cassette in Hindi, signed 'VHP—New Delhi' and entitled 'Ram Shila Pujan'.

25. *Muslim India* 103, December 1991: 557.

26. *Economic and Political Weekly,* 4 May 1996: 1055.

27. K. Chaudhuri, 'A Commission Divided: Who Was Behind the Bhagalpur Riots?', *Frontline,* 11 August 1995: 33.

28. *India Week,* 3 November 1989: 2; *The Times of India,* 4 November 1989: 1.
29. *Economic and Political Weekly,* 4 May 1996: 1058.
30. Quoted in *India Week,* 3 November 1989: 3.
31. *Hindu Vishva* 25 (12), August 1990: 62.
32. *Frontline,* 27 October 1990: 31–4.
33. In Gujarat, militant Hindu nationalists had made use of the processions associated with the Ganesh festival, which occurred shortly before the *Ram Jyoti yatra.* In five towns (above all in Baroda, Anand and Surat), they organized processions with insulting slogans directed against Muslims. Officially, the Hots caused sixteen deaths (Engineer 1990: 2234–5). For more on the rioting in Baroda, where hundreds of thousands of persons took part in a procession and *gulal* was thrown at a mosque, see 'Communal Riots in Baroda,' *Economic and Political Weekly,* 24 November 1990: 2584-5.
34. A similar phenomenon was observed in Madras, when the decision by V.P. Singh to recognize the birth anniversary of the Prophet Muhammad as a holiday provoked the anger of the militant movements of the Hindu Munnani (Hindu Front formed after the conversions of 1981). On 2 September, the Vinayak (Ganesh) Chaturthi procession slowed in front of a mosque at the time of prayer. According to official sources, the ensuing riot, in which Dalits took part, resulted in three deaths (Geetha and Rajadurai 1990: 2122–3).
35. These figures and orders of magnitude were provided by police reports issued to the press at the time of the events (*vide,* for example *The Indian Express,* 1–5 November 1990). Either the government did not take this wave of riots into account when it drew up the balance of violence for the year in the Rajya Sabha (*Muslim India* 103, July 1991: 323), or it was deliberately underestimated, since it certainly could not have been ignored; the rioting in Jaipur, then, must have resulted in about 100 deaths (*Frontline,* 10 November 1990: 106) and not fifty-one as officially indicated.
36. Field observations made at Shivpuri (Madhya Pradesh), corroborated by reports published in the press.
37. *India Today,* 15 January 1991: 28–9.
38. These figures come from the Ministry of Home Affairs. Note for Consultative Committee Meeting on Communal Situation (*Muslim India,* December 1995: 558).
39. *Frontline,* 6 October 1995: 30–2.
40. The testimony of this British administrator illustrates the parallel that one can establish between the situation created by Hindu processions and Muslim processions:

    The last day of the festival (of Muharram) . . . was always an anxious one for the police. The whole city turned out to see the *taziyas;* sightseers crowded streets and the roofs of the houses. The mourners, excited by the onlookers and fortified with drugs, worked themselves up to a final pitch of fervour and frenzy, which the most trifling incident might turn to blind fury. It was during the early part of the day, when the *taziyas* were still moving about in the crowded walled city, that the danger was the greatest. At some places rival processions had to pass close to one another; the routes of several lay right through the centre of the Hindu quarter of the city. An angry word or a slight mischance might easily precipitate a riot . . . there was a long tale of Muharram riots. . . . One year the top of a large *taziya* stuck against a telegraph wire; a small bit was broken off and fell on the ground. In a few minutes a rumour spread through the crowds that a Hindu had thrown a stone at a *taziya*. Hindus and Muslims fell upon one another, hooligans set fire to buildings, houses were looted, and for several days there was an orgy of bloodshed. On another occasion, just as the *taziyas* were being lined up on the circular road, it was heard that four Muslims had been stabbed by Hindus on the other side of the city. Dropping their *taziyas* on the road, the mourners and bearers rushed back into the city to loot the Hindu shops and murder any Hindu they might meet on their way (Moon 1944: 88).

41. As usual, everybody gave different versions but three press reports coverge: *The Sunday* and *The Hindustan Times*, cited in *Muslim India* 163, July 1996: 323–4 and *India Today*, 15 July 1996: 17.
42. Regarding British Policy, see Robb 1986: 285–319.
43. *The Organiser*, 9 May 1992.
44. *Dainik Bhaskar*, 21 October 1989.
45. Smita Gupta, 'Riots and Election Strategy', *The Independent*, 12 October 1989.
46. Interview in *Communalism Combat*, February 1995.
47. *India Today*, 31 January 1993: 31–7.
48. When he was Chief Minister of Uttar Pradesh, Mulayam Singh Yadav, true to his reputation for conspicuous concern for the Muslims, 'asked the CID to launch prosecution against 19 PAC and other police personnel who had been indicted for involvement in the killing of innocent persons in May 1987 in Meerut,' but 'nothing has happened beyond the order to the CID to prosecute the accused' (*PUCL Bulletin*, Vol. 15, No. 8, August 1995: 1).
49. On this point, see the comments of retired police officer N.S. Saxena (1990: 20).
50. 'Recalling Bhagalpur: Aftermath of 1989 Riots', *Economic and Political Weekly*, 4 May 1996: 1057.

# References

Banerjee, Ashish (1990), 'Comparative Curfew: Changing Dimensions of Communal Politics in India', in Veena Das (ed.), *Mirrors of Violence: Communities, Riots and Survivors in South Asia*, Delhi: Oxford University Press.

Bayly, C.A., 'Patrons and Politics in Northern India', *Modern Asian Studies*, Vol. 7, No. 3.

——— (1975), *The Local Roots of Indian Politics: Allahabad 1880-1920*, Oxford: Clarendon Press.

Bharti, I. (1989), 'Bhagalpur Riots and Bihar Government', *Economic and Political Weekly*, 2 December.

Bose, P.K. (1981), 'Social Mobility and Caste Violence: A Study of the Gujarat Riots', *Economic and Political Weekly*, 18 April.

Brass, Paul R. (1993), 'The Rise of the BJP and the Future of Party Politics in Uttar Pradesh', in H. Gould and S. Ganguly (eds.), *India Votes: Alliance Politics and Minority Governments in the Ninth and Tenth General Elections*, Boulder: Westview Press.

Cashman, Richard I. (1975), *The Myth of the Lokamanya: Tilak and Mass Politics in Maharashtra*, Berkeley and Los Angeles: University of California Press.

Chandra, Sudhir (1996), 'Of Communal Consciousness and Communal Violence:

Impressions form Post-Riot Surat', in J. McGuire, P. Reeves, and H. Brasted (eds.), *Politics of Violence: From Ayodhya to Behrampada*, New Delhi: Sage.

Chiriyankandath, James (1992), 'Tricolour and Saffron: Congress and the New Hindu Challenge', in S.K. Mitra and J. Chiriyankandath (eds.), *Electoral Politics in India: A Changing Landscape*, New Delhi: Segment Books.

Dale, Stephen (1975), 'The Mappila Outbreaks: Ideology and Social Conflict in Nineteenth Century Kerala', *Journal of Asian Studies*, Vol. 35, No. 1.

Engineer, Asghar Ali (1982), 'The Guilty Men of Meerut', *Economic and Political Weekly*, 6 November.

——— (1984), *Communal Riots in Post Independence India*, Hyderabad, India: Sangam.

——— (1986), 'Gujarat Burns Again', *Economic and Political Weekly*, 3 August.

——— (1988), 'Meerut: Shame of the Nation', in Asghar Ali Engineer (ed.), *Delhi-Meerut Riots: Compilation, Documentation and Analysis*, Delhi: Ajanta.

——— (1991), 'Making of the Hyderabad Riots', *Economic and Political Weekly*, 9 February.

——— (1995a), 'Communalism and Communal Violence in 1994', *Economic and Political Weekly*, 4 February.

——— (1995b), 'Communalism and Communal Violence in 1995', *Economic and Political Weekly*, 23 December.

——— (1996), 'Bhagalpur Riot Inquiry Commission Report', *Economic and Political Weekly*, 15 July.

Freitag, Sandria (1990), *Public Arenas and the Emergence of Communalism in North India*, Delhi: Oxford University Press.

Gaborieau, M. (1985), 'From Al'beruni to Jinnah', *Anthropology Today*, Vol. 1, No. 3.

Gordon, R. (1975), 'The Hindu Mahasabha and the Indian National Congress: 1915 to 1926', *Modern Asian Studies*, Vol. 9, No. 2.

Jaffrelot, Christophe (1996), *The Hindu Nationalist Movement and Indian Politics, 1952 to the 1990s*, New Delhi: Viking/London: Hurst/New York: Columbia University Press.

Jog, N.G. (1979), *Lokamanya Bal Gangadhar Tilak*, New Delhi: Government of India.

Kelkar, N.C. (1967 [1928]), *Life and Times of Lokamanya Tilak*, translated from Marathi by D.V. Divekar, Delhi: Anupama Publications.

Kesavan, M. (1990), 'Communal Violence and its Impact on the Politics of North India: 1937-39', *Occasional Papers on History and Society*, second series, New Delhi: Nehru Memorial Museum and Library.

Madan D.P. (n.d.), *Report of the Commission of Inquiry into the Communal Disturbances at Bhiwandi, Jalgaon and Mahad in May 1970*, Vol. 1, n.p.

Masselos, Jim (1996), 'The Bombay Riots of January 1993: The Politics of Urban Conflagration', in J. McGuire, P. Reeves, and H. Brasted (eds.), *Politics of Violence: From Ayodhya to Behrampada*, New Delhi: Sage.

Mathew, G. (1982), 'Politicization of Religion: Conversions to Islam in Tamil Nadu', *Economic and Political Weekly*, 19 June.

——— (1983), 'Hindu-Christian Communalism: An Analysis of Kanyakumari Riots', *Social Action*, October 1983.

Michael, S.M. (1986), 'The Politicization of the Ganapati Festival', *Social Compass*, Vol. 33.

Moon, Panderel (1944), *Strangers in India*, London: Faber and Faber.

Noorani, A.G. (1987), 'Amnesty Reports on Meerut Killings', *Economic and Political Weekly*, 12 December.

Pandey, Gyanendra (1978), *The Ascendancy of Congress in Uttar Pradesh*, Delhi: Oxford University Press.

Parmanand (1985), *Mahamana Madan Mohan Malaviya*, Benares: Banaras Hindu University.

Patel, S. (1985), 'Violence with a Difference', *Economic and Political Weekly*, 7 July.

Prakash, I. (1938), *A Review of the History and Work of the Hindu Mahasabha and the Hindu Sangathan Movement*, New Delhi: Akhil Cheratiya Hindu Mahasabha.

Rajgopal, P.R. (1987), *Communal Violence in India*, New Delhi: Uppal Publishing House.

Robb, P. (1986), 'The Challenge of Gau Mata: British Policy and Religious Change in India, *1880-1916*', *Modern Asian Studies*, Vol. 20, No. 2.

Robinson, Francis (1973), 'Municipal Government and Muslim Separatism in the United Provinces, 1833 to 1916', *Modern Asian Studies*, Vol. 7, No. 3.

Saksena, N.S. (1990), *Communal Riots in India*, Noida: Trishul.

Sundaram, V.A. (1942) (ed.), *Banaras Hindu University 1916-1942*, Benares: R. Pathak.

Tambiah, S. (1996), *Leveling Crowds: Ethnonationalist Conflicts and Collective Violence in South Asia*, Berkeley: University of California Press.

Van der Veer, Peter (1987), 'God Must Be Liberated! A Hindu Liberation Movement in Ayodhya', *Modern Asian Studies*, Vol. 21, No. 2.

# Chapter 17

# The 2002 pogrom in Gujarat
# the post-9/11 face of
# Hindu nationalist anti-Muslim violence

Violence between Hindus and Muslims is a structural feature of Indian society. One finds its traces very early in the country's history,[1] a fact that can drive the analyst to explain the phenomenon by referring to the incompatibility of Hindu and Muslim cultures.[2] However, those historians interested in the phenomenon have always emphasized the economic dimension of the rivalry between Hindus and Muslims, which springs from conflicts about real estate or commercial competition (Bayly 1995: 190–1). Among sociologists and political scientists, this approach has found favour with many authors more or less inclined to Marxist categories (Ahmed 1984: 903–6; Engineer 1984: 34–41).

The interpretation of violence between Hindus and Muslims that I have suggested is very different (Jaffrelot 1996). It emphasizes the role of politics in two complementary aspects, the impact of a militant ethno-religious ideology and the exploitation of communal issues by political parties.

Indeed, research on communal riots in India after 1947 suggests that these riots largely originate from a distorted idea of 'the Other' among Hindus who, though representing an overwhelming majority, often perceive the Muslims as a 'fifth column' threatening them from within Indian society. After independence, Hindu-Muslim riots became one *classicus locus* of Indian politics largely because the Hindu nationalist parties—the Jana Sangh and then the Bharatiya Janata Party (BJP)—resorted to anti-Muslim violence to polarize the electorate and solidify the Hindu 'vote bank'. This process culminated in the Ayodhya movement through which the *Sangh Parivar*—the 'RSS family', i.e. the network of organizations developed by the RSS, including the BJP—reclaimed one of the mosques of Uttar Pradesh, the Babri Masjid by claiming that it was built on the birthplace of Lord Ram. This movement was marred by recurring riots which reached their climax in 1992 when Hindu nationalist activists destroyed the Babri Masjid.

This explanatory model of Hindu-Muslim riots combining ideological and electoral dimensions was verified again in the light of the Gujarat riots of 2002.

Indeed, these riots also commit us to reconfirm the role of the Hindu nationalist politicians. The latter has to be weighted even more heavily in Gujarat for they held political power in that province. This state of things explains the rather exceptional intensity of the Gujarat riots. This time, Hindu-Muslim violence was not so much a reflection of the routinized logic of communal riots in India, but rather the result of an organized pogrom with the approval of the state apparatus of Gujarat acting not only with the electoral agenda in mind, but also in view of a true ethnic cleansing. Besides, the intensity of the riots has also demonstrated that this kind of violence has triggered a feedback in society even among groups hitherto less inclined to ethnic nationalism, such as, for example, the tribals. But there is an effect of yet another political strategy at work, which reminds us of the ideological core of our explanatory model: the more and more thorough diffusion of Hindutva in Gujarat in reaction to a fear of Jehad.

## Godhra, 27 February 2002: A Riot Provoked

Gujarat has long been known for its communal violence.[3] The riot in Ahmedabad in 1969, which left approximately 630 dead, remained the most serious riot in India after Partition until the Bhagalpur riot, 20 years later, which was part of the wave of clashes between Muslims and Hindus from the *Ramjanmabhoomi* Movement. But this same movement also brought Gujarat to the fore: throughout the 1980s to 1990s, this state counted the most riot victims per inhabitant. In 1990, L.K. Advani's *Rath yatra* sparked riots that left about 220 dead in this state. In 1992, the demolition of the Babri Masjid also set off a wave of violence that killed 325 people, mostly Muslims. The heightening of this phenomenon in the 1990s already reflected nationalist Hindu activism. The clashes in 2002 must also be analysed as a political phenomenon.

Violence broke out on 27 February in Godhra, a district headquarters in eastern Gujarat. Fifty-seven Hindus were killed, including 25 women and 14 children, who were burned alive aboard the Sabarmati Express. The train was carrying back from Faizabad (Uttar Pradesh) nationalist Hindu activists who had travelled to Ayodhya to build a temple dedicated to the god Ram on the ruins of the Babri Masjid. A campaign to build this temple had been instigated by the Vishva Hindu Parishad (VHP), within the context of the election campaign in Uttar Pradesh, where the BJP was attempting to retain power by all possible means. The undertaking had once again been postponed through Central Government mediation and the judges' vigilance, a recurrent process since the demolition of the Babri Masjid in 1992, which had increasingly frustrated the *karsevaks* (literally 'servers-in-action'), Hindu nationalist activists who had come to Ayodhya to erect the temple.

Those who were originally from Gujarat and were returning home aboard the Sabarmati Express had gathered together in a few coaches. They chanted Hindu nationalist songs and slogans throughout the entire journey, all the while harassing Muslim passengers. One family was even made to get off the train for refusing to utter the *karsevaks'* war cry: 'Jai Shri Ram?' (Glory to Lord Ram!). More abuse occurred at the stop in Godhra: a Muslim shopkeeper was also ordered to shout

'Jai Shri Ram!' He refused, and was assaulted until the *karsevaks* turned on a Muslim woman with her two daughters. It seems that one of them was forced to board the train before it started going again.

The train had hardly left the station when one of the passengers pulled the emergency chain. It was yanked several times, until the train came to a halt in the middle of a Muslim neighbourhood inhabited by Ghanchis, a community from which many of the Godhra street vendors hail. According to Hindu nationalist activists, hundreds of Muslims surrounded the coaches occupied by the *karsevaks* and attacked it with stones and torches. Coach S6 caught fire, killing 57 people (Vardarajan 2002). But the Justice U.C. Banerjee Commission, a one-man commission which had been appointed in September 2004 by the Union Government, held that the fire which occurred aboard the Sabarmarti Express at the Godhra Railway Station was accidental and started from inside. This assessment was first spelled out by this former Supreme Court judge in his interim report submitted in January 2005 and was confirmed in the final report one year later in March 2006.

Whatever the initial cause,[4] the aftermath of the events clearly showed that the violence reached unprecedented proportions because of the political strategy employed by Hindu nationalists.

## From Riot to Pogrom: State-sponsored Violence

Narendra Modi, the BJP Chief Minister in Gujarat, is a former cadre member in the RSS which spawned the Hindu nationalist movement, and where most of the VHP and BJP leaders began their career. Whereas Godhra District Collector, on 27 February, had spent the day explaining that the incident was not premeditated, Modi declared that very evening that it was a 'pre-planned violent act of terrorism' (Communalism Combat, 2002). And that very evening too, on the government's orders, the bodies of those who had died in Godhra were taken to Ahmedabad for a post-mortem and public ceremony. The arrival of the bodies at the Ahmedabad station was broadcast on television, causing considerable agitation among the Hindus, all the more so since the bodies were exhibited merely covered with a sheet. The following day, the VHP organized the shutdown of the city (*bandh*) with the support of the BJP. This mobilization established the conditions for a Hindu offensive in Ahmedabad.

However, in addition to Godhra and Ahmedabad (two cities with histories steeped in communal strife),[5] other towns in Gujarat where such riots had not developed previously experienced clashes. On the evening of 28 February, Gandhinagar, the capital of Gujarat, located 30 km from Ahmedabad, was the scene of Hindu-Muslim rioting for the first time in its history. Twenty-six towns in all were subject to curfew. Ahmedabad and Godhra saw the most serious clashes, with 350 and 100 victims respectively in early March, according to official figures. After these two cities came Mehsana (50 dead) and Sabarkantha (40 dead).

Reviewing the sequence of events, even in a condensed version, gives an idea of the power of destruction that came over Gujarat during those few days. On 28 February, in Ahmedabad, in the Naroda Gaon and Naroda Pattiya areas an armed hoarde of several thousand people attacked Muslim houses and shops, killing 200. Six other neighbourhoods in the city were subject to similar attacks on a lesser scale. Three other districts, Vadodara, Gandhinagar and Sabarkhanta, were host to comparable violence. In the latter district, several settlements were the scene of clashes. Elsewhere, too, but to a lesser degree, the previously spared rural areas were involved. The next day, on 1 March, mainly rural districts were added to the list of hotspots: Panchmahal, Mehsana, Kheda, Junagadh, Banaskantha, Patan, Anand and Narmada. On 2 March, Bharuch and Rajkot, which had yet to be affected by communal violence, were hit in turn. On 4 March riots broke out in Surat, a town that had seen considerable Hindu-Muslim violence in the 1990s and was much less affected this time.

## PREMEDITATED AND COORDINATED CLASHES

The clashes in Gujarat could not have spread so quickly and taken on such proportions unless they had been orchestrated by well-organized actors and the attackers' plan had been prepared prior to the events in Godhra. As early as 28 February, 24 hours after the attack on the Sabarmati Express, and shortly after Modi's repatriation of the bodies had caused such extreme distress, the VHP *bandh* degenerated into an orgy of violence: nothing was left to chance; it was a far cry from the spontaneous rioting Modi later described to excuse the Hindus.[6]

Actually, everything went according to a military-like plan in Ahmedabad and elsewhere.[7] The troops were perfectly disciplined and incredibly numerous: groups of attackers often included thousands of men. These squads generally arrived in the Muslim neighbourhoods by truckloads. They wore a basic uniform— the RSS khaki shorts and a saffron headband—and carried daggers and pitchforks as well as bottles of water to quench their thirst en route. The lists that the ringleaders had in hand attest to the premeditated nature of the assault: these indicated Muslim homes and shops, some of which bore Hindi names, thereby proving that investigation had actually been undertaken before hand to ascertain the owner's identity. These lists—on computer print-outs had obviously been drawn up on the basis of voter registration lists.

That the entire plan had been carefully organized can also be inferred from the assiduous use the aggressors made of cellular telephones. They apparently reported regularly to a central headquarters and received their instructions from this same centre. It is not entirely impossible that these headquarters had been set up simply in the police stations of the towns involved, or of the state itself because a number of Hindu nationalist leaders took up residence there throughout the period of violence. Several senior civil servants—on condition of anonymity— admitted to National Human Rights Commission investigators that on 28 February, the Gujarat Interior Minister and Health Minister directed the advance of the assailants from the 'City police control room' of Ahmedabad.[8] At the same time, the Urban Development Minister had set up his headquarters in the Gujarat 'State police control room' in Gandhinagar. All gave the police forces orders not to intervene.

The attackers were organized and well equipped. This was obvious in the use of gas cylinders that they had shipped to their attack sites. The typical scenario of this new-style violence involved looting Muslim shops then blowing them up with these makeshift but extremely powerful bombs. Not only do these operations show carefully planned organization, but they also indicate official state support. It would be impossible to transport that many men (and gas cylinders) with that many trucks without the benefit of state logistic support. Above all, the protected nature of the clashes over days, weeks, and even months can only be explained by active government cooperation.

This bias was tested beforehand by the Hindu nationalist activists, after their leaders had given them assurances: they set fire to a few automobiles in the vicinity of police stations to make sure their schemes could be carried out with no fear of punishment. This was almost always the case, given that the leaders of the party in power, the BJP, had quickly occupied central police headquarters. The administration was paralyzed. But in any event, since their rise to power in Gujarat, Hindu nationalists had already penetrated deep into the state apparatus, starting with the police. Hence the standard response they gave to the Muslims who called them to their rescue: 'We have no order to save you' (Human Rights Watch 2003).

Local BJP and VHP leaders were out in the streets alongside the attackers. Victims of their violence gave names and descriptions about which there can be no mistake. On the basis of these, the editor-in-chief of *Communalism Combat,* a secularist publication, revealed that charges had been filed against a BJP MP and four city councillors.[9] No tangible effective action was taken.

An indication that the government wanted to see the clashes last was that the army, which was already in the vicinity on 1 March—12 columns with 600 men were stationed at the time in Ahmedabad and other hotspots in Gujarat—was not sent to the places where it could have been the most useful. Aside from a few 'flag marches', it had to settle for remaining on stand-by because allegedly no 'official' was available to accompany the troops.

The state partiality also appeared in the treatment inflicted on the Muslims who took shelter in refugee camps. At the height of the violence, there were as many as 125,000 refugees in these camps. Officially, they still numbered 87,000 in April 2002, 66,000 of them in Ahmedabad alone. In three months, the government registered the return home of 73,500 refugees (52,500 in Ahmedabad) to pretend that law and order had been restored and that elections could be held. In any case, the authorities never took the necessary steps to help the refugees: most of the aid came from Muslim NGOs.

## CLASHES IN RURAL GUJARAT: THE
## COMMUNALIZATION OF TRIBAL ZONES

Riots between Hindus and Muslims have traditionally been an urban phenomenon. This was all the more true in Gujarat where there are, moreover, proportionally more Muslims in cities than in the countryside (the share of Muslims living in rural areas is only 42 per cent in Gujarat compared to 65 per cent for the national average).[10] Yet the violence in 2002 spread to the villages and so in many cases, to villages where very few Muslims resided. The districts of Mehsana and Gandhinagar, for instance, which have only 6.6 per cent and 2.9 per cent Muslim residents respectively according to the 2001 census, were heavily affected, even in the rural areas.

This singularity can be largely explained by the fact that the small Muslim minority is made up mainly of shopkeepers and moneylenders: unlike their coreligionists in the rest of India, the Muslims have a small, fairly successful economic elite in Gujarat. This social class is primarily from the Bohra, Khoja and Memon castes. In many villages, these groups own several businesses and are the main moneylenders (*sahukar*), to whom peasants become indebted, sometimes to pay their daughter's dowry, sometimes to buy seed for the year. These Muslims were one of the attackers' prime targets. Often this target was pinpointed by Hindu nationalist activists who had come from the city. They exploited the peasants' resentment toward this small economic elite; they raised their hopes of financial reward in the form of looting shops. This has led Dipankar Gupta to interpret the spread of rioting to rural areas in Gujarat as due mainly to economic reasons (Gupta 2002). The study conducted by Bela Bhatia in Sabarkantha partly corroborates this analysis. The author in fact observes a shift in the violence from cities to villages between 28 February—the date when the cities of Khedbrahma and Bhilodas were hit—and the evening of 1 March, when it spread to the villages (see Bhatia). The agents of this spread were Hindu nationalist activists from the city or nearby towns. These *tolas* (groups), whose members were wearing the saffron-coloured headband and chanting anti-Muslim slogans, entered the villages on tractors or in jeeps. Most of them were from the Patel caste—a caste of landed peasants who had prospered in farming before going into trade and industry to such an extent that the urban economy in Gujarat today is as much in their hands as those of the traditional merchant castes in the region. These assailants proved to be perfectly organized: divided into three groups, *todwavalla* (those who were destroying), *lootwavalla* (those who were looting) and *baadwavalla* (those who were burning), they went through several villages. In all, 2,161 houses, 1,461 shops, 71 workshops and factories and 38 hotels were looted and entirely or partly destroyed in the district of Sabarkantha. In addition, 45 places of worship underwent the same fate, which suggests that beyond the purely economic aspect, the violence reflected xenophobic feelings. In fact, one of the most repeated slogans was: *Muslai ne gaam ma thi kado?* (Run the Muslims out of the village), a slogan chanted by local villagers as well as activists from outside the village.

Altogether, over 1,200 villages were affected, particularly in the districts of Panchmahal, Mehsana, Sabarkantha, Bharuch, Bhavnagar and Vadodara. In this latter district, the army had to be called in on 5 March. Some 2,500 Muslims from 22 different villages were evacuated and moved to refugee camps. These villages no longer had a single Muslim according to the District Magistrate.[11]

But the most surprising development still, lies elsewhere: of the villages involved, many of them were in the tribal zone, the eastern 'tribal belt', bordering Madhya Pradesh, from Ambaji to Narmada. Never before had there been such massive participation of indigenous peoples (*adivasis*) in the anti-Muslim riots alongside Hindu nationalist activists.

This phenomenon has usually been interpreted by local observers in the same way villager involvement has, the *adivasis* being a subgroup of them. Bela Bhatia's study in Sabarkhanta—a district where tribes make up 17 per cent of the population—thus leads her to conclude that the *adivasis* 'were used by upper caste and class Hindus in their pogrom against the Muslims' (see Bhatia). Testimonies gathered by Bhatia in the field among Muslim survivors even made excuses for the aggressions the *adivasis* perpetrated, considering that it was not surprising to see them loot Bohra, Khoja and Memon shops, given the drought they had long suffered and the atmosphere created by the riot.

## Election-oriented Violence

The government's involvement in Hindu-Muslim violence—a fact that largely explains its exceptional scope—is part of an unavowed but easily reconstructed political strategy. There is great suspicion that the BJP, and the Hindu nationalist movement on the whole, honed this strategy between 1989 and 1991 when their activists worked at provoking anti-Muslim riots as election time approached. This violence in effect polarizes society along a religious line of cleavage, which generally leads the Hindu majority, with a heightened sense of Hindu identity, to vote more in favour of the BJP. This explains the correlation between the election calendar and the cycle of riots. Steven Wilkinson has thus shown that 'both riots and deaths do tend to cluster in the months before elections, and then drop off sharply in the months after an election is held' (Wilkinson 2000: 132).

This analysis began to lose some of its relevance in 1993 when the BJP was defeated in state assembly elections in Madhya Pradesh, Himachal Pradesh and Delhi precisely due to excessive violence: too many riots tend to cancel out the impact of what is gained in terms of votes, because even the Hindu elite suffers from the anarchy resulting from repeated violence and curfews. Shopkeepers and industrialists—from whom the BJP traditionally draws a lot of support—are particularly at risk when violence is heavy and drawn out. The violence of the 1992-3 riots following the demolition of the Babri Masjid in Ayodhya on 6 December 1992 exceeded anything India had yet experienced since Partition.

Afterward, the BJP was also dissuaded from using riots as a strategy by the mere fact of its rise to power in New Delhi in 1998, since it was henceforth responsible for public order and it had to accommodate coalition partners who did not share its ideology. However, this new rule of conduct was challenged by many party activists and cadres as the BJP was declining. At the end of the 1990s, the party in fact started losing local and state elections one after the other. The most radical members then suggested doing away with the moderate official line and returning to a strategy of ethno-religious mobilization, of which communal violence was a key element, so as to win the elections again.

In Gujarat, elections were not scheduled until 2003, but the rioters' high level of organization suggests that the Hindu nationalist movement was already preparing for this date with strong-arm tactics. Nothing could be more logical. First, the state was accustomed to pre-election riots (between 1987 and 1991, 40 per cent of the 106 Hindu-Muslim riots that afflicted Gujarat took place at election time). Second, the BJP had stacked up repeated electoral setbacks here as elsewhere: in December 2000, the party lost two cities in municipal elections (one of which was Ahmedabad) out of the six it had held up to then, and above all, it was marginalized in nearly all the *zila parishads* (district councils) whose elected officers were being renewed at the same time (Shah 2002: 4838–42).

The *Sangh Parivar* thus used Godhra as an opportunity to unleash violence upon which it hoped to capitalize during early elections. It was to provoke early elections that Modi decided to recommend that the governor—S.S. Bhandari, another RSS activist—dissolve the Gujarat assembly on 19 July. At the same time, he resigned as Chief Minister, while remaining at the helm to handle routine proceedings. And he immediately set about calling for early elections. These tactics were all the more shocking since the violence had far from subsided everywhere.[12]

In such conditions, James Michael Lyngdoh, Chief Election Commissioner, who visited 12 of the state's districts between 31 July and 4 August, was reluctant to organize any poll, especially since many voters, a vast majority of them Muslims, were still living far from their homes in refugee camps. So Modi and the BJP strove to demonstrate that calm had been restored, leading them first to hurriedly close the refugee camps or lower the number of their occupants reported in official statistics, and argue that in accordance with Article 174 of the Constitution, the time between dissolving the assembly and holding new elections could not exceed six months. National BJP leaders—starting with deputy prime minister L.K. Advani—joined in the call for early elections. Given the objections of the Election Commission, which preferred that President's Rule be declared because the election could not be organized under proper conditions and because, in this case, article 174 did not apply, the BJP brought the case before the Supreme Court. The Court refused to express an opinion, referring to the Election Commission's decisions. In early November, the Commission set a date for the elections to begin on 12 December.

On 8 September, Modi relaunched the campaign he had started in the immediate aftermath of the violence, in preparation for the elections. He then undertook a tour of the state that was highly reminiscent of L.K Advani's *Rath yatra* in 1990. Like this huge political pilgrimage that left from the Somnath Temple in Gujarat, Modi's *Gaurav yatra* left from the Bhathiji Maharaj Temple in Phagval (Kheda district). This tour instantly met with great popular success. On 9 September in Himmatnagar, for instance a huge crowd gathered along the roadside and at the place where Modi was to hold his rally, which he did not even reach until 2 a.m.

Throughout this entire tour, Modi's speeches were peppered with anti-Muslim references. In Becharaji, he referred to Muslims as abiding by the motto *hum paanch, hamare pachchees* (We are five—an allusion to Muslim polygamy—we will have 25 children—an open criticism of the high Muslim birth rate that many Hindus fear). The VHP distributed thousands of copies of this speech. The BJP and the VHP carefully divided up the work: Modi was bound by the Election Commission's model code of conduct obliging political parties to maintain a certain reserve, whereas Togadia, VHP international general secretary, used all means at his disposal: he held 220 rallies during the election campaign, taking 'jehadi terrorism' as his main target. The VHP not only handed out CDs describing the massacre in Godhra, but also had T-shirts printed stating: 'We will not allow our area to be converted into Godhra'.

The Election Commission was obliged to react. It demanded that Modi take the necessary steps to end the *Vijay yatra* that the VHP had begun in mid-November. Modi had Togadia and 42 other VHP militants arrested when their movement set off on 17 November from a temple in Ahmedabad. The VHP initiated another movement called *Jan Jagaran*, a mass awareness campaign. The government settled for denying Togadia access to Panchmahal of which Godhra is the district headquarters. Many suspected that this gesticulating fooled no one: Modi and Togadia had divided up the work for an extremely aggressive election campaign.

Not only was the BJP campaign rife with anti-Muslim references, but it was also based on an obvious equation between Islam and terrorism. One of the BJP's television commercials began with the sound of a train pulling into a station, followed by the clamour of riots and women's screams before the ringing of temple bells was covered by the din of automatic rifle fire. After which, Modi's reassuring countenance appeared, hinting to voters that only he could protect Gujarat from such violence. The BJP election manifesto pledged to train Gujarat youth, particularly those living on the Pakistani border, in anti-terrorist tactics. Self-defence militia would be set up in border towns where large numbers of retired servicemen would be brought in. Special gun permits would be issued to the lifeblood of a nation under siege. Not only to the BJP did Muslim mean terrorist, but the equation went a step further by establishing an equivalence between 'Muslim' and 'Pakistani' as well: any adept of Islam was potentially a fifth-column

Pakistani. This explains the attention devoted to attacks against Musharraf in Modi's election campaign. He, for instance, declared at a rally in Ahmedabad on 1 October—for 'Anti-Terrorism Day': 'India will continue to refer to him as Mian Musharraf. If the pseudo-secularists don't like it, they can go and lick Musharraf's boots. I dare him to send more terrorists to Gujarat, we are prepared this time. *Arey mian, taari goli khuti jashe* (Mian, your bullets will get exhausted)' (Desai 2002).

Modi spared no efforts throughout his campaign to spread this anti-Muslim security-based obsession which developed in the specific context created by the 9/11 events but also by the attack on the Indian Parliament in December 2001. He covered 4,200 km during the *Gaurav yatra*, which began on 8 September and ended at the same time as the election campaign. He held 400 rallies in 146 of the state's 182 constituencies. He did what he could to discredit his main opponent, the Congress, accusing it in particular of being the 'mother of terrorism' during a rally in Bhuj on 4 December. The outcome was in his favour: 63 per cent of the registered voters took the trouble to go out and vote and the BJP garnered a majority of seats for the third time in a row (unprecedented elsewhere in India) with a record score of 126 seats out of 182 (compared to 117 in 1998) and about 50 per cent of the votes cast. As for the Congress, it won only 51 seats (2 fewer than in 1998 despite a slight increase in votes, 38 per cent compared to 34 per cent). Only the violence made this landslide possible: the BJP won 42 out of the 50 seats in the three districts most heavily affected by this violence, Panchmahal, Dahod and Vadodara. This is what allowed it to transcend caste cleavages and attract the Hindu masses. An exit poll mentioned for instance that while 76 per cent of the upper castes and 82 per cent of the Patels voted for the BJP, Other Backward Classes (OBC) castes supported this party too—between 54 and 61 per cent according to the *jat* (Kumar 2003: 275). Another survey showed that 59 per cent of the respondents did not wish to have someone from another community as a neighbour, indicating just how deep the divide is and calling forth explanations other than mere electoral tactics on the part of politicians (*India Today*, 16 December 2002: 27).

## The Communalization of a Society and the *Jehad* Syndrome

The political strategy of a movement solidly entrenched in the state apparatus and desperate for electoral gains is not enough to explain the scope and intensity of the violence in Gujarat. These methods must be placed in a broader context: that of a reactivation of the Hindu majority's inferiority complex caused by Islamist attacks, and, more generally speaking, that of the communalization of the state of Gujarat and its society.

Since the 1990s, Gujarat has become the main stronghold of Hindu nationalists, to such an extent that today it is the state where the BJP is in power for the longest period, a situation which enabled the party to reshape the administration. One of the BJP government's favourite targets was the police. Muslim police officers have systematically been barred from executive positions. Of the 65 'IPS Officers' on active duty in the state in 2002, only one of them still fulfilled such a role as Deputy Superintendent of Police. All the others had been transferred to railway surveillance, organization of computer-training programmes, etc. (Communalism Combat, 2002: 119). At the same time, a vast number of Hindu nationalist activists and sympathizers were recruited by the Gujarat Home Guards, a form of municipal police in important cities of the state.

In addition to the police, the state machinery seems to have been infiltrated by Hindu nationalists and to have bowed to BJP influence. Otherwise how could one explain that the rioters had access to documents that could only come from the state administration? They were thus able to identify, and torch, a shop in Ahmedabad that did not have a Muslim name but of which 10 per cent of the capital was owned by a Muslim, as well as a factory owned by a Hindu who had just secured a contract in the Middle East. The aggressors could not have identified these targets without documents supplied by the administration.

Hindu nationalist control over the state apparatus is a determining factor in explaining the violence in Gujarat, but the collective psychology is an equally significant variable.

## THE NEW DOMINANT IDEOLOGY: HINDUTVA AGAINST *JEHAD*

In August 2002, a survey conducted among a sample of 17,776 citizens spread over 98 parliamentary constituencies showed that for a relative but nearly absolute majority of respondents, the Gujarat riots were not due to the state government or Hindu nationalists or even to local rabble-rousers, but to 'Muslim fundamentalists' and Muslims aggressors from Godhra (29 per cent and 20 per cent of the answers respectively) (*India Today*, 26 August 2002: 33). Moreover, many of the respondents rated Modi highly, ranking him in second place among the chief ministers in terms of popularity, with 45 per cent of favourable opinions (compared to 22 per cent six months earlier in a similar survey) (ibid.: 42).

The notion that the Hindus were in a position of self-defence and that Islamism was the guilty party can be explained by the context on 13 December 2001, when a suicide commando gained entry to the Lok Sabha, killing 15 people. This tragic event which targeted the core of the polity of India has been its 9/11 in a way. But other, less publicized attacks happened elsewhere, including in Jammu and Kashmir where a massive explosion killed 50 people in front of the state assembly of Srinagar on 30 September 2001.

These attacks reactivated the feeling of vulnerability Hindus have experienced toward Muslims periodically throughout the twentieth century (Jaffrelot 1996): in the 1920s, the Khilafat Movement gave rise to the first Indian Muslim show of pan-Islamism and in return triggered the creation of the RSS during a series of communal riots; in the 1980s, Islamic proselytism, which appeared in a more fundamentalist light since the Iranian revolution, fuelled a Hindu nationalist counter-mobilization—which ended up focalizing on the Ayodhya incident and several riots; the terrorist attacks of 2001 made the same impact since they enabled the Hindu nationalist movement to capitalize on the feeling of some threat. A tract distributed during the riots opened with this characteristic assertion: 'Today the minority community is trying to crush the majority community' (Communalism Combat, 2002: 136). Another declaration, made by the Bajrang Dal, began the same way: '50 years after independence it appears that Hindus are second [class] citizens of this country. Religious conversions, infiltration terrorism and bomb blasts have surrounded Hindustan.' This sense of insecurity is justified a little further on by designating a culprit: 'Jehad is being carried out in order to establish an Islamic state in Hindustan' (ibid.: 137).

A VHP tract distributed in Ahmedabad goes into detail on this point:

America found Laden alone too much whereas we have in our lanes and by-lanes thousands of Ladens . . . and two lakhs [200 000] mullah-maulvis who poison one lakh [100 000] madrassas and mosques day and night with terrorist activities. Organisations like SIMI [a Muslim student union], Lashkar-e-Toiba [a Pakistani Islamist movement active in Kashmir and other places in India] and ISI [the Pakistani secret service] with the support and help of Pakistan, are carrying on terrorist activities. They train lakhs of terrorists in thousands of institutions. They have formed an army of single, unemployed Muslim youth of India by paying high salaries. The terrorist and traitorious Muslims of this country get weapons from more than 50 Muslim nations to carry out their religious war. They are supplied with AK-56 and AK-47 rifles, automatic machine guns, small canons, rocket launchers and several kilos of RDX. . . . When Pakistan attacks India, the Muslims living here will revolt (ibid.: 77–8).

Which led Pravin Togadia to comment: 'What is happening in Gujarat is not communal riots but people's answer to Islamic Jehad' (*Asian Age*, 2002). A leaflet distributed by Bajrang Dal activists during the Gujarat riots went one step further since it requested the Hindus to 'reply in the same language that is used for Jehad'.

This strategy of stigmatizing and *imitating* the Other, who, by his assumed strength, represents a danger to the Hindus has been the brand mark of Hindu nationalism since its inception (Jaffrelot 1996). For long it fuelled an ethnic nationalism that did not preclude community cohabitation: Muslims were required to pledge allegiance to the majoritarian Hindu culture, even publicly assimilate it, although they could continue to practise their religion in private. But a new juncture was arrived at in 2002 in Gujarat. Then, the nationalist Hindu discourse openly advocated elimination of the Muslims.

## TOWARD ETHNIC CLEANSING: SADISM AND SAVAGERY

Over and above the geographic and social extent of the violence, the intensity and savagery of the rioting of Gujarat is what was most striking. The countless accounts gathered by spontaneous NGO investigations and more official inquiries all concur: never has Hindu-Muslim violence reached such extremes in both the systematic nature and duration. This analysis could leave things at that and drape a veil of discretion over these unbearable scenes, but instead of shying away from this violence, it must be told. Putting a damper on the survivors' accounts would boil down to denying what for some could have been their last wish: to recount the unspeakable. What happened? Entire families were electrocuted in their houses, which were first flooded by the murderers. Children were forced to drink kerosene before a match was set to their mouths. Foetuses were cut from the bellies of pregnant women and held up to see. Women, again, were gang raped before being mutilated and burned alive before their children's eyes. No one was safe. Not even former Ahmedabad MP, Ehsan Jafri a Muslim of the Congress Party. Holed up in his home, he repeatedly called the police for help as the hoardes besieging him continued to grow. Dragged outside and delivered up to public condemnation, he was covered with wax and burned alive along with his brother-in-law, the latter's wife and their two sons.

As it is now obvious, women were not spared by the rioters, on the contrary. For example, in the mass grave dug by the Naroda Pattiya victims in Ahmedabad, 46 of the 96 bodies buried there were women. And never had communal violence reached such heights of sexual cruelty vis-à-vis women. Among the Hindus, it harks back to an ancient obsession: Muslims have always appeared more virile to them, partly because of their diet (meat-eating) and their ritual animal sacrifices. Hindu women themselves tend to see Muslims as threats. As explained by Nonica Datta, 'The imaginary suspicion of the Muslim as an aggressor and a sexual predator continues to haunt the Hindu nationalist's psyche' (2002: 408), including that of women who sympathize with this ideology. The widespread practice of gang rape in the course of clashes in Gujarat no doubt reflects a desire to equal and even surpass Muslims in the sex act. But there is much more than that. First, the desire to dishonour and destroy an entire community by raping and torturing its women, which of course also aims to destroy their reproductive capacity (Sarkar 2002: 2872–6)—a method akin to the rationale of ethnic cleansing.

Another tract distributed during the riots of Gujarat, entitled 'Jehad' and written in Gujarati in the form of a poem is most edifying in this respect (ibid.):

> The people of Baroda and Ahmedabad have gone berserk
> Narendra Modi you have fucked the mother of *miyas* [derogatory term for Muslims]
> The volcano which was inactive for years has erupted
> It has burnt the arse of *miyas* and made them dance nude
> We have untied the penises which were tied till now

Without castor oil in the arse we have made them cry
Those who call religious war, violence, are all fuckers
We have widened the tight vaginas of the 'bibis' [term referring to married Muslim
women]
Now even the *adivasis* have realized what Hinduism is
They have shot their arrow in the arse of mullahs
Wake up Hindus there are still *miyas* left alive around you
Learn from Panwad village [a village in Panchmahal district that was the
scene of serious rioting] where their mother was fucked
She was fucked standing while she kept shouting
She enjoyed the uncircumcised penis
With a Hindu government the Hindus have the power to annihilate *miyas*
Kick them in the arse to drive them out of not only villages and cities but
also the country.

The violence in Gujarat, due to its very geographic scope and unbearable
intensity, in fact marks the first example of ethnic cleansing targeting Muslims since
India's Partition in 1947: the aim here was not only to loot and destroy private
property, even if such events also took place, but indeed to murder and run off
those perceived as intruders. In Sabarkantha, Hindus of Khetbrahma, the district
headquarters, after having emptied the place of its Muslim inhabitants, wrote on
a sign at the entrance to the town: 'Muslims not allowed' (Balagopal 2002:
2119).

A tract distributed in Gujarat during the riots says it plainly:

We do not want to leave a single Muslim alive in Gujarat. . . . Annihilate Muslims from
Bharat . . . when there were kings, the Muslim kings forced Hindu brethren to convert and
then committed atrocities against them. And this will continue to happen till Muslims are
exterminated. . . . Now the Hindus of the villages should join the Hindus of the cities and
complete the work of annihilation of Muslims (ibid.: 135).

This obsessive desire to eradicate Islam from India also explains the many
attacks against Muslim places of worship. Though it is widely thought that the
official figures regarding the casualties of the Gujarat riots and these destructions
have been underestimated, they provide some valuable indications: between 27
February and 1 April, the official number of Muslim victims was 536 and Hindus,
95; the number of Muslim wounded was 1,143, Hindus, 529. (These figures are
considerably lower than those published by *Muslim India*, which reports the total
number killed in Gujarat as 1,071 and wounded, 1,973) (*Muslim India*, 2002: 305).
In fact, the total number of casualties was most certainly over 2,000 dead. As for
places of Muslim religion, they were attacked at least as repeatedly as Muslim shops,
an indication that these symbolic targets were also of major importance. Altogether,
527 mosques, madrasas, cemeteries and other *dargahs* were damaged or destroyed
(ibid.). Most places of worship that were demolished were 'replaced' by a statue
of Hanuman and a saffron-coloured flag.

The very fact that communal violence in Gujarat acquired such large proportions forces us to resort to explanations other than the instrumentalist one: the Hindu activists were not only trying to polarize the society according to a religious line of cleavage; nor did the rioters target the Muslims only for looting. Their actions were over-determined by an obsessive fear of the Muslim 'Other' and an uncontrollable desire to annihilate Islam. The systematic dimension of the pogroms is an indication of the unprecedented responsiveness of society to this deep-rooted xenophobia. In a way, the pervasiveness of this feeling was evident from the incredible passivity of all actors in the public sphere, with the exception of a few NGOs and newspapers. The debate organized at the Lok Sabha shows to what extent anti-Muslim violence has become part of everyday life and how much the political class has become accustomed, or even sympathetic, to this fact. The regional parties which had joined the BJP-led ruling coalition under the condition that the BJP should moderate its Hindu nationalist rhetoric because they were sworn secularists and counted Muslims among their electoral supporters (such as the Telugu Desam Party) protested only as a matter of form. It is mainly for this reason that one can agree with Ashis Nandy's statement that 'The Gujarat riots mark the beginning of a new phase in Indian politics' (Nandy 2002). The violence in Gujarat reflects the dissemination of hatred of the 'Other' that had never before reached such intensity or had ever been so widespread—extending even into the tribal areas, a place to test these assertions.

## THE MILITANT HINDUIZATION OF THE *ADIVASIS*

It is a limited interpretation to view the riots as spreading to the tribal zones only because Hindu nationalist activists from the city exploited the *adivasis* by luring an impoverished community jealous of Muslim merchants' wealth with the mirage of looting their riches. Such an analysis disregards how the *adivasis* appropriated the riots. If, at the start, the violence came from the outside, was exported, so to speak, by city-dwelling activists, the *adivasis* devised their own version of it. This process was particularly obvious in the first tribal village in Gujarat to be affected, Tejgadh, in the district of Panchmahal. There again, the first shops were torched by outsiders, but 'once the first attack was over, other villagers joined in on their own with no further need for instigation and the looting continued', writes Ganesh Devy, who observed the riots in the field for the most part. To Devy, from that point on it was clear that rioting 'was not included in the master plan of violence'. It became 'leisurely': one or two shops were torched every day. Twelve days after the outbreak of violence, one house was burned down, then another the next day, and another the day after: 'It was cold-bloodedness in slow-time. This ritual quality was a clear indication that at this end of the Gujarat riots, the theme of communalism was taking a back seat, having been taken over by the norms of tribal culture'. This process of tribal takeover was even more clearly illustrated in Panwad, a village 30 km from Tejgadh where about 200 *adivasis* took part in the violence, armed with their ceremonial bows and arrows.

Although Devy is convincing when he temporizes the instrumentalization of the *adivasis*, his emphasis on the influence of visible marks of tribal culture during the violence poses a problem. Outer signs of culture, such as bows and arrows, are not enough to make the violence the expression of that culture. Actually, the *spontaneous* involvement of the *adivasis* in the rioting reflects the Hinduization of their culture under the influence of a campaign led by the RSS, VHP, BJP and especially the Vanavasi Seva Sangh.

This organization is one of the regional branches of the Vanavasi Kalyan Ashram created in 1952. The very name of this 'ashram' for the welfare of 'forest (*vana*) dwellers' translates both the vision that Hindu nationalists have of tribals and the strategy they have developed towards them. Hindu nationalists refer to tribals as 'those who live in the forest' (*vanavasis*) rather than 'those who were there first' (*adivasis*), simply because to them, 'first' among the people of India can only be Hindus. But the *vanavasis* are nevertheless a target group, for the Hindu nationalists are determined to compete within this milieu against Muslim and Christian missionaries.

They first sought to pit tribals against Christians to counter the latter's evangelizing efforts among these animist tribes, which had met with a degree of success since the nineteenth century: the conversion rate of tribals to Christianity was particularly high in the Chhattisgarh tribal belt where the RSS set up the Vanavasi Kalyan Ashram (VKA). Its strategy of gaining access to the tribes was simply to imitate the Christian missionaries' approach, which owed its popularity to its social work. The organization in fact set up branches in nearly all states in India over the years, a development confirmed by the name change to *Bharatiya Vanavasi Kalyan Ashram* in 1977.

In Gujarat, this movement was known as Vanavasi Seva Sangh (VSS). The name well reflects its primary vocation: social work. There, as in other places, the VSS strove to attract tribals by duplicating the missionaries' charity strategies, at the same time stigmatizing Christians all the better to Hinduize them. Their most ordinary form of Hinduization involved free distribution of statuettes of Lord Ganesh, to encourage the tribals to worship him. Another, strategy was to build temples devoted to Hanuman all over *adivasi* villages.

In the end, Devy is obliged to remark that 'the VSS and the BJP have achieved a measure of success in providing the tribals a political agenda of hatred'. So tribal culture has indeed been altered under the influence of Hindu nationalist propaganda. One must emphasize the receptivity of certain Bhils to Hindu nationalist ideas in the districts of Panchmahal and Sabarkantha, through propaganda from the RSS and its sister organizations. As a matter of fact, other tribes refer to these tribals somewhat ironically as 'Ramayana Bhils', a name coined from the great classic in Hindu literature, the *Ramayana*.

The last communal violences are bound to accentuate this trend, not only because Muslims—from whom tribals used to borrow funds—do not trust *adivasis* as much as before, but also because these *adivasis* have realized that they could draw dividends from riots in terms of looting and exerting power (Lobo 2002: 4848). For Lobo, the *adivasis* are even more attracted to Hindutva than before, and their culture has been irreversibly affected. Indeed, more than one-third of the Scheduled Tribes have voted for the BJP during the Gujarat election according to the Centre for the Study of Developing Societies (CSDS) exit poll.

If Hindu nationalist propaganda prospers, as we believe it does, on the instrumentalization of an increasingly widespread Hindu sense of insecurity, the rise in terrorist attacks attributed to Islamic militants is in danger of rekindling Hindu activism and fuelling a literally infernal spiral of which the Muslims will ultimately be the victims.

The violence in Gujarat has already put the Muslims in this state in an unbearable situation. Since Partition no riot had yet equalled this pogrom, either in the number of victims or the savagery of the violence; no government had to this extent sided with the assailants—to the point of becoming an aggressor itself; no administration, from the bureaucracy to the police, had ever shown such open complicity with the attackers. Whom can the Muslims turn to? The media? The English language press—whether it is national or regional—demonstrated its support and criticized the abuses, but the Gujarati press continually fanned the fire. For instance, on 1 March the daily newspaper *Sandesh* published an entirely fabricated story claiming that two Hindu women in Godhra travelling on the same train as the *karsevaks* had been attacked by Muslims, raped, mutilated, then murdered (Chenoy 2002: 5). The story proved to be unfounded. Alone and traumatized, the Muslim community became entrenched in camps forming ghettos and continued to be harassed by the police after the riots. When Nivedita Menon came to Ahmedabad from Delhi, like so many other human rights and minority rights activists, she recounted that in June

every day the police would raid Juhapura, the Muslim ghetto, to try to round up 'suspects', they would be resisted by the residents, there would be police firing, and the papers were full of front-page photographs of 'Muslim mob marching towards Juhapura police station'. The photograph clearly showed an unarmed, peacefully marching demonstration (Menon, 'Surviving Gujarat', e-mail communication).

And Menon added: 'Every Hindu knows full well that what was perpetrated there is beyond human endurance. They have looked into the void—will there not come a moment when the void will look back?' (ibid.)

The moment of 'Muslim backlash' finally arrived in September 2002. On the 23rd, a makeshift bomb hidden in a bus in Ahmedabad wounded five. But the most spectacular operation took place the next day, on 24 September, in Gandhinagar, when two armed men entered the Akshardham Hindu temple, a huge complex that can accommodate up to 5,000 worshippers. With AK-56s they shot at everything that moved and launched grenades, killing 28 people. They holed up in the temple until a National Security Guard commando flushed them out the next morning. Three members of the police forces were killed in the siege.

Modi immediately declared that the terrorists were from Pakistan but the fact that it was an act of vengeance was made clear by the notes found in the two men's pockets, in which they claimed, in Urdu, to belong to a group called 'Tehreek-e-Kasas'. Addressing 'thousands of conscienceless enemies of the Muslim of India', they declared: 'We will never rest in peace if we do not take revenge for the killings of our people' (Desai 2002).

This act is indicative of the risk of escalation India may face if the Muslims are still subjected to unbearable abuse. Till now Gujarat has not been brought back to normalcy. Not only are riots still a recurring phenomenon—in Vadodara, a riot killing eight persons occurred in May 2006 after the Municipal Corporation decided to demolish a *dargah*—but in riot-hit areas of 2002, there's no *status quo ante*. Dealing with the villages which had been affected by the 2002 communal clashes, A.A. Engineer wrote recently:

Those who have returned live in fear and total isolation. No one talks to them, no one invites them, no one even looks at them. So scorned they find it difficult to live there. Villages are small units of population and quite interdependent. In big cities one can live in such a situation but not in small villages (Engineer 2006).

A ray of hope may come from the judiciary. The Gujarat government had closed down all the cases soon after the events, arguing that there was no evidence. But the Supreme Court has reopened more than 2,000 of them. The guilty men now need to be punished, otherwise Gujarat may never fully recover from this trauma.

## Notes

1. See, for example, the description of Ibn Battutta dating from the fourteenth century (Battutta 1969: 80).
2. Louis Dumont is not far from a culturalist reading of this kind when evoking 'l'hétérogénéité sociale définitive des deux communautés' (1966: 382).
3. Between 1970 and 2002, Gujarat experienced 443 Hindu-Muslim riots.
4. The Hindu nationalists naturally offer a different interpretation. In 2004 I found a very revealing publication in the bookstore of the RSS headquarters in Delhi. It reads:

    On the 27 February 2002, innocent, unarmed *karsevaks* including women and children were burnt alive in S6 compartment of Sabarmati Express. From information available so far, the whole episode was preplanned. Had the train reached there as per its scheduled time, it was planned to burn the whole train near village Chanchelav. A mob of 2,000 strong men with petrol bombs, enough quantity of kerosene, can not be mustered all at once. As per the investigating agencies, it is felt that the threads of all this operation appear to be pointing towards ISI [Inter Services Intelligence—the Pakistani military intelligence service] involvement here .... The mastermind behind this plan are those people of terroristic mentality who had the courage to carry out an attack on Parliament House. Their intention was not only to burn the *karsevaks* but in a wider effect, they wanted to spread unrest in the country and to destabilize it through insurrections within the country. The army be required to be shifted from the Indo-Pak boarders and to tarnish the international image of Bharat as also to increase the inimical rift between the Hindus and Muslims. All this was a wisely planned action (*Godhra: Terrorism Unmasked*, 2002: 1).

5. With 1,119 victims of Hindu-Muslim riots between 1950 and 1995, up to then Ahmedabad ranked just behind Bombay (1,137 dead) in this grim classification. It most likely took the lead in 2002 (see Varshney 2002: 7).

6. He even justified the most violent doings among them with these words: 'The violence in Godhra was communal violence, the violence after that was "secular violence"'.

7. The VHP president in Gujarat in fact stated that the Muslims' shops in Ahmedabad were divided up the morning of 28 February. He added that the most active thugs in the violence were Waghri Untouchables—which recalls the use of Untouchables as real mercenaries during previous riots in the 1980s; the 'payoff' came in the form of looting Muslim shops (<http://www.rediff.com 12 March 2002>).

8. The National Human Rights Commission's interim report, interim order and final report on Gujarat are reproduced in Dayal 2003: 182–231.

9. Letter of Teesta Setalvad to Election Commission of India, 26 July 2002. E-mail communication.

10. Hindu-Muslim riots for a long time remained basically an urban phenomenon in Gujarat and elsewhere: from 1950 to 1995, 80 per cent of the victims of all the rioting in Gujarat were in Ahmedabad and Vadodara (Varshney 2002: 7).

11. These figures come from a confidential report of the National Human Rights Commission, following its March 2002 investigation in Gujarat.

12. Several months after the paroxysm of late February to early March, skirmishes were still claiming victims: on 21 April, the death of a policeman in Ahmedabad led to acts of vengeance—six Muslims were shot down by men in uniform. On 20 July, the day after the assembly was dissolved, two people were killed and 14 others wounded by stone-throwing and police gunfire, again in Ahmedabad. On 13 August, still in Ahmedabad, sporadic clashes wounded three. On 17 September, violence again broke out in Borsad (a small town in Anand district) after a Muslim motorcyclist accidentally hit a young Hindu. Shops owned by Muslims were torched in retaliation. The riot left one dead and 13 wounded. The town had to be put under curfew. On 29 September, a makeshift bomb exploded, wounding one person in Godhra. On 2 October, the festivities organized to celebrate Gandhi's birthday (Gandhi Jayanti) gave rise to violence in Bhavnagar (where the police had to open fire to disperse the attackers), Vadodara and Piplod, where police forces had to use teargas. On 6 October the police again had to intervene, leaving two wounded, after Hindu-Muslim clashes. On 15 October, a makeshift bomb exploded in a bus in Godhra, wounding six. The following day another bomb went off in a bus in Lunawada (Panchmahal district), wounding two people.

# References

Ahmed, I. (1984), 'Political Economy of Communalism in Contemporary India', *Economic and Political Weekly*, Vol. 2, No. 6.

*Asian Age* (Delhi edition), 2 April 2002.

Balagopal, K. (2002), 'Reflections on "Gujarat Pradesh" of "Hindu Rashtra"', *Economic and Political Weekly*, 1 June.

Battutta, Ibn (1969), *Voyages d'Ibn Battuta*, Paris: Anthropos.

Bayly, C. (1995), 'The Pre-history of "Communalism"? Religious Conflict in India, 1700-1800', *Modern Asian Studies*, Vol. 19, No. 2.

Bhatia, B., 'A Step Back in Sabarkantha', *Seminar*, No. 513. Available at <http://www.india-seminar.com/2002/513/513%20bela%20bhatia.htm>

Chenoy, K.M. et al., (April 2002), *Gujarat Carnage 2002: A Report to the Nation.*

*Communalism Combat* (March/April 2002), Vol. 8, pp. 77–8.

Dumont, L. (1966), *Homo Hierarchicus*, Paris: Gallimard.

Dayal, J. (ed.) (2003), *Gujarat 2002: Untold and Retold Stories of the Hindutva Lab*, Vol. 1, Delhi: Media House.

Datta, N. (2002), 'On the Anti-Muslim Ethos of Hindu Women in Gujarat', *Muslim India*, No. 237, September.

Desai, D. (2002), 'That Missing Healing Touch', *Outlook*, 10 October.

—— (2002), 'Temple Terror', *Outlook*, 7 October.

Devy, G., 'Tribal Voice and Violence', *Seminar*, No. 513. Available online at: <http://www.india-seminar.com/2002/513>

Engineer, A.A. (1984), 'The Causes of Communal Blots in the Post-partition Period in India', in A.A. Engineer (ed.), *Communal Riots in Post-independence India*, Bombay: Sangam Books.

—— (2006), 'They Hate Us, We Fear Them: The Situation in Gujarat', csss@vsnl.com (accessed 2 March 2006).

*Godhra: Terrorism Unmasked* (2002), Ahmedabad: Vishva Samvad Kendra.

Gupta, D. (2002), 'The Limits of Tolerance: Prospects of Secularism in India After Gujarat', Prem Bathia Memorial Lecture, 11 August.

Human Rights Watch (April 2003), *India, 'We have no order to save you': State Participation and Complicity in Communal Violence in Gujarat*, Vol. 14, No. 3.

*India Today*, 26 August and 16 December 2002.

Jaffrelot, C. (1996), *The Hindu Nationalist Movement and Indian Politics: 1920s to the 1990s*, New York: Columbia University Press.

Kumar, S. (January 2003), 'Gujarat Assembly Elections 2002: Analysing the Verdict', *Economic and Political Weekly*, Vol. 25.

Letter of Teesta Setalvad to Election Commission of India, 26 July 2002, e-mail communication.

Lobo, N. (2002), 'Adivasis, Hindutva and Post-Godhra Riots in Gujarat', *Economic and Political Weekly*, 30 November.

*Muslim India* (2002), No. 235, July.

Menon, N., 'Surviving Gujarat', e-mail communication.

Nandy, A. (2002), 'Obituary of a Culture', *Seminar*, No. 513. Available online at <http://www.india-seminar.com/2002/513>

Sarkar, T. (2002), 'Semiotics of Terror: Muslim-Children and Women in Hindu Rashtra', *Economic and Political Weekly*, 13 July.

Shah, G. (2002), 'Contestation and Negotiations: Hindutva Sentiments and Temporal Interests in Gujarat Elections', *Economic and Political Weekly*, 30 November.

Vardarajan, S. (2002) (ed.), *Gujarat: The Making of a Tragedy*, New Delhi: Penguin India.

Varshney, A. (2002), *Ethnic Conflict and Civic Life: Hindus and Muslims in India*, New Haven/London: Yale University Press.

Wilkinson, Steven I. (Winter 2000), 'Froids calculs et foules déchaînées, Les émeutes intercommunautaires en Inde', *Critique Internationale*, No. 6.

# Chapter 18

# Gujarat: the meaning of Modi's victory in 2007

The 2007 elections in Gujarat revealed that Narendra Modi was not only a new kind of politician, he also represented a new kind of politics. By playing on notions of Gujarati nationalism and pride, by sustaining an anti-Muslim mood and by building a personality cult that appealed to both the urban middle class and the 'Gujarati' voter, Modi seemed to be reinventing politics. Is Gujarat a forerunner of politics in all of India?

In December 2007, the ruling party, the Bharatiya Janata Party of Narendra Modi escaped the usual anti-incumbency reflex of the voters to win a comfortable majority in the Gujarat assembly. This unprecedented performance was even more surprising as the outgoing chief minister had been attacked in the press before the campaign started because of his role in the 2002 pogrom. His success may be attributed to his economic factors, but the election campaign revealed that other factors—which may be more significant—must be taken into account.

## 'Vikas Purush' and Hindutva

The BJP election manifesto, that was released in October 2007 focused on development issues and good governance (*The Indian Express*, Ahmedabad edition, 22 October 2007). Gujarat being one of the best performing Indian states in terms of per capita revenue, Modi publicized his economic achievements in the first weeks of his election campaign and projected himself as the 'vikas purush' (development man). He clearly did so to avoid any reference to the 2002 pogrom, but the media did not let him go away with it.

One of the *Tehelka* reporters, Ashish Khaitan, who had managed to approach *Sangh Parivar* leaders involved in the riots by pretending that he was a sympathizer doing a Ph.D., succeeded in recording their interviews with a hidden camera. Babu Bajrangi, who had played a decisive part in the violences of Naroda Patiya, one of the Ahmedabad neighbourhoods where 89 Muslim were killed on 28 February 2002 confessed (Jaffrelot 2007):

It has been written in my FIR that I ripped open the womb of a pregnant Muslim woman and flung the baby away with the sword. After killing Muslims we felt like Maharana Pratap.

After killing them, I called up the home minister (Gordhan Zadaphiya) and also Jaideep Patel (a Vishva Hindu Parishad leader). I told the home minister we have killed so many people, please take care of us. He told me to flee the spot, hide somewhere and save myself. . . . We were doing a running commentary for the home minister from the field when the riots were on. Modi also helped me in many ways. He asked me to flee and kept me in hiding in Abu, and, finally, when I was arrested he ensured the transfers of three lower courts judges to facilitate bail for me. No one can do what Modi did. He came to Naroda Patiya, saw our enthusiasm and thanked us.

According to *India Today*, Modi's agenda was not compatible with a visit to Naroda Patiya (*India Today*, 12 November 2007: 30), but the fact that Bajrangi is on bail remained quite embarrassing for the Gujarat government.

Last but not least, Arvind Pandya, the government counsel in the enquiry commission that had been appointed after the riot, the Nanavati-Shah Commission told Khaitan:

The report of the Nanavati-Shah Commission is going to come in the government's favour because Shah is our man and Nanavati can be swayed by money. Modi was so enraged by the Godhra carnage that had he not been a [chief] minister, he would have himself gone and thrown bombs in Juhapura.

After this interview was broadcast by *Aaj Tak*, a TV channel, Pandya resigned and then the collector of Ahmedabad censored the channel. However, an opinion poll that was made soon after showed that 55 per cent of the interviewees—60 per cent of whom were urban dwellers—considered that 'The government's performance in the last five years is more important than the Godhra riots'—20 per cent of them disagreed with this proposition and 25 per cent did not know how to respond (*DNA*, Ahmedabad edition, 24 November 2007: 2).

This survey was a clear indication that the Congress would focus its election campaign on the communal issue at its own risk. Some Congressmen even claimed that *Tehelka* report had been planted by the BJP in order to increase Modi's popularity!

## Congress Schizophrenia

This time the anti-Modi political forces decided to present a common front for a change in Gujarat. The Congress agreed to have some seat adjustment in 10 constituencies with the Nationalist Congress Party, for instance. And its leaders, though locked in personal rivalries, did not fight each other as much as faction chiefs often make in the Congress Party: Bharat Solanki, the state party president, Arjun Mohwadia, the leader of the opposition in the state assembly and Shankarsinh Waghela, the union minister for textiles, did not project themselves as chief ministers in waiting.

So far as its election campaign was concerned, the state Congress was keen not to identify itself with the Muslim cause by recalling the 2002 pogrom. When asked, in late November, about the issues the Congress were focusing on, Mohwadia replied:

First, law and order: fear psychosis, kidnapping of women, children and businessmen, misuse of the police, general insecurity, fake cases and encounters, misuse of investigating agencies; second, privatisation of education; third, deprivation of health; fourth, farmers issues, including indebtedness; fifth, unemployment, especially within the youth. (interview by Christophe Jaffrelot with Arjun Mohawadia, 25 November 2007 in Gandhinagar)

It is only after I asked him about communal harmony that he added to his list 'to sponsor riots for political purpose'. Moreover, the Congress nominated only seven Muslim candidates and welcomed a dozen BJP dissidents who, in some cases, had indulged in anti-Muslim actions in 2002.

The Congress was therefore proceeding in the same vein as in the 1990s when the party had, for instance, co-opted Shankarsinh Waghela. Besides, the state Congress canvassed on the same ground as the BJP. In newspaper ads figuring a terrorist covering his face, he denounced the complacency of Vajpayee's government on four grounds: first, the liberation of Masood Azhar, the Pakistani Jehadist who was to found Jaish-e-Mohammad, after the December 1999 Indian Airlines hijacking; second, the attack of the Akshardham Temple of Gandhinagar in 2001; third, the destruction of Jammu and Kashmir temples and; fourth, the assault against Hindu pilgrims in Amarnath.

The Congress was trying to exploit the same latent anti-Islamistic sentiment of the Gujarati Hindus as the BJP. The national leaders of the Congress who campaigned in Gujarat articulated a different discourse. Sonia Gandhi launched the official campaign of the party on November 3 in Anand by a meeting intended for women which stood in stark contrast:

We all know the misdeeds committed during his [Modi's] rule in 2002. The truth makes us hang our heads in shame. Which civilised society would want such a ruler? . . . After all we all are mothers, wives and daughters of those who have been killed and jailed.[1] We have to raise our voice against barbarians. 'Maujuda kushasan badalne ka mauka hain' (We have the opportunity to change the present government). (*The Indian Express, Newsline*, Ahmedabad edition, 4 November 2007)

In her second tour a few days before the polls, Sonia Gandhi repeated untiringly the same argument. On 7 December she said during her Amreli meeting: 'The Gujarat election is not about one election, but about the protection of democracy, rule of law and humanity itself' (*The Indian Express*, Ahmedabad edition, 9 December 2007). And she added that Gujarat had been known as the place were the belly of pregnant women was split open. Soon before, she had argued, in Navsari and Rajkot, that 'those who run the government are liars, corrupt and peddlers of religion and death' (ibid.). Local Congressmen suggested that the latter comment was not aimed at Modi, but Digvijay Singh, the secretary general of Congress insisted that a 'Hindu terrorist' had misbehaved in 2002 in Gujarat and Abhishek Singhvi, the Congress spokesperson, went even further by demanding that Modi should be judged by an international court. Modi immediately exploited this new context.

## Modi's Ultimate Radicalization

Till then, Modi's campaign had focused on purely economic issues. But he was perfectly aware that his Hindu nationalist-cum-anti-Muslim image was more of an asset than a liability. Incidentally, he had already started to refer to Ram Setu in a recurring manner during his election meetings. He hit back immediately after Congress national leaders attacked him on the communal terrain. He first intensified his propaganda on security issues. He had one placard published in the English press under the title: 'In 4 years, acts of terror claimed 5,619 lives in India. But in Gujarat, only 1'.[2] Citizens were then invited to restore a safe India 'by trouncing soft-on-terror Congress'. Among other things, the ad criticized the repeal of POTA.

In a meeting in Godhra, Modi harangued the crowd in a typical way: 'The Congress says you are terrorists. Are you terrorists? This is an insult to Gandhi's and Sardar Patel's Gujarat. Teach the Congress a lesson for calling the people of Gujarat terrorists. . . . Sonia Behn, it is your government that is protector of merchants of death. In Gujarat, we have eliminated the merchants of death [that is the Muslims in 2002]. . . . Sonia Behn, if you cannot hang Afzal, hand him over to Gujarat. We will hang him' (*The Times of India*, Ahmedabad edition, 6 December 2007).

Afzal Guru had been condemned to the death sentence in 2006 because of his implication in the 13 December 2001 attack against the Lok Sabha. He pleaded for presidential mercy but the head of the state never replied and at present is serving death row.

A few days before the first round of elections, Modi further communalized the campaign by mentioning Sohrabuddin. This militant of the Islamist Pakistan-based movement Lashkar-e-Toiba, according to the Gujarat police, but a small-time extortionist according to independent media reports, had been killed in 2005 on the border between Gujarat and Rajasthan. To begin with, Modi's government had argued that he had been a casualty of the Rajasthani police on the Rajasthani side in some encounter. But his brother had argued that it was a fake encounter and that Sohrabuddin's wife too had been killed in cold blood by the police who, then, had her body burnt. During his meetings in south Gujarat on 4 December Modi referred to this case on a very aggressive tone:

I am thumping my chest and declaring that Sohrabuddin's encounter took place on the 'dharti' of Gujarat. If I have done something wrong, hang me. But these people [Congressmen], next they will offer a 'chadar' at Sohrabuddin's grave. (ibid.)

This was a way to claim full responsibility for the crime in order to receive all the credit for this 'achievement'. But such a strategy was in contradiction with the previous line of conduct of Modi whose government had, so far, considered Sheikh Sohrabuddin's death as a mistake by the police, had put the guilty men behind bars and had informed the Supreme Court on 23 March 2007.[3]

So far as trial by an international court was concerned, Modi declared in his Godhra meeting: 'Why not a court in Pakistan? The centre talks of imposing Article 356 in Gujarat but the Gujaratis will give me an AK-56 to fight it' (ibid.). Soon after, while campaigning in Rajkot, he termed Manmohan Singh's government 'the Delhi Sultanate' (*The Indian Express*, 9 December 2007).

The shift in Modi's campaign was duly noticed in the media, though it was never interpreted as a response to the campaign of national Congress leaders.[4] This new context resulted in the mobilization of *Sangh Parivar* activists who had played a rather marginal part in the BJP's campaign so far. Now Modi appeared once again—like in 2002—as the rallying point of the anti-Congress and anti-'Muslim appeasement' forces. In early December, a thousand of the RSS cadres joined the BJP campaign in an active manner (*DNA*, Ahmedabad edition, 10 December 2007).

The Modi Phenomenon Hindutva is not the only mainstay of what may be called 'Moditva'. The 2007 election campaign was very revealing of two other saliant features of this phenomenon: an extreme personalization of power and a managerial style of governance (or, at least, some taste for it). 'Modi Is Gujarat and Gujarat Is Modi', 'High Tech' Populism: the 2007 election campaign had been fully organized around the personality of Modi.

The BJP state president in Gujarat, Purshottam Rupala, himself admitted that his party had a one-point programme: Modi.

Not only did the iconographic material on which the BJP propaganda was based show Modi in a systematic manner, but the chief minister displayed a narcissist taste for photography. Vivek Desai, one of the men who portrayed Modi with his camera, explained in the press that he was very particular about each and every detail, dress, colour, attitudes which could carry some specific meaning—he never showed the palm of his right hand because this is the Congress electoral symbol, for instance [Dayal 2007]. His website, that he had contracted to a private company, comprised 373 photographs of Modi.

In August 2007, two months before the campaign started, he hired an American firm specializing in the communication of public figures, Apco Worldwide, which had already worked for the Nigerian dictator, Sani Abacha, the life-president of Kazakhstan, Nazarbaiev and the former Russian oligarch, Mikhail Khodorkovsky. This company reshaped the image of Modi for 25,000 dollars a month (*The Times of India*, 17 November 2007).

Modi officially launched his electoral campaign on 22 October 2007 by pretending that he was the only 'full-time CM in the country' since he had no wife and children to take care of, he hereby suggested that Gujarat was his family (*The*

*Indian Express*, Ahmedabad edition, 23 October 2007). He then made a point to occupy the public space. He succeeded in being on the front page of newspapers almost everyday, not only because of his speeches and achievements, but as a private individual.

Let us take the example of the front page of *The Times of India* on four successive days. On 23 November one article recalls, on the basis of testimonies by old teachers of Modi, how good he was as an actor in the theatre plays organized in his village school. On 24 November the newspaper narrates the fact that, as a child he liked to swim in the lake near his house amidst crocodiles—he even brought back a baby crocodile to his home once, but he obliged his mother when she asked him not to do it. On 25 November, one of the front page articles of the newspaper is devoted to one of the sentences found on Modi website: 'I can digest any kind of poison'.

The journalist who authored this piece then compares Modi and one sultan of Ahmedabad who had similar power. On 26 November, we learn that Modi, when he was 10, helped his father sell tea on the platform of a small railway station.

In addition to Modi's omnipresence on the public scene, he tried hard to maintain a direct relation with all the citizens of Gujarat. For that purpose he made a point to use the latest technology. Having three laptops—one in his office, one at home and one for travelling—he is supposed to spend about 4 hours a day to read the 200–50 emails he receives everyday from citizens of Gujarat. He allegedly responds to 10 per cent of them and lets the bureaucracy take care of the others (*The Times of India*, 14 November 2007).

Modi's campaign has used this channel—the internet—and the mobile phone too, Gujaratis being very well equipped with mobile phones compared to the rest of India (14 million people—out of 52 inhabitants—had one cellphone in 2007). Such phones enabled Modi to send thousands of SMS and MMS to potential voters as well as party cadres.

Modi not only tried to establish a direct relation with every citizen of Gujarat but also made a point to be identified with Gujarat. His main slogan was 'Jitega Gujarat!', as if his victory could only be the victory of Gujarat. He tried hard, indeed, to appear as the protector of the Gujaratis.

One of his video clips broadcast on the internet starts off with a bomb blast, followed by sirens, dead bodies strewn about and Modi threatening unseen terrorists with 'int no jawab patthar thi'—a stone for every brick (*The Times of India*, 19 November 2007).

His techniques remind us of Indira Gandhi's modus operandi. In the 1970s she could reach every Indian home by using All India Radio and projecting a similar propaganda whose motto was 'Indira is India and India is Indira'. Modi did the same in 2007, as evident from the name of his TV channel, *Vande Gujarat* (adapted from *Vande Mataram*) and from the fact that his supporters canvassed while wearing a mask of him—as if hundreds of Modis were campaigning together![6]

Like Indira Gandhi, Modi is authoritarian, but Gujaratis do not mind too much.

A survey by the Centre for Study of Developing Societies (CSDS) of early November 2007, showed that 34 per cent of the interviewees (and, among them 37 per cent of BJP voters) considered that Modi's style was 'dictatorial'. But 48 per cent of those who disapproved of his 'dictatorial style of leadership' were ready to vote for his party, whereas among those who approved of this style, 61 per cent were about to do the same (*The Indian Express*, 27 November 2007).

These figures reflect an increasing rejection of parliamentary democracy and an increasing interest in non-democratic forms of governance.

The managerial culture of politics of Modi is very popular among businessmen,[7] including those who are at the helm of multinational companies and who take part every year in the Vibrant Gujarat Investors' Summit. Mukesh Ambani said about him: 'Narendrabhai is a leader with a grand vision . . . amazing clarity of purpose with determination . . . strong ethos with a modern ourlook, dynamism and passion' (*The Indian Express*, 27 November 2007). His brother, Anil, said, 'Narendrabhai is one of India's biggest leaders, a man who inspires loyalty and attracts followers wherever he goes...a political visionary' (ibid). K.M. Birla went even further: 'Gujarat is vibrant because of its political leadership and Modi is a fulltime chief minister of the state and genuinely the chief executive officer of Gujarat'. (ibid.)

The fact that Modi behaves like a CEO is of course to the liking of CEOs. It proves that even the political system admits that it should be ruled according to their principles.

Indeed, Modi believes in a market economy and has accelerated the retreat of the state. He has reduced the state spending which had not been part of the five-year plans by 9 per cent and reformed the Gujarat State Electricity Board. This SEB which was in the red regained some financial health once it started to have power paid by the consumers, including in the villages. Last but not the least, the Industrial Disputes Act was amended in order to make the labour laws more flexible in the state's special economic zones.

Besides, Modi 'has shown the possibilities of an alternative approach to politics', according to Swapan Dasgupta, because he claimed that he would adopt efficacy as the only criterion of his action, like in business (Dasgupta 2007). Going by these principles, Modi sidelined a record number of 33 outgoing MLAs (out of 127) because they had not delivered, according to him.

## What Electoral Basis?

Modi's policies are well in tune with the natural inclinations of the urban middle class which developed because of the economic reforms. This social milieu also has strong reservations vis-à-vis the state's interventions in the economy, simply because the private sector is supposed to perform better. This group is also critical of the traditional political personnel who are described as not only ineffective but also corrupt—a liability which is not affecting Modi, it seems.

Such a political culture explains the rising anti-parliamentarianism of the urban middle class and its growing lack of interest in elections: the turnout is very low indeed in urban middle class residential areas. The alternative style of governance that this milieu is longing for borrows its main features from the corporate sector: the political system must deliver the same way, and no one really cares if it goes along with a dose of authoritarianism.

The hidden face of this political culture lies in communalism. Modi's authoritarianism is largely praised or accepted by the Hindu urban middle class also because it has brought results vis-à-vis the Muslims who, as I heard so often in perfect English, have been taught the lesson they deserved in 2002.

Gujaratis adhere to what is known as Modi's 'marut', a form of virility which is associated with Modi because he never apologised for what happened in 2002, in contrast to Advani who said that the demolition of the Babri Masjid on 6 December 1992 had been the saddest day in his life.

Gujaratis get identified with him even more since the rest of the whole world is pointing a finger at Gujarat. The US which has refused Modi a visa and the centre—via Sonia Gandhi have hurt the Gujaratis who, therefore, have tended to display some solidarity with their chief and have highlighted their economic achievements as a major source of pride (incidentally one of the rubriques of *The Times of India* in Gujarat is called 'Gujarati Pride'). But to highlight economic achievements is often a way to legitimize one's support for Modi—whereas this sympathy is in fact deeply rooted in communal feeling.

The urban middle class, therefore, is one of the nucleus of supporters on which Modi relies, as evident from the CSDS survey made a few weeks before the elections, between 31 October and 6 November. Potential voters (number: 3,983) were interviewed in 60 constituencies. The results showed that the richer the interviewees were, the more favourable they were to Modi's party (Table 18.1).

TABLE 18.1: Voting Pattern of Different Socio-Economic Groups (In %)

| Socio-economic groups | BJP | Congress |
|---|---|---|
| Rich | 62 | 28 |
| Intermediary | 50 | 35 |
| Low | 43 | 40 |
| Poor | 36 | 49 |
| Very Poor | 36 | 50 |

Source: *The Indian Express*, 15 November 2007: 4.

The break-up shown in Table 18.1 is further documented by the voting pattern by caste and religious community (Table 18.2).

TABLE 18.2: Voting Pattern of Castes and Religious Communities

| Castes and communities | BJP | Congress |
|---|---|---|
| Upper castes Brahman | 64 | 20 |
| Rajput | 50 | 37 |
| Intermediary castes Patidar | 66 | 20 |
| OBCs Koli | 30 | 48 |
| Mer | 47 | 38 |
| Other cultivating OBCs | 46 | 35 |
| Scheduled castes | 30 | 56 |
| Scheduled tribes | 45 | 43 |
| Muslims | 13 | 74 |

*Source:* Ibid.

Though Modi is from an OBC caste, he is well in tune with the upper caste ethos, largely because of his RSS training. Moreover, he projects himself as an ascetic fully devoted to the cause of the people, a 'Karmayogi', like so many *pracharaks*. In a book that was forthcoming at the time of the 2007 elections, and whose title was precisely *Karmayog*, he gives a spiritualist interpretation of the caste system which was likely to maintain the social status quo. In some of the pages which have leaked to the press, he pays attention to the Dalits and more precisely to the Bhanghis (scavengers)—whose sanskritized name is 'Valmikis':

I do not believe that they [the Valmikis] have been doing this job just to sustain their livelihood. Had this been so, they would not have continued this type of work generation after generation. . . . At some point of time, somebody must have got the enlightenment that it is their duty to work for the happiness of the entire society and the Gods; that they have to do this job bestowed upon them by Gods; and that this job of cleaning up should continue as an internal spiritual activity for centuries.

This should have continued generation after generation. It is impossible to believe that their ancestors did not have the choice of adopting any other work or business.[8]

Such an interpretation of some of the worse forms of untouchability is typical of the RSS and carries also some Gandhian connotations.

Society is presented as potentially harmonious and permeated by the legacy of its divine origins. Each group is supposed to fulfil complementary functions without suffering from any hierarchical arrangement. Modi's views were strongly rejected by Dalits who asked for a ban of the book. Its release was postponed officially because to do so a few weeks before the polls would have contradicted the electoral code of conduct.

## New Face of BJP Politics?

Narendra Modi not only embodies a new style of politics in India, as evident from the main features of his 2007 election campaign, but also, to some extent, a new type of BJP politician. Generally speaking, the *Sangh Parivar* leaders are not supposed to develop such a personality cult. The Hindu nationalist movement has always functioned in such a way as the organization comes first and men afterwards.

Second, the RSS had to prevail in all strategic moves, the *Sangh* giving, absolute priority to institutional considerations in comparison to personal equations. Modi, while he was a staunch follower of Hindutva and, therefore, could hardly be criticized by the RSS on this ground, tried to free himself from this organization. For instance, he did not submit the list of candidates nominated by the BJP to the RSS headquarters as state party leaders routinely do in such circumstances. He also reduced the coordination with the state *prant pracharak* to a minimum. As a result, one of the RSS strongmen in the Gujarat unit of the organization, Mukund Deobhankar, declared in the press that this time his organization would not get involved in election work (*The Times of India*, 6 November 2007).

One of his colleagues, Pravin Maniar, explained in an interview that indeed the RSS would adopt a different attitude than in 2002: 'This time around, we have not asked our workers to get involved in any poll related work. . . . We have always extended our support for the cause of Hindutva. But we are wedded to an ideology and not any individual . . . None of the *Sangh Parivar* organisations have benefited from this government' (*DNA*, Ahmedabad edition, 25 November 2007).

The RSS was clearly reproaching Modi with his personalization of power and resented the fact that he had not done much for the other components of the *Sangh Parivar*, which had helped him so much in 2002. The Vishva Hindu Parishad (VHP) and the Bharatiya Kisan Sangh (BKS) felt especially alienated. The BKS is rooted in that part of Gujarat—the villages—to which Modi paid little attention. Not only did the government implement a pro-capitalist policy by focusing on the industry and services, but it asked the peasants to pay for their electricity in places where they had never done so.

The VHP was even more hostile to Modi since its leaders considered that he had won largely because of the organization's support in 2002 but never repaid his debt. Pravin Togadia, one of the VHP leaders in Gujarat, let his brother canvass in favour of the Congress Party. Devendra Das, the secretary general of the Akhil Bharatiya Sant Parishad and of the Ram Janmabhoomi Nyas Raksha Samiti accused Modi of killing 1,00,000 cows. He propagated a staunchly anti-Modi slogan in his stronghold of Baroda: 'Narendra Modi is not the protector of Hindus, but their destroyer' (*The Indian Express*, Ahmedabad edition, 11 December 2007).

The vice president of the Sant Parishad, Swami Avilchaldasji Maharaj, who was also the leader of the Gnan Sampradaya, one of the most popular sects of Gujarat justified his rejection of Modi in three words: 'We feel cheated' (ibid). The anti-Modi mobilization of these religious figures did not have any political fallout. Uma Bharti, the BJP dissident who had launched her own party, the Bharatiya Jan

Shakti, received the support of many former colleagues and supporters of Modi but she eventually gave up the idea of opposing him. In the end, the central headquarters of the VHP, BJP and RSS have closed ranks and demanded their members fully support Modi. Such an evolution was partly due to the communal turn of his campaign. As soon as the Congress projected itself as the defender of secularism—and, therefore, as the protector of the Muslims from the *Sangh Parivar's* point of view—the Hindutva Movement could not take the risk of weakening Modi, who had returned to his Hindutva plank.

Nonetheless, Modi was not the first choice of the *Sangh Parivar* and he remains atypical compared to other Hindu nationalist leaders. But he may have inaugurated a new style of leadership in the BJP, based on personal appeal rather than the *Sangh Parivar's* network. Where the BJP has become really big as in Gujarat, the party leader may be able to rely on his personal popularity and emancipate itself from the RSS. Similar developments may occur at a pan Indian level too. Interestingly, L.K. Advani has managed to remain leader of the opposition in the Lok Sabha and to appear as the National Democratic Alliance's candidate for prime ministership at the time of the next general election in spite of the RSS' eagerness to replace him after the 2004 defeat.

The BJP does not need the RSS and its other affiliates as much as before. It does not need *swayamsevaks* going door to door to convey the party's propaganda as much as before. It can develop populist strategies by relying on new communication techniques and it raises money for its own expenditures—including from the diaspora which, in the case of Modi, was a great help.

Certainly, the 'revelations' made by *Tehelka* in October 2007 launched the Gujarat 2007 election campaign. But far from sealing Modi's political fate, they have contributed his electoral success and the national leaders of the Congress further helped him by referring to the 2002 riots during their meetings and interviews.

Such a strategy paradoxically led the voters to identify themselves more with their chief minister and to accept more the way he tried to get associated with the state of Gujarat by virtue of a new form of Gujarati pride. Gujarati patriotism and anti-Muslim feelings played a significant part in Modi's success, development and economic achievements being a very convenient fig leaf for the middle class which wanted to find more legitimate arguments for justifying their vote for the BJP.

Gujarat's election results throw up new interrogations regarding not only Gujarat but the rest of India too. What kind of treatment will the Muslims meet in the state, especially those staying in the 'relief colonies' having resulted from the 2002 pogroms? What kind of justice and reconciliation is now possible—if any? These questions acquire a new meaning if Gujarat, one of the most modern states, is reinventing politics along lines of what the new middle class wants. Is Gujarat's trajectory announcing similar inflexions elsewhere?

## Notes

1. Here Sonia Gandhi alludes to the arrests of so many Muslims after the Godhra events especially under POTA.
2. Note here that Modi speaks as if Gujarat was not in India.
3. K.T.S. Tulsi, the lawyer representing Modi to the Supreme Court let it immediately be known that he was withdrawing from the case: 'On the one hand, the Gujarat government has filed a number of affidavits in the Supreme Court saying that it's a cold-blooded murder and it has filed a chargesheet against its own police officers and is prosecuting them for murder. And now the chief minister says that the murder is justified. In this situation, the stand of the government and the chief minister is completely contradictory. I cannot defend such a case. I cannot accept that any police officer has the right to murder anyone. It's a mockery of law' (*The Times of India*, Ahmedabad edition, 6 December 2007).
4. See, for instance, *DNA*, Ahmedabad edition, 10 December 2007.
5. He said, for instance, in November: 'Local issues are not important during the campaign in the forthcoming polls. There is just one issue with us—Modi' (cited in Rajiv Shah, 'Modi Only Mascot for BJP: Rupala', *The Times of India*, 5 November 2007).
6. An astute commentator indeed observed: 'Modi is not just a man or (a) chief minister, but an 'event' in Indian politics after Indira Gandhi to present that sole authoritative model of leadership. With wider vision of brand building and systematic strategies of image positioning than Indira. So, in a way Gujarat has seen non-stop round the clock election campaign by him in the past five years' (*The Times of India*, 11 December 2007).
7. The Gujarat Chamber of Commerce and Industry organized a function in honour of Modi during the election campaign. Interestingly he seized this opportunity for improvising a very harsh speech, showing that he felt he was in the company of hard core Hindutva supporters: 'Anti-Gujarat lobby has been propagating that I killed Sohrabuddin. If AK-57 rifles are found at the residence of a person, do I go to take their advice or should I ask the lawyers, you tell me what I should do, should I not kill them?', and the crowd responded by shouting, 'Kill them! Kill them!' (*The Times of India*, Ahmedabad edition, 18 November 2007).
8. Cited in Rajiv Shah, ' "Karmayogi" Swears by Caste Order', *The Times of India*, Ahmedabad edition, 24 November 2007.

## References

Dasgupta, S. (2007), 'Modi, Inept Pragmatist', *The Indian Express*, 24 November.
Dayal, Prashant (2007), 'Shutter-Bug's Delight and Fit for the Ramp', *The Times of India*, Ahmedabad edition, 27 November.
Jaffrelot, C. (2007), 'The 2002 Pogrom in Gujarat: The Post-9/11 Face of Hindu Nationalist Anti-Muslim Violence', in R. King (ed.), *Mirrors of Violence*, London and New York: Routledge.

# IV

## The Rise of the Lower Castes

# Chapter 19

# The plebeianization of
# the Indian political class

Political theories tell us that there are two kinds of representation—one which is based on the election of individual deputies by abstract citizens, and the other which emphasizes the social identities of the represented and the representatives, namely, mirror-representation (Pitkin 1967). Historically, the former has been epitomized by the French experience since 1789: in post-revolutionary France, any elected member of the national assembly was supposed to represent the nation as a whole. The link between the representatives and their local electors was so tenuous that when France lost Alsace-Lorraine to Germany, the members elected in this province continued to participate in the deliberations as part of the 'representation nationale'. The French parliamentary system relied on territorial constituencies, but the way it operated calls to mind the 'scrutin de liste'.

The second ideal-type of representation is best exemplified, among the democratic trajectories of the world, by the British case. Here, in contrast to the French tradition, the social identity of the represented and the representative—and the relationship between both—mattered so much that, originally, groups were entitled to forms of statutory representation (Beer 1957). In the nineteenth century, the British tradition of representation took for granted that the people at the university, the gentry, the merchants, etc., were entitled to some political representation. In a way, this approach harked back to the medieval form of representation—which was based on guilds and orders—that the French Revolution had deliberately attempted to eradicate.

Unsurprisingly, the British tended to introduce a group-based form of representation in India when they began to democratize the institutions of the Raj. Not only did universities, landlords and merchants get their special representatives, but religious minorities (Muslims, Sikhs) as also caste groups (non-Brahmans, Marathas, Scheduled Castes, etc.) got separate electorates or reserved seats. Naturally, these special representations were granted to these groups by the government as a result of their political pressures as interest groups. But the British tradition laid themselves to such pressures and predisposed the government to be responsive. This policy was of course in tune with the Raj's strategy of 'divide and rule'.

However, these special representations did not cover the majority of the electorate; they were compensatory schemes since the abstract citizen remained the basis of the political system. And, this embryonic form of mirror-representation was further reduced after independence. The debates in the Constituent Assembly bear testimony to the fact that any system of separate electorates had become illegitimate simply because the partition of India was attributed to the original privilege that the Muslims got in terms of such separate electorates. But other schemes were abolished too: non-Brahmans, Marathas and other non-Dalit castes lost their reserved seats. The Scheduled Castes and Scheduled Tribes alone continued to benefit from quotas in the assemblies.[1]

The removal of institutional provisions which were intended, under the British, to improve the representation of non-elite groups was justified in the name of universalistic values. The Indian Constituent Assembly attempted to erase socioeconomic distinctions on behalf of the fundamental equality of all the citizens. However, under the cover of such ideological commitments, this orientation reflected the hegemonic design of the dominant, classes which occupied the upper layers of the Congress Party. Be they from the state bureaucracy, the capitalist milieu or from the landowners, these 'dominant proprietary classes' (Bhardan 1984) were keen to establish, as much as they could, their monopoly over the political representation of India. The Congress Party, therefore, came to consist of huge clientelistic networks through which these groups maintained their domination, by resorting to votebank politics: the party fielded candidates from these social categories at the time of elections and had them returned to the assemblies largely because of their local influence as notables—be they big merchants (and moneylenders) or landowners (and moneylenders). The common point of all these elite groups was their social background: they all belonged to the upper castes.

The domination of the upper castes over the Indian society traditionally relied on several factors. In ritual terms, the upper *varnas*—Brahmans, Kshatriyas and Vaishyas—are known as the *dvijas* (twice-born) or *savanas* and, therefore, enjoy the reputation of being purer than the *varna* below, the Shudras and, of course, the Untouchables (or Scheduled Castes), better known as Dalits today. In the Hindu worldview, as codified in the Sanskrit literature by the Brahmans themselves, these three groups which are ordered in a ritual hierarchy are supposed to exert a moral authority over the rest of society—at least, they expect greater respect because of the caste into which they are born.

While the caste system is obviously organized according to the notion, of status, what Max Weber called 'stand' (2003: 110–27), the domination of the upper castes did not rely on their ritual position alone. It had also much to do with their social position in socioeconomic terms and their occupation which were largely related to the ritual status of each caste: Brahmans, as literati, were bound to administer power; Kshatriyas, as warriors, exerted power—at least as landlords or maharajas in the territory they (or their ancestors) had conquered and Vaishyas, as merchants and moneylenders, became industrialists who largely controlled the economy.

Certainly, caste and class (defined in socioeconomic terms) never coincided. But they have always broadly overlapped and they still do, as evident from the National Sample Survey 2000 which shows a remarkable correlation between caste and one's standard of living. According to this survey, more than 60 per cent of the urban upper caste Hindus had a per capita monthly consumption expenditure of Rs 775 or more, whereas less than 25 per cent of the urban Other Backward Classes (OBC) and less than 18 per cent of the urban Scheduled Castes (SC) were in such a position. Similarly, among the urban rich whose per capita consumption expenditure is more than Rs 1,500, 59.8 per cent were from the upper caste Hindus, 14.6 per cent from the OBC and 3.8 per cent from the SC (Deshpande 2003: 112–13). Unsurprisingly, castes and occupations coincide to a large extent. According to a survey achieved thanks to the Centre for the Study of Developing Societies (CSDS) database, 24.5 per cent of the upper castes belong to the 'salariat' and 20.4 per cent to 'business', as against 9.5 and 10.1 per cent respectively for the OBC and 10.9 and 5.3 per cent respectively for the SC (Kumar 2002: 4095).

However, Shudras have also exerted power in the past, when they could assert their authority and even rule society. The case in point is the dominant castes, peasant Shudras, who have occasionally risen to power because of their hold over land and their sheer number.[2] In history, the dominant castes which were the most successful in their attempt at conquering power managed to be recognised as Kshatriyas by Brahmans who invented genealogies for them. According to M.N. Srinivas, the Kshatriya category was the most open of the caste system (1978: 238). The very existence of the 'dominant' castes show that the Brahmanical view of society may describe (or prescribe) an ideal-type in the Weberian sense, but not the reality of power relations: *swarnas* may not be at the top of the socio-political hierarchy. But, sometimes, ritual status and power position coincide when a *savarna* group is also a dominant caste, like the Rajputs in several regions of the Hindi belt. For us, the main point to bear is that caste remains a key variable of the Indian social structure, and especially so when compared to class, for instance.

## Regional Contrasts and Systemic Evolutions

Caste groups are not equally distributed in every region. In fact, the *varna* system never existed in a full-fledged manner outside the Hindi belt. Elsewhere, there is always a missing category, like the Kshatriyas (in Bengal or Maharashtra) or the Vaishyas (in Maharashtra). As a result, the arithmetic of caste is very different from one region to another. In the Hindi belt where *savarnas* are all represented, the upper castes form about one-fifth of the society with the Brahmans topping 10 per cent of the total population in Uttar Pradesh, for instance. By contrast, in the south of the Vindhyas, the upper castes represent a very small minority of less than 10 per cent—with the Brahmans, the largest of all the upper castes, culminating at about 3 per cent of society.

Besides, anthropologists and sociologists have shown that the ritual dimension of caste hierarchies based on the notion of the pure and the impure was eroding quickly, especially in urban settings as also in the countryside (see Srinivas, 1996; Gupta, 2000). And political scientists have joined hands with them to explain, with the help of qualitative methods, the changing socio-political landscape of India.[3] As argued by Rajni Kothari, 'It is not politics that gets caste-ridden; it is caste that gets politicized' (1970: 20). The Kshatriyas of Gujarat are a case in point since this new category—bearing an old name—was born out of the need that some caste leaders (Rajputs, who are upper castes, and Kolis, who are Shudras) felt to add up their demographic strength in order to play a more effective role in the political arena, especially at the time of elections.[4]

The main objective then is to study how India's caste-based social diversity translated into politics in a dynamic perspective, over more than 60 years, at the state level. Indeed, in India's state politics, caste plays a major part today. But if its importance is increasing, it has always been a significant factor. This is why the relation between caste and politics needs to be scrutinized in a historical perspective.

In some regions, caste has been a vehicle for socio-political change; in others, it has preserved a deep-rooted status quo. Our study helps to build a typology based on most of the large states of the Indian Union, some of the case studies being more detailed and comprehensive than others.

This typology of the Indian states based on the social background of their MLAs studied over more than half a century has led me to identify seven categories to which we shall now turn.

A HINDI BELT PATTERN

The region which has always attracted a lot of attention so far as politics is concerned in India, is the Hindi belt. That is fair enough since it was weighted more than any other: about 40 per cent of the total population of the country lived there; as a result, the same proportion of Members of Parliament (MPs) was returned from this area. For decades, the prime minister of India invariably came from this area, and more precisely from Uttar Pradesh, the largest state of the country.

For decades too, the Hindi belt was the stronghold of conservative Congressmen from the upper castes who cultivated a clientelistic modus operandi. The opposition parties were hardly more plebeian. This is well reflected in the caste background of the MPs returned in Uttar Pradesh, the Hindi-speakers-dominated constituencies of Punjab as also Haryana, Chandigarh, Madhya Pradesh, Rajasthan, Bihar and Delhi. In 1952, the upper caste MPs represented 64 per cent of the total (Table 19.1). They remained in majority till 1977, when the defeat of the Congress for the first time was the occasion of a significant decline

TABLE 19.1: Caste and Community of MPs in the Hindi Belt, 1952–2004 (%)

| Castes and communities | 1952 | 1957 | 1962 | 1967 | 1971 | 1977 | 1980 | 1984 | 1989 | 1991 | 1996 | 1998 | 1999 | 2004 |
|---|---|---|---|---|---|---|---|---|---|---|---|---|---|---|
| Upper Castes | 64.00 | 58.60 | 54.90 | 55.50 | 53.90 | 48.20 | 40.88 | 46.90 | 38.20 | 37.11 | 35.30 | 34.70 | 35.40 | 33.00 |
| Intermediate Castes | 1.00 | 1.43 | 1.88 | 2.75 | 4.11 | 6.64 | 5.33 | 5.31 | 8.00 | 5.43 | 7.53 | 8.90 | 7.90 | 7.10 |
| OBC | 4.45 | 5.24 | 7.98 | 9.64 | 10.10 | 13.30 | 13.74 | 11.10 | 20.87 | 22.60 | 24.80 | 23.60 | 24.00 | 25.30 |
| SC | 15.76 | 18.10 | 19.72 | 18.35 | 18.26 | 17.70 | 17.78 | 17.26 | 17.78 | 18.10 | 18.14 | 18.20 | 18.60 | 17.80 |
| ST | 5.42 | 6.90 | 7.04 | 7.80 | 7.31 | 7.08 | 7.56 | 7.52 | 7.56 | 8.14 | 7.52 | 7.60 | 7.50 | 8.40 |
| Muslims | 5.42 | 4.76 | 4.23 | 3.67 | 4.57 | 5.75 | 11.56 | 9.73 | 5.78 | 4.52 | 3.54 | 5.30 | 5.00 | 7.10 |
| TOTAL | 96.05 | 95.03 | 95.75 | 97.71 | 98.25 | 98.67 | 96.85 | 97.82 | 98.19 | 95.90 | 96.83 | 98.30 | 98.40 | 98.70 |

Source: Survey by author.

of the percentage of the upper castes among the Hindi belt MPs—from almost 54 per cent to about 48 per cent. Then they remained above 40 per cent till 1989— the date of the second defeat of the Congress at the centre and the second milestone in terms of the caste background of the MPs. This turning point, which was due to the success of the Janata Dal—a peasant and low caste-oriented party—was reconfirmed during the 1990s: election after election, the percentage of the upper caste MPs continued to decrease (to end up with 33 per cent in 2004) whereas the share of the OBC continued to grow. While the percentage of the OBC MPs had increased by only 3 percentage points in 1977, the first milestone, it almost doubled in 1989, from 11 to 21 per cent and continued to grow afterwards— whichever party be in office. This change was largely due to the impact of the Mandal affair, when upper caste students (and others) opposed the granting of a quota of 27 per cent of the posts in the administration to the OBC. OBC leaders orchestrated counter-mobilizations and their followers started to vote for candidates from their own milieu in order to defend their interests and also simply because they got politicized and were eager to emancipate themselves from the vertical, old clientelistic system of the Congress Party.

V.P. Singh, who decided to implement the recommendations of the Mandal Report, called this process a silent revolution, and I borrowed the term from him because a non-violent transfer of power had indeed begun to take place—plebeians dislodging elite groups from power.[5]

The evolution of the caste profile of the Hindi belt MPs shows a distinctive pattern: the growing politicization of the OBC, largely due to their mobilization

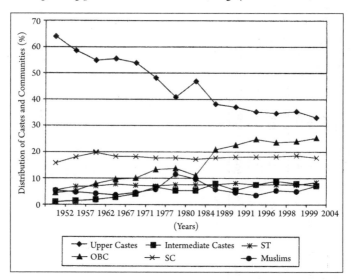

FIGURE 19.1: Castes and Communities of MPs in the Hindi Belt, 1952–2004

*Source:* Survey by author

in favour of reservations, resulted in a transfer of power from upper castes to OBC politicians.

This process is even more pronounced at the state level among some of the largest states of the Hindi belt. Indeed, the state assemblies of the core of the Hindi belt formed by Uttar Pradesh, Madhya Pradesh and Bihar emulate the development mentioned above regarding the MPs. In all these states, the proportion of the upper caste MLAs has steadily declined from about 40–55 per cent in the 1950s to about 25–35 per cent today while the share of the OBC grew from 10–20 per cent to about 20–40 per cent.

Here, Bihar shows the way: between 1952 and 2005, the proportion of OBC MLAs has doubled from 20 to 42 per cent—slightly more than their share in the population according to the 1931 Census, 38.5 per cent—whereas the percentage of the upper caste MLAs was halved, from 46 to 26 per cent (twice their share in the population, 13.7 per cent).[6] The trends are exactly symmetrical and, interestingly, both graphs crossed each other in 1990, the Mandal year. At that time, the proportions of OBC MLAs and upper caste MLAs were still the same at 35 per cent and then the pace of change got accelerated. The pioneering role of Bihar, was partly due to the long tradition of socialist politics in the state: Lohia's socialists were keen to promote affirmative action programmes for the OBC in Bihar and mobilized the lower castes rather early in this very perspective. No other state in the Hindi belt can compete with Bihar so far as the rise of OBC MLAs is concerned, but two of them, Uttar Pradesh and Madhya Pradesh, comply with the Hindi belt pattern anyway. In both states, upper caste MLAs still represented more than one-third of the assemblies in the late 1990s, whereas the OBC represented between one-fifth and one-fourth of the total. In Madhya Pradesh, where the upper castes represent 13 per cent of the population, the share of the upper caste MLAs was still more than 37 per cent in 2003, whereas the OBC MLAs were less than 20 per cent in a state where they form more than 41 per cent of the population. But the OBC have jumped in 1977 and have continued to grow steadily since as early as 1980. In Uttar Pradesh, where the upper caste represent more than 20 per cent of the population, 'their' MLAs represented more than 35 per cent of the population after the 2002 elections, and the OBC MLAs reached 27.5 per cent in a state where OBC are almost 42 per cent of the population. However, figures do not vary significantly according to which party wins the election. When the BJP performs well, the upper castes display a great resilience whereas the OBC—and the Muslims—surge when the Samajwadi Party and/or the Bahujan Samaj Party get good results.

## A NORTH-WESTERN PATTERN

On the western border of this core group—Uttar Pradesh, Madhya Pradesh and Bihar—three states, namely, Punjab, Rajasthan and Gujarat, introduce a variant to the so-called Hindi belt partem. There, upper castes are almost at the same level among the MLAs as those in the Hindi belt (between one-fifth and one-third), but the dominant castes, the Jats in Punjab and Rajasthan and the Patidars in Gujarat, are as strong as the upper caste MLAs and on the rise in most cases. In contrast with the Hindi belt, the OBC remain rather low, except in Gujarat.

In Punjab, where the Jats represented 21.3 per cent of the state in 1931, they have always represented between 35 and 52 per cent of the MLAs over the last 15 years. This domination of the Jats went on par with the erosion of the upper castes (from 27 per cent in 1992 to 19.7 per cent in 2002) and the embryonic mobilization of the OBC whose MLAs never represented more than 5 per cent of the MLAs! The Dalit MLAs form a large contingent thanks to a quota of 25 per cent of the seats for the Scheduled Castes. But they are not in a position to compete with the Jats.

In Rajasthan—a Hindi-speaking state which, from my point of view here, does not belong to the Hindi belt but to north-west India because of the growing role played by the Jats—the upper castes (who represent about 20 per cent of the population) have met the same fate as those in Uttar Pradesh and Madhya Pradesh. 'Their' MLAs fell from 51 per cent in 1952 to 32 per cent in 2003, but the OBC (about 40 per cent of society) have not benefited from their decline; they still represented less than 10 per cent of the MLAs in 2003. The Jats, less than 10 per cent of the population, on the contrary, have been able to assert themselves. In 1995, they peaked at 30 per cent of the MLAs and remained around 29 per cent in 2003. Jats—a dominant caste—and upper castes remain in command of Rajasthan politics.[7]

This pattern is closely followed by Gujarat, one of Rajasthan's neighbouring states. Here too, a dominant caste, that of the Patidars, 13 per cent of the population, established its strength as early as the 1960s. Like the Jats in Rajasthan, the Patidars of Gujarat represent between one-fifth and one-third of the MLAs since the 1963 elections. And like in Rajasthan, the upper castes—also 13 per cent of the population—show a strong resilience. In both states; their representation has declined by 15 percentage points since the early 1960s but they were still 20–30 per cent of the MLAs—till 2007 when their share declined in Gujarat. The main difference between Gujarat and Rajasthan concerns the OBC which have mobilized early in the former. As a result, the proportion of OBC in the State Assembly has jumped from 8 to 34 per cent between 1962 and 2007.

WHERE THE DOMINANT CASTES ALONE RUN THE SHOW:
THE DECCAN PATTERN

Three states of the Deccan plateau—Maharashtra, Karnataka and Andhra Pradesh—show the unchallenged rule of the dominant castes. In these three states, peasant proprietary castes have always represented between 40 and 60 per cent of the MLAs and their share is not on the decline.

In Maharashtra, the Marathas—who represent 32 per cent of the population—remain in control, though they have never won more than 45 per cent of the seats. While Maharashtra belongs to western India, it can be included in the Deccan belt owing to the major role traditionally played by the Marathas, a dominant caste comparable to those in Andhra Pradesh and Karnataka. In this state, the Maratha MLAs are slightly less numerous than their alter egos of the dominant castes in the bordering Dravidian states, but they tend to increase from 39 per cent in 1985 to almost 45 per cent in 2004. Correlatively, the share of the upper castes—less than 7 per cent of the population—is eroding, but it has always been very low anyway: from less than 6 per cent in 1967 to less than 3 per cent in 2004. Maharashtra is the only state of this group where the OBC (almost 30 per cent of the population) represent more than 20 per cent of the MLAs; but this percentage remains the same since the 1960s.

In Karnataka, Lingayats and Vokkaligas—who represent 26 per cent of the population—have always been in majority in the State Assembly. In 1999, they still represented 58.9 per cent of the MLAs, 0.6 percentage points more than in 1952! Certainly, the share of the OBC—32.5 per cent of the population—was almost doubled in the meantime, but it remained very low, passing from 7 per cent to about 12 per cent. The share of the upper castes—3.5 per cent of the population—remained almost stable but also very low, it decreased from 9 to 8 per cent.

In Andhra Pradesh, Kammas and Reddys—who represent also 26 per cent of the population—are increasingly more prominent since 1990—they represent more than 50 per cent of the MLAs since this date—at the expense of the upper castes and the OBC, 6 and 36 per cent respectively of the population. From the 1970s to the 2000s, they have jumped from 42.5 per cent of the MLAs to 59.2 per cent. At the same time, the share of the upper caste MLAs dropped from more than 9 per cent to 2 per cent and that of the OBC MLAs declined from 19.5 per cent to 18.3 per cent.

## THE FORGOTTEN *ADIVASI*

In 2000, three new states were carved out in the Indian Union: Uttaranchal (now Uttarakhand), Jharkhand and Chhattisgarh. The last two resulted partly from the demands of tribal movements which were eager to give the local *adivasi* states that they could call their own. Indeed, the percentages of Scheduled Tribes in Jharkhand and in Chhattisgarh are among the highest in India (with the exception of the north-east) with 26.3 per cent and 31.8 per cent respectively according to the 2001 Census. In both states, tribals represent 36–39 per cent of the MLAs but the upper castes are still very influential. In Jharkhand, they represent 4 per cent of the population and 11 per cent of the MLAs whereas in Chhattisgarh they represent 3.3 per cent of the population and 25.5 per cent of the MLAs. The main difference lies in the share of the OBC who are only 20 per cent of the Jharkhand population but represent 30 per cent of the MLAs whereas they form 50 per cent of the population of Chhattisgarh, but only 23.3 per cent of the MLAs. More importantly, in neither state could the tribals really seize power owing to their marginalization within the apparatus of the main parties and within state governments.

While the four patterns just identified can be associated with regions—the Hindi belt, the north-west, the Deccan and the tribal belt of central India—the other ones are found in states which are not at all contiguous.

## WHERE THE UPPER CASTES RESIST WELL:
## WEST BENGAL AND KERALA

The fifth group is made of two states—West Bengal and Kerala—which have no borders in common but have something else in common: a remarkable share of upper caste MLAs in their assemblies. In none of these states, this percentage is below 37 per cent whereas in fact, upper castes are not present in large numbers in the population.

West Bengal and Kerala are strongholds of communism for years. Kerala was the first state where the Communist Party of India (CPI) rose to power in 1957 and West Bengal is governed by the Communist Party of India (Marxist) or CPI(M) since 1977. There is probably no contradiction between the upper caste social profile of the political personnel of these two states and their communist leanings simply because the upper caste communist elites believe more in class than caste and have implemented socioeconomic reforms accordingly. They have managed to retain power—or to stage repeated comebacks—not mainly by opening up to the lower castes, but by being associated with progressive measures like land reforms.

West Bengal represents a trajectory on its own. This is the only state where the percentage of the upper castes MLAs has increased over the last 20 years, from 38 per cent in 1972 to 50 per cent in 1996. Lately, the trend has been reverted in 2001, when the percentage of the upper caste MLAs fell just below 38 per cent, but upper caste ministers were still more than 51 per cent in the state government. This very uncommon route is partly due to the fact that over the same period, the Congress and the CPI(M)—two upper caste dominated parties—remained the main political forces. But it is also due to the sheer absence of OBC movements in this region.

The situation of Kerala is very similar. Here, the percentage of the upper caste MLAs decreased from 49 per cent in 1957 to 38 per cent after the last elections. Kerala, however, has a large number of OBC MLAs due, mainly, to the sizeable Izhavas community and their well-established organization, the Shree Narayana Dharma Paripalana Yogam (SNDPY) which has strong relations with the communist movement. Indeed, the CPI(M) is more plebeian than the Congress, one of the most elitist state branches of the party in India.

## THE REIGN OF PROPORTIONALITY

In Himachal Pradesh and Delhi too, upper caste MLAs represent the largest share of the state assemblies. In Himachal, their share is slightly eroding, from 68 per cent in 1967 to 61.8 per cent after the last elections; but it remains quite comfortable. The OBC, by contrast, have never represented more than 10 per cent of the MLAs. Delhi tells a similar story. In this state, for which data are available for only three elections—1993, 1998 and 2003—the upper caste MLAs are not in majority any more since their share fell from 54 per cent to 46 per cent, but this is a rare achievement anyway, especially because the Jats are still below 10 per cent of the MLAs since the 2003 elections and the OBC at 7 per cent.

However, this trajectory is different from that of West Bengal and Kerala for the simple reason that in these two states, small elites were over-represented at the top whereas in Himachal Pradesh and Delhi they are represented in a quasi-proportional way. Indeed, upper castes represent 48 per cent of the population of Himachal Pradesh according to the 1931 Census and 38 per cent of Delhi population according to surveys conducted by the Centre for the Study of Developing Societies (CSDS) in the state.

## TAMIL NADU: THE SUBALTERNIST TRADITION

Tamil Nadu is another case of quasi-proportionality. According to the Backward Classes Commission, the OBC represent 67 per cent of the population and, indeed, the OBC MLAs have never been less than 56 per cent of the state assembly and have reached 66 per cent once. But it is a very different situation from that of Himachal Pradesh and Delhi for the obvious reason that it is easier for a large elite group to retain power than for plebeian groups—even when they are large groups—since, to begin with, they were not in office. The Tamil trajectory clearly harks back to the history of the region. In the Madras Presidency, during the British Raj, the plebeians mobilized early against the Brahman power and organized social movements such as the non-Brahman movement and established political parties such as the Justice Party—which seized power in the 1920s. As a result, programmes of positive discrimination have been implemented in a big way for the upliftment of the lower castes. After independence, the Congress was obliged to promote a low caste leader, Kamaraj, as replacement for C. Rajagopalachari, a conservative Brahman, but it was not sufficient for defusing the rising popularity of the Dravidian parties which had inherited some of their legitimacy from the non-Brahman movement.

To sum up, the sociology of the political personnel has followed several different routes in India. The Hindi belt pattern is marked by the rise of the OBC at the expense of the upper castes; the north-western trajectory is a variant of the previous one since the main beneficiaries of the erosion of the upper castes, here, are dominant castes; the Deccan distinguishes itself with the continuation of the dominant castes in command; so-called 'tribal states' of the Hindi belt have, in fact, not let the *adivasis* seize power (which remains in the hands of upper castes); states with a communist tradition—West Bengal and Kerala—epitomize a typical resilience of the upper castes. Such a domination is also evident from the social profile of the MLAs elected in Himachal Pradesh and Delhi, but this is a case of proportionality; Tamil Nadu is a similar case, but in favour of plebeian groups which have had to struggle to gain their share of power.

The great variety of trajectories reflected in this typology suggests that the 'silent revolution pattern' largely identified with the Hindi belt, is not that dominant. Certainly, the states embodying this pattern—Uttar Pradesh, Bihar, Madhya Pradesh—are among the largest in India. But one must recognise that beyond the Hindi belt, there are other dynamics at work. The dominant caste-oriented trajectory is indeed a strong challenger because it does not only prevail south of the Vindhyas but also in Punjab, Rajasthan and Gujarat although to a lesser extent. In fact, one may argue that the south and the west have become less progressive than some of the northern states in terms of the lower caste people's rise to power.

Such a view needs to be qualified though. First, the state which has played a really pioneering role is Tamil Nadu, a southern state par excellence. Second, the increase of the OBC MLAs in state legislatures does not necessarily mean that the influence of the OBC has increased. To measure this influence, one must not contend oneself with studying the MLAs but must also look at the posts low caste people may occupy within the apparatus of the parties and in state governments; some portfolios carry more weight than other. Third, caste does not say everything. For instance, the *Who's Who* do not always have information on the occupation or education of MLAs. But the data show anyway that, by and large, peasants are increasingly becoming numerous in the assemblies, that the level of education of the MLAs is rising, and that women tend to be more numerous in the assemblies now.

## Notes

1. However, post-independence reservations were not likely to mirror the interests of these groups as much as before, under the British, since the system of primaries had gone. Till 1947, the Scheduled Caste citizens had to vote in order to select the three candidates who would be allowed to stand before the general electorate. But after independence, just any candidate could contest elections for those reserved seats provided he or she was a member of the Scheduled Castes.
2. The notion of dominant caste has been introduced in the vocabulary of Indian studies by M.N. Srinivas (1995).
3. The two-volume book edited by F. Frankel and M.S.A. Rao (1989 and 1990) remains a landmark in this respect.
4. As Ghanshyam Shah showed in his seminal work (1975).

5. For more details on this process, see Jaffrelot (2003).
6. In this chapter, the 1931 Census is the source I have used to present the share of caste groups in state population, except for Delhi and Tamil Nadu.
7. Although the Jats were classified as OBC before the 2003 elections, they have been included in the Intermediary Castes category in the statistical survey in order to compare figures over a longer period of time.

## References

Beer, S.H. (1957). 'The Representation of Interests in British Government: Historical Background', *The American Political Science Review*, Vol. 51, No. 3, pp. 613–50.

Bhardan, Pranab (1984), *The Political Economy of Development in India*, Oxford: Blackwell.

*Census of India, 1931* (1933), Government of India, Rajputana Agency, Nagpur.

Deshpande, Satish (2003), *Contemporary India: A Sociological View*, New Delhi: Penguin.

Frankel, F. and M.S.A. Rao (1989, 1990) (eds.), *Dominance and State Power in Modern India*, 2 Vols., Delhi: Oxford University Press.

Gupta, D. (2000), *Interrogating Caste: Understanding Hierarchy and Difference in Indian Society*, New Delhi: Penguin.

Jaffrelot, C. (2003), *India's Silent Revolution: The Rise of the Lower Castes in North Indian Politics*, Delhi: Permanent Black.

——— (2007), 'Caste and the Rise of Marginalized Groups', in S. Ganguly, L. Diamond and M. Plattner (eds.), *The State of Indian Democracy*, pp. 67–88, Baltimore and Washington: The Johns Hopkins University Press.

Kothari, R. (1970), 'Introduction: Caste in Indian Polities', in R. Kothari (ed.), *Caste in Indian Politics*, pp. 3–25, New Delhi: Orient Longman.

Kumar, S., A. Heath and O. Heath (2002), 'Changing Patterns of Social Mobility: Some Trends over Time', *Economic and Political Weekly*, Vol. 37, No. 40, pp. 4091–6.

Pitkin, H.F. (1967), *The Concept of Representation*, Berkeley: University of California Press.

Shah, G. (1975), *Caste Association and Political Process in Gujarat*, Bombay: Popular Prakashan.

Srinivas, M.N. (1978), 'The Future of the Caste System', *Economic and Political Weekly*, Vol. 7, No. 8, p. 238.

——— (1995), *Social Change in Modern India*, New Delhi: Orient Longman.

——— (1996) (ed.), *Caste: Its Twentieth Century Avatar*, New Delhi: Viking.

Weber, Max (2003), *Hindouisme et Bouddhisme*, Paris: Flammarion.

# Appendix 1

EVOLUTION OF THE UPPER CASTE MLAs (STATE-WISE %)

| States | Percentage in the State Population[a] | 1952 | 1955-57 | 1960-63 | 1967 | 1969-70 | 1971-74 | 1975-79 | 1980-83 | 1984-85 | 1987-90 | 1991-92 | 1993-95 | 1996-2000 | 2001-05 | 2007 |
|---|---|---|---|---|---|---|---|---|---|---|---|---|---|---|---|---|
| *Type 1* | | | | | | | | | | | | | | | | |
| Uttar Pradesh[b] | 20.5 | 58.0 | 55.0 | 58.0 | 45.3 | 43.9 | 37.8 | 35.2 | 41.3 | 39.7 | 35.7 | 39.0 | 26.7 | 34.6 | 35.4 | – |
| Madhya Pradesh[b] | 12.9 | – | 41.2 | 48.4 | 44.9 | – | 49.6 | 46.6 | 40.3 | 40.7 | 40.9 | – | 37.1 | 35.6 | 37.7 | – |
| Bihar[b] | 13.7 | 46.1 | 46.1 | 46.1 | 44.8 | 42.0 | 42.8 | 40.6 | 36.6 | 38.5 | 34.6 | – | 21.8 | 25.1 | 25.9 | – |
| *Type 2* | | | | | | | | | | | | | | | | |
| Punjab | 14.7 | – | – | – | – | – | – | 17.9 | – | – | – | – | – | 15.4 | 19.7 | – |
| Rajasthan | 20.6 | 51.2 | 47.1 | 45.6 | 45.6 | – | 42.1 | 32.5 | 31.9 | 35.7 | 22.0 | 27.4 | 32.5 | 31.1 | 32.1 | – |
| Gujarat | 13.0 | – | – | 34.0 | 40.0 | – | 30.0 | 27.0 | 21.0 | 25.0 | 25.0 | – | 21.0 | 21.0 | 20.0 | 14.0 |
| *Type 3* | | | | | | | | | | | | | | | | |
| Maharashtra | 6.6 | – | – | – | 5.9 | – | 6.6 | 6.9 | 5.2 | 4.8 | 4.5 | – | 4.1 | 2.7 | 3.4 | – |
| Karnataka | 3.5 | 9.4 | 10.0 | 9.1 | 8.8 | – | 7.7 | 9.8 | 8.2 | 7.3 | 5.8 | – | 5.2 | 5.4 | – | – |
| Andhra Pradesh | 6.0 | – | 9.1 | 9.3 | 5.9 | – | 9.4 | 6.1 | 4.8 | 4.4 | 4.4 | – | 3.2 | 3.4 | 2.0 | – |
| *Type 4* | | | | | | | | | | | | | | | | |
| Jharkhand[c] | 3.9 | – | – | – | – | – | – | – | – | – | – | – | – | 17.3[e] | 11.1[f] | – |
| Chhattisgarh[d] | 3.3 | – | – | – | – | – | – | – | – | – | – | – | – | – | 25.5[g] | – |
| *Type 5* | | | | | | | | | | | | | | | | |
| West Bengal | 5.7 | 45.4 | 50.0 | 49.2 | 40.0 | 41.8 | 38.2/38[j] | 45.9 | 43.2 | 45.2 | 45.3 | 45.0 | – | 50.0 | 37.5 | – |
| Kerala | – | – | 49.0 | 46.0 | 42.0 | 43.0 | 52.0 | 41.0 | 42.0 | 44.0 | 43.0 | – | – | 40.0 | 38.0 | – |

| | | | | | | | | | | | | | | | | | |
|---|---|---|---|---|---|---|---|---|---|---|---|---|---|---|---|---|---|
| *Type 6* | | | | | | | | | | | | | | | | | |
| Himachal Pradesh | 48.0 | – | – | – | 68.3 | – | 67.6 | 66.2 | 64.7 | 66.2 | 61.8 | – | – | 61.8 | 58.8 | 61.8 | – |
| Delhi | 38.0ʰ | – | – | – | – | – | – | – | – | – | – | – | – | 54.0 | 46.0 | 46.0 | – |
| *Type 7* | | | | | | | | | | | | | | | | | |
| Tamil Nadu | – | – | – | 17.9 | – | 18.8 | 17.9 | 20.5 | 18.4 | 11.9 | 12.4 | – | 11.6 | – | – | | |

*Source:* Survey by author.

*Note:*   a   Based on Census 1931.
      b   As till year 2000.
      c   Scheduled Tribes (ST) represent 26.3 per cent of the population according to Census 2001.
      d   ST represent 31.8 per cent of the population according to Census 2001.
      e   ST represented 35.8 per cent of the MLAs.
      f   ST represented 37 per cent of the MLAs.
      g   ST represented 38.9 per cent of the MLAs.
      h   Based on surveys of the CSDS Data unit.
      i   *Source:* Jaffrelot (2007)
      j   The two percentages refer to the two elections held in 1971 and 1972 respectively.

# Appendix 2

EVOLUTION OF THE INTERMEDIATE/DOMINANT CASTE MLAs (STATE-WISE %)

| States | Percentage in the State Population[a] | 1952 | 1955–57 | 1960–63 | 1967 | 1969–70 | 1971–74 | 1975–79 | 1980–83 | 1984–85 | 1987–90 | 1991–92 | 1993–95 | 1996–2000 | 2001–05 | 2001–2007 |
|---|---|---|---|---|---|---|---|---|---|---|---|---|---|---|---|---|
| *Type 1* | | | | | | | | | | | | | | | | |
| Uttar Pradesh[b] | 2.0 | 3.0 | 3.0 | 2.0 | 0 | – | 1.4 | 1.2 | 1.2 | 2.1 | 2.6 | 3.1 | 3.1 | 3.7 | 4.7[f] | – |
| Madhya Pradesh[b] | 1.1 | – | 1.1 | 0.6 | 0.6 | – | 0.3 | 0.9 | 0.9 | 0.3 | 0.3 | – | 0.6 | 0.9 | 2.6 | – |
| Bihar[b] | – | 0 | 0 | 0 | 0 | – | 0 | 0 | 0 | – | 0 | – | 0 | 0 | – | – |
| *Type 2* | | | | | | | | | | | | | | | | |
| Punjab | 21.3 | – | – | – | – | – | – | 47.9 | – | – | – | 39.3 | – | 52.2 | 35.9 | – |
| Rajasthan | 9.2 | 15.9 | 17.7 | 23.3 | 16.7 | – | 17.2 | 40.0 | 20.7 | 14.3 | 26.0 | – | 29.9 | 18.5 | 28.6 | – |
| Gujarat | 13.0 | – | – | 27.0 | 21.0 | – | 23.0 | 27.0 | 21.0 | 21.0 | 25.0 | – | 24.0 | 22.0 | 25.0 | 28.0 |
| *Type 3* | | | | | | | | | | | | | | | | |
| Maharashtra | 32.0 | – | – | – | 43.1 | – | 43.1 | 40.9 | 42.7 | 39.2 | 44.7 | – | 45.4 | 43.0 | 44.7 | – |
| Karnataka | 26.1 | 58.3 | 50.8 | 55.8 | 58.5 | – | 53.2 | 52.6 | 57.5 | 60.4 | 54.8 | – | 60.2 | 59.8 | – | – |
| Andhra Pradesh | 26.0 | – | 53.6 | 47.7 | 48.4 | – | 42.5 | 45.2 | 47.6 | 46.9 | 52.0 | – | 58.5 | 56.8 | 59.2 | – |
| *Type 4* | | | | | | | | | | | | | | | | |
| Jharkhand[c] | – | – | – | – | – | – | – | – | – | – | – | – | 0 | 0 | 0 | – |
| Chhattisgarh[d] | 0.2 | – | – | – | – | – | – | – | – | – | – | – | – | – | 0 | – |
| *Type 5* | | | | | | | | | | | | | | | | |
| West Bengal | 35.0 | 4.6 | 7.5 | 5.9 | 6.0 | 8.2 | 7.5/6.5[g] | 9.5 | 7.5 | – | 7.5 | 5.0 | 3.0 | – | 5.0 | – |

| | | | | | | | | | | | | | | | |
|---|---|---|---|---|---|---|---|---|---|---|---|---|---|---|---|
| Kerala | — | — | — | — | — | 0 | — | 0 | 0 | 0 | 0 | 0 | 0 | — | — |
| *Type 6* | | | | | | | | | | | | | | | |
| Himachal Pradesh | 0 | — | — | — | — | 0 | — | 0 | 0 | 0 | 0 | — | 0 | 0 | — |
| Delhi | 5.0[e] | — | — | — | — | — | — | — | — | — | — | — | 9.0 | 13.0 | 9.0 |
| *Type 7* | | | | | | | | | | | | | | | |
| Tamil Nadu | — | — | — | — | — | 0 | — | 0 | 0 | 0 | 0 | 0 | 0 | — | — |

*Source:* Survey by author.

*Note:*  [a]  Based on Census 1931.

  [b]  As till year 2000.

  [c]  Scheduled Tribes (ST) represent 26.3 per cent of the population according to Census 2001.

  [d]  ST represent 31.8 per cent of the population according to Census 2001.

  [e]  Based on surveys of the CSDS Data unit.

  [f]  *Source:* Jaffrelot (2007)

  [g]  The two percentages refer to the two elections held in 1971 and 1972 respectively.

# Appendix 3

EVOLUTION OF THE OBC MLAs (STATE-WISE %)

| States | Percentage in the State Population[a] | 1952 | 1955–57 | 1960–63 | 1967 | 1969–70 | 1971–74 | 1975–79 | 1980–83 | 1984–85 | 1987–90 | 1991–92 | 1993–95 | 1996–2000 | 2001–05 | 2007 |
|---|---|---|---|---|---|---|---|---|---|---|---|---|---|---|---|---|
| *Type 1* | | | | | | | | | | | | | | | | |
| Uttar Pradesh[b] | 41.7 | 9.0 | 12.0 | 13.0 | 29.2 | 26.8 | 18.3 | 16.8 | 13.4 | 19.6 | 24.2 | 27.1 | 32.4 | 24.8 | 27.5 | – |
| Madhya Pradesh[b] | 41.5 | – | 4.7 | 9.1 | 9.4 | – | 9.5 | 14.3 | 16.1 | 18.6 | 18.7 | – | 22.7 | 22.0 | 19.5 | – |
| Bihar[b] | 38.5 | 20.6 | 19.4 | 24.4 | 26.6 | 27.9 | 25.7 | 28.3 | 30.4 | – | 34.9 | – | 46.8 | 40.3 | 42.0 | 34.0 |
| *Type 2* | | | | | | | | | | | | | | | | |
| Punjab | – | – | – | – | – | – | – | 3.4 | – | – | – | 5.1 | – | 3.4 | 3.4 | – |
| Rajasthan | 40.0 | 3.7 | 2.5 | 4.4 | 2.2 | 5.5 | 2.5 | 7.4 | 8.0 | 12.0 | – | 5.2 | – | 6.6 | 8.9 | – |
| Gujarat | 40.0 | – | – | 8.0 | 11.0 | – | 16.0 | 15.0 | 24.0 | 24.0 | 26.0 | – | 21.0 | 21.0 | 29.0 | 34.0 |
| *Type 3* | | | | | | | | | | | | | | | | |
| Maharashtra | 29.8 | – | – | – | 22.3 | – | 21.4 | 23.2 | 19.7 | 24.6 | 26.0 | – | 23.2 | 23.6 | 23.9 | – |
| Karnataka | 32.5 | 7.3 | 13.1 | 14.1 | 11.2 | – | 12.6 | 13.0 | 13.0 | 10.1 | 13.9 | – | 12.8 | 12.5 | – | – |
| Andhra Pradesh | 36.0 | – | 8.7 | 13.0 | 14.3 | – | 19.5 | 19.0 | 20.7 | 20.1 | 11.9 | – | 12.9 | 11.9 | 18.3 | – |
| *Type 4* | | | | | | | | | | | | | | | | |
| Jharkhand[c] | 19.7 | – | – | – | – | – | – | – | – | – | – | – | – | 27.2[e] | 29.7[f] | – |
| Chhattisgarh[d] | 50.4 | – | – | – | – | – | – | – | – | – | – | – | – | – | 23.3[g] | – |
| *Type 5* | | | | | | | | | | | | | | | | |
| West Bengal | – | 0 | 0 | 0 | 0 | 0 | 0 | 0 | 0 | 0 | 0 | 0 | 0 | – | – | – |

| | | | | | | | | | | | | | | | |
|---|---|---|---|---|---|---|---|---|---|---|---|---|---|---|---|
| Kerala | — | 27.0 | 26.0 | 33.0 | 30.0 | — | 20.0 | 26.0 | 27.0 | 28.0 | 25.0 | — | 29.0 | 31.0 | — |
| *Type 6* | | | | | | | | | | | | | | | |
| Himachal Pradesh | 10.5 | — | — | 1.7 | — | 2.9 | 7.4 | 5.9 | 7.4 | 7.4 | — | 10.3 | 7.4 | 7.4 | — |
| Delhi | 14.0[b] | — | — | — | — | — | — | — | — | — | — | 7.0 | 7.0 | 7.0 | — |
| *Type 7* | | | | | | | | | | | | | | | |
| Tamil Nadu | 63.6 | — | — | 66.2 | — | 61.6 | 59.0 | 57.7 | 56.9 | 61.5 | 62.4 | — | 62.0 | — | — |

*Source:* Survey by author.

*Note:* [a] Based on Census 1931.
[b] As till year 2000.
[c] Scheduled Tribes (ST) represent 26.3 per cent of the population according to Census 2001.
[d] ST represent 31.8 per cent of the population according to Census 2001.
[e] ST represented 35.8 per cent of the MLAs.
[f] ST represented 37 per cent of the MLAs.
[g] ST represented 38.9 per cent of the MLAs.
[h] Based on surveys of the CSDS Data unit.
[i] *Source:* Jaffrelot (2007).

# Chapter 20

# The changing identity of the Jats in north India: kshatriyas, *kisans* or backwards?

Students of nationalism and ethnic conflicts have generally come to the conclusion that there is nothing permanent in collective identities based on language or religion. The frontiers of linguistic groups or religious communities are not given—as the 'primordialists' tend to claim—but are ever-changing.[1] The question is not 'if' but, why and how do identities transform themselves into something different? Psycho-sociologists argue that identities can only change at the time of crisis. Erik Erikson, for instance, looks at adolescence as the crisis period leading to identity transformation par excellence (Erikson 1972). Interestingly his analysis is not confined to the individual's inner conflicts. According to him, the adolescence crisis develops in interaction with the 'other'. This is a keyword for approaching the 'why' dimension of our threefold question: as Paul Ricoeur has shown, the identity formation process unfolds itself in a dialectic relation with others.[2] But how? I have addressed this question in the case of a religious community—the Hindus of India—in an attempt at explaining the Hindutva Movement (Jaffrelot 1999a). I would like to address the same question here vis-à-vis a specific caste, that of the Jats. While Alice Thorner has not paid attention to this particular group, her work, with Daniel Thorner, on the Indian peasantry is related to some of the issues the Jats had to deal with—such as land reforms and the process of class formation in rural India.[3] The (often self-proclaimed) spokesmen of this caste have projected three very different kinds of identity over the last one hundred years. First, they claimed that Jats were Kshatriyas, then that they were *kisans* (peasants) and finally that they belonged to the 'backward castes'. These three identities overlapped in the course of time but stood in clear succession within the discourse of the caste leaders. I hypothesize that this evolution was due to the changing relation of the Jats vis-a-vis other dominating groups and the state. The political arena played a very important role indeed in these identity-(trans)formation process.

## An Intermediate Caste Claiming the Rank of Kshatriyas

The Jats are especially numerous in the Punjab plain, in west Uttar Pradesh and in Rajasthan. Technically, they belong to the *varna* of the Shudras. However, till the mid-twentieth century, they claimed a Rajput descent (Datta 1999: 37), such a propensity to Sanskritization being largely reinforced by the influence of the Arya Samaj.

## THE SANSKRITIZING INFLUENCE OF THE ARYA SAMAJ

The Arya Samaj has been too often regarded as confined to the urban middle class.[4] In fact, it was popular among the Jats of rural Punjab and today's Uttar Pradesh. Jat leaders especially appreciated the way Dayananda questioned the authority of the Brahmans[5] and praised their caste for forcefully resisting the Brahmans' 'popish' attitudes (Saraswati 1981: 436). His discourse was also popular among the Jats because it had affinities with the Sadh's credo.[6] However, Dayananda's indictment of the Brahmans did not imply a rejection of the caste system. What he condemned was the hereditary caste. He specifically recommended that the 'fixture of the *varnas* according to merits and actions should take place at the sixteenth year of girls and twenty-fifth year of boys.[7] Accordingly, he considered that a Brahman needed only to eat food prepared by caste fellows because 'The nature of genital fluids made in a Brahman's body due to special kind of fooding is different from that made in *chandalas* body on account of bad diet. The body of the *chandalas* is full of rotten particles due to rotten diet' (ibid.: 334).

The first Jats who joined the Arya Samaj were those of Hissar District where Lala Lajpat Rai—a senior Arya Samajist—practised law, Ramji Lal Hooda, a medical practitioner, was attracted to the movement in 1883 by Lajpat Rai's father, Radha Krishan, who was his teacher in Persian.[8] He played a major role in organizing Jat Sabhas (and the Jat Mahasabha) and in spreading, via this channel, the Arya Samajist ideology among his caste fellows. In 1921 he became president of the Arya Samaj in Hissar and then contributed to the development of *Shuddhi*[9] Sabhas which played a major role in the attempt of Sanskritizing the lower castes. These *Shuddhi* Sabhas 'purified' Jats—and lower castes—in large numbers supposedly in order to transform them into 'twice borns'.

However, *shuddhi* instead of promoting equality, fit in the logic of Sanskritization.[10] Nonica Datta emphasizes that the 'Jats were told not to consume alcohol or meat, minimize the expenditure on wedding and ceremonial displays, and refrain from singing cheap songs and watching lewd pictures during the fairs' (Datta 1999a: 71). The Arya Samaj exerted over the Jats such a strong Sanskritization effect that a man like Hooda opted for a vegetarian diet (Juneja and Singh Mor 1989: 159). Datta points out that the Arya Samaj presented the Jats as Kshatriyas in order to counter the colonial discourse, which had described the Jats as 'lowly or Indo-Scythians, not Aryans...' (Datta 1999a:79). The All-India Jat Mahasabha, 'an offshoot of the Arya Samaj, formed in Muzaffarnagar in 1905' (ibid.: 76), developed the same discourse under the auspices of Jat princes since the Maharajas of Bharatpur and Dholpur—both of them Jats—were particular about stressing the Kshatriya identity of their caste.[11]

This caste association, however, had a very ambivalent discourse. On the one hand, it claimed that Jats were Kshatriyas and exhorted the Jats to give up the consumption of alcohol and meat and recommended that severe restrictions should be 'imposed on the movement of women'. On the other hand, invoking the social backwardness of the Jats, it asked for a special treatment from the government.[12] The growing intervention by the state in society has therefore given birth to an alternative idiom emphasizing the needs of an underprivileged caste for positive discrimination. A third identity began to take shape around the same time, the one based on the professional skill of the Jats as a cultivating caste.

## The Jats' Industrious Ethos

The Arya Samaj, with its strong emphasis on the notion of self-help had affinities with a specific character of the Jats, their sense of industry. The Arya Samajists have early displayed a marked spirit of enterprise—partly due to the fact that many of them came from the business community, partly due to their nationalist concern for self-sufficiency. They were the first, in the 1880s, to set up indigenous enterprises, which were the precursors of the Swadeshi Movement. Mul Raj, the founder-president of the Lahore Arya Samaj set up associations selling only *deshi* (made in India) clothes (Joshi 1965: 96). The following year he initiated the first bank with purely Indian capital, the Punjab National Bank (Tandon 1989: 152). This sense of enterprise was well in tune with the industrious ethos of the Jats.

The agrarian system of the Jats laid itself to such a production-oriented lifestyle. This system was known under the name of *bhaichara* because 'customs (*chara*) were observed by a community (*bhaia*) for the management and distribution of land' (Singh 1992: 10). But far from implying any collectivist modus operandi, or any hierarchical arrangement, this system had truly individualist connotations. Jagpal Singh emphasizes that: 'under this system the peasant-proprietors had individual and hereditary rights on the land' (ibid: 11).[13] The *bhaichara* system in contrast with the other agrarian arrangements of north India—offered the suitable context for the development of the Jat industriousness. The Jat Arya Samajists shaped their own identity of emancipation from their relatively subordinate condition by combining this work culture and the teaching of the Arya Samaj. Chhotu Ram is a case in point.

## Chhotu Ram, or the Transition from the Jat Kshatriyaness to *Kisanness*

Chhotu Ram was born in 1881. The son of an illiterate small Jat peasant proprietor in a village of Rohtak District, he was initiated to public life by Ramji Lal Hooda. Remarkably intelligent, he studied in Delhi in St Stephen's High School and then in St Stephen's College. He passed his LL.B, set up his practise in Agra and then in his home district, Rohtak, in 1912. Chhotu Ram was, therefore, one of the first Jat peasants who became part of the intelligentsia but he never severed his links with his original milieu and never ceased to advocate its cause. He was the first politician who articulated in analytical terms the opposition between rural and urban India. This attitude initially resulted from the cultural shock he felt while he came to Delhi:

My seven years of study at Delhi brought me into close contact with students from the highly cultured sections of Delhi society. My relations with them were always entirely cordial, but, in friendly banter, these urban comrades always styled their school and college fellows from the countryside as rustics, clowns and pumpkins. Jats came in for particularly heavy share of these epithets. (cited in Gopal 1977: 16)

In 1907, he wrote in *The Imperial Fortnightly* an article entitled 'The Improvement of Indian Village Life' in which he contrasted the quickly changing town and the stagnant village (Ram 1996: 71). Chhotu Ram wanted that the individual deploy his sense for entrepreneurship and that was to be one of the basic principles of the ideology of the *kisan*, that is of the peasant-proprietor. This entrepreneurial individualism was supported by the Arya Samajist allegiance of Chhotu Ram.[14] But his quest for the peasants' emancipation led him to question the role of the organization in Punjab.

He dissected the Arya Samaj by criticising its main figure, the *banya*. He emphasized that 'Servility, selfishness, and greediness were his characteristic' (Yadav 1996: 74). Simultaneously, he defended the interests of his group. In the mid-1930s he published a series of 17 articles in the *Jat Gazette* under the title 'Bechara Zamindar'[15] where the 'zamindar' is in fact the poor peasant suffering from exploitation by urban upper castes, cited in Datta (1999a: 104). Chhotu Ram wanted first to protect the peasants from the traders who did not buy the agricultural products at their fair price and acted as greedy moneylenders.

Chhotu Ram had joined the Congress in 1917 but discovered that the party was in the hands of the urban Arya Samajists and more especially of the *banyas*. Hence his rapprochement with Mian Fazl-i-Husain, a Muslim leader who was equally eager to organize the peasants in Punjab. They formed the National Unionist Party (NUP) in this perspective. After the electoral success of the NUP, Fazl-i-Husain became Chief Minister of Punjab and Chhotu Ram Minister of Agriculture. He was then largely responsible for amending the Land Revenue Act so as to fix the term or a normal settlement at a minimum of 40 years and the state's share at a maximum of 25 per cent of the net assets for passing the Regulation of Accounts Bill. The bill which protected the debtor against the malpractise of the moneylenders and made the Punjab Land Alienation Act still more favourable to the 'agricultural tribes', a phrase coined by the British but a key word in the Jats' quest for a *kisan* identity. The NUP government also reduced the water rates from

7.5 million to 6 million so that the cultivators got better conditions for irrigation. Last but not least, the Punjab Agricultural Produce Marketing Act reformed the marketing committees of the *mandis* (marketplace for agricultural products), with two-thirds representation to the peasants and one-third to the traders. Gokul Chand Narang, an Arya Samajist notable who ran several sugar mills protested that 'through this legislation, penny worth peasants would sit alongside millionaire *mahajans* [Banyas] in the committee'. And Chhotu Ram replied: 'The Jat deserves no less respect than the Arora mahajan [Aroras are Banyas from Punjab]. . . . The time is not far off when the hardworking peasant would leave the worshippers of money far behind' (Datta 1999a: 108).

This reply is very revealing of the way Chhotu Ram shifted from the notion of 'Jats' to that of 'peasants', suggesting that an equation could be established between both.

Chhotu Ram therefore played a pioneering role in introducing an ideological distinction between rural and urban India, what was to be known at a later stage as the famous 'Bharat versus India' leitmotif. He has invented a new idiom of politics, *'kisan* politics', which emphasizes socio-economic cleavages. This agenda was bound to offer the cultivating castes an alternative identity towards social emancipation. Another Jat, Charan Singh articulated this *kisan*-based ideology in a more sophisticated way after independence.

## Charan Singh and the Jat as a *Kisan* par excellence

Charan Singh[16] displayed a sharp awareness of the latent conflicts between rural and urban India as evident from his policy as the minister in charge of land reform in Uttar Pradesh (Goyal 1978: 6–7). As early as 1939, he wrote:

In our country the classes whose scions dominate the public services are either those which have been raised to unexampled prominence and importance by the British, e.g. the money-lender, the big *zamindar* or *taluqdar*, the *arhatia* or the trader, or those which have been, so to say, actually called into being him—the *vakil* [advocate], the doctor, the contractor. These classes have, in subordinate cooperation with the foreigner, exploited the masses in all kinds of manner during these last two hundred years. The views and interests of these classes, on the whole, are, therefore, manifestly opposed to those of the masses. The social philosophy of a member of the non-agricultural, urban classes is entirely different from that of a person belonging to the agricultural rural classes. (C. Singh 1986: 203)

Charan Singh equated the exploited masses with the cultivating classes. Like Chhotu Ram, he tried to promote the *kisan* as a group.

Though he was proud of being a Jat, he attempted to subsume caste identities into a feeling of peasant solidarity. This approach undoubtedly was partly dictated by the fact that the Jats occupied an intermediary position and did not account for large numbers. Though, technically, they have to be classified as Shudras, their dominant caste status are often the root cause of conflict with other Shudras. Second, in Uttar Pradesh they represent 1.2 per cent of the population. Therefore, Charan Singh had good reasons for forging a *kisan* identity emphasizing the opposition between the peasants and the town-dwellers in order to submerge caste divisions into a new group feeling—a group of *kisans* of which the Jats would be the leaders. He was above all a political entrepreneur eager to shape an electoral coalition.

As revenue minister in-charge of the land reform in Uttar Pradesh after independence, Charan Singh tried to promote a middle class peasantry, hence the moderate and selective character of the Uttar Pradesh land reform, which consisted mainly in abolishing the zamindari system, and then his conflict with Nehru. In 1959, in the Nagpur session of the Congress he vigorously opposed the project of agricultural cooperatives announced by the latter.[17] He even published a book called *Joint Farming X-rayed: The Problem and its Solution,* where he proposed an alternative strategy of global development.[18] In a way *Joint Farming X-rayed* is the first manifesto of *kisan* politics in post-independence India. Questioning the need for a rapid, state-sponsored industrialization as advocated by Nehru, Charan Singh proposed to give priority to agriculture and to promote it by developing small farmer holdings, the only way according to him to generate the surpluses that were needed for industrial investment.[19] For him, agricultural cooperatives would have limited the productivity gains resulting from the elimination of the zamindar-like intermediaries because this would have jeopardized the independence of the farmers:

The thought that land has become his [the peasant's] and his children's in perpetuity, lightens and cheers his labour and expands his horizon. The feeling that he is his own master, subject to no outside control, and has free, exclusive and untrammelled use of his land drives him to greater and greater effort. . . . Likewise any system of large-scale farming in which his holdings are pooled must affect the farmer, but in the reverse direction. (Singh 1959: v-vi)

Obviously, for Charan Singh, economic rationality is not the only reason for rejecting agricultural cooperatives. Indeed he defends a way of life in addition to vested interests. According to him, 'The peasant is an incorrigible individualist; for his avocation, season in and season out, can be carried on with a pair of bullocks in the solitude of Nature without the necessity of having to give orders to, or, take orders from anybody' (ibid.: 104). Charan Singh spells out a very romantic view, even a mystique of the *kisan,* as the man in communion with Nature (a word that he writes with a capital n) and the only one able to sustain its harmony, first of all because being a *kisan* implies the use of bullocks which will produce the manure that the earth needs.

Charan Singh defends the way of life and the interests of the peasant-proprietors exclusively of those of other social groups, especially the landless peasants (ibid.: 88). He is against any land reform applying too low a ceiling and aiming at giving some land to everybody because it would multiply the non-economic exploitations and weaken the peasant-proprietor pattern. The average ceiling should be fixed at about 30 acres because this is the optimum surface one man can manage (ibid.: 90); this proposition is revealing of Charan Singh's attempt of sheltering a whole class of well-off farmers from expropriation.

In spite of this selective defence of the rural folk, Charan Singh systematically attempted to project himself as the spokesman for village India, against the city-based and parasitic elite. Therefore he presented the village community as forming a harmonious whole. He claimed that a village 'was always a stronger moral unit than a factory. The sense of the community was a vital thing among the peasantry, providing a natural foundation for collaboration or co-operative action' (ibid.: 270).

Thus, Charan Singh completed the identity shift of the Jats towards *kisanness* that Chhotu Ram had initiated. However, Charan Singh's identity as an individual and that of the Jats as a group was not only *kisan*-oriented. Singh paid more and more attention to the changing identity of the lower castes which emphasized their 'backwardness' in order to benefit from the help of the state.

## FROM *KISANNESS* TO 'BACKWARDNESS'

Initially, Charan Singh did not pay much attention to caste. He was explicitly in favour of the abolition, pure and simple, of the caste system.[20] However, his marginalization within the Uttar Pradesh (UP) Congress led him to promote a rapprochement with Other Backward Classes (OBC) leaders who based their claim on caste considerations.

Even though he remained a minister of the UP government almost without any interruption in the 1950s and 1960s, Charan Singh was repeatedly prevented from implementing the measures he was most interested in. One of his rivals within the Congress, the Rajput leader, Thakur Hukam Singh, opposed the large-scale land regrouping which Charan Singh undertook as revenue minister because this process served above all the interests of the middle farmers whose productivity suffered most from the scattered land parcels (Johnson 1975: 57, 103). Finally Thakur Hukam Singh replaced Charan Singh as revenue minister in 1959 and held the post until 1967.

In 1967, Charan Singh was also very bitter because he had political ambitions and resented the way upper-caste Congressmen frustrated them. C.B. Gupta had been preferred to him as chief minister even though he had twice lost an election to the Assembly during the current term, 1957–62, and was not even a Member of the Legislative Assembly (MLA) at that time. In 1963, the post had been offered to Sucheta Kripalani who was not even from UP and after the 1967 elections, which the Congress won by a small margin, C.B. Gupta was again preferred to Charan Singh for the post of chief minister.

He left the Congress with 16 MLAs which in majority belonged to non-upper-caste groups: 9 were OBCs (mainly Yadavs and Kurmis) and 2 were from the Scheduled Castes. This defection was large enough for causing the fall of Gupta's government and for enabling Charan Singh to become the chief minister with the help of opposition parties, with which he formed a coalition called Sanyukta Vidhayak Dal. For the first time in UP it was not a 'twice-born' Hindu who occupied the highest post of the state. In addition, 43 per cent of the ministers and state secretaries came from the intermediary, lower and Scheduled Castes, whereas in the previous government, 9 out of 11 ministers belonged to the upper castes (Government of Uttar Pradesh 1977: 95).

The coalition supporting Charan Singh included communists, socialists, Republican Party of India members and Jana Sanghis. It was so heterogeneous that the bones of contention were many and the government fell in February 1968. The rapprochement with the socialists, however, continued in the 1970s and it reflected Charan Singh's growing interest in OBC politics: the socialists had always supported affirmative action programmes for the lower castes and Charan Singh gradually rallied around aspects of this quota politics.

His party, the Bharatiya Kranti Dal (Fickett 1971: 201–3), contested the elections for the first time in 1969. It won 21.3 per cent of the votes in UP, partly because of the full support of the Jats from the western part of the state.[21] In 1974, it won more seats than in 1969—106 as against 98. Paul Brass has convincingly demonstrated that the BKD got most of its supporters from peasants who used to vote for independents so far (Brass 1980: 31). However, Charan Singh's emphasis on *kisanness* got diluted in the mid-1970s. Under Raj Narain and Charan Singh's influence in 1974, a fraction of the SSP and the BKD merged to form the Bharatiya Lok Dal with Charan Singh as president. Gradually, the BLD rallied around the notion of quota politics. In 1974, the party's election manifesto had a very revealing paragraph on this question:

While the socially and educationally backward classes, other than Scheduled Tribes and Castes, both Hindu and Muslim, constituted more than half of our people, they have little or no place in the political and administrative map of the country . . . . While, therefore, BLD regards any kind of reservation as a vicious principle, it has, at long last, come to the conclusion that there is no way out but that a share in Government jobs, say 25 per cent, be reserved for young men coming from these classes, as recommended by the Backward Classes Commission . . . (*An Observer* 1984: 62)

Indeed the Kalelkar Commission, the first Backward Classes Commission had been appointed in 1953 to identify the Other Backward Classes which were in need of affirmative action programmes. It established a list of low caste people and submitted its report in 1955, recommending reservations for the OBCs in the education system and in the administration. The report was rejected by the Home Minister, G.D. Pant (see Government of India 1953).

The BLD supported quota politics even more openly after the Janata Party took over in 1977. Charan Singh, as deputy Prime Minister was partly responsible for the appointment of the second Backward Classes Commission, known as the Mandal Commission because of the name of its Chairman, B.P. Mandal. The report of the commission recommended that 27 per cent of the posts in India's central administration be reserved for OBCs. It was submitted to Indira Gandhi's government in December 1980 but was laid on the table of the Lok Sabha on 30 April 1982 only. The most vehement speakers were lieutenants of Charan Singh, whose party had been renamed Lok Dal after the disintegration of the Janata Party (Lok Sabha Secretariat 1982: Col. 359). The Lok Dal Members of Parliament (MPs) could not make any impact and the Congress government put the Mandal Commission report in cold storage. But the tabling of the Mandal Commission report before the Lok Sabha—which had been scheduled for mid-February and then postponed—marked the conversion of Charan Singh to the notion to quota-politics. He launched a movement that was very revealing of his new interest in caste-based reservations (and politics):

The Janata Party appointed the Mandal Commission as per the provisions of the Constitution to review the situation and make appropriate recommendations for the welfare of the backward castes. The Congress (I) Government at the centre has been in possession of the said report for the last one year but has not yet published it despite its repeated assurances in the Parliament to put it on the table of the House. It seems the recommendations of the Mandal Commission would meet the same fate as the previous Kaka Kalelkar Commission Report unless the backward castes start a massive people's movement to compel the Government to implement them. (cited in Ray 1984: 5–6)

On 18 February 1982, Charan Singh held a meeting outside the Lok Sabha to put pressure on the MPs for the adoption of the report's recommendations. However, Lok Dal leaders were not all equally interested in demanding the implementation of the Mandal Commission report. According to Rashid Masood, one of the general secretaries of the Lok Dal, during the Janata phase, many of Charan Singh's lieutenants had supported the appointment of the Backward Classes Commission because they 'thought then that all the *kisans* would benefit from it, including Jats'.[22] The Jat identity was changing once again. Charan Singh had largely diluted his *kisan* identity for tactical reasons: that is in order to include low castes leaders advocating quota politics. But this tactical move, for some of his supporters, went hand-in-hand with a redefinition of the Jat identity: some politicians now claimed that Jats were backward castes.

The projection of the Jats as a caste suffering from social backwardness is not a complete innovation since we came across such a line of argument in the discourse of the Jat Mahasabha in the early twentieth century. This approach had then developed in response to the growing role of the colonial state: most of the non-elite groups began then to expect some help from the administration. About one hundred years later, the demands to the state had become much more vocal because of the steady enlargement of its affirmative action policies.

## The Jats as OBCs

This third identity shift—in terms of distribution of emphasis—was therefore largely due to material incentives: quota politics was gaining momentum and the Jats were attracted by the prospects of reservations. This trend became most obvious in the late 1980s and early 1990s. The Janata Dal of V.P. Singh which won the general elections in 1989 had presented the implementation of the Mandal Commission report as one of the remedies to the social backwardness of the lower castes. The party was prepared to show the way and promised to allot 60 per cent of the tickets in the general elections to 'the weaker sections of society'. Before that, V.P. Singh had promised to apply this 60 per cent reservation to the party apparatus. This 60 per cent quota was an old socialist idea that Lohia had propagated in the 1960s. It could not be implemented at the time of the nomination of the Janata Dal state party presidents because of the opposition of Devi Lal (Mustafa 1995: 115).

Devi Lal was a Jat leader from Haryana who had been one of Charan Singh's lieutenants.[23] He had left Congress in 1973 because the party was ignoring the *kisans*. He had then launched the Kisan Sangharsh Samiti. Subsequently, he joined the Janata Party and then Charan Singh's Lok Dal. Charan Singh had expelled him in 1982 largely because he opposed the rise of his son, Ajit Singh, in the party apparatus, but he continued to represent the same brand of *kisan* politics as Charan Singh and in 1989, his party merged in the Janata Dal, along with that of Ajit Singh's LD(A)—('A' stood for Ajit). However, these Jat leaders, who remained imbued with the old *kisan* ethos, had reservations vis-a-vis the quota politics of the Janata Dal.

Devi Lal had been appointed by V.P. Singh as chairman of a committee for the implementation of the Mandal Commission report but, according to the latter, he had not taken 'much interest [in it]' (Mustafa 1995: 171). He would have felt stronger motivations, had the Jats been classified as OBCs in the report.[24] It seems that he tried to have this change accepted by the government but in vain.[25] Devi Lal, therefore, did not convene more than a couple of meetings to prepare the implementation of the report and V.P. Singh decided to ask the minister of social welfare, Ram Vilas Paswan, a Dalit leader, to do the job. All the Jat ministers strongly objected that their caste group should be included in the list of the OBCs.[26] A signature campaign was organized among the MPs and 107 signatures were collected among Jat and Muslim leaders who also wanted that some of their coreligionists should be recognized as OBCs.[27] According to Satpal Malik, V.P. Singh was 'very clever and asked Surjeet Singh (the General Secretary of the CPI[M], a party of the ruling coalition) to write against it. Surjeet Singh wrote a letter saying that the Jats could not be backwards because they had been kings in Patiala and Bharatpur.'[28] V.P. Singh made a vague promise 'but nothing came' and he announced the implementation of the Mandal Commission report on 7 August 1990 a few days after Devi Lal resigned from his government.

Devi Lal perceived V.P. Singh's reforms as posing a threat to the *kisans'* interest, since they were bound to promote the assertiveness of tenants and agricultural labourers from the lower castes. Devi Lal's resignation in fact consummated the falling apart of the Charan Singh coalition. Indeed, V.P. Singh was criticized by disciples of the Chaudhury for the way he divided the *kisan* (Brass 1980: 2090). Eventually, quota politics has prevailed over *kisan* politics, and Devi Lal had to recede in the background.

## THE BKU, THE LAST JAT PROPONENT OF *KISAN* POLITICS?

Immediately after the Mandal affair, the Jats not only favoured *kisan* politics but looked at themselves as closer to the upper castes. Correlatively, they moved towards the BJP. This trend was well illustrated by the attitude of the Bharatiya Kisan Union (BKU).

The BKU, which represents the last incarnation of *kisan* politics (outside party politics), is, in fact, a Jat movement. Its chief, Mahendra Singh Tikait, is a Chaudhury—the chief of a Jat clan—from west UP (Rana 1994: 41ff) who owns 15 acres of land, a large herd of cattle and a tractor. Tikait's horizons broadened from 1978 under the influence of Charan Singh, who was then member of the central government. They founded the BKU at that time. Tikait took over this organization and ensured its growth in the 1980s. Its first major action occurred in 1986–7, in reaction to power cuts and an increase in the electricity rates, while peasants were increasingly in need of electricity to operate the growing number of the irrigation pumps (Gupta 1988; 1997). Its programme reflected the concerns of the landed farmers who had benefited from the Green Revolution and from the recent irrigation works in west UP.[29] The BKU in fact owed its influence in the region to the importance of the medium and big farmers.

Even though it projects itself as a 'union', the BKU presents many characteristics of a caste association as evident from its desire to reform Jat social practises such as child marriage and dowry.[30] The BKU has obviously inherited many characters of the Jat panchayats (caste councils).

In 1989, the BKU campaigned for the Janata Dal, because Devi Lal and Ajit Singh had then joined hands with V.P. Singh. Two years later, it supported the BJP in the tenth general elections because the Jats disapproved of the implementation of the Mandal Commission Report. They looked at themselves as upper-caste

Hindus. They tended to revert to the old Sanskritization strategy by stressing their Hindu identity, as evident from the fact that they took active part in the Ayodhya movement. Simultaneously, they continued to emphasize their *kisan* identity which was well in tune with the ethos projected by the urban middle class, the strongest supporters of the BJP. Both groups presented themselves as the custodians of a demanding work culture, in contrast to the lower castes which relied on reservation policies. The Jats did not project this identity for very long.

## Jats are 'Backwards' . . . and Vote BJP—Rajasthan and Beyond

While the Mandal Commission had not classified the Jats as OBCs, state commissions had reached a different conclusion. In Haryana, the Gurnam Singh Report (1991) favoured the inclusion of the Jats on the list of the OBCs, for instance. Similar state commissions made the same recommendations in Rajasthan, Uttar Pradesh and Delhi. Immediately, parties politicized this issue. In Rajasthan, where the Jats constitute the largest caste with 9 per cent of the state population, according to the 1931 Census, the Congress explained that Jats were backward indeed, and should therefore benefit from reservations. The party aroused the expectations of the Jats in its 1993 election manifesto by promising their reclassification as OBCs if voted to power. It did the same in 1998 and won the elections partly because of the Jats' support. However, the Jats were very upset by the appointment of an OBC, Ashok Gehlot, as chief minister since many of their leaders had more or less implicitly applied to the post. Gehlot appointed a new commission to look into the demand of the Jats, who looked at this move as a delaying tactic. They were now fully mobilized in favour of their inclusion amongst the OBCs.

The Jat Mahasabha was at the forefront. The reservation issue was 'converted into "a battle for Jat identity" by the Jat Mahasabha whose leadership is today in the hands of professional lawyers, doctors and retired bureaucrats' (Lodha 1999).[31] The Jats are not only peasants any more. Cashing on their growing affluence as farmers, the older generation has given an ever better education to the Jat youth. They have also benefited from their number, so much so they can help to elect an ever larger proportion of their leaders as MLAs—the Jats represented about one-fourth of the members of the state assembly of Rajasthan in the 1990s. They evidently pretended to form an underprivileged group in order to benefit from reservations. The grievances of the Jats are not unfounded since, as Nonica Datta emphasizes, 'the Rajput *jagirdari* elite continues to enjoy monopoly on land-ownership and the symbols and rituals of social deference' (Datta 1996c). But to present the Jats as 'backward' is highly arguable, simply because as Nonica Datta herself admits that 'Jats cannot be categorized, objectively speaking, as a unified and homogeneous entity' (ibid.). The Jat Mahasabha even started negotiations with the Dalit-based Bahujan Samaj Party (BSP) in order to make some alliance before the 1999 general elections. The state BSP chief described the coming together of the 'oppressed castes' [*sic*] as 'a new awakening for social justice' (*The Hindu*, 28 July 1999). This coalition of the highest and the lowest among the rural folks was in fact directed against the OBCs who had, now, a protector at the top in the person of Gehlot. The Jat Mahasabha targeted him during the election campaign. A massive Jat rally organized in Jaipur resolved that the priority was to vote Congress out because of its 'treachery' vis-à-vis the caste in question. The ruling party promised to honour its word but it was too late: the BJP had already captured the imagination of the Jats. The Prime Minister, Atal Behari Vajpayee, himself, while canvassing in Rajasthan promised the Jats that his government would accede to their demand if voted to power (*The Hindu*, 25 August 1999). According to the election survey of the Centre for the Study of Developing Societies, 65 per cent of the Jats voted for the BJP in Rajasthan in 1993 (*Frontline*, 10 December 1999: 43). They were, therefore, largely responsible for the success of the BJP which won 16 seats out of 25, as against 9 seats which went to the Congress. By supporting the BJP, the Jats of Rajasthan joined hands mostly with upper-caste voters. According to the survey of the Centre for the Study of Developing Societies, 98 per cent of the Rajputs and 62 per cent of the Brahmans voted for the BJP in Rajasthan whereas 72 per cent of the Scheduled Castes voted for the Congress (*Frontline*, 10 December 1999: 43). Clearly, the Jats pretended to be 'backward' and had made an alliance with the Dalits for purely tactical reasons: they sided with the upper castes and voted accordingly for the BJP.

The Jats of Rajasthan were included in the list of the OBCs immediately after the elections at the behest of Vajpayee. In UP also the BJP tried to woo the Jats by acceding to their claim of backwardness. Soon after the launch of the Jat Mahasabha's campaign in Rajasthan, four Jat organizations merged to form the Jat Arrakshan Sangharsh Samiti in UP. This organization attracted political leaders from different parties ranging from the BJP to the Samajwadi Party of Mulayam Singh Yadav. It resolved that in the future the Jats would vote for the party which would help them to get reservations (*The Times of India*, 5 November 1999). The BJP Chief Minister, Ram Prakash Gupta agreed to include them in the list of the OBCs in early 2000.

Our survey of the changing Jats' identity over more than one century has provided us with relevant examples of the malleability of collective identities and more especially of the ways identities transform themselves in relation to others. This process is inherent in the caste system since the mechanisms of Sanskritization consists, for a low caste, in emulating the upper castes and in differentiating itself from those ranked 'below'. Hence what Olivier Herrenschmidt called the 'Hindu obsession with small differences' (Herrenschmidt 1996: 14). That was the key to the identity formation process of the Jats in the late nineteenth century-early twentieth century under the influence of the Arya Samaj when they claimed that they were Kshatriyas.

Then Jat leaders reinterpreted the identity of their caste by emphasizing their conflicting relation vis-à-vis another 'other', the upper castes, mainly Banyas and Brahmans. These people, who monopolized business and state power, were described as the real exploiters of the Jat peasants. Chhotu Ram played a pioneering role in highlighting the contrast between rural and urban India and in projecting the Jats as the embodiment of the former. The allies of yesterday, the upper caste-Arya Samajists became rivals whereas Muslim peasants became friends. This peasant-based repertoire crystallized under the aegis of Charan Singh. Even more than Chhotu Ram, Charan Singh was power hungry and regarded the ideology of the *kisan* as the most relevant device for federating and mobilizing cultivating castes behind him. Obviously, the Jat identity was transformed by political entrepreneurs not only because of the caste's hostility vis-à-vis others, but also because of the rationale of the democratic competition for state power.

Hence the second conclusion of this case study: collective identities transform themselves also in relation to the state whenever the state-building process asserts itself. This is most obvious when the state exerts a direct intervention on society, for instance through programmes of affirmative action which lead groups to coalescence (under the OBC umbrella, for instance), or to oppose each other (like in the Jats vs OBCs scenario). But the social impact of the state-building process is also evident from the competition for power that it generates, especially in a democratic context where leaders and parties need to identify groups and mobilise them for shaping winning coalitions. The politization of caste (or casteification of politics) is a good example of this phenomenon. Here again, the impact of state politics may take different forms in the course of time, as evident from our case study.

Charan Singh derived rich dividends from his *kisan* strategy in the 1960s-1970s but he had to adjust himself once again in the 1980s because of the growing mobilization of the lower castes. These castes, which had been part of the *kisan* repertoire so far, began to form a new coalition after the state which had classified them as OBCs, started to grant them reservations. To begin with, Charan Singh was very reluctant vis-à-vis this alternative repertoire of the non-elite groups. But gradually he realized that its attractiveness was so powerful that he should rather use it. Jat leaders who appeared as Charan Singh's political heirs, including his son, Ajit Singh, stuck to *kisan* politics but did the same after V.P. Singh decided to implement the Mandal Commission Report. They began to claim that their caste fellows also were 'backwards'. Once again, the competition in the political arena affected the Jat identity. They agitated for the inclusion of their caste amongst the OBCs for electoral reasons for wooing the Jat voters. They did not look at the Jats as 'backwards' is reality, as is evident from the fact that they supported an upper-caste-dominated party, the BJP

Finally, this study suggests that identity transformations do not come in clear succession but overlap in the course of time. The notion that Jats were primarily *kisans* was already prevalent in the nineteenth century. The idea that they were 'backward' and needed the help of the state was also present in the writings of Chhotu Ram. Identities are not mutually exclusive but multi-faceted. The Jats have not only experimented with the three repertoires we studied in our survey, but have also occasionally emphasized the Hindu dimension of their identity under the influence of the Arya Samaj or of BJP leaders during the Ayodhya movement. It seems to me, however, that this propensity to occasionally embrace militant Hinduism has often been determined by their eagerness to be recognized as being part of the upper castes.

## Notes

1. I have developed this critique of primordialism and reviewed alternative theories of nationalism in 'Of Nations and Nationalism'. See Jaffrelot (1996).
2. P. Ricoeur (1990). This dialectic is also the core argument of James Clifford (1988).
3. As a young student of Indian society, I learnt a great deal in Alice's article, 'Semi-Feudalism or Capitalism: The Contemporary Debate on Classes and Modes of Production in India' (Thorner 1982: 19–72).
4. This is the main limitation of the otherwise path-breaking book by Kenneth Jones (1976).
5. For Dayananda the Brahmans were responsible for the decay of Hinduism because of their lack of morality and their use of superstitions for maintaining society in their dependence.
6. The Sadhs were a sectarian movement with strong anti-Brahman overtones. N. Datta emphasizes that 'Their rituals and ceremonies at weddings and funerals had no place for the Brahmans' (Datta 1999a: 38). Their rejection of the Brahmans as religious intermediaries had much in common with Dayananda's credo.
7. Dayananda Saraswati, 1981: 115. He adds that this task should be handled by 'a syndicate of learned persons' who would 'decide after examination as to which is Brahman, which Kshatriya, which Vaishya and which Shudra' (ibid: 483).
8. In his diary he says 'I owe every good thing in my life since 1881 to him' (Juneja and Singh Mor 1989: 47).
9. Traditionally, the word *Shuddhi* designates a ritual of purification that upper caste Hindus have to perform whenever they have been 'polluted' by some impure contact. The Arya Samaj reinterpreted this ritual of purification in order to transform it into a ritual of (re)conversion for the Hindus who had become Christians, Muslims or Sikhs. It also used it for allegedly transforming low caste people into 'twice-born' Hindus. This move was perfectly in tune with the spirit of Sanskritization.
10. For more details, see C. Jaffrelot (1996).
11. See Datta (1999a: 161, 165). The Maharaja of Dholpur, while he was president of the Jat Mahasabha in 1917–18, supported the development of the Arya Samaj in his state (Juneja and Singh Mor 1989: 198).
12. In 1916 it sent a memorandum to the Lieutenant Governor of the Punjab asking for the employment of more Hindu Jats in the administration (ibid: 108).

13. M.C. Pradhan points out: 'In the *bhaichara* system, land was especially divided among the lineage (*thoks*) of the founding ancestors of original conquerors. This system of land tenure was a Jat idea because Jats did not acknowledge the rights of their chiefs to the sole proprietorship of land conquered and colonized by them' (Pradhan 1966: 34).

14. Chhotu Ram entered 'Vedic' in the column against religion specified in the admission form of the Intermediate examination to show that he fully adhered to Dayananda's doctrine (Yadav 1996: 14).

15. He pointed out that 'in some provinces *zamindars* are different from peasants. But in the Punjab, the two are synonymous. Here the agriculturist who has proprietary rights in land is the one who actually ploughs it' (cited in Datta 1999a: 97).

16. For an overview of Charan Singh's political thought, the best source is G. Raval (1985).

17. For Charan Singh, Nehru epitomized this elitist urban-oriented approach of Indian society:

> This supreme city dweller administrator had no knowledge whatsoever about life conditions of the millions of helpless Indians who live in the villages of India. He, who had only knowledge of the Western principles of economy learnt in the Oxbridge university education system, was given the charges of administering the growth of the country. He got carried away towards these ready-made theories and concepts, which promised comparatively higher national production. He had imagined that by a public ownership of the industries the country could get a high level of production (cited in G. Raval 1985: Chapter 8).

18. Charan Singh wrote this book while he was out of the Uttar Pradesh government. He had resigned in April 1959 because of several disagreements with Sampurnanand, the chief minister. He was replaced as revenue minister by Thakur Hukum Singh (Johnson 1974).

19. Charan Singh spells out this argument rather late in the book but it is his starting point: 'Industrialization cannot precede but will follow agricultural prosperity. Surpluses of food production above farmers' consumption must be available before non-agricultural resources can be developed' (1959: 251).

20. *An Observer, Who is a Casteist*, New Delhi, The Kisan Trust 1984, p. 21. Similarly, he proposed in 1951 that 'no Congressman shall either be a member or participate in the proceedings of an organization whose membership is confined to a particular caste or castes or indulge in spreading hatred against other castes' (Cited in *An Observer, Who is a Casteist?*, op. cit.: 27).

21. In Aligarh district R.I. Duncan has established a clear correlation between the Jat domination and the BKD vote, which was positive almost in all the constituencies (Duncan 1979: 156, 175).

22. Interview with Rashid Masood, New Delhi, 28 October 1998.

23. For more information on Devi Lal, see the rather agiographic biography by Raj Pal Singh (1988).

24. Interview with Ajay Singh—one of the Jat ministers in V.P. Singh cabinet—New Delhi, 28 October 1997.

25. Interview with P.S. Krishnan, New Delhi, 4 April 1998. P.S. Krishnan was Secretary to the Ministry of Social Welfare. He prepared the implementation of the Mandal Report for Ram Vilas Paswan.

26. Satpal Malik claims that he was the first minister to ask for the inclusion of the Jats in the OBC list (interview with S. Malik, New Delhi, 25 October 1998).
27. Interview with Rashid Masood.
28. Interview with S. Malik.
29. Meerut, Bulandshahr, Muzzaffarnagar and Aligarh Districts experienced an annual growth rate of 4.5 per cent of agricultural production between 1960-6 and 1970-2. This increase was due mainly to the increase in the area covered by irrigation. At the end of the 1970s, 71 per cent of the farms were completely or partly irrigated (Hasan 1989: 2663).
30. The BKU's genesis cannot be dissociated from caste considerations. This organization, an *avatar* of the Jat-dominated Kisan Sangharsh Samiti (KSS) had been created in 1978 to protest against the distribution of 120 acres of land by the government to untouchables, in a west Uttar Pradesh village, in the context of the policy on positive discrimination. This KSS published a manifesto on this occasion, where the demand for better prices was secondary to the demand for the suppression of government reservation quotas for untouchables in the administration. According to the KSS, these quotas should have been applied on the basis of socio-economic criteria, and not on the basis of caste (Rana 1994: 16).
31. The Jat Mahasabha chief, Gyan Prakash Pilania is a former Director-General of Police (*The Hindu*, 23 August 1999).

# References

*An Observer* [Anonymous] (1984), *Who is a Casteist?*, New Delhi: The Kisan Trust.

Brass, P. (1980), 'The Politicisation of the Peasantry in a North Indian State: Part 2', *The Journal of Peasant Studies*, Vol. 8, No. 1, p. 31.

Clifford, J. (1988), *The Predicament of Culture: Twentieth Century Ethnography, Literature and Art*, Cambridge, Massachusetts: Harvard University Press.

Datta, N. (1999a), *Forming an Identity: A Social History of the Jats*, Delhi: Oxford University Press.

——— (1999b), 'Backward Caste Movement Gains Ground', *Economic and Political Weekly*, p. 2630.

——— (1999c), 'Jats: Trading Caste Status for Empowerment', *Economic and Political Weekly*, p. 3172.

Duncan, R.I. (1979), 'Levels, the Communication of Programmes, and Sectional Strategies in Indian Politics with Reference to the Bharatiya Kranti Dal and the Republican Party of India in Uttar Pradesh and Aligarh District (UP)' Ph.D. thesis, University of Sussex.

Erikson, E.H. (1972), *Adolescence et Crise. La Quête de L'identité*, Paris: Flammarion.

Fickett Jr., L.P. (1971), 'The Politics of Regionalism in India', *Pacific Affairs*, Vol. 44, No. 2, pp. 201–3.

Gopal, M. (1977), *Sir Chhotu Ram: A Political Biography*, Delhi: B.R. Publishing Corporation.

Goyal, S.S. (1978) (ed.), *Profile of Chaudhary Charan Singh*, New Delhi: Ompal Singh.

Government of India (1953), *Report of the Backward Classes Commission Vol. 1*, New Delhi: Government of India Press.

Government of Uttar Pradesh (1977), *Report of Most Backward Classes Commission*, Lucknow: Government of Uttar Pradesh (Hindi).

Gupta, D. (1988), 'Country-Town Nexus and Agrarian Mobilisation: Bharatiya Kisan Union as an Instance', *Economic and Political Weekly*, 17 December, pp. 2692–3.

—— (1997), *Rivalry and Brotherhood: Politics in the Life of Farmers in Northern India*, Delhi: Oxford University Press.

Hasan, Z. (1989), 'Self-Serving Guardians: Formation and Strategy of the Bharatiya Kisan Union', *Economic and Political Weekly*, p. 2663.

Herrenschmidt, O. (1996), '"L'inégalité gradée" ou la des inégalités: L'analyse de la société: hindoue par Ambedkar', *Archives Européenne de Sociolgie*, Vol. 37, No. 14.

Jaffrelot, Christophe (1996), 'Of Nations and Nationalism', *Seminar*, Vol. 442, pp. 31–6.

—— (1999a), *The Hindu Nationalist Movement and Indian Politics*, New Delhi: Penguin.

——(1999b), 'Militant Hinduism and the Conversion Issue (1885–1990): From *Shuddhi* to *Dharm Parivartan*: The Politicization of an Invention of Tradition', in J. Assayag (ed.), *The Resources of History: Tradition and Narration in South Asia*, pp. 127–52, Paris: Ecole Française d'Extrême Orient.

Johnson, M. (1975), 'Relation Between Land Settlement and Party Politics in Uttar Pradesh', Ph.D. thesis, University of Sussex.

Jones, Kenneth (1976), *Arya Dharm: Hindu Consciousness in Nineteenth Century Punjab*, Berkeley: University of California Press.

Joshi, V.C. (1965) (ed.), *Lajpat Rai: Autobiographical Writings*, Delhi and Julundhur: University Publishers.

Juneja, M.M. and K. Singh Mor (1989) (eds.), *The Diaries of Dr Ramji Lal Hooda*, Hissar: Modern Book Co.

Lodha, S. (1999), 'Election 1999: Rajasthan, Caste and Two-Party System', *Economic and Political Weekly*, p. 3347.

Lok Sabha Secretariat (1982), *Lok Sabha Debates Vol. 31*, New Delhi: Government of India Press.

Mustafa, S. (1995), *The Lonely Prophet, V.P. Singh: A Political Biography*, New Delhi: New Age International.

Pradhan, M.C. (1966), *The Political System of the Jats in North India*, London: Oxford University Press.

Ram, Chhotu (1996), 'The Improvement of Indian Village Life', Appendix to K.C. Yadav (ed.), *The Crisis in India: Reflections of Sir Chhotu Ram*, Kurukshetra: Haryana Historical Society.

Rana, M.S. (1994), *Bharatiya Kisan Union and Ch. Tikait*, Meerut: Paragon Publication.

Raval, G. (1985) (ed.), *Chaudhury Charan Singh: Sukti aur Vichar* (Hindi), New Delhi: The Kisan Trust.

Ray, R. 'Preface (2)', in *An Observer, Who is a Casteist*, pp. 5–6, New Delhi: The Kisan Trust.

Ricoeur, P. (1990), *Soi-Même Comme un Autre*, Paris: Le Seuil.

Saraswati, Dayanand (1981), *The Light of Truth: English translation of Swami Dayanand's Satyarth Prakash*, Allahabad: Dr Ratna Kumari Svadhyaya Sansthana.

Singh, Charan (1959), *Joint Farming X-rayed: The Problem and its Solution,* Bombay: Bharatiya Vidya Bhavan.

Singh, C. (1986), 'Why 50 per cent of Government Jobs should be Reserved for Sons of Agriculturists', in Charan Singh, *Land Reforms in UP and the Kulaks,* New Delhi: Vikas.

Singh, Jagpal (1992), *Capitalism and Dependence: Agrarian Politics in Western Uttar Pradesh, 1951–1991,* Delhi: Manohar.

Singh, Raj Pal (1988), *Devi Lal: The Man of the Masses,* Yamuna Nagar: Veenu.

Tandon, P. (1989), *Banking Century: A Short History of Banking in India and the Pioneer, Punjab National Bank,* New Delhi: Penguin.

Thorner, Alice (1982), 'Semi-feudalism or Capitalism: The Contemporary Debate on Classes and Modes of Production in India', in J. Pouchepadass (ed.), *Caste et Classe en Asie du Sud, Purushartha,* Vol 6, pp. 19–72.

Yadav, K.C. (1996), *The Crisis in India: Reflections of Sir Chhotu Ram,* Kurukshetra: Haryana Historical Society.

# Chapter 21

# Sanskritization vs. ethnicization in India changing identities and caste politics before Mandal

In the 1970s, the Janata Party-led state governments of Bihar and Uttar Pradesh launched new reservation policies for lower castes. The controversy surrounding these policies came to a fore when upper castes resisted the implementation of the Mandal Commission Report in 1990. While reservation policies played a role in the crystallization of the low caste movements in south and west India, their momentum was sustained by the ideology of 'pre-Aryanism' or Buddhism in these regions. In the north, however, the state policies were more or less the starting point of the whole process. This essay will discuss the crystallization of lower caste movements in India, arguing that the mobilization of the lower castes was delayed and did not imply any significant change in caste identities: the emancipatory and empowerment agenda in India materialized without any prior ethnicization.

## Historical Background

The north-south divide is a *locus classicus* of Indian studies, partly based on cultural—and more especially linguistic—differences. It also derives from economic and social contrasts. First, the kind of land settlement that the British introduced in India was not the same in these two areas. While the zamindari (intermediary) system prevailed in north India, the raiyatwari (cultivator) system was more systematically implemented in the south.[1] Second, these two regions always had a different caste profile. In the Hindi belt, the caste system is traditionally the closest to the *varna* model with its four orders (Brahmans, Kshatriyas, Vaishyas, and Shudras) and its Untouchables. In the south, the twice-born are seldom 'complete' because the warrior and merchant castes are often absent or poorly represented, as in Maharashtra and Bengal. Correlatively, the upper *varnas* are in larger numbers than in the north. According to the 1931 census, the last one asking about caste, upper castes represented from 13.6 per cent (in Bihar) up to 24.2 per cent (in Rajasthan) of the population. In the south, the proportion of the Brahmans and even of the twice-born is often low. In Andhra Pradesh, for instance, the Brahmans and the Kshatriyas represent respectively 3 per cent and 1.2 per cent of the population. In Maharashtra, a bridge state between the north and the south, the twice-born were only marginally a larger number with 3.9 per cent Brahmans, 1 per cent Kshatriyas, and 1.69 per cent Vaishyas.

However, the factor of caste does not explain the north/south divide only for arithmetic reasons. In fact, the caste system underwent a more significant and early change out of the Hindi belt. The caste system has been analysed by anthropologists as a sacralized social order based on the notion of ritual purity. In this view, its holistic character—to use the terminology of Louis Dumont (Dumont 1966)—implies that the dominant, Brahmanical values are regarded by the whole society as providing universal references. Hence, the central role played by Sanskritization, a practise that M.N. Srinivas has defined as 'the process in which a "low" Hindu caste, or tribal or other group, changes its customs, ritual, ideology and way of life in the direction of a high, and frequently, "twice-born caste", that is the Brahmans, but also the Kshatriyas or even the Vaishyas' [Srinivas (1995 [1966]): 6]. Low castes may for instance adopt the most prestigious features of the Brahmans' diet and therefore emulate vegetarianism.

The caste system underwent transformations because of the policies of the British Raj. Among them, the introduction of the census made the most direct impact because it listed castes with great detail. As a result, castes immediately organized themselves and even formed associations to take steps to see that their status was recorded in the way they thought was honourable to them. Caste associations were therefore created to pressure the colonial administration to improve their rank in the census. This process was especially prominent among the lower castes.

In turn, caste associations were secularized when the British started to classify castes for usage in colonial administration. These associations claimed new advantages from the state, principally in terms of reservations (quotas) in educational institutions and in the civil service. Caste associations—even though they often lack a resilient structure—therefore not only played the role of pressure groups, but also that of interest groups. Subsequently, they also became mutual aid structures. They also founded schools as well as hostels for the caste's children and created cooperative movements for instance. Lloyd and Susanne Rudolph have aptly underlined the modern character of these caste associations (Rudolph 1966). They argued that caste associations behaved like a collective enterprise with economic, social, and political objectives, in a way, which brings to mind the modern image of lobbies.

In addition to the concessions they could get from the British, the most important social change that these associations have achieved concerns the unity of the caste groups. They have successfully incited the sub-castes to adopt the same name in the census and to break the barriers of endogamy. It seems to me, however, that intermarriages are only one aspect of the ethnicization of caste. The subjective representation of the collective self plays a crucial role in this transformation. Caste is largely a mind-set and a belief system. Those who live in such a society have internalized a hierarchical pattern relying on the degree of ritual purity. Therefore the primary implication of ethnicization of caste consists in providing alternative nonhierarchical social *imaginaires*. This is a key issue so far as the emancipatory potential of the low caste movements is concerned since in their case, the ethnicization process provides an egalitarian alternative identity. Besides intermarriages, the ethnicization of the low castes, for efficiently questioning social hierarchies, therefore, must imply the invention of a separate, cultural identity and more especially a collective history. While such an ethnicization process endowed the lower castes and even the Untouchables of south and west India with egalitarian identities, such a mental emancipation did not occur to the same extent in the north. I hypothesize that this north/south-west contrast is largely due to the resilience of the ethos of Sanskritization in the Hindi belt.

## The ethnicization of caste in west and south India

The ethnicization process that took place in west and south India was largely due to the impact of the European ideas, as propagated by the missionaries and the schools. Certainly, castes have always been perceived by the historian Susan Bayly as being 'kingroups or descent units' (Bayly 1999: 10). British orientalism gave purely racial connotations to caste and linguistic groups in the nineteenth century. Colonial ethnography equated the 'Aryans' with the upper castes and the Dravidians with the lowest orders of the Indian society. This perception prepared the ground for the interpretation of castes in ethnic terms in west and south India. Caste leadership played an important part in this process. Jyotirao Phule and B.R. Ambedkar are two of the most prominent lower caste leaders of their time.

Jyotirao Phule (1827–90) was probably the first of the low caste ideologues in the late nineteenth century. Phule's endeavour had a pioneering dimension since he was the first low caste leader who avoided the traps of Sanskritization by endowing the lower castes with an alternative value system. As early as 1853, he opened schools for Untouchables. He projected himself as the spokesman of the non-Brahmans at large and, indeed, kept targeting the Brahmans in vehement pamphlets where he presented them as rapacious moneylenders and corrupt priests.

Phule was also the first low caste organizer. In 1873, he founded the Satyashodak Samaj in order to strengthen the sentiment of unity among the low castes. He narrated so-called historical episodes bearing testimony of the traditional solidarity between the Mahars and Shudras and protested against the Brahmans' stratagems for dividing the low castes. At least in the late nineteenth and early twentieth centuries, the Satyashodak idiom embraced rich peasants as well as agricultural tenants who belonged to very different castes including Untouchables.

Another social activist from Maharashtra, precisely from an Untouchable caste, Bhim Rao Ambedkar (1891–1956) gave a larger dimension to the theory of Phule, whom he regarded as one of his mentors. Ambedkar is known as the first

Dalit leader and for his work as chairman of the Drafting Committee of the Indian Constitution. He was a thinker as much as a political leader. In fact, his political activities were based on a sociological analysis of the caste system that he developed early as a student in the U.S. He argued that the system was based on a peculiar kind of hierarchy and domination. First the lower castes emulate the Brahmans because they believe in the same value system and therefore admit that the Brahmans are superior to the others. Ambedkar identified the mechanisms of Sanskritization and understood their role in maintaining the lower castes in a subservient position. Second, for Ambedkar no other society has such 'an official gradation laid down, fixed and permanent, with an ascending scale of reverence and a descending scale of contempt' (Ambedkar 1990: 26) that prevents the lower castes from uniting themselves against the elite domination.

Ambedkar was the first low caste politician to offer such an elaborate condemnation of the caste system. Moreover, he deplored the division among the lower castes, especially the Dalits. He lamented that the latter formed 'a disunited body . . . infested with the caste system in which they believe as much as does the caste Hindu. This caste system among the Untouchables has given rise to mutual rivalry and jealousy and it has made common action impossible' (ibid., 1989: 266). Ambedkar, on the basis of his sociological analysis endeavoured to ethnicize the identity of the Untouchables for enabling them to get united around a separate, specific identity.

While his aim and Phule's were similar, Ambedkar adopted a different viewpoint since he rejected the racial theory underlying the origins of the caste system. According to this account, the Untouchables descended from a group of indigenous people subjugated by the Aryan invaders. In his book, *The Untouchable: Who Were They and Why They Became Untouchables,* Ambedkar explained that each and every society is subjected to invasions by tribes appearing to be more powerful than the local ones. Suffering from a process of dislocation, the latter give birth to new groups that Ambedkar called the 'Broken Men' (Dalits in Marathi). Ambedkar argued that after the conquering tribes became sedentary, they used the services of the Broken Men against the still unsettled tribes to guard the villages. Therefore, they established themselves at the periphery of clusters of habitations, also because the villagers did not want them as neighbours. These Broken Men became the first and most fervent adepts of Buddha and they remained so even though most of the other converts returned to the mainstream of Hinduism.

Ambedkar tried to endow the Untouchables with a Buddhist identity, a separate and prestigious culture. Eventually, he even converted to Buddhism and invited his castemates to do the same in large numbers. They were bound to acquire in this way a strong ideological basis for questioning their subordinate rank in the caste system, all the more so as Buddhism offered them an egalitarian doctrine.

Hence, Maharashtra gave to India her first Shudra leader with Phule and her first Untouchable leader with Ambedkar. While the former insisted on the common pre-Aryan identity of the bahujan samaj (untouchable society), the latter, rejecting the racial theory, tried to endow the Dalit with a Buddhist identity. A similar pattern developed in the south where the Dravidian movement was even more solidly established on the ground of ethnicity.

## FROM NON-BRAHMANISM TO DRAVIDIANISM

In south India (particularly in the Madras presidency), the non-Brahman movement was instrumental in engineering forms of caste fusion and succeeded in endowing the lower castes with an ethnic identity that relied on two grounds: they were not only presented as the original inhabitants of India, as Phule had already argued, but also as former Buddhists based on Ambedkar's interpretation. By the turn of the twentieth century, an equation had crystallized between the non-Brahmans and the Dravidians, defined as the original inhabitants of India.

One of the most influential proponents of the Dravidian ideology was M.C. Rajah (1883–1947), a Pariah who became secretary of the Adi-Dravida Mahajan Sabha in 1916 and later presided over the All India Depressed Classes Association. As a nominated member of the Madras Legislative Council since 1920, Rajah moved in 1922 that a resolution recommending that the terms 'Panchama' and 'Parya' be deleted from the government records and the terms Adi-Dravida and Adi-Andhra substituted instead.

This identity-building process was led one step further by Ramaswami Naicker, alias Periyar, a religious mendicant of the Self-Respect movement. The movement argued that the Dravidian-Buddhists had been traditionally ill-treated by the Aryan-Hindus because they opposed caste hierarchy. In 1944, Periyar also founded a political party, the Dravida Kazhagam (DK). Through its mouthpiece, *Viduthalai*, Periyar advocated the coming together of the Christians, Muslims, and low caste Hindus (particularly the Untouchables and Shudras). Such a rapprochement eventually took place, since Nadars and Adi-Dravidas (Untouchables) formed the backbone of the Self-Respect movement and the DK.

This ethnicization process was fostered by the British policy of compensatory discrimination based on the reservation of seats in the bureaucracy and in the assemblies. The very decision to grant such and such statutory representation to such and such group in these assemblies contributed to the crystallization of new social categories that resented their non- (or their under-)representation. In Madras, British officials explicitly fostered the non-Brahman movement to counterbalance the growing influence of the Brahman-dominated Congress. The non-Brahmans asked for more seats in the Madras assembly because they were 'different'. During the 1920 election campaign, their leaders requested 'all non-Brahmans in this presidency to immediately organize, combine and carry on an active propaganda so as to ensure the return to the reformed Council of as many non-Brahmans as possible' (Justice 1920). This tactic yielded dividends since the Justice Party won the elections. In their plea to the British, the non-Brahmans also emphasized their marginality in the state services and the 'disabilities' from which they were suffering. This discourse fitted well, too, with the British approach since the government also regarded political representation as a means for compensatory discrimination. The case of the non-Brahman movement of south India exemplified the way positive discrimination helped forge a coalition, defined negatively (as non-Brahmans), of a wide array of castes. This process—which resulted from state engineering—went hand-in-hand with the invention of a Dravidian identity of the lower castes. Both processes mutually reinforced each other. The Dravidian identity gave the lower castes a cultural umbrella under which they can coalesce for defending their common interests vis-à-vis the state.

In south and west India, caste associations marked the first stage of a much larger ethnicization process. They have not only promoted caste fusion, their discourse on autochthony and the Buddhist origins of the lower castes endowed them with a prestigious identity. In north India, none of these processes reached their logical conclusion, even though the British policies of positive discrimination had created the same context as in the south and in the west.

## What Low Caste Movement in the Hindi Belt?

In north India, while caste associations took shape at an early date, they did not prepare the ground for a resilient ethnicization process but operated within the logic of Sanskritization. These shortcomings are well illustrated by three cases chosen among the Shudras and the Untouchables, respectively the Yadavs and the Chamars.

### THE YADAV MOVEMENT: AHIRS AS KSHATRIYAS

The 'Yadav' label covers a great number of castes. The common function of all these castes was to take care of cattle as herdsmen, cowherds, and milk sellers. In practice, however, the Yadavs have been spending most of their time tilling the land. While they are spread over several regions, they are more specially concentrated in the Ganges plain where they represent about 10 per cent of the population. They form one of the largest castes in Bihar and Uttar Pradesh with respectively 11 per cent and 8.7 per cent of the population.

The Yadavs reportedly descend from immigrants from Central Asia, the Abhiras, who established kingdoms in north India. From the 1930s onward, intermarriage-based fusion was made easier when north Indian Yadavs started to migrate from their villages to towns. But this ethnicization process remained largely unachieved because the Yadav movement remained imbued with the ethos of Sanskritization.

The Yadavs lent themselves to such Sanskritization because they had a special relation to the Hindu religion, owing to their association with the Arya Samaj. The

Arya Samaj is an association too often regarded as purely Punjabi and confined to the urban middle class. The Arya Samaj did not hesitate to mobilize lower caste people against the Brahmans, but not against the caste system. In fact, they followed the path of Sanskritization. Their campaigns were especially successful in Uttar Pradesh and Bihar.

## The 'Aryanization' of the Yadavs

The propensity of the Yadavs toward Sanskritization is evident from their attempt at 'Aryanizing' their history. The first history of the Yadavs was written by Kithal Krishna Khedekar in the late nineteenth century. This work was finalized by his son, R.V. Khedekar, and published in 1959 under the title *The Divine Heritage of the Yadavs*. The book situates the origins of the Yadavs in the Abhiras and then the ruling dynasties mentioned as Yadavs in the *Mahabharata* and the *Puranas*. Most of these caste histories try to demonstrate that Abhiras were of Aryan origin and that Rewari is the last representative of the Abhira kingdoms.

This narrative certainly aimed at giving the Yadavs an ethnic identity, but this ethnicization process was embedded in the Sanskritization logic. In contrast to the lower caste leaders of Maharashtra and south India—who tried to invent a *bahujan* or a Dravidian identity that presented the Shudras and Untouchables as the original inhabitants of the country *against* the Aryans—the Yadavs claim that they *are* Aryans in order to enhance their status *within* caste society. Thus, the Yadavs, largely because of the influence of the Arya Samaj, remained imbued with the ethos of Sanskritization. It prevented them from developing an emancipatory identity like in the west or in the south. The same kind of reasoning can be made about the Untouchables' movement.

The Untouchables of north India were also exposed to the influence of the Arya Samaj at the turn of the twentieth century. This is evident from the Jatav movement in Uttar Pradesh. Jatavs are Chamars, Untouchable leather workers, who claim descent from the Yadu race, which, allegedly, entitled them to be known as Kshatriyas like the Yadavs, and once again the Arya Samaj missions were responsible for propagating these views. They were especially successful through their schools among the sons of Agra Chamars who had become rich thanks to the leather trade. They were drawn by the teachings of Swami Manikchand Jatavaveer (1897–1956). He was one of the founders of the Jatav Mahasabha in 1917. He was a teacher in an Arya Samaj-run school of Agra. Together with Sunderlal Sagar (1886–1952) and Swami Prabhutanand Vyas (1877–1950), they all preached moral reform, vegetarianism, teetotalism, and temperance for achieving a cleaner status. That was also the first inclination of Swami Achhutanand (1879–1933), who was to become a major Untouchable leader of the United Provinces in the 1920s–30s.

Swami Achutanand worked with the Arya Samaj, from 1905 until 1912, but then he revolted against the Arya Samaj and adopted a new name, Swami Achutanand (deriving from *Achut,* Untouchable). He spelled out his Adi-Hindu philosophy for the first time in 1917 in a collection of poems and couplets. According to him, the Untouchables were the first inhabitants of India and the rightful owners of this land. The Aryans came from outside, as refugees who, by resorting to tactics and strategies, captured power and subordinated the autochthonous people. Swami Achhutanand maintained that the Adi-Hindus had their roots in the Indus Valley civilization. The Adi-Hindu philosophy was well designed for promoting the unity of the Shudras, the Untouchables, and the Tribals since it endowed those three groups with a common—cultural and ethnic—background.

However, Swami Achutanand's attitude toward the caste system remained ambivalent. Instead of trying to eradicate them, Swami Achutanand recognized castes among the Untouchables. More importantly, his egalitarian discourse was largely framed in a religious mould drawing its inspiration from the *bhakti* (devotion) tradition. Basically, Swami Achutanand discovered social equality in religion. Swami Achutanand, therefore, represented an old tradition. Besides Sanskritization, low caste groups have indeed explored avenues for upward mobility through the *bhakti* movements and the sectarian model. Hindu gurus have recurrently questioned the caste system on behalf of the fundamental equality of individuals before god. Their disciples who were initiated into monastic orders forgot about their caste to form new fraternities. Far from establishing a separate identity that would situate the Untouchables out of the caste system, the Adi-Hindu movement used their so-called original identity as a means for promoting their status *within* the system. And correlatively, the *bhakti* resurgence did not imply a radical questioning of their belonging to Hinduism. They questioned Brahmanism by adhering to a virtually subversive religious cult but it had the same modus operandi as the Hindu sects of the *bhakti*—whose egalitarian impact has always been otherworldly.

The movement also suffered from the weaknesses of its structures. By 1924, local Adi-Hindu Sabhas had been set up in only four cities of U.P. (Kanpur, Lucknow, Benares, and Allahabad). The Adi-Hindu movement remained chiefly confined to Agra and Kanpur. Out of the 23 Dalit leaders of the United Provinces, almost half of them were from these two cities (eight from Agra and two from Kanpur). In addition to these limitations, the movement also failed to unite the Untouchables in terms of communality or otherwise. Its leaders tried to organize inter-dining ceremonies but did not meet very enthusiastic responses.

The Adi-Hindu movement eventually failed to endow the Untouchables with a separate identity. Its *bhakti*-like, inspiration and recognition of castes prevented the Chamars, its main supporters, from emancipating themselves from the Sanskritization ethos. The Jatav movement could therefore rely on the same kind of ethnic ground as the Dalit movement in Maharashtra or the Dravidian movement in Tamil Nadu. According to Owen Lynch, for the Jatavs, 'political participation' became a 'functional alternative' to Sanskritization, in the sense that they tried to achieve social mobility through access to power (1969: 7). This empowerment process was fostered by the British policies of positive discrimination and gradual democratization since they both incited the caste to assert itself as a collective body. However, such a change was confined to the Jatavs of Agra. Except for the president of the Scheduled Castes Federation of the United Provinces, Piarelal Kureel (1916–84), who was a Kureel from Unnao District, most of the supporters of Ambedkar were Jatavs from Agra.

This chapter about the changing identity of the low castes before independence in India suggests that the low caste movements can be regrouped in three categories: the reform movements operating within the caste system and relying on the mechanisms of Sanskritization; those which draw their inspiration from the Hindu sect of the *bhakti* and do not attack the caste system, either; and finally those which are based on an ethnic ideology with a strong egalitarian overtone.

The rise of egalitarian movements, stemming from the ethnicization of caste was more prevalent in the south and in the west. In these two mega-regions the ethnicization of caste did not rely only on caste fusion. This process, fostered by caste associations, prepared the ground for a more radical transformation based on new *imaginaires*. In Maharashtra, Phule invented a pre-Aryan pedigree for the Shudras while Ambedkar endowed the Untouchables with a Buddhist identity. In Tamil Nadu, the Dravidian identity of the non-Brahman movement borrowed from both sources of inspiration. This ethnicization process provided the lower castes with an alternative, egalitarian sub-culture. In contrast, in pre-independence India, the Yadav movement can be classified in the first group of the typology presented here and the Adi-Hindu movement in the second one. None of them really challenged the caste system. Obviously, it is not just by chance that both of them have a north Indian origin because in this area Sanskritization continued to exert a strong influence and contributed decisively to the divisions of the lower castes according to the mechanisms of 'graded inequality', to use the words of Ambedkar.

In contrast to the situation prevailing in the south and west India, the mobilization of the lower castes stopped with caste associations. They could not establish their claim on ethnic grounds, which prevented them from shaping large coalitions like the Dravidian non-Brahman groupings. In fact, they started to move toward the formation of larger fronts only when the state extended its compensatory discrimination policy to what became known as the 'Other Backward Classes'. The OBCs, then, became, a relevant unit and low castes started to rally around this administrative category in order to defend their quotas in the bureaucracy from the state (Jaffrelot 2000: 86–108).

In this essay I have discussed the crystallization of lower caste movements in India. The essay argued that the mobilization of the lower castes was delayed and did not imply any significant change in caste identities. Instead, the emancipatory and empowerment agenda materialized without any prior ethnicization. Nevertheless, although contemporary reservation policies may have played a role in the crystallization of the low caste movements in south and west India, I have argued that this process was sustained by the ideology of 'pre-Aryanism' or Buddhism. In contrast, in north India, state policies were more or less the starting point of the whole process.

## Note

1. In north India, when the colonizer went to levy estate taxes, they often used intermediaries, mainly zamindars, who had already been used for similar tasks under the Mughal Empire. In the south, where the Mughul administration had not been as powerful, the British did not find such a dense network of zamindars (or the equivalent). The tendency then was to select individual farmers as land proprietors and direct taxpayers: hence the system raiyatwari, from raiyat (cultivator). The latter was more conducive to the formation of a relatively egalitarian peasantry than the zamindari system.

## References

Ambedkar, B.R. (1990), 'Who Were the Shudras? How They Came to Be the Fourth Varna in the Indu-Aryan Society', in *Dr. Babasaheb Ambedkar: Writings and Speeches*, Vol. 7, Bombay: Government of Maharashtra.

——— (1989), 'Held at Bay', in *Dr. Babasaheb Ambedkar: Writings and Speeches*, Vol. 5, Bombay: Government of Maharashtra.

Bayly, Susan (1999), *The New Cambridge History of India*, Vol. 4, Cambridge: Cambridge University Press.

Dumont, L. (1966), *Homo Hierarchicus*, Paris: Gallimard.

Jaffrelot, C. (2000), 'The Rise of the Other Backward Classes in the Hindi Belt', *Journal of Asian Studies*, Vol. 59, No.1, February.

*Justice* (1920), 29 March, in Indian Office Library and Records, L/P&J/9/14.

Lynch, Owen (1969), *The Politics of Untouchability*, New York: Columbia University Press.

Rudolph, Lloyd I. and Rudolph, Susanne Hoeber (1966), 'The Political Role of India's Caste Associations', in *Social Change: The Colonial Situation*, (ed.), Immanuel Wallerstein, New York: J. Wiley.

Srinivas, M.N. (1995 [1966]), *Social Change in Modern India*, Hyderabad: Orient Longman.

# Chapter 22

# The rise of the Other Backward Classes in the Hindi belt

The rise of the Other Backward Classes (OBCs) is certainly one of the main developments in the Hindi-belt politics over the last ten years. The OBCs are castes in the Indian social system that are situated above the Untouchables but below the forward castes (the 'twice-born') and the intermediate castes (mostly peasant proprietors and even dominant castes). They form the bulk of the Shudras—the fourth category (*varna*) of the classical Hindu social arrangement. The OBCs, whose professional activity is often as field-workers or artisans, represent about half of the Indian population, but they have occupied a subaltern position so far. Their rise for the first time seriously questions upper caste domination of the public sphere.

The over-representation of these elite groups in the political sphere has always been more pronounced in the Hindi-speaking states than anywhere else. In the south, and even in the west, the upper castes lost ground early, largely because they were smaller in number—in Tamil Nadu Brahmans account for only 3 per cent of the population whereas they constitute almost 10 per cent in Uttar Pradesh (a state where the upper castes altogether represent one-fifth of society). But the upper caste remained politically dominant in the Hindi belt also because of the pattern of land ownership that enabled them, especially the Rajputs, to consolidate their grasp over the countryside as zamindars, jagirdars, or taluqdars under the British and to retain some of their influence in spite of the efforts toward land reform after 1947.

In fact, these notables were the backbone of the Congress Party's network, and for decades the social deficit of democracy in north India resulted from the clientelistic politics of this party. The Congress co-opted vote-bank 'owners', who were often upper caste landlords, and Untouchable leaders, whose rallying around the ruling party deprived their group of some important spokesmen. There were even fewer lower caste leaders within the Congress Party, the lower castes being closer to the opposition parties, especially the Socialists, or the 'independents' (Brass 1980); they remained marginalized also for this reason. Until the early 1970s, the upper caste Members of Parliament (MPs) represented more than 50 per cent of the north Indian MPs as against less than 5 per cent for intermediate castes and, at the maximum, 10 per cent for the Other Backward Classes.

Historically, in north India two kinds of approaches have prevailed among those who attempted to dislodge the upper caste, urban establishment from its positions of power. The first one concentrated on their mobilization as peasants (*kisans*). It was initiated by members of cultivating castes such as Chhotu Ram (a Jat) in Punjab between the 1920s and the 1940s (Gopal 1977), and Swami Sahajanand (a Bhumihar) who became a leading figure of the Bihar Kisan Sabha in the 1930s.[1] The second one relied more on caste identities and was primarily articulated by socialist leaders such as Rammanohar Lohia, who regarded caste as the main obstacle towards an egalitarian society. While the 'kisan school' endeavoured to gather together all those engaged in cultivating work on the basis of socio-economic demands, the caste-oriented Socialists attempted to form an alliance of the non-elite groups mainly on the basis of affirmative action techniques: they asked for caste-based quotas, especially in the administration. The social groups represented by these two approaches had much in common but did not coincide. The proponents of 'kisan politics' came primarily from the rank of peasant-proprietors who tried to mobilize 'the peasants'—as if that were a social category without internal differentiation—to promote their own interest and maintain lower castes under their influence. The caste-based approach was rather conceived for defending the latter.

Over the last decades, these two strategies have contributed to the rise of first the middle caste peasants and then the OBCs in north Indian politics. The first significant changes occurred in the 1960s when they entered the Bihar and Uttar Pradesh legislative assemblies in massive numbers under the auspices of the socialist parties and Charan Singh. *Kisan* politics asserted itself in the 1970s and 1980s, thanks to Charan Singh and his lieutenants. But in the late 1980s and 1990s, the anti-establishment agenda was taken over, on the political scene, by heirs of the socialist movement within the Janata Dal, whose quota politics culminated in the implementation of the recommendations of the Mandal Commission Report. As a result, the *kisan* front broke down along caste lines, the peasant proprietors from the intermediate castes distancing themselves from the OBCs. But do the latter have more coherence and can they resist the new upper caste dominated, BJP-led ruling coalition?

## Quota Politics and *Kisan* Politics

Few men and political parties in north India have tried to promote the cause of the lower castes since independence. The Congress Party was dominated, at the Centre, by progressive leaders a la Nehru who did not regard caste as a relevant category for State-sponsored social change, and it relied anyway on a network of conservative potables. None of them was truly interested in acknowledging the needs of the Other Backward Classes even though this expression was originally used by Nehru in his first speech, on his Objectives Resolution, on 13 December 1946, before the Constituent Assembly. He announced that special measures were to be taken in favour of 'minorities, backward and tribal areas and depressed and other backward classes' (*Constituent Assembly Debates*, 1989, Vol. 1: 59) but did not elaborate further and, interestingly, senior Congressmen such as K.M. Munshi resisted any effort to clarify who these OBCs were (1: 697). Article 340 of the Indian Constitution voted on 26 January 1950, merely stated:

The President (of the Republic) can by decree nominate a Commission formed by persons he considers to be competent to investigate, within the Indian territory, on the condition of classes suffering of backwardness as well in social as in educational terms, and on the problems they meet, the way of proposing measures which could be taken by the Central or a State Government in order to eliminate difficulties and improve their condition. (Government of India, n.d.: 178)

The first Backward Classes Commission was appointed on 29 January 1953 under the chairmanship of a former disciple of Gandhi, Kaka Kalelkar (Government of India 1955). Its report relied heavily on the concept of caste for defining the Other Backward Classes. Caste was not the only criterion but it was a key element and the Commission, therefore, established a list of 2,399 castes, representing about 32 per cent of the Indian population, as forming the bulk of the 'socially and educationally backward classes' that needed affirmative action programmes.

The report was rejected by Nehru's government. G.B. Pant, the Home Minister, objected that 'With the establishment of our society on the socialist pattern . . . , social and other distinctions will disappear as we advance towards that goal' (*Memorandum*, n.d.: 2). Second, he disapproved of the use of caste as the most prominent criterion for identifying the backward classes. He considered that 'the recognition of the specified castes as backward may serve to maintain and even perpetuate the existing distinctions on the basis of caste' (ibid.). The report was tabled before Parliament accompanied by a Memorandum by Pant on 3 September 1956, but was not even discussed (Government of India 1980: 2). In May 1961, the Nehru government eventually decided that there was no need for an all-India list of the OBCs—and that, consequently, there would be no reservation policy at the Centre. Even though they were responsible for Article 340 of the Constitution, Congressmen were obviously reluctant to cater to the needs of the lower castes, either because of sheer conservatism or socialist ideas.

So far as the communists were concerned, they were very reluctant to take caste into account, holding the view that this social category was bound to be submerged by that of class. For a long time the Socialists were the only ones to consider the lower castes as a pertinent social and political entity.

## THE SOCIALISTS AND POSITIVE DISCRIMINATION
## FOR THE LOWER CASTES

The first to recognize the importance of the lower castes was probably Rammanohar Lohia. Although he was from a merchant caste and had been influenced by

Marxism, Lohia decided to fight for the cause of the lower castes. To those who favoured an analysis in terms of class, he objected that 'caste is the most overwhelming factor in Indian life' (Lohia 1979: 79).

Many socialists honestly but wrongly think that it is sufficient to strive for economic equality and caste inequality will vanish of itself as a consequence. They fail to comprehend economic inequality and caste inequality as twin demons, which have both to be killed. (ibid.: 20)

Lohia therefore became one of the staunchest supporters of positive discrimination—what he called 'unequal opportunities'—not only in favour of the Scheduled Castes but also of the backward castes:

When everybody has an equal opportunity, castes with the five thousand years old traditions of liberal education would be on top. Only the exceptionally gifted from the lower castes would be able to break through this tradition. . . . To make this battle a somewhat equal encounter, unequal opportunities would have to be extended, to those who have so far been suppressed. (ibid.: 96)

According to him, the Marxist views about revolution or Nehru's policy of nationalizing private properties amount to 'vested-interest socialism' because none of these things would change Indian society:

Workers with the brain are a fixed caste in Indian society; together with the soldier caste, they are the high caste. Even after the completed economic and political revolution, they would continue to supply the managers of the state and industry. The mass of the people would be kept in a state of perpetual physical and mental lowliness, at least comparatively. But the position of the high caste would then be justified on grounds of ability and in economic terms as in is now on grounds of birth or talent. That is why the intelligentsia of India which is overwhelmingly the high caste, abhors all talk of a mental and social revolution of a radical change it respect of language or caste or the bases of thought. It talks generally and in principle against caste. In fact, it can be most vociferous in its theoretical condemnation of caste, so long as it can be allowed to be equally vociferous in raising the banner of merit and equal opportunity. What it loses in respect of caste by birth, it gains in respect of caste by merit. Its merit concerning speech, grammar, manners, capacity to adjust, routine efficiency is undisputed. Five thousands years have gone into the building of this undisputed merit. (ibid.: 96–7)

Lohia did not entertain any romantic idea of the Indian plebe—'the Shudra too has his shortcomings. He has an even narrower sectarian outlook' (ibid.: 13)—but in spite of this for Lohia, the Shudra deserved special treatment, especially in one direction: he should be 'pushed to positions of power and leadership' (13). He did not regard affirmative action in the education system as desirable[2] but emphasized the need for quotas in the administration and for the election candidates. Obviously, reservations were intended to give a share of power to the lower castes; it was an empowerment scheme. In 1959, the third national conference of the Socialist Party expressed the wish that at least 60 per cent of the posts in the administration be reserved for Other Backward Classes (ibid.: 135). This recommendation was reiterated at the fifth annual session of the party, in April 1961, a few months before the third general elections (ibid.: 142). Subsequently, the programme or election manifestos of Lohia's party promoted the notion of 'preferential opportunities', which was justified by the special nature of caste society, as in the programme adopted by the first Conference of the Samyukta Socialist Party (SSP) held in April 1966:

It should be remembered that equality and equal opportunity are not synonymous. In a society characterised by a hierarchical structure based on birth, the principle of equal opportunity cannot produce an equal society. The established, conventional notions about merit and ability must result in denial of opportunities in actual practice for backward castes, harijans [Scheduled Castes], adibasis [Scheduled Tribes], etc. The principle of preferential opportunities alone will ensure that the backward sections will catch up with the advanced ones in a reasonable period of time. (Mohan et al., 1997: 258–9)

This document again recommended a quota of 60 per cent for the backward sections of society—comprising then the Scheduled Castes, Scheduled Tribes, OBCs, and women—but extended it to 'all spheres', not only the administration, but also the education system and the assemblies. The weakness of the 'people's movement', according to the document, resulted from its divisions, and also from 'the preponderance of upper caste leadership in [the] major political parties' (ibid.: 260). To show the way, the SSP nominated a large number of candidates from non-elite groups, and the socialists had a larger number of OBC Members of Legislative Assemblies (MLAs) elected than other political parties in the states where they achieved their best scores, in Uttar Pradesh and Bihar. In the latter state, in the 1967 elections, the SSP had almost 40 per cent of its MLAs coming from the lower castes (as against 22 per cent on the Congress side) (Mitra 1992: 120).

Obviously, Lohia's strategy bore its most significant electoral fruits in Bihar, the birthplace and cradle of socialism in India since the foundation of the Congress Socialist Party in the state capital in 1934. In 1967, Lohia's party, the Samyukta Socialist Party (SSP), the communists, and the Jana Sangh formed a majority coalition called the Samyukta Vidhayak Dal (SVD). However, the socialist leaders were, in a way, victims of their own strategy of promotion and mobilization of the lower castes. While this policy largely explained their success and the election of a large number of lower caste MLAs, especially Yadavs whose number had increased so much as to be just behind the Rajputs (14.8 per cent as against 24.1 per cent) (Blair 1980: 68), this group did not display much commitment to the SSP. Soon after the elections, Bindeshwari Prasad Mandal, a Yadav who was to preside over the second Backward Classes Commission in 1979, defected and formed the Shoshit Dal, 'the party of the oppressed' with 40 lower caste MLA dissidents from different sides, including the SSP. Madhu Limaye, one of Lohia's lieutenants, lamented that 'as soon as power came, SSP men broke up into caste groups. They equated . . . [Lohia's] policy with casteism! . . . Ministers developed affinities on caste lines. Castemen belonging to other parties were felt to be closer than one's own Party comrades belonging to other castes' (Limaye 1988: 155–6).

In fact, these developments had some positive aspects. Castes, eventually, got transformed into interest groups, which meant that lower caste people could not be integrated in vertical linkages as easily as during the heyday of the Congress Party domination. The lower castes may have lent themselves to manipulations by political entrepreneurs like B.P. Mandal, but greater caste consciousness also implied a stronger rejection of vertical arrangements and a growing solidarity between lower caste MLAs from different parties. These phenomena had become so pronounced that to topple the SVD government the Congress had no other choice but to support one of the Shoshit Dal leaders; thus in February 1968 B.P. Mandal became the first OBC chief minister of Bihar. He was to be followed by other non-elite leaders. Out of the nine chief ministers who governed the state from March 1967 to December 1971, only two belonged to the higher castes.

## Charan Singh and the Mobilization of the Farmers

Besides the socialist approach recognizing caste as a lever of social domination and the corollary caste-based mobilization and affirmative action, north India saw in the late 1960s the shaping of an alternative strategy by Charan Singh which aimed at empowering the peasantry. The fact that 'the Chaudhuri', a title held by Jat leaders, became influential in the late 1960s is largely explained by the relative economic growth which, at that time, benefited the middle-class farmers of north India. This growth resulted from two cumulative phenomena. First, the land reform, even though it had remained incomplete, enabled many tenants to become peasant-proprietors. Second, the Green Revolution served the interests of those among these landowners who had some investment capacity. This 'revolution' stemmed from the introduction of high-yielding seeds between 1965 and 1966, but also from the development of irrigation and the use of chemical fertilizers.

Charan Singh always identified himself with the interests of the peasants. In 1939, before the executive committee of the Congress parliamentary group in the Uttar Pradesh assembly, where he had been elected for the first time in 1937, he proposed a 50 per cent quota in public administration in favour of the sons of farmers. He framed his project in terms of a latent 'urban India versus rural India' conflict:

In our country the classes whose scions dominate the public services are either those which have been 'raised to unexampled prominence and importance' by the Britisher, e.g. the money-lender, the big *zamindar* or *taluqdar*, the *arhatia* or the trader, or those which have been, so to say, actually called into being by him—the *vakil* [advocate], the doctor, the contractor. These classes have, in subordinate cooperation with the foreigner, exploited the masses in all kinds of manner during these last two hundred years. The views and interests of these classes, on the whole, are, therefore, manifestly opposed to those of the masses. The social philosophy of a member of the non-agricultural, urban classes is entirely different from that of a person belonging to the agricultural rural classes. (Singh 1986: 203)

The All-India Jat Mahasabha supported his proposal, but Charan Singh did not value caste affiliations very much. He tried, rather, to subsume caste identities into a feeling of class or at least into one of a peasant movement. This approach was partly dictated by his own caste background, since the Jats occupy an intermediary position: though technically they have to be classified as Shudras, their dominant caste status is often the root-cause of conflicts with lower castes. In addition, their number is comparatively small in Uttar Pradesh (1.2 per cent of the population). Therefore Charan Singh had good reasons for forging a *kisan* interest group that the Jats would be leading, and for promoting an identity opposing the peasants to the town-dwellers in order to subsume caste divisions into a new group feeling. Even though OBC leaders rallied around the Chaudhuri, his scheme was not designed for emancipating their group but for promoting the interests of those who owned some land and could sell their surplus crops. In fact, it was likely to reinforce the Jats' hegemony over the lower castes.

As revenue minister in-charge of land reform in Uttar Pradesh after independence, Charan Singh promoted the interests of what he called the middle peasantry by abolishing the *zamindari* system.[3] The bulk of this class was to come from the intermediary castes, including his own, the Jats. This approach largely explains the selective character of Uttar Pradesh land reform and his later conflict with Nehru. In 1959 he vigorously opposed the project of agricultural cooperatives announced by the Prime Minister in the Nagpur session of the Congress. He immediately published a book called *Joint Farming X-Rayed: The Problem and Its Solution,* in which he proposed a strategy of global development radically opposed to that of Nehru.[4] Questioning the need for a rapid, state-sponsored industrialization as advocated by Nehru, Charan Singh proposed to give priority to agriculture and to promote it by developing small farmer holdings, the only way to generate the surpluses that were needed for industrial investment.[5] For him, agricultural cooperatives would annul the productivity gains resulting from the elimination of the *zamindar*-like intermediaries because they would jeopardize the independence of the farmers:

The thought that land has become his [the peasant's] and his children's in perpetuity, lightens and cheers his labour and expands his horizon. The feeling that he is his own master, subject to no outside control, and has free, exclusive and untrammelled use of his land drives him to greater and greater effort. . . . Likewise any system of large-scale farming in which his holdings are pooled must affect the farmer, but in the reverse direction. No longer will he be his own master; he will become one of the many; his interest will be subordinated to the group interest. (Singh 1959: v–vi)

Obviously, economic rationality is not the only reason for rejecting agricultural cooperatives. Charan Singh admits that 'Ultimately it is not a question of economic efficiency or of form of organization, but whether individualism or collectivism should prevail' (1959: 107). Indeed, he argues, 'The peasant is an incorrigible individualist; for his avocation, season in and season out, can be carried on with a pair of bullocks in the solitude of Nature without the necessity of having to give orders to, or, take orders from anybody' (ibid.: 104). Charan Singh spells out a very romantic view of the *khan,* even a mystique of the peasant, as the man in communion with Nature (a word that he writes with a capital n) and the only one able to sustain its 'nutritional cycle' (ibid.: 266).

On landless agricultural labour, Charan Singh's views are worth noting, too. Referring, *en passant,* to the labourers' condition, he notes that 'If wages have at all to be paid, in view of the fact that a large supply of idle labour is almost always available, the wages paid need only be subsistence wages' (1959: 168). Indifferent to the condition of the landless labourers, Charan Singh was against too low a ceiling in the land reform programme which could have benefited them because it would multiply the noneconomic exploitations and weaken the peasant-proprietor pattern.

In spite of this selective defence of the rural folk, Charan Singh systematically attempted to project himself as the spokesman for village India. He presented the village community as forming a harmonious whole and claimed that it 'was always a stronger moral unit than a factory. The sense of the community was a vital thing among the peasantry, providing a natural foundation for collaboration or co-operative action' (1959: 270). He completely ignored the deep social contradictions and class antagonisms between landowners, tenants, sharecroppers, and labourers. While Charan Singh is of course the representative of peasant-proprietors, his whole strategy consists in forging a *kisan* identity in which all the people working in the fields may be able to recognize themselves. He insisted on the dichotomy between the cities and the countryside in this very perspective.

There has always been lack of equilibrium, rather a sort of antagonism between cities and the countryside. This is particularly so in our land where the gulf of inequality between the capitalist class and the working class pales into insignificance before that which exists between the peasant farmer in our village and the middle-class town dweller. India is really two worlds—rural and urban. The relationship between the countryside and the cities is, therefore, a vital problem to us. (1984: 212)

Charan Singh's *kisan* politics was successful to a certain extent, since he was able to gradually evolve a coalition of cultivating castes from different social ranks. This coalition came to be known as AJGAR, an acronym where A stood for Ahir (or Yadav), J for Jat, G for Gujar and R for Rajput. While there was no representative of the (often landless labourers) untouchable castes in this grouping, it covered a wide range of status from OBC to intermediate and upper castes. For instance,

Mulayam Singh Yadav was among the followers Charan Singh attracted in the 1960s. Yadav was elected MLA for the first time in 1967 on a ticket of the Bharatiya Kranti Dal, Charan Singh's party. Interestingly, he was introduced to the Chaudhuri by another OBC, Jairam Verma (Lal and Nair 1998: 32), who was a Kurmi, a sign that Charan Singh attracted cultivating castes even beyond the AJGAR coalition.

## The Janata Party at the Confluence of Quota and *Kisan* Politics

The fact that both strategies, quota politics and *kisan* politics, persisted during the 'JP movement' and the subsequent Janata phase is evident from the discourse then promoted by Madhu Limaye and Charan Singh, who became Deputy Prime Minister and Home Minister in 1977. The former, as convener of the J.P. Movement Programme Committee in 1975, drafted a document where one could read the following statements:

Caste hierarchy based on birth is the biggest obstacle in the path of achieving social equality. In an unequal society, the doctrine of judicial equality and equal opportunity cannot by itself remove caste disabilities. The doctrine of preferential opportunity, therefore, had to be invoked in order to enable the backward sections to come up to the level of the upper castes. Reservation in the services that we have today had not enabled us to over come the disabilities from which our suppressed communities suffer . . . This must change, and these people and other backward classes should be enabled to secure, through preferential opportunities and reservation, the substance of power. (Limaye 1997: 314)

Madhu Limaye emphasized the empowerment dimension of affirmative action schemes the same way as his mentor, Lohia, did. Charan Singh regarded the 'three decades of Congress rule in post-independence India as essentially elitist and urban oriented' and argued that the Janata Party had to maintain 'its live links with the villages, with agriculture, with cottage and village industries, and generally with the uplift of our Kisans' (1997: 325, 327). Two major components of the Janata, the former Congress (O) of Prime Minister Morarji Desai and the Hindu nationalist Jana Sangh 'were unwilling to concede primacy' to Charan Singh (Varshney 1995: 104). Dismissed by Desai on the ground of indiscipline, he organized a huge peasant rally of about one million people in December 1978 and then rejoined the government as Senior Deputy Prime Minister in-charge of Finance. His 'kulak budget', to use the pressmen's words in 1979, reduced several indirect taxes on mechanical tillers, diesel for electric water pumps, and chemical fertilizers, by 50 per cent for some of them; it 'lowered interest rates for rural loans; increased subsidy of minor irrigation and earmarked funds for rural electrification and grain-storage facilities' (ibid.: 105). The Janata did not last long enough to implement all these measures, but Charan Singh had raised the peasants' issues in such a way that they arrived centrestage; so much so that they were taken up by farmers' movements in most of the states (T. Brass 1995), amongst which the Bharatiya Kisan Union of Tikait and the Shetkari Sangarhana of Sharad Joshi in Maharashtra were especially noticeable for their attempt at projecting their apolitical character.

The Janata government was too heterogeneous a coalition to have a consistent affirmative action policy. The Jana Sangh, representative primarily of the urban and upper caste middle class, was reluctant to move in the direction of affirmative action. The differences showed clearly at the subnational level, when Karpoori Thakur, the socialist chief minister of Bihar, and Ram Naresh Yadav, his socialist counterpart in Uttar Pradesh, tried to introduce quotas in the state administration. Yet Desai yielded to OBC pressures and appointed the second Backward Classes Commission, whose principal terms of reference were 'to determine the criteria for defining the socially and educationally backward classes' and 'to examine the desirability or otherwise of making provision for the reservations of appointments or posts in favour of such backward classes of citizens which are not adequately represented in public services . . .' (*Government of India*, 1980, Vol. 1: vii). The Commission, whose Chairman was B.P. Mandal, concluded from its survey that the OBCs were coterminous with low castes, representing 52 per cent of the population, and that their backwardness justified a quota of 27 per cent of the posts being reserved for them in the bureaucracy and the public sector. The Mandal Commission Report was submitted in late 1980, more than a year after the fall of the Janata government. Indira Gandhi and then Rajiv Gandhi were not interested in implementing measures that might affect the upper caste supporters of the Congress or, at least, damage its image of a 'catch-all party'. The report was finally made public by the Janata Dal when it took power from the Congress in 1989.

## The Janata Dal and the Empowerment of the Lower Castes

The Janata Dal, which was officially founded on 11 October 1988, amalgamated the legacies of Lohia and Charan Singh, as evident from the identity of the parties it incorporated. On the one hand, the Lok Dal (A) of Ajit Singh, son of Charan Singh, and the Lok Dal (B) of Devi Lal, another Jat leader from Haryana, merged in the Janata Dal. On the other hand, many socialist old-timers from the Janata Party, such as Madhu Dandavate (who was to become Finance Minister in V.P. Singh's government), George Fernandes (who was to hold the portfolio of Railways), and Surendra Mohan (a member of the Janata Dal Executive Committee who shaped its election manifesto), took an active part in it. This amalgamation had inner problems, as the controversy over the naming of the party quickly demonstrated. Until the last minute the party was to be called Samajwadi Janata Dal, but Devi Lal strongly objected to the term socialist and it had to be removed (Mustafa 1995: 110).

Yet the party's discourse on social justice remained heavily loaded with socialist references, and its affirmative action programme drew most of its inspiration from Lohia's modus operandi. The party's president, V.P. Singh, was a late convert to this brand of socialism. Descending from a Rajput lineage which had been the ruling family of a small princely state near Allahabad, the 'Raja of Manda'—as he came to be called rather ironically—had shown some early interest in the Sarvodaya movement, but had then been co-opted by the Congress Party to become, as MLA and then MP, one more 'notable' in the vote-bank pyramid. He was expelled from the Congress in July 1987 because of his accusation that Congress Party leaders were corrupt. The party he founded then with other Congress dissidents, the Jan Morcha, was small, but it played a pivotal role in the foundation of the Janata Dal and became the rallying point of other opposition parties with which it formed the National Front. The day after he was sworn in as Prime Minister, on 3 December 1989, in his First Address to the Nation, Rammanohar Lohia and Jayaprakash Narayan were the only names he mentioned as his guides (V.P. Singh 1997: 357). This shift from Congress to a mixed brand of socialist politics reflected V.P. Singh's old commitment to Sarvodaya but also his dependence upon socialist leaders.

The Janata Dal indeed tended to adopt the socialist programme for social justice: it concentrated its attention less on class than on ascriptive groups and turned towards affirmative action as the main remedy. The programme adopted by the party during its inaugural session promised that 'Keeping in view special needs of the socially and educationally backward classes, the party [if voted to power] shall implement forthwith the recommendations of the Mandal Commission' (ibid.: 343). The patty was prepared to show the way and promised to allot 60 per cent of the tickets in the general elections to 'the weaker sections of society'. Before that, V.P. Singh had promised to apply this 60 per cent reservation to the party apparatus. The 60 per cent quota was an old socialist idea that Lohia had propagated in the 1960s. It could not be implemented allegedly because of the opposition of Devi Lal (Mustafa 1995: 115). Once again, the socialist approach was opposed by a Jat who tried to appear as the heir of Charan Singh.

The JD, indeed, represented the aspirations of the proponents of *kisan* politics as well. Devi Lal, the then Chief Minister of Haryana, had won the 1987 state elections largely because he had promised to waive the cooperative loans up to Rs 20,000 (Varshney 1995: 141). The 1989 election manifesto of the National Front promised to do the same with 'Loans up to Rs 10,000 of small, marginal and landless cultivators and artisans' (ibid.: 143). Most of the items regrouped under the headline 'Rural Economy' were in favour of the peasant-proprietors:

Not less than 50 per cent of the investible resources will be deployed for the development of rural economy. Farmers will be assured of guaranteed remunerative prices for their produce, a countrywide network of godowns and warehouses, remission of debts, provision of cheap credit, removal of unreasonable restrictions on movement of agricultural produce, crop insurance, security in land holding and strict implementation of land reforms and improved access to water resources. (ibid.: 26)

The only promise which directly concerned the agricultural labourers was the one about the land reform, which was not implemented. On the other hand, Devi Lal who became Deputy Prime Minister with the Agriculture portfolio, and Sharad Joshi one of his advisors, with a cabinet rank, waived 'all agricultural loans under central jurisdiction up to Rs 10,000' (Varshney 1995: 143).

Yet, *kisan* politics was not as resolutely pursued by the V.P. Singh government as the 'quota politics', probably for two reasons. From a pragmatic point of view, V.P. Singh was more eager to cater to the needs of the lower castes than to those of the middle peasants. The latter constituency was already won over by Ajit Singh and Devi Lal. V.P. Singh was more interested in broadening his base among the OBCs. From a more ideological point of view, like most of the old socialist leaders, V.P. Singh believed less in economic and financial support than in the reform of the power structure within society, for which affirmative action appeared to be the most relevant method. The 1989 National Front election manifesto underlined that 'Implementation of reservation policy will be made effective in government, public and private sector industrial undertakings, banking institutions, etc., by resorting to special recruitment drives so as to fulfil their quotas within the shortest possible time' (*National Front Manifesto*, 1989: 26) and that 'The recommendations of the Mandal Commission will be implemented expeditiously' (ibid.: 27). While the government did not dare to extend the reservation system to the private sector, it did implement the Mandal Report recommendations.

V.P. Singh announced this decision in a one-and-a-half page *suo motu* statement in both Houses of Parliament on 7 August 1990. He justified it in his Independence Day address on 15 August by the need to give 'a share to the poor in running the Government' (Mohan et al., 1997: 360):

We believe that no section can be uplifted merely by money. They can develop only if they have a share in power and we are prepared to provide this share. In this year of justice, in memory of Dr. Bhimrao Ambedkar the Government has recently taken a decision to give reservation to the backward classes in the jobs in Government and public sector. It is being debated as to how many persons would get benefit out of it. In a sense, taking into account the population of this country, the Government jobs account for only one per cent [of the total] and out of this one per cent if one fourth is given to anyone, it cannot be a course for his economic betterment though it may have some effect. But our outlook is clear. Bureaucracy is an important organ of the power structure. It has a decisive role in decision-making. We want to give an effective share in the power structure and running of the country to the depressed, downtrodden and backward people. (ibid.: 361)

As it was for most socialists before him, the caste system was also a target for V.P. Singh, and he analysed the caste system based on power relations. This approach could not please the proponents of *kisan* politics. Devi Lal had been appointed by V.P. Singh as chairman of a committee for the implementation of the Mandal Report recommendations, but, according to the Prime Minister, he 'did not take much interest' (cited in Mustafa 1995: 171). He had strong reservations concerning the report because the Jats had not been included among the OBCs (interview with Ajay Singh, Jat minister in V.P. Singh's cabinet, New Delhi, 28 October 1997). Devi Lal tried to have the Jat's inclusion accepted by the government, but in vain.[6] Finally, V.P. Singh decided to ask Minister of Social Welfare Ram Vilas Paswan, a Dalit leader, to do the job.

The Prime Minister announced the implementation of the Mandal Commission Report recommendations only a few days after Devi Lal resigned from his government. Though there were other issues also leading to the rupture, the views and interests of V.P. Singh and Devi Lal could not coincide. Indeed, the social potential of V.P. Singh's reforms was perceived as posing a threat to Jat interests insofar as it could promote the assertiveness of tenants and agricultural labourers from the lower castes.

Devi Lal's resignation signalled the breakdown of Charan Singh's coalition. For partisans of 'quota politics', such a breakdown was for the better because *kisan* politics, in their view, merely served the economic interest of the peasant-proprietors and maintained the social status quo in the countryside. The old socialist and Ambedkarite approach based on an anti-caste discourse and affirmative action was considered more promising.

## Caste Polarization around Mandal

The main achievement of V.P. Singh was to make a broad range of castes coalesce under the OBC label. In fact, he made it a relevant category for the lower castes, as per the quotas recommended by the Mandal Commission Report. Many of those who were earlier known as 'Shudras' internalized this administrative definition of their identity in the early 1990s. The OBC category also crystallized for a while because the upper castes militantly resisted such reservations in the administration. The cleavage between upper castes and lower castes was suddenly reinforced by a collective, open hostility on the part of the former and by the unleashing of violence.

Soon after V.P. Singh announced the implementation of the Mandal Commission Report recommendations, upper caste students formed organizations such as the Arakshan Virodhi Sangharsh Samiti and the Mandal Ayog Virodhi Sangharsh Samiti in Uttar Pradesh. Students who were from the upper castes but from the lower middle class protested against a new quota that would deprive them of some posts in the administration. They wanted to 'abolish all reservations including reservations for the Scheduled Castes' (Hasan 1998: 155), a demand that brought the Dalit and OBC leaders closer. At the same time, the students 'feared that their hopes of government patronage would be thwarted by a coalition of lower castes' (ibid.: 155), which they were largely shaping themselves by provoking a new cleavage between forward castes (including Jats)[7] and lower castes.

Immediately, leaders from the Janata Dal organized a countermobilization. Sharad Yadav, one of the Ministers of V. P. Singh, launched the movement in Delhi. 'We will,' he said, 'show them within 15 days how many people are behind us if they don't come back to their sense . . .' (cited in *The Hindustan Times*, 3 September 1990). V.P. Singh went to Patna for an anti-upper caste rally. Thus, the early 1990s were marked by an exacerbation of the cleavage between upper castes and lower castes, an atmosphere which explains *at that time* the emotional value of the OBC as a social category.

Their new unity helped the OBC to organize themselves as an interest groups outside the vertical, clientelistic Congress-like patterns. The aim was to benefit from its main asset, its massive numbers (52 per cent of the Indian population), at the time of elections. Indeed, the share of the OBC MPs increased in the Hindi belt because lower caste people became more aware of their common interests and decided no longer to vote for upper caste candidates. In south and west India such a silent revolution had already started before independence and bore fruits soon after. By contrast, in the states of the Hindi belt—Uttar Pradesh, Bihar, Madhya Pradesh, Rajasthan, Haryana, Himachal Pradesh, Delhi, and Chandigarh—politics was still almost monopolized by the upper castes until the 1980s, as suggested by the caste background of the MPs returned to the Lok Sabha (the lower house of Parliament).

As Table 22.1 shows, the share of intermediate-caste and OBC MPs really started to increase in 1977, thanks to the Janata Party's victory, when the proportion of the upper caste MPs fell below 50 per cent for the first time. But the decline of the upper castes benefited more the upper layer of the peasantry, especially the Jats, and the return of the Congress Party in the 1980s brought back a large number of upper caste MPs, especially in 1984. The percentage of OBC MPs increased again after the Congress lost power in 1989, doubling from 11.1 per cent in 1984 to 20.9 per cent in 1989, when the share of upper caste MPs fell below 40 per cent for the first time, largely because the Janata Dal, the winner of the ninth general elections, had given tickets to a considerable number of OBC candidates. Interestingly enough, the proportion of the OBC MPs continued to grow in 1991, in spite of the Congress Party's comeback in 1996, when the BJP became the largest party in the Lok Sabha and in 1998 when the coalition it was leading was able to form the government. This evolution was continuously pursued at the expense of the upper castes. Most political parties, it would appear, had started giving a larger number of tickets to OBC candidates.

However, the rise of the OBCs has been rather uneven in the states of the Hindi belt. In Rajasthan the share of OBCs among the MPs has remained stable at 12 per cent between 1984 and 1998, whereas over the same period it has increased from 11 per cent to 20.8 per cent in Uttar Pradesh and from 7.5 per cent

TABLE 22.1: CASTE AND COMMUNITY OF THE MPs ELECTED TO THE LOK SABHA IN THE HINDI BELT IN 1952-98 (IN %)

| Castes and communities | 1952 | 1957 | 1962 | 1967 | 1971 | 1977 | 1980 | 1984 | 1989 | 1991 | 1996 | 1998 |
|---|---|---|---|---|---|---|---|---|---|---|---|---|
| *Upper Castes* | 64 | 58.6 | 54.9 | 55.5 | 53.9 | 48.2 | 40.88 | 46.9 | 38.2 | 37.11 | 35.3 | 34.67 |
| Brahman | 30.54 | 21.9 | 19.25 | 22.48 | 28.31 | 16.37 | 18.22 | 19.91 | 12.44 | 16.29 | 15.49 | 12.44 |
| Rajput | 8.87 | 13.33 | 15.49 | 13.76 | 13.7 | 13.27 | 11.56 | 15.49 | 15.11 | 14.03 | 14.03 | 13.33 |
| Bhumihar | 3.45 | 2.38 | 3.76 | 3.21 | 2.28 | 3.1 | 3.11 | 2.65 | 2.22 | 1.81 | 1.77 | 1.78 |
| Banya/Jain | 10.34 | 9.52 | 7.51 | 8.26 | 5.48 | 8.4 | 4.89 | 5.31 | 3.11 | 1.81 | 1.77 | 3.56 |
| Kayasth | 8.37 | 8.57 | 4.69 | 2.75 | 2.28 | 3.1 | 0.89 | 1.33 | 2.22 | 1.81 | 1.33 | 1.78 |
| Other | 2.46 | 2.87 | 4.23 | 5.05 | 1.83 | 3.98 | 2.21 | 2.21 | 3.1 | 1.36 | 0.89 | 1.78 |
| *Intermediate Castes* | 1 | 1.43 | 1.88 | 2.75 | 4.11 | 6.64 | 5.33 | 5.31 | 8.00 | 5.43 | 7.53 | 8.00 |
| Jat | 1 | 1.43 | 1.88 | 2.75 | 4.11 | 5.75 | 4.89 | 4.87 | 6.67 | 5.43 | 6.64 | 7.11 |
| Maratha | | | | | | 0.89 | 0.44 | 0.44 | 0.89 | | 0.89 | 0.89 |
| Other | | | | | | | | | 0.44 | | | |
| *OBC* | 4.45 | 5.24 | 7.98 | 9.64 | 10.1 | 13.3 | 13.74 | 11.1 | 20.87 | 22.6 | 24.8 | 23.56 |
| Yadav | 1 | 1.9 | 4.69 | 4.59 | 6.39 | 6.19 | 5.33 | 6.19 | 9.33 | 7.69 | 8.41 | 6.67 |
| Kurmi | 1.48 | 2.86 | 2.35 | 1.83 | 2.28 | 3.98 | 4.44 | 1.77 | 7.11 | 9.95 | 7.08 | 7.56 |
| Lodh | | | | | | | 0.44 | 0.44 | 1.78 | 1.36 | 1.77 | 1.78 |
| Koeri | | | | | | | 0.44 | | 0.44 | 0.91 | 0.44 | 1.33 |
| Gujjar | | | | | | | | 0.89 | 0.44 | 0.91 | 0.44 | 0.89 |
| Mali | | | | | | | 0.44 | 0.44 | 0.44 | 0.45 | 0.89 | |
| Panwar | | | | 0.46 | 0.46 | | 0.89 | | 0.44 | 0.91 | 0.44 | |
| Jaiswal | | | | | | | | | | | 0.89 | |
| Other | 0.49 | 0.48 | 0.94 | 2.76 | 0.92 | 3.09 | 1.76 | 1.32 | 0.89 | 0.45 | 4.41 | 5.32 |
| SC | 15.76 | 18.1 | 19.72 | 18.35 | 18.26 | 17.7 | 17.78 | 17.26 | 17.78 | 18.1 | 18.14 | 18.22 |
| ST | 5.42 | 6.9 | 7.04 | 7.8 | 7.31 | 7.08 | 7.56 | 7.52 | 7.56 | 8.14 | 7.52 | 7.56 |
| Muslim | 5.42 | 4.76 | 4.23 | 3.67 | 4.57 | 5.75 | 11.56 | 9.73 | 5.78 | 4.52 | 3.54 | 5.33 |
| Other minorities | 1.48 | 0.96 | 0.94 | 0.46 | 0.46 | 0.44 | 0.89 | 0.44 | 0.44 | 0.9 | 0.89 | 0.89 |
| Sadhu | | 0.47 | 0.46 | 0.46 | | | 0.44 | | | 0.9 | | |
| Unidentified | 2.96 | 4.76 | 2.82 | 1.38 | 1.3 | 0.89 | 0.89 | 2.21 | 0.89 | 1.36 | 2.21 | 0.89 |
| TOTAL | 100 | 100 | 100 | 100 | 100 | 100 | 100 | 100 | 100 | 100 | 100 | 100 |
| | N = 203 | N = 210 | N = 213 | N = 218 | N = 219 | N = 226 | N = 225 | N = 226 | N = 225 | N = 221 | N = 226 | N = 225 |

*Source:* Fieldwork.

to 20.5 per cent in Madhya Pradesh. In Bihar, the share of OBC MPs rose from 17 per cent to 43 per cent between 1984 and 1996. The figures concerning the Vidhan Sabhas confirm these trends. In Uttar Pradesh, the share of upper caste MLAs decreased from 58 per cent in 1962 to 37.7 per cent in 1996, whereas the proportion of OBCs grew from 9 per cent to 30 per cent in 1993—before declining to 24 per cent in 1996 due to the BJP's success (Jaffrelot and Zerinini-Brotel 1999: 80). In Madhya Pradesh, the share of upper caste MLAs decreased from 52 per cent in 1957 to 33 per cent in 1998, while the proportion of OBCs rose from 7 to 21 per cent (ibid.). In Bihar, the share of the upper castes in the state assembly decreased from 42 per cent in 1967 to 33 per cent in 1990, while that of the OBCs rose from 26 per cent to 35 per cent in the same period.[8]

The OBCs' rise to power, in conjunction with the increasing electoral participation of the lower castes, has been called a 'second democratic upsurge' by Yogendra Yadav, who further considers that 'The expression "OBC has . . . travelled a long way from a rather careless bureaucratic nomenclature in the document of the Constitution to a vibrant and subjectively experienced political community' (Yadav 1996: 96, 102). While the 'Mandalization' of Indian politics has certainly contributed to the democratization of a traditionally conservative democracy the capacity of OBCs to sustain the kind of unity that is needed in forming a 'political community' is very doubtful.

## Are the OBCs a Community?

In 1996, one member of the Uttar Pradesh Backward Classes Commission observed that 'Political change is now leading to social change. The OBC which was a constitutional category has now become a social category' (cited in Hasan 1998: 164). This comment, which reflects a widely held view, is questionable. While lower caste solidarity increased during the Mandal affair, when caste polarization was at an extreme, such solidarity has been declining since the mid-1990s.

### GRASSROOT MOBILIZATION OR YADAV MANIPULATION?

The rise of the OBCs is first of all the rise of the Yadavs and the Kurmis, as their share among the MPs testifies. Together, they represent about 15 per cent of north Indian MPs in the 1990s, as much as the Brahman or the Rajput MPs. Certainly, Table 22.1 shows almost graphically that, while the Yadavs and Kurmis alone had representatives in the Lok Sabha until the 1970s, new castes joined the political arena in the 1980s (Lodhs, Koeris, Gujars, Malis) and 1990s (such as the Jaiswals, the Telis, and the Kacchis—I have classified the latter two castes among the 'others' in Table 22.1). However, the share of the Yadavs and the Kurmis has grown too, so much so that each one of these castes represents about one-third of the OBC MPs of north India since 1989.

Even though the Kurmis organized themselves as early as the Yadavs through caste associations,[9] the Yadavs have been at the forefront of the OBC mobilization since the very beginning. The leader of the All-India Backward Caste Federation in the 1960s and 1970s, Brahm Prakash Chaudhury, was a Yadav. B.P. Mandal himself was a Yadav, and Yadav leaders have consistently paid greater interest to his report. After the Janata Dal took over in 1989, they mobilized in favour of implementing the Mandal Commission Report. Sharad Yadav, the Minister for Textile and Food Processing in V.P. Singh's government, was among the most vocal. After the anti-Mandal agitation started, he was at the forefront of the counter-mobilization in Delhi and elsewhere in the country, until he launched his Mandal Rath Yatra in late 1992 and early 1993 in reaction to the Supreme Court's decision regarding the exclusion of the 'creamy layer' of OBCs from the quotas. The Court used this expression to designate the elite among the OBCs who did not need any help from the State and, therefore, should not be entitled to any quotas. The Janata Dal, with Laloo Prasad Yadav as President and Sharad Yadav as leader of the legislative group in the Lok Sabha, then lobbied for excluding the well-off peasants from the 'creamy layer'. They were obviously defending the interests of their caste since many Yadavs had become relatively rich. Eventually, the pressure exerted by the Yadavs—and other OBC leaders—proved to be effective, and the 'creamy layer' was defined in a rather loose way. It comprised only the OBC applicants from establishment families, or those whose fathers owned land beyond 85 per cent of the actreage permitted by ceiling laws.

When the 27 per cent reservation was eventually implemented at the Centre after the Supreme Court decision of November 1992, the upper castes did not resist it any more. They resigned themselves to the rule of numbers. Moreover, the liberalization of the economy also began to make careers in the private sector, to which affirmative action laws did not apply, more attractive. Simultaneously, having won the battle over quotas, the lower castes did not feel an acute need for solidarity any more. The very notion of the OBCs started to lose its edge.

The general OBC category was, in fact, often used by a Yadav elite to promote its interests. Such an elite manipulation was not uncommon in the past since the *kisan* identity promoted by Charan Singh was also perceived by many Jats as a means to mobilize a large social base and Lohia had deplored it already in the 1960s: 'Ever and even again, the revolt of the down-graded castes has been misused to upgrade one or another caste . . .' (Lohia 1979: 90). Lohia had already seen the Yadavs as the main protagonists for such a strategy (ibid.: 103).

## YADAV POLITICS IN BIHAR AND UTTAR PRADESH

The way Yadav leaders used the Janata Dal reservation policy for promoting their caste interests is evident from the strategies of Mulayam Singh Yadav and Laloo Prasad Yadav after they became Chief Ministers, in November 1989 and March 1990, respectively, of Uttar Pradesh and Bihar. Mulayam Singh Yadav lost power in 1991 but governed the state again between 1993 and 1995. Laloo Prasad Yadav won both the 1990 and the 1995 state elections, and is still at the helm through his wife, Rabri Devi, who took over from him in 1997, when he was indicted for corruption in the infamous 'fodder scam'.

Even before V.P. Singh's reservation policy was announced, Mulayam Singh Yadav, the new Uttar Pradesh Chief Minister, had promulgated an ordinance providing the OBCs with a quota of 15 per cent in the state administration (Hasan 149). Though he came from the Lok Dal, Charan Singh's party, Mulayam Singh Yadav decided 'to place a far greater emphasis on the collective identity of the backward classes than the Lok Dal had ever done' (Duncan 1997: 262). That was well in tune with what Lohia had taught him in his early career. In fact, Yadav was initiated into politics by Lohia when the latter came to his village for a 'jat todo' (break caste) meeting (Lal and Nair 1998: 32). He then took part in the canal rate agitation launched by Lohia in 1954.

The Samajwadi Party—which Mulayam Singh Yadav founded after severing his links with the Janata Dal in 1990—contested the 1993 state elections in association with the Bahujan Samaj Party (BSP), a Dalit-led party, and highlighted the cleavage between the upper castes and the lower castes. Its election manifesto promised a quota of 27 per cent for the OBCs in the state administration, and it implemented the quota once Yadav became chief minister for the second time through the Uttar Pradesh Public Services (Reservation for Scheduled Castes, Scheduled Tribes and Other Backward Classes) Act of 1994. This new measure, while it was under discussion, was strongly resented in Uttarakhand where the OBCs represent only 2 per cent of the population. Yadav severely repressed this protest movement. His government at that point had only three 'representatives' of the upper castes but as many as twenty members of the OBCs and Dalits (and two Muslims) (Duncan 1997). Upper caste bureaucrats were transferred to non-essential posts. The number of Additional District Magistrates from the upper castes decreased from 43 (out of 63) to only thirteen in only six months. The Chief Secretary, a Brahman, was replaced by a Kayasth. These decisions, which were publicized on purpose, were partly made under the pressure of the BSP. But they accorded well with Mulayam Singh Yadav's strategy.

A similar scenario unfolded in Bihar. Already during the 1990 election campaign, the JD assured voters that it was the only party prepared to reserve posts

TABLE 22.2: Distribution, According to Caste, of
DMs and DDCs in Bihar in 1995

|  | *District Magistrates* | *Deputy Divisional Commissioners* |
|---|---|---|
| OBCs | 26 | 30 |
| Minorities | 4 | 4 |
| Forward Castes | 20 | 16 |
| TOTAL | 50 | 50 |

*Source: India Today,* 28 February 1995: 100–7.

for the OBCs in the State administration and at the Centre. Once voted to power, it increased the quota for the OBCs up to 27 per cent. In August 1993 the Patna University and the Bihar University Amendment Bill was passed, according to which 50 per cent of the seats would be reserved for the OBCs in the universities' senate and syndicate (Chaudhary 1999: 193). In 1993, a member of the Indian Administration Service (IAS) from the Scheduled Castes replaced a Brahman as Chief Secretary and an OBC took over the charge as Director General of Police from another Brahman. A large number of OBC bureaucrats were transferred from the sidelines to the main department, and the number of the District Magistrates (DM) and Deputy Divisional Commissioners (DDC) positions—two strategic positions—belonging to the OBCs increased. The number of OBC DMs and DDCs exceeded those from the upper castes (see Table 22.2).

In 1993 the Bihar Vidhan Sabha passed the Panchayati Raj Bill according to which 'the Panchayats with majority of the people belonging to backward classes will be reserved for them only and in these Panchayats upper castes will be debarred from even contesting elections' (ibid.: 226). This bill was unanimously passed by both houses of the state legislature.

The Yadavs benefited more than any other lower caste groups from the policies followed in Uttar Pradesh and Bihar, the two states in which they form the largest component of the OBCs with respectively 8.7 and 11 per cent of the state population (according to the 1931 census). In Bihar, the largest caste (after the Chamars) they had one-fifth of the MLAs in 1990 and more than one-fourth of the MPs in 1996. In Uttar Pradesh, where they form the third largest caste after the Brahmans and the Chamars with 8.7 per cent of the population (according to the 1931 census), they represented more than one-fourth of the MLAs in 1993 (as much as the Rajputs and more than the Brahmans).[10] The governments of Mulayam Singh Yadav and Laloo Prasad Yadav were more and more identified with the Yadavs, so much so that it became obvious that the notion of the OBCs had been used by this caste to its own advantage right from the beginning.

Of course, the Yadavs were likely to be among the first beneficiaries of the quotas because they are more numerous and relatively more educated than the other OBCs. But they were also favoured by the governments of Mulayam Singh and Laloo Prasad Yadav. In Uttar Pradesh, out of 900 teachers appointed by Mulayam Singh Yadav's second government, 720 were Yadavs. In the police forces, out of 3,151 newly selected candidates, 1,223 were Yadavs (*India Today*, 15 October 1999: 37). Such a policy alienated the BSP, the SP's ally, but also the Kurmis, the second largest OBC caste of the state, which was well represented in the BSP. Sone Lal Patel, the Secretary General of the party, who presided over the Uttar Pradesh branch of the All-India Kurmi Mahasabha, organized a Kurmi Rajnitik Chetna Maha Rally in Lucknow to protest against the Yadavization of the State one year after the formation of Mulayam Singh Yadav's government (*India Today*, 15 December 1994).

The SP does have Kurmi leaders, but it has not been able to project itself as a party representing the second largest OBC caste of Uttar Pradesh. In 1993, more than one-third of its MLAs were Yadavs (as against 8 per cent Kurmis) and in 1996, almost one-fourth (as against less than 3 per cent Kurmis) were Yadavs ( J. Zerinini-Brotel database). In 1996, a pre-assembly election opinion poll by the Centre for the Study of Developing Societies showed the extent to which the OBCs were politically divided in Uttar Pradesh. While 75 per cent of the Yadavs remained strongly behind the SP, the Lodhs supported the BJP of Kalyan Singh, a Lodh himself, and the Kurmis divided their votes chiefly between the BJP (37 per cent) and the BSP (27 per cent).[11] A *summa divisio* took shape within the OBCs, with the Lower OBCs (or Most Backward Castes) expressing a strong preference for the BJP and a more limited inclination in favour of the SP (25 per cent) and the BSP (19 per cent).

The BSP has thus become a strong contender for the vote of a substantial section of the OBC. In contrast with its Dalit image, in Uttar Pradesh and in Madhya Pradesh the party has gained some following among the OBCs and especially the Most Backward Castes (MBCs) (Jaffrelot 1998a). The poll showed that, while only 4 per cent of the Yadavs were prepared to vote for the BSP, 27 per cent of the Kurmis and 19 per cent of the 'lower backward' supported this party in Uttar Pradesh. Indeed, BSP's leader, Kanshi Ram, regarded the MBCs as his main target in 1996: 'There are 78 Most Backward Castes in Uttar Pradesh. 26 per cent of the UP population are from the MBCs and the maximum tickets I have given to the MBCs' (interview with Kanshi Ram, New Delhi, 12 November 1996). This strategy is well illustrated by the social profile of the BSP candidates in the 1996 Assembly elections: 30 per cent of the candidates were OBCs (more than half of them MBCs), whereas 29 per cent were Scheduled Castes, 16 per cent from the upper castes, and 16 per cent Muslims.[12]

The political division of the OBCs is also most obvious in Bihar where, again, the main cleavage is between Kurmis and Yadavs. In this state, too, the Kurmis resented Laloo's bias in favour of his caste fellows. For instance, Yadavs were appointed as heads of important boards such as the Bihar Public Service Commission, the Bihar Secondary Education Service Commission, the Bihar State Electricity Board, and the Bihar Industrial Development Corporation. Kurmi leaders felt sidelined, and one of the most prominent of them, Nitish Kumar, left the Janata Dal in 1994 and sponsored the creation of the Samata Dal along with George Fernandes. This party made an alliance with the BJP in the mid-1990s and cashed in on the Kurmi vote in all subsequent elections.

Obviously, the very notion of the OBCs as 'a political community' needs to be qualified because of the rivalry between major castes such as the Yadavs, the Kurmis and the Lodhs. Castes classified as OBCs might have coalesced in the early 1990s because of the Mandal affair, but this cementing force declined subsequently.

The internal divisions, however, do not mean that the rise of the lower castes can be taken lightly. They may not form a social—or even a political—category, and the *jatis* classified as OBCs may be divided themselves in their political choices, but the members of these castes have acquired a new political consciousness that leads them to vote more than before for candidates from their own milieu. This has forced political parties to pay more attention to the OBCs in selecting their candidates, instead of relying on rather old clientelistic and paternalist vertical linkages. The growing importance of the lower castes in the public sphere shows that they have gained a new influence. Even though he regretted the 'casteist' attitude of B.P. Mandal in 1967–8, Madhu Limaye drew similar conclusions from this episode:

> If the [socialist] caste policy had not been there, the factional abuse would have taken some other form. But this does not prove that the general policy was wrong. Throughout the zigzag and tortuous course of this policy, the rising consciousness among the Scheduled Castes, Scheduled Tribes and OBCs had been a fact of life. It was still not what Lohia called a 'resurrection of India—the destruction of caste'. . . . : Still it was a step forward of sorts towards equality. (Limaye 1998: 163–4)

## The BJP's Reluctant Mandalization

While Limaye's comment earlier may sound relevant even for today, one must finally consider the implications of the rise of Hindu nationalism for OBC politics. There is a kind of dialectic between both phenomena. Many upper caste people and non-OBC Shudras, like the Jats, became supporters of the BJP and took part in the Ayodhya movement because that was the only party that initially showed some reluctance towards caste-based reservations, while trying to subsume the lower castes versus upper castes cleavage by resorting to ethnoreligious propaganda.

The Hindu nationalist movement has always been known for its upper caste, even Brahmanical character. The Hindutva ideology relies on an organic view of society where castes are seen as the harmonious limbs of the same body (Jaffrelot 1996: Ch. 1). The RSS has concentrated on attracting to its local branches Hindus who valued this ethos, either because they belong to the upper castes or because they want to emulate them. The technique of 'conversion' of lower caste people to Hindutva relies on the same logic as what M.N. Srinivas called 'Sanskritization' (Srinivas 1995: 7).

However, the upper caste character of Hindu nationalism has gradually become a liability for the BJP because of the growing political consciousness of the lower castes. The 1993 election results, when the BJP lost both Uttar Pradesh and Madhya Pradesh partly because of the OBC and Dalit voters, led the party leaders to promote a larger number of lower caste people in the party apparatus.

K.N. Govindacharya, one of the BJP General Secretaries, was the main advocate of this policy, which he called 'social engineering'. Murli Manohar Joshi, a former president of the BJP, opposed this move and even implicitly questioned the notion of 'social engineering' in general by asking 'what social justice has been brought in the name of social engineering? Rural poverty has increased and most of the rural poor continue to be Dalits' (interview in *Sunday*, 26 January 1997: 13).

As the 1996 election approached, the party evolved a compromise between these conflicting views. The party's manifesto put a stress on social harmony[13] but also admitted that the existing quotas in favour of the Scheduled Castes and the OBCs could not be questioned 'till they are socially and educational [sic] integrated with the rest of society'. This compromise reflected the debate within the BJP between the advocates of 'social engineering' and those who wanted to abstain from acknowledging caste conflicts.

Up to the late 1990s, the BJP opted for what I have called 'indirect Mandalization' (Jaffrelot 1998b), that is, the making of alliances with parties representing lower castes (such as the Samata Party in Bihar or even the BSP in Uttar Pradesh). However, its leaders seem now prepared to resign themselves to a more direct brand of Mandalization, inducting a growing number of lower caste cadres in the party executive committees and the nomination of more OBC candidates at the time of elections. While the share of OBCs among the BJP MPs returned in the Hindi belt—the party's stronghold—is lower than among the Congress and Janata Dal's MPs, it increased from 16 per cent in 1989 to 20 per cent in 1998, while the proportion of its upper caste MPs dropped from 52.3 per cent in 1991 to 43.4 per cent in 1998 (Jaffrelot 2000). The state units of the BJP show the way. In Uttar Pradesh, even though the share of the OBCs among the BJP MLAs marginally increased from 18 per cent to 22 per cent from 1991 to 1996, the share of the OBCs in the governments of Kalyan Singh—himself a Lodh—jumped from 22 per cent in 1991 to almost 32 per cent in 1999 (Jaffrelot, Zerinini, and Chaturvedi (forthcoming)).

True, OBC candidates from the BJP are not projected as Backward Caste leaders, which is largely due to the Hindu nationalist ideology: the RSS and its offshoots insist on the need to put the emphasis on the Hindu sense of belonging to an organic community, the 'Hindu nation', rather than to particular castes. According to Uma Bharti, a prominent OBC leader of the BJP, the acceptance of such an outlook has given lower caste leaders of the BJP a 'Brahman's mentality'. She even complains that the 'BJP OBC candidates have an upper caste mentality. They do not show their caste' (interview with Uma Bharti, 12 February 1994).

However, the BJP has been led to co-opt an ever-increasing number of OBC and Scheduled Castes leaders from other parties, including the Samajwadi Party and the BSP, in order to cope with the need for 'Mandalizing' itself and in view of the rise of lower caste parties. Many of its cadres and election candidates do not have any RSS background today. On the contrary, they import 'subversive' references: for example, a BJP Scheduled Caste MLA from Agra West originally from the BSP adopts Ambedkar's discourse (interview with Ram Babu Harit, Agra, 3 November 1998), and an OBC MLA from Bhopal, even though trained in the RSS *shakhas,* displays the photograph of Lohia in his office and forcefully articulates egalitarian arguments (interview with Babulal Gaur, Bhopal, 23 October 1998). This dilution of the sanskritization ethos may well accentuate the 'Mandalization' of the BJP in the near future.

Traditionally, political mobilization against the urban, upper caste establishment has followed two routes in north India. One route—that of quota politics—came from Lohia, who attributed most of social inequality to caste and favoured affirmative action programmes. The other route—that of *kisan* politics—came from Charan Singh, who promoted peasants' solidarity against urban India. The former strategy eventually prevailed over the latter in the political arena when it was adopted by the Janata Dal. It proved to be doubly effective since, first, it emancipated the OBCs from the hegemonic strategy of the proponents of *kisan* politics—mainly the Jats whose interests did not fully coincide with that of the OBCs and, second, it contributed to getting an OBC vote-bank crystallized after the implementation of the recommendations of the Mandal Commission report, the most important decision ever made in the framework of the 'quota politics'. For the first time, lower caste people have started to vote en masse for leaders belonging to their own milieu. It means that the political class is changing with the replacement of an upper caste oligarchy by rather plebeian newcomers. This silent revolution has probably opened the second age of Indian democracy as Yogendra Yadav convincingly argued.

But the OBC phenomenon is also something of a myth because the Other Backward Classes do not represent a cohesive social category. There was unity when the battle lines were drawn over the Mandal Commission's recommendations, when the castes classified as OBCs had to mobilize to overcome the resistance from the upper castes. But this solidarity declined when the battle was won—partly because the upper castes gave up, all the more easily as the 1991 liberal turn opened for them better opportunities in the private sector than in the bureaucracy—and it soon appeared that the OBCs were stratified, the less backward of these caste groups, the Yadavs especially, instrumentalizing this category to promote their own interests. The policies of Mulayam Singh and Laloo Prasad, as well as the fragmentation of the so-called OBC vote, bear testimony of the cleavages between the castes classified as OBCs.

The rise of the OBCs has met another adversary in Hindu nationalism, which remains upper caste dominated and whose OBC politicians have little affinities with the value system of lower caste movements. The Hindu nationalist movement, however, is experiencing a tension between sanskritization and 'social engineering', a strategy which is leading the BJP to co-opt a larger number of OBC leaders without any RSS background among its election candidates; at the same time, those who have one, like Kalyan Singh or Babulal Gaur, are asserting themselves and tend to project themselves as lower caste leaders.

Obviously, the rise of the lower castes in north Indian politics, though substantial, will have a more transformative effect if two conditions can be fulfilled in the future: (1) if OBC leaders of the BJP take over the party apparatus on behalf of more egalitarian values, and (2) if the Most Backward Castes (MBCs) unite and gain their share of power against the dominant OBCs. The former move is very likely to be resisted by the RSS and, were it to happen, likely also to undermine the ideological cohesion of the *Sangh Parivar*. The latter possibility is one of the challenges before the lower caste parties.

They will have to overcome many more difficulties than their southern counterparts which have been pursuing this strategy for decades. In Tamil Nadu, for instance, the Dravida Kazhagam and its successors, the DMK and then the AIADMK, could rely on the Dravidian identity as a cementing force, since the Brahmans, who were smaller in number than in the north anyway, were seen as the Aryan invaders. By fighting them, the lower castes were promoting a regional identity transcending caste cleavages. Such an ideological basis is missing in the north, where the notion that the lower castes are descendants of the original inhabitants of India can never prevail in the same way. In the Hindi belt, lower caste discourse has always been influenced by the categories of sanskritization. For instance, the Ahirs (who call themselves 'Yadavs') and the Kachhis (who have adopted the name of another Rajput dynasty, the Kushwahas) claim a Kshatriya ancestry. Instead of developing horizontal solidarities, they are engaged in competition based on the criterion of status. Deprived of a common identity, the OBCs may join hands because of their growing awareness of common interests regarding the reservation policy, but this route is bound to be longer than the one used by the Dravidian parties.

## Notes

1. See his book *Khet Mazdoor* in Hauser 1994.
2. He tried to justify this stand in 1958 by saying: 'Let the backward castes ask for two or three shifts in schools and colleges, if necessary, but let them never ask for the exclusion of any child of India from the portals of an educational institution' (1979: 104).
3. This system, which had been established by the British, combined property rights and fiscal aspects: the zamindars, like the taluqdars and the jagirdars, were both landowners and tax agents since they collected the land revenue.
4. Charan Singh wrote this book while he was out of the Uttar Pradesh government. He had resigned in April 1959 because of several disagreements with Sampurnanand, the chief minister (Johnson 1975: 145).
5. Charan Singh spells out this point rather late in the book but it is his basic argument: 'Industrialization cannot precede but will follow agricultural prosperity. Surpluses of food production above farmers' consumption must be available before non-agricultural resources can be developed' (Singh 1959: 251).
6. Interview with P.S. Krishnan, New Delhi, 4 April 1998. P.S. Krishnan was Secretary to the Ministry of Social Welfare who prepared the implementation of the Mandal report recommendations for Ram Vilas Paswan.

7. The Bharatiya Kisan Union (BKU) was explicitly against caste-based quotas and favoured, like the BJP, an economic criterion for job reservations.
8. I am most grateful to Anand Kumar (CSSS, JNU) for providing me with these data.
9. On the Kurmis early entry into the public sphere, see Verma 1979 and on the Yadavs, Rao 1987.
10. I am most grateful to Jasmine Zerinini-Brotel for these figures.
11. *India Today,* 31 August 1996: 53; A. Mishra, 'Uttar Pradesh: Politics in flux', *Economic and Political Weekly,* 1 June 1996: 1300, and 'Uttar Pradesh—Kurmis and Koeris: Emerging 'Third' Factor', op. cit., 4 January 1997: 22–3.
12. These data have been compiled on the basis of lists published in *Bahujan Sangathak,* 11 November 1996.
13. The manifesto said: 'The task is nothing short of rekindling the lamp of our eternal *'Dharma,'* that *Sanatan* thought which our sages bequeathed to mankind—a social system based on compassion, cooperation, justice, freedom, equality and tolerance' (Bharatiya Janata Party 1996: 5).

## References

Bharatiya Janata Party (1996), *For a strong and prosperous India: Election Manifesto,* New Delhi.

Blair, Harry (1980), 'Rising Kulaks and Backward Classes in Bihar', *Economic and Political Weekly,* Vol. 15, No. 2, 12 January.

Brass, Paul (1980), 'The politicization of the peasantry in a North Indian state: Part 2', *The Journal of Peasant Studies,* Vol. 8, No. 1, pp. 3–36.

Brass, Tom (1995) (ed.), *New Farmers' Movements in India,* Ilford: Franck Cass.

Chaudhary, S.N. (1999), *Power-Dependence Relations: Struggle for Hegemony in Rural Bihar,* New Delhi: Har-Anand.

Duncan, Ian (1997), 'Agricultural Innovation and Political Change in North India', *The Journal of Peasant Studies,* Vol. 24, No. 4, pp. 246–65.

——— (1997), 'New Political Equations in North India: Mayawati, Mulayam and Government Instability in Uttar Pradesh', *Asian Survey.*

Gopal, Madan (1977), *Sir Chhotu Ram: A Political Biography,* Delhi: B.R. Publishing Corporation.

Government of India (n.d.), *The Constitution of India (As Modified up to the 15th August 1983),* n.p.

——— (1955), *Report of the Backward Classes Commission,* Vol. 1, Delhi.

——— (1980), *Report of the Backward Classes Commission,* Vols. 1 and 2, New Delhi.

———, *Constituent Assembly Debates, Lok Sabha Secretariat,* 1989, Vols. 1 and 2, New Delhi.

———, Ministry of Home Affairs, n.d., *Memorandum on the Report of the Backward Classes Commission,* Delhi.

Hasan, Zoya (1998), *Quest for Power: Oppositional Movements and Post-Congress Politics in Uttar Pradesh,* Delhi: Oxford University Press.

Hauser, Walter (1994) (ed.), *Sahajanand on Agricultural Labor and the Rural Poor,* Delhi: Manohar.

Jaffrelot, Christophe (1996), *The Hindu Nationalist Movement and Indian Politics: 1925 to 1990s,* New York: Columbia University Press.

—— (1998a), 'The Bahujan Samaj Party in North India: No Longer Just a Dalit Party?', *Comparative Studies of South Asia, Africa and the Middle East*, Vol. 18, No. 1.

—— (1998b), 'The *Sangh Parivar* between Sanskritisation and "Social Engineering"', in *The BJP and the Compulsions of Politics in India*, (ed.), Thomas Blom Hansen and Christophe Jaffrelot, Delhi: Oxford University Press.

—— (2000), 'Inde: De l'acclimatation du modèle anglais à la fin de la démocratic conservatrice', in *Démocraties d'ailleurs: Démocratie et démocratisation hors d'Occident*, ed. Christophe Jaffrelot, Paris: Karthala.

Jaffrelot, Christophe and Jasmine Zerinini-Brotel (1999), 'La montée des basses castes dans la politique nord-indienne', *Pouvoirs*, October, No. 90.

Jaffrelot, Christophe and Jasmine Zerinini-Brotel with Jayati Chaturvedi (forthcoming), 'The BJP and the Rise of the Dalits in Uttar Pradesh', in *Uttar Pradesh 2000*, (ed.), R. Jeffry and J. Lerche.

Johnson, M. (1975), 'Relation between Land Settlement and Party Politics in Uttar Pradesh', Ph.D. thesis, University of Sussex.

Lal, P. and Nair, T. (1998), *Caste vs Caste: Turbulence in Indian Politics*, Delhi: Ajanta.

Limaye, Madhu (1988), *Birth of Non-Congressism*, Delhi: B.R. Publishing Corporation.

—— (1997), 'Socio-economic Program of JP Movement', in *Evolution of Socialist Policy in India*, (ed.), S. Mohan et al., New Delhi: Bapu Kaldate.

Lohia, Rammanohar (1979 [1964]), *The Caste System*, Hyderabad: Rammanohar Lohia Samata Vidyalaya.

Mitra, R. (1992), *Caste Polarisation and Politics*, Patna: Syndicate Publications.

Mohan, Surendra, Hari Dev Sharma, Vinod Prasad Singh, and Sunilam (1997) (eds.), *Evolution of Socialist Policy in India*, New Delhi: Bapu Kaldate.

Mustafa, Seema (1995), *The Lonely Prophet: V.P. Singh, A Political Biography*, New Delhi: New Age International.

*National Front: Lok Sabha Elections 1989 Manifesto* (1989), V.P. Singh, Convenor, National Front, New Delhi.

Rao, M.S.A. (1987), *Social Movement and Social Transformation*, Delhi: Manohar.

Singh, Charan (1959), *Joint Farming X-Rayed: The Problem and Its Solution*, Bombay: Bharatiya Vidya Bhavan.

—— (1964), *India's Poverty and Its Solution*, New York: Asia Publishing House.

—— (1986), *Land Reforms in UP and the Kulaks*, Delhi: Vikas.

Singh, V.P. (1997), 'The Emergence of Janata Party: A Watershed in Post-independence Politics', in *Evolution of Socialist Policy in India*, (ed.), S. Mohan et al., New Delhi: Bapu Kaldate.

Srinivas, M.N. (1995 [1966]), *Social Change in Modern India*, New Delhi: Orient Longman.

Varshney, Ashutosh (1995), *Democracy, Development, and the Countryside: Urban, Rural Struggles in India*, Cambridge: Cambridge University Press.

Verma, K.K. (1979), *Changing Role of Caste Associations*, New Delhi: National Publishing House.

Yadav, Yogendra (1996), 'Reconfiguration in Indian Politics: State Assembly Elections 1993-95', *Economic and Political Weekly*, 13 January.

# Chapter 23

# The subordinate castes⬜revolution

India claims to be a democracy—indeed, the world's largest democracy—and there are serious reasons to accept that claim. It is certainly one of the few countries in the south to have established a stable parliamentary system with regular free and fair elections. One may object that India's democracy lacks substance, since the institutional mechanisms of the state are superimposed on a social system that is dominated by the logic of castes, which seems incompatible with the values of democracy. A normative commitment to equality, after all, would seem necessary for a 'real' democracy. This essay explores the explicit and growing role of caste-based political parties in India and how their commitment to affirmative action fits with the evolving Indian democratic polity.

In the classic Sanskrit literature dealing with castes, Hindu society is divided into four *varnas:* the Brahmans, the Kshatriyas, the Vaishyas, and the Shudras.[1] The 'Untouchables', who are now officially designated as Scheduled Castes (SCs), are not part of the *varna* system but exist beneath it. Their name reflects the fact that they not only occupy the bottom of society but suffer from the most pronounced stigma of impurity. Ritual purity is a key element of the system of *jatis*, which are the real castes, in contrast to the *varnas*, which ignore the Untouchables. The word *jati* derives from *jano*, 'to be born', and the endogamous nature of the *jati* system indeed reflects the name: one is born into the caste one's parents belong to. The *jatis* are organized in a hierarchical way based on their status, defined in terms of ritual purity along a continuum ranging from the Brahmans to the Untouchables.[2] This hierarchy of inherited statuses goes with economic activities. For instance, Brahmans avoid manual work as much as possible, especially if it implies forms of violence (as does agriculture, which destroys microorganisms); non-violence is a Brahmanical ideal that also manifests itself in a vegetarian diet. On the contrary, the Chamars, one of the main Untouchable *jatis*, are leather workers who are particulary impure because they not only treat organic matter but also work with cattle skin, and the cow is a sacred animal par excellence in Hinduism.

The rationale of caste does not lend itself to the egalitarian values of democracy but to the persistent domination of a small, ascriptive elite. Certainly, representative democracy does not imply that the assemblies reflect the composition of society like a mirror, but the exclusion of entire large groups over a long period of time is an insuperable impediment simply because the interests of large sections of the population are not defended efficiently. For decades in India, politicians coming from the upper layers of society and representing their interests have competed through different parties or factions and alternated in power in a kind of closed circuit. The large number of parties in competition in the political arena has masked a great social homogeneity: representatives of the social elite have always dominated the mainstream parties. India may therefore be a case of political democracy without any social democracy, because the plebeians have never been able to get access to political responsibilities, at least not in north India.

One needs to distinguish, indeed, the situation prevailing in the north from that of the south. The first sections of this essay will highlight this contrast between the south and the north, with a focus on the conservative overtone of the system institutionalized by the Congress Party, for many years the dominant party in India. Then the essay will examine the impact of affirmative action programmes in order to show that, while they were implemented in north India much later than in the south, they played a major role in the political mobilization of the lower castes there, especially after the Mandal affair of 1990. In this context, the essay will scrutinize the rise of the low-caste-dominated political parties in Uttar Pradesh and Bihar, their two main strongholds. The last section will qualify this phenomenon by arguing that, though all the political parties pay some lip service to the lower castes, they are not promoting their cause in the same way.

## The Progressive South: The Ethnicization of Caste and Affirmative Action

The over-representation of the social elite in the political sphere has always been more pronounced in the Hindi-speaking states than anywhere else. In the south, the upper castes lost ground early. There was an element of class in this diverging trajectory. The kinds of land settlement that the British introduced in India were not the same in these two areas. While the zamindari system (and its variants such as the taluqdari, malguzari, and jagirdari systems) prevailed in north India, the raiyatwari system was more systematically implemented in the south. In the north, when the colonizers went to levy estate taxes, they often used zamindars who had been established under the Mughal Empire; these intermediaries of the central authority, who were often upper caste Rajputs or Muslims of aristocratic dement of a tribute. They were recognized as landowners by the British in exchange for the privilege of collecting taxes in the rural area. In the south, where the Mughal administration had not been as powerful, the British did not find such a dense network of zamindars (or the equivalent). They tended to select individual farmers as land-proprietors and direct taxpayers. This raiyatwari system (from raiyat, 'cultivator') was more conducive to the formation of a relatively egalitarian peasantry than the zamindari system.

For another thing, these two megaregions have always had different caste profiles. In the Hindi belt, the caste system has traditionally been the closest to the *varna* model, with its four orders and its Untouchables. In the south, the twice-born are seldom 'complete', since the warrior and merchant castes are often absent or poorly represented. Correlatively, members of the upper *varnas* are fewer in the south than in the north: according to the 1931 census, they represented about 20 per cent of the population—including 10 per cent Brahmans—in the United Provinces (today Uttar Pradesh) and 24.2 per cent in Rajputana (today Rajasthan), whereas in the south, the proportion of the Brahmans and even of the other twice-born was and still is low. In Tamil Nadu and Andhra Pradesh, for instance, the Brahmans represented about 3 per cent of the population according to the 1931 census, and the other upper castes were marginal, which is still the case.

In addition, the caste system underwent an earlier and more significant change in south India. The caste system has often been analysed by anthropologists as one based on the typically Hindu notion of ritual purity, which explains the domination by the custodians of this value system, the Brahmans, who occupy the most prestigious position in the social order. This hierarchical arrangement explains the central role played by Sanskritization, a practise that M.N. Srinivas has defined as 'the process in which a "low" Hindu caste, or tribal or other group, changes its customs, ritual, ideology and way of life in the direction of a high, and frequently, "twice-born caste" that is the Brahmans, but also the Kshatriyas or even the Vaishyas' (Srinivas 1995: 6). By adopting the most prestigious features of the upper castes' ethos, the lower castes explicitly acknowledge their social inferiority.

Things changed early in the south, primarily in reaction to the census operations organized by the British and their decision to establish the rankings of the castes (*jatis*) within the *varnas*. Caste associations were created to put pressure on the administration in order to improve the castes' rank in the census tables. This move was in keeping with the logic of Sanskritization, since the objective was not to opt out of the system but to rise within it according to its own rules and values. However, caste associations became secularized when the British started to classify castes on, for instance, the basis of the concept of martial races in order to recruit these groups into the colonial army. The associations also claimed new advantages from the state through quotas in the education system and in the administration. Caste associations therefore became interest groups.[3] In terms of social transformation, the most remarkable achievement of these associations concerns the unity of the caste groups. They have successfully incited the subcastes to adopt the same name in the census and to break the barriers of endogamy, a process that was especially successful in the south.[4] S. Barnett has convincingly argued that this kind of fusion tended to transform castes into ethnic groups (Barnett 1977: 401). This evolution was consummated with the claim by the lower castes of south India that they were Dravidians, a community with distinctive language and common racial bonds.

The primary implication of this ethnicization of caste lies in its provision of alternative, non-hierarchical social imaginaries with a remarkable emancipatory potential. During the Madras Presidency, the low caste leaders launched a non-

Brahman movement that portrayed the lower castes as the original inhabitants of India (Geetha and Rajadurai 1998: 43). The movement obviously drew its inspiration from British Orientalism, since Reverend Caldwell (1819–91) had already suggested that Brahmans were colonizers whereas the original inhabitants had been Dravidians who spoke Tamil, Telugu, and so forth (Ram 1979: 377–402). This identity-building process crystallized with Ramaswami Naicker, alias Periyar, who founded the Self-Respect movement in the 1920s and the Pravidar Kazhagam in 1944. These organizations attracted low caste people as well as Untouchables into a kind of Dravidian front.

Affirmative action programmes played a key role in the making of the Dravidian movement. The British implemented their first affirmative action measures during the Madras Presidency in the 1870s in order to promote the education of what they called the Backward Classes. While the list of Backward Classes increased and widened from 39 to 131 communities in the 1920s, the Untouchables claimed the right to be treated as a distinct class, which led to the 1925 decision to parse out the 'backward' designation between Depressed Classes (Untouchables and tribals) and Castes Other than Depressed Classes (Radhakrishnan 1990: 509–17). In addition to establishing quotas in the education system that favoured the Backward Classes, the British reserved a large number of seats (28 out of 65) for the much larger 'non-Brahman' category in the framework of the 1919 constitutional reform. This measure helped the Justice Party—an explicitly anti-Brahman party—to win the 1920 elections. The new government immediately developed a third area of affirmative action, the establishment of quotas in the administration. The First Communal Government Order, in 1921, asked the chiefs of all administrative services, the collectors, and the district judges to issue every six months a list of their recruits classified into six categories: Brahmans, non-Brahman Hindus, Christian Indians, Muslims, Europeans and Anglo-Indians, and others.[5] From the second half of 1921, a readjustment took place as the administration recruited 22 per cent of its staff from Brahmans, 48 per cent from non-Brahman Hindus, 10 per cent from Christian Indians, 15 per cent from Muslims, 2 per cent from Europeans and Anglo-Indians, and 3 per cent from other groups. This move by the Justice Party's government confirmed that the quest for empowerment was one of the driving forces sustaining the non-Brahman movement in Madras. The movement exemplifies the way affirmative action helped forge a coalition of a wide array of castes. The scope of this coalition, however, must not be exaggerated. The Panchamas (an Untouchable caste), for instance, were left out by the Justice Party as soon as it gained power; the other, higher-level non-Brahmans had used them for electoral power gain only to drop them soon after (Irschick 1969: 188, 192).

The rise to power of the Dravidian/non-Brahman movement challenged the Congress Party to democratize itself to retain power. As everywhere else, the party had been dominated by Brahmans. In the 1930s, however, Congress leaders began to realize that the Justice Party and the self-respect movement were forces to reckon with. They made 'attempts to incorporate even the lowliest groups under their leadership' (ibid.: 145). They focused first on the lowest castes, the Untouchables, but they were also able to attract other low castes such as the Nadars. The rise to power of Kamaraj Nadar epitomized this new, accommodating attitude of the Congress Party. C. Rajagopalachari, a Brahman, was then the towering figure of the Congress in Tamil Nadu. He became chief minister in 1937 and again in 1947, but Kamaraj succeeded him in 1954. At that time, the Brahmans represented only 5 per cent of the members of the legislative assembly (MLAs), compared with 17.2 per cent in 1937 (Saraswati 1974; Baker 1976: 586) which means that by the early 1950s the representation of the Brahmans in the assembly was almost proportionate to their population share.

## North India: The Resilience of Sanskritization and Conservative Democracy Under the Congress Raj

In this chapter, north India is most often used as a synonym for the 'Hindi belt'. One may wonder to what extent the six states of the Hindi belt—Uttar Pradesh, Bihar, Madhya Pradesh, Rajasthan, Haryana and Delhi—form a relevant unit. As mentioned above, these areas had a type of land settlement in common (since the zamindari system prevailed in most of these places) and had the same kind of caste system (since the twice-born were all represented and were in large numbers). Another feature was the comparatively high proportion of princely states: two of the most important states of the Hindi belt, Rajasthan and Madhya Pradesh, were largely born from the merging of former princely states. These were all factors inhibiting the forces of social change.

In this context, the caste system did not change in the way it had in the south. Caste associations did not prepare the ground for any significant ethnicization process but instead remained within the framework of Sanskritization, partly because of the influence of the Arya Samaj. This socio-religious reform movement, for instance, canvassed for the adoption of the sacred thread by the Yadavs, cowherds who form the largest Shudra *jati* in Uttar Pradesh and Bihar. In so doing, the Arya Samaj sought to empower lower castes socially by including them in the Hindu twice-born groups, signified by the sacred thread. But the organization was still paying allegiance to the traditional caste structure. The Arya Samajists also enrolled the Yadavs in the cow protection movement. This movement, initiated in 1893 and relaunched at several points during the first two decades of the twentieth century, attracted many Yadavs who were anxious to emulate the upper castes (Pandey 1983: 104). The propensity of the Yadavs toward Sanskritization is evident from their attempt to 'Aryanize' their history. The first history of the Yadavs was written by Kithal Krishna Khedekar in the late nineteenth century. This work was finalized by his son, R.V. Khedekar, and published in 1959 under the title *The Divine Heritage of the Yadavs*. The book situates the origins of the Yadavs in the Abhiras and then in the ruling dynasties mentioned as Yadavs in the *Mahabharata* and the Puranas. The caste history tries to demonstrate that the Abhiras were of Aryan origin and that Rewari was the last representative of the Abhira kingdoms (Michelutti 1996: 16). This narrative certainly aims at giving the Yadavs an ethnic identity, but in this case the ethnicization process is embedded in the Sanskritization logic. In contrast to the lower caste leaders of south India who tried to invent a Dravidian identity that presented the Shudras and Untouchables as the original inhabitants of the country against the Aryans, the Yadavs claim that they are Aryans in order to enhance their status within caste society.

The Untouchables of north India were also exposed to the influence of the Arya Samaj at the turn of the twentieth century. This is evident from the Jatav movement in Uttar Pradesh. The Jatavs are Chamars, untouchable leather workers, who claimed descent from the Yadu race, which allegedly entitled them to be known as Kshatriyas, like the Yadavs; once again, the Arya Samaj missions were responsible for propagating these views. They were especially successful through their schools among the sons of Agra Chamars who had become rich in the leather trade (Lynch 1969: 68–9). The Jatav Mahasabha, which was founded in Agra in 1917, preached moral reform, vegetarianism, teetotalism, and temperance to achieve a cleaner life and higher status. The resilience of Sanskritization helped the upper caste to maintain its social hegemony and its political domination of the Congress Party.

Upper caste notables remained the backbone of the Congress Party's network, and for decades the social deficit of democracy in north India resulted from the clientelistic politics of this party. The Congress selected its candidates from among vote-bank 'owners', who were often upper caste landlords or businessman who could gather the support of those who depended on them at election time (Weiner 1967: 15). Many of the landlords were former rulers (maharajas or nawabs). The typically Indian notion of vote-banks is a key element in this pyramid of power. The system has been convincingly defined as depending on the votes 'that can be delivered by local potentates acting as political intermediaries between the parties and the electorate, and a personalised and particularistic structure of political support' ('Voting Behaviour in a Developing Society: A Working Paper,' in *Party System and Election Studies* 1967: 280). This sociopolitical domination relied on class relations[6] but also on caste, since the 'personalised' rapport in question had to do with reverence and fear vis-à-vis the superior. Class and caste largely coincided in this power structure. The clientelistic dimension of the Congress fit with the vertical arrangement of society, as is evident from the caste background of the Members of Parliament (MPs) from the Hindi belt in the 1950s and 1960s. As shown in Table 23.1, in 1952, 64 per cent of the MPs belonged to upper castes, and that was still the case of 55.5 per cent of them in 1967; over the same period, the intermediate and low castes rose from 5.5 per cent to only 12.5 per cent of the total and the Scheduled Castes and Tribes rose from 21 per cent to 26 per cent because of reservations.[7] Like the SCs (the official designation for the Untouchables), the Scheduled Tribes (STs—the official

TABLE 23.1: CASTE AND COMMUNITY OF THE MPs ELECTED IN
THE HINDI BELT, 1952–67 (IN %)

| Castes and communities | 1952 | 1957 | 1962 | 1967 |
|---|---|---|---|---|
| Upper castes | 64.00 | 58.60 | 54.90 | 55.50 |
| Intermediate castes and OBCs | 5.45 | 6.67 | 9.86 | 12.39 |
| SCs/STs | 21.18 | 25.00 | 26.76 | 26.15 |
| Muslims | 5.42 | 4.76 | 4.23 | 3.67 |
| | N = 203 | N = 210 | N = 213 | N = 218 |

*Source:* Database compiled by the author on the basis of interviews.

*Note:* This table relies on the figures concerning Uttar Pradesh, Bihar, Rajasthan, Madhya Pradesh, Delhi, Chandigarh, and the Hindi-speaking districts of Punjab (which were to form Himachal Pradesh and Haryana).

designation for the tribal population) benefit from quotas in proportion to their number.

In spite of these quotas, the SCs and STs were marginalized in north India after independence, preventing them from emerging as a political force, as the fate of Bhim Rao Ambedkar's political parties testifies. Ambedkar, the first pan-Indian leader of the SCs, launched three political parties: the Indian Labour Party (1936), the Scheduled Castes Federation (1942), and the Republican Party of India, whose concept he defined just before he died in 1956. None of these parties really took off. First, they did not succeed in transcending the deep cleavages that divided the SCs. Therefore, the parties remained confined to one or two groups, such as the Jatavs in north India and the Mahars—Ambedkar's caste—in Maharashtra. Second, the Congress had become adept at co-opting SC leaders who were known for their moderation, such as Jagjivan Ram in Bihar, or who toned down their militancy once they were accommodated in the power structure, such as B.P. Maurya in Uttar Pradesh. This strategy was one of the reasons the Congress succeeded in attracting SC voters who tended to cast their votes for individuals and follow their advice, irrespective of the party they belonged to. As a result, the ruling party tended to attract voters who were poles apart in the social structure and presumably in their political interests: besides a large number of members of the upper castes (especially Brahmans), many SC people voted for the party. For this reason, the Congress support base has been presented as a 'coalition of extremes' (Brass 1980: 3–36).

Naturally, the parties that were competing with the Congress indicted this approach to society and politics. Historically, in north India, two kinds of strategies have prevailed among those who have attempted to dislodge the upper caste, urban establishment from its position of power. The first strategy concentrated on the mobilization of peasants (*kisans*). It was initiated by members of cultivating castes, such as Chhotu Ram—a Jat—in Punjab in the 1920s–1940s and Swami Sahajanand—a Bhumihar—who became a leading figure of the Bihar Kisan Sabha in the 1930s. The second strategy relied more on caste identity and was primarily articulated by socialist leaders such as Rammanohar Lohia, who regarded caste as the main obstacle to an egalitarian society. While the 'kisan school' endeavoured to gather all those engaged in cultivation on the basis of socioeconomic demands, the caste-oriented socialists attempted to form an alliance of nonelite groups on the basis—mainly of affirmative action techniques: they asked for caste-based quotas, especially in the administration, in favour of the Other Backward Classes (OBCs). Indeed, affirmative action played a key role in the polities mobilization of the lower castes in north India.

## The Political Impact of Affirmative Action

Under the British Raj, as the Madras Presidency played a pioneering role in the making of the policies of affirmative action, the central administration gradually moved in the same direction and eventually tried to harmonize the local classifications. The time-honoured expression the central government used to designate the lower and intermediate castes had first been Depressed Classes, a group for which seats in local and national assemblies were reserved from 1919 on. However, after the 1935 Government of India Act, the Untouchables were designated as SCs, and the denomination spread throughout the provinces of British India. The Untouchables continued to be designated as SCs even after independence, when the lower castes were designated as OBCs. While the former received a quota of 15 per cent—their share in the general population—in the education system, the assemblies, and the administration, the latter were not treated the same way. Their very definition was a problem, as evident by the use of the word *class* instead of *caste* in 'Other Backward Classes', though the term was used to designate the lower castes other than the SCs. How is it that caste was the relevant criterion for identification in one case and class in the other? One must go back to the Constituent Assembly debates to understand this.

On 13 December 1946, Jawaharlal Nehru, in his first speech before the Constituent Assembly on his objectives resolution, announced that special measures were to be taken in favour of 'minorities, backward and tribal areas and depressed and other backward classes' (*Constituent Assembly Debates*, Vol. 1, 1989: 59 [hereafter *CAD*]). He did not elaborate further and, interestingly, senior Congressmen such as K.M. Munshi resisted any effort to clarify what these OBCs were (ibid., Vol. 7: 697). Article 340 of the Indian Constitution, voted on 26 January 1950, stated, 'The President [of the Republic] can by decree nominate a Commission formed by persons he considers to be competent to investigate, within the Indian territory, on the condition of classes suffering of backwardness as well in social as in educational terms, and on the problems they meet, the way of proposing measures which could be taken by the Central or a State Government in order to eliminate difficulties and improve their condition.'

The first Backward Classes Commission was appointed on 29 January 1953, under the chairmanship of a former disciple of Mohandas K. Gandhi, Kaka Kalelkar

(Report of the Backward Classes Commission, 1955, Vol. 1). Its report relied heavily on the concept of caste to define the OBCs, so much so that it established a list of 2,399 castes representing about 32 per cent of the Indian population, that formed the bulk of the 'socially and educationally backward classes'. The OBCs' were therefore defined as those castes that, in the Indian social system are situated above the Untouchables but below the upper castes and the intermediate castes that are predominantly made up of peasant-proprietors. The OBCs form the bulk of the Shudras, and their professional activity often consists of working in the field or as artisans. In order to redress the socioeconomic and educational malaise of the OBCs, the Kalelkar Commission formulated two main recommendations. First, the OBCs should benefit from a 70 per cent quota in technical education institutions [including the disciplines of applied sciences, medicine, agriculture, veterinary studies, and engineering (ibid.: 125)]. Second, quotas had to be reserved for them in the central and state administrations: 40 per cent of the vacancies in classes III and IV, 33.3 per cent in class II, and 25 per cent in class I (ibid.: 140). The Indian administration is divided into four categories—like the *varna* system—ranging from the elitist class I, where one finds the Indian Administrative Service, to the plebian class IV, where one finds sweepers, who come mostly from the SCs.

The report was rejected by Nehru's government. G.B. Pant, the home minister, objected that 'with the establishment of our society on the socialist pattern . . . , social and other distinctions will disappear as we advance towards that goal' (Memorandum on the Report of the Backward Classes Commission, n.d., 2). He also disapproved of the use of caste as the most prominent criterion for identifying the Backward Classes. He considered that 'the recognition of the specified castes as backward may serve to maintain and even perpetuate the existing distinctions on the basis of caste' (ibid.). The report was presented before Parliament accompanied by a memorandum by Pant on 3 September 1956, but was not even discussed (Report of the Backward Classes Commission: First Part, 1980, Vols. 1 and 2: 2). In May 1961, the Nehru government decided that there was no need for an all-India list of the OBCs and that consequently there would be no reservation policy for them at the Centre. Even though they were responsible for Article 340 of the Constitution, Congress people were obviously reluctant to cater to the needs of the lower castes, either because of sheer conservatism or because of a deliberate negation of the role of caste as opposed to the Marxist category of class. They did support positive discrimination programmes in favour of the SCs, probably because these were in the most pitiable condition and because they would not be in a position to pose a threat to the upper caste establishment even after the implementation of such programmes. In fact, this policy enabled the Congress Party to patronize SC leaders in a clientelistic manner.

The socialists—especially the followers of Lohia—remained the main proponents of affirmative action in favour of the OBCs. The adepts of *kisan* politics, including Charan Singh, were also gradually attracted to it to a lesser extent (Jaffrelot 2000: 86–108). Over the last decades, these two groups have contributed to the rise of middle caste peasants and then of the OBCs in north Indian politics. The first significant changes occurred in the 1960s when the middle castes and OBCs massively entered the Bihar and Uttar Pradesh legislative assemblies under the auspices of the socialist parties and Charan Singh. *Kisan* politics asserted itself in the 1970s and 1980s, thanks to Charan Singh and his lieutenants. The two traditions merged in 1977 in the Janata Party.

On 20 December 1978, Prime Minister Morarji Desai announced the government's decision to appoint the Second Backward Classes Commission, whose terms of reference were close to those of the first one: it had to determine the criteria defining the OBCs and to recommend measures, such as reservations in the administration, that could contribute to their social uplift (Report of the Backward Classes Commission, First Part, vii). In contrast to the Kalelkar Commission, this commission did not include any members of the upper castes; it included only OBC members, three out of five of whom were MPs or ex-MPs. The chairman of the commission, Bindhyeshwari Prasad Mandal, was a Yadav who had been elected MP in Bihar in 1967 on a socialist ticket and who had been chief minister of this state for a month in 1968. He played an important part in the Janata Party and in 1980 he became a member of the party's central election committee. Unsurprisingly, the Mandal Commission advocated the socialist approach of affirmative action: 'To treat unequals as equals is to perpetuate inequality. When we allow weak and strong to compete on an equal footing, we are loading the dice in favour of the strong and holding only a mock competition in which the weaker partner is destined to failure right from the start' (ibid.: 21).

The Mandal Commission argued that in India the caste system was the root cause of structural inequality. It had therefore no inhibition against recognizing caste as the main factor in the backwardness of the OBCs. The members of the commission considered that this social category was made up of castes—mostly of low ritual status[8]—that represented 52 per cent of the Indian population. After identifying the OBCs, the Mandal Commission investigated their needs and recommended in its report that 27 per cent of the posts in the central administration and in public sector undertakings should be reserved for them. This recommendation reflected an Ambedkarite and socialist-like approach of compensatory discrimination, since the objective was to give the OBCs access to power, not to give them jobs. The report read, for instance, 'By increasing the representation of OBCs in government services, we *give them an immediate feeling of participation in the governance of this country*' (Report of the Backward Classes Commission, First Part, 57. Emphasis mine).

The report was submitted to Indira Gandhi's government in December 1980, but it was not laid on the table of the Lok Sabha until 30 April 1982, and then there was barely a quorum in the house, a clear indication of the ruling party's priority. The most vehement speakers were MPs from the Lok Dal, the party Charan Singh had created some time after the breakup of the Janata Party. One of them, Chandrajit Yadav, emphasized that the main finding of the Mandal

Commission Report was that 'the other backward classes constituted 52 per cent of our population' (*Lok Sabha Debates*, 1982, Vol. 31, Col. 359). OBC leaders were obviously realizing that the 'community' was in a majority and could form an Unbeatable constituency. The seniormost representative then in the house, Defence Minister R. Venkataraman, considered that the Mandal Commission Report, which had identified 3,743 castes, contradicted the findings of the Kalelkar Commission, which 'identified somewhere 2,000 and odds' such castes. A few days after the Lok Sabha debate, the Home Minister, Giani Zail Singh, gravely declared that 'the Central Government have forwarded the Report of the Commission to the various State Governments for obtaining their views' (*Memorandum Explaining Action Taken on the Report of the Second Backward Classes Commission*, 1982: 5–6). That was the only action taken by the Congress.

The presentation of the Mandal Commission Report before the Lok Sabha marked the partial conversion of Charan Singh to the notion of quota politics. In 1982 he held a meeting outside the Lok Sabha to put pressure on the MPs for the adoption of the report's recommendations, however, the Lok Dal was not in a position to continue its fight for the implementation of the Mandal Report. There were many reasons for this: First, *kisan* leaders were not interested in demanding the implementation of the Mandal Commission Report when they did not belong to an OBC caste. The Jats, for instance, were in this situation. Second, the party was increasingly suffering from caste-based differences. In 1987, the split of the Lok Dal into two parties—Lok Dal (A) and Lok Dal (B)—resulted partly from the desire of Yadav leaders; such as Mulayam Singh Yadav, who joined Lok Dal (B), to emancipate themselves from Jat tutelage. The tension remained prevalent within the Janata Dal, but this party's policy consummated the triumph of quota politics, not only within the party but at an all-India level. In fact, what was at stake was north India: in the south, the upper castes had already been displaced from their seat of power, while in the north this process really began in the late 1980s within the framework of affirmative action policies.

## THE JANATA DAL AND THE EMPOWERMENT OF
## THE OBCs IN THE HINDI BELT

Twenty years after the first Janata experiment, a second one started with the rise to power of the Janata Dal in 1989. Once again, this success was due to north Indian voters: 101 of the 143 seats won by the Janata Dal came from the four largest states of the Hindi belt. It was a significant achievement for a party that had been founded one year before, on 11 October 1988. But the Janata Dal had not been developed from scratch. In north India, it relied on the local network of the Janata Party, the Lok Dal (A) of Ajit Singh and the Lok Dal (B) of Devi Lal— another Jat leader who had taken over the party and become chief minister of Haryana. All these parties merged in the Janata Dal. While the Janata Party had been a heterogeneous coalition-like party whose followers ranged from socialists to Hindu nationalists, the Janata Dal primarily amalgamated only two currents of Indian politics, that of the socialists and that of Charan Singh.

The discourse of the party chief, V.P. Singh, was heavily loaded with socialist references. The 1989 National Front election manifesto promised that 'implementation of reservation policy will be made effective in government, public and private sector industrial undertakings, banking institutions, etc., by resorting to special recruitment drives so as to fulfil their quotas within the shortest possible time' (Singh 1989: 26) and that 'the recommendations of the Mandal Commission will be implemented expeditiously' (ibid.: 27). V.P. Singh became prime minister in December 1989, and he announced this decision in a one-and-a-half-page suo motu statement in both houses of Parliament on 7 August 1990. He justified it in his Independence Day address on 15 August by the need to give 'a share to the poor in running the Government' (Sharma, Singh and Sunilam 1997: 360). As the Mandal Commission had, he looked at the administration as a power institution: 'Bureaucracy is an important organ of the power structure. It has a decisive role in decision-making. We want to give an effective here [*sic*] in the power structure and running of the country to the depressed, downtrodden and backward people' (ibid.: 361).

This approach could not please the proponents of *kisan* politics. All the Jat ministers strongly objected to the notion that their caste should be included on the list of OBCs.[9] A signature campaign was organized among the MPs and 107 signatures were collected from Jat and Muslim leaders who also wanted some of their coreligionists to be recognized as OBCs (Rashid Masood, interview by the author, New Delhi, 28 October 1998). V.P. Singh made a vague promise but refused to dilute the Mandal scheme. He announced the implementation of the Mandal Commission Report only a few days after Devi Lal resigned from his government.

The new quota of 27 per cent did not represent many jobs. Of the 204, 288 recruitments that had been made in 1988, 55,158 jobs would have been given to members of OBCs according to the new reservation policy. In fact, the number of posts was declining (from 2,26,781 in 1985 to 2,04,288 in 1988) whereas the candidates were more and more numerous [from 2.4 million in 1985 to 2.9 million in 1988 (*India Today*, 15 September 1990: 36–7)]. But the quota was for that very reason even more strongly resented by the upper caste people who regarded administration as their—already shrinking—monopoly. In 1980, the OBCs represented 12.55 per cent of the central services and the SCs and STs 18.72 per cent (the OBCs represented less than 5 per cent in class I services, as against the high castes' 90 per cent).[10] Besides, quotas for the SCs and STs often remained unfilled.

Soon after V.P. Singh announced the implementation of the Mandal Commission Report, upper caste students set up organizations such as the Anti-Mandal Commission Forum, based at Delhi University. The agitation started in Delhi, where students burned degrees, carried away the corpse of 'merit', and damaged about 60 buses on 24 August 1990 (Prasad 1997: 58–9). Generally speaking, north India was the epicentre of this agitation not only because of the upper caste students' mobilization but also because of the behind-the-scenes activities of the Bharatiya Janata Party (BJP), the Congress Party, and Devi Lal in Haryana. Immediately after the first anti-Mandal demonstrations, leaders from the Janata Dal organized a countermobilization. V.P. Singh went to Patna for a rally at which slogans such as 'Brahman saala desh chhado!' (Bastard Brahman, get out of the country!) were shouted. Thus, 1990 was marked by an exacerbation of the cleavage between upper and lower castes, an atmosphere that explains the emotional value of the OBCs as a social category at that time. The main achievement of V.P. Singh was therefore to make a broad range of castes coalesce under the OBC label and, consequently, to contest the elite groups' domination more effectively than before. 'Other Backward Classes' had become a relevant category for the lower castes because they had a vested interest in it, namely, the quotas promised by the Mandal Commission Report. Many of those who had been known as Shudras had internalized this administrative definition of their identity in the early 1990s simply because they thought they could derive benefits from it. However, the category also crystallized because of the attitude of the upper castes that had rejected reservations in the administration. The cleavage between upper and lower castes had suddenly been reinforced by a collective, open hostility on the part of the former and even by the unleashing of violence. The low castes began to share a political identity that was expressed in terms of the OBCs versus the upper castes: caste had become the building block of a larger social coalition.

The OBC phenomenon helped the low castes to organize themselves as an interest group outside the vertical, clientelistic Congress-like pattern. This enabled the low castes to benefit from their main asset, their massive numbers, at the time of elections. A similar process had already taken place in the south. In states such as Tamil Nadu, Andhra Pradesh, and Karnataka, the upper castes had been dislodged from power in the 1960s and 1970s. Their demographic weakness had been largely responsible for their decline, whose main beneficiaries had been 'upper

TABLE 23.2: CASTE AND COMMUNITY OF THE MPs ELECTED
IN THE HINDI BELT, 1980-99 (IN %)

| Castes and communities | 1984 | 1989 | 1991 | 1996 | 1998 | 1999 |
|---|---|---|---|---|---|---|
| Upper castes | 46.90 | 38.20 | 37.11 | 35.30 | 34.67 | 30.90 |
| Intermediate castes | 5.31 | 8.00 | 5.43 | 7.53 | 8.89 | 6.40 |
| OBCs | 11.10 | 20.87 | 22.60 | 24.80 | 23.56 | 22.20 |
| SCs | 17.26 | 17.78 | 18.10 | 18.14 | 18.22 | 17.80 |
| STs | 7.52 | 7.56 | 8.14 | 7.52 | 7.56 | 7.30 |
| Muslims | 9.73 | 5.78 | 4.52 | 3.54 | 5.33 | 5.00 |
| | N = 226 | N = 225 | N = 221 | N = 226 | W = 225 | N = 221 |

Source: Database compiled by the author on the basis of interviews.

Shudras', such as the Kammas and the Reddys in Andhra Pradesh. In this state, the percentage of Brahman MLAs declined from 7.6 per cent in 1957 to 4 per cent in 1978, while that of the upper Shudras rose from 36 per cent to 39 per cent and that of the OBCs from 13 per cent to 19 per cent.[11] The transition in the Hindi belt began only in the late 1990s, as Table 23.2 shows. Indeed the percentage of OBC MPs from north India increased in the late 1980s and early 1990s because low caste people had become more aware of their common interests and had decided not to vote any longer for upper caste candidates but instead to cast their ballots for those from their own social milieu. Now, the OBCs represent 52 per cent of society and form in many constituencies an unbeatable majority.

The percentage of OBC MPs from north India doubled from 11.1 per cent in 1984 to 20.9 per cent in 1989, largely because the Janata Dal, the winner of the ninth general elections, had offered a larger number of candidacies within the party to OBC candidates. The proportion of upper caste MPs fell below 40 per cent for the first time. Interestingly, the percentage of OBCs among the MPs continued to grow in 1991, in spite of the Congress Party's comeback, and in 1996, when the BJP became the largest party in the Lok Sabha. This evolution took place at the expense of the upper castes, because all the political parties were now giving larger numbers of tickets to OBC candidates. That was precisely the goal V.P. Singh had been pursuing. He was to declare in a lecture at Harvard University, 'Now that every party is wooing the deprived classes, with every round of elections more and more representatives of the deprived sections will be elected. This will ultimately be reflected in the social composition of the local bodies, state governments, and the central government. A silent transfer of power is taking place in social terms' (Vishwanath Prasad Singh in Prasad 1997: 316–17).

This approach of social change eventually prevailed at the expense of *kisan* politics: Jats reacted strongly to Singh's policy and deserted the Janata Dal. But lower castes rallied around the party and its regional offshoots in north India, especially in key states such as Uttar Pradesh and Bihar. In these states, two Janata Dal leaders from the caste of the Yadavs, Mulayam Singh Yadav and Laloo Prasad Yadav, took over in 1989-90 and promoted the interests of their own group by implementing new affirmative action programmes.

UTTAR PRADESH AND BIHAR: THE KEY STATES

Uttar Pradesh and Bihar deserve special mention not only because they are the two largest Indian states in terms of population (and, therefore, in terms of Lok Sabha seats—85 and 54 out of 542, respectively) but also because the rise to power of the lowest castes has been more dramatic in these states than anywhere else in north India. Bihar has been governed by an OBC chief minister since 1990. In Uttar Pradesh Mulayam Singh Yadav occupied the post twice—in 1989-91 and in 1993–5—and an SC-dominated party, the Bahujan Samaj Party (BSP), has achieved unprecedented electoral performances. The root cause of this socio-political change is well known since it unfolded in the post-Mandal context. But what are the main consequences of this silent revolution, and how has it materialized?

As chief minister of Uttar Pradesh in 1989-91, Mulayam Singh Yadav issued an amending ordinance giving the OBCs of the state the same reservations—27 per cent—as the Mandal Commission Report had recommended. After he formed the government once again on 4 December 1993, as the leader of a coalition with the BSP, his first decision was to implement the 27 per cent quota. Then the government voted in the Uttar Pradesh Public Services (Reservation for Scheduled Castes, Scheduled Tribes and Other Backward Classes) Act on 22 March 1994. This new law reserved 21 per cent of the posts for the SCs, 2 per cent for the STs, and 27 per cent for the OBCs.

Reservations were introduced in the *panchayati raj* institutions along the same pattern as in the administration. While the Seventy-Third Amendment to the Indian Constitution, in 1993, made the reservation of seats for SCs (in proportion to their demographic weight) and for women (33 per cent) mandatory at all levels of the *panchayati raj* system, in June 1994, the Mulayam Singh government amended the Uttar Pradesh Panchayat Act of 1947 to include these changes and added one more modification: it granted a 27 per cent quota to the OBCs (Lieten and Srivastava 1999: 250).

In addition to the administration and local body reservations, Mulayam Singh made provisions for 27 per cent reservation for OBCs in medical colleges and educational institutions teaching engineering and management.[12] This decision was strongly resented in Uttarakhand, where the OBCs made up only 2 per cent of the population (Mawdsley 1996: 205–10). The agitation there was judged illegitimate and politically motivated by Mulayam Singh Yadav, who decided to repress it and launched a countermobilization. He emphasized that he was fighting for the 95 per cent deprived people against the 5 per cent privileged ones.

In order to strengthen his image as a low caste leader, he transferred upper caste bureaucrats to non-essential posts. The number of district-level bureaucrats from the upper castes decreased dramatically. These decisions—which were intentionally publicized—were made partly because of pressure from the Bahujan Samaj Party, but they were in tune with Mulayam Singh Yadav's strategy. Mulayam Singh 'pampered' his fellow caste members in the administration. Out of 900 teachers appointed under his second government, 720 were Yadavs. In the police forces, out of 3,151 newly selected candidates, 1,223 also belonged to this caste (*India Today*, 15 October 1994: 37). This policy alienated the Kurmis, the second-largest OBC caste of the state (Jaffrelot 2000).

However, the performance of Mulayam Singh's party in the general elections of the 1990s in Uttar Pradesh suggests that he has succeeded in broadening his base. From about 13 per cent of the valid votes in 1991, Mulayam's party reached about 21 per cent in 1996–8 and then 24 per cent in 1999, only 3.6 percentage points fewer than the 'winner', the BJP. As in Uttar Pradesh, the rise of the OBCs in Bihar is primarily the rise of the Yadavs. The Yadavs represented the largest caste group among the Bihar MPs in 1991, after the Mandal affair (17.3 per cent as against 7.7 per cent for the Rajputs). In 1996, they represented twice the percentage of the second-largest group, the Rajputs, at 22.2 per cent as against 11.1 per cent. Laloo Prasad Yadav, a Janata Dal leader who became chief minister of Bihar in March 1990, deliberately introduced a new style of politics highlighting the rustic qualities of the low caste people of Bihar. For instance, he made a point of speaking the Bhojpuri dialect. Once voted into power, he increased the quota for the OBCs from 20 per cent to 27 per cent, and this was voted into law in 1992. In August 1993, the Patna University and Bihar University Amendment Bill was passed, according to which there would be 50 per cent reservation of seats for the BJECs in the senates and syndicates of these universities.[13] Most of the vice-chancellors and directors of these educational institutions have since been selected from among the OBCs. Still, in 1993, a member of the Indian Administrative Service from the SCs replaced a Brahman as chief secretary, and a member of the OBCs took over the charge of director general of police from another Brahman. Three years after Laloo Prasad Yadav took over, 70 upper caste officials had sought—and obtained—transfer to the centre because of the humiliation and ill treatment they suffered in Bihar. In addition to these voluntary shifts, the state government has transferred twelve out of thirteen divisional commissioners and 250 of the 324 returning officers in order to have more lower caste people at the helm at the local level.

The government has also given jobs to a larger number of members of the OBCs. In 1996, the University Service Commission of Bihar recruited 1,427 lecturers for the universities and their constituent colleges in the state. Protests were immediately lodged because most of the candidates were OBC members, and more precisely Yadavs. In 1993, the Bihar Vidhan Sabha passed the Panchayati Raj Bill, according to which 'the Panchayats with majority of people belonging to backward classes will be reserved for them only and in these Panchayats upper castes will be debarred from even contesting elections'.

The fact that the lower castes have partly taken over power in Bihar is evident from the social profile of the governments of Laloo Prasad and his wife, Rabri Devi, who succeeded him in 1997 after he had to resign because of a charge of corruption registered against him. The percentage of ministers from the OBCs increased from an already high 46.5 per cent in 1990–5 to 64.47 per cent in 1995–2000. Significantly, this empowerment went almost exclusively to the upper OBCs—including the Yadavs—whose share rose from 35.2 per cent to 57.89 per cent, whereas the percentage of the lower OBCs decreased from 11.3 per cent to 6.58 per cent.

Similar to the case in Uttar Pradesh, the Kurmis resented the bias of Laloo Prasad Yadav in favour of his caste fellows when he appointed Yadavs as heads of important boards such as the Bihar Public Service Commission, the Bihar Secondary Education Service Commission, the Bihar State Electricity Board, and the Bihar Industrial Development Corporation (Chaudhary 1999: 242). Kurmi leaders felt sidelined, and one of the most prominent of them, Nitish Kumar, left the Janata Dal in 1994 to sponsor the creation of the Samata Dal with George Fernandes. This party made an alliance with the BJP in the mid-1990s. In spite of the division of the OBCs, the Rashtriya Janata Dal (RJD) of Laloo Prasad Yadav retained power thanks to the support of the Muslims and a large section of the SC voters. In Bihar, the party rose from an already high 27 per cent of the valid vote in 1998 to 28 per cent in the 1999 general elections and the 2000 assembly elections.

The OBCs, and more specifically the Yadavs, have thus benefited more than any other low caste groups from the policies followed by Mulayam Singh and Laloo Prasad in Uttar Pradesh and Bihar, two states in which the Yadavs form the largest component of the OBCs. The OBCs, however, are not the only ones to have benefited from the post-Mandal mobilization. The Dalits, or 'broken men'—to use the name that people of the SCs tend to apply to themselves nowadays—have also profited by it.

## A NEW PARTY OF THE DALITS:
## THE BAHUJAN SAMAJ PARTY

The main political party advocating the cause of the Dalits, the Bahujan Samaj Party (BSP), which was officially founded on 14 April 1984, has made rapid progress on the electoral front. Its growth from 2.07 per cent of the valid vote in 1989 to 3.64 per cent in 1996 enabled the party to obtain from the Election Commission the status of a national party after the 1996 elections, and it went on to get 4.7 per cent of the valid vote in 1998. This growth chiefly resulted from the organizational efforts of the party's founder, Kanshi Ram, who had first launched trade unions of low caste civil servants (Jaffrelot 1998). But it was also due to the electoral strategy of the BSP and the post-Mandal context, especially in Uttar Pradesh. While the BSP has reached double digits in another state—Punjab—Uttar Pradesh is the only state in which it has made real inroads in the last ten years, going from 9.93 per cent of the valid vote in the 1989 general elections to 20.9 per cent in 1998.

According to the Centre for the Study of Developing Societies (CSDS) opinion polls of 1996 and 1999,[14] most of the supporters of the BSP come from the SCs, and more precisely from the Chamars (the largest caste of Uttar Pradesh, with about 13 per cent of the population of that state). In the 1990s, three-fourths of the Chamars voted for the BSP, according to the surveys.

The leap forward that the BSP achieved between 1993 and 1996 in Uttar Pradesh enabled the party to reach power through coalitions. The mobilization of the upper castes against the implementation of the Mandal Commission Report had triggered a countermobilization that cut across low caste cleavages. Not only did the OBCs discover the need for more solidarity and more activism, but the Dalits felt the same, especially when the very notion of reservations—including for the SCs—started to be questioned by some upper caste movements. The BSP was even more clearly a potential ally of the OBCs because Kanshi Ram acknowledged their need for quotas in the administration. The context created by the Mandal affair was therefore conducive to the alliance between the new party of Mulayam Singh Yadav, the Samajwadi Party (SP), and the BSP in 1993. However, this alliance also responded to tactical considerations fully in keeping with the pragmatic nature of Indian electoral politics. Kanshi Ram explicitly admitted, 'The reason why concluded alliances with Mulayam Singh Yadav is that if we join our votes in U[ttar] P[radesh] we will be able to form the government' (Interview, *Sunday*, 16 May 1993: 10–11).

In the 1993 assembly elections, the Samajwadi Party won 109 seats out of 425, and the BSP won 67. The two parties formed the government thanks to the Congress Party's support. Mulayam became chief minister, and the BSP obtained eleven ministerial portfolios in a government of twenty-seven. Relations between the two partners, however, soon deteriorated. First, the BSP was becoming worried about the 'Yadavization' of the state. Second, the OBCs, who were anxious to improve their social status and to keep the SCs in their place, reacted violently to the Dalits efforts to achieve social mobility. The OBCs and the Dalits class interests are clearly antagonistic in Uttar Pradesh since the latter are often landless labourers or cultivators with very small plots who work for the former. Conflicts over the wages of the agricultural labourers and disputes regarding landownership have always been acute, but they have become even more frequent since the Dalits and the OBCs grew more assertive following the 1993 elections. These bones of contention partly explain the increasing number of atrocities against the Dalits (Mishra 1994: 409).

The breakup of the SP-BSP coalition showed how difficult it was to associate OBCs and SCs. It had been possible in 1993 because of the Mandal affair, but ties between the two parties began to weaken once the battle for quotas had been won. The 1993 assembly elections had been the culminating point of the anti-high caste mobilization. Yet the divorce between the SP and the BSP did not bring the latter back to square one. In fact, the BSP put an end to the coalition with the SP only to become actively involved in another alliance, in an even more favourable position. On 3 June 1995, Mayawati, Kanshi Ram's closest associate in Uttar Pradesh, became chief minister of the state with the BJP's support. This alliance was primarily directed against Mulayam Singh Yadav, whom the BSP and the BJP wanted to keep in check because of his increasing political influence that reflected the growing assertiveness of the OBCs, and especially the Yadavs. The alliance of the BSP with the BJP epitomized the convergence of the Dalit and upper caste leaders against the OBCs.

With Mayawati as chief minister, the largest state of India was for the first time governed by a member of the SCs, a Chamar.[15] For many members of the SCs, she became a source of pride. Mayawati's accession to Uttar Pradesh's top post therefore played a major part in the consolidation of the BSP's main vote-bank. This consolidation also resulted from the benefits Mayawati granted to members of the lower castes. For example, the Ambedkar Villages Scheme, which had been started by Mulayam Singh Yadav to allot special funds for socioeconomic development for two years to villages whose populations were at least 50 per cent Dalit, was revised to include villages with at least 30 per cent Dalit (and even 22 per cent in certain areas). Mayawati gave special treatment to the Dalits of these villages since 'all the roads, handpumps, houses, etc., have been largely built in their bastees [neighbourhoods]' (Pai 1997: 2314). Grants were created for Dalit children attending classes between levels one and eight. As for the OBCs, Mayawati announced that they were to benefit from 27 per cent of the state budget and that the quotas introduced by Mulayam Singh Yadav would be implemented as soon as possible.

Mayawati also altered the composition of the bureaucracy. She appointed supporters to key positions. More than 1,500 transfers took place in Uttar Pradesh during the 136 days of her government. This allowed her to post an SC district magistrate at the helm of almost half of the districts (*Frontline*, 1 December 1995: 31). Her empowerment policy went much further than the Mandal scheme had. The BJP became worried because the BSP was reinforcing its local implantation, and the party withdrew its support from Mayawati on 18 October 1995.

The BSP decided to stand alone six months later, in the 1996 Lok Sabha elections. Yet the party doubled its share of valid votes in Uttar Pradesh, from about 10 per cent in the 1989, 1991, and 1993 elections to 20.6 per cent (9,483,739 votes, 50 more than the SP received). The Mayawati government had obviously enabled the party to broaden its base among the lower castes by showing that Dalits could occupy the seat of power (in itself a very strong symbol) and exercise it to the profit of the downtrodden. The BSP was especially successful in consolidating the SCs behind its candidates. According to the aforementioned CSDS survey, during the 1996 assembly elections, 63.4 per cent of the SCs voted for the party, as against 26 per cent of the non-Yadav OBCs, 4.3 per cent of the Yadavs, 4.7 per cent of the Muslims, and less than 1 per cent of the upper castes (Chandra and Parmar 1997: 215).

Immediately after the 1996 elections in Uttar Pradesh, the BSP leaders announced that they would form a coalition with any political force willing and able to allocate the chief ministership to Mayawati. After six months of President's Rule, the BJP accepted their conditions. This decision can once again be explained by the apprehensions that Mulayam Singh Yadav generated in the BJP and the BSP.[16] According to the BJP-BSP agreement, Mayawati would be chief minister for six months, followed by a BJP leader, and the two would then function in rotation. As for the government, it would be made up half by BJP and half by BSP ministers. The BSP, therefore came back to power thanks to a new reversal of alliances.

During her six-month tenure, Mayawati transferred 1,350 civil and police officials (*The Times of India*, 18 September 1997). Only two days after taking power, she announced that 250 constable-clerks would soon be recruited from among the

SCs and STs (ibid., 23 March 1997). She also revived the Ambedkar Villages Scheme under her direct supervision and stated that she was focusing her political tenure 'on one section of society', the Dalits (interview, *India Today*, 11 August 1997: 33). The Rs. 3.5 billion (Rs. 350 crore) scheme covered 11,000 villages. Mayawati also implemented the Scheduled Castes and Scheduled Tribes (Prevention of Atrocities) Act of 1989 in a more drastic way than any of her predecessors.

After six months in office, Mayawati turned the post of chief minister over to Kalyan Singh from the BJP, but the BSP immediately criticized the government order he issued stating that the Act mentioned above should not be misused and withdrew its support from him. However, contrary to Kanshi Ram's expectations, the Kalyan Singh government did not fall, because the BJP had attracted a sufficient number of defectors from the Congress Party and the BSP to stay in power. The breakaway group from the BSP consisted of twelve MLAs, all of whom were rewarded with ministerial berths in Kalyan Singh's cabinet.[17] The BSP contested the 1998 Lok Sabha elections on its own in Uttar Pradesh, and it polled almost the same number of votes as in 1996.

While the BSP has consolidated its base in Uttar Pradesh, it is on the decline everywhere else, largely because of organizational difficulties, including factionalism: as Ambedkar had, Kanshi Ram tended to concentrate power in his own hands, depriving his party of a strong structure and causing much jealousy. The BSP is also affected by the reaction of upper caste-dominated political parties, as is evident from the co-option of some of its MLAs by the BJP in Uttar Pradesh and by the Congress in Madhya Pradesh.

The rise of the OBCs and Dalits to power in north India, in conjunction with the rising electoral participation of the low castes, has led Yogendra Yadav to consider that India has experienced a 'second democratic upsurge' in the 1990s (1996: 96). A transfer of power is certainly taking place, but this analysis needs to be qualified from three points of view. First, this phenomenon has not spread evenly across the Hindi belt; states such as Rajasthan, for instance, lag behind. Second, the OBCs and the Dalits are still very much divided, with those benefiting from the ongoing social democratization of Indian political democracy forming a new elite that comes from only a few castes, as is evident from the quasi-hegemonic role of the Yadavs and Chamars. Finally, the main political parties, the Congress and the BJP, have undertaken to counter this 'silent revolution'. As the first two issues have been dealt with elsewhere (Jaffrelot 2000), this chapter will now turn to the third one.

## The Congress, the BJP, and Mandal

In the late 1990s, for a brief period, three of the four largest states of the Hindi belt were governed by OBC chief ministers: Kalyan Singh in Uttar Pradesh, Rabri Devi in Bihar, and Ashok Gehlot in Rajasthan. Madhya Pradesh alone had an upper caste chief minister, Digvijay Singh. Interestingly, the three OBC chief ministers belonged to three different parties: the Bharatiya Janata Party, the Rashtriya Janata Dal, and the Congress Party. Certainly, this is an indication of the rise to power of the lower castes in north India, but while the RJD is naturally committed to the cause of the OBCs, the other two parties may be more eager to defuse the mobilization of the lower castes than anything else.

The way the Janata Dal and its offshoots—the Samajwadi Party and the RJD—on the one hand and the Bahujan Samaj Party on the other hand consolidated their bases among the OBCs and the SCs, respectively, in the 1990s posed a threat to the Congress and the BJP in north India. Until then, the former had owed most of its success to its catch-all party profile, while the latter, like its earlier incarnation, the Jana Sangh, not only had upper caste members at its helm but primarily represented the urban middle class of north India, which could hardly compete with the OBCs in terms of numbers. Both parties had to adjust to the Mandal challenge.

## THE CONGRESS PARTY'S NOSTALGIA FOR THE 'COALITION OF EXTREMES'

The implementation of the Mandal Commission Report generated a debate within the Congress. Low caste leaders of the party—such as then treasurer of the Congress Sitaram Kesri, a Banya from Bihar, where his caste is classified with the OBCs—were favourably inclined toward the report (Yadav 1994: 91). But these leaders were rather isolated. V.P. Singh's decision to implement the recommendations of the Mandal Report was strongly criticized in the Lok Sabha by Rajiv Gandhi, then Congress president and leader of the opposition, on 6 September 1990. He considered that a 'national consensus' had to be evolved (Mustafa 1995: 206) and that caste-based reservations could only divide Indian society.[18] Alternatively, he suggested, the quotas should be based on economic criteria and 'assistance should be given to the truly poor, to the landless, to the people falling in the poorest category' (*The Indian Express*, 8 September 1990). Obviously, the Congress tried to maintain its 'coalition of extremes' by indirectly promising quotas to the poor Brahmans and new concessions to the SCs. The party, therefore, continued to display indifference toward the OBCs, at the risk of further alienating this group. The Congress regained power, though without securing a clear-cut majority, after the May-June 1991 general elections. Soon after, on 25 September, Prime Minister Narasimha Rao issued an office memorandum that amended that of V.P. Singh by reserving 10 per cent of the posts in the government services to 'economically backward sections of the people' who were not covered by the existing quotas; the poor from the upper castes were to benefit from this scheme. The Congress was still attempting to blur the cleavage between the upper castes and the lower castes and to recapture the allegiance of the former. The change in reservations was declared invalid by the Supreme Court in a November 1992 judgement in which the judges emphasized that economic criteria could not be used in the definition of 'backwardness' under Articles 15 and 16 of the Constitution. The Congress had to resign itself to the centrality of caste in the identification of OBCs, and it began to adjust to their rise. This was evident from the way the government negotiated the 'creamy layer' issue. This issue crystallized when the Supreme Court asked the government to exclude from the list of OBCs eligible for quotas those who did not need any help from the state—the 'creamy layer' of the OBCs. The Prasad committee appointed by Rao to do this considered that the progeny of farmers who owned irrigated land that represented more than 65 per cent of the statutory area fit this category. The Janata Dal protested that the criterion was too strict. Subsequently, the welfare minister, Sitaram Kesri, displayed a conciliatory attitude during an all-party meeting he organized himself, and the proportion of land was increased to 85 per cent in August 1993. Later, he even invited private sector enterprises to establish quotas for the OBCs (interviews in *Sunday*, 2 October 1994 and *The Times of India*, 4 July 1995). During the 1996 election campaign, the Congress tried to project itself as the spokesperson of the OBCs. Its manifesto argued:

Reservations for the Backward Classes was an idea of the Congress. Jawaharlal Nehru made this into a Constitutional Principle in 1952. . . . In 1990, due to its ham handed and opportunistic approach, the Janata Dal Government triggered a virtual caste war in several parts of India.

The election of a Congress Government in 1991 brought peace to a society that was threatened with disruption by caste strife.

Quietly but firmly, Shri P.V. Narasimha Rao's Government implemented the recommendations of the Mandal Commission. (*Election Manifesto: General Election 1996*, 1996: 11–12)

The Congress was still trying to appear to be a consensus party and, at the same time, was attempting to project itself as the defender of the OBCs. However, the party was not able to attract more than about one-fifth of the OBC vote in 1996 and 1998. It had to wait until 1999 for a significant improvement in its electoral presence among the OBCs (35 per cent) and the SCs (40 per cent) (Yadav, Kumar and Heath 1999: 40). The Congress is still an upper caste party in north India, and this regional characterization reflects a more general reality, as is evident from the social profile of the Congress Working Committee, shown in Table 23.3.

Until the late 1980s, the upper castes represented more than 50 per cent of the Congress Working Committee members. Ten years later, their percentage had substantially declined, so much so that they formed slightly more than one-third of the total. However, the OBCs did not profit by this dramatic erosion; their share remained around one-tenth of the total. Its main beneficiaries were the SCs and STs, an indication of the persistent coalition of extremes pattern.

TABLE 23.3: CASTE AND COMMUNITY OF THE MEMBERS OF
THE CONGRESS WORKING COMMITTEE

| Castes and communities | 1981 | 1987 | 1998 |
|---|---|---|---|
| Upper castes | 11 | 11 | 10 |
| Intermediate castes | 1 | 0 | 3 |
| OBCs | 3 | 3 | 3 |
| SCs/STs | 1 | 0 | 5 |
| Muslims | 2 | 2 | 3 |
| Christians | 1 | 1 | 2 |
| Sikhs | 1 | 1 | 0 |
| Unidentified | 2 | 1 | 2 |
| TOTAL | 22 | 19 | 28 |

*Source:* Fieldwork at the AICC office, New Delhi.

## THE BJP'S EFFORTS TO DEFUSE
## THE 'SHUDRA REVOLUTION'

The situation is somewhat different in the case of the BJP. The Hindu nationalist movement has always been known for its upper caste, even Brahmanical, character. This specificity stems from the content of Hindutva, or the Hindu nationalist ideology, itself: shaped by Brahmans, it relies on an organic view in which castes are seen as the harmonious components of society (Jaffrelot 1999: Ch. 1). Since its creation in 1925, the Rashtriya Swayamsevak Sangh (RSS), has grown by attracting to its *shakhas* Hindus who value this ethos, either because they belong to the upper castes or because they want to emulate them. Therefore, the technique of 'conversion' of low caste people to Hindutva relies on the logic of Sanskritization.

The RSS immediately criticized the announcement by V.P Singh on 7 August 1990 that the recommendations of the Mandal Commission Report would be implemented. Reacting to the 'Raja's caste-war', *The Organiser* attacked not only the politics of quotas favouring the OBCs, denounced as the pampering of vote banks, but also the policy of affirmative action itself from the RSS' traditional organicist angle: 'The havoc the politics of reservation is playing with the social fabric is unimaginable. It provides a premium for mediocrity, encourages brain-drain and sharpens caste-divide' (*The Organiser*, 26 August 1990: 15). On the implicit assumption that it was virtually harmonious, the 'social fabric' was regarded in this case as in need of preservation from state intervention.

*The Organiser* came to embrace the cause of the upper castes publicly when one of its columnists wrote, 'There is today an urgent need to build up moral and spiritual forces to counter any fall-out from an expected Shudra revolution' (Kamath 1994: 20). The RSS high command followed more or less the same line as *The Organiser*. Rajendra Singh, then the chief of the RSS, considered that 'there should be a gradual reduction in the job quotas' (*The Organiser*, 18 December 1994: 20). In response to the new caste-based politics, the RSS launched a new programme in January 1996 called *samarasya sangama*, 'confluence for harmony', which provided that each RSS worker should adopt one village to contribute to its development in order, in the words of Rajendra Singh, to promote 'social harmony between various sections of the society and social assimilation' (*The Organiser*, 14 January 1996: 7).

The BJP, however, did not react to the Mandal affair and the rise of the low castes in the same way. The party leaders did not dare openly attack V.P. Singh's decision regarding the implementation of the Mandal Commission Report because they were apprehensive of alienating OBC voters. They instead fostered the students' anti-Mandal agitation behind the scenes. When one of the party's Rajya Sabha members, J.K. Jain, began a fast against the implementation of the Mandal Report, he was criticized by the high command and had to fall into line (Jaffrelot 1999: 431). The BJP was cautious about projecting its views. The upper caste character of Hindu nationalism had become a greater handicap for the BJP in the 1990s because of the growing political consciousness of the low castes, as the 1993 elections testified.

Those election results, when the BJP lost both Uttar Pradesh and Madhya Pradesh at least partly because of OBC and Dalit voters, led the party leaders to promote a larger number of low caste people in the party apparatus. In January 1994, Hukumdev Narain Yadav was appointed as special invitee to the party's national executive board, and Uma Bharti, a Lodh, became chief of the Bharatiya Janata Yuva Morcha. The main advocate of the inclusion of an increasing number of low caste members at all the levels of the party apparatus was K.N. Govindacharya, himself a Brahman and then one of the BJP general secretaries. He called this policy 'social engineering'. However, this strategy was opposed by some of his colleagues and by RSS leaders, who objected on principle to any artificial transformation of the so-called social equilibrium and did not want to give a new importance to caste as a result of pressures from the Mandal affair. Murli Manohar Joshi, a former president of the BJP, opposed the move and even implicitly questioned the notion of social engineering in general by asking, 'What social justice has been brought in the name of social engineering? Rural poverty has increased and most of the rural poor continue to be Dalits' (interview, *Sunday*, 26 January 1997: 13).

In a way, the BJP fell into line with the mother organization, the RSS, during the all-party meeting on reservations that was held in 1995 under the auspices of the then union welfare minister, Sitaram Kesri. At that meeting, the BJP representative, Atal Behari Vajpayee, alone opposed the extension of reservations for SCs and STs and refused to express a willingness to increase the ceiling of 50 per cent reservation for these two categories and the OBCs.[19] However, as the eleventh general elections approached, the BJP amended its earlier position on the reservation issue. Before the 1991 elections, the BJP had expressed very general

views: 'Reservation should . . . be made for other backward classes broadly on the
basis of the Mandal Commission Report, with preference to be given to the poor
amongst these very classes and . . . [a]s poverty is an important contributory factor
for backwardness, reservation should also be provided for members of the other
castes on the basis of their economic condition' (*Towards Ram Rajya* 1991: 27).

In 1996, the BJP retained the social harmony discourse[20] but made precise
promises to the OBCs:

1. Continuation of reservations for the Other Backward Classes till they are
   socially and educational [*sic*] integrated with the rest of society;
2. A uniform criteria [*sic*] for demarcating the 'creamy layer';
3. Flow of reservation benefits in an ascending order so that the most
   backward sections of the OBCs get them first;
4. Ten per cent reservation on the basis of economic criteria to all
   economically weaker sections of society, apart from the Scheduled Castes/
   Scheduled Tribes and the Other Backward Classes (*For a Strong and
   Prosperous India*, 1996: 62).

The BJP had admitted the inevitability of quotas for the OBCs but tried to
combine the criterion of caste with socioeconomic criteria. This compromise
reflects the debate within the BJP between the advocates of 'social engineering' in
favour of the low castes and those who want to abstain from acknowledging caste
conflicts and amending the supposedly harmonious structure of society.

Another dimension of this compromise was the BJP's strategy of indirect
'Mandalization': the party did not promote low caste people (either as election
candidates or office bearers) but made alliances with parties having a base among
the OBCs, such as the Samata Party, a Kurmi-dominated breakaway of the Janata
Dal in Bihar. While the BJP had received only 16 per cent of the vote in 1991,
largely because it remained identified with the upper castes and the tribal belt of
the south, its alliance with the Samata Party enabled it to make inroads in northern
and central districts thanks to that party's base among the Kurmis and the Koeris
(another OBC caste). In several constituencies, these low castes were allied with
upper castes (Brahmans, Rajputs, Bhumihars, and Kayasths), which helped the
BJP a great deal. The party won eighteen seats, as opposed to five in 1991. The
BJP admitted the need to become more rural and even to 'Mandalize' itself, but
only indirectly.

After the 1998 elections, the BJP formed a coalition, the National Democratic
Alliance (NDA), that enabled Vajpayee to become prime minister. This alliance
was formalized before the 1999 elections to such an extent that the party did not
prepare an election manifesto for itself; there was only one manifesto for the entire
NDA. As it was now the pivotal force of a larger coalition whose components were
often less upper caste-oriented than the BJP itself, the party tended to dilute its
stand further regarding the reservation issue. In the NDA election manifesto, one

could read, 'If required, the Constitution will be amended to maintain the system of reservation. . . . We are committed to extending the SC/ST reservation for another 10 years. Reservation percentages above 50 per cent, as followed by certain states, shall be sanctified through necessary legislation measures' (National Democratic Alliance, 1999: 8).

Vajpayee himself, while campaigning in Rajasthan, declared that his government 'would implement the reservation policy in right earnest' (cited in *The Hindu*, 25 August 1999). Obviously, the BJP leaders had become more responsive to the OBCs' demands not only because of their coalition partners but also in order to attract more OBC voters. However, the BJP remains an upper caste party, as is evident from the social profile of its MPs and office bearers, shown in Table 23.4.

TABLE 23.4: Caste and Community of the BJP MPs
Returned in the Hindi Belt (In %)

| Castes and communities | 1989 | 1991 | 1996 | 1998 | 1999 |
|---|---|---|---|---|---|
| Upper castes | 53.13 | 52.33 | 46.28 | 43.40 | 37.96 |
| Intermediate castes | 1.56 | 4.65 | 4.96 | 6.61 | 7.4.1 |
| OBCs | 15.62 | 15.10 | 17.40 | 20.50 | 16.67 |
| SCs | 17.20 | 18.60 | 21.50 | 18.80 | 19.40 |
| STs | 7.80 | 5.80 | 7.40 | 6.73 | 8.34 |
| Muslims | 1.56 | | | 0.83 | 0.93 |
| Sikhs | 1.56 | 1.16 | 0.83 | 0.83 | |
| Sadhus | | 2.33 | | | 1.85 |
| Unidentified | | | 1.65 | 2.48 | 7.41 |
| | N = 64 | N = 86 | N = 121 | N = 122 | N = 108 |

*Source:* Fieldwork by the author.

The last five elections have shown a steady erosion of the percentage of members of the upper castes among the BJP MPs of the Hindi belt, from 53 per cent in 1989 to 43 per cent in 1998 and 38 per cent in 1999. However, those who benefit from this trend are less the OBCs than the dominant castes (mainly the Jats) and even the Dalit candidates, who are often elected with the support of upper caste BJP voters. Indeed, the decrease in upper caste MPs does not coincide with diminishing attractiveness of the party to the upper caste voters or with growing attractiveness to the OBCs and the SCs and STs. Besides, the efforts of the party to woo the OBCs are real but limited; the rise in OBC MPs probably reflects the increasing number of OBC candidates fielded by the party, but by and large the OBCs' share remains around 20 per cent. (Incidentally, this is also the percentage of OBC voters who support the BJP, according to the 1999 CSDS survey.) Moreover, while the party is steadily giving more tickets to OBCs election after election, it does not make much room for this group in the party apparatus. In 2000, the removal of Kalyan Singh from the post of Uttar Pradesh chief minister under pressure from the upper caste lobby and the appointment of Bangaru Laxman as party president even suggests that the BJP may follow the Congress Party strategy of building a coalition of extremes (see the afterword to Hansen and Jaffrelot 2001).

India has come a long way since the early days of its conservative democracy. The political system of the 1950s and 1960s was characterized by the domination of elite groups (the upper caste intelligentsia, the business community, and the landowners) that maintained the clientelistic arrangement of the 'Congress system'. This system was democratic in the sense that there were frequent, competitive elections, the press was free, and the judiciary was independent, but its beneficiaries all came from the same upper caste groups. Paradoxically, Indian democracy has acquired a social dimension through caste—an institution based on hierarchy but undergoing transformation. South India led the way from the late nineteenth century, when low caste groups began to emancipate themselves from the rigid hierarchy of Indian society through an ethnicization process and affirmative action policies. In north India, attempts at ethnicizing caste were hindered by the pervasive ethos of Sanskritization, but the policies of affirmative action led to the same result as in the south several decades later.

Indeed, the main landmark in the low castes' ascendancy to power in north India in the late 1980s and early 1990s was the implementation of the recommendations of the Mandal Report. The lower castes mobilized throughout north India and formed a front against the upper castes' vocal hostility to the new scheme of reservations. As a result, OBC leaders were elected in large numbers to Parliament and took over in Uttar Pradesh and Bihar. In the wake of this mobilization, the Dalits deserted the Congress for a new party, the Bahujan Samaj Party, which aggressively fought upper caste domination in north India. In 1997, growing recognition of the SCs in the Indian political system found expression in the election of K.R. Narayanan, a Dalit from Kerala, as president of the country.

India is therefore experimenting with a silent revolution. Power is being transferred from an upper caste elite to plebeian groups without much violence. Certainly, riots took place during the Mandal affair, but violence remained limited. The relative quiescence is primarily due to the fact that the whole process is incremental: the upper castes are still in command, with people of the OBCs forming a second line of leadership, a new generation in waiting. The educational and social limitations of the lower castes are such that they will probably not be in a position to generate a full-fledged new elite for years. Second, the rise to power of the lower castes has been very uneven. They have taken over in Bihar, but they remain in a subaltern position in Rajasthan, for instance. Third, the conflict is not based on clear-cut political opposition, since upper caste-dominated parties have low caste people among their ranks and vice versa (even the BSP has upper caste office bearers). Fourth, the upper castes are losing ground in the political sphere and in the administration, but the liberalization of the economy—which, like the Mandalization process, began in the early 1990s—has opened new opportunities to them in the private sector; they may not regret losing their traditional monopoly over the bureaucracy so much when they see these greener pastures.

Fifth, and more important, the rise to power of the lower castes is not irreversible and linear. There is clearly a trend, but there are also several handicaps to overcome. The lower castes suffer from a structural lack of unity. The divorce between the Samajwadi Party and the Bahujan Samaj Party in 1995 showed that an alliance between the OBCs and the Dalits is very difficult to maintain, partly because these two groups have conflicting class interests. Besides, the SCs and the OBCs themselves do not really form social categories.

Finally, the rise to power of the lower castes is also hindered by the response of the upper castes to their new assertiveness and ambitions. Mainstream political parties are resorting to old techniques in this regard. The traditional Gandhian discourse on the organic unity of society is still articulated by the RSS in order to weaken Dalit militancy, and the Congress Party is still using its old strategy of co-option to build a 'coalition of extremes'. The BJP has adopted the latter to a certain extent. It also endeavours to defuse the mobilization of the OBCs by diluting the social cohesiveness of this already not so homogeneous social grouping. In the late 1990s, BJP politicians successfully advocated the inclusion of the Jats on the list of OBCs toward this very end.

The extension of the social groups benefiting from quotas may well be the favourite tactic of the BJP for making 'quota politics' non-operational. This tactic may take on an even larger dimension with the introduction of quotas for women in the elected assemblies: if 33 per cent of the seats are reserved for women, the upper castes may well be the first beneficiaries of the reservations—a rather ironical conclusion that brings to mind that in Europe the conservatives were responsible for enlarging' the franchise in order to exploit their influence over 'their' peasant voters. However, the peasants in question eventually emancipated themselves from their patrons, and in India, too, this tactical move may only slow down the silent revolution in the making.

## Notes

1. Brahmans, Kshatriyas, and Vaishyas are all considered 'twice-born', or *dvija*.
2. However, qualitative leaps exist in this gradation since the *varna* system gives structure to the profusion of *jatis*. Each *jati* belongs to a specific *varna*. The *jatis* of the twice-born *varnas* naturally enjoy a higher status than those of the Shudras, and those of the Untouchables are the lowest of all.
3. Susanne Hoeber Rudolph and Lloyd I. Rudolph have underlined the modern character of caste associations in 1966: 448.
4. This has been observed by Robert Hardgrave in the case of the Nadars of Tamil Nadu. Their caste association, the Nadar Mahajana Sangam, was founded in 1910, and it

promoted what he calls 'caste fusion' as 'the unit of endogamy expanded' (Hardgrave Jr. 1968: 1065–70 and 1969).

5. For the complete text, see Irschick 1969: 368.

6. Pranab Bardhan has identified three 'dominant proprietary classes' in India: industrial-capitalists, rich farmers, and white collars/professionals. See Bardhan 1984.

7. In 1952, the percentage of MPs whose caste I could not identify was 3 per cent, and 1967 it was 1.5 per cent.

8. Brahman and Rajput subcastes that suffered from economic deprivation were classified as OBCs, too.

9. Satpal Malik claims that he was the first minister to ask for the inclusion of the Jats (interview by the author, New Delhi, 25 October 1998).

10. These figures are based on replies furnished by thirty central ministries and departments and thirty-one attached and subordinate offices and public sector undertakings under the administrative control of fourteen ministries (for the complete statistical figures, see *Report of the Backward Classes Commission*, 42).

11. Adapted from C. Ram Reddy 1987: 305.

12. In 1994 his government had also passed another reservation scheme, the Uttar Pradesh State Universities Reservation in Admission for Scheduled Castes, Scheduled Tribes and Other Backward Classes, which provided a 21 per cent quota for the SCs, a 2 per cent quota for the STs, and a 27 per cent quota for the OBCs.

13. This and the information in the two following paragraphs is from S.N. Chaudhary 1999.

14. The main results of these surveys have been published in *India Today*, 31 August 1996; Kumar 1999; and *Frontline*, 19 November 1999: 41.

15. Before Mayawati, there had been only three Dalit chief ministers, and none of them had been a woman: D. Sanjiviah in Andhra Pradesh, Ram Sunder Das in Bihar, and Jagannath Pahadiya in Rajasthan.

16. As a cabinet minister in the Deve Gowda government, Mulayam Singh had indeed acquired a strong influence over the governor of Uttar Pradesh, Romesh Bhandari.

17. The BSP petitioned the speaker, K.N. Tripathi, since this breakaway group represented less than one-third of the BSP legislative group and its members, therefore, should have been disqualified. But Tripathi—a senior BJP leader—argued in his 148-page report that the breakaway group had initially had twenty-six members.

18. On the following day, Rajiv Gandhi accused V.P. Singh of conducting 'the country to the edge of caste war' (*The Indian Express*, 8 September 1990).

19. Kesri consulted the political parties before bringing before Parliament a constitutional amendment bill designed to nullify the 50 per cent ceiling imposed by the Supreme Court on reservations and a bill seeking the extension of reservations for the SCs and STs in government jobs beyond 1997. Addressing a convention of SC and ST MLAs, ministers, mayors, deputy mayors, members of municipal corporations, and *panchayat* office bearers in Bhopal, he denounced the BJP as the biggest enemy of the SCs, STs, and OBCs on the basis of Vajpayee's stand (*National Mail*, 19 May 1995).

20. The manifesto also said, 'The task is nothing short of rekindling the lamp of our eternal "*Dharma*" that *Sanatan* thought which our sages bequeathed to mankind—a social system based on compassion, cooperation, justice, freedom, equality and tolerance' (Bharatiya Janata Party 1996: 5).

# References

Baker, C. (1976), 'The Congress and the 1937 Elections in Madras', *Modern Asian Studies*, October.

Barnett, S. (1977), 'Identity Choice and Caste Ideology in Contemporary South India', in K. David (ed.), *The New Wind: Changing Identities in South India*, The Hague: Mouton.

Bardhan, Pranab (1984), *The Political Economy of Development in India*, Oxford: Blackwell.

Brass, Paul (1980), 'The Politicization of the Peasantry in a North Indian State', *Journal of Peasant Studies*, Vol. 8.

Bharatiya Janata Party (1991), *Towards Ram Rajya: Mid-Term Poll to Lok Sabha, May 1991—Our Commitments*, New Delhi.

——— (1996), *For a Strong and Prosperous India: Election Manifesto 1996*, New Delhi.

Centre for the Study of Developing Societies (1967) (ed.), 'Voting Behaviour in a Developing Society: A Working Paper', in *Party System and Election Studies*, Bombay: Allied Publishers.

Chandra, Kanchan and Parmar, Chandrika (1997), 'Party Strategies in the Uttar Pradesh Assembly Elections', *Economic and Political Weekly*, 1 February.

Chaudhary, S.N. (1999), *Power-Dependence Relations: Struggle for Hegemony in Rural Bihar*, New Delhi: Har-Anand.

*Constituent Assembly Debates* (1989), Vols. 1 and 7, New Delhi: Lok Sabha Secretariat.

Geetha, V. and Rajadurai, S.V. (1998), *Towards a Non-Brahman Millennium: From Lyothee Thass to Periyar*, Calcutta: Samya.

Hansen, Thomas B. and Jaffrelot, Christophe (2001) (eds.), 'Afterword', in *The BJP and the Compulsions of Politics in India*, 2nd edn, Delhi: Oxford University Press.

Hardgrave, Robert L. Jr. (1968), 'Caste: Fission and Fusion', *Economic and Political Weekly*, July.

——— (1969), *The Nadars of Tamilnad*, Berkeley and Los Angeles: University of California Press.

Indian National Congress (I) (1996), *Election Manifesto: General Election 1996*, New Delhi: AICC(I).

Irschick, Eugene F. (1969), *Politics and Social Conflict: The Non-Brahman Movement and Tamil Separatism, 1916–1929*, Bombay: Oxford University Press.

Jaffrelot, C. (1998), 'The Bahujan Samaj Party in North India: No Longer Just a Dalit Party?', *Comparative Studies of South Asia, Africa and the Middle East*, Vol. 18.

——— (1999), *The Hindu Nationalist Movement and Indian Politics: 1925 to the 1990s*, 2nd edn, Delhi: Penguin.

——— (2000), 'The Rise of the Other Backward Classes in the Hindi Belt', *Journal of Asian Studies*, Vol. 59.

Kamath, M.V. (1994), 'Is Shudra Revolution in the Offing?', *The Organiser*, 1 May.

Kumar, P. (1999), 'Dalit and the BSP in Uttar Pradesh: Issues and Challenges', *Economic and Political Weekly*, 3 April.

Lieten, George K. and Srivastava, Ravi (1999), *Unequal Partners: Power Relations, Devolution and Development in Uttar Pradesh*, New Delhi: Sage.

*Lok Sabha Debates* (1982), Vol. 31, New Delhi: Lok Sabha Secretariat.

Lynch, Owen (1969), *The Politics of Untouchability: Social Mobility and Social Change in a City of India*, New York: Columbia University Press.

Mawdsley, E. (1996), 'Uttarakhand Agitation and Other Backward Classes', *Economic and Political Weekly*, 27 January.

*Memorandum on the Report of the Backward Classes Commission* I (n.d.), Delhi: Ministry of Home Affairs.

*Memorandum Explaining Action Taken on the Report of the Second Backward Classes Commission* (1982), New Delhi: Ministry of Home Affairs, Government of India.

Michelutti, L. (1996), 'Ahirs-Yadavs Between Society and Politics', paper presented at the Fifteenth Conference of the Association for Modern South Asian Studies, Copenhagen, September.

Mishra, A. (1994), 'Challenge to the SP-BSP Government', *Economic and Political Weekly*, 19 February.

Mustafa, Seema (1995), *The Lonely Prophet: V.P. Singh, a Political Biography*, Appendix 1, New Delhi: New Age International.

National Democratic Alliance (1999), *For a Proud, Prosperous India: An Agenda, Election Manifesto, Lok Sabha Election, 1999*, New Delhi: Printed and published at the Bharatiya Janata Party, for and on behalf of the National Democratic Alliance.

Singh, V.P. (Convenor) (1989), *National Front: Lok Sabha Elections 1989 Manifesto*, New Delhi: National Front.

Pai, Sudha (1997), 'Dalit Assertion in UP: Implications for Politics', *Economic and Political Weekly*, 13 September.

Pandey, Gyanendra (1983), 'Rallying Round the Cow: Sectarian Strife in the Bhojpuri Region, c. 1888-1917', in *Subaltern Studies II*, (ed.), Ranajit Cuha, Delhi: Oxford University Press.

Prasad, Anirudh (1997), *Reservational Justice*, New Delhi: Deep and Deep.

Radhakrishnan, P. (1990), 'Backward Classes in Tamil Nadu: 1872–1988', *Economic and Political Weekly*, 10 March.

Ram, N. (1979), 'Dravidian Movement in Its Pre-Independence Phases', *Economic and Political Weekly*, February.

Reddy, C. Ram (1987), 'The Politics of Accommodation: Caste, Class and Dominance in Andhra Pradesh', in *Dominance and State Power in Modern India*, (eds.) Francine Frankel and M.S.A. Rao, Vol. 1, Delhi: Oxford University Press.

*Report of the Backward Classes Commission* (1955), Vol. 1, Delhi: Government of India.

——— (1980), Vols. 1 and 2, New Delhi: Government of India.

Rudolph, Susanne Hoeber and Rudolph, Lloyd I. (1966), 'The Political Role of India's Caste Associations', in *Social Change: The Colonial Situation*, (ed.), Immanuel Wallerstein, New York: J. Wiley.

Saraswati, S. (1974), *Minority Politics in Madras State*, Delhi: Impex.

Sharma, S.M.H. Dev, Singh, V. Prasad and Sunilam (1997) (eds.), 'Justice for the Poor', in *Evolution of Socialist Policy in India*, New Delhi: Bapu Kaldate.

Singh, Vishwanath Prasad (1997), 'Power and Equality: Changing Grammar of Indian Politics', in Anirudh Prasad, *Reservational Justice*, New Delhi: Deep and Deep.

Srinivas, M.N. (1995), *Social Change in Modern India*, 3rd edn, Hyderabad: Orient Longman.

Weiner, Myron (1967), *Party Building in a New Nation: The Indian National Congress*, Chicago: Chicago University Press.

Yadav, Yogendra (1996), 'Reconfiguration in Indian Politics: State Assembly Elections 1993-95', *Economic and Political Weekly*, 13 January.

———, Sanjay Kumar, and Heath, Oliver (1999), 'The BJP's New Social Bloc', *Frontline*, 19 November.

Yadav, K.C. (1994), *India's Unequal Citizens: A Study of Other Backward Classes*, Delhi: Manohar.

# Chapter 24

# The impact of affirmative action in India more political than socioeconomic

India was probably the first field for experimentation with positive discrimination policies. Christian missionaries and British colonial authorities, inspired by utilitarians, wanted to improve the human condition through programmes for the advancement of the underprivileged (Stokes 1989 [1959]). As early as the late nineteenth century, the first beneficiaries of these policies were found among the victims of India's inherently inegalitarian system of castes. At the top of this social system are the 'twice-born', including the Brahmans, and at the bottom the Untouchables, ostracized out of a belief that they were impure from birth.[1] According to the census taken every ten years since 1871, this segment of the population made up about one-tenth of India's inhabitants by the end of the nineteenth century. Untouchables, then, were the logical first targets of the colonial positive discrimination policy, which in the course of time was to take the form of quotas, known as 'reservations'. This policy became even more systematic when India achieved independence, but it brought only limited results. By contrast, its extension to the castes ranked just above the Untouchables sparked fierce debate and had a major political impact disproportionate to its socioeconomic effect, which has remained inconsequential. Hence the two paradoxes on which this chapter focuses: first, Dalits 'benefited from' their very low status in the sense that caste, in their case, was immediately identified as the relevant criterion for positive discrimination, whereas it took decades to reach the same conclusion in the case of the caste groups situated just above them; second, while the political scene has been profoundly transformed, at least in north India, by the controversial implementation of reservations for these low castes, in practise these measures did not produce any substantial socioeconomic changes.

## Reservations for the Untouchables: A Non-Issue

The British census rigidified the contours of Indian society by outlining three main groups: the 'twice-born', making up the three upper *varna*, the lower castes (Shudras), and the Untouchables. These groups no doubt pre-existed, but their frontiers were fuzzy until then and certainly had never been quantified.[2] Those

*A shorter version of this article has been published in French: Inde: l'avènement politique de la caste, *Critique Internationale*, No. 17, October 2002: 131–44.

ranked at the bottom immediately contested this exercise in social engineering, but the Untouchables posed the least problem of all. Their case was plain: their impurity, which for generations excluded them from temples and all public places where others feared 'pollution' from contact with them, put them at the bottom of the social pyramid.[3] Such stigmas were always combined with demeaning occupations, from the butchering of dead animals to that of day labourer, the most common activity among the Untouchables, who for the most part were landless peasants.

The British first set up a positive discrimination programme that aimed to advance the education of Untouchables. In 1892, they established special schools for them because the public system, due to wholesale rejection by teachers and pupils' parents, was unable to accommodate them. These institutions managed to bring the level of literacy of the 'Depressed Classes', the official term for Untouchables until 1930, up to 6.7 per cent for boys and 4.8 per cent for girls in 1921. Gradually a scholarship policy was developed: in 1944, a five-year budget of Rs. 3,00,000 was set aside for pupils of these 'classes' (Sharma 1982: 18–19). The British went further still by introducing hiring quotas in the civil service when it turned out that despite education, the Untouchables still were not finding jobs.[4] In 1934, 8.5 per cent of the civil service vacancies were reserved for them. This share was raised to 12.5 per cent in 1946 to reflect the proportion of Untouchables in the population.

The British also introduced quotas in political representation. Ten years after the 1909 reform setting up provincial legislative councils, a system was instituted whereby seats were reserved for the Depressed Classes on these councils as well as in the central legislative assembly that convened in New Delhi. Another reform was undertaken in 1928, aiming to give an opportunity for the increasingly outspoken Untouchable leaders to air their demands. Thus, at the 1930 Round Table Conference, Dr. B.R. Ambedkar—the first Untouchable leader to have a pan-Indian influence—called for a system of separate electorates that would have allowed the Depressed Classes to choose their representatives to elected assemblies, as had been the case for Muslims since 1909.

This demand was immediately met by opposition from the Congress Party and, more especially, from Gandhi, who viewed it as a seriously divisive factor for Hindu society. Gandhi, like the notables in the Congress and the movement's leaders—except of course the progressive elite gathered around Nehru—often took a conservative stance on the issue of the caste system. For him, this form of social organization was not based primarily on a hierarchical principle, but on one of complementarity: each caste fulfilled a socioeconomic function that helped to guarantee the harmony of the whole. He would crusade against untouchability, certainly, but by reforming mentalities to better integrate the Depressed Classes into the bosom of Hinduism, not by accentuating cleavages, which granting a separate electorate for the Untouchables would have done (Jaffrelot 2003: Ch. 1). He thus resorted to his preferred weapon, the hunger strike, when the British agreed to Ambedkar's demand for a separate electorate. Ambedkar was forced to yield to pressure and make do with a system of reserved seats which no longer involved allowing the Untouchables to choose their representatives in elected assemblies. Instead, a certain number of constituencies were reserved for Untouchable candidates. The difference was significant, because all voters were qualified to vote for one candidate or another, and in any given constituency Untouchable voters were never a majority.

Affirmative action programmes in favour of Untouchables were routinized after independence: so long as they took the form of reservations, they were never seriously challenged. Indeed, the system of reserved seats in favour of Untouchable castes—renamed 'Scheduled Castes', another bureaucratic euphemism, in 1935—was maintained in the Constitution adopted in 1950, with minor differences. First, the system of proportional representation led the state to raise the proportion of reserved seats to 15 per cent, the new figure for Scheduled Castes according to the 1951 census (this figure would continue to vary and thus alter the quota: the threshold of 17 per cent was passed in 1991). Next, the 'reservation' policy was extended in a systematic manner to tribal peoples, which represented 7 per cent of the population in 1951.

The impact of this policy turned out to be considerably limited. Not having received their mandate from their caste fellows—always a minority in the reserved constituencies (see Table 24.1)—elected officials in these constituencies were not very keen to defend their interests in the assemblies to which they were elected. On the contrary, performing a delicate balancing act, they sought to satisfy both their rank and file and their party, most of these elected officials being members of the Congress. This party in fact not only attracted politicians seeking office, but had also become skilled at drawing off cadres from the Untouchable party Ambedkar had founded, the Republican Party of India, which was divided into multiple factions and had lost most of its political clout by the early 1970s.

As it turned out, the reservation system did little to provoke social change with regard to its two other facets, educational advancement and hiring quotas in the civil service. This failure arose from the simple fact that the quotas were never

TABLE 24.1: DISTRIBUTION OF CONSTITUENCIES RESERVED FOR THE SCHEDULED CASTES BY POPULATION SHARE IN 1961*

| % of Scheduled Castes | Number of constituencies |
|---|---|
| 0–10 | 4 |
| 10–20 | 25 |
| 20–30 | 33 |
| 30–40 | 10 |
| 40–50 | 3 |

*It should also be noted that in the 1970s, only 25 per cent of the Untouchables lived in a reserved district.
Source: Galanter 1979: 438–9.

filled, due to a lack of qualified candidates . . . or a lack of willingness on the part of those in charge of filling them. In 1961, Untouchables made up fewer than 2 per cent of graduates of any given age bracket (Galanter 1994: 61). As for hiring quotas, they were only filled in a significant way in the 1980s for the upper employment ranks (Classes 1 and 2), as can be seen in the distribution of Scheduled Castes in the central administration (Table 24.2). This meant that, for decades, the greater percentage of Scheduled Castes in the national bureaucracy were employed in low-level menial positions, which would seem to defeat the purpose of the reservations.

TABLE 24.2: DISTRIBUTION OF SCHEDULED CASTES IN THE
CENTRAL ADMINISTRATION (PERCENTAGES)

| Year | 1953 | 1961 | 1963 | 1967 | 1974 | 1980 | 1987 |
|---|---|---|---|---|---|---|---|
| Class 1 | 0.53 | 1.2 | 1.78 | 2.08 | 3.2 | 4.95 | 8.23 |
| Class 2 | 1.29 | 2.5 | 2.98 | 3.1 | 4.6 | 8.54 | 10.47 |
| Class 3 | 4.52 | 7.2 | 9.24 | 9.33 | 10.3 | 13.44 | 14.46 |
| Class 4 | 20.52 | 17.2 | 17.15 | 18.18 | 18.6 | 19.46 | 20.09 |

*Sources:* Dubey and Mathur 1972: 167; Mendelsohn and Vicziany 1988: 135.

It is impossible not to draw a comparison between the four classes of Indian administration and the caste system hierarchy, given the crushing over representation of upper castes in the higher classes and the Dalits in the lower classes. Class 4 includes mainly public sanitation workers, which is why the quotas of jobs reserved for the Scheduled Castes have always been so well filled: the Untouchables traditionally assigned these tasks continue to perform them; now they simply wear a government uniform and enjoy civil servant status.

The policy of reservation in favour of the Scheduled Castes was thus implemented very early on and very systematically—the three dimensions, education, hiring quotas and political representation, being complementary—but this potentially revolutionary ambition was so well accepted by the Indian elites and especially the Congress establishment because the Untouchables could never challenge them. None of these measures threatened their domination, all the more so as quotas were not filled. This situation continued to prevail until the 1980s, a time when anti-reservation feelings developed among the upper castes as evident from the recurrent clashes between Dalit and upper caste students in Gujarat (Bose 1981; Desai 1981 and Baxi 1990: 215–39). The case of the other lower castes, however, involved a completely different dynamic.

## The Invention of the 'OBCs', or
## the Concealment of Caste

The expression 'backward classes' appeared for the first time in the 1870s in Madras Presidency. The Tamil region was then the crucible of a non-Brahman movement made up of lower castes except for the Untouchables. Most of them were Shudras, a massive category which includes fairly clean and noble castes, such as farmers who, due to their status as small- or medium-sized landowners and their demographic proportions, sometimes even exercise domination of the local society—at which time they are referred to as the 'dominant caste' (Srinivas 1995)—and very impure castes, such as launderers and barbers, who are few in numbers and therefore vulnerable, and whose situation can scarcely be distinguished from that of the Untouchables. For this reason, British colonial authorities in Madras grouped together both Shudra and Untouchable castes under the label 'backward classes', swelling their numbers from 39 to 131 between 1870 and 1920. This classification had no other aim than to identify the groups eligible for positive discrimination. But the stigma of untouchability decidedly made the Depressed Classes a separate group, whereas the 'Castes other than Depressed Classes', an awkward expression indeed, finally became a separate category in 1925 (Radhakrishnan 1990: 509–17).

When India achieved independence, Nehru rechristened them, divorcing their name from the notion of caste. He called them 'Other Backward Classes',[5] such a social category including groups 'other' than the Untouchables and tribals. But the key word here is 'classes': even if he was not the first to use it, Nehru was clearly intending to distance himself from an approach in terms of caste.

The Constituent Assembly did not enter into this debate. It merely designed a clause, Article 340, stipulating that the president was entitled to appoint a commission to identify the 'socially and educationally backward classes' and suggest measures to improve their condition. But by emphasizing their 'backwardness' in social and educational terms, the Constituent Assembly further complicated the task of those who would have to define the contours of this new social category, the 'OBCs', to use the abbreviation commonly employed in India.

The first Backward Classes Commission was appointed in 1953. After working for months, it came to the conclusion that its four main criteria for social backwardness—degraded status, lack of education, under representation in the civil service, and secondary and tertiary sectors—all came down to one common denominator: caste. The Commission thus drew up a list of 2,399 so-called OBC castes, which made up 32 per cent of Indian society on the basis of the 1931 census (Report of the Backward Classes Commission, 1955, Vol. 1). The Commission in fact had to go back to the last detailed census (that of 1941, organized during the Second World War, was abbreviated) that took caste into account, because the Indian government had eliminated this factor from the 1951 census, feeling that it underlay divisions that might jeopardize the unity of the young Indian nation.

The resolutely modernist attitude that permeated Jawaharlal Nehru's government partly explains why his home minister, G.B. Pant, rejected the Commission's report. He in fact argued that development efforts—which he saw as embodied in the First Five-Year Plan—would lead to 'the establishment of our society on the socialist pattern', an evolution with which 'social and other distinctions will disappear' (*Memorandum on the Report of the Backward Classes Commission* n.d.: 2). Pant added another argument in 1961 when he informed each of the state-level government heads of Nehru's decision not to conduct the specific policy in favour of OBCs on the federal level. The rationale then was that positive discrimination measures would have the drawback of penalizing the most capable (and deserving) people, and would therefore hinder efficiency in the administration and business.[6]

This last argument was a direct reaction to the Commission's recommendations, which included several measures in favour of the OBCs, ranging from a 70 per cent admissions quota in vocational training institutions to a 25 to 40 per cent reservation of vacant positions in the civil service, depending on the class. The argument of merit—and its corollary, that of efficiency that flows from competence—reflected the aspirations of independent India's leaders, but also the dread of the upper castes (to which these leaders all belonged) of seeing OBCs gain more jobs in the civil service, considered by the educated elites as their private sinecure.

As for the argument against caste criteria, it reflected the preponderance of the notions of class and class struggle among an intelligentsia influenced by Marxism as well as Gandhi's utopia of a conflict-free society. This twofold line of thinking preferred to deny the existence of caste but by doing so it maintained the social status quo.

The Indian elites' eclipsing of caste thus came to challenge decades of positive discrimination in favour of lower castes—except the Untouchables—both in India and the princely states. The princely states were vast territories (two-fifths of the area of the Raj) in which the British had left the Hindu maharajas and the Muslim nawabs to manage their principalities autonomously. Too often these states are considered to have been repositories of tradition, particularly because, in an effort to guard their privileges, the princes had resisted allowing the Congress Party a toehold in their land. This view is too simplistic. In fact, some of these princely states played a pioneering role in implementing positive discrimination, for the simple reason that their sovereign had come from a Shudra caste. In Maharashtra, the ruling dynasty of Kolhapur was of the Maratha caste (a caste of farmers). At the turn of the century the ruling prince applied an egalitarian quota policy: Shahu Maharaj, after assuming the throne in 1895, had by 1902 reserved 50 per cent of the vacant positions for backward castes out of a concern that Brahmans might dominate his administration (Mudaliar n.d.: 21).

The princely state that experimented with the most extensive positive discrimination policy was Mysore. Here again, a sovereign from the Shudra caste had sought to combat Brahman over representation in his administration. He charged Leslie Miller, the British president of the state's high court, with assessing the problem and making suggestions to remedy it. As a result, the 1918 Miller Commission was the first of a long series of Backward Classes Commissions. The term 'backward classes' was, in any event, used to refer to the lower castes, for which it recommended reserving half the highest civil service positions (Manor 1977: 60; Reddy 1990, Vol. 1: 11–12), a quota that the Mysore sovereign was to implement in 1921.

At the same time, the British were striving to improve representation of these groups in elected assemblies with ever-increasing powers. The 1919 reform thus brought the government to reserve seven seats of the Bombay Legislative Council for Marathas and 28 of the 65 seats of the Madras Council for 'non-Brahmans', a category created by grouping the Untouchable castes and the Shudra castes together to combat Brahmanical hegemony. This comfortable quota of reserved seats allowed the Justice Party to win the 1920 regional elections and in 1921 the government thereby formed had introduced a 48 per cent quota in the Madras administration for non-Brahmans (Irschick 1969: 369).

These quotas based on caste criteria were all called into question after independence in a move parallel to the rejection of the first Backward Classes Commission Report. The state of Mysore, a pioneer in the matter, was the first hit: pursuing the momentum begun in the 1920s, by 1959 it had set a 59 per cent quota for backward classes in civil service jobs. The state's high court immediately objected that this quota had been attributed to groups identified on a caste basis, which was in breach of the Constitution. The government therefore appointed a Backward Classes Commission, which concluded that there were no other viable solutions and recommended reserving 50 per cent of government jobs for backward classes, still defined by caste criteria. These quotas were added to those already granted to the Scheduled Castes and Scheduled Tribes, so that over two-thirds of the state civil service jobs were subject to quotas. Upper caste opponents brought this positive discrimination policy before the Indian Supreme Court, which rendered its decision in 1963 in the famous *Balaji* v. *Mysore* State judgement. The measures passed by the state of Mysore were repealed, first because they were based on an unconstitutional definition of OBC, giving too much weight to caste criteria and, second, because the judges felt that having over 50 per cent of jobs subjected to quotas was contrary to the spirit of the Constitution, particularly because it penalized individual merit.

The *Balaji* v. *Mysore* State judgement challenged all regional positive discrimination policies in favour of OBCs. In Kerala, the 40 per cent OBC reservation for civil service jobs was repealed by the state high court in 1964. The same occurred in Andhra Pradesh—a state created by redrawing the boundaries of Madras in 1953—three times, in 1963, 1968, and 1972, each time with the rationale that the beneficiaries were defined in terms of caste. But a new turning point was reached in the 1970s. In Tamil Nadu, the state high court, acting on a complaint brought before it by upper caste members validated the 31 per cent OBC reservation for regional government jobs in 1971. In Karnataka, after a tug-of-war lasting several years, a 26 per cent quota for OBC in the civil service was also validated in 1985 (a quota recommended by the umpteenth state Backward Classes Commission ten years earlier), although it brought the total quota to 66 per cent.

The situation did not evolve as clearly in the north where, traditionally, upper castes strongly resisted positive discrimination measures. Caste demography partly explains this difference. In the north, the 'twice-born' comprise one-fifth of the population on average, as opposed to less than 5 per cent in most southern states. In Bihar the high court invoked the Balaji decision to invalidate the OBC list that the state had drawn up in 1951—although Bihar had never used the list at all. No Backward Classes Commission had ever, in fact, been appointed in any of the northern states until the 1970s, which prevented the judges from having to invalidate their recommendations! This situation can probably be explained by the inhibiting effect of the Balaji judgement and the demographic weight of the upper castes, but even more so by the social elite's identification with the Congress Party, dominant in the region until the 1970s–80s, whereas, in the south, the creation of both the Justice Party and regional, even regionalist, parties, had continued to develop, both of which defended the cause of the lower castes.

Due to the deadlock situation, OBC populations in northern India became particularly important for opposition parties, including the socialists. Their efforts evolved into a strategy that boiled down to using quotas both as a political tool and as a lever for social advancement.

## The Political Coming-of-Age of Caste, or the Instrumentalization of Positive Discrimination

In northern India more than elsewhere, rejection of the report by the first Backward Classes Commission provoked intense debate, beginning in the 1950s, on the place of caste in Indian society and the role of positive discrimination policies. The socialists were the avant-gardes of such reflection. Drawing his inspiration as much from Ambedkar as Marx, 1950s–60s Socialist Party thinker Rammanohar Lohia maintained that caste, much more so than class, was the basic unit of Indian society and that Nehru's version of socialism would not be enough to combat inequalities (1964). Lohia worried that nationalizing industries and collectivizing land would never revolutionize the social order, simply because upper castes would continue to exercise real social domination on the basis of skills handed down from father to son 'for thousands of years' (to use Lohia's expression). Against this, the lowest castes were in need not only of socioeconomic redistribution but also of a way to shed their feelings of inferiority. A policy of positive discrimination was therefore indispensable. In 1959, the Socialist Party passed a resolution in favour of reserving 60 per cent of civil service jobs for the OBC (Mohan, Sharma, Singh and Sunilam 1997: 258–9).

In the late 1960s, the electoral breakthrough made by the socialists in Bihar put such pressure on the Congress that in 1971 the government—with a Congress majority—finally appointed the first Backward Classes Commission in the state. Its report, which recommended a 26 per cent OBC quota for government jobs, nevertheless had no effect as long as the Congress remained at the helm. In 1977, however, Congress was relegated to the opposition—nationally as well as in most of the northern states—by a new group, the Janata Party, formed by the unification of the former main opposition parties, including the socialists. In Bihar, the latter finally managed to impose a 20 per cent quota for the 'backwards' in the civil service in November 1978, in keeping with the 1971 Commission recommendations. This measure only affected 1,800 posts per year, but the upper castes took to the streets in protest, bringing down the government.

Uttar Pradesh, Bihar's neighbour and the most populous state in India, experienced a similar scenario. The first Backward Classes Commission, which the Congress had resignedly appointed in 1975, recommended allocating 29.5 per cent of civil service posts to OBCs (*Sarvadhik Pichhra Varg Ayog*, 1977: 75). The Janata Party implemented 25 per cent reservations in the state. Immediately, street demonstrations broke out that were largely responsible for bringing down the government. Here, more clearly than in Bihar, the return of the Congress to power resulted in cancellation of the reforms underway.

In view of the sociopolitical roadblocks before the lower classes of northern India, their representatives in the Janata Party devised a new strategy. In December 1978, their representatives in the party managed to have a second Backward Classes Commission appointed, presided over by a lower caste leader, B.P. Mandal. His report, completed two years later, again considered caste as the relevant criteria for positive discrimination: 'Caste is also a class of citizens and if the caste as a whole is socially and educationally backward, reservation can be made in favour of such a caste . . .' (Report of the Backward Classes Commission: First Part, 1980: 21).

On this basis, the Mandal Commission identified 3,743 castes that it found to form India's other backward classes, representing 52 per cent of the country's population. Noting that OBCs only occupied 12.5 per cent of civil service posts, the Mandal Commission recommended that 27 per cent of the posts of the public sector be reserved to the OBCs. This figure was not proportional so as to spare the ire of the judges, who, since the Balaji decision, were concerned with keeping quota totals below 50 per cent. (These 27 per cent were in addition to the 15 per cent in favour of the Scheduled Castes and the 7.5 per cent in favour of the Scheduled Tribes). The authors of the report justified their recommendations in new terms:

It is not at all our contention that by offering a few thousands jobs to OBC candidates we shall be able to make 52 per cent of the Indian population as forward. But we must recognise that an essential part of the battle against social backwardness is to be fought in the minds of the backward people. In India Government service has always been looked upon as a symbol of prestige and power. By increasing the representation of OBCs in government services, we *give them an immediate feeling of participation in the governance of this country*. When a backward class candidate becomes a Collector or a Superintendent of Police, the material benefits accruing from his position are limited to the members of his family only. But the psychological spin off of this phenomenon is tremendous; the entire community of that backward class candidate feels socially elevated. Even when no tangible benefits flow to the community at large, the feeling that now it has its 'own man' *in the 'corridors of power'* acts as morale booster. [Report of the Backward Classes Commission/ibid.: 57 (emphasis added)]

The rationale behind this project was therefore not as much social as it was political: the issue was not primarily to improve the socioeconomic condition of a disenfranchized population, but to make it gain new confidence in its relationship to power, even to mobilize it politically.

Congress was unable to rise to the challenge contained in the Mandal Report. Returning to power in 1980 after the Janata interlude, Indira Gandhi, instead of implementing its recommendations, swept them under the carpet. Not only did she deprive herself of OBC support, but she gave up this trump card to her opponents. In 1989, the Janata Dal, distant heir of the Janata Party, once again ousted Congress from power. Its leader, V.P. Singh announced the implementation of the Mandal Commission Report a few months later. In his Independence Day speech on 15 August 1990, Singh espoused the rationale of the report:

We believe that no section can be uplifted merely by money. They can develop only if they have a share in power and we are prepared to provide this share. In this year of justice, in memory of Dr. Bhimrao Ambedkar the Government has recently taken a decision to give reservation to the backward classes in jobs in Government and public sector. It is being debated as to how many persons would get benefit out of it. In a sense, taking into account the population of this country, the Government jobs account for only one per cent and out of this one per cent if one-fourth is given to anyone, it cannot be a course for this economic betterment though it may have some effect. But our outlook is clear. *Bureaucracy is an important organ of the power structure. It has a decisive role in decision-making. We want to give an effective [sic] here in the power structure and running of the country to the depressed, downtrodden and backward people.* (Singh 1997a: 361 [emphasis added])

'Empowerment' was the watchword of this political programme. Hiring quotas did not have a redistributive vocation in favour of these underprivileged categories, but were instead intended to give them access to the management of public affairs and mobilize them politically. For V.P. Singh, Mandal was not an employment scheme. The number of posts that were at stake was very low anyway. Of the 204,288 appointments that had been made in the bureaucracy in 1988, 55,158 jobs would have been given to OBCs according to the new reservation policy. In fact, the bureaucracy was shrinking, with the number of posts declining from 226,781 in 1985 to 204,288 in 1988.

In 1990, the upper caste students, reacting against Mandal, protested against both their loss of job opportunities and the challenging of a socio-political order they had always dominated (quotas in favour of the Untouchables having hardly affected them). Street demonstrations multiplied, students set themselves on fire (there were 63 such self-immolation cases), and the Supreme Court finally ordered the announced measures to be suspended.

This upper caste resistance gave rise to countermobilization among the OBCs, which for the first time formed a common front to defend the quotas they were in danger of losing. This abstract administrative category, 'the OBCs', thus acquired political substance not from the inside, but under the influence of external opposition, by being faced with the Other, the upper castes. In such a context of social polarization, Untouchables, who feared paying the price of a more generalized hostile reaction to the rationale of positive discrimination, sided with the OBCs. This new social coalition resulted in the development of new political parties, such as the Samajwadi Janata Party and the Bahujan Samaj Party, both of which claimed to represent the OBCs and the Scheduled Castes. Beginning with the 1991 elections, these groups, and of course the Janata Dal, fielded larger numbers of candidates and were increasingly successful at the polls. The OBCs, which in northern India form at least a relative majority, voted for their own and no longer for upper caste notables, following the clientelistic rationale once practiced by the Congress Party. In north India, the proportion of OBC elected representatives rose from 11 per cent in 1984 to 25 per cent in 1996, whereas that of the upper caste elected officials fell from 47 per cent to 35 per cent.[7] V.P. Singh's prognosis thus proved true since he had proclaimed that:

Now that every party is wooing the deprived classes, with every round of elections more and more representatives of the deprived sections will be elected. This will ultimately be reflected in the social composition of the local bodies, state governments, and the central government. A silent transfer of power is taking place in social terms. (Singh 1997b: 316–17)

This silent revolution, still underway, naturally resulted in newfound legitimacy for caste in the public space. The OBC front that crystallized over the 'Mandal affair' was nothing other than a collection of castes. And the increased weight of caste in the political arena was bound to return, like a boomerang, into the field of positive discrimination. The Supreme Court, before which an upper caste opponent to the Mandal Report brought a complaint, finally validated caste as a legitimate criterion for identifying OBCs within the framework of positive discrimination programmes, thus cancelling 30 years of jurisprudence based on the Balaji decision. In December 1992, in fact, the judges solemnly declared: 'A caste can be and quite often is a social class in India' (Summary of Issues, 1997: 308). Symmetrically, the Supreme Court put a stop to the Congress government's attempts to implement positive discrimination on the basis of criteria other than caste. In 1991, Prime Minister P.V. Narasimha Rao had introduced a 10 per cent quota of national civil service jobs for 'economically backward' people. In their December 1992 decision, the judges objected that economic backwardness could not be a sufficient criterion and so repealed the Rao decree.

The Balaji decision was also questioned from a different viewpoint: the Supreme Court no longer considered a 50 per cent threshold to be a glass ceiling, due to the very high percentage of OBCs, Scheduled Castes and Scheduled Tribes populations in certain states. All states thus began to raise quotas. Today Tamil Nadu reserves the largest percentage of civil service positions, with nearly four-fifths of the civil service posts subject to quotas.

The Indian practice of positive discrimination is in many respects paradoxical. The deep-rootedness of this tradition, over a century old, contrasts with the slimness of the results achieved. Reservations have not significantly improved the fate of the most destitute, at least until the 1990s when things took a different, more political turn. This is partially due to the real misuse of positive discrimination measures for Untouchables. Very early on they benefited from fairly generous quotas simply because they were easily identified, too destitute to threaten the upper castes, and bound to remain unthreatening because the quotas would never be filled. Those who were able to take advantage of the quotas ended up forming a relatively influential Untouchable elite, but it took decades of political consciousness-raising to persuade them to resist parties led by the upper castes, the Congress foremost, before they began backing the Bahujan Samaj Party and other parties with an uncompromising Dalit agenda.

Another paradox lies in the difference in treatment accorded to the Untouchables. Identifying them by caste did not pose a problem. Yet the other lower castes, which, as the expression 'Other Backward Classes' well indicates, were for decades fated to be identified and branded by other criteria. In a way, they suffered from the fact that their caste identity was not sufficiently tidy. While the stigma of untouchability placed the Scheduled Castes in a separate category, the castes directly above them were scarcely less impure and went hand in hand with sometimes-comparable segregation. In fact, the unfavourable treatment of OBCs can be explained by the upper castes' fear of being overwhelmed by groups that were far more consequential demographically and economically than the Untouchables. This explains efforts by the Congress and the judiciary to subvert caste-based identification, thereby preventing this administrative category from giving rise to a coalition of castes.

However, the most paradoxical outcome still lies elsewhere: whereas positive discrimination aims at social transformation, in India it made first and foremost a *political* impact. Contrary to the Congress attitude and that of the establishment in general, the strategy of the northern India socialists and of the main parties in southern India involved making OBC a *political* category based on caste, a major source of social oppression for Lohia and his associates. For them, positive discrimination measures were primarily a pretense for a caste alliance capable of influencing or even dislodging those in power. Hiring quotas in the public sector have never managed—or even intended—to equalize socioeconomic conditions. But the quotas have transformed the OBCs' relationship to power in two respects: first, now that their 'own kind' hold office, such role models offered psychological encouragement to go further, to fight for political power. Second, the lower castes started to form sociopolitical coalitions in the 1990s after realizing the extent of upper caste resistance to positive discrimination programmes. These programmes did not do much to change their socioeconomic condition, but they provided good reasons to mobilize together, challenge existing clientelistic networks, and seek power on their own. The fact that caste was at stake—in street demonstrations as well as before the judiciary—played an important role here because it made of this social institution the building block of large sociopolitical coalitions. Without caste, it would have been much more difficult to aggregate and articulate the interests of the plebeians.

In northern India today, all the major states are governed by OBC chief ministers, whether from a socialist tradition (Mulayam Singh Yadav in Uttar Pradesh), associated with the BJP (Nitish Kumar in Bihar) or from the BJP itself (Shivraj Singh Chauhan in Madhya Pradesh). No party can ignore the OBCs anymore—although this does not mean that they form a homogeneous category (Jaffrelot 2003: 363–86). Today, OBC empowerment does not leave their socioeconomic condition unaffected. On the contrary, the low caste leaders in office generally seek strong redistributive impact, not only by developing reservation policies, but also by appointing their own people in the administration, irrespective of quotas. For instance, Mulayam Singh Yadav and Laloo Prasad Yadav have recruited many from their caste into the police and other state services. Therefore, socioeconomic change may result from the rise to power of the lower castes in an indirect way. As usual in India, where; everything is so political, politics plays the mediating role.

## Notes

1. The key word to designate castes in India, *jati,* has the same root as *jana,* 'to be born'.
2. The impact of the census on the caste system was highlighted by Bernard Cohn in the 1970s. See Cohn 1987.
3. The relationship to ritual purity, which Louis Dumont saw as the dominant criteria of the caste system, is highly relevant here. See Dumont 1966.
4. The first Untouchable ever to have earned a Ph.D., Ambedkar was never able to find clients after he started practicing law as an advocate. See Jaffrelot 2005.
5. See Nehru's inaugural speech before the Constituent Assembly on 13 December 1946. (*Constituent Assembly Debates,* 1989, Vol. I: 59).
6. Quoted in the letter from Jawaharlal Nehru to the Chief Ministers, 27 June 1961 in Nehru 1989, Vol. 5: 456–7.
7. These figures come from a database I have compiled over the last ten years, the main findings of which were first presented in Jaffrelot 2000: 86–108.

## References

Baxi, Upendranath (1990), 'Reflections on the Reservations Crisis in Gujarat', in Veena Das, (ed.), *Mirrors of Violence: Communities, Riots and Survivors in South Asia,* Delhi: Oxford University Press.

Bose, P.K. (1981), 'Social Mobility and Caste Violence: A Study of the Gujarat Riots', *Economic and Political Weekly*, 18 April.

Cohn, Bernard (1987), *An Anthropologist among the Historians*, Delhi: Oxford University Press.

*Constituent Assembly Debates* (1989), Vol. I, New Delhi: Lok Sabha Secretariat.

Desai, I.P. (1981), 'Anti-reservation Agitation and Structure of Gujarat Society', *Economic and Political Weekly*, 15 May.

Dubey, S.N. and Mathur, U. (1972), 'Welfare Programmes for Scheduled Castes: Content and Administration', *Economic and Political Weekly*, 22 January.

Dumont, Louis (1966), *Homo Hierarchicus*, Paris: Gallimard.

Galanter, M. (1979), 'Compensatory Discrimination in Political Representation', *Economic and Political Weekly*, Annual Number, February.

——— (1994), *Competing Equalities: Law and the Backward Classes in India*, Delhi: Oxford University Press.

Irschick, E.F. (1969), *Politics and Social Conflict in South India: The Non-Brahman Movement and Tamil Separation, 1916-1929*, Bombay: Oxford University Press.

Jaffrelot, Christophe (2000), 'The Rise of the Other Backward Classes in the Hindi Belt', *Journal of Asian Studies*, Vol. 59, No. 1, February.

——— (2003), *India's Silent Revolution: The Rise of the Lower Castes in North India*, New York: Columbia University Press.

——— (2005), *Dr. Ambedkar and Untouchability: Analysing and Fighting Caste*, New York: Columbia University Press.

Lohia, Rammanohar (1964), *The Caste System*, Hyderabad: Rammanohar Lohia Samata Vidyalaya.

Manor, James (1977), *Political Change in an Indian State: Mysore, 1917-1955*, Delhi: Manohar.

*Memorandum on the Report of the Backward Classes Commission* (n.d.), New Delhi: Ministry of Home Affairs.

Mendelsohn, O. and Viciziany, M. (1988), *The Untouchables: Subordination, Poverty and the State in Modern India*, Cambridge: Cambridge University Press.

Mohan, S., Sharma, H.D. , Singh, V.P. and Sunilam (1997) (eds.), 'The Socialist Program', in *Evolution of Socialist Party in India*, New Delhi: Bapu Kaldate, abridged from the programme adopted by the 1st Conference of the Samyukta Socialist Party held at Kota from 3–6 April 1966.

Mudaliar, Chandra (n.d.), *The Kolhapur Movement*, Kolhapur: Shivaji Vidhyapith.

Nehru, Jawaharlal (1989), *Letters to the Chiefs Ministers, 1947-1964*, Vol. 5, Delhi: Oxford University Press.

Prasad, A. (1997), 'Summary of Issues, Judgement and Directions in Indra Sawhney v. Union of India', *Reservational Justice to Other Backward Classes*, New Delhi: Deep and Deep.

Radhakrishnan, P. (1990), 'Backward Classes in Tamil Nadu, 1872–1988', *Economic and Political Weekly*, 10 March.

Reddy, O. Chinnappa (1990), *Report of Karnataka Third Backward Classes Commission*, Vol. 1, Bangalore: Government of Karnataka.

*Report of the Backward Classes Commission* (1955), Vol. 1, New Delhi: Government of India.

*Report of the Backward Classes Commission: First Part* (1980), New Delhi: Government of India.

*Sarvadhik Pichhra Varg Ayog* (1977), (Hindi), Lucknow: Uttar Pradesh ki sarkar.

Sharma, B.A.V. (1982), 'Development of Reservation Theory', in B.A.V. Sharma and M.K. Reddy, (eds.), *Reservation Policy in India*, New Delhi: Light and Light Publishers.

Singh, V.P. (1997a), 'Justice for the Poor', in S. Mohan, H.D. Sharma, V.P. Singh, and Sunilam, (eds.), *Evolution of Socialist Party in India*, New Delhi: Bapu Kaldate.

—— (1997b), 'Power and Equality: Changing Grammar of Indian Politics', in A. Prasad, *Reservational Justice to Other Backward Classes*, New Delhi: Deep and Deep.

Srinivas, M.N. (1995), *Social Change in Modern India*, New Delhi: Orient Longman.

Stokes, Eric (1989 [1959]), *The English Utilitarians and India*, New Delhi: Oxford University Press.

# Chapter 25

# The Bahujan Samaj Party in north India no longer just a Dalit party?

From the 1930s to the 1950s, Dr Ambedkar evolved a new kind of leadership combining socio-religious work at the grassroots level with political action 'from above'. He became convinced that his caste fellows should convert to a new religion because Hinduism inherently condemned them to endure an everlasting oppression and at the same time he wanted to fight for their cause politically. He eventually converted to Buddhism a few months before his death in 1956 and thousands of his followers—mainly from his caste, the Mahars—did the same. Simultaneously he prepared the ground for a new political party, the Republican Party of India (RPI), which was to take roots in his native state, Maharashtra, and to develop pockets of influence in Uttar Pradesh and Punjab. However, the party started declining in the early 1970s, largely because of factionalism and the cooperation of some of its leaders by the Congress.

Almost 30 years after the launch of the RPI, a new party founded by Scheduled Caste members took shape and started making headway in north India. Its chief, Kanshi Ram had first tried to organize the non-elite groups through social work but had never contemplated conversion as a means to emancipate them. For him, such a move does not make sense unless the bulk of the lower castes is prepared to do it: 'Whatever religion we adopt, it should be in crores, not in lakhs. It may take some time. It may be possible in the 21st century. Mahars have become Buddhists, but they remain as they were' (interview with Kanshi Ram, 12 November 1996). Gradually, Kanshi Ram began to stress purely political activities and especially the building of a party, the Bahujan Samaj Party. Whether as a social worker or as a party leader, however, he emphasized the need to reach beyond the Dalit milieu. To what extent this attempt has been consistently pursued and how successful it has been are the two issues I address in this essay.

## From 'Assertiveness' to 'Empowerment': Kanshi Ram's Political Strategy for Shaping the Bahujan Samaj

Kanshi Ram was born in 1932 in a Scheduled Caste family in rural Punjab—his native village Khwaspur is situated in the district of Ropar (Parliament of India,

*I am most grateful to Owen Lynch for his comments on an earlier version of this article.

1992: 326). His exact origin is subject to controversy but he seems to have been originally from a Ramdasia *jati*—Chamars converted to Sikhism (*Sunday*, 13 February 1994: 23–31). Without talking of his religious affiliation, he underlines that his early environment was not as oppressive as the one Untouchables suffered elsewhere:

> Because of the Sikh religion, also because most of the Chamars have adopted the Sikh religion, there was some upward mobility. The teaching of the [Sikh] gurus is more egalitarian. (interview with Kanshi Ram)

Like Ambedkar's family, Kanshi Ram's benefited from the military jobs that the British reserved for Untouchables.[1] His father was the only man of the family who did not leave for the front during World War II because at least one man had to stay behind. The army not only provided a good salary, it also raised the self-esteem of the Untouchable soldiers. This social and family context, which one generally does not find in the Hindi belt, explains why Kanshi Ram was able to attend college.

After getting his B.Sc., he left the Punjab in 1958 to work as a chemist's assistant at the Explosive Research Defence Laboratory set up by the Ministry of Defence in Kirkee, near Poona in Maharashtra. Kanshi Ram is clearly a representative of the small Untouchable elite who have benefited from the reservation policy in the public sector. The miserable life of the Mahars in Poona, whose condition contrasted with the Scheduled Castes of Punjab, came as a shock to Kanshi Ram.

> I was first exposed to the miseries of the Mahars and Mangs [an even lower Untouchable caste] and then I read *Annihilation of Caste* and *What Gandhi and the Congress have done to the Untouchables*. These are the two books, which have influenced me most. Later I came to know about Mahatma Jyotirao Phule. (interview with Kanshi Ram)

He resigned in 1964 when a Dalit colleague was suspended for having protested the cancellation of a two-day leave so that he could attend two celebrations dear to Untouchables—the birthday celebrations of Ambedkar and Valmiki (the author of the *Ramayana*, whom many Untouchable Bhangis [sweepers] regard as their ancestor).[2] Since then, Kanshi Ram devoted his time to raising the consciousness of his caste fellows and to developing their assertiveness. He severed all links with his family and abandoned the idea of getting married, although he was already engaged. At that time he discovered the thought of Ambedkar and became a member of the Republican Party of India. Seven years later he resigned because he regarded the party, which was more and more fragmented and paralyzed by faction conflicts, as a vassal of the Congress.

## 'I STARTED BUILDING THE BAHUJAN SAMAJ IN 1971'[3]

Kanshi Ram inaugurated a new type of movement when he founded, on 14 October 1971, 'The Scheduled Castes (SCs) and Scheduled Tribes (STs), Other

Backward Classes (OBCs) and Minority Communities Employees Association.' This association was limited to the district of Poona but prefigured Kanshi Ram's future organizations since he already endeavoured to federate employees of Dalit, Tribal, low caste and religious minority background. Amongst the five vice-presidents who assisted Kanshi Ram were one Mahar, one Tribal, one Mali (gardener–OBC), one Muslim and one Christian. They were representatives of what Kanshi Ram considered the 'bahujan samaj'.

This expression literally means the community of those who are in great numbers, in a majority. The 'bahujans' are like the plebeians in the Roman sense, the second estate, in opposition to the patricians. However, in the Indian context, the 'bahujan' hardly form a *samaj*, i.e. a 'community' because of caste and class divisions as well as ethnic, religion, and language-based—cleavages. In fact these groups are also affected by sub-divisions. Ambedkar himself was not able to rally to his political parties the Scheduled Castes in their entirety: while his caste fellows, the Mahars, supported him more or less *en bloc*, the Chambhars (leather workers) and the Mangs (basket and rope makers) tended to vote for the Congress largely to differentiate themselves from the Mahars (Zelliot 1992: 106–7). The caste system, as Ambedkar once said, is not only a division of labour but also a division of the labourers. To transform the subaltern castes and communities into a relatively cohesive force was a colossal task that Kanshi Ram assigned to himself. To begin with, in Poona he focused on the elite of these groups, those who like him, were the product of the reservation system.

The association launched in 1971 became a federation in 1973, and went beyond the limits of Poona. Kanshi Ram left the town three years later and created a new movement soon after. On 6 December 1978 he officially founded the All-India Backward (SC, ST, OBC) and Minority Communities Employees Federation (BAMCEF) whose aim was to organize the elite of the bahujan samaj, essentially wage earners with intellectual qualifications who had benefited from quotas. BAMCEF could make rapid headway and reach a kind of critical mass because of the growing number of educated Scheduled Caste members in the administration. In Uttar Pradesh, for instance, the Scheduled Castes' literacy rate increased from 7.1 per cent in 1961 to 10.2 per cent in 1971, 15 per cent in 1981 and 27 per cent in 1991, which partly explains the growing number of Scheduled Caste members in the administration, even if the quotas are only filled in the lower rungs of the bureaucracy.[4] Today in Uttar Pradesh the Scheduled Caste Indian Administrative Service (IAS) officers 'form the largest number next to the Brahmans and Kayasuhs' (Ramaseshan 1995: 73). Yet these officers feel frustrated because they are denied 'important posts in the districts as well as the state capital' (ibid.).

Kanshi Ram travelled for years all over India to convince these officers from the bahujan samaj to get organized within the BAMCEF.[5] Gradually he built a network of activists who carried this message in the countryside.[6] In the early 1990s, BAMCEF had almost 200,000 members, amongst whom were 15,000 scientists and 3,000 MBBS graduates (Omvedt 1994: 163). The government

TABLE 25.1: BSP ELECTORAL PERFORMANCES DURING THE 1989, 1991 AND 1996 GENERAL ELECTIONS

| Year | Seats contested | Seats won | Forfeited deposits | Votes polled | % of votes polled |
|------|-----------------|-----------|--------------------|--------------|-------------------|
| 1989 | 246 | 3 | 222 | 6,215,093 | 2.07 |
| 1991 | 231 | 2 | 211 | 4,420,721 | 1.61 |
| 1996 | 117 | 11 | 47 | 12,184,038 | 3.64 |

Sources: Election Commission of India 1990: 7; Election Commission of India n.d.: 9; and Election Commission of India 1996.

became concerned about the organization's progress because of the risk of politicization of the Scheduled Caste employees. BAMCEF cadres—Kanshi Ram estimated them to be about 1,000 in the mid-1980s—were continuously transferred and harassed.[7] This led Kanshi Ram, in 1985, to transform BAMCEF into a shadow organization:

It has no office-bearers. There are no records of these thousands of office-bearers. Only we know the workers. They provide us brain power and money power. They can contribute. Most of the BSP offices are run by BAMCEF people. (interview with Kanshi Ram)

The vice-president of the BSP unit of Madhya Pradesh, I.M.P. Verma defines today's BAMCEF as being made of those 'who can pay money, mind and time for their community?' (interview with Indra Mani Prasad Verma, Bhopal). Its (former) members evidently form the backbone of the party. While BAMCEF endowed Kanshi Ram with a core group of followers, he did not really regret its official dissolution since he no longer regarded it as his priority to do social work among the employees:

I started with the idea of social transformation and economic emancipation. I still want my people to advance socially and economically. But I have realized that unless we have political clout, we cannot advance much on those sides. (interview with Kanshi Ram)

Kanshi Ram was following in the footsteps of Ambedkar who also thought that the lower castes not only needed to become aware of their rights and organize but had also to seize power. In Kanshi Ram's vocabulary, it implied a shift from 'assertiveness' to 'empowerment'.

## IN THE ARENA OF PARTY POLITICS

Kanshi Ram founded the Dalit Shoshit Samaj Sangharsh Samiti (Committee to fight for the community of the exploited and the oppressed) on 6 December, 1981—Ambedkar's death anniversary. This organization dispensed with the official euphemisms (Backward Classes, Scheduled Castes, etc.) preferring instead the words, Dalit and Soshit that politicized Untouchables use more frequently to designate themselves. However, Dalit does not refer here to the Untouchables only, as it is often the case, especially in Maharashtra. The English-language publication of the DS-4, as the movement came to be known, *The Oppressed Indian*, repeatedly published editorials propagating an historical vulgate in which the Shudras (OBCs) and Ati-shudras (Untouchables) were bracketed together and went on to include Tribals as well:

The history of India is full of the daring stories of the Shudras and Ati-Shudras. There are number of instances in which the Shudras and Ati-Shudras (*the oppressed and the exploited*) [emphasis added] set examples of bravery in the field of battle at the cost of their life for the sake of others. Thousands of years back they were the rulers of this land. Sikander the Great had a taste of the bravery of the Shudra Army when he was advancing to conquer India. He had to go back when confronted with the tribals of the land. Unfortunately, the high caste historians of this land who pose as the custodians of the culture and literature distorted the facts and wrote the history in such a way that for all time Shudras and Ati-Shudras were projected as very helpless and hopeless creatures. ('Marching to Awaken the Ambedkarite Masses', *The Oppressed Indian* 1983: 16)

On the eve of the fiftieth anniversary of the 1932 Poona Pact that the Congress was preparing to celebrate with great pomp, Kanshi Ram published a booklet, *The Chamcha Age*, where he denounced this agreement as sealing the alienation of the Untouchables. He argued that the system of reserved seats that had been forced on Ambedkar, who favoured a system of separate electorates, had helped the high castes dominate Congress, co-opt Dalit candidates who were mere sycophants (*Chamcha*) of the Congress since the Scheduled Castes were not in a majority in any single reserve constituency. Facing such a situation, the DS-4 had to act as a political party and contest elections. It was the only way out since, 'A tool, an agent, a stooge of *Chamcha* is created to oppose the real, the genuine fighter' (Ram 1982: 90). The DS-4 presented 46 candidates for the assembly elections of Haryana in 1982, without making much of an impact.

The Bahujan Samaj Party (BSP), officially founded on 14 April 1984, Ambedkar's birthday, took over from the DS-4.[8] It did not imply much more than a change of name but by rechristening his organization that way, Kanshi Ram consummated his shift from social work to party politics. The BSP has made rapid progress on the electoral front. During the general elections of 1984, it received more than one million votes. This number was multiplied sixfold in 1989 when the party got 6,215,093 votes, 2.07 per cent of the recorded votes and obtained three seats in the Lok Sabha. In 1991, it won only two seats and 1.61 per cent of the votes but five years later it gained 11 seats with 3.64 per cent of the votes.

The growth of the BSP enabled the party to obtain the statute of National Party from the Election Commission after the 1996 elections. This growth resulted chiefly from Kanshi Ram's continuous efforts to get the bahujan samaj organized since the 1960s. The title of the BSP mouthpiece, *Bahujan Sangathak* (the organizer—in the sense of unifier—of the masses) bears testimony to the priority given to organizational aspects. Today, thanks to the activists trained by the BAMCEF and the DS-4, the BSP has committees in all the districts of Uttar Pradesh. In Madhya Pradesh, in the mid-1990s only six districts (Panna, Vidisha, Betul, Jabalpur, Ujjain and Khandwa) did not have a BSP unit. However, the rise of the BSP has also much to do with the party's implantation and mobilization techniques and their actions while in office.

## The BSPs Implantation and Mobilization Techniques

The BSP inherited from the DS-4 not only a leader and his network, of activists, but also a range of mobilization techniques. For instance, between 15 March and 17 April 1983 the DS-4 organized a 3,000 km cycle march—bicycles being the main means of locomotion for the poor, as Kanshi Ram observed—covering seven states in order to 'educate the oppressed and the exploited people that they need to build up their own organization and independent movement' ('Marching to Awaken the Ambedkarite Masses', *The Oppressed Indian* 1983). The following year, the DS-4 launched a similar but bigger movement with processions of cyclists leaving from five peripheral provinces of India to converge on Delhi, which recalled, oddly enough, the form of the *Ekatmata yatra*, organized shortly before by the Vishva Hindu Parishad. This hundred-day campaign allowed 7,000 meetings to be held all over India (Joshi 1986: 115). It concluded in Delhi with a huge meeting from which emerged the Bahujan Samaj Party.

For Kanshi Ram and his party—the DS-4 and then the BSP—these demonstrations were intended to deliver an ideological message. This discourse was symbolized by the oft-repeated metaphor of the ball-point pen, used by Kanshi Ram on platforms and before cameras: the top of the pen represents the upper castes who, though being only 15 per cent of the population rule the country while the pen itself represents the remaining 85 per cent who have to become aware of their fate and of their numerical strength. This logic is omnipresent in the slogans, often extremely aggressive,[9] designed by the BSP for political as well as educational purposes:

(1) Jiski jitni samkhya bhari uski utni bhagidari
The highest number has to be the best represented.
(2) 85 par 15 ka raj nahin chalega, nahin chalega
85 per cent living under the rule of 15 per cent, this will not last, this will not last.
(3) Vot hamara, raj tumhara, nahin chalega, nahin chalega
We have the votes, you have the power, this will not last, this will not last.
(4) Tilak, taraju aur talvar isko maro joote char
The tilak [emblem of the sectarian affiliation of the Hindus which is applied on the forehead and symbolizes the Brahman], the balance [symbol of the merchant castes]

and the sword [symbol of the warrior castes], hit them with their shoes [symbol of the work of the Chamars, the principal Untouchable caste of North of India, who work with leather].

(5) Tilak, taraju aur talvar, unhe pade joote char [Down with the Brahmans, Thakurs and Banias].[10]

Kanshi Ram has tried to emerge as a spokesman for the bahujan samaj by advocating the interests of all its sub-groups. He clearly expressed this concern in a speech at the Vidhan Sabha of Haryana that was made during the election campaign in 1987:

The other limb of the Bahujan Samaj [in addition to the Scheduled Castes] which we call OBC or Other Backward Classes, needs this party badly. Thirty-nine years after independence, these people have neither been recognised nor have they obtained any rights. Improvements have been introduced in the legislation for the Scheduled Castes and the Scheduled Tribes, but nothing similar has happened for these people. The truth is that the government of this country is not ready to recognise them and we see that according to section 340, which was included in the Constitution by Dr. Ambedkar for the welfare of these people, and in respect of it the Kaka Kalelkar and Mandal Commissions were constituted. The reports of both the commissions were thrown in the waste paper basket on the pretext that there are 3,743 castes that can be called Other Backward Castes. But our central government is not ready to recognize any of these castes. When these castes are not even recognized, where is the question of obtaining their rights?

The religious minorities also badly need this party. The religious minorities have many problems and their problems are increasing day by day and are becoming more and more difficult. But we think that the biggest problems are the riots done against them. The Muslim minority is a big community and is about 11 to 12 per cent of the whole population. Against these people, in the 365 days of the year, at least 400 disturbances happen or are created against them. In this way whatever progress or betterment they achieve with hard labour is destroyed by these riots. (Ram 1992: 23)

Kanshi Ram thus admitted quite readily that in some respects the conditions of the Scheduled Castes were better than those of other components of the bahujan samaj. For example, he admitted that the Scheduled Castes and the Scheduled Tribes had a larger presence than the OBCs because of the quota system and that a special effort had to be undertaken in their favour. One of the BSP's slogans has been 'Mandal ayog lagu karo, ya kursi khali karo' (Implement Mandal or vacate the seat). Kanshi Ram has repeatedly emphasized the under-representation of OBCs in the administration:

In this country, out of the 450 District Magistrates more than 125 are from SCs/STs but those from the OBCs are very few. . . . The number of OBC is 50 to 52 per cent but we don't see any of them as District Magistrate. The issue, which is special for us, is that reservation is not a question of our daily bread, reservation is not a question of our jobs, reservation is a matter of participation in the government and administration. We want participation in the government and administration of this country. There is democracy in this country. If in the republic 52 per cent of the people cannot participate, then which is the system in which they can participate?[11]

Kanshi Ram's tours or election campaigns have provided him with excellent opportunities for aggressively propagating this discourse of empowerment. It is primarily aimed at shaping the bahujan samaj on a pan-Indian basis and relies on administrative categories such as the Scheduled Castes, Scheduled Tribes and Other Backward Classes. This canvassing was systematically accompanied by references to Ambedkar whose portraits served as a symbol of the anti-caste movement.[12] For decades, the Ambedkarites have stylized 'Baba Saheb' by representing him as always impeccably dressed and groomed. His portraits are quite often flanked by those of Mahatma Jyotirao Phule and Lord Buddha, so much so that a kind of pan-Dalit or even pan-bahujan iconography has been evolved in the course of time. However, the BSP has been able to combine these pan-Indian images with vernacular cultures and even local caste identities. This was evident in the use of street theatre, a technique of conscientization that the Dalit movement had perfected over a long period in Maharashtra. The BSP-sponsored theatre groups display in a dramatic form the sufferings of the Dalits at the hands of the upper castes and attract much attention, especially in villages. The BSP has therefore become adept at using elements of folk cultures to project new notions such as that of the bahujan samaj.

In Madhya Pradesh, the DS-4 and then the BSP, similarly utilized the traditions of the Satnamis. Initially the Satnampanth was formed in the early nineteenth century by Ghasidas, a Chamar from Chhattisgarh who came to be recognized as a guru. He initiated a new faith whose devotees ignored the Hindu deities but believed in satnam (true name). Eventually, 'Satnampanth developed a stock of myths, rituals and practices which were associated with the gurus' (Dube 1993: 385) especially Ghasidas. His followers and their descendants—who have come to be known as Satnamis—have remained Scheduled Castes but have always actively challenged the caste system (Dube 1998). Kanshi Ram attended the yearly Satnami fair in Chhind in the early 1980s probably because it was a good opportunity to meet thousands of Dalits. The DS-4 had an exhibition on Ambedkar in Raigarh, displaying his achievements such as the burning of the Manusmriti in Mahad and so on. R.K. Jangde, a Satnami who became chief of the DS-4 of Raipur district in 1984, joined the movement at this juncture (interview with R.K. Jangde, Bhopal, 19 October 1995). Today, the Satnamis have the largest number of Scheduled Caste members—including the president, Daulat Ram Ratnakar—in the MP Executive Committee.

In Uttar Pradesh, the BSP has exploited the emotional dimension of caste histories and myths. The Pasis, who traditionally raise pigs, regard themselves as descendants of medieval kings or soldiers of Rajput kings. Folk tales narrating the martial achievements of Maharaja Bijli Pasi, Raja Trilok Chand, Raja Madari Pasi and Raja Satan stress the bravery of the Pasis in their fight against the British. The

BSP has cashed in on this oral culture to gain greater acceptance within a caste that tends to be more favourably inclined towards the Janata Dal because of Ram Vilas Paswan. For instance, Mayawati declared in an interview:

The people who wrote our history wiped out all traces of Dalit raja-maharajas. For a long time our history has been wiped out. The social system is such that someone like Bijli Pasi found no mention in our history books while there is evidence that the Pasis at one time were ruling this area. So I am not inventing history, I am only highlighting history that has been consciously suppressed. (*India Today*, 11 August 1997: 33)

In Bundelkhand, the BSP often refers to Jhalkaribai, a member of the female battalion (called Durga Vahini) of the Rani of Jhansi who is still very popular for her role in the 1857 rebellion against the British. Jhalkaribai was a Kori, an Untouchable whose rank was not much above the Chamars, but folk stories stress the fact that she had special access to the queen, whom she taught archery, wrestling and shooting (Tiwari 1998). She is also presented as exceptionally courageous. In 1996, in Bundelkhand the BSP fielded a candidate whose virtues were compared to Jhalkaribai, so that the party could cash in on the popularity of her story.

TABLE 25.2: Percentage of Votes Polled by the BSP in Five North India States During the 1989, 1991 and 1996 General Elections

| Year | Haryana | Punjab | Uttar Pradesh | Madhya Pradesh | Jammu & Kashmir |
|------|---------|--------|---------------|----------------|-----------------|
| 1989 | 1.62 | 8.62 | 9.93 | 4.28 | 4.06 |
| 1991 | 1.79 | no election | 8.70 | 3.54 | no election |
| 1996 | 6.6 | 9.35 | 20.61 | 8.18 | 6 |

Thus, in the 1980s, the BSP tried to take root in north India by utilizing two kinds of resources: (a) in terms of party-building, the leadership of Kanshi Ram and, at the local level, the network of cadres he had shaped through BAMCEF and the DS-4; (b) in terms of conscientization and mobilization of supporters, a combination of the bahujan discourse and local traditions. These resources did not enable the party to implant itself evenly in north India. It carved out pockets of influence where the context was especially favourable—e.g. regions where a new bahujan middle class had developed as a result of the reservation policy—and in localities whose special characteristics made them receptive to the BSP ideology and programme.

## The BSP in Uttar Pradesh and Madhya Pradesh

The states where the BSP has made inroads in the last 15 years are mainly Punjab, Uttar Pradesh and Madhya Pradesh.

The rise of the BSP in the Punjab has been systematically studied by Kanchan Chandra who points out that it was helped in part by the previous attempt at mobilization of the Scheduled Castes such as the Adharm movement (1998: 20) which had already prepared the ground for the Scheduled Caste Federation and the RPI. I shall focus on Uttar Pradesh and Madhya Pradesh where the BSP benefited from local traditions of Dalit militancy. In Uttar Pradesh, the Jatav movement in the Agra region which started in the 1920s prepared the ground for the RPI and then the BSP (Lynch 1969). In Madhya Pradesh the Satnami movement in Chhattisgarh and socialist parties in Vindhya Pradesh played a similar role, though to a lesser extent. In both states the intensity of caste conflicts as reflected in the large number of 'atrocities'—murder, rape, violation and plunder—against the Scheduled Castes contributed to Dalit militancy.

In Uttar Pradesh and Madhya Pradesh the BSP also owed its rise to its capacity to reach beyond the Dalit milieu.

## LOCAL IMPLANTATIONS

In Uttar Pradesh, the electoral presence of the BSP began to be felt in 1984, especially in the by-elections held in the mid- and late-1980s, when the party secured the second position in most of the constituencies. In 1985 Mayawati contested in Bijnor and lost to Meira Kumar (the daughter of Jagjivan Ram) but got 65,000 votes. In 1987 she contested in Haridwar and lost again to the Congress candidate but came second before Ram Vilas Paswan who could not save his deposit. The following year Kanshi Ram lost in Allahabad against V.P. Singh but made an impact. In 1989 the BSP emerged as a force to reckon with, when it polled 9.3 per cent during the Ninth General Elections—as against 7.4 per cent to the BJP. In the late 1980s-early 1990s, the BSP's zones of strength remained confined to Bundelkhand and, later, eastern Uttar Pradesh but since the mid-1990s, its influence has been more evenly distributed, as evident from Table 25.4.

In contrast to the situation prevailing in Uttar Pradesh, the BSP has not been able to spread its influence evenly in the different regions of Madhya Pradesh. In 1996, the region-wise electoral table compiled by the Centre for the Study of Developing Societies showed discrepancies between Vindhya Pradesh and the other areas (see Table 25.5).

The figure concerning Malwa needs to be disaggregated because in the northern districts of Morena, Bhind and Gwalior, the BSP is at least as strong as in Satna and Rewa, its two strongholds in Vindhya Pradesh. In fact, besides Bilaspur district in Chhattisgarh, the BSP has taken root mostly in the districts bordering Uttar Pradesh, partly because of the influence from this state where the party started its career earlier but also because of caste conflicts.

In Vindhya Pradesh, for instance, the upper castes account for about one-fifth of the population—roughly the same proportion as in Uttar Pradesh and the

TABLE 25.3: The Atrocities Against the Scheduled Castes by State

| State | 1984-5 |
|---|---|
| Total | 16,586 |
| Uttar Pradesh | 4,200 |
| Madhya Pradesh | 6,128 |
| Rajasthan | 1,648 |
| Bihar | 1,845 |
| Gujarat | 690 |
| Tamil Nadu | 689 |
| Maharashtra | 579 |

*Source:* Tatu 1991: 131.

Brahmans, more than 13 per cent of the total, are especially oppressive. This has enabled the left, from the Praja Socialist Party to the Janata Dal, to acquire some influence in this area but they have gradually lost ground because of factional fights and a lack of organizational strength. When the BSP emerged as a force in Rewa district, the OBC votes were automatically transferred from the socialists to the BSP.[13] Indeed, in 1991 the BSP candidate who won the Rewa Lok Sabha seat was a Kurmi who could draw on the votes of the Scheduled Castes and the Kurmis, who were united against the upper castes. In reaction, the latter launched a Savam Samaj Party, the party of the community of the forward castes, which polled 13.5 per cent of the valid votes in Rewa constituency in 1996, as against 27 per cent to the BSP candidate who won the seat. In this area the BSP obviously benefited from the polarization between the upper castes and the lower castes. In Madhya Pradesh at large, the BSP can try to project itself as the spokesman for the bahujan all the more as it does not suffer from OBC-dominated competitors such as the Samajwadi Party, the Samata Party or the Janata Dal.

In addition to local traditions and caste conflicts, the BSP's rise in Madhya Pradesh and Uttar Pradesh stem from their capacity to attract low caste voters in addition to the Dalits.

MORE THAN A DALIT PARTY

In the 1993 Vidhan Sabha elections in Madhya Pradesh, only 31 per cent of the BSP candidates belonged to the Scheduled Castes, not much more than the OBC (23.5 per cent) and Tribal candidates, while 9 per cent of these candidates were Muslims (Muslims are 4.96 per cent of the population of this state). Similarly, in Uttar Pradesh, during the 1996 state elections, the Scheduled Castes were only 28 per cent of the total BSP candidates, with the OBCs making up 24 per cent and the Muslims 18 per cent, while 16.6 per cent were from the upper castes! 

The social background of the BSP cadres is very similar to that of its candidates. While Dalits (often from the BAMCEF) form the hard core of the party apparatus, the BSP includes many OBCs, Tribals and Muslims amongst its cadres and even its state leaders. A Kurmi and a Pal have been past presidents of the UP unit. Similarly, the Vice President of the MP unit is a Nai (barber).

Kanshi Ram has endeavoured to co-opt leaders enjoying personal support among non-Dalit groups. In Madhya Pradesh where the Scheduled Tribes represent 23.27 per cent of the population, he recruited Arvind Netam, a former minister of Indira Gandhi and Narasimha Rao who had been elected MP in Kanker, Bastar district, five times. In 1996 the Congress refused to give him a ticket as he was facing corruption charges, but his wife stood in his place and won. He then decided to shift to the BSP in 1997. However, he lost in the 1998 Lok Sabha elections and rejoined the Congress, even though he had been given responsibilities in the BSP. In the same way Kanshi Ram recruited Arif Mohammed Khan, a former minister of Rajiv Gandhi government who was elected MP from Bulandshahr (Uttar Pradesh) in 1989. He won the Lok Sabha seat of Bahraich in 1998. Kanshi Ram also solicited the support of Imam Bukhari of the Great Mosque of Delhi but was disappointed by his impact on the Muslim voters during the Uttar Pradesh assembly elections in 1996.

In fact, Kanshi Ram's efforts to expand his party beyond the Dalits have not been entirely successful. In Uttar Pradesh, the BSP had more OBC MLAs in 1996 (23 as against 20 SCs and 11 Muslims). However these candidates won because of Dalit voters who tend to follow the party leaders' advice in such a way that they

TABLE 25.4: REGION-WISE VOTE SHARE OF THE BSP IN THE 1991, 1993 AND 1996 UTTAR PRADESH ELECTIONS

| Regions | 1991 Assembly elections (in %) | 1993 Assembly elections (in %) | 1996 Lok Sabha elections (in %) | 1996 Assembly elections* (in %) |
|---|---|---|---|---|
| Uttarakhand | 3.5 | 4.2 | 10.1 | 21.5 |
| Ruhelkhand | 5.9 | 2.7 | 20.5 | 27.2 |
| Upper Doab/Western UP | 3.5 | 5.7 | 18.5 | 29.7 |
| Awadh/Central UP | 8.8 | 5.6 | 18.8 | 33.2 |
| Lower Doab | 10.2 | 9.9 | 22.8 | |
| Bundelkhand | 20.3 | 26.1 | 25.8 | 35.8 |
| Poorvanchal/Eastern UP | 13.5 | 21.9 | 20.2 | 27.45* |

*Sources: Frontline,* 3 December 1993; 24, 28 June 1996 and 15 November 1996: 22.
*For these elections, the region-wise vote share of the BSP has been analysed on the basis of six regions only, Uttarakhand, Ruhelkhand, Western UP, Central UP, Bundelkhand and Eastern UP.

TABLE 25.5: REGION-WISE ELECTION RESULTS OF THE BSP IN MADHYA PRADESH (IN %)

| | Vindhya Pradesh | Chhattisgarh | Mahakoshal | Malwa |
|---|---|---|---|---|
| 1996 Lok Sabha elections | 19.6 | 7.4 | 2.9 | 1.2 |

*Source: Frontline,* 28 June 1996: 85.

now form a transferable vote bank. The BSP receives a fraction of its votes from the OBCs. A poll carried out by the Center for the Study of Developing Societies before the 1996 state elections in Uttar Pradesh showed that while only 4 per cent of the Yadavs and 5 per cent of the Muslims (two categories who support the Samajwadi Party of Mulayam Singh Yadav) were going to vote for the BSP, 27 per cent of the Kurmis and 19 per cent of the lower OBCs intended to do so. However, those figures remain much lower than the 65 per cent of Dalits who expressed their preference for the BSP (*India Today*, 31 August 1996: 53). Today Kanshi Ram considers the conquest of the Most Backward Castes the utmost priority of the BSP, particularly in Uttar Pradesh: 'There are 78 Most Backward Castes in Uttar Pradesh. Twenty-six per cent of the UP population are from the MBCs and the maximum tickets I have given to the MBCs' (interview with Kanshi Ram). He did not quite go that far but gave more than 51 (17.8 per cent) of the tickets to candidates from the MBCs and was well advised in doing so since 16 of them won, a far better rate of return than from any other category, including the Scheduled Castes (19 successful candidates out of 83).

Thus, the BSP took root in parts of north India not merely because of Kanshi Ram's organizational work and charisma. The niches it carved out for itself in Uttar Pradesh and Madhya Pradesh coincided with areas known for long-standing Dalit movements and, perhaps more importantly, the BSP could attract some support among the OBCs because it fielded candidates and gave responsibilities to cadres from these caste groups. But the leap forward that the BSP achieved between 1993 and 1996 in Uttar Pradesh can also be explained by its tactical alliances.

## Using Ladders to Reach Power:
## A Factor of Growth, But for How Long?

Kanshi Ram refused for a long time to make electoral alliances that could distract him from his main aim, namely the organization of the bahujan samaj. But since the founding of the DS-4 his priority was to get access to power and, like Ambedkar, he learned quite soon that expedients were necessary to foster the rise to power of the low castes. In 1993, the BSP formed a pre-election pact with the Samajwadi Party of Mulayam Singh Yadav. This alliance responded more to tactical than to ideological considerations, as Kanshi Ram explicitly admitted: 'The reason why I concluded an alliance with Mulayam Singh Yadav is that if we join our votes in U[ttar] P[radesh] we will be able to form the government.'[14]

In the 1993 Assembly elections, the Samajwadi Party won 109 seats out of 425 and the BSP 67. Both parties formed the government thanks to the Congress' support. Mulayam Singh Yadav became Chief Minister and the BSP obtained 11 ministerial portfolios in a government of 27. During the first month of this coalition, the BSP and the SP faced down the BJP and some members of the Congress who vehemently protested the implementation in Uttarakhand—a sub-

TABLE 25.6: Social Profile of the BSP Candidates and MLAs in the Assembly
Elections of Madhya Pradesh (1993) and Uttar Pradesh

| (1996) Castes and communities | Madhya Pradesh (1993 candidates) (in %) | Uttar Pradesh (1996 candidates) (in %) | Uttar Pradesh (1996 MLAs) (in %) |
|---|---|---|---|
| *Upper castes* | | 48 (16.4) | 9 (13.5) |
| Brahman | | 11 (3.8) | 3 (4.5) |
| Rajput | | 24 (8.3) | 4 (6) |
| Banya | | 4 (1.3) | |
| Khattri | | 2 (0.7) | |
| Bhumihar | | 2 (0.7) | 1 (1.5) |
| Kayasth | | 1 (0.3) | |
| Kashyap | | 3 (1) | 1 (1.5) |
| Other | | 1 (0.3) | |
| *Intermediate castes* | | 5 (1.7) | 1 (1.5) |
| Jats | | 5 (1.7) | 1 (1.5) |
| *Other Backward Classes* | 69 (23.5) | 87 (30.4) | 26 (38.8) |
| *Backward castes* | 25 (8.5) | 36 (12.6) | 10 (15) |
| Kurmi | 16 (5.5) | 21 (7.3) | 8 (12) |
| Ahir/Yadav | 8 (2.7) | 10 (3.4) | 1 (1.5) |
| Lodh | 1 (0.3) | 5 (1.7) | 1 (1.5) |
| *Most Backward castes* | 44 (15) | 57 (17.8) | 16 (24) |
| Pal | | 8 (2.8) | 4 (6) |
| Teli | 12 (4.1) | 1 (0.3) | |
| Kachhi/Kushwaha | 9 (3) | 5 (1.7) | 2(3) |
| Kirar | 2 (0.7) | | |
| Gujjar | 2 (0.7) | 3 (1) | |
| Nai | 2 (0.7) | | |
| Rawat | 1 (0.3) | | |
| Mali | 1 (0.3) | | |
| Marar | 1 (0.3) | | |
| Kallar | 1 (0.3) | | |
| Gadariya | 1 (0.3) | | |
| Nishad | | 6 (2) | 3 (4.5) |
| Baghela | | 1 (0.3) | 1 (1.5) |
| Kumhar | | 1 (0.3) | 1 (1.5) |
| Sunar | | 1 (0.3) | |
| Chaurasia | | 1 (0.3) | |
| Rajbhar | | 7 (2.4) | 2(3) |
| Shakya | | 4 (1.3) | 1 (1.5) |
| Saini | | 4 (1.3) | |
| Maurya | | 9 (3) | 2(3) |
| Others | 12 (4) | | |
| *Scheduled Castes* | 91 (31) | 83 (29) | 19 (28.4) |
| Chamar/Jatav | 33 (11) | 59 (20.6) | 11 (16) |
| Satnami | 26 (9) | | |
| Mahar | 12 (4) | | |

| Bhangi/Balmiki | 2 (0.7) | 3 (1) | |
| Balai | 2 (0.7) | | |
| Kori | 1 (0.3) | | 1 (1.5) |
| Dhobi | | 2 (0.7) | 1 (1.5) |
| Khatik | | 1 (0.3) | 1 (1.5) |
| Pasi | | 13 (4.5) | 5 (7.5) |
| Katheriya | | 2 (0.7) | |
| Kuril | | 2 (0.7) | |
| Others | 15 (5) | 1 (0.3) | |
| Scheduled Tribes | 75 (26) | | |
| Muslim | 26 (9) | 51 (18) | 11 (16) |
| Sikh | | 2 (0.7) | |
| Christian | | 1 (0.3) | |
| Unidentified | 30 (10) | 9 (3) | 1 (1.5) |
| TOTAL | 291 (100) | 286 (100) | 67 (100) |

Sources: For Madhya Pradesh, interviews at the BSP office of Bhopal; for Uttar Pradesh, *Bahujan Sangathak*, 11 November 1996.

region of Uttar Pradesh where the OBCs represented only two per cent of the population—of the quotas designed after the Mandal Report.

The relations between the two partners, however, soon deteriorated. First, the BSP was getting worried about the advancement of Yadavs in the administration.[15] Second, the Backward Castes, who were anxious to improve their social status and to keep the most subaltern groups under their domination, reacted violently to the Dalits' efforts towards social mobility. Conflicts over the wages of the agricultural labourers,[16] disputes regarding the proprietorship of land and clashes over expenditures on wedding processions that Untouchables can or cannot afford in the eyes of the OBCs, have always been acute. However, they have increased since both groups, the Dalits and the OBCs, have become more assertive since the 1993 elections. These bones of contention partly explain the increasing number of 'atrocities'. The Commission of Scheduled Castes and Scheduled Tribes enumerated 11,719 cases of 'atrocities' in its 1989-90 report; five years later, it listed 35,262 such cases in its report of 1995, with Uttar Pradesh being the most violent state (see Table 25.8).

The recrudescence of atrocities in Uttar Pradesh was often caused by the upper castes, more particularly the Rajputs, who were worried about the increasing political influence of the Dalits (Swami 1994: 4–12). However, the OBCs—and especially the Yadavs—who became more self-confident after the formation of Mulayam Singh Yadav's government, were also prompt to harass the Untouchables.[17]

The BSP workers reacted by intensifying their efforts to set up statues of Ambedkar in mohallas and villages. This idea, which had apparently been suggested by Radhey Lal Boudh, a leader of the Dalit Panthers (Mukerji 1994: 60), served several purposes. It was hoped that it would enable the BSP to propagate the

TABLE 25.7: Caste and Community Background of the BSP Executive
Committees in UP and MP after the 1997 Party Elections

| Caste and communities | Madhya Pradesh | Uttar Pradesh* |
|---|---|---|
| Upper castes | | 4 |
|   Brahman | | 3 |
|   Banya | | 1 |
| Other Backward Classes | 15 | 13 |
|   Yadav | | |
|   Kurmi | 4 | 1 |
|   Lodh | | 1 |
|   Teli | 2 | |
|   Nai | 1 | 1 |
|   Kachi | 3 | 1 |
|   Gujar | 2 | 1 |
|   Kirar | 1 | |
|   Mallah | 1 | |
|   Kalar | 1 | |
|   Gadarya | | 1 |
|   Saini | | 1 |
|   Bharbhunja (Rajbbar) | | 2 |
|   Manihar | | 1 |
|   Kumhar | | 1 |
|   Nishad | | 1 |
|   Bind | | 1 |
| Scheduled Castes | 11 | 5 |
|   Chamar | 7 | 3 |
|   (Satnami) | (4) | |
|   (Jatav) | (1) | (1) |
|   (Ahirvar) | (1) | |
|   Pasi | | 1 |
|   Mahar | 2 | |
|   Basoh | 1 | |
|   Balai | 1 | |
|   Khatik | | 1 |
| Scheduled Tribes | 6 | |
|   Gond | 2 | |
|   Bhil | 1 | |
|   Mina | 1 | |
|   Urav (Christian) | 1 | |
|   Bhilala | 1 | |
| Muslim | 4 | 3 |
| Unidentified | | 4 |
| TOTAL | 36 | 28 |

*The office bearers alone are taken into account.

TABLE 25.8: ATROCITIES AGAINST THE SCHEDULED CASTES BY STATE

| State | 1989–90 | 1995 |
|---|---|---|
| Uttar Pradesh | 1,067 | 14,966 |
| Madhya Pradesh | 5,592 | 2,717 |
| Rajasthan | 1,501 | 5,204 |
| Bihar | 434 | N.A. |
| Gujarat | 710 | N.A. |
| Tamil Nadu | 334 | N.A. |
| Maharashtra | 426 | N.A. |
| TOTAL | 11,719 | 35,262 |

*Sources:* For 1989-90, *Lok Sabha Debates,* Vol. 8, 1990: 622–30 and for 1995, Hanumanthappa, Vol. 2, 1997: 9.

Ambedkarite iconography likely to generate a kind of pan-Indian bahujan 'imagined community'. It was also a means to assert the bahujans' control over land and correlatively the building of such statues could be 'rituals of provocation' that could trigger riots and polarize the upper and lower castes, much as building temples or sufi tombs often serve to set off communal (Hindu-Muslim) riots and can be used for crystallizing communal solidarities (Gaborieau 1985).

In March 1994, in Meerut, Dalits demonstrated against the removal of one of these statues from a public park. The police dispersed them and killed two demonstrators. In Fatehullapur (Barabanki district) Yadavs protested the installation of a bust of Ambedkar on a plot they had been occupying for a long time. In a span of four months about 60 incidents linked to the installation of statues led to 21 deaths amongst the Dalits (*India Today,* 10 April 1994: 56). The BSP insisted that Mulayam Singh should take all necessary measures to stop these 'incidents' but they continued. For Kanshi Ram the growing number of atrocities was the main reason for the divorce between the BSP and the SP.[18]

However, the immediate reason for this divorce was Kanshi Ram's feeling of having been betrayed by his ally. During the local elections, the SP and the BSP did not carry out seat adjustments and the SP often preferred to support Janata Dal candidates. The BSP won only one chairmanship of a district committee (Zila Parishad), while the BJP gained one-third and the SP one-half of them (Mishra 1995: 1356). Moreover, Mulayam Singh did not hesitate to welcome BSP dissidents into his party, and probably even encouraged their defection. In June 1994 several of its leaders—Dr Massod Ahmed, Minister of State for Education; Mohammed Islam, general secretary of the BSP in Uttar Pradesh; Sheikh Suleiman, leader of the parliamentary group of Lucknow—left their posts to protest the authoritarianism of the BSP's leaders and their indifference towards the Muslims (*The Times of India,* 24 June 1994). Kanshi Ram accused Mulayam of being responsible for these defections. The chief minister preferred not to accept the support of the BSP dissidents. One year later, he established a privileged relationship with the resident of the BSP of Uttar Pradesh, Raj Bahadur, and this 'axis' fostered Kanshi Ram's distrust vis-à-vis his partner. On 2 June 1995, the BSP withdrew its support to the government and its 11 ministers resigned. The following day Raj Bahadur and 12 other BSP MLAs joined the SP.

The break up of the SP-BSP coalition shows how difficult it is to build an alliance of OBCs and the Scheduled Castes. It had been possible in 1993 because of the Mandal affair but the momentum receded once the battle of quotas had been won. The 1993 Assembly elections had been the culminating point of the anti-high caste mobilization. Yet, the divorce between the SP and the BSP did not bring the latter back to square one as its rise to power testifies.

The BSP put an end to the coalition with the SP to become actively involved in another alliance, in a more favourable position, since on 3 June 1995 Mayawati became Chief Minister of the Uttar Pradesh government with BJP support. This alliance was neither more nor less tactical than the one with the SP. It was primarily directed against Mulayam Singh Yadav whom the BSP and the BJP wanted to keep in check because of his growing political influence which, in turn, reflected the increasing assertiveness of the OBCs, especially the Yadavs. The alliance of the BSP with the BJP epitomized the convergence between Dalit and upper castes leaders against the OBCs and, above all, against the Yadavs who now posed as much of a threat to the Scheduled Castes as to the elite landowners and civil servants, because of Mulayam Singh Yadav's reservation policy. This rapprochement of groups poles apart in the social structure was justified by Kanshi Ram in the following terms:

We can take the help of the BJP to advance our national agenda. We feel that the upper castes will be more amenable to social transformation than the intermediate castes. (interview with Kanshi Ram in *Frontline*, 28 June 1996: 35)

The fact that the upper castes seem more conciliatory towards the Untouchables than towards the OBCs is quite plausible because they regard the former as posing a relatively minor threat to their continued social and economic dominance. Yet, keeping the Yadavs away from power was not the main reason for the BSP's association with the BJP; this alliance was especially valued because it enabled the BSP to be in office.[19] The ends justified the means and this approach was substantiated by Mayawati's first experiment in power.

Mayawati is a Chamar from Uttar Pradesh (her native village, Badalpur is located in the district of Gautam Buddh Nagar). At the time of her birth in 1956 her father was employed in the telephone department (he retired as an MTNL supervisor). Mayawati was successful in her studies in Meerut (B.A. and B.Ed.) and in Delhi (LL.B.) where her family settled when she was two years old. She became a schoolteacher in 1977. Having experienced the typical discrimination that even educated Scheduled Castes routinely endured at that time—and still endure occasionally—'she took to reading Dr. Ambedkar and soaked up his writing like blotting paper' (Singh 1995). Her first political experience took place in 1977, apparently within the Janata Party; but this episode of her life remains rather obscure. Three years later while preparing for the IAS examination she met Kanshi Ram who persuaded her to enter politics. In 1984 she left her job to devote herself to the BSP.[20] Apparently Kanshi Ram had been impressed by her verbal skills and indeed Mayawati made a name for herself through aggressive, even provocative speeches. For instance, she declared that Gandhi was 'the biggest enemy of the Dalits. If Harijans means children of God, should it be considered that the Mahatma was the son of Satan?' (Singh 1995).

With Mayawati as chief minister, the largest state of India was for the first time, directed by a Scheduled Caste; and one who aggressively advocated the cause of the bahujan samaj. For a very large number of Scheduled Castes she became a source of pride, a role model. Mayawati's accession to Uttar Pradesh's top political post played a major part in the consolidation of the BSP's vote banks.

Such a consolidation also resulted from the special treatment Mayawati granted to subaltern groups. The Dalits were the first to benefit from it. Mayawati started with a series of name changes, Agra University being renamed Dr. Bhimrao Ambedkar University and the one at Kanpur, Chhatrapati Shahuji Maharaj University. A new district was carved out and was called Dr. Bhimrao Ambedkar Nagar, Agra stadium was named Eklavya, and so on. Dozens of Ambedkar statues were put up across the state. The acme of this symbolic conquest of public space was the Periyar Mela that the Mayawati government organized in Lucknow on 18 and 19 September 1995 in honour of E.V. Ramaswamy Naicker, or 'Periyar'. This Tamil leader, who was more or less the alter ego of Ambedkar in south India until his death in 1973, had been declared *persona non grata* in Uttar Pradesh after the translation into English of his book, *The Ramayana: A True Reading,* where he presented Ram and Sita in a way that many upper caste Hindus in the so-called native state of this divine couple considered blasphemous.[21] The Periyar Mela aimed at rehabilitating his name, mobilizing Dalits and provoking the upper castes, as Kanshi Ram did on this occasion by making derogatory remarks about Gandhi.

The Scheduled Castes also benefited from some concrete measures during the four-and-a-half months of Mayawati's first government. The Ambedkar Villages Scheme, which had been started by Mulayam Singh Yadav, to allocate special funds for socioeconomic development under the IRDP, JRY, etc., for a period of two years to villages with a 50 per cent Dalit population, was revised to include those with 30 per cent (and even 22 per cent in certain areas) Dalits. Mayawati gave special treatment to the Dalits of these villages; as a result 'all the roads, handpumps, houses, etc., have been largely built in their bustees [neighbourhoods]' (Pai 1997: 2314). Grants were created for Dalit children to attend classes between level 1 and 8; those for Bhangi children were doubled. The Bhangis (or Balmikis), who tend to vote for the BJP, received special treatment as Mayawati announced a programme of rehabilitation to help them go beyond their traditional jobs as sweepers. Finally, an ambitious plan to equip 10,000 villages with schools and roads was undertaken.

As far as the OBCs were concerned, Mayawati announced that they were to benefit from 27 per cent of the state budget, and that the quotas introduced by Mulayam Singh Yadav would be implemented as soon as possible. Some caste groups that had been neglected by the administration were included in the OBC list and the Nishad (boat-people also called Mallah or Kevat) got the privilege of hiring plots of sandy land running alongside the rivers.

Finally, Muslims were designated to receive the same grants as Scheduled Caste children and Mayawati implemented the recommendations of the UP Backward Classes Commission which insisted, in a report of 11 July 1994, that low caste Muslims should benefit from reservations in the state administration. Mulayam Singh Yadav had not been in favour of such a measure because it was bound to reduce the quotas of the Hindu OBCs. Mayawati granted the Muslims 8.44 per cent of the 27 per cent due to the OBCs. A comparable proportion, 8 per cent, of the police officers' posts also was reserved for the Muslims. Muslims equally appreciated the Mayawati government's resistance to the Vishva Hindu Parishad's attempt at organizing in September 1995 an important event on Krishna's 'birthday' at Mathura, his supposed place of birth. There is a historic mosque at this site and the VHP's intention was, as in Ayodhya, to mobilize Hindus in order to 'reconquer' a Muslim space. Mayawati allowed the VHP's function on the condition that it was held more than 3 km away from the mosque.

The BSP government appointed its supporters to key positions in the administration. More than 1,500 transfers took place in Uttar Pradesh during the 136 days of Mayawati's government.[22] Scheduled Caste District Magistrates ended up at the helm of almost half of the districts (*Frontline*, 1 December 1995: 31). This policy produced a lot of resentment among non-Dalit bureaucrats. The BJP was also worried because the BSP was reinforcing its local implantation, which was confirmed in December 1995 during the local elections when the BSP took control of one municipal corporation (out of 11 of the biggest city councils), nine middle-size municipalities and 22 small towns (as against 1, 82 and 100 for the BJP and 1, 27 and 45 for the SP respectively). The BJP, which already disapproved of the quotas for the Muslims, and resented the way Mayawati countered the VHP in Mathura, withdrew its support on 18 October 1995. The fall of the Mayawati government led New Delhi to declare President's Rule in Uttar Pradesh.

The BSP decided to stand alone, six months later, in the 1996 Lok Sabha elections. The party doubled its share of valid votes in Uttar Pradesh, from about 10 per cent during the 1989, 1991 and 1993 elections to 20.6 per cent (9,483,739 votes, 50 more than the SP). Undoubtedly, the actions of the Mayawati government contributed to this new-found popularity. The party was able to broaden its base amongst the bahujan samaj by showing that Dalits, OBCs and Muslims could occupy the seat of power (in itself a very powerful symbol) and exercise it to their profit (something Mayawati barely had the time to do—many of her promises did not materialize). Yet, the BSP was especially successful in consolidating the Scheduled Castes behind its candidates. According to the CSDS post-poll survey, 63.4 per cent of them voted for the party, as against 26 per cent non-Yadav OBCs, 4.3 per cent Yadavs, 4.7 per cent Muslims and less than 1 per cent upper castes (Chandra and Parmar 1997: 215). The BSP leaders were utterly disappointed by their inability to attract Muslim voters but the fact that the party received two-thirds of the Scheduled Caste vote, representing 21 per cent of the state's population, and more than one-fourth of the non-Yadav OBCs was quite an achievement which could only be explained by the BSP's rise to power. Mayawati appeared as the party's most efficient crowd-puller during the election campaign. A study of four villages in Meerut district showed that:

Mayawati is popular and acceptable to the jatav villagers because during her tenure as CM a number of welfare measures for Dalits where undertaken. . . . In the Ambedkar villages . . . the land 'pattas' which had been allotted to Dalits during the emergency but not given, were actually distributed among them 'pucca' roads linking the villages to the main road, construction of houses, drinking water pumps and toilets in the SC sections of the villages; pensions for old persons; panchayat 'ghars', installation of Ambedkar statues, etc., were some of the schemes implemented. (Pai and Singh 1997: 1358)

The developments of June 1995 to June 1996 therefore confirmed Kanshi Ram in the opinion that any coalition was worth considering provided it allowed the BSP to come to power. The BSP was approached by several potential allies in view of the Uttar Pradesh Assembly elections due in September 1996. The United Front, under leader Deve Gowda, that had just come to power at the Centre, was the first to propose to Kanshi Ram an alliance with BSP, but in terms that did not satisfy him.[23] Eventually, the BSP worked out a seat adjustment with the Congress. On 25 June P.V. Narasimha Rao, as Congress President, and Kanshi Ram presented the details of their agreement at a highly symbolic press conference, as for the first time the Congress agreed to be the junior partner of a party representing the bahujan samaj (Congress would contest the elections in only one-third of the constituencies against 300 for the BSP). The Congress also agreed that it would support Mayawati as Chief Minister, should the alliance win a majority. The reason why the BSP decided to enter into such an alliance with the Congress was again purely pragmatic. As Kanchan Chandra and Chandrika Parmar argue, it was '(1) a short run strategy to catapult the party into a position to form a government in U.P. and (2) . . . a means to capture Congress' remaining Dalit and backward vote in U.P. and in other states' (Chandra and Parmar 1997: 216). Even though the BSP repeated its score of the Lok Sabha elections (20 per cent of the votes) and obtained the same number of MLAs (67) as in 1993 (when associated with a stronger partner, the SP), the alliance only won 100 seats out of 425. None of the political parties won a majority or was willing to form an alliance with one of its rivals and, therefore, New Delhi imposed President's Rule.

The BSP leaders announced straightaway that they would form a coalition with any political force in a position to give the Chief Ministership to Mayawati. After six months of President's Rule, the BJP accepted BSP's conditions. This decision could once again be explained by the apprehension that Mulayam Singh Yadav generated in the BJP and the BSP. Being a Cabinet Minister in the Deve Gowda government, Yadav had indeed acquired a strong influence over the Governor of Uttar Pradesh, Romesh Bhandari. According to the BJP-BSP agreement, Mayawati would be chief minister for six months, followed by a BJP leader and they would then function in rotation. The BJP and the BSP would each supply one-half of the ministers. The BSP therefore came back to power thanks to a new reversal of alliances. Mayawati declared:

Our rank and file has no problems about the new political line. They know that we have to change tactics from time to time to achieve social change. (interview in *Frontline*, 18 April 1997: 15)

Within the government the BSP and the BJP had eight ministers and 12 ministers of state each, as Mayawati kept 33 departments from 24 ministerial portfolios.[24] During her six-month tenure, Mayawati transferred 1,350 civil and police officials (*The Times of India*, 18 September 1997). (Two days after taking over she announced that 250 constable clerks would soon be recruited from amongst the Scheduled Castes and Scheduled Tribes) (*The Times of India*, 23 March 1997). The Ambedkar Villages Scheme was revived in a big way under the direct supervision of the chief minister who admitted that by doing so she was focusing her attention 'on one section of society', i.e. the Dalits (interview in *India Today*, 11 August 1997: 33). The Rs. 350-crore-scheme covered 11,000 villages. In addition, 15,000 Ambedkar statues were installed all over Uttar Pradesh, one of them, in Lucknow, at an estimated cost of Rs. 250,000. Also in Lucknow, the Rs. 120-crore Ambedkar Udhyan (park) assumed colossal dimensions with five 12 feet tall bronze statues of Ambedkar. Mayawati also implemented the Scheduled Castes and Scheduled Tribes (Prevention of Atrocities) Act, 1989 in more drastic ways than any of her predecessors.

After six months in office, she left the post of chief minister to Kalyan Singh of the BJP but the BSP immediately criticized the government order he issued to the effect that the SC/ST (Prevention of Atrocities) Act should not be misused. The BSP then withdrew its support to the government. A few weeks earlier Kanshi Ram had prepared the ground for such a move:

My aim is that the BSP should move forward. At any given point, I'll enter into a tactical alliance with another party if I feel it will strengthen the BSP. And it is what I have done in the past I did not enter into an alliance with the BJP because of any ideological common ground—in fact we are poles apart. My opinion about the party is the one I had stated in 1988—that it is a cobra. I have never left any party, whether it is the BJP, Congress or whoever in the dark. We entered into an understanding with the BJP last year to increase the base of the BSP and when we feel we are not benefiting any longer, we'll end it . . . I'm only looking for a suitable ladder. (*The Times of India*, 21 August 1997)

However, contrary to Kanshi Ram's expectations, the Kalyan Singh government did not fall because the BJP attracted sufficient number of defectors from the Congress and the BSP to stay in power. The breakaway group from the BSP was made of 12 MLAs who, according to Kanshi Ram, had been lured by an attractive financial offer of Rs. 50,00,000.

The BSP contested the 1998 Lok Sabha elections on its own in Uttar Pradesh and Madhya Pradesh and it polled almost the same number of votes as in 1996 in both states. It suffered setbacks in Punjab, where it had made an alliance with the Congress, and in Bihar (where its seat adjustment with Laloo Prasad Yadav did not really bear fruit). The 1998 elections revealed the weaknesses of the BSP policy regarding party alliances. This policy has certainly enabled the party to consolidate its Dalit vote bank by giving it access to power but it has other limitations. First, with 20 per cent of the votes, the BSP cannot reach power alone but it has alienated potential partners, at least for some time. Second, the BSP has been striving so hard for power that it has not hesitated to co-opt criminals and recruit politicians who were not as committed as people with a BAMCEF or DS-4 background. Kanshi Ram says that he is aware of the inherent risks in this aggregative party-building pattern:

The risk is there of diluting our identity, but for the sake of our growth we have to take that risk. We want a quicker growth and the empowerment of the oppressed. We do not give them [the new comers] any responsibility within the party apparatus, but only field them as our candidates. The organizers are from the DS-4, 95 per cent of them. And we are also giving them tickets. (interview with Kanshi Ram)

However, old leaders from the Dalit movement resent the fielding of newcomers during the elections, especially those from the upper castes, such as wealthy industrialists. During the 1998 elections, in Meerut district, BSP activists resigned from the party to protest the issuing of a ticket to former mayor Arun Jain.

Constant changes in alliances for the sake of winning power have led to a decline in party discipline: the BSP is all the more exposed to defections from its members who want to stay in power as their leaders have promoted a political culture based on the occupation of power. Over the last five years, the BSP has also been repeatedly affected by dissidence and defections resulting from weak party structures. BSP does not enjoy great democratic legitimacy: until 1997, it had never held party elections, the office bearers being designated by higher-ranked persons. Kanshi Ram appointed presidents in the states and they, in turn, chose the leaders of the district committees. In 1997 the chiefs of the state units were elected but they continue to select the members of the state executive committees and the district bodies. More importantly, Kanshi Ram and Mayawati do not hesitate to displace presidents of state units; for example, they unceremoniously removed Bhagwat Pal from party presidentship in Uttar Pradesh in May 1997.[25] This authoritarianism and personalization of power is most certainly a weakness. Kanshi Ram founded the party and dominates it thanks to his historical legitimacy, and charisma, but his succession might be difficult to organize and already some cadres and activists are worried about his idiosyncratic way of exercizing power. However, Kanshi Ram did announce soon after the disappointing 1998 elections that he would not contest elections over the next five years in order to concentrate on consolidation of the party. It might be a salutary return to his initial focus on organization.

\* \* \*

Over the last 15 years the BSP has been almost constantly on an upward trend, a rise largely based on the groundwork of the BAMCEF and the DS-4, the organizational skill of Kanshi Ram, his efforts to reach groups beyond the Dalits and the dividends of Mayawati's governments. However, in 1998, the BSP reached a plateau. This state of things can be explained from different viewpoints. First, one can argue that Mayawati's governments have not been altogether positive for the party. As Chief Minister she emptied the coffers of Uttar Pradesh and has been branded, for that reason, totally irresponsible and utterly corrupt. Rumours about her supposedly long-term affair with Kanshi Ram have adversely affected the BSP leadership. Yet, to my mind, the actual and symbolic power of gaining office had a greater effect on Dalits: Mayawati's assumption to the Chief Ministership showed other castes that they could do it.

The BSP's weaknesses rather lay in its narrow social basis. Despite Kanshi Ram's efforts to forge a 'bahujan front', his party has not been able to attract a large number of low caste supporters. It is no longer exclusively a Dalit party, but it is not a party of the low castes either since a mere fraction of the OBCs has joined its ranks. In addition, the BSP is not even the party of the Scheduled Castes. For instance, it has relatively few followers among the rural labourers because it paid little attention to land reform. When asked about their programme in this respect, BSP state leader soften reply by referring to the party slogan, 'Jo Zamin sarkari hai, voh zamin hamari hai' (the government land is ours), but the land mentioned here is often urban land and this slogan is generally used by Dalit movements when they look for a place to instal Ambedkar statues. The BSP is also often identified with the Chamars, just as the RPI tends to be 'a Mahar party' in Maharashtra. Khatiks, Balmikis and Pasis vote for other parties, partly to distinguish themselves from the Chamars whose hegemony is feared. Besides, the BSP recruits most of its supporters from the younger generations while their parents still vote for the Congress (as in Chhattisgarh among the Satnamis, for instance). The BSP may therefore grow incrementally in the long run and, in the meantime, use its young partisans to convince their parents.

However, broadening its base may not be useful if the BSP's organization is not strengthened and if its policy regarding alliances is not more consistent. A first step in this direction may well consist in the setting up of a more collective, democratic leadership and the exploration of some rapprochement with like-minded parties such as the RPI, the other organization claiming the Ambedkarite pedigree.

## Notes

1. Kanshi Ram still comes from the lower classes: two of his sisters got married to landless labourers in Punjab, a third one to a civil servant of the fourth category and the fourth one to a soldier. His first brother is welder at the thermion factory at Ropar, and the second one cultivates the 1.5 acre family farm. (*Sunday*, 13 February 1994: 28–31).
2. According to another source, the birthday celebration of Lord Buddha was the reason (*Sunday*, 7 July 1996: 16).
3. Interview with Kanshi Ram.
4. In the central administration the share of Scheduled Castes has increased from 3 and 4 per cent for the groups A and B respectively to 10 and 12 per cent between 1972 and 1992. (Group A comprises under secretary to secretary level officers and group B, section officers.) *India Today*, 30 April 1994: 32.
5. One of the Congress MPs from the Scheduled Tribes in Madhya Pradesh, Ajit Jogi, who joined the Indian Administrative Service before turning to politics, testifies that when Kanshi Ram called on him, as Collector in Sidhi district (Vindhya Pradesh), 'He looked very determined and dearly there was a messianic zeal in the work he was doing?' (cited in *Sunday*, 7 July 1996: 16).
6. In Bilaspur, Daulat Ram Ratnakar, who was to become the BSP chief in Madhya Pradesh, was approached while an undergraduate by T.R. Khunte, an engineer in NPTC who had come from Delhi on behalf of BAMCEF (interview with D. Ratnakar, Bhopal, 2 November 1997).
7. Kanshi Ram bears a grudge against Rajiv Gandhi for this and refused to ally with the Congress during the 1989 elections when, on the contrary, his party aggressively attacked the then ruling party (interview with Kanshi Ram).
8. The DS-4 has not been dissolved. BSP workers told me that it was now the party's youth wing, in charge of agitations such as the one in favour of reservations. But no action has been held on behalf of the DS-4 over the last 15 years.
9. Kanshi Ram also began many of his public speeches with an injunction to the upper castes who happened to be present, to leave the meeting-place.
10. Some of these slogans come from Kanshi Ram (1992: 67).
11. 'Azadi ke 44 sal bad bhi bahujan samaj (anusuchit jati, janjati, pichre varg va dharmic alpasankhyak) anyaya atyachar ka shikar' in ibid.: 58.
12. One of the BSP slogans says: 'Baba [Saheb Ambedkar] tera mission adhura Kanshi Ram karenge pura' (Baba your unfinished work will be fulfilled by Kanshi Ram).
13. Interview with I.M.P. Verma, a Nai (barber) who has been returned MLA from Mauganj (Rewa district) in 1993.

14. Interview in *Sunday,* 16 May 1993: 10–11. With the elections won he admitted the tactical character of the alliance: 'Up until new, neither Mulayam Singh nor me can stand alone in U[ttar] P[radesh]. That's why we are together' (interview in *Sunday,* 13 February 1994: 26). Therefore, one cannot follow Sudha Pai when she writes that the BSP was converted 'from a social/cultural movement to an opportunistic party' in 1995 when it made an alliance with the BJP; the party had started making tactical alliances in 1993 and its move reflected more pragmatism than opportunism (See Pai 1997: 2314).

15. In the educational sector 720 teachers out of 900 appointed in the districts of Garhwal and Kumaon had been chosen from among the Yadavs, according to a Congress MP whose information had been collected district by district. In the police, of the 6,000 officers recruited, according to the BJP and the Congress whose figures appeared in the press, 4,200 were said to have been Yadavs. Similarly, 70 per cent of the 3,500 policemen recruited by the Uttar Pradesh police were Yadavs (*India Today,* 15 October 1994: 35). This way of acting particularly exasperated the Kurmis whose votes were coveted by the BSP (*Frontline,* 13 January 1995: 35).

16. The OBCs and the Dalits' class interests are clearly antagonistic since the Untouchables are often landless labourers or cultivators with a very small plot working for the OBCs.

17. Mishra 1994: 409, and Chandra 1994: 10–13. In March 1994, *The Times of India* cited an intelligence report according to which 27 out of 54 cases of atrocities perpetrated against Untouchables were carried out by OBCs—half a dozen of them involved Yadavs (*The Times of India,* 2 March 1994).

18. 'BSP withdrew support in 1995 because Mulayam [Singh Yadav] tried to attract some of our people and because of atrocities against the Scheduled Castes, especially by the Yadavs. That was the main reason. I tried to warn him but he could not or did not want to do anything' (interview with Kanshi Ram).

19. Ambedkar himself thought pragmatically that the Scheduled Castes should try to reach power in many ways—including collaboration with the British—because they should not have any inhibition in the conduct of their fight against untouchability.

20. The same year her family converted to Buddhism.

21. The book had been proscribed there in 1969.

22. During his first term, Mulayam Singh Yadav transferred 419 officers of the Indian Administrative Service and 228 officers of the Indian Police Service between December 1989 and June 1991. His BJP successor Kalyan Singh transferred 460 IAS and 319 IPS between June 1991 and December 1992. Mulayam Singh Yadav during his second term reversed the proportions with respectively 321 IAS and 493 IPS transferred between December 1993 and June 1995. After one month of exercise of power, Mayawati had already transferred 82 IAS and 96 IPS (*India Today,* 31 July 1995).

23. The results of the general elections had to serve as a base for seat adjustment at the elections in Uttar Pradesh, but the Samajwadi Party—a constituent part of the United Front—had reached the top (or was second) in a large number of constituencies, and if the SP could present more candidates than the BSP it would give the advantage to Mulayam Singh Yadav in the race for Chief Ministership because this post, in application to the agreement, would go to the United Front's party having the largest number of MLAs.

24. Such as home, general administration, finance, power, information, civil aviation, excise, forest, justice, planning, industrial development export promotion, vigilance, secretarial administration, appointment, administrative reforms, small-scale industries, estate and Ambedkar villages development.
25. *National Mail,* 24 May 1997. Pal was subsequently rehabilitated.

## References

BSP (1996), *Mukhya lakshay evam apil,* New Delhi.

Chandra, K. and Parmar, C. (1997), 'Party Strategies in the Uttar Pradesh Assembly Elections', *Economic and Political Weekly,* 1 February.

Chandra, K. (1998), 'Why does the Bahujan Samaj Party (BSP) Succeed? A Case Study of the BSP in Hoshiarpur', paper prepared for presentation at the Annual Meeting of the Association for Asian Studies, Washington D.C., 28 March.

Chandra, S. (1994), 'Dalits versus the OBCs', *Sunday,* 27 February.

Dube, S. (1993), 'Idioms of Authority and Engendered Agendas: The Satnami Mahasabha, Chhattisgarh, 1925–1950', *The Indian Economic and Social History Review,* Vol. 30, No. 4.

—— (1998), *Untouchable Pasts: Religion, Identity and Pawer among a Central Indian Community, 1780–1950,* Albany: State University of New York Press.

Election Commission of India (1990), *Report on the Ninth General Elections to the House of the People in India,* 1989, New Delhi: Government of India Press.

—— (1996), *Statistical Report on General Elections, 1996 to the Eleventh Lok Sabha,* Vol. 1, New Delhi.

—— (n.d.), *Report on the Tenth General Elections to the House of the People in India,* 1991, New Delhi.

Gaborieau, M. (1985), 'From Al-Beruni to Jinnah: Indian Ritual and Ideology of the Hindu-Muslim Confrontation in South Asia', *The Anthropologist,* Vol. 1, No. 3, January.

Hanumanthappa, H. (1997), 'Dalits in India: A Status Report', in *Dalit International Newsletter,* Vol. 2.

Joshi, B. (1986) (ed.), 'First phase of 100 Days Social Action Concludes in Delhi', *The Oppressed Indian,* cited in *Untouchable! Voice of the Dalit Liberation Movement,* New Delhi: Selectbook Service Syndicate.

Lynch, O. (1969), *Politics of Untouchability: Social Mobility and Change in a City of India,* New York: Columbia University Press.

'Marching to Awaken the Ambedkarite Masses', *The Oppressed Indian,* Vol. 5, No. 1, April 1983.

Mishra, A. (1994), 'Challenge to SP-BSP Government', *Economic and Political Weekly,* 19 February.

—— (1995), 'Limits of OBC-Dalit Politics', *Economic and Political Weekly,* 10 June.

Mukerji, D. (1994), 'In the Name of Ambedkar', *The Week,* 24 April.

Omvedt, G. (1994), 'Kanshi Ram and the Bahujan Samaj Party', in K.L. Sharma (ed.), *Caste and Class in India,* Jaipur and New Delhi: Rawat.

Pai, S. (1997), 'Dalit Assertion in UP', *Economic and Political Weekly,* 13 September.

—— and Singh, J. (1997), 'Politicization of Dalits and Most Backward Castes', *Economic and Political Weekly,* 7 June.

Parliament of India, *Tenth Lok Sabha Who's Who*, Delhi: Lok Sabha Secretariat, 1992.

Ram, Kanshi (1982), *The Chamcha Age: An Era of the Stooges*, New Delhi.

——— (1992), *Bahujan Samaj ke lye asha ki kiran*, New Delhi: Bahujan Publications.

Ramaseshan, R. (1995), 'Dalit politics in UP', *Seminar*, January.

Singh, Gurmukh (1995), 'Power of Maya', *The Times of India*, 11 June.

Swami, P. (1994), 'Conflicts in UP', *Frontline*, 11 March.

Tatu, V. (1991), *Politics of Ethnic Nepotism*, New Delhi: Sterling Publishers United.

Tiwari, Badri Narayan (1998), 'Symbol, Memory and Politics: A Social Documentary Paper, presented in the international seminar, 'Popular Culture and Social Action', Pune, 2-8 January, organized by the Centre for Cooperative Research in Social Science.

Zelliot, E. (1992), *From Untouchable to Dalit*, Delhi: Manohar.

# Chapter 26

# The Bahujan Samaj Party in Uttar Pradesh: whose party is it?

Dr Ambedkar oscillated between two different strategies so far as party-building was concerned.[1] To begin with, he founded a party aiming at the rural and urban workers, the Independent Labour Party (1935). Then he focused not on a socioeconomic class any more, but on a status group, the Dalits, by launching the Scheduled Castes Federation (1942). And finally he reverted to a mixed approach that was intended to woo all the depressed categories of the lower castes by initiating the Republican Party of India (1956), which came into existence after Ambedkar's death in 1957.

Kanshi Ram, who inherited some of the legacy of Dr Ambedkar, followed a similar political trajectory. He first established the Dalit Shoshit Samaj Sangharsh Samiti (DSSSS), a party in whose name the word 'Dalit' had the strongest connotations. The DSSSS was immediately associated with the Untouchable castes. But three years later, he built the Bahujan Samaj Party which aspired to represent the 'Bahujans'.

In practise, Ambedkar could never attract support from large groups, except from his own caste, the Mahars of Maharashtra. But the BSP, while it has largely remained confined to one state only, Uttar Pradesh, seems to have become more than the party of one *jati* and even more than a Dalit-only party.[2]

## Party of the Dalits, or Party of the Chamars?

While Ambedkar's party remained identified with the Mahars, the BSP's core group may not even be the Dalits, but the Chamars, the largest Untouchable caste of north India. Kanshi Ram himself was born in 1932 in rural Punjab (Parliament of India 1992: 326)[3]—in a family of Ramdasias, Chamars converted to Sikhism, though he made a point to keep his caste a secret. In an interview he gave me 10 years ago, without disclosing his caste, he underlined that his first environment was not as oppressive as the one Untouchables suffered elsewhere 'because of the Sikh religion, and more especially because most of the Chamars have adopted the Sikh religion;[4] there was somewhat upward mobility'.[5]

AN ATTEMPT AT CONSTRUCTING
A DALIT VOTE BANK IN UTTAR PRADESH

The other major figure of the BSP, Mayawati, is also a Chamar. Though she was brought up in Delhi, Mayawati was successful in her studies in another UP town, Meerut (where she did her B.A. and B.Ed.) before returning to Delhi for her LL.B. She became a schoolteacher in 1977 and her first political experience took place during the same year within the Janata Party. Three years later, she was preparing for the Indian Administrative Service examination when she met Kanshi Ram[6] who persuaded her to enter politics. In 1984, she left her job to devote herself to the BSP. She became chief minister of UP for the first time in 1995—she was to occupy this post two more times.

The BSP projected Mayawati as a source of pride after she became chief minister of UP. Her accession to the topmost position in UP was part of a deliberate strategy: considering this first short-term as CM, she declared in an interview: 'my biggest achievement has been consolidation of the Dalit vote bank' (*The Pioneer,* 23 October 1995: 9). She became an icon and also became adept at manipulating symbols especially the pan-Dalit symbol that Ambedkar is today all over India. Agra University was re-named Dr Bhimrao Ambedkar University. New districts were carved out and renamed after Dr Bhimrao Ambedkar and Mahamayana, the mother of Buddha. The Agra stadium was named Eklavya, etc. More importantly, dozens of statues of Ambedkar were put up across the state to impose Dalit presence all over the public space.

But the consolidation of the BSP's Dalit vote bank also resulted from the special treatment Mayawati granted to the Dalits. They benefited from some concrete measures during the four-and-a-half-months of Mayawati's first government. Originally, the Ambedkar Villages Scheme allotted special funds for socioeconomic development for one year to villages which had a 50 per cent SC population. Then Mayawati extended this programme in June 1995 to those villages which had a 22–30 per cent SC population and on top of it, in 1997–8, 10 villages with SC population of 30 per cent or more were selected in each assembly constituency. All in all, 25,434 villages were included in the Ambedkar Villages Scheme. The Dalits of these villages received special treatment since roads, handpumps, houses, etc., were built in their neighbourhoods.[7] Sudha Pai underlines the fact that 'The Jatavs in our sample villages, described the 1995 Mayawati government as "our government" and were quick to point out the benefits they had received' (2002: 129–30). When Mayawati came back to power in 1997, the Ambedkar Villages Programme (AVP) was revived in a big way under the direct supervision of the chief minister, who admitted that she was focusing her attention 'on one section of society', that is, the Dalits.[8] The Rs 3,500 million scheme covered 11,000 villages. In addition, 15,000 Ambedkar statues were installed throughout

UP, one of them, in Lucknow at an estimated cost of Rs. 250,000. Also, in Lucknow, the Rs 1,200 million Ambedkar Udhyan (park) assumed colossal dimensions with five 12 feet tall bronze Ambedkar statues. But has the BSP reached out to all sorts of Dalit groups, or has it remained confined to the Chamars—also known as the Jatavs in UP—as suggested by Pai?

## CAPITALIZING ON THE JATAV MOVEMENT

The BSP borrowed a large part of its political culture from the Chamars, not only because its leaders came from this caste, but also because the Chamars have been the largest caste group in UP (12.5 per cent of the population according to the 1931 Census, as against the Brahmans who form 9.2 per cent of the population) and the most politicized caste of Dalits in northern India since the 1920s (see Briggs [1920] and Kshirsagar [1994]). To begin with, they remained imbued with the ethos of Sanskritization, as evident from the religious style of Swami Achutananda, the first Dalit leader of north India and the founder of the Adi-Hindu movement (see Jigyansu [1960] and Gooptu [1993]). Their craze for Sanskritization found its clearest expression in the name Chamar activists gave to their caste at the turn of the twentieth century: 'Jatavs', from Yadu, the founding father of a dynasty of Kshatriyas.[9] Owen Lynch points out that, at that time, 'The Jatavs were not attempting to destroy the caste system; rather they were attempting to rise within it in a valid, though not licit, way' (1969: 75). But the influence of Ambedkar made a strong impact on the Jatav movement in the 1940s, including in terms of conversions from Hinduism to Buddhism—so much so that the 'Buddhist identity has replaced Sanskritic Kshatriya identity' (ibid.: 206, see also p. 93). This process was especially strong in west UP where, unsurprisingly, the RPI made electoral inroads in the 1960s. As a result, the RPI won 8 MLA seats in 1962 and 10 in 1967, as against respectively 3 and 5 in Maharashtra, the party's original stronghold. The RPI performed so well thanks to the grassroot work of dedicated activists such as B.P. Maurya, who, however, defected to the Congress in the early 1970s.[10]

Thirty years later, the BSP recaptured the same segments of the Dalit population. For instance, it carved a niche for itself in Agra. During the 1995 municipal elections, the BSP won 32 seats out of 80. The BSP absorbed parts of the Jatav culture to such an extent that one of the mottos in which its ideology got encapsulated, was: 'Tilak, taraju aur talvar isko maro joote char', which means, 'The tilak [emblem of the sectarian affiliation of the Hindus which is applied on the forehead and symbolizes the Brahman], the balance [symbol of merchants castes] and the sword [symbol of warriors castes], hit them with their shoes [that is, with the symbol of the Chamars who work the leather]' (Kanshi Ram 1992a: 67).

## THE CHAMAR CORE GROUP OF A DALIT NEBULAE

The BSP has attracted the UP Chamars in large numbers because this caste owned a small elite which could not find a niche for itself in any other party. The Census of India shows that in UP the literacy rate among the SCs rose from 7.14 per cent in 1961 to 10.2 per cent in 1971, 15 per cent in 1981 and 27 per cent in 1991. The Chamars benefited more than any other caste from the progress made by the SCs in terms of education, not only because they were the largest Dalit caste (they constituted 56.6 per cent of the SC population of UP in 1991, as against the Pasis, who formed 14.6 per cent of the SC population), but also because they modernized more quickly.

This modernization process was partly due to the relative affluence resulting from their activity as shoemakers. Some of the leather workers became artisans or even traders. But this upward social mobility was boosted after independence by the reservation system which enabled thousands of Dalits to join university and the public services in even larger numbers. In Uttar Pradesh, among the cadres from the IAS, the SC officers 'form the largest number next to the Brahmans and Kayasths' (Ramaseshan 1995: 73). Yet, these officers felt frustrated because they were denied 'important posts in the districts as well as the state capital' (ibid.). The BSP cadres came first from this new, frustrated Dalit elite which had already been the main supporters of the BAMCEF. Pai has shown that the BSP activists belonged to a new generation of young, educated Dalits. Out of 66 BSP MLAs in 1993, 16 had a B.A., seven had an M.A., 15 had an LL.B. and one a Ph.D.; three years later, out of 67 MLAs, 24 had a B.A., two had an M.A., 19 had an LL.B. and one had a Ph.D. (Pai 2002: 96). But why did these young Dalit activists opt for the BSP? Kanchan Chandra argues convincingly that they did so because 'each of these men was seeking better economic opportunities and higher status recognition than his parents, and each found these in politics' (2004: 185ff). But why not in other, more established parties? The Congress, the first choice of the Dalits after independence, should have been a more natural avenue for upward socio-political upward mobility. But the party has remained upper caste dominated till today, as evident from the social composition of the party apparatus as well as the status of its elections candidates (see Jaffrelot 2003).[11]

In contrast, the new Dalit leaders who captured the most important posts within the BSP were Chamars. According to Kanchan Chandra, 85 per cent of the state-level posts of the BSP in UP were cornered by Chamars in 1995–6. None of them went to the Pasis or leaders from any other Dalit caste (Ibid.: 189). In fact, Pasis (pig herders), Balmikis (sweepers), Khatiks (meat-cutters) and others dislike the Chamars because of their socioeconomic and political ascent. They also resent the way they cornered the reservation quotas. Such an alienation of minor Dalit *jatis* recalls the reaction of non-Mahar Dalit groups vis-à-vis Ambedkar's parties in Maharashtra: the Mangs and Chambhars preferred to vote for the Congress or other parties (including the Shiv Sena) instead of joining hands with the Mahars, a group whose domination they resented a lot. Similarly, in UP, the Balmikis support the Congress or the BJP, partly because of their leaning towards Sanskritization and partly because they offer an alternative to the BSP (see Jaffrelot et al., 2002). Chandra insists that the BSP 'does not do well among Chamars because Chamars are naturally attracted to it. Rather, it obtains the support of Chamar voters only when it supersedes the competition as channel to office for Chamar elites from across subdivisions among Chamars, and not otherwise' (Ibid.: 170). I would propose a different view. Certainly, the key element in the attractiveness of the BSP for the educated Chamar leaders was the opportunities it offered them; but so far as the voting pattern of the Dalits of UP is concerned, the identification of the BSP as a Chamar or a Jatav party played a role in attracting more Chamar/Jatav voters and for repulsing Dalits from other *jatis*. Identity politics and political cultures keep some explanatory potential in this context and a rational choice-oriented interpretation is bound to underestimate this potential. In fact, a purely rational choice-oriented kind of interpretation, which would ignore the impact of sentiments of belongingness, could not explain the scope of the pro-BSP Chamar vote.[12]

Indeed, surveys indicate that most of the voters of the BSP come from the Chamars who were already the mainstay of the RPI when the party made some incursion in UP in the 1960s. (In 1962, the electoral slogan of the RPI was 'Jatav Muslim bhai bhai, Hindu kaum kahan se aye?'—'Jatavs and Muslims are brothers, where do the Hindus [community, nation] come from?' [cited in Duncan 1979: 286]). Table 26.1 shows that in the second half of the 1990s, when the BSP really took off electorally, about three-fourths of the Chamars voted for it.

In 1996 and 1999, to get three-fourths of the Chamar votes was a major achievement in a state where this group represented the largest caste. But confining itself to the Chamars was also a dangerous limitation. The BSP seemed to be facing the same difficulty as Ambedkar's political parties since the Independent Labour Party (ILP), the Scheduled Castes Federation (SCF) and the RPI had not been able to significantly attract voters beyond the Mahars in Maharashtra and the Chamars in Uttar Pradesh.

However, the BSP is not a Chamar party only, as evident from the fact that more than 45 per cent of the Pasis voted for its candidates in the 1996 Lok Sabha elections. It is not even a Dalit only party: in the same election 24.7 per cent of the Koeris voted for it and in the assembly elections, 27 per cent of the Kurmis did the same. Interestingly, in 2004, 9 per cent of the Yadavs—the vote bank par excellence of the Samajwadi Party (SP)—supported the BSP and 16 per cent of non-Yadav OBCs as well as 17 per cent of the MBCs (Most Backward Castes) did the same.

In 1999, however, the BSP received only 13 per cent of the non-Yadav OBC votes. At that time, the Kurmis had deserted the party[13] largely because of the splits orchestrated by Kurmi leaders such as Raj Bahadur and Jung Bahadur who formed

TABLE 26.1: CASTE AND COMMUNITY OF THE BSP VOTERS (IN %)

| Castes and communities | 1996 Vidhan Sabha elections | Lok Sabha elections | | |
|---|---|---|---|---|
| | | 1996 | 1999 | 2004 |
| Upper castes | | | | |
| Brahman | - | - | 2 | 5 |
| Rajput | - | - | 1 | 4 |
| Banya | - | 2.9 | | |
| Others | - | 2.9 | 5 | 10 |
| Intermediate castes | - | 1.9 | | 11 |
| OBC | | | | |
| Yadav | 4 | 4.3 | 4 | 9 |
| Kurmi | 27 | - | | |
| Koeri | - | 24.7 | | |
| Pal/Gadaria | | 11.8 | 13 | |
| Others | Lower OBCs: 19 | Peasant: 16.7; Artisan: 14.9; Others: 20.6 | | Other OBC: 16; MBC: 17 |
| Scheduled castes | 65 | | | 71 |
| Chamar | | 73.8 | 74 | |
| Pasi | | 45.7 | | |
| Others | | 60.6 | 39 | |
| Muslims | 5 | | 5 | 10 |
| Muslim (low) | | 6.5 | | |
| Muslim (high) | | 3.1 | | |
| Others | | 23.1 | | |

Sources: CSDS Data Unit, India Today, 31 August 1996: 53; Kumar 1999: 822 and Frontline, 19 November 1999: 41 and The Hindu, 20 May 2004.

respectively the BSP (R) and the Bahujan Samaj Dal, while another Kurmi leader from the BSP, Sone Lal Patel created the Aapna Dal. But a significant section of the Koeris supported it.

Sudha Pai argues that these splits resulted from inner tensions between Kanshi Ram and the OBC leaders of the BSP. According to Pai, in the mid-1990s, 'Kanshi Ram holds that lower backwards are not as politicised as the Dalits and lack both a strong leadership and an understanding of the need to unite and fight the savarnas' (Pai 2000: 40). As a result, the BSP allegedly developed a Dalit-oriented policy: 'In its post-bahujan phase, social justice has been defined not only as retributive but also *exclusive*, i.e. meant only for the Dalits and not the entire bahujan community' (ibid.: 42). According to Sudha Pai, the BSP changed its strategy once again in 1999 when 'the leadership decided to broaden the base of the party by giving tickets to carefully selected candidates belonging to the Muslim community, upper and backward castes, in the 1999 Lok Sabha elections thereby increasing its share of seats' (1999: 3100). This reading of the BSP's electoral strategy is not entirely convincing. In fact, the BSP had always tried to attract OBCs by giving them tickets at the time of elections, including in what Sudha Pai calls the party's 'post-bahujan' phase.

## The BSP, also a party of the OBCs and the Muslims

When he lived in Maharashtra, Kanshi Ram was very critical of the RPI's tendency to work only among the Dalits and even more especially among the Buddhist Mahars: 'Nothing can be achieved in a democracy by working with a particular community.'[14] For him, the RPI by focusing so much of its attention on the Dalits was betraying Ambedkar. His reading of *Annihilation of Caste* had convinced him that any organization based on one particular community would fail.[15] As Gail Omvedt emphasizes, Ambedkar considered that Dalits, tribals and Backward Castes were 'natural allies' against the *savarnas* (upper castes) and that the Dalits needed to make alliances with these other subalterns (1998: 224).

However, for suggesting an alternative strategy he drew his inspiration not so much from Ambedkar as from Phule who used the Aryan theory to his own advantage: the fact that the origins of the upper castes could be traced from Aryan conquerors enabled him to argue that they descended from foreigners and that their culture, including the caste system, was alien to India's original people who, for him, were the ancestors of the low castes, those who he called the bahujan samaj (Phule 1991).

Kanshi Ram drew his inspiration from this theory for endowing the lower castes with an ethnic identity. He transposed the motif of the Aryan invader versus the oppressed bahujan samaj in the democratic context of India:

In a democracy, the one with the larger number of votes forms the government. The bahujan samaj accounts for 85 per cent of the votes. It is a shame that the foreign Aryans constituting 15 per cent are ruling over the 85 per cent . . . . The Aryans have exploited us. An Aryan ruler can never work for our betterment . . . . When our ancestors from the bahujan samaj were ruling over his country, India was known worldwide for its prosperity. The bahujan samaj can rule this country even today. . . . (Kanshi Ram 1997)

Right from the beginning, Kanshi Ram included the religious minorities in his definition of the bahujan samaj since, even though those who did not descend from low caste converts did not belong to the pre-Aryan society, they suffered from the same oppression of the upper caste Hindus. On 14 October 1971, Kanshi Ram created 'The Scheduled Castes and Scheduled Tribes, Other Backward Classes and Minority Communities Employees Association'. Kanshi Ram, considered, at that time, that the most urgent need of the bahujan samaj was to organize its elite, which was, like him, a product of reservation in the education system and largely employed in administration. He then defined the bahujan samaj in opposition to the twice-born upper castes, the savarna, whom he also called the 'Manuwadi', those who follow the *varna* system as codified by Manu's *Dharmashastra*.[16]

Capitalizing on this organization he had set up in Maharashtra, Kanshi Ram created in 1978 an all-India association called the All-India Backward (SC, ST, OBC) and Minority Communities Employees Federation (BAMCEF) whose aim was still to organize the elite of the bahujan samaj, wage earners having intellectual qualifications and benefiting from quotas. BAMCEF made rapid headway and reached a degree of critical mass because of the growing number of educated SC civil servants. But it was not intended to organize the Dalits only. Kanshi Ram did not content himself with a unionist kind of strategy either: he wanted to play a political role too. In 1996 he told me, 'I still want my people to advance socially and economically. But I have realised that unless we are having political clout, we cannot advance much on those sides'.[17] Kanshi Ram was walking in the footsteps of Ambedkar, who also considered that capturing power had to be a priority.

Kanshi Ram launched the DSSSS in this perspective. In spite of its name, the party was not supposed to target the Dalits specifically. In fact, in addition to Shudras and tribals, the DSSSS also tried to attract Muslims, especially in UP. Dr Mahsood Ahmed, a temporary lecturer at Aligarh Muslim University became one of the full-time organizers of the DSSSS in 1983 (Mendelsohn and Vicziany 1998: 224–5) in order to serve this expansion scheme. In 1987, the launch of the BSP amounted to a change of name more than a change of strategy. Kanshi Ram continued, indeed, to defend the interests of the OBCs as much as those of the Dalits.

### KANSHI RAM AND THE OBCS

Even before the Mandal affair exploded in 1990, when the debate (in the Lok Sabha and outside) on the Mandal Commission Report was gaining momentum, Kanshi Ram emphasized the claims of the OBCs. This is evident from one of his speeches during the election campaign for the Vidhan Sabha of Haryana in 1987:

The other limb of the Bahujan Samaj [in addition to the Scheduled Castes] which we call as OBC or Other Backward Classes, needs badly this party [the BSP]. Thirty-nine years after independence, these people have neither been recognised nor have they obtained any rights. Improvements have been introduced in the legislation for the Scheduled Castes and the Scheduled Tribes, but nothing similar has happened for these people. The truth is that the government of this country is not ready to recognise them. In accordance with section 340 of the Constitution, which was drafted by Dr. Ambedkar for the welfare of these people, the Kaka Kalelkar and Mandal Commissions were constituted, but the reports of both the commissions were thrown in the waste paper basket on the pretext that they had identified 3,743 castes which could not be called Other Backward Classes. Our central government is not ready to recognise any of these castes. When these castes are not even recognised, where is the question of obtaining their rights? (Kanshi Ram 1992b: 23)

Kanshi Ram thus admitted that in some respects the condition of the SCs was better than those of the OBCs. He thus recognized that the SCs and the STs had a larger presence in the bureaucracy than the OBCs because of reservations:

In this country, out of the 450 District Magistrates more than 125 are from SCs/STs but those from the OBCs are very few. . . . The number of OBC is 50 to 52 per cent but we don't see any of them as District Magistrate. The issue, which is special for us, is that reservation is not a question of our daily bread, reservation is not a question of our jobs, reservation is a matter of participation in the government and administration. We want participation in the government and administration of this country. There is democracy in this country. If in the republic 52 per cent of the people cannot participate, then which is the system in which they can participate? (Kanshi Ram 1992c: 58)

Similarly, he noted in 1994, that of some 500 IAS officers in UP, 137 were SCs whereas there were only seven OBCs (six of them were Yadavs) (Mendelsohn and Vicziany 1998: 224). One of the BSP's slogans has been 'Mandal ayog lagu karo, ya kursi khali karo' (Implement Mandal Commission [Report] or vacate the seat [of power]). This was part of Kanshi Ram's strategy of constituting the bahujan samaj into a political force and therefore the BSP undoubtedly benefited from the atmosphere created by the 'Mandal affair' and tried to tap the OBC vote at the time of elections.

After gaining power in 1995, Mayawati announced that the OBCs would benefit from 27 per cent of the state budget. Some castes that had been neglected by the administration and which belonged to the lower stratum of the OBCs—popularly known as Most Backward Classes—were included in the OBCs' list and the Nishads (boat-people also called Mallahs or Kewats) got the privilege of hiring plots of sandy land running alongside the rivers.

Similarly, the Muslims were designated for receiving the same grants as SC children and Mayawati implemented the recommendations of the UP Backward Classes Commission which insisted, in a report of 11 July 1994, that the low caste Muslims should benefit from reservations in the state administration. Mulayam Singh Yadav had not been in favour of such a measure because it was bound to reduce the quotas which the Hindu OBCs tended to monopolize. Mayawati granted the Muslims 8.44 per cent of the 27 per cent due to the OBCs. A comparable proportion—8 per cent—of posts of police officers were also allegedly reserved for Muslims.[18]

## ELECTORAL AND PARTY POLITICS:
## BEYOND THE DALIT THRESHOLD

The BSP's ambition to become more than a Dalit party became clear in the 1980s when it nominated non-SC candidates at the time of elections in UP. In 1989, when BSP MLAs were elected for the first time, a majority of its successful candidates were not Dalits (four Muslims, three OBCs and five SCs). In 1991, the results were even more striking since none of the BSP Dalit candidates were returned to the assembly whereas 11 OBCs and one Muslim joined the Vidhan Sabha on a BSP ticket. Since then, the electoral outcomes have been more balanced. But in 1993 and in 1996, the OBC MLAs were still 10 percentage points ahead of the SC MLAs (44.7 per cent as against 34.3 per cent and 38.6 per cent as against 29.5 per cent in 1993 and 1996 respectively). Though the percentage of the Muslim BSP MLAs is declining, from 16.4 in 1993 to 10.9 in 2002, their share remains high (see Table 26.2).

TABLE 26.2: CASTE AND COMMUNITY OF THE BSP MLAs (1989-2002)

| Caste and community | 1989 | 1991 | 1993 | 1996 | 2002 |
|---|---|---|---|---|---|
| *Upper castes* | | | 1.5 | 13.5 | 16.2 |
| Brahman | | | 1.5 | 4.5 | 6.8 |
| Rajput | | | | 6 | 6.8 |
| Banya | | | | | 1.3 |
| Bhumihar | | | | 1.5 | 1.3 |
| Kayasth | | | | 1.5 | |
| *Intermediate castes* | 22.8 | 91.4 | | 1.5 | 1.3 |
| Jat | | | | 1.5 | 1.3 |
| *Other Backward Classes* | | | 44.7 | 42 | 39.7 |
| Yadav | 7.6 | 16.6 | 14.9 | 1.5 | 2.7 |
| Kurmi | 7.6 | 16.6 | 7.5 | 12 | 10.9 |
| Lodh | | | 1.5 | 1.5 | 4.1 |
| Koeri | | | | | 1.3 |
| Shakya | | | | 1.5 | 1.3 |
| Rajbhar | | 8.3 | 2.9 | 3 | 1.3 |
| Saini | | | | | 2.7 |
| Pal/Gadaria | | | | 6 | 2.7 |
| Kashyap | | | | | 1.3 |
| Kushwaha | | | 1.5 | 6 | 2.7 |
| Muraon/Maurya | | | | 3 | 2.7 |
| Nishad | | 8.3 | 1.5 | 4.5 | 1.3 |
| Bhagel | | | | 1.5 | 1.3 |
| Gujar | | | | | 1.3 |
| Other | 7.6 | 41.6 | 14.9 | 1.5 | 2.7 |
| *Scheduled Castes* | 38.4 | | 34.3 | 27.2 | 25.9 |
| Jatav | | | | 16.6 | 20.5 |
| Passi | | | | 7.6 | 4.1 |
| Khatik | | | | 1.5 | |
| Other | | | | 1.5 | 1.3 |
| *Muslim* | 30.7 | 8.3 | 16.4 | 16.6 | 10.9 |
| *Non-identified* | | | 2.9 | | |
| TOTAL | 100 | 100 | 100 | 100 | 100 |
| | N = 13 | N = 12 | N = 67 | N = 64 | N = 64 |

However, one should not look only at the caste break-up of its MLAs, but also at the social profile of the candidates to analyse the strategy of the BSP. I did this research for the 1996 Assembly elections (see Table 26.3). Then the SC candidates were only 29 per cent of the total number, whereas the OBCs were 34

TABLE 26.3: CASTE AND COMMUNITY OF THE BSP CANDIDATES
IN THE 1996 ASSEMBLY ELECTIONS IN UTTAR PRADESH

| Caste and community | % |
|---|---|
| *Upper castes* | 17.5 |
| Brahman | 4 |
| Rajput | 8.2 |
| Banya | 1.3 |
| Khattri | 1.6 |
| Bhumihar | 06 |
| Kayasth | 0.9 |
| Others | 0.9 |
| *Intermediate castes* | 1.6 |
| Jat | 1.6 |
| *Other Backward Classes* | 34.4 |
| *Backward castes* | 11.8 |
| Kurmi | 6.3 |
| Yadav | 1.9 |
| Lodh | 1.9 |
| *Most backward classes* | 22.6 |
| Pal/Gadariya | 1.9 |
| Teli | 0.3 |
| Kachhi/Kushwaha | 2.3 |
| Gujjar | 0.9 |
| Nai | |
| Nishad | 1.9 |
| Baghela | 0.6 |
| Kumhar | 0.3 |
| Sunar | 0.3 |
| Chaurasia | 0.3 |
| Rajbhar | 2.3 |
| Shakya | 1.6 |
| Kashyap | 0.6 |
| Prajapati | 1.3 |
| Chaukan | 0.9 |
| Vora | 0.3 |
| Saithwar | 0.9 |
| Bair | 0.3 |
| Saini | 1.6 |
| Maurya | 2.3 |
| Others | 1.3 |
| *SCs* | 28.3 |
| Chamar/Jatav/Dhore | 19.1 |

(*Table 26.3 contd.*)

TABLE 26.3 (*Continued*)

| Caste and community | Per cent |
|---------------------|----------|
| Kori | 0.9 |
| Pipil | 0.3 |
| Dhobi | 0.6 |
| Khatik | 0.3 |
| Dusadh/Pasi | 4.2 |
| Katheriya | 0.3 |
| Kuril | 0.6 |
| Chilpkar | 0.3 |
| Balmiki | 0.9 |
| Others | 0.3 |
| *Muslim* | 17.5 |
| *Christian* | 0.3 |
| *Non-identified* | 0 |
| TOTAL | 100 |
| | N = 303 |

*Sources:* Interviews in the BSP office of Agra, *Bahujan Sangathak*, 11 November 1996; *National Mail*, 20 September 1996.

per cent and the Muslims 18 per cent. Interestingly, the OBC candidates of the BSP were relatively more successful since there were almost 40 per cent OBCs among the party MLAs and only 28 per cent among the SCs. This gap suggests that the BSP owns a fully transferable Dalit vote bank and get an additional support from the OBC voters when the party candidate belongs to the OBC category. Interestingly, this interpretation does not apply to the Muslims who may adopt more systematically a strategic vote in order to beat the BJP candidate.

The share of the OBCs is even more important among the state party office bearers than among the BSP candidates to the assembly elections (see Table 26.4). By contrast, the Dalit office bearers are almost as few as the upper castes! Interestingly, the president of the Uttar Pradesh BSP has been an OBC for years, ever since Sone Lal Patel (a Kurmi) was replaced by Bhagwat Pal (a Gadariya), who was himself replaced by Dayaram Pal, another Gadariya.

A majority of the lower caste leaders of the BSP come from the MBC and not from larger, dominant BC such as the Yadavs. In fact, Yadavs were important till the mid-1990s but their role diminished after the SP—a Yadav-dominated party—and the BSP developed hostile relations. The relations between the BSP and the SP deteriorated soon after their electoral success in 1993. First, the BSP was worried about the 'Yadavization' of the state initiated by Mulayam Singh Yadav. Second, the Yadavs, who were anxious to improve their social status and to keep the Untouchables in their place, reacted violently to the Dalits' efforts to achieve social mobility. The OBCs and the Dalits' class interests are clearly contradictory in some regions of UP. While in east UP 'the OBCs and the Scheduled Castes labourers have a common enemy: the old elite' (Lerche 1998: A-33) made up of

TABLE 26.4: Caste and Community of the BSP Office
Bearers in Uttar Pradesh (1996-2000)

| Castes and communities | Office bearers of the Executive Committee of the BSP in UP | |
|---|---|---|
| | 1996 | 2000 |
| Upper castes | 13.7 | 14.3 |
| Brahman | 10.3 | 10.7 |
| Banya | 3.4 | 3.6 |
| Other backward classes | 44.2 | 46.5 |
| Backward castes | 6.8 | |
| Kurmi | 3.4 | 3.6 |
| Lodh | 3.4 | 3.6 |
| Most backward castes | 37.4 | 39.3 |
| Pal/Gadariya | 3.4 | |
| Kachhi/Kushwaha | 3.4 | |
| Gujjar | 3.4 | 3.6 |
| Nai | 3.4 | 3.6 |
| Nishad | 3.4 | 7.1 |
| Kumhar | 3.4 | 3.6 |
| Rajbhar | 6.8 | |
| Saini | 3.4 | 7.1 |
| Others | 6.8 | 7.1 |
| Scheduled castes | 17.2 | 21.4 |
| Chamar/Jatav/Dhore | 10.5 | 3.6 |
| Khatik | 3.4 | 3.6 |
| Dusadh/Pasi | | 10.7 |
| Others | | |
| Muslim | 10.5 | 7.1 |
| Non-identified | 13.7 | 10.7 |
| TOTAL | 100 | 100 |
| | N = 29 | N = 28 |

*Source:* Interviews in the BSP office of Agra.

the upper caste ex-landlords, elsewhere the Untouchables are often landless labourers or cultivators with a very small plot who work for OBC farmers: their class interests then are virtually antagonistic. Conflicts about the wages of agricultural labourers and disputes regarding land ownership have always been acute, but became more frequent since both groups—the Dalit and the OBCs—had become more assertive after the 1993 elections.

The situation was almost the same with the Kurmis. Their position has remained influential within the party, but their presence has also decreased after the splits mentioned earlier. Obviously, these OBCs do not belong to the same world as the Dalits. They often employ—and exploit—the Dalits as labourers whereas the MBCs and Muslims have a similar class status.

To cope with the rise of the OBCs and more especially with the party of the Yadavs, that is, the SP, the BSP developed two strategies. First, it joined hands with the BJP, an upper caste dominated party which was equally anxious to sandwich Mulayam Singh Yadav. When the BSP put an end to the coalition with the SP, it became actively involved in another alliance with the BJP, in an even more favourable position since on 3 June 1995 Mayawati became chief minister of the UP government with the BJP's support. The alliance of the BSP with the BJP epitomized the convergence between Dalit and upper caste leaders against the OBCs and above all against the Yadavs, who were now posing a threat as much to the SCs as to the elite landowners and civil servants because of Mulayam Singh Yadav's reservation policy.[19]

Second, the BSP decided to focus on the MBCs. As a result, the list of the BSP candidates started to include people from many small, dominated castes such as the Nishads, Sainis, Shakyas, Baghels, Kashyaps, Rajbhars, etc. The MBC MLAs and office bearers of the BSP of UP come today from a dozen different *jatis*, whereas its SC MLAs are almost all Jatavs. But the former are in larger numbers anyway.

To sum up: even though within the UP branch of the BSP, power always laid in the hands of a Chamar, Mayawati, the BSP's image as a 'Dalit party' needs to be amended since the SCs do not represent the largest number of office bearers and party candidates (or MLAs) in UP. This picture, however, is more in tune with the social profile of its electoral basis which suggest that the BSP may be less a Dalit party than a Chamar party.

## The BSP, New Catch-All Party?

Kanshi Ram, like Ambedkar, promoted the formation of a socio-political coalition gathering together ascriptive groups with similar social and economic status. Ambedkar had oscillated between this position and the defence of the Dalits alone, but had opted for a larger front in the end. Kanshi Ram did the same on behalf of the bahujan samaj and, in contrast to Ambedkar, succeeded in partially uniting the SCs—mostly Chamars—and in rallying around this core group some OBC castes—mostly MBCs—and some Muslims whose socioeconomic condition has declined, especially among the *ashlaf* (lower castes). The party's social basis remains relatively narrow anyway. It is not exclusively a Dalit party any longer, but it is not a party of the low caste either since a mere fraction of the OBCs vote for its candidates. In addition, the BSP is not even the party of the SCs. It is still identified with the Chamars, just as the RPI tended to be 'a Mahar party' in Maharashtra.[20] Balmikis and Pasis vote for other parties, partly to distinguish themselves from the Chamars whose hegemony they fear—the former for the BSP, the latter for the Janata Dal because of Ram Vilas Paswan.[21]

In order to further broaden the social basis of the party, the BSP leaders have decided to approach the upper castes too. Since the mid-1990s, the party has made it a point to give tickets to a significant number of upper caste candidates and to appoint a similar number of office bearers from the upper castes too. In both cases, the percentage of the upper castes in question approximates their share in the total population, that is, 15–20 per cent. This is in tune with Kanshi Ram's assumption that assemblies should reflect the composition of society, a principle which echoes the theory of mirror representation.[22] In the 1999 Lok Sabha elections, the BSP continued with this policy. Kanshi Ram decided explicitly to nominate candidates in proportion to the caste and community break-up of society. Out of 85 candidates, he fielded 17 Muslims (20 per cent), 20 SCs (23.5 per cent), 38 OBCs (45 per cent) and 10 upper castes (12 per cent)—five Brahmans and five Rajputs (*The Hindu*, 11 August 1999: 9). In 2002, the BSP did the same during the UP Assembly elections: it gave tickets to 37 Brahmans, 36 Rajputs and 86 Muslims. In 2004, this strategy started to bring some dividends since 5 per cent of the Brahman voters, 4 per cent of the Rajputs and 10 per cent of the Muslims cast their votes in favour of the BSP according to a CSDS survey.

Among the upper castes, the Brahmans seem to be the favourite target of the BSP. In May 2005, the party coined a new slogan 'Brahman-Dalit bhai-bhai' and Mayawati decided to set up 'Bhaichara samiti' (brotherhood committee) in all the assembly constituencies with Brahmans as presidents and Dalit as secretaries! (*Central Chronicle*, 16 May 2005).

Satish Chandra Mishra, the new general secretary of the BSP, is the main architect of this policy. But Mayawati has invested a lot of time and energy into it, as evident from the series of 'Brahman sammelans' she has organized across UP, including in Lucknow where the 'Brahman maha rally' marked the culmination of 50 'Brahman jodo sammelans' (Brahman enrolling conferences). Interestingly, in Lucknow, Mayawati was greeted with Brahmanical rituals, a group of priests chanting Vedic hymns while she was presented with a silver axe, the mythical weapon of Lord Parashuram—a Brahmanical icon (*The Hindu*, 10 June 2005).

At the same time, the BSP targeted Mulayam Singh Yadav's social stronghold, the Yadavs, by organizing 'Yadav sammelans' at all major places in UP. The party even set up a Yadav Vikas Manch (*The Hindu*, 22 January 2005).

Generally speaking, the OBCs were bracketed together with the Dalits during the new campaign Mayawati launched in the fall of 2005 for the fulfilment of quotas and the introduction of reservations in the private sector, not only for Dalits and OBCs, but also for the tribals (*The Hindu*, 20 September and 6 October 2005).

The BSP is trying its best to broaden its social basis beyond its traditional Dalit support by reaching out to new groups. For Mayawati, this needs to be done for presenting the party as a credible alternative to the other party in the fray in UP. In a way, she is oscillating the same way as Ambedkar did more than half a century ago. The fate of Dalit politicians remains the same, but the BSP may have accumulated enough strength for achieving more than its predecessors. On top of it, the party seems to be in a position to overcome the transition to a new leader, Mayawati, who became party president in 2003, after Kanshi Ram—who died recently—suffered a terrible stroke. The political resilience of Mayawati is remarkable so far, but the judiciary may hinder her career anyway.

# Appendix: The Electoral Performance of the BSP

TABLE A.1: PERCENTAGE OF VOTES POLLED BY THE BSP DURING
THE LAST SIX GENERAL ELECTIONS

| Year | Candidates | Winning candidates | % of valid votes |
|------|-----------|--------------------|------------------|
| 1989 | 246 | 3 | 2.07 |
| 1991 | 231 | 2 | 1.61 |
| 1996 | 117 | 11 | 3.64 |
| 1998 | 251 | 5 | 4.7 |
| 1999 | N.A. | 14 | 4.2 |
| 2004 | 435 | 19 | 5.3 |

*Sources:* Election Commission of India (1990: 7; n.d.: 9; 1996), Rao and Balakrishnan (1999) and Yadav and Kumar (1999: 120–6).

*Note:* The growth of the BSP enabled the party to obtain from the Election Commission the status of national party after the 1996 elections.

TABLE A.2: ELECTORAL PERFORMANCE OF THE BSP IN FIVE STATES
OF NORTH INDIA DURING THE GENERAL ELECTIONS OF 1989-99
(IN PERCENTAGE OF VALID VOTES)

| States | Haryana | Punjab | Uttar Pradesh | Madhya Pradesh | Jammu & Kashmir |
|--------|---------|--------|---------------|----------------|-----------------|
| % of SCs in | | | | | |
| 1991 | 19.75 | 28.31 | 21.05 | 14.5 | N.A. |
| 1989 | 1.62 (0) | 8.62 (1) | 9.93 (2) | 4.28 (0) | 4.06 (0) |
| 1991 | 1.79 (0) | No election | 8.70 (1) | 3.54 (1) | No election |
| 1996 | 6.6 (0) | 9.35 (3) | 20.61 (6) | 8.18 (2) | 6 (0) |
| 1998 | 7.7 (1) | 12.7 (0) | 20.9 (4) | 8.7 (0) | 5 (0) |
| 1999 | 1.7 (0) | 3.8 (0) | 22.1 (14) | 5.2 (0) | 4.8 (0) |
| 2004 | 4.9 (0) | 7.7 (0) | 24.7 (19) | 4.7 (0) | 2.2 (0) |

*Note:* Numbers in parenthesis indicate seats.

TABLE A.3: PERFORMANCE OF THE BSP IN THE ASSEMBLY ELECTIONS OF UP

| Year of elections | 1989 | 1991 | 1993 | 1996 | 2002 |
|-------------------|------|------|------|------|------|
| Seats | 13 | 12 | 66 | 67 | 98 |
| Percentage of votes | 9.4 | 9.3 | 11.1 | 22.6 | 23.1 |

TABLE A.4: REGION-WISE VOTE SHARE OF THE BSP IN THE
ELECTIONS OF THE 1990s (IN %)

| Regions | Assembly elections | | Lok Sabha elections | |
|---------|------|------|------|------|
| | 1991 | 1993 | 1996 | 1999 |
| Uttarakhand | 3.5 | 4.2 | 10.1 | 6.7 |
| Rohilkhand | 5.9 | 2.7 | 20.5 | 22.6 |

| Upper Doab/West UP | 3.5 | 5.7 | 18.5 | 23.8 |
|---|---|---|---|---|
| Awadh/Central UP | 8.8 | 5.6 | 18.8 | 22.8 |
| Lower Doab/Central East UP | 10.2 | 9.9 | 22.8 | 22.8 |
| Bundelkhand | 20.3 | 26.1 | 25.8 | 28.9 |
| Poorvanchal/East UP | 13.5 | 21.9 | 20.2 | 23.6 |

*Sources: Frontline,* 3 December 1993: 24; 15 November 1996, 22 and 19 November 1999: 41.

## Notes

1. I have made this argument in my book, Jaffrelot (2005).
2. In 1998, I argued that the BSP was more than a Dalit party, but this interpretation needs to be revisited because the statistical basis for such an interpretation was then based on a couple of elections only. See Jaffrelot (1998).
3. Mendelsohn and Vicziany give another date for Kanshi Ram's birth—1934 (Mendelsohn and Vicziany 1998: 219).
4. In fact, the proportion of the Hindu Chamars is still very high in Punjab. In the 1931 Census, they were 62.1 per cent, as against 14.4 per cent of Sikh Chamars.
5. Interview with Kanshi Ram, New Delhi, 12 November 1996.
6. The same year her family apparently converted to Buddhism.
7. The best account of the AVP, with special references to Meerut district, is Pai (2002: 126–49).
8. Interview in *India Today,* 11 August 1997: 33.
9. After the publication of the white paper which was to be the basis of the 1935 Government of India Act, the Agra-based Jatav Conference sent a memorandum to the deputy secretary to the Government of India where it was said:

    The Jatavs are the descendants of Yadu, the founder of Jadav [*sic*] tribe, from which the great Hero of Maha Bharat, Lord Krishna, came. But this position of superiority could not remain intact. Our community fell down from that great height to this degraded status in the Hindu fold . . . our present position is the outcome of the age-long inhumane oppressions of Brahmanism on the Kshatriyas. We, Kshatriyas of the past, are labouring under various sorts of disabilities, restrictions and religious injunctions imposed on us by the Orthodox Hindus . . . . But we are at loss to understand the exclusion of our (Yadav) Jatav community from the list of the Scheduled Castes given in the White Paper. The result of this horrible negligence would, no doubt, be the sacrifice of the interests of our community. (Memorandum of Jatav Conference of Agra, in IORL/P&J/9/108)

    Such a discourse suggests that, while the Jatavs were eager to benefit from reservations for the SCs, their movement was still operating in the framework of Sanskritization.
10. Interview with B.P. Maurya in Delhi, 7 November 1997.
11. K. Chandra underlines that 'Congress leaders themselves readily acknowledge that the representational blockage for Scheduled Castes elites in their own party pushed them towards he BSP' (Chandra 2004: 187).
12. K. Chandra argues that the 'Chamars' do not really exist and cannot, therefore, be motivated by such an identity: 'The category "Chamar" is an aggregate rather than an

individual category, no different from the category "Scheduled Caste" [*sic*]' (Chandra 2004: 168). It is now common knowledge that all identities are constructed not only with some cultural symbols, but also with some material interests in mind. But once the identity-building process has reached a certain stage, people believe in this construction. Chamars or Jatavs consider they form a group in today's UP, like Muslims in spite of even more dramatic status-based divisions.

13. Till the mid-1990s, the BSP succeeded in attracting Kurmis of the region between Faizabad and Banda.

14. Cited in Kanshi Ram (1997). Kanshi Ram had appreciated Maurya's attempts at federating the SCs and the Muslims under the banner of the RPI in UP.

15. One of the BSP slogans is: 'Baba tera mission adhura Kanshi Ram karenge pura' (Baba [Saheb Ambedkar] your unfinished work will be fulfilled by Kanshi Ram).

16. Kanshi Ram talks of 'Manuwadi' versus 'Manavwadi', those who believe in men as human beings. His hostility to Manu led him to ask for the removal of the statue of Manu from the premises of the Jaipur High Court (*The Hindu*, 5 September 1998: 4).

17. Interview with Kanshi Ram.

18. BSP (1996). The Muslims also appreciated the way the Mayawati government resisted the Vishva Hindu Parishad's attempt at organizing an important event at Mathura for Krishna's birthday in September 1995. On this site, that the VHP claimed to be Krishna's birthplace, stands a mosque and the VHP's intention was, like in Ayodhya, to mobilize the Hindus in order to 'reconquer' a Muslim space. Mayawati allowed the VHP's function to take place provided that it was held more than 3 km away from the mosque.

19. This rapprochement of groups which were poles apart in the social structure was justified in those terms by Kanshi Ram: '... we can take the help of the BJP to advance our national agenda. We feel that the upper castes will be more amenable to social transformation than the intermediate castes' (interview of Kanshi Ram in *Frontline*, 28 June 1996: 35).

20. Mayawati, while confessing that she feared for her life, declared in late 1998: 'If I am killed, members of the Chamar community would create a havoc' (*The Hindu*, 12 December 1998).

21. Besides, the BSP recruits most of its supporters from the younger generations while their parents still vote for the Congress. But the party may therefore grow incrementally in the long run and, in the meantime, use its young partisans to convince their parents.

22. Political theories tell us that there are two kinds of representation, one which is based on the returning of individual deputies by abstract citizens to houses of representatives and the other which emphasizes the social identities of the represented and the representatives—mirror-representation (see Pitkin [1967]).

# References

Ambedkar, B.R. (1936), *Annihilation of Caste*, Jalandhar: Beema Patrika Publications.
Briggs, G.W. (1920), *The Chamars*, Calcutta: Association Press.

BSP (1996), *Mukhya Lakshay Evam Apil* (in Hindi), New Delhi: BSP.

Chandra, K. (2004), *Why Ethnic Parties Succeed: Patronage and Ethnic Head Counts in India*, Cambridge: Cambridge University Press.

Duncan, R.I. (1979), 'Levels, the Communication of Programmes, and Sectional Strategies in Indian Politics, With Reference to the Bharatiya Kranti Dal and the Republican Party of India in Uttar Pradesh State and Aligarh District (UP)', Ph.D. thesis, University of Sussex.

Election Commission of India (1990), *Report on the Ninth General Elections to the House of the People in India, 1989*, New Delhi: Government of India Press.

——— (n.d.), *Report on the Tenth General Elections to the House of the People in India, 1989*, New Delhi: Government of India Press.

——— (1996), *Statistical Report on General Elections, 1996 to the Eleventh Lok Sabha*, Vol. 1, New Delhi: Government of India Press.

Gooptu, N. (1993), 'Caste and Labour: Untouchable Social Movements in Urban Uttar Pradesh in the Early Twentieth Century', in P. Robb (ed.), *Dalit Movements and the Meaning of Labour in India*, Delhi: Oxford University Press.

Jaffrelot, Christophe (1998), 'The BSP in North India: No Longer Just a Dalit Party', *Comparative Studies of South Asia, Africa and the Middle East*, Vol. 18, No. 1, pp. 35–51.

——— (2003), *Indian Silent Revolution: The Rise of Lower Castes in North Indian Politics*, New York: Columbia University Press.

——— (2005), *Dr Ambedkar and Untouchability: Analysing and Fighting Caste*, New York: Columbia University Press.

Jaffrelot, Christophe, Zerinini, J. and Chaturvedi, J. (2002), 'The BJP and the Rise of Dalits in Uttar Pradesh', in R. Jeffrey and J. Lerche (eds.), *UP 2000*, pp. 128–46, New Delhi: Manohar.

Jigyansu, C.P. (1960), *Swami Achhutanand*, Lucknow: Bahujan Kalyan Prakashak.

Kshirsagar, R.K. (1994), *Dalit Movement in India and its Leaders*, New Delhi: MD Publications.

Kumar, P. (1999), 'Dalit and the BSP in Uttar Pradesh', *Economic and Political Weekly*, Vol. VIII, No. 2, 3 April, p. 822.

Lerche, J. (1998), 'Agricultural Labourers, the State and Agrarian Transition in Uttar Pradesh', *Economic and Political Weekly*, Vol. XIV, No. 3, 28 March, A-33.

Lynch, O. (1969), *The Politics of Untouchability: Social Mobility and Social Change in a City of India*, New York: Columbia University Press.

Mendelsohn, O. and M. Vicziany (1998), *The Untouchables: Subordination, Poverty and the State in Modern India*, Cambridge: Cambridge University Press.

Omvedt, G. (1998), 'Peasants Dalits and Women: Democracy and India's New Social Movements', in M. Mohanty, P.N. Mukherji and O. Tornquist (eds.), *People's Rights: Social Movements and the State in the Third World*, pp. 86–102, New Delhi: Sage.

Pai, S. (1999), 'BSP's New Electoral Strategy Pays Off', *Economic and Political Weekly*, 30 October, p. 3100.

——— (2002), *Dalit Assertion and the Unfinished Democratic Revolution: The Bahujan Samaj Party in Uttar Pradesh*, New Delhi: Sage.

——— (2004), 'The BSP in Uttar Pradesh', *Seminar*, No. 471, p. 40.

Parliament of India (1992), *Tenth Lok Sabha Who's Who*, New Delhi: Lok Sabha Secretariat.

Phule, J. (1991), *Slavery: Collected Works of Mahatma Jotirao Phule*, Vol. 1, Bombay: Government of Maharashtra.

Pitkin, H.F. (1967), *The Concept of Representation*, Berkeley: University of California Press.

Ram, Kanshi (1992a), *Bahujan Samaj ke lye Asha ki Kiran*, New Delhi: Bahujan Publications (Hindi).

———— (1992b), 'Bahujan Samaj Party aur Haryana Pradesh ke Chunav', in Kanshi Ram, *Bahujan Samaj ke lye Asha ki Kiran*, New Delhi: Bahujan Publications (Hindi).

———— (1992c), 'Azadi ke 44 sal bad bhi bahujan samaj (anusuchit jati, janjati, pichre varg va dharmic alpasankhyak) anyaya tyachar ka shikar', Kanshi Ram, *Bahujan Samaj ke lye Asha ki Kiran*, New Delhi: Bahujan Publications (Hindi).

———— (1997), *Aajke neta: Alochnatmak adhyayanmala*, New Delhi: Rajkamal Prakashan (Hindi).

Ramaseshan, R. (1995), 'Dalit Politics in UP', *Seminar*, January, p. 73.

Rao, G.V., Narasimha, L. and Balakrishnan, K. (1999), *Indian Elections: The Nineties*, New Delhi: Har-Anand.

Yadav, Y. and Kumar, S. (1999), 'Interpreting the Mandate', *Frontline*, 5 November, pp. 120–6.

# V

## The Political Culture (of Voting) in India

# Chapter 27

# Voting in India: electoral symbols the party system and the collective citizen

The Republic of India is often described as 'the largest democracy in the world' chiefly because of its ability to organize free elections at regular intervals. In the period from 1951 to 2004 fourteen elections were held to renew the lower house in New Delhi, the Lok Sabha. However, the country's socio-cultural and demographic conditions complicate the electoral process. The electorate grew, in just over three decades, from 173 million in 1952 to nearly 400 million in 1984, and voter participation progressed, during the same period, from 45.7 per cent to 64.1 per cent. In 1989 the right to vote was extended to include young people aged eighteen to twenty-one, increasing the electorate further, to 499 million people, from which a total of 298.3 million cast their votes. Furthermore the electorate grew at each of the following six elections, from 491 million in 1991 to 670 million in 2004. Over the same period the turnout rate peaked at 62 per cent in 1998 and then decreased marginally to 58 per cent in 2004. Still the number of voters remained high, at about 389 million in 2004.

The difficulties linked to the sheer size of the electorate are exacerbated by widespread illiteracy (in 1990 nearly 52 per cent of the population still could not read), which hinders the domestication of the act of voting for the very simple reason that many Indian citizens cannot read the names of the candidates. According to the 2001 census, 34.7 per cent of the population did not know how to read and write. Thirty years earlier—when India was already the largest democracy in the world—that was roughly the percentage of people that were literate (to be precise, 34.5 per cent according to the 1971 census). Matters are further complicated by the huge number of candidates contesting elections. Despite the small size of the lower house—with 543 members it is no larger than the French National Assembly, but represents a population more than seventeen times larger—the number of candidates is incredibly high: it peaked in 1996 with 13,952 individuals. It has decreased since then, but with 5,436 candidates in 2004 the average number of candidates per constituency remained above ten.

India has tried to grapple with the low level of education of its electorate and the large number of candidates by employing enormous material means at each election (in 1999 more than 1.7 million ballot boxes were despatched across the country so that the vote could take place over the space of a few days in 773,708 polling stations,[1] and in 2004 more than 700,000 stations were equipped with electronic voting machines, while 4 million civil servants supervised the electoral process in and around the polling stations); and second, by developing an electoral procedure that allows citizens to cast their votes under auspicious conditions. Voting takes place through the recognition of electoral symbols, whose growing role has in turn contributed to institutionalizing the party system. In addition to using symbols, the Election Commission, an independent administrative body responsible for the electoral process, has tried to surround the act of voting with as many guarantees as possible (concerning voting secrecy and measures against outside influences) so as to create the conditions for rational and independent voting. However, the sophisticated measures taken to this effect have had unintended consequences.

## The Use of Electoral Symbols and the Party System

India inherited its voting system, among many other political institutions and practices, from methods introduced by the British. In the latter part of the colonial era an increasing number of Indians obtained the right to vote through constitutional reforms in 1909, 1919 and 1935 (by which time 30 million Indians, or one-sixth of the adult male population, were enfranchized). The British administration tried to avoid the obstacle of illiteracy, which became increasingly serious as the right to vote spread, by instituting two procedures, depending on the region: either polling station officials 'helped' hesitant voters to write the name of the candidate across their ballot paper (which violated voting secrecy laws), or ballot boxes were painted a different colour for each candidate, enabling the voter to identify the correct box without needing to know how to read the candidate's name (Butler, Lahiri and Roy 1989: 15). After independence India tried to build on the second system through the use of electoral symbols, depicted first on the ballot boxes and later on the ballot papers themselves.

### FROM THE BALLOTING SYSTEM TO THE MARKING SYSTEM

In the 1950s the Election Commission considered that 'the percentage of literacy in India being in the neighbourhood of 16.6 per cent only, it would have been impossible for the vast majority of voters who are illiterate to mark their votes on the ballot papers with the names of the contesting candidates printed on it'.[2] The elections of 1951–2 and those in 1957 were organized using the balloting system procedure, which consisted in distinguishing ballot boxes not by colour but by symbols associated with each of the candidates. In 1951 the Election Commission published a list of symbols; each candidate in a constituency was asked to choose three, ranked in order of preference. The local representative of the Election Commission, having assembled the lists, assigned a different symbol to each candidate to use during the campaign (Graham 1983: 72). Every polling station in the constituency had a room, closed off by a curtain, containing ballot boxes for each candidate. Voters picked up ballot papers at the polling station entrance and deposited them in the boxes of their choice. There were two kinds of papers—green and pink—because elections for the New Delhi Lower House and for the legislative assemblies of the federal states took place simultaneously. Each voter thus had at least two ballot papers to be placed in two different ballot boxes.

In certain constituencies the situation was still more complex as some electoral seats were reserved for members of Scheduled Castes (Untouchables) or Scheduled Tribes. The Constitution of 1950 set aside seat quotas in the electoral assemblies for these disadvantaged populations. These quotas were—and still are—proportionate to the percentage of the national population represented by these communities for the central Parliament, and proportionate to the percentage of the population in each federal state for the state legislative assemblies. In certain so-called double (or triple) constituencies, where these populations were particularly sizeable, voters had to elect one candidate for the 'general seat', one Untouchable and/or one Scheduled Tribe member. Each party could put forward a candidate for each of these seats and independents could also run. The ballot boxes for candidates for the reserved seats were marked with the same symbols as those for other candidates of the same party, but with the symbol circled in black (Election Commission 1959: 92).

Partly because elections at the national and state level were held simultaneously and partly because of the double or triple constituency system, the electoral procedure, intended to be simple enough to allow illiterate voters to vote, turned out to be too complex. The sheer number of ballot boxes in polling stations led to mistakes: voters confused ballot boxes for the candidates to Parliament with those for candidates to the legislative assemblies. The same confusion arose with the ballot boxes for Untouchable or Scheduled Tribe candidates. In 1957 in one constituency in West Bengal 133,063 ballots out of 990,800 were declared spoiled because they had been placed in the wrong ballot box (ibid.: 164). This electoral system had two other drawbacks. First, candidates could accuse returning officers of switching ballot papers from one ballot box to another after voting was closed, as the papers had no distinguishing marks. Second, a secret ballot was not absolutely guaranteed since the curtain behind which the ballot boxes were placed did not completely hide the movements of the voter in front of the row of boxes. This voting procedure was thus replaced by another at the beginning of the 1960s.

The marking system was used for the first time in the late 1950s in by-elections, then on a regular basis starting with the General Elections of 1962. Ballot boxes with electoral symbols disappeared. Instead symbols appeared on the ballot papers themselves, next to the candidates' names, to help those voters who otherwise could not decipher the ballot. There was one ballot for elections to Parliament and another for elections to the state legislative assembly, printed with the name and corresponding symbol of each candidate (Fig. 27.1). Voting took place as follows:[3] (1) In a polling station the first voting officer identified the voter's name on the electoral roll, which was annually updated, and wrote the number of the voter's ballot paper for the state legislative assembly elections in a ledger, before passing it on to a colleague; (2) The colleague did the same with the ballot paper for the elections to Parliament and passed both along to a third official; (3) This third official gave the two ballot papers to the voter and marked the index finger of the voter's left hand with indelible ink in order to spot without difficulty any attempts to vote a second time; (4) A fourth official took the ballot papers from

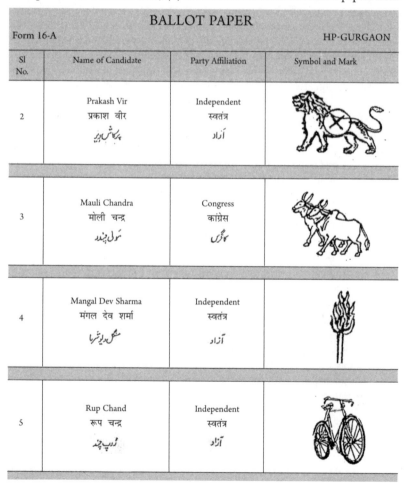

## BALLOT PAPER

Form 16-A                                                    HP-GURGAON

| Sl No. | Name of Candidate | Party Affiliation | Symbol and Mark |
|---|---|---|---|
| 2 | Prakash Vir<br>प्रकाश वीर<br>پرکاش ویر | Independent<br>स्वतंत्र<br>آزاد | |
| 3 | Mauli Chandra<br>मोली चन्द्र<br>مولی چندر | Congress<br>कांग्रेस<br>کانگرس | |
| 4 | Mangal Dev Sharma<br>मंगल देव शर्मा<br>منگل دیو شرما | Independent<br>स्वतंत्र<br>آزاد | |
| 5 | Rup Chand<br>रूप चन्द्र<br>روپ چند | Independent<br>स्वतंत्र<br>آزاد | |

FIGURE 27.1: Ballot Paper Used During 1957 By-Elections

*Source:* Election Commission 1959: Vol. 1.

the voter and explained how to mark the ballot paper next to the name and symbol of the chosen candidate, using a rubber stamp lent to the voter for the purpose. The official then gave the ballot paper for the legislative assembly back to the voter and passed the ballot for Parliament to a fifth official. The voter went into the voting booth to stamp the first ballot in secret; (5) The voter then collected the second ballot from the fifth official and stamped it as well, before dropping both ballots into a single ballot box.[4]

This method of voting, codified by the Election Commission,[5] has changed little, except that since 1971–2 elections for Parliament and for the state legislative assemblies no longer take place together. The marking system simplified the act of voting, which was the main aim of the Election Commission. However, the use of symbols has had significant repercussions for the political system in that it has contributed strongly to the institutionalization of political parties.

## ELECTORAL SYMBOLS AND
## THE IDENTIFICATION OF POLITICAL PARTIES

The adoption of the system of electoral symbols led parties to demand that they be assigned their own distinctive symbols. Also the Election Commission itself wanted to see all the candidates of a given party use the same symbol, to simplify its own work. In 1951 fourteen parties were recognized as having the right to their own symbols. The headquarters of each party were then required to communicate to the Election Commission the names of the candidates who could be assigned the party's symbol. As Bruce Graham (1983: 74) writes:

... by instituting this procedure the Commission accepted the principle that endorsement by a central party organisation was the essential determinant of party affiliation; in other words the Commission had virtually agreed to accept the appearance of a candidate's name on a party list as adequate proof of his attachment, and took little if any account of other evidence of allegiance, such as the candidate's own views and statements, his endorsement by informal associations and by local party branches and his membership of groups in the outgoing legislature. It was a principle which reduced the complexity of candidatures to two relatively simple categories, mutually exclusive groups of party nominees on the one hand and an undifferentiated mass of independents on the other, and it greatly strengthened the recruiting power of the central party organisations in the process.

The impact of this procedure was reinforced by the 1953 decision of the Election Commission to extend the right to a symbol, at the national level, only to those parties receiving more than 3 per cent of the popular vote in parliamentary elections. Only four parties met this criterion. However, there was a separate list for parties having attained the same threshold in legislative assembly elections, for which these state parties kept the right to their symbol (Fig. 27.2). Parties which came in under these thresholds lost an excellent means of affirming their existence and making their identity known: their candidates were attributed those 'free' symbols which were not reserved for the recognized parties and which could change from one election to the next. This procedure thus served the purposes of the major parties whose identity, reinforced by unchanging India-wide symbols, grew stronger: all the more so as in 1968 the thresholds were raised from 3 to 4 per cent. The Chief Election Commissioner offered as a partial justification for the symbol system and the new thresholds the fact that they would serve to limit the number of parties (Graham 1983: 78). However, it did not limit the number of candidates, quite the contrary: parties set up candidates even in constituencies where they had no standing, simply to attain the required 4 per cent.[6]

The major parties quickly became associated with their symbols, which they in turn constantly promoted. Party slogans referred, and still refer, explicitly to the

DESIGNS OF SYMBOLS                DESIGNS OF SYMBOLS FOR STATE PARTIES
FOR ALL INDIA PARTIES                  AND INDEPENDENT CANDIDATES

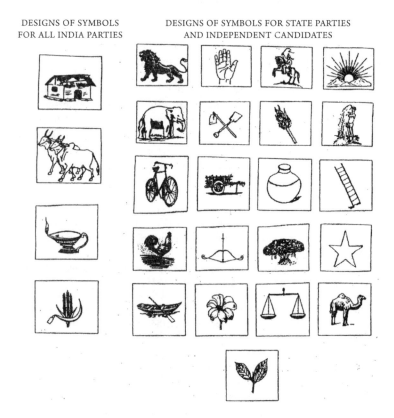

FIGURE 27.2: Electoral Symbols Reserved by the Election Commission for the Four National Parties and for Other Parties in 1957

*Source:* Election Commission 1959: Vol. 1.

party symbol. Ever since the hand was adopted as the symbol of the Congress Party, Congress has called on voters to 'give a helping hand' or to 'lend a hand', while the nationalist Hindu party Jana Sangh invited voters to be 'guided' by its long-time symbol, the lamp. Major parties quickly mobilized their workers to teach voters how to recognize the symbol on a ballot paper. Fake ballots on which only the symbol of the party in question is real are used for instructional purposes [see Fig. 27.3, a fake ballot used in Bhopal prior to elections in 1989 by extremist elements of the Bharatiya Janata Party whose symbol is the lotus flower].

| क्र | नाम | निशान | क्र. | नाम | निशान | क्र. | नाम | निशान |
|---|---|---|---|---|---|---|---|---|
| १ | हनीफ खाँ | | १४ | राधावल्लभ | | १७ | वहीद भाई | |
| २ | चन्द्र मोहन | | १५ | चुन्नीलाल | | २८ | प्रकाशचंद्र | |
| ३ | अब्दुल सत्तार | | १६ | सुलेमान | | २९ | राधेश्याम | |
| ४ | शकुन्तला | | १७ | मधुकांत | | ३० | महेशकुमार | |
| ५ | रामफूली बाई | | १८ | घनश्याम दास | | ३१ | ईश्वर सिंह | |
| ६ | अफजल मियाँ | | १९ | दीपचन्द | | ३२ | हाकम सिंह | |
| ७ | बख्तियार | | २० | रंजीत कुमार | | ३३ | शिवनारायण | |
| ८ | बालाराम | | २१ | बाबूलाल | | ३४ | चंद्रशेखर | |
| ९ | मोहम्मद अली | | २२ | हीरालाल | | ३५ | राम औतार | |
| १० | योगेन्द्र सिंह | | २३ | श्याम लाल | | ३६ | प्यारे मियां | |
| ११ | हरनाम सिंह | | २४ | प्रेमनारायण | | ३७ | सुशीलचंद्र वर्मा | |
| १२ | रामलाल | | २५ | रामचन्द्र | | ३८ | सेंट जॉन | |
| १३ | तेजेन्द्र सिंह | | २६ | ओमप्रकाश | | ३९ | अशरफ खाँ | |

FIGURE 27.3: Fake Ballot Paper used by BJP Activists to Teach Potential Voters to Recognize their Party's Symbol, the Lotus Flower

The importance electoral symbols had acquired in the functioning of the Indian democracy became clear after the first Congress Party split in 1969. The group that seceded from the Congress Party under Indira Gandhi, Congress O (for 'Organization'), hoped to be attributed the spinning wheel symbol. Congress R (for 'Ruling') protested that this was too close to the national flag, which bears a wheel, the symbol for *dharma* as well as Buddhism. Congress R requested for itself the symbol of a child. The Election Commission's decision was to grant each party its second choice: a woman working at a spinning wheel for Congress O and a cow with her calf for Congress R. Opposition parties objected that this latter symbol had religious connotations attractive to Hindu voters, given the sacred nature of the cow in Hinduism (Election Commission 1972: 67). In 1977, when four opposition parties (Congress O, the Socialists, the Hindu nationalists and the Bharatiya Lok Dal—BLD, a peasants' party) joined to form the Janata Party, they began by using the electoral symbol of Congress O in the Tamil south and the BLD symbol (a ploughman within a wheel) in the north.

A similar conflict had earlier opposed the two Congress factions created in 1978, the Congress U (named after its leader Devraj Urs) and Congress I (for Indira Gandhi). Both claimed the cow and calf symbol, which the Election Commission withheld. Congress I was finally assigned the hand symbol and Congress U the spinning wheel (Election Commission 1980: 42). These examples of conflict over electoral symbols reveal the importance of such symbols in identifying political parties; the more so as parties usually manage to obtain symbols reflecting their ideology or their social base, or to introduce relevant elements: for communist parties, for example, a sickle would appear with sheaves of wheat or with a hammer or the Maoist star, while peasant parties always managed to place a ploughman on their electoral symbol. Other cases are, however, more subtle. Congress initially used a pair of oxen as its symbol, alluding both to the use of oxen as draught animals by the peasants and to Hindu respect for the cow. This latter allusion was even more clearly echoed by the symbol of the cow and the calf. The spinning wheel, also favoured by certain Congress factions, recalls the prestige of Gandhi, who liked to spin thread and encouraged India to seek self-sufficiency in this way. The Hindu nationalist party, the Jana Sangh, which was assigned the lamp symbol in 1951, presented it as the instrument used in temples to illuminate the deity within and to carry out morning and evening prayers.

In sum, the electoral procedure which linked a symbol to each candidate and reserved specific symbols for parties overcame the obstacle of illiteracy but was not without political implications: institutionalization of the party system resulted in large part from this modus operandi which, therefore, had rather unintended consequences. The efforts of the Election Commission to develop a procedure to surmount the obstacle of under-education are, however, part of a larger design, the goal of which is to create the conditions for electors to vote in an independent and reasoned way.

## Searching for an Individual, Reasoned Act of Voting

The Election Commission has always sought to improve voting conditions to ensure that voting is an individual, voluntary act in conformity with the Western model that inspired the Indian Republic. Thus attention has been given to three elements in particular: the secret ballot, the verification of voter identity and the struggle against external influence.

In the former procedure, despite the screening curtain, it was still possible to tell in front of which ballot box the voter paused to vote. The marking system nonetheless also had its weaknesses: the returning officer would note the number printed on the ballot next to the voter's name in the electoral roll, it was thus possible during the count to check the ballot paper against the roll to see how a given voter had voted. Starting with the 1971 electrons a ballot book was introduced from which individual ballot papers were detached. The voting officer would detach a ballot paper from the book, write down on the ballot stub the number under which the voter was listed in the electoral roll, ask the voter to countersign the stub, and then underline the voter was listed in the electoral roll, ask the voter to countersign the stub, and then underline the voter's name in the roll to indicate that a ballot had been received. After vote counting the stubs and ballots were sealed and stored and could only be unsealed by court order, for instance for a recount. To match votes to voters three documents were thus required, not two: the ballot, the stub (which had the same serial number) and the electoral roll, which had the voter's number that had also been inscribed on the stub at the moment the ballot was distributed (Election Commission 1972: 203–5). These precautions to ensure secrecy of the ballot were aimed at freeing voters from the control of any external authority. However, more direct measures to protect electors from the influence of local power-mongers were also put in place from the 1950s onward.

## THE STRUGGLE AGAINST OUTSIDE INFLUENCES

For local notables the most common way to win voters' favour was to convey them to polling stations. The Representation of the People Act of 1951 therefore stipulates that 'the hiring or procuring, whether on payment or otherwise, of any vehicle or vessel by a candidate or his agent or by any person for the conveyance of any elector (other than the candidate himself, the members of his family or his agent) to or from any polling station is a corrupted practice' (quoted in Viraraghavan 1956: 129). As breaches of this clause continued to take place, in spite of the fines incurred, the Election Commission decided to reduce the risk by increasing the number of polling stations and so reducing the distance the average voter had to travel. In 1962 it was 3 miles, except in sparsely populated areas; in 1971 it was reduced to 1.25 miles. As Untouchables were the most vulnerable to external influence, the Election Commission ensured that polling stations were set up in their neighbourhoods (whether in reserved constituencies or not) to counter any possible intimidation from upper castes (Election Commission 1965: 35; 1972: 201). In 1980 the Election Commission recommended that this rule be applied even if the Untouchable neighbourhood in question numbered fewer than 750 voters, until then the minimum size required for a polling station (Election Commission 1980: 70). For the same reason, it was decided in 1971 that ballots would not be counted in polling stations, but rather would be centralized for counting in district headquarters (the districts roughly corresponded to the constituencies of the state Lok Sabha). The Election Commission explained that this innovation 'eliminated to a large extent pre-election intimidation and post-election victimisation of voters belonging to the weaker, poorer and smaller sections of the community' (Election Commission 1972: 203). Indeed vote counting in polling stations made clear the voting patterns of large communities in the area in question. Losing candidates—if they came from upper castes or wielded any sort of power (economic or politico-administrative)—could exact reprisals.[7] Removing vote counting from their local base effectively suppressed one of the means of control they exercised over the local voters. This decision was reversed in the late 1970s under pressure from local notables of all the parties, but the Election Commission reimpsed a similar modus operandi in 1996.

IMPERSONATION AND VOTER IDENTIFICATION

The Election Commission also sought to reduce sources of fraud regarding voter identification. The system in place in the 1950s consisted of marking the index finger of the left hand of those who had voted to prevent them from voting more than once. From the outset this procedure proved to be unreliable.[8] After the 1957 elections identity cards (at that point not obligatory) were considered as a solution. The experiment was first attempted in Calcutta, where the administration decided to photograph voters at their own homes, keeping one photo for the electoral roll and putting the other on the identity card. The operation failed three times out of eight: women refused to be photographed and many voters could not be found at home. The cost of the operation was also exorbitant. The only improvement, in 1962, consisted in authorizing any polling station official (either independent or from a political party) to question the identity of a voter, at a cost of a deposit of Rs. 2 with the president of the polling station (Election Commission 1965: 73). A further step was taken in the 1971 elections, when the Election Commission recommended the appointment of women officials in voting stations where veiled women were numerous (essentially in Muslim neighbourhoods), which facilitated identity checks (Election Commission 1972: 75).

For the 1980 elections the identity card system was introduced on an experimental basis in the state of Sikkim. However, the citizens proved largely suspicious and only 70 per cent of the population of this very small state were registered. Yet the Election Commission still hopes to generalize this system. To try and overcome the distrust of Indian citizens the Commission has proposed that the same card should serve as a social security card, ration card, university admission card and hiring card and for the registry or sale of real estate (Election Commission 1980: 37). The efforts to make the cards attractive are revealing of the suspicion aroused by the state (which is primarily viewed as a tax-collecting entity in a country where tax evasion is widespread). Above all it confirms the lack of differentiation of separate domains of the public sphere: voting is no more the foundation of citizenship than any other aspect of social life.

The Election Commission has thus in general striven to promote the secret ballot and a safe voting process free of external influence. Its concern for rigour, its perfectionism even, are evident in some very sophisticated recommendations and measures: for instance, because the stamp used to mark ballot papers sometimes left a trace next to another symbol if the paper was folded before the ink dried, a new stamp was introduced in 1971, designed with lines curving in a clock-wise fashion, which permitted the correct mark to be distinguished from any possible imprint (Election Commission 1972: 202). Other signs of the same attention to detail are evident: polling booths were to be installed, where possible, in public buildings with a courtyard of at least 20 square metres (Election Commission 1980: 69); polling stations had to offer a waiting line reserved for women; it was recommended that the sale of alcohol be forbidden on the day of the election; and the Election Commission regularly published its advice to voters on posters and in newspapers: Nonetheless there was an obvious contrast between the efforts of the Election Commission to guarantee conditions for reasoned and independent voting, uncompromised by any faults of form, and the actual conditions surrounding the act of voting.

## Caste-ism, Communalism and Fraud

In the West the act of voting has gradually become more individualistic in nature. Dalton and Wattenberg (1993: 212–13) convincingly argue that there has been 'a shift away from the previous style of decision-making based on social group and/ or party cues towards a more individualised and inwardly oriented style of political choice. Instead of depending upon party elites and reference groups, more citizens now attempt to deal with the complexities of politics and make their own political decisions.' In India, only in the Westernized circles of the largest cities can voting really be considered, sometimes, a personal act.

### THE MYTH OF THE INDIAN INDIVIDUAL VOTER— OR THE INVENTION OF THE RATIONAL COLLECTIVE VOTER

While doing fieldwork in India on the 1980 elections James Manor came to the conclusion:

. . . most rural dwellers seem to have decided how, to vote not out of excitement or inspiration by any individual leader, but after careful, and in a great many cases, sceptical deliberation. These deliberations tended to be a group activity, and voting decisions appear in an overwhelming number of cases to have been taken collectively, not individually. A large majority of these choices were very strongly, usually decisively, influenced by 'opinion leaders' who were very different figures from the powerful landed magnates who once used intimidation to dictate to villagers at elections. They tended to be people with a secondary or university education and some appreciation of the workings of government and the legal system. They were very often people who had assisted villagers in dealing with supra-local authority in some way, whether in minor matters like filling in forms or in more serious cases defending villagers' interests in disputes or in gaining them a small share of government largesse. Many opinion leaders lived in or travelled often to towns in the vicinity of the village. They were often schoolteachers, clerks, voluntary association and co-operative society workers, development board members or employees or—apparently less often—small town lawyers. (Manor 1983: 98)

This long quotation is revealing of two phenomena. First, it testifies to the emancipation of the villagers from the ascendancy that local notables (landlords, moneylenders, etc.) exerted over them for three decades after India's independence in the framework of a Congress-dominated clientelistic system. In 1980 this development was mature enough because of the impact of positive discrimination policies and the Green Revolution, as I have shown elsewhere.[9] Second, Manor's analysis is a good illustration of the persisting tendency of political scientists to overlook the role of ascriptive identities in political phenomena, such as the act of voting. Certainly some 'opinion leaders' sometimes led villages to vote *en bloc* for the same party or candidate in order to create a special relationship with the local representative in the assembly. Subrata Mitra (1979: 288–9) recalls that in 1974 three villages of Orissa where he was doing fieldwork 'had coordinated their electoral strategies', an experience which 'had shown them the benefits of making a deal whereby they pooled votes and then shared out resources'. But, for the most part, the collective decision of voting is increasingly determined by collective considerations linked to membership of a caste or a religious community.

Religious communities tend more and more to withdraw into themselves when it comes to voting. Muslims have traditionally preferred to vote for representatives from their own community, to ensure representation in Parliament and in the legislative assemblies. They have been especially good at developing a 'tactical vote'. Though they represent, according to the 2001 census, 12.12 per cent of the Indian population, they play a major role in 75 Lok Sabha constituencies (out of 545), where they are concentrated and even, in a few of them, in a majority. This 'tactical vote' has been developed in order to cope with the growing threat posed by the Hindu nationalist Bharatiya Janata Party (BJP). From the early 1990s the Muslims' motto became 'Vote for the strongest anti-BJP candidate' (Fazl 1996: 19). In some states they have found relevant parties for implementing such a strategy. In Uttar Pradesh (UP), where they represented 20–50 per cent of the voters in 23 constituencies out of 85 in the 1990s, the Muslims have tended to join hands with the Samajwadi Party (SP) of Mulayam Singh Yadav, a low caste Hindu leader, to fight against the BJP. Yadav captured power in 2003 partly because of the Muslims' support. In 2004, 62 per cent of the UP Muslims voted for the SP, according to the exit poll survey of the Centre for the Study of Developing Societies.[10]

The same phenomenon holds true for castes. All parties examine the caste composition of a constituency before appointing their candidates. The party leaders tend to select their candidates from the locally dominant caste, that is, the one that is the most numerous (though rarely in the majority); however, it can also be tactically wise to choose someone of another caste who will attract the votes of all the less numerous castes, who may be hostile to the dominant caste. These strategies reflect a larger phenomenon: in many cases, within the sub-caste (the local members of a caste), the vote is subject to deliberation. In Uttar Pradesh G.K. Lieten (1996: 1412) noticed that among the Jats—one of the state's dominant castes—'the vote is decided collectively, according to the general tendency in the Jat *viradari* [local sub-caste]'. Lieten even shows that in 1991 the Jats delinked their vote to the state assembly and their vote to the Lok Sabha in order to keep the two main factions of the caste happy: the Jats decided to vote for the Bharatiya Janata Party in the general elections, and for the Congress in the state elections.

Voting appears here to be both a collective and a rational act. Though external influence is still at play, it no longer comes from traditional power sources; it makes itself felt through the advice that the group in question has sought in order to vote in its own best interests. The array of measures implemented by the Election Commission to guarantee a secret and reasoned vote has promoted the development not of an individual rational voter but of a collective and rational voter. However, one must go a step further by looking simultaneously at the two conclusions we drew from Manor's quote. Indeed, the procedures implemented so strictly by the Election Commission for creating an *individual voter* exerting his free will are largely responsible for the political emancipation of the lower castes and their capacity to exert *collective voting*. This paradoxical outcome is well illustrated by many testimonies—including that of Viramma, a woman of the Pariah caste (the largest caste of Untouchables in Tamil Nadu) from Pondicherry. To begin with she voted for the Communist Party, but the local notable, the 'Grand Reddi', came to know about it and she had to vote for him. She explained this shift to the communist candidate:

The party has good ideas, but I've got children to feed. I need work, my son does as well. All my family are serfs at the Reddiar's and we eat the *kuj* he gives us. I depend on him completely. I have to run to his house to borrow when we've got nothing to eat, or when we have to celebrate an important event. I don't want to provoke his anger and we must vote for him. (Viramma and Racine 1997: 263)

The communist local leader replied that all he asked her was that one person in the family give him his vote. Viramma's family acted accordingly and the whole Untouchable neighbourhood where she lived did the same. As a result the area received electricity, running water and ration cards thanks to the intervention of the Grand Reddi, their patron who was returned repeatedly from their constituency. This clientelistic arrangement translated into ritual-like attitudes and material gratifications. For instance, before the elections the Grand Reddi distributed fake ballot papers on which his name and election symbols were highlighted and then organized a function for 'his' electors: 'There was a big party, a meal for all the voters and loudspeakers playing music. It was like a wedding!' (Viramma and Racine 1997: 274) In addition, the Grand Reddi distributed saris to the women voters (and probably alcohol to the men). Gradually, however, the patron-client relationships loosened because the dependents, like Viramma, realized the act of voting was secret:

We had five parties at one time. The ploughmen's party [that is the party whose election symbol was a ploughman] gave twenty rupees and a bottle of brandy; the two leaves party twenty-five rupees and a very brightly coloured factory sari; the cow and the calf party twenty-five rupees and some groundnut oil; the spinning wheel party fifteen rupees, and another one gave fifteen as well. We tell them all we'll vote for them and we take their money. But anyway, everybody's only got one vote. . . (Viramma and Racine 1997: 275)

However, those who paid for but did not receive the votes of the Untouchables could find out so long as the ballot papers were scrutinized at the local level. Hence the assaults against the recalcitrant Untouchables' neighbourhoods that candidates who had lost sometimes launched in retaliation.[11] Matters changed when the ballot papers polled in a segment started to be mixed and made into bundles for the purpose of counting at the district level. Then the secret ballot enabled the Untouchables to vote for whom they wanted, but they did it as groups, not as individuals.

The Dalits and the lower castes indeed prefer to remain united in order to use their demographic weight to act as interest groups during elections. In Uttar Pradesh, for instance, the Chamars—shoemakers who form the largest Untouchable caste—support the Bahujan Samaj Party (BSP) almost unanimously. In 2004, 71 per cent of the Dalits voted for the BSP (according to a very reliable opinion poll) while 72 per cent of the Yadavs, a caste of cowherds, supported the Samajwadi Party. In Bihar 77 per cent of the Yadavs voted for another regional party, the Rashtriya Janata Dal, in 2004.[12] Naturally voters claim they vote according to programmes, but one of the most determining factors is caste and community. In fact the upper castes also tend to vote *en bloc* for 'their' parties. In 2004, 77 per cent of the Vaishyas (merchant caste) voted for the BJP in UP. As a result the Congress could not remain the dominant 'catch-all party' that it was in the 1950s–60s. It continues to attract voters from different sections of society, but not to the same extent.

Indians tend not to vote as individual citizens but as members of religious minorities or caste groups, be they from the upper or from the lower castes. However, the two last categories must not be bracketed together because they are not on the same footing: if the lower castes can vote for the candidates of their liking, it is because of the procedures established by the Constitution of India and the Election Commission, even though these rules of the game were introduced for promoting an individual voter. The Untouchables' collective act of voting for candidates of their liking is really the unintended consequence of procedures designed for other purposes.

## FRAUD AND VIOLENCE

The sophistication of the measures taken by the Election Commission to surround voting with the best possible guarantees (as far as a secret ballot and voter identification are concerned) seemed also out of place for years when contrasted with the basic conditions under which elections are held, in terms of fraud and violence around the polling stations. While the act of voting itself may be surrounded by guarantees, the same could not be said for ballot boxes until the 1990s. The most common electoral fraud (for those candidates or parties who sense, on election day, that victory is not assured) consisted for a long time in hiring the services of an armed gang to grab one or more ballot boxes in a constituency. In 1971 the Commission counted eleven acts of 'booth capturing', including eight in Bihar, a state known for political violence (Election Commission 1972: 81). In 1980 nearly 60 polling stations—including 21 in Bihar, 12 in Uttar Pradesh and 19 in Kashmir—saw, similar incidents or faced tensions that led to the cancellation of voting (Election Commission 1980: 113–14). In addition to these practices there were often incidents around polling stations, such as clashes between party activists and unrest aimed at interrupting the voting procedure. In 1989 electoral violence caused a hundred deaths. In 1991 460 detachments of the Central Reserve Police Force were deployed around polling stations after campaign violence had already claimed 75 victims, including 50 in Bihar.[13]

The new head of the Election Commission, T.N. Seshan, then reacted with proper firmness. He decided to allow new elections to take place in polling stations that had fallen victim to fraud, in a more systematic fashion than in the past. In 1991 new elections took place in 2,614 voting stations (1,177 in Bihar and 876 in Uttar Pradesh, the two states most subject to political violence). Then the Election Commission did not hesitate to postpone an election in order to deploy additional police personnel to reduce the risk of booth capturing and other forms of violence which generally occurred around the polling stations. In 1996 the Election Commission sent 1,500 observers (an average of three per constituency) to supervise the polls.[14] Approximately 600,000 policemen were deployed to enforce law and order around the polling booths, which were manned by 1.5 million agents of the state, supervising the polls. More than 300,000 people were arrested as a preventive measure (125,000 in Uttar Pradesh[15] and 59,000 in Madhya Pradesh, where 87,000 arms were seized).[16] These measures enabled the state to control unrest around the booths, as elections were countermanded and then reorganized in 1,056 polling booths, as against 1,670 in 1989. A little less than half of them

(471) were in Bihar, 231 in Andhra Pradesh, 96 in Assam, 31 in Rajasthan, 43 in Uttar Pradesh and 22 in Orissa.[17] Furthermore the number of violent incidents at the polls declined from 3,363 in 1991 to 2,450 in 1998 and the number of deaths from 272 in 1991 to 213 in 1996, 65 in 1998 and 32 in 1999, including 29 people who were killed in landmine blasts engineered by Naxalites in Bihar,[18] and 18 in 2004.[19] Election-related violence is geographically concentrated, mainly in Bihar and in Uttar Pradesh. The strict policy of the Election Commission was partly responsible for a higher participation rate (+10 points in Uttar Pradesh), the security around the booths attracting more voters, especially those of the Scheduled Castes, whom the party thugs could not intimidate quite so easily as before. A fifty-year-old man from the caste of the Dhobis (washermen) recounts how things have changed in his village in Bihar:

When I first tried to vote some 30 years ago, I was told by them [the upper castes of the village] that I and other members of my community did not have votes. We realised later that they were casting our votes for their candidate. Then we resolved that we would cast our votes. Initially we used to go to the polling booth only to be beaten up and were forced to run away. But our resolve grew stronger with each election and we started reacting to their physical assaults in their own coin. I have been voting without getting beaten up in the last four elections [which include both Assembly and Lok Sabha polls since 1996]. (Quoted in Ramakrishnan 2004)

## Are Electronic Voting Machines Good for Democracy?

The Indian culture of voting underwent a significant change in 2004 with the systematic use of electronic voting machines (EVMs) during the general elections. The Election Commission first contemplated instituting an electronic voting system in 1977. The experiment, conducted in several by-elections from 1982 onwards, was abandoned in 1989 for reasons of cost (Butler, Lahiri and Roy 1989: 16) and because of the objections of the opposition, who feared being tricked by the government. The Election Commission nonetheless announced, after the 1991 elections, that this method of voting would enter into force for the next elections. The whole process was delayed but by the end of the decade in 1999, EVMs were introduced in 46 Lok Sabha constituencies spread over 17 states. And in 2004 they dislodged ballot papers everywhere. This new technology obliged the parties to adjust and even to reinvent their campaigns: they even ordered model EVMs to conduct demonstrations of their functioning during their house-to-house visits.

Indeed the citizens needed to be initiated into this new act of voting. According to the website of the Election Commission of India, 'instead of issuing a ballot paper, the Polling Officer in-charge of the Control Unit will press the Ballot Button. This will enable the voter to cast his vote by pressing the blue button on the Balloting Unit against the candidate and symbol of his choice'.[20] The symbol system has been retained by the Election Commission for an obvious reason: to cope with the persistently high rate of illiteracy. This modernization of the act of voting has been hailed 'as a bold and progressive decision' in the media. But things may not be as positive as the zealots of this technological modernization expected. According to the Election Commission, the EVM has four main advantages:

The EVMs will reduce booth capturing in the case of 'miscreants intimidating the polling personnel and stamping the ballot papers on the symbol and escaping in a matter of minutes ... because the EVMs are programmed in such a way that the machines will record only five votes in a minute.'

The EVMs will dispense the state from the printing of millions of ballot papers since 'only one ballot paper is required for fixing on the Balloting Unit at each polling station instead of one ballot paper for each individual elector.'

The EVMs will quicken the pace of polling since the voter has simply to press the button next to the symbol and name of his or her chosen candidate for registering his vote, instead of having to 'unfold the ballot paper, mark his preference, fold it again, go to the place where the ballot box is kept and drop it in the box'. Because of this long process, in the 1990s the voters queuing to cast their votes were sometimes counted in hundreds.[21] The EVMs also make the counting of votes faster.

Use of EVMs will reduce the number of invalid votes due to the stamping in between two candidates on the ballot paper. According to the Election Commission, 'in every General Election, the number of invalid votes is more important than the winning margin between the winning candidate and the second candidate, in a number of constituencies' (In Karnataka on an average there were 30,000 invalid votes for each parliamentary constituency and 5,000 for each Assembly constituency [Raghava 2004]).

While the EVMs were supposed to go some way toward remedying some of the most blatant frauds, like booth capturing, in fact during the 2004 elections gangs were able to take away some of the machines. Snatching of EVMs was especially prominent—though residual in terms of numbers—in states where Maoist groups tried to enforce some boycott of the elections: Andhra Pradesh, Bihar, Jharkhand, Chhattisgarh, etc. For instance, in Andhra Pradesh Maoist activists from the People's War Party 'kidnapped' two EVMs.[22]

Besides, the EVMs introduced new kinds of fraud. For instance, the ballot papers, which are inserted underneath the machines' glass-panes, with the names and symbols of the candidates—different in each constituency—had been printed in such a way, in some parts of Andhra Pradesh, that the election symbols of the Congress and other opposition parties were unduly hazy and small in size compared to the ruling party, the Telugu Desam Party. As a result, and in reaction to complaints lodged by Congress supporters, the Election Commission had to withdraw 45,000 'ballot papers'.[23] In addition to these defects the use of sophisticated technology, instead of reassuring the ordinary citizens, aroused new fears. In Andhra Pradesh, again, 'opposition parties, especially the Congress, and citizen groups' questioned the safety of votes recorded by the EVMs:

Their worst fear is about the software part of the machine which, they allege, can be 'preset' or influenced by polling officials or anybody for that matter to favour a party/candidate. The Congress leaders have been contending that the machine, depending on the type of pre-setting, can ensure every fourth vote being cast to a rival party, say, Telugu Desam, and open up to vulnerability after ensuring that a certain number of votes go to different parties. (Rao 2004)

Unsurprisingly a scientific innovation, instead of inspiring trust, is perceived as opaque and conducive to manipulations. However, in addition to irrational fears the EVMs are an objective cause for concern for one reason at least: the counting of the votes is now made at the level of the polling station. As a result voting patterns EVM-wise and, therefore, polling station-wise are revealed in the EVMs themselves at the time of counting of votes, and are known by the contestants immediately through their agents since they take part in the counting operations. The victimization of hostile voters—including Untouchables—by frustrated candidates with muscle power may once again become the order of the day, all the more so as EVMs can record a maximum of 3,840 votes. Today the total number of electors in a polling station is even less—it does not exceed 1,500—which means it is very easy to identify the voting pattern of very precise groups, who can therefore be readily harassed, except in the many regions where low caste people and Dalits have organized themselves.

India developed an electoral procedure to overcome the widespread problem of illiteracy: the symbol system, perfected over the course of many elections, which allows voters to cast their ballot under conditions guaranteeing independence, adequate information and secrecy. This procedure had unintended consequences since it contributed to institutionalizing the party system, which is an important illustration of the effects the procedural aspects of elections can have. But the perfection, or even refinement, of the electoral procedure promoted by the Election Commission and inspired by Western practices has had other unintended consequences: while the whole array of measures taken by the state aimed at ensuring an individual act of voting, they also enabled the crystallization of a collective vote among the lower strata of society, including the Dalits who sometimes dared to vote against the local notables only because the ballot was strictly secret.

By Western, liberal standards the community or caste dimension of voting contradicts democracy since this political system relies on the free will of individual citizens. Certainly members of the group—women for instance—may be forced to vote for candidates they would not have selected, but otherwise the collective dimension of voting strengthens democracy inasmuch as community-based or caste-based aggregations of individual preferences enable dominated religious minorities and lower castes to gain some leverage in the public sphere. This ethnicization of politics is in fact a major factor in the democratization of Indian democracy.[24] Similarly one need not worry too much about the degradation of the electoral procedures given the growing watchfulness of the Election Commission.

This vigilance has already borne fruit, as the declining intensity of violence at the time of elections testifies. However, the new EVMs may not be the panacea for remedying the plague of booth capturing, and they may even help local notables to regain their lost influence over recalcitrant voters—though such a regression may only happen in the few places where the lower castes are not yet organized.

## Notes

1. In 1998 for the first time polling for the Lok Sabha elections was held in five phases, spread over a month in order to give sufficient time for the paramilitary forces to move from one state to another. Hence the cost of the elections: Rs. 7,50,00,000 were spent in organizing the general elections, as against Rs. 6,00,00,000 in 1996 (A.K. Sinha, 'The Price of Democracy', *Outlook*, 22 December 1997: 68). In 2004 the Lok Sabha elections were held in five phases spread over three weeks between 21 April and 10 May. The cost of the 2004 General Elections was estimated at Rs. 12,00,00,000 for the Indian state (*India Today*, 8 March 2004: 34).
2. Election Commission, *Report of the First General Elections in India 1951–52*, Vol. I (General), New Delhi, 1955: 80 (quoted in Bharadvaja 1972: 56).
3. For a more detailed description of voting modalities, see Hauser (1986: 951–6).
4. Double or triple constituencies had disappeared. There was henceforth only one elected representative per constituency; some constituencies were reserved for Scheduled Castes and Scheduled Tribes.
5. The above reconstitution of the voting procedure comes from the guidelines of the Election Commission (1965: 66–7).
6. Interestingly the introduction of a deposit that each candidate had to pay for contesting and which he forfeited if he could not get a minimum number of the valid votes did not dissuade parties from fielding hordes of candidates. This is one of the reasons for the huge amount of money spent by the political parties at the time of elections (for more details, see Jaffrelot 2002).
7. On the victimization of 'deviant' Dalit voters by upper castes in Uttar Pradesh, see Maheshwari (1980: 99).
8. In 1957 the idea of replacing ink by a smallpox vaccination whose scar would long remain visible was envisaged (Election Commission 1959: 106). This suggestion is revealing of the confusion surrounding the official view of electoral activity in India: it is seen as a sign of civic duty, as are vaccinations.
9. See Jaffrelot (2003).
10. The main results of the CSDS exit poll were published in *The Hindu* supplement 'How India Voted', 20 May 2004. On Uttar Pradesh, see p. AE-5.
11. It happened once in Viramma's village (Viramma and Racine 1997: 278–9).
12. *The Hindu* supplement 'How India Voted', 20 May 2004, pp. AE-5, AE-6.
13. *National Mail*, 8 May 1991.
14. Video cameras were used to film the election campaign in order to exert psychological pressure on candidates and their supporters (*The Economic Times*, 14 March 1996).
15. *National Mail*, 2 May 1996.

16. *Madhya Pradesh Chronicle*, 7 May 1996.
17. *Madhya Pradesh Chronicle*, 4 and 5 May 1996; *The Times of India*, 5 May 1996; and *National Mail*, 30 April 1996.
18. *The Hindu*, 30 August 1999 and *National Mail*, 19 September 1999.
19. Among these eighteen casualties—all of which occurred during the first phase of polling—were seven Naxalites and four paramilitary personnel in charge of a polling station (*The Hindu*, 21 April 2004).
20. Election Commission of India, 'Frequently asked questions—Electronic Voting Machines (EVMs)'. Available at (<http://www.eci.gov.in/faq/elecvtmach.htm>).
21. Some parties have been known to send underage activists, who cannot in fact vote, to swell the queues in polling stations where candidates are vulnerable, in the hope of making legitimate voters lose patience and leave before voting.
22. 'EVMs become the target', *The Hindu*, 27 April 2004.
23. 'EC withdraws 45,000 "ballot papers"', *The Hindu*, 16 April 2004.
24. This is one of the main arguments of my book: Jaffrelot (2003).

# References

Bharadvaja, B. (1972), 'Election Symbols in Polities', *The Indian Political Science Review*, Vol. 6, No. 1, October.

Butler, D., Lahiri, A. and Roy, P. (1989), *India Decides: Elections 1952–1989*, New Delhi: Living Media.

Dalton, R.J. and Wattenberg, M.P. (1993), 'The Not So Simple Act of Voting' in A.W. Finifter (ed.), *Political Science: The State of the Discipline*, Washington DC: APSA.

Election Commission (1959), *Report on the Second General Elections in India, 1957*, New Delhi.

———(1965), *Report on the Third General Elections in India, 1962*, Vol. 1, *Narrative and Reflective Part*, New Delhi.

———(1972), *Report on the Fifth General Elections in India, 1971–72*, *Narrative and Reflective Part*, New Delhi.

———(1978), *Report on the Sixth General Elections to the Lok Sabha*, New Delhi.

———(1980), *Report on the General Elections to the House of the People*, Vol. 1, *Narrative*, Jaipur: Government Central Press.

Fazl, O. (1996), 'Muslims need better Strategy for next Polls', *Radiance*, No. 2, June.

Graham, B. (1983), 'Electoral Symbols and Party Identification in Indian Politics', in P. Lyon and J. Manor (eds), *Transfer and Transformation: Political Institutions in the New Commonwealth*, Leicester: Leicester University Press.

Hauser, W. and Singer, W. (1986), 'The Democratic Rite: Celebration and Participation in the Indian Elections', *Asian Survey*, Vol. 26, No. 9, September, pp. 951–6.

Jaffrelot, C. (2002), 'Indian Democracy: The Rule of Law on Trial', *India Review*, Vol. 1, No. 1, January, pp. 77–121.

———(2003), *India's Silent Revolution: The Rise of the Lower Castes in North Indian Politics*, London: Hurst.

Lieten, G.K. (1996), 'Inclusive View of Religion: A Rural Discourse in Uttar Pradesh', *Economic and Political Weekly*, No. 8, June.

Maheshwari, A.C. (1980), 'Uttar Pradesh: Rigging in Practice', *Economic and Political Weekly*, No. 19, January.

Manor, M. (1983), 'The Electoral Process amid Awakening and Decay: Reflections on the Indian General Elections of 1980', in P. Lyon and J. Manor (eds.), *Transfer and Transformation: Political Institutions in the New Commonwealth*, Leicester: Leicester University Press.

Mitra, S.K. (1979), 'Ballot Box and Local Power: Elections in an Indian Village', *Journal of Commonwealth and Comparative Politics*, Vol. 3, No. 17, November.

Raghava, M. (2004), 'EVMs May Eliminate Invalid Votes, Change Poll Outcome', *The Hindu*, 9 March.

Ramakrishnan, V. (2004), 'A Dalit Village's Struggle to Vote', *The Hindu*, 26 March.

Rao, M. (2004), 'EVMs Continue to Raise Hackles', *The Hindu*, 20 April.

Viramma, J. and Racine, J.L. (1997), *Viramma: Life of an Untouchable*, London and New York: Verso.

Viraraghavan, V.C. (1956), 'Election Law and Procedure' in R.V. Krishna Ayyar (ed.), *All India Election Guide*, Madras: Oriental Publishers.

# Chapter 28

# ⟨Why should we vote?⟩ the Indian middle class and the functioning of the world⟨s⟩ largest democracy

The political culture of the Indian middle class has often been analysed in terms of partisan orientations. From its inception till the 1950s, the Congress Party was looked at as a creation of the middle classes, resulting from the process of 'macaulayisation' (see Seal 1968; Broomfield 1968).[1] In the 1960s, the Jana Sangh appeared as 'the party of small industry and commerce' (Graham 1990: 158), largely because its traditionalist—even corporatist—ideology led its leaders to defend family-based economic. Twenty years later, the 'middle-classes were keen supporters of Rajiv Gandhi' (Hasan 2002: 159) who then embodied a promising form of modernity epitomized by his motto 'to prepare India's entry into 21st century' (Weiner 1989). Then in the 1990s, the Indian middle class was attracted by Hindu nationalism once again. They contributed to the Bharatiya Janata Party's (BJP) rise to power in 1998 and the re-election of its coalition, the National Democratic Alliance (NDA), in 1999.

While the party got 19.7 per cent of the valid votes in 1999, it received 23.8 per cent of middle class votes, according to the figures of the CSDS Data Unit. They became the cornerstone of what Yogendra Yadav, Sanjay Kumar and Oliver Heath (1999) called the 'BJP's new social bloc'. In the BJP, writes Suhas Palshikar (2002: 172):

the middle classes could find almost everything they dreamt of: a frankly market-oriented economic policy, a foreign policy striving to befriend the Americans, a suave middle-of-the-road prime minister (A.B. Vajpayee) along with a strong home minister (L.K. Advani); all coupled with an appropriate dosage of chauvinistic cultural-nationalist assertion.

In the BJP, the middle classes also found an undeclared hostility to positive discrimination on behalf of individual merit and strong reservations vis-à-vis parliamentarianism. Hindu nationalism was never fully reconciled with parliamentarian democracy, a regime borrowed from the West (see Jaffrelot 2000). The party believed more in a presidential system with authoritarian overtones. Its leader, A.B. Vajpayee, declared in the 1996 'Desraj Chowdhary Annual Memorial

*I am grateful to the CSDS Data Unit and more, especially, to Sanjay Kumar for providing me with many of the survey data on which this essay is based.

Lecture' that 'the present system of parliamentary democracy has failed to deliver the goods' and that his first choice was a presidential system. In his view, such a system would emancipate India from the rule of parties and enable the country to replace politicians by bureaucrats and technicians.[2] This anti-parliamentarianism was well in tune with the political culture of the middle classes. In 1993, an opinion poll conducted by MARG in Bombay, Delhi, Calcutta, Madras and Bangalore revealed that 58 per cent of the interviewees agreed with the proposition: 'If the country is to progress it needs a dictator' (*Sunday* 1994: 59).

The anti-parliamentarian inclination of the Indian middle classes not only results in their proximity vis-à-vis the BJP, but also explains the distancing of this social milieu from the institutional functioning of the world's largest democracy. The most obvious symptom of this alienation—that may amount to a real depoliticization—lay in the declining electoral participation of the middle classes. Yet, this notion needs to be qualified because such an assessment applies only to the upper caste segment of these classes.

## The Declining Electoral Participation of the Urban Middle Classes in India

At first glance, electoral participation is on the rise in India. From a meagre 45.7 per cent in 1952, the turnout rate has increased steadily to peak in 1984 at 64.1 per cent. This was an exceptional achievement due to the tragic circumstances of the assassination of Indira Gandhi. But since then, turnout has never dropped below 58 per cent at the time of general elections. However, this general picture dissimulates important geographical and social disparities. North and west India do not vote as much as south and east; the turnout rate of women remains much below that of men; voter turnout is higher in villages than in cities and towns.

This is a new development, as evident from Table 28.1, which shows that in 1977, rural constituencies had a lower turnout rate than urban ones (57.2 per cent as against 61.4 per cent), whereas this order was reversed in 1991 when the rural

TABLE 28.1: TURNOUT ACCORDING TO THE CONSTITUENCY CATEGORIES

| Year of elections | Urban | Rural |
|---|---|---|
| 1977 | 61.4 | 57.2 |
| 1980 | 58.3 | 53.9 |
| 1984 | 64.0 | 63.0 |
| 1989 | 61.3 | 60.8 |
| 1991 | 53.8 | 56.1 |
| 1996 | 54.6 | 57.8 |
| 1998 | 57.6 | 61.5 |
| 1999 | 53.7 | 60.7 |
| 2004 | 53.1 | 58.9 |

*Sources:* For 1977-99, *Journal of Indian School of Political Economy* (2003). For 2004, CSDS Data Unit.

constituency turnout remained at 56.1 per cent while the urban turnout fell to 53.8 per cent.

This trend has continued since then, so much so that the difference between the rural and the urban turnout rate has never been less than 3 percentage points and has increased as much as 6/7 percentage points, with rural constituencies registering a rate of almost 59 per cent in 2004 whereas urban constituencies fell to almost 53 per cent, the lowest ever. The cities of India vote less because the urban middle class votes less.

## THE ATYPICAL INDIAN PATTERN OF ABSENTEEISM

In most democracies—if not all—electoral abstention is positively correlated with social and educational backwardness (to use terms the Indian Constitution is familiar with). Hence the popular expression, 'the disenfranchized' which is used to designate those who had no right to vote in the past—because of their low income—and who continue not to vote today because of their socioeconomic condition. In the United States, the correlation is perfectly linear: in November 2002, for the mid-term elections, 78 per cent of those who earned less than US\$ 5,000 a year did not vote, compared to 43.4 per cent of those who earn more than US\$75,000 a year. Those who voted less were the unemployed (abstention rate: 72.8 per cent), whereas those who voted the most were government workers (40.9 per cent) and the self-employed (51 per cent) (US Census Bureau 2004). Similarly, 63.5 per cent of those who earned US\$10,000 did not vote in 2004 for the presidential elections, while only 21.7 per cent of those who earned more than US\$150,000 abstained, the correlation being perfectly linear too—the richer you were, the more you voted (US Census Bureau 2004). In Britain also, the proportion of those who voted was higher for self-employed people (71 per cent) during the 2001 general elections than for employed people (66 per cent); unemployed people were the least likely to vote—only 48 per cent voted (see <http://www.statistics. gov.uk/cci nugget_print.asp?ID=1008>). In France, only 40.4 per cent of unemployed people and 40.2 per cent of the workers voted in the 2002 elections, whereas 58.8 per cent of the 'Cadres et professions intellectuellei supérieures' (executives and higher intellectual professions) did so (Octant 2005: 5).

In stark contrast with this dominant pattern, in the world's largest democracy, the poorer one is, the more one votes and the richer one is, the less one votes. This is evident from Table 28.2, which shows that during the last Lok Sabha elections, 59.3 per cent of the very poor people the CSDS agents interviewed in the exit poll survey said that they had voted, whereas only 56.7 per cent of the rich said the same.

This unusual pattern is especially pronounced in big cities. Delhi is a case in point. During the 2003 state elections, the gap between the turnout of the 'rich'

TABLE 28.2: Turnout According to Class during the 2004 Lok Sabha Elections
(CSDS Post Poll Survey Weighted by Actual Turnout)

| Social class | Voters (in %) | Non-voters (in %) |
|---|---|---|
| Very poor | 59.3 | 40.7 |
| Rich | 56.7 | 43.3 |
| Average | 58.1 | 41.9 |

*Source:* CSDS Data Unit.

TABLE 28.3: Turnout According to Class during the
2003 State Assembly Elections in Delhi (CSDS Post Poll
Survey Weighted by Actual Turnout)

| Social class | Voters (in %) | | Non-voters (in %) | |
|---|---|---|---|---|
| Very poor | 77.5 | 60 | 22.5 | 40 |
| Poor | 57 | | 43 | |
| Lower middle | 53.5 | 53.6 | 46.5 | 46.4 |
| Middle | 53.8 | | 46.3 | |
| Rich | 45.8 | 48.3 | 54.2 | 51.7 |
| Very rich | 57.5 | | 42.5 | |
| Average | 53.4 | | 46.6 | |

*Source:* CSDS Data Unit.

and the turnout of the 'very poor' was almost 32 percentage points, even though
the difference was not so great so far as the 'poor' were concerned (see Table
28.3).

If one aggregates the 'very rich' and the 'rich' into a single category, it is quite
clear that this class is the only one where those who do not vote are more numerous
than those who do.

## WHY DO THE URBAN RICH VOTE LESS?

To answer this question, one must explore several hypotheses which reflect—each
in its own way—the multi-faceted identity of this category that we call the middle
classes. The most trivial explanations have much to do with the materiality of the
voting process: voting is painful because one has to stand in the queue and wait
for hours under the sun or the rain—something rich people are not used to. This
is an excuse I have heard repeatedly, but it is not as convincing as it might have
been in the past because the Electronic Voting Machines have substantially reduced
the queues in front of the booth.[3]

Another aspect of the voting process invoked by the middle class to explain
why they do not go to the polling booth concerns the voters list. These lists are
criticized because many names are missing from them, an anomaly that is generally
attributed to the ruling party's malpractises. Impersonation is another related issue.

A university lecturer protests: 'Many a times when you go to the polling booth, you find that your vote has already been cast'. Though this is hard to believe given the computerization of voter lists and the checking of IDs as well as the marking of one finger of every voter with indelible ink, this phenomenon may have reached massive proportions in some towns and cities. But then the question is: why has it dissuaded middle class people to vote and not others?

Middle class people are not so easy to reach during the election campaigns. In India, more than in any Western democracy, party activists canvass by going door to door. This method cannot be really effective in the case of an urban middle class, which is eager to protect its privacy. In contrast, the plebeians are more accessible and some political activists may even take them to the booth collectively (in trucks or buses), though this is strictly forbidden by the law. The Representation of the People Act of 1951 stipulates that 'the hiring or procuring, whether on payment or otherwise, of any vehicle or vessel by a candidate or his agent or by any other person for the conveyance of any elector (other than the candidate himself, the members of his family or his agent) to or from any polling station is a corrupt practice' (cited in Viraraghavan 1956: 129). But, these are rather common practises in the countryside till today, which may partly explain the gap between the turnout rates of urban India and rural India. While these parameters and the 'gift' (saris, alcohol, and so on) offered to the poor may explain why they go to the polling booths, they do not explain why the rich do not go.

In fact, most of the arguments based on the materiality of the voting process are allegedly for justifying attitudes which are not legitimate in a democracy where voting is a duty as well as a right. Obviously, one must look for more profound explanations.[4] One of them lies in a strong rejection of the political personnel— there is no need to vote because MPs and MLAs form a political class known for its corruption and its unethical arrangements. One of the faculty members I interviewed in Jammu University in March 2005 says it plainly:

Well firstly, I would quote the definition of democracy which is 'Of the people, by the people, for the people'. In the context of the Indian democratic system, I will quote that it is a democracy which is 'OFF the people, FAR the people and BUY the people'.... As far as the Indian polity is concerned, it is totally dominated by money and commercial elements. So, as far as the politics of Indian politics is concerned, it is a politicization of criminals, corruption, the caste system and communalism. So where is this political system going? Only a few politicians are deciding the future of the country. According to their vested interests, they are misguiding the people. Now we have the coalition politics. They have contested the elections separately, and they formed the coalition without uniting in principle and ideology. So this is a democracy decided by the polity. In the Indian context, that is why I say that democracy is not working properly as far as the masses are concerned.

The era of coalition which India entered in the 1990s has apparently aggravated the discredit of the political personnel because the outcome of the elections regarding who will form the government has not been decided by the voters but through behind-the-scenes negotiations. This happened in 1996 and 1998. Since then, however, *pre-electoral* alliances have been able to take over power—in 1999, the BJP-led NDA and in 2004, the Congress-led UPA.

In addition to their lack of morality, politicians are rejected because of their ineffectiveness. This argument is recurrently made by executives who are used to the rules of management applied in the corporate sector. A Bhopal-born senior executive at Indian Oil who works seven days a week and does not even find the time to visit his parents 800 km away declares in this vein:

This is an opportunistic democracy. In the name of democracy we have lost all sense of discipline. The army and, to some extent, the judiciary are the only disciplined institutions in this country. Corruption is everywhere. People have no sense of public interest. Nobody pays taxes—except we, the salaried people. In the name of democracy we have let rural India escape all taxes. They don't even pay for electricity. This is the bane of democracy. The party which makes the peasants pay taxes and electricity bills will be out of power for ten years.

This corporate executive targets the populist dimension of Indian democracy, which results in demagogic, anti-economic and inequitable decisions. Interestingly, he praises a more disciplined brand of polity. Such an attitude, which originates from the booming private sector, has become very common among the new middle class. These people are not so much calling for a military regime as for a more managerial democracy on behalf of efficiency. One remembers the heading of the homepage of the website of N. Chandrababu Naidu, the then chief minister of Andhra Pradesh who tried to make Hyderabad a high tech city but was voted out by the peasants he had thoroughly neglected—'Chandrababu Naidu: CEO, Andhra Pradesh', showing him typing on his laptop (see <http://members.tripod.com/chandrababu/>).

The 'State of Democracy in South Asia' survey that the CSDS coordinated in 2005 shows converging results. When asked whether 'We should have a strong leader who does not have to bother about elections', 38 per cent of the interviewees from the 'elite' agreed and 30 per cent of the interviewees from the masses agreed. However, only 15 per cent of the interviewees from the 'elite' felt 'The country should be governed by the Army' whereas 80 per cent felt that 'All major decisions about the country should be taken by experts rather than politicians' (CSDS 2008). This is a clear indication of the development of a new political culture that believes more in managers than in parliamentarians. This shift is not unrelated to economic liberalization and the growth rate of the economy, which is attributed to a more managerial style of conducting public affairs. It found its first vocal expression in the summer of 2005 when monsoon floods were considered as badly handled by the administration in Mumbai. The local middle class them called for the replacement of the state apparatus by people trained in the corporate sector. This move was naturally supported by the role big firms had already played in reconstructing Gujarat after the 2002 earthquake.

There is no denying that some urban middle class people do not vote because they no longer trust parliamentary democracy. However, another major explanation for this new attitude lies in the dynamics of caste politics.

## The Key Element of Caste

Indian sociologists have tended to de-link caste and class as much as they could, be it from a Marxist perspective or from a Weberian one. For the Marxists, of course, there is nothing compared to class, as a social category defined by the position of the people vis-à-vis the ownership of the means of production—one belonged either to the proprietary classes or to labour. B.R. Ambedkar exposed this flawed perception as early as the 1930s, showing that caste solidarity cuts across class sentiments simply because the 'caste system is not merely division of labour. *It is also a division of labourers*' (Ambedkar 1990 [1935]: 47, emphasis original).[5] The neo-Weberians, who acknowledge the importance of status in social relations, have constantly tried to maintain a distinction between class situation and status situation. André Béteille (1996: 513) argued along these lines:

a major contribution of analytical sociology has been to formulate and explore systematically the distinction between class and status. It is true that sociologists differ on how the distinction should be made, just as they differ on what they mean by status and by class. Nevertheless, they would agree upon the need to maintain as consistently as possible some kind of distinction between the two.

For me, it is not possible, and certainly not desirable, to distinguish class and caste simply because both categories are closely connected, as André Béteille (2002: 74) himself has suggested recently when he wrote: 'It will be impossible to understand the morphology, leave alone revalues, of the Indian middle class without taking account of the pre-existing differentiation of Indian society on the basis of language, religion and caste.' To look at caste and class separately would be an artificial exercise amounting to some wishful thinking that caste belongs to the past and that India has entered the era of class. This is what Jayaram assumes when he writes:

The combination of caste and class status is no more a sociological axiom—the decline of the Jajmani system and the commercialisation of agriculture, the implementation of land reforms, the release from bondage of serfs, and the consequent changes in agrarian relations; and the rise of the land-owning 'upper-Shudra' caste groups, have all profoundly altered the economic bearing of the caste system. (1996: 82)

Certainly, India has changed—though the land reforms have been stillborn in many states. Caste and class do not coincide any more, but they are still closely related anyway. Indeed, the 2000 National Sample Survey shows a remarkable correlation between caste and one's standard of living. According to this survey, more than 60 per cent of the urban upper caste Hindus had a per capita monthly consumption expenditure of Rs 775 or more, whereas less than 25 per cent of the urban Other Backward Classes (OBCs) and less than 18 per cent of the urban Scheduled Castes (SCs) were in such a position. Similarly, among the urban rich who spend more than Rs 1,500 of per capita consumption expenditure, 59.8 per cent are from the upper caste Hindus, 14.6 per cent from the OBCs and 3.8 per cent from the SCs (cited in Deshpande 2003: 112–13). Unsurprisingly, castes and occupations coincide to a large extent. According to a survey conducted thanks to the CSDS Data Unit, 24.5 per cent of the upper castes belong to the 'salariat' and 20.4 per cent to 'business', as against 9.5 and 10.1 per cent for the OBCs and 10.9 and 5.3 per cent for the SCs respectively (Kumar 2002: 4095).

One may object that standards of living and consumption patterns do not say everything—caste and class are also mindsets and even though the rich may come from the upper caste, they might have emancipated themselves from the hierarchical ethos of their original status group. Indeed, Béteille argues that:

Middle-class values are often contradicted by the values of caste and community, and the same individual is pulled in opposite directions. Individuals frequently act in ways that they condemn in others, justifying their own conduct by the press of circumstance. (2002: 74)

I beg to differ again and rather consider that, far from being schizophrenic, middle class people combine rather easily both value systems to make one integrated new synthesis. A core element of this socio-political culture lies in the typical middle class value of individual merit and the correlative rejection of positive discrimination—the recurrent setting to fire of 'the corpse of merit' in anti-reservation protests is the most pictoral illustration of this correlation. Now, the defence of merit, which occupies the front row in the middle class repertoire, is well in tune with the hierarchical ethos of the upper caste Hindus. This is due to the fact that positive discrimination is largely based, in India, on the criterion of caste and, indeed, this major feature of the upper caste middle class worldview became prominent during the Mandal affair in the early 1990s. But this is also due to the elective affinities between the upper castes' ethos and the middle class value system. Commenting upon the book by Amitav Ghosh, *The Hungry Tide*, Sankaran Krishna shows that one of the characters, Kanai, 'an urbane, single and successful male entrepreneur from Delhi' can only oscillate 'between an ideational commitment to egalitarian values and an inability to practise it in reality', something the author implicitly attributes to caste consciousness or subconscious:

so long as the subaltern's desire for a better life remains mimetic, aspirational and ultimately futile. . ., Kanai can be both indulgent and supportive. And yet, the minute it threatens the sedimented hierarchy of *an enduring social order,* he turns vicious, and a repressed inner-self surfaces with incredible hatred towards the subaltern.[6] (2006: 2328, emphasis mine)

It is very difficult to prove that this defence of hierarchy is rooted in caste feelings because no middle class man would confess that his behaviour is still dictated by the illegitimate social institution that is caste. But, here, political scientists could help sociologists understand what is going on. The starting point for such an analysis, once again, must be the Mandal affair. To my mind this affair made a bigger impact over the political culture of the urban middle class than the almost simultaneous decision to liberalize the Indian economy because of the changes in the polity that it entailed. New political parties emerged, which found their roots in two separate milieus, Dalits and OBCs. The Bahujan Samaj Party, the Samajwadi Party and the Rashtriya Janata Dal are cases in point. The rise to power of these parties, which have governed Uttar Pradesh and Bihar over the last 15 years, permanently or intermittently, has transformed (north) Indian politics. It not only reflects the growing political awareness of the subalterns but also affects mainstream parties. For instance, the Congress and the BJP have given tickets to an ever larger number of OBC candidates. So much so that the declining presence of the upper castes among the MPs has taken them to their lowest points so far. This socio-political transformation results from the changing political attitude of the low caste voters. When they were included in clientelistic networks, they voted for their patrons—be they landlords, bosses or moneylenders on whom they depended. But after the upper castes objected to the reservation policies, as they did in the streets in 1990 during the anti-Mandal demonstrations, they joined hands in a move towards horizontal solidarity and they now vote for their own caste fellows, be they candidates nominated by explicitly low caste parties or by mainstream parties.[7] This shift was bound to make a big difference to Indian politics given the sheer number of the lower castes: Dalits (17 per cent of the population) and OBCs (52 per cent) represented almost 70 per cent of Indian society. In 2004, upper caste MPs represented only one-third of all the MPs returned in the Hindi belt whereas the OBC MPs are almost one-fourth of the total (Jaffrelot 2007a).

This plebianization of Indian politics has alienated the urban middle class from two points of view—first, the new social profile of the candidates is not to their liking because the nominees come more and more from the lower castes; second, they have started to wonder what difference their vote could make, given their small numbers. When I asked her why the middle class people of Delhi abstained from voting is such large numbers, Sheila Dikshit, the Chief Minister of the state since 1998, replied:

Now there is a kind of cynicism about how is it going to make a difference if we go to vote or do not go to vote. They talk about politics most of them. But their attitude is 'I am not ready to try and make a difference', because they feel that they are not in number adequate enough to bring about a change.[8]

Things were different in the past when the addition of middle class votes could garner the plate of a candidate of their own milieu for whom plebeians had been requested to cast their vote according to a classic clientelistic pattern.

Caste politics is, therefore, largely responsible for the growing indifference of the middle class towards elections. In fact, instead of focusing on class as the more relevant variable, one should pay more attention to caste. Indeed, the difference between the electoral participation of the upper castes and the Dalits is even more significant than the difference between the electoral participation of the rich and the poor.

The idea that caste may be the most important variable when we try to understand the voting pattern of the middle class, is supported by the chronology of the change in turnout rates mentioned in Table 28.4. Indeed, the voters of the towns and cities of India where the upper caste middle class is concentrated started to vote less in 1991, precisely when low caste politics took off in the context of the Mandal affair.

TABLE 28.4: Turnout According to Caste During the 1999 and the 2004 Lok Sabha Elections in India (CSDS Post Poll Survey Weighted by Actual Turnout)

| Caste groups | Voters | | Non-voters | |
|---|---|---|---|---|
| | 1999 | 2004 | 1999 | 2004 |
| Dalits | 60.6 | 63.3 | 39.4 | 36.7 |
| Upper castes | 58.0 | 57.7 | 42.0 | 42.3 |

*Source:* Adapted from data provided by the CSDS Data Unit.

Moreover, if we now turn to the Dalit middle class, we do not find the same apathy so far as voting is concerned and nor do we find the same rejection of parliamentary democracy. The notion of a Dalit middle class, though rather new, is not at all irrelevant, given the progress SCs have made in terms of education and socio-professional mobility thanks to the reservation policies in the university and the public sector. As pointed out earlier, the share of the Dalits in the salariat is bigger than that of the OBCs (and also of the Muslims), 10.9 per cent against 9.5 per cent (and 10.7 per cent) (Kumar, Heath and Heath 2002: 147). According to Gopal Guru, this Dalit elite has distanced itself from its original milieu:

The Dalit middle class keeps a safe distance from their caste people who normally reside in the slums of major cities. They have undergone a complete change in the value structures. Their past life has become so disgusting that they do not want to be reminded about it. (2002: 147)

I do not share Guru's pessimism. Certainly, many Dalit *parvenus* lay themselves to the old co-option process that the Congress manipulated so well during the golden age of clientelistic democracy. And many of them probably do not visit the slums where their caste fellows continue to live. But it does not mean that they have severed their links with their original milieu. I do not agree with Guru's assessment that 'the Dalit middle class has nothing to do with the ideology of

Ambedkar' (ibid.). Many Dalit civil servants and students have read some of his books and try to propagate his social as well as political views, as is evident from the social background of the members of the Backward and Minority Communities Employees Federation (BAMCEF), a union that has been the crucible of the BSP. These Dalit middle class people have lost no interest in electoral politics, on the contrary!

In order to explore the political culture of the Dalit middle class, I conducted dozens of interviews over the last 10 years. I shall reproduce below the main results of the one I conducted on 25 February 2005. It was a group interview with 18 Dalit students of Jawaharlal Nehru University (JNU), Delhi, coming from 10 different states.[9] The students definitely belonged to the middle class so far as their standard of living was concerned. Incidentally they were all fluent in English except one Hindi-speaking girl. I posed them a single twofold question: 'What is your assessment of Indian democracy and is it useful to vote?' Except one proponent of the naxalite ideology, they were all enthusiastic about the functioning of Indian democracy and positive about the act of voting. One of the interviewees said:

My own assessment is that the Indian democracy is working quite well, and is moving towards being more participative and giving power to the lower caste. And it is through this movement that the lower caste is asserting themselves. So I think it is within our reach through democracy only to upset that hegemony of the upper caste.

This respondent was not at all isolated. Most of the others were satisfied with Indian democracy insofar as it permitted the empowerment of the lower castes—they approved of a form of *democracy by caste*. One of them even declared:

From the 1990s what we are seeing is that along with the Hindu nationalist forces, we are also seeing regional parties, different caste parties, and local parties; there is a kind of resurgence of protest against the Congress or against Hindu fundamentalist forces. There is a kind of resurgence of protest. That is again a part of the Indian democracy which from the last 20 years has been coming up. And of course caste politics and caste participation is compulsory in that.

These young Dalits of the intelligentsia very pertinently suspected that the upper castes were now giving a bad name to democracy because they were losing power in comparison to the lower castes. One of them made this very perceptive comment:

There are moves now to subvert democracy. There has been a sense that in the early part since Indian independence, India was the only functional democracy in the third world, that its democratic values were great, etc. . . . But what happens when lower caste groups start coming into power, then the whole discourse starts being built up saying that democracy is fraud, the State is doing funny things, that people are grabbing, using the State to grab more than what they require through non-democratic means. Politics becomes something dirty suddenly. The whole point, even of this survey itself, is very interesting at what time it comes up. When democracy was in shambles in the beginning of the 1940s–1950s, Indian democracy was portrayed as the shining light of the world. And now when it is actually coming into its own, when people are participating, people are beginning to voice what they feel, then democracy becomes something on which we have surveys being conducted about if it is good to vote or not.

Another Dalit student made a very similar analysis by paying more attention to the strategy of the upper caste middle class:

I feel the group of the upper caste and middle class who used to hold the political power, has moved to two spheres: NGOs and the media. It is through the media that the sense is created that politics is dirty. If you clearly analyse the media, where the upper caste is moving, especially the English media, the way Laloo Prasad Yadav is portrayed, Mayawati is portrayed, there is a sense amongst the middle class-upper caste, that Laloo Prasad Yadav is a criminal and corruption personified. And that Mayawati is another factor that should not come to politics. So the other option for them is military rule because democracy is not functioning. I am perfectly happy with the way Indian society and Indian democracy is functioning. And it is getting more and more democratized. NGOs also. You move to NGOs, and they say that politicians are bad and that it is not functioning, etc., etc. So I will vote. Definitely I will vote.

In this perspective, voting is important. In fact all the respondents, except the follower of the Naxalite strategy, said so. One of them expressed this view very well:

Social and economic democracy is not functioning in the Indian social structure, basically OBCs and SCs/STs communities. Still, if you consider OBCs and SCs/STs politics, they are asserting themselves in the parliament in a political way. Politics or the democratic way is the only way that they can assert themselves. Democracy is the only structure in which they can bargain and justify themselves. So voting is the only way to assert themselves.

Another interviewee made the same point in one sentence: 'you cannot make a change in this country without voting'.

The declining interest in elections among the urban upper caste middle class of India can primarily be explained by its growing rejection of brand the existing form of democracy and the rise of a new plebeian brand of politics. There, caste plays an important part—the urban middle class which abstains from voting is upper caste. The Dalit middle class people do vote and very much appreciate the empowering potential of democracy.[10]

The contrasting attitude of the upper castes and the lower castes regarding the act of voting partly explains one of the puzzling results of the CSDS 2005 'State of Democracy in South Asia' survey where we find that the percentage of those who considered that their vote had some effect increased, whereas the percentage of those who considered that it made no difference increased as well (see Table 28.5):

TABLE 28.5: Responses to the Question: 'Do You Think Your
Vote has an Effect on how Things are Run in this Country?'

|                    | 1971 | 1996 | 2005 |
| ------------------ | ---- | ---- | ---- |
| Has an effect      | 48.4 | 58.7 | 61.7 |
| Makes no difference| 16.2 | 21.4 | 26.1 |

*Source:* CSDS State of Democracy in South Asia Survey, 2005, New Delhi (roneo).

My hunch is that those who consider that their vote has an effect come more from the lower castes whereas those who think that it makes no difference come more from the upper castes. But is the upper caste middle class the real loser in India? Pawan Varma (2002: 90) argues that 'The middle class is no longer in the driver's seat in Indian politics'. At the same time, the urban upper caste middle class is benefiting more than any other group from economic liberalization. The 40 million people or so who earn US$1,000 a month form a group that increases by 10 per cent every year. The middle classes are powerful—so much so that they may think they do not need to vote to get what they want; they do not need to vote because they get the phone! One of the faculty members I interviewed elaborates very convincingly on this theme:

They think that they have accessibility, they are part of the governing system, and that they can influence and that they can get things done if the need be. So they are relatives or friends of a *neta* (political leader) or IAS (civil servant) or PCs (Police Constabularies). So they have their channels through which they can get their work done. So what is the need to go and vote for this leader or that leader?

Indeed, this is another major reason of the declining turnout of the upper caste middle class—it is so influential that it does not need to vote!

This point needs to be looked at in a wider perspective, beyond the focal point of this chapter that is the political culture of the upper caste middle class. If we take this larger view, we may argue that the way this social category abstained from voting substantiates a widespread view that it wants to secede 'from the rest of India' (Krishna 2006: 2327). Krishna, for instance, argues that 'one of the existential realities of being a middle class Indian is an inescapable desire to escape the rest of India' (ibid.). Given the fact that the upper caste middle class remains in command even though it does not vote as much as before, I would qualify this escapism. This class wants to escape from the growing influence of the plebeians—in order to continue to rule the country.

## Notes

1. In 1920, 64.4 per cent of the delegates to the annual session of the Indian National Congress were lawyers, 7.4 per cent were journalists, 7.4 per cent were businessmen,

3.7 per cent were medical practitioners and 3.1 per cent were teachers (see Krishna 1966: 422).

2. In an interview to *India Today,* the middle class newsmagazine par excellence, Vajpayee declared in 1997 that 'where political parties are unable to form a government at the Centre, the President should carry on the administration with the help of advisers' (*India Today* 1997).

3. On the act of voting in India, see Jaffrelot (2007b).

4. Yet, there is one element of the material process of voting which is relevant here, and that is the absence of 'none' or 'nil' on the Indian ballot papers (or on the screen of de EVMs)—the voters who are not willing to vote for any of the candidates (be they independents or supported by political parties) should be able to register a vote for none of them. The French system, for instance, makes this vote of protest, which may reflect the quest of some alternative, possible. It is known as a 'vote blanc' or a 'vote nul'. Interestingly, in France, the 'blanc' et nuls' are increasing, along with the erosion of the mainstream parties and the rise of the extremes, both phenomena being symptoms of the growing rejection of the political parties.

5. For more details, see Jaffrelot (2005).

6. This article is primarily a fascinating review of the biography of the late nuclear scientist Raja Ramanna.

7. I have studied this process in a *longue durée* perspective in Jaffrelot (2003).

8. Interview with Sheila Dikshit, New Delhi, 5 March 2005.

9. On the method of group interview, see Duchesne and Haegel (2004).

10. The idea that the support for democracy was widespread in the general public had already been substantiated by Peter Mayer in the 1970s (see Mayer 1972).

## References

Ambedkar, B.R. [1990 (1935)], *Annihilation of Caste,* New Delhi: Arnold Publishers.

Béteille, A. (1996), 'The Mismatch between Class and Status', *British Journal of Sociology,* Vol. 47, No. 3, pp. 513–25.

——— (2002), 'The Social Character of the Indian Middle Class', in I. Ahmad and H. Reifeld (eds.), *Middle Class Values in India and Western Europe,* New Delhi: Social Science Press.

Broomfield, J.H. (1968), *Elite Conflict in a Plural Society: 20th Century Bengal,* Berkeley and Los Angeles: California University Press.

CSDS (2008), *State of Democracy in South Asia,* Delhi: Oxford University Press.

Deshpande, S. (2003), *Contemporary India: A Sociological View,* New Delhi: Penguin.

Duchesne, S. and Haegel, F. (2004), *L'enquête et ses méthodes: L'entretien collectif,* Paris: Nathan/SEJER.

Graham, B.D. (1990), *Hindu Nationalism and Indian Politics,* Cambridge: Cambridge University Press.

Guru, Gopal (2002), 'Dalit Middle Class Hangs in the Air', in I. Ahmad and H. Reifeld (eds.), *Middle Class Values in India and Western Europe,* New Delhi: Social Science Press.

Hasan, Z. (2002), 'Changing Political Orientations of the Middle Classes in India', in I. Ahmad and H. Reifeld (eds.), *Middle Class Values in India and Western Europe,* New Delhi: Social Science Press.

<http://members.tripod.com/chandrababu/>, consulted on 15 September 2006.
<http://www.statistics.gov.uk/cci/nugget_print.asp?ID=1008>
*India Today* (1991), 15 May.
―――― (1997), 15 May.
Insee, 'Enquêtes participation électorale', *Octant*, No. 102, juillet 2005, p. 5 (www.insee.fr).
Jaffrelot, C. (2000), 'Hindu Nationalism and Democracy', in F. Frankel, Z. Hasan, R. Bhargava and B. Arora (eds.), *Transforming India: Social and Political Dynamics of Democracy*, Delhi: Oxford University Press, pp. 352–78.
―――― (2003), *India's Silent Revolution: The Rise of the Lower Castes in North India*, Delhi: Permanent Black.
―――― (2005), *Dr. Ambedkar and Untouchability: Analysing and Fighting Caste*, New Delhi: Permanent Black.
―――― (2007a), 'The Democratisation of Indian Democracy: The Rise to Power of the Plebeians', in S. Ganguly (ed.), *India, the World's Largest Democracy*, Baltimore and Washington: The John Hopkins University Press.
―――― (2007b), 'Voting in India: Electoral Symbols, the Party System and the Collective Citizen', in R. Bertrand, J.L. Briquet and P. Pels (eds.), *Cultures of Voting: The Hidden History of the Secret Ballot*, London: Hurst, pp. 78–99.
Jayaram, N. (1996), 'Caste and Hinduism: Changing Protean Relationship', in M.N. Srinivas (ed.), *Caste in its Twentieth Century Avatar*, New Delhi: Viking.
Journal of Indian School of Political Economy (2003), *Political Parties and Elections in Indian States, 1990–2003*, Special Issue, Vol. 15, Nos. 1 and 2.
Krishna, G. (1966), 'The Development of the Indian National Congress as a Mass Organization, 1918–1923', *Journal of Asian Studies*, Vol. 25, No. 3.
Krishna, S. (2006), 'The Bomb, Biography and the Indian Middle Class', *Economic and Political Weekly*, Vol. 41, No. 23.
Kumar, S., A. Heath and O. Heath (2002), 'Changing Patterns of Social Mobility: Some Trends over Time', *Economic and Political Weekly*, Vol. 37, No. 40.
Mayer, P.B. (1972), 'Support for the Principles of Democracy by the Indian Electorate', *South Asia*, Vol. 2, pp. 24–32.
Palshikar, S. (2002), 'Politics of India's Middle Classes', in I. Ahmad and H. Reifeld (eds.), *Middle Class Values in India and Western Europe*, New Delhi: Social Science Press.
Seal, A. (1968), *The Emergence of Indian Nationalism: Competition and Collaboration in the Later 19th Century*, Cambridge: Cambridge University Press.
*Sunday* (1994), 9 January.
U.S. Census Bureau (2002), *Current Population Survey*, Available online at www.census.gov., accessed on 28 July 2004.
―――― (2004), *Current Population Survey*, available online at www.census.gov., accessed on 25 May.
Vajpayee, A.B. (1996), 'Challenges to Democracy in India', Desraj Chowdhary Annual Memorial Lecture, *The Organiser*, 24 November, p. 4.
Varma, P. (2002), 'Middle-class Values and the Creation of a Civil Society', in I. Ahmad and H. Reifeld (eds.), *Middle Class Values in India and Western Europe*, New Delhi: Social Science Press.

Viraraghavan, V.C. (1956), 'Election Law and Procedure', in R.V. Krishna Ayyar (ed.), *All India Election Guide*, Madras: Oriental Publishers.

Weiner, M. (1989), 'Rajiv Gandhi: A Mid-term Assessment', in A. Varshney (ed.), *The Indian Paradox*, New Delhi: Sage, pp. 293–318.

Yadav, Y., S. Kumar and O. Heath (1999), 'The BJP's New Social Block', *Frontline*, 19 November.

# Chapter 29

# Indian democracy: the rule of law on trial

Corruption has become an all-pervasive phenomenon in contemporary India. A 1997 study showed that in large cities like Chennai, Ahmedabad and Bangalore, 20–33 per cent of slum dwellers—not to speak about the middle class—had to pay 'a bribe for getting a service or solving a problem with a public agency' (Paul and Shah 1997: 152). Over half of the 1,556 persons responding to a 1995 six-city poll stated that bribes were required for obtaining even basic services such as a driving licence or an electricity connection (*The Times of India*, 14 January 1995: 1). Rural India is not spared either. In 1989, Rajiv Gandhi admitted that only 15 per cent of rural development subsidies reached their intended beneficiaries. The *patwaris,* who maintain village records, are notorious for malpractices such as favouring landlords who are likely to bribe them during the transfer or partition of land. This essay critically examines the challenge of and responses to political corruption in India.

The chapter first examines alternative explanations for political corruption. Corruption has often been interpreted through culturalist overtones. Some authors argue that the lack of moral concern about it stems from the very conception of sin or the selfishness of the individual that are inherent in India's culture and social system.[1] Such an analysis is not convincing because it fails to explain the increase in corruption over the last ten years: culture and society have certainly not changed in the same proportion as the rising graph of black money. A conservative estimate suggests that 'the black economy as a percentage of the national income (GDP) is supposed to have grown from 3 per cent in the mid-fifties to 7 per cent by the end-sixties to 20 per cent by 1981, [then] to around 35 per cent by 1990–1 and 40 per cent by 1995-6' (Kumar 1999: 2). Other analysts explain the evolution of corruption over the last 50 years by the personality of the successive Prime Ministers of India. For example, three chapters of S.S. Gill's book on this issue are named after Jawarhalal Nehru, Indira Gandhi, and Rajiv Gandhi. Shiv Visvanathan and Harsh Sethi also emphasize the role of one man, Narasimha Rao, who, according to them, 'liberalized corruption and made it a signature of citizenship' (Vishnavathan and Sethi 1998: 11). Certainly, the importance of men in history must not be underestimated, but I would argue that, so far as corruption in India is concerned, socioeconomic and political dynamics played a more crucial part. The corruption boom of the 1980s and 1990s—the doubling of the black economy in 15 years—was largely due to liberalization measures and the growing integration of India into the global market.

This essay also notes the need to go beyond the study of corruption alone, and to pay more attention to a related topic, the criminalization of the state. Accordingly, the second section focuses on the links between the criminalization of politics and the politicization of criminals. It explores the diversification of the crime industry, the Bombay mafia, and the question of why politicians need criminals. It points out that the interdependence between politics and the underworld is growing rapidly, and that these developments are a direct threat to the democratic polity of India. I then analyse reasons for this increased criminalization—reasons such as the legacy of the Emergency, the role of mafias as social agencies, the communalization of the underworld, and the transformation of musclemen into politicians. The essay concludes by discussing institutional responses to the challenges of corruption and criminalization. It analyses the role of commissions of inquiry, the judiciary, judicial activism, and India's Election Commission in checking the criminalization of politics.

## From Corruption to Criminalization of Politics

The twofold commonplace assumption about corruption in India is that this is a very old story which is simply getting worse, and that India's political leaders have generally been responsible for it. This process is certainly contemporary with the emergence of the political class. In fact, the Congress indulged in corrupt practices when the party formed ministries in 1937 under the 1935 Government of India Act. The Constituent Assembly brought up and tried to remedy the issue by keeping a check on the assets of government representatives. But it eventually gave up because it felt that they were too easy to dissimulate and left it to public opinion to marginalize dishonest politicians. (*Constituent Assembly Debates* [henceforth *CAD*], 1948: 1180–9).

India's political leaders appear to be responsible for the development of corruption in post-independence India, not only because of their leniency during the Constitution-making process but also when they assumed power. Among them, Nehru is often regarded as especially guilty of laxity. Gill, for instance, even though he acknowledges that Nehru was 'undoubtedly the cleanest politician you could imagine', underlines that 'it was his handling of this disease which turned it into an epidemic' (Gill 1998: 45).

### WHOSE RESPONSIBILITY: NEHRU'S OR THE 'NEHRUVIAN SYSTEM'S'?

Nehru certainly tended to protect Congressmen who indulged in corrupt practices. This is evident from the way he reacted to the misconduct of his friend, Krishna Menon, as early as 1948. Menon, the Indian High Commissioner in London, had been asked urgently to buy 4,000 jeeps for the Indian army which was fighting the

Pakistanis in Kashmir. Not only was the contract he signed not in the standard form, but only 155 jeeps reached India in March 1949—and they were declared unserviceable by the army. Harsh critics emerged in the press and in Parliament. The Public Account Committee recommended that the matter be examined by the High Court, but Nehru's government rejected the proposition and pronounced the case closed in 1955. Five months later, Menon was made a minister. The Congress Parliamentary Sub-Committee Report was never published. A.G. Noorani, in his book *Ministers' Misconduct,* concludes that as early as the 1940s Nehru created the impression that 'the corrupt could get away with it if they were on the side of the rulers' (Noorani 1973).

Noorani also points out that Nehru defended his Minister of Finance, T.T. Krishnamachari, when he was indicted by the Chagla Commission in the Mundhra affair.[2] Krishnamachari resigned but the Prime Minister wrote to him that, 'despite the clear finding of the commission, so far as you are concerned, I am convinced that your part was the smallest and that you did not know what was done.' Similarly, Nehru resisted for years an inquiry into the activities of his Minister for Mines and Fuel, K.D. Malaviya, who was suspected of having issued licences to the managing partner of a mining company, Mohammed Serajuddin, against substantial bribes. While the Attorney General recommended a full-fledged inquiry, Nehru simply asked a sitting Supreme Court judge to pursue the investigation and he chose not to publish the resulting report in which Malaviya was indicted. Nehru's partisan attitude was even more evident from his backing of Pratap Singh Kairon, the Congress Chief Minister of Punjab since 1956, who was suspected—two years later—of having illegally allocated his son a plot of land in Chandigarh for building a cinema. At a 1958 press conference, Nehru declared that the charges were 'fantastic, frivolous and absurd'. After a long delay, Nehru was forced to appoint a Commission of Inquiry in 1963 because of mounting pressure from opposition parties. The S.R. Das Commission, however, submitted its report after Nehru's death. It was not published.

Nehru is also regarded as responsible for the spread of corruption because of his lack of interest in various inquiry commissions which were appointed in the 1950s to assess and check corruption in the bureaucracy and the public sector. In 1951, the Gorwala Commission submitted its 'Report on Public Administration' and four years later J.B. Kripalani did the same as chairman of the Railway Corruption Inquiry Committee. They both failed to attract his interest: to him they were like 'the mumblings of old prophets' (Visvanathan 1998: 23) at a time when he was confident that the new state he was building would soon be free from such legacies. He was wrong because, in reality, this state was the very crucible of corruption, as a third inquiry commission, the Santhanam Commission, was to show in 1962. The Commission pointed out that between April 1957 and December 1962, 44,238 civil servants had been penalized for corruption.

These findings directly challenge the explanations focusing on Nehru: they show that his leniency alone could not be responsible for such widespread corruption. This phenomenon resulted from the system itself. Increased state control over the economy through nationalization and the 'licence raj' gave bureaucrats and politicians much more power. Businessmen depended upon them for running their firms, to diversify or increase production; they bribed these decision-makers, often simply to give priority to their files. This led to the emergence of a triad of capitalists, bureaucrats, and politicians (Kumar 1999: 12). The Congress Party, which was the ruling party for 30 years between 1947 and 1977, was largely financed through donations which were, in reality, bribes. For instance, Malaviya had asked Serajuddin to give Rs. 10,000 to the party. Thus, one must look beyond Nehru and pay attention to domestic structural (or systemic) factors to explain post-independence corruption.

These structures became still more rigid under Indira Gandhi. On behalf of socialism, she enacted the Monopolies and Restrictive Trade Practices (MRTP) in 1970 and the Foreign Exchange Regulations Act in 1973 to regulate the economy further. These new rules enabled the Congress to receive additional bribes from the corporate sector. For instance, in 1971, the Indian Cotton Mills Association was allowed to import 100,000 tonnes of cotton—provided it gave Rs. 30 per bale to the ruling Congress (Noorani 1973: 262). Shiv Visvanathan points out that 'Socialism created the dominance of the 'filariat'. It enshrined the divine right of clerks. . . . Grossly underpaid, the policeman and clerk got a bigger bite of the cake through the bribe' (1998: 7). This picture would not be complete without the politician, the custodian of socialism, from which the clerk and the policeman take their orders. Among Indira Gandhi's fund raisers, L.N. Mishra, her Minister of State for Commerce, 'made full use of the "licence-quota-permit raj" and attached a price-tag to every licence, permit or clearance that he issued. He collected huge amounts of money, and disbursed like a king' (Gill 1998: 69). This is what Stanley Kochanek has called 'briefcase politics' (1987: 1290), which is the core element of what is popularly known as the 'Congress culture'.

The conclusion we have reached—the structures of the 'Nehruvian system' are more likely to explain corruption than the personalities in power—has been shared by several scholars who then conclude that economic liberalization policies would eradicate corruption. An anonymous contributor to *Foul Play* argues that

> To some extent the abolition of the licensing raj for setting up industries and the removal of several restrictions in the import policies and exchange control rules has [*sic*] loosened the stranglehold on industry. As a corollary, they have breathed easier and obviously the payouts have been less. But this is only a drop in the ocean. Unless the systems are drastically changed along with the basic culture and attitude of government to provide a free environment industry will have to continue to pay the price.

This is an unconvincing explanation. Certainly, Indian entrepreneurs who are freed from the licence raj do not have to pay the bureaucrats and the politicians as before, but liberalization is not the solution to the corruption issue. This anonymous author laments that the excise officers 'who are "on the payroll" of each factory' should be given less power, like the custom officers, whom businessmen have also to bribe, as before. Incidentally, this is the recipe that the IMF recommends against corruption. In a 1997 document titled 'Pourquoi faut-il s'inquiéter de la corruption' ('Why we must worry about corruption'), the IMF regarded trade regulations and administrative restrictions as the main factor behind corruption in the world (*Le Monde Economie*, 21 October 1997: iii). But such recommendations ignore the impact of the liberalization policy on corruption.

## LARGE SCALE CORRUPTION AS A BY-PRODUCT OF LIBERALIZATION AND GLOBALIZATION

Instead of checking corruption, India's economic liberalization policy has corresponded with the dramatic increase of this disease. Arun Kumar comments:

When the nineties are compared to the eighties, the amounts involved in the scams have grown exponentially. The biggest scam of the eighties was Bofors involving a sum of Rs. 65 crores [650 million] but there were at least a dozen scams involving larger sums in the nineties, the largest being the securities scam involving Rs. 3,000 crore [*sic*—30 billion]. The number of scams reported in the eighties was 13 while the number for the nineties till 1996 was 26. (Kumar 1999: 243–4)

Among these scandals, the securities scam, the privatization of tele communications, and the 'hawala affair' are revealing of the impact of India's liberalization policy on corruption.

The securities scam, exposed in 1992, has been associated with Harshad Mehta, one of the brokers involved in it, but there were many other guilty parties: once again, what is at stake is the system, not the few persons. The system in question derived from the first liberalization measures and the mentality accompanying it. In July 1991—when the first liberal package was announced— Indian banks were in a peculiar situation. On the one hand, they had large securities (the Reserve Bank of India ordered that nearly 60 per cent of their deposits be placed in government bonds) and their deposits, which were already high, continued to grow. On the other hand, they could not lend any more to the government—a usual borrower which had to spend less to oblige the IMF—or to the corporate sector which was then affected by an economic slump. At the same time, enterprises feared a decline of their shares in the stock market because of the new, liberalized free market environment which made takeovers easier. (NRIs were seen as a threat to Indian enterprises, for instance.) Brokers then came to the rescue of banks and firms. They borrowed from the former—illegally, at a very low rate—against securities such as shares in Indian firms, which they may not actually possess. With this money, brokers bought shares in Indian firms whose rate therefore increased, benefiting these firms whose takeovers thereby became more difficult. Banks lent more money to brokers who bought more shares whose rate continued to increase.

Harshad Mehta, who handled about one-third of the State Bank of India's securities trade, indulged in such a business with the help of corrupt bank officers who gave him bank receipts (BRs) backed (or not backed) by securities. He was therefore able to buy with suspect BRs an enormous number of shares whose rate artificially increased. When the State Bank of India management found that he owed them Rs. 5 billion, he sold his shares to finance these payments. Others did the same and the market dropped: in April-May 1992, the Bombay Stock Exchange Sensitive Index lost 1,500 points and investors—including those with low savings lost millions of rupees.

Does this episode justify more liberalization or more regulation? Any regulating agency, like the French Commission des Operations de Bourse, would have reacted to the dramatically rising share prices. The Indian government could have done so, but in 1991 it was decisively for liberalism: it viewed the stock exchange boom as resulting from expectations of a favourable post-reform economy, which was a good thing in itself.

The link between liberalization and scams is even more obvious in the telecommunications case. In August 1996, police discovered Rs. 36.6 million in former Communication Minister Sukh Ram's residence. His National Telecom Policy, indeed, had allowed private enterprises to enter the telecom sector in spite of the strong opposition by trade unions. The demand for this sector was so high—the telecom sector grew 20 per cent each year over the 1990s—that it attracted large numbers of investors. The Department of Telecommunications alone had to choose between them, since it was the sole buyer of telecom equipment in the country. After it reached a decision, Sukh Ram did not hesitate to ignore its conclusions in favour of those who had asked him to place more orders for them—probably against large payments.[3] Once again, the liberalization process gave opportunities for more corruption rather than antidotes to the disease.

This scam illustrates a new mentality in the Indian government which draws its legitimacy from the liberalization motto. Ministers forego the advice of bureaucrats and experts and bypass old procedures, and instead seek quick decisions under the liberal spirit of deregulation. As a result, they deal directly with Indian and foreign firms and get their percentage without intermediaries—or any serious control. Indeed, the scope of this scandal may reflect the fact that telecommunications attracted rich foreign operators such as AT&T, to which a Rs. 7.85 billion contract was awarded for network management systems, and Siemens, which got a Rs. 3 billion contract for trunk automatic exchange. Indeed, the international ramifications of such liberalization based scams need to be scrutinized.

The argument that I am trying to refute regarding the impact of liberalization as a good means to get rid of 'licence raj'-related corruption very often has an international corollary. Namely, if India opens up and integrates with the world market, it will have to conform to the norms observed by the corporate sector worldwide, otherwise foreign investors will remain cautious. The advocates of such a globalization-based approach to corruption often invoke the rating of international agencies such as Transparency International (TI). According to a 1997 TI poll, in which executives from multinational companies were interviewed, India was ranked forty-fifth by increasing order of corruption—just before Indonesia and Pakistan, the most corrupt Asian countries (*Dawn*, 3 August 1997: 21). Besides invoking the TI reports, the Indian authorities commissioned surveys to its local branches. In March 2001, the government of Delhi commissioned Transparency International India to study its ten leading departments and indicate comparative corruption rates (*The Hindu*, 13 March 2001). To be under the scrutiny of the West, or Western-inspired agencies, appears as the best remedy to corruption.

While globalization has therefore been presented as the best antidote to corruption, I would argue that this process, rather, offers new opportunities for corruption. Recent reports of the Central Bureau of Investigation point out that 'the current revelation of "corrupt money", to a large extent, is associated with foreign currency' (Bhattacharyya and Ghose 1998: 2795). The liberal turn of 1991 and the expansion of the Indian market have attracted an ever increasing number of foreign firms which were prepared to pay bribes to get administrative clearance and establish themselves in India. But there are many other channels through which globalization fosters corruption.

The 'hawala affair' is a case in point.[4] In this scandal, money came mainly from foreign firms in the context of Rajiv Gandhi's policy of (a then still very limited) economic liberalization. This money was channelled through Indian businessmen specializing in export-import transactions. Diaries belonging to one of them, Surendra K. Jain, identified French, Swedish, and Russian firms as having used his services to pay off about 60 politicians.[5]

S.K. Jain initially made his fortune in foreign exchange, by getting around foreign exchange control regulations to take advantage of the differences in the interest rates. Many Indian operators, especially those who try to 'launder' black money, use these mechanisms, called *hawala*, particularly in dealings with the United States and Hong Kong. Once rich, S.K. Jain resorted to the most common form of corruption in India, bribing high government officials who were in a position to award contracts. Some 65 political leaders from all parties—with the exception of the communist and allied parties—figured in his diaries seized by the police, with the amounts paid. The largest sum was presumably paid to Rajiv Gandhi; a total of Rs. 655 million was distributed from 1988 to 1991.[6]

To sum up, one of the root causes of the rising level of corruption in India may well be the liberalization and globalization process, which has aggravated this phenomenon rather than reduced it (Kumar 1999: 681–94). This is an important factor of corruption on the supply side. But one needs to scrutinize the demand side too. Here, a major element is the rising cost of political competition.

## THE CHANGING FACE OF ELECTION-BASED CORRUPTION

Over the years, politicians have had to find increased funding for election campaigns. These became increasingly expensive because of greater competition between parties and the growing awareness of their bargaining power on the part of voters and opinion leaders. Until the late 1960s, the Congress Party remained dominant while relying on the influence of local notables. This Congress system was affected by the 1969 schism, which obliged the ruling Congress of Indira Gandhi, the Congress (R), to promote new faces against the old guard of the Congress (O) and to reach out to voters directly. Since then, elections have become increasingly competitive. The Congress Party lost power in 1977 and, after a stable—but difficult—decade in the 1980s, alternation in power was a routine phenomenon in the 1990s. The cost of elections correlatively increased.

In constituencies where competition is stiff, candidates largely exceed the ceiling on campaign expenditure fixed by the Election Commission. In 1984, the ceiling was Rs. 150,000 expenditure in a parliamentary constituency and Rs. 50,000 in a legislative assembly constituency. In 1994, it was fixed at Rs. 450,000 for a parliamentary constituency. In 1997, the Election Commission got the government's authorization to further increase the ceiling limits to Rs. 600,000 for the Assembly elections and Rs. 1.5 million for the Lok Sabha elections. But the actual financial outlay for a high profile or hotly disputed Lok Sabha seat could be anything from Rs. 1.5 million to Rs. 8 million.[7] Arun Kumar, who interviewed 14 Lok Sabha candidates in 1998, concluded that their average election campaigns cost about Rs. 12.9 million. Though his respondents probably underestimated their expenditure, the disaggregate figures supplied by Kumar's respondents are most interesting. Costs of manpower represented a large percentage: in one case, 5,000 activists were used daily for canvassing. Meetings with voters and local leaders have also become expensive. Some candidates had to organize 20 meetings daily, the smaller ones costing Rs. 2,000–Rs. 5,000 each, and larger ones costing Rs. 50,000–Rs. 200,000 each. Dummy candidates are also costly. In one case, eight 'dummies' were supported by one candidate at the cost of Rs. 7.5 million. The day before polling, gifts have to be distributed. In one case Rs. 900,000-worth of liquor, saris, and blankets were distributed (Kumar 1999: 274–6). In some slums, residents 'sell' their votes for up to Rs. 100. In this way 'donors' hope to curry favour with the voters, though they are well aware that voters may cast their vote independently in the privacy of the polling booth.

All major political parties have followed the example of the Congress Party and resorted to 'briefcase politics' for funding election campaigns. They have also diverted public funds. Laloo Prasad Yadav and Jayalalitha have given recent examples of these corrupt practises. Yadav, Chief Minister of Bihar in 1990-7, has been indicted for the Fodder Scam, a scandal resulting from malpractises which had been initiated much earlier, in the early 1980s, by officials of the state's Animal Husbandry Department (AHD). In 1983-4, the AHD exceeded its budget. The department's officials then operated more systematically by forging state documents. The money from this fraud was shared with civil servants and politicians who protected them. Laloo Prasad Yadav became the most prominent of these patrons after he assumed office in 1990. So far as Jayalalitha is concerned, one of her sources of 'income' was the TV schema: as Chief Minister of Tamil Nadu, she distributed 45,000 TV sets to those living below the poverty line, at the cost of Rs. 85 million. She allegedly retained a substantial percentage of proceeds in this process. In 1995, her foster son's marriage, which had 150,000 invitees, reportedly cost Rs. 1 billion.

While the domestic sources of this corruption have always been more prominent, it acquired a new dimension during the 1980s when politicians began to funnel 'black money' from abroad.[8] At this time Congress started collecting large commissions from foreign contracts (Sahai 1996: 253). Since the liberalization of the economy was not sufficiently advanced to attract foreign firms, the source tapped was still largely arms dealers. In 1981, while Prime Minister Indira Gandhi also held the Defence portfolio, India placed orders for four submarines with the German shipyard, HDW. A seven per cent commission was allegedly paid at that time, according to V.P. Singh, who made this revelation as Rajiv Gandhi's Defence Minister in 1987. He resigned soon after.

The Bofors affairs hit the headlines two years later and once again tarnished the image of the Gandhi family. Rajiv Gandhi's coterie and the Prime Minister himself were accused by the press of having received around 50 million dollars in front-end commissions from a Swedish armaments firm, Bofors, in 1986, for the purchase of heavy artillery guns amounting to 1.12 billion dollars.[9] The 'Bofors affair', which contributed to Rajiv Gandhi's defeat in the 1989 elections, was, apparently, a classic case of greasing palms to secure a government contract.

The fact that defence procurement was open to irregularities was even more evident in the following years. Politicians have regularly accused their rivals of corruption—or at least have hinted that their opponents had accepted bribes. For instance, former Prime Minister H.D. Deve Gowda questioned the probity of the T-90 battle tank acquisitions, and George Fernandes, when he was Defence Minister, had done the same vis-à-vis the Sukhoi Su-30 deal. These irregularities were referred to by former Chief of the Naval Staff Admiral, Vishnu Bhagwat, after he was dismissed by George Fernandes in 1999. Bhagwat, for instance, stated that Rear Admiral Suhas Purohit's promotion to the rank of Vice Admiral had been delayed because of pressure from arms dealers who feared he would limit their influence over the Indian Navy's procurement operations. Bhagwat also mentioned that Admiral S.M. Nanda and his son, Lieutenant Commander Suresh Nanda, were known for facilitating such operations. 'The Nandas' have been frequently mentioned in the context of the Tehelka affair.

This affair came as confirmation, in 2001, that arms procurement remained a major source of corruption in India and showed that military officers were increasingly involved in such malpractices. Journalists of the website *Tehelka.com*, who presented themselves as arms dealers, first met officers from the Ordnance and Supply Division; they offered to 'provide information on Army indents for spare parts, the price at which procurements were last made and the possible scheduling of future orders' (*Frontline*, 13 April 2001: 4). Another officer, who explained the army's procurement procedure to *Tehelka* journalists, was then caught receiving Rs. 100,000; as Additional Director General, Weapons and Equipment Wing, this officer was on a select panel, headed by the Defence Secretary, that briefed the Chief Vigilance Commission before it began investigating corruption in defence deals. Officials on the civilian side of the Defence Ministry also played a key role as they gave the *Tehelka* team access to politicians who influenced the decision-making process. A Deputy Secretary introduced them to a self-styled 'national trustee' of the Rashtriya Swayamsevak Sangh, who was not, in reality, occupying such a position, but was able to fix an appointment with the BJP president Bangaru Laxmon for Rs. 2.5 million. The *Tehelka* journalists met the party president twice; they gave him Rs. 100,000 and promised more, while he indicated his preference for dollars. Another political leader, president of the Samata Party, a partner of the ruling coalition, accepted Rs. 200,000. On 13 March 2001, the *Tehelka* tape was broadcast over a satellite television network. Both party presidents immediately explained that the money was not for them but for their party, but the scandal caused them to resign. George Fernandes, the Minister of Defence and the most senior member of the Samata Party, also resigned from government. The Congress Party seized this opportunity to launch a campaign against the government: 10,000 copies of the *Tehelka* tape were distributed.

Naturally, the *Tehelka* affair made such a big impact because security issues are especially sensitive. On 17 March, Prime Minister Vajpayee made a public statement emphasizing that

> The Government shall do everything necessary to bring everyone guilty to account—howsoever high or low. Its only concerns are (i) That the country's security apparatus remains strong as ever; (ii) That our soldiers retain the fullest confidence in it; (iii) That institutions of governance and our political system regain their health; (iv) That our people's trust and faith in them are fortified. (*The Hindu*, 17 March 2001)

Strategic concerns came first and, indeed, the worst affected victim of the scam was probably the Indian Army. For the army, the scam came as a shock; the accused officers were suspended, and three commissions of inquiry were appointed. The *Tehelka* affair almost coincided with the submission, by the Central Vigilance Commission (CVC), of the report that Defence Minister Fernandes had commissioned in February 2001. This report asked the CVC to investigate 75 defence deals that had been signed since 1989. The Commission submitted its report on 3 March 2001 and, though it remained confidential, the media noted that it had identified scores of irregularities and involved numerous intermediaries. The fact that military personnel were accused—and sometimes found guilty—of corruption is a new development. But the key role that arms deals play in the illicit financing of politicians is one of the most traditional sources of corruption.

Corruption, therefore, has increasingly affected the Indian political system in the 1980s and 1990s for two different reasons. On the supply side, the liberalization policy, far from abolishing the vices of the 'licence raj', offered new opportunities to make black money from the old triad (businessmen, bureaucrats, and politicians), especially after foreign firms began entering the Indian market. On the demand side, the increasingly competitive electoral landscape led politicians to spend more in their campaigns. They raised what they needed from Indian businessmen, but also from foreign investors. The Congress Party, under increasing political pressure in the 1980s, took bribes from arms dealers—who were often the most important foreign players in the politico-economic game before the 1990s—and then increasingly took advantage of the entry of multinationals—for instance in the telecom sector. In fact, most of the scams of the 1990s have foreign ramifications. The son of Narasimha Rao, Prabhakar Rao, was involved in scandals concerning the import of sugar and urea. Rao himself, via his 'guru', Chandraswami, bargained with NRIs such as a pickle manufacturer who allegedly gave him US$ 100,000 to obtain government contracts for the import of newsprint and paper pulp. One may argue that these affairs reflect Rao's personal inclinations, but they are part of a more general trend: corruption has become 'globalized' even more quickly than the economy.

Corruption, when it assumes such proportions, becomes a negation of democracy. It subjects citizens to the law of money which eludes all constitutional regulations, as well as the poll verdict. The elite voted to power appears to be in the hands of others, whether the bureaucracy or the large business houses. This alarming development in recent years has gone hand in hand with the criminalization of politics. This partly needs to be seen in the same perspective as the new pervasiveness of corruption, as a means for vulnerable politicians to retain power. But it also allows the entry of criminals into the political sphere.

## The Criminalization of Politics or the Politicization of Criminals?

The links between the mafia and the politicians are long standing, with the two groups mutually serving each other's ends. Several aspects of these links are worth exploring—the diversification of the crime industry, especially in Mumbai, and the question of why politicians need criminals, but also why criminals embrace a political career.

### THE DIVERSIFICATION OF THE CRIME INDUSTRY

Gangs need protection for their nefarious activities. These practices involving trafficking in drugs, arms, and other illicit activities have increased hundred fold in recent years. This is partly due to the growing production of opium in Afghanistan, where the United Nations Drug Control Programme estimated a record production of 4,500 tonnes in 1999. Hence the ever increasing (and unprecedented) seizures of heroin on the India-Pakistan border, from 640 kg in 1997 to 750 kg in 1999 (Krishnan 2000: 60). In south India, which till the 1990s had been relatively free of drug trafficking, a staggering 26 tonnes of narcotics were seized in 1995 (against 1.21 tonnes in 1991).[10]

Hooch or illicit liquor has also become very profitable, especially in states with prohibition, such as Gujarat. This resulted in a network of clandestine distilleries, with bootleggers in cahoots with politicians quite willing to extend their protection to traffickers in exchange for a cut.[11] Another flourishing activity is the prostitution racket. In 1995, Human Rights Watch denounced the nexus between politicians and pimps in Mumbai, where the activities of thousands of prostitutes (estimates vary between 20,000 and 50,000) generate considerable earnings (*The Statesman* (Delhi), 26 September 1995).

Arms traffic also soared in the 1990s, in tandem with regional conflicts. The biggest arms hauls were made in Jammu and Kashmir and Punjab, where drug and arms traffics were carried on side by side.[12] But the insurgents of these regions were not the only ones interested in the arms trade, which has spread all over India. More than 5,300 illegally held firearms were confiscated in Uttar Pradesh in 1997. They were manufactured in 434 clandestine workshops which were shut down the same year (interview of K.L. Gupta, Additional Director General, Crime, in *The Sunday Times of India*, 22 June 1997).

Finally, gold trafficking remains lucrative. While India's gold production is negligible, the demand has always been high and continues to increase (gold inflows were 190 tonnes in 1990-1 and 815 tonnes in 1998). Till 1992, gold imports were banned and therefore smuggling flourished. Even though gold can be legally imported since 1992, smuggling continues because it is cheaper than paying customs duty (Kumar 1999: 28).

Racketeering, euphemistically termed 'protection money', and kidnapping constitute another increasingly important mafia activity, especially in Bihar and Uttar Pradesh. Initially, the expression 'protection money' referred to the percentage that the better armed gangs levied per week on traffickers (dealing either in illicit liquor or video cassette piracy). Today, the scale of operations has grown. In the new classic scenario, a rich industrialist is asked for a large sum of money and threatened with violence if he does not comply. If the threat is not obeyed, the industrialist, or a member of his family, is kidnapped and a ransom demanded. The victim's family often prefers to pay the ransom rather than alert the police, whose competence and honesty are increasingly suspect. In 1994, because of their frequency, kidnappings and demands for ransom were placed in a separate category by the Indian Penal Code. As a result, more data is now available. While kidnappings appear to have declined from 1,371 in 1994 to 1,136 in 1996, for the investigators this is in fact a sign that victims tend not to alert the police for various reasons, including their lack of confidence and their fear of retaliation.[13] One may easily understand these reasons since, for the ninety-odd kidnappings which took place in Delhi between 1992 and 1997, 194 persons were arrested, but not one was brought to trial.

In Uttar Pradesh and Bihar, the two most affected states, the number of kidnappings rose respectively from 178 in 1997 to 83 in the first six months of 1998 and from 291 in 1991 to 342 in 1997 (*India Today*, 4 May and 7 September 1998: 32, 30). As a result, rich businessmen have begun to move to other places, including Gujarat. The UP government has decided to be more liberal in issuing arms licences to traders. The rising graph of kidnappings also explains the growing number of private security agencies. More policemen are being lured to these agencies by their higher salaries (Halankar et al., 13).

## MUMBAI, CAPITAL OF CRIME

Mumbai, the economic capital of India, has also become the capital of crime, with the first gangs emerging in the 1960s–70s under the aegis of Haji Mastan, Karim Lala, and Varadaraja Mudaliar. The underworld first developed closer links with the film industry of Bollywood (Mumbai's Hollywood). It made some early inroads because the Mumbai producers, not content with large-scale tax evasion, habitually accepted 'donations' from local godfathers, who in this way managed to recycle 'black money' and make huge profits (Wright 1978: 5–6). In the 1980s, the gang of Dawood Ibrahim, a second-generation don, is said to have invested heavily in 'Bollywood'.[14] Today an estimated 30–40 per cent of the share of 'Hindi films' is believed to be financed by the mafia (*The Times of India*, 17 August 1997, and *India Today*, 25 August 1997: 31). Moreover, fiction and reality have come dangerously close in recent films where 'the villain' is idealized under the guise of a muscleman, inspired by the underworld culture of crime. Some scripts are rewritten by godfathers, who also decide whom to cast (*The Hindu*, 19 December 2000).

In addition to the film industry, land and real estate procurement is a lucrative area for the Mumbai mafia. In a city where prices are sometimes on a par with Tokyo, builders are immensely interested in having lands vacant (and vacated). Criminals offered their services for intimidating reluctant tenants, businessmen whose factories were centrally located, or slum dwellers. Eventually, gangsters became builders: they purchased old buildings, removed the tenants, demolished the buildings, and constructed higher buildings which were then rented. The illegal dimension of such operations was twofold. First, muscle power was used to make landlords sell their buildings and tenants vacate them. Second, new buildings either exceeded the authorized height or were constructed on land reserved by the civic authorities for public purposes (Bhatt 1998: 109–17).

In Mumbai, protection money was primarily extorted from builders and film personalities (in 1997 film producer Gulshan Kumar was killed and in 2000 film producer Rakesh Roshan was shot at, apparently because both refused to pay protection money). But this disease has gradually affected businessmen and rich professionals. The spread of racketeering is such that an extraordinary ruling of the High Court, in 1998, declared that extortion paid to gangsters would be exempted from tax—something the income tax department immediately challenged. (Anandan 1998: 26). During the first 11 months of 1998, 713 complaints were registered with the Mumbai police, against 251 in 1997 (Aiyar 1998: 32).

Gangs have thus acquired considerable assets, and they need political patronage to shield their activities from police investigation. For instance, in Mumbai, the Chief Minister in the mid-1980s was alleged not only to have granted to builders land reserved for civic purposes, but also to have protected gangsters operating in the building business. The Shiv Sena, after its victory at the Bombay Municipal Corporation in 1985, reportedly did the same. But the politicians were not only interested in mafia money.

## WHY POLITICIANS NEED CRIMINALS

While the mafia seeks the protection of politicians, the latter also require mafia services for activities such as organizing electoral fraud. A losing candidate may, for instance, resort to the most common fraud, *booth capturing*. The practice involves engaging an armed gang to seize ballot boxes. During the 1971 general elections, 11 such cases were registered, of which eight were in Bihar (Election Commission 1972: 81). In 1980, nearly 60 polling booths—of which 21 were in Bihar, 12 in Uttar Pradesh, and 19 in Jammu and Kashmir witnessed incidents of violence or tension leading to the countermanding of the particular election (Election Commission 1980: 113–14). A repoll was ordered in 265 polling booths in 1984, and in 1,670 booths in 1989 (Sethi 1990: 42). The exponential progression of these figures is only partly explained by the fact that earlier violations of the law were concealed, while today this is not so easy. Incidentally, in Bihar, gangs 'bill' booth capture at the rate of Rs. 50,000 to Rs. 100,000 per booth, which adds to the financial outlay of politicians and consequently induces further corruption.

Other types of election-related problems also take place. Most common are clashes between party activists, but there is also violence by gangs who enforce a poll boycott when their 'boss' fears losing a vote. Such violence claimed 33 lives in 1984, 130 in 1989, and 198 in 1991 (*National Mail*, 8 May 1991; Gill 1998: 190). Violence against candidates has also increased, even if it is still quite rare. In 1989, a Congress opponent in the Uttar Pradesh Legislative Assembly elections, standing from Rajiv Gandhi's constituency, was shot in the stomach. In 1991, Shankar Guha Niyogi, a labour union leader who had launched the Chhattisgarh

Mukti Morcha, a virtually political movement, was killed. In 2000, Gurudas Chatterjee, another trade unionist working in the coal mine of Dhanbad (Bihar) and who had been returned twice to the Legislative Assembly in 1995 and 2000 was assassinated: the Dhanbad mafia were notorious for financing his main opponents, 'But having failed to finish him politically, they decided to finish him physically' (Roy 2000). In Bihar at large, the number of political killings averaged about 50 every year. (The Police Department cited in *India Today*, 29 June 1998: 25).

Apart from electoral fraud, politicians use gangs during communal riots. This type of violence often involves Hindu nationalist activists, but members of other groups are also involved (Jaffrelot 1992: 25–53). The Congress chiefs were thus able to 'manage' this violence when the need arose. For instance, Congressmen excluded from power tried to corner the party's ruling faction in the state government by taking part in or inciting a riot, thus demonstrating that the state government was incapable of maintaining 'law and order'. A state government might also delay intervention by the police or the army for three sets of reasons: to appease the community behind the riot, as in Hyderabad in 1990 when the Chief Minister held back from intervening for many days, resulting in 120 deaths; to allow the agitation against a minority to become a full blown riot and then to intervene by presenting oneself as the indisputable champion of the minority community—a role which the Congress has always claimed; or 'to teach a lesson' to a minority, if it had refused its support to the ruling party during the previous elections.

Whether these objectives are attained or not, their pursuit lays the administrative cadres open to interference from local politicians. In 1981, police and government officials saw them as a major cause of their inability to prevent or control riots quickly (Gani 1987: 18). But this is also a convenient excuse, particularly on the part of the north Indian state police, for example, the Provincial Armed Constabulary (PAC) (which is responsible to the Uttar Pradesh government) whose anti-Muslim bias is well known.

The means employed to control communal violence reflects the decline of the rule of law, the direct consequence of which is the growing criminalization of politics. On the one hand, interfering with the logic of the forces of law and order is a way of abetting—at the very least—the growth of riots; on the other, the eruption of riots in the context of a power struggle implies that the politicians who are behind it are employing thugs from criminal gangs, who need protection from over-zealous policemen.

The Bhagalpur (Bihar) riots in 1989, which caused a thousand deaths, is a good example. The violence was initiated by Hindu nationalists trying to polarize voters along communal lines some weeks before legislative elections. However, these incidents were immediately fuelled by gangs working with a local politician who had lost the previous election. For the former, it was a means of getting the new local police chief transferred for incompetence, as he was more active against the gangs than his predecessors. For the latter, it was a way of 'teaching a lesson' to the Muslims who had not supported him in the last election.

With the growth in the financial outlay of politicians, money has become another major reason for collaborating with the underworld. Politicians, for instance, play an important role in the protection money business since they profit by protecting gangs.[15]

## FROM OSMOSIS TO SYMBIOSIS

The classic configuration of the criminalization of politics in India therefore rests on a collaboration between the mafia and politicians, who need gangs for their operations (especially in and around the polling booths). The nexus between gangs and politicians is not, however, the only form of 'criminalization' since one now finds mafioso in politics and politicians behaving as criminals—the two milieux can hardly be distinguished sometimes.

The latter configuration is well illustrated by the case of Chautala. In 1990, Om Prakash Chautala, the son of then Deputy Prime Minister, Devi Lal, was involved in pre-election violence in Meham constituency. He needed to win the seat to retain the post of Chief Minister.[16] In 1995, a commission of inquiry concluded that Chautala's actions were responsible for the death of one candidate (*India Today*, 31 January 1995: 16). It took many secret machinations before the party whip of the Janata Dal, Chautala's party, finally secured his resignation.

While politicians behave as criminals, a growing number of criminals have entered politics; some even get elected while in police custody (Bhatnagar 1997). The Representation of the People Act, 1951 makes an important distinction between 'convicted criminals'—who are not systematically disqualified (they would not be so if the conviction is for less than six months, for instance)—and 'chargesheeters' who can stand for elections, even if they are accused of important crimes (Dhavan 1999: 10). Parliament is still relatively safe, even if five MPs elected in 1996, for instance, were accused of murder (*The Times of India*, 7 July 1997), but the criminalization of politics has reached disquieting proportions at the state level. The 1993 Legislative Assembly elections in Uttar Pradesh marked a new step in this process because, out of the 425 MLAs elected, 126 had had a brush with the law or had connections with the local mafia.[17] All parties were involved: 49 members from the BJP were on this list, 41 from the Samajwadi Party, 16 from the BSP, 11 from the Janata Dal and 9 from the Congress (a figure which is small due to the electoral rout of the party).[18]

The then Chief Minister, Mulayam Singh Yadav, abrogated the Anti-Goonda Act, a law passed by the previous BJP government in 1991–2 to facilitate the fight against the mafia by strengthening the hands of the police. Yadav's party, the Samajwadi Party, incorporated criminals like any other. Arun Shukla, alias Annaa, a gang leader charged with 79 crimes and misdemeanors since 1973, was appointed as party secretary. In 1990, the party backed Shukla's brother and brother-in-law, as a result of which the latter became the deputy mayor of the state capital, Lucknow. Members of another gang, Swami Charan and Kamesh Pathak, were also promoted by the SP. The first became vice-president of a local section of the party, and the second a member of the upper house in the UP assembly. In all likelihood, Pathak had been released from prison in 1986 on Mulayam Singh Yadav's intervention. His relationship with Annaa was of the same nature, which prompted the latter to say: 'When I met Mulayam Singh Yadav, I was nothing. He helped me when the government, the police and the Congress were all after me. Now, any time he wants me, I will be there' (*India Today*, 30 June 1990).

The 1996 Legislative Assembly in Uttar Pradesh did not reverse but may have increased the 1993 trend. Not only did the BJP, the BSP, and the SP give tickets to dozens of candidates against whom legal proceedings had been instituted (33, 18, and 22 respectively), but a certain number of BJP, BSP, and Congress MLAs amongst them became ministers when the BJP formed the government, first jointly with the BSP, then alone, from October 1997. This was achieved by recruiting dozens of MLAs from the BSP and the Congress (and offering up to a few hundred thousand rupees per MLA), with a ministerial post for each. Thus, the Uttar Pradesh cabinet comprised 92 members.[19] The BJP Chief Minister, Kalyan Singh, tried to project himself as clean and set up a Special Task Force (STF) in 1998 to capture or liquidate criminals. However, public enemy number one, then, was Shri Prakash Shukla, who appeared to have colluded with at least eight ministers of Kalyan Singh's government; they protected him, making the task of the STF more complicated (Mishra 1998: 52).

Uttar Pradesh is not the only state where the entry of the mafia into politics has accelerated in the last few years. Bihar is certainly as seriously affected as UP. In 2000, 31 Legislative Assembly candidates had cases registered against them for crimes ranging from murder to dacoity. Most of them contested as 'Independents', but there were BJP, Congress, RJD, and Samata candidates as well.[20] Maharashtra is also suffering from the same disease. During the municipal elections in 1997, 150, 72, and 50 candidates with past or present difficulties with the law (Godbole 1997) were fielded from Mumbai, Nagpur, and Pune respectively.[21] Andhra Pradesh is not lagging behind, since in 1999 an NGO called Lok Satta Election Watch released a list of 46 candidates contesting elections to the Lok Sabha or the Legislative Assembly with, allegedly, some criminal background (*The Hindu*, 3 September 1999: 5).

Delhi is also new in this circle of the most criminalized states. In fact, Delhi is gradually taking over from Mumbai as the crime capital of India. This city-state tops the list of number of crimes per head, with 527 in 1996 (against 121 in Bihar) and, in terms of percentage change, with +55 per cent change in 1996 over the quinquennial average of 1991–5 (Swami 1998: 17). In 1998, 32,016 crimes were reported in Delhi, against 14,644 in Mumbai (Joshi 1999: 19). This trend was largely due to gangs such as Dawood Ibrahim's shifting their activities because they had been affected by Mumbai's market recession and slump in real estate. This change found expression in the criminalization of Delhi politics too. Out of 815 Legislative Assembly candidates in 1998, 120 had more than two criminal cases registered against them, and out of 69 MLAs, 33 had criminals cases against them (*The Hindustan Times*, 26 October 1998; *The Hindu*, 23 November 1998).

## Why the Criminalization of Politics?

While the rising cost of election campaigns partly explains the growth of corruption and the criminalization of politics, the latter phenomenon also reflects a profound transformation of the political and social systems, and not only the role of a few individuals or the impact of a key period—the Emergency.

### THE EMERGENCY, A MILESTONE: INDIRA GANDHI, SANJAY, AND THE CRIMINALIZATION OF POLITICS

The Emergency period of 1975–7 is often looked at as a turning point in the rise of corruption and the starting point of the criminalization of politics in India. S.S. Gill, for instance, writes:

Mercifully, the nineteen month long nightmare of the Emergency came to an end in January 1977. But the damage it had done to institutions and the administrative culture of the country was by then permanently embedded in the tissues of the system. Good traditions are easy to destroy, but bad habits diehard. The tidal wave of corruption which rolled over India during the Emergency could never be fully rolled back. (Gill 1998: 65)

This sea change is generally attributed to the suspension of democracy and the personality of the new autocrats. Certainly, the fact that democratic rule was not operating enabled the government to monopolize power and plunder the state without fearing retaliation: the press was submitted to censorship and the judiciary much weakened. In this context, it was quite legitimate to interpret the Emergency as the rule of a group 'that had privatized the state and turned the lower bureaucracy into a supine instrument of its whims' (Visvanathan and Sethi 1998: 54). Bansi Lal, the Chief Minister of Haryana, could give 445 acres of land to Sanjay Gandhi for setting up a Maruti car factory. Sanjay Gandhi could also resort to musclemen— who were rather new in politics at that time for ordering and achieving unauthorized demolitions under the garb of anti-encroachment drives in Delhi and elsewhere. Forced sterilizations were also masterminded by Sanjay Gandhi. It is therefore commonly considered that the criminalization of politics, which developed during the Emergency was largely due to his personal role. The editors of *Foul Play*, for instance, emphasize that 'Sanjay Gandhi gave this lumpenization a Nehruvian imprimatur. Goons were "in". Sanjay signalled the further process of deinstitutionalization of corruption as an era of Goebellian quick fixes' (Visvanathan and Sethi 1998: 10).

Certainly, personalities play a role in history, especially in such extraordinary phases, and the political context—in that case authoritarianism—made corruption and criminalization more (or less) easy to spread. Yet, in 1977 parliamentary democracy was restored for good and in 1980 Sanjay died, but corruption and criminalization of politics continued to flourish, which suggests that other more permanent factors than the Emergency and the role played by Sanjay Gandhi need to be taken into consideration.

### FROM VERTICAL TO HORIZONTAL POLITICS

For decades, until the late 1970s, India was under the 'Congress Raj' which initiated a form of clientelistic, vertical politics. The ruling party dominated the political arena mainly because it was adept at co-opting local magnates who could get themselves elected by virtue of their prestige, economic standing (as businessmen or landlords), or their capacity to coerce. Recourse to physical force was obviously not excluded in obtaining electoral support, but it was not the only factor to be considered: economic dependence and the interiorization of the social hierarchy often engendered a spontaneous submission to dominant groups, and violence— physical as well as symbolic—when it was needed, rarely involved gangs.

The vertical principles that structured these social relations began to disintegrate in the 1970s, along with the emancipation of lower castes and small peasants who have benefited from the Green Revolution as well as other aspects of the modernization process. Today's violence is reciprocal, as evident from the caste and class conflicts in Bihar where 'jati senas' (caste armies) multiply and, even where the situation is not so tense, votes are not as easy to come by as in the past. Candidates therefore resort to financial inducement—which increases their expenditure—and to gangs for the intimidation of voters, unless it is they themselves who issue the threats.[22]

### MAFIAS AS SOCIAL AGENCIES

Socioeconomic changes have also prepared the ground for the underworld in a very different way. The growing cities with their hoardes of unemployed have also been a fertile recruitment ground for the gangs. The mafias offer jobs to thousands of idle youths. In Mumbai, at least 10,000 people live on their activities (Bhatt 1998: 110). According to the criminology department of the Tata Institute of Social Science, the new recruits increasingly come from the middle class (*India Today*, 18 January 1999: 54–5). For them, gangs offer short cuts to material success, a very powerful incentive since they crave for the consumption-oriented lifestyle that has been promoted in the social *imaginaire* by economic liberalization.

Besides, gangs have their own code of honour, or at least a discourse over this code, which make them more attractive and legitimate. They present themselves as fighting against the real, bigger crooks who are involved in smuggling and other crime. For instance, a Dubai-based don explained to *Outlook:* 'We target only those who have dealings with the underworld—those who have earned money overnight through unfair means like drug smuggling and have links with the underworld . . . We deliver instant justice. . . . We settle matters worth Rs. 50–Rs. 60 crores in a month. We take our percentage which can be anything between 20 to 40 per cent' (*Outlook*, 7 December 1998: 28). In addition, the mafia engages itself in an understudied strategy of social welfare[23] to gain supporters. They are all the more successful as the state is shrinking and gives up some of its social programmes, and as slums spread over entire inner suburbs of India's cities. In the 1980s, already, the Munbai don Vardarajan Mudaliar projected himself as the Robin Hood of Dharavi (Asia's largest slum). Today, Arun Gawli, another former Mumbai mafia boss holds court daily in Pune (Raval 1999: 26).

The social welfare dimension of the Indian mafia is especially obvious in other cases.[24] In Ahmedabad, the economic capital of Gujarat, the mafia is largely dominated by 'barons' who appear to be committed to the welfare of their community, against political support. Abdul Latif, a bootlegger who had made his debut in the 1970s, chose his men from among the unemployed, delinquent youth of his community. After the communal riots of 1985, he helped the Muslim victims and acquired a reputation as a Robin Hood. In consequence he was elected as the municipal councillor of Ahmedabad in 1986 (although he was behind bars at the time of the polls). He was perceived as a benefactor by many of his co-religionists, for whom he procured jobs, though mostly illegal ones. Latif was not troubled for a long time because politicians such as Chiman Bhai Patel, Chief Minister of Gujarat in the early 1990s, preferred him as an ally to use his popularity among the Muslims. This advantage was lost when Hindu-Muslim relations became so strained that most politicians preferred not to alienate the majority community by taking an ambiguous stand. Muslim godfathers were even less in a position to exploit the trump card in their hands, as they had themselves been involved in the communal riots.

## THE COMMUNALIZATION OF THE UNDERWORLD

The politics of communalism which developed in the 1990s has been another reason for the rise of crime. This trend peaked in 1992 when Hindu nationalist activists demolished the Ayodhya mosque. In the wake of this event, Muslim godfathers were to be found in the forefront of the retaliatory operations. The most spectacular occurred on 13 March 1993, when a dozen bombs exploded in Mumbai at such symbolic places as the Stock Exchange and the Air-India headquarters. These criminal attacks, which caused more than 200 deaths, were the work of

Dawood Ibrahim's gang which operated from Dubai, where Ibrahim had taken refuge in the late 1980s (subsequently, he moved to Karachi). Since the demolition of the Ayodhya mosque, Ibrahim has not hidden his militant solidarity with his 'Muslim brothers' (see his interview in *The Indian Express*, 24 October 1997: 5). The Mumbai blasts were not favoured by some of Ibrahim's Hindu lieutenants, including Chhota Rajan who severed his links with his mentor and settled down in Malaysia. From there he apparently killed Salim Kurla, involved in the blasts, in 1998. In retaliation, the gang of Ibrahim made two unsuccessful attempts at killing Milind Vaidya, former Shiv Sena mayor of Bombay who took part in the anti-Muslim riots of 1992–3. These gang wars are adding a new dimension to politico-criminal violence since the mafia, which used to be secular, is now deeply divided along communal lines.

## THE TRANSFORMATION OF THE *AKHARAS*: 'MUSCLEMEN FOR SALE'

The criminalization of politics dovetails with the transformation of the *akharas*, the recruiting centres of many musclemen. Initially, the *akhara* was a place where a physical activity such as wrestling or weight lifting (Alter 1992) was practiced under the guidance of a guru (the *akhara*, which was often affiliated to a temple). But these seats of Indian martial arts have been transformed; as muscular exercise is the legitimate activity of these centres, they attract young men drawn to violence and who are keen on physical exploits, but in a manner that is very different from what existed traditionally. Film heroes, armed to the teeth in an imitation of Rambo, but drawing some of their features from Ram, are the new icons of youth. The latter, vulnerable because of unemployment, find further incentives to join gangs because they provide them with an identity. Naipaul has perfectly captured the way in which some of them are influenced by the mannerisms of the rich and powerful, and the lifestyle of the gang leaders of their district, who have never had to foot the bill. For the young delinquents, joining an *akhara* (a gang) is a means of vindicating some male honour or *izzat*, to reconquer some male virility threatened by failure (Naipaul 1992: 89).

While Indian politicians have been in the habit of selecting their muscle power from this milieu and especially from the *akharas*, yesterday's thugs are gradually throwing off their tutelage to enter the electoral arena themselves. They have an inclination for strong-arm tactics, as they have to fight prominent personalities of dominant groups to make themselves heard. Famous wrestlers have become gang leaders and/or politicians by virtue of the popularity they gained during tournaments (interestingly, Mulayam Singh Yadav was a popular wrestler before turning to politics).[25] Prior to an election, politicians recruit their bodyguards from among the *akhara* wrestlers, and may use them to intimidate voters or rig ballot boxes.[26]

The conclusions to which this survey leads us are evidently disturbing. India is increasingly affected by corruption because of the new opportunities that liberalization (and globalization) offer and because of the ever increasing financial pressures for political activities. In addition, the criminalization of politics is also galloping, first, because politicians not only need money but also gangs (to get more money and muscle power); and, second, because mafias are flourishing and need political protection. Besides, it is as much a case of criminalization of politics as a case of politicization of criminals since an increasing number of gang leaders contest elections and become ministers. The triad politician/bureaucrat/ businessman may be gradually replaced by another, politician/criminal/ businessesman, in which the key player is the criminal in the sense that he may be a politician and a businessman as well. The critical question that remains is how well India's political system and the rule of law can handle the criminalization of politics.

## The Political Personnel and its Judges: A Trial of Strength

Is the rule of law in India ineluctably rotten? We would be tempted to respond positively to this question if we limited our scrutiny to the actions of politicians who, though they have been making solemn promises, have taken no serious remedial measures. Narasimha Rao's government set up a commission to study the nexus between businessmen and the mafia, but the Vohra Commission Report was presented to Parliament in a watered down and summarized version.[27] The report, though it officially concurred, after a certain fashion, with the criminalization of politics in India (on the basis of statements made by the chiefs of police in particular), did not mention any name other than that of Dawood Ibrahim (Vohra Committee Report, n.d.). In view of this lacuna, it proposed setting up a special cell under the Home Ministry, which would complete the investigation. But this new body set up by the Rao government has yet to show results.[28]

### COMMISSIONS OF INQUIRY AND *LOK AYUKT* AS POLITICAL WEAPONS

Generally speaking, commissions of inquiry have given disappointing results. The Commissions of Inquiry Act 60 of 1952 suffered from obvious lacunae as it left the appointment of a commission to the discretion of the government or the Lower House of the legislature, central or state: the party in power therefore monopolized the capacity of initiating commissions.[29] As a result, the inquiry commissions have not played a very prominent role. Certainly, the Chief Minister of Punjab, Pratap

Singh Kairon, was forced to resign because of the findings of a commission (Bhargava 1974: 165ff). But most commissions were gradually politicized. For instance, Bakshi Ghulam Mohammed, the former Chief Minister of Jammu and Kashmir, was accused of corruption and a commission of inquiry was appointed because Bakshi, now in the opposition, was proving an embarrassment for the Srinagar government (Noorani 1973: 64–5). This was to become a recurring phenomenon: commissions of inquiry, generally presided over by a retired judge, were formed by those in power against those who had been in office before and continued to pose a threat in opposition.

Unsurprisingly, therefore, the first wave of 'revelations' came after the 1967 elections, which witnessed a Congress defeat in many states. The parties which took power ordered many commissions of inquiry, two of them in Bihar (Pandhy 1986). The Congress retaliated when it staged its comeback. This happened in 1968 in Bihar, in 1972 in Orissa (where an enquiry commission was set up in 1973 to examine the misuse of power by the incumbent Chief Minister from 1967 to 1971) (ibid.), and in 1976 in Tamil Nadu, where an inquiry was ordered against the former Chief Minister, Karunanidhi.

Another series of inquiry commissions were set up after the Congress defeat in 1977. The Shah Commission was appointed to examine government misdoings during the Emergency. This time, it was not simply a matter of corruption. However, another national commission was set up to measure the extent of influence peddling in the Maruti case. Nevertheless, the report of the Gupta Commission did not result in any legal action, as Indira Gandhi returned to power in 1980. A third national commission was appointed by the Janata government to investigate contracts awarded to foreign firms by the then Defence Minister Bansi Lal. Even though the report concluded that the minister was partially guilty, no action was taken. If the inquiry commissions often disclosed instances of corruption, their credibility was nevertheless doubly undermined because, first, they were nominated by the political opponents of the accused, and, second, their findings did not result in any legal action. As A.G. Noorani emphasizes, 'the initiation of an investigation into crime or an inquiry into charges of corruption or maladministration must not depend on the wishes of the men in power. If it does, it ceases to be government according to the rule of law' (Noorani 1997a: 221).

In addition to the inquiry commissions, another agency has been imagined by the state for defending the citizens against corrupt politicians and officers, the *Lok Pal* and *Lok Ayukt*. These institutions were suggested in the report of the Administrative Reforms Commission headed by Morarji Desai, the *Interim Report on Problems of Redress of Citizens Grievances*, in 1966. It proposed establishing one *Lok Pal* at the Centre and a *Lok Ayukt* in each state. These independent institutions would investigate cases of 'injustice, corruption or favoritism' in an informal manner (Noorani 1997b: 192). Several Lok Pal Bills have been introduced—mostly in vain—in the Lok Sabha (Kashyap 1997), and several states have established their own *Lok Ayukt*. Each state has followed its own modus operandi, but, in general, the *Lok Ayukt* who has been appointed is a respected senior fellow. For instance, in Madhya Pradesh, where the Lok Ayukt Act was passed in 1991, Justice Faizanuddin, who was appointed in 1997 for a six-year term, is a former Supreme Court judge. The complaints he received led him to register cases against three ministers of the state government for 'misuse of office and criminal conspiracy to help someone' (*Madhya Pradesh Chronicle*, 3 April 1998). However, his report was not tabled in the state assembly and he bitterly complained that the provision for permission from the state executive before prosecuting any government official made his work almost impossible (interview with Faizanuddin, in Bhopal, 7 November 1998).

While politicians are probably unable to re-establish the rule of law, partly because it would be to their own disadvantage, India can rely on other institutions for doing so.

## THE JUDICIARY, ON THE
## SOLID GROUND OF THE CONSTITUTION

While Sudipta Kaviraj convincingly argued that, in India, liberalism was short-circuited in the ideology of the Congress during the freedom movement itself because of Gandhi's conservatism and Nehru's socialism (Kaviraj 1996: 151ff), the values of liberalism are at the root of a long-standing interest in law—whether it is the rule of law or the rights of the individual. Does not the Indian Constitution begin with a list of 'Fundamental Rights', concerning as much the freedom of speech as that of association and respect for human dignity? One could object that these declarations of principle have remained totally abstract and immaterial, but such an interpretation would be exaggerated since the Constituent Assembly gave Indian courts the means to implement them by instituting a strict separation of powers. This decision partly reflected the fact that the concepts of law, as well as the judiciary, have played a crucial role in Indian society ever since the colonial period. Members of the new 'middle class' became lawyers in large numbers. This career offered interesting opportunities, especially after the introduction by the British of the principle of private property, till then alien to India, gave rise to numerous law cases. Courts gradually became critical arenas of public life. Statistically speaking, there was one lawyer for every 4,290 people in 1952, that is to say many more than in France where the ratio was one to 5,769 in 1958, and in Japan where it was on to 14,354 in 1960 (Galanter 1992: 279). Today, India has the largest legal profession in the world after the United States, with 500,000 advocates.[30]

Quite soon lawyers began to dominate the Congress and the freedom movement at large, predisposed as they were to debate and the defence of individual and collective rights. They began to form the core group of the emerging political class at a very early stage. In 1916 they were already occupying one-third of Imperial

Legislative Council seats and 48 per cent of the provincial legislative councils ones, despite the advantage of quotas and separate electorates granted by the British to the landowners and merchants (Montagu and Chelmsford 1918: 54). The large percentage of lawyers in the Congress during the colonial era was reflected in the composition of the Constituent Assembly, which partly explains the great interest shown by this body in the judicial system. On 21 May 1947, a committee of lawyers, members of the Constituent Assembly, which had been charged with the task of setting up the judicial system, submitted their report, in which the independence of the judiciary was presented as an imperative.[31] The system finally adopted for inclusion in the Constitution designated the Supreme Court as the apex body (inspired by the American model), with the High Courts (courts dealing with litigation at the state level) under it. All lower courts, the states and the central government frequently referred questions of law to the Supreme Court for settlement. The latter is also the appellate court to which a plaintiff can refer an appeal against a High Court ruling. Judges in the Supreme Court are appointed by the President of the Republic after consultation with the existing members of the Supreme Court as well as the High Court judges. This principle was intended as a safeguard against political pressure, as also was the rule that judges could not be dismissed, in case of misdemeanor or incapacity, except by Parliament according to a very cumbersome impeachment procedure.

The judiciary itself did not escape the taint of corruption, including within the Supreme Court. In 1998, 108 MPs had voted an impeachment motion against a judge, V. Ramaswami, who was supposed to have misappropriated large sums in his earlier position as Chief Justice of Punjab and Haryana. The matter was finally hushed up, probably because most MPs were afraid that by voting to lift the judges' immunity a precedent would be created which might one day rebound on them. In 1999, the government of Prime Minister Vajpayee proposed the setting up of a National Judicial Commission that would have the power to 'appoint, transfer and remove erring judges, including the Chief Justice of the Supreme Court' (Ahmed 1999: 27). Probably to pre-empt such a move, chief justices of various high courts met in Delhi and announced a 16-point code of conduct, one of the items commanding the judges not to give interviews to the media. But the judiciary remains cleaner than most Indian institutions and it was therefore the most appropriate institution for reacting to the rise of corruption and the criminalization of politics.

## 'JUDICIAL ACTIVISM', AND AFTER?

The Supreme Court appeared to be especially determined in the 1990s, so much so that the media coined the phrase 'judicial activism' to describe its growing influence in the public sphere.[32] The judges justified their 'activism' on the basis of the unprecedented corruption and criminalization of politics. In February 1996, the Chief Justice, A.M. Ahmadi, declared that 'the Court had to expand its area of competence' because 'members of Parliament have become less representative of the will of the people' and that each one feels 'increasingly frustrated by the democratic process' (extracts from Justice Ahmadi's Zakir Hussain Memorial Lecture, quoted in *Frontline*, 3 May 1996: 98). A discourse of this type can be interpreted as dangerous for representative democracy since it may reflect the increasing reservations of judges vis-à-vis parliamentary institutions.[33] But it was not that Ahmadi and the Chief Justice who succeeded him in 1997, J.C. Verma, were aspiring to a government of judges; they were simply reminding the political class of its responsibilities.

The media spoke about 'judicial activism' in the second half of the 1990s, after Justice Ahmadi's term as Chief Justice began in October 1994, in the context of the 'Hawala affair', of which the public would not have known without the intervention of the Supreme Court. The Central Bureau of Investigation (CBI), one of the primary police organizations, had seized the diaries of S.K. Jain in 1991 in which details of bribes were noted. The affair, which made headlines at that time, did not result in substantive prosecutions, no doubt because many ministers and an ex-Prime Minister figured on the list. It was only when two journalists took the matter to the Supreme Court in 1993 that it was able to demand clarification from the CBI on the investigation (*India Today*, 15 February 1996: 34).

Thereafter, the Supreme Court continued to spur CBI action, either by admonishing or praising the investigators, depending on the results. The revelations made in the early 1990s compelled seven ministers and two state governors to resign, including the leader of the opposition in the Lok Sabha, the Chief Minister of Delhi and the leader of the opposition in the Bihar Assembly. The scandal affected all parties, with the exception of the communists.

A February 1996 opinion poll on a random sample of 2,334 adults from nine large Indian cities highlights the positive response of the urban population to 'judicial activism': 78 per cent of the respondents considered that the Supreme Court 'was just doing its job'. But 55 per cent thought that it would not affect the working of governments present and future in any way (*The Times of India*, 2 March 1996: 1). Five years after the 'Hawala affair' it is to be feared that this opinion has some justification even though the achievements of 'judicial activism' must not be underestimated. The results of the judges' action in this affair were in fact mitigated. For lack of proof, other than the Jain diaries, the Supreme Court discharged the accused. Kalpnath Rai, a former Congress minister sentenced to ten years' imprisonment by the Delhi High Court for his supposed links with Dawood Ibrahim's lieutenants, was also pardoned by the Supreme Court on appeal because of the tenuous nature of the evidence. The absence of proof is not, however, the only drawback that 'judicial activism' has had to contend with; political obstruction also prevents justice from functioning smoothly.

After having been pushed against the wall, the executive took the initiative again and once more began to cross swords with judges. Although Prime Minister I.K. Gujral had solemnly declared on the occasion of the fiftieth anniversary of Indian independence that the country's biggest failure since 1947 was the rise in corruption,[34] he did nothing to facilitate the Supreme Court's task, in fact quite the opposite. In July 1997, he shifted Joginder Singh, the CBI director, who was working on a number of sensitive investigations, giving him an inoffensive job (the affairs of pensioners and freedom fighters), and in his place appointed a man known for his compliance. This unprecedented decision was no doubt an attempt to slow down important investigations such as the Bofors affair and the fodder scam. As a matter of fact, in February 1997, the Swiss authorities had given the Indian courts information regarding the accounts in which the Swedish bribes had been deposited. The Congress, afraid that the revelations could tarnish Rajiv Gandhi's image, took full advantage of its crucial support to the ruling party to put pressure on Gujral.[35] The latter probably ceded more easily to pressure, as his own party, the Janata Dal, was directly targeted by 'judicial activism'. Laloo Prasad Yadav, the then party president and chief minister of Bihar, had been forced to resign after the CBI, prompted by the Supreme Court, investigated massive misappropriation of the state's agricultural subsidies budget in the fodder scam. For the first time, an acting chief minister was jailed (Laloo Prasad Yadav remained at the helm by proxy since his wife took over). This affair also led to his Congress predecessor, Jagannath Mishra, being remanded in police custody. Judicial activism thus bore fruit,[36] but found itself open to riposte on the part of the executive.

Patna High Court dared to instruct a joint director of the CBI, U.N. Biswas, to bypass his superiors and report directly to the court on the Bihar fodder scam because he had claimed that senior officers were protecting Laloo Prasad Yadav. And the Supreme Court reacted to Gujral's decision in December 1997 by issuing a very important judgement that was bound to loosen the government's grip over the CBI. The CBI director could not be appointed by the government's discretion as before. He had to be chosen from three candidates recommended by a committee headed by the Central Vigilance Commissioner. The Supreme Court also 'quashed a 1997 government order which prohibited the CBI from initiating investigations into officers above the rank of joint secretary [a mid-level position in the bureaucracy] without prior sanction from the government' (Mitra 1998: 21).

The December 1997 Supreme Court judgement had far-reaching consequences for the Central Vigilance Commission (CVC). The CVC had been founded in 1964, in the wake of the Santhanam Report, to check corruption in the administration. But in 1997 it was given superintending power over the CBI and the capacity to initiate an inquiry on its own. The first Central Vigilance Commissioner who enjoys these statutory powers, N. Vittal, has gradually asserted himself. In early 2000 he launched an aggressive campaign against corrupt bureaucrats. The names of 88 corrupt Indian Administrative Service officers and 21 Indian police superintendents against whom the CVC had sought criminal or departmental proceedings were publicized on the Commission's website. Vittal listed also the names of 78 Central Service officers who were notoriously corrupt.

'Judicial activism' in India has often been compared to the *manu pulite* (clean hands) operation in Italy (ibid.: 44). Certainly, for the first time, high-profile politicians have been convicted and even arrested. Because of the Hawala affairs, several ministers of Narasimha Rao's government resigned in early 1996.[37] Rao himself received a three-year jail sentence in 2000 over the Jharkhand Mukti Morcha bribery case. But this is not the simple result of judicial activism. In July 1993, while the Congress had only 251 MPs in the Lok Sabha, whose actual strength was then 528, Rao had apparently sought to bribe four JMM MPs on a no-confidence motion. Narasimha Rao and Buta Singh were convicted but the four JMM MPs were acquitted because they were immune from legal action: under article 105(2), 'No MP shall be liable to any proceedings in any court in respect to any vote given by him in Parliament'. The notion that bribe givers are guilty whereas the bribe takers are innocent somewhat diminished the impact of the case, but it remains significant that a former Prime Minister was for the first time sentenced to jail.

At the state level, the Supreme Court disenfranchized Bal Thackeray—the Shiv Sena leader whom few had dared to confront before then—in 1999 for inciting religious passions during the 1987 Maharashtra elections. (*Bal Thackeray v. Shri Prabhakar Kashinath Kunte* [J.S. Verma], *Judgements Today*, S.C. 609-S.C. 686, and Cossman and Kapur 1997: 115–70). In Kerala one former minister, R. Balakrishna Pillai, has been sentenced to five years' imprisonment.

But the total number of politicians tried or convicted is rather limited and their appearance before judges and/or their jailing has not hurt most of their careers. Almost all the Hawala tainted leaders were re-elected to Parliament in 1996 or 1998 (for instance, Madhav Rao Scindia and L.K. Advani), or had their wives elected (for instance, Kamal Nath and Arvind Netam). Then they were acquitted on appeal. Kalpnath Rai contested his seat from behind bars and retained it, before being acquitted on appeal for lack of proof. Brij Bushan Sharan Singh, who was jailed along with Rai on the same charge, had his wife successfully contest his seat. Sukh Ram retained his seat too. At the state level, Chautala returned to power in 2000 and Laloo Prasad Yadav retained power through his wife, Rabri Devi, after his party won the 2000 state elections. The fact that politicians can still exert power at the state level, even when there are cases against them, has been reconfirmed with the victory of Jayalalitha's party, the AIADMK, in Tamil Nadu in May 2001. Jayalalitha had been acquitted in the 'Rs. 10.16-crore colour TV scam' in 2000; there were other cases against her and the Election Commission debarred her from contesting elections, even though she became Chief Minister in spring 2001 and only stepped down several months later. The comparison with Italy holds since Silvio Berlusconi has been re-elected in spite of the many cases against him.

Indian judges seem to be very isolated in their 'activism', not only because the voter does not consider their findings or suspicion as being sufficient reason for not supporting corrupt politicians, but also because they often have great difficulty in collecting the relevant testimonies against suspects. An obvious reason for that is fear: politicians or criminals intimidate those who could lodge complaints. For instance, the victims of Romesh Sharma are very reluctant to file reports and the CBI failed to establish a murder charge against Paltan Mallah, the man who was most probably responsible for the killing of Niyogi. All the accused in this murder case were acquitted in 1998. In order to overcome the difficulty, Justice Dhingra, Delhi High Court judge who sentenced Kalpnath Rai to ten years' imprisonment, suggested that statements before police officers should have the status of a confession and be admissible as legal evidence. This was because 'Terrorists, even if confined in jail, have got sufficient gang strength outside to order execution of witnesses. Witnesses are killed. "The Terror" is the reason for non-association of public witnesses' (Visvanathan in Visvanathan and Sethi 1998: 144).

The Supreme Court has also attacked the growing role of money in politics with mixed results. Some weeks after the revelations in the Hawala affair, and in view of the coming elections of April-May 1996, the judges reinterpreted section 77 of the 1951 Representation of the People Act of 1951, which imposed a ceiling on the election expenditure of a candidate. In 1974, the Supreme Court had ruled that the ceiling on a candidate's expenditure was constituted by the sum of the resources from his pocket, and the funds given by his party or other private individuals (Ganesan in Guhan and Paul 1997: 31–2). Indira Gandhi had counter-attacked by having an 'explanation' attached to Section 77, according to which only the candidate's private funds came under the ceiling. This interpretation was endorsed by the Supreme Court in 1985 (Sridharan 1966: 2731). Ten years later the same body became concerned about the consequences of this step, for election expenditure just went on increasing due to black money injected into the process. To overcome the hurdle that the 1985 jurisprudence represented, the Supreme Court decreed on 4 April 1966 that parties not declaring their income to the income tax authority, as required by the Income Tax Act, would not be able to claim their candidate's expenses. This meant that in all probability the candidate would exceed the ceiling. In fact, during the last few years, the communist and affiliated parties were the only national parties to have declared their income.[38] (Moreover, a communist leader, Inderjit Gupta, was appointed in 1998 at the helm of a multi-party parliamentary committee on the issue of money in elections. It recommended that the expenditures of candidates of the recognized parties should be funded by the state.)

The Supreme Court could not, however, act alone in this undertaking, for it depended *inter alia* upon the Election Commission as the enforcing agency. The Commission is certainly the other institution which, over the last ten years, has constituted the other pillar of the rule of law.

## THE ELECTION COMMISSION:
## THE WATCHDOG OF THE POLLS

The Election Commission was conceived as an independent body by the legislators to monitor the organization of polls. Even before independence, in July 1947, the idea of a commission of this type was proposed by the sub-committee charged with reflecting upon fundamental rights (*CAD*, Vol. 1: 918). Article 324 of the

Indian Constitution provides that the preparation of electoral lists, and the process of national and local elections, should take place under 'the supervision, direction and control' of the Election Commission. This body is composed of a Chief Election Commissioner and of as many members as India's President may deem necessary. Such appointees would remain in office till their retirement and cannot be removed except by means of the same procedure as that followed for the judges, that is, impeachment. Before each election, the President would also appoint, in consultation with the Chief Election Commissioner, state election commissions to supervise voting operations in the states. The task of this institution has become increasingly important and delicate because of the criminalization of politics.

In the 1990s, the Election Commission reacted to this trend under the impetus of T.N. Seshan, who was appointed as Chief Election Commissioner in 1990, and then of his successor, M.S. Gill. Seshan was first accused of partiality because during the 1991 elections he deployed a special zealousness in strongholds of the Janata Dal—the ruling party. Elections were either postponed or countermanded on one pretext or another (for instance, in Bihar), sometimes absolutely baseless ones. On the whole, Seshan behaved unpredictably. For instance, he cancelled the state assembly elections in Punjab some hours before the polls were to begin, which prompted the Governor's resignation. But Seshan's firmness yielded results. He reduced violence around the polling booths by preparing the ground for the deployment of police and paramilitary forces in a much more systematic way than before. His decision to strictly implement the 'model code of conduct' that the political parties had accepted years before enabled the Election Commission to make the November-December 1993 state elections much more disciplined in the Hindi belt. Politicians refrained from using official cars for canvassing and had to accept that transfers of officials before elections was prohibited (Govindan Kutty 1995: 221). Seshan alienated most of them, but they were not prepared to unite and impeach him. Instead, the government appointed two other election commissioners alongside Seshan, M.S. Gill and G.V.G. Krishnamurthy, to dilute his powers. But this multi-member structure has, in fact, enabled the Election Commission to fight even more strongly for reforming the electoral process.

The Election Commission did not hesitate to postpone an election to deploy additional police personnel to reduce the risk of booth capturing and other forms of violence around polling stations. In 1996, the Election Commission sent 1,500 observers (an average of three per constituency) to supervise the polls.[39] Approximately 600,000 policemen were deployed to enforce law and order around polling booths, which were manned by 1.5 million agents of the state. More than 300,000 people were arrested as a preventive measure (125,000 in Uttar Pradesh (*National Mail*, 2 May 1996: 1) and 59,000 in Madhya Pradesh, where 87,000 arms were seized (*Madhya Pradesh Chronicle*, 7 May 1996)). This apparatus enabled the state to control unrest; elections were countermanded and had to be reorganized in 1,056 polling booths, as against 1,670 in 1989. A little less than half of them

(471) were in Bihar, 231 in Andhra Pradesh, 96 in Assam, 31 in Rajasthan, 43 in Uttar Pradesh, and 22 in Orissa (Ibid., 4 and 5 May 1996; *The Times of India*, 5 May 1996; and *National Mail*, 30 April 1996).

The incidence of poll violence declined from 3,363 in 1991 to 2,450 in 1998 and the number of deaths from 272 in 1991 to 213 in 1996, 65 in 1998, and 32 in 1999, including 29 killed in landmine blasts engineered by Naxalites in Bihar (*The Hindu*, 30 August 1999; *National Mail*, 19 September 1999: 1). Election-related violence is increasingly geographically concentrated, mainly in Bihar (where re-polls were ordered in about 5,000 polling stations in the 1998 Lok Sabha elections) and in Uttar Pradesh. The policy of the Election Commission was partly responsible for a higher participation rate (up by ten points in Uttar Pradesh), with the security around the booths attracting a greater number of voters, especially Scheduled Castes, whom party thugs could not intimidate quite so easily as previously.

The Election Commission tried to limit electoral expenditure when, in April 1996, the Supreme Court mandated it to proceed in this field. It therefore ordered the parties to submit their accounts for examination after the polls. It also attempted to 'decriminalize' Indian politics. In September 1997, G.V.G. Krishnamurthy declared that 1,500 of the 13,952 candidates in the 1996 general elections had a criminal record. This was also true of 40 MPs and 700 MLAs (*The Times of India*, 21 August 1997). Seshan's successor to the Commission, M.S. Gill, directed the Commission's representatives in the states to reject candidates who had had a brush with the law. Strictly applying Section 8 of the Representation of the People Act, the Election Commission now demands that the candidates file an affidavit stating whether he or she has been convicted for an offence specified in the RPA. It recommends that candidates who have been convicted should not be allowed to contest, even if they are on appeal, since the appeals process is very lengthy. In Madhya Pradesh, a candidate was barred from contesting on the basis of his affidavit. But in Tamil Nadu, Jayalalitha simply ignored all recommendations. The feasibility of the Election Commission's step remains to be proved.

The unprecedented rise of corruption and the criminalization of politics that India is experiencing pose a direct threat to India's democratic regime. The power of money tends to prevail upon that of the citizens. The voter is subject to the law of the two 'Ms', money and muscle, with more and more criminals contesting elections. This evolution is not due to the personality of the key figures of post-independence India, Jawaharlal Nehru, Indira (and Sanjay) Gandhi, or Narasimha Rao, as a superficial understanding of the issue would like to make us believe. Corruption stems from socioeconomic and political conditions: the 'licence raj' led the businessmen to bribe bureaucrats and politicians to get their projects cleared; its dismantling in the framework of the new liberalization policy generates even more corruption since the Indian economy is more attractive, and offers more opportunities for Harshad Mehta and Sukh Ram to amass huge benefits. Besides the impact of these changing economic structures, the rising cost of elections in the context of an increasingly competitive polity exacerbates the politicians' search for money.

India is not only affected by corruption; the criminalization of the state has become another serious chronic disease over the last two decades. Once again, no single leader is personally responsible for this—even if Indira and Sanjay Gandhi are considered to have prepared the ground for it during the Emergency period. This process derives from structural conditions. First, the development of illicit trade and practices has transformed the mafia into a power to reckon with. Second, politicians have sought its collaboration because they require greater funding for contesting elections and power to exert influence over voters—who were emancipating themselves from the clientelistic arrangement of the notables-based Congress system. In the 1990s, India's political scene took a step backward, beyond the criminalization of the politicians, with the entry of criminals into the political arena.

This assessment, however, needs to be seen in a comparative perspective. The situation is not as bad as in some states of Latin America or Africa. In Africa, Jean-François Bayart, Stephen Ellis, and Beatrice Hibou have identified several major indicators of the criminalization of politics: the use for private purposes of the legitimate organs of state violence by those in authority; the existence of a hidden, collective structure of power which surrounds and even controls the official occupant of the most senior political office, and which participates in economic activities considered to be criminal under international law; and the involvement in such economic activities of international crime networks (Bayart, Ellis and Hibou 1999: 26–7). While in India the police force is certainly one of the most corrupt institutions at the local level—so much so that criminals can operate from jail, and bribes are also used to secure police postings in areas of high criminal activity so as to take advantage of mafia payoffs[40]—conditions are not that bad in the upper echelons of the police, and the army is certainly not used for private purposes. Second, there is no cohesive structure behind the occupant of power, even if the political networks of Chandraswami or Romesh Sharma, and their links with mafia dons, suggest that there is a kind of nebula taking shape with loose but numerous interconnections. Third, even though the international network of Dawood Ibrahim suggests that India is now well integrated in the international political economy of crime, its inclusion in the global economy is still modest.

More importantly, the criminals and/or politicians are not in a position to control power in India because the rule of law still has defenders. The institutional basis designed by the Constitution has endowed the country with a robust judiciary and a virtually independent Election Commission. The 'judicial activism' on which the former embarked in the 1990s has certainly not been as successful as some commentators suggest, but it has made some impact.[41] The Election Commission has also taken seriously its role in protecting the public scene from the gangrene of crime. These institutions have not been able to clean up the political arena because of the resistance of their first target, the politicians,[42] but also because public opinion has not been responsive to the extent of ostracizing the guilty. Why have the hawala-tainted leaders and Jayalalitha, for instance, been voted to power again? I do not believe that it was only because they could intimidate the citizens or because they had more money than the other candidates. Their return to power was also due to the fact that their powers and fortunes fascinated the masses, and also perhaps to the fatalism of the voters. For them, all politicians may well appear dirty, so 'dirt' is not a major criterion in choosing candidates.

The media, which have already played an important role in exposing corruption in the Indian establishment, must educate the public in this regard. The worrying factor here lies in the growing infection of the press by the very disease they should fight. The 14 Lok Sabha candidates interviewed by Arun Kumar mentioned that they paid journalists for covering their election campaign and proprietors of local press were paid by the column centimetre (Kumar 1999: 275). There are other channels through which corruption finds its way into the media because newspaper owners have commercial interests that can be promoted through good relations with politicians. The fact that the press proprietors are often businessmen is, in itself, a factor of corruption, especially when it corresponds with their official entry into politics. For instance, the Managing Director of *Nav Bharat* group of newspapers, Prafulla Maheshwari, was elected to the Rajya Sabha on a Congress ticket in March 2000. The corruption of mediapersons was exposed in Uttar Pradesh when, in 1994, Chief Minister Mayawati leaked lists of journalists who had benefited from the Chief Minister's relief fund set up by her predecessor, Mulayam Singh Yadav. But such denunciation may not be sufficient to clean up the profession.

Change may possibly come from below. Some individuals have already made an impact. In the early 1990s, G.R. Khairnar, the former Deputy Municipal Commissioner of Bombay denounced the nexus between Congress politicians, mafioso and other bureaucrats in the business of land in Mumbai. However, he has been suspended and the case has been in the High Court for years. Anna Hazare, a former army truck driver who converted to Gandhism and became a tireless crusader against corruption, launched his campaign against the irregularities of the Maharashtra government in 1996. While Jayaprakash Narayan had been able to mobilize thousands of demonstrators against corruption in the 1970s, similar developments are less likely today, largely because corruption is so widespread among the political personnel that no party is prepared to support such a campaign by individuals like Hazare. V.P. Singh tried to be 'to Congress what JP was to the Janata' (Thakur 1989: 4), but the Congress Party was not open to such transformation—and no party appears to be so.

The relevant pressures against corruption probably need to come from below and through collective rather than individual enterprises. Leaders are needed, certainly, but they must have organizations behind them too. The most encouraging developments, in that respect, come from grassroot associations such as the Mazdoor Kisan Shakti Sangathan (MKSS), which fights against corruption at the local level in Rajasthan,[43] or the Chhattisgarh Mukti Morcha (CMM), which continues its struggle in spite of Niyogi's assassination. Instead of focusing on deregulation, international institutions like the IMF and the World Bank should pay more attention to these antidotes to corruption and criminalization.

## Notes

1. Chandan Mitra: 'The Hindu belief that, while the commission of *paap* (sin) is inevitable in one's lifetime, its effects can be neutralized for the afterlife by acts of *punya* (piety), probably explains why this delightful hypocrisy enjoys a remarkable, even if unstated, degree of social sanction' (1998: 6). Emphasizing the impact of social structures, S.S. Gill underlines that in the Indian society 'there is caste ethics and there are group norms, but there is no such thing as Indian social norms. Thus there are hardly any criteria of right and wrong, honest and dishonest, permissible and impermissible applicable across the board' (1998: 252).

2. Haridas Mundhra, a businessman facing serious financial difficulties had, apparently, convinced Krishnamachari to make the Life Insurance Corporation buy shares representing more than 12.5 million rupees of several of his concerns.

3. For more details, see 'Right Connections: Telecom', in Visvanathan and Sethi 1998: 195–207.

4. The career of V. Krishnamurti—the former chairman of Maruti—in the 1980s would also be interesting to scrutinize since it shows how a prestigious civil servant launched his own business to play the role of middleman between foreign investors and the Indian bureaucracy to his own advantage. See Visvanathan 1998: 151–70.

5. See his deposition to the police, reproduced in *Frontline*, 23 February 1996: 12.

6. The data regarding the 'hawala affair' are appended to an otherwise rather journalistic book: Kapoor 1996.

7. Hardgrave and Kochanek 1993: 330. According to another source, the initial investment that a candidate to the State Assembly and to the Lok Sabha has to make is respectively, 1 and 5 million rupees (*Sunday*, 27 November 1994: 36). A more recent estimate published in *India Today* sets at 2 to 3 million rupees the capital needed for a parliamentary seat and at Rs. 500,000 to Rs. 600,000 that for a state assembly seat (*India Today*, 31 March 1996: 13).

8. These 'innovations' do not exclude old forms of corruption such as the embezzlement of public money. The anti-poverty programmes launched by Rajiv Gandhi, called Jawahar Rozgar Yojna, is a telling example, as only 25 per cent of the funds earmarked for spending in 1995 reached their destination. Either the money was misappropriated by politicians, or it was simply not used (*The Hindu*, 21 October 1995). In the beginning of 1997, the National Council of Applied Economic Research concluded that only 15 per cent of this financial assistance to the poor effectively reached them (*Monthly Public Opinion Survey*, February 1997: 43–4).

9. See the testimony of the Indian Ambassador to Sweden at the time of the incident, B.M. Oza (1997).

10. Satyamurti, 1996: 77–8.

11. In Karnataka, after the sale of illicit liquor by bootleggers, in which 298 people died in Bangalore, a Congress member proved quite influential in preventing the Chief

Minister from applying the National Security Act against the barons directing this traffic. Another—perhaps the same one—managed to have the gang leader released after his arrest (Manor 1993: 143–5).

12. According to official sources 10,000 AK-47 rifles, 29,000 grenades, 30,000 detonators, 15,000 explosives, 5,500 anti-tank missiles, 7,200 revolvers and 3,000 rockets were seized in Jammu and Kashmir between 1989 and 1997 (*The Times of India,* 15 September 1997).

13. Halankar, Chakravarty and Koppikar, 1997: 14. The total amount of protection money and ransom from kidnappings was estimated at six billion rupees for 1996.

14. The film world of Mumbai is so called by analogy with Hollywood.

15. Uttar Pradesh police chiefs blame politicians for the situation. In their opinion, without them, organized crime would not be able to defy the police so effectively (on the situation in Lucknow and in the west of the province, where ransoms vary between Rs. 20,000 and Rs. 6,000,000, see *India Today,* 30 November 1994: 108 and 28 February 1995: 207).

16. It boiled down to intimidating certain voters, or rather dissuading them from going to the polling booth.

17. This figure was given by *Sunday* (8 May 1994: 67). However, according to *The Times of India,* 130 MPs are incriminated.

18. *Sunday,* 8 May 1994: 67. These figures have to be compared with the total number of elected members in each party: 177 in the BJP, 105 in the SP, 71 in the BSP, 25 in the Congress and 23 in the Janata Dal.

19. This information was collected during a field mission in November 1997.

20. Among the Independents, the most famous criminal turned MLA was Suraj Bhan Singh, who has 26 cases against him, including murder, kidnapping and extortion (Tewary 2000: 26).

21. Amongst them, Arun Gawli deserves special mention. After being involved in gold trafficking in the Middle East for many years, Gawli became the leader of one of the Mumbai gangs in 1988. He was arrested two years later for the murder of one of the lieutenants of Dawood Ibrahim, the leader of a rival gang. On his release from prison in 1997, Gawli founded a political party and ran for local elections, prior to being arrested again for the murder of N.M. Desai, a promoter—the fifteenth in three years in Bombay—who had given protection money to Dawood Ibrahim. Bhandare 1997 and *The Times of India,* 20 and 21 August 1997.

22. In 1985, a candidate to the state elections in Madhya Pradesh, and a well known 'goonda', had for a slogan: 'Mohar lagegi hathi par, nahi to goli chhati par, lash milegi ghati par' (Put the stamp on the elephant [his electoral symbol on the ballot papers] otherwise your chest will be pierced by bullets and your body found in the ravine). Quoted in *India Today,* 15 April 1990: 32.

23. On the implementation of this strategy by Hindu nationalists, see Jaffrelot (1994).

24. If Naipaul's last travelogue, *India: A Million Mutinies,* is to be believed, the Muslim godfathers of Bombay patronize a mutual aid organization based on religion, created after the communal riots of 1984. In Indore (the economic capital of Madhya Pradesh), the mafia is also dominated by Muslim barons, of whom Bala Baig stood for elections in the beginning of the 1990s before being sentenced to three years' imprisonment in 1997.

25. On many occasions he was the district champion and was even selected to represent the state.

26. In Delhi, hiring an *akhara* wrestler for booth capturing and rigging the ballot boxes, costs between Rs. 20,000 and Rs. 25,000; a minimum of five men are needed for the operation to succeed. *Delhi Times,* 2 April 1996.

27. The final report has only 12 pages whereas the minister, V.C. Shukla, had described it as having a few hundred pages.

28. It was necessary for the government to calm the spirits as the situation was a very explosive one. The Narasimha Rao government held back the report for one and a half years before reluctantly producing it in Parliament, under pressure from the Opposition and public opinion, after the 'Tandoor affair'. Sushil Sharma, a Youth Congress leader from Delhi, had killed his wife (before stuffing her body inside a *tandoor,* an oven) who, according to him was having illicit relations with two ministers. This event gave the press an opportunity to stress the links that Congressmen, of whom Sharma was one, had with the mafia, and their dubious morals.

29. The Commissions of Inquiry (Amendment) Act 19 of 1990 enabled the legislative houses (the Rajya Sabha or State Legislative Councils), which can be dominated by opposition parties, to initiate such commissions, but their composition would nevertheless be determined by the government.

30. N.R. Madhava Menon, a member of the Law Commission, explained such a plethora in not very flattering terms, by the fact that 'Law remains the cheapest and, perhaps, easiest professional degree anybody can obtain anywhere with little inclination and minimum enterprise!' (*The Hindu,* 26 October 1999).

31. In the plenary session, the mode of appointment of judges became the topic of lively discussion. Some suggested that the nomination of the Chief Justice of the Supreme Court be submitted to Parliament for approval or the opinion of the Council of State be sought (*Constituent Assembly Debates* [hereafter *CAD*], 1989: 229–67). Representatives were concerned about certain provisions that could lead to a government of judges (ibid.: 397).

32. As Upendra Baxi points out, judicial activism, in fact, took shape in the 1970s, when judges tried to resist Indira Gandhi's attempts at asserting her domination over the judiciary. Baxi 1997: 345.

33. Some days after Ahmadi's conference, this sentiment was clearly expressed by a Delhi High Court magistrate (see extracts from the written reply made by Shiv Narain Dhingra to Kalpnath Rai, reproduced in the *Frontline* of 22 March 1996: 18).

34. He also declared, the next day, before an audience of businessmen: 'I know that you give money [to bureaucrats and politicians]. You tell me in private, but you do not dare saying it publicly' (*The Sunday Times,* 17 August 1997: 1).

35. In 1997, the Congress had decided to support the government from outside, i.e. without participating in it.

36. The former Minister of Oil and Natural Gas in the Rajiv Gandhi government, Satish Sharma, was also ordered in November 1996 to pay a fine of 5 million rupees (about 140,000 dollars) for having attributed public sector service stations to more than 80 friends and relations.

37. On Chandraswami and the dubious role of the Tantrics in politics, see Jaffrelot 2001: 75–94.

38. The law is faulty on many points: the parties do not have to declare the donor's identity within the limit of Rs. 10,000, nor give an account of the sums spent for 'propaganda or distribution of the election programme'; lastly, the 1974 text did not only prevent a candidate's campaign from being financed by his party, but also by individuals, and this last provision still holds. Among individuals, farmers are not obliged to render accounts to the Income Tax authorities with regard to their budget, as they are exonerated from paying taxes.

39. Video cameras were used to film the election campaign in order to exert psychological pressure on candidates and their supporters (*The Economic Times*, 14 March 1996).

40. A senior police officer told Arun Kumar that 'more police stations mean more crime' because the criminals had to earn more for giving their share to the local policemen. In the 'constituency' of each police station, there is prostitution, encroachment for housing, black marketing, etc., but policemen often agree to look the other way against the payment of a sum of money they collect every week, hence its name, 'hafta' (Kumar 1999: 256).

41. For Mitra, the assertion of the judges has 'emaciated Indian politicians who today find themselves powerless to wield the stick on the judiciary, much the same way as Italian parliamentarians have been frustrated in their attempts to rein in activist judges there' (Mitra 1998: 58).

42. Arun Jaitley, the then Union Minister of State for Information and Broadcasting declared that judicial activism was welcome but that 'over-assertiveness' of the judiciary would affect the balance of the different institutions (*The Hindu*, 27 December 1999).

43. Rob Jenkins and Anne Marie Goetz point out that the MKSS 'demands and frequently obtains access to official expenditure records which citizen-activists then cross-check in a kind of people's audit' (Jenkins and Goetz 1999a: 39. See also Jenkins and Goetz 1999b: 603–22).

## References

Ahmed, F. (1999), 'Judging Judges', *India Today*, 20 December.

Aiyar, V. Shankar (1998), 'Ransom City', *India Today*, 30 November.

Alter, J.S. (1992), *The Wrestler's Body. Identity and Ideology in North India*, Berkeley: University of California Press.

Anandan, S. (1998), 'Who's next. . .', *Outlook*, 9 November.

Anonymous (1998), 'Bribes and Industry', in Vishvanathan and Sethi (eds.), *Foul Play: Chronicles of Corruption, 1947-1997*, New Delhi: Banyan Books.

Bayart, J.F., Ellis S. and Hibou, B. (1999), *The Criminalization of the State in Africa*, Oxford: James Currey.

Baxi, U. (1997), 'Judicial Activism: Usurpation or Re-democratization?', *Social Action*, Vol. 47, No. 3, October-December.

Bhandare, N. (1997), 'The Return of the Don', *Sunday*, 5 January.

Bhargava, G.S. (1974), *India's Watergate: A Study of Political Corruption in India*, New Delhi: Arnold Heinemann.

Bhatnagar, R. (1997), 'A Prisoner Can't Vote But May Become An MP', *The Times of India*, 15 July.

Bhatt, M. (1998), 'Land to the Killer', in Visvanathan and Sethi (eds.), *Foul Play: Chronicles of Corruption, 1947–1997*, New Delhi: Banyan Books.

Bhattacharyya, D.K. and Ghose, S. (1998), 'Corruption in India and the Hidden Economy', *Economic and Political Weekly*, 31 October.

*Constituent Assembly Debates* (1989), Debate of 31 December 1948, Vol. 7, Delhi: Lok Sabha Secretariat.

———, Debate of May 24, 1949 and Debate of May 27, 1949, Vol. 8, New Delhi: Lok Sabha Secretariat.

———, Debate of July 29, 1947, Vol. 1.

Cossman, B. and Kapur, R. (1997), 'Secularism's Last Sigh? The Hindu Right, the Courts, and India's Struggle for Democracy', *Harvard International Law Journal*, Vol. 38, No. 1, Winter 1997.

Dhavan, Rajeev (1999), 'Criminals or MPs?', *The Hindu*, 16 July.

Election Commission (1972), *Report of the Fifth General Election, India 1971–1972, Narrrative and Reflective Part*, New Delhi.

——— (1980), *Report on the General Elections to the House of the People*, Vol. 1, *Narrative and Reflective Part*, Jaipur: Government Central Press.

Galanter, M. (1992), *Law and Society in Modern India*, Delhi: Oxford University Press.

Ganesan, K. (1999), 'Corruption in the Political Process: A Case for Electoral Reform', in Guhan and Paul (eds.), *Corruption in India: Agenda for Action*, New Delhi: Vision Books.

Gani, H.A. (1987), *Problems of Minorities in Contemporary India*, Nanded: Sharda Prakashan.

Gill, S.S. (1998), *The Pathology of Corruption*, New Delhi: Harper Collins.

Godbole, M. (1997), 'Crime and Blandishment My Thug is Better than your Thug', *The Times of India*, 18 April.

Hardgrave, R.L. and Kochanek, S.A. (1993), *India-Government and Politics in a Developing Nation*, Fort Worth: H.B. Jovanovitsh.

Halankar, S., Chakravarty, S. and Koppikar, S. (1997), 'Fear in the City', *India Today*, 6 October.

Jaffrelot, C. (1992), 'Les émeutes entre hindous et musulmans. Essai de hiérarchisation des facteurs culturels, économiques et politiques', *Cultures et conflits*, No. 5, Spring.

——— (1994), 'Oeuvres pies et rationalité économique', in J.F. Bayart (ed.), *La Réinvention du capitalisme*, Paris: Karthala.

——— (2001), 'Guru et politique en Inde: Des éminences grises à visage découvert?', *Politix*, No. 54.

Jenkins, R. and Goetz, A.M. (1999a), 'Constraints on Civil Society's Capacity to Curb Corruption', *IDS Bulletin*, Vol. 30, No. 4, October 1999.

——— (1999b), 'Accounts and Accountability: Theoretical Implications of the Right-to-information Movement in India', *Third World Quarterly*, Vol. 20, No. 3.

Joshi, R. (1999), 'Blood in the Street', *Outlook*, 29 March.

Kapoor, S. (1996), *Bad Money, Bad Politics: The Untold Hawala Story*, New Delhi: Har-Anand.

Kashyap, S.C. (1997) (ed.), *Judicial Activism and Lok Pali*, New Delhi: Uppal Publishing House.

Kaviraj, S. (1996), 'Démocratic et développement en Inde', in J.F. Bayart (ed.), *La greffe de l'Etat*, Paris: Karthala.

Kochanek, S.A. (1987), 'Briefcase Politics in India: the Congress Party and Business Elite', *Asian Survey*, Vol. 27.

Krishnan, M. (2000), 'The Road to Dusty Death', *Outlook*, 21 February.

Kumar, A. (1999), *The Black Economy in India*, New Delhi: Penguin.

Kumar, A. (1999), 'The Black Economy: Missing Dimensions of Macro Policy-Making in India', *Economic and Political Weekly*, 20 March.

Kutty, K. (1995), *Govindan Seshan: An Intimate Story*, Delhi: Konark Publishers.

Manor, J. (1993), *Power, Poverty and Poison: Disaster and Response in an Indian City*, New Delhi: Sage.

Mishra, S. (1998), 'Criminal's Bedfellows', *India Today*, 26 October.

Mitra, C. (1998), *The Corrupt Society: The Criminalization of India from Independence to the 1990s*, Delhi: Viking.

Montagu, E. and Chelmsford (1918), *Report on Indian Constitutional Reforms*, Calcutta: Superintendent Government Printing.

Naipaul (1992), *L'Inde, un million de revoltes*, Paris: Plon.

Noorani, A.G. (1973), *Ministers' Misconduct*, Delhi: Vikas.

—— (1997a), 'Commissions of Inquiry', in S. Guhan and S. Paul (eds.), *Corruption in India: Agenda for Action*, New Delhi: Vision Books.

—— (1997b), 'Lok Pal and Lok Ayukt', in Guhan and Paul (eds.), *Corruption in India: Agenda for Action*, New Delhi: Vision Books.

Oza, B.M. (1997b), *Bofors: The Ambassador's Evidence*, Delhi: Konark Publishers.

*Outlook* (2000), 'Son of the Soil', 20 March, p. 6.

Pandhy, K.S. (1986), *Corruption in Politics: A Case Study*, Delhi: B.R. Publishing Corporation.

Paul, S. and Shah, M. (1997), 'Corruption in Public Service Delivery', in S. Guhan and S. Paul (eds.), *Corruption in India: Agenda for Action*, New Delhi: Vision Books.

Raval, S. (1999), 'Mobile Underworld', *India Today*, 15 March.

Roy, A.K. (2000), 'Fighting the Dhanbad Mafia', *Economic and Political Weekly*, 13 May.

Sahai, S. (1996), 'Hawala Politics: A Congress Legacy', *Economic and Political Weekly*, 3 February.

Satyamurti, K. (1996), 'A Southern High Alarming Rise in Narcotics Trafficking', *Frontline*, 29 November.

Sethi, Harsh (1990), 'Notes on Electoral Violence', *Seminar*, No. 368, April.

Sridharan, E. (1966), 'State Funding of Elections', *Seminar*, April.

Swami, P. (1998), 'Crime Fiction', *Frontline*, 23 October.

Tewary, Amarnath (2000), 'Partners in Crime', *Outlook*, 14 February.

Thakur, J. (1989), *V.P. Singh: The Quest for Power*, New Delhi: Warbler Books.

*The Times of India* (1997), 'Should Lawbreakers be Lawmakers', 7 July.

Vishvanathan, S. (1998), 'By Way of a Beginning', in S. Visvanathan and H. Sethi (eds.), *Foul Play: Chronicles of Corruption, 1947–1997*, New Delhi: Banyan Books.

——, 'The Early Years', in Vishvanathan and Sethi (eds.), *Foul Play*.

——, 'Hero of the Public Service', in Visvanathan and Sethi (eds.), *Foul Play*.

——, 'Revisiting the Shah Commission', in Visvanathan and Sethi (eds.), *Foul Play*.

——, 'Inadmissible Evidence', in Visvanathan and Sethi (eds.), *Foul Play*.

Visvanathan, S. and Sethi, H. (1998) (eds.), 'Right Connections: Telecom', *Foul Play: Chronicles of Corruption, 1947–1997*, New Delhi: Banyan Books.

*Vohra Committee Report* (n.d.), 'An Eye-Opening Account of Crime-Politics Nexus and Right to Information Sawant Committees Proposal for a Bill', New Delhi: Lok Shakti Abhiyan.

Wright, T.P. (1978), 'Muslim Mobility in India through Peripheral Occupations: Music, Sports, Cinema, Smuggling', in *Asie du Sud, traditions et changements*, Paris: CNRS.

# Chapter 30

# India and Pakistan: interpreting the divergence of two political trajectories

While relations between India and Pakistan have been the subject of numerous studies, few inquiries have compared their political trajectories. One of them, from Ayesha Jalal, concludes that the two countries are converging (Jalal 1995). For Jalal, India suffers from such centralization of power that its democracy is largely 'formal', while Pakistan is gradually emerging from its authoritarian tradition. Jalal formulated this interpretation at a moment when Pakistan was indeed engaged in a phase of democratization, while India, caught up in ethnic tension, was showing an increasing tendency towards authoritarianism. However, when placed in the context of the last 50 years, this reading no longer stands up to scrutiny.

Instead, what is striking is the divergence of the political trajectories of India and Pakistan over the medium term of the last half-century. India, with the exception of its state of emergency from 1975 to 1977, has managed to uphold the same constitution since 1950 and a parliamentary democracy largely inherited from the British. This stability owes a great deal to the Nehru-Gandhi line that gave three prime ministers to India: Jawaharlal Nehru, from 1947 to 1964; Indira Gandhi, in the post from 1966 to 1977 and then from 1980 to 1984, and Rajiv Gandhi, from 1984 to 1989. Nonetheless, this was in no way a dynasty, as is sometimes claimed, since the Nehru-Gandhis were always subject to universal suffrage and in fact lost power twice through the ballot box (in 1977 and 1989), making India part of the small circle of democratic countries familiar with shifts in power.

For its part, Pakistan has had three constitutions and three military *coups d'état*. In 1958, the putsch of General Ayub Khan put an end to eleven years of constitutional debate, in the course of which the political class had failed to bring about the democratic system of government it had called for. General Yahya Khan, who succeeded him in 1969, set about organizing the elections that finally brought Zulfikar Ali Bhutto to power in 1971. But Bhutto was overthrown in 1977 by a new military *coup d'état* orchestrated by General Zia ul-Haq. Zia ul-Haq remained in power for eleven years before his death in an air accident. The process of democratization that this triggered was marked by the ascension of Benazir Bhutto to the post of Prime Minister. For eleven years, she alternated power with Nawaz Sharif, who was finally overthrown by General Musharraf in 1999.

Yielding to the simplifying charms of culturalism, many commentators have tried to explain these contrasting political developments by stressing a basic incompatibility of Islam and democracy (Ziring 1980: 7), while others, on the Indian side, have striven to discern affinities between Hinduism and democracy (Kothari 1988: 155–6). This chapter will take a different approach in focusing on the genesis of this divergence in the period 1940–50.[1] First it will be necessary to explain why democratic convergence was not possible, although in 1947 both countries were meant to be democratic. On 9 June 1947, a few weeks before independence, Mohammed Ali Jinnah declared during a meeting of his party, the Muslim League, that the constitution of Pakistan would be of a 'democratic type' (McGrath 1998: 42). As for India, Jawaharlal Nehru, who had become Prime Minister in 1946, in the Objectives Resolution that he introduced in the first session of the Constituent Assembly, started from the principle that India would be a republic; that it would be democratic was for him self-evident (*Constituent Assembly Debates* [hereafter *CAD*] 1989: 62). India realized this goal, while Pakistan's efforts have been in vain. To explain the political divergence of the two countries following their independence, this essay proposes to test five hypotheses in subjecting the two countries to a point-by-point comparison: (1) India and Pakistan, though both issued from the same colonial womb, were not, in 1947, heirs to the same political experience. (2) The priority given to national security pushed the question of the nature of the regime to the background in Pakistan, while India was, for a long time, little concerned with external threats. (3) While the arithmetic of ethnic groups acted as a brake on the growth of democracy in Pakistan, it aided the process in India. (4) India and Pakistan have never been equally endowed with respect to political parties. Finally, (5) Indian and Pakistani societies are not structured in the same way, the lack of organization being much more pronounced on the Pakistani side than in India, where caste, for instance, has paradoxically helped aggregate interests.

These five hypotheses call for an analysis that is simultaneously synchronic and diachronic: on the one hand, it is important to identify the key moments of divergence between India and Pakistan (which will lead to a concentration on the 1950s); on the other hand, this point-by-point comparison must be re-situated against the medium-term backdrop of the first three decades of the existence of the two countries, to give the trajectories their historic substance.

## The Geographic Limits of Colonial Parliamentary Democracy

Comparing India and Pakistan might seem a relatively simple undertaking, given their common colonial experience. After all, the two states derive from the same political entity, British India, which had subjected the region to the same political rules for close to two centuries. However, one cannot start from the assumption that the historical variable is controlled by this fact alone: the regions of the British Raj—the name given to the Empire by the Indians—which were to form Pakistan in 1947 had not, in fact, been administered in the same way as those which would constitute India.

From a macro point of view, it is clear that the guiding line of British policy from the nineteenth century onward was dominated by the gradual devolution of power to Indians at the local, and then regional level. The starting point of this process, the 1882 Self-Government Act, allowed a local political arena to take shape by enlarging the scope of competence of municipalities and introducing, at this still limited level, the electoral principle. The provinces were the second administrative level to enjoy a degree of power, starting in 1909. However, the real turning point was just after the First World War, when the reform of 1919 accorded legislative autonomy to the provincial legislative councils and, in particular, the power to remove ministers from office. Finally, the Government of India Act of 1935 established a degree of parliamentary democracy at the provincial level. The British governors, appointed by the Viceroy, kept important ruling prerogatives (which they could moreover extend through recourse to emergency procedures), but much of the essence of ministerial portfolios was now in the hands of Indians working under the authority of a chief minister. These governments were responsible to legislative councils elected by a broader, poll-tax-paying electorate, the electoral body having grown from 2.8 per cent to 14.1 per cent of the population of British India.

The Indian constitution, promulgated on 26 January 1950, was a direct extension of the institutions of the British Raj: 250 of its 380 articles were drawn from the Government Act of 1935. They reproduced the general structure of that document, in reaffirming more broadly the federal principle, and, above all, in the choice of a British-style parliamentary democracy. The constituents thus accorded the same preponderant weight to the government, and especially to the Prime Minister, as in the British cabinet system. Though India did not explicitly inscribe the separation of legislative and executive powers in its constitution, it did create 'a climate of separation of powers' (Morris-Jones 1964: 198).

The British transplant did not similarly take root in Pakistan, for reasons that stem in part from the geography of early colonial parliamentarism. The whole territory of the Raj did not benefit in the same way from the colonial apprenticeship of democracy. The provinces that would later become the principal components of Pakistan were among the least solidly anchored in this tradition. Certainly Bengal and Sindh, two zones conquered early on, were administered by the British much as were those that would make up India after 1947, but this was not the case with the other constituent entities of Pakistan. Punjab, the pivotal province of the country, was the last to be conquered by the British, in 1849 when British troops finally overcame the resistance of Ranjit Singh, a Sikh prince. Conquered only after a struggle, Punjab 'benefited' from special treatment, all the more so as it lay on the edges of Central Asia along a traditional invasion route and in contact with an expansionist Russia. The province was thus more militarized than others, and became a real laboratory for the bureaucracy and in particular for the Indian Civil Service, the elite corps of the colonial public service seen by all observers as the 'steel frame' of the British presence in India. District Magistrates literally reigned over their territories, where they were responsible not only for tax collection but for the administration of justice. The Lawrence brothers, who administered Punjab after its annexation, embodied better than anyone this mixture of paternalism and authoritarianism.

The deficit of political participation in Punjab, which contrasted sharply with the colonial parliamentary democracy prevalent further east within the frontiers of the Raj, was also the case in the other provinces of the northwest involved in the Great Game.[2] These included the North-West Frontier Province (NWFP), an administrative entity created out of whole cloth by the British in 1901 to organize the defence of the Raj against possible attacks from Central Asia. This zone formed the security perimeter of the Empire in its efforts to contain the Russian southward thrust. Strategic considerations thus led the British to exclude the region from the fledgling democratic practices applied elsewhere in order to concentrate better their authority and even to militarize the zone—which was not without impact on the local society.

Farther south, the British had created the province of Baluchistan during the Second Afghan War (1878-80), and in this region electoral practices were confined to the municipality of Quetta. (Baluchistan did not elect its provincial assembly by universal suffrage until 1972.) In addition, Baluchistan contained numerous princely states, which became, as in the rest of colonial India, curators of the aristocratic ethos.

The weight of militarism in Punjab and the NWFP is not explained solely by the deployment of troops for security reasons, but also by the fact that these two regions soon became sources of recruitment for the army. The British had classed the Punjabis—in particular the Muslim Jats—and the Pashtun tribes among the 'martial races' of the Empire. As a result, entire villages embraced military careers. In 1947, Punjabis constituted 77 per cent of the Pakistani army, while Pashtuns made up 19.5 per cent of the troops,[3] whereas they represented, respectively, 25 per cent and 8 per cent of the total population. Naturally, their political culture leant more towards keeping order than towards democracy. The Punjabis were the most powerful ethnic group in the state, and after the creation of Bangladesh in 1971 the most numerous.

## The State and Security: Preconditions of Democracy

### INDIA'S SELF-CONFIDENT, UNINTERRUPTED STATE

In India, the state survived partition almost intact. The administrative machinery functioned: New Delhi, the capital, remained the centre of power; the army and the bureaucracy were hardly affected by the departure of the Muslim military personnel and civil servants who chose Pakistan. As for the Treasury, it was divided in proportion to the respective populations, and India was far larger than Pakistan in demographic terms. This advantage also extended to the continental area of the country.

India drew an assurance from its weight and size that Nehru exploited well on the international stage. He succeeded first in establishing the country as an Asian power, as was evident from the 1947 Asian conference held in Delhi, and also from the Bandoeng meeting in 1955. Then he opted for non-alignment, a strong indication that India was self-confident enough to stand on its own. Indeed, Nehru rejected the alliance system of the early Cold War and, instead, strove to maintain the best possible relations with numerous partners, including the United States, the USSR and China. This policy, linked to a visceral anti-militarism, explains in large part the little interest Nehru accorded to security questions, until the warning shot of the Chinese invasion in 1962.

Yet, even this war did not fundamentally question the previous assumptions: India did not feel that insecure. No political movement or army chief came to think that democracy was putting the nation in jeopardy due to lack of discipline or unresponsiveness to challenge. In fact, the government did react: Nehru decided to make a deliberate effort in military terms, including on the nuclear front, and India gradually played the game of the blocs by 'non-aligning itself' with the Soviet Union, a process that culminated in the 1971 friendship treaty.


## PAKISTAN: THE INSECURE STATE TO BE BUILT

Pakistan, in comparison, saw itself as fragile, despite its two wings, one on each side of India, which gave the country the illusion of encircling its hereditary enemy. The state had virtually to be built from scratch. To be more precise, it had to be constructed on the foundation of provincial administrations that had been suddenly deprived of their decision-making centre, the ex-capital, Delhi, from which they had always taken their lead. Pakistan was a migrant state that the Mohajirs installed in a ghost capital, Karachi, where the newcomers set themselves up within walls deserted by Hindus.

There, Jinnah orchestrated the birth of a new nation to which he wished to give a clear-cut identity. Certainly, his two-nation theory implied that, for him, the people of Pakistan already formed a nation. But he was perceptive enough to realize that this religious unity was superimposed on many ethnolinguistic cleavages. Therefore he wanted to build a Pakistani nation through language too. In his view, Urdu, which only a small minority of Pakistanis, his fellow Mohajirs—Urdu speakers who had migrated from India to Pakistan in 1947—spoke at the time, had to become the idiom of the nation—an over-ambitious objective given, in particular, the linguistic patriotism of the Bengalis.[4] The project was further complicated by the fact that the 'country of the pure' was, from the outset, in a relationship of conflict with its large Indian neighbour.

The very circumstances of Partition locked both countries in a more or less low-intensity war-like situation. Indeed, Kashmir was from the outset a bone of contention, the Pakistanis considering that this province had to be theirs because it harboured a population with a Muslim majority. The notion that partition remained 'unachieved' with Kashmir on the Indian side led to the first India-Pakistan war in 1947–8. Pakistan lost because it was weaker. It looked upon itself as more vulnerable and became security obsessed.

Jinnah's authoritarianism, from the very early days of Pakistan, can be explained in large part by this sentiment. While New Delhi, following the practice of other Commonwealth dominions, named C. Rajagopalachari, a respected personality but with little political authority, to the post of Governor General, in Pakistan, Jinnah himself decided to take on this function and combine it with that of President of the Constituent Assembly, a unique situation in the annals of the British dominions. This concentration of power in the hands of a single man was constantly justified by the weakness of the new state compared with India, particularly in military matters. The troops that Pakistan inherited on partition represented only 36 per cent of the British Indian army, or 140,000 men out of 410,000, which left New Delhi at a considerable advantage (Jalal 1990: 42). The government approved an exceptional financial expenditure to build up the army and modernize its equipment. On average, military expenditures represented more than half the annual state budget from 1947 to 1959. The army quickly acquired considerable influence. Simultaneously, the inability of politicians to give the country a constitution put the viability of Pakistan's parliamentary democracy into question. Ayub Khan, the Commander in Chief of the army from 1951, of Pashtun origin and born in Punjab, was convinced by 1947 that the survival of Pakistan depended on the army. He rose to the position of President following a *coup d'état* in 1958.

## The Arithmetic of Ethnolinguistic Groups

Relations among ethnolinguistic groups exercised very different influences on the political trajectories of India and Pakistan. While India utilized its ethnolinguistic diversity as one basis for political pluralism and reinforced, thereby, its democratic framework, Pakistan suffered from the competition for power between a limited number of such groups among which the less numerous ones were *de facto* exert power in 1947—an unfavourable configuration for democracy.

### THE ANTI-MAJORITY SYNDROME IN PAKISTAN

In Pakistan, the arithmetic of linguistic groups inhibited democratic development. In contrast to India, the country had in 1947 only a small number of ethnolinguistic communities. Bengalis were clearly in the majority, representing 55 per cent of the population in the 1951 census. Punjabis were only in second place with about a quarter of the total population, followed by Sindhis, Pathans, Mohajirs and Baluchis. This ethnic equation led Bengalis to demand the establishment of a democratic system, with which they were already familiar given the early development of colonial parliamentary democracy in Calcutta province. Yet power was in the hands of the Mohajirs who had followed Jinnah to Pakistan, mainly to Karachi, the capital until 1961, and of the Punjabis, who held the army. The mass of the population may have been in the East, but the ruling elites were in the West and they were consequently loath to opt for a system in which one person equalled one vote.

The Constituent Assembly saw many clashes between Bengalis and the Mohajir/Punjabi coalition. The first constitutional project that Liaquat Ali Khan, the Mohajir Prime Minister of Pakistan, submitted to the Assembly in September 1950 sparked immediate protest on the part of Bengali representatives who were worried not only by the elevation of Urdu to the status of national language, but also by their under-representation in the institutions that were being formed: Bengalis would only have held the same number of seats as the other administrative entities of West Pakistan (Punjab, NWFP, Baluchistan, Sindh and Karachi) in the upper house. This logic of parity was even more prejudicial to their interests in that the two assemblies were to enjoy the same legislative capacities.

Faced with Bengali opposition, Liaquat Ali Khan withdrew his proposal in November 1950. But his assassination in 1951, the circumstances of which are still unclear, allowed Ghulam Mohammed to take over the post of Governor General, thus confirming the accession to power of bureaucrats at the expense of politicians, and of Punjabis at the expense of Bengalis and even Mohajirs. Minister of Finance under Liaquat Ali Khan, Ghulam Mohammed had begun his career in the Indian Civil Service and was a Punjab-born Pathan.

From his years as a high-ranking civil servant of the Raj he had retained nostalgia for the British 'steel frame', a widespread sentiment in his region of origin, Punjab. Moreover, Punjabis, whom he represented at the very summit of the state, had everything to lose from the development of institutions based on the law of numbers, given their demographic weakness vis-à-vis the Bengalis. Ghulam Mohammed fired two Bengali Prime Ministers in succession, Nazimud-din and Bogra, and then in 1954 prevented the adoption of a constitution that would have established a real parliamentary system in Pakistan by declaring a state of emergency. This then brought about the election of a second Constituent Assembly in 1955.

Though the text the Assembly drafted included many attributes of parliamentary democracy, it gave the President prerogatives that were incompatible with that type of system. In the middle of the 1950s, Pakistani parliamentary democracy ran aground on the demographic power politics between Bengalis and Punjabis who refused the law of numbers.

## CONVERTING ETHNOLINGUISTIC DIVERSITY
## INTO POLITICAL PLURALISM IN INDIA

Conversely, in India, where ethnolinguistic divisions were especially numerous, they contributed instead to political pluralism and to a decentralization of power. Though Hindus represented 85 per cent of the population (which was less than 10 per cent Muslim), they were crisscrossed by multiple lines of linguistic division. The constitution of 1950 recognized 15 official languages. With the exception of English, these were regional languages to which the local populations were very attached. Language-linked patriotism fed authentic ethnic regionalisms in certain provinces of the Dravidian south, as, for example, in the Tamil land. These movements penetrated the Congress Party and influenced it from within. They managed in this way to contest the all-powerful nature of the central state inherited from the British, and served as a source of support for political pluralism without putting the nation's integrity into question, as illustrated by the decisive episode of the reordering of the States of the Indian Union along linguistic lines.

Within the Constituent Assembly, partisans of such a reorganization had argued sporadically in the years 1946–50 that the administrative borders inherited from the Empire were artificial, since they did not correspond to any linguistic reality.[5] Nehru, prime minister since 1946 and the strong man of the country, was hostile to these claims because he feared that recognition of regionalisms would hinder the process of nation building (Gopal 1979: 262). He was also particularly concerned with keeping a strong state, not just because the British had bequeathed him one and no one lightly reduces one's own power, but also because his brand of socialism required that he have a powerful administration at his disposition. However, the idea of 'linguistic states' gained ground within the local branches of his party, Congress, because regional identities, to which language was often the key, were taking hold throughout India on the rubble of the 'all English' system imposed by the British. On 15 December 1952, Potti Srisamullu, a former disciple of Gandhi, who called for the formation of a province, 'Andhra', to be constituted from the division of Madras Province, died as a result of a hunger strike. His death aroused such emotion that Nehru resigned himself to announcing the formation of Andhra Pradesh, whose frontiers coincided with the extent of the Telugu language. This new entity was to be followed by several other linguistic states. The Prime Minister decreed on 22 December 1953 the creation of a commission charged with setting out 'the broad lines according to which states should be reorganised'.[6] He received the report of the States Reorganisation Commission on 30 September 1955. This text recommended the replacement of the 27 existing states by three Union Territories administered by New Delhi and 16 states, of which only three would be created along linguistic lines. This provoked violent demonstrations, notably in Maharashtra, where Marathi speakers sought to free themselves from the domination of the Gujaratis to whom they found themselves bound, artificially to their eyes, within the Bombay Presidency. The reorganization of the majority of states on a linguistic basis was agreed to in 1956. Maharashtra and Gujarat were created in 1960.

The debate on linguistic states and its outcome reveal the weight locally based politicians had achieved within Congress. For the most part, they had managed to draw support from a regional linguistic identity. Whole regions wound up identifying with political personalities. Linguistic pluralism served as a springboard for political pluralism and democracy in that it forced the central power to negotiate with the provinces and seek compromise—such as that which resulted in the creation of linguistic states. Nehru, who sought to transmit his policies via these regional leaders and in particular the chief ministers, to whom he wrote on average once a fortnight, had to accord them, reluctantly, a margin of manoeuvre. They used it to the point of becoming regional political bosses, spokesmen for authentic ethnocultural communities.

This dynamic took on even greater momentum when parties designed to articulate the interests of linguistic groups developed first on the edge of Congress, and then in opposition to it. The Dravida Munnetra Kazhagam (DMK)—a Dravidian party in Tamil Nadu—was thus joined by a multitude of ethnic parties that, after having been sometimes tempted by separatism (like the DMK itself), decided to play the political game, recognizing that the federal framework allowed them to manage their province themselves. Far from wrapping themselves up in nationalism and rejecting the system, these groups went into politics and fought in elections from the 1950s on. In so doing, they facilitated the representation of groups outside the English-speaking elite in the public sphere. Ethnicity thus showed it could function, in the interests of democracy, at least in its linguistic form; conflicts among religious communities could spill over into violence, as shown by the example of Punjabi Sikhs.

This evolution can be explained first by the splintered nature of the ethnolinguistic groups: none had a majority. Hindi speakers constituted less than 40 per cent of the population in 1951 and did not form a bloc, since the language consisted of several dialects. Because of this, no group could, as in Pakistan, make others fear that it would one day hold absolute power following a democratic vote. Each group could only hope to gain limited access to power through engaging in coalitions, which had endlessly to be negotiated and re-negotiated because they were not stable, but rather shifted in their makeup. Thus Congress gradually resigned itself to allying with Dravidian parties that had split from the DMK. Another difference with Pakistan was that the ethnolinguistic group that enjoyed a demographic advantage was also that which historical circumstances had placed in power: Nehru and Rajendra Prasad (the first President of the Republic) were from the 'Hindi Belt'—a zone that was not in a majority, but the most populated anyway.

## Political Parties: Missing or Key Elements of Democracy

Even if not quite as important as relations between ethnic groups, the very different role played by political parties in India and Pakistan can also explain some of the divergence between the political trajectories of the two countries. A party system came into being very early on in British India owing to the constitutional reforms mentioned earlier. The Indian National Congress, founded in 1885, began gradually to contest elections while at the same time seeing itself as the spearhead of the independence movement. The Muslim League, which would call for the creation of Pakistan under Jinnah's leadership in 1940, was officially founded in 1906 and consistently presented candidates for elections. From the 1930s, an internal faction of Congress, the Hindu Mahasabha of Hindu nationalist obedience, formed a party. On the left-wing of Congress, the Communist Party, created in the early 1920s, chose not to run in elections for ideological reasons, but two other parties with similar programmes did so: the Indian Labour Party, founded in 1937 by Bhim Rao Ambedkar, the first Untouchable leader of national importance, and the Congress Socialist Party, created within the Indian National Congress in 1934. None of these parties could rival Congress, but they did contribute to the organization of the political sphere.

## INDIA'S CONGRESS SYSTEM AND MULTIPARTY SYSTEM

By 1947, Congress had acquired certain attributes of a party of mass appeal (Manor 1990: 29). Its transition in status from a party of notables to a mass party had hitherto been incomplete, given the role that local notables still played, but accelerated under Gandhi. Once he had asserted himself at the head of Congress in 1920, the Mahatma decided to reform its structures. Until then, the movement had been essentially an elite circle with little existence beyond its annual plenary session. Gandhi wanted to anchor Congress in the rural substratum of British India. Each village with five or more Congress members was considered an antenna of the movement. Above that, the party was organized at the canton (*taluk* or *tehsil*) level, and at the district level. Districts were important, since the District Congress Committees designated the Provincial Congress Committees, from which proceeded delegates to the All India Congress Committee, the body that elected the Party President.

Gandhi put these structures at the service of popular mobilizations, which became increasingly powerful in 1920–2 through the Non-Cooperation Movement, in 1930–1 during the Civil Disobedience Movement and in 1942 during the Quit India Movement. Contrary to those that preceded them, these campaigns transcended provincial boundaries. Congress thus took on the airs of a mass party, which was useful in a democratic sense in that it helped it to integrate new citizens into the political process after 1947. The participation rate in the elections of 1951–2, for example, was as high as 46 per cent—ten points higher than in Pakistan in 1997 in the most recent general elections organized in the country.

In 1947, India could thus make its institutions work thanks to a system of parties built around the Congress, something Rajni Kothari was to appropriately call 'the Congress system' (Kothari 1964: 1161–73). All the more so because many

Congress members had acquired a real popularity owing to their involvement in the anti-colonial struggle for which they had made many sacrifices, starting with Nehru, who had spent nine years of his life in prison.

## PAKISTAN'S FAILED PARTY SYSTEM

In the Pakistani case, the political party that embodied the national movement, the Muslim League, was from its origin a defence movement for a minority fearful of the majority rule (a principle on which democracy is built). This movement first began in regions with a Hindu majority, in particular in the United Provinces (today Uttar Pradesh), which had a Muslim elite, heirs to the aristocracy of the Mughal Empire who were gradually being replaced by the rise to power of the Hindu intelligentsia (Robinson 1974). Initially it represented an anti-democratic reaction. The beginnings of democratization had worried this elite since the implementation of the Local Self-Government Act in 1882. Syed Ahmed Khan (1817–98) was the first to be alarmed by this development in his city of Aligarh, where he created a university to train the intellectual elite who later founded the Muslim League (Lelyveld 1978). The announcement by the British of the introduction of Legislative Councils at the provincial level in 1906 led the Aligarh intelligentsia, in conjunction with the aristocratic elite of East Bengal, to demand the Viceroy, Lord Minto, to create a separate electorate for Muslims: another attempt to get around the law of numbers.

This legacy of the colonial era was responsible for the reticence with which the Muslim League, of which Mohammed Ali Jinnah had taken leadership in the 1920s, approached democratic structures after the creation of Pakistan. League leaders were resistant to democracy to the point of deliberately thwarting the activities of political parties, including their own. Liaquat Ali Khan became the head of the Muslim League in 1950, but he did not acknowledge the existence of other parties and did very little for his own. His mistrust of politicians was evident in his support for the Public and Representative Officers Disqualification Act (PRODA) on 26 January 1950. This law permitted the Governor General, provincial governors and even ordinary citizens to bring charges against a minister or other elected official suspected of corruption, nepotism, favouritism or bad management. Politicians prepared to risk Rs. 5,000—the deposit required to launch the process—freely used PRODA against their rivals.

Beyond its mistrust for other parties, the Muslim League had too weak a structure to breathe life into parliamentary democracy. The party had never been as well organized as Congress. It had long been little more than a tiny elite group representing the landed aristocracy and the intelligentsia, who had none of the prestige of the Congress leaders who had done time in British jails: Muslim League leaders had, on the contrary, chosen to collaborate with the colonizers. This microcosm only managed to mobilize the masses in the months preceding Partition. Its first breakthrough came only during the elections of 1946, when it campaigned on the theme of 'Islam in danger'. After independence, Jinnah and Liaquat Ali Khan primarily used the party as a conduit of power. National representatives never opposed the leaders, including when they came under the influence of Ghulam Mohammed (Sayeed 1967: 83). As for local cadres, the centralized decision-making process inspired them less to work in their regions than to throw themselves into factional in-fighting.

The weakness of the Muslim League and the party system in general deprived the governing powers of an essential channel of communication with society which would have been in keeping with the democratic approach they claimed. In spite of their ostensible democratic interests, their priorities actually lay elsewhere in the construction of the state.

## Two Contrasting Political Societies

The notion of 'political society', which we owe to Juan Linz and Alfred Stepan, seems to be more relevant here than that of 'civil society' to describe those institutions that bring together the interests of social groups in the political sphere (Linz and Stepan 1996: 8). In this category Linz and Stepan put, primarily, political parties, which were examined earlier; for my part I would include unions, associations, the press and even the judicial apparatus insofar as it acts as an obstacle to the omnipotence of the executive power. One might object that it is an integral part of the state, but Indian judges, unlike their Pakistani counterparts, managed to occupy a place apart shortly after independence in 1947.

### THE PAKISTANI WEAK POLITICAL SOCIETY

The social structures of India and Pakistan seem at first glance to be equally ill suited to the development of democracy. Castes and tribes—two social formations present in both countries—were ordered, each in their own way, according to an extremely inegalitarian hierarchy; the individual was not recognized as the basic element of society. Though this social configuration is not, in principle, crippling in and of itself, in Pakistan it weighed in favour of maintaining authoritarian structures, given the coincidence of its internal divisions with other class-based divisions. This superimposing of divisions shored up a 'feudal' socioeconomic structure, to use the standard Pakistani phrase. This 'feudalism'—which has little in common with the European model—rests on the absolute power of absentee landowners who enjoy a superior status similar to the chief of a clan or tribe. While the system of the Sardars and the Khans in Baluchistan and the Pathan region are varieties of this new feudalism, its archetype is in Sindh, where the *wadera* play a role comparable to Latin American *latifundia* owners. Punjab underwent a Green Revolution in the 1960s, which allowed in some places the rise of a middle-ranking peasantry outside of the traditional structures. But the domination that landowners, business circles and the military caste continued to exercise in the Punjabi countryside after independence prevented the development of a real peasant movement, just as it hampered the growth of unions. More generally, the anti-communist policy of the 1950s disorganized the workers' movement in a lasting and even irreparable way. Class solidarity was further prevented by the vertical nature of the caste and tribe system that prevailed in Punjabi villages and elsewhere.

In the cities, the middle classes produced an intelligentsia open to the outside world, owing to studies abroad or contacts with the diaspora. This elite became involved in associations, to the point where it became synonymous with 'civil society'. It also displayed a strong critical spirit, which rapidly found an echo in the press. Though the Urdu press tended to be conservative and conformist in nature, English-language newspapers considered it a point of honour to denounce the corruption and authoritarianism of the governing class. This intellectual pole did not, however, find any corresponding partners within political parties and the judicial apparatus.

The submission of judges to the executive power became evident in the 1950s. They did not react to the provocation of the dissolution of the Constituent Assembly in 1954. One of the few to object was the President of the Assembly, Tamizuddin Khan, who brought his case before the High Court of Sindh. The tribunal unanimously decided in his favour, considering that the Assembly was a sovereign institution, but the government appealed the decision before the Supreme Court, which confirmed the actions of the Governor General on 21 March 1955. The Chief Justice of the Supreme Court, Munir, a Punjabi named by the Governor General a few months previously, shared his views concerning the Bengali threat. He justified the state of emergency in the name of a new doctrine, the 'civil law of necessity' (Newberg 1995: 66–7). The same law would be invoked during each new military *coup d'état*. In 1977, when the wife of Zulfikar Ali Bhutto contested the imprisonment of her husband by General Zia, the Supreme Court dismissed her case using the same doctrine, rebaptized 'state necessity' for the occasion. The judges also confirmed Zia in his capacity as administrator in charge of martial law, with the power to make legislation and amend the constitution.

## INDIA'S RULE OF LAW AND
## PARADOXICAL CASTE-BASED CIVIL SOCIETY

In India, judges have always acted more independently, despite the pressures exerted by the executive power, to such a degree that they can be seen as the guardians of democracy. This is largely because they could rely on the status granted them by the Constituent Assembly, which is sometimes overlooked in the analysis of Indian democracy. The many lawyers in Congress during the colonial era were naturally present at the Constituent Assembly, which explains in part the great interest of this body for the judicial system.[7] The structure finally enshrined in the constitution was headed by a Supreme Court, inspired by the American model, supported by the High Courts (tribunals treating disputes at the state level). Under the constitution, the President of the Republic names the members of the Supreme Court after consultation with the other existing Supreme Court judges and those on the High Courts. This principle is intended to shelter them from political pressure, as is the fact that judges cannot be removed from the court, except by Parliament in case of wrongdoing or incapacity, following a very complex impeachment procedure.

The judiciary was required very early on to oppose the executive branch, whose authority was restricted as a result. This was, for example, the case in the 1950s, when Nehru, in the opinion of the Supreme Court, seemed to infringe property rights in his land redistribution policy. Certain aspects of agricultural reform were not, as a result, implemented. An even more serious conflict erupted at the beginning of the 1970s when the Supreme Court condemned Indira Gandhi for her use of sound equipment and vehicles belonging to the state during her 1971 election campaign—an offence that Pakistani judges would certainly never have dared pursue, but which obliged Indira Gandhi to choose between resigning her post as member of parliament, and thus as Prime Minister, or confronting the legal branch. She chose the latter path, declaring a state of emergency in 1975. The state of law was suspended for 18 months from 1975 to 1977. But the damage was repaired in 1977 when Indira Gandhi, condemned by voters, lost power. The Supreme Court launched further attacks on politicians in the 1980s and especially the 1990s, engaging in a kind of 'judicial activism', which destabilized several ministers. In 1996, to take an example, seven ministers were forced to resign following their conviction on corruption charges. The Supreme Court's actions— whose efficacy should not be exaggerated, for it has served purely as a safeguard— have always had the backing of the press which has long been remarkable for the freedom it exercizes, in both English and the vernacular languages. The fourth estate in India acts as an effective opposition.

The judiciary and the press are only two of the more obvious pillars of Indian political society, which is organized in such a way that it prevents the concentration of all the power in the hands of the same establishment people. The peasant classes have formed a number of associations since the colonial era—the All India Kisan Sabha was founded in 1936—and there are also unions—the first of which, the All India Trade Union Congress, was founded in 1920. However, these were inventions of Congress, which sought ties to the countryside and to workers. Moreover, the large trade unions settled for organizing only the working class elite and employees, who were easier to incorporate. Other workers began to organize in unions in the 1980s but their movements, more violent than the institutional syndicates, were often broken up by employers' militias with the state's blessing.

The peasant movements underwent significant transformation in the 1960s. They had initially represented middle-ranking peasants who owned a small plot of land and sold a part of their output. These were the first beneficiaries of the Green Revolution, which had been organized to obtain from the state lower agricultural costs and revalued agricultural commodity prices. These movements were based on caste structures. In the north, the principal movement of this type, the Bharatiya Kisan Union (BKU), which won several showdowns with the government over electricity costs, wheat and sugar cane prices, arose out of the Jat caste. The fact that caste could serve as the basis of a movement like the BKU demonstrates the role it could play in enlarging the social foundations of Indian democracy.

Changes in the caste system have strengthened democracy. When the British undertook a census and classification of the castes, associations were formed to improve or defend the ranking of various castes in the administration's double-entry table. They then acted as mutual aid societies, setting up schools and cooperatives and demanding new advantages from the state. Colonial parliamentary democracy further favoured a politicization of castes because it was not constructed on an individualist basis, but on concepts of representation inherited from the Old Whigs, who gave communities, including castes in the Indian context, pride of place (Beer 1957: 613–50). The granting of seat quotas and separate electorates to these groups led the interested parties, and those who were denied these privileges, to organize in order to assert their rights better. The reform of 1935 accorded seats to the Untouchables who were grouped euphemistically under the name 'Scheduled Castes' (SC). Immediately, in each province, associations of Untouchable castes excluded from the quotas mobilized to claim their due, thereby becoming politically involved. After independence the Scheduled Castes continued to benefit from quotas, not only in the elected assemblies and the administration, but also in the educational system.

Just as the granting of quotas to the Untouchables was one of the driving factors behind the formation of a front grouping all the Scheduled Castes, this tendency to group together was accentuated after the invention of a new administrative category following independence, the Other Backward Classes (OBCs). This category was inscribed in the constitution of 1950 to designate social groups who should benefit from particular state aid. In several southern Indian states, quotas in favour of the OBC were immediately introduced and/or extended in local administrations and certain schools and universities. This practice spread throughout India as soon as the middle-ranking peasant classes, who were often in the avant-garde of the OBC, benefited from a certain increased prosperity following the Green Revolution of the 1960s. They understood by then the advantage their numbers gave them and tended to group together behind political parties such as the Socialist Party and the Bharatiya Kranti Dal of Charan Singh, founded in 1969, which would become the Bharatiya Lok Dal in 1974. At the end of the 1970s, these formations took a share of power as part of the Janata Party, with which they had merged in 1977. A first step had been taken to broaden the system's social foundation.

The impact caste transformations had on Indian political society—principally the emergence of caste fronts like the SC and the OBC—certainly reinforced democracy in that country. At any rate, they contributed to the democratization process. Indian democracy was long conservative given the role played by the Congress Party, which up until the 1970s tried to choose its candidates from the upper caste elite (urban as well as rural). In the villages the dominant castes rarely voted as a bloc, owing to factional conflicts, but a faction head could draw on a comfortable reservoir of votes and wielded solid influence through his tenant farmers, his day labourers or his debtors. This clientelism was further strengthened by the splintered nature of the low castes, each of which linked itself to a different higher caste or 'boss'. It began to weaken once the lower castes became conscious of the benefits to be gained by greater horizontal solidarity, as clearly seen in the rise to prominence of the OBC, illustrated on a national scale by the victory of the Janata Party in 1977.

Far from depending on a hypothetical cultural determinism, the multi-factorial interpretation of the divergence of the political trajectories of India and Pakistan that was proposed follows two temporalities. The first, which is purely political, allows us to apprehend the failure of the democratic regime in Pakistan and the entrenchment of parliamentary democracy in India in the ten years that followed independence in 1947 on the basis of four factors: the inheritance of colonial parliamentary democracy, applied differently in different regions; the inhibiting or multiplying effect of ethnic pluralism; the political culture and breadth of the Congress and the Muslim League; and, finally, the existence of a state machinery on which to build democracy: present in India and absent in Pakistan, which led to priority being given in Pakistan to its construction and to national defence, an orientation that made the army the country's key institution. Though in India the army remained apolitical, in Pakistan it took on a preponderant role, including during the phases of civilian rule. This hypothesis explains in large part the country's inability to democratize itself, as witnessed by the political destiny of Z.A. Bhutto in the 1970s.

The impact of social factors on the political system in the two countries has also been underlined in a less narrow chronological framework. The mediocre structure of political society in Pakistan—from the weaknesses of the judiciary to the predominance of statutory hierarchies—contrasts with its vitality in India, though only really confirmed by the emergence of the Other Backward Classes. The democratization of the political game and of society took a significant step in 1977 with the victory of the Janata Party, which this chapter will take as a concluding point—aware that it is also the year when the first attempt to redemocratize Pakistan failed with Zia's *coup d'état*.

Though this chapter concentrated on the early years (or decades) of existence of these two countries, the relevance of such a historical assessment for understanding today's situation and even for predicting the future is obvious. Such an extrapolation is implicit in the nature of the trajectory-focused approach that has been adopted in this chapter. The political trajectory of 'new countries' like the

Indian Union and Pakistan derives from structural data, such as the political culture inherited from the colonial experiment or the arithmetic of ethnic groups. The course of their political life is not entirely conditioned by these data—to support such views would lead to cultural and historical determinism and would ultimately ignore the impact of exterior influences. However, no country can emancipate itself from its previous itinerary and this very past indicates some direction. After 50 years, Pakistan is still dominated by the Punjabi ethos that penetrates its praetorian state. It still feels vulnerable vis-à-vis India—even more since the conquest of Kabul by friends of New Delhi in 2001. Its party system is still underdeveloped and failed to make democracy work from 1988 to 1999. Last but not least, Pakistani society is still affected by the conservative influence of dominant groups such as the feudal lords, the business families and the Islamist groups.

In contrast, India has built a democratic tradition upon the colonial parliamentarian one. It does not suffer from any real vulnerability complex—including vis-à-vis China, especially since its 1998 nuclear test. Its ethnolinguistic diversity is largely integrated in the institutional process, including in Punjab after the defusing of Sikh separatism (the only two remaining exceptions are Kashmir and Assam). The party system is deep-rooted and rather stable despite the development of new regional parties. Finally, political society is becoming stronger and stronger, not so much because of the assertiveness of the judiciary and the press, but rather because of the ever-increasing politicization of the lower castes. In both cases, India and Pakistan, the parameters that I have identified in the 1950s are still valid for analysing their diverging political trajectories today.

There is a very important caveat, however, so far as India is concerned: will its democracy survive the institutionalization of Hindu nationalism? After four years in office at the Centre, the Bharatiya Janata Party has shown its true colours in 2002 when turning its back to its previously moderate attitude. It has engineered a state-sponsored anti-Muslim pogrom in Gujarat, one of the states it is ruling. Why? Most probably because its local leaders thought it was the best means to polarize the electorate along communal lines of cleavages and retain power by consolidating its Hindu majority vote bank. Such a strategy has come as a confirmation that the BJP's ethnic brand of nationalism was incompatible with democracy (Jaffrelot 2000: 353–78). Will India become aware of the threat it poses to its democratic system before it is too late?

## Notes

1. Ian Talbot has adopted a similar framework, covering pre- and post-independence issues, in a stimulating book: Talbot 2000.
2. The 'Great Game' is an expression designating the competition between Russia and Great Britain in Central Asia.

3. Today, the vast majority of military personnel still come from three districts within Punjab (Rawalpindi, Jhelum and Campbellpur) and two districts of the NWFP (Kohat and Mardan). See Cohen 1998: 44.
4. In 1951 the Mohajirs were about seven million out of a total population of 76.5 million Pakistanis. See Callard 1975: 156.
5. Such was, for example, the case of N.G. Ranga. *Constituent Assembly Debates* 1989: 351, debate of 9 November 1948.
6. Gopal 1979: 373. However, he let his worries be known to the chief ministers. On this see the letter of 24 December 1954 in Parthasarathi 1988: 116. See also the letters of 20 May 1955: 181 and 2 August 1959: 224.
7. Their efforts to establish an independent justice system were supported by the Prime Minister. Nehru proclaimed, as early as 1948, to a euphoric Assembly, 'I can say without hesitation that, as far as the government is concerned, the separation of judicial and executive functions is entirely agreed (applause). I can add that the sooner the better' ('Debate of 6 November 1948', *Constituent Assembly Debates*, 1989: 589).

# References

Beer, Samuel H. (1957), 'The Representation of Interests in British Government: Historical Background', *American Political Science Review*, Vol. 51, No. 3.

Callard, K. (1975), *Pakistan: A Political Study*, London: Allen & Unwin.

Cohen, S. (1998), *The Pakistan Army*, Karachi: Oxford University Press.

*Constituent Assembly Debates* (1989), Vol. 5, New Delhi: Lok Sabha Secretariat.

———, Debate of 9 November, 1948, Vol. 7 and Debate of 6 November 1948, Vol. 7, Book 2.

Gopal, S. (1979), *Jawaharlal Nehru: A Biography, Vol. 2 (1947-1956)*, London: Jonathan Cape.

Jaffrelot, C. (2000), 'Hindu Nationalism and Democracy', in F. Frankel, Z. Hasan, R. Bhargava and B. Arora (eds.), *Transforming India: Social and Political Dynamics of Democracy*, Delhi: Oxford University Press.

Jalal, A. (1990), *The State of Martial Rule: The Origins of Pakistan's Political Economy of Defence*, Cambridge: Cambridge University Press.

——— (1995), *Democracy and Authoritarianism in South Asia*, Cambridge: Cambridge University Press.

Kothari, R. (1964), 'The Congress "System" in India', *Asian Survey*, December.

——— (1988), *The State against Democracy*, Delhi: Ajanta.

Lelyveld, D. (1978), *Aligarh's First Generation: Muslim Solidarity in British India*, Princeton: Princeton University Press.

Linz, J. and Stepan, A. (1996), *Problems of Democratic Transition and Consolidation*, Baltimore: The Johns Hopkins University Press.

Manor, J. (1990), 'How and Why Liberal Representative Politics Emerged in India', *Political Studies*, Vol. 28.

McGrath, A. (1998), *The Destruction of Pakistan's Democracy*, Karachi: Oxford University Press.

Morris-Jones, W.H. (1964), *The Government and Politics of India*, London: Hutchinson.

Newberg, P.R. (1995), *Judging the State: Courts and Constitutional Politics in Pakistan*, Cambridge: Cambridge University Press.

Parthasarathi, G. (1988) (ed.), Letters of 24 December 1954, 20 May 1955 and 2 August 1959 in *Jawaharlal Nehru: Letters to Chief Ministers*, Vol. 4 (*1951-1957*), Delhi: Oxford University Press.

Robinson, F. (1974), *Separatism among Indian Muslims*, Cambridge: Cambridge University Press.

Sayeed, Khalid B. (1967), *The Political System of Pakistan*, Boston: Houghton Mifflin.

Talbot, Ian (2000), *Indian and Pakistan: Inventing the Nation*, London: Arnold.

Ziring, L. (1980), *Pakistan: The Enigma of Political Development*, Boulder: Westview Press.

# VI

---

## India and the World

# Chapter 31

# The cardinal points of Indian foreign policy

The oldest Indian text on the art of governing, the *Dharmashastra*, is attributed to Kautilya, considered the Indian Machiavelli. In it, Kautilya advises the Prince to become allies with the neighbours of India's closest neighbours so that he may manipulate alliances, independently of any cultural or social affinity. While the *Dharmashastra* suggests that there is a tradition of cynical, realpolitik political thought in India, there is a countervailing tradition that eschews direct intervention in foreign nations in favour of the 'soft power' of ideas. In this tradition, India has not valued power in itself. It has never waged war outside of its 'natural' borders, formed by the Himalayan Arc and the Indian Ocean. Indeed, it seems that throughout its history, India has paid scant attention to events beyond this perimeter. At the same time, India has long believed that it carried a message for all of humanity, one it propagated in Southeast Asia from time to time, though never through violent means.[1]

The notion that India could conquer its aggressors—and beyond them, the world—through the sheer force of its ideas re-emerged in full force during the British colonial era. During the 1893 Parliament of World Religions in Chicago, the reformer Vivekananda presented India as a land of spirituality, superior to an ailing West drowning in materialism. Some fifteen years later, Gandhi contrasted the East and West in the same way in *Hind Swaraj*, as part of his effort to bring about a change of heart in the British through non-violent means, and in doing so to spread an ethos rooted in Hindu civilization.

Since 1947 India's relationship with the rest of the world appears to have been dictated both by a keen and at times Machiavellian sense of strategy and an expansionist but non-coercive universalism. However, this framework for understanding Indian foreign policy must be combined with another—the regional and the global, between which India's foreign policy priorities have shifted intermittently. India's foreign policy is therefore best understood as a set of strategies shifting between positions along two axes: realism/idealism and the regional/the global.

## Nehru's 'Practical Idealism', or the Pursuit of Nationalism by Other Means

### INDIA IN THE ERA OF NON-ALIGNMENT

Following its independence in 1947, India began playing the diplomatic score composed by Gandhi. Nehru's foreign policy motto was, quite naturally, 'non-alignment'. The word itself brought to mind Gandhi's expression of 'non-violence' and the philosophy behind it as well. For Nehru, taking sides and choosing one of the two blocs formed in 1945 would be tantamount to endorsing a conflictual approach to international relations, which he rejected. As a loyal follower of Gandhi, he aspired for peace and general disarmament.

Nehru was also repelled by militarism because of the way it regimented men. His mistrust of the Japanese after World War II stemmed in part from this distaste. Like Gandhi's non-violence, however, non-alignment is not synonymous with withdrawal or passivity; indeed it requires commitment and courage. Non-alignment is neither neutralism nor isolationism, but rather a proactive approach described initially by Nehru as stemming from five principles, the *Panchsheel*,[2] which he introduced during negotiations for a treaty on trade in Tibet signed by India and China in 1954.

Nehru's main foreign policy goal was to create a coalition of states that could promote this principle to the rest of the world. In a way, non-alignment was the latest ideological manifestation of India's expansionist universalism. India focused on exporting non-alignment to Asian countries that had followed and in some cases imitated India's fight against colonialism. Nehru began reaching out to these states even before India officially gained independence from British rule on 5 August 1947. Indeed in March 1947, he organized an Asian Relations Conference in New Delhi, where he delivered a stirring speech in which he presented India as a guide for an Asia destined to lead the world first to peace and eventually to enlightenment. India's sense of authority and leadership stemmed from the pioneering role it played in the general trend toward decolonization. Nehru believed India had a special responsibility as the first country to free itself from colonial rule. It was with this sense of responsibility in mind that he organized a conference among Asian states in 1949 in order to put pressure on the Netherlands to grant Indonesia its independence.

The Bandung Conference of 1955 marked a decisive step in India's efforts to rally Asian and African states behind a project to promote peace and freedom. Twenty-nine countries attended the conference, most of which were emerging from a long period of colonization. The Non-Aligned Movement began to take form the following year, in the wake of the Bandung Conference and following an encounter between Nehru, Tito, and Nasser in Brioni. The movement's first summit was held in Belgrade in 1961, during a period of growing tension between the East and the West that was marked by the breakdown of Cuban-American relations, the collapse of the Four Power summit meeting in Paris, and resumption of thermonuclear testing by the USSR. The summit also took place at a time when decolonization was growing increasingly violent, both in Algeria and sub-Saharan Africa, for example with the Congo crisis and assassination of Patrice Lumumba.In India, 1961 was marked by the failure of negotiations between New Delhi and Lisbon over Goa and the armed liberation of the Portuguese enclave. This event marked the end of India's battle for independence. In this context, the non-aligned countries strove to promote peaceful conflict resolution through the UN, where they represented a powerful pressure group. Their strength lay in a sort of Afro-Asian solidarity, which was defended by Nehru in the name of anti-colonial struggle and as a tribute to Gandhi, whose efforts in South Africa remained vivid in the minds of Indians.

## UNIVERSALISM'S NATIONALIST DIVIDENDS

Nehru's foreign policy was more than the promotion of pacifism and anticolonialism; it was also a form of realpolitik. After the Bandung Conference, he described the participants' approach to international relations as a form of 'practical idealism',[3] an expression that most certainly applies to India more than any other country. Nehru argued for a foreign policy that would balance idealism and realism: 'If [a policy] is not idealistic, it becomes one of sheer opportunism; if it is not realistic, then it is likely to be adventurist and wholly ineffective.'[4] Nehru's statement suggests that nothing can be accomplished, even in the realm of ideas, if it is not implemented with a degree of realism. The statement also implies, albeit in a subtle manner, that it is in India's national interest to promote the ideals of non-alignment. Nehru hinted at this strategy when he wrote, 'non-alignment is a policy that is nationally profitable for any country'.[5] It was indeed above all the best way to consolidate national independence. From Nehru's point of view, allies of the USSR and the United States relinquished part of their sovereignty by joining coalitions that imposed various constraints on them, such as the hosting of military bases and strategic or diplomatic coordination. India, on the other hand, chose to identify with a group of countries united by their desire to remain independent—a stance that reinforced their national sovereignty.

Moreover, the group saw itself as a champion of lofty values, lending Nehru a certain moral authority as the group's spokesman. Thus India's voice was one that mattered; it was considered credible when it offered to serve as mediator before the Korean War in 1950 or when it presented its view on Indo-China at the 1954 Geneva Conference. Because of his independence and prestige, Nehru was seen as a valuable partner by the major world leaders with whom he met on a regular basis.

One can see in this a continuation by other means of a nationalist quest that began with the independence movement. In this respect, Nehru is a true disciple of Gandhi. Gandhi was aware of his country's limits in his quest to rid India of the British and used non-violence because he believed it was the most effective weapon available. Non-violence proved to be a powerful weapon, allowing Gandhi to mobilize huge crowds and eventually to guilt a colonizer into leaving. In the same manner, Nehru, the nationalist movement's heir, was realistic in his quest to affirm

India's place in the world. Although he was proud of his country's great civilization, he knew that it lacked military and economic power. Thus Nehru opted for an alternative path, which, like Gandhi's, proved to be highly effective. India's moral prestige gave it a position on the radar of international diplomacy that may seem disproportionate to its economic and military clout at the time. In this sense, India's 'moralpolitik' was a form of realpolitik.

## Back to Reality—and the Regional Scale—After Nehru?

### 1962 AS A TURNING POINT

The debacle of the India-China war of 1962 signalled the death of Nehru's idealism. Nehru always had mixed feelings about China. Whereas he had little respect for Japan, viewing it as a pale copy of its Chinese and Korean neighbours, he was fascinated by China and its ancient civilization that seemed to him so much like India's. At the same time, Nehru so feared China that his many friendly gestures towards the Chinese can be interpreted as a tactic to defuse Chinese hostility, which seemed more threatening before its entry into the UN Security Council in 1971. Nehru may have initially pursued this strategy as a way to 'civilize' India's large neighbour, but the tactic backfired. Nehru recognized this in 1962, and began to question a policy that began to appear more utopian than idealistic given the military weakness it implied. In 1963, Nehru began modernizing the Indian army, increasing the defence budget from less than 2 per cent of GDP to 4.5 per cent in 1963–4 and 3.8 per cent in 1964–5. Yet there was no real shift in India's policy of non-alignment until Nehru's death in 1964.

### NON-ALIGNED WITH THE USSR?

Indira Gandhi brought India one step further along the path to realism during the 1971 war between India and Pakistan over the creation of Bangladesh. Gandhi concluded during this period that India's strategy of non-alignment had resulted in a sort of weak isolation. New Delhi realized that Pakistan's network of alliances with the United States and China gave it a strategic advantage. Thus Indira Gandhi decided to sign a Treaty of Friendship with the USSR on 9 August 1971, just a few months before attacking Pakistan in December. When Washington and Beijing responded mildly to the Indian offensive, she attributed their passivity to the treaty with the USSR.

The Non-aligned Movement also declined in importance in the 1970s because of the growing strength of the oil-producing countries following the oil and energy crises of 1973 and 1978.

## THE 'INDIRA DOCTRINE'

The 'Indira doctrine' was characterized above all by a withdrawal of sorts from the global stage and a renewed focus on the South Asian region. The early years of Indira Gandhi's leadership were marked by two wars (in 1965, shortly before she took office, and in 1971) that pitted India against its regional rival, Pakistan. In this context, it was only natural for her to turn her attention towards the regional sphere.[6] Moreover, Gandhi was concerned by the fact that the major world powers were intensifying their presence in South Asia. For example, the United States established a naval base on Diego Garcia island, a British territory in the middle of the Indian ocean. This superpower encroachment constituted a threat to her plans to strengthen India's role as regional power and reinforced her focus on the South Asian region.

Nehru viewed Asia as a regional base that India could depend on for support. For his daughter, South Asia constituted India's sphere of influence, the only arena where the country's size gave it a natural advantage. But asymmetry also had its drawbacks, since India's smaller neighbours were naturally tempted to band together or even to seek ties with more distant and powerful allies in order to act as a counterweight. India's neighbours had all the more reason to be wary of its ambitions after it annexed the tiny Himalayan kingdom of Sikkim in 1974, to the chagrin of China, which shared a border with this territory.

## THE 'RAJIV DOCTRINE'

Rajiv Gandhi succeeded his mother in 1984, and his foreign policy was a direct continuation of her own. The Indo-Sri Lanka agreement he signed with Jayawardene, which outlined a plan to end the conflict between the Tamils and the Sinhalese, stipulated that the two parties would take all necessary steps to ensure that their territory is not used for 'activities prejudicial to the unity, integrity and security of the other party'. The clause was designed to prevent Colombo from allowing the US to use the much-coveted deep-sea port of Trincomalee and was rapidly denounced by the Sri Lankan opposition as a shameful relinquishment of sovereignty. More generally, the agreement reflected India's ambition to become the regional policeman. Indeed, it provided for the dispatch of an Indian Peace Keeping Force (IPKF) to facilitate the demilitarization of the island's northern and eastern portions, then in the hands of the Liberation Tigers of Tamil Eelam (LTTE). This mission proved to be a resounding failure. India lost more than a thousand men in two years and was forced to withdraw, without having contributed to a resolution of the conflict. Moreover, Rajiv Gandhi was assassinated in 1991 by an LTTE militant in retaliation for his interference through the IPKF.

In 1988, the 'Rajiv doctrine' also took the form of military intervention in the Maldives to save the authorities from a coup organized by a handful of mercenaries. Once again, a major strategic issue was at stake; India did not want the Gan naval base, abandoned since the British retreat of 1976, to fall into unfriendly hands.

## THE JANATA EPISODES,[7] OR THE GOOD NEIGHBOUR POLICY

Indira and Rajiv Gandhi placed the region at the heart of their international strategy by acting as the region's policeman. Opponents of the Congress maintained the same regional priority but adopted a more conciliatory and constructive attitude towards India's neighbours.

In 1977, the first opposition party victory in India's history brought to power the Janata Party, which was determined to improve relations with India's neighbours. The party's efforts were successful in the case of Bangladesh, with whom it signed an agreement on the operation of Farakka Barrage. The dam had been constructed despite heavy criticism from Dhaka in order to flush out the silt at the Calcutta port by diverting a branch of the Ganges River that originally ran through Bangladesh.

The Congress' second electoral defeat in 1989 brought the Janata Dal to power.[8] Following the Janata Party's example, Janata Dal placed South Asia at the heart of a 'good neighbour' policy. I.K. Gujral was the central figure of the policy, acting first as foreign minister then as Prime Minister. Gujral negotiated a treaty with Bangladesh that allowed for the sharing of the Ganges and Brahmaputra Rivers, organized the first visit of Chinese president Jiang Zemin to India in November 1996, and renewed dialogue with Pakistan during the South Asian Association for Regional Cooperation (SAARC) summit in the Maldives. The strategy also led to the creation of a new regional economic cooperation body called Bangladesh-India-Sri Lanka-Thailand Economic Cooperation (BISTEC).

From Indira Gandhi to I.K. Gujral, India's foreign policy tended to concentrate on the regional level, shifting from a rather aggressive stance when the Congress Party was in power, to a more conciliatory approach when it was replaced by the opposition. This contrast should be nuanced, however, as it was Rajiv Gandhi who went to Islamabad and Beijing to restart talks with Pakistan and China. His leadership was nonetheless tainted by the Sri Lankan affair, which came to represent the failure of his regional strategy.

## Return to the Global: India in Search of Power

A new era began in the late 1990s that raised New Delhi's ambitions from the regional level to the global one. India understood—and probably knew all along—

that it would have a very hard time convincing its neighbours to recognize it as a regional power. Despite its weight in the region, SAARC was not advancing, in part because of the latent (and sometimes open) conflict between India and Pakistan. Furthermore, India could seek a larger role on the international scene because of the financial and military means it now had at its disposal.

## NUCLEAR NATIONALISM

The 1998 elections represented a turning point in Indian politics. First of all, they brought to power people that, unlike Desai and Gujral, had never been members of the Congress Party. Moreover, these people preached a radically different ideology that can be qualified as Hindu nationalism. Their movement, which emerged in the 1920s as a reaction to the 'Muslim threat' and the Gandhi method, rejects the principle of non-violence. It sees power as being measured not in terms of influence but of strength, and considers any compromise as a sign of weakness. Gandhi's assassin was recruited from this milieu precisely because he believed his act would rid India of an internal enemy. While Hindu nationalists targeted Nehru because of his idealism in the domain of foreign policy, they lauded Indira Gandhi for her determination during the 1971 war. Justifications for the use of force became even more prominent in Hindu nationalist discourse during this period, as they saw India as being threatened by both Pakistan and the 'fifth column' formed by Indian Muslims—and by China. This worldview developed into an all-out 'encirclement complex' when Beijing and Islamabad formed an alliance that led to the transfer of nuclear technology from the former to the latter in the 1980s-90s.

In 1998, the election manifesto of the Bharatiya Janata Party promised to pursue a new form of power politics in order to increase India's influence in world affairs. Their ambitions included winning a permanent seat on the UN Security Council and the addition of nuclear weapons to the Indian arsenal, as well as the accelerated development of the Agni ballistic missile, whose range and precision the BJP wanted to increase. The government of Atal Behari Vajpayee, one of the BJP's seniormost leaders in power until 2004, thus proceeded with five nuclear tests on 11 and 13 May 1998, less than three months after he took office. In his statement about the nuclear tests, Vajpayee argued that they were an important step of India's progression 'towards a new millennium [in which] India will take its rightful place in the international community'.

## POWER FOR WHAT PURPOSE?

In addition to becoming a nuclear power, India has gradually acquired the financial means to carry out its new ambitions thanks to the country's unprecedented economic growth. It spent 23.933 billion dollars on defence in 2007, compared with 10.740 billion in 1992, a 'lean' year during which spending nevertheless represented the same proportion of Indian GDP, 2.8 per cent. India purchased, for example, a Falcon AWACS aircraft under American licence from Israel for one billion dollars, and an aircraft carrier currently undergoing repairs from Russia. It is also completing its already extensive panoply of ballistic missiles, the latest of which, the Agni-3, has a range of 3,000 km.

Why is India accumulating so much military might? To date, no official document or authorized speech has spelled out the strategic vision of an emerging India. But an examination of its foreign policy in recent years leads to the hypothesis that the country is seeking influence beyond South Asia, along a meta-regional arc stretching from the Persian Gulf to Southeast Asia and including the Indian Ocean to the south and Central Asia to the north.

New Delhi is working to increase its influence in the Gulf for obvious energy-related reasons, since the bulk of its oil and gas supply comes from the Middle East. The country's preoccupation with energy security explains in part why it is so careful to maintain its long-standing friendly ties with Iran. New Delhi has no desire to see Tehran acquire a nuclear weapon. In fact it voted twice against Iran at the International Atomic Energy Agency in the 2000s, probably responding to pressure from the United States. However, it is clear that India wants to maintain good relations with a country that, in addition to its vast energy resources, is an important ally against Pakistan.

In the Indian Ocean, India clearly aims to play the role of policeman, in keeping with an updated version of the 'Indira doctrine'. The Navy, whose budget has traditionally been the smallest among India's military branches, has seen its share of the defence budget grow since the late 1990s. This budget increase is intended in part to help secure India's transportation routes for hydrocarbons.

Central Asia is more difficult to penetrate under the vigilant eyes of China, Russia and even Pakistan. Still, India has managed to shore up its presence in Afghanistan, where it has opened several consulates and uses Afghan-Pakistani antagonism to its advantage, and in Tajikistan, where it has established a military base with two MiG-29 squadrons. India was also awarded observer status from the Shanghai Cooperation Organization in 2005 and played a significant role during the Moscow summit in June 2009.

India's prospects seem more promising in Southeast Asia. The 'Look East policy' initiated in the early 1990s by Prime Minister Narasimha Rao finally allowed India to become a 'full dialogue partner' of the Association of South-East Asian Nations (ASEAN) and to establish an annual India-ASEAN summit in 2001. India was also invited to the first East Asia Summit in 2005. These political developments have coincided with economic ones; bilateral economic (mainly commercial) ties with many of the region's countries like Singapore are growing closer.

This meta-regional expansion has naturally attracted the attention of the world's major powers, including that of the United States, with which India has managed to increase its influence over the past few decades. The rapprochement between the US and India should be viewed within the context created first by the collapse of the Soviet Union and then by the turning point of 11 September 2001. Both events prompted India to reconsider its international strategy, but each time it decided to continue in the same direction. 1991 was a watershed year both internally and externally. Internally, India's balance of payments crisis led it to begin liberalizing its economy. Externally, it was forced to accept the disappearance of its Soviet partner (if not ally), which had provided most of its weapons, and turned to East Asia (the 'Look East policy') and, more discreetly, the United States, with a detour through Israel. After years of defiance tied to its pro-Arab and in particular pro-Palestinian policy, New Delhi opened an embassy in Tel Aviv and vice versa.

The 1998 nuclear tests stalled the rapprochement with Washington, but efforts were renewed in March 2000 with Bill Clinton's visit to India, the first in 22 years by an American president. The events of 9/11 then had a significant impact on this process. Initially, the US sought stronger ties to Pakistan because it needed to use the country as a base for attacking Al-Qaeda and the Taliban in Afghanistan. Islamabad—which had not quite relinquished its ties with the Taliban—quickly revealed itself to be nothing more than a tactical ally. India, on the other hand, presented itself as a strategic ally.[9] Atal Behari Vajpayee explained to George Bush that the same networks targeting Kashmir and the United States were targeting India. New Delhi thus managed to convince Washington that the two countries were in a similar situation before a new public enemy number one, Islamism. Moreover, the US and India shared the same concerns about a rising China. The growing weight of the Indian community in the US, comprising 1.5 million highly successful people, drew the countries even closer together.

The post-9/11 Indo-American rapprochement was not based solely on security considerations, but also on the idea that the US, India and Israel and the civilizations they represented had a common, increasingly menacing enemy: Islamism. In a much-noted trip to Washington in May 2003, Brajesh Mishra, Prime Minister Vajpayee's right-hand man and special security adviser, called for a new form of coalition: 'India, the United States and Israel have some fundamental similarities. We are all democracies, sharing a common vision of pluralism, tolerance and equal opportunity. Stronger India-US relations and India-Israel relations have a natural logic. . . . The US, India and Israel have all been prime targets of terrorism. They have to jointly face the same ugly face of modern terrorism.' The speech was delivered in Washington during the American Jewish Committee Annual Dinner, which highlights another dimension to the Indo-American-Israel rapprochement: the weight of the Indian and Jewish diaspora communities, which have assumed an important role in these ongoing diplomatic processes.

Defying predictions made by many observers, the rapprochement between the US and India did not suffer from the electoral defeat of the BJP and the Congress Party's return to power in 2004. The new Prime Minister, Manmohan

Singh, justified the maintenance of an initiative launched in January 2004 by Bush and Vajpayee, the 'Next Step in the Strategic Partnership' (NSSP), from a purely realpolitik perspective. Replying to communists who reproached him for congratulating George W. Bush too warmly the day after his reelection, he replied, 'One must face up to reality. International relations are a matter of power and powers are not equal in worth. One cannot escape from reality. The international context has to be used to the best of our interest. It is indispensable to become closer to the United States. The United States plays a leadership role in global economy and international politics. We cannot ignore this fact.'[10]

Signs of continuity in Indo-American relations are numerous. The two countries have accelerated the practise of joint military exercises, and in June 2005 they concluded a ten-year cooperation agreement providing for the joint production of military equipment, heightened collaboration for missile defence and joint peace-keeping interventions in unstable regions. The 'New Framework for the US-India Defence Relationship' agreement stated that the two countries were inaugurating a new era reflecting 'common principles and shared national interests'. Finally, one of the major areas of the NSSP,[11] cooperation in civilian nuclear programmes, led to a much-discussed agreement in August 2007 in which the United States agreed to the transfer of sensitive technology previously denied to India because of legislation tied in part to sanctions imposed in 1998.

India is of great geo-strategic value to the US. Washington views it as a potential counter-weight to China and is sensitive to its influence in the crisis-prone meta-region stretching from the Persian Gulf to Southeast Asia. From the American point of view, India could be a super swing state that could play an important role in stabilizing the region. However, India does not see itself as an instrument of US foreign policy. Raja Mohan, an eminent member of the Indian National Security Advisory Board, emphasized that India could become a partner—not ally—of the US, as long as they shared two main priorities:[12] the 'containment' of China and the fight against Islamist movements, which are now targeting its territory not just in Kashmir but in major urban centres such as Mumbai in November 2008. This partnership is also conditional on Washington's recognition that India has ample room to manoeuvre in its foreign policy, and that it will not be an American pawn. Such a scenario may change if the US under President Obama regards China in a different light or if it pursues a new, more diplomatic approach with the Muslim world.

This analysis offers only a partial response to the question of the role India wants to play in the world, as it only provides a basic realpolitik vision of Indian foreign policy. India is ready to join forces with the United States in order to fight its enemies more effectively. One could add—still from a realist perspective—that it intends to reap material and strategic benefits from this alliance in the form of economic and military collaboration. Nonetheless Raja Mohan's words say nothing of how India intends to use its fiercely guarded autonomy or whether it still sees itself as possessing a message for the world.

## An Emerging Country in Search of a Global Message

India is no longer one of the leaders of the under-developed world, but is still an emerging country whose economic interests often diverge from those of the US and the European Union. This evolution can be clearly seen from its positions in the WTO, where it has allied itself with China, Brazil and South Africa against the US and Europe. This position was formalized with the creation of the BRIC group, which held its first summit in Russia in 2009, and with that of the IBSA group, formed by India, Brazil and South Africa. The idea for the IBSA trio was conceived in 2003 by Brazilian foreign minister Celso Amorim and his South African counterpart, Nkosazana Dlamini-Zuma. Dlamini-Zuma in turn discussed the idea with India's top diplomat, Yashwant Sinha, who travelled to Brasilia six months later. The IBSA's first summit was held in the Brazilian capital in September 2006. On this occasion, Manmohan Singh made a bilateral visit, decades after the last official encounter at this level by Indira Gandhi in 1968. The goals of the trio formed by Lula, Mbeki and Singh were to reinforce economic trade in order to decrease their dependence on industrialized nations; to strengthen cooperation in the sectors of agriculture, defence, aeronautics, information technology, civil aviation, etc.; and finally, to work together to democratize multilateral organizations such as the WTO and the UN. Manmohan Singh qualified the visit as 'historic' and called the IBSA an 'innovative' alliance.[13] The first summit of the BRIC countries can be seen in the same light, perhaps even more so given that it represents the first time non-Western countries have dared to consider financial and monetary alternatives to the current system and challenge the dominant currencies.

India thus continues to see itself as a part of the 'South', as an emerging country that can help the poorest countries, and as a non-aligned state. It demonstrated its independence from Washington when Manmohan Singh participated in the Non-Aligned Movement summit in Cuba following his stay in Brasilia. At this summit he met with Fidel Castro, and then the Venezuelan and Iranian presidents—two of the US' major foes at the time—for discussions deemed very positive. Manmohan Singh thus sees himself as remaining faithful to the spirit of non-alignment.[14] Compared with the Nehru/Gandhi years, however, India has, as an emerging and non-aligned country, acquired a new level of influence. The question remains, however: How does it intend to use it?

## From Moralpolitik to Realpolitik

Sunil Khilnani suggests that India's position between two worlds—the West and the South—allows it to play a privileged role in the promotion of peace, both as mediator and facilitator.[15] Although the idea seems credible, there are no signs that India has attempted to play such a role in South Asia.

In Sri Lanka, India preferred to stand by and watch Colombo crush the LTTE at the cost of significant civilian casualties rather than work to promote a political solution. India's hesitation can be explained in part by the failure of the Indian Peace Keeping Force in 1987 and the assassination of Rajiv Gandhi by the Tigers in 1991. Still, few countries of that size would have allowed such bloodshed to occur at its border without intervening. Whether or not India is now prepared to work in favour of some Sinhalese/Tamil agreement remains to be seen.

In Afghanistan, India is contributing to state building and democracy promotion. It not only financed the new building for the Afghan parliament, but also provides training in New Delhi to Afghan civil servants in parliamentary procedures such as the drafting of legislation. The Indian Law Institute of New Delhi is also training Afghan judges and prosecutors. These activities demonstrate India's expertise in nation building and democracy training but remain relatively limited, given the brevity of the training sessions and the small number of trainees. It is unclear how much more India can contribute, however, since the US has asked New Delhi to keep a low profile in Afghanistan in order to avoid provoking Pakistan. And indeed, India's presence beyond the Durand line would most certainly make Pakistan feel encircled.

India's stalled reaction during the Nepalese revolution is symptomatic of a still unfinished process of strategic thinking on how best to use its growing influence. New Delhi continued to advise the Nepalese king to make concessions in order to stay in power up until the very last moment. The Indian government backed the last plan proposed by King Gyanendra to save the monarchy on 21 April 2006, when it was clear the monarchy was about to be swept out of power by the masses. In doing so, India followed the American position, according to which it was sufficient for the king to stick to the 1990 Constitution rather than to call a constitutional assembly in Nepal, for example. New Delhi and Washington were forced to make an abrupt about-face when it became clear that such an assembly could, in fact, be the primary instrument for integrating Maoists into the democratic process. India seems to have simply followed the American position rather than attempt to work with other aid donors that had considerable influence in Nepal. Thus India announced it would provide financial assistance unilaterally even though other major players wanted to create a consortium.[16] Furthermore, India backed the fall of the popular Prachanda government, which it feared would get too close to Beijing. As a result, New Delhi contributed to a return of instability in the young Himalayan republic, where Maoists could easily take up arms again.

The case of Indo-Burmese relations is not very different. After having denounced the Junta's dictatorship for years, the Indian government began normalizing relations, first so that Rangoon would help New Delhi suppress rebellious tribes in border regions, then to gain access to Burma's energy resources. India has invested 150 million dollars in a gas deposit on the Arakan coast, and two public companies, Oil and Natural Gas Corporation and Gas Authority of India Ltd, have acquired 30 per cent of shares in an offshore gas deposit. When

Buddhist monks demonstrating against the Junta were repressed, India remained silent. India even rejected a proposal by the US and the EU to impose sanctions on Burma, claiming that such a move would be counterproductive.

Half a century after Nehru's flamboyant reign, India is back on the world stage. The high number of conflicts in South Asia between the 1960s and the 1980s obliged Nehru's immediate successors to shift their focus to the regional level. While Nehru viewed the world from a global and rather idealistic perspective, his daughter's and grandson's realistic perspectives led them to focus more on the region. Since the 1990s, India has been governed by leaders who have wanted to increase India's power—especially its military power—and who have the means to pursue a global policy. They have opted to do so in a realist fashion that appears to be at odds with Nehru's approach.

This seemingly stark contrast should be qualified, however. It is true that Nehru's commitment to a people's right to self-determination would have led him to become more involved in Sri Lanka, Nepal and Burma than the current set of leaders. It is also likely that Nehru would have been loath to get as close to the US as they have in the recent years. He would have probably disapproved of India's failure to capitalize on its newfound influence, which gives the impression that its quest for power has become an end unto itself. But the common thread running through all of these periods, and going back before Nehru (and perhaps up to Kautilya!) reflects a basic continuity: the desire for a level of national independence befitting of a great country with a unique civilization. This national sentiment— perhaps we should call it nationalism—forms a foundation common to all of India's contemporary political forces. Communists on the left and Hindu nationalists on the right find themselves united today in condemning a nuclear agreement with the US that, from their standpoint, undermines national independence. But Manmohan Singh, who signed the agreement, is not willing to compromise this national independence either. To him, it is not a question of relinquishing national sovereignty, but rather, obtaining the support of the United States in order to accelerate India's ascent to power.[17] Manmohan Singh is less of a realist than a pragmatist. If this position does not represent a rupture with Nehru, it certainly does with Gandhi, for whom the end never justified the means.

## Notes

1. Long-distance traders were the first to take interest in the outside world. From the dawn of the Common Era, they set off for Orient and established new kingdoms there. Faint echos of these kingdoms remain in the vestiges of Angkor and Borobudur.

2. The Pancha Shila is composed of the following five principles—mutual respect for each other's territorial integrity and sovereignty, mutual non-aggression, non-interference in each other's internal affairs, equality and mutual benefit, and peaceful coexistence.

3. Jawaharlal Nehru, 'Bandung, l'espoir du tiers monde', *Manière de voir*, August-September 2007, p. 52.

4. Michael Brecher, *Nehru,* op. cit., p. 217.

5. Ibid.

6. This was also China's goal. By supporting Pakistan, it sought to limit India to its western border, or at least to keep it in the region.

7. The Janata Party took power in 1977. It was created out of a coalition of Indira Gandhi's main opponents, from socialists to Hindi nationalists to Congress dissidents. The highly-mixed party-coalition would only remain in power until late 1979.

8. Founded by a Congress dissident, V.P. Singh, the Janata Dal was less heterogeneous than the Janata Party but remained a minority party in Parliament. As such, it relied on the support of parties on opposite sides of the political spectrum: the communists of the CPI(M) and the Hindi nationalists of the BJP. V.P. Singh's government lasted less than a year, and the Janata Dal was defeated in the 1991 elections. It then found itself at the centre of a new coalition called the 'Third Force', which took power in 1996 and remained there until 1998.

9. The sanctions imposed by the United States on India and Pakistan following their 1998 nuclear tests were lifted on 22 September 2001.

10. *The Hindu,* 8 November 2004.

11. There are four greater collaboration in civilian nuclear activities, civilian space programmes, and high technology trade, and expanded dialogue on missile defence.

12. C. Raja Mohan, 'India and the balance of power', *Foreign Affairs,* Vol. 85, No. 4, pp. 29–30.

13. PM's statement at the Plenary Session of the First IBSA Summit, in *Visit of Prime Minister Dr. Manmohan Singh to Brazil and Cuba, 10–18 September 2006,* New Delhi: Ministry of External Affairs, Government of India, 2006, pp. 35–7.

14. PM's onboard press conference enroute to Brasilia, in *Visit of Prime Minister Dr. Manmohan Singh to Brazil and Cuba, 10–18 September 2006,* New Delhi: Ministry of External Affairs, Government of India, 2006, p. 78.

15. Sunil Khilnani, 'India as a bridging power', in P.K. Basu, B. Chellaney, P. Khanna and S. Khilnani, *India as New Global Leader,* London, The Foreign Policy Centre, 2005, p. 9.

16. See *Nepal: From People Power to Peace?, A policy report of the International Crisis Group,* No. 115, 10 May 2006, p. 20.

17. PM's onboard press conference en route to Brasilia, op. cit., p. 80.

# Chapter 32

# The *Sangh Parivar* and the Hindu diaspora in the west: what kind of long-distance nationalism?*

Benedict Anderson's theory outlined under the ingenious expression of 'long-distance nationalism' suggests that a strong and nearly automatic allegiance binds members of an ethnic diaspora to their homeland. According to Anderson, immigrants continue to feel toward their native land identical sentiments to those nourished in the context of 'traditional' nationalism. The political positions of the 'long-distance nationalists' serve to protect an ethnic identity that is threatened either within their country of origin or sometimes in the host society. The only specific feature that Anderson recognizes in this variant of nationalism has to do with its irresponsibility, which sanctions extreme radicalism. In fact, the long-distance nationalist 'need not fear prison, torture, or death, nor did his family' (Anderson 1998: 74).

In our opinion, the main weakness of this approach lies in its indifference to nationalist organizations operating in the homeland that attempt to mobilize its offspring abroad. This type of transnational action has been studied in detail with regard to religious movements such as the Tabligh-i-Jamaat, which advocates the re-Islamization of Muslims who have migrated to the West. But the role of ethno-nationalist movements, which have many similarities, has not sparked the same interest, as if the flow of diasporas with regard to the homeland was one-directional. In fact, 'long-distance nationalism' is at least as much the product of a reverse flow of political entrepreneurs from the mainland generating nationalist aspirations among the diaspora. Indeed, the very notion of diaspora often results from the deliberate action by a centre vis-à-vis its periphery (Ragazzi 2004; Dufoix 2005). The case of India allows one to test this hypothesis in relation to Hindu nationalism, a movement directed since 1925 by a key organization, the Rashtriya Swayamasevak Sangh.

Hindu nationalism is an exclusive form of ethno-religious nationalism which thrived in the first years of the twentieth century in reaction to the 'threat' the West (Christian missionaries as well as British colonizers) and the Muslim minority (allegedly related to a pan-Islamic movement rooted in the Middle East) were

---

*This chapter has been co-authored by Ingrid Therwath.

posing to the Hindus. This movement, which quickly became the largest Hindu nationalist organization, was intended not only to propagate the Hindutva ideology but also to infuse new physical strength into the majority community (Jaffrelot 1996).

Indeed, the RSS has adopted a very peculiar modus operandi relying on the development of local branches (*shakhas*). In 1939, it had 500 *shakhas*, and now there are 44,417 in 30,988 places, with some cities and towns having more than one (*The Organiser*, 2007: 67). Moreover, the RSS developed front organizations after independence, its aim no longer being merely to penetrate society directly through *shakhas* but also to establish organizations working amidst specific social categories. Hence in 1948, RSS cadres based in Delhi founded the Akhil Bharatiya Vidyarthi Parishad. In 1951, the movement created a political party today known under the name Bharatiya Janata Party (BJP). In 1964, in association with Hindu clerics, it set up the Vishva Hindu Parishad, a movement responsible for grouping together the heads of the various Hindu sects to lend this very unorganized religion a sort of centralized structure. Lastly, in 1979, the RSS founded Seva Bharati, to penetrate the slums through social activities (free schools, low-cost medicines, etc.). Taken together, these bridgeheads are presented by the mother organization as forming the *Sangh Parivar*, 'the family of the Sangh', that is of RSS (Jaffrelot 2005).

The RSS' strategy of reaching out to the diaspora consisted in reproducing abroad the modus operandi of the organization in India. This voluntarist approach explains the rise of the Hindutva Movement outside India at least as much as the diaspora's alleged 'long-distance nationalism'. If the latter was latent, there is no doubt that it was the RSS that activated it. But such an undertaking would have been doomed to fail if the host societies hadn't played along through a peculiar mixture of racism and multiculturalism, and if the international context, dominated by 'the Islamist threat', hadn't mirrored certain features of the situation in India: Hindu nationalist discourse was thus able to acquire relevance on a global scale. This is particularly true in three countries: the United Kingdom, the United States, and Canada.

## Hindu Nationalism Beyond Hindustan

Hindu nationalism is not naturally inclined to overflow India's borders. Its deep-seated nature is ethno-religious and it therefore coincides with a people and a civilization. It is indissociable from a territory, the sacred land (*karmabhoomi*) of eternal India. Why and how, then, has this 'ism' been able to broaden its radius of action beyond the 'black water' (*kala pani*)[1] of the Indian Ocean?

One reason is that Hindu migrants have gradually formed communities in the four corners of the world. These ethnic bridgeheads have justified an overseas expansion of Hindu nationalist movements because they formed fragments of India abroad which, without them, were in danger of being denatured. The promotion of Hinduism in diaspora was the primary motivation of the Arya Samaj *upadeshaks* (activists) in the first movement of this school of thought founded in 1875, which followed the waves of immigration in the colonial nineteenth century in South Africa and the Caribbean.[2]

The RSS later took up the flame according to the same logic. One of its leaders, M.S. Golwalkar, who became head of the movement in 1940, in fact devoted an entire passage of his famous book, *Bunch of Thoughts*, to overseas Hindus, calling on them to act as ambassadors for their nation:

The first point to be borne in mind by our brothers and sisters living abroad is to keep alive in their day-to-day behavior a spirit of intense national self-respect. And for this, a keen awareness of the glorious heritage that our forbears have left for us should ever be present in our minds. (Golwalkar 1980: 450)

He added that Hindu migrants should serve 'the Cause' abroad:

And in order to do this the one supreme conviction that we are a great people charged with a World Mission, should be ever vibrant in our breasts; that a sacred duty and trust is cast upon us of bringing home to the entire humanity the sublime truths embedded in our Dharma [religion] and that the various ills and challenges being faced by it could be met successfully on the basis of the all-comprehensive scientific yet spiritual outlook of Hinduism. (Sadashivrao 1980: 456)

Golwalkar therefore recommended Hindu migrants to teach their children Hindu civilization, to build temples and not to alienate the host society. His successor, Balasaheb Deoras—who took the lead of the movement in 1973—crossed another threshold by entrusting diaspora Hindus with part of the RSS mission. In his message to the 1989 UK Virat Hindu Sammelan—one of the largest Hindu nationalist events organized in the West—he stated:

Inspired by sublime thought and feeling, countless great personalities of Bharat have propagated and promoted this cultural vision in many countries, seeking nothing but the welfare of the entire humanity. The Hindus who have settled in several countries all over the world have contributed significantly to the all-round development of social, economic and cultural life of the countries of their residence. Present times demand that they carry on constructive and social welfare activities with greater zeal with harmonious cooperation of the local people to make universal brotherhood a reality. (cited in Seshadri 1990: 13)

The RSS thus gradually wished to rely on Hindu communities abroad to spread its message. To this end it created a special branch for Hindus overseas, the Antar Rashtriya Sahayog Parishad, in 1978. It was, moreover, this very development strategy that involved creating sister organizations which gave rise to the expression 'Sangh Parivar': the RSS—or *Sangh*—forms a 'family' that it lords over and of which the multiple branches are its children.

According to the official RSS history, the first *shakha* to have been created outside of India formed spontaneously in 1946 aboard a ship linking Bombay to Mombasa in Kenya:

One evening, on a tempestuous day, two passengers, both in Khaki [*sic*] shorts, accidentally met on the deck of the ship. One of them was from Punjab and the other from Gujarat, both unknown to each other. But a popular Hindi song that one of them was singing *sotto voce*, attracted the other towards him with raised eyebrows; and they recognized each other as belonging to the common Sangh family. Facing towards the Motherland, both of them together then sang 'Namaste Sada Vatsale Matrubhoome' [Hail to Thee O Motherland!]. Thus was born the first Sangh *shakha* off-shore! (Rashtriya Swayamsevak Sangh 1992: 1)

Kenya was indeed the country in which the first non-Indian *shakha* was officially created in 1947 by these *swayamsevaks* once they located other Hindus there. Kenya and Uganda were the host countries for Indian immigration in which the RSS expanded the most rapidly in the 1950s and 1960s under the label of Bharatiya Swayamsevak Sangh. The BSS was an important locus of socialization for the Hindu minority, as much through its athletic activities as through cultural events. It was also one of the crucibles for the Hindu Council of Kenya, which was to become the main political organization for the defence of Hindus in that country. A similar development also occurred in Uganda (Bhatt 2000: 577).

These East African beginnings are not irrelevant to our comprehension of the development of the *Sangh Parivar* in the West, because many full-time cadres that would operate in Great Britain and North America first went through Uganda or Kenya. The African experience of nearly one-quarter of the Hindu community living in Great Britain has considerably influenced British Hinduism and has given it a strong diasporic dimension. The same African and Caribbean detour can be found among many Canadian Hindutva adherents.[3] When Rajendra Singh, the successor of Deoras, went to Kenya in 1997 to commemorate the golden jubilee of the development of the RSS overseas, he emphasized:

Outside Bharat, Kenya is the place where Sangh work is established thoroughly according to our technique. Last time when I came, I visited a *shakha* the *Karyavaha* [activist in charge] of which could give full particulars of the families of all the 16 or 17 *swayamsevaks*. Our relationship should be with the entire family of *swayamsevaks*. Then only a *swayamsevak* can develop properly and through him a change will come even in the family. Such *shakhas* exist in Kenya from where *swayamsevaks* went out and started *shakhas* in England, Canada, etc. We meet *karyakartas* [activists] who say 'I am a *swayamsevak* for the last 50 years, made in Kenya'. (Rajaram Mahajan 1997: 5–6)

The RSS operated under still a different name, the Hindu Swayamsevak Sangh in Great Britain and then in the United States, Canada, the Netherlands, Trinidad, and Hong Kong. To begin with, the HSS gave absolute priority to multiplying the number of *shakhas,* as the RSS had done in the years from 1925 to 1948. In Great Britain *shakhas* were thus rapidly created in cities such as Birmingham and Bradford where they attracted Hindu immigrants eager to convey Hindu culture to their children (Burlet 2001: 13).

The organization of the *shakhas* was nevertheless adapted to the diaspora population. Less time was spent reciting prayers, and team sports replaced martial arts training. Moreover, certain *shakhas* are mixed and meet on Sunday or during school vacation in order to attract the largest possible audience. Despite these variations, the HSS *shakhas* attest to the transposition of the Indian model of the RSS in diaspora. Another common feature lay in the fact that an important network of temples offered the HSS a logistic base, the same way as the RSS had benefited from the support of the Hindu temples in India when it developed its organization.

The HSS took on new importance in the eyes of the 'mother organization' during the Emergency in 1975–7. During these 18 months when the rule of law was suspended by Indira Gandhi, the RSS was banned for the second time in its history (the first dated back to the assassination of Mahatma Gandhi by a former movement member). It then found in its international affiliates valuable advocates of its cause and an alternative source of funding. The RSS headquarters in Nagpur at that time kept a secret register of *swayamsevaks* who had applied to emigrate, putting them in contact with those already settled in the destination country and encouraging them to join a *shakha* or to start one (Goyal 1979: 106, note 91).

In 1976, *swayamsevaks* settled in Great Britain founded the Friends of India Society whose primary aim was to organize and defend Hindutva principles abroad. This organization is still very active in Great Britain and continental Europe, particularly in Paris (Andersen and Damle 1987: 212–3). The existence of family links has sometimes helped a lot in the development of this network.

Like the RSS in India, the HSS in the United Kingdom adopted a centralized structure divided into geographic sections each headed by a movement cadre. The highest leadership council, the Akhil UK Pratinidhi Sabha (a copy of the Akhil Bharatiya Pratinidhi Sabha) meets once a year like its Indian counterpart, and the Kendriya Karyakari Mandal every 3 months like its Indian counterpart and homonym. Likewise, every year the HSS holds training camps for the movement cadres: Instructors' Training Camps for *shakha* leaders, Officers' Training Camps for those of a higher rank. These weeklong camps also decide on the content of the 'teachings' delivered daily in the *shakhas*. The duplication of the RSS modus operandi is all the better insured since emissaries are regularly sent from Nagpur to oversee the camps, or even to hold standard training sessions.[4]

Reflecting the RSS strategy which, after having created a network of *shakhas,* gave rise to a multitude of affiliates forming a so-called family—the *Sangh Parivar*— the HSS created a network of sister organizations. The Vishva Hindu Parishad UK was founded some 8 years after the VHP in India, in 1972, as an affiliate of the

VHP in the United Kingdom (Bhatt 2000: 559). The Overseas Friends of the Bharatiya Janata Party (OFBJP) became the correspondent for the BJP in the country. The Rashtra Sevika Samiti—the women wing of the RSS founded in 1936 in India—also has an alter ego in Great Britain in an organization of the same name. The main Hindu student union in Great Britain, the National Hindu Students Forum (NHSF), is likewise the official correspondent for the ABVP. Lastly, Bharat Sewa is the functional equivalent of the RSS affiliate devoted to social work, Sewa Bharti.

Like their Indian counterparts, the various components of the British Sangh are in constant contact but strive to mask the links they have with the RSS to avoid being overtly stigmatized by too strong an ideological branding and thereby circumvent the legislation in force. Indeed, the British Charity Commission prohibits the funding of political and sect activities, while section 5 of the Indian Foreign Contribution (Regulation) Act of 1976 (FCRA) forbids the RSS and its affiliates from receiving funds from abroad without prior authorization from the central government on a case-by-case basis. It is thus of the utmost importance for the components of the *Sangh Parivar* to distinguish themselves from transnational political movements which would be illegal to fund. Thus, the Press Officer of the NHSF stated in November 2005 that 'we have no direct link with them [HSS UK]; we are not funded or bonded to them, but there is a moral affiliation as with every other Hindu organization'.[5]

This tactical distance nevertheless conceals real collaboration that AWAAZ, a network of anti-communal individuals and organizations based in India and the United Kingdom and set on exposing the illegal foreign funding of the *Sangh Parivar*, sets out to demonstrate in its report.[6] It points out that the leader of the HSS sits on the board of directors of the VHP UK, whose representative for religious education issues is also a leader of the HSS and the former editor-in-chief of *Sangh Sandesh,* an HSS publication. The same interpenetration can also be observed among grassroots activists. The homology between the RSS and the HSS is thus mirrored in the networks formed by the *Sangh Parivar* in India and Great Britain.

In the United States, Hindutva adherents reproduced the same system, except that the first organization to have been created on American soil was not the local equivalent of the RSS but the Vishva Hindu Parishad of America. This is totally atypical as the RSS generally comes first. Founded in 1971, at the time when a wave of qualified emigrants arrived in the United States, the VHP-A today is one of the most active branches of the Sangh with 40 operational sub-branches and over 10,000 members.[7] In May 1990, the Hindu Students Council (HSC) was formed, and today claims some 50 branches in universities throughout the United States and Canada (Rajagopal 2000: 476). Its growth is remarkable given that the first HSC chapter was founded only in 1987 at Northeastern University in Boston. As for the alter ego of Sewa Bharti, in the United States it is called the India Development and Relief Fund.

Canada followed the same path as the United States. VHP-Canada was created in 1970 and built a temple in Vancouver the following year. It was only later, in 1973 on the recommendation of M.S. Golwalkar that L.M. Sabherwal, an RSS member since his youth who had arrived in Canada in the early 1970s, founded the HSS (initially under the name of Bharatiya Swayamsevak Sangh) (Jain 1998: 19). Throughout the entire 1980s and 1990s the American *swayamsevaks* attempted to reproduce the development of the *Sangh Parivar* in Canada. VHP-Canada, of little importance until then, got a second wind in 1987 (Lele 2003: 85). Similarly, the HSC in Canada came about with the help of activists from the neighbouring United States. Thus still today, the VHP and the HSC, together with Sewa International, the charity arm equivalent locally to Sewa Bharti, constitute the pillars of Canadian Hindutva.

The *Sangh Parivar* has thus managed to reproduce most of its structure abroad, except that the HSS is not at the system's hub: the centre continues to be the RSS. Hindu nationalist movement affiliates either in India or abroad therefore swear allegiance to the same decision-making centre, which certainly makes this movement qualify as a network. Not only do the members of the British Sangh regularly attend events organized by the Indian Sangh, but reports on the RSS activities in India are also presented in meetings of the HSS UK. More importantly, Rajendra Singh, the leader of the RSS from 1994 to 2000, presented his organization's 'Code of guidelines to workers', to HSS members in London on 21 April 1995.[8] Interestingly, the RSS has divided the world into geographical areas, one of its senior cadres being in charge of each of them.[9] Similarly, since 1984, the VHP centre in Delhi has been exercising its jurisdiction over the entire organization all over the world.[10] It is thus to India that the overseas components of the *Sangh Parivar* look for their material and ideological leadership.

## Adapting the RSS modus operandi abroad

*Sangh Parivar* representatives working outside India have naturally sought to reproduce the modus operandi that were successful in the homeland. And so the functioning of *shakhas* was transposed overseas: *swayamsevaks* in other parts of the world are also supposed to get together morning or evening, if possible dressed in the standard uniform, for physical training sessions including the virtually military raising of the flag and ideological get together that vary according to circumstances but the targets of which are usually the Muslims in the West and whose heroine is always eternal Hindu India. However, we shall see in this section that the RSS has been obliged to adapt its techniques to the new environment.

As for the VHP, its effort to unify Hinduism in diaspora uses some of the methods employed in India: this involves the construction of 'Pan Hindu temples' destined to welcome all sects and castes and the organization of Dharma Sansad throughout the world. These assemblies bring together Hindu religious figures that have come from local ashrams and temples and who strive to establish and disseminate a Hindu code of conduct by inventing a sort of catechism.

Like in India, the British, American, and Canadian branches of the VHP also hold huge rallies in the form of ethno-religious events. The first such gathering was probably the Virat Hindu Sammelan which took place in Milton Keynes, in the suburbs of London, in 1989. For the first time in Great Britain the VHP had managed to bring together hundreds of Hindu organizations (officially 300) and from 50 to 100,000 participants. In United States an even larger rally took place in 1993 to celebrate the hundredth anniversary of the arrival of Vivekananda—a religious reformer with nationalist leanings—in Chicago and his famous speech to the world parliament of religions in 1893 in which he had criticized the materialistic West and praised the virtues of a spiritual Orient. This gathering was called 'Global Vision 2000', which was an apt reflection of the international ambitions of Hindutva adherents.

Although from traditional *shakhas* to ethno-religious mobilization campaigns, Hindu nationalists in diaspora seem to reproduce the initial model of the *Sangh Parivar*, they function in a highly specific manner.

## THE PRIMACY OF RELIGIOUS FIGURES

The role of religious figures in the *Sangh Parivar* abroad is much more significant than in India. The fact that the VHP-America and VHP-Canada were founded before the North American equivalent of the RSS is not by chance; it reflects the long-standing presence of Hindu gurus in the United States and Canada and the strength of their networks. In North America—but also in Great Britain—the Hindu nationalist movement therefore relied on the action of various sects founded by gurus recognized abroad, like the Arya Samaj, established in 1875 by Swami Dayanand Saraswati, the Ramakrishna Mission, founded in 1897 by Vivekananda, the Swaminarayan movement, which was created shortly afterwards and to which we shall return below, the Divine Life Society founded in 1936 by Swami Shivananda, the Chinmaya Mission founded in 1953 by Swami Chinmayanand, the Sri Aurobindo Society founded in 1960 and the International Sai Organization founded in 1972 by Sathya Sai Baba. Interestingly, in 1973, M.S. Golwalkar, still at the helm of the RSS, wrote to a young *swayamsevak* who had migrated to Canada, that he should 'meet the holy men who leave our country to spread our religion' and that he 'would gain a lot from these acquaintances' (Golwalkar 1973).[11]

Swami Chinmayanand, the co-founder of the VHP—the movement was created in 1964 in his Bombay ashram—enjoyed such a popularity in the West that he became an international entrepreneur in religion. After a world tour in 1965, he decided to invest his energy in the United States where he started to go every year from 1968 onwards. The first Chinmaya Spiritual Camp outside India was held in 1973 in California. Six years later, Swami Chinmayanand started 'an ashram-school' (Patchen 1989: 238) in northern California. Though the Chinmaya Mission had many branches[12] out of the United States, this country was its stronghold and Swami Chinmayanand therefore played a major role in establishing the VHP, America (McKean 1996: 178). Another guru, Satyamitranand Giri, also contributed to the movement's development in Great Britain in a decisive manner. In fact, the VHP-UK is officially placed under the patronage of this man who was first known for his religious activities aiming to federate Hinduism in India. In 1983 in the holy city of Haridwar, he thus founded a Bharat Mata Mandir, of which each of the seven stories brings together figures that symbolize aspects of the Hindu nation (*Dharma Marg* 1984: 39–41).

Beyond this guru, the *Sangh Parivar* finds in the Swaminarayan movement a most valuable ally in Great Britain.[13] In 1995 the building of a huge temple in Neasden, in the London suburbs, reflected the growing influence of the Swaminarayan movement in England, especially among the affluent Gujarati community. Not only does this temple present all the deities of the Hindu pantheon as does Satyamitranand Giri's Bharat Mata Mandir, but its permanent exhibit entitled 'Understanding Hinduism' adopts a very nationalistic tone, the faithful being informed of the fact that Hindus not only discovered the zero, but also geometry, astronomy, plastic surgery and quantum physics! (Mukta 2000: 461).

Beyond the channel offered by the Swaminarayan movement, the Gujarati milieu—most of whose members subscribe to this movement—has given Hindu nationalism countless specific advantages. First of all communication relays: a radio station, *Radio Sunrise*, three newspapers, *Garavi Gujarat*, *Gujarat Samachar* and the weekly *Asian Voice*, all media serving to echo the debates concerning the Christian 'threat' constituted by the conversions of tribals in India. Second, it wields considerable financial clout, as we will see further on.

### DRAFTING A NEW CATECHISM AND EDUCATING YOUTH

If the religious factor plays such a considerable role in the promotion of Hindutva abroad, it is not only due to the influence of gurus and sectarian movements like the Swaminarayans, but also to the demand for Hinduism. Hindu migrants want their children to know their religious tradition. One Hindu leader thus explained in *The Organiser*:

The American Hindu is perpetually concerned that his children are brought up in the Hindu tradition, that he gets acquainted with the Hindu gods and goddesses. Some of the parents are highly exercised over their children being tainted by the Western culture. Some they are now repenting at leisure that in their blind pursuit of wealth they had abandoned their children to absorb the Western culture. Others have awakened to the danger. (*The Organiser*, 1996: 40)

The difficulties that young people encounter when they have to justify aspects of their culture that arouse astonishment or sarcasm partly helps to understand the success of the VHP. Here is an organization able to explain the Hindu 'catechism' clearly to the young generations. It has even undertaken to train teachers. The VHP-UK published *Explaining Hindu Dharma: A Guide for Teachers* in 1996. In the United States in 2005, the VHP-A sought to influence the rewriting of history textbooks in the state of California, giving rise to a debate among experts between community representatives and India scholars opposed to this fallacious rewriting for ideological ends (Jaffrelot 2007).

The VHP-UK follows the same line. Seeta Lakhani's textbook, for instance, pretends drawing its inspiration from Hinduism to pronounce negative opinions on cloning, contraception, precocious sexual intercourse, divorce, adultery, and homosexuality. The author's efforts to fashion the mentality of second and third generation Hindu youths go so far as to warn this population against the BBC and what she deems its partial treatment of Hinduism. Her map of India naturally encompasses the portion of Kashmir under Pakistani control, as per Hindu nationalist ideology (Lakhani 2005: 58, 105–6).

To appeal to the youth, the Hindutva movement often has recourse to apparently inoffensive activities such as summer camps or language courses (Mukta 2000). They also offer student cultural evenings such as *Mastana*, a student night of 'fun' organized on the campus of the Cambridge University, UK.

In the United States and Canada many temples also host VHP classes aiming to explain their culture to children and to inculcate a Hindu pride that denies the diversity or even the ambiguities of Hinduism. The situation, however, is not the same in all the countries under review. In the United States as well as in Great Britain, various offshoots of the *Sangh Parivar* focus on the most affluent Hindus. The high rate of academic success among young Americans and British of Indian stock, mainly Hindus, and from more affluent families than the rest of Asia, is often held up as proof of an intrinsic superiority. This justifies the campaign to dissociate Hindus from the mass of 'Asians' conducted in various *Sangh* publications that target a young audience. In Canada, where the Indian community has been firmly established since the early twentieth century, the HSC has on the other hand adopted an inclusive strategy aiming to highlight the numerical—and therefore political—significance of Hindus in the country, and the universal and encompassing dimension of Hinduism. But the Hindu nationalist propaganda in Great Britain and in the United States is not always the same. The adaptation of certain moral codes to make room for homosexuality, living out of wedlock, and divorce, for instance, and the negation of caste distinctions constitutes a major difference of British and American Hindutva with respect to its Indian version.

However, aside from these exceptions, the causes and ideology defended by the pro-Hindutva movement in Great Britain, United States, and Canada have been imported from India and these organizations claim inspiration from the same mentors. And indeed the same idea of a besieged community prevailing in India is found here and the low proportion of Hindus in the British and North America populations lends it even greater strength.

## CYBER HINDUTVA

If the HSS was founded after the VHP-A in the United States, it is not only because of the religious demand emanating from the Hindu community; it is also due to the lack of enthusiasm of the latter for the modus operandi of traditional *shakhas*. There was no way that business executives, the prime HSS target, were going to get up at dawn to salute the saffron flag reciting a Sanskrit anthem—and even less do calisthenics in khaki shorts! It is thus also because the HSS has had to adapt to a new sociology that, instead of emphasizing the classical functioning of *shakhas,* it has invented *cybershakhas*.

The Hindu nationalist movement has thus multiplied Internet websites enabling its members to remain in contact, to keep informed of *Sangh Parivar* actions and to follow its analysis of current events. The most important of these sites in the United States is probably the *Global Hindu Electronic Network* (<http://www.hindunet.org>). As for the most radical of them, it is beyond a doubt *Sword of Truth* (<http://www.swordoftruth.com>) which includes a blacklist of 'anti-Hindu' people. These websites also offer instant answers to the questions the Hindu diaspora is confronted with, as evidenced by headings such as 'Eternal Hindu Values' or 'Hindu Customs'. Besides, several blogs backing the *Sangh Parivar* have cropped up in the past few years. Most of the pro-Hindutva blogs inventoried on 25 September 2006 using the *Google* search engine are either anonymous or originate from enterprises such as *Dharma Today*. Bloggers who identify themselves are moreover, all men.

## The Key Role of Fund Raising

The importance of fund raising in the activities of the *Sangh Parivar* abroad is naturally explained by the spectacular financial and social success of the diaspora. In United States, the 2000 census revealed an average income of $67,000 for Indians as opposed to $30,000 average overall income. Such an accomplishment gives Indians—and especially the Hindus among them—the sense that they form a model minority. In Great Britain, over 30 per cent of Hindus aged from 16 to 30 years hold a university degree, and 5 per cent of the Hindus in any age brackets are doctors.[14]

These achievements make them the preferred target of fundraisers based in India. The *Sangh Parivar* managed to tap these resources for the first time in 1989 when it undertook a huge fundraising campaign aiming to finance the (re)construction of the Ram Temple in Ayodhya. The *Ram Shilas* funded by gifts from abroad were carried to Ayodhya with great care and placed in display cases.

Indians in the United States had sent $350,000 to India to rebuild the Ram Mandir in the year following the demolition of the Babri Masjid, on 6 December 1992 by Hindu nationalist activists.

Since that time the main source of *Sangh* funds has come from abroad, as shown by the 2002 report on the India Development and Relief Fund (IDRF) and the one published in 2004 by the AWAAZ network, a humans rights organization in South Asia, entitled *In Bad Faith? British Charity and Hindu Extremism*, on Sewa activities in the United Kingdom.[15] The authors of these two reports, which caused a scandal in India, the United States, and Great Britain, lay bare the whole foreign financing structure of the *Sangh Parivar* through the IDRF and Sewa-UK, and reveal the institutional and personal relations that link the Hindu diaspora in these countries to the *Sangh.*

The Maryland-based IDRF, conveyor belt for *Sangh*-destined funds in the United States, presents itself to its donors as a nonprofit charity NGO. It collects funds throughout the United States for development projects in India. This organization has been presided since its inception by a former economist at the World Bank, Vinod Prakash. From 1990 to 1998 it raised $2 million and the Hindu Heritage Endowment that it formed in 1994 raised $2.6 million in pledges (Biju and Prashad 2000: 529). According to another source, from 1995 to 2002, it raised $5 million that it distributed to 284 organizations involved in social programme in India. IDRF rules stipulate that 20 per cent of the funds that it collects are earmarked for beneficiaries whose name is been specified by the donors, whereas 80 per cent of the remaining donations are distributed at the movement's discretion. As it turns out, among the 75 organizations affiliated with the IDRF—the primary beneficiaries of this gold mine of $5 million between 1995 and 2002—60 of them were *Sangh Parivar* affiliates, including the Sewa Bharti, the Vanavasi Kalyan Ashram or other affiliates of the Hindu nationalist movement. As it turns out, four of the six IDRF vice presidents at the time were HSS members and one of them belonged to the VHP-A National Governing Council.[16]

Once again, the Hindu nationalists have managed to hide their hand, this strategy being made easier by the multiplication of screen companies constituted by the countless offshoots of the *Sangh.* Although the *Sangh Parivar's* fundraising activities abroad have particularly taken off in the United States, drives also take place in Canada, via Sewa International (also known as Sewa-Canada), and in Great Britain. According to Sat Wadhwa, the founder and secretary-general of Sewa-Canada, this organization came about in the early 1990s and raised $225,000 in 2005. He sends a sizable check on behalf of Sewa-Canada (the sum was $150,000 in February 2006) earmarked for seven or eight projects in India. Some of these projects are directly managed by Sewa Bharti and others, particularly in the tribal zones, by the VKA. Fundraising is mostly done 'by word of mouth. We put our leaflets in various temples and in one gurudwara [sikh temple].'[17]

Although it is still difficult to evaluate the scope of Canadian funding of the *Sangh* for lack of complete reports on this subject, the British contribution is well known now thanks to the AWAAZ investigation.[18] Sewa-UK, the main Hindu nationalist fundraising agency in Great Britain, proved to be extremely effective following the Bhuj earthquake in Gujarat in 2003, the Gujaratis forming the most solid Hindu nationalist support network in England. Altogether, Sewa-UK has allegedly collected £2.3 million nearly all of which—£1.9 million of it—was transferred to the Gujarati branch of Sewa Bharti. A third of these funds apparently served to build Hindu nationalist schools, particularly in the tribal areas, whereas it was supposed to go to rebuilding destroyed villages.

These revelations sparked great indignation in the United States and Great Britain where many donors totally ignored the final destination of their donations. It would appear nevertheless that in the United States many of them have a clear conscience about the ideological orientation of the IDRF. Its director in fact had to apologize to them after having given money to victims of a fire in a mosque at Mecca![9] Whether the donors had consented or not it is obvious that one of the specificities of Hindu nationalism in the United States has to do with its function as a 'money pump'.

This dimension is naturally highly appreciated by the BJP whose funding needs are constantly growing due to the rising costs of election campaigns.[20] It is therefore not surprising that the party has given pride of place to Non-Resident Indians rather early, in its 1996 election manifesto, at a time when other Indian political parties largely disregarded the diaspora. Besides, BJP leaders—Vajpayee, Advani, etc.—toured the United States several times to raise funds among wealthy Indians during gala dinners completely at odds with the ideal of austerity advocated by the RSS. The financial stakes now represented by the Indian diaspora in the United States is clearly reflected by the attraction this destination holds for the political class. It is precisely to prevent Ashok Gehlot, Digvijay Singh, and Sheila Dikshit—all Congress Chief Ministers—from poaching on its preserves that the Vajpayee government denied them permission in 2003 to travel to the United States. These three Congress heads of state governments wanted to look for handouts in North America before elections in their state.[21]

Vijay Prashad considers that the Hindu diaspora's 'generosity' can be explained by ulterior motives. According to him, 'at least their advertisements and their cringing servility would, they hoped, earn them a few contracts and investment deals when Hindutva began the "privatization" fire-sale of India's public sector assets' (Prashad 1997: 9, 2002: 10). Others see it as a means of assuaging the conscience of those who, having been successful abroad, feel a certain sense of guilt at having left the other poor country where they were initially educated. One is wary, however, of such instrumentalist and psychological interpretations that tend to conceal other substantial factors.

## The Mechanisms of Success

Throughout the 1990s the *Sangh Parivar* developed considerably among the Hindu diaspora, especially in Great Britain and the United States. In this country where the HSS was virtually non-existent in the 1980s, it grew rapidly throughout the following decade. In the late 1990s, the states of New York, New Jersey and Connecticut alone already counted 150 *shakhas* (Rajagopal 2000: 480). These inroads, which were long in coming, are not only explained by factors internal to the Hindu milieu, but also by features of the host societies.

## INTERNAL FACTORS

Arvind Rajgopal explains the attraction of Hindu nationalism for the Indian diaspora in the United States by their sociological characteristics. Hindus in America count among their ranks a growing number of computer scientists and small business owners that come from the 'little-exposed strata of Indian society, completely bypassing the usual socialization of the bigger cities' (2000: 482). Certainly, the core of Hindu nationalism has been historically recruited among what Bruce Graham has called the 'middle world' of the Hindi belt, small business executives and professionals, all who come from upper castes (1990: 158). But to attribute the Hindu nationalist leanings of a new wave of migrants to their lack of cosmopolitanism is not convincing when the most cosmopolitan ones are no less attracted by the *Sangh Parivar*. Indeed, since the end of the 1980s, the *Sangh Parivar* has made its way into the upper middle class in big cities.

Jayant Lele suggests another interpretation of the development of the *Sangh Parivar* in Canada. Whereas most of the Indians who came to this country before the Second World War were workers and farmers, the more recent wave of immigration, particularly beginning in the 1960s, was mainly made up of members of the upper middle class. According to Lele, these affluent Indians find in the Brahmanical, unifying and flattering dimension of Hinduism as it is presented by the *Sangh Parivar* confirmation of their dominant position within Canadian society and within the Indian community (2003: 93–8).

These two opposite readings suggest that the internal factors of the Hindu nationalist movement's success may still lay elsewhere. First of all in the consolidation of its network in the course of time and in an increased mobilization drive on the part of the *Sangh Parivar*. This could be seen in the Milton Keynes (1989) and 'Global Vision' (1993) rallies, but also in Rajendra Singh's 1995 tour and those of his successor, K. Sudarshan. The importance of these tours has been considerably overlooked. Never before had an RSS leader travelled outside of India. Neither Golwalkar nor Deoras had felt the need to set out into the world to which they had nevertheless decided to extend the *Sangh Parivar*. Rajendra Singh's visit to Europe thus marked a turning point. The RSS leader presented his ideas in a very moderate tone, which suited what was basically an exercise in public relations. At the School of Oriental and African Studies in London, for instance, he gave a provocatively entitled speech, 'The 21st Century: A Hindu Century', but the content was reassuring. He claimed to be open to a third way between socialism and capitalism, true to the holistic qualities of Hinduism, a model, if he were to be believed, of social cohesion and fraternity (Raj 2000: 549). Singh's visit showed a new style that is better suited to international relations that the RSS' usual lectures peppered with references to a glorious Hindu past.

The second factor of success that one can attribute to the *Sangh Parivar* has to do with the 'mainstreamization' of the Hindu nationalist movement. From the mid-1990s onwards, particularly after the 1996 elections that gave the BJP the largest number of seats in the Lok Sabha, Hindutva gained respectability. As a result, the diaspora was less afraid to show its face during its rallies and fundraising drives.

The third factor, internal not to the movement but to the Hindu diaspora, has to do with its political culture, which indeed became more radical in the 1990s. For the first time the *Sangh Parivar* was no longer popular among the diaspora merely because it met a religious demand, but also because of its ethnic nationalist project. Why did the Hindu diaspora prove receptive to this ideology at that point of time in its history? To understand this, specific factors having to do with the situation in countries of immigration must be taken into account.

## ISLAMISM, RACISM, AND MULTICULTURALISM
## IN THE HOST SOCIETIES

The radicalization of the Hindu diaspora is partly a reaction to the epitome of the Other that is the Muslim, in India as well as abroad. In India, the conversions that took place in 1981 in Meenakshipuram—a little town in southern India where thousands of Dalits (ex-Untouchables) 'went over to Islam'—and the Shah Bano incident in 1985 prepared the ground for the Hindu nationalist mobilization in the 1980–90. Abroad, the Rushdie affair of 1989 and Hizb ut Tahrir's campaigns had a similar impact, especially on university campuses where cohabitation among students from different communities was becoming more and more problematic. At the SOAS in London, for instance, Hindu and Jewish students joined efforts to get the Hizb banned. At the same time they also led a campaign against the conversion of young Sikh and Hindu women to Islam when they marry a Muslim (Raj 2000: 555, notes 15 and 19).

Besides, Hindu nationalist organizations have cashed in on a very specific socio-political context in Great Britain and in North America, two countries which, especially in the 1980s-90s, combines a certain amount of ordinary racism and a strong sense of multiculturalism. Such alchemy tends to exacerbate communitarian mobilizations as Peter Mandeville has shown Muslim movements (Mandeville 2001).

In the United States multiculturalism has fostered the organization of the Indian minority, first because of the affirmative action policy underlying it. In 1977 the Association of Indians America fought to include Indians as 'minorities' expressly 'to benefit from the modest affirmative action provided by the state in its contracts' (Biju and Prashad 2000: 519–20). In 1982, the US Small Business Administration accepted a petition from the National Association of Asian Indian Descent requesting that Indians be recognized as a 'socially disadvantaged minority in need of special preferences' (Leonard 1995: 83). In 2000, the United States census gave Indians a specific category, enabling them no longer to be tallied together with Pakistanis.

In Canada, known for its social-mosaic rather than melting-pot ideal, the federal and provincial authorities, confronted with the demands of French-speaking Canadians, strengthened community groups by granting them tax advantages and giving them a role in the decision-making process at the municipal level. Thus, in both Great Britain and in North America, Hindus benefited from communitarian policies. In these three countries, Hindutva adherents seek to assert their 'genteel multicultural presence' to use Arvind Rajagopal's expression and take on the most ordinary attributes in order to appear harmless (Rajagopal 1997: 47, 51–65).

But alongside multiculturalism Anglo-Saxon style, British, American, and Canadian societies have multiplied forms of discrimination. Here, it is important to distinguish between the xenophobia of extreme right-wing movements and everyday expressions of ordinary racism. Bhatt and Mukta point out that 'the American and British New Right language of the 1980s . . . carried similar themes of "majority discrimination" and an attack on minority rights and protection' (Bhatt and Mukta 2000: 437). And thus Senator Pat Robertson slammed Hinduism, which he described as diabolical in the context of a campaign aiming to reduce the flow of Indian immigrants in a 'dominantly Christian' country.

Besides, these political developments, one must not overlook more benign forms of racialism. Children are the first victims of this refusal of otherness. How many second-generation immigrants in primary or secondary school have been the butt of classmates who were taken aback not only by the colour of their skin but by Hindu customs such as vegetarianism, cow worship, arranged marriages, wearing the sari, or the sacred rope worn by upper caste men?

This cultural context explains the founding of Hindu defence organizations not belonging to the *Sangh Parivar*. For instance in the United States the Federation of Hindu Associations vehemently protested against Sony's and Gap's use of Hindu deities in their advertising campaigns. Both companies had to cancel the ads and apologize for them. Similar protests were levelled at the American series *The Simpsons*, when in one of its episodes one of its characters threw peanuts at a statue called Goofy Ganesh. The scale of the challenge posed by these practices in the eyes of militant Hindus prompted them to create the American Hindu Anti-Defamation Coalition (AHADC) in 1997, modelled after the Anti-Defamation League initially founded to combat anti-Semitism. The primary aim of the AHADC is to monitor that the iconography and vocabulary used regarding

Hinduism does not convey prejudice against it. This approach was only possible because American law—in keeping with the official multiculturalism—-recognizes everything dear to the followers of one religion as worth protecting.

Across the border, several organizations such as Canadian Hope and the Hindu Conference of Canada pride themselves in monitoring and protecting Hindus' image in the national media.[23] The Hindu Conference of Canada has also set itself the aim of increasing the number of visas granted to Indians and facilitate the establishment of Indian and Hindu managers by granting degree equivalences. Moreover, it publicly backed the conservative party in the 2006 federal elections.[24] This example thus shows that multiculturalism enables communitarian defence groups to form associations, which quickly turn into ethnic lobbies.

Great Britain provides the most accomplished example of this evolution. Since September 2003, Hindutva organizations resolutely present themselves as ethnic lobbies. On this date, some of them, including Hindu Forum UK, as well as several MPs of Indian stock launched an 'Operation Hindu Vote' modelled after the 'Operation Black Vote'. This campaign sought at once to identify Hindu population centres and people who openly support a nationalist and extreme vision of Hinduism, in order to supply them with the necessary lobbying material, such as press packets.[25] This national lobbying effort is combined with growing participation in local politics. The NHSF, for instance, strongly encourages its members to be active in the National Union of Students and in student politics. The penetration of champions of Hindutva in student unions enables this ideology to benefit from legitimate forums. British Hindutva activists see in these various sources of political support, fostered by a policy of multiculturalism and a lack of information on Hindu extremism, a means of legitimation and a way to position themselves as spokespersons for the entire Hindu community, even the entire Indian community in the country.

The case study just explored enables us to qualify, even invalidate Benedict Anderson's theory of long-distance nationalism. Far from being the product of a one-way flow moving from the diaspora to the homeland, the migrants' ethno-religious mobilization is also the result of concerted action on the part of very well structured organizations. Western Hindu community involvement in Indian politics for the sake of promoting the majoritarian culture owes much to the way in which the RSS and its affiliates have established themselves overseas and orchestrated a veritable process of 're-Hinduization'. To expand its network overseas the RSS has been obliged to adapt its modus operandi, without denaturing it though. But its success was also due to the very specific context of host countries combining racism and multiculturalism.

These conclusions rehabilitate the role of political actors in a field where social forces are often analysed as largely autonomous and almighty. Arjun Appadurai, for instance, defines the 'ethnoscapes' resulting from the intensification of migrations as the creations of the diasporas alone. By ignoring the role of political agencies such as the *Sangh Parivar*, one takes the risk of disregarding new forms of overseas nationalism to conclude that diasporas belong to a post-national world, simply because they are incapable of giving a territorial dimension to their national imaginaire (see Appadurai 1997).

Our approach does not only re-evaluate the role of ideological movements but of another actor too, the state. Not only the nature of the state of the host countries matters, as evident from the impact of multiculturalist public policies mentioned above, but the role of the state of the original nation must be taken into account here. Indeed, the state can stimulate the national allegiance in those who have left their homeland, as well as their offspring. In the case of India, such a phenomenon clearly manifested itself when the Hindu nationalists came to power in 1998. The Hindu diaspora then became a target and a major resource for the ruling BJP. It now appeared not only as a bridgehead in the RSS millenarist mission or, more prosaically, a source of funding, but also a source of influence, a lever for Indian diplomacy. Jaswant Singh, BJP minister in the Vajpayee government, for instance considered that the Indians of the diaspora 'now . . . have to carry the message that India is preparing to be in the forefront as a global power to reckon with—not in the combative or confrontationist sense—but as a cultural and economic superpower' ('Conclusion' in Singh 2000). This message warranted dissemination first throughout the United States, the first world power where ethnic lobbying was accepted practice. For Brajesh Mishra, the then security advisor of Vajpayee, the 'brain drain' feeding the American economy with a supply of Indian engineers and doctors was an investment he readily consented to because it gave India the means of influencing American public opinion—particularly in Congress. He appreciated the fact that to do so, the Hindu diaspora had to follow the example of the Jewish lobby.[26]

The Vajpayee government experience was thus the framework of an attempt to instrumentalize the diaspora. This time the instrumentalization was not the work of an ideological group but of the Indian state itself. For the authorities it was not only a matter of using the diaspora as a new group ambassador, but also to attract new investors. This is the spirit in which the Pravasi Bharatiya Divas, the 'Overseas Indians Day', an annual event organized for the first time by the Government of India in January 2003 and presented as a meeting of NRIs with the Indian authorities, was started. Interestingly, Manmohan Singh's Congress alliance government pursued the approach undertaken by the Vajpayee regime after the 2004 alternation in power, not only by continuing the Pravasi Bharatiya Divas meetings, but by appointing a Minister of Overseas Indian Affairs, Jagdish Tytler, whose ideas are very close to those of his predecessor, the Hindu nationalist L.M. Singhvi.

Whatever the colour of the government in New Delhi, the Indian state is thus a party to the rise of the diaspora's 'long-distance nationalism'. This notion, indeed, must be analysed as the outcome, not only of social forces, but also of political actors, ideological minded organizations and the state itself.

## Notes

1. The Ocean waters are thus named in Hindu orthodoxy for to cross them means taking the risk of no longer being able to comply with Hindu rituals and especially, to expose oneself to impure contacts that cannot be washed away if one is far from places of purification such as the Ganges.

2. Bhai Parmanand, for instance, travelled through southern Africa and Guyana at the turn of the twentieth century as an Arya Samaj *updeshak* (see Parmanand 1982: 27ff).

3. Kavita Sukhu, vice-president of the Hindu Student Council (HSC), local student branch of the *Sangh Parivar*, at the University of Toronto, Saint George Campus, is a good illustration of this. Her grandparents, originally from the north of India, belonged to the Sanatan Dharma Sabha, an orthodox Hindu organization, and her grandfather was a priest. They finally settled in British Guyana. The following generation then migrated to Canada (interview with K. Sukhu in Toronto, 27 March 2006).

4. The founding of the VHP Overseas (led by B.K. Modi, also president of VHP, India) in November 2002 to coordinate VHP activities throughout the world fits within this same logic.

5. Interview with Rujuta Roplekar, 22 November 2005, London.

6. AWAAZ—South Asia Watch Limited (2004: 14, 51) http://www.awaazsaw.org/ibf/index.htm (accessed on 6 May 2004).

7. See the VHP website.

8. AWAAZ—South Asia Watch Limited, op. cit., 13, 50.

9. Ibid., 46.

10. Ibid., 51.

11. For more information see Therwath (2007).

12. The mission, all in all had 97 branches in India and abroad in the 1990s.

13. Its founder, the ascetic Neelkanth, born in 1781, emphasized social work in cities and villages, monotheism rather than idolatrous polytheism and superstition, and to counter the christian missionaries he structured the seat into dioceses according to the model of christian churches. See William (1984, 2001).

14. National Hindu Students Forum UK, 'Focus on religion folder', op. cit.

15. *The Foreign Exchange of Hate: IDRF and the American Founding of Hindutva*, Bombay: Sabrang Communications Private Limited.

16. *The Foreign Exchange of Hate*, op. cit. See also The South Asia Citizens Web, <http://www.stopfundinghate.com>, 20 November 2002.

17. Interview with Sat Wadhwa, Toronto, 29 March 2003.

18. AWAAZ—South Asia Watch Limited, op. cit.

19. Sword of Truth website: <http://wwv.swordoftruth.com/sworoftruth/archives/oldarchives/bjprss.html>.

20. Keeping in mind that the BJP is obliged to go through other branches of the *Sangh Parivar* to receive funds from the diaspora because the law forbids an Indian political party from receiving contributions from abroad.

21. The BJP spokesperson in Rajasthan moreover justified its refusal to Gehlot by explaining that 'the real purpose of Gehlot's visit to the US is to raise funds from expatriate Marwaris [merchant caste] for the forthcoming elections' (cited in S. Mishra, 'BJP sniffs cash stink in trip', *The Telegraph*, 1 July 2003).

22. This incident involved a Muslim woman repudiated by her husband by virtue of Koranic law, who, through the courts obtained maintenance payments despite the opposition of Muslim organizations for which this decision challenged the status of the Sharia as a source of law in India. In 1986, Rajiv Gandhi had a constitutional amendment passed exempting the Muslim community from the article of the Criminal Code by virtue of which the Supreme Court had ruled. He did this in order to ensure the continued support of Muslim opinion leaders. But his tactic resulted in a resurgence of Hindu nationalist activism.
23. See the Canadian Hope website: <http://www.canadianhope.org/aboutus.html>.
24. See the website of the Hindu Conference of Canada: <http://www.hccanada.com/media/HCCEndorsement.pdf>.
25. <http://www.redhotcurry.com/archive/news/2003/hindu_vote.html>.
26. Interview with Brajesh Mishra in Paris, Summer 2001.

# References

## PRIMARY SOURCES

### NGO Report

Awaaz—South Asia Watch Limited (2004), *In Bad Faith? British Charity and Hindu Extremism*, London.
Rajaram Mahajan Sharad (1997) (ed.), *Sarsanghchalak Rajendra Singh's Tours of Mauritius, S. Africa & Kenya in 1997*, Nagpur: Bharatiya Vichar Sadhana.
Seshadri, Hongasandra Venkataramaiah (1990), *Hindus Abroad: Dilemma—Dollar or Dharma?*, New Delhi: Suruchi Prakashan.

## OFFICIAL DOCUMENTS

Reeves, Terrance J. and Bennett, Claudette E. (2004), 'We the People: Asians in the United States', Census 2000 Special Reports, No. 17, December 2004. Available at the US Census Bureau website: <http://www.census.gov> (accessed January 2007).

### Confidential Document

Golwalkar, M.S. (1973), Private Correspondence Sent to L.M. Sabherwal, 9 March 2000.

### Pro-Hindutva Movement Documents

*Dharma Marg* (1984), January 1984, Vol. 1, No. 4.
Golwalkar, Madhavrao Sadashiv (1980[1966]), *Bunch of Thoughts*, Bangalore: Jagarana Prakashana.
Hindu Conference of Canada, <http://www.hccanada.com/media/HCCEndorsement.pdf> (accessed 15 February 2007).

Hindu Forum UK, <http://www.hinduforum.org/Default.aspx?sID=784&cID=36&IID=0> (accessed 12 October 2006).

Lakhani, Seeta (2005), *Hinduism for Schools*, London: London Vivekananda Centre.

National Hindu Students Forum UK, Souvenir (2003/2004), *Vision in Action*, National Hindu Students Forum.

National Hindu Students Forum UK (2004), *Challenge Yourself*.

National Hindu Students Forum UK (2005), *Hindu Concepts of Relationships: The Global Quest for Unity*, Leicester: De Montfort University, 26 November.

National Hindu Students Forum UK (Summer 2005), *HUM*.

Rashtriya Swayamsevak Sangh (1992), *Widening Horizons*, New Delhi: Suruchi Prakashan.

Singh, Jaswant (2000), *Pioneers of Prosperity: Contributions of Persons of Indian Origin*, New Delhi: Antar-Rashtriya Sahayog Parishad.

*The Organiser*, Republic Day Special, 28 January 1996.

———, 25 March 2007, p. 67

Vishva Hindu Parishad, <http://www.vhp.org/englishsite/d.Dimensions_of_VHP/qVishwa%20Samanvya/vishvahinduparishadabroad.htm> (accessed 8 May 2006).

## SECONDARY SOURCES

### Books

Andersen, Walter K. and Damle, Shridhar, D. (1987), *The Brotherhood in Saffron: The Rashtriya Swayamsevak Sangh and Hindu Revivalism*, Westview Special Studies on South and Southeast Asia, Boulder, Colorado: Westview Press.

Anderson, Benedict (1998), *The Spectre of Comparisons: Nationalisms, Southeast Asia, and the World*, London: Verso.

Appadurai, Arjun (1990), 'Disjuncture and Difference in the Global Cultural Economy', *Theory, Culture and Society*, Vol. 7, Nos. 2-3, July, pp. 295–310.

Bhatt, Chetan (2000), '*Dharmo Rakshati Rakshitah*: Hindutva Movement in UK', *Ethnic and Racial Studies*, Vol. 23, No. 3, May, pp. 559–93.

Bhatt, Chetan and Mukta, Parixa (2000), 'Hindutva Movements in the West: Resurgent Hinduism and the Politics of Diaspora', *Ethnic and Racial Studies*, Vol. 23, No. 3, May.

Biju, Mathew and Prashad, Vijay (2000), 'The Protean Forms of Yankee Hindutva', *Ethnic and Racial Studies*, Vol. 23, p. 3.

Burlet, Stacey (2001), 'Re-awakenings? Hindu Nationalism Goes Global', in Roy Starr (ed.), *Asian Nationalism in the Age of Globalization*, Richmond, Surrey: Japan Library (Curzon Press), pp. 1–18.

Dufoix, Stephane (2005), 'Notion, concept ou slogan : qu'y a-t-il sous le terme «diaspora»?', in L. Anteby-Yemeni, W. Berthomiere and G. Scheffer (eds.), *Les diasporas, 2000 ans d'histoire*, Rennes: Presses Universitaires de Rennes, pp. 53–78.

Goyal, Des Raj (1979), *Rashtriya Swayamsevak Sangh*, New Delhi: Radhakrishna Prakashan.

Graham, Bruce Desmond (1990), *Hindu Nationalism and Indian Politics: The Origins and Development of the Bharatiya Jana Sangh*, Cambridge: Cambridge University Press.

Jaffrelot, Christophe (1996), *The Hindu Nationalist Movement and Indian Politics*, New York: Columbia University Press.

—— (2005) (ed.), *The Sangh Parivar: A Reader*, Delhi: Oxford University Press.

—— (2007) (ed.), *Hindu Nationalism: A Reader*, Princeton, NJ: Princeton University Press.

Jain, Ajit (May 1998), *Genesis and Growth of HSS in Canada*, India Abroad.

Katju, Manjari (2003), *The Vishva Hindu Parishad and Indian Politics*, Hyderabad: Orient Longman, Delhi: Oxford University Press, pp. 429–35.

Lele, Jayant (2003), 'Indian Diaspora's Long-Distance Nationalism: The Rise and Proliferation of *Hindutva* in Canada', in S.J. Varma and R. Seshan (eds.), *Fractured Identity: The Indian Diaspora in Canada*, New Delhi: Rawat Publications, pp. 66–119.

Leonard, Karen (1995), *The South Asian Americans*, Westport CT: Greenwood Press.

Mandaville, Peter G. (2001), *Transnational Muslim Politics: Reimagining the Ummah*, New York: Routledge.

McKean, Lise (1996), *Divine Enterprise: Gurus and the Hindu Nationalist Movement*, Chicago: Chicago University Press.

Mukta, Parita (May, 2000), 'The Public Face of Hindu Nationalism', *Ethnic and Racial Studies*, Vol. 23, No. 3, pp. 442–66.

Parmanand, Bhai (1982), *The Story of My Life*, Delhi: S. Chand & Co.

Patchen, Nancy (1989), *The Journey of a Master: Swami Chinmayananda: The Man, The Path, The Teaching*, Berkeley: Asian Humanities Press.

Prashad, Vijay (1997), *The Karma of Brown Folk*, Minneapolis: University of Minnesota Press.

—— (2002), 'Ayodhya's Anniversary: NRI Donations for Barbarism', *Himal: South Asia*, Vol. 15, No. 12, December, p. 10.

Raj, Dhooleka Sarhadi (2000), 'Who the Hell Do You Think You Are?' Promoting Religious Identity Among Young Hindus in Britain', *Ethnic and Racial Studies*, Vol. 23, No. 3, May, p. 549.

Rajagopal, Arvind (1997), 'Hindu Immigrants in the US: Imagining Different Communities?, *Bulletin of Concerned Asian Scholars* 1997, Vol. 6, pp. 51–65.

—— (2000), 'Hindu Nationalism in the US: Changing Configurations of Political Practice', *Ethnic and Racial Studies*, Vol. 23, May, p. 3.

Ragazzi, Francesco (2004), *Looking at the Diasporic Field in International Politics: Diaspora As a Performative Utterance,* presentation before the Standing Group of International Relations, European Consortium of Political Research, The Hague, The Netherlands, 9-11 September.

Rashtriya Swayamsevak Sangh (1992), *Widening Horizons*, New Delhi: Suruchi Prakashan.

Therwath, Ingrid (2007), 'L'Etat face à la diaspora: stratégies et trajectoires indiennes', Unpublished dissertation, Institut d'Etudes Politiques, Paris.

Williams, Raymond Brady (1984), *A New Face of Hinduism: The Swaminarayan Religion*, Cambridge: Cambridge University Press.

—— (2001), *An Introduction to Swaminarayan Hinduism*, Cambridge: Cambridge University Press.

# Chapter 33

# India's Look East policy: an Asianist strategy in perspective

[In Southeast Asia], there is often some contempt for India because of her dependent condition; and yet behind all this there is a feeling of respect and friendship for India, for old memories endure and people have not forgotten that there was a time when India was a mother country to these and nourished them with rich fare from her own treasure-house. Just as Hellenism spread from Greece to the countries of the Mediterranean and in Western Asia, India's cultural influence spread to many countries and left its powerful impress upon them.

– Jawaharlal Nehru, *The Discovery of India*, 1989: 209–10

Our imagination is now riveted on the Asia-Pacific Century that is knocking at the door of human kind . . . Pan-Asian regionalism will take some time to emerge as a stable international phenomenon; when it does, it will truly change the world. Jawaharlal Nehru foresaw even in the late forties and the early fifties this great historical turn-around casting its silhouette on the horizon. For three and a half centuries Europe and America have dominated the world; almost the whole of Asia was a colony. Now in the 21st century Asia and the Pacific rim are likely to be the West's true peer in wealth, in technology and in skilled human resources.

– I.K. Gujral, External Affairs Minister, *India Digest*, Vol. IV, August 1996: 5

Historically, India has exerted a great cultural influence on East and Southeast Asia. One is reminded of Indianized kingdoms such as Khmer, Sailendra, Funan, Sri Kshetra, Sri Vijaya, and Majapahit through the splendour of Angkor, Borobudur, Bagan, and Lara Djonggrong. More importantly, India was the birthplace of Buddhism, which was later to spread throughout Asia. Although today Buddhists form only a small minority of the Indian population (0.76 per cent in 1991),[1] it is in this land that the Buddha began his teaching, and the Chinese travellers who came to India from the fifth through seventh centuries emphasized the vitality of this Buddhism.

This Indian influence can be witnessed even now by the popularity of the *Ramayana* in Southeast Asia. In 1992, a Kuala Lumpur-based organization produced a ballet entitled *The Ramayana: An Asian Confluence*, which fused a variety of Asian dance forms originating from several different countries including India and Indonesia. For Indian commentators, such a performance not only revealed the popularity of the *Ramayana* from South Asia to Southeast Asia, it also reflected the emergence of a new 'Asianism' (*India Today*, 31 December 1996: 102).

The notion of Asianism is not something new in India. As early as the inter-war period, some of the spokesmen of the Indian nationalist movement who were proud of this heritage displayed an 'Asiatic' identity. Nehru, for instance, expressed a desire to come closer to China[2] and other Asian countries in the name of common values explicitly in opposition to the West. This first Indian Asianism had much to do with the affirmation of nationalist feelings in the framework of an anti-colonial movement. While it would be reductionist to deny any role to ideas—to the notion of cultural affinities between Asian countries—Indians largely promoted the Asianist ideology because it suited their national interests. Moreover, this repertoire almost vanished after the failure of India's first attempt at propagating its brand of Asianism in the 1950s. This setback marked the beginning of a long period of retreat from Asia that ended in the 1990s.

The Asianist sensitivity that became visible in India in the 1990s responds to economic imperatives: Indian leaders eagerly invoke their cultural affinities with East Asia in their efforts to join this new pole of growth. Thus, the instrumentalization of these themes is again above all determined by national interest. Besides, the anti-West dimension of this turning toward Asia partly goes hand in hand with the rise of Hindu nationalism on the political scene. India, which had been for so long isolationist as if its huge size and population allowed it to be self-sufficient, is now opening up to East and Southeast Asia. It is doing so willingly, as this part of the world is perceived as an extension of India's own civilization and the birthplace of an alternative, non-Western model of modernization.

## India's First Asianism:
## A Nationalist Interest for the East

One cannot understand the relationship of India toward the rest of Asia without first studying the ideological characteristics of India's national identity. Certainly the freedom movement that crystallized against the British was not ideologically homogeneous. While the main strand of nationalist thought tended toward universalism, others advocated the affirmation of an ethnic—mainly Hindu or Muslim—sentiment. Yet all of these trends proceeded from a common reaction to Western colonialism: if, in the nineteenth century, some of the intelligentsia's socio-religious reform movements undertook to 'modernize' Indian culture along European patterns, this reformist zeal gradually weakened. By the early twentieth century, most Indian nationalist leaders were determined to affirm the value of indigenous traditions. Western materialism was then stigmatized in comparison to the spiritual vitality of India. In articulating such views, Indian ideologues were emulating the Orientalists' stereotype of the East. In that sense, nationalism was 'a derivative discourse' (Chatterjee 1986).

Mahatma Gandhi, more than anyone else, expressed this anti-colonial ideology in terms of a civilizational conflict. In *Hind Swaraj*, published in 1909, he did not try to link India's struggle against Western materialism with other Asian cultures,[3] but his nationalism later prepared the ground for a form of Asianism. Indeed, he fought against the West on behalf of values that were presented as being typically Asian, such as a spiritually based non-violent approach to politics and a non-individualistic sense of social harmony. Moreover, he changed his views and, eventually, advocated the notion of an Asian federation, eulogizing 'Asia's special international message of spiritual enlightenment' at the Asian Relations Conference in New Delhi in 1947 (Keenleyside 1982: 212, 216). Other Indian nationalist leaders developed an Asianist discourse even earlier and more explicitly than the Mahatma.

## ASIANISM AS AN OFFSPRING OF ANTI-COLONIALISM

Rabindranath Tagore regarded Asia as the only continent where real civilization was still alive[4] and defined this 'Eastern mind' with the same criteria as did Gandhi: 'spiritual strength', 'love of simplicity', and 'recognition of social obligation' (Tagore 1992: 22). These common features, according to Tagore, made the Asian countries one; in fact they had been the foundation of the unity of Asia in the past, an historical development that Tagore mentions without providing an accompanying date.[5] The characteristics of this Asian identity strongly contrast with the West, known for its materialism and its individualistic, anomic society. In fact, the whole Asianist discourse is built in opposition to the West. In the long run, the East would win out over the West because 'The East with her ideals, in whose bosom are stored the ages of sunlight and silence of stars, can patiently wait till the West, hurrying after the expedient, loses breath and stops' (Tagore 1992: 27). The rationale and themes of Tagore's Asianism are more or less the same as those of Gandhi's nationalism.

While Tagore tends to deal with Asia as a bloc, Nehru, another Indian leader who promoted the idea of an Asiatic identity during the inter-war period, did not consider all Asian countries in the same way. Nehru emphasized the affinities between India and China. He had come into close contact with Chinese nationalist leaders as early as 1927, when he had taken part in the Congress of Oppressed Nationalities in Brussels. The Indian and Chinese delegations at the Congress published a joint statement which Nehru played a role in drafting. The statement read that, 'From the days of Buddha, to the end of the Moghul period and the beginning of British domination in India, [the] friendly intercourse [of 'more than three thousand years' between both countries] continued uninterrupted' (*The Indian Quarterly Register*, 1927: 207). Subsequently, Nehru's visit to China in 1939 confirmed his views on the need for a rapprochement with that country.

During his imprisonment from 1930 to 1933, Nehru wrote most of the letters to his daughter Indira in the form of lessons in world history. These letters, which were later published in the book *Glimpses of World History*, reveal Nehru's admiration for China. He continually establishes a parallel between the long history inherited by contemporary China and that which India received as its legacy (1989: 28) in part because these countries enjoy a historical continuity which has no equivalent in Europe:

In Europe [with the coming of the Dark Ages] we see the end of a civilization and the early beginnings of another which was to develop slowly into what it is to-day. In China we see the same high degree of culture and civilization continuing without any such break. . . . So also in India. . . . [This culture] spreads from India to the other countries of the East. It absorbs and teaches even the barbarians who come to plunder. (ibid.: 111)

The continuity that Nehru emphasizes here is not only temporal but also geographical, since, for him, India is responsible for having provided the East Asian civilization with a solid basis. Nehru's Asianism does not involve any cultural disowning; on the contrary, it shows India in the role of moulding Asian cultures. Buddhism—whose message, as Nehru admits, has been adapted by East Asian countries according to their national characteristics—was the main factor responsible for this cultural influence, which, while promoting an Asian identity, enables him to extol the glory of India (ibid.: 113). In a later book, Nehru writes:

Probably China was more influenced by India than India by China, which is a pity, for India could well have received, with profit for herself, some of the sound commonsense of the Chinese, and with its aid checked her own extravagant fancies. China took much from India but she was always strong and self-confident enough to take it in her own way and fit it in somewhere in her own texture of life. (ibid.: 199)

Thus, in Nehru's view, Chinese culture owes much to the Indians (an argument the latter can use in their nationalist discourse), but China is a great civilization in its own right. The main point to be made concerns the opposition between, on the one hand, these two giants from Asia and, on the other hand, the West. Moreover, while Nehru heaped praise on the grandeur of China's classical civilization, he took care to present China as the representative of Asia[6] and as surpassing Europe.[7] Nehru's Asianism epitomizes a form of anti-Western nationalism or 'civilizationalism'. For him, India and China shared a philosophy of life that set them apart from the materialistic West, notably because of the notion of harmony with nature that both of them preached.[8]

While he admired China, Nehru was very critical of Japan. He considered Shintoism as a religion prone to legitimating social hierarchies and blind obedience to priests, whereas the Buddha had rebelled against this kind of attitude (ibid.: 119). According to him, the Japanese were characterized simultaneously by a rare capacity for being self-centered (ibid.: 271–3) and by the ability to imitate, indeed to copy, first from China (ibid.: 169) and then from the West. Nehru felt that the Westernization of Japan partly explained its expansionism: 'Japan not only followed Europe in industrial methods, but also in imperialistic aggression' (ibid.: 457).

Tagore had more or less the same opinion after his visit to Japan in 1916. He found in that country 'the same features of material greed, mechanical organization and imperialist aggression' (Thompson, 'Introduction', in Tagore 1992: 10), as were evident in the West. Before an American audience, he regretted that Japan 'thinks she is getting powerful through adopting Western methods but, after she has exhausted her inheritance, only the borrowed weapons of civilization will remain to her. She will not have developed herself from within'.[9]

By contrast, Lala Lajpat Rai, a colleague (and at times rival) of Jawaharlal Nehru's father, Motilal Nehru, was one of the first Congressmen to give a substantial account of his trips to Japan in 1915-6. He first emphasized a point that everybody had in mind since the war of 1905, after Japan had shocked European observers by defeating Russia: Japan 'has reached a stage in her evolution which entitles her to a place in the list of world powers' (Rai 1990: 110). Interestingly, Lajpat Rai justified this rise to a powerful position by the fact that Japan 'has falsified the croakings of her Western critics and their dictum that Western wine could not be put into Eastern bottles' (ibid.). In other words, Japan was a model because it had succeeded in borrowing from the West what it needed to modernize without losing its identity. While this view has gained many supporters today, it remained marginal at the time and could not make the same impact as the adverse judgements of Gandhi, Tagore, and especially Nehru, who was to be in command for a long time.

Nehru's stress on the special relationship between India and China was mainly aimed at showing Asian superiority over the West. By contrast, his Asianist discourse about Southeast Asia was more intended to support Indian nationalism, by developing the theme that India had been a dynamic and expanding force. Nehru had obviously been impressed by the archaeological discoveries of Angkor and Borobudur, which revealed how deep the Indian influence in this area had been, something he could not help being proud of:

The military exploits of these early Indian colonists are important as throwing light on certain aspects of the Indian character and genius which have hitherto not been appreciated. But far more important is the rich civilization they built up in their colonies and settlements and which endured for over a thousand years. (Nehru 1989: 201)

On the same page, Nehru even writes that Southeast Asia 'is sometimes referred to as Greater India'. Many Indian scholars in the 1940s repeated this notion. It was especially popular within the nationalist historiography (Keenleyside 1982: 213), but the Indian National Congress occasionally mentioned it, as well (*The Indian Quarterly Register,* 1926: 305-6). This 'big uncle'-like attitude stoked apprehensions among the countries of Southeast Asia.

The notion of Greater India was especially widespread in Hindu nationalist circles, which often emphasize India's historical link with Buddhism. This ideological milieu always considered the religions that had first appeared on Indian soil, including Buddhism, as having been acquainted with Hinduism, a belief they based upon their equation that Indianness equalled Hinduness. For instance, in the early 1950s, Shyama Prasad Mookherjee, founder of Jana Sangh, the most active Hindu nationalist party after independence, went on a tour in Southeast Asia in his capacity as president of the Mahabodhi Society of India. He carried with him the relics of the two main disciples of the Buddha, which Britain had just returned to India.[10] After having allowed millions of Buddhists to pay homage to the relics, first in Thailand and then in Vietnam, Cambodia, and Laos, Mookherji declared on his return: 'Many of these countries in Southeast Asia, after attaining independence, are striving hard to receive the highest elements of Buddhist cultural and religious thought. In this respect India occupies the role of their spiritual mother' (Madhok 1969: 187).

His call for Asian nations to come together under the leadership of India was directed against the West; in the context of decolonization it meant drawing sustenance from Asian traditions and founding a world different from the international order dominated by Western imperialism.

To sum up, as an ideology, the first Indian versions of Asianism did not regard all Asian countries in the same way. While China was an object of fascination that Nehru considered as India's peer and partner, Japan was generally poorly thought of because of its Westernization. Southeast Asia was often looked upon as an extension of India, the notion of Greater India reflecting a sense of nationalist expansionism. In fact, all the varieties and facets of Asianism had a common nationalist foundation. If these nationalist leanings are more obvious in the case of 'Greater India', they are in evidence when Indian leaders dwell on the superiority of Asia's spiritual mind over the lifestyle of the materialistic West. This discourse looks like a mere extrapolation of the nationalist language many Indian ideologues already used against the British to regain their self-esteem. Undoubtedly, many of them sincerely believed in the cultural affinities between Asian countries, but Asianism also flourished under the British Raj because it gave more weight to the nationalist discourse. The ambivalence of the formative phase partly explained the difficulties the Indian version of Asianism encountered after 1947.

A FAILED ASIAN PROJECT

In 1947, when India became independent, the leaders of the nationalist movement looked on Asia as 'their' region, a region where, Nehru thought, India's new status should endow it with some kind of leadership (Keenleyside 1982: 210–30). Nehru's sister, Vijaya Lakshmi Pandit, participated in the first United Nations conference in San Francisco and denounced the under-representation of other Asian countries. In 1947, she argued in the Constituent Assembly for the idea that India should assure its place as Asia's leader.[11] In January 1947, in the same assembly, Nehru declared that the Indian Constitution that was in the process of being formalized and

will lead also to the freedom of the countries of Asia, because in a sense, however unworthy, we have become—let us recognise it—the leaders of the freedom movement of Asia, and whatever we do, we should think of ourselves in these larger terms . . . we shoulder . . . the responsibility of the freedom of 400 million people in India, the responsibility of the leadership of a large part of Asia, the responsibility of being some kind of guide to vast numbers of people all over the world. (*Constituent Assembly Debates*, Vol. 1, 1989: 322)

In March 1947, when Indian independence had been acquired in principle but had not yet become effective, New Delhi organized a Conference on Asian Relations, bringing together 250 delegates from 25 countries, some of them still under colonial rule.[12] India then proclaimed itself the leader of Asia's march towards independence and confirmed this ambition during the Special Conference on Indonesia, which was organized in Delhi in January 1949 and which brought together 15 countries.

From the Indian point of view, the 1955 Bandung Conference of the non-aligned countries was the continuation of these first contacts. Nehru, through the doctrine of non-alignment, attempted to keep Asia away from the US—and Soviet-led blocs, as well as to make India one of Asia's leaders on the basis of shared cultural affinities. This approach was to be applied in particular to India's relations with China. In 1954, Nehru set forth his doctrine of *Pancha Shila*[13] in the Sino-Indian Panchashila Agreement, where India recognized China's sovereignty over Tibet. Chou Enlai warmly supported the inclusion of this notion in the 1954 agreement, and the Bandung Conference enthusiastically rallied to it. Parallel to this, New Delhi, which had recognized the People's Republic of China as early as January 1950, lobbied for China's admission in the UN, so that it could be party to great power discussions on settling the Korean issue.

Nehru's conciliatory approach to China was partly due to the Sino-Soviet alliance: in that context, a conflict between Delhi and Beijing would have probably pushed India toward the United States, a move Nehru wanted to avoid at any cost because, at that time, the Americans were close to India's main opponent, Pakistan—which had signed the Mutual Defence Assistance Agreement in May 1954. Besides, India was fundamentally attached to the non-aligned movement. To integrate China into the world diplomatic game, to treat it as a regular and trustworthy member of the international community, was also a means to oblige it to behave itself.[14]

Yet Asianism quickly lost most of its efficacy. The ideal of Asianism had been shaped against the imperialistic West. After decolonization, the notion of pan-Asian solidarity did not appear as relevant as it had previously: like pan-Arabism, pan-Asianism could hardly overcome the diverging interests of the new nation-states. To begin with, many Southeast Asian countries harboured a fear of India, especially as Nehru seemed anxious to transform his nation into a kind of regional leader. During the Conference on Indonesia in 1949, he had suggested that India might 'possibly play a fairly important part in bringing Asian countries together'. (Keenleyside 1982: 224). The Southeast Asian countries, which already had a sizeable Indian community, also feared that New Delhi favoured an emigration policy. Besides, many Southeast Asian countries showed greater interest in China than in India. This inclination was clear in Bandung, where Nehru was almost humiliated by the way Southeast Asian delegates ignored India and tended to rally around China's leadership. Finally, the Indian version of Asianism was not only jeopardized by the rivalry between Beijing and New Delhi for Asian leadership, but also by their bilateral conflict. The action taken by China in 1959 to put down dissent in Tibet and the Sino-Indian war of 1962 put an end to the warm relations between Beijing and New Delhi. China's influence in this zone prevented the countries of this region—with the exception of Malaysia—from supporting India during the 1962 war.

Other geo-strategic developments tended to cut India off from the rest of Asia. The Cold War logic did not leave any room for Asianist partisans inspired by the ideals of non-alignment to manoeuvre; Asia proved to be the site for some of the 'hotter versions' of this proxy war conducted through intermediary allies (Gupta 1964: 51). In the name of non-alignment, and because of its opposition to a substantial American presence in Asia, India strongly criticized the entry of several Asian countries (including Pakistan) into strategic alliances of Western inspiration, such as SEATO (Southeast Asian Treaty Organization, founded in 1954).

In the 1950s and 1960s, several Southeast Asian countries showed themselves open to a rapprochement with New Delhi. The newly born city-state of Singapore was among the first countries to take side in favour of India when the 1965 Indo-Pakistan war broke out; Malaysia supported the Indian position in the United Nations. Even so, when Singapore soon after sought India's assistance in setting up its army, New Delhi did not respond (Suryanarayan 1996: 16). The Association of South-East Asian Nations (ASEAN) was created without India in 1967 (Ayoob 1990: 11), and most Southeast Asian countries subsequently resented the strengthening of ties between India and the USSR in 1971.[15] Yet Malaysia served twice as the main arbiter of a more positive approach of the ASEAN toward India when in 1975 and 1980 Kuala Lumpur invited New Delhi to take part in a dialogue with the ASEAN. The Indian leadership showed indifference, even hostility, toward an association that it ultimately perceived as being the West's Trojan horse.

India's position in Southeast Asia was further complicated by the situation in Indochina. In 1980, as India was about to recognize the Hanoi-installed government of Heng Samrin in Cambodia, Indian Foreign Minister Narasimha Rao declined the Malaysian invitation to participate in the ASEAN Foreign Ministers' meeting. This last-minute decision, motivated partly by a concern to strengthen Vietnam vis-à-vis China and partly by a concern not to offend the Soviet Union, alienated India from the Southeast Asian governments. Thus the development of Western-led alliances, the growing ties between Pakistan and China and the Indo-Soviet alliance all served to cut India off from Southeast Asia for decades. Japan, a close ally of the United States during the Cold War, also kept some distance vis-à-vis India.

In short, Nehru's 'Asian' dream had slowly withered away from the mid-1950s. From then until the late 1980s India was largely isolated from all Southeast Asian nations except for Vietnam. In the late 1980s and early 1990s, however, India was forced to rethink its foreign policy because of the collapse of the Soviet bloc and its own domestic economic liberalization. To Indian liberalizers, East and Southeast Asia appeared to be a model of success, and Asianism could be revived under a different garb to serve new purposes.

## The Look East Policy of the 1990s

The collapse of the Soviet system deprived India not only of a valuable partner—(the Rupee Trade Area accounted for about one-fourth of its exports, and the USSR always supported India diplomatically through UN votes and militarily through arms sales) but also of an important (if flawed) model of centralized economic planning. The Indian establishment and the members of the intelligentsia who wanted to escape Westernization then became more favourably inclined toward Asianism as an alternative to the American capitalist model.

The balance of payments crisis in July 1991, which persuaded India to liberalize its economy under the authority of the International Monetary Fund (IMF), certainly proved to be another catalyst in its decision to open up to the world market. At the same time, the development of apprehensions (sometimes amounting to an inferiority complex) vis-à-vis East Asia, and particularly vis-à-vis an on-the-rise China,[16] has contributed to India's effort since 1991 to emulate its Asian neighbours. A number of Indians have held important posts in international organizations (for example, Manmohan Singh, the then Finance Minister and the architect of the Indian economic reforms, had been Secretary General of the South Commission of the UN in Geneva from 1987 to 1990) and these positions had helped them to compare the situation of their country to others before calling for the imitation of the East Asian 'models' in India. Manmohan Singh often repeated that Korea and India had the same GDP per capita in the 1950s and that South Korea could be emulated.[17] In September 1995, he declared, in the same vein: '[T]he economic policies of India take into account the dynamism of this region [Asia-Pacific], which shall soon be the tiger-economy of the world. We want to be participants in this process'.[18] Gautam S. Kaji, one of the Managing Directors of the World Bank, expressed the same view in April 1995, when he told a gathering of Indian financiers in Mumbai:

Certainly, the East Asian nations are still grappling with some of the same problems as India, albeit on a lesser scale. But they have demonstrated that with the right commitment, it is possible to move very far. With the same kind of commitment, I am convinced that there can be an 'Indian miracle.' (1995)

The Indian desire to draw inspiration from the East Asian path of development and to become more closely associated with this zone in economic terms was officially declared by Narasimha Rao (by this time Prime Minister) in 1994 during his visit in Singapore:

The Asia-Pacific could be the springboard for our leap into the global market place . . .

I am happy to have had this opportunity to enunciate my belief in this vision of a new relationship between India and the Asia-Pacific from Singapore, which I consider the geographic and symbolic centre of the Asia Pacific.

I trust this vision will be realized . . . and that the next century will be a century of partnership for us all. (1996: 23)

Two concerns underpin this discourse: on the one hand, India's efforts to come closer to East Asia and Southeast Asia through the organization of regional economic cooperation and foreign investment from this part of the world and, on the other, the imitation of methods employed by the East Asian countries. Each of these two options in its own way implies conferring value to an Asian identity of which India would be a participant.

## HOW TO WOO EAST ASIA?[19]

### Diplomatic Activity

In 1991, the government of Narasimha Rao claimed that Japan was one of the partners likely to help India in its new economic policy. In his autobiography, J.N. Dixit, then Foreign Secretary, recalls that 'Japan was identified as one of the most important sources of both investment and technology by the Government of India' (1996: 254). Japan, indeed, was the first country to send a substantial business delegation to India in December 1991. However, this delegation expressed reservations and even submitted a 21-point memorandum proposing further reforms that would make India a really attractive investment destination.[20] Narasimha Rao then went to Japan in 1992 for a weeklong visit, one that proved to be largely fruitless.[21] This is probably one of the main reasons for India's increased interest in Southeast Asia.

At the diplomatic and economic level, India had shown an interest in joining ASEAN since 1987. Such membership would have helped the timid policy of economic liberalization initiated by Prime Minister Rajiv Gandhi; it would have reinforced its effects by developing trade between India and other member countries and by encouraging confidence among investors. The ASEAN countries, however, expressed reservations that New Delhi should pay for the support it gave to the Heng Samrin regime, and feared that if India were to become a member of ASEAN Pakistan would try to follow suit. The ASEAN members were apprehensive about the destabilizing effect that the tensions between the two countries would bring to the organization, even though India had always promised that she would not introduce bilateral issues into ASEAN (Pillai 1995: 1911).

Nonetheless the economic reforms initiated by India in 1991 met with the approval of the ASEAN countries. In 1992, they granted India the status of 'sectoral dialogue partner' for tourism, commerce, investments, and science and technology. Around that time, Narasimha Rao accorded a new priority to Southeast Asia. In the second half of 1992, he placed the Foreign Secretary himself directly in charge of this region, which had previously been dealt with by one of the secretaries of the Ministry for External Affairs (Dixit 1996: 266). In October 1995, a member of the Secretariat for Economic Affairs of the Ministry for External Affairs declared: 'ASEAN is at the heart of our reworked strategy' (*India Today*, 15 October 1995: 138). Two months later, during the fifth ASEAN summit, India, along with China and Russia, was given the status of a full dialogue partner of the organization.

The possibility of a change of policy was opened up by the defeat of Congress (I) in the Indian general elections of May 1996, but the left-wing government eventually formed by H.D. Deve Gowda continued with earlier efforts to come to terms with East Asia. I.K. Gujral, the first Minister for External Affairs to attend an ASEAN conference (July 1996, in Indonesia), expressed there the government's approval of the new relationship in the following emphatic terms:

We see the full dialogue partnership with ASEAN as the manifestation of our Look East destiny. This is because we are geographically inseparable, culturally conjoined and now more than ever before, economically and strategically interdependent and complementary. . . . What the Look East policy really means is that an outward looking India is gathering all forces of dynamism—domestic and regional—and is directly focussing on establishing synergies with a fast consolidating and progressive neighbourhood to its east in the mother continent of Asia . . . [India] would work with ASEAN as a full dialogue partner to give real meaning and content to the prophecy and promise of the 'Asian century' that is about to draw upon us. (*The Times of India*, 25 July 1996)

The full dialogue membership made India an *ex-officio* member of the ASEAN Regional Forum (ARF), the body dealing with security issues. Besides obvious economic reasons, the full dialogue membership granted to India by ASEAN can be explained by considerations of geostrategy, mainly concerns—above all Singaporeans'—over Chinese assertiveness. In the mid-1960s, after China's successful nuclear test, premier Lee Kuan Yew had said he would welcome an Indian naval presence in Southeast Asia, and had even invited India to hold a nuclear test (Ghoshal 1996: 96). In the 1970s and 1980s, for several reasons mentioned above, including the Indo-Soviet alliance, India was not seen any longer as a potential protector. This perspective changed in the 1990s. The Southeast Asian countries became worried about China's power again, mainly because of China's nuclear tests, its claim over the Spratly Islands in the South China Sea and its aggressive attitude at the time of the Taiwanese elections in 1996. Fearing that the collapse of the Soviet Union could lead the United States to withdraw from strategic locations in Asia and free China from its previous constraints, East and Southeast Asian countries were eager to play it safe by establishing vital sea-lanes of communications, such as the Taiwan, Malacca, Sunda, and Lombhok Straits. In this context, ASEAN countries could well regard India as a useful partner to balance China given the former's nuclear capacity (implicit since 1974) and its naval forces, the largest in the Indian Ocean.[22]

Joint Indian naval exercises took place with Indonesia and Malaysia in 1991 and Singapore in 1993. Although Singapore had once considered the Indian navy to be a threat to the security of its region, in 1996 it concluded an agreement with India on military cooperation that included anti-submarine warfare exercises and allowed Singapore to test certain missiles with Indian naval installations. Similarly, in 1993 Malaysia signed a Memorandum of Understanding with India on defence cooperation providing training to MiG-29 fighter pilots, supplying spare parts, and servicing these aircraft (Naidu 1995: 17, and Naidu, 'India Strategic Relations with Southeast Asia', p. 32). Thus, proponents of Asianism such as Malaysian Prime Minister Mahathir Muhammad and Lee Kuan Yew certainly welcomed India in the great Asiatic family because of cultural affinities, but for other reasons as well.

Parallel to its diplomatic offensive aiming at becoming a member of the ASEAN,[23] India sought to intensify its bilateral economic relations with East Asian countries. From 1992 onward, Narasimha Rao sought closer ties with East and Southeast Asian countries by visiting them regularly. On each visit he was accompanied by an impressive delegation of businessmen: in Indonesia in 1992, Singapore, Thailand, Malaysia, Vietnam, and South Korea[24] in 1993, Singapore again in 1994, and Malaysia again in 1995. Similarly, President Suharto of Indonesia visited India twice in 1993, Prime Minister Mahathir of Malaysia came three times (in 1993, 1994 and 1996), Prime Minister Goh Chok Tong of Singapore was the chief guest in the Republic Day of India in 1994, and Lee Kuan Yew (still a dominant force in Singapore despite his political retirement) is a regular visitor.

These visits gave many opportunities to the Indian prime ministers and their Southeast and East Asian counterparts to develop an 'Asianist' discourse. Singapore and Malaysia are two of the Southeast Asian countries with which India probably had the oldest tradition of warm relations, because of the strong presence of an Indian community and old economic ties. Yet the common experience of colonialism and its intellectual outcomes were obviously not the cultural aspects that Indian officials liked to emphasize,[25] instead they preferred to put forward their respect for Asian values. Thus, during his visit to Kuala Lumpur in 1995, Narasimha Rao declared before Dr Mahathir that the deepening of Indo-Malaysian relations would favour the emergence of 'an Asian identity' (*The Hindustan Times*, 4 August 1995. Approved investments from Malaysia rose from US$1.8 million in 1991 to US$1 billion in 1995.) The same comments applied to the relations between India and Singapore, since, according to a well-informed student of Indian foreign policy, 'Both countries believe that exchanges with each other will be less threatening to traditional values than [will exchanges] with Western countries.'[26] The reference to 'Asian values' here is not only intended to intensify diplomatic relations while keeping the West aloof; it is also used by India to attract a benevolent attitude from East and Southeast Asia in terms of investments.

Buddhism is used to this effect, as was illustrated by the 1995 visit of Bihar's Chief Minister Laloo Prasad Yadav, who underlined the fact that the place where the Buddha obtained enlightenment, Bodh Gaya, was situated in his state. The trees grown from cuttings of the fig tree beneath which this event took place are objects of worship throughout the Buddhist world, and Bodh Gaya itself harbours temples financed by Thai, South Korean, and Japanese Buddhists. Laloo Prasad Yadav accompanied his discussions with leaders and businessmen of Thailand and South Korea with a video cassette showing the Buddhist sites of Bihar. He even opened up the negotiations by declaring that his state was the cradle of the 'powerful emperor Ashoka, who spread the message of the Buddha far and wide in the countries of Asia'.[27] This use of Buddhism is not limited to Bihar alone, since Uttar Pradesh, the neighbouring state which also has some Buddhist sites, set up shuttle flights in 1995 allowing East Asian pilgrim-tourists to visit them. The Japanese government has undertaken to contribute 20 to the development of tourist infrastructure for the 'Buddhist circuits'.[28]

Buddhism, however, is not the only common reference that advocates of Asianism put forward to justify the rapprochement between India and other Asian countries. In February 1996, Kim Young Sam, in the first official visit of a South Korean president to India, expressed happiness about the ongoing reconciliation between the two countries in the name of Asian values. He underlined the fact that he included in those values those upheld by Mahatma Gandhi, whose writings had largely contributed to fashion his own philosophy (*The Times of India*, 24 February 1996: 11).

## The Economic Outcome

The results of Indian efforts to attract East and Southeast Asian capital and to develop commercial links have not been negligible. Of course, the Americans and the British remained the main investors for the period from August 1991 to October 1994 (the United States representing 34.5 per cent of foreign investments and the United Kingdom 10.3 per cent); but Japan followed with 6.3 per cent and Hong Kong, Thailand, and Singapore were among the next fifteen investors (*Asia Newsletter*, December 1994: 2).

Japan, while it has remained among the top investors in India, did not show as much enthusiasm as New Delhi had hoped in the early 1990s. Initially, India benefited from the increasing presence of Japanese firms in Asia. Suzuki, which had played a pioneering role in the automobile sector by founding, in collaboration with the Indian government, a joint-venture called Maruti as early as 1983, took advantage of the economic liberalization to obtain a 50 per cent share in a company that produced 81 per cent of the 425,000 personal and utility vehicles produced in 1996–7. Honda and Toyota have also joined with Indian groups to make vehicles. (In the latter's case, total investment in the project is estimated at US$263 million to US$439 million) (*Nikkei Weekly*, 6 January 1997). Sony is one of the rare foreign firms that has a wholly owned Indian subsidiary, and Fujitsu, Hitachi, and Sanyo have been also attracted to India because of the size of its market and its educated work force (Prakash et al. 1996: 239).

Nonetheless, the presence of Japanese firms remains well below Indian expectations. Of the 4,299 Japanese firms operating in Asia in 1991, only 110 were doing business in India (Kesavan 1996: 99). In the 1990s, while Maruti occupied the seventh place on the list of Japanese firms operating abroad in terms of sales, the second Japanese undertaking working in India ranked ninety-seventh and the third at 142.

Japanese investments in India represented US$95 million in 1994–5, US$61 million in 1995–6, and US$96 million in 1996–7, which meant that Japan remained the fourth or sixth largest foreign investor, depending on the year under consideration and that its investments represented 4–5 per cent of total foreign direct investments (FDIs) entering India every year. These rather low figures are not difficult to explain. The Japanese were worried about the continued existence of bureaucratic restrictions and the uncertainties that weighed on the continuation of the programme of economic liberalization.[29] Japanese diplomats were not shy of justifying the hesitations of their investors by arguing, as the Japanese Ambassador did in February 1997, that Thailand, Malaysia, and the Philippines 'provide a somewhat better business environment' (interview in *International Times*, 7 February 1997: 3).

Similarly, while Japan remained the second trading partner of India in the mid-1990s, its market absorbed only 7.7 per cent of the Indian exports in 1994–5 as against 10.7 per cent in 1985–6 (Government of India 1996: 88). Thus, while the Japanese showed interest in India in the 1990s, they were clearly waiting and watching for a consolidation of the economic liberalization. As a result, they prefer to put stress on overseas development aid (ODA) rather than on direct investment.

In comparison, South Korean multinationals showed greater enthusiasm. The investments of the fifty-two South Korean companies operating in India went up from US$12 million in 1994–5 to US$333 million in 1996, making this country the third largest investor in India. As a result, in 1997, Japan and South Korea were neck-and-neck in terms of investments in India over the post-liberalization period (1991–7): with about Rs 62,000 million, Japan was the fourth foreign investor, and South Korea came immediately after with almost Rs 57,000 million. Given the low level of the South Korean presence in 1991, this was revealing of a voluntarist strategy. The chaebols (large Korean conglomerates) were naturally the main architects of this strategy. In 1995, Daewoo 'decided to transfer to India a part of its Chinese budget because it seemed there was a greater freedom for investment'. In 1996, it increased its equity holding in DCM–Daewoo Motors Ltd., the joint-venture originally set up with Toyota, from 51 per cent to 75 per cent, and then to 92 per cent in 1997. The other South Korean automobile maker, Hyundai, 1995, has been able to create a wholly owned subsidiary for a total investment of US$700 million. In contrast with most of the foreign manufacturers, which established plants in India in order to gain access to the domestic market, the South Korean firms largely use India as a 'work shop' country with lower labour costs. This strategy marks a new step in the process of industrial shift in concentric circles, which had given birth to the so-called 'flying geese' investment pattern originating in Japan.

The share of the investments coming from ASEAN countries has jumped from almost nothing in 1991 to US$2.5 billion in the late 1990s (Mattoo 2001: 111). The three leading countries have been Malaysia (US$1.3 billion in 1991–8), Singapore (US$833 million) and Thailand (US$612 million). The symbol of the growing presence of Southeast Asian countries in India is the US$150 million Technology Park Project of Bangalore, financed by Singapore. If one looks at cumulative investments from 1991 to 1997, the city-state ranks fourteenth among the foreign investors in India. Malaysia is ahead, occupying the eighth rank with US$36 billion. The role played by Singapore and Malaysia can be partly explained by their large Indian minorities, since in 1981 they had respectively 167,000 and 1.2 million inhabitants of Indian origin, or, respectively, 8.5 per cent and 6.7 per cent of their populations (Lardinois 1996: 307). While New Delhi tended to neglect these components of the Indian diaspora for a long time, in the 1990s successive governments attempted to attract investments from these Non-Resident Indians (NRIs). Several NRI groups from Singapore are investing in India today (Bhattacharyya 1996: 59). In a symmetric way, Indian firms are establishing joint-ventures in Southeast Asia, sometimes with the help of NRIs. In 1993, out of 430 joint-ventures with an Indian participation abroad, 98 were located in Malaysia, Singapore, Thailand, and Indonesia (ibid.: 57). Most of them, however, are small in scale.

Moreover, the ASEAN investment projects approved by the Indian government did not represent more than 5 per cent of the total in 1995. Similarly, the volume of trade between India and the ASEAN countries almost tripled between 1992–3 and 1996–7 (rising from Rs 71,500 million to Rs 205,000 million in 1996–7), but in 1995 the European Union still absorbed 27 per cent of Indian exports, as against 7 per cent for the ASEAN market (Asia at large represented 14 per cent of the total). One therefore had to look at the actual figures and the trend separately. Unfortunately, the trend could not be sustained in the late 1990s because of the Asian crisis and other turbulences.

## LATE 1990S TURBULENCES: INDIA, THE ASIAN CRISIS, AND 'POKHRAN II'

India's 'Look East policy' has been badly affected by the Asian crisis after 1997. From 1996–7 to 1998–9, the ASEAN share in Indian exports fell from 8.5 per cent to 4.7 per cent, the Japanese share from 6 per cent to 4 per cent, and the South Korean share from 1.5 per cent to 0.8 per cent.

East and Southeast Asian investments in India also suffered. South Korea's investments fell from US$33 million in 1997–8 to US$8 million in 1999–2000. While Hyundai succeeded in capturing 10 per cent of the automobile market in a very short time, Daewoo sank and was even for sale in late 2002. Malaysian investments have also been reduced drastically between 1997 (Rs 21,000 million) and 1999 (Rs 1,100 million). Japanese firms were the only ones to resist. They even increased their investments, from $US 96 million in 1996–7 to US$142 million in 1999–2000.

Despite the increasing Japanese economic presence in India, relations between India and Japan became very tense after India's Pokhran II nuclear tests in May 1998. Tokyo was the first to react: overseas development aid was suspended, and Japanese authorities cancelled the meeting of the Aid India Consortium and vetoed any financial support from the multilateral institutions in which Tokyo had a say. Keizo Obuchi, then Japan's Foreign Minister and later to become Prime Minister, initiated a 'Tokyo forum', in which nineteen countries took part and whose aim was to build support against the development of nuclear weapons. In November 1998, Tokyo lifted some of the sanctions it had imposed upon Pakistan after its nuclear tests; India had to wait few more months to benefit from the same treatment. Not surprisingly, the Hindu nationalist press was annoyed by such an attitude:

Japan has been generous, if not 'reckless' in investing in Pakistan. Japan has been equally stingy and reluctant while investing in India, though the Western media have called Japan's attitude towards India 'caution'. Japan is currently the biggest bilateral donor to Pakistan. . . . There is a hidden political agenda behind this so-called 'caution' approach. Japan fears India as a competitor in international politics. (Sharma 1998: 15)

In November 1999, Prime Minister Obuchi told Jaswant Singh, the Indian Foreign Minister, that the normalization of the relations between both countries could not occur, before India signed the Comprehensive Test Ban Treaty (CTBT), a condition that was ill received by New Delhi.

Relations between India and ASEAN were also affected by the nuclear tests. In July 1998, during the Manila summit, two schools of thought emerged: those who wanted to impose sanctions over India (Japan, Australia, Canada, and New Zealand) and those who recommended a more benign attitude (Singapore, Vietnam, Malaysia, and Indonesia). Eventually, the final resolution expressed 'the grave concern' of the country members and 'strongly deplored the nuclear tests in South Asia, which exacerbated tensions in the region and raised the spectre of a nuclear arms race.' This was a rather weak condemnation, in which India was not even explicitly mentioned. In fact, one excerpt of the resolution harked back to an old Indian stand, since it 'strongly urged the nuclear-weapon States to take concrete and timely measures towards the total elimination of nuclear weapons in compliance with the positions of the NPT (Nuclear Non-Proliferation Treaty)'. One of the most influential Indian experts on security issues, the journalist Raja Mohan, wrote in *The Hindu:*

> In stopping the Anglo-Saxon brigade from condemning India for its recent nuclear tests at the annual security conclave here [Manila] this week, the South-East Asian nations have once again demonstrated their genuine commitment to a deeper relationship with India. . . . The collapse of the Soviet Union and the rise of China at the turn of the 1990s fundamentally transformed the Asian landscape. As India embarked on the path of economic reform and renewal in the mid-1990s, the ASEAN was quick to see the potential for a positive Indian role in the evolution of Asian balance of power. As a consequence they rushed to bring India into the ARF by end of 1995. . . . It is the solid support from Singapore, Indonesia, Malaysia, Vietnam and Laos that allowed India to emerge relatively unscathed from the ARF meeting here. (1998: 11)

Indo-South Korean relations were even less affected by the Pokhran II tests because of the growing awareness in Seoul, that Pakistan—the country posing the most direct nuclear threat to India—was giving nuclear technology to North Korea, their own arch enemy.[30]

Thus, India's Look East policy has certainly suffered from the 1998 nuclear tests and even more from the Asian crisis. But its limitations also stem from the ambiguous conception of Asia that India, and more especially, the Hindu nationalist movement, is propagating.

## Emulating Asia, or Influencing Asia? The Syndrome of Great(er) India

### An 'Asianization' Focusing on the Ambivalent Emulation of Japan

From the outset, India's Look East policy was Japan-oriented, not only because New Delhi expected more investment from that country, but also because in the early 1990s it appeared as the first success story of Asia: a country which epitomized a non-Western version of modernity—not only democracy, something India already knew, but also economic prosperity. In the early 1990s, opinion polls (which are increasingly reliable although restricted to the urban middle class) showed a real fascination with Japan. In 1993, it was by far the most popular country in the polls of the *Monthly Public Opinion Surveys:* 49.9 per cent of the respondents had a very good opinion of Japan (against 30.2 per cent for the United States, which came next), 36.6 per cent had a good opinion (against 39.8 per cent) and 7.9 per cent had neither a good nor a bad opinion (against 18.9 per cent) (*Monthly Public Opinion Surveys*, February–March 1993: v). In 1995, India's relations with Japan were perceived in a similar way, since 43 per cent considered them to be 'very good' and 50.7 per cent 'quite good'. The highest scores were among the more educated people, notably students, professionals, businessmen, and executives.

(ibid., July 1995: xi). In 1996, Japan again proved to be the most popular country, with three-fourths of the interviewees displaying a positive image of the country (50.8 per cent had a 'very good opinion' of Japan and 34.2 per cent a 'good opinion').[31]

The first group to become enthusiastic about promoting a Japanese-oriented 'Asian culture' was the business sector. During the Deve Gowda government, the man who most explicitly represented business interests was Finance Minister P. Chidambaram. He declared in 1997 that India could become an economic giant like Japan within a lifetime and that India 'will now Asianise itself': 'It is time now for India to learn from the Asian experience, pull herself up, step up efficiency and demand its rightful place in the world' (*The Times of India*, 15 February 1997: 14 and 8 March 1997: 1).

Since the early 1990s, India has been in the process of rediscovering capitalism within the framework of economic liberalization. Economic supplements within newspapers are proliferating—such as *Ascent,* which appeared for years every week in *The Times of India*—and one could detect in them an increasing interest in 'Japanese methods'. This is implicit when it is a question of enhancing the value of family environment in the enterprise (Balakrishnan 1995: 1), but most often the Japanese inspiration is announced right from the first lines of the article, whether the question be productivity or adaptability supposedly inspired by Zen Buddhism.[32] Books on Japanese methods are also being published and are reviewed in the specialized press (Bhattacharyya 1995; *The Economic Times*, 29 October 1995). In practice, the major Indian companies subject to increasing competition are showing increasing willingness to import Japanese techniques such as total quality management, *kaizen* (a technique by which the worker is continuously helped to improve his performance), and *kanban* (a similar technique used for managerial tasks) (Rattanani 1995: 66–7). More than 3,000 Indian executives have already been trained by correspondence courses to apply these methods.

This fascination with Japan can be explained by the fact that, while a large part of the Indian elite is not shy of emulating the West (as opinion polls suggest), an equally large fraction is looking for a model of capitalism which is not purely Western. India's tradition of fighting against imperialism, which had been shaped by the nationalist intelligentsia and the state during Nehru's era, have created a broad-based anti-Americanism, which becomes more prevalent at times of tension such as the Gulf War of 1991 and its replay in 2003. Moreover, taking inspiration from Japan can be seen as India not disowning itself but re-establishing links with its own timeless traditions. India's Asianism, of which the enthusiasm for Japan is only one aspect, constitutes in many ways a means to regenerate India's own culture. This point is well illustrated by the indigenization of the Total Quality Management technique suggested by one of the executives of Eischer, an Indian firm that applied Japanese methods:

This is quite similar to the Hindu concept of the attainment of spiritual objectives through Karma Yoga (the selfless pursuit of one's duties). Total Quality Management requires that we serve all our external and internal customers with a substantially diminished sense of our own importance, or our own indispensability. (Lal 1992; and 'How to Woo Japan?', p. 48)

The 'Japan' supplement published in November 1994 by *The Times of India* offers a corpus of texts that are revealing in this regard. All the authors underline the sense of work and discipline of the Japanese and then go on to highlight the cultural affinities which should allow India to follow the same path:

Research shows that there is a striking similarity between the Indian and Japanese psyches. Both are familial (not individualistic) but the Japanese psyche extends beyond the family itself, unlike the Indian psyche. The orientation of the Japanese is collectivistic, characterized by the commitment to achieve the specified goals by cooperating with group members. Then to what extent can we practise Japanese management elements in our country? (Vijaykumar 1994: 9)

Here India and Japan are brought together on the basis of the classic distinction between the individualistic West and an East where social solidarity is still strong. But Japan has succeeded in channelling its sources of social cohesion towards economic success, and it is there that India has to learn from Japan, all the more so because that does not mean betraying one's culture. As another contributor points out: 'Of all our trading partners, Japan has the closest cultural and spiritual ties with India. . . . The Japanese have studied our civilization and absorbed its values. We would be well advised to study their civilization and assimilate its values' (Palkhivala 1994: 1).

Presenting things in such a way is equivalent to saying that for the Indian elite to emulate Japan is to rediscover the essence of India.[33] The limitation of this brand of Asianism is quite obvious: India thinks of itself as the centre of Asian cultural influence because of its ancient civilization and because of the fact that Buddhism appeared on its soil. This inclination, which calls to mind India's first pre-independence Asianism, goes hand in hand with the recent rise of Hindu nationalism.

## ASIANISM AND HINDU NATIONALISM

While we have dwelt on the affinities between Asianism and Indian nationalism before independence, we have not studied closely the relationship between this 'ism' and another nationalist ideology, Hindu nationalism. In contrast with Nehru, Hindu nationalist leaders always strongly mistrusted the People's Republic of China, partly because of its Communism, but more importantly because of its expansionism. In the 1950s Hindu nationalists were quick to denounce China's policy in Tibet (Jaffrelot 1996: 178–9). The 1962 war heightened their hostility toward this country. The leader of the Rashtriya Swayamsevak Sangh (RSS) even resorted to a racist repertoire:

. . . in Communist China we have the explosive combination of two aggressive impulses. It is a case of 'Already a monkey, moreover drunk with wine'. We would therefore only be deluding ourselves and taking false steps in our preparation to face it if we attribute Communist China's aggressiveness only to its racial nature and not to its present Communism also. . . . [The Chinese] do not possess even normal human qualities like kindness, pity or respect for human life. (Golwalkar 1966: 381–2)

While the Hindu nationalists did not feel, like Nehru, that China had a civilization comparable to that of India. To say the least, they always regarded Buddhism as a great religion of India. In the beginning of the century, the Hindu Mahasabha—the first political organization propagating this ideology—welcomed into its ranks Sinhalese Buddhist revivalists, such as Anagarika Dharmapala. Certainly, a number of Hindu nationalist ideologues lamented that Buddhism was responsible for introducing within India a spirituality removed from caste-based duties, and that such a spirituality therefore served to weaken societal links (Jaffrelot 1995). Nevertheless in 1956, when B.R. Ambedkar and several hundred thousand other Dalits converted to Buddhism to escape the caste system, Hindu nationalists were satisfied with this choice because Buddhism was another Indian religion. (They had feared that Ambedkar would opt for Islam or Christianity, both of which faiths had been actively considered by the Dalit leader.) In 1964, the founding of the Vishva Hindu Parishad was accompanied by the establishment of links with Buddhist movements. In 1979, the second Hindu national conference organized by the VHP was inaugurated by the Dalai Lama, perhaps the most widely recognized Buddhist leader in the world. Such a background explains the stand of the Bharatiya Janata Party (BJP).

Since the 1990s, the Hindu nationalists have been favourably inclined towards the Congress-initiated 'Look East policy'. In 1996, the electoral manifesto of the BJP, on the occasion of an election that was to make it the first political force in Parliament, announced as the objective of its foreign policy 'the promotion of Asian solidarity' (Bharatiya Janata Party 1996). Hindu nationalists also seem still to find the Japanese model especially attractive because Japan shows that it is possible to become modern without becoming Westernized (D'Costa 1995: 12). The upper middle class and the economic elite sharing this body of opinion also form the core base of the BJP.

Members of the middle class are indeed concerned about modernization, not only because they fear that India could be left behind in the race for international power (behind China for instance), but also because of their new consumerism. At the same time, sectors of the middle class show some disenchantment toward Westernization.[34] The Hindu nationalist movement thus sees in Japanese methods an inspirational source for its own anti-Western campaigns. Its leaders obviously find some common ground between the Japanese industrial ethos and their own concern for promoting a typically Indian sense of entrepreneurship, such as what they call the 'Bhakti model' which is 'based on the parental relationship existing between a mother and a child' and which, therefore, conceives of 'the manager's role as mother giving nurturing love to the subordinates' (*The Organiser*, 2 February 1997). Besides, the Hindu nationalist leaders have found in Japan arguments supporting some of their protectionist stances. At the end of 1993, India's signing of the General Agreement on Tariffs and Trade (GATT) was the occasion for them to launch a campaign against the 'selling out' of India to international capitalism. In fact, the purpose of this campaign was to oppose the entry of multinationals into India's market of consumer goods. This campaign was cleverly conducted under the banner of *swadeshi*, a word first used during colonial times to designate the boycott of British goods, and one whose emotional resonance was still powerful. P. Ghate, the leader of the Bharatiya Mazdoor Sangh, the labour union associated with the BJP which had recently overshadowed a major union affiliated to the Congress Party, regarded Japan as a 'model of *swadeshi*'. He appreciated the way in which Eisuke Sakakibara (then the head of the Japanese Ministry's International Finance Bureau) and Takeshi Umehara (a philosopher and anti-American eulogist of the Japanese way of development) had rejected Western capitalism. Ghate described the United States as the great lesson-giver that has lost its human face. Against American hegemony, Asian values were presented as the best alternative to Westernization:

Highly Westernized outwardly, Japan has kept its tradition and culture alive in its heart to develop its own indigenous economic model. It should be an eye-opener to those countries which have been either forced to follow the capitalist model of the west or are feeling helpless in the wake of the onslaught of free market economy . . . Umehara thinks that replacement for liberalism will be drawn from Asian values. Japan's Shintoism involves nature worship and Buddhism holds that plants and mountains deserve as much respect as people. Confucian ethics encourage respect for authority. All these principles become guidelines for economic development, he feels. In the Japanese view, developing countries should treat the free market advice of western economists with caution . . . This is the Japanese swadeshi economy. There is much for India to learn from it. (1995)

Ghate probably puts in the mouths of the Japanese more than they have said (regarding economic liberalization, for instance), but it is revealing of the Hindu nationalists' view of Japan. They are all the more attracted to the Japanese model as they see in it a method by which India can modernize in the face of the West without betraying its identity. Further, the notion of Asianism probably attracts them on the condition that Hinduism plays the role of the bonding agent and guiding principle. Moreover, they are willing to see their nationalist objective diluted within an Asianist thrust to the extent that it will be able to affirm Hindu identity, indeed Hindu primacy (at least in historical terms). In 1969, Balraj Madhok, the former president of the Jana Sangh, wrote that, for his predecessor and mentor, S.P. Mookerji, 'Buddhist thought and culture, which is essentially

Indian or Hindu in its inspiration and essence, could act as a great unifying factor to bind together the Buddhist world, particularly the Southeast Asian countries, with India' (Madhok 1969: 183).

This kind of nationalism still seems to be prevalent today. It clearly reflects the persistence of the notion of Greater India that had always been a liability for New Delhi in its relations with Southeast Asia. As an Indian academic who worked in Indonesia puts it:

An important assumption underlying our attitude to the region is that we understand Southeast Asia because it is like India. It is believed that the culture of the region is an extension of the culture of India. This close cultural affinity, it is assumed, will help us in building up a good working relationship with the people of Southeast Asia. (Dasgupta 1996: 81)

In fact, the author adds, this kind of Indo-centric view of Southeast Asia is bound to provoke a nationalist reaction. Cultural affinities can be instrumentalized in the framework of an Asianist discourse, but an excessively India-centred use of it could alienate the countries of this area. This is one of the risks inherent in the Hindu nationalist version of Asianism that tends to revive the concept of Greater India. While *The Organiser,* the Hindu nationalist weekly, is now publishing articles on the Indian diaspora, these often focused on its Hindu rituals (*The Organiser,* 2 March 1997) and regard the countries where it is well represented as part of 'Farther India'. Claiming, for instance, that the Hindus of Malaysia 'have preserved their centuries-old culture and values', one of the columnists explains that 'On account of the large number of temples in the country Malaysia looks like another Hindusthan' (Kumar 1995).

The Indian case probably offers a good illustration of both the scope and the limits of Asianism. Asianism is not a phenomenon that can be interpreted through a culturalist approach; we are not witnessing a joining together of societies that have discovered some fundamental cultural affinities and consequently aspire to a closer political, economic, or other collaboration. Culture here is manipulated in order to achieve precise objectives. The existence of common traditions is thus invoked to establish economic links more easily or to enter into regional organizations. Furthermore, traditions are polysemic and can be reinterpreted.

As a result, a Muslim country like Pakistan could cash in on the large presence of Islam in East and Southeast Asia in its attempt at being co-opted by ASEAN. In Pakistan, too, columnists are fascinated by the Asian miracle (Haqqani 1997) and officials are striving to become another of ASEAN's full dialogue partners (Baabar 1997). Logically enough, the Pakistanis present this attempt, and those intending to become part of the new Asian pole of growth, with references to 'the enduring force of Asian values in the face of moral collapse in the West' (Irfani 1997).

A comparison between the first Indian Asianism and the version recently developed shows interesting variations corroborating the need for a non-culturalist approach to this ideology. In the inter-war period, China exerted a strong fascination over Indian leaders, whereas Japan was despised for its Westernization. Today, China is more feared than admired and Japan seems to be regarded as a model by many Indians. These changes reflect the impact of important historical events (such as the 1962 War) and international developments (the economic assertiveness of Japan). They also draw from an alteration in the balance among different Indian nationalist schools. While the universalist brands of nationalism (represented by Gandhi, Tagore, and Nehru) valued the spiritual image of India, the Hindu nationalist movement was more interested in strengthening and even militarizing India; it approved of the way the Japanese imitated the West to become more powerful (as Lajpat Rai in the 1920s testifies). It is perhaps not simply by chance that today the growing influence of the Hindu nationalist movement in India is on a par with Japan's popularity.

Second, Asianism is primarily used to unite Eastern countries vis-à-vis the West. From this point of view, it has strong nationalist connotations. Indian Asianism—whether that of the 1940s and 1950s or of the 1990s—aims at redressing the balance of power in favour of the East. For Nehru, strengthening ties with China meant setting up an alternative to the dominant civilization based on capitalism and individualism. For the Hindu nationalists today, taking inspiration from Japan should in the same way allow India to escape Americanization. The relationship with the West is thus consubstantial with Indian Asianism, and perhaps with Asianism in general.

How can we assess India's Look East policy, and what can be its future? New Delhi's expectations were high; they have not been met, but important progress has been made. Japan has disappointed India, but it may in the end become one of India's solid trading partners. In 2000, the rapprochement between the countries has been accelerated on two different fronts. Security issues have led Tokyo to pay more attention to Delhi's views. Japan, which depends on import inflows (mainly oil) using the sea routes of the Indian Ocean, is highly sensitive to safety concerns in this region. Tokyo knows that India can help Japan in this respect. Japan has, accordingly, been granted a post of special observer within the board of the Indian Ocean Rim. Another factor that may contribute to the rapprochement between Japan and India is—paradoxically, it seems—the latter's technological capacity. In March 2000, Eisuke Sakakibara, one of the advisors to the Japanese Minister of Finance, emphasized the need for the two countries to collaborate in order to 'leapfrog into the IT revolution and catch up with the US'. In a purely Asianist vein, he added: 'Asian countries, especially India, had the skills required and Indian talent has been extensively tapped by the US in transforming its economy into the 'cyber capitalism' mode' (*The Hindu*, 28 March 2000). In fact, Japan wanted to imitate the US and also attract Indian software engineers. In May 2000, *Asahi Shimbun* pointed out that the Japanese government wanted to recruit 10,000 of them to Japan. This question was at the centre of the discussions during the visit to India of Prime Minister Yoshiro Mori in August 2000. In Bangalore, India's high-tech city, where he went prior to arriving in New Delhi, Mori described India and Japan as complementary, because the former has 'high software technology that leads the world and embraces rich and prominent human resources. Japan has one of the largest markets in the world and high technology in manufacturing' (*The Hindustan Times*, 23 August 2000: 1). Mori announced a special training programme for 1,000 Indian software engineers. Whether this offer appears more attractive than the opportunity to work in the US remains to be seen. Mori repeated that Japan wanted India to sign the CTBT, but that it was no longer a priority.

India's capacity in the high-tech sector was also an important element in the relaunching of relations between India and the Southeast Asian countries after the peak of the Asian crisis was over. Once again, Singapore showed the way: Prime Minister Goh Chok Tong came to Bangalore in January 2000 to inaugurate the International Technology Park. Speaking from an Asian(ist) point of view, he said in his speech that 'e-business was experiencing explosive growth in Asia as evidenced by a large number of "dot-com" companies. The Indian IT companies would find Singapore an excellent launching pad into the Asian e-business market' (*The Hindu*, 22 January 2000). Later, in New Delhi, he declared to Prime Minister Atal Behari Vajpayee: 'India is losing some people to the Silicon Valley [in the United States] and I hope you would lose some to Singapore' (*The Hindu*, 19 January 2000).

As these quotes demonstrate, Asianism seems closely linked to the phenomena of globalism and regional economic integration. As India becomes more globalized, it can be expected not merely to cast its vision to the economies of the US and Europe, but increasingly to 'Look East' as well.

## Notes

*I am most grateful to the anonymous referee who commented upon the first draft of this article in a very well informed and supportive way.

1. The Buddhist population of India consists largely of inhabitants of Ladakh and other Himalayan regions, Tibetan refugees, and Dalit followers of B.R. Ambedkar who converted in the first decade following independence in order to escape the Hindu hierarchy of the caste system.

2. Unless otherwise noted, the term 'China' refers to the Peoples' Republic of China rather than the Republic of China (Taiwan).

3. In *Hind Swaraj*, Gandhi's survey of grand civilizations is very revealing: 'I believe that the civilization India has evolved is not to be beaten in the world. Nothing can equal the seeds sown by our ancestors. Rome went, Greece shared the same fate, the might of the Pharaohs was broken, Japan has become westernized, of China nothing can be said, but India is still, somehow or other, sound at the foundation' (Gandhi 1919: 63).

4. In 1916, he said, in a different way from Gandhi: 'The lamp of ancient Greece is extinct in the land where it was first lighted; the power of Rome lies dead and buried under the ruins of its vast empire. But the civilization, whose basis is society and the spiritual ideal of man, is still a living thing in China and in India' (Tagore 1992 [1917]: 25).

5. 'I cannot but bring to your mind those days when the whole of eastern Asia from Burma to Japan was united with India in the closest tie of friendship, the only natural tie which can exist between nations. There was a living communication of hearts, a nervous system evolved through which messages ran between us about the deepest needs of humanity' (ibid.: 23).

6. Nehru 1996. On p. 166, he writes: 'So China was well in the van of civilization in those days, and could, with some justification, regard the Europeans of the time as a set of semi barbarians. In the known world, she was supreme.'

7. Nehru writes: 'China at the end of the fifteenth century was far ahead of Europe in wealth, industry, and culture. During the whole of the Ming period, no country in Europe or elsewhere could compare with China in the happiness and artistic activities of its people. And remember that this covered the great Renaissance period in Europe' (Nehru 1996: 268).

8. 'Having gained some control over the forces of Nature, they [the Europeans] became arrogant and overbearing to others. They forgot that civilized man must not only control Nature but also control himself' (ibid.: 450). In a letter he wrote to his daughter in 1943, Nehru highlights the idea that 'Harmony in personal relationships is the key . . . to the larger good of society. Ancient societies like India and China . . . tended to concentrate on the cultivation of those virtues which made the individual less self-centred and willing to cooperate—tact, poise, balance were essential' (Jayakar 1992: 130).

9. Thompson, 'Introduction', in Tagore 1992: 83–4. While Tagore's visit to Japan was not a success, his poetry was well received—and is still popular—in Korea, a country which he regarded as 'the light of the East' (Hoffman 1993: 12). Today, Malaysian propagandists of Asianism, such as Anwar Ibrahim, regard Tagore (along with Jose Rizal and Muhammad Iqbal) as 'The progenitors and early protagonists of the Asian Renaissance' (Ibrahim 1996).

10. The relics of Sari-Putta and Maha-Moggalana had been recovered from the stupa of Sanchi, near Bhopal, by Director General of the Archaeological Survey Sir Alexander Cunningham in 1851 and given to the British Museum. After independence, Britain returned them to India. Nehru handed them over to S.P. Mookherji during a solemn ceremony on 14 January 1949, and the later displayed them in Southeast Asian countries whose governments wanted to show them to the population. On 30 November 1952, Nehru and Mookherji met again to solemnly replace the relics in the stupa of Sanchi.

11. 'Of all the Asiatic countries, India alone has stood for democracy throughout the years. . . . Unless Asia comes into its own, the world cannot function as a whole' (Constituent Assembly Debates, 1989, Vol. 1: 277).

12. The others could not but appreciate the repeated appeals of Nehru to the Indian labourers who had been deported to Southeast Asian colonies by the British, to become one with their new countries (Nehru 1961: 127–31). However, while India hereby earned some goodwill in diplomatic terms, it caused some resentment among the Indian diaspora and probably prevented the country from relying on its 'overseas nationals' the same way as China did.

13. These five principles, shaped by the so-called 'oriental philosophy', were mutual respect for the sovereignty and the territorial integrity of the other; non-aggression; non-interference with the domestic affairs of another state; equality; and mutual help and

pacific coexistence. In Buddhist doctrine, *Pancha Shila* signifies the five virtues when one has overcome the five obstacles. The same term (*panchasila*, in Bahasa Indonesia), standing for a different five principals, became the touchstone of postcolonial Indonesian identity.

14. Kripa Sridharan convincingly argues: 'It was not as if Prime Minister Nehru was unaware of the challenge China posed to the states in South and Southeast Asia. But he proposed the taming of China by tying it down with pledges instead of confronting it with defence pacts. It was this reasoning, especially in the wake of the Sino-Indian Panchsheel Agreement (1954) that led him to take the lead in convening the Bandung Conference. He used the occasion to introduce China into the Afro-Asian conclave as a respectable member of the Afro-Asian community and thereby to keep it honest' (Sridharan 1996: 25).

15. Ibid.: 41. Indonesia was the only nation, before the upset of Vietnam, not to join the Western camp from which India had resolutely backed away after signing the friendship treaty with Soviet Union in 1971. Indonesia towards the end of Sukarno's period had come close to Pakistan, to the extent of supporting it during the war that pitted it against India in 1965.

16. One of the Bhopal-based English dailies newspapers published a suggestive editorial under the title 'China Meets the Challenge of 21st Century': 'While we have been making so much noise about taking our country into the 21st century without evolving any concrete action plan for doing so, China has decided to meet the challenge by increasing three times the present level of funding for scientific research and development' (*National Mail*, 11 August 1995).

17. This kind of discourse tends to become commonplace today (see, for instance, Basu 1997).

18. *The Asian Age*, 24 September 1995: 13. *The Asian Age*, a daily newspaper founded in the early 1990s and published in both London and Delhi, devotes at least one page every day to East and Southeast Asia.

19. This sub-heading is borrowed from a special issue of an Indian journal, *Seminar*, *Wooing Japan* (*Seminar*, No. 397).

20. Among other things, the Japanese Economic Mission wanted multinationals to be allowed to set up wholly owned subsidiaries in several sectors, that the customs duties were substantially reduced and that the tax system was restructured (Iqbal, 'Attracting Investments', in *Wooing Japan*, p. 27).

21. Somewhat bitterly, Dixit concludes his chapter on Japan by regretting that for this country, 'relations with India occupy a secondary priority' (Dixit 1996: 262).

22. This is the argument of G.V.C. Naidu, who points out that 'The Indian Navy is the only navy in Asia which possesses medium-sized aircraft carriers . . . and a fairly modern submarine force' (Naidu 2000: 182).

23. Delhi has also applied to join the Asia-Pacific Economic Cooperation (APEC) forum, without any success so far. Wanting to join a regional zone of economic cooperation, and quite aware of the limits of South Asian Association for Regional Cooperation (SAARC) despite the setting up of a free-trade agreement, in December 1995, the South Asian Preferential Treaty Arrangement, India, in 1995 launched the idea of an 'Indian Ocean' zone extending from South Africa to Australia, including South Asia. (The inaugural meeting took place in Mauritius in March 1995. Delegates from Australia, South Africa, Oman, Singapore, Kenya, and India took part in it. In June of

the same year, 23 countries were invited in the second meeting in Australia.) This project, however, is still embryonic, and the priority of India remains on the side of ASEAN.

24. It was the first ever visit of an Indian Prime Minister to this country.

25. Except that, during one of his official visits in New Delhi, Lee Kuan Yew emphasized the existence of a real judicial system, inherited from the British, which made investments in India safer than in other countries. *The Times of India,* 6 January 1996.

26. Thakur 1994: 242.

27. *India Today,* 31 August 1995. Yadav also said: 'If you invest in Bihar, you not only partake of the state's prosperity, but also come closer to hallowed Buddhist sites.' *The Times of India,* 5 August 1995.

28. *Pioneer,* 13 October 1995. In the first half of the 1990s, the Union tourism and civil aviation minister visited Japan, South Korea, Thailand, etc., to promote 'Buddhist tourism', while the Uttar Pradesh government invested Rs 10 million to develop the needed infrastructures (*National Mail,* 11 November 1996). These initiatives attracted many tourists. Unfortunately, the attempts to 'commercialise Lord Buddha' led to serious clashes between businessmen and the monks (*India Today,* 15 August 1996: 15) and the influx of tourists attracted miscreants: in 1996, a coach with 60 Taiwanese tourists aboard was attacked on its way to Gaya (*The Times of India,* 16 October 1996).

29. In late 1996, Suzuki suggested to the government of India, its equal partner in Maruti, to divest 24 per cent of its shares in the joint venture, a figure based on the intentions displayed by the Minister of Finance regarding privatizations. However, the government proved to be reluctant, which prevented the company from pursuing with its plans of raising funds for modernization. There has been a substantial increase in Japanese overseas development aid (ODA) to India since 1991. Japan has become the largest donor of ODA; in 1993, the Japanese aid represented 40 per cent of the total aid received by India. However, it ranked fifth among those receiving Japanese developmental aid, with 3.62 per cent of the total, far behind China (16.54 per cent), Indonesia (14.07 per cent), the Philippines (9.29 per cent), and Thailand (4.29 per cent). India did move up to the fourth place in 1995, with US$470 million, and in 1996–7 it received US$1.1 billion (133 billion Yen) to fund 11 projects in the power and transports sectors (*Japan's ODA Annual Report,* 1995: 111).

30. In August 2000, South Korea's Foreign Ministry declared in Delhi: 'India and South Korea are now fully conscious of the new security linkages between the subcontinent and the Korean peninsula. There have been disturbing reports, over the recent years, of nuclear and missile cooperation between Pakistan and North Korea. Such cooperation would have adverse implications for security on the Korean peninsula' (cited in Raja Mohan 2000).

31. *Monthly Public Opinion Surveys,* August-September 1996: 27. The relative enthusiasm for East Asia tended to include even China since in 1996 only 7.3 per cent of the interviewees had a bad or a very bad opinion about this country, 35.8 per cent had a good or a very good opinion of it and the remainder, 49.5 per cent did not express any opinion. Sino-Indian relations were considered good or very good by 72.7 per cent of the interviewees in 1994 and by 80.5 per cent of them in 1995; a majority of

people considered that these needed to be improved. To the question, 'Which country is helping our economy by investments?' 33.1 per cent of the interviewed people answered the United States, 29.3 per cent Japan, 8 per cent Germany, and 7.2 per cent Great Britain, whereas Japan then was far behind Great Britain on the list of foreign investors—but it is true that its presence is being increasingly felt as it is concentrated in consumer goods (*Monthly Public Opinion Surveys*, August 1995: iv).

32. Khare 1995 and Maitra 1995. Several authors recommended a 'corporate ethics programme' drawing its inspiration, more or less directly, from the 'oriental philosophy' (see Pattanayak 1996: 23).

33. The title of the other front-page article of this supplement is also very telling: 'A Country to Be Proud of', as if India need not be ashamed of its offspring!

34. The Indian middle class, the Hindu nationalist movement and some of the ASEAN's advocates of Asianism also have in common a certain reluctance towards democracy. In 1993, an opinion poll revealed that 58 per cent of the 1,715 persons interviewed in Mumbai, Delhi, Kolkata, Chennai, and Bangalore (many of whom were probably from the middle class) agreed with the following proposition: 'If the country is to progress it needs a dictator.' Simultaneously, in the early 1990s, the BJP reaffirmed its faith in a presidential form of government (see Jaffrelot 1996: 432).

# References

Ayoob, M. (1990), *India and Southeast Asia: Indian Perceptions and Policies*, London: Routledge.

Baabar, M. (1997), 'Pakistan Hopes to become ASEAN's Full Dialogue Partner', *The News*, 12 March.

Balakrishnan, G. (1995), 'A Brave New World', *Ascent*, weekly supplement to *The Times of India*, August.

Basu, K. (1997), 'Seoul's Successes: Indolence Keeps India Behind', *The Times of India*, 23 January.

Bharatiya Janata Party (1996), *For a Strong and Prosperous India: Election Manifesto 1996*, New Delhi.

Bhattacharyya, B. (1996), 'Indo-ASEAN Investment Relations', in S. Prakash, V. Ray, and S. Ambatkar (eds.), *India and ASEAN*, New Delhi: Gyan Publishing House.

——— (1995), 'Winning the World Market', in *Ascent*, weekly supplement to *The Times of India*, 25 October.

Chatterjee, Partha (1986), *Nationalist Thought and the Colonial World: A Derivative Discourse?*, London: Zed Books.

*Constituent Assembly Debates* (1989), Vol. 1, New Delhi: Lok Sabha Secretariat.

Dasgupta, A. (1996), 'Intellectual and Academic Cooperation Between India and Southeast Asia', in B. Ghoshal (ed.), *India and Southeast Asia: Challenges and Opportunities*, Delhi: Konark.

Dixit, J.N. (1996), *My South Block Years: Memoirs of a Foreign Secretary*, New Delhi: UPSB.

D'Costa, A.P. (1995), 'Why Doesn't India Look East for Growth?', *The Organiser*, 10 September.

Gandhi, M.K. (1919 [1909]), *Indian Home Rule*, Madras: Ganesh and Co.

Ghate, P. (1995), 'Japanese Model of Swadeshi', *The Organiser,* 19 March.

Ghoshal, B. (1996), 'India and Southeast Asia: Prospects and Problems', in B. Ghoshal (ed.), *India and Southeast Asia: Challenges and Opportunities,* Delhi: Konark Publishers.

Golwalkar, M.S. (1966), *Bunch of Thoughts,* Bangalore: Jagarana Prakashana.

Government of India (1996), *Economic Survey, 1995-96,* Delhi.

Gujral, I.K. (1996), 'Foreign Policy Objectives of India's United Front Government', reproduced in Embassy of India, *India Digest,* Vol. IV, August, Paris, September.

Gupta, Sisir (1964), *India and Regional Integration in Asia,* Bombay: Asia Publishing House.

Haqqani, Husain (1997), 'Learning from Korea', *The Friday Times,* 14 March.

Hoffman, D.M. (1993), 'Culture, Self and "Uri": Anti-Americanism in Contemporary South Korea', *Journal of Northeast Asian Studies,* Vol. 12, No. 2, Spring.

Ibrahim, Anwar (1996), *The Asian Renaissance,* Kuala Lumpur: Times Books.

Ito, H. (1995), 'East Asia Joins India Investment Caravan', *The Nikkei Weekly,* 25 September.

Irfani, S. (1997), 'A Pluralist Asian Age is Coming', *Dawn,* 21 February.

Iqbal, B.A., 'Attracting Investments', *Wooing Japan,* a special issue of *Seminar,* No. 397.

Jaffrelot, Christophe (1995), 'The Concept of Race in the Writings of the Hindu Nationalist Ideologues: A Concept Between Two Cultures', in P. Robb (ed.), *The Concept of Race in South Asia,* Delhi: Oxford University Press.

——— (1996), *The Hindu Nationalist Movement and Indian Politics, 1925 to the 1990s: Strategies of Identity-building, Implantation and Mobilization,* New York: Columbia University Press.

*Japan's ODA Annual Report: 1994* (1995), Tokyo: Ministry of Foreign Affairs.

Jayakar, P. (1992), *Indira Gandhi: A Biography,* Delhi: Viking.

Kaji, G.S. (1995), 'What East Asia Has Achieved, India Too Can Emulate', *The Times of India,* 13 April.

Keenleyside, T.A. (1982), 'Nationalist Indian Attitudes towards Asia: A Troublesome Legacy for Post-independence Indian Foreign Policy', *Pacific Affairs,* Vol. 55, No. 2, Summer.

Kesavan, K.V. (1996), 'Japan's Investment Interest in India and Southeast Asia', S. Prakash, V. Ray, and S. Ambatkar (eds.), *India and ASEAN,* New Delhi: Gyan Publishing House.

Khare, A. (1995), 'In the Nick of Time', *Ascent,* weekly supplement to *The Times of India,* May.

Kumar, Pramod (1995), 'Hindus in Malaysia', *The Organiser,* 3 December.

Lal, Vikram (1992), 'A Learning Experience', *Seminar.*

Lardinois, R. (1996), 'Transition démographique et croissance de la population', in C. Jaffrelot (ed.), *L'Inde contemporaine—De 1950 à nos jours,* Paris: Fayard.

Madhok, B. (1969), *Portrait of a Martyr: Biography of Dr. Shyam Prasad Mookerji,* Bombay: Jaico.

Maitra, A.K. (1995), 'Zen and the Organisation', *Ascent,* weekly supplement to *The Times of India,* 10 May.

Mattoo, Amitabh (2001), 'ASEAN in India's Foreign Policy', in F. Grare and A. Mattoo (eds.), *India and ASEAN: The Politics of India's Look East Policy,* Delhi: Manohar.

Naidu, G.V.C. (1995), 'India and Pacific Asia in the Post-Cold War Era: Some Observations', *The Japan Foundation Newsletter*, Vol. 23, No. 1.

—————— (2000), *Indian Navy and Southeast Asia*, Delhi: Knowledge World.

Nehru, Jawaharlal (1989 [1946]), *The Discovery of India*, Delhi: Oxford University Press.

—————— (1989 [1933-34]), *Glimpses of World History*, Delhi: Oxford University Press.

—————— (1961), *India's Foreign Policy: Selected Speeches, September 1946–April 1961*, New Delhi: Ministry of Information and Broadcasting.

Palkhivala, N.A. (1994), 'Eternal Friends, Natural Partners', *The Times of India*, 25 November.

Pattanayak, B. (1996), 'The Panchsheel Programme', *Ascent*, weekly supplement to *The Times of India*, 25 December.

Pillai, M.G.G. (1995), 'India and South-East Asia: Search for a Role', *Economic and Political Weekly*, 29 July.

Rai, Lala Lajpat (1990), 'The Evolution of Japan', in S.R. Bakshi (ed.), *Lajpat Rai, Swaraj and Social Change, 1907-1918*, Vol. I, Delhi: H.K. Publishers.

Raja Mohan, C. (1998), 'India's Gains from the ARF Meet', *The Hindu*, 29 July.

Rao, V.V. Bhanoji (1996), 'India and Southeast Asia: New Partnership', in S. Prakash, V. Ray, and S. Ambatkar (eds.), *India and ASEAN*, New Delhi: Gyan Publishing House.

Rattanani, L. (1995), 'Borrowing from Tokyo', *India Today*, 15 September.

Sharma, J.K. (1998), 'Japan's Hidden Agenda', *The Organiser*, 2 August.

Sridharan, K. (1996), *The ASEAN Region in India's Foreign Policy*, Aldershot: Dartmouth.

Suryanarayan, V. (1996), 'Looking Ahead: India and Southeast Asia in the 1990s: New Perspectives, New Challenges', in B. Ghoshal (ed.), *India and Southeast Asia: Challenges and Opportunities*, New Delhi: Konark Publishers.

Tagore, Rabindranath (1992 [1917]), *Nationalism*, Calcutta: Rupa.

Thakur, R. (1994), *The Politics and Economics of India's Foreign Policy*, New York: St. Martin's Press.

*The Organiser* (1997), 'Industrial Houses to Achieve Optimum Production through Bhakti Model', 2 February.

—————— (1997), 'Thaipusam: The Hindu Festival of Singapore', 2 March.

*The Indian Quarterly Register* (1927), Vol. 1, Calcutta.

—————— (1926), Vol. 2, Calcutta.

Thompson, E.P. (1992 [1917]), 'Introduction', in Tagore, *Nationalism*, Calcutta: Rupa.

Vijaykumar, P. (1994), 'Creating Human Space in Management', *The Times of India*, 25 November.

# Chapter 34

# Does Europe matter to India?

India and post-Cold War Europe[1] share at least three characteristics: democracy (India's electorate of 600 million voters is slightly bigger than the entire population of Europe, including Turkey), diversity (India's 22 official languages, 28 states and seven union territories make it more varied than Europe) and internal differences (on issues ranging from governance models, market economy, reservations [affirmative action] to minorities, immigration, terrorism and their respective roles in the emerging world order). Yet, despite these common traits and a long common history, Europe has only recently re-discovered India (Acharya et al., 2004; Gnesotto and Grevi 2006; Islam 2008). However, despite Europe being a popular destination for Indian tourists, India has still to re-discover Europe in any significant way. This begs the question: does Europe matter to India?

The short answer would have to be that Europe matters far less to India than the United States, the Russian Federation or East Asia. This is primary on account of several economic, political, conceptual, security and institutional factors. First, in economic terms, East Asia (which includes the burgeoning Sino-Indian trade) has overtaken Europe as India's largest partner. Similarly, the United States remains India's largest single nation trading partner and the biggest source of foreign direct investment (FDI). Thus, in economic terms the 27-nation bloc of the European Union (EU) has diminished in significance, particularly as only a handful of countries (France, Germany, the United Kingdom and Italy) account for the bulk of the EU's trade, FDI, joint ventures and technology transfers.

Second, in political and strategic terms, the United States, through a 2004 bilateral agreement, offers a significant strategic military and non-military partnership to New Delhi. The jewel in the crown of this enlarging security and political partnership is the US-India Civil Nuclear Cooperation Initiative (CNCI), which seeks to provide for India's civil nuclear energy needs. In contrast, Europe has been far more ambivalent about providing access to such strategic dual-use technology, even though some countries have been more forthcoming. Moreover, as India moves from non-alignment towards multi-alignment in the emerging multi-polar world and enters into a variety of bilateral and regional arrangements, it simply does not consider Europe to be a reliable partner, although it has entered into a 'strategic partnership' (European Commission 2004) with the EU. Events

---

*This chapter has been co-authored by W.P.S. Sidhu.

of the past few years have confirmed to New Delhi that Europe is unable to stand united against either the United States, Russia or China. Thus even though several European countries are individually considered to be reliable strategic partners, collectively Europe is not considered as one of the potential 'poles' in the evolving multi-polar world (Raja Mohan 2002: 63).

Third, conceptually, independent India is justifiably regarded as a 'modern state' which emphasizes sovereignty, territoriality and *raison d'état*. In contrast most states occupying the European space are considered to be 'post-modern' as they do not emphasize sovereignty or the separation of domestic and foreign affairs and increasingly regard borders as irrelevant. Thus, the European Union, which epitomizes the post-modern state, 'has become a highly developed system for mutual interference in each other's domestic affairs, right down to beer and sausages' (Cooper 2002). The difference between the conceptual outlook of India and the European Union might also explain the inherent discomfiture of a modern India in engaging with a post-modern entity like the European Union. In contrast, India is more comfortable in dealing with the individual nation states that constitute the European Union, particularly the bigger states, than the collective Union. Perhaps that is why New Delhi is most at ease in its interactions with the United States, which embodies the ideal modern state.

Fourth, despite common traits, challenges and perspectives, Europe and India have divergent approaches to addressing security issues. For instance, the EU has formalized an elaborate Common Foreign and Security Policy (CFSP), a European Security and Defence Policy (ESDP), and even a European Security Strategy (European Council 2003) while India has not formally articulated a national security strategy. It needs a more deductive and interpretive approach to discern India's security and defence policies from the few statements of its decision-makers. Besides, unlike the EU, India does not believe in promoting its secular, pluralistic, and democratic ideology to other states (Bendiek and Wagner 2008).

Finally, Europe with its multiplicity of complex organizations is considered to be over-institutionalized and over-bureaucratised and, therefore, far less attractive to engage with than powerful countries, such as the United States, the Russian Federation, Britain or France, or less-institutionalized regional organizations, such as the Association of South-East Asian Nations (ASEAN) or the Shanghai Cooperative Organization (SCO). Ironically, even as EU-India relations struggle to gain traction, Indo-UK and Indo-French relations continue to grow by leaps and bounds. The latter trend is evident not only in the visits by both the British Prime Minister, Gordon Brown, and the French President Nicholas Sarkozy to New Delhi in January 2008 but also the depth of the strategic, economic and political cooperation which is simply not reflected in India's dealings with the EU. For instance, while the Joint Communiqué issued at the end of the ninth EU-India summit in September 2008 merely 'reaffirmed their commitment to promote energy security and energy efficiency', France and India signed an 'agreement for civil nuclear cooperation' at their bilateral summit around the same time (EU-India

2008; France-India 2008). In many ways, these bilateral interactions have done more to promote Indo-European cooperation than has the EU.

To address the question of whether Europe matters to India, the chapter begins with a short historical overview of Indo-European relations including the policies and approach of independent India to Europe during the Cold War. This first part also looks at the shift in India's perspective and policies in the post-Cold War period. The second part examines the present Indian worldview and the relative insignificance of Europe as a hard and soft power to India, in comparison to the United States. The third part analyses the widening social and economic gap between India and Europe and its impact on relations between the two.

## India and Europe: the Evolution of Ties

### A BRIEF HISTORY OF INDO-EUROPEAN RELATIONS

Indo-European relations date back to at least 326 BC when Alexander of Macedonia first reached the banks of the Indus River but developed significantly only after AD 1500 when India became the central focus of European explorers, traders and, eventually, colonizers. It could be argued that since then Asia in general and China and India in particular have mattered to Europe. In the 1500s Asia accounted for over 55 per cent of the global Gross Domestic Product (GDP) (Ming China 25 per cent; India 24.5 per cent; and the Far East 8.4 per cent) and until the 1800s China and India accounted for well over 45 per cent of the global GDP (China 32.9 per cent and India 16 per cent) (Maddison 2003). It was only in the 1850s (after the Opium Wars when the British forcibly sold Indian opium to China to pay for Chinese tea which was in great demand in Europe) that the European share of global GDP reached 24.1 per cent and exceeded that the India and China. During this period Europe mattered to India to the extent that India and Indians sought to free themselves from the European colonial economic and political yoke. By the time of India's independence in 1947 its share in the 'global output had plummeted to less than 4 per cent' (Mukherjee 2007). Indeed, one key tenet of current Indian strategic thinking is to regain its position as a major global economy and, as a corollary, reclaim the share of global GDP it boasted in the 1500s.

Ironically, it was Europe that also provided the norms, ideas and education to Indians who would lead the independence struggle against the European colonial empires and establish an independent India based on European enlightenment and related liberal structures. Indeed, not only did Britain shape most of the Indian institutions during the British Raj (rule), but most of the Indian leaders who have ruled the country since independence have been trained in Europe. As a result, one of the most precious achievements of India so far, pluralistic democracy, is a by-product of the intimate relationship of India with Europe. When Prime Minister Manmohan Singh (2005) was made a Doctor Honoris Causa of Oxford University in 2005, he made that point clear:

The idea of India as enshrined in our Constitution, with its emphasis on the principles of secularism, democracy, the rule of law and, above all, the equality of all human beings irrespective of caste, community, language or ethnicity, has deep roots in India's ancient civilization. However, it is undeniable that the founding fathers of our republic were also greatly influenced by the ideas associated with the age of enlightenment in Europe. Our Constitution remains a testimony to the enduring interplay between what is essentially Indian and what is very British in our intellectual heritage.

This 'soft' contribution notwithstanding, Europe (with the exception of the United Kingdom) played a limited 'hard' political, security or economic role in independent India until the 1980s. This was on account of the desire of India not to be dependent on external powers (especially the former colonial powers) for its security and economic well being. Thus while imbibing European ideals India sought to insulate itself, especially from the raging Cold War, by embarking on a policy of non-alignment. This meant that India would not formally align itself with the two Cold War blocs and would seek self-reliance to ensure its own defence. In addition, India also opted for a mixed planned economy model comprising of state-led enterprises and over-regulated limited private sector enterprises governed by the so-called 'Licence Raj'[2] which effectively closed the Indian market to the world. Simultaneously the decolonization process in Asia and Africa led to the withdrawal of Europe and European powers from the rest of the world to their own continent. This was coupled with the growing European preoccupation with the Soviet Union during the Cold War. Finally, the absence of appropriate European institutions, except for the North Atlantic Treaty Organisation (NATO), which non-aligned India abhorred, meant that Europe could not be an effective security actor on its own.

Ironically, although India professed non-alignment it became closely connected with the Soviet Union for a number of political, security and economic reasons. However, following the Soviet intervention in Afghanistan in 1979 and the arrival of the Cold War on India's doorstep, an uncomfortable New Delhi turned to Europe to diversify its military and economic base. Interestingly, it was the extravagant military purchases made from Europe in the 1980s (aircraft carriers and aircraft from Britain, aircraft from France, submarines from Germany, missiles and torpedoes from Italy and artillery guns from Sweden) that drove India bankrupt and compelled its leaders to embark on far-reaching economic reforms in 1991. These reforms coincided with the collapse of the Soviet Union and the end of the Cold War and were particularly significant for New Delhi's ensuing strategic shift (Baru 2007).

## POST-COLD WAR STRATEGIC SHIFT

In the post-Cold War period while the underlying objective remained to ensure India's autonomy of action in the emerging world order, New Delhi made three significant shifts in its strategic perspective to achieve this goal (Sidhu 2002). The first shift was to reluctantly but progressively dismantle the 'Licence Raj', unshackle the Indian economy and link it more closely with the global economy. This paved the way for a more pragmatic and economically driven foreign policy (Schaffer 2002: 37). Today, with an annual growth rate of around 8 per cent India is already the world's third largest economy in terms of purchasing power parity (after United States and China) (International Monetary Fund 2007; World Bank 2007).

Initially, Europe played a significant role in this early phase of India's economic liberalization, evident in the former's emergence as the single largest trade partner of India. However, by 2005, as bilateral trade between China and India continued to grow, Europe was displaced from its leading position both with India as well as in the global economy. Indeed, by 2025 the Indian economy is projected to be about 60 per cent the size of the US economy and by 2035, it will be only marginally smaller than the US economy but larger than that of Western Europe (Virmani 2005). Thus, by the middle of the twenty-first century, India (along with China and East Asia) is likely to relegate Europe's share of the global GDP to the pre-1500s level.

The second shift in India's strategic perspective was from non-alignment to multi-alignment which was premised on the perception of the emergence of a multi-polar world. 'Where leadership among the non-aligned once was the principal means of gaining international status', Teresita Schaffer and Mandavi Mehta note, 'India now seeks a seat at the high table, the United Nations Security Council and the "nuclear club", with China illustrating the standing India wants' (Schaffer and Mehta 2001). In such a scenario India has two aspirations: first to emerge as a 'pole' in its own right in this multi-polar world (Ministry of Defence 2006: 2) and, second, to align with other 'poles' which could both contribute to India's own rise and recognition as a global decision-making pole and to counter potential threats from other decision-making poles. The nuclear tests conducted in 1998 were a manifestation of the first aspiration and announced the arrival of India as an autonomous actor on the world stage. Significantly, the European Parliament (May 1998), while acknowledging that India faced serious external security problems, condemned the nuclear tests and asked India to sign and ratify the Comprehensive Test Ban Treaty (CTBT) and the Nuclear Non-Proliferation Treaty (NPT), to support and actively contribute to the negotiations on a Fissile Material Cut-off Treaty (FMCT) and to prevent material, equipment and technology that can be used for the production of weapons of mass destruction being exported from India to other countries.

Subsequently, however, key EU states, notably the two nuclear states—France and Britain—embarked on strategic dialogues with India which tacitly acknowledged India's nuclear status and practically countermanded the EU declaration.[3] In 2005, France even sponsored the resolution supporting G4 (Germany, Japan, India and Brazil) membership in an enlarged UN Security Council, further undermining the EU declaration. These mixed signals from Europe were in contrast to the consistent Indo-US nuclear dialogue which evolved into the Indo-US nuclear deal in 2005.

It would appear that in the aftermath of the nuclear tests New Delhi was taken more seriously than before. In line with the second aspiration, India also embarked on a series of strategic partnerships with the United States, the EU, Britain, France, Germany, Russia, Japan, and ASEAN. However, clearly, some of these partnerships are more strategic than others.

Not surprisingly, the third shift was the emergence of the United States as a dominant focus of India's foreign policy and, perhaps, as New Delhi's most important strategic partner. This was a dramatic reversal from the Cold War period when the United States and India had remained 'estranged democracies' (Kux 1993). There were several political, economic and societal factors that facilitated this shift. At the political level the recognition of India as a key emerging player by successive administrations, especially the George W. Bush administration, provided a tremendous impetus for enhancing strategic relations. At the economic level, despite Europe's significant role, the United States remains India's single largest trade partner and source of FDI. Finally, the huge and influential Indian diaspora in the United States further provided an impetus for improving relations. This societal driver in particular contrasted poorly with the impression of 'fortress Europe' being closed to immigrants, including Indians.

In line with these strategic shifts, India views the world in three concentric strategic circles: first the immediate neighbourhood comprising members of the South Asian Association for Regional Cooperation (Afghanistan, Bangladesh, Bhutan, the Maldives, Nepal, Pakistan and Sri Lanka), China and Myanmar; second the extended neighbourhood, stretching from the Persian Gulf to the Straits of Malacca and from Central Asia to the Indian Ocean, which is often described as Southern Asia; and third the global stage which would include other parts of the globe where India is involved, such as Africa, Latin American and the Far East as well as institutions and organizations such as the UN, the Commonwealth and the Non-Aligned Movement. Both the United States and Russia are present in all three circles because of their physical presence in the local neighbourhood as well as their global reach. While Europe too could have been part of all three circles (given the presence of European institutions and troops in the local neighbourhood), it is curiously not considered in all three circles. In fact, Europe has been relegated to the distant global circle but is not regarded as a global player.

In the first circle, India ideally seeks primacy and veto over action of outside powers but in reality is willing to work with external powers as long as its own interests are ensured. This is evident in New Delhi's tacit endorsement of both the US and NATO presence in Afghanistan. In the second circle, India seeks to balance the role of other powers with the support of outside powers in the short-term and by itself in the long-term. At the global level, India seeks to become one of the 'poles' in a multi-polar world and a key player in international peace and security membership of key global decision-making structures, such as a permanent seat on the UN Security Council and membership of an enlarged G8. In addition, as one of the top five contributors of military personnel and civilian police to UN peace operations (UN website 2007), India was elected as a member of the UN Peacebuilding Commission and is expected to have a greater say in UN peace missions.

In addition to these areas of strategic interest, there are several issues of similar interest for New Delhi. These are described as the 'four deficits' by Indian officials and include the historical deficit (the need to reconnect economically and politically with the Gulf region, Central Asia and Southeast Asia); the security deficit (the need to deal with proliferation, proxy wars and terrorism); the economic deficit (the need to ensure access to energy and dual-use technology); and the global decision-making deficit (the need to be part of the global decision-making architecture, including the UN Security Council) (Mukherjee 2005).

## Europe versus the United States: India's Preferences

### THE CHARADE OF A STRATEGIC PARTNERSHIP

Against this backdrop, how does India see the role of Europe and the various European organizations in addressing the four deficits? While there are at least three European institutions of substance—NATO, the EU and the Organisation for Security and Cooperation in Europe (OSCE)—India has only developed relations with the EU. In June 2000, the first ever EU-India summit was held in Lisbon with the objective of fostering closer political ties. In doing so, India joined the small and elite club of countries (United States, Canada, Japan, Russia and China) with whom the EU holds annual summits. Since then nine EU-India summits have been held, the latest one in September 2008 in Marseille. In June 2004, as part of this process, the European Commission (2004) presented its communication regarding an 'EU-India strategic partnership', and India (India 2004) delivered its response paper in August and identified five areas of cooperation:

- multilateral cooperation in the area of conflict prevention, anti-terrorism, non-proliferation, the promotion of democracy and the defence of human rights;
- strengthening economic cooperation, especially jointly drafted regulatory policies;
- development cooperation to enable India to achieve the UN-set Millennium Development Goals;
- increasing cultural and intellectual exchange;
- enhancing the institutional framework of Indo-European relations.

However, the implementation of this programme has been mixed. The biggest achievement has been in the sphere of science and technology with the participation of India in both the ITER (International Thermonuclear Experimental Reactor Project) and the GALILEO satellite programmes. In contrast, progress in the political, economic and societal spheres has stalled.

In its response paper India extols the virtues of multilateralism and highlights the central role of the UN while simultaneously making a strong pitch for India's candidacy for permanent membership of the UNSC with the expectation that the EU would support its bid. The paper also proposes a joint India-EU group on the Middle East peace process as well as the political and economic reconstruction of Iraq and of Afghanistan but makes no mention of the Kashmir dispute. While India asserts its commitment to 'uphold human rights and fundamental freedoms', it also insists that the 'issue of human rights is solely within the national domain' and calls on the EU and itself to 'avoid a prescriptive approach' (European Commission 2004).

Similarly, the Mittal-Arcelor affair (examined in detail later) showed India the limits of doing business with and in Europe. The differences over the International Criminal Court and the convention against anti-personnel mines are also indicative of the limits in improving political relations between the two. As Rajendra Jain notes, India does not see the EU as a

credible counterweight to the United States given the structural difficulties of making multipolarity work effectively apart from the inherent constraints of an evolving CFSP in a more diverse and heterogeneous Union. India remains sceptical about the EU's political and foreign policy capabilities. (Jain 2005)

Besides, Lorenzo Fioramonti (2007: 2) notes that

the EU is associated with the rest of the so-called First World (particularly, the United States). . . . When it comes to the political discourse in multilateral venues, the EU and the United States are seen as two faces of the same coin.

Not surprisingly then the EU-India Joint Action Plan (JAP) (European Commission 2005) announced at the New Delhi Summit in 2005 has seen very little action, especially when contrasted with the US-India Civil Nuclear Cooperation Initiative. The JAP focuses on five areas:

- strengthening dialogue and consultation mechanisms;
- political dialogue and cooperation;
- bringing together peoples and cultures;
- economic policy dialogue and cooperation; and
- developing trade and investment.

It is apparent that the JAP is a misnomer and instead of seeing action is likely to remains a mere talking-shop with emphasis on dialogue for the sake of dialogue. One possible reason for this could be that the EU is not considered to be a sovereign entity by New Delhi and, therefore, unable to deliver in any of these areas, except in terms of norms and principles. Another possible factor could be the perceived inability of the EU to speak in one voice on many of these issues and the tendency of individual EU members to negotiate bilaterally with India sometimes in disregard of the stated EU policy on the subject.

## EUROPE: A SPENT FORCE
## COMPARED TO THE UNITED STATES?

A significant section of the Indian elite, proud of the country's newly acquired power, does not bother to hide its disdain for a Europe seen as paralyzed by its divisions and far too discreet in world affairs. According to Karine Lisbonne de Vergeron (2006: xii), for the Indian elite, 'Europe lacks a strategic vision and ranks at the bottom of list of partners in India's multipolar understanding of the future geometry of world affairs.' Raja Mohan, one of the most influential Indian experts in international affairs, contrasts the situation of the EU and that of the United States. India's relations with Europe have been limited by the fact that New Delhi is fairly unimpressed with Europe's role in global politics. It senses that Europe and India have traded places in terms of their attitudes towards the United States: while Europe seethes with resentment of US policies, India is giving up on habitually being the first, and most trenchant, critic of Washington. As pessimism overtakes Europe, growing Indian optimism allows New Delhi to support unpopular US policies (Raja Mohan 2006: 25).

Indeed, besides the Delhi-based strategic community the whole Indian middle class supports the Bush administration. Certainly, most of the newspapers, true to their leftist inclinations, are highly critical of the India-US rapprochement. Editorials arraign a policy selling out the independence of the country; front-page articles long for the previous non-aligned tradition; columnists attack the imperialist attitude of the United States. These are to no avail: Indian society, at least the urban middle class, remains favourably inclined towards the United States. India is the only country recording such a high opinion of the United States, after five years of war in Iraq—a war which has led to a moral divorce, of America by so many European societies. In India, the level of positive opinion regarding the United States was even higher in 2005 than in 2002.

The 2005 Pew Global Attitudes survey (Pew Research Center 2005) found that 71 per cent of Indians had a favourable view of the United States, as against 54 per cent in 2002. Only 17 per cent expressed an unfavourable opinion, compared to 38 per cent in Great Britain. Of course, this opinion partly resulted from the fact that they saw this country as a land of opportunity: asked where they would recommend that a young person move in order to lead a good life, 38 per cent of Indians chose the United States—this is a figure no other country, among those surveyed, could match. Poland came a distant second with only 19 per cent.

More importantly, the United States is also appreciated in India because of its foreign policy. Fifty-four per cent of the interviewees appreciate the way George Bush was handling the world affairs. Of the 16 countries surveyed on this question, India was the only one—aside from the United States—in which a majority expressed some confidence in the American president. Revealingly, when asked whether the United States takes into account the interest of 'countries like yours',

63 per cent of Indians answer in the affirmative—more than in any other country. On Iraq, India is the only country other than the United States in which a plurality—45 per cent—believed that the removal of Saddam Hussein from power has made the world safer—and Indians are even less likely than the Americans to say that the Iraq War has made the world more dangerous. However, just over half—52 per cent—of the respondents favoured US-led efforts to fight terrorism, a level of support similar to many European countries.

Other opinion polls give similar results. A poll conducted by the Indian weekly *Outlook* revealed that 66 per cent believed that Bush was a friend of India, 54 per cent felt that India needs the United States, 46 per cent 'love' America and the same number said that they would not mind emigrating to the United States (*Outlook*-AC Nielsen Opinion Poll 2006).

The positive view of the United States that a majority of Indians entertain can be explained from two points of view. First, so far as American society is concerned, it is seen as an efficient model for economic dynamism, social mobility and multiculturalism—as evident from the success story of the Indian minority living there. Second, so far as world affairs are concerned, the surveys mentioned above reflect the Indian appreciation of what the United States has done for India (in terms of nuclear collaboration for instance) as well as the belief that India and the United States are in the same camp today. For decades they have been adversaries because of the Cold War, but the world has changed, the fight between communism (or socialism) and capitalism is no longer of order of the day. If the key conflict may be expressed in terms of clash of civilizations, then India and the Untied States have a common enemy: terrorism. Though they are not reported as much as they should be in the West, bomb attacks are more and more pervasive in India. Every six months they kill dozens—if not hundreds—of people in big cities like New Delhi (62 casualties in October 2005) (*BBC News* 2005), Mumbai (188 casualties in July 2006) (*BBC News* 2006), on the India-Pakistan Samjhauta Express train in February 2007 (*BBC News* 2007a), Jaipur (56 killed in May 2008) and Ahmedabad (49 killed in July 2008) (Sengupta 2008). For the Indian government and for the Indians as well, these terrorist actions are due to Islamist groups based in Pakistan. Therefore, India and the United States are perceived as in the same fold and as allies in the fight against terror.

Logically enough, when George Bush paid on official visit to India in March 2006, he was most warmly welcomed by the Vishva Hindu Parishad, a Hindu nationalist outfit, on the ground that he was heading a nation which was boldly fighting 'Jehadi terrorism' (United News of India 2006).

## EUROPE: NOT CONSIDERED A SERIOUS SECURITY ACTOR

Given Europe's own experience with 'Jehadi terrorism' with the Madrid attack in March 2004 and the London attack in July 2005, the involvement of several

European states in the so-called 'war on terror' in Iraq and in Afghanistan under the NATO-led International Security Assistance Force (ISAF), it would have been logical to expect not only greater convergence but also operational interaction between Indian and European organizations—be they strictly European like the EU or Euro-Atlantic like NATO. However, in reality this is not the case. While the Indo-EU joint statement following the eighth India-EU summit commits both sides to continue 'their cooperation on counter-terrorism' as 'one of the priority areas for the EU-India Strategic Partnership', they have still a long way to go before practical joint and anti-terrorism operations are embarked upon (India and the EU, 2007: §22).

On Iraq, the Indian Parliament passed a resolution criticizing the US-led war as unacceptable on the grounds that this action was taken without the sanction of the UN Security Council. Subsequently, New Delhi also rejected Washington's demand for Indian troops for Iraq (Pattanayak 2005) on the same grounds. In reality, the Indian position on Iraq had little to do with the absence of a UN mandate (although this was a convenient stratagem) and more with the fact that such a war was not in India's interest. After all, New Delhi had intervened in East Pakistan (now Bangladesh) in 1971 and Sri Lanka in 1987 without a UN mandate. Given the large Indian diaspora population in Iraq and the fact that Iraq was one of the biggest oil suppliers for India often supplying the vital resource at 'prices lower than the benchmark of OPEC' (Pattanayak 2005), New Delhi was opposed not only to the war but also the UN sanctions. However, India was more than willing to respond to the UN appeal for humanitarian relief and subsequent reconstruction of the war-torn country and eventually contributed around US$40 million for this purpose.

Similarly, on Afghanistan, while both India and the EU 'reaffirmed their sustained commitment to assist the Afghan Government in the stabilisation and rebuilding of Afghanistan' there is no reference for joint action or closer bilateral cooperation (India and the EU, 2007: §16). Indeed, in January 2008 visiting European Commissioner for External Relations Benita Ferrero-Waldner reminded Indians that 'with global influences come not only rights, but also responsibilities' and called on New Delhi to '[u]se your influence in the neighbourhood. You are a stable democracy here' (Press Trust of India 2008). Interestingly, while the ISAF presence has paved the way for India's engagement with the reconstruction and development of Afghanistan and its US$700 million aid has been 'widely appreciated, including by the NATO allies' (Minuto-Rizzo 2007), India has been reluctant publicly to acknowledge the role of NATO or ISAF let alone forge closer ties with them. Indeed, scholarly assessments of India's role in Afghanistan do not even mention ISAF or NATO (see D'Souza 2007).[4] While there is certainly a case for greater Indian dialogue and, perhaps, engagement with the various European security structures, there is also great hesitation on the part of New Delhi to embark on this path.

Clearly, the clarion call for the establishment of a 'global NATO' by American policy-makers and scholars is likely to go unheeded in New Delhi (Daalder and Goldgeier 2006). On the contrary, Indian scholars caution that 'the worry of NATO being labelled as a Global Police Force will loom large and its "Out-of-Area" Operations will remain controversial' (Rane 2005). There are several reasons why India might be reluctant to establish formal ties with European security structures like NATO or the nascent EU force. First, although a vibrant pluralistic, multi-ethnic, democracy itself, India is reluctant to spread democracy through the barrel of a gun as a matter of principle. Non-promotion of the Indian model of democracy remains a distinct trait of India's foreign policy. Second, although it has embarked on a strategy of multi-alignment, India is unlikely to enter into formal arrangements with military alliances. This would be against the very spirit of its desire to ensure autonomy of decision-making and action. Third, there is concern that such alliances undermine the UN, especially if the alliance commitment calls for action even without a UN mandate. Fourth, given the evolving strategic partnership between India and the United States, New Delhi might consider Washington to be its informal partner in NATO. Finally, with a few notable exceptions (such as strategic airlift, global positioning and state-of-the-art communications) the over one million-strong professional Indian military (the second largest in the world) with its decades-long experience in peace operations as well as counter-insurgency operations has greater capacity than the nascent EU force and, therefore, New Delhi does not see any particular advantage in such an alliance. While India would certainly benefit from the superior military technology and is willing to acquire it, New Delhi is unwilling to acquire it at the cost of entering into formal military alliances or partnerships.

These reservations notwithstanding, there is certainly a greater need for more discussion these issues between India and Europe as the former has significant experience which might be of use to the latter. In this context, the joint workshop on 'Asian, European and African Policies, Practices and Lessons Learnt in Peace Operations in Africa' was a promising start (von Gienanth 2007). The workshop, held in New Delhi in June 2007 was the first Indian-European Dialogue on peacekeeping and was organized in the context of the German EU Presidency. It brought together leading Indian and European peacekeepers who had worked together in UN peace operations in Africa and provided a forum to exchange views on peacekeeping. This workshop was in line with one of the recommendations of the JAP, which calls for more dialogue on UN peacekeeping and peacebuilding to exchange perspectives on conceptual and operational aspects of peacekeeping operations, including post-conflict reconstruction and rehabilitation. While the prospects of fielding a joint Indo-European peace operation are still a long way off, such joint workshops are a useful first step. In a similar vein, New Delhi might also consider participating in the Partnership for Peace Programme (which includes Russia and neutral Switzerland as members) to bitter understand NATO policies even if it is opposed to them.

# The Widening Gap

## THE EUROPEAN ECONOMY:
## PROTECTIONIST AND DOOMED TO DECLINE

The Indians middle class tends to look at Europe as mired in economic stagnation and content with the bourgeois comfort of its welfare state. For this section of Indian society, Europe is a 'has-been' because of its demographic decline and ageing population. As Lisbonne de Vergeron notices in her study (2006: xiii), 'Europe is simply unattractive to India, especially by comparison with the United States. Many Indians regard it as "socially and culturally protectionist", and as offering interest only on account of its "exotic tourist appeal". This perception crystallized during the Arcelor/Mittal affair which for the first time concerned the acquisition of a European firm—Arcelor—by an Indian tycoon, Lakshmi Mittal. Arcelor was born in 2002 of the merger of Arcelia from Spain, Arbed from Luxemburg and Arcelor from France. Mittal Steel, one of the largest steel companies in the world, was registered in Rotterdam in the Netherlands but was associated with India in the common man's perception because it is the birthplace of its chief executive officer, Lakshmi Mittal. On 27 January 2006, Mittal Steel made a bid of US\$22 billion on Arcelor which was considered by Arcelor to be hostile. Guy Dolle, Arcelor's French chief executive officer, argued that 'Arcelor made perfume while Mittal Steel made *eau de cologne*'. French politicians like Dominique Strauss-Khan (former socialist minister of finance and now director general of the International Monetary Fund) described this bid as the *OPA du Tiers monde* (a Third World bid) and others suggested that Arcelor's shareholders might be paid in *monnaie de singe* (monkey's money). After three months, Mittal increased his bid by 38.7 per cent and succeeded in acquiring the firm. But by that time, the Indian media and the government had started to hit back. The Indian Minister for Commerce and Industry, Kamal Nath, warned the European Commission that opposition to the bid violates norms of the World Trade Organization and nobody in Europe paid attention to Mittal's argument that his firm and Arcelor were European companies which should better join hands to resist China's ambitions. The Indian media had a field day in vilifying the double standards of the EU, ever ready to play the capitalist game when it suits them, but refusing to play it when it does not. After all India saw no objections in allowing Lafarge to become a giant of the Indian cement industry. Why should this not be possible with the reverse scenario in the steel industry? Interestingly, the European Commission sided with the Indian government, on behalf of the principles of economic liberalism and against the economic nationalism displayed by the French and others.

At the same time France was accused of treating India as a giant garbage bin by carelessly sending the aircraft carrier *Clemenceau*, laden with undisclosed but significant amounts of asbestos, lead, mercury and other toxic chemicals, to be broken up in the scrapmetal yards of Gujarat instead of within Europe. Following several court cases in France and activities by Greenpeace, President Jacques Chirac finally recalled the ship from India and ordered an investigation.

## THE RISING TIDE OF RACISM

In contrast to the positive outlook towards the United States, the Indian perception of the arrogant attitude of the Europeans was reinforced by the racial discrimination many Indians can suffer in Europe.

Alongside multiculturalism, the British society has multiple forms of discrimination. Here it is important to distinguish between the xenophobia of extreme right-wing movements and everyday expressions of ordinary racism (Bhatt and Mukta 2000: 437).[5] Children are the first victims of this refusal of otherness. How many second-generation immigrants in primary or secondary school have been the butt of classmates who were taken aback not only by the colour of their skin but by Hindu customs such as vegetarianism, cow worship, arranged marriages, wearing the sari or the sacred rope worn by upper caste men? In Britain, the 'Shilpa Shetty affair' was revealing of this benign form of racism: a reality show of *Channel Four*[6] invited Shilpa Shetty, a Bollywood starlet, for a 26-day-long show in January 2007. Things turned sour when, after three weeks, the three white celebrities turned against Shilpa, criticizing her diet and saying that she would prefer to be white since she bleached her facial hair. More than 40,000 complaints about racism were sent to *Channel Four*, mostly by Indians, and politicians had to apologise publicly. Ken Livingstone, the Mayor of London, declared that such marks of racism were unbearable, and Keith Vaz, the Leicester MP, raised the issue in the House of Commons. Gordon Brown himself had to reassert that Britain was tolerant country and needed to remain so, during an official visit to India (*BBC News* 2007b).

Indians have been victims of xenophobia in a more extreme way in Germany. In August 2007, eight Indian men were the victims of a racist attack when they were beaten and chased through the streets of Leipzig by a mob of 50 shouting 'Foreigners out!' even as the townsfolk looked on. The incident not only raised the spectre of the prevalence of right-wing extremism but also of an anti-Indian bias (*Spiegel* 2007).

The case of France is different. Not only are racist attitudes commonplace there, but in contrast to the British context, the French Republic is hostile to any form of multiculturalism. The most significant measure that has been taken by the states in this respect concerned the exterior signs of religious affiliation. In 2005 it was decided that none could be worn either by the pupils or by the teachers in the premises of schools and universities. Besides the Muslim girls who wear the veil, the Sikh boys were directly affected by this new rule. Their family objected that the turban was part of their cultural attributes, to no avail. The Indian resentment vis-à-vis this regulation dominated the press coverage of the official visit Prime Minister de Villepin paid to India in September 2005.

Europe has always mattered to India in terms of norms, concepts and ideas. Therefore India will remain drawn to Europe's soft power. But will Europe continue to be a norm generator and norm upholder or will it be relegated to becoming a norm follower, espousing the ideas developed elsewhere? If it is the latter, then Europe will become even less significant to India.

In economic terms, Europe will matter. But here too unless Europe can prove to be as competitive, attractive and open, it might continue to lose out to the United States and East Asia. Economics is also likely to be the most contentious issue between India and Europe, and Europe will have to become more attractive and open for business. Europe also needs to play on its industrial strengths to re-launch its cooperation with India. Two areas here are of primary importance, infrastructure and environmental protection. Given Europe's sensitivity to environmental questions as well as its technological capabilities, this is one area where Europe can offer solutions to India's problems. In the sphere of infrastructure, energy is a priority area for India which is experiencing serious shortages of and over-dependency on oil and coal—two of the most polluting fossil fuels. India's quest for gas supplies and nuclear energy are a consequence of this resource crunch. This is another area for Europe to step up its cooperation with India.

In political and hard power terms, Europe, sadly, matters the least to India. There is certainly sympathy and expectations for Europe as a potential alternative to the United States. 'Several officials agreed that "India would benefit from a tilt of the balance of power from the United States towards the EU", for this would ensure "more stable multipolar geopolitics in the future"' (Lisbonne de Vergeron 2006: 14). However, so far this potential has remained unrealized. Were Europe to emerge as a real alternative to Washington and play a more activist role in ensuring the elevation of India to the rank of a permanent member of the UN Security Council, as well as its inclusion in an enlarged G8, it would matter to India. Besides, it might strengthen the cause of multilateralism not only in India but also at the international level by democratizing the global decision-making institutions. It remains to be seen if Europe lives up to these expectations or becomes increasingly irrelevant to the rising powers in Asia and the emerging world order.

## Notes

1. In the official Indian perspective 'Europe' comprises the 27 member states of the European Union (EU), the North Atlantic Treaty Organisation (NATO) members (except the United States and Canada) as well as Switzerland and the Balkan states. Significantly, India does not regard the Russian Federation as a part of Europe but locates it in 'Eurasia' along with the Central Asian republics. Thus, by extension, while the EU and NATO are regarded as European institutions, the Organization for Security and Co-operation in Europe (OSCE), due to the geographic breadth represented by its 56 participating states, and despite its name, is not really considered to be a European institution. See Ministry of External Affairs 2007: v-viii.

2. 'Licence Raj' refers to an elaborate system of controlling private sector enterprises by issuing official licences and imposing strict rules and regulations for the conduct of their business. It resulted in red tape, corruption, protectionism and fettered Indian entrepreneurship.

3. This approach of France and Britain was not dissimilar to that of the other permanent members of the UN Security Council (China, Russia and the United States), all of whom established strategic dialogues with India, which was against the spirit of UNSC resolution 1172 (which also condemned the Indian and Pakistani nuclear tests and called on New Delhi and Islamabad to sign the NPT and the CTBT and start negotiations on the FMCT).

4. Interestingly, in the last five years, *Strategic Analysis,* India's leading security journal, has not featured a single article on Indo-European security relations.

5. Bhatt and Mukta point out that 'the American and British New Right language of the 1980s . . . carried similar themes of "majority discrimination" and an attack on minority rights and protection'.

6. 'Celebrity Big Brother', which consists of locking together so-called celebrities for four weeks and inviting the public to vote to eliminate them.

# References

Acharya, A., Biato, M.F., Diallo, B., Gonzalez, F.E., Hoshino, T., O'Brien, T., Olivier, G., and Wang, Y. (2004) (eds.), 'Global Views on the European Union', *Chaillot Papers* 72, Paris: EU Institute for Security Studies.

Baru, S. (2007), 'Strategic Consequences of India's Economic Performance', in Baldev Raj Nayar (ed.), *Globalization and Politics in India*, Delhi: Oxford University Press.

*BBC News* (2005), 'Who is behind the Delhi bombings?', 31 October.

——— (2006), 'Mumbai Train Attacks', 30 September.

——— (2007a), 'Dozens dead in India train blasts', 19 February.

——— (2007b), 'Politicians enter Big Brother row', 27 January.

Bendiek, A. and Wagner, C. (2008), 'Prospects and Challenges of EU-India Security Cooperation', in Shazia Wuelbers (ed.), *EU India Relations: A Critique*, New Delhi: EuroIndia Centre and the Academic Foundation.

Bhatt, C. and Mukta, P. (2000), 'Hindutva in the West: mapping the antinomies of globalization', *Ethnic and Racial Studies*, Vol. 23, No. 3, pp. 407–41.

Cooper, R. (2002), 'The Post-Modern State', in M. Leonard (ed.), *Re-Ordering the World*, London: Foreign Policy Centre.

Daalder, I. and Goldgeier, J. (2006), 'Global NATO', *Foreign Affairs*, Vol. 85, No. 5, pp. 105–13.

D'Souza, S.M. (2007), 'India's Aid to Afghanistan: Challenges and Prospects', *Strategic Analysis*, Vol. 31, No. 5, pp. 833–42.

EU-India (2008), 'EU-India Joint Press Commniqué', Marseille, 29 September.

European Commission (2004), 'An EU-India Strategic Partnership', Communication from the Commission to the Council, the European Parliament and the European Economic and Social Committee, COM(2004) 430 final, Brussels, 16 June, and annex.

——— (2005), 'EU-India Joint Action Plan', Brussels.

—— (not dated), *The European Union and India: A Strategic Partnership for the 21st Century*, brochure. Online, available at: www.ec.europa.eu/external_relations/library/ publications/25_india_brochure.pdf (accessed 24 May 2008).

European Council (2003), 'A Secure Europe in a better world', *European Security Strategy*, Brussels, 12 December.

European Parliament (1998), 'Resolution on the Communication from the Commission on EU-India Enhanced Partnership', COM (96)0275-C4-0407/96, 25 May.

Fioramonti, L. (2007), 'Report on India', *The External Image of the European Union*, Garnet Working Paper, March.

France-India (2008), 'Joint Statement issued on the occasion of the France-India Summit meeting', 30 September.

Gnesotto, N. and Grevi, G. (2006), *The New Global Puzzle: What World for the EU in 2025?*, Paris: EU Institute for Security Studies.

India (2004), 'An EU-India Strategic Partnership: India's Response', 27 August.

India and the EU (2007), *India-EU Joint Statement*, New Delhi, 30 November.

Islam, S. (2008), 'Europe Looks East-Part F', *Yale Global Online*, 30 January. Online, available at: http://yaleglobal.yale.edu/display.articlePid-10272 (accessed 24 May 2008).

International Monetary Fund (2007), *World Economic Outlook Database*, October.

Jain, R.K. (2005), 'India, the European Union and Asian Regionalism', paper presented at the EUSA-AP conference on 'Multilateralism and Regionalism in Europe and Asia-Pacific', Tokyo, December.

Kux, D. (1993), *India and the United States: Estranged Democracies 1941-1991*, New Delhi: Sage.

Lisbonne de Vergeron, K. (2006), *Contemporary Indian Views of Europe*, London: Chatham House and Foundation Robert Schumann.

Maddison, A. (2003), *Historical Statistics for the World Economy: 1-2003 AD*, Paris: OECD.

Ministry of Defence (2006), *Annual Report 2005-2006*, New Delhi: Government of India.

Ministry of External Affairs (2007), *Annual Report 2006-2007*, New Delhi: Government of India.

Minuto-Rizzo, A. (2007), 'NATO's Changing Role in the Post-Cold War Period', speech at the Institute for Defence and Strategic Analyses (IDSA), New Delhi, 20 April.

Mukherjee, P. (2005), Speech at Carnegie Endowment for International Peace, Washington DC, 27 June. Online, available at: www.carnegieendowment.org/files/Mukherjee_ Speech_06-27-051.pdf (accessed 24 May 2008).

—— (2007), Remarks at the Council on Foreign Relations, New York, 1 October. Online, available at: <http://www.cfr.org/publication/14339/> (accessed 24 May 2008).

*Outlook*-AC Nielsen Opinion Poll (2006), '66 per cent say Bush is India's Friend', 6 March. Online, available at: www.outlookindia.com/full.asp?fname=Cover% 20Story6 cfodname=20060306&sid=1 (accessed 24 May 2008).

Pattanayak, S. (2005), 'Regime Change in Iraq and Challenges of Political Reconstruction', *Strategic Analysis*, Vol. 29, No. 4, pp. 629–52.

Pew Research Center (2005), 'US Image up Slightly, but Still Negative. American Character Gets Mixed Reviews', Washington DC, 23 June.

Press Trust of India (2008), 'India should use influence for neighbourhood peace: EU', 8 January.

Raja Mohan, C. (2002), 'India, Europe and the United States', in R. Jain (ed.), *India and the European Union in the 21st Century,* New Delhi: Radiant Publishers.

——— (2006), 'India and the balance of power', *Foreign Affairs,* Vol. 85, No. 4, pp. 17–32.

Rane, P. (2005), 'NATO Enlargement and Security Perceptions in Europe', *Strategic Analysis,* Vol. 29, No. 3, pp. 470–90.

Schaffer, T. (2002), 'Building a New Partnership with India', *Washington Quarterly,* Vol. 25, No. 2, pp. 31–44.

——— and Mehti, M. (2001), 'Rising India and US Policy Options in Asia', *South Asia Monitor,* Vol. 40, No. 1, pp. 1–6.

Sengupta, S. (2008), 'Facing a wave of violence, India is rattled', *New York Times,* 28 July.

Singh, M. (2005), Address by Prime Minister at Oxford University, 8 July. Online, available at: www.hinduonnet.com/thehindu/nic/0046/pmspeech.htm (accessed 24 May 2008).

Sidhu, W.P.S. (2002), 'La stratégie de l'Inde: un changement de paradigme?', *Politique Étrangère,* Vol. 67, No. 2, pp. 315–33.

*Spiegel Online International* (2007), 'After attack on Indians, Germany fears for its reputation', 22 August.

United Nations Website (2007), 'Monthly Summary of Contributors of Military and Civilian Police Personnel', December. Online, available at: www.un.org/Depts/dpko/dpko/contributors/ (accessed 24 May 2008).

United News of India (2006), 'VHP welcomes Bush visit', 4 March.

Virmani, A. (2005), 'World Economy: From uni-polar to tri-polar', *The Hindu Business Line,* 8 February. Online, available at: www.thehindubusinessline.com/2005/02/08/stories/2005020800030800.htm (accessed 24 May 2008).

Von Gienanth, T. (2007), 'Asian European and African Policies, Practices and Lessons Learned in Peace Operations in Africa', Report 08/07 of joint seminar organized by Centre for International Peace Operations and the United Services Institute of India-Centre for United Nations Peacekeeping, New Delhi, June. Available at: www.zif-berlin.org/Downloads/Analysen/Veroeffentlichungen/ ReportJndien_finaL22.08.2007.pdf (accessed 24 May 2008).

World Bank (2007), *World Development Indicators database,* September. Online, available at: http://siteresources.worldbank.org/DATASTATISTICS/Resources/ GDP_PPP.pdf (accessed 24 May 2008).

# Chapter 35

# The India-US rapprochement: state-driven or middle class-driven?

The years 1998 to 2004 of Vajpayee's government saw a turning point in India-US relations. Although the first major decision this government made—the 1998 nuclear testing—brought on immediate sanctions from Washington, the warming detectable afterwards has not waned, so much so that in January 2004, the two countries launched a joint initiative, baptized the Next Step in the Strategic Partnership (NSSP).

Lesser than six months later, the coalition backing the Vajpayee government conceded power to a new Congress-led alliance, the United Progressive Alliance (UPA), which installed Manmohan Singh as prime minister. There was much speculation then about a return to the doctrine of non-alignment, at least of a stauncher defence of multilateralism and, indeed, the government was composed of enough Congressmen in their seventies to lend some credence to this theory. All the more so as the UPA government depended upon the outside support of communist MPs who were nostalgic of India's former foreign policy and hostile to the Indo-American rapprochement.

But nothing of the sort occurred, and beyond mere continuity, one could even see a deepening of relations between the United States and India. This process, at first sight, can be attributed to the strategic thinking of a small group of Indian statesmen and their advisers who wanted to place India on the global map and themselves had ties with the American establishment. Certainly, this foreign policy shift has been decided 'in camera', the Indian Parliament being largely sidelined: It is a government-led transformation, as evident from the manifestations of the strategic partnership between India and the US, which multiplied in 2004–8 and culminated, on the latter year, in the 123 Agreement about civil nuclear energy. However, in the second part of this essay, I will try to show that this rapprochement also has to do with factors reaching beyond strategic and diplomatic considerations that pertain to the economy and to the societal ties currently linking the two countries. Even more interestingly, it is in tune with the approach of international affairs displayed by the Indian public opinion—at least by the new middle class.

## An Executive-Led Rapprochement

The capture of the decision-making process by the neo-conservatives in the US has shown, in the first years of the twenty-first century, that the international agenda—including radical turns—of a great democracy could be shaped by a small group of highly motivated politicians and experts. A similar development unfolded itself in India so far as the Indo-American rapprochement was concerned, since it has primarily been brought about by a mix of senior politicians, strategic advisers and bureaucrats. This shift called to mind the 'modus operandi' of the Indian government during the 1991 economic reform when matters were not debated in the Parliament either. Here again, the real parliamentary debate occurred very late, during the summer of 2008. Certainly, Congressmen were not unanimously in favour of this rapprochement. But those who showed the stronger reluctance have been sidelined (Foreign Minister Natwar Singh left the government in 2005 and Mani Shankar Aiyar was shifted to another portfolio, from the strategic ministry of Gas and Petroleum to the more innocuous one of Panchayati Raj). Certainly, the communist MPs who supported the UPA government since its inception rejected the most significant component of this rapprochement—the nuclear deal—but Prime Minister Manmohan Singh resigned himself to lose their support during the summer of 2008 in order to go ahead with the deal.

## TOWARDS A STRATEGIC PARTNERSHIP

Besides the 123 Agreement, the government-led Indo-American rapprochement relied on many other pillars, which need to be taken into account. One year after the formation of the UPA government, Pranab Mukherjee, the then Defence Minister, set in place a Defence Framework with his counterpart Donald Rumsfeld on 28 June 2005. This 'framework' set out the common interests of both countries in maintaining security and stability, combating terrorism, protecting the free flow of commerce and preventing the spread of weapons of mass destruction and associated material, data and technologies. It read:

The United States and India will work to conclude defence transactions, not solely as ends in and of themselves, but as a means to strengthen our countries' security, reinforce our strategic partnership, achieve greater interaction between our armed forces and build greater understanding between our defence establishments.[1]

This framework was fleshed out in a highly substantial manner by arms sales and joint manoeuvres. Till date, the US had lagged behind Russia, Israel and European countries in terms of military procurement. Things are changing. Among the most significant Indian acquisitions, one finds six C-130J 'Super Hercules' cargoes (at the cost of US$1 billion), a US$2.2 billion contract—still under negotiation as far as the price is concerned—regarding eight P-81 Poseidon long-range maritime patrol/strike aircraft to the Indian Navy and the procurement of the Landing Platform Dock, Jalashwa, the Indian Navy's second-largest combat platform after the aircraft carrier Viraat. Simultaneously, discussions have been held about selling F-35 Lightening II, the American fifth-generation fighter, and ballistic missile defence systems. The Americans had also offered to sell the Indians F-16s or F-18, 'Hornets', when they announced the sale of F-16s to Pakistan.[2]

Joint military manoeuvres involving the army, the navy and the air force had already become commonplace under Vajpayee's government, but they have gained momentum under Manmohan Singh. For instance, in October 2004, joint exercises—called 'Malabar', involving the navies of India, Canada and the US, took place in Goa. For the first time, the United States engaged P3C Orion aircraft, specialized in maritime surveillance, in these operations. In 2005, the first phase of 'Malabar 05' involved aircraft carriers of the two navies—US pilots flew in Indian Sea Harriers and Indian pilots did the same on F-18s. The second phase concentrated on submarine warfare. However, the biggest-ever naval exercise in the Bay of Bengal took place in September 2007, involving three aircraft carriers— two American and one Indian—and five countries: India, the US, Japan, Australia and Singapore.

In the field of space exploration, which is also very much strategic and government-led, National Aeronautics and Space Administration (NASA) and its alter ego, Indian Space Research Organisation (ISRO), signed an MoU (Memorandum of Understanding) implying that India's first unmanned lunar mission, Chandrayaan I, should carry two NASA instruments to map the moon. The mission took place on 21 October 2008. Other scientific joint programmes developed in different domains under the framework of the umbrella agreement on cooperation in the field of science and technology, which the Union Minister for Science and Technology, Kapil Sibal, and Condoleezza Rice signed in October 2005. For instance, India and the US have launched a 'knowledge initiative on agriculture' with a three-year financial commitment of US$100 million in 2006 and technical collaborations are taking place in the realm of energy to make Indian coal cleaner.

As far as civil aviation is concerned, the United States and India concluded an 'open skies' agreement in January 2005. This agreement, replacing the 1956 Air Service Agreement, allows any Indian or American airlines to establish service between any city in the two countries. Air-India immediately announced it would increase its scheduled flights from 28 to 37 a week, a telling sign of the intensity of exchanges. The company bought 68 aircraft from Boeing, which, in 2006, sold almost US$14 billion worth of aircraft to India—more than its sales to any other country in the world that year.

Other diplomatic moves bore testimony of the growing strategic rapprochement between India and the US. For instance, India hastened to join the coalition of donors initiated by the United States after the tsunami on 26 December 2004. This coalition, which included Japan and Australia as well, did not last, but it nevertheless demonstrated India's propensity to follow US initiatives rather than adhere to a purely multilateral rationale.[3] The contrast with the Arab–Latin America summit held in Brasilia in May 2005 is striking: in this context, about thirty countries in these two regions went so far as to denounce the unilateralism of the US policy. One year later, Manmohan Singh announced a US$5 million contribution to the US Red Cross for relief and rehabilitation of the victims of Hurricane Katrina.

Similarly, India refrained from declaring sanctions against the United States when the latter delayed repealing the Byrd Amendment[4] after the WTO (World Trade Organization) ruled it to be illegal. Indian complacency was all the more significant since New Delhi had referred a complaint to the WTO to denounce Washington's payment of anti-dumping duty proceeds to US industries and that Canada, co-complainant, had imposed sanctions (*The Hindu,* 4 September 2005b).

Last but not least, the Indian-Israeli rapprochement has also followed its course. This is not unconnected to India-US relations. The Indian initiative of establishing diplomatic relations with Israel in 1991 was in part aimed at Washington: It was a way of 'getting at' the United States via Tel Aviv. Initiated by the Congress government in 1991–2 with the opening of an Indian embassy in Israel and vice versa, this process was continued by the NDA. It culminated in September 2003 with Ariel Sharon's visit to New Delhi. The Congress was, then, highly critical of the Indo-Israeli rapprochement and the communists were appalled by it. Under Manmohan Singh, though, nearly nothing has changed: military cooperation between the two countries has not slackened[5] and the government has not really readjusted its relations with the Middle East in favour of its old Arab allies. It is significant that the only Indian official to have made the trip to attend the funeral of Yasser Arafat—a close friend of the Nehru/Gandhi family—was Natwar Singh, Minister of Foreign Affairs. The communists secured the suspension of joint military manoeuvres between the Indian and Israeli armies, but this was the only concession that was made to them and these activities were resumed after the withdrawal of their support to the UPA government. In October 2008, 'The Indian and Israeli Special Forces [we]re in the process of finalizing plans to conduct their first ever round of joint counter-terrorism manoeuvres. . .' (Bedi 2008).

## AMERICAN AND INDIAN MOTIVES: IDEALISM VS PRAGMATISM?

The motives underlying the Indo-American rapprochement are not always the same in New Delhi and Washington and, therefore, India may not be interested in going as far as the US would like to take her.

On the American side, after decades of mistrust, the US is willing to transform India into a strategic partner not only because nobody can afford to ignore it any more—in strategic as well as economic terms—but also, and more positively, because India can be useful to the US. In his 'Anatomy of a partnership', Henry Kissinger considered in 2006 that China, Southeast Asia and Islamic terrorism were the three main reasons why India and the US had to join hands

(Kissinger 2006). From the US point of view, the first and the third factors are probably the highest on the list of priorities.

As an Asian power, India may help the US to balance China. Such an approach will never be spelled out explicitly, in order not to irritate Beijing, but some officials can't seem to help mentioning it. For instance, Evan Feigenbaum, Deputy Assistant Secretary for South and Central Asian Affairs declared, while briefing the Harvard University Weatherhead Fellows:

> . . . those of us who try to be forward-thinking about the role of India in the world are starting to think about India not [j]ust as a South Asian power, but as an Asian power—and about the role of India, China and Japan, these three large Asian powers, and their relations with each other in this larger . . . Asian space. So we spend a lot of time dunking about India vis-à-vis China, China vis-à-vis India. That doesn't mean China is the rationale for the interest in US—India relations. Despite what some people say, I can think of 63 good reasons why we should have improved our relations with India a long time ago. But I won't deny that it's in the background, it's a factor. (Feigenbaum 2008)

The second most important factor relates to the search for partners in the fight against Islamic terrorism. For the US, India is a natural ally in such a fight, given the fact that the country has suffered from Jehadist movements for decades in Kashmir. John Negroponte, Director of American National Intelligence, has made this point explicitly (Baruah 2007). As a result, the Indo-American rapprochement had been boosted by the post-9/11 scenario under Vajpayee. Brajesh Mishra, then prime minister Vajpayee's right-hand man and national security adviser, expressed a desire for an alliance of three democracies—India, the US and Israel—in a famous speech given during a highly publicized visit to Washington in May 2003. The argument was a simple one:

> India, the United States and Israel have some fundamental similarities. We are all democracies, sharing a common vision of pluralism, tolerance and equal opportunity. Stronger India-US relations and India-Israel relations have a natural logic . . . . The US, India and Israel have been prime targets of terrorism. They have to jointly face the same ugly face of modern day terrorism.[6]

While the words have changed under Manmohan Singh's governance, the ideas have remained more or less the same, at least on the American side. The US is convinced that India will even more strongly join hands with them in the global war on terror, as its cities are now increasingly targeted by bomb attacks. In late 2006, Republican King addressed the New York chapter of the Global Organization of People of Indian Origin (GOPIO) in the following terms:

> Vibrant democracies such as the US and India share common goals and should count on each other for support and cooperation . . . . As in the US, India is working hard to head off, stop and minimise any attack on itself as we are in this struggle together against global terrorism.[7]

This discourse partly resulted from the American assessment of Pakistan's policy as being fundamentally ambivalent, which made the country appear less reliable in the fight against terrorism. Certainly, Islamabad was a partner in the global war against terror, but Pakistan had become a tactical ally, when India had reached the status of a strategic ally. In 2007, again, James Clad, Deputy Assistant Secretary of Defence for South and Southeast Asia, declared: 'India simply must, as a long-term consideration, matter more for us than Pakistan' (*The Hindu*, 1 January 2007a).

The Chinese and Islamic factors hark back to something bigger that the Indians have apparently missed so far, that is the meta-strategic and even the civilizational stake the US have invested in the Washington/New Delhi axis. Indians often ask (themselves or publicly) with suspicion: 'why do they want us so much?'[8] For the BJP, Washington wants to reduce the Indian military independence, while the communists denounce, in a similar vein, 'American imperialism'; but they are probably both wrong. The American motivations are part of a long-term agenda with civilizational overtones. In 2004, the National Intelligence Council published a report, *Mapping a Global Future*, where one could read:

The likely emergence of China and India, as well as others, as new major global players— similar to the advent of a united Germany in the 19th century and a powerful United States in the early 20th century—will transform geopolitical landscape, with changes potentially as dramatic as those in the previous two centuries. In the same way that commentators refer to the 1900s as the American Century, the 21st century may be seen as the time when Asia, led by China and India, comes into its own.

Now, the US fears China almost as much as the Muslim world because the Middle Empire does not share the same interests and values, whereas India has much in common with America: the oldest and the largest democracies in the world believe, at least officially, in the rule of law, multiculturalism and a form of secularism very accommodating so far as the role of religion in the public sphere is concerned. The US establishment appreciates the Indian stand of entrepreneurship promoted by Indian capitalism since the 1991 reform too. Both countries are, theoretically at least, 'multicultural market democracies'. The Bush administration, therefore, aspired to build a kind of civilizational partnership in a somewhat Huntingtonian way. As George W. Bush said in 2006 to his Indian counterpart: '...the partnership between our free nations has the power to transform the world.'[9] The task, obviously, is colossal. This is why its main actors always situate their policy in a long-term perspective. The Under Secetary of State for Political Affairs, Nicholas Burns said, for instance, in 2007: 'The nuclear deal is done. We hope that will happen. I think Americans might be able to say, 20 years from now, India is one of our two or three most important partners in the world' (*The Hindu*, 4 April 2007b).

The main explanation for the nuclear deal lies in this long-term approach, the search for allies against the axis of evil of the future, of which China or the

Muslim countries—or both!—may well be part of. Without keeping this element in mind, it is very difficult to understand the very persistent way in which the Bush administration has had a large body of legislation revised, and has pressurized the reluctant members of the NSG[10] (Nuclear Suppliers Group) to get the nuclear deal materialized.

While the American motives behind the India-US rapprochement sounds rather idealistic, New Delhi's attitude vis-à-vis the US seems to rely on rather pragmatic calculations. In fact, Manmohan Singh's programme in foreign policy is overdetermined by a strong sense of 'realpolitik'. In response to communists who objected to the warmth of tone with which he congratulated George Bush on his re-election in 2004 he replied:

. . . we have to look at the realities of the world. International relations are, in the final analysis, power relations. And we are living in a world of unequal power. We cannot wish away the realities of this situation. We have to use the available international system to promote our interests. And, therefore, we have a necessity to engage the US. The US plays a very important role in the world economy, the political world system and we cannot wish that away. (*The Hindu,* 11 August 2004)

Such a discourse keeps coming back in his speeches about foreign policy. It seems to be at odds with Nehru's idealism and his Third World-oriented non-alignment, but it is not entirely so. Certainly, the moral dimension has gone—hence, the ambivalence regarding Myanmar or Tibet—but the obsession with national independence remains: like the proponents of non-alignment, Dr Singh defends the promotion of national interest at any cost; he simply does it from an economist's point of view and in a more candid way, as before the 2006 IBSA (India, Brazil, South Africa) meeting:

I've always said that foreign policy is essentially a device to widen our development options. The foremost problem before our country is to get rid of chronic poverty, ignorance and disease which still afflict millions of people. We need a strong economy. We need a fast growing economy. We need a pattern of growth which creates a lot more jobs. Whether it's improving relations with the US or improving relations with China or choosing the potential of cooperation with other developing countries whether in Africa or in Latin America, I think it fits into the over-all picture of making use of all opportunities to expand our economic and other multi-faceted contacts with other countries. (GoI 2006: 80)

Such a definition of national interest as the alpha and omega of foreign policy is bound to limit the US-India relations. As Raja Mohan underlined: India 'will never become another US ally in the mould of the United Kingdom or Japan. But nor will it be an Asian France, seeking tactical independence within the framework of a formal alliance' (Raja Mohan 2006). In fact, India will probably remain a good partner so long as it gains in terms of economic development—Manmohan Singh's pet subject—and/or strategic advancement, military equipment, for instance. For Manmohan Singh, economic development being a key priority, the nuclear deal met some of his major concerns. By making an exception for India, the US won India's trust, and this achievement was reconfirmed by the way Washington put pressure on the reluctant members of the NSG during the summer of 2008. Before signing the 123 Agreement in Washington, Pranab Mukherjee declared in Washington:

> In signing the agreement between India and the United States of America for cooperation on peaceful uses of nuclear energy, we have brought to fruition three years of extraordinary effort by both our governments. This agreement is the more visible sign of the transformed relationship and partnership that our two countries are building together. (US Department of State 2008)

At the same time, Mukherjee insisted, in the interviews he gave to the Indian media, that New Delhi had not eroded national sovereignty at all. For instance, he said to *India Today* that 'we did not want any condition imposed on us that we would not be permitted to conduct a test' (22 September 2008).

The Indo-American rapprochement has delivered on another front: It has helped New Delhi loosen the ties re-created between the United States and Pakistan in the aftermath of 11 September 2001. Certainly, the American aid secured by Islamabad remains substantial—about US$100 million a month—but it has been made conditional by the Congress after the 2006 mid-term elections. Undoubtedly, the Indian caucus has played a part in this shift. And while Pakistan was named as one of its 'Non-NATO allies' by the United States in 2004, the US-Pakistan relations have soured, especially after American troops entered the FATA (Federally Administered Tribal Areas) from Afghanistan to fight Talibans.

## Non-state Factors of the India-US Partnership

While the Indo-American rapprochement may look vulnerable because of the keenness of India to retain its national independence, in addition to the marginalization of anti-American pressure groups such as the communists and old Congressmen such as Natwar Singh, the thickness of societal relations makes this relation much more enduring than it may appear. Indeed, beyond the diplomatic and strategic compensations that India gets from the US, its goodwill towards the US can be explained more structurally by the expansion of economic and social ties linking the two countries.

### AN ECONOMIC RELATIONSHIP WITH A
### STRONG HIGH-TECH CONTENT

In terms of trade and investments, the expansion of the Indo-American ties is recent—it dates from the economic reform undertaken in 1991—but vigorous. In ten years, US exports to India more than doubled—from US$2.8 billion in 1991–2 to US$6.4 billion in 2001–2—and almost doubled again in the five years between 2001–2 and 2006–7, reaching US$12.6 billion (GoI 2008: A-92). More importantly, American imports of Indian goods multiplied by 3.5 times—from US$4 to 14 billion between 1991–2 and 2001–2; it reached US$18.8 billion in 2006–7 (ibid.: A-97). In 2006–7, the US remained India's more important trading partner with 14.9 per cent of its exports being directed towards India.

In the field of investments, the US is the second-largest foreign investor—after Mauritius, through which many American NRIs' investments are channelled for tax reasons—with 9.37 per cent of the total in cumulated figures since 1991 (ibid.: 201). The number of American corporations in India has multiplied by fourteen since 1991, numbering now over a thousand.[11]

Alone with the mass-consumer products sold by McDonald's, Dominos, Pizza Hut, Pepsi, Coca-Cola, Reebok, Nike and Avon—which are changing the lifestyle of Indians, especially among the youth—American investments are also made in strategic areas of high technology, including in the defence sector of activity.[12] The computer engineers that India produces on a large scale are a specific asset given their expertise and still meagre salaries compared to labour costs in the United States.

Driven out of India by a wave of hostility towards US multinationals in the 1960s-70s, IBM is back again; now the company employs 23,000 people in India (*The Hindu*, 15 June 2005) and has developed a partnership with three of the best Indian Institutes of Technology, those in Delhi, Kanpur and Chennai, which supply it with internationally qualified engineers. In June 2005, IBM inaugurated its Global Delivery Centre near Hyderabad.

Hewlett-Packard, since it bought out Compaq in India, employed 10,000 in 2005 and had a network staking its presence in 120 cities. Microsoft, whose largest foreign investments—other than industrial—have been made in India, has established its software development offices in Hyderabad.

American computer companies have all set up major R&D offices in India. For instance, 80 per cent of Oracle's 5,000 Indian employees work in its Indian Development Centre—the first centre of this type outside of the US for the firm was set up in Bangalore in 1994. By the same token, Adobe's development centre was set up in Noida (near Delhi) in 1998. This is where Acrobat Reader was developed. As for Apple, its famous iPod was designed at the centre that the company owns in Hyderabad—before being mass-produced in factories in Taiwan. The Texas Instruments R&D centre in Bangalore—approximately 900 engineers—had already filed for 225 patents, mainly for computer chips, in 2005. Another industry giant, Intel, is also based in Bangalore. The largest American company R&D centre in India, however, is General Electrics, which employed 22,000 people in 2005, including 1,800 computer engineers in Bangalore, which enabled 95 patents to be filed in the US. It did business worth US$2 billion in India in 2006.

In the spring of 2005, the Indo-US Science and Technology Forum decided to set up R&D centres in India in various sectors, including design engineering, energy and eco-informatics. A centre devoted to this specialized field has already opened in Bangalore.

The magnitude of less sophisticated outsourcing has further increased the interlocking of Indian-US business activities. Many banks, such as American Express and Citibank, and automobile manufacturers—Ford, General Motors, for instance—have their accounting and much of their back office activity done in India. And the number of call centres is constantly on the rise. The largest US company in the field, Convergys Corps, employed over 5,000 people in India in 2005, although it only set up its first offices there in 2001.

The entertainment industry may well be the next area for collaboration. In April 2008, the USIBC (US-India Business Council) and FICCI (Federation of Indian Chambers of Commerce and Industry) launched a Bollywood-Hollywood initiative in order to fight against counterfeiting and piracy.

## THE ROLE OF THE DIASPORA AND
## THE STUDENT COMMUNITY

In addition to business activities, social ties play an extremely important role in the Indian-US rapprochement. The primary factor in these is the Indian diaspora in the US, a demographic mass that has doubled in ten years to 2 million people. The flow of legal Indian immigrants is now greater than that of the Chinese. In 2006, a record number of 84,681 Indians got green cards, as against 50,228 in 2003 and 70,151 in 2004. Many of them come to study computer engineering. If Oracle established offices in India so early on, it is because among its management there are many Indians. Similarly, Adobe decided to set up an office in India on an initiative by its Indian managers of the company in the US.

The number of Indian students on American campuses has risen from 30,000 in 1996–7 to 75,000 in 2003–4[13] and 80,000 in 2005–6, 2006–7 and 2007–8.[14] Since 2002–3, the contingent of Indian students has been larger than any other group of foreign students.[15] In May 2005, the US Citizenship and Immigration Services (USCIS) announced it would grant an additional 20,000 H1B visas[16] to foreign graduates of American universities with a Master's or higher level and specialized in state-of-the-art technology. This measure, aimed, primarily at meeting the demands of US corporations in terms of computer engineers, works to the great benefit of Indian students seeking a job in the US.

These students, like their elders, are successful in the US (when they do not return home). The US year 2000 census, in fact, shows that Indian-Americans have an average per capita income of US$60,093 compared to the national average of US$38,885 (only 6 per cent of them reportedly live below poverty level), which can be explained by the fact that three-quarters of this community have attended university.[17] In 2006, India was very proud of Indra Nooyi, a Chennai-educated

NRI in her 40s who became the CEO of PepsiCo. The Indian diaspora is, thus, in a position to act as a lobby—particularly by financing the 'Indian Caucus' in the House of Representatives and the Senate—but also as a showcase for India, whose image has changed considerably in the United States: the age-old cliché of destitute poverty has been done away with. The Indian Caucus was instrumental in making American aid to Pakistan conditional and in strengthening the India-US relations on behalf of the global war on terror.[18] Lalit Mansingh, the Indian ambassador to the US confessed in 2007: 'I am convinced that the nuclear deal could not have passed with 85 per cent support in the Congress without the efforts of the Indian American community'.[19]

## A PRO-AMERICAN MIDDLE CLASS

Besides these economic and diasporic links, the Indian middle class is playing a significant part, since it is increasingly supporting a rapprochement between New Delhi and Washington.

In 2008, India was the only country recording such a high opinion of the US, after five years of the war in Iraq—a war which led to a moral divorce of America by many European societies. The 2008 Pew Global Attitudes survey, like the previous ones, found that a large majority of the Indian interviewees, 66 per cent (as against 59 per cent in 2007 and 56 per cent in 2006) had a favourable view of the US, compared to 50 per cent in Japan, 31 per cent in Germany and 33 per cent in Spain (Pew 2008: 21). Interestingly, there were more Indians than Americans and the British who believed that the 'efforts in Iraq will succeed', 59 per cent as against 54 per cent and 52 per cent, respectively; no country except Nigeria (72 per cent) matches India on that front (Ibid.: 28). This is related to the fact that 55 per cent of the Indian interviewees showed a lot or some confidence in George Bush (as against 37 per cent in the US, 25 per cent in Japan, 16 per cent in Britain and 14 per cent in Germany).

In the 2005 Pew survey, of the sixteen countries surveyed on this question, India was the only one—aside from the US—in which a majority expressed a lot or some confidence in the American president. Revealingly, when asked whether the US took into account the interest of 'countries like yours', 63 per cent of Indians answered in the affirmative—more than in any other country. On Iraq, India was the only country other than the US in which a plurality—45 per cent—believed that the removal of Saddam from power had made the world safer, and Indians were even less likely than the Americans to say that the Iraq War has made the world more dangerous. However, just over half (52 per cent) of the respondents favoured US-led efforts to fight terrorism.

The positive view of the US that a majority of Indians entertain can be explained from two points of view. As far as the American society is concerned, at least till the recent crisis it was looked at as an efficient model for economic dynamism, social mobility and multiculturalism—as evident from the success story of the Indian minority over there. As far as world affairs are concerned, the surveys mentioned above reflect the Indian appreciation of what the US does for India (in terms of nuclear collaboration, for instance) as well as the belief that India and the US are in the same camp today: For decades, they have been adversaries because of the Cold War; the world has changed, the fight between communism (or socialism) and capitalism is not the order of the day any more; today, the key conflict may be expressed in terms of clash of civilizations. The Islamist bomb attacks, which have multiplied over the last five years in India, have reinforced this feeling. Logically enough, when George Bush paid an official visit to India in March 2006, he was most warmly welcomed by the General Secretary of the VHP (Vishva Hindu Parishad), on the grounds that he was heading a nation that was fighting boldly 'Jehadi terrorism' (*The Hindu*, 4 March 2006). Bush then said candidly: 'I have been received in many capitals, but I have never seen a reception as grand as the one we have just received' (*The International Herald Tribune*, 6 March 2006).

The rapprochement between India and the US, which has translated in so many collaborations and strategic deals, seems to be partly based on some quid pro quo basis, if we go by what governments say. On the one hand, Washington would like to transform India into a long-term ally to defend the American interests and values; on the other hand, New Delhi seems to be willing to partner with the US as long as this relationship serves its interests in economic and strategic terms.

New Delhi, for instance, may not join hands with the US in the WTO at all as long as the issues regarding American protectionism and subsidies in agriculture remain. India may also resist American attempts to instrumentalize her against China and Iran.

For the US, China has emerged as the number one enemy of the coming years. For India, it is more an enemy of the past, though it is still perceived as a threat and has not helped India get the needed consensus in the NSG: so far as the civil nuclear issue is concerned. Today, the Sino-Indian trade is booming and the cross-investments may follow suit. Simultaneously, 66 per cent of Indians have a good opinion of China, only one-third of them expressed apprehensions about its economic rise and 56 per cent of them do not view China's military modernization as a threat.

A still more delicate issue has to do with Iran and the energy crunch India is faced with. To alleviate this obstacle, India does not hesitate to do business with countries more or less ostracized from the international community, not only Sudan[20] and Myanmar, a country with which India will soon be linked via a gas pipeline, but Iran as well, this country being an old friend, and the heir of a prestigious civilization with which India is most familiar. In January 2005, the state-owned Indian Oil Corporation contracted with the Iranian company Petropars to exploit natural gas resources from Pars, an area which has the largest natural gas reserves in the world known to date. Such an energy supply contract would strengthen the ties between India and Iran, the two countries already having entered into a strategic partnership two years ago. Not only is India helping Iran build a deepwater port in Chabahar to compete with Gwadar in Pakistan, but military cooperation between India and Iran is allegedly about to take on a rather sophisticated technological dimension, with the development of submarine batteries that could allow Tehran to forego Russian technology, which is ill-suited to warm waters. Such a rapprochement bothers Washington, which is doing its best to isolate Tehran so as to dissuade Iran from pursuing its nuclear programme. But can India afford to alienate Iran if the US asks her to sever some of the existing links?

The future will tell whether tensions in the WTO and the Indian relations with China and Iran should become insuperable obstacles. But the economic and societal links that have been built between India and the US may make it difficult for the Indian government to backtrack, even if it wishes. In fact, the deepening of such links may well be part of the American strategy: By letting them develop, Washington is indeed making difficult any roll-back process. Evan Feigenbaum (2008) argues, for instance:

... the most interesting thing about the bilateral relationship to me ... is that it's sort of moving forward in spite of government. And in fact the most interesting and exciting things are happening outside of government. Its this very dynamic private sector. It's happening in terms of investment both ways: Indian investments into the United States, not just American investment into India, in fact now branded Indian investment in the linked States. It's students, business people citizens. There are 80,000 Indian students in the United States, more than from any country in the world. There are about three million Indian-Americans who are kind of a 'human bridge' between the two countries.[21]

What may well be at stake is nothing else than the autonomy of the state vis-à-vis non-state interests ranging from the corporate sector to the new Indian middle-class.

The economic crisis, which started affecting the US and India in a more or less severe manner in 2008, may have an impact on the relationship between both countries in a significant way. The nature of this effect will largely depend upon the duration of the slump. If it lasts a few years, the prestige of the American model may be eroded among the Indian middle too.

## Notes

1. Cited in S. Krishnaswami, *The Hindu*, 30 June 2005.
2. However, the Indian Army has always been reluctant to purchase American equipments because of the fickleness of the US Congress, which is quick to accuse its clients of misconduct and impose sanctions on them and, hence, stop delivery of spare parts. As soon as the American offer regarding fighters was made public, former Air Force Chief, Anil Yeshwant Tipnis, and former Army Chief Shankar Roychowdhury, separately made known to the government, in general, and the defence minister, in particular, their hostility to such a revolution in Indian military procurement. In September 2005, the former Chief of the Army Staff, General (retd.) S. Padmanabhan declared that it would

be better develop military relationship with Russia and China instead of the US (*The Hindu*, 1 September 2005).

3. In an interview granted to *India Today* during her first visit to India—as also Asia—as Secretary of State, Condoleezza Rice expressed great satisfaction with the way in which India had joined the US initiative three months earlier (*India Today*, 28 March 2005: 64).

4. This amendment directs the US government to distribute the anti-dumping and anti-subsidies duties to the US companies that brought forward the cases.

5. The third meeting of the Joint Working Group on military cooperation was held in Jerusalem in December 2004. Joint development of a ballistic missile was allegedly on the agenda.

6. Speech available on http://www.indianembassy.org/indusrel/2003/nsa_ajc_may_8_03.htm.

7. Cited in the *Central Chronicle*, 23 December 2006.

8. See the convoluted introspection of Raj Chengappa 2007.

9. Cited in *Central Chronicle*, 18 June 2006.

10. On the first phase of this process, see D. Mistry 2006.

11. Most American companies established in India have grown at a highly satisfactory rate. McDonald's, which, for instance, did not open in Delhi until 1996, had 40 sales points in India seven years, later, in 2003, and had sold 45 million burgers in the country.

12. In 2007, as many as 52 US corporations such as Boeing, Lokheed-Martin, Ratheon, Honeywell and General Electric had set up offices in India.

13. It doubled between 1998–9 and 2002–3, in five years.

14. See, Jaffrelot 2009: 76–89.

15. They already made up 13 per cent of total 74,603 out of 586,323, in 2002–3.

16. A quota of 65,000 visas in this category had already been decided earlier in the year.

17. To temper the enthusiasm these figures incite, it is worth reading. Khagram, M. Desai and J. Varughese, 2001: 258–84.

18. On the role of USINPAC (US-India Political Action Committee), see I. Therwath, 2008: 111–24.

19. The Third Annual SAPRA Seminar on Indo-US Relations: 2007 'Can Business Interests Shape a Strategic Partnership?'.

20. New Delhi invested US$750 million there in the Greater Nile Oil Project.

21. Richard Boucher, Assistant Secretary for South and Central Asian Affairs, made almost the same speech in front of the American Association of Physicians of Indian Origin: 'Together, you comprise a "living bridge", spanning two cultures and two countries. And the bridge is growing. Last year we issued more than 725,000 non-immigrant visas in India and the number will likely be even higher this year—a clear indication that US-India relations are not simply among governments' (Boucher 2008).

# References

Baruah, A. (2007), 'India a "Reliable Ally" Against Global Terrorism: U.S. Report', *The Hindu*, 13 January.

Bedi, R. (2008), 'Israeli Army Chief Made a Hush-hush Visit to Kashmir', *Covert*, 1–14 October.

Boucher, R. (2008), 'US-India Relations', *U.S. Department of State,* http://www.state. gov./p/sca/rls/2008/106476.htm. (accessed on 17 October 2008).

C. Jaffrelot, 'India's Emergence', in C. Jaffrelot (ed.), *The Emerging States: The Wellspring of a New World Order,* New York: Columbia University Press.

*Central Chronicle* (2006), 18 June.

———— (2006), 23 December.

Chang, Gordon H. (2001) (ed.), *Asian Americans and Politics,* Washington: Woodrow Wilson Center/Stanford University Press.

Chengappa, Raj (2007), 'Why US Wants the Deal', *India Today,* 19 November, pp. 36–7.

Feigenbaum, E. (2008), 'Strategic Context of US-India Relations', US Department of State, http://www.state.gov/p/sca/ris/2008/10/3809.htm. (accessed on 17 October 2008).

GoI (2006), 'PM's Onboard Press Conference Enroute to Brasilia—11 September, 2006', in *Visit of Prime Minister Dr Manmohan Singh to Brazil and Cuba (First IBSA Summit and XIV NAM Summit),* New Delhi: Government of India.

———— (2008), *Economic Survey: 2007/08,* Delhi: Oxford University Press.

Indian Embassy (2003), Speech available at: http://www.indianembassy.org/indusreiy2003/ nsa_ajc_may_8_03.htm. (accessed on 18 June 2008).

*India Today* (2005), 28 March.

————, 'Interview: Pranab Mukherjee', 22 September, p. 22.

Kissinger, H. (2006), 'Anatomy of a Partnership', *The Herald Tribune,* 11–12 March.

Khagram, Desai, M. and Varughese, J. (2001), 'Seen, Rich but Unheard? The Politics of Asian Indians in the United States', in Gordon H. Chang (ed.) *Asian Americans and Politics.*

Krishnaswami, S. (2005), 'India, U.S. Sign Framework for Defence Cooperation', *The Hindu,* 30 June.

Mistry, D. (2006), 'Diplomacy, Domestic Politics, and the US-India Nuclear Agreement', *Asian Survey,* Vol. XLVI, No. 5 (September-October), pp. 675–98.

National Intelligence Council (2004), *Mapping a Global Future,* Washington: US Government.

Pew (2008), *24-Nation Pew Global Attitudes Survey* (June), Pew Global Attitudes Survey, available at http://pewglobal.org. (accessed on 10 July 2008).

Raja Mohan, C. (2006), 'India and the Balance of Power', *Foreign Affairs,* Vol. 85, No. 4, pp. 29–30.

*The Hindu* (2004), 11 August.

———— (2005a), 15 June.

———— (2005b), 1 September.

———— (2005c), 4 September.

———— (2006a), 4 March.

———— (2007a), 'India Matters More than Pakistan, says U.S. official', 1 January.

———— (2007b), 4 April.

———— (2007c), 'India will be Key Ally in 20 Years', 4 October.

*The International Herald Tribune* (2006), 6 March.

Therwath, I. (2008), 'La diaspora aux Etats Unis comme acteur international', in C. Jaffrelot (ed.), *New Delhi et le monde: Une puissance entre realpolitik et soft power,* Paris: Autrement, pp. 111–24.

*The Third Annual SAPRA Seminar on Indo-US Relations* (2007), 'Can Business Interests Shape a Strategic Partnership?', *SAPRA India Bulletin,* February, p. 12.

US Department of State (2008), 'Secretary of State Condoleezza Rice and Indian Minister of External Affairs Pranab Mukherjee at the Signing of the US-India Civilian Nuclear Cooperation Agreement', http://www.state.gov/p/sca/rls/2008/10/l 10916.htm. (accessed on 17 October).

# Select Bibliography

The following is a list of the author's publications in English.

## Books

Jaffrelot, Christophe (1996, 1999), *The Hindu Nationalist Movement and Indian Politics, 1925 to the 1990s*, New York: Columbia University Press; London: Hurst; New Delhi: Penguin India.

—— (2003), *India's Silent Revolution: The Rise of the Lower Castes in North India*, New York: Columbia University Press; London: Hurst; New Delhi: Permanent Black.

—— (2005), *Dr Ambedkar and Untouchability: Analysing and Fighting Caste*, New York: Columbia University Press; London: Hurst; New Delhi: Permanent Black.

## Edited Volumes

Jaffrelot, Christophe and Hansen, T.B. (eds.) (1998), *The BJP and the Compulsions of Politics in India*, Delhi: Oxford University Press.

Jaffrelot, Christophe (2002), *A History of Pakistan and its Origins*, London: Anthem Press.

—— (2002), *Pakistan: Nationalism Without a Nation?*, Delhi: Manohar; London/New York: Zed Books.

—— (2005), The *Sangh Parivar: A Reader*, Delhi: Oxford University Press.

—— and Dieckhoff, Alain (eds.) (2005), *Revisiting Nationalism: Theories and Processes*, London: Hurst; New York: Palgrave.

Jaffrelot, Christophe (2007), *Hindu Nationalism: A Reader*, New Delhi: Permanent Black; Princeton, NJ: Princeton University Press.

Jaffrelot, Christophe and Van der Veer, P. (eds.) (2008), *Patterns of Middle Class Consumption in China and India*, New Delhi: Sage.

Jaffrelot, Christophe and Gayer, L. (2009), *Armed Militias of South Asia: Fundamentalist, Maoists and Separatists*, London: Hurst; New York: Columbia University Press; New Delhi: Foundation Books.

Jaffrelot, Christophe (2008–9), *Emerging Powers: The Wellspring of a New World Order*, London: Hurst; New York: Columbia University Press.

—— and Kumar, S. (eds.) (2009), *Rise of the Plebeians? The Changing Face of Indian Legislative Assemblies*, New Delhi: Routledge.

## Chapters in Books

Jaffrelot, Christophe (1993), 'The BJP in Madhya Pradesh: Networks, Strategy and Power', in *Hindus and Others: the Question of Identity in India Today*, ed. G. Pandey, New Delhi: Penguin.

———— (1995), 'The idea of the Hindu race in the writings of Hindu nationalist ideologues in the 1920s and 1930s: a concept between two cultures', in *The Concept of Race in South Asia*, ed. P. Robb, Delhi: Oxford University Press.

———— (1998), 'The Sangh Parivar between Sanskritization and Social Engineering', and 'The BJP and the Challenge of Factionalism in Madya Pradesh', in *The BJP and the Compulsions of Politics in India Today*, ed. T.B. Hansen and C. Jaffrelot, Delhi: Oxford University Press.

———— (1998), 'The Politics of Processions and Hindu-Muslim Riots', in *Community Conflicts and the State in India*, ed. A. Kohli and A. Basu, Delhi: Oxford University Press.

———— (1999), 'The Vishva Hindu Parishad: Structures and Strategies', in *Religion, Globalization and Political Culture in the Third World*, ed. J. Haynes, London: Macmillan.

———— (1999), 'Militant Hindus and the Conversion Issue (1885–1990): From *Shuddhi* to *Dharm Parivartan*, The Politization and the Diffusion of an "Invention of Tradition"', in *The Resources of History: Tradition and Narration in South Asia*, ed. J. Assayag, Paris: EFEO.

———— (2000), 'The Hindu Nationalist Movement in Delhi: From "Locals" to Refugees— and Towards Peripheral Groups?', in *Delhi: Urban Space and Human Destinies*, ed. V. Dupont, E. Tarlo and D. Vidal, Delhi: Manohar.

———— (2000), 'Hindu Nationalism and Democracy', in *Transforming India: Social and Political Dynamics of Democracy*, ed. F. Frankel, Z. Hasan, R. Bhargava and B. Arora, Delhi: Oxford University Press.

———— (2001), 'Hindu Nationalism and the Social Welfare Strategy', in *Modern Roots: Studies of National Identity*, ed. A. Dieckhoff and N. Gutierrez, Aldershot: Ashgate.

———— (2001), 'The Vishva Hindu Parishad: A Nationalist but Mimetic Attempt at Federating the Hindu Sects ', in *Charisma and Canon: Essays on the Religious History of the Indian Subcontinent*, ed. V. Dalmia, A. Malinar and M. Christof, Delhi: Oxford University Press.

———— (2001), 'The Rise of Hindu Nationalism and the Marginalization of the Muslims in India Today', in *The Post-Colonial States of South Asia*, ed. Shastri and A.J. Wilson, Richmond: Curzon.

———— and Dieckhoff, A. (2001), 'From the Nation-State to Post-Nationalism', in *The New International Relations: Theory and Practice*, dir. Smouts (Marie-Claude), London: Hurst; New York: Palgrave.

Jaffrelot, Christophe, Zerinini-Brotel, J. and Chaturvedi, J. (2002), 'The BJP and the rise of Dalits in Uttar Pradesh', in *UP 2000*, ed. R. Jeffrey and J. Lerche, Delhi: Manohar.

Jaffrelot, Christophe (2002), 'The subordinate caste revolution', in *India Briefing: Quickening the Pace of Change*, ed. A. Ayres and P. Oldenburg, New York: M.E. Sharpe.

———— (2004), 'Epilogue: Musharraf and the islamists: from support to opposition after September 11', in *A History of Pakistan and its Origins*, ed. C. Jaffrelot, London: Anthem Press.

———— and Zerinini-Brotel, Jasmine (2004), 'Post-"Mandal" Politics in Uttar Pradesh and Madhya Pradesh', in *Regional Reflections: Comparing Politics Across India's States*, ed. Rob Jenkins, Delhi: Oxford University Press.

Jaffrelot, Christophe (2004), 'Composite Culture is not Multiculturalism: A Study of the Indian Constituent Assembly Debates', in *India and the Politics of Developing Countries, Essays in Memory of Myron Weiner,* ed. A. Varshney, New Delhi: Sage.

————— (2004), 'From Indian Territory to Hindu *Bhoomi*: The Ethnicization of Nation-State Mapping in India', in *The Politics of Cultural Mobilization in India*, ed. John Zavos, Andrew Wyatt and Vernon Hewitt, Oxford/New York: Oxford University Press.

————— (2005), 'Introduction', in *The Sangh Parivar: A Reader*, ed. C. Jaffrelot, Delhi: Oxford University Press.

————— (2005), 'The BJP and the 2004 elections: dimensions, causes and implications of an unexpected defeat', in *Coalition Politics and Hindu Nationalism*, ed. Katharine Adeney and Lawrence Sàez, New York: Routledge.

————— (2005), 'For a theory of nationalism', in *Revisiting Nationalism*, ed. A. Dieckhoff and C. Jaffrelot, London: Hurst.

————— and Dieckhoff, A. (2005), 'The invert U curve of nationalism?', in *Revisiting Nationalism: Theories and Processes*, ed. A. Dieckhoff and C. Jaffrelot, London: Hurst; New York: Palgrave.

Jaffrelot, Christophe (2006), 'The 2002 Pogrom in Gujarat: The Post-9/11 Face of Hindu Nationalist Anti-Muslim Violence', in *Religion and Violence in South Asia*, ed. J. Hinnels and R. King, London and New York: Routledge.

————— (2006, 2007), 'Introduction: The invention of an ethnic nationalism', in *Hindu Nationalism: A Reader*, ed. C. Jaffrelot, New Delhi: Permanent Black; Princeton, NJ: Princeton University Press.

————— (2007), 'Caste and the rise of marginalized groups', in *The State of India's Democracy*, ed. S. Ganguly, L. Diamond and M.F. Plattner, Baltimore and Washington: The Johns Hopkins University Press.

————— (2007), 'The BSP in Uttar Pradesh: party of the Dalits or of the Bahujans—or catch-all-party?', in *The Dalits of India*, ed. M. Sebastian, New Delhi: Sage.

————— and Gupta, Smita (2007), 'The Bajrang Dal: The New Hindu Nationalist Brigade', in *Living with Secularism: The Destiny of India's Muslims*, ed. Mushirul Hasan, Delhi: Manohar.

Jaffrelot, Christophe (2007), 'Voting in India: Electoral Symbols, the Party System and the Collective Citizen', in *Cultures of Voting: The Hidden History of the Secret Ballot*, ed. R. Bertrand, J.L. Briquet and P. Pels, London: Hurst.

————— and Van der Veer, P. (2008), 'Introduction', in *Patterns of Middle Class Consumption in India and China*, ed. C. Jaffrelot and P. Van der Veer, New Delhi: Sage.

Jaffrelot, Christophe (2008), 'Why Should We Vote?': The Indian Middle Class and the Functioning of the World's Largest Democracy', in *Patterns of Middle Class Consumption in India and China*, ed. C. Jaffrelot and P. Van der Veer, New Delhi: Sage.

————— (2008), 'Hindu nationalism and the social welfare strategy', in *Development, Civil Society and Faith-Based Organisations: Bridging the Sacred and the Secular*, ed. G. Clarke and M. Jennings, New York: Palgrave.

————— (2008), 'Containing the lower castes: The Constituent Assembly and the reservation policy', in *Politics and Ethics of the Indian Constitution*, ed. R. Bhargava, Delhi: Oxford University Press.

————— (2008–9), 'Introduction' and 'India, An Emerging Power, but How Far?', in *Emerging Powers: The Wellspring of a New World Order*, ed. C. Jaffrelot, London: Hurst; New York: Columbia University Press.

Jaffrelot, Christophe and Sidhu, Waheguru Pal Singh (2009), 'Does Europe Matter to India?', *European Security in a Global Context: Internal and External Dynamics*, dir. Thierry Tardy, London: Routledge.

Jaffrelot, Christophe (2005), 'Introduction', 'The uneven rise of lower castes in the politics of Madhya Pradesh', and C. Robin, 'Towards Jat empowerment in Rajasthan', in *Rise of the Plebeians? The Changing Face of Indian Legislative Assemblies*, ed. C. Jaffrelot and S. Kumar, New Delhi: Routledge.

——— (2006), 'India and the European Union: The charade of a strategic partnership', in *Rising India: Europe's Partner?*, ed. K. Voll and D. Beierlein, Berlin: Weissensee Verlag.

——— with Gayer, L. (2009), 'Introduction', 'The Militias of Hindutva: Communal Violence, Terrorism and Cultural Policing', with L. Gayer, 'Conclusion', in *Armed Militias of South Asia: Fundamentalist, Maoists and Separatists*, ed. L. Gayer and C. Jaffrelot, London: Hurst; New York: Columbia University Press; New Delhi: Foundation Books.

——— with Gayer, L. and Maheshwari, M. (2010), 'Cultural policing in South Asia: an anti-globalization backlash?', in *Cultural Expression, Creativity and Innovation*, ed. H. Anheier and Y.R. Isar, Los Angeles.

Jaffrelot, Christophe (2009), 'Gujarat: The Meaning of Modi's Victory', in *Political Marketing: An Overview*, ed. S.V. Menon, Hyderabad: The Icfai University Press.

## Articles in Journals

Jaffrelot, Christophe (1992), 'Hindu nationalism: strategic syncretism in ideology building', *Indian Journal of Social Science*, Vol. 5, No. 42, August.

——— (1993), 'Hindu nationalism: strategic syncretism in ideology building', *Economic and Political Weekly*, Vol. 28, Nos. 12–13, 20 March.

——— (1995), 'The genesis and development of Hindu nationalism in the Punjab: From the Arya to the Hindu Sabha (1875-1990)', *The Indo-British Review*, Vol. 21, No. 1.

——— (1996), 'Madhya Pradesh I: Setback to BJP', *Economic and Political Weekly*, Vol. 31, Nos. 2–3, 13 January.

——— (1996), 'Of nations and nationalism', *Seminar*, No. 442, June.

——— (1998-9), 'Interpreting ethnic movements in Pakistan', *The Pakistan Development Review*, Vol. 37, No. 4, Winter.

——— (1998), 'The Bahujan Samaj Party in North India: no longer just a Dalit party?', *Comparative Studies of South Asia, Africa and the Middle East*, Vol. 18, No. 1.

——— (2000), 'The Rise of the Other Backward Classes in the Hindi Belt', *The Journal of Asian Studies*, Vol. 59, No. 1, February.

——— (2000), 'Sanskritization vs. Ethnicization in India: Changing Identities and Caste Politics before Mandal', *Asian Survey*, Vol. 60, No. 5, September–October.

——— (2000), 'Indian democracy: the rule of law on trial', *Indian Review*, Vol. 1, No. 1, January.

——— (2002), 'India and Pakistan: interpreting the divergence of two political trajectories', *Cambridge Review of International Affairs*, Vol. 15, No. 2, July.

——— (2003), 'India's look east policy: an asianist strategy in perspective', *Indian Review*, Vol. 2, No. 2, April.

——— (2005), 'The Politics of the OBCs', *Seminar*, No. 549.

——— (2006), 'The impact of affirmative action in India: more political than socioeconomic', *Indian Review*, Vol. 5, No. 2, April.

——— with Therwath, Ingrid (2007), 'The Sangh Parivar and the Hindu diaspora in the West: what kind of "long-distance nationalism"?', *International Political Sociology*, Vol. 1, No. 3, September.

——— (2008), 'The Hindu nationalist reinterpretation of pilgrimage in India: the limits of *Yatra* politics', *Nations and Nationalism*.

———, 'Hindu Nationalism and the (Not So Easy) Art of Being Outraged: The *Ram Setu* Controversy', *South Asia Multidisciplinary Academic Journal*, Special Issue No. 2, 'Outraged Communities': Comparative Perspectives on the Politicization of Emotions in South Asia. Available at: http://samaj.revues.org/document1372.html.

——— (2008), 'The Meaning of Modi's Victory', *Economic and Political Weekly*, 12 April.

——— (2008), 'The uneven plebeianization of Madhya Pradesh politics', *Seminar*, November.

——— with Virginie Dutoya, Radhika Kanchana and Gayatri Rathore (2009), 'Understanding Muslim voting Behaviour', *Seminar*, No. 602.

——— (2009), 'The cardinal points of Indian foreign policy', *Mondes*, No. 1, Autumn.

——— (2009), 'The India-US Rapprochement: State-Driven or Middle-Class Driven', *India Quarterly*, Vol. 65, No. 1.

——— with Verniers, G. (2010), 'India's 2009 elections: the resilience of regionalism and ethnicity', SAMAJ, No. 3.

## Working Papers

Jaffrelot, Christophe (2003), 'For a theory of nationalism', Paris, FNSP-CERI, June.

——— (2003), 'Communal riots in Gujarat: the state at risk?', *Heidelberg Papers in South Asian and Comparative Politics*, No. 13, May.

——— (2009), 'Dr. Ambedkar's strategies against untouchability and the caste system', Indian Institute of Dalit Studies, Working Papers Series, Vol. III, No. 4.

# Index